W9-BRI-539

Gun Digest®

1987/41st Annual Edition

EDITED BY KEN WARNER

DBI BOOKS, INC.

ABOUT OUR COVERS

The Front Cover

It's this year's most "newsworthy" firearms event. It's the announcement of Sturm, Ruger's *first* centerfire, semi-auto pistol—the double-action P-85™ in 9mm Luger. We are delighted to have the P-85™ grace the front cover of this, the 41st edition of GUN DIGEST.

The P-85™, indeed, serves to give truth to past public and industry rumors about a "new 9mm semi-auto handgun" en route from the folks at Southport. At this point, it must also be said that the P-85™ seen on our front cover is an advanced pre-production prototype.

Keeping in mind that the cover gun is prototypical in nature, and that minor changes may take place prior to its approximate on-sale date ("late 1986"), here is a list of P-85™ specifications we received from Sturm, Ruger just prior to going to press:

P-85™ Specifications

Mechanism Type	Recoil operated, semi-automatic
Breech Locking Mode	Tilting barrel, link actuated
Action	Double-action
Ammunition	Cal. 9x19mm
Magazine Capacity	15 rounds
Weight (Magazine Empty)	2.0 lbs.
Weight (Magazine Loaded)	2.38 lbs.
Barrel Length	4.50 in.
Height	5.63 in.
Width	1.125 in.
Overall Length	7.84 in.
Sight Radius	5.80 in.
Sights	Fixed square notch rear adjustable for windage, square post front. Both front and rear have white dot inserts.
Catalog Number	P-85
Suggested Retail Price	$295.00

Prices and specifications subject to change at Sturm, Ruger's discretion without notice.

Also, be advised that the magazine release, located at the bottom-rear of the trigger guard is of the full-time ambidextrous type. With the exception of the frame, which is investment cast of lightweight aluminum alloy, the P-85™ is of solid-steel construction. (The grips are made of a G.E. material called "Xenoy." Note the heavy, non-slip ribs.) Lastly, the take-down aspects of the P-85™, at least on the prototype we had, were indeed *unique*.

The Back Cover

On our back cover is another new Ruger handgun, the GP-100™. The GP-100™ is the first of a new revolver series which will be made in three frame sizes to handle everything from 22 rimfire up through 44 Magnum. Ruger's primary goal was to come up with a double-action revolver that would be both attractive, *and* rugged. They've succeeded with the GP-100™.

Ruger advised us that, having been initially introduced in 357 Magnum, the GP-100™ is designed from the outset to successfully withstand the stresses imposed by the repeated use of 357 Magnum ammunition in all factory loadings.

The GP-100™ has, as you can see, a pair of readily visible (new) features. The ejector shroud runs stylishly out to the end of the barrel and should help to tame muzzle whip. The grips are totally new. They're called the Ruger Cushioned Grip System (Patent Pending). The perimeter is of black, live rubber, the interior being of polished Goncalvo Alves. The contrast, as you can see, is *very* attractive. The new Ruger Cushioned Grip System is also functional in that it helps soften recoil and presents the shooter with a secure, non-slip surface to hang on to.

Options include a 4- or 6-inch barrel and solid (wraparound) walnut grips. The front sight system is of the "interchangeable-blade" type. The rear sight is, of course, fully adjustable.

Photos by John Hanusin

GUN DIGEST STAFF

EDITOR-IN-CHIEF
Ken Warner
SENIOR STAFF EDITOR
Harold A. Murtz
ASSOCIATE EDITOR
Robert S. L. Anderson
ASSISTANT TO THE EDITOR
Lilo Anderson
CONTRIBUTING EDITORS
Bob Bell
Dean A. Grennell
Rick Hacker
Edward A. Matunas
Layne Simpson
Larry S. Sterett
Hal Swiggett
Ralph T. Walker
D. A. Warner
J.B. Wood
EUROPEAN CORRESPONDENT
Raymond Caranta
GRAPHIC DESIGN
Jim Billy
Stephen Johnson
MANAGING EDITOR
Pamela J. Johnson
PUBLISHER
Sheldon L. Factor

EDITOR EMERITUS
John T. Amber

DBI BOOKS, INC.

PRESIDENT
Charles T. Hartigan
VICE PRESIDENT & PUBLISHER
Sheldon L. Factor
VICE PRESIDENT—SALES
John G. Strauss
TREASURER
Frank R. Serpone

Copyright © MCMLXXXVI by DBI Books, Inc., 4092 Commercial Ave., Northbrook, IL 60062. All rights reserved. Printed in the United States of America.

No part of this publication may be reproduced, stored in a retrieval system, or transmitted in any form or by any means electronic, mechanical, photocopying, recording, or otherwise, without the prior written permission of the publisher.

The views and opinions contained herein are those of the authors. The editor and publisher disclaim all responsibility for the accuracy or correctness of the authors views.

Manuscripts, contributions and inquiries, including first class return postage, should be sent to the Gun Digest Editorial Offices, 4092 Commercial Ave., Northbrook, IL 60062. All material received will receive reasonable care, but we will not be responsible for its safe return. Material accepted is subject to our requirements for editing and revisions. Author payment covers all rights and title to the accepted material, including photos, drawings and other illustrations. Payment is at our current rates.

CAUTION: Technical data presented here, particularly technical data on handloading and on firearm adjustment and alteration, inevitably reflects individual experience with particular equipment and components under specific circumstances the reader cannot duplicate exactly. Such data presentations therefore should be used for guidance only and with caution. DBI Books, Inc. accepts no responsibility for results obtained using this data.

Arms and Armour Press, London, G.B., exclusive licensees and distributors in Britain and Europe; Australia; Nigeria, South Africa and Zimbabwe; India and Pakistan; Singapore, Hong Kong and Japan.

ISBN 0-87349-001-0   Library of Congress Catalog #44-32588

IN THE BLACK ◉

USRAC's Sticking

It was bad news-good news for the company that makes Winchesters in America. January 16, 1986: USRAC filed for reorganization under chapter 11 of the Bankruptcy Code. Then, February 14: USRAC recalls production workers; the court and new money put them back in business. At press-time it was coming up roses and there can still be Winchesters in your future.

Browning's Biggie

The two millionth Browning Auto-5, the one naughty Richard Nixon didn't get, was auctioned on behalf of the National Shooting Sports Foundation's wildlife programs and brought $50,001 and big grins to both Browning and NSSF. William Henkel of Winchester, VA, got the gun.

Aussies Vote AUG

The Australian military has adopted the Austrian bull-pup infantry rifle, the AUG, which they will make. We're told the Australians hope to be supplying the rifle to others around the Pacific Rim.

RECALLS

Federal wants some 85-gr. Premium 243 ammo back—it's a little hot. Needed are lots marked 5A or 5B, together with any of the following—4592, 4593, 4594, 4595, 4598 (5A-4592, for example)—in a white area on the back panel of the box. Federal will pay for the ammo and shipping.

Ruger wishes to replace the trigger overtravel adjustment set screw on any M-77 (not 77/22, 10/22, No. 1 or 3, or 44 Carbine) that does not have a "T" on the underside of the bolt handle. There is no charge. Write Dept. M-77 at 140 Guild Rd., Newport, NH 03773.

T/C Skeet Anyone?

Take your Thompson Contender and its 45/410 or 44 Magnum Hot Shot barrel to the Point Moinllee Shooting Range in South Rockwood, Michigan and run some 25-bird races if you wish. No, they've modified the course—no doubles.

Or you could join the T/C Association formed at the 1986 SHOT Show. Write Joe Wright, its president, at P.O. Box 792, Northboro, MA 01532.

A high-ticket auction in Manhattan by Christies to benefit the Arms and Armor Department of the Metropolitan Museum of Art saw this Paterson and this guitar donated by Johnny Cash among a great many guns from other notables.

SHOT Show Stuff

Rock Rohlfing, who invented the show, saw his last one as boss in 1986. He's now President of NSSF and Bob Delfay has become Executive Director. Rohlfing is to retire in earnest at year's end, 1986.

The big show has kept on getting bigger as usual. This last time it had 1,100 exhibitors in well over 200,000 square feet of exhibits. There were 22,000 people from 40 countries. The show, which is a private trade show, will be in New Orleans in 1987, in Anaheim in 1988.

This is now officially a $201,000 rifle, having sold at auction at that price. David Miller and a number of associates made it; Safari Club International commissioned it and sold it.

M. L. Brown
1934-1985

Two-time winner of the Townsend Whelen award, Lee Brown was well-known for his well-researched articles and books. Indeed, an M. L. Brown article appears in this issue of GUN DIGEST. His death was unexpected and he will be missed.

Bell Writes Fiction, Too

A collection of 32 stories by contributing editor Bob Bell has just been published by Northwoods Publications, Inc., 2101 N. Front St., S-206, Harrisburg, PA 17110. Riflemen and hunters will greatly enjoy the collection, priced at $21.00 postpaid. The title is *Even The Last Six*.

Gary Cob got his *Airgun News & Report* off and running from, of all publishing centers, Comanche, TX.

James E. Serven
1894-1985

Author of several seminal volumes on gun collecting, Jim Serven wrote for this publication and many others—more than 100 magazine articles, in fact. An Easterner, Serven chose the West in 1935, both intellectually and in his lifestyle. He is survived by his wife Frances, two sons, seven grandchildren and three great-grandchildren. His absence from the firearms scene will be felt.

CONTENTS

Silver-mounted duelling pistol with octagonal barrel and hair trigger by Twigg and Bass. The short length of this partnership pinpoints the pistol between 1788 and 1790. Though the butt has the look of the holster pistol, the angle has steepened, and it has fine diamond checkering.

Those who were Quick did not become Dead, given a good gun . . .

the essence of the dueller

by WILFRID WARD

These pistols fought a famous duel, when The Duke of Wellington, then Prime Minister, fought The Earl of Winchelsea over Catholic Emancipation. (From an anonymous private collection)

THE ONLY safe definition of a duelling pistol is "one of two pistols—as near identical as possible—with which a duel might have been fought." Rules of conduct for duels existed, such as The Clonmell Rules and the British Code of Duel, and were strictly applied, but they did not lay down what pistols were to be used.

Though my definition tells one little about the pistols themselves, it emphasizes the vital attribute—equality. The assumption of the time was that the fairness in the duel and identicality of weapon were the same thing. This proposition does not really stand up to examination. The 18th century duelling pistol could not, any more than Colonel Sam Colt's equalizer, make fair the difference between good and bad shots; and in duelling,

as in the West, the Fast soon became the Quick and the Slow the Dead. Nonetheless, this was the view of the time. Strangely enough, if a man stated on his Honour that he was no swordsman, he could avoid his opponent's choice of weapon and use pistols, but I have heard of no example of the reverse being applied.

The nature of the pistols was, of course, closely related to the conditions under which the duel itself was fought. Neither was decided all at once but by a process of evolution. While the most active period in this process was between 1765 and 1800, changes and improvements went on throughout the period of duelling in Britain.

Duels were normally conducted at 12 yards. All the details of the en-

counter were agreed beforehand between the seconds. Examples can be found varying from pointblank to 30 yards. Mr. Best, as one example, shot Lord Camelford at this latter distance, selected because the parties were such good shots. The whole procedure was directed towards fairness and this was one reason why seconds were appointed. They had to look after the interests of their principals and above all to reconcile them if this was possible.

The normal limit of exchanges was two if neither party was hurt. In exceptionally bad cases, such as the seduction of a wife or dependent female, three shots were permitted. If a pistol failed to fire for any reason this counted as a shot. Thus one of the most vital features of the pistol had to be reli-

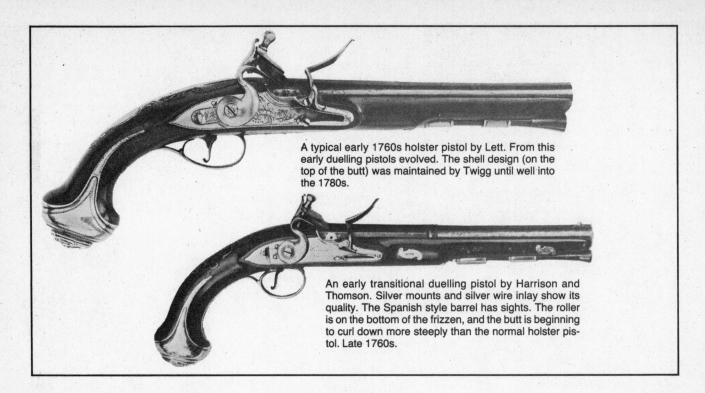

A typical early 1760s holster pistol by Lett. From this early duelling pistols evolved. The shell design (on the top of the butt) was maintained by Twigg until well into the 1780s.

An early transitional duelling pistol by Harrison and Thomson. Silver mounts and silver wire inlay show its quality. The Spanish style barrel has sights. The roller is on the bottom of the frizzen, and the butt is beginning to curl down more steeply than the normal holster pistol. Late 1760s.

ability.

In later days, when both parties fired together, this was marginally less important because by the time an opponent had realized that one's own pistol had misfired he would have fired himself. In earlier days, when the first shot was decided by tossing a coin such knowledge was of great importance, as one knew that one was out of danger for the time being at any rate.

The signal to fire was normally the dropping of a handkerchief. When it was given the shot had to be taken immediately and without deliberate aim. This was the same, whether one or both parties were firing. Aiming, or firing too slowly, was cheating; and if a murder trial followed, might be the difference between life or death for the survivor. After the duel, the seconds produced a written and agreed statement setting out the causes and conduct of the encounter. If there were any breaches of etiquette these were set out, so that these too would be brought before the court.

It can be seen from this outline that the best type of pistol for such an affair was a reasonably light and well-balanced one which handled well. The ideal was that it should point where the firer looked. Bearing in mind the distances involved, both the coexistent holster pistol and, to a lesser extent, the military pistol already had these qualities. The former was by no means a sophisticated weapon, probably about 28-bore, or larger, with a barrel between 8 and 12 inches long. Nonetheless, its capacity to point

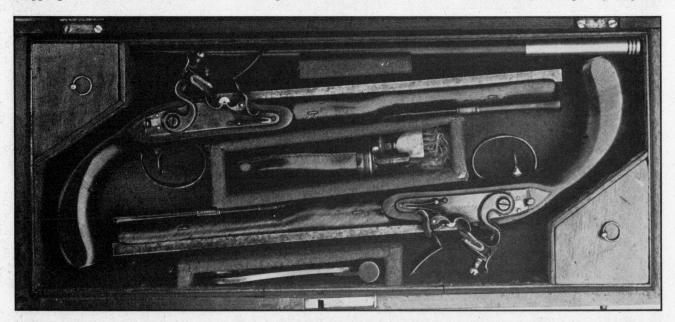

This pair of full-stocked 30-bore flintlock duelling pistols by Wogdon, *ca.* 1780, has 10-in. octagonal barrels. The roller is on the frizzen. The finials are of acorn design. The case is inscribed "Capt. Munro, 79th Highland (or Ross-shire Buffs) Regt."

made it the weapon from which the duelling pistol evolved. When one adds the fact that such pistols were normally made in pairs, another ready-made feature is supplied—that of equality. Such pistols were carried in holsters on a rider's saddle. Though they would have been loaded, primed, and at half cock, safety was still an important feature, so heavy trigger pulls were installed. Safety bolts would also have been present on most examples. There would have been no backsight, and foresights where they

younger man, Tow, into partnership.

Barrels were either round, or in the Spanish style—part octagonal for a few inches from the breech and round for the rest. The lock might be fitted with a hair trigger, though many of the early pistols were of such simplicity that they had not sights, safety bolts, nor hair triggers.

Thus it can be seen that the very early duelling pistols (often called "transitional") could well be confused with high grade holster pistols. Such pistols would have probably have

often thought that being in a case means that a pistol must be a duelling pistol. Aside from early trunk-like boxes for protection on a journey, cases were probably used for duelling pistols before other kinds of pistols, but the practice soon spread to all types. The reason that the cases were employed for duelling pistols in the first place was that it enabled all the necessities for the pistols to be got and kept together in one place. Even when such cases were used, the outfit was quite often forgotten and before the

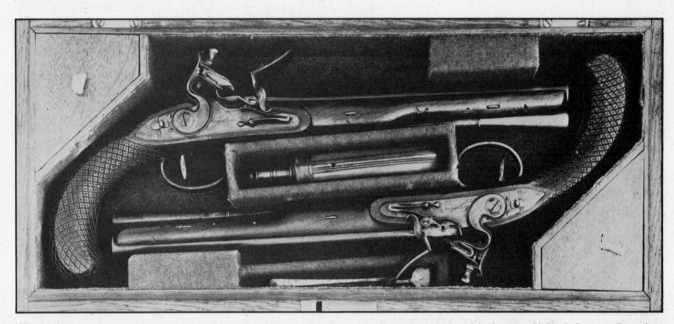

Wogdon believed in extreme simplicity. This pair of duelling pistols, dating from the mid-1780s, has 9-in. barrels with Nocksform configuration. The rough baize is typical of that used in early casings. Note the similarity of Wogdon's checkering to that used by Egg.

were fitted, would have been rudimentary. Normally, one just pointed and pulled as quickly as possible, hoping the highwayman would either be hit or go away.

Griffin, a prominent maker of sporting guns, probably made the first pistols which posterity and the gun trade have labeled as duelling pistols. Externally, there was probably little obvious difference from holster pistols. Just as shotguns had been fitted to the customer to enable him to bring the gun to his shoulder and point straight to the mark, so this feature of "pointability" was transferred to these very early duelling pistols. The locks were speeded up and sometimes very simple sights added. Most significant of these changes was the adding of an anti-friction roller to the frizzen. It was later transferred to the feather spring. This was certainly done on some pistols during the 1760s and had become an established (though not invariable) practice by the early 1770s, when Griffin took a

been kept in woven bags of material similar to high grade blanket material, usually with cheerful colored patterns.

I well remember, when I was at Oxford, such a pair of holster pistols by Collis of Oxford being discovered from behind an ancient chest in the Bursary of All Souls College. They were in near-perfect condition, still in their original bags, and had been the holster pistols of the "riding bursar," whose duty it was to collect rents from outlying farms and who accordingly was in need of protection. They were in immaculate condition, doubtless because of the bags, and are almost identical to the pistol which I illustrate. The latter has sadly become separated from its bag. Both were examples of the immediate predecessor of the duelling pistol and date from about 1760.

Individual bags gave way to wooden cases, and to them can be attributed many of the popular misconceptions about the duelling pistol, for it is

introduction of cases the risk of something being left behind at such a time of stress was vastly increased.

The practice of casing pistols was well established by 1770, and had probably begun rather earlier. In the cases were every necessity for a duel from screwdriver to powder and ball. The presence of the original case can add as much as a third to the value of a set of pistols (whether duelling or others). The actual cases themselves were simple boxes made in the style of good quality furniture makers of the time. As can be seen from my illustrations, no space was wasted. In particular, *the cases were fitted to the pistols*. Indeed if a pair of pistols is loose in its case, it is a fair, though not infallible, indication that the combination is not an original one.

The various accessories all had their places. One finds one or more corners used to make small compartments for items likely to be lost, such as flints or spare balls, with sometimes more unusual items. I once saw

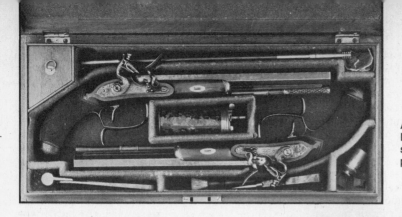

A typical pair of D. Egg duelling pistols of about 1795. Note how Egg has removed his old trade card and substituted a more up-to-date version (doing a rather poor repair job on the baize at the same time).

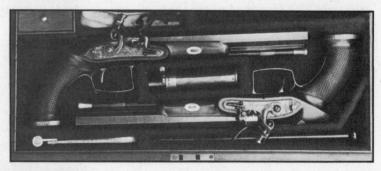

These half-stocked, saw-handle, 32-bore flintlock duelling pistols by Tatham and Egg, *ca.* 1804, have 9-in. barrels, French cocks, and rainproof pans. This pair is very similar to, though not identical with, the pair used in the Best/Camelford duel in 1804. The latter had "wire" style hair triggers.

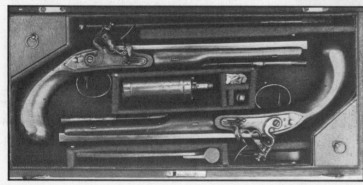

These 18-bore duelling pistols by Barton (Wogdon's surviving partner) have swamped barrels and hair triggers. Barton worked alone after 1805. This emphasizes how old styles, even the slab-sided butt, continued despite advances by other makers.

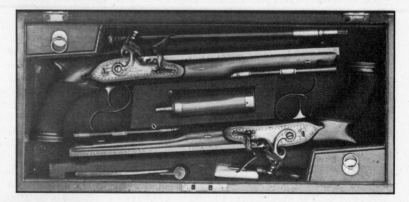

These full-stocked flintlock duelling pistols (*ca.* 1810) by W. H. Mortimer and Son have French cocks and rollers on the feather springs, but not hair triggers. The trade card proclaimed the firm as "Maker to His Majesty, The United States of America, and the Honble East India Comp."

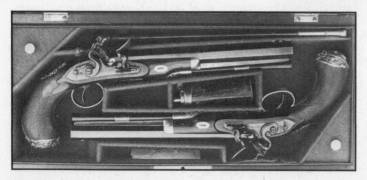

Some duelling pistols had heavy silver furniture. This pair, which belonged to the Marquis of Hertford, is typical of John Manton's finest work. Despite the beautiful work they have seen plenty of use.

a device about two inches long, the size of the bore, with four blades on a short stalk. It was only when beneath some cleaning tow I found a quartered ball that I realized that its purpose was to split the ball, when still warm, into segments. These could be loaded into the pistol, and fired like bird shot as an anti-burglar load. Charity and the likelihood of discovery makes me feel that this was its only purpose; but as it was in a case of pistols made by a user of "secret rifling," of which more later, one can never tell. These cases are a study by themselves, and readers who wish to follow the subject further are referred to Neal and Back: *British Gunmakers, Their Trade*

From about 1775, cases were made of oak, and were generally lined with rough baize. Sometimes wallpaper was used. On the top, an ordinary drawer handle was provided for lifting, while the lid was secured with hooks. These cases were simple examples of the furniture of the time. With the import of mahogany, the new wood displaced oak. By about 1785, the inconvenient drawer handles had given way to ones which folded flat into the lid of the case. Upon these handles, or their brass surrounds, the crests or names of the owners were engraved. Later the handle was replaced by a circle of brass, which gave greater scope to the engraver, and the

most famous ones. This is related by Sir Jonah Barrington in his *Sketches of His Own Time*. Writing in 1812, he tells how in the 1790s a young barrister was about to set out from Dublin to contest an election case. By chance he met the opposing barrister, who said that he hoped that he had Wogdon's case at his fingertips, for he was sure that it would be needed. Expressing his gratitude the greenhorn hunted unsuccessfully for the Wogdon report. Eventually, he sought the advice of a colleague, who enlightened him by explaining that he needed a gunshop rather than a bookseller, as the case in question contained a pair of duelling pistols.

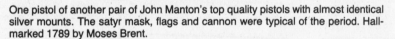

One pistol of another pair of John Manton's top quality pistols with almost identical silver mounts. The satyr mask, flags and cannon were typical of the period. Hallmarked 1789 by Moses Brent.

Cards and Equipment.

Heraldry was such a part of 18th century England that it featured even on a man's gun or pistol cases. It also justified the imposition of a tax on the use of arms on carriages and table silver. Technically, being a gentleman meant the right to use a coat of arms. Likewise, one could only be called upon to fight an equal. It was customary, therefore, to carry a copy of one's grant of arms when traveling in case they were needed to prove one's status. Likewise, the arms or perhaps a crest alone, were engraved on one's pistols and often the case as well. Though open to forgery in the cases of the arms of the famous, such devices are of considerable assistance to the collector in tracing the history of weapons.

The earliest cases date from about 1760 and were of white wood covered with leather. Sometimes they were decorated with patterns of brass nails.

lifting was done with an incorporated handle which folded flat into its edge. Finer baize was also used on the later cases.

In the lid of the case the maker placed his label, strictly referred to as his trade card. By a remarkable usage it was accepted that if another maker took in the pistols for overhaul or repair, he could, and did replace the card with his own. Original makers sometimes updated their cards. The pair of D. Egg pistols which I illustrate (ca. 1795)—though flintlocks—have a card which advertises Egg's products under the detonating system (about 1825). The cards themselves varied between simple dignity and considerable ostentation. This can be seen by contrasting the simple choice of John Manton with the almost billboard-like preference of his brother Joseph.

Before leaving the subject of cases mention must be made of one of the

Gradually, the practise of casing pistols spread so that by 1790 casing was merely a way of protecting the pistols from damage in transit. Quite frequently, one will find not only officers' pistols, but even double-barrelled pistols cased like duellers. The only outside indication of the difference would be the depth of the case. On occasions, one will also find two pairs of pistols in one case; either all on the same level or one on top of the other. In this event, one pair will usually be duellers and the other pocket pistols. All this was a question of convenience and does not really go to the true nature of the duelling pistol. Perhaps because they are so rare, one finds few, if any, of the transitional duelling pistols in cases of their original period. The early pair of Egg duelling pistols which I illustrate date from about 1775. They have been recased by John Manton and the casing can be dated about 1785.

This oak case for a pair of Wogdons is typical of the style of the period 1770-1785. The drawer handle and keyhole surround might equally have been encountered on a chest or desk of the time.

A mahogany case with inset carrying handle, *ca.* 1795. Though in fact it contained duelling pistols, it could equally well have housed officers pistols.

Twigg was the first to use octagonal barrels for his duelling pistols. He started to do so in the late 1760s. This form not only received general support, but continued throughout the existence of the duelling pistol in Great Britain. To start with barrels were as long as 12 inches, but gradually were reduced to 10 inches. Wogdon set his own rules and many of his early pistols had barrels of only 9 inches. He was also slow to adopt the octagonal shape. Henry Nock and Durs Egg both set up their own businesses in 1772. Nock introduced his own barrel shape, known as Nocksform. This had a flat sighting plane along the top and was rounded beneath to fit the stock. It achieved considerable popularity for some years and was used by both Egg and Wogdon as well as Nock. It must have appealed to the Prince of Wales, later George IV, for there are a number of pairs of duelling pistols with barrels in this form in the Royal Collection.

For the most part these early Nocksform barrels have the normal duelling bore diameter of half an inch. By degrees, however, the octagonal shape gained preference and Nocksform barrels fell into disuse except for officers' pistols. For those it remained popular until the advent of the revolver rendered single-barrelled pistols obsolete. The distinction between an officer's pistol with barrel of either shape, and a duelling pistol is really largely one of size and weight. The normal dueller would have had a longer barrel (10-in.) and smaller bore. Officers' pistols very often had belt hooks. Occasionally they also had short sliding bayonets. Here, however, one must remind oneself that many such pistols were used in duels, because they were the only pair of weapons available.

H. W. Mortimer, another holder of the Royal Warrant, made most of his pistols with large bores. Such pistols were very popular among officers and looked exactly like duelling pistols in

Double-barreled pistols—definitely not duellers—were also cased with accessories. When in use, they would have been carried in holsters.

all other respects. The Nocksform barrels were introduced at quite an early stage, before the vogue for very heavy barrels. They were light and easy to point in duelling bore. Indeed the hallmark of a good pistol of the early period was its lightness and pointability. The skill of Wogdon in particular became so famous, that tradition had it (probably wrongly) that if the user of one of his pistols were blinded in the duel, he could still kill his man because of the amazing pointing qualities of his pistols. Be this as it may, any pistol shot who handles a Wogdon seems to be immediately sure that he could hit his target with it.

Duelling pistols had not attained the ultimate in accuracy which they were in due course to achieve. They were well suited to a fast shot. In particular the capacity to point where the

firer looked was incorporated from the shotgun via the holster pistol. It survived the period of ultra-heavy barrels initiated by Joseph Manton in the 1790s and can be traced to the high speed "pointing" revolver shooting of the trench warfare of 1914. Signs of it can even be discerned in the concepts behind the "instinct" shooting training given to the various "special" forces during the 1939-45 war. Wogdon was the maker most associated with the duel in the public mind, and was also one of the most prolific makers. The true reason for all this fame was probably his capacity to fit the pistol and its owner to each other.

Hair triggers—a device which enables the main trigger merely to discharge a subsidiary spring which is already cocked, and so releases the main lock with a much lighter trigger pull—had been known since the 17th century. They were incorporated into the duelling pistol early in its development. Wogdon used both the normal shape and short wire-like ones. The latter are reminiscent of some modern free pistol triggers. The ideal

sights. The rear sight would be the larger, being about $\frac{9}{16}$-in. wide and $\frac{1}{10}$-in. above the barrel. Foresights were about the same height and perhaps $\frac{1}{32}$-in. wide. The latter were roughly $\frac{1}{4}$-in. long. The only concession to accuracy was that the back-

sporting guns of the period. While it would be an overstatement to say that its presence was taken for granted, it could be provided for only a small extra percentage of the cost. Just as there were specialist casemakers, so there were specialist silversmiths for the needs of the gun trade. Silver mounts, known as furniture in the trade, had been highly popular on the cannon-barrelled pistol, and quite usual on holster pistols. Many of Griffin's duellers were likewise silver mounted; so too were those of Twigg and their various successors and partners. Nonetheless, it is a fact that by degrees plain silver furniture was falling from general use. The generally accepted reason for this is not the extra cost of the silver, but the widely held theory of the time that the presence of silver on one's pistol gave an opponent something to aim at. Brief thought on this will demolish it. The distance made it unnecessary. To wait until the opponent's pistol showed its trigger guard or butt cap and then to aim at it was to wait until the pistol pointed at you. At 12 yards this was little short of suicide. All the same this is almost certainly what was believed at the time, so it is what mattered. What it probably tells us is why *plain* silver mounts fell from use. Those which survived gradually became the highly decorated ones.

By 1820, apart from presentation pieces, silver mounts had become very much the exception. A good many silver-mounted duellers had been made, particularly by Durs Egg, who really was the Prince of Wales' gunmaker as opposed to a mere holder of his warrant. Egg's taste, doubtless influenced by his continental origins, was very rich. Both he and John Manton turned out such duelling pistols. Both had their particular styles, Egg with pillared trigger guards and his own style of finial; Manton with ultraheavy sideplates and butt masks decorated with warlike themes. Both makers seem to have retained the same designs over the years, though examination of the individual pieces shows that the individual casts differ in execution. Apart from the silver, the pistols were made and cased in exactly the same way as ordinary duelling pistols; and some of them have seen considerable use. Though more pistols of this style are found dating from 1780s than the 1800s, while the Prince Regent was an active and enthusiastic patron who liked that style, the trade continued to cater for him and his friends with enthusiasm.

Presentation pistols, in both duel-

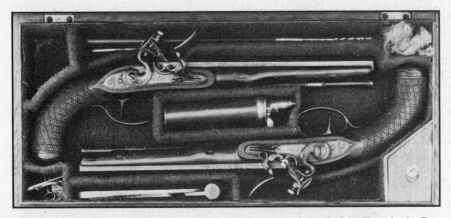

This pair of early (*ca.* 1780) Egg pistols appear in the case to be typical duelling pistols. Further examination shows them to have 9-in. barrels, and belt hooks on the reverse side. They clearly might have served a dual role, of course.

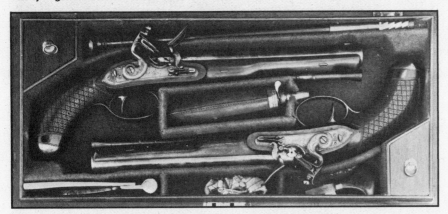

This pair of Durs Egg officers pistols are cased exactly like duelling pistols. The barrels are Nocksform and fire a 16-bore ball, distinctly oversize by the Code.

was always the perfection of the shooter/butt relationship. The ideal for the dueller required not only a quick discharge but a controlled one—as every modern pistol shooter knows.

A high proportion of the earliest duelling pistols had no sights at all. Before long, however, as part of the progression to greater accuracy simple sights were fitted. These took the form of a bar rear sight, which was let into the top of the barrel. Horizontal adjustment was possible by tapping the bar in the desired direction. A notch on the top of the bar, usually in the shape of a U or a V, enabled the shooter to align with the foresight. The foresight was completely fixed and usually of gold or later of silver.

To a modern pistol shot, the most remarkable feature is the exceptionally small size of both front and rear

sight was set so that it shot centrally on the horizontal plane. If vertical adjustment was needed, it could only be by the provision of a higher or lower foresight or backsight.

There were some alterations to the style of sights, but only marginal ones, in the direction of fitting bigger sights of the same shape. Though bead foresights are occasionally encountered on British duelling pistols, there were few fundamental differences, apart from size, between the sights which I have described and those used on the last of the duelling/target pistols.

Once the shape of the pistols had settled down, as they had by 1770, gunmakers were able to exercise their art by embellishing their products in ways compatible with their main purpose, i.e. successful use in a duel. Silver was found on a great many of the

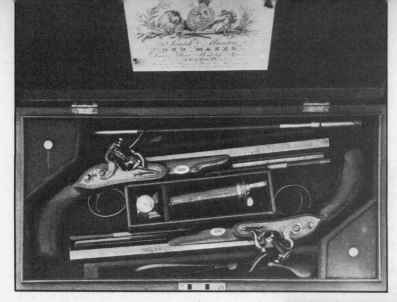

Half-stocked flintlock duelling pistols by Joseph Manton show a flamboyant label in contrast to the business-like simplicity of the pistols themselves. The heavy barrels, waterproof pans, and fast locks mark this pair as typical of the great maker's later flintlocks.

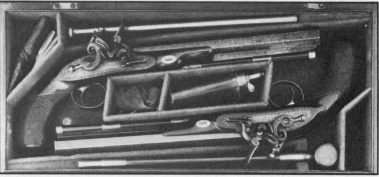

John Manton persevered with the perfection of the flintlock until the end. This pair (ca. 1819) has French cocks and waterproof pans. Note the flint in the fired position is right over the pan, thus ensuring fast ignition and the frizzen actually fits into the pan, producing an even more watertight closure. These were the fastest flintlocks made.

ling and holster forms continued to be made, often for the Near Eastern market. These were heavily encrusted with silver and sometimes semiprecious stones. They cannot really be classed as duelling pistols, since they were hardly ever used for duelling or anything else. Mere decoration, however, will not exclude a properly made pistol from the class. Work of makers such as Brunn of Charing Cross are good examples of this principle, for while their decoration is as lavish as that used by the great Directeur Artiste Boutet of Versailles, Brunn's were pistols capable of serious use in a duel.

Change is usually heralded as progress. In the evolution of the duelling pistol the same was true. It is certainly arguable that the pistol used in 1780 was more suitable for fighting the true duel than any of its more accurate successors. At the distances used, the chance of wounding an opponent was 6:1 and of killing him 14:1. It seems very improbable that most duellists really wanted to kill opponents. Accordingly, one may well ask why there was a movement away from the early form of pistol to the heavier and more accurate ones produced by Joseph Manton and his contemporaries. The answer lies in several different directions. First it was natural for a client to judge a pistol by its accuracy. Though the real need was to take a fast shot to hit a target the size of a small pillow case, as the weight of both pistols would be the same, it was entirely understandable that the client would choose one which could hit a folded handkerchief if he was offered it. Secondly, though the trade was small, the market for top-grade duellers was smaller still, so many alterations were merely sales puffs. Finally where one's life was at stake any improvement, real or imagined, was welcome.

This state of affairs among very rich buyers may have led to some wasted money. It also added an element of competition and urgency, which in its turn led to real improvements to the flintlock. Locks were speeded up, made to perform more efficiently and, above all, more reliably. The premium on reliability was immense, and the gun trade led by Joseph Manton was ever active in its pursuit. With practicing at targets no longer being regarded as cheating (except immediately before a duel) heavier barrels were adopted. Half-stocks were introduced about 1795, so giving some compensation for the increased barrel weight. In Ireland though the heavy barrels were adopted, they were shorter and not so heavy.

The semi-waterproof lock of the 1790s was eventually succeeded by the waterproof pan about 1795. John Manton's inventions in the last days of the flintlock produced a lock which was very nearly as efficient as its percussion successor. By getting the spark into the powder by the shortest route possible the lock speed had been increased to its maximum. All these refinements appear on both sporting guns and duelling pistols, some, such as the final versions of his pans and frizzens, coming after the percussion system was well established.

There is a tremendous interrelation between correct loading procedures and accuracy in any form of shooting. In the case of the muzzle-loading pistol, this is especially true, and it did not fail to escape the notice of our 18th century ancestors.

The quality of powder used made a big difference, for coarse powder did not facilitate accurate measuring. The early pistols were loaded direct from the flask, but by Wogdon's time a measure on the end of a rod carried an exactly measured charge. The rod was held vertically, and the inverted pistol lowered upon it. The pistol and rod were then reversed and the loading process continued as normal.

As powders improved, charges became lighter. The ball was contained in either a waxed linen or a paper patch, thus obtaining a tight fit and a good grip into the rifling (if any). How far the reduction of charges became possible through these improvements, or how much mere experience showed that a light charge gave the best results is hard to say. Whatever the reason, this is certainly what happened. A comparison between the nozzle of the flask of the Wogdon pair illustrated, and that of the pair of percussion Purdeys gives graphic illustration of this point.

Joseph Manton was largely responsible for the introduction of very

which was a survival of this feature. Wogdon, who had been a great exponent of the slab-sided butt, abandoned it before Manton did, so he must have believed that he could control the line by other means. Twigg and Bass in their short partnership (1788-1790) kept the flat sides but checkered them all over. Only Mortimer made a complete transformation from "slab sides" to "walking stick handle" in a minimum of time. Egg had gone the same route even earlier.

Joseph Manton's stocks somehow seem "obvious." His was the simplicity of Twigg, of Wogdon, and all the really great makers. In his stocks, as in his lightly adorned locks, this made his great workmanship look effortless. It was not, though it seemed to

be. The change from fullstock to halfstock in about 1795 was a fundamental one. It not only lightened the pistols but improved balance. At the same time the way was opened for the ultimate target/duelling stock which had no provision for a ramrod. Such pistols were pioneered by James Purdey in the 1820s, but later the shape was generally adopted. Eventually it became the basis of the design which was adopted on the continent.

Earlier, however, one of the changes which altered the appearance of the duelling pistol most was the introduction of the saw handle stock. First seen in about 1805, these represented the ultimate in fit, and were the ancestors of the orthopedic grips of today. As the name implies,

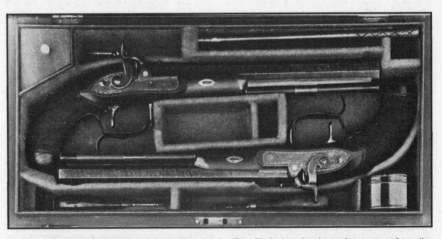

This duelling pistol by Forsyth & Co. was made for The Earl of Fife about 1823. It has sliding primer ignition. Photo courtesy W. Keith Neal.

heavy barrels. At the same time, however, he avoided ridiculous lengths and weights. This was not always the case. The marks of Joseph Manton's work were simplicity and efficiency. Overlong barrels would have impaired efficiency. He never fell into this trap though lesser makers did. The cult of the target pistol, which I have long suspected to be *largely* interchangeable with the duelling pistol, aggravated this difficulty in the 1800s, though makers such as Purdey and Lang saw the trap and gradually led the fashion away from it.

Apart from the basic need to point properly, and the foibles of the different styles of checkering adopted by the various makers, there seems to have been little about the butt (or handles as they were then called) which really went to the essence of the duelling pistol. The two exceptions to this are slab-sided grips in the early days and the saw handle, of which more later, near the end.

The slab-sided butt must, I always think, have been a great assistance in getting the pistol to fit its owner in terms of line. John Manton kept the style, in all grades of his pistols, much later than other makers. Even in about 1800, there was still a flat strip on the side of the butt of his pistols

Comparing these Egg percussion duellers to the Egg flintlock pair, shows how, apart from the ignition system, the pistols hardly changed. The flint pair has the earlier type of safety, while the percussion has a standard bolt.

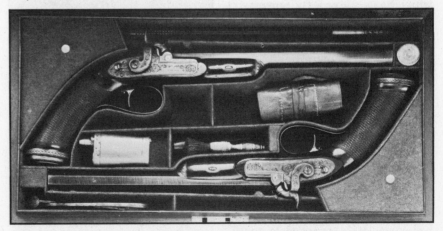

This pair of pistols by Purdey was made about 1826. They are heavily rifled, and so may have been target pistols. Note the powder measure under the barrel of the lower pistol. That small nozzle threw a small charge. In later years rifled pistols *were* used for duels, as they always would have been where no others were available.

the grip not only extended under the heel of the hand, but also back over the web. The result was a greatly improved fit for the owner of the pistol. On the other hand an opponent, who could have held an ordinary duelling pistol might well have been unable to get his hand into the grip. W.H. Mortimer was a great exponent of such pistols, many of which have the large bores which he so favored.

It was with such a pistol made by Tatham and Egg that Mr. Best shot Lord Camelford. The style was more popular in Ireland than England, where 9-inch rather than 10-inch barrels were favored, but in due course was superseded by Purdey's new style of pistol. The well-made saw handle incorporated the qualities of good pointing to an even greater degree than the early pistols. The pointing was, however, harder to produce in them because of the tighter fit needed to make this style of pistol effective. In Ireland sawbacks continued to be made well into the 1830s. The famous Rigby of Dublin produced many in both flint and percussion as did Cavanagh.

Though the discovery of the percussion ignition represented the biggest improvement in firearms of them all, surprisingly it was not widely used by duellists until a very late stage. Early percussion locks are, for the most part, found on sporting guns and sometimes pocket or holster pistols, but seldom duelling pistols. The full story of the evolution of percussion ignition can be read in Neal and Back's *Forsyth and Co Patent Gunmakers.* Suffice it to say that the tables of surviving weapons in that book confirm, not only that Forsyth made few duelling pistols, but that they represent only a small proportion of his output which has survived. By courtesy of Mr. Neal, I illustrate the Earl of Fife's Forsyth duelling pistol.

Why this was the case is hard to say. The early percussion arms, pistols or sporting guns, were only reliable when they received proper care and cleaning. They did not always get this with the results that there were many misfires and occasional burst locks. The rest of the trade were only too ready to belittle the Rev. Dr. Forsyth's invention—though many of them were equally willing to try to infringe his patents—and this can have done little to improve the public's view of the subject. Joseph Manton had immediately perceived its significance and made repeated efforts to evade the patent. Patch locks, pellet locks, pill locks and tube locks all

flowed from his inventive mind. All were contraventions or near contraventions of the Forsyth patent, but, as reference to the appropriate table in *The Mantons: Gunmakers* (by the same authors) will bear out, these inventions were not widely supported as far as duellists were concerned. Many flintlock duelling pistols existed; and it was not until it was abundantly clear that the system was a great deal better than flint ignition that the duellist was prepared to fight with its successor.

The merits which percussion held over flintlock were greater speed of ignition and, in its final form, greater reliability than flint, particularly in wet conditions. Though these merits were accepted in the end, there was nothing about its introduction which really changed anything about the duel. Apart from the ignition the pistols were identical. If there was a difference, it was that they were marginally more deadly, (because they shot faster and more easily); but as we have seen in the vast majority of instances, all duelling pistols were far more accurate than was necessary anyway.

Another similar "improvement" was the introduction of "secret rifling." Ordinary rifling was prohibited under the rules—though Lord Cardigan used a rifled pistol and was acquitted of malpractice because "He most probably imagined when he brought those pistols to the field with him, that one of them would be directed against his own person." (Lord Cardigan's Case p.18) Secret rifling was—of its nature—trying to steal a march on an opponent. It came in two

Author Ward duels himself, according to the Code UIT, and is shown here at Bisley, ca. 1985, taking his best shots with a 32-caliber FAS, uncased.

kinds. Either the pistol was rifled from the breech but the rifling stopped well away from the muzzle, or it was "hair" rifling made with very fine lines. Either form was invisible from the muzzle. Who invented it is not (understandably?) revealed. Both Manton brothers used it. Though they would have said the customer's word was law, this is surprising in reputedly honorable men. Whatever the position of the gunsmith, that of the duellist was clear. It was *cheating*, as much as the wearing of a cuirass (early body armour) would have been.

By the time percussion duelling pistols were eventually accepted in about 1825 the end of the British duelling was in sight. Though young bloods still fought one another, there was a strong anti-duelling movement. The law had always been clear: to kill in a duel was murder, whether the duel was fairly conducted or not. More pressure came for the law's strict enforcement. Gradually people refused to duel. Captain Ross, without doubt one of the finest pistol shots of all time, was one of these.

Though duelling pistols by British makers were shown at the Great Exhibition in 1851, these can have been little different to those made in the 1830s. Target pistols were being made—and doubtless where duels were fought they would have been brought into service. The inventiveness and above all the demand which had brought the British duelling pistol to the unrivaled hegemony of Europe had deserted it. Paris, with makers such as Le Page and Gastinne Renette; and Prague with Lebeda, had taken over.

The pistol as the primary weapon of the duel had lasted less than 100 years in Britain. The existence of this specialized form of shooting caused the production of an equally specialized, highly accurate, pistol, which in its turn evolved into the free pistol of Olympic shooting. During the period of development a gun not dissimilar to a horse pistol acquired such precision it could drive nails at the 12 yards duelling distance. Such was the achievement of the gunmakers: some made fortunes. Many duellists died; but collectively their story is what gives fascination to the essence of the dueller.   ●

My illustrations, except where specifically acknowledged, come from private collections, the owners of which, in these unhappy times, prefer to remain anonymous. I thank them for their help.
                              Wilfrid Ward

by JIM THOMPSON

The Radom . . .

. . . toughest 9mm ever.

An early war Radom can often outshoot new 9s, and will always out-tough them.

THE LOCALS all called him "Dynamite Dave." His idea of a starting point reload was where the reloading manuals left off. He was always bemoaning the lack of denser propellants . . . read that: he was upset that nitroglycerine leaked out of his brass, and that there were no nuclear powders. He was the only man I ever saw open up a Ruger Blackhawk, peeling the cylinder and sending the top strap to some other dimension.

Dave's particular passion was developing what he called "load limits" for automatics. That meant destroying them as rapidly as possible. I sold him my Smith & Wesson Model 39 when the constant jams became a chronic annoyance. I even lost money. Two weeks of Dave's handloads reduced that jinxed pistol to a collection of fractured and distorted parts.

The next gun I passed on to Dave, way back in 1970, was a splendid prewar Polish Radom, a pistol he'd never heard of before. So far—as this is written, 15 years later—that venerable Polish classic is still intact and working in those same very badly scarred hands. Perhaps Dave will find a way to polish off this pistol, too, as he has so many others; but the overload required may be sufficient to send both him and the pistol to that last, great reloading bench in the sky.

To those who've been fortunate enough to own Radoms in good shape, their toughness is legend. Yet, it's a pretty safe bet that most American shooters never even heard of the gun.

Born as the result of Polish rearmament policy in the '20s, the Vis Model 35 was one of the last sidearms hatched by practitioners of the ancient and, then, still honorable cavalry mentality. The pistol basically combines a Browning Hi-Power slide with Colt M.1911 frame. There's a grip safety, a firing pin-retracting hammer drop, the half-cock, and no other safety.

The hammer drop and even the takedown lever, located where a 1911 safety would normally be, are all located where the right thumb can reach them. A horseman, after all, has to handle the reins with his left hand. All Radoms, even the crude, rough pistols the Nazis had finished by Steyr in Austria, have lanyard loops. A cavalryman cannot drop his pistol.

The Poles had access to Fabrique Nationale technology, yet apparently rejected double-row magazines as used in the Hi-Power. All this went to make a heavy (37-38 ounces) long-but-thin-profiled service pistol whose strong points were sturdiness and reliability. In terms of gross bulk, the Radom is the largest service 9mm pistol ever designed.

The Nazis were sufficiently impressed to place the Radom into German service as the P.35(p) and to reinstitute its manufacture at Radom arsenal almost immediately. Most of the captured Radoms I've seen which could be traced or whose captures were witnessed seem to have been taken from paratrooper or Waffen S.S. officers, and these captures include quite a number of very high quality pre-war guns.

Radom pistols fall into four basic groups, the eldest invariably being the best:

First, we have 1935-'39 "eagles"—always have an eagle on user left side of slide, always display complete set of Polish proofs, always have shoulder stock slot in mainspring housing, and are of superb fit, finish and quality. These guns have individually fitted barrels of "national match" style, and are tight, solid, and durable. Steels appear to be high chrome and vanadium content ordnance steels; heat treated in the area of 38-42 on the Rockwell C scale. Barrels run softer, 28-32, and are numbered to match the guns, unless they are later replacements.

Second are 1939-early '41—units made from finished Polish parts, sometimes with the stock slot, mostly without. These all have the takedown at frame rear, are fairly well-fitted, parts are properly heat-treated and finished at about the level of a modern commercial pistol. Some bear traces of the Polish eagle, and a very few have complete sets of Nazi and Polish proofs. These are solid guns, but barrels are not fitted as securely as pre-

The shrouded, round Radom hammer offers most of the advantages of a "bobbed" hammer, yet still allows thumb cocking. It is unlikely to snag on anything or get in the way, cannot cut the thumb web, but still can be reached in a hurry.

The controls of the Radom are all located in cavalry positions for the right thumb. Slide stop and magazine release are like the Model 1911; that's the hammer drop just below the sight, and the takedown is just below and behind the drop lever, on the frame.

What appears to be a safety on the Radom is, in fact, the takedown lever, which is shown here in its detent in the slide, ready to disassemble. The hammer drop is directly above the takedown lever in this picture.

war pistols, so they are not quite as accurate.

The third range—mid '41-early '43—some made from Polish parts, some new-made parts, always with very rough black-finished magazines which appear painted (some are), loose-fitting barrels, but almost identical with group two except for general deterioration in fit and quality. Hardness levels of major parts run 18-25 on the Rockwell C scale, indicating no heat treating at all. Most obvious presence of tool marks/sloppy finish on recess in slide below barrel ferrule, behind recoil guide rod. Never has stock slot in mainspring housing.

And then fourth are mid-'43/mid-'44. These are the Nazi "last gasp" units, parts made mostly by slave labor, much of it in the Warsaw ghetto on a subcontract basis. These mostly lack the takedown lever. No heat treating of any parts. Very sloppy fit. Recoil spring assemblies often misaligned, some observers think intentionally sabotaged. Always show Steyr assembly/inspection "WA 77." There seems to be a small group of Radoms assembled either by the Russians or by the Polish insurgents or interim government which use the same parts, but show slightly better fit and finish.

While all issue Radoms are in 9mm, there were prototypes, one of which still exists in Scandinavia, in 30 Luger. Rumors persist of prototypes in 38 ACP/9mm Steyr and 45 ACP. The "Pat. Nr. 15567" on the slide tends to suggest intended commercial sales and export. The shoulder stock appears to have never been actually produced, though there must have been a prototype. It's likely a Radom in 45 would have been popular in the U.S., and were the gun made now, it would likely be popular in its original 9mm Parabellum caliber.

The partially submerged round hammer gives most of the advantages of a "bobbed" hammer, but can still be easily thumb-cocked. The pistol's inherent accuracy is such that, recently, with a group of I.P.S.C. shooters, an old, worn-out Radom from "group four," whose bore looked like old tracks on a muddy road, shot near the middle of the pack. "The pack" was a bunch of very expensive custom 45s and 38 Supers from America's finest pistolsmiths.

A lot of this, on the speed-shooting course, had to do with handling. The tapered grip is very comfortable, and recoil is dampened both by the grip and by the massive double recoil spring. A lot of it also has to do with the 8.81mm bore on that old war horse, tight by wartime standards, and about .002-in. tighter than most 9s.

The old pistol also shot quite well from improvised rests, which was absolutely amazing to me, turning in about 2-inch groups at 25 yards. Later, I shot a pre-war pistol, with its original but burned-out barrel and with an Ordnance Improvement match-grade Radom barrel which John Student fitted to the gun. Groups were even tighter with the original barrel and went to genuine match quality with the new stainless tube fitted. It seems the Radom's long ferrule to barrel contact area, extraordinarily heavy springs, and secure lockup make for rather exceptional stability. Even on junkers, the bores run tight, and the basic system is good enough that even relative dogs shoot fairly well.

Passed around to about 20 Government Model buffs, they all said that my 9mm Commander "felt better" than the Radom. They all shot better with the Radom, despite its fairly miserable 1930s-style V-notch tiny sights. They also shot it faster.

None of this really surprises anyone who knows the pistol's pedigree. It's a cross between features of the U.S. Model 1911 and the Browning Hi-Power, prepared with consultation from Fabrique Nationale on the lock

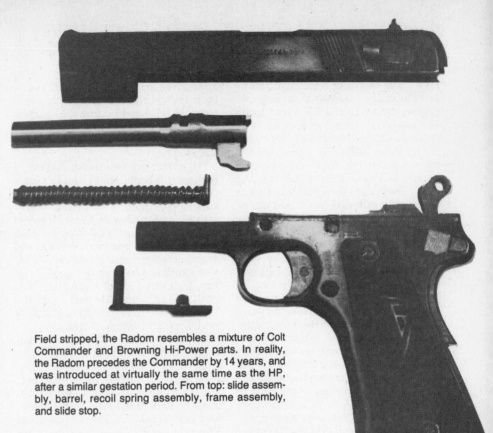

Field stripped, the Radom resembles a mixture of Colt Commander and Browning Hi-Power parts. In reality, the Radom precedes the Commander by 14 years, and was introduced at virtually the same time as the HP, after a similar gestation period. From top: slide assembly, barrel, recoil spring assembly, frame assembly, and slide stop.

The Radom lends itself to currently popular two-hand holds; its original purpose was one-handed fire from horseback. The ergonomics are Polish and no joke—the gun feels good.

system, similar to the P35 Browning, but simpler. The ergonomics seem to be original with the Poles, and designers Wilneiwcyc and Skrzypinski also appear to be responsible for the sturdy recoil system, with its beefy double springs and guide rod, whose design is remarkably similar to some 1970s aftermarket independent items for the Government Model Colt. The Poles seem to have distrusted the topside slide/barrel lock, and made the springs sufficiently strong to restrain the slide even if some breakage or misalignment caused the locks to fail to engage. It's hard to imagine such a malfunction—and if the barrel failed to lock to the slide, timing, ejection, and feeding would probably be seriously compromised. But the cammed bottom lug would still partially function, and the purpose of the comparatively powerful spring setup seems to be to allow fairly safe blowback operation. I've heard one collector, Howard Tokarsky, suggest that an alternative spring to the 22-pound units (when new) was issued, or was planned. But no one can say for sure.

The Poles definitely distrusted the barrel bushing, link and pin, and spring/plunger assemblies on the Colt. They wanted a pistol easier to strip, without self-propelled parts. Yet, they retained almost all the frame-based features of the Colt—the stirrup trigger, slide stop position (albeit without the plunger tube—the Poles used the recoil spring and bottom strut to hold the slide stop in place), separable grip safety and mainspring housing. Rejected were those Hi-Power features which complicate things—the hinged trigger and magazine disconnector, in particular. And the double-row magazine, which also fattens the grip. The Radom magazine holds only eight rounds.

Amazingly to me, considering the tension of the recoil system, I've never encountered a Radom that wouldn't digest anything from PMC or U.S. 9mm, which is fairly soft, to super-hot IMI-Samson ammo marked "carbine" and actually intended for use in the UZI. Nor, unlike a lot of other commercial 9s I've shot, does the pistol's inertia-type firing pin have any difficulty with hard military primers. Wartime guns, though, especially the later ones, should have their feed ramps polished if a user intends to shoot any jacketed hollow points or flat-nosed bullet configurations. Pre-war guns or those with new commercial barrels generally have no such worries, though Radom magazines are quite another matter.

A lot of original Radom magazines appear to have been intentionally sabotaged. Ground-through followers, erratic crimp marks on feed lips, tweaked springs, and serious dents are far more common than even 40 years' use could account for. After 1942, the magazines seem to have been made in the Warsaw ghetto. Apparently, the slave laborers knew what their masters had in mind, and in their small way, wished to return the favor.

I've had excellent luck with R.H.L. magazines, ordered from R.H.L., P.O. Box 650323, Miami, FL 33165. They're not as elegant as the many-component, custom-looking pre-war Radom magazines, but they work, and they're not expensive.

Many surplus dealers stock some Radom parts.

Ordnance Improvement, P.O. Box 3356, Northridge, CA 91323, sells both tight drop-in and slightly oversized (in hood and bottom lug) barrels of new manufacture in 4-16 stainless. I ought to know. I'm the President of the company.

On about my twentieth Radom, I became infuriated that I couldn't get a replacement barrel for an otherwise superb specimen. I contacted nearly every barrel maker in America to get one made. Finally, I found a machine shop with barrel experience and asked how much one would cost. After near cardiac arrest at the quoted figure, I inquired about quantities, and with a fond "what the hell," had the barrels made in two configurations. It really wasn't that much more.

It was an interesting process which taught me much about the gun. The first thing I found out was that the Nazi original barrels were little better than junk, about twenty-thousandths undersized all over the place, and just barely capable of function. The pre-war Polish units were a bit soft, but brilliantly cut and precisely finished and detail-fitted to individual guns. Added to that, the ferrules where the barrels peek through the slide vary in size about $\frac{1}{16}$th of an inch. So we built a tube way better than the German-supervised units, yet not as massive as the oversized pre-war Polish ones. And all because I wanted one barrel for one gun. If I'd opted for a specification similar to the pre-war Polish units, whatever the barrel cost, a consumer would have to add $50.00 to $90.00 to have a custom 'smith fit an $87.50 barrel.

Handling the Radom is basic Browning stuff. One merely has to remind oneself that that lever isn't a safety, and otherwise in shooting follow standard Model 1911 procedure.

Field stripping is way simpler than the Government Model. Making sure that the gun is unloaded and magazine removed, draw the slide back so that the notch just below and in front of the firing pin retard hammer drop can engage the claw of the takedown lever. Push the takedown lever up. The slide stop may be pulled or pushed from the right side for removal; since the recoil spring bears against the stop, a slight tug forward on the guide rod will make this easier. Once the slide stop is removed, return the takedown lever to its "down" position and draw the slide forward and off the frame. The recoil spring assem-

bly can then be wiggled from its place below the barrel, intact. There's nothing here to stick in your forehead, unless you try to disassemble the recoil spring system. If so, watch out for the pin holding the small tube. It tends to get lost. It's also a good idea to do that work with the spring assembly in a vise. The barrel can be plucked from the slide with a tug on the strut.

Detail stripping is very much like the 1911, but simpler, because there is no safety. The firing pin stop forms a right angle, and is massive compared to the Colt unit. They often require considerable strength to remove. Part of it is tucked under the firing pin. Some odds and ends of Colt parts will fit. Grip screws and bushings and mainsprings, for example, fit directly, and some pins and springs can be adapted without undue work. There is very little difference in the rear sight dovetail of a Radom and a Government model, and aside from the tiny, checkered "rib"—the word "line" seems more appropriate—atop the slide, the top side of the gun is very "Coltish," and even front sights could be easily modified to fit.

A word of caution is in order to the shooter. A pre-war specimen, or even an exceptional wartime gun with all matching parts, should not be modified in any way which cannot be more or less instantly reversed. These guns are valuable, especially "eagle" specimens, which can fetch over $500 in sound condition.

At this writing, I've begun the slow assembly of parts for a custom "pin gun" based on the Radom. This will be a massive, compensated 9mm "major" unit, and I'll have to have rough wartime parts heat-treated, then hard-chromed. It'll look very much like one of Jim Boland's or Jimmy Clark's compensated *Star Wars* pistols, only it'll be more comfortable to me than anything Colt began. Sure, the newest Radom is now over 40 years old, but quality commercial guns are just beginning to equal it for comfort and balance.

It's been 20 years now since one of my old customers and friends, Bob Benson, now of Des Moines, ordered a Radom from me, which I acquired from Interarms. I thought he was crazy. Who, after all, shoots—who, indeed, is ever even *seen*—with, of all things, a Polish pistol? I had promised to testfire it and the other pistols ordered for him. This I approached with considerable trepidation, not to mention perspiration. However, once begun, this testfiring continued for some time. It's still going on, in fact. ●

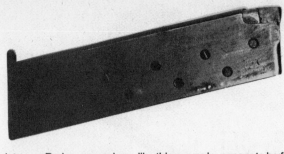

Many late-war Radom magazines, like this example, appear to be finished with black paint. Many also show signs of sabotage, like this one. Spring has an internal crimp, the follower is cut so thin the spring has come through it, and a big dent appears to have been made with a punch. It still works.

The Radom recoil spring guide rod is intended to stabilize the slide's travel, much like the units currently in vogue on expensive pistolsmithed match 45s. This captive unit is very robust, and seldom distorts, even the rough late-war units.

Thompson's Ordnance Improvement M35 Radom barrel is shown for size comparison next to, from top, a 7-in. 38 Super, 38 Super 6-in. low tang, and a 7-in. 45 Pin Gun Special. It is fundamentally simpler in design than most other Browning barrels, yet some specs are very demanding.

The author shown working on a Model 1911 Colt, a gun which—together with the Browning Hi-Power—taught him much about the even more rugged Radom.

A reasonably good-looking Radom like this one often shows *no* signs of having ever been heat-treated. Major assemblies here ran as soft as 18 on the Rockwell "C" scale. Good Eagle parts seldom dip below 35, and major moving parts run 40-44 on most Polish-built and assembled guns. Already-refinished parts guns, with cheap fake grips, are the only Radoms to modify. The others, especially with matched numbers, are too valuable as collector's guns.

Cal. 50

by KONRAD F. SCHREIER, JR.

The Brophy super sniper built on the Russian PTRD action. This Brophy rifle was 69.5 inches long and weighed 45 pounds. (From U.S. Army report photo *ca*. 1955)

SUPER SNIPERS

The cal. 50 Brophy experimental super sniper rifle in action in the Korean War, then Capt. Brophy at the controls. This experimental super sniper rifle is the only one ever combat tested and it was effective. (Photo courtesy LtC Brophy)

SNIPER rifles in today's U.S. Army and Marine Corps are proven accurate to 1,000 meters—1,100 yards—and more. They were effective at even longer ranges in combat in Viet Nam. Military riflemen quite properly want super sniper rifles with doubled (and more) range, and these are under current development.

But the super sniper rifle is not a new idea. Neither is the 50-caliber Browning ammunition being fired in some guns under current development. In fact, we have 70 years of history here.

It all began way back in the middle of World War I. The British and French introduced tanks, and the Germans had to find a way to fight them. To do this the Germans invented antitank guns, and one such was the 13mm T-Gewehr—"Tank Abwehr Gewehr" or antitank rifle. It was first fired against British tanks on the Somme in July, 1918, and knocked some of the British mechanical monsters out of action.

The T-Gewehr was a huge single-shot version of the standard German Mauser infantry rifle. Its 13mm—52-caliber—cartridge was 5.5 inches long and fired 805-grain bullets at a muzzle velocity of 2,440 feet per second (fps). The rifle was 67 inches long—as long as an average man is tall. It weighed 37.5 pounds, or about as much as a light machine gun of the time. It punched holes through the ½-inch armor of early tanks, and it was accurate.

The T-Gewehr was not a very successful weapon for several reasons. The thing had an incredible kick—some 80 foot pounds of recoil. For comparison, the 30-06 Springfield only offers 20 pounds or so. And the T-Gewehr had nothing to protect the shooter. Most German soldiers were terrified of the huge rifle once they saw it fired. I, among many people, have refused offers to fire it.

The 50 Browning cartridge is a virtual scale-up of the 30-06. The two are among the select few "most successful cartridge cases."

Although the Germans observed the T-Gewehr's accuracy and suggested it for sniping, the rifle's sights were very coarse and only calibrated to 500 meters. After the war the German military rated the rifle a failure, but it led to another development in the U.S.A.

The U.S. Army had carefully observed weapons development in World War I, and in early 1918 it decided it needed a new heavy machine gun firing a very high-power cartridge in about a ½-inch bore size. When the T-Gewehr became known, it led the U.S. Army to develop its new super-heavy machine gun with a 50-caliber cartridge firing at about 2,600 fps giving a range of some 6,000 or so yards—3.4 miles. The great John M. Browning and Colt developed the machine gun for use as a dual-purpose ground and anti-aircraft machine gun. The Browning 50 was adopted by the U.S. Armed Forces in 1921, and first issued in 1922.

Although the 50 Browning machine gun was pretty well perfected in 1921, its ammunition was not. And the Army, which handled the ammunition development, needed a single shot test gun on which to mount a machine gun barrel. Among captured German ordnance from World War I, the U.S. Army found just the thing: the T-Gewehr. It had been the Mauser Antitank Rifle; now it was the "caliber 50 Test Rifle, Mauser Action."

That test rifle worked so well that it is still in use. Like most ammunition test guns, it is fired from a machine rest, and not the shoulder, but when it was first adopted it sometimes was fired from the shoulder. And from the first use about 1920, people have frequently observed that it can be extremely accurate at very long ranges with some ammunition.

From the early days, it has shot many lots of 50 Browning ammunition into an 8-in. circle at 600 yards, and that's excellent. Maj. Gen. Julian S. Hatcher, who was in on the development, suggested it could make a great sniper caliber, as did others. Unfortunately the U.S. Army had to put its very limited development funds into other projects and sniper rifles were not developed.

However, work on the machine gun and its ammunition *was* given priority, and a set of new, improved models was adopted in 1932. One was the 45-in. barrel water-cooled model now no longer used, and another was the 36-in. barrel aircraft model which is still in service. And the most important was the 45-in. barrel M2-HB which is not only still in use, but also still in

A mid-1930s 50 Browning M2-HB with the periscopic long-range telescopic sight. In this version, which author has fired, the machine gun could be used to snipe at ranges up to 2,000 yards. (U.S. Army photo—*ca.* 1935)

The World War I German 13.2mm Mauser "T-Gewehr" antitank rifle, 52-caliber monster, was 67 inches long, weighed 37.5 pounds, and scared its own shooters. But it worked.

This is one of the many attempts to make a Browning machine gun into a sniper. The result is a semi-automatic weighing about 107 pounds and over 69 inches long, too big and clumsy. (U.S. Army photo *ca.* 1948)

manufacture.

The M2-HB 50 could fire full or semi-automatic, and it had a 2,000-yard optical periscope sight. Firing the gun semi-automatic with the optical telescopic sight, it was a cinch to hit point targets at a 1,000-1,500 yards range. I have done it. At longer ranges—2,000 or so yards—it can hit any target which can be seen, but they must be large—the size of a pick-up truck or so. Unfortunately, that telescopic sight hasn't been standard issue since the end of the Korean War.

Ammunition for the 50 was perfected in 1940 and has changed little since. The bullets weigh around 700 grains, or 4½ times the weight of a standard 7.62-mm NATO rifle bullet. In a 36-in. barrel, the muzzle velocity is 2,800 feet per second; in a 45-in. it's 2,900 fps. That is hot. Production ammo must group in a 16-in. circle at 500 yards and in an 18-in. circle at 600 yards. That is far from gilt-edged, but most of the ammunition will shoot much better than the requirement. Most of it is fired in machine guns where pin-point accuracy isn't required, so this is perfectly acceptable. In fact, dispersion is an advantage in machine guns.

Of course the idea of a 50-caliber super sniper rifle occurred to the U.S. Army during World War II. What is more, the U.S. Army was procuring the British caliber 55 Boys Antitank Rifle from which a sniper rifle could be made. This Canadian-made weapon was closely related to the World War I Mauser antitank rifle, but much improved. It was a 64-in. long bolt action on a bipod mount. Unlike the Mauser, it had a recoil system, muzzle brake and butt padding to ease its recoil. It fired a 930-grain bullet at a whopping 3,100 fps, but the load was never developed to give very good accuracy. And, of course, the rifle had the kick of an enraged mule.

A number of attempts were made in War Two at converting the Boys into a U.S. Army super sniper rifle by re-barreling and adding a telescopic sight. Most of these were unofficially made and tested, and it is said some of them showed fine accuracy out to 1,500 and 2,000 yards. There is no record of them having been fired in combat, and they were never considered for adoption—the U.S. Army was having too much trouble getting its 30-06 sniper rifles working right.

When the usefulness of good sniper rifles was demonstrated in the Korean War, the super sniper naturally came up again. One idea was to make one out of a Browning M2-HB machine gun by adding a telescope sight, bipod, butt rest, padded butt and pistol grip trigger. This resulted in an impractical 69-in. long, 110-pound rifle which a man could fire, but not carry into action. And during the Korean War, one U.S. Army Ordnance officer who was an expert rifleman worked on sniper rifles to such good effect in combat that he was twice decorated for it. He was Capt., later Lt. Col., William S. Brophy, now the Senior Technical Manager of Marlin Firearms and a distinguished writer of arms history.

Brophy began using his own 30-06 target rifle, mounting a telescopic sight. While he could hit hostile targets up to 1,000 yards, beyond that range he was unable to do much to them. But Capt. Brophy had a better idea.

Brophy took a captured Russian 14.5mm PTRD antitank rifle and converted it into a 50-caliber super sniper rifle. To the bolt-action of the PTRD, he adapted a 45-in. Browning M2-HB machine-gun barrel, and on it he mounted a 20x scope sight. The gun had a bipod support, butt support, and a butt pad.

Brophy proved in combat that this experimental super sniper rifle could consistently hit targets out beyond 1,000 yards. The official U.S. Army reports state they were "individual targets," which means hostile individuals. There is another challenge in using a sniper rifle at these extremely long ranges. The military term is "time of flight"—the time it takes the bullet to reach the target. For 50-caliber ammunition at 2,000 yards, it is about 3.75 seconds. In that time, a man walking at a normal pace can cover 15 to 20 feet.

On returning to the United States, now-Major Brophy was authorized to run a series of sniper rifle tests, and he issued his final report on this in 1955. In these well-done tests, Brophy compared his experimental super sniper rifle with the 30-06 sniper rifles the Army was then issuing. The Brophy rifle got 23 out of 50 hits at 1,000 yards, while the best 30-06 got only 6 out of 50. His rifle was good, but not good enough, and Brophy knew the reason.

The ammunition fired in Brophy's tests was standard issue 50-caliber M2 Ball, loaded for machine gun use. There is good reason to believe the Brophy rifle was capable of much better accuracy than the ammunition it fired.

Maj. Brophy's 1955 report concludes: "It is recommended that consideration be given to development of a cartridge-rifle-telescopic sight combination having properties minimizing the effect of atmospheric variation and errors in sighting and range estimation, but having characteristics suitable for use as a shoulder weapon of practical dimensions." And "Generally, neither the caliber 50 nor the caliber 30 cartridges and none of the weapons and telescopes tested possess all the characteristics desired for use in a sniper's weapons."

Although Brophy did an excellent job, and nobody could have summed up the situation better, when he left the Army his ideas for a super sniper rifle pretty well fell off the table.

During Viet Nam, the U.S. Army did a lot of work on sniper rifles firing 7.62mm NATO ammunition of what is called "match target grade"—ammunition made to have "gilt edge" accuracy. These perform out to 1,000 yards, and over 1,500 under ideal conditions, and they are current Army and Marine Corps issue.

The idea of the super sniper rifle has never really died, probably because a lot of people had heard of Brophy's combat experiences. Since 1980 or so, interest has revived, and there are a number of current commercial and experimental models including:

The Barrett Model 82, a short recoil-operated semi-automatic magazine-loaded rifle for the 50 MG. It is about 64 inches long and weighs about 35 pounds. It has a scope sight, a bipod mount, and its recoil is suppressed by its semi-automatic action, a muzzle brake and a padded butt. This appears to be a practical rifle, and it has shown accuracy to 2,000 yards and more.

Another is the Research Armament Industries Special Application Sniper Rifle, a much simpler single-shot bolt action. It is about 46 inches long and weighs around 30 pounds, and has a scope sight, bipod mount, padded butt and muzzle brake. It also appears to be a practical rifle with the desired long-range characteristics.

Other models include the Stroessner & Hunting Firearms caliber 50 Horstkamp rifle which looks like a modernized Mauser antitank rifle, and another rifle they have worked on with a single shot dropping block action like the old-time Sharps rifle. There is also the VMP Model T80E1 which is a "bull pup" with the action beside the shooter's face—a place where most riflemen don't like it to be.

All these experimental super sniper

A British "desert rat" shows how to pack a 55 Boys in 1942. The Boys actually defined the useful limits of size and weight for carrying a super sniper rifle in combat. (British Press Service photo *ca*. 1942)

A British soldier with a Boys in training in England about 1940. The British soldier appears to be a good sized man and a little too cheerful to have ever fired the hard-kicking gun. (British Press Service photo *ca*. 1940)

The Aimstar super sniper rifle, a simplified bolt-action single shot, 46 inches long, and about 30 pounds. The bolt is removed from the receiver for loading. (Photo courtesy Research Armament Industries, Inc.)

rifles are being offered for military and police use. They are all in the very expensive price range—$2,000.00 up to as much as $5,000.00 each. And they all face the same problem in the U.S. Armed Forces: the military have no serious requirement—no formally acknowledged desire—for a super sniper rifle.

Given that the idea of a super sniper rifle has merit, there remain problems to be overcome:

The primary one is the ammunition. First, it should be the U.S. Army standard caliber 50 which is used everyplace, and not a special caliber which could orphan the rifle in the supply line. And, while it *could* fire the standard rounds, it will need a special target load to get the best range and accuracy possible. Present 7.62-mm NATO rifle caliber match target ammunition is made for sniper rifle, and in the past, 30-06 National Match Grade ammunition was issued, so there is precedent.

Another factor which would help a super sniper rifle from being a complete logistic orphan and get the best possible performance out of it would be the use of selected 45-in. M2-HB Browning machine gun barrels. So much work has been done with the ammunition in this length barrel that it is the most efficient in the caliber. Selecting "match target" barrels from regular rifle barrel production has been done for over half a century, so there is reason to believe the same sort of thing could be done with machine gun barrels.

But probably the single most important factor is the man. The super sniper rifle must be a rifle a man can carry, handle, and shoot with relative ease, and even comfort. For that last, it will be necessary to control and suppress the rifle's recoil. A muzzle brake is not desirable. All muzzle brakes kick up clouds of dust in very visible and unmistakable "signatures."

Of course the scope sight will have to be something special—at least a 20x with super precise optics and mount, and rugged enough to take both the rifle's recoil and field service abuse. The sight should be of the ART—Adjusting Range Telescope—type now used on the 7.62mm NATO M21 and other sniper rifles.

The super sniper rifle concept should be encouraged. Marksmen are no longer winning battles, they say, but marksmen with such rifles as these could deny an opposing force easy travel over square miles of ground possibly more cheaply than any other infantry weapon. Maybe that's how to sell it. ●

The Barrett Model 82 super sniper rifle, one of the current experimental models. This is a short recoil-operated semi-automatic, weighing around 35 pounds and about 64 inches long, shown here in sniper mode. (Photo courtesy Barrett Firearms Mfg., Inc.)

The Barrett can be employed from a standard tripod for the Browning machine gun M2-HB. The tripod, while it fits the gun better to perform some static roles, is not an ideal sniper accessory. (Photo courtesy Barrett Firearms Mfg., Inc.)

The Mauser T-Gewehr with a cartridge in the action. This massive single shot is mechanically an enlarged version of the '98 Mauser.

This Boys antitank rifle's bolt is open; the hole on the top is for the magazine. Sniper modifications put the scope there.

The action of a Russian PTRD like that the Brophy rifles were built on. It is single shot, and loads through the slot in the top.

Solving the Problem of

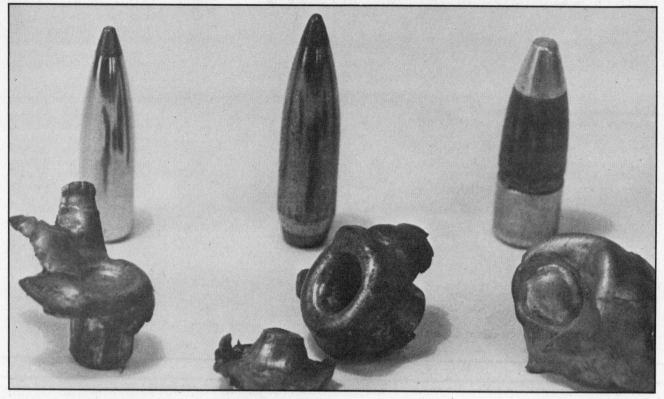

It's what gets inside that counts. The 100-gr. Nosler (left) took a facing buck in the shoulder knuckle, and still went through both lungs. The other two did not perform so well.

THE WESTERN RIFLE

It's not the terrain, nor even the cartridge—it's the targets.

by JOHN BARSNESS

AFTER school, the weeks before my first big game season were spent in two ways: listening attentively during my Wednesday night hunter safety class, and making a pest of myself down at the local sporting goods store. The first was required of anyone under 18 who wanted to hunt in Montana, but the flimsy excuse for the second was a Lee Loader I'd ordered for my sporterized 7.62mm Russian Moisin-Nagant. This was back in the mid-'60s when $10 Moisin-Nagants were a big item among those of us dependent on paper routes.

The loader didn't come in for a few weeks, so I'd walk down to the Powder Horn every afternoon, find out my Lee hadn't arrived, then hang out for an hour or so listening to gun talk. Back then most of Montana was still divided among 30-06, 270 and 30-30, but several new calibers had recently arrived, and one guy would be saying it was *obvious* that the 100-grain 243 was better than the 257 Roberts because 6mm bullets would have a higher ballistic coefficient in any given weight. Another guy said he "just couldn't feature" how anyone could claim the '06 was still an elk rifle when the new 7mm Remington Magnum sent a 175-grain bullet out faster than any '06 big game load. In between, a few quiet types would sneak in, grab a box of 30-40s or 348s and leave before anyone could engage them in any damnfool arguments.

In the 20 years since, I've gained some actual experience in the pursuit of pronghorn, mule deer and elk, the three game animals the Powder Horn Club constantly discussed, experience that's helped me realize that a lot of the talk down there was *just* talk, because everybody started with a given caliber and worked their argument from there. Two factors more important than caliber, I've found, are the animal and the bullet. Just as not all game animals are created equal, each caliber is limited by *what's actually available,* either in factory shells or handloads. Once we understand the bullets and the game, we can make a more realistic choice in cartridges.

The choice may still be a 30-06, but at least we'll know why.

We'll try it here, animal by animal:

Pronghorn

The first thing you'll notice is that antelope aren't shy about standing around in the open. The second is that they're not very big. The largest ever killed in Montana weighed 121 pounds field dressed, or about the size of a big whitetail doe. I've never taken one over 100 pounds and a trophy buck my wife shot two seasons ago barely broke 70 pounds, about what most full-grown pronghorn does will weigh.

Despite their size, they can be tough. A mature pronghorn has a heart the size of the heart in a 150-pound deer, and even with severe wounds they'll sometimes go amazing distances. I once watched a doe, hit in the diaphragm-liver area with a 165-grain 30-06 bullet, go ½-mile before the hunter caught up with her. He put another bullet through both lungs and the doe staggered and fell, then *got back up* and stood around for 15 seconds before going down for good. Jack O'Connor once wrote that he'd never seen a hoofed big game animal get up after falling from a solid lung hit, and I never had either until that 70-pound pronghorn doe did it.

The small size and the big heart

would seem to indicate an almost explosive bullet for pronghorn, one designed to expand on light resistance and tear up vascular tissue. That's why some hunters choose varmint loads like the 22-250, the 80-grain 243 and 87-grain 25-06. If put into a pronghorn's *ribs,* any of these kill spectacularly, but studies have also shown that the pronghorn's other bones are 8-10 times as strong, on a per-weight basis, as those of domestic cattle, which makes sense considering the stresses involved in running 60 miles per hour. I once watched a buck disappear on three legs after an 87-grain 25-06 varmint load hit him in his "fragile" shoulder.

Even the lightest big game bullets in any caliber aren't always the most effective on pronghorn, primarily because of wind drift. With most modern pronghorn calibers, wind can be an even bigger problem than trajectory. Range is pretty easy to estimate if you use a scope with a duplex reticle; for years I've used a 6x Bushnell that's just about perfect because the distance from the intersection of the crosshairs to the point of the thicker part of the reticle subtends 15 inches at 250 yards, and that is about what a pronghorn measures from brisket to back. If a pronghorn fits in that space I know it's within range of about any high-velocity cartridge using spitzer

bullets. With the near-standard 3-inch-high sighting at 100 yards, a variety of cartridges from the 6mms on up to the 200s will take pronghorn nicely out to 350 yards or more, as long as the load is accurate and the wind isn't blowing too hard.

Wind is harder to judge than range, and there's a big difference in how well some loads hold up in the stiff breezes that blow around Casper, Wyoming. The accompanying chart indicates that the theoretic ideal is a medium magnum shooting the heaviest spitzer available at 3000 fps or more. But over the years I've found that even less than "ideal" calibers can be better pronghorn tools than some of the traditional choices like the 130-grain 270. The 30-06, loaded with the 200-grain Nosler at 2700 fps, is better in the wind than the 243 or 270 or several other "flat" calibers, and the big bullet also kills pronghorn cleanly at extended ranges, partly because the front portion of the jacket is so thin, and partly because a 30-caliber is bigger than a 6mm or 270 in the first place. I know this not because of any theory but because I've shot pronghorn with all three calibers, and a variety of bullets between 100 and 200 grains, out past 200 yards.

If you must have the absolute flattest trajectory possible in your pronghorn rifle, however, please note that muzzle velocity is the biggest factor affecting trajectory of spitzer bullets out to 300 yards. Past 300 yards, high ballistic coefficient begins to make a difference, but even pronghorn are not often taken past that magic range. The 257 Roberts is lots more gun over the sage flats than the 243, for instance, because even though some 6mm bullets have higher numbers than most 100-grain 25s, you can get an extra 200 fps or more out of a 257, usually with less pressure. The 257 will still be ahead in trajectory, energy and wind-drift out at 500 yards, which is farther than you or I should ever shoot.

Mule Deer

The smallest mule deer, either buck or doe, are as large as the biggest pronghorn, and the biggest muley can be pretty damn big. My heaviest weighed 232 pounds after he'd hung in my garage for 5 days, maybe something over 340 when first killed, and that is a lot of deer. Try dragging one on dry ground or flinging it over a horse sometime.

Occasionally you'll have to take them at long range, but usually not; they'll hide in the thick stuff, but real-

Pronghorn are small but not really fragile; their bones are 8-10 times as strong as those of domestic cattle, and their cardio-vascular capacity would shame a marathoner. And then there are those near-constant pronghorn country winds.

ly prefer more open country than whitetails or even elk. I've never shot at one past 250-300 yards, even on the plains of Montana, and since they're so much bigger than pronghorns, they're that much easier to hit.

Aside from size, the biggest difference between mule deer and pronghorn is skin. Antelope have thin, almost papery hide, but mule deer skin is much thicker, and rubbery in texture. It's also thickest where you want to shoot them, across the neck, chest and spine. Over the years I've recovered more bullets from mule deer than pronghorn or elk, probably because pronghorn won't stop many bullets and all except one elk were taken with heavy Noslers. Two of the bullets particularly interested me, because they came apart on the *skin;* I found the jackets right at the entrance hole while skinning out the carcasses. One was a 130-grain 270 boat-tail Sierra, the other a 105-grain Speer from a 243. Both had entered at an angle, came apart when they opened up, and plowed angling through the hide. A 40-grain piece of core from the 270 Sierra went into one lung and killed that deer, and the core of the 243 Speer broke the other's spine; I was lucky in each case. I also have the jacket base of a 150-grain Silvertip that blew up completely on the shoulder knuckle of a buck 200 yards away, and this not from a 300 Magnum but an '06 factory load. I found the deer ½-mile further on and put another through his lungs; none of the first bullet got past his ribs.

At the other extreme are two 100-grain Noslers, examples of the classic mushroom, both pulled from mule deer. One is a Partition from a 257 that took a facing buck in the shoulder knuckle; the bullet continued through the chest, popped through the diaphragm, then slid between hide and belly muscle for a foot. The other is a 6mm Solid Base from a 243 that angled into a buck from the rear of the rib cage, going through both lungs and stopping in the far shoulder. Both weigh just over 60 grains now, or 50 percent more than what was left of that 130-grain 270 bullet.

Nosler doesn't make the same claims for the Solid Base as for the Partition, but I've used it a lot in the 243 and 30-06 and found it just as reliable as other "semi-controlled-expanding" bullets like the Hornady Interlock and Remington Core-Lokt. You have to shoot lengthwise through the spine, or hit both the shoulder and spine, to make any of the three come apart on deer, and none have come apart on the skin. On the other hand,

Mule deer does are the size of monster pronghorn bucks; big mule deer bucks can go 300 pounds. Penetration is important on mule deer.

almost all the Sierra boat-tails and lighter Silvertips I've dug out of deer have separated jacket from core to some extent. The heavier Speers are better than the lighter ones. All of which is why I'd rather hunt mule deer with a 100-grain Nosler or 130-grain Interlock than some of the others in 150-165-grains. It's not how much the bullet weighs in the chamber of your rifle, but how much gets inside the deer, that counts.

The real bone problem in shooting elk isn't the shoulder blade but the shoulder "knuckle," which is exactly what's facing you here on this bull if you try to place a bullet in his lungs. All except the rear third of the lungs is blocked by big bone.

Elk

Once again, young cow and bull elk are just a bit bigger than the largest mule deer. This past season I killed the smallest elk of my life, a 1½-year-old cow that went around 250-260 pounds field dressed. The cow's skinned quarters weighed just about the same as those of that big mule deer, but the elk's bones were perhaps 25 percent more massive. Mature bulls average twice as large, or even more.

Despite their mass, big elk are about 15 inches wide through the rib cage. Even a 243 or 257 will kill them

From left—270 Winchester, 7x57 Mauser, 7mm Remington Magnum, 308, 30-06 and 300 Winchester Magnum. All will do the job on elk—if you understand elk anatomy and use the right bullet.

dead if the bullet goes broadside into the ribs, and elk are such big targets that some hunters do this consistently. My own grandmother used a 257 for years, taking her last elk sometime in her 60s, but that was 30 years ago, back when there were fewer hunters and cow elk were generally legal. Things are different today; most elk are bulls shot in anything *but* a broadside position, and usually in thick timber, which means you'll have to put a bullet through some bone or perhaps part of the paunch. The big bone problem is not the shoulder blade itself (one Wyoming friend claims he's shot through both blades with a 150-grain Hornady from a 30-06) but the shoulder knuckle and "arm" bones. The paunch is just a lot

of thick, semi-liquid resistance. Both take more bullet than you'll ever need on anything outside of brown bear or Cape buffalo.

My first elk was a cow that jumped out of an alder creek bottom and started up the far hillside, 50 yards away. I was in one of my "all-around" stages, using the 270 on everything, and the Speer Grand Slam had just appeared to glowing press reports. I put a 150-grain at the rear of the cow's rib cage to angle it up into the lungs, a shot I'd made on many deer. The cow never flinched and we found it by chance a day later and a ½-mile away. There

was no blood and the ground was dry. The Grand Slam never made it past the liver, having come apart soon after entry. Is the 270 a lousy elk cartridge? No, but you have to pick your shots or use the very toughest bullets you can find. I'd avoid tough angling shots even with the Core-Lokt, Interlock or Nosler Solid Base, especially with the 130-grain.

Dr. Philip Wright, professor emeritus of zoology at the University of Montana and one of the honchos in the Boone & Crockett Club, wrote up a report on elk control shooting at the National Bison Range years ago. The cartridges were the 30-06 and 375, using 220-grain and 300-grain Silvertips respectively. Dr. Wright tabulated 24 elk, a dozen taken with each caliber, all well-hit, mostly mature bulls. The 375 put elk down in an average of 13 seconds, versus 21 seconds for the '06, and created a wound channel twice the diameter. The professor summed up the evidence by noting that the biggest advantage of the 375 was in complete penetration, leaving a good blood trail for tracking, but he also said the 30-06 showed up "surprisingly well," none of the elk traveling far enough to make recovery difficult even without a blood trail. I've discussed the article with Dr. Wright and asked him what elk rifle he uses, since he's a noted big game hunter. The answer: a 7mm Remington Magnum, using some squirreled-away 175-grain Bitterroot Bonded Cores, loaded to 3000 fps.

I've never used the 375 on game, but have some experience with the 338-06 wildcat, and know folks who use various over-30s from the 358 Winchester to the 340 Weatherby. All

The 30-06 will still do it all, but better these days. The two bullets are a 165 Nosler Solid Base and 200 Partition, the author's choices in maximum handloads.

kill elk quickly, and with the right bullet usually leave a blood trail. I finally went back to the 30-06, however, primarily because Nosler finally put a point on their old round nose 200-grain 30, bringing the ballistic coefficient up from .358 to an astronomical .584. Now, a jump like that *does* make some difference, enough that my load, which starts off at 2700 in a 22-inch barrel, shoots as flat and retains as much energy at 300 yards as a 210-grain Nosler started at 2900 from a 338. The load just about exactly matches Wright's 7mm load at the same range, but drops about 3 inches more, I'd guess. It's a much better load over game ranges than my old 338-06's 210 at the same velocity.

The 338 would be "better" with 250-grain bullets, but the 250 Nosler comes with a round nose, like the old 200-grain 30, and drops off at long range. There's no real reason for the round nose, but we're stuck with it. Again, theory is nice, but the reality is that we're limited to what's available, so my 338-06 has been relegated to black timber use only.

What we also confront in the over-30s is recoil. A decade ago Dave Petzal of *Field & Stream* warned me that recoil tolerance declines with age. I was a rifle madman in my early 20s, shooting everything from the 243 to the 375 and not minding it, while Dave had been abusing his 34-year-old shoulder with a 340 Weatherby for a while. I'm now 33 and find that sticking a sandbag between my 30-06 and my shoulder is the only thing making those 200-grain loads tolerable off the bench. Thanks for the warning, David.

Jack O'Connor liked his 270. He shot most of his elk in open timberline country, where he had a chance to pick his shot, and used stout handloads with good bullets. Elmer Keith liked various over-30's, because he did most of his hunting in thick timber and liked that blood trail. Most of the rest of us do just fine with something in between 270 and 338, like Wright's 7mm Magnum or the 30-06, or something like my old 338-06 or the 358 Winchester if we hunt where we *know* no shot will be much beyond 200 yards. Just choose the right bullet.

Rifles

The good news is that finally rifles are getting lighter and shorter and harder for game to see. We're finally getting a *choice,* rifles with dull finishes and even a few factory fiberglass stocks, surrounding fine barrels and excellent triggers. My wife is crazy about her new Browning A-Bolt 270, for example, dull all over from barrel to matte-finished Bushnell 4x. They took metal out of the action, rather than the barrel; the whole outfit only weighs 7½ pounds and put early three-shot groups into an average of ¾-in. with Remington factory loads. So we're also getting light, dull-finished rifles that *shoot.*

The rifle is like the bullet; it's more important than the cartridge (within certain broad limits) because it's what we have to carry around the hills. It doesn't do much good to choose the right load for the game, if the animal spooks at a flashy stock, or we're worn out after climbing half the mountain under a 9-pound rifle, or the rig doesn't hold zero under *hunting* conditions. My Ruger '06 is practically invisible under use-scratches, only weighs 8 pounds, and puts 200-grain Partitions or 165-grain Solid Bases into the same place month after month. But that fiberglass sure got tempting the last week of last November, when the elk finally came down to where they were reachable with a mere 1500-foot climb. Maybe next year. ●

RECOMMENDED WESTERN LOADS

Caliber	Bullet	BC	Muzzle Velocity	Bullet Impact @ 300 yards with +3" sight @ 100	Approx. drift @ 300 yards in 20 mph crosswind
243 Win.	100 Sierra	.445	3000	−2	12.8
243 Win.	100 Nosler SB	.381	3000	−3	15.0
6mm Rem.	100 Sierra	.445	3100	−1	12.2
6mm Rem.	100 Nosler SB	.381	3100	−2	14.0
257 Rob.	100 Sierra	.400	3200	0	13.2
257 Rob.	100 Nosler PT	.409	3200	0	13.2
257 Rob.	120 Nosler SB	.471	3000	−2	13.1
25-06	117 Sierra	.438	3200	+1	11.9
25-06	120 Nosler SB	.471	3200	+1	11.3
264 Win.	120 Nosler SB	.422	3300	+1	12.2
264 Win.	140 Sierra	.541	3100	0	10.0
270 Win.	130 Sierra	.426	3100	−1	12.8
270 Win.	150 Nosler SB	.513	2900	−2	11.9
7mm-08 & 7x57	140 Sierra	.490	2900	−2	12.2
280 Rem.	140 Sierra	.490	3000	−1	11.5
280 Rem.	160 Nosler PT	.508	2800	−2	12.6
7mm Rem.	140 Sierra	.490	3300	+2	10.1
7mm Rem.	160 Sierra	.561	3100	+1	9.5
7mm Rem.	175 Sierra	.654	3000	0	8.4
7mm Rem.	175 Nosler PT	.484	3000	−2	12.1
308 Win.	150 Sierra	.409	2900	−3	15.3
30-06	150 Sierra	.409	3100	−1	13.4
30-06	165 Nosler SB	.446	2950	−2	13.5
30-06	180 Sierra	.534	2800	−3	11.5
30-06	200 Nosler PT	.584	2700	−3	11.2
.300 Win.	165 Nosler SB	.446	3300	+2	11.5
.300 Win.	180 Sierra	.534	3100	+1	10.0
.300 Win.	200 Nosler PT	.584	3000	0	9.8
.338 Win.	210 Nosler PT	.386	2900	−4	16.3
.338 Win.	250 Nosler PT	.364	2700	−5	19.3
.338 Win.	250 Sierra	.570	2700	−3	11.3

This table was prepared assuming the use of maximum safe handloads in each caliber, in standard sporting length barrels available for each caliber, with data from the author's tests, the *Nosler Reloading Manual Number Two,* the *Sierra Bullets Reloading Manual,* and Bob Hagel's excellent book, *Game Loads and Practical Ballistics For The American Hunter.*

Tough talk over good guns could be the highlight of any day John Amber had.
(Anderson photo)

REMEMBERING JOHN

JOHN AMBER's life may be plainly seen to have had three parts—an unimportant time of childhood, a young manhood which permitted him to learn something of the world and firearms, and then 40-odd years when firearms were his life, his passion and his work, full-time and virtually unfettered. That this life spanned two World Wars, a Great Depression, several other wars, a deal of deluxe travel, had some impact on Amber, the man, but none whatever on Amber, the gun nut.

There just wasn't anything about guns John Amber didn't like. He preferred the exotic, the classy, the expensive—and regarded anyone who didn't a fool—but when he was not near the guns he loved, he loved the guns he was near.

And he also liked all the things one can do with guns—study, shoot, hunt, fondle, buy and trade. He didn't like selling, not personal guns. Of all of it, he especially enjoyed talking about guns.

A lot of the people he talked with remember him that way.

Dave Petzal of *Field & Stream* recalls, "I'll always remember the sight of John Amber and Warren Page strolling along Madison Avenue in New York at noon. It was raining lightly, and Warren held a pink and lacy parasol over them both. They were unaware of the stares—they were discussing guns, and who cared?"

Dick Dietz, who works for Remington, remembers, "Conversation about firearms brought out the Amber I liked best—the patient, interested teacher, hoping you are as interested as he is. He also created the textbook for his course—GUN DIGEST."

Bob Brownell recalls, "He could give a gun man a lot of thrills, but the most thrilling, I think, was to ride with him down The Outer Drive in Chicago during rush hour when he was expounding on something gun-related, oblivious to the time, the place, and the traffic."

Amber's friends and colleagues do remember talk of other things.

"We were sitting on a couch in a hospitality suite and getting close to exhausting my meaningful input on guns," recalls George Martin, of *Guns & Ammo* once and NRA now, "when I drew some sort of tentative parallel between guns and shooting and the racing of sporty cars. John brightened and with near glee pounced upon the subject. That conversation, with breaks of months at a time, lasted for the next 25 or so years."

For Jim Carmichel, of *Outdoor Life*, cars were a common ground, too. He remembers, "We both loved guns, but also automobiles, especially sports cars, cameras and anything else that was mechanical. We spent long hours, even days, discussing anything that required talented workmanship.

"He loved to walk and we often set out early in the morning walking the streets of such places as London, Copenhagen, Paris or Moscow. John would invariably become involved in long conversations with shop owners or resident craftsmen. John wanted to know about everything."

Amber *was* exhaustive and exhausting in his effort to wring all the available information out of every encounter. That's how a lot of those who wrote for him remember him.

"Chatting over coffee, even," recalls ballistician Ed Yard, "he asked as many questions as he did in his letters."

Jerry Rakusan of *GUNS* wrote, "The several years I spent on GUN DIGEST were a grand mixture of excitement, frustration, anxiety and just plain hard work. In spite of his temper tantrums and his unyielding demand for perfection, John offered me an opportunity for learning editorial skills and amassing gun lore available nowhere else."

Ken Waters, he of *Pet Loads* and so many years in GUN DIGEST, began to know Amber in 1956. "John was a veritable encyclopedia of firearms. Knowledgeable, incisive, censorious—he was all of those—but humorous and kindly as well."

Dean Grennell, who called Amber Mr. Fossilresin in a private language, says, "He was a great editor to work for: generous in praise if you did good things for him and scaldingly corrosive if you let him down. I recall rewriting a piece he wanted boiled down. In the process, I wound up with half-again as many words and sent it to him, anyway. He read it over, gulped bravely and proceeded to run it as rewritten."

Frank Barnes worked with Amber on the first three editions of CARTRIDGES OF THE WORLD, and has written: "I remember John; I always will; I loved the man because we shared the same general philosophy and love of guns, shooting and the outdoors. He was something of a perfectionist and set high standards, which irritated me sometimes. I hate to do anything over."

It is not difficult to find those who found John T. Amber—the full style

according to P. M. Dickey is John Thomas Kirk Patrick Amber—helpful in their careers and, indeed, on a larger stage.

"Every gun engraver owes John Amber a debt that cannot be paid," says E. C. Prudhomme. "The first list of gun engravers that ever appeared anywhere appeared in the 9th edition of GUN DIGEST.

"As for me, he was my friend and could not have been better to me had he been my father. I benefitted with all of you for his having passed this way."

That was not a purely subjective as-

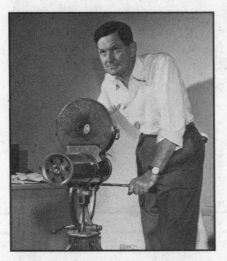
Already in a heyday to last for decades, a clean-shaven Amber kept a Gatling near his desk. (Kufrin photo)

sessment, for Prudhomme also says, "He was a hard nut. You had to show him."

Geoffrey Boothroyd writes from England, "I remember John, not because he published something, but because he didn't. I sent an article and he sent a cheque and a letter in criticism and instruction and my start as a professional writer/photographer dates from that letter. I believe him an immortal."

And for many years John Amber had a friend in France, the man who is still GUN DIGEST's European Correspondent, Raymond Caranta. Caranta is also Editor of *GUILLAUME TELL*, a Gallic GUN DIGEST, but in 1952 he was a French jazz freak. He tells it . . .

"In France, after World War II, there were plenty of guns, few connoisseurs and only a handful of gun books. In Paris in 1952, besides Sidney Bechet's clarinet and Claude Luther's cornet, I found my first GUN

DIGEST—a bonanza.

"Soon, John T. Amber became one of my gods. When in 1967 I had the idea to write, in English, my history of handguns in France, I could hardly submit it to somebody else, and the miracle arose—I won the Townsend Whelen Award in 1969.

"Since then, there has been something of John Amber in each of 19 editions of my books. To European eyes, he represented a typical American character of a glorious epoch.

"I remember his office in Chicago's Loop where he welcomed me in front of an American flag surmounting a magnificent pile of firearms, and Creedmoor Farm, where he lived among a crowd of birds he used to feed every morning, and his folkloric returns from Africa with the trophies and rifles we had painfully to release from the customs . . ."

Nearer at hand, Don Johnson of Milwaukee wrote a letter to Editor Amber in 1953, a letter Amber said should become an article. Again, Amber cursed and cajoled performance, and again, in Don Johnson, he pushed someone to new horizons.

J. B. Wood clearly remembers his first call from John Amber. It became an article, and other articles became a book, and Jay writes for GUN DIGEST

Once settled in at his place in Marengo, IL, Amber gave little thought to moving, and never did. (Murtz photo)

today. Now, Wood writes, "The last time I saw John, I told him none of us were getting any younger, and while we were both still around, I wanted to say how much I appreciated his recognition of me as a writer. I'm glad I got it said."

Dave Wolfe has had no small career in gun publishing and no small relationship with John. He tells it:

"I was starting a gun magazine, to be called *Shooting Times,* and I asked John Amber if he'd be my editorial advisor. 'Hell, yes!' he answered.

"In 1960, John introduced me to Col. Townsend Whelen, and the ensuing discussion (mostly between them) is a golden memory. Another 'goldie' is a full day in 1967 going through John's collection.

"At our last contact, he seemed pensive, much more serious than usual, but he returned to normal by closing the talk with an abusive remark and I said 'Thanks, you crusty old bastard.'

"He laughed, but I know John Amber took pride in his brashness. He would like to be remembered by friends as a 'crusty old bastard'—even though he wasn't."

Regardless of those honestly held sentiments, John T. Amber was not an angel. "A monument, maybe, but no angel" someone put it.

For Dick Dietz, it was, "I knew and worked with John, shared hotels and hunting camps with him, for some 25 years. He could be and was at times warm, witty, charming and highly entertaining. Also, remote, sardonic, cantankerous and, sometimes, downright rude. That was John. You either bought the sum of John Amber or rejected it."

For Ashley Halsey, sometime Editor of *The American Rifleman,* Amber was mostly a fellow collector. He remembers him that way:

"To witness John with a fine single shot rifle in his hands left one with a memorably vivid portrait of a most happy man.

"As with other honest coinage, there was another side. In his indefatigable gun collecting he resembled, to some, an affable version of a steel trap.

"Let it be said, however, that he never shot a dollar on the ground."

Val Forgett of Navy Arms remembers the collector, too, believing Amber to be "one of the few people in the world that thoroughly loved and understood guns. All kinds of guns, big guns, little guns, expensive guns, inexpensive guns, rifles, pistols, shotguns and anything to do with them."

Ted McCawley labored at Remington for much of Amber's tenure, and the countless meetings came down to, "Whenever our paths crossed, I had the feeling that John was genuinely glad to see me. I know the sentiment was reciprocated. He was genial, witty, and above all, knowledgeable, but he had little tolerance for cant and could be acerbic in its presence."

Maxine Moss of the NMLRA believes "John Amber's high ethical standards as Editor of GUN DIGEST set a precedent that will long be remembered in the industry. He was a gentle man in a gentleman's sport."

With Turner Kirkland, Chairman of the Dixie Gun Works Board, Amber often shared sleeping quarters (Kirkland's, of course) in Friendship. Kirkland says, "He would always be the last one to go to bed and he'd wake up early in the morning squirrely-eyed and bushy-tailed . . . one of the most amicable persons I have ever known."

Jerry Fisher, noted stockmaker, wrote just three sentences. Two of them were: "John Amber was eloquent, knowledgeable, honest, and had just enough humility to be considered a true gentleman. I fear he was one of the last of a vanishing breed."

Skeeter Skelton and John Amber had a great mutual friend in Bill Ruger and met often, so Skeeter says, "Rather than in a writer/editor relationship, John and I became fast friends because we liked one another. In spite of his hardnosed image, John Amber was one of the most generous, thoughtful, and genial men I have ever known."

John Falk of Winchester had a long experience of John Amber. He says, "Funny, but all my memories of John are of lighthearted moments, little quips, quick jokes and lots of eyetwinkling. Serious though he could be, his witty, fun-loving side is the John Amber I'll always think of . . . ten to one, that would please him most."

Bill Jordan observed that John Amber "seemed always to make a business of enjoying life right to the top."

Jordan was once part of a crew dealing with Amber's pacemaker—they were on a celebrity hunt and it was nip-and-tuck getting Amber out. "Didn't faze him much," Jordan says. "He just kept taking his pulse."

G. T. Garwood of Devon—the famous Gough Thomas—also knew Amber in a medical emergency. Amber visited the Garwoods only to collapse and stay weeks. At 87 himself, Garwood comments, "Eighty-two was *good* for him and he never would have

attained it but for his rare combination of humour and courage. Mildred marked it well when she saved his life those years ago."

Hal Swiggett knows firmly what he knows and he says of John Amber: "He had a heart of gold, in spite of the tough, grouchy, demanding image he seemed to prefer. I know because of a personal relationship with him for more than a quarter of a century that inside he was a caring, warm-hearted man and that's the way I will always remember him."

Col. Jim Crossman found spending time around Amber to be "a real privilege, not to mention education. When he took over GUN DIGEST, he picked just the right combination of articles and reference information. He set high standards. I clearly remember, after an argument, trotting to the dictionary to prove John wrong, but he was right."

Colin Greenwood, Editor of *GUNS REVIEW* in England, felt "John Amber's finest gift may well have been his ability to crystallize what it was about the world of guns that attracted a wide range of people right across the world. Through GUN DIGEST he extended my interest in guns and opened up for me, and I am sure for countless others, a wider, more interesting and more exciting world."

Alex Bartimo is another who found Amber a giant. "John Amber did it one way, the *best* way," Bartimo believes. "He sought perfection, reflected in GUN DIGEST and the publishing empire he helped build."

For Larry Sterett, Amber was rather avuncular: "He often phoned around 11 PM, saying 'Well, young man, how are things with you?' and then get right at it—with criticism, an assignment, even questions."

R. L. Wilson, the collecting authority, was, quite simply, impressed by Amber: "He knew guns and gunmaking from the 14th century to today. It was a pleasure, an honor and often a challenge knowing this supremely capable and talented *genuine expert.*"

John Amber made close friends, more than those who saw him as curmudgeon thought possible. From time to time, he fought with and parted from those friends.

Fred Huntington hunted with John and Ray Speer early on. His view is: "John was honest in his convictions and thoughts, but not always right. He and I almost parted company several times. I found him a bit cantankerous, for instance, about my musical snoring. We ended up good friends, though."

Collector Louis A. Ostendorp was not a collector when he met Amber selling antique guns in 1944. And has no idea why Amber spent 20 years educating him, but will always be grateful. All the memories are good ones.

Jim Carmichel and Amber kicked up their heels here and there over the years, but it wasn't all high jinks. Carmichel recalls:

"A few months before John's death Linda and I visited him and found a mess. Linda tackled mops and broom, while I mowed both his lawn and shooting range. Linda spent three hard days making the house habitable, but John couldn't stop raving about having the range operational.

"Even when he had only a few weeks to live—as far as he was concerned his life still lay before him."

One close friend not in the gun business was John Corry. He says, "Although John had an acid tongue, he was not without honor. During the past decade, I saw John alienate, by varying degrees, many of his former acquaintances, but this did not seem to bother him. He often stated 'My mother always said I was half Irish and half son-of-a-bitch.'

"He loved to tell stories at other peoples' expense. For one, there was the time Elmer Keith visited Creedmoor Farm and, shooting a big bore British rifle, was knocked to the ground.

"Underneath his tough shell and cryptic manner, John loved cats and dogs and could even have generous moments. He always loved a bargain though, and when he sold a gun to a hard bargainer at full retail price, he crowed 'I got the bastard.' "

Roger Barlow recalls that Amber often greeted latecomers to various festivities with a stentorian and theatrical, "Here comes the Prince now." And so, Roger believes . . . "somewhere, on January 1st, 1986, a group of former shooters perhaps named O'Connor, Page, Wynne, among many others, might well have chorussed 'Here comes the Prince NOW!' as John Amber, to our loss and their gain, joined them."

Les Bowman often hunted with John Amber and his friend Breezy Wynne in the company of Len Brownell. He and Martie Bowman thought the group more family than clients, and more sportsmen than most.

Bob Steindler has great tales of the quintessential Amber, the fellow who arrived with chronographs and rifles, but no ammo, and hid out in the library while Steindler's 30th wedding anniversary celebration went a-glimmering.

Jack Lewis of *Gun World* has one fond and revealing memory: "John Amber had a reputation for being crotchety and unkind most of the time even to his friends. Shortly after I met him, we were discussing firearms in general, and some specifically. I marvelled at his knowledge and he offered a sly smile.

'I read about that yesterday,' he admitted, 'and I've been looking for a chance all day to impress someone.'

'There's a big difference,' Amber added, 'between having a good library and being brilliant. A lot of people tend to confuse the two.' "

Pete Dickey, once of Firearms International and now of *The American Rifleman,* has a clear and direct view:

"Much of JTA's vast knowledge of guns and gunning will benefit sportsmen and students as long as plagiarists and libraries exist. His personal friends will benefit more from the recollection of his good fellowship, fascinating conversation and, above all, his sense of humor."

Louis G. Hector, Esq. was, in latter days, John Amber's attorney and his friend, fascinated as almost all of us, by this lion in the living room. He found Amber "precise in his thought, as well as in his oral or written expression of that thought.

"I think I may have received the last, or one of the last, letters John wrote. It is dated December 30th, 1985 and reads:

"Dear Lou,

Thank you for your consideration and for all your help.

Forgive my brevity—I'm in awful shape—this long cold spell has got me down, and God knows how I'll get by the rest of winter. It's a damn good thing that Jim Sweet and Bill H. are usually around when I need them.

The very best for 1986, and we must get together soon—if we don't it may be too late.

John"

The Jim Sweet of that letter is James E. Sweet, D.D.S., of Marengo who, over 20 years, whiled away, he puts it, many an unstructured hour with Amber, along with neighbor and good friend Bill Hunziker.

"My offices are across the street from John's, and we got along, mostly famously, all those years. John didn't care that I was no expert; he told me about guns anyway.

"I know he admired craft above all else, and viewed himself as a craftsman in words and ideas. And I believe he was that.

"Toward the end, John fought fatigue of the body, but not the mind. His last words at parting over the years were almost always 'See ya', kid.' and so it was the last time I saw him.

"I said then and I say now—see ya', John."

John Amber was a working editor. He worked a whole career with one firm and with a lot of people not mentioned here yet.

Milt Klein, who originated the GUN DIGEST and who hired John Amber, remembers meeting him first when Klein sold books to Amber, then book buyer for the Marshall Field & Co. sporting goods department. It became an association rich in memory, in conflict and in profit for them both.

Amber's secretary of long decades, Lilo Anderson, preserves a proper, even prim, silence about her old boss. He was, obviously, both an interesting experience and a great occasional trial. "Definitely unique" is as far as Lilo goes, laughing because John Amber did not like the indiscriminate use of that word.

Charles T. Hartigan, now president and an owner of DBI Books, has a clear memory of this editor he has called "the most interesting man I ever met."

"John T. Angry, we called him. He was difficult on a *good* day; impossible in the final weeks of an edition of GUN DIGEST.

"He could never understand how I knew so little about firearms after having been exposed to them so many years. We found a common ground outside the office in the simple beauty of the martini. He'd talk for hours, tongue loosened by the juniper berries.

"His voice grew louder with each martini and his language leaned to the ribald, so the tables immediately surrounding ours were often empty. When we'd leave, since I was the younger, I'd fetch the car. I sometimes returned to find him unconcernedly watering the gutter at the feet of an astonished doorman.

"He left us, I'm sure, because it was his turn to buy."

John Strauss, long DBI's sales manager and now also an owner, absolutely admired Amber's mastery of the story—any story:

"What Scheherazade was to the bedroom, John T. Amber was to the gun room and the locker room. He never met a story he couldn't tell . . . and leave you begging for more.

"Across the desk, across the bar,

across the *years*, John Amber had a way of telling people what he knew and felt . . . and making them care."

Sheldon Factor worked with Amber early on and late. Now Vice President and Publisher, he had his differences with Amber, but concedes that in one respect, the Editor was in fact legendary:

"When he actually threw a wrench into a printing press to stop it when no printer would push the button,

Warren Page came to Amber's somewhat early 1975 retirement party. (Swiggett photo)

Amber and Chuck Hartigan shared many glasses and chuckles. (Swiggett photo)

John Amber achieved instant fame in Midwestern printing circles. They all remember him."

It takes more than executive staff to make books. It takes other editors and those who worked with Amber remember him.

Pam Johnson is now Managing Editor of DBI Books. Her memory of Amber has her neither very managerial nor very editorial:

"I never was sure John Amber *really* knew my name. He usually referred to me as 'Hey' or 'Hey, you,' and both years I worked on GUN DIGEST, I was noticed. John and I battled those years over commas.

"Who won is not important. What is important is that John Amber *cared* about those commas."

Harold A. Murtz has his own GUNS ILLUSTRATED and is a senior editor of GUN DIGEST these days, but confesses to intimidation in 1972 when he first saw Amber and the Marengo office.

"Some folks didn't care much for John, what with his irascible character, sometimes corny sense of humor and his general demeanor, and I guess I didn't either, at first. Above all else he was fair, however, and though he had a pretty short fuse, he did spend a

fair amount of time with me.

"John Amber came as close to being my mentor as anyone."

For Bob Anderson, also on the GUN DIGEST staff and now Editor of the GUN DIGEST HUNTING ANNUAL, there is an inspired quid-pro-quo to remember about John:

"We were in Amber's barn and I spotted the distinctive forend of a Remington Model 11 autoloader—a fairly pedestrian discovery, consider-

ing John's reputation. As I picked it up, John said, 'I used to keep that loaded and next to my desk down in the old Chicago office.'

To make a long, warm story short, he soon also said, 'Why don't you take it and use it?' Then: 'Why don't you keep it?'

I went home with that prize, cleaned it up and went back out there. As I got out of the car I said, "Got a present for ya!"

"The hell ya say!" came the reply.

"John didn't have one and I had

three. As I took the old Winchester Model 57 rimfire out of the scabbard, JTA's eyes lit up. He was as much surprised and elated as I had been over the gift of the Model 11.

"Ten minutes later we were shooting that gun, with 45-year old EZXS. At 100 yards, we got well under 2 inches and JTA was beaming.

"I like remembering that."

Bob Bell goes back, as they say. He worked in that fabled and crowded second-floor office. Now he gives the hunters of Pennsylvania their *Game News* each month, and he remembers things:

"Late one night last December, the phone rang. I answered, and a voice said, 'Bell? This is Ambrose.'

" 'John,' I said. 'How you doing?'

"He grunted. 'Better not to talk about it.'

"But we did. Quite awhile. About something I'd written and something he hadn't, about some personal things, about guns. We always talked guns.

"Things were never simple around Ol' John. He was far too complex for that, his personality too volatile. He could charm a hoot owl out of a tree, but had an explosive temper. I once saw him smash his phone on the floor, then calmly use mine to tell the company to come replace it.

"We often argued. He couldn't admit he was wrong. The only way I could win was to make notes, then show them to him when he later chewed me out for doing it. He'd just mumble and change the subject.

"But I learned more useful stuff from John than I did in college, and he had more influence on me than any other man except my father, and I still can't accept that he's gone."

To Grits Gresham of *Sports Afield*, who thinks Amber was indeed unique, Amber spoke quite clearly on the subject of Amber in 1978:

"I'm ending my reign of terror—they call me John T. Angry at the Gun Digest—at the end of this month. I've put in 30 years, doing the job that I exactly wanted to do. That I love doing. As I said before, I think I made a reasonable success out of it—GUN DIGEST."

And that is true, but perhaps an uncharacteristic understatement. He actually made a hell of a success of it.

And as for me—Ken Warner—why, I owe him, too, as do you. He was everything they all say he was, and less, and more. Remembering John is a complex business.

—Ken Warner

"IS IT POSSIBLE for a bullet to be fired from a 300 Winchester Magnum, 30-06, 308, 270 or 25-06 into an animal's chest, kill the animal instantly, yet not go through far enough even to touch a rib on the far side of that chest cavity?"

I wrote that paragraph in 1972 and it was published in the now-extinct *GUNSport* Magazine in May, 1973. The next paragraph read: "Is it possible for a big game bullet to miss its target, yet to be absolutely ricochet-free once that bullet has touched ground, rock or water?"

The answer to both questions was yes—still is yes—and the bullet is the fabulous Glaser Safety Slug.

Colonel Jack Canon developed his famous Safety Slug with the help of his long-time friend Armin Glaser of Zurich, Switzerland, in whose honor the projectile was named. In those days the Glaser Safety Slug consisted of a Sierra bullet jacket filled with Teflon-coated Number 12 shot held in place with a 25% glass-impregnated Teflon nose plug. Crude they were, by any standards, but extremely effective. Each was handmade by Colonel Canon in his garage in Louisiana—one at a time on a Hollywood press.

If ever a "Soldier of Fortune" existed, Colonel Jack Canon was one. He was his own man. Scrapes and conflicts during his military career bear positive testimony to the fact. Before he ever contacted me about the virtues of his bullet, those attributes had been proven over and over again and not in theory, not on paper, but with flesh, blood and bone where and when it counted.

Colonel Canon's effort was first towards rifle bullets but that soon changed and was shortly dropped in favor of handgun slugs. I still have a good many of those first Safety Slugs, both rifle and handgun.

Colonel Canon tested the 308 caliber bullets in most every 30-caliber cartridge, up through 300 Winchester Magnum. He made a few 270s and 25-06s and tested them himself. He was content that results were comparable to 30's, but discarded them as impractical compared to the much more popular 308 diameter used in the 30-caliber rifles. He settled entirely on 30-06 and 308 Winchester cartridges since these were by far the most popular.

It was here this writer came into the picture.

Those first projectiles—I received the grand total of twelve—weighed 133 grains and were intended for use in 30-06 cases. The Colonel suggested—that isn't exactly true; he ordered—a charge of 51 grains of H335

The early labels were printed on bright orange paper.

by
HAL
SWIGGETT

The Glaser
Safety Slug Story

Colonel Jack Canon, the man behind the now famous Glaser Safety Slug.

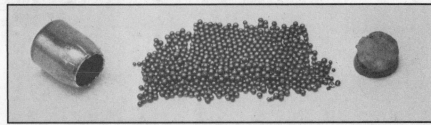

The Glaser Safety Slug is a simple assembly for the internal delivery of #12 shot. This is a current 140-gr. 45 slug.

These are early rifle bullets produced by Col. Canon, and they killed game quick.

and CCI Magnum primers. I haven't the vaguest idea as to velocity, but fired three into a 1½-inch group using my Steyr-Mannlicher and its double-set triggers. They printed an inch and a half high with no scope adjustment.

The first animal shot was a Corsican ram on the world-famous Y.O. Ranch. It was about 90 yards and I aimed to place the bullet squarely in the center of the chest, as per Colonel Jack's orders. Harvey Goff was my guide, watching with 8x binoculars. Recoil obscured my view, but Harvey said the ram was obviously instantly dead before it ever dropped and that it really didn't drop but was driven down into its tracks. It weighed probably 125 pounds before field dressing.

Shortly later I received a batch of 308 bullets weighing 145 grains and was told to load them the same way. Three whitetails, three mule deer,

This old Hollywood tool made all of Col. Jack Canon's Glaser Safety Slugs and the early ones turned out by Kurt Canon. Kurt said he got up to 200 an hour once he got the hang of it.

This Y.O. ibex is mounted life-size and on display in the Y.O. Ranch Lodge. It fell in its tracks from a Glaser "mid-stream" 308 bullet.

Heinz Sander took this blackbuck on the Y.O. with the writer's 30-06 and a Glaser Safety Slug.

and another Corsican ram fell to those Glaser Safety Slugs using my same 30-06 Steyr. One mule deer, shot at about 165 yards, lunged forward and as his feet touched the ground started walking slower each step until he dropped, a total of five or six steps. The Corsican took off in a "dead" run and collapsed less than 20 yards from where he had been hit. All three whitetails and the other two mule deer literally collapsed in their tracks.

I did not do all this shooting. Since I also guide a good deal, my hunters had a hand in the project as I watched with binoculars. This, by the way, is a lot better than actually firing the shot because moment of impact can be observed. It's impressive, too.

One 300-pound wild hog gave up at the moment of impact and wild hogs aren't noted for such action. They are solid critters with not only a layer of thick hide but a layer of thicker fat to penetrate. His demise both decisive and instant.

The next batch of bullets weighed 150 grains. These were shot in 30-06, 308, and 30-30. Only one bullet failure occurred. A sheep, shot at about 70 yards, was penetrated completely with the bullet going through both shoulders. The jacket obviously never ruptured, which must happen to produce the effectiveness. Those 600 tiny Number 12 pellets disperse

At 15 feet, a 44 Magnum Glaser Safety Slug literally drives the bottle away from the water. Note here how the water is still suspended, has barely started to fall.

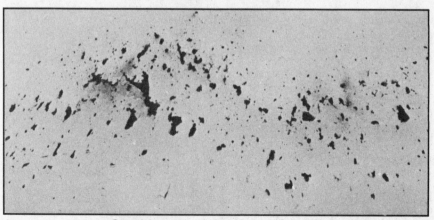

One of the very early 357 Magnum Safety Slugs was fired into hard ground at 10 yards and produced a shower of dirt and a few mild pellet strikes on this poster board.

throughout the immediate area, but don't go far because of their lack of weight. It's the shock, the total devastation of lung and heart tissue that kills the animal instantly.

Back in those beginning days I broke down 10 Glaser Safety Slugs listed at 148 grains. The average, before tearing them down, was 149.5 grains. Tops was one at 150.4 and the lightest was 148.1 grains. The Teflon nose plugs averaged 5.25 grains and I believe it was here most of the variation in weight took place as they definitely were not the same thickness. Actual pellet count settled on an average of 592 for the ten dissected.

Colonel Canon had definite ideas on how to get the most out of one of his Safety Slugs. Quoting from a letter: "The best place to shoot a heavy animal is just about the middle of the ribs on a side shot. On a quartering shot from the rear, hit just aft of the rib cage. Both shots seem to rupture the diaphragm muscle, as well as main arteries, and cause heart and lungs to hemorrhage. No animal is going far without a diaphragm muscle."

Since I'm a handgun hunter at heart, a batch of those 148-150-grain bullets were loaded in 30-30 cases and fired in my Thompson/Center Contender with its 2x Leupold scope. Using 29 grains of 4198, they proved deadly on jackrabbits out to about 75 yards. None beyond that were tried. It couldn't be said "they died in their tracks" because they were sitting in every instance but it could be said "they died in their seats." Collapsed might be a better word. None moved; they just settled.

By then the Colonel was sending bullets for 38/357s weighing 77 grains. These used a Speer jacket. Also, he sent loaded ammo in 38 Special cases stuffed with 10 grains of Unique, magnum primers, and specific instructions on shooting them in 357 Magnum guns only. He claimed 1-inch accuracy at 25 yards out of a 6-inch Colt Python using his Deadeye Handgun Stock (another of Colonel Canon's inventions—a legal handgun stock since it did not attach to the gun). I was never able to duplicate that, but could stay consistently in 2½ to 4 inches with either a 2½-inch M19 S&W or my 4⅝-inch Ruger Blackhawk.

Glaser Safety Slugs for rifles soon disappeared. I was never really told why but assumed two reasons: Range was an important factor and Jack had no control over hunters taking longer shots, then maybe blaming the bullet, and 2) I think maybe time had a lot to do with it. Making each bullet by

hand meant only a given few could be turned out in a day and his interest became more directed towards police use.

Once deep into handgun bullets, Glaser Safety Slugs were announced as available only to police departments and that policy was stuck to—NO exceptions. I had them, along with eventually a few other writers, but no civilians other than our exceptions. One occasion concerning this always comes to mind whenever Glaser Safety Slugs are mentioned. The Colonel called me right after it happened. A big black car pulled up across his driveway and two men walked back to his garage shop. With no introduction or formality whatever one said, "We understand you make a very deadly handgun bullet and we want to buy 5,000."

Jack quickly shot back, "I don't have 5,000 but I have five right here which you are going to get if you don't get out of here."

He produced a Chiefs Special from his pocket and they left.

During his tenure, Canon had a standing offer to police officers using his product: "If you get a single shot of return fire after hitting your target any place in the torso I will give you a new 357 Magnum revolver."

I will never forget one instance using a 357 Glaser Safety Slug. A Corsican ram had been dropped by a hunter. It was on the ground but not dead. He was about to finish it off when I suggested he use my 4-inch 357 Magnum instead. "Where should I shoot it," he asked?

"Right behind the shoulder," was my answer.

He did. From only a few feet, life could be seen instantly going out of that animal. I mean that bullet hit and it was over. On examining the chest cavity not a single mark was on the far side. Not one.

Another similar incident with a wild hog, this time with my Thompson/Center 30-30 pistol: the shot was maybe 15 yards; the hog was running along a trail slightly above where I was standing. Swinging along with him I slapped the trigger shotgun style. I caught him with his leg forward, so the bullet entered the chest directly below the heart, went through it, and killed the hog in the middle of his jump. He dug a deep furrow with his nose as he hit head first. The heart and lungs were gone, just a mass of jelly. The only marks on the other side of the inner rib cage were tiny red specks sort of like measles.

I tried, back in those days (I was sports photographer for a large metro-

politan daily with appropriate reaction capabilities) several times to get a photograph of plastic bottles being blown up with rifle bullets but could never time the exposure close enough. Only a spray of water could be seen. Cans were exploded with handgun bullets, always tearing out the front and seldom ever making any marks at all on the back.

One series of tests were run putting white poster board 18 inches behind a flat rock. Shooting from 10, 15, and 25 yards never once was there anything but tiny pellet holes in the cardboard. Glaser Safety Slugs did not and would not ricochet.

The last shipment of ammo from Colonel Canon included this note: "Enclosed 34 44 Mag, 15 44 Special, 6 45 ACP, plus 3 sighting shots for 44 Mag. Both 44 will be low and require sight elevation. Light projectiles. The 45 ACP is right on. Maybe a little high depending on your sight picture. All will drop anything you have on ranch with one body hit. Recommend 44 Mag for bear on your hunt. Should put down a black with it anywhere in body."

As can be seen he had loaded up special ammo for a bear hunt I had scheduled. I went on that hunt and stayed a week, but I never saw a bear. I had proper ammunition, though.

Glaser Safety Slugs as built by Colonel Jack Canon were not things of beauty. In fact, no two ever looked alike. But they did their assigned job to perfection. It has been said, "All things must come to an end." And it seemed like that might be true of Glaser Safety Slugs when Colonel Canon died. Nothing more was heard about the Safety Slug. I knew there was a son and tried to contact him but did not connect.

Then came the 1984 SHOT Show in Dallas. Glaser Safety Slug had a booth and it was staffed by Kurt and Marilyn Canon, Jack's son and daughter-in-law. They made me feel real good by remembering I had written the first piece on their dad's bullet. They made me feel real good too in knowing the Glaser Safety Slug wasn't gone.

But it wasn't the same!

Their new bullet was a thing of beauty, every one identical to the next, loaded identically, packaged beautifully, and accompanied by a handsome full color brochure.

Kurt automated the process of building Glaser Safety Slugs. I happened to be in his part of California a few months later and spent most of a day with him seeing how his modern version of the Glaser Safety Slug was produced. Kurt's father was a rugged individualist and it showed in his product. Kurt is a business man and this shows in his product. What a team they would have made had they been able to work together.

Glaser Safety Slugs are not sold as components at the moment and I honestly don't know that they ever will be. So far as I know Jack never sold them that way himself. He just sent me bullets knowing I would load them the way he said which saved him time and effort. And expense.

During Jack's last days of production he loaded most popular handgun calibers from 380 on up. Kurt has added 25 ACP to the list which includes 380, 9mm, 38 Super, 38 Special, 357 Magnum, 44 Special, 44 Magnum, 45 ACP and 45 Colt.

The little 25-caliber auto handles a 40-grain slug at 1,000 fps from 2½ inches of barrel. The 380 uses a 70-grain bullet at 1,350 fps from a 3½-inch barrel. Next up the list 9mm, 38 Super, 38 Special and 357 Magnum all use the same 80-grain Safety Slug at 1,700 fps for the 9mm and 38 Special, 1,750 fps for 38 Super and 1,800 fps for 357 Magnum.

Both 44s use the same bullet; Special at 1,350 fps and Magnum 1,850 fps. It weighs 130 grains. Same for 45s; the ACP puts the 140-grain bullet out at 1,400 fps and the big Colt case at 1,350.

Kurt also markets two rifle cartridges—308 Winchester and 30-06. Both use the same 125-grain projectile at 3,000 fps in the 308 and 3,100 in the '06.

Glaser Safety Slugs' current claim is 1½-inch groups at 15 yards with handguns and at 100 yards for rifles. This has been close to my figures and I've been shooting a good many 357 Magnum, 44 Special, 44 Magnum, 45 ACP and 45 Colt. I've not shot all that many rifle cartridges but enough to know they will do the job. Most have been 30-06 and most of them through my Thompson/Center single shot rifle. My best group was 1⅛ inches for three shots, though most were closer to the 2-inch mark.

The biggest animal taken with these new Glaser Safety Slugs dropped in its tracks from one 125-grain 30-06 bullet in the lungs. It was a white-tailed gnu (wildebeest). I talked a hunter into using my rifle and cartridge on the Y.O. Ranch. Several whitetails, jackrabbits, javelina, one ibex, one black bear and one blackbuck antelope went down with a single shot. The bear wasn't large, but seldom have I seen any bear dropped in its tracks like this one.

Early 30-30 and 30-06 Glaser Safety Slugs (center) compared with conventional bullet counterparts.

New 308 and 30-06 Glasers use the same 125-gr. Safety Slug. Bullets are hollow pointed.

Glaser Safety Slugs now produced are consistent in appearance and weight. Here are, from left—38 Special, 357 Magnum, 44 Magnum, 45 ACP, 45 Colt.

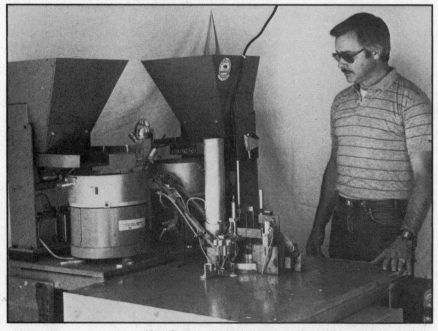

Kurt Canon with his custom-made machine which turns out Glaser Safety Slugs by the hundreds with the flip of a switch.

Plastic gallon jug of water hit by a Glaser Safety slug simply blows apart in a pattern no other bullet produces.

It is obvious these late Glasers were still hand-made because of the tip variations you can see. This lot is 38 Special.

Kurt Canon shows off his neat Glaser Safety Slug packaging with six identical rounds in each bubble container.

Countless gallon plastic jugs have been exploded with handguns, and I do mean exploded. In every instance only the front was blown out—never the back. Smaller cartridges sometimes leave a few pellets in what's left of the jug. One afternoon of shooting saw a bystander rather thoroughly soaked from more than 30 feet in front of the container. Another 15 yards in front had water splashed on his jeans. Handling the camera from 25 feet and alongside the jug more than once has put water spots on the lenses.

How are Glaser Safety Slugs made? Not by hand, that's for sure. Kurt had the machine custom built. One huge hopper dispenses jackets, another nose plugs, and the third Number 12 shot. Colonel Canon used to pull the handle—Kurt did too when he first picked up the business—of a Hollywood press to make each bullet. Now Kurt just flips a switch to make hundreds of Glaser Safety Slugs.

All those many years ago, I had taken a batch of original Safety Slugs apart and checked each component for weight, so one of Kurt's 45s was treated likewise. I did only one because I could see no reason to waste any more. Each step was automated. Nose plugs were obviously identical. I saw hundreds lying there in bulk Those 45 slugs are listed at 140 grains. The one I dissected weighed 139.6—which broke down to 37.9 grains for the jacket, 6.3 grains for the nose plug, and 95.4 grains for the 582 (I counted each one) Number 12 pellets.

Glaser Safety Slugs, in those early days, were obviously different than conventional rounds. They were handmade. They looked handmade. They looked sinister. Kurt's production looks like any other round. The nose plug is blue (there is a black-nosed round made specifically for police use and sold only to law enforcement agencies) but this isn't noticeable so there is little chance for anyone not extremely knowledgeable on the subject to know it is not a conventional cartridge.

The cartridges are put together by a custom loader in a nearby community. Packed six to a bubble package they are attractively displayed. And, even better yet, they are available to all who want them. They are not inexpensive. Priced at $15.70 for 38 Special; $16.45 for 357 Magnum; $18.60 for 44 Magnum; and $17.70 for 45 ACP. This is for a package of six (6) rounds. Rifle cartridges, 308 Winchester or 30-06, list at $23.60 per six-round package. These are prices cur-

rent at this writing.

Colonel Jack Canon started it in his garage in Louisiana, one at a time. Son Kurt has upgraded the product to automated production. Often automation lessens quality but not in this case. Colonel Jack's bullets never, ever, had the same shape nose plug—nor the same weight. Kurt's are identical—meaning they can and do shoot identical. At least as identical as any one bullet can shoot against another.

If there is a flaw, and it isn't really that, because of distances involved, Glaser Safety Slugs *do not* shoot to the same point of impact as conventional handgun bullets. At law enforcement distances or personal protection distances, this is no problem, but 15 yards makes a difference and 25 yards make a decided change in the point of impact. So try a couple when you get yours.

Jack Canon had a dream. A dream of peace officers being able to control a situation and endanger no one but the trouble maker. Glaser Safety Slugs do exactly that. Many police officers, right now, are carrying them. Maybe they have no more than one because of department rules, but that one Glaser Safety Slug chambered as the second cartridge up could save their life, or the life of a citizen, in a situation where nothing else would be so swiftly effective.

During his last years Canon spent a good deal of time at Wilford Hall Hospital here in San Antonio at Lackland Air Base. I don't believe Jack ever discovered he could call me before eleven o'clock at night. Many calls came to my phone about that time and lasted, sometimes, more than an hour. He just wanted to talk, and told tales I have no reason whatever to doubt because—I didn't know it then but do now—they were tales of a dying man, a man who had been there. He told of early days testing Glaser Safety Slugs by haunting city dumps and shooting stray dogs.

He talked about other things, too, like the night his conversation started with a laugh. It seems one of the Air Force doctors determined there was a bit of a kidney problem. After extensive testing the young doctor discovered Canon had only one kidney. After telling me about it Jack said, "I could have told him that, but he didn't ask. I got stabbed and lost it."

Yes, Colonel Jack Canon was his own man just as his Glaser Safety Slug is its own distinctive bullet. I'm glad it's alive and well and I wish he was so he could call again. ●

FIREPOWER!
The Machine Gun Comes of Age

by M. L. BROWN

THE GREAT 1914-1918 war was at that point in history the most devastating conflict ever fought in terms of human sacrifice. And it has been estimated more than half of the 7,000,000 killed fell to the deadly firepower of a technologically sophisticated weapon seen for the first time in a major role in warfare—the machine gun.

Twenty-eight nations were allied against Germany, Austria-Hungary, Bulgaria, and Turkey aligned as the Central Powers. The seven principal Allies—Belgium, France, Great Britain, Italy, Roumania, Russia, and the United States—sustained 15,836,109 casualties, while Central Powers dead and wounded are estimated at 11,788,000.

In just 19 months from April 6, 1917, until the Armistice of November 11, 1918, the American Expeditionary Force (AEF) lost 53,169 to combat deaths and disease. Another 179,625 were wounded, while 3,323 were counted as captured or missing.

Automatic weapon systems, initially represented by machine guns, are the product of cumulative technology. Technological warfare began when

primitive man first used for defense a means other than his own physical prowess.

With the gradual introduction of gunpowder weapons to northern Europe from the Arabic sphere in North Africa and Spain during the late thirteenth century (ca. A.D. 1275), military tactics and weaponry dramatically changed as the Old World powers struggled for ascendancy, engendering a frenetic arms race which continues to escalate.

By 1390 European armorers and gun-founders, seeking the ultimate weapon, had introduced a number of radical concepts including various kinds of multi-shot firearms and breech-loading cannon, while by 1500 revolving breech firearms appeared. All of those ancient weapon systems were intended to increase firepower.

Puckle machine gun, 1718, used the revolving breech principle dating from antiquity to fire 63 shots per minute and was the predecessor of machine guns emerging nearly two centuries later. Author's sketch.

MLB '84

The early 18th century saw the predecessor of the manually operated machine gun.

On May 15, 1718, James Puckle of Sussex, England, patented a refined application of the early revolving breech principle, describing it as "... a portable gun or machine that discharges so often and so many bullets, and (can) be so quickly loaded as renders it next to impossible to carry any ship by boarding."

Puckle's innovative weapon displayed a single, smoothbore barrel with sights and an elevating mechanism, the whole mounted on an adjustable tripod. The breech, containing the powder and projectile chambers, was rotated by a crank. Depending on the chamber shape, the projectiles were round or square. Matchcord or a flintlock mechanism ignited the powder. A 1722 London exhibition held in a driving rain saw

the Puckle gun deliver 63 shots in seven minutes despite the downpour—an amazing nine rounds every sixty seconds which was then nothing short of phenomenal.

Firepower notwithstanding, few Puckle guns were sold and there is no record of them used in battle. The Puckle gun faded quickly into obscurity, possibly because no one had confidence in a repeating weapon designed by its inventor to employ round bullets against Christians and square ones on infidels.

Of potentially more significance to machine gun evolution than Puckle's weapon was the appearance in France of a revolutionary manufacturing concept. In 1785, Parisian arms-maker Honoré Blanc began mass-producing firearms with interchangeable components made entirely by machines. Blanc's concept, however, was generally ignored in Europe and, like

Blanc himself, was subsequently lost in the bloody tumult of the French Revolution (1789-1795).

Not until 1798 was the concept resurrected when Eli Whitney of New Haven in Connecticut entered the arms-making trade. Simeon North, Asa Waters, and other U.S. firearms manufacturers adopted Whitney's techniques shortly thereafter. During the War of 1812 (1812-1814) those techniques were expressed on a limited scale in the national armories at Springfield, Massachusetts, and Harper's Ferry, Virginia. By 1825, interchangeability had been perfected at Harper's Ferry Armory with the manufacture of the first martial breech-loading firearm adopted by any nation—the U.S. Rifle, M1819 (Hall).

The fulminous 19th century ushered in another radical innovation which rendered more feasible the machine gun concept—percussion ignition. After 1814, when Joshua Shaw invented the percussion cap, that system gradually superseded flintlock ignition which had been the standard for nearly two centuries.

Shaw, a British citizen residing in Philadelphia, applied the system to breech- or muzzle-loading firearms, the small copper cap seated on a hollow nipple projecting from a drum or bolster threaded into the breech. A minuscule amount of mercury fulminate—a volatile explosive—was sealed in the cap by a waterproof foil liner. When the hammer struck the cap the fulminate detonated, flashing through the hollow nipple to ignite the powder charge.

All of the technological elements requisite for the invention of the machine gun had appeared by 1850, a decade before the first practical model was introduced. All of the machine guns originating in the 1860-1883 period were manually operated, utilizing a revolving or a reciprocating breech or rotating barrel system, but they were practical.

With the advent of the American Civil War (1861-1865) there was an inordinate demand for weapons. Many arms inventors approached the belligerents and among the first was Wilson Ager, a U.S. citizen living in England. Ager there patented in 1860 a machine gun based on the venerable revolving breech principle although it displayed a feed system which radically accelerated firepower.

The Ager gun, also known as the Union Repeating Gun—the term "machine gun" not as yet entering the vernacular—offered a hopper-type

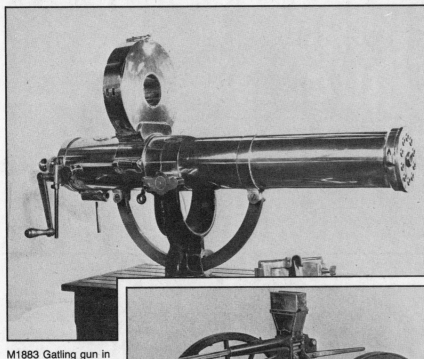

M1883 Gatling gun in standard U.S. 45-70 caliber with Accles feed drum; the design is the basis for high-firepower guns today. *U.S. Military Academy Museum, West Point, NY photo.*

The Union repeating gun, or Coffee Mill Gun, was invented in 1860 and was the first practical machine gun used in an armed conflict. *Library of Congress photo.*

magazine situated atop the rotating breech; the breech designed with lateral grooves instead of chambers and aligned with a single, rifled barrel. The gun was therefore not limited by the number of chambers as were the revolving cylinder handguns of the period.

Mounted on a wheeled carriage, the Ager used the standard 58-caliber U.S. military musket cartridge, the powder and the projectile secured in a paper wrapper. Paper cartridges or bullets with loose powder were loaded in special steel cases provided at the base with percussion nipples. The cases were gravity-fed from the hopper into the breech grooves as fast as the operating handle was turned, a cam forcing the hammer to strike the percussion caps seated on the nipples.

With the 58-caliber bullet backed by a 75-grain black powder charge, the Ager had a maximum effective range of 1,000 yards and it attained the astonishing firing rate of 100 to 120 rounds per minute.

President Abraham Lincoln, seeking any means to resolve the conflict quickly and having a particular affinity for ordnance, witnessed the dawn of a new age in weaponry when he attended an Ager gun demonstration in June, 1861. Amazed, he likened the discharge of the expended cases from the breech to coffee beans ground from a mill and dubbed it the Coffee Mill Gun, which it was called throughout the war. In July, Lincoln personally authorized the immediate purchase of ten guns, and on December 19 he ordered a reluctant Ordnance Department to procure 50 more. Although never officially adopted, Coffee Mill guns were also purchased independently by several Union generals.

Despite their awesome firepower, fewer than 100 Agers saw service. The U.S. Ordnance Department's negative policy regarding machine guns and other repeating arms mirrored the philosophy of Brig. Gen. James Wolfe Ripley, Chief of Ordnance.

A more progressive attitude was displayed by Major Josiah Gorgas, Chief of Ordnance, CSA, who early recognized firepower as a means to compensate for the predominantly agrarian Confederacy's lack of manpower, natural resource procurement, and mechanized arms-making facilities. The Confederate Ordnance Department enthusiastically received the 1.25-inch breech-loading machine gun invented by Capt. D.R. Williams, CSA, and patented November 5, 1862.

The carriage-mounted Williams gun featured a single barrel with a reciprocating breech. Combustible paper cartridges, hand-fed into the receiver, were chambered by the breech block when the operating crank was turned. The crank also cammed an exposed hammer which struck a percussion cap seated on a nipple protruding from the side of the breech chamber. The explosive force of the powder charge drove the breech block rearward, reciprocating the forward movement, and that novel innovation would be taken a step farther in the automatic weapon systems subsequently devised by others.

The Williams gun, despite its hand-feed system, achieved a firing rate of 65 rounds a minute and had a maximum effective range of 2,000 yards. Employed in battery strength, the firepower was devastating, attested to by Union forces facing the guns at Seven Pines, Virginia, on May 3, 1862. Forty-two Williams guns were made—seven batteries of six guns each—and they served effectively throughout the conflict.

In addition, the Confederates used several kinds of revolving breech cannon emulating the common revolver design, a volley-firing gun with multiple barrels known as the Vanden-

Capt. Charles D. Chandler, USA (left) was the first to fire a machine gun—a Lewis—from an aircraft, June 7, 1912. *Library of Congress photo.*

berg, and experimented with other repeating arms such as the 18-shot, 1.25-in. machine gun invented by Chief of Ordnance Gorgas.

The Gorgas gun had a smoothbore barrel and the flat, circular breech rotated horizontally, turned by a lever rather than a crank. The breech chambers were loaded with combustible paper cartridges ignited when the hammer, also operated by the lever, struck the percussion caps at the breech chamber base.

On November 4, 1862, the day before the Williams gun was patented, Dr. Richard Jordan Gatling received a U.S. patent for what is currently re-

Austria-Hungary's 8mm Schwarzlose heavy machine gun, here with its crew during Italian mountain campaigns, was accurate to 500 yards, fired 400 rounds per minute. *Library of Congress photo.*

The French 8mm Lebel Chauchat light machine gun purportedly delivered 400 shots per minute; it was so unreliable, U.S. Marines simply threw it away. *Library of Congress photo.*

The dreaded German M08/15 Maxim heavy machine gun in action somewhere on the Western Front, 1917; note the armor-plate shields. *Library of Congress photo.*

Canadian gunners in Flanders setting up their heavy, water-cooled Maxim-Vickers machine gun. *Library of Congress photo.*

garded as the most sophisticated machine gun ever designed. The Gatling was subsequently perfected to the point where it ultimately superseded the late 19th century automatic machine guns which had rendered it obsolescent by 1911, for it is the antecedent of the 20mm Vulcan aircraft cannon and other devastating multibarrel guns.

The first Gatling, like the Ager, was mounted on a wheeled carriage, initially used steel cases gravity-fed from a hopper, and was crank-operated; however, the similarity stopped there. Rather than a breech rotating around a single barrel, the design incorporated six rifled barrels rapidly revolving around a central axis.

The Gatling exhibited several features which overcame many of the problems associated with other rapid-firing guns developed during and after the Civil War, among them overheating as exemplified by the single-barreled Ager and Williams. The 1-to-6 firing sequence of the early Gatling models gave each barrel time to cool between shots, while misfires were eliminated by positive ejection, whether or not the cartridge fired.

Gatling, like Ager, had difficulties convincing the U.S. Ordnance Department of the need for a reliable machine gun although, as with the Ager, several were purchased by individual unit commanders such as Gen. Benjamin F. Butler, USA, who paid $1,000 each for 12 guns.

Gatling eventually arranged for an official trial of his invention at the Washington (D.C.) Arsenal in January, 1865. Then Chief of Ordnance Brig. Gen. Alexander B. Dyer, USA, having a more liberal attitude toward repeating arms, was greatly impressed by the gun's performance, suggesting that it be modified to use a 1-in. metallic cartridge.

The first practical metallic cartridges, based on an 1848 Walter Hunt innovation improved in 1856 by Horace Smith and Daniel B. Wesson, consisted of a copper tube or case incorporating the powder, the projectile, and the fulminate ignition agent; the latter sealed in a rim at the case base. Self-contained rimfire cartridges were superior to paper and were successfully used early in the war with the 44-caliber Henry rifle and the 56-caliber Spencer rifle and carbine, each of them breechloaders.

The Civil War ended before the cartridge Gatlings were delivered; however, tests were completed and on August 24, 1866, the Gatling became the first manual-type machine gun adopted by any nation. The Ordnance Department then ordered 100 additional guns, 50 chambered for the 1-in. rimfire cartridge and the remainder chambered for the newly adopted 50-caliber rimfire rifle cartridge. The Gatling gun was further improved, employing 5-to-10 barrels and chambered for the superior centerfire cartridges devised by Col. Hiram Berdan, USA, and Col. Edmund M. Boxer, Chief of British Ordnance.

In 1865 the average firing rate of the Gatling was 1,000 rounds per minute with a maximum effective range of 1,000 yards. By 1880, the range exceeded 2,000 yards and the firing rate accelerated to 1,200 rounds a minute. In 1893, a gun driven by an electric motor delivered an astonishing 3,000 rounds in a single minute.

By 1883 the Gatling had been adapted to the Accles drum (dough-

ever, Capt. John H. Parker, USA, organized and trained a Gatling gun battery and it was used in Cuba as the defensive and offensive infantry weapon its rapid-fire capability had suggested to him, thereby establishing the fundamentals of future machine gun employment.

Until 1884, all machine guns were operated manually, a turn of the hand crank performing such mechanical functions as chambering the cartridge, firing it, and then extracting the spent cartridge from the chamber and ejecting it.

In automatic machine guns, the operating cycle was accomplished by either of two methods, each relying on the explosive force of the powder when the cartridge fired: recoil operation or gas operation.

In recoil-operated machine guns,

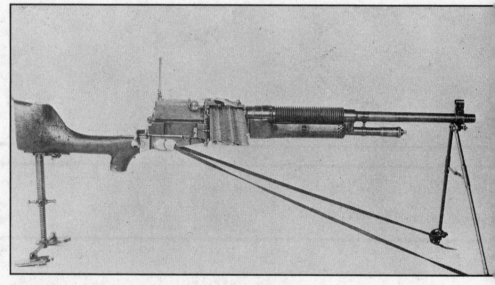

The M1909 Benét-Mercié light machine gun or machine rifle was co-invented by Laurence V. Benét, son of Brig. Gen. Stephen Vincent Benét, U.S. Chief of Ordnance from 1874 to 1891. It served with U.S. forces in Mexico in 1913 and 1916; later, it was used as an aircraft gun. *U.S. WDGS, National Archives photo.*

nut) magazine and three years later the vertical "stick" magazine invented by L. F. Bruce. Before the turn of the century the Gatling had been adopted by several nations, achieving a worldwide reputation.

Eighty U.S. manual-type machine guns had been patented by 1883, among them weapons devised by Fortune L. Bailey, DeWitt Clinton, W.B. Farwell, William Gardner, Benjamin Berkeley Hotchkiss, James P. Taylor, and Elihu Wilder. The Gatling remained superior to them all.

Following the Civil War, the Gatling and other manual-type machine guns had been equated with artillery and likewise employed. During the Spanish-American War (1898), how-

the explosive energy of the powder charge in the cartridge expanded against the face of the breech block forcing it rearward. Components automatically working in conjunction with the movement extracted the expended cartridge from the chamber and ejected it. As the breech block was thrust forward by a heavy spring, other components automatically fed the cartridge into the mechanism and chambered it; thus, each time a cartridge fired, the operating cycle was rapidly repeated until the ammunition in the feed system was expended or the trigger released.

With gas-operated machine guns, the gases produced by the combustion of the chambered cartridge followed the bullet down the bore and some of it was tapped off, expanding against the head of a spring-actuated piston which, in turn, drove the breech block to the rear. As in recoil operation, the components automatically performed the operating cycle in reciprocal concert with the breech block movement.

The first automatic-firing, recoil operated machine gun was patented in the U.S. on April 22, 1884 by Hiram Stevens Maxim of Brockway's Mills, Maine. Maxim was a brilliant, self-educated electrical and mechanical engineer with no arms-making experience. Visiting England in 1882, he was told a fortune could be made by devising a practical machine gun other than the manual type, and that nobody had yet succeeded.

Maxim accepted the challenge, staying in London where in 1883 he

The M1917 Marlin machine gun was designed as a belt-fed infantry weapon, later modified for aircraft use. Two thousand reached the AEF before war's end. *U.S. WDGS, NARS photo.*

discovered the recoil principle when at target practice his shoulder began to ache from the heavy kick delivered by his rifle. Inspired, he used recoil energy to create the following year the prototype of a machine gun which came to be sold in large numbers throughout the world.

The M1884 Maxim used the British 45-caliber Gatling gun cartridge, the cartridges inserted in a cloth belt as with the innovative feed system devised in 1874 by U.S. inventor Fortune L. Bailey. With that arrangement the gun delivered 600 r.p.m., the single barrel cooled by a surrounding water jacket. Displaying a reciprocal, toggle-joint breech block, the mechanism could be set to fire one shot a

minute or short bursts of 10, 20, or 100 r.p.m. Weighing 60 pounds without the tripod mount, the M1884 Maxim could be rapidly disassembled and reassembled without tools.

Despite superior design features, the Maxim machine gun was not instantly accepted because most nations had an abundant supply of Gatlings and other manual-type guns. The U.S. Ordnance Department ignored Maxim after an 1888 demonstration and American manufacturers refused to produce the gun, some scoffing at the design.

In 1886 the Maxim was adapted to use cartridges loaded with nitrocellulose ("smokeless") powder introduced a year earlier in France. The new propellant improved the gun's performance because it left no residue in the bore, thus reducing the need for frequent cleaning mandated by black powder.

On July 20, 1888, Maxim and industrialist Albert Vickers formed Vickers Sons and Maxim, Ltd. In 1904 the firm substituted aluminum and a superior steel for making many of the components, producing a gun weighing 18.5 pounds less than the M1884.

Germany, which had adopted the Maxim machine gun in 1899, was the first nation to recognize the potential of the automatic weapon and expanded its role in her armed forces. In the aftermath of the Russo-Japanese War (1904-1905), in which large numbers of machine guns were used in combat for the first time, most European nations decided to replace their manual-

type machine guns with automatic weapons. The Maxim filled the technology gap until those nations produced machine guns of their own.

At Spandau Arsenal, the Germans developed a heavy machine gun based on the Maxim design which used the 7.92mm Mauser cartridge chambered in the standard infantry rifle and it was adopted in 1908. The M1908 was the machine gun Germany relied on throughout World War I. It was modified in 1915, known thereafter as the Model 08/15.

In 1889, five years after Maxim introduced the recoil operated machine gun, John Moses Browning, the genius gun designer of Ogden, Utah, discovered the principle of gas operation while duck hunting, observing that the muzzle blast from his shotgun violently disturbed a tall stand of marsh grass. He reasoned that the energy released by the powder gases escaping from the gun muzzle could be harnessed to operate the mechanism. On August 20, 1895, nearly six years later and after several experiments, Browning received a U.S. patent on the gas operation principle and made arrangements for his machine gun to be produced by Colt's Patent Fire Arms Manufacturing Co.

In January, 1896, the U.S. Navy tested Browning's M1895 "Potato Digger" machine gun—so called because of the unusual movement of the gas actuator rod suspended beneath the barrel—and purchased 50 of them chambered for the standard naval service 6mm Lee cartridge. With that order the M1895 Browning became the first automatic machine gun adopted by the U.S.

Belt-fed like the Maxim, the M1895 Browning had a cyclic firing rate of 400 r.p.m. and a maximum effective range of 2,000 yards. The gun weighed 40 pounds without its tripod mount and proved its mettle in the Spanish-American War, earning the sobriquet "Peacemaker," and in the Boxer Rebellion (1900). In 1906 the Browning was altered to take the 30-06 cartridge used in the U.S. Magazine Rifle, M1903 (Springfield), the basic infantry weapon used by the AEF in World War I.

The years immediately preceding the Great War saw numerous attempts to develop machine guns employing the Maxim recoil principle or Browning's gas operation system, many of them successful. France adopted a gas operated machine gun designed by U.S. inventor Benjamin B. Hotchkiss in 1897 and it was improved in 1914. Another French machine gun, the St. Étienne, emerged in 1907. Austria-Hungary adopted the 8mm Schwarzlose recoil-operated machine gun in 1907 and an improved version was introduced as the M1907/1912. The Danish Madsen machine gun appeared in 1903 and the recoil mechanism was improved in 1914, the same year Italy adopted the recoil-operated Revelli machine gun.

It was also during the 1900-1914 period that several light machine guns and machine rifles appeared, each of them air rather than water-cooled. Among them were the M1902 Bergmann and M1912 Dreyse developed in Germany, as well as the M1913 Parabellum. France adopted the gas-operated Berthier machine rifle in 1909, the same year that the U.S. Army adopted the M1909 Benét-Mercié gas-operated machine rifle and its 30-round strip magazine.

While those innovative machine guns and machine rifles were originally designed for infantry use, either as individually or crew-served weapons, many of them were subsequently employed as aircraft guns, for in the Great War the airplane and the machine gun complemented each other as tactical weapons.

One of the most popular light machine guns utilized as an infantry or aircraft weapon was designed in 1910 by Lt. Col. Isaac Newton Lewis, USA. The air-cooled, gas-operated Lewis gun was introduced in 1911, delivering a rate of fire estimated at 750 r.p.m. as fed from a horizontal drum magazine, the larger holding 96 and a small one 47 30-06 cartridges.

The Lewis gun has the distinction of being the first machine gun fired from an aircraft, the event transpiring June 7, 1912 at College Park, Maryland, in a Type B Wright "pusher" piloted by Lt. T. DeWitt Milling. Capt. Charles DeForest Chandler, acting as the gunner, that day wrote the first chapter in aerial warfare.

Like other U.S. machine gun pioneers, Col. Lewis was ignored by the Ordnance Department. In 1913 he established a factory to produce his guns in Liège, Belgium. With war clouds gathering on the horizon, Lewis prudently relocated in Birmingham, England, where his guns were made in 303 caliber by the British Small Arms Co., then the world's largest small arms manufacturer.

The seemingly deliberate refusal of the U.S. to accept modern machine guns saw the nation completely unprepared in that respect when in 1914 hostilities erupted in Europe. Worse, nothing had been done to rectify the abysmal lack of suitable automatic weapons by 1917 when the AEF departed for France.

A top secret memoranda circulated among key U.S. military personnel on April 6, 1917, the very day Congress declared war, intimated that a minimum of 100,000 machine guns would be required to meet that eventuality. The U.S. then had available 1,010 obsolescent guns of various kinds: 158 M1895 Brownings, 282 M1904 Maxims, and 670 M1909 Benét-Merciés.

Germany entered the war with 12,500 improved Maxim machine guns and her armament factories had orders to make 50,000 more. With the initial German onslaught repulsed with horrendous casualties to both sides at the Marne (September 6-10, 1914), the conflict thereafter stagnated into a savage, bloody contest in which neither the Allies nor the Central Powers significantly gained much of the muddy, cratered ground between rusty barbed wire entanglements and a heavily fortified, confusing maze of trenches thickly studded with machine gun emplacements.

Massive artillery bombardments were the rule of the offensive, supported by equally massive infantry assaults, but the bloody, mutilated earth was murderously defended by the "little angels of death."

In World War I machine guns, as infantry, tank, and aircraft weapons, wrote *finis* to the horse cavalry steeped in ageless tradition, fulfilling the prophesy of an astute British military observer in the Russo-Japanese War who declared ". . . the only thing the cavalry could do in the face of entrenched machine guns was to cook rice for the infantry."

Great War machine gunners contributed numerous tricks and stunts to the terrible carnage they wrought, some of them so adept at manipulating their weapons that they "sang" popular tunes and communicated in Morse code with staccato bursts of fire. Gunners also devised a method of locating opposing emplacements at night, firing short bursts until the bullets struck the enemy's protective barbed wire, "getting the sparks" as they called it.

To prevent detection when night-firing—muzzle flash a deadly beacon—gunners erected two stakes about five feet apart and two feet from the muzzle, stretching between them sandbag burlap soaked to keep it from catching fire when the thus masked gun shot through it. During a sustained fire-fight when a red-hot barrel steamed away the gun's cooling jacket water and none was available to replenish it, gunners and crewmen urinated in the empty water chest which fed the jacket. The same method was occasionally used to dampen the ground in front of the gun to prevent the dust stirred by muzzle blast from revealing its position.

By 1915 the initial reconnaissance role relegated to aircraft early in the conflict had been radically altered, the aerial bomb and the rapid-firing machine gun imparting offensive and defensive capability. Machine guns, mounted singly or in pairs, soon appeared on the wings and fuselage of many aircraft.

As early as February, 1915, French air ace Roland Garros installed a M1909 Benét-Merié in front of his cockpit, attempting to fire it through the spinning propeller which had been fitted with steel blade guards to deflect the bullets. Garros flamed two German scout planes with that primitive arrangement before a ruptured fuel line forced him to make an emergency landing. He and his single-seater Morane were captured.

The Germans immediately grasped the significance of his innovation, shipping the Morane to Berlin for study the next day. Within 48 hours Dutch-born engineer Anthony H.G. Fokker, the instrument responsible for Germany's air superiority early in the war, designed and built a simple device synchronizing the gun's firing rate with propeller blade rotation; thus the bullets passed harmlessly between the blades, eliminating the need for steel guards.

Unknown to Fokker, he reinvented a device by which August Euler had theoretically solved the problem in 1910, while other equally ignored solutions had been perfected in 1913 and 1914. Fokker's synchronized firing system quickly altered the complexion of the air war and a variety of methods were shortly thereafter adopted by the Allies.

Confederate Gen. Nathan Bedford Forrest's strategy for winning battles was to simply "Git thar fustest with the mostest!" That dictum has been too long forgotten in respect to U.S. machine gun procurement. AEF doughboys often found themselves with unsuitable guns or none at all. They employed captured German guns or were armed with weapons provided by their allies, France offering a recoil-operated Chauchat M1915 light machine gun notorious for malfunctioning.

John M. Browning had continued to experiment with automatic weapons, developing in 1901 a water-cooled, recoil-operated gun with a firing rate of approximately 600 rounds per minute. The M1901, in modified form, was resurrected as the M1917 when wartime exigency goaded the U.S. into recognizing the desperate need.

Also under development at the time was the Marlin M1917 gas-operated machine gun designed by Swedish inventor Carl G. Swebilius and produced by the Marlin-Rockwell Corp., New Haven, Connecticut. The Marlin M1917 delivered 630 rounds per minute.

At last given direction, the astounding productivity of U.S. industry was galvanized into action. Marlin-Rockwell manufactured 23,000

now widely known by its initials B.A.R. The Browning automatic rifle was gas-operated, firing from a 20-shot magazine which emptied in 2½ seconds. Beginning in February, 1918, Colt, Winchester, and Marlin-Rockwell had delivered 52,000 B.A.R.'s by the end of the war.

The B.A.R. also arrived in France with the 79th Division which took it into action September 13, 1918. The 80th Division was the first unit already in France to be armed with B.A.R.'s, and they were demonstrated in combat by Lt. Val Browning, the inventor's son.

Though Browning-designed machine weapons contributed little during the Great War, they became the backbone of the automatic weapon

paign engendered among the adversaries 719,324 casualties. Thus, in merely two instances, 1,437,360 lives were cut short, many—perhaps most—by the deadly curtains of lead spewing forth from the powder-blackened muzzles of rapid-firing machine guns. The machine gun truly came of age in the merciless blood baths of The Great 1914-18 War. ●

(It is with regret we note that M. L. Brown has died since writing this article. Editor.)

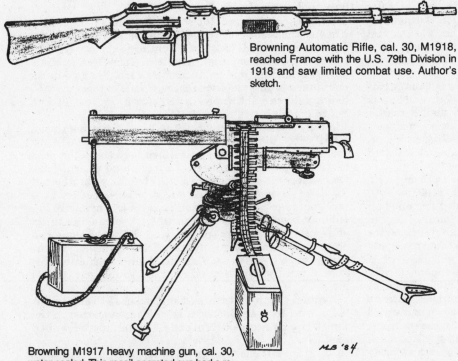

Browning Automatic Rifle, cal. 30, M1918, reached France with the U.S. 79th Division in 1918 and saw limited combat use. Author's sketch.

Browning M1917 heavy machine gun, cal. 30, water-cooled. This recoil-operated gun had a reciprocating breech. Water tank and hose were standard. Basic mechanism still in service. Author's sketch.

M1917 machine guns and 2,000 reached France a month before the Armistice, too late to see action.

The M1917 Browning fared slightly better. Three contractors had made 43,000 prior to the end of the war: Westinghouse making 30,150; Remington producing 12,000; and Colt fabricating 850. The guns arrived in France with the 79th Division and were taken into combat September 26, 1918, merely forty-six days before hostilities ceased.

It was also in 1917 that John M. Browning introduced a machine rifle

systems employed by the U.S. and other allied nations in World War II (1939-1945) and Korea (1950-1954), while they also served in Vietnam and are currently used by many emerging Third World powers.

In terms of producing huge casualty figures in World War I, the machine guns were greatly supported by incompetent leadership. The fiery cauldron of the 1916 Somme offensive produced casualties on both sides totaling 718,036. The senseless carnage which came to Belgium with the July-December, 1917, Flanders cam-

BIBLIOGRAPHY

Brodie, Bernard and Fawn. *From Crossbow to H-Bomb*. New York, 1962.

Brown, M.L. *Firearms in Colonial America: The Impact on History and Technology, 1492-1792*. Washington, 1980.

Browning, John and Gentry, Curt. *John M. Browning, American Gunmaker*. New York, 1964.

Bruce, Robert V. *Lincoln and the Tools of War*. Indianapolis, 1956.

Chinn, Lt. Col. George M., USMC. *The Machine Gun, History, Evolution, and Development of Manual, Automatic, and Airborne Repeating Weapons*. Vol. I. Washington, 1951.

Empey, Arthur Guy. *Over the Top*. New York, 1917.

Fredericks, Pierce G. *The Great Adventure, America in the First World War*. New York, 1960.

March, Francis A., Ph. D. *History of the World War, An Authentic Narrative of the World's Greatest War*. Philadelphia, 1919.

Millis, Walter. *Arms and Men, A Study in American Military History*. New York, 1956.

Moorehead, Alan. *Gallipoli*. New York, 1956.

Peterson, Harold L., ed. *Encyclopedia of Firearms*. New York, 1964.

Smith, W. H. B. *Small Arms of the World, A Basic Manual of Military Small Arms*. Harrisburg, 1952.

Stallings, Laurence. *The Doughboys, The Story of the AEF, 1917-1918*. New York, 1963.

Tschappat, Lt. Col. William, USA. *Text-Book of Ordnance and Gunnery*. London, 1917.

Tuchman, Barbara W. *The Guns of August*. New York, 1962.

War Department Annual Reports, 1916. Vol. I Washington, 1916.

Wolff, Leon. *In Flanders, The 1917 Campaign*. New York, 1958.

It started in Kentucky...

IN MANY places in America today, good citizens who own firearms are treated like common criminals. Massachusetts will jail you for one year minimum if you have a pistol without a permit. If you're passing through New Jersey with a shotgun or rifle with no permit, you're a criminal. And forget about a pistol license in Morton Grove, Illinois—there aren't any because pistols are banned.

When this nation was founded, the only firearms laws on the books required all free males to own muskets, rifles, or pistols and swords. To be sure, Tories who were tarred and feathered in the Revolution were also disarmed. And slaves were generally disarmed by law, although in practice many were allowed to hunt. But not one law existed anywhere which restricted the possession of firearms by free citizens.

How we ever got to the present condition is a complex question, but for starters we might ask what was the first restrictive firearms law passed, and why? It took place in the most unlikely place, and for a most unlikely reason when judged by today's way of thinking.

In 1813, Kentucky became the first state to ban the carrying of concealed weapons. The unprecedented act read: "Any person in this commonwealth, who shall hereafter wear a pocket pistol, dirk, large knife, or sword in a cane, concealed as a weapon, unless when travelling on a journey, shall be fined in any sum not less than one hundred dollars...."

While no jail time was allowed, debtor's prison was a real possibility in those days for a minimum $100 fine with no set maximum. Moreover, the act provided that one half of the fine would go to the informer—a dazzling sum in that period, which was beset with financial disaster caused by the War of 1812. This provision could have only encouraged perjury and spying among neighbors.

Why would Kentucky ban concealed weapons, and in the midst of war at that? Concealed weapons had never been the subject of any English law, from the statutes of King Alfred, written in 871-899 A.D., on down and would not be until the early twentieth century. To the contrary, in England it was an offense to carry arms openly in such matter as to terrify the King's subjects by brandishing them or committing an affray.

At the end of 1791, Virginia ratified the federal Bill of Rights, which then became part of the U.S. Constitution. The Second Amendment recognized that "the right of the people to keep and bear Arms, shall not be infringed."

Just a few months later, Kentucky entered the union with a Bill of Rights copied from Pennsylvania, including a declaration "that the right of the citizens to bear arms in defence of themselves and the state, shall not be questioned."

Kentucky's later law of 1813 is the first reference in Anglo-Saxon legal or political literature to classify concealed weapons as criminal. While today we may have rationalizations as to why carrying hidden weapons in public should be illegal, it is by no means obvious that the Kentucky legislature was motivated by the same reasons.

The Kentucky law was passed on February 3, 1813. While the Library of Congress has only one Kentucky newspaper around that date (see below), there is no doubt that the law sparked a howl of protest. It was probably not respected or enforced any more than the laws against billiard tables, gaming, or duelling.

When the law passed, the state capitol was reeling from a defeat the month before where Indians allied with the British scalped and massacred Kentuckian prisoners. The North Western campaign in which Kentuckian soldiers played a leading role ended as a failure. A gun control measure was an unlikely panacea from Kentuckians who had fought the Shawnees in 1811, and would continue fighting until New Orleans in 1815.

A copy of the Georgetown *Telegraph* dated a month and a half after the law passed included news of military events, Indian atrocities, an editorial stressing the need for training with firelock and bayonet, and militia calls. "Remember the dreadful fate of your butchered brothers at the River Rasin," it implored. An editorial signed by "Citizen Volunteer" noted: "Sacred is the object of a wise Republican government—personal liberty, personal security, and enjoyment of private property..... The sword alone, can protect us from foreign invasion." No crimes or disturbances were reported such as would have warranted passage of what was in those days a draconian gun control law.

Kentucky's gun culture, as displayed in 1815 at New Orleans with Andrew Jackson, is well remembered in the song "The Hunters of Kentucky," which includes such lines as:

> But Jackson, he was wide awake,
> And wasn't scared at trifles;
> He knew what deadly aim we take
> With our Kentucky rifles.

Ironically, when the Kentucky militia arrived at New Orleans, General Jackson reported: "Not one man in ten

by STEPHEN P. HALBROOK

Our First Gun

was well-armed and only one man in three had any arms at all." When first learning of this situation, Jackson exclaimed, "I don't believe it. I have never seen a Kentuckian without a gun and a pack of cards and a bottle of whiskey in my life."

Some of the militia men had their own private arms, but most were conscripts, substitutes, poor or just released from prison on enlistment. No state arms were ever supplied. The citizens of New Orleans contributed their personal guns and rifles to arm the more than one thousand Kentuckians who would hold their fire until they saw the whites of the Redcoats' eyes.

If it is surprising that politicians elected to represent "the Hunters of Kentucky" would pass the first prohibition in America on carrying concealed weapons, it is less surprising that the state's highest court would declare the law void within less than a decade. Its decision was the first published judicial opinion in America on the right to bear arms.

The Kentucky Bill of Rights of 1792 declared "that the right of the citizens to bear arms in defence of themselves and the state, shall not be questioned." In *Bliss v. Commonwealth* (1822), the Appellate Court held the act to be unconstitutional and reversed a conviction for carrying a sword cane.

Rejecting the prosecutor's distinction between regulation versus prohibition of the right, the court ruled that "whatever restrains the full and complete exercise of that right, though not an entire destruction of it, is forbidden by the explicit language of the constitution."

The court continued:

> And can there be entertained a reasonable doubt but the provisions of the act import a restraint on the right of the citizens to bear arms? The court apprehends not. The right existed at the adoption of the constitution; it had then no limits short of the moral power of the citizens to exercise it, and it in fact consisted in nothing else but in the liberty of the citizens to bear arms. Diminish that liberty, therefore, and you necessarily restrain the right; and such is the diminution and restraint, which the act in question most indisputably imports, by prohibiting the citizens wearing weapons in a manner which was lawful to wear them when the constitution was adopted. In truth, the right of the citizens to bear arms, has been as directly assailed by the provisions of the act, as though they were forbid carrying guns on their shoulders, swords in scabbards, or when in conflict with an enemy, were not allowed the use of bayonets; and if the act be consistent with the constitution, it cannot be incompatible with that instrument for the legislature, by successive enactments, to entirely cut off the exercise of the right of the citizens to bear arms. For, in principle, there is no difference between a law prohibiting the wearing concealed arms, and a law forbidding the wearing such as are exposed; and if the former be unconstitutional, the latter must be so likewise.

No high court since the above has had the courage to interpret the right to bear arms in this literal way. Yet the Kentucky court asked questions which no sophistry can explain: what if the open carrying of weapons was prohibited? Would the right not be violated because one could still carry a weapon concealed? "The absurd consequence would thence follow, of making the same act of the legislature, either consistent with the constitution, or not

Law

"I have never seen a Kentuckian without a gun and a pack of cards and a bottle of whiskey in my life," in the words of Old Hickory. *Above*: the Andrew Jackson Kentucky Pistol, as recreated by the United States Historical Society, Richmond, VA. (Katherine Wetzel photo)

so, according as it may precede or follow some other enactment of a different import."

For almost three decades after the above decision, Kentuckians were free to bear arms openly or concealed. There is no evidence that the bonds of the social order were torn asunder by thus allowing exercise of the right so explicitly recognized by the Constitution. But in 1849 authorization was given to the legislature to prohibit carrying concealed arms.

The Kentucky constitutional convention of 1849 voted 50 to 39 to add to the right-to-bear-arms guarantee, "but the General Assembly may pass laws to prevent persons from carrying concealed arms." The biggest issue at the convention was a proposal that would require officeholders and lawyers to swear that they had never sent or accepted a challenge or fought a duel with deadly weapons.

"Duelling is the fairest mode of fighting known," argued William C. Bullitt. "Where the duel is resorted to, men do not find it necessary to carry arms, and consequently, in case of a sudden quarrel, resort cannot be had to them on the instant." By permitting the duel, "you will avert the evil consequences of carrying concealed weapons." "Each man amongst us, must mainly rely on his own arm for protection of his person," but the duel provided rules and fairness. Providence did not design that the weak should "submit to insult and injury, else why permit the invention of the revolver, which very nearly reduces the strong to the level of the weak."

Another opponent moved to require politicians and attorneys to swear that they had never "worn any concealed deadly weapon except for self-defence." "I ask gentlemen which has produced most misery and mourning in Kentucky, the duel or the bowie knife?" The duel was a necessary evil, urged still another, because "if a man, influenced by a keen sense of honor, meets his adversary face to face, and scorns the use of the bowie knife and concealed weapons, where do you place him?"

Ben Hardin, who had drafted Kentucky's law against duelling back in 1811, spoke out against the proposed oath that one had never carried a concealed weapon other than for self-defense. "But says one gentleman, we must have a provision against the carrying of concealed weapons if we desire to guard against this terrible shedding of human blood. I should have no objection to that if it were possible to carry it fairly out, but we all know how indefinite such a provision would be. Here is a miserable old penknife that I carry, and it is a weapon."

Hardin recalled an instance where a man had been killed instantly with a penknife. His observations give a glimpse of life at that time: "street murders" were "being committed now all over the country;" many young men practiced with sword and pistol constantly; and no one in Kentucky had ever been punished for duelling. On one occasion, two duellists used shotguns at twenty yards; in another, it was muskets with three balls apiece, at eight feet! "I am against the carrying of concealed weapons *for aggressive purposes,*" he concluded, but "would not here make it a disqualification for office."

Speaker after speaker noted that public opinion favored the *code duello.* However, the "concealed carry" folks won over the duellists in the convention and the only oath required was that one had never duelled another Kentuckian. This allowed Kentucky's delegates to Congress to protect their honor against Congressmen from other states "who would avail themselves of any opportunity . . . to insult a Kentuckian."

The 1849 convention debates suggest that concealed weapons had been prohibited in 1813 because they violated the rules of the *code duello.* Duelling was the lesser of the two evils because it provided procedures for a fair fight; the same weapons, a specific starting time, and seconds and referees, all out of the presence of the ladies (whose honor the duel was often intended to uphold). Duelling was far superior to litigation to protect one's good name and reputation.

In contrast with Kentucky, certain other states with right-to-bear-arms guarantees never authorized the legis-

Stephen P. Halbrook, Ph.D., J.D., is author of *That Every Man Be Armed: The Evolution of a Constitutional Right* (University of New Mexico Press 1984), the most comprehensive history of the Second Amendment ever published. He is a practicing attorney located in Fairfax, Virginia.

lature to regulate concealed weapons, and yet the courts in some of the states upheld such legislation. The examples of Indiana, Texas, and Pennsylvania are instructive.

In 1816, Indiana entered the union with a Bill of Rights which declared "that the people have a right to bear arms for the defense of themselves and the State." Just four years after its legislature passed the same concealed-carry ban as Kentucky, but setting a maximum fine of one hundred dollars which would go to the county seminaries(!). The Supreme Court of that state upheld the law in 1833, though it gave no reasons for its opinion.

Yet Indiana's constitutional convention of 1850 rejected motions to add to the guarantee, "in an open and unconcealed manner" or to change it to: "No person shall be restricted in the right to carry visible arms." The latter's proponent thought the existing provision "gave a direct license to every desperado and ruffian in the State to carry concealed weapons." A sarcastic delegate responded: "I hope the gentlemen will modify his amendment, by adding after the word 'arms' the words 'or eyes.' (Great laughter.)" Today's joke about arming bears has an early counterpart about bearing "visible arms or eyes."

When Texas adopted its statehood constitution in 1845, the convention included in its Bill of Rights: "Every citizen shall have the right to keep and bear arms in the defense of himself or the State." The convention rejected provisions that the legislature could "pass laws prohibiting the carrying of deadly weapons, secretly," or regulating "the practice of bearing arms concealed, in the private walks of life." Based on this guarantee, the Texas Supreme Court some 15 years later declared that "the right of a citizen to bear arms, in lawful defense of himself or the State, is absolute."

After the War Between the States, the minority Republican government added the qualification, "under such regulations as the legislature may prescribe." This allowed the carpetbaggers in power to pass and selectively enforce a law to disarm ex-Confederates.

In 1876, when the federal troops were removed and the white majority regained power, the limitation was changed to "but the Legislature shall have power by law to regulate the wearing of arms, with a view to prevent crime." This was calculated to prohibit former slaves from carrying arms.

The Pennsylvania Declaration of Rights of 1791 stated: "The right of the citizens to bear arms in defence of themselves and the State, shall not be questioned." At the constitutional convention of 1873 an attempt was made to rephrase it to read, "openly to bear arms," because some judges were recognizing a right to carry pistols concealed. (Actually, the only gun control laws at the time were local ordinances which prohibited carrying concealed weapons with wrongful intent.)

"I believe in the right of self-defence of the weak against the strong," urged one opponent, a short man who could not see "why the Constitution should prohibit a man from carrying weapons to defend himself unless he carries them openly, why you should require him to sling a revolver over his shoulder." Another delegate noted that in recent labor unrest " no man's life would have been safe had it not been well understood that every man carried concealed weapons."

The convention overwhelmingly defeated addition of the word "openly." Despite this, after Pennsylvania prohibited carrying concealed firearms in the early twentieth century, the courts upheld the legislation.

While the Southern and Western states passed laws against concealed weapons before the War Between the

States, most of the Northeastern states had no such laws until the early twentieth century.

New Jersey banned duelling after Aaron Burr laid Alexander Hamilton to rest in 1804, but did not prohibit concealed weapons until 1905. Ironically, some of these Northeastern states now have the most stringent gun laws in the country.

When *Outlawing the Pistol* was the debate topic in 1926, the manual with that title noted: "The failure of the laws against carrying concealed weapons is pointed out as a warning, for it is a well known fact that the courts of many states have refused to enforce this law." While today crime-free Vermont is the only state not to prohibit concealed weapons, in most states the law is not stringently enforced although horror stories (often involving overzealous prosecutors and incompetent defense counsel) abound.

Kentucky's 1813 ban on arms not open to common observation was America's first Morton Grove: it was a shocking infringement on the right to bear arms, nullified by civil disobedience and, eventually, a high court. Still, it was the first such inroad in an Anglo-Saxon freedom never before violated in a thousand years of legal history. ●

Curiously, our first anti-gun law was as much a defense of duelling as anything else.

The Care & Feeding of *PISTOL MAGAZINES*

A charger-loaded Mauser military pistol, caliber 7.63mm Model 1896, has the charger in the feed position; built-in magazine shown disassembled.

by
DONALD M. SIMMONS

IN FIREARMS there are three terms that are sometimes confused. They are the words *magazine, clip* and *charger:*

A *magazine* is a device for storing loaded cartridges under integral spring tension. There are two distinct types of magazines, removable and built-in. This self-contained unit will continue to raise cartridges to its feed lips until all are expended.

A *clip* holds a group of loaded cartridges within a firearm. The raising of each cartridge is accomplished by a separate and independent follower and spring.

A *charger* holds a group of loaded cartridges external to a firearm. By finger pressure, the cartridges can be stripped from the charger and deposited into the magazine of the firearm.

These are my own definitions and I am sure there are exceptions to my three rules. The big point is that magazines should not all be called clips as is so often the case. Also the words "stripper clip" really mean "charger."

Let's look at examples of all of the above:

A built-in magazine will be found on most Mauser Military pistols.

A removable magazine is found on the Colt Model 1911/1911 A-1.

A clip, quite rare in automatic pistols, is found on Bergmann pistols. A clip-operated arm will not function correctly without its clip in place.

A charger is used to feed the built-in magazine in a Mauser Military pistol. The pistol can be made to function without the charger.

Probably the most common malfunctions in self-loading pistols involve their magazines. The new cartridge either doesn't rise to the feed lips or, stripped from the magazine, does not enter the chamber. Usually, the feed lips are bent wrong or the magazine's sides have been crushed. So a good rule of thumb, if you are having this kind of trouble, is to try a new magazine.

By carefully making a laminated steel mandrel, dents in the body of a magazine can be removed. If you are careful, you can reform feed lips with round nose pliers. If at all possible, though, use a new magazine.

People often ask me if a magazine works if it has been left fully loaded for year. The answer is yes, it will work, but if the pistol is being used for defense, don't bet your life on it. I would unload and reload it at least every six months.

The Japanese Nambu Type 14 (late) shows this ingenious method of loading, often miscalled a "magazine derattler."

In a well-made magazine, you will find the feed lips a great deal harder than the rest of it. You will also find the steel in the magazine's body near $\frac{1}{32}$ of an inch thick. If you have a non-shooting pistol—part of a collection—with a missing magazine, then a non-original replacement magazine will fill the hole, but to shoot a pistol, try to obtain an original magazine.

One of the hardest pistols to find *working* magazines for is the Luger because of the angle of the Luger's grip to the line of its bore. While giving an ideal grip, it unfortunately makes a very hard gun to magazine feed.

The very earliest repeating or automatic pistols were clip-fed. These would be the Bergmann pistols, the Bitner and Schonberger. With the advent of the first really successful automatic pistol, the Borchardt, we find the removable magazine. This magazine is covered by a German patent dated September 9, 1893. The pioneer automatic of John M. Browning, the

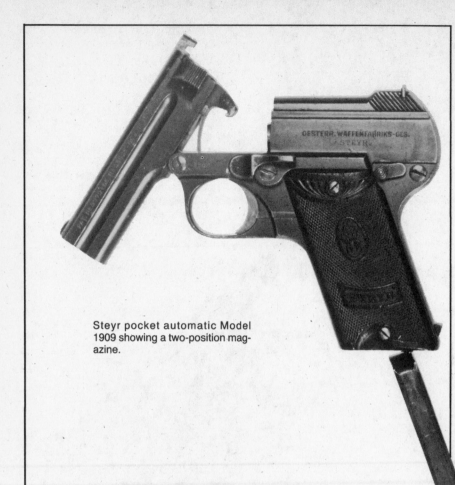

Steyr pocket automatic Model 1909 showing a two-position magazine.

At left is a Borchardt magazine; at right, a Colt Model 1900 38 ACP type.

Colt Model 1900, had a removable magazine. The 1900 Colt's magazine was patented by Louis Diss in September of 1884. These magazines, although made before the turn of the century, look contemporary today. Both exhibit cartridge counting holes, for instance.

An automatic pistol can get too big, so really large magazines have never been popular because of their unwieldiness. Certainly, one of the smallest would be the 9-shot magazine for the Austrian Lilliput 4.25 mm pistol. Still, large capacity magazines have been made for every successful pistol. The long-barreled Luger with shoulder stock, used as a carbine in World War I, had a 32-round snail drum magazine. The popular Colt Model 1911 also has had, over the years of its dominance, extra capacity magazines. These magazines tend to make either pistol awkward.

When you have been shooting and decide to stop before you have emptied a magazine, you should remove the magazine and EJECT THE CHAMBERED ROUND. The counting holes in the magazine body—when present—quickly tell you how many rounds are left and how many cartridges are needed.

Some magazines have just an open slot on one side as in the 1903 Browning in 9mm Browning Long; others have open slots on both sides like most Berettas. Some have a series of slots like the Savage Models 1907, 1915, and 1917. Some have in-line holes like the Walther P38, some have staggered holes like the Webley &

A magazine-loaded Colt Model 1911 shown ready to have a loaded magazine inserted. Notice the lips have the top cartridge pointed slightly to expedite feeding.

Mannlicher 7.63mm Model 9103 may be either charger- or magazine-loaded.

Scott Model 1913 455 automatic. Some high-capacity modern magazines only show the 5th, 10th and 15th round. In the case of the Astra A-80, these holes are stamped with the appropriate number. For the Star Model 28DA, the holes are there, but unnumbered. The Heckler & Koch P-7 has the number of each round from "2" through "8" stamped on BOTH sides—really foolproof. The Llama OMNI 9mm has the counting holes in the rear face of the magazine. There are, of course, some magazines like the Browning High Power's which have no counting holes at all.

There are basically two types of floorplates, the fixed or pinned type, and the removable type. One of the periodic types of care needed by a magazine is a thorough cleaning. The removable floorplate makes this cleaning much easier. The most common such plate is secured in place by a dimple in a second floorplate protruding through a hole. The floorplate slides off when the dimple is pushed. The Walther P.38 has just this type of conveniently removable floorplate. The Colt Model 1911/1911 A-1 has the fixed type of floorplate and usually goes uncleaned throughout its life. Some few military magazines will be found with a lanyard loop on their floorplate. Two examples are the Colt Model 1911 and the Russian Tokarev automatic pistol.

I know that everyone knows how to load a magazine, but still I ask: "Do they?" So at the risk of boring some of you, let me give a blow-by-blow description of how it is done:

1. Find a nonscratching surface; failing all else, sit down and use your knee. Hold the magazine in your left hand with the left index finger over the magazine's lips; pointing in the direction of the bullet's flight.

2. Insert the first cartridge by placing its back end on the front of the follower; then depress the cartridge which will in turn depress the follower until the cartridge can be slid to the rear under the lips of the magazine.

3. On each subsequent insertion of a cartridge, press with your left forefinger at the rear of the already inserted cartridge; this will facilitate the insertion of the next round. The new high-capacity double-stacked magazines are pretty hard to load the last four or five rounds, but using this procedure will make it a lot easier.

Some new high-capacity magazines have feed lips like those in a Mauser rifle; that is, the lips are further apart than the diameter of a cartridge. Both the Steyr GB 9mm and the Heckler & Koch 9mm VP700Z are like this. The followers in these magazines have one high side which keeps the top cartridge held in place by the single lip, first on one side and then the other. Such magazines are loaded by forcing cartridges down through the feed lips from directly above, using the left thumb to force the new cartridge down. Sometimes pushing the right thumb down on top of the left thumb is needed.

Magazines like the 32-round drum for the Luger pistol require a loading tool to set a full load. These tools snap around the top of the magazine and by working a lever, push the rear of the last cartridge to be loaded down enough so that the new cartridge can be slid into place. The lever arm replaces the left forefinger, which perhaps couldn't do it anyway.

Designers no sooner finish an automatic pistol than someone comes along and invents a loading aid. Perhaps this started with the Model 1910 Glisenti, which has an open-sided magazine and finger grooves on the follower one can actually grip. This represents the simplest most direct aid. The follower of the short-lived Whitney Wolverine was drilled to hold a 22 Long Rifle cartridge or empty crosswise to help depress the magazine follower. The Lahti Model 1939 offers a hoop made of steel, which is also a screwdriver; this special tool is carried in every Lahti holster. The Colt Woodsman, like many other 22 automatics, has just a knurled button to be thumb depressed to help in loading. (A day of loading this type of magazine can lead to a lacerated thumb and a lot of four-letter words. I find that by folding the cardboard cover to a box of 22 Long Rifle cartridges over the magazine button, a lot of the wear and tear can be reduced.)

The Luger pistol has a button connected to its magazine's follower, but the Luger was usually issued with a little combination screwdriver and loading tool which slipped over this button to make loading a lot easier. That's the right-angled tool carried in a pocket on the inside of the holster cover flap.

The early Japanese Nambu Model 14 had a hole in the magazine follower for the end of the cleaning rod. Later Nambus are even more ingenious. The follower is depressed fully either with the thumb or with the cleaning rod as described above; in the front of the magazine there is a hole into which the forward edge of the follower locks. The magazine can then be loaded with no resisting spring tension and thus inserted into the pistol. When the shooting hand depresses an S-shaped spring on the foregrip, the follower is released and the cartridges are under spring tension.

Contrary to what is taught on a combat course, you don't slam a magazine into a pistol, not for long anyway! If the pistol has a button magazine latch like the Colt 1911/1911 A-1, the magazine is pushed into its well firmly until it is latched in place. This process can be greatly facilitated if the thumb of the shooting hand depresses the magazine latch until the end of the magazine's movement. This will save wear on the latch and drag marks on the wall of the magazine. In the case of the bottom magazine latch like that found on the Walther P.38, the insertion is made by hooking the forward nose of the magazine in the well and then straightening out the magazine

Removable floorplates, from left—early Mauser 1910, caliber 6.35mm; late Mauser HSC, caliber 7.65mm; Savage Model 1907, caliber 32 ACP; Czechoslovakian Model 27, caliber 7.65mm; Browning FN Hi-Power Model 1935; Walther P.38; Whitney, caliber 22; Glisenti Model 1910; Japanese Type 94 8mm Nambu; Lahti Model 1939; Tokarev Model 1933, caliber 7.62mm; High Standard G-380, caliber 380 ACP; Bergmann-Bayard Model 1908, caliber 9mm Bergmann-Bayard.

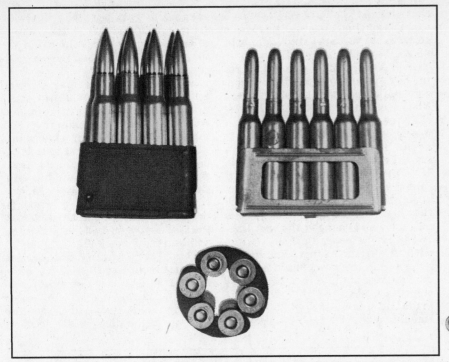

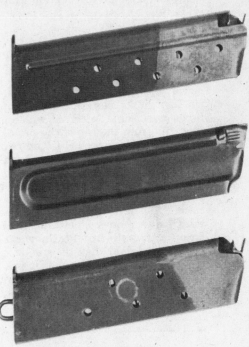

Clips look like this: at left is an M-1 rifle 8-round clip, caliber 30-06; at right, an Italian Mannlicher-Carcano clip in 6.5mm; at bottom are half-moon clips for a Colt or Smith & Wesson Model 1917 45 ACP revolver.

A family of magazines—different calibers for the same frame.

which will at the same time force back the latch. The magazine is then again pushed firmly into place with the palm of the left hand.

Today we find, due again to combat course shooting, a type of magazine latching system which when pushed forcefully ejects the magazine which in turn hits the ground—the example here would be again the Colt 1911/1911 A-1. This is all very well in real combat or play, but it is hell on magazines. Normally, one should catch the magazine, even the padded ones.

The bottom magazine latch system requires a slightly different release. Holding the pistol in the right hand as though shooting and with the forefinger clear of the trigger, push the latch to the rear with the left thumb while at the same time hooking the forward section of the floorplate with the left index finger. The left hand can then completely withdraw the magazine.

Both the insertion and the withdrawal of either type of magazine seem simple, but watch on the firing line someday and see how many really do it right. It seems there are never any instructions any more from the manufacturer on how to do these basic things because the manufacturer has to issue so many safety instructions—not just about his product but about all shooting—that he runs out of paper before he can get to the basics.

In the early days of automatic firearms, there was a great fear that unseasoned troops would fire the entire contents of their weapon's magazine before the crucial moment in the battle. Because of this fear, most turn-of-the-century arms were supplied with cut-offs which kept the contents of the magazine intact until rapid fire was needed, allowing only single shot firing until then. A few automatic pistols inherited this feature. The Webley & Scott Model 1913 automatic has two lock-up notches on its magazine's rear wall; the highest one will not allow the slide to pick up the next round and makes the pistol a single shot. The Steyr Model 1909 7.65mm also has the two-notch magazine but goes one step further and has a tip-up barrel to facilitate single loading.

Another very unusual automatic pistol is the Mannlicher 7.63mm Model 1903. It has a detachable magazine which is top loading like the Steyr GB and the H&K VP 70Z previously discussed; further, it can also be loaded by a charger without removing the magazine.

Some magazines serve dual purposes. Two examples are the German Dreyse and the German Jager. On the Dreyse the floorplate on its forward end has a hook-like projection which is used to depress the recoil spring during disassembly. The Jager

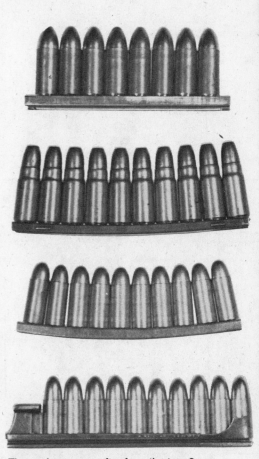

These chargers are for, from the top: 9mm Steyr, 8 rounds; 7.63mm Mauser military, 10 rounds; 7.65mm Mannlicher 1901, 10 rounds; 8mm Roth-Steyr Model 1907, 10 rounds, with a sliding thumb rest.

also has an awl-like projection which will act as a special drift to disassemble the entire pistol.

One last oddity is worth mentioning. Usually, a detachable grip-mounted magazine is inserted from the bottom of the grip—usually, but not always. The Austrian-made "Little Tom" has a magazine with a bottom conventional latch but which is inserted from the top of the pistol. First, the slide is locked in the rear position, then the magazine is inserted through the ejection area.

Usually a firearms manufacturer starts production chambering just one caliber in a new automatic pistol; as sales mount, requests inevitably come for different calibers. If the new cartridges are larger than the standard, then a lot of redesign may be required. However, if the new cartridge is smaller, maybe only magazine and barrel changes will be required. The

Colt Model 1911/1911 A-1 is a good example of this. Originally made in 45 ACP, it was soon asked for in both 38 ACP and 22 Long Rifle rimfire. The 38 Auto version was made into the 38 Super Auto and left the magazine well in the frame the same size as when used with a 45 ACP. The 22 version has a magazine with outer dimensions those of the 45 magazine.

The Savage Arms Corporation started with a 32 ACP caliber auto in 1907; by 1913 demand for a 380 ACP caliber was answered. The 32 used a double-stacked magazine; for the 380, they just reduced the capacity of the magazine and changed the width between feed lips and off they went without a frame change. Remington Arms began their excellent Model 51 automatic pistol line in a 380. When they decided to add a 32, they just made the single-stacked 380 magazine into a slightly double-stacked 32

magazine getting away without frame changes. All those caliber changes require that the different magazines be marked to avoid misuse.

Not so with the German Ortgies automatic pistol. They use the same magazine for both 32 ACP and 380 ACP. The right side is marked "7.65 mm" and has seven cartridge counting holes to indicate eight rounds capacity. The left side of the same magazine is marked "9mm" and has only six counting holes—pretty ingenious. No matter which caliber an Ortgies is, the same magazine can be used. Yes, the space between feed lips is loose on a 32 and tight on a 380.

The only real way to get a magazine clean is to strip and clean it. If it has a removable floorplate like most European magazines, it's easy. A loaded cartridge is inserted, bullet first, into the hole in the floorplate. The floor-

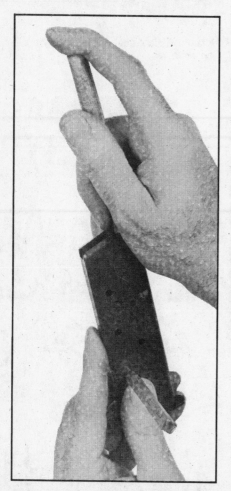

Stripping a magazine that has a fixed floorplate.

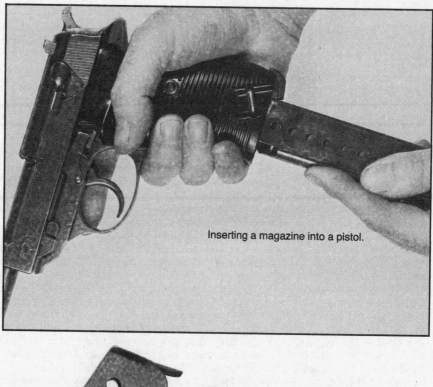

Inserting a magazine into a pistol.

The dual caliber Orgies magazine is 7.65mm on one side and 9mm Kurz (380 ACP) on the other.

plate is then slid off forward at the same time the index finger holds back the follower spring. The spring and the follower may now be removed and all parts can be given a thorough cleaning. The body can be cleaned with a bore-cleaning brush.

If the floorplate is crimped or pinned to the bottom of the magazine, the disassembly is a little more difficult but still can be done with simple tools. With a dowel or even a pencil, the follower is depressed until it can be just seen in the lowest cartridge counting hole. A drift is then inserted between the follower and the spring. The follower is now free to fall out through the lips of the magazine. By turning the top of the magazine upside down into a piece of cloth while removing the drift, the follower spring can be expelled without being lost. The parts can now be cleaned. When reassembling, the dowel must

Loading a Luger snail drum, among others, requires technical assistance.

Removing a magazine from a pistol.

Loading a magazine can be an easy manual job, done correctly.

have a greater diameter than the spring's coils, but not too big to avoid expanding the walls of the magazine. A clean magazine with well-formed feed lips and no dents in its wall will give good service.

Magazines perform a very important task in an automatic pistol; they not only store externally a load of cartridges but they also act to feed these cartridges to the auto during firing. A cheaply made magazine with easily bent feed lips and easily dented sides is less than worthless. This is particularly true of a magazine used in a firearm that may have to defend its own-

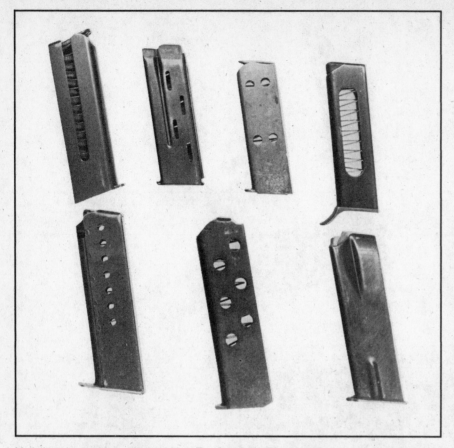

Variations in cartridge counting holes: Top from left—Browning Model 1903 9mm Browning Long; Savage Model 1907, caliber 32 ACP; Oriental caliber 7.65mm Browning; Beretta Model 1934, caliber 9mm Browning Short; and at bottom, from left—Walther P.38; caliber 455 W & S auto; Browning Hi-Power Model 1935.

The Luger Artillery Model 1917 32-round drum, the Lilliput 4.25mm magazine, and a 20-round special magazine for Colt Model 1911/1911 A-1 are all extra-capacity units.

er's life. Don't use gypsy magazines; get a new one from the manufacturer of the gun.

If the gun is no longer made and the manufacturer's supply of spare magazines is exhausted, get the best used magazine you can find as a replacement. Even if one is just plinking, it is a pain to have to stop shooting periodically to clear a jam caused by a malfeeding magazine. Take good care of your original magazine and there is no reason why it won't last as long as its original gun.

Luger magazines that work well are hard to find. It has been my experience that the best ones are those made during the initial years of World War II—that is, 1936 through 1939—with plastic or aluminum floorplates and extruded bodies. If you can find one of these, it can be used in any Luger you have and will give good results.

If an automatic pistol comes with a second magazine, alternate the use of these two magazines and reduce the wear in half on each one. If you have two original magazines and plan to leave a loaded automatic around for defense, load one magazine and then six months later, unload it and load the alternate one. This will be easier on the magazine's springs.

At gun shows, when I don't find any pistols I can't live without, I buy up a few magazines. Someday, you may get a chance to buy a magazineless gun at a bargain price and you, and only you, know that you have its correct magazine sitting at home in a drawer.

Can you tell if a magazine has been fired a lot? Yes, you can even if the blue is excellent. Look at the front edge of the magazine and you will see the little bumps that the rounds in the magazine make after lots of rounds have been shot through them. These bumps are only found on magazines used with hard ball ammo.

If you are going to load a lot of magazines in a caliber similar to ones also found in submachine guns, you can often buy a loading device used for the full automatic arm which will work for you with no or only a little modification. As an example, the loading device for an MP-40 can be used, with minor modification, to load many double-stacked 9mm pistol magazines. It makes a much quicker job of the work.

When a magazine is out of its pistol, it is very vulnerable. Don't put weight on its side walls and protect its feed lips. Over the the long haul, take care of your magazines and they will perform their duties faithfully. ●

Five Shiloh Sharps percussion models, from top: 1863 Sharps carbine, Sharps Confederate Robinson carbine, 1859 Military carbine, Military rifle and the Sporting percussion rifle, produced by Shiloh from 1972 until 1980.

Making Mr. Sharps' Rifles TODAY

by BILL BIGELOW

THE SHARPS rifle has been an enduring piece of Americana since its introduction in 1849. For more than ten years now, it has been "re-manufactured" in America under the loving guidance of Wolfgang Droege and his Shiloh Sharps Manufacturing Co.

This particular story perhaps starts with Wolf Droege rather than Christian Sharps and as any student of the Sharps rifle will attest, it is typical of the wild, on-again-off-again story of Sharps rifles.

Wolf Droege is an American-born son of German parents, who returned as a child to Germany before WW II. He grew up in Nazi Germany and made his way back to his homeland, the USA after 1945. Wolf had learned his trade as a highly skilled machinist and toolmaker during the war years.

For many years, he supervised construction of machine tools. Later he operated a tool shop in New York specializing in highly technical aircraft parts. Wolf also spent a good part of his career building and repairing machine tools for a manufacturer. All this background was present when one day a friend asked Wolf if he could re-create a Sharps rifle.

"I wanted to do something that seemed more worthwhile than aircraft parts, and I was searching for something else to do with my machines. When my associate asked, 'Why don't you manufacture the Sharps?' I will be very honest with you, I asked, 'What is the Sharps?'

"I went to Dixie Gun Works in Union City, Tennessee and I looked at the originals there. I looked, and looked, and looked some more. I went back three months later to look again and I bought one.

"I bought a carbine, the percussion carbine. I started taking it apart. It took me six months to get it on paper, checking dimensions and making

Wolf Droege, Shiloh Sharps founder, takes a shot from the cross-sticks while author looks on. The rifle is a #1 Sporting style with tang rear and windgauge front sights.

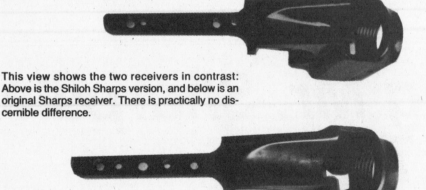

This view shows the two receivers in contrast: Above is the Shiloh Sharps version, and below is an original Sharps receiver. There is practically no discernible difference.

hand drawings. At that time I was still making aircraft parts.

"Because I was making other black powder accessories at that time, it seemed right to get into the gun business. I said, 'Let's go with this thing and see if we can make some money.' Well, little did I know how much it was going to cost!"

He made some of the first moulds at the tool shop then and some of the moulds were made by a specialty shop in New England. As Wolf was still manufacturing aircraft parts, the whole project would have taken too long if not for the outside supplier of investment casting moulds working from Wolf's drawings.

At that point he looked around for a barrel source. Six to eight months later he really started to move on the project. They finished the moulds and had some sample parts on hand.

The total cost of the tooling at that time was $96,000. That is a lot of $500 rifles, none of which had been made or sold yet. He then had to set up his machinery to make gun parts. It took a little over a year to get the first gun out from the time he started the drawings on paper to the time he had one in hand.

Droege made four complete receivers by hand. That is, not from a casting but machined from solid blocks of steel. He still has three of those re-

ceivers. He took them to the National Sporting Goods Association (NSGA) Show at Chicago and walked out with 150 orders for guns.

At that point, Droege started carrying the gun project and was slowly dropping the aircraft parts. He made the first gun, or prototype in 1972. It was a carbine and over a year later the percussion rifle appeared. The cartridge gun followed less than a year later in 1974. Exactly 100 years after the introduction of the Model 1874 Sharps, Shiloh Sharps was re-creating the '74.

Typical of Wolf Droege's attitude is this statement, "The perfection of the tooling was only completed about two months ago. We now feel we have things under control after ten years!!"

That was in 1984.

If you read Frank Sellers' book on the Sharps you will become familiar with the gas check problem on the percussion guns of the original Sharps. Sharps himself tried everything, including a platinum gas check ring on the breech-block face to stop erosion, but never solved the problem. Shiloh Sharps has found a way to reduce the problem and prolong breech-block life over the originals, but this is 130 years later. In their Model 1874, Shiloh Sharps Manufacturing has at last solved the firing pin problem inherent in the Sharps original design, 110 years later.

Today people are using smokeless powders in the Sharps cartridge rifles. This called for a smaller firing pin due to metal flow of the primers on firing. Wolf tried all sorts of new materials, but finally changed the pin to a two-piece arrangement. The old "dogleg" pin would fatigue due to side pressure. The two-piece pin eliminates that fatigue.

Any Shiloh Sharps with the small firing pin can be retro-fitted with the two-piece pin and it will work. The old original large firing pin Sharps which the Shiloh company produced can be switched to the modern 2-piece pin by getting a new breech block. The newer smaller one-piece firing pins must have the breech block returned to the factory for retrofit of the two-piece firing pin. The new pin is an inertial type, which eliminates fatigue and disperses the harmonic pressures of being struck by the hammer.

Shiloh Sharps is using the original Sharps rifling configuration, but the manufacturing technique is vastly different from the way Robbins and Lawrence did it. Shiloh's barrels are button-rifled in the Shiloh factory. The gun drilling is done at high speeds and precision reaming to a polish finish inside the barrels is considered highly important. In a 34-in. barrel, total runout of the hole from end to end is never allowed to exceed .025-in. Many barrels are produced with a minimum of runout.

The original Sharps barrels were cut-rifled by the traditional method, yet high degrees of accuracy were obtained in the originals. A look inside a new Shiloh barrel, compared with the inside of an original, quickly tells the story. A mirror-like finish appears brightly in the Shiloh barrels. This is accomplished due to modern gun barrel metallurgy in the steel that Shiloh uses, plus the high speed machining techniques, reaming and polishing for the button rifle method.

Today, Sharps receivers are investment castings, finish machined. Originals were forged and machined. The original receivers were threaded on a lathe using a point-to-point method, the thread a flat 10-pitch style. This approach was very time-consuming. It would take at least ten minutes in the old factory of Robbins and Lawrence. Today, Shiloh does barrel threading in one minute.

Today, the investment cast receivers are put on a surface grinder and the castings are cleaned up and shaped with a specially shaped grinding wheel. Then the remainder of the surfaces are trued or squared up for a few more machining operations. The breech block, lever, lever pin and such are considered separate parts. They, too, are investment cast, sanded and polished.

Today's investment casting techniques bear some discussion. Casting

From left: Shiloh Sharps Bridgeport style Long Range rifle; the Shiloh Long Range Express rifle; an original Sharps Creedmoor as manufactured at Bridgeport, CT, in the 1870s. (Original rifle courtesy C. Sharps Arms Co. collection)

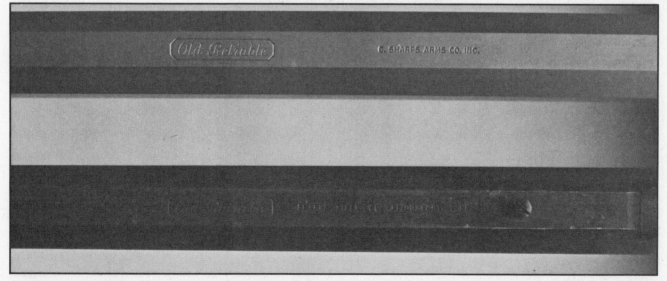

The Shiloh Sharps barrel (top) as made recently showed the C. Sharps Arms Co., Inc. name stamped into the barrel—C. Sharps was the sole sales agent for the Shiloh Sharps Manufacturing Co. An original barrel as manufactured by Robbins & Lawrence for Sharps Rifle Co. is also shown. The "Old Reliable" trademark is used on both the recreation and the original.

requires cleanup of such things as sprues and fins, if any. Banking surfaces must be established for machining and different fixtures are used in the milling and grinding processes to bring the casting to the fine tolerances of the finished part.

In the simpler parts, it is suggested that forging might be superior to casting, since hammer forgings would be more nearly to size and some machining operations would be eliminated. The investment casting method is far more efficient in the long run, despite these factors.

Perhaps Wolf Droege has stated the situation best: "Today our materials are better. When you talk about method, in the old days they were first rate. It is very hard to follow in their footsteps with only finished guns for a map. I want to get as close as possible to what Christian Sharps did. Mr. Sharps really knew what he was doing!"

The manufacturing concern of Robbins and Lawrence also knew what they were doing and were the people behind Sharps' design that made it work. Robbins and Lawrence did the actual gunmaking starting in 1851.

". . . Robbins and Lawrence, who more than any other New England manufacturer can be credited with being the fathers of the machine tool industry, thus making a reality of Whitney's dream of true interchangeability. Robbins and Lawrence undoubtedly did not invent all the machines or the machine shop practices which they employed, but they did use intelligence and initiative in bringing together the skills, the know-how, and the machines. They were not working on the theoretical level. (I.e. as was Sharps himself.) They built machine tools for the British and they, equipped, owned, and operated the first factory in Hartford to produce the famous Sharps rifle." (From: Dreyup, Felicia Johnson; *Arms Makers of the Connecticut Valley 1790-1870*. Smith College Studies in History, Vol. 33, Northampton, Mass. 1948.)

The Robbins and Lawrence Manufacturing Co. did the actual gunmaking starting in 1851. By 1850, iron bed lathes were being manufactured in New Haven, Connecticut, with interchangeable gears. These allowed greater accuracy and flexibility in machining operations necessary to fine gunmaking. Robbins and Lawrence were well recognized for their excellent quality machine tools of all

Original Sharps Production

Perhaps clearer pictures are obtained by looking at production figures.

The total Sharps production of all models and designs was approximately 164,700 rifles and carbines plus about 400 shotguns as near as I can calculate.

Model 1849	Less than	200			
Model 1850		200			
Model 1851	Carbine	1,650	Sporting Rifles	400	
Model 1852	Carbine	4,500	Sporting Rifles	560	
Model 1853	Carbine	10,300	Sporting Rifles	2,950	
			Military Rifles	204	
Model 1855	Carbine	700	Sporting Rifles	12	
			U.S.N. Rifles	263	
Model 1855 British Carbines		6,000			
New Model 1859, 1863 & 1865 Carbines and Rifles		All types	115,000		
New Model 1869 Rifles and Carbines		925			
Altered Model 1870		1,300			

Model 1874

Sporting Rifle	6,500	Mid-range #3	4
Military Rifle	1,769	Long Range #1	87
Military Carbine	456	Long Range #2	258
Hartford Rifle	592	Long Range #3	75
Creedmoor #1	134	Long Range #4	9
Creedmoor #2	12	Business Rifle	1,604
Creedmoor #3	3	Schuetzen	69
Mid-range #1	102	A Series	700
Mid-range #2	71		

Model 1877 Rifle	100
Sharps-Borchardt 1878 Rifle	8,700

GRAND TOTAL of approximately 164,705*

*Sellers, Frank; Sharps Firearms, Beinfeld Publishing, Inc. North Hollywood, CA., 1978 (pages 31, 33).
*Flayderman, N., Flayderman's Guide to Antique American Firearms. DBI Books, Inc., Northbrook, IL (pages 158-168).

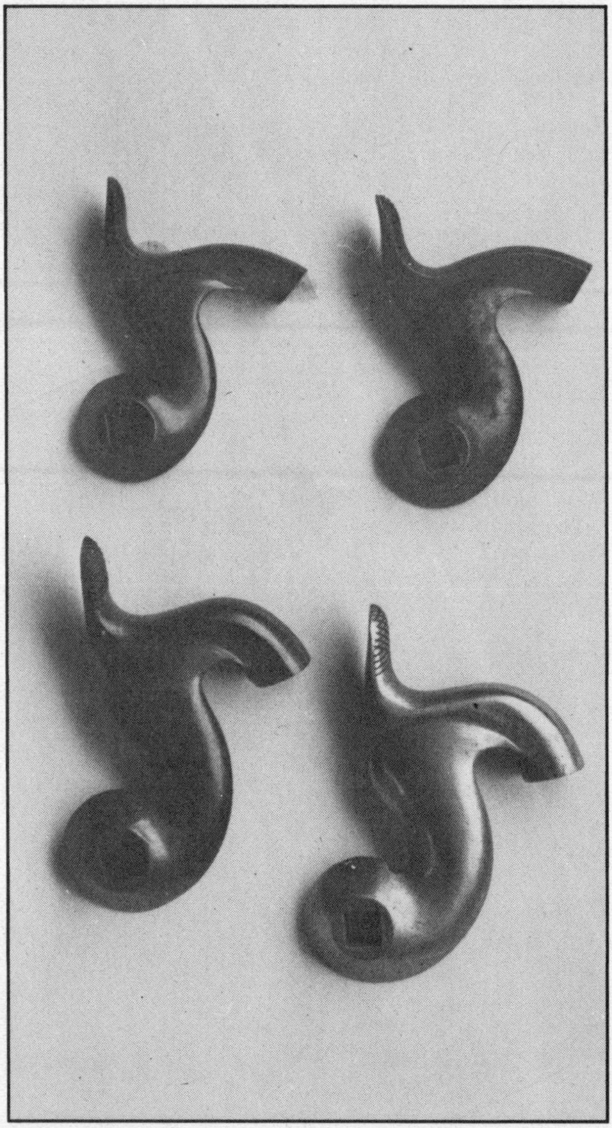

Two hammer styles are necessary—one for percussion models, one for cartridge models. The hammers on the left are the Shiloh versions; original hammers are shown to the right.

Two percussion style lockplates, the original Sharps above with C. Sharps Inc., Oct. 5th, 1858 marking, plus the R. S. Lawrence, April, 1860, marking near the primer feed device. The lower plate is Shiloh's New Model with the Farmingdale, New York, address.

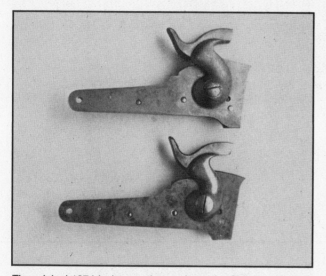

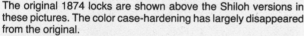

The original 1874 locks are shown above the Shiloh versions in these pictures. The color case-hardening has largely disappeared from the original.

Serial Numbers of the Shiloh Sharps

The Shiloh Sharps serial numbers begin with #200, issued from the original factory site at 37 Potter Street in Farmingdale, New York. Numbers of Model 1863 and 1874 are interspersed except for the first few hundred numbers, which are all percussion. Therefore, there is no practical way to tell from the records which receivers are percussion and which were shipped from the factory as cartridge guns.

Production started in 1972 and ran, by October 31, 1984, to serial number 6,999.

From 1973 through December, 1978, serial numbers up to 1,999 were stamped. By September of 1979, serial number 3,189 had been produced, and by December of 1979 serial number 3,517 was stamped. Then, to May of 1980 numbers get through 3,793, followed by number 4,315 being shipped in September of 1980. By January of 1981, number 4,388 had been marked. In January, 1982, serial number 5,257 was shipped.

Records show that by July, 1982 serial numbers through 5,257 were shipped and in December of 1982, serial number 5,656 was shipped. By December of 1983, production had reached the 6,000 level and in January of 1984 the first rifle produced at Big Timber, Montana, #6,122 was shipped. At the time of this writing, October 1984, numbers through 6,999 had been stamped on receivers for December shipping.

Some receiver castings were rejected and destroyed over the years after numbering due to imperfections discovered upon normal inspection, plus normal breakage. Also, early records are not available due to a fire at Farmingdale. Therefore, neither consecutive order on receiver numbers nor exact quantities can be documented.

Of the above numbers we do know some few particulars. There are a few Shiloh Sharps that vary from the above numbering. In 1982 a "D" series under the Drovel Tool Co. name was produced during a period of reorganization. These were 66 guns only and run D-1000 through D-1065.

In addition, there are the Confederate Robinson Sharps numbered from #201 - 409 only. These were produced by special order over a period of several years. A few are still available on special order only.

There are several presentation guns in the percussion sporting model that carry serial numbers between 202 - 298. These were produced in 1979. Matched pairs of carbines and rifles range from #200 - 242 with C and R respectively in the number.

Wolf Droege holds the #200 Robinson carbine and the number 102 1863 carbine in his personal collection.

Some additional presentation rifles were produced as follows:

54 caliber: 238, 240, 242, 246, 252, 254, 256, 268, 270, 274, 276, 278, 282, 284, 286, 294, 296, 298, 304, 306, 308, 316, 318, 320, 328, 332, 334.
50 caliber: 244, 258, 260, 262, 264, 266, 272, 280, 288, 302, 310, 322, 326.
45 caliber: 248, 250, 290, 292, 300, 312, 314, 324, 330, 336.

There were only eight saddle rifles made, in the #1 pattern, four in the #3 pattern, all 40-caliber.

All this jumping around with numbers and models fits exactly the pattern of the orignal Sharps companies. The originals were started in Mill Creek, Pennsylvania and manufactured by the Albert S. Nippes Co. on the 1848 patent in the year 1849. Then, the patent sold to George Pembroke who organized the Sharps Rifle Manufacturing Co. in 1851 in Hartford, Connecticut. And so on.

This shows about a third of the Shiloh Sharps production facility now located in Big Timber, MT.

Tapered flats are milled on six barrels at a time after they have been bored, reamed, rifled, turned and chambered.

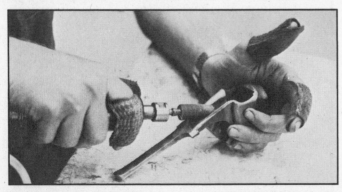

Among many hand operations in casting cleanup is polishing out the loading ramp of the Shiloh receiver.

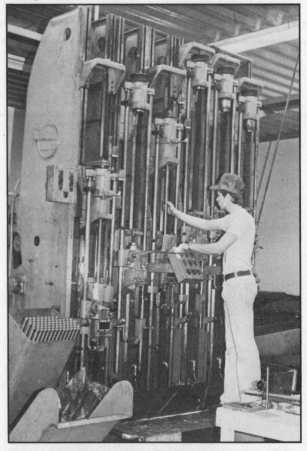

Vertical gun drilling operation in Big Timber can produce six barrels at a time. Reaming and button rifling operations are performed on special machines.

types and probably were the recognized premier manufacturer in the U.S. at that time.

Today's Shiloh Sharps rifles are manufactured using techniques available worldwide to the machine tool industry. However, the Sharps original design does not lend itself to complete automatic machine shop production. There is a very necessary amount of hand-fitting and filing and other operations, particularly on the smaller parts and the wood. This is where the costs of production rise sharply. Droege says the cost of the rough-turned wood stocks as they are received from the supplier amount to ⅓ of the total material cost. So, production efficiencies in the machining end are what keep the Sharps rifles down in cost to a reasonable level. Even so, by standards that most American shooters enjoy, the price is higher than for typical American-made modern rifles.

Nearly all major pieces of the Shiloh rifles require machining and cleanup. Lockplates are both milled to appropriate shapes and drilled. The receivers are surface ground, milled and drilled plus threaded. Barrels in the rough are fitted to receivers and marked, then disassembled for further finishing operations such as milling flats, chambering, etc. Many smaller parts are belt-sanded then hand-filed. Approximately 35 different screws are required between the two models (1863 and 1874). These are made with original sizes and threads.

Today's Shiloh Sharps parts are in many respects faithful reproductions of the originals. Some may even be interchangeable with the originals. This is both good and bad. Sometimes it takes the resident expert at the factory to tell the sample original parts from the production parts. Mould marks of one sort or another are the giveaway. However, diligent hand filing can erase even this clue. It is possible to restore old damaged rifles with new Shiloh parts. Collectors should be aware of this, even though the factory does not suggest their parts are suitable or interchangeable for originals.

The final result is, just as the originals, offered in a plethora of calibers and barrel lengths and styles. So are the Shiloh models. There are carbines, sporting rifles, military rifles and business rifles. These are all produced to be compatible with original Sharps offerings. All this is in keeping with Wolfgang Droege's desire to "... follow Mr. Sharps." ●

Shiloh Sharps employees hand-assemble and hand-fit production rifles before testfiring.

A close-up view of the chamber reaming operation. The C-clamp will be replaced with a permanent fixture.

Typical screws produced for the Shiloh Sharps in the Big Timber plant.

IN DEFENSE OF
THE MAGNIFICENT BB

Out at 50 yards, over 200 patterns change a ballistician's mind.

The best BB loads all have three things in common: copper-plated shot; granulated polyethylene buffer; and a plastic shot sleeve.

by EDWARD A. MATUNAS

THE MOST misunderstood and frequently misapplied shot size is the giant BB. Too small to be called buckshot and so large as to be beyond the traditional numbering system used to identify relative sizes, the BB has been both cursed and honored by shotgunners for a long time.

Unfortunately, BB size shot is often used by gunners who insist on shooting at waterfowl or large small game at ranges well beyond that which could be called sporting; often 100 yards or more. These unsportsmanlike hunters reason that just one lucky pellet will bring the bird or game down if that pellet is a large BB. The result of such action often is that birds (which might have eventually flown into gun range of a careful hunter) are driven even higher into the heavens by these sky busters who open up on birds that other hunters would hardly give a second glance. Also, some hunters have attempted to use BB's to replace buckshot for short range deer hunting. These abuses of BB size pellets have become so widespread that the mere possession of shells loaded with BBs will often bring accusing glances and comments. Indeed, the stigma of BBs has become so great that in some jurisdictions possession or use afield is, by legislation, illegal. And this stigma often keeps hunters from realizing that, when properly applied, the BB can be the ideal shot size for a number of applications. In fact, BBs can make it possible to shotgun hunt small game that is normally hunted only with a rifle.

It is important to first set aside any thoughts that the BB should be compared to buckshot. Even the smallest buckshot offer enormous energy and penetration compared to the BB. There are no applications of buckshot that overlap with the BB. Tables 1 and 2 will clearly point out the comparatively huge size of the smallest buckshot (#4 Buck) compared to BBs. It should be noted that most authorities consider #4 buckshot much too small for deer hunting, favoring instead 00 Buck for such purposes.

To understand the potential effectiveness, as well as the shortcomings, of the BB, one needs to consider physical size and downrange ballistics alongside other large shot. As can be seen from the accompanying table (No. 1), BBs are big, weighing considerably more than other standard large shot. This means that when a given charge weight of BBs is started out at the same velocity as a smaller size pellet, each BB pellet will have notably more energy at any given range. The actual downrange ballistics of various large size pellets are listed in Table No. 2. At the 60-yard mark a BB will deliver more than twice the energy of a No. 2 pellet; almost four times the energy of a No. 4 pellet; and about five times the energy of a No. 5 pellet. This is due to the BB's greater mass and its ability to retain more of its original velocity. The exterior ballistics tables are one of the best possible ways to compare BBs and other shot sizes.

What larger size and greater energy means to the hunter is that in order to deliver the same energy to the target as with a single BB pellet the target would have to be stuck with 2.1 No. 2 pellets, or 3.7 No. 4 pellets, or 5.3 No. 5 pellets. Yet, with a given weight of shot charge this is improbable, since the number of pellets in a given charge of the varying sizes does not allow for this. Based on a given charge weight there will be only 1.8, 2.7, or 3.5 pellets respectively of Nos.

2, 4 or 5 shot for each BB. This means that on a mathematical basis, No. 2s can deliver only 86% of the energy of BBs, with No. 4 or No. 5 size shot delivering only 74% and 67% of the BBs' energy to a target area.

Of course, such an analysis would prove meaningless in attempting to anticipate the performance of the various shot sizes if the actual number of pellets striking game in the field varied notably from these suggestions. Therefore, I carefully patterned a number of different BB, 2, 4, and 5 loads on silhouette outline targets at 50 yards. The actual number of smaller pellets striking a given 30″ target for each BB hit was close, but somewhat less than the analysis would indicate. Compared to an equal charge weight, 1.6 No. 2 pellets hit the target for each BB. No. 4 pellets scored only 2.5 and 5s only 3.3 hits for each BB.

But even if the shooter were able to find a load that would pattern sufficiently dense with smaller shot to put enough pellets into the target to deliver energy to equal the BB's performance, the results would not be the same on the larger small game or birds. This is due to the fact that the individual pellet energy is what gives each pellet the ability to penetrate and reach the vitals. On large birds, such as geese or turkey, a BB has sufficient energy to exit the far side on a broadside hit. On angles where deep penetration might be required the BB will almost always ensure sufficient depth to reach vitals even at 60 yards. The lesser size shot simply are not always up to this task. Frequently, especially at the longer ranges, smaller pellets will fail to completely penetrate big bones and muscle, let alone reach the vitals. Based on input from a number of shooters, we know even No. 2 shot will not always exit the far side of a 40-yard, 20-pound+ turkey.

An obvious disadvantage of BBs is the fewer number of pellets available per given shot charge weight. As stated, there are 1.8 No. 2s for each BB in a given weight of shot. Thus for smaller targets it might be impossible to score any hits at all with BBs when multiple hits are possible with smaller pellets. Obviously, then, for all its merits the BB is not the right shot size for any of our smaller game or birds. In fact, it takes a fairly large target to insure that BBs can perform well. Geese, turkey, fox, woodchuck and similar size game are examples of supposed proper matching of shot size and game when BBs are employed by hunters. Smaller targets might be completely missed when well-centered in the pattern of BB size shot at

all but extremely short ranges.

Another disadvantage often associated with large pellets is their ability to travel for greater ranges thus increasing the risk of bodily harm or property damage to some person or thing unnoticed due to the great distance separating them from the shooter. A No. 5 pellet started at 1330 fps (feet per second) can travel 290 yards; a No. 4—310 yards; and a No. 2—340 yards. A BB started at the same speed can travel 390 yards. Thus, if you choose to use BB size shot you should keep in mind the shot's ability to travel greater distances than lesser size pellets.

Just how effective any shotgun can be with any specific loading varies somewhat with the individual gun. Most full choke guns will shoot BBs quite well. A few will not pattern the big pellets satisfactorily. Only actual shooting will determine if a specific shotgun barrel will perform well with BBs. It is interesting to note that in my testing the differences between the degrees of barrel choking were much less noticeable with BBs than with smaller size shot.

The ability of a choke to pattern well varies when shot larger than 6s are employed. Big pellets are less liquid in their passage through the choke and it is not uncommon for more choke to mean greater deformation of the large size pellets. And, deformed pellets do not fly as true as round pellets. Therefore, more choke could sometimes mean a less dense pattern. With one load of BBs, an improved cylinder choke actually averaged patterns as tight as a full choke barrel. However, the load in question (1⅞ ounces) was not the best performing BB load (see Table No. 6). Whenever using shot sizes of No. 5 or larger, it is essential to check the gun's performance with the load to be used at the maximum ranges at which you will shoot. If one load does poorly, another might do quite well. It pays to try more than one brand of shell and more than one charge weight.

For this review, I obtained two boxes of each 12-gauge BB load currently being offered to the shooter by the three major ammunition manufacturers as noted in Table 5. Five shells of each load were carefully cut open and the average pellet count was recorded along with the average weight of each pellet. This inspection revealed a number of points. One was that the pellet count, in general, was slightly higher than anticipated. This was due to the fact that all of the loads inspected had average pellet weights somewhat below the nominal. It also

Turkeys are best hunted with BBs. However, not every locale allows the use of this effective pellet size. Here Ed displays the 10-in. beard of a 22-pound gobbler dropped cleanly with a load of 1½ ounces of BBs from a full choked Remington 870. The range was 55 of 6′3″ Ed's paces.

The author has used BBs, whenever permissible, for geese for many years. His investigation of the performance of BBs has explained why some shots had devastating effects and others let birds escape unharmed.

was of interest to note how many shells were at the maximum possible pellet count for the total charge weight indicated by the manufacturer. Of the 16 loads inspected, five had a full count of pellets and seven were only one pellet short of the count that would have brought the charge weight to the maximum without exceeding the manufacturer's indicated charge weight. Two loads were two pellets light, while one load was three

isfied that none of the ammo was above or below the nominal expected results, I then proceeded with the patterning tests.

To determine the actual exact average pattern performance of a load takes about 40 patterns. However, 10 patterns will give a good, solid, overall view that will come quite close to the results that 40 patterns would generate. Therefore, to keep the testing manageable, I decided to use 10

pecially on goose-only hunts.

To provide a realistic picture of the pattern results, I selected the load that averaged the best results in four different shotguns (two guns for 3″ shells). This is not overstating each load's performance since every shooter should try several brands of loads before deciding which one patterns the best in his gun. Thus, I selected eight different loads (one from each basic category) and added my favorite

Not all BB loads will pattern identically. One of the differences in premium grade ammunition is the granulation size of the polyethylene buffer used. Winchester's "grex" (lower left) is much coarser than either Federal's (right) or Remington's (top). Federal uses the finest granulation. Some guns will simply pattern one load better than another.

Not all BBs are created equal. The perfectly round dark color pellets are steel BBs, light colored ones are copper-plated and range from excellent quality to less than perfect. The rest are unplated lead BBs which vary in quality as well. The best-formed shot will deliver the most uniform patterns, but small imperfections are meaningless.

pellets short and another four pellets short of a full count. In general, the overall quality of the ammo, with respect to pellet count, was quite good. Five rounds of each load were then fired over the chronograph to see if any of the ammo contained any notable deviations. Again, all the ammo proved quite uniform and velocities were all within the expected range; that is, within plus or minus 35 fps of the load's nominal velocity. Thus satisfied that none of the ammo was

patterns with each load as my basis of comparison. I began by hanging up 5′×5′ sheets of photographer's background paper and firing patterns with each load in four different guns (with three different chokes). Because of not being able to shoot 3″ shells in the 2¾″ chambered guns and other considerations, I actually finished the test firing with 260 patterns to evaluate. A few surprises were in store for this writer, who has often favored BBs, es-

1½-ounce BB reload to the group.

I drew a 30″ circle around the center of each pattern and then reduced the 5′×5′ sheets of paper to 3′×3′ in order to make handling and pattern evaluation a bit easier to accomplish. All patterns were fired at a measured 50 yards because the users of BBs are most often interested in long range performance. Too, 50 yards is about as far as a good shotgunner can consistently hit game. The pattern percentages obtained are shown in Table 6, while Table 7 shows the actual number of pellets in each 30″ circle.

Many shooters have noted that 1⅞ ounces of shot in a 12-gauge 3″ gun often will not pattern as evenly as 1½ ounces of the same shot size. The heavier shot charges frequently show a tendency to cluster, leaving large areas free of pellets. The 1½-ounce charge, however, will often provide quite even coverage of the pattern

was required.

I had to wait a month to obtain one of my needs for that evaluation, a turkey carcass. As things go, I was fortunate enough to bag a 22-pound turkey during a Vermont hunt. This bird was carefully laid on a piece of cardboard and positioned somewhat as he might stand on a quartering away shot. I then traced his outline onto the paper.

Getting a goose was no problem as the freezer held a nice 12-pound bird

fired, a target moving some distance from him. Therefore, I determined the least number of hits possible, as well as the greatest number, depending upon the target's location by selective orientation of the silhouette within the 30″ circle. The results of this analysis are shown in Table 8 for the turkey and in Table 9 for the goose.

One could well question my choice of specific silhouette size or the use of a quartering away profile. Admittedly, a bird could present a full side view or the smaller profile of a going-directly-away-position. But the profile used does represent at least one position at which game will be shot in the field. The profiles were based on large specimens, thus the results are realistic expectations of what might well occur in the field under reasonably good conditions when mature birds are fired upon. Smaller birds would obviously receive fewer hits.

TABLE 1
Hard Lead Pellet Specifications*

Size	Wgt. (grs.)	Diameter (inches)	Pellets per oz.
#4 Buck	19.51	.23	22
BB	8.75	.18	50
2	4.97	.15	88
4	3.24	.13	135
5	2.50	.12	175

*Actual weight and pellets per ounce can vary with density of shot used. Soft shot will weigh somewhat more and contain a few pellets less per ounce.

TABLE 2
Exterior Ballistics For Lead Pellets

Pellet Size	Velocity in ft/s:							Energy in foot pounds:						
	3 yds.	10 yds.	20 yds.	30 yds.	40 yds.	50 yds.	60 yds.	3 yds.	10 yds.	20 yds.	30 yds.	40 yds.	50 yds.	60 yds.
#4 Buck	1330	1200	1100	1025	965	910	865	76.7	62.4	52.4	45.5	40.4	35.9	32.4
BB	1330	1195	1085	995	915	850	790	34.4	27.8	22.9	19.2	16.3	14.0	12.1
2	1330	1170	1045	945	860	790	725	19.5	15.1	12.1	9.9	8.2	6.9	5.8
4	1330	1150	1010	905	815	745	680	12.7	9.5	7.3	5.9	4.8	4.0	3.3
5	1330	1135	990	880	790	715	650	9.8	7.2	5.4	4.3	3.5	2.8	2.3

Pellet Size	Time of Flight in sec. to:							Drop in inches at:						
	3 yds.	10 yds.	20 yds.	30 yds.	40 yds.	50 yds.	60 yds.	3 yds.	10 yds.	20 yds.	30 yds.	40 yds.	50 yds.	60 yds.
#4 Buck	—	.024	.050	.079	.109	.141	.175	—	0.1	0.5	1.1	2.1	3.4	5.1
BB	—	.024	.050	.079	.111	.145	.182	—	0.1	0.5	1.2	2.4	4.0	6.4
2	—	.024	.051	.082	.115	.151	.191	—	0.1	0.5	1.3	2.6	4.4	7.0
4	—	.024	.052	.084	.119	.157	.199	—	0.1	0.5	1.4	2.7	4.8	7.7
5	—	.025	.053	.085	.121	.161	.205	—	0.1	0.5	1.4	2.8	5.0	8.1

area, making it impossible for most large game or big birds to be in the pattern without receiving multiple hits. This tendency was quite notable during my testing.

It was obvious, in counting pellet holes, that the patterns of any given load were not always uniform. In each group of 10 patterns there was always at least one and sometimes two or three patterns which were notably inferior in pellet count or in the uniformity of pellet spread. Likewise, there were always several patterns which were particularly good with respect to both pellet count and spread. Obvious also was the fact that a simple statement as to pattern percentage or pellet count could not accurately reflect on the true game-taking capability of a particular load. A better method of performance evaluation

which one of my sons was intending to mount. The goose was also outlined in a quartering away position.

After the tracings were made, I eliminated from each enough to allow for feathers, down and non-vital tail and leg areas. The resulting outlines were then cut out to be placed over the pattern sheets to determine the actual number of hits possible with each pattern. It is highly unlikely that a gunner would center, in each pattern

TABLE 3
Energy Delivery At 60 Yards

Pellet Size	No. of Pellet To Deliver Equal Energy	Actual No. of Pellets Delivered	Actual Energy Delivered
BB	1.0	1.0	100%
2	2.1	1.8	86%
4	3.7	2.7	74%
5	5.3	3.5	67%

As expected, the BB patterns proved extremely effective for turkey; each pattern placed a minimum of 4 and a maximum of 29 pellets on the turkey silhouette when a full choke was used. The 2¾″, 1½-ounce load provided better results than the big 3″ shells loaded with 1⅞ ounces of shot. Also, buffered loads using a filler of granulated polyethylene provided better performance than non-buffered loads. And, because of a high initial pellet count compared to lead, steel shot loads scored very well indeed. In fact, a 1¼-ounce load of steel shot provided the same approximate number of hits as a 1⅞-ounce load of lead shot. Steel pellets do not deform in their

The BB loads tested by Ed were all on the market in December, 1984.

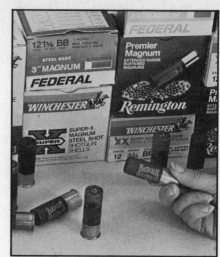

TABLE 4
Maximum Pellet Range* In Yards

Size	1330 ft/s	Muzzle Velocity 1220 ft/s	1100 ft/s
#4 Buck	485	470	460
BB	390	380	370
2	340	330	320
4	310	300	290
5	290	280	275

*Approximate horizontal distance to point of first impact for leading pellets of shot string with no allowance for balled shot.

TABLE 5
Current (12/84) Factory BB Loadings For 12 Gauge

Brand	Type of Shot	Shell Length in inches	Dram Equiv.	Wgt. of Shot in ounces	Actual Pellet Count	Shell Type	Actual Pellet Wgt. in ounces	Pellet Variation From Nominal
Remington	lead	3	MAX	1⅞	98	Nitro Magnum-Buffered	8.34	0
Federal	lead	3	4	1⅞	96	Premium-Buffered	8.55	0
Federal	lead	3	4	1⅞	95	Hi-Power Super Magnum	8.49	−1
Winchester	lead	3	4	1⅞	97	Super Double-X-Buffered	8.34	−1
Winchester	lead	3	4	1⅞	95	Super-X Magnum	8.51	−1
Winchester	steel	3	MAX	1½	104	Super-X Steel	6.15	−2
Federal	steel	3	MAX	1⅜	100	Steel Shot Load	5.90	−1
Remington	lead	2¾	MAX	1½	78	Nitro Magnum-Buffered	8.34	0
Federal	lead	2¾	4	1½	77	Premium-Buffered	8.40	−1
Federal	lead	2¾	3¾	1½	76	Hi-Power Super Magnum	8.55	0
Winchester	lead	2¾	MAX	1½	76	Super Double-X-Buffered	8.47	−1
Remington	lead	2¾	3¾	1¼	64	Express	8.41	−1
Federal	lead	2¾	3¾	1¼	64	Hi-Power	8.51	0
Federal	steel	2¾	MAX	1¼	86	Steel Shot Load	6.10	−3
Winchester	lead	2¾	3¾	1¼	59	Super-X	8.55	−4
Winchester	steel	2¾	MAX	1¼	87	Super-X Steel	6.12	−2

passage through the bore and hence ensure more retained pellets in the pattern than lead shot.

Even improved cylinder and modified choked barrels showed that they could be successfully used on turkey. When reviewing the charts showing the number of pellets on a bird, it is best to place more value on the minimum number of pellets that could have struck the target (first number) rather than the maximum (second number). Based on my field experience, six BB pellets on a turkey at 50 yards would seem to insure a minimum of several hits in the vital area. Thus, any load that will consistently put six or more pellets into the target should be considered a prime choice. Two loads, the 3", 1½-ounce steel BB load and the 2¾", 1½-ounce lead buffered BB load meet this requirement even with the improved cylinder gun. It is evident that you need not refrain from turkey hunting with your favored open bored upland gun *if* BBs are legal where you hunt, and if you restrict your maximum range to 50 yards.

TABLE 6
50-Yard 30″ Circle Percentages
12 gauge Shotgun and Choke

Load	3″ I.C.	2¾″ Mod.	3″ Full	2¾″ Full	Comments
3″-1⅞-BB	35%	—	33%	—	buffered
3″-1⅞-BB	28%	—	29%	—	non-buffered
3″-1½-BB	41%	—	50%	—	steel
3″-1⅜-BB	N.T.	—	44%	—	steel
2¾″-1½-BB	39%	49%	58%	78%	buffered
2¾″-1½-BB	33%	41%	50%	68%	non-buffered
2¾″-1½-BB	32%	43%	49%	67%	reload
2¾″-1¼-BB	32%	39%	50%	67%	non-buffered
2¾″-1¼-BB	41%	N.T.	48%	51%	steel

I.C. = improved cylinder. **N.T.** = not tested

TABLE 7
50-Yard 30″ Circle Pellet Count
12 gauge Shotgun & Choke

Load	3″ I.C.	2¾″ Mod.	3″ Full	2¾″ Full	Comments
3″-1⅞-BB	34	—	32	—	buffered
3″-1⅞-BB	27	—	28	—	non-buffered
3″-1½-BB	43	—	52	—	steel
3″-1⅜-BB	N.T.	—	44	—	steel
2¾″-1½-BB	30	38	45	60	buffered
2¾″-1½-BB	25	31	38	52	non-buffered
2¾″-1½-BB	24	32	37	50	reload
2¾″-1¼-BB	21	25	32	43	non-buffered
2¾″-1¼-BB	36	N.T.	42	44	steel

I.C. = improved cylinder. **N.T.** = not tested

From left to right are BB loads: 1¼-oz. lead; 1¼-oz. steel; 1⅜-oz. steel; 1½-oz. lead; 1½-oz. steel and 1⅞-oz. lead. Note the steel shot loads contain far more pellets than equivalent or heavier loads of lead pellets.

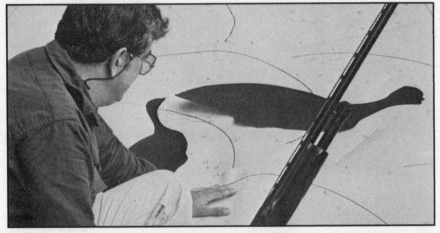

Ed's testing convinced him that BBs are a top choice for turkey or fox, but a poor selection for geese—information worth shooting (ouch) and counting (yech) over 200 patterns.

TABLE 8
Minimum & Maximum 50-Yard Turkey Silhouette Pellet Count
12 gauge Shotgun & Choke

Load	3" I.C.	2¾" Mod.	3" Full	2¾" Full	Comments
3"-1⅞-BB	4 / 15	—	7 / 17	—	buffered
3"-1⅞-BB	4 / 12	—	5 / 15	—	non-buffered
3"-1½-BB	8 / 23	—	9 / 21	—	steel
2¾"-1⅜-BB	N.T.	—	8 / 19	—	steel
2¾"-1½-BB	7 / 13	7 / 16	8 / 21	13 / 29	buffered
2¾"-1½-BB	5 / 11	5 / 12	6 / 15	8 / 20	non-buffered
2¾"-1½-BB	2 / 9	3 / 12	4 /13	5 / 15	reload
2¾"-1¼-BB	3 / 9	4 / 11	6 / 14	7 / 15	non-buffered
2¾"-1¼-BB	4 / 11	N.T.	7 / 18	9 / 18	steel

I.C. = improved cylinder. **N.T.** = not tested

TABLE 9
Minimum & Maximum 50-Yard Goose Silhouette Pellet Count
12 gauge Shotgun & Choke

Load	3" I.C.	2¾" Mod.	3" Full	2¾" Full	Comments
3"-1⅞-BB	0 / 10	—	0 / 9	—	buffered
3"-1⅞-BB	0 / 4	—	0 / 5	—	non-buffered
3"-1½-BB	0 / 14	—	0 / 15	—	steel
3"-1⅜-BB	N.T.	—	0 / 11	—	steel
2¾"-1½-BB	0 / 7	1 / 11	1 / 14	2 / 17	buffered
2¾"-1½-BB	0 / 3	0 / 5	0 / 8	1 / 10	non-buffered
2¾"-1½-BB	0 / 3	0 / 4	0 / 7	0 / 7	reload
2¾"-1¼-BB	0 / 3	0 / 4	0 / 4	0 / 5	non-buffered
2¾"-1¼-BB	0 / 4	N.T.	0 / 9	0 / 7	steel

Do not interpret the high pellet counts of steel shot loads to mean equal or superior performance to lead. Due to the decrease in weight, it takes more steel pellets to deliver energy equal to lead. Too, the steel pellets run out of steam before the lead ones!

Of course BB size shot is also offered in 10-gauge shells. Loads currently available include 3½" shells with both 2¼ and 2 ounces of lead pellets and 3½" shells with 1¾ and 1⅝ ounces of steel pellets. While these loads were not tested for this effort it is reasonable to expect results similar to those of the 12 gauge. That is to say, I would anticipate the best patterns to occur with buffered 2-ounce loads. BBs are not loaded in smaller gauges by any of the various U.S. factories. Those interested in the use of BBs with a 10-gauge gun would do well to pattern their individual gun and load combinations before assuming too many conclusions.

The test results were unexpectedly different when the goose silhouette was placed over the same patterns. In fact, I was shocked by the high frequency with which I could position the goose outline so that not a single pellet would fall into the target area. Seven loads supplied patterns with which not a single hit could be scored when the outline was positioned in the obvious gaps between shot holes. The 1½-ounce 2¾" buffered lead shot load was the only one that *consistently* put at least one pellet on the target when modified or full choke was employed. But that one pellet frequently struck the target in what could easily be considered a non-vital or at least not immediately vital area. In my opinion, it takes three striking BBs to consistently knock geese out of the air, based on my own field experience. The best load in the densest patterning gun averaged only two pellets on the target when the worst-condition-positioning was selected. Yet, an average of 17 hits was recorded with the same load and gun when the target was positioned to maximize the number of possible hits. At best, this is erratic performance clearly indicating that BBs are not a good selection for geese (even big Canada's) when the ranges reach 50 yards. I now understand why frequently in the past I have felt I did everything right and yet never put a pellet into a high flying goose; and at other times have wreaked havoc on a bird under similar circumstances.

My opinion now is, assuming the use of a 1½-ounce buffered load, that BBs are not all I thought for goose

When counting hits Ed determined the number of pellets in the 30-in. pattern circle, shot at 50 yards, and then, after positioning the silhouette, he counted the number of hits that could still be seen. It took extensive positioning and recounting to accurately determine the minimum and maximum hits possible with a specific pattern.

A 1⅞-oz. load of BBs in an Improved Cylinder choke got at least four hits and as many as 15 consistently, proving you can effectively use open-bored guns with BBs, even at 50 yards.

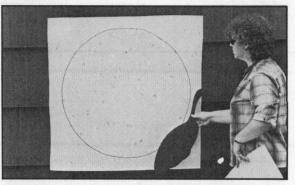

Debbie Matunas deliberates the possible positioning of a goose silhouette to obtain the fewest possible hits. Simply sliding it into the pattern circle looks as though only perhaps one pellet would be placed on the target. Over 200 patterns were checked this way for turkey, geese, duck, fox and woodchuck potential.

Only the 1½-oz. premium loads (this target fired with Federal brand) would consistently allow at least two hits at 50 yards on the goose silhouette if a Full choke was used.

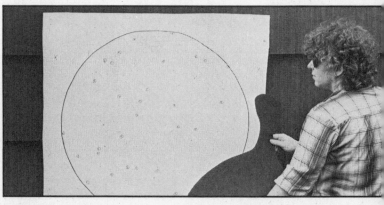

This Improved Cylinder 50-yard pattern with 1½-oz. of BBs using a premium-style load scored a minimum of 7 hits and a maximum of 13 hits on the turkey silhouette, making it at least the equal of a 1⅞-oz. load from the same gun.

hunting unless the ranges do not exceed a maximum of 40 yards. I am now equally convinced that No. 2 lead shot is the best choice for geese.

When the same kind of checks were made using a fox outline, the results were as favorable as they were with the turkey silhouette. On the other hand, a woodchuck silhouette produced results similar to the goose test, bearing out actual field experience. I have hunted woodchucks not infrequently with a shotgun for a number of reasons, the first of which was to accommodate a farmer who wanted no high powered rifle bullets whizzing about on land used by his cattle. This experience also quickly proved that a shotgun is actually a preferred choice when the grass is above your knees and it's a walk-up-and-jump-a-chuck at 20 yards or so or no shooting at all. I quickly learned that No. 2 shot would not stop a chuck at ranges past a dozen yards or so. And all too often No. 4 Buck proved a crippler, putting only perhaps a single pellet into a non-vital area if ranges exceeded 15 or 16 yards. The effective range of BBs proved about 20 yards, past which cripples would occur.

It is obvious that the BB is a magnificent pellet size for the large small game or our largest bird. In fact, for turkey hunting it has no peers, laws prohibiting it not withstanding. A 1½-ounce load of BBs will put plenty of hits on a 50-yards distant turkey, especially if a buffered load is used. Most often each of these hits will completely, or very nearly, penetrate the off-side of the bird, resulting in a turkey that goes down for keeps. Ditto for the performance of BBs on fox. Indeed, I have stopped more than 50 fox quite cleanly with BBs. With a good patterning gun matched to the right ammo, kills on turkey or fox are very realistic at a range to 60 yards, if the shooter is capable of reasonably centering his quarry in the pattern at such a range.

Surprisingly, the BB's performance proved not well-suited to long range goose shooting as the test results indicate. At 40 yards BBs would perform satisfactorily on the big waterfowl. But so will No. 2 shot. And the No. 2 pellets will consistently kill geese right up to 50 yards when there are 1½ ounces of them in the pattern. So, when BBs are maligned for goose hunting, I now will have to take the side of those who claim they are less than ideal. In that heavier loads provided less dense patterns I doubt that 2-ounce or 2¼-ounce 10-gauge loads would change my opinion in this mat-

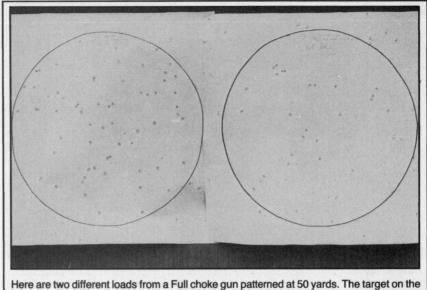

Here are two different loads from a Full choke gun patterned at 50 yards. The target on the left was fired with a 1½-oz. load and the target on the right with a 1⅞-oz. load. Note the better density of the lighter 1½-oz. load.

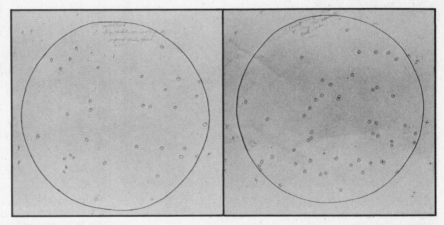

Typical pattern results with 3-in., 1½-oz. steel shot load as assembled by Winchester. Target at left is an Improved Cylinder pattern and target at right is a Full choke pattern—both fired at 50 yards.

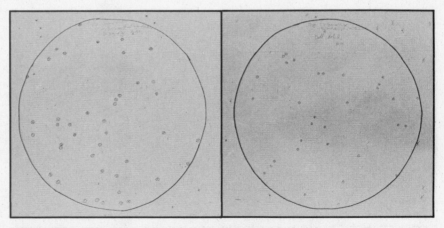

Typical pattern results with a 3-in., 1⅞-oz. load as assembled by Winchester. Target at left is an Improved Cylinder pattern and target at right a Full choke pattern. Note the similarity in patterns despite the wide differences in chokes. Both fired at 50 yards.

BBs and foxes do mix. The author displays a red fox pelt taken with 1½ ounces of BBs at a very long 58 paces. Five hits were made, three in fatal areas.

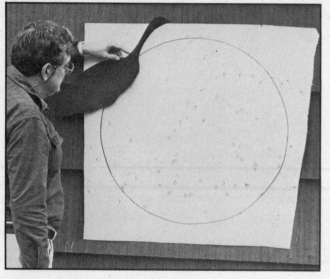

Ed found 1½ ounces of steel BBs from a Full choke would allow the goose silhouette to be positioned with but a few hits out at 50 yards.

This Improved Cylinder 2¾-in. gun, with 1½-oz. Federal Premium (fired in 3-in. chamber) BBs provided good results for big targets at 50 yards.

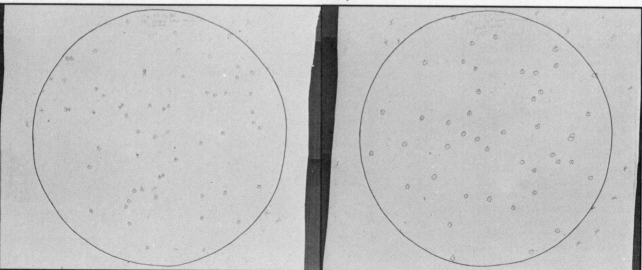

With Full choke 2¾-in. gun, 1½ oz. Federal Premium makes a good pattern (left), better than the same load fired in a 3-in. chamber (right).

ter by any notable degree.

But for turkeys or fox the BB's performance is nothing less than magnificent. However, before you run off to buy a box for your next turkey or fox hunt, do be certain to check the laws of the locale in which you will hunt. Some jurisdictions do prohibit the use of BB pellets. This perhaps because the lawmakers have heard the BB maligned as the pellet size used by those who cast sportsmanship aside and shoot at targets well beyond range, hoping for that one lucky pellet to strike a vital zone; or perhaps the local lawmakers just don't feel the need to allow such an efficient load as 1½ ounces of BBs to be let loose among the state's turkey population. But where legal, the magnificent BB will allow you a definite edge on turkey or fox, enabling you to kill these critters at ranges perhaps 10 yards further than you could hope for with less efficient loads. And, if you can get reasonably close, they are just devastating on woodchucks.

Handloaders who might want to consider loading BBs in the 16-gauge or a 3″ 20-gauge shell will be somewhat disappointed. Accepting that 1¼ ounces of shot is an absolute minimum for practical use of the BB, you will note that it simply is not possible to get 1¼ ounces of these large pellets (although 1¼ ounces of smaller sized pellets can be used) into the case using existing recipes for powder and wads. Thus, BBs are practical only for the 10 and 12 gauge reloader.

Finally, do not attempt to over-match BBs to the quarry. For example, penetration tests using plywood and pine boards quickly proved that BBs have only about one-third of the penetration potential of No. 4 Buck and do not begin to approach 00 Buck's capability. For deer hunting, or use on other large species where buckshot seems to work, BBs will prove to be, at best, inadequate.

But as my tests have proven, don't be misled into believing that more BBs are better. The 1⅞-ounce loads, while certainly effective at 50 yards, proved less desirable than the 1½-ounce loads. And do consider the use of the buffered loads as they are indeed to be preferred over the non-buffered variety. By restricting your shots to a maximum of what you feel is 50 yards, you will, despite the errors often made in the field, keep your target well within the killing range of your BB-sized pellets. And a turkey or fox at 50 yards is a very satisfying accomplishment; one consistently possible with the magnificent BB. ●

This brace of geese was bagged with BBs, but author doesn't now like BBs for geese if ranges exceed 40 yards.

Even the biggest ducks can fly through a pattern of BBs without being hit, so they're not an all-purpose waterfowl load.

For turkeys, Matunas shoots premiums, with 1½ ounces of copper-plated BBs and polyethylene buffer. That load in a Full-choke gun is a real confidence builder.

THIS YEAR, the muzzle-loading business is concentrating on the beginning shooter and the esoteric aficionado. The in-between frontstuffer, as far as this year's new products are concerned, is ignored. It's the newcomer or the buckskinner-who-has-everything.

Most noteworthy in the latter class is the new Dance Confederate percussion six-shooter by **Southwest Muzzleloaders Supply.** Advanced students of arms used during the War of Northern Aggression (as it is called in certain parts of the country) may be vaguely familiar with the scant number of 36-caliber revolvers put out in Texas by J. H. Dance & Brother in 1862 and 1863. Closely resembling the pattern 1851 Colt Navy, the Dance featured a turned, Dragoon-style barrel and the complete absence of a recoil shield, giving the back part of the frame a rather flat look. There were only an estimated 250 guns produced by this short-lived Confederate armory and Dance revolvers are quite rare today. Likewise, although a number of replica firms are producing copies of Confederate sidearms, up until this year there had not been a copy of the little-known Dance wheel-gun.

All that has changed since Tony Gajewsky located serial #10 of a Dance revolver in his hometown of Angelton, Texas, and proceeded to have the gun re-created by well-known Italian replica manufacturer, Aldo Uberti. There will be 500 cased and specially engraved Dance revolvers for the collectors, but the real attraction is the unlimited (and much lower priced) regular shooter. Here is a scarce replica, the likes of which hasn't been seen since the days of Shiloh, to pack on those skirmishes.

Another frontloader for the shooter who has everything is the appropriately-named "Boomer" Christmas celebration pistol, imported by **Euroarms of America.** This is one gun that I am truly sorry did not arrive in time for me to shoot and for you to see, for it must be experienced to be believed. Physically, the Boomer looks like a pregnant pirate pistol, complete with percussion lock, chunky brass barrel and thick, bulky wooden stock. The single shot pistol is so oversized it even comes with its own carrying strap.

There is some history behind all this: it seems that in certain parts of the Continent, such pistols as these were hauled out on ceremonial occasions, most notably Christmas, loaded to the maximum (with or without ball), and then fired across the valleys of the Alps to echo in the Nativity, the New Year, or just another star-filled night. In short, it was a celebration pistol and EOA has re-created this hefty hand cannon for those who wish to carry such revelry on into the Twentieth century. Seems like just the thing to announce the arrival of your mother-in-law.

Getting down to serious introductory muzzleloading, **CVA** has come a long ways towards providing quality products for the new black powder shooter. Most noteworthy is CVA's new 410 double-barreled shotgun. At 6 lbs. 4 oz., this would seem to be the ideal scattergun for women, children, and those of us who don't always like the bone-bruising recoil of the bigger gauges. CVA has also introduced Blazer II, a scaled-down version of their straight-line ignition percussion single shot with shorter barrel, the lighter weight, and a lower price tag. Not traditional in styling by any means, either Blazer is an economical way to get started in muzzleloading.

The Allen Fire Arms Hawken, shown above, now comes in 50-caliber and shoots fine.

I recall having high hopes for CVA's 50-caliber double rifle last year, but expressed concern over the obviously required expensive hand regulation of barrels. I was right. It took a year, and no doubt some money, but modern technology, mainly using laser beams, will now make the bullets converge at approximately 75 yards. We shall see.

What I consider to be the most graceful of all the original Colt pistols, the 36 Pocket Police, is now being produced in a brass-framed version by CVA. And there is now a Presentation Grade series of elegantly engraved and nickeled guns, including their 12-gauge Shotgun, Hawken Rifle and various combinations of their cap and ball revolvers.

The rest of the muzzleloaders for the 1986-87 scene are variations on a theme. For example, **Navy Arms** has purchased the entire black powder division of the defunct Harrington & Richardson and is now producing their single shot Stalker hunting rifle. Navy is also creating a truly unique frontloading scattergun—a 20-gauge single shot with interchangeable chokes. The gun will come with its own wrench, and will be rather spartan in appearance, with no checkering or forend cap. Navy has also issued an authentically "improved" version of their 1858 Remington 44-cal. More historically correct than the other replicas on today's market, they say, the Navy Remington features progressive rifling (with a slower twist at the breech than at the muzzle) and the iridescent charcoal blue of yesteryear's guns.

Allen Firearms has long been known for their 54-caliber Hawken, and they are now importing this same rifle in 50 caliber. Unlike the 54 (which actually is a true 52 caliber) the 50-caliber will take the proper .490-in. patched round ball. Also new to Allen is a 32-caliber Squirrel Rifle, featuring brass furniture, case-hardened lock and adjustable sights. This halfstock sporter is available in either flintlock or percussion.

Thompson Center's big news this year is the introduction of their single shot 12-gauge New Englander straight grip shotgun, with open choke and brass bead front sight. This frontloader will also take a special T/C 50-caliber drop-in barrel, rifled 1 in 48-in. twist for Maxi-balls. Thompson Center is also producing a 1 in 66-in. twist drop-in barrel for their popular Hawken and Renegade hunting rifles, for those who wish to use patched round balls.

Mowrey Gun Works, makers of

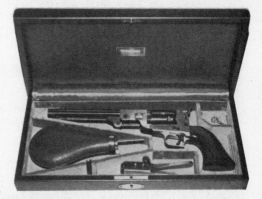

An unlimited number of "shooter's" guns will be made, and also 500 cased sets, with each revolver etched in gold across the top flat of the barrel, bearing special serial numbers, and furnished with the right accessories.

Southwest Muzzleloader's Supply is importing this well-made replica of the rare 36-caliber Confederate Dance revolver. The Dragoon-style barrel, square-back trigger guard, and the lack of recoil shield are all authentic features.

Close-up of the Dance revolver, showing how simple the job of making the revolver frame became without that recoil shield.

Trail Guns Armory is honoring the 150th Anniversary of Texas Independence with a special presentation version of the 50 caliber Alamo Rifle. With the exception of the lockplate and barrel, all metalwork will be plated in sterling silver, with special commemorative inscriptions on the lockplate and barrel. Only 1,836 Alamo Rifles will be made.

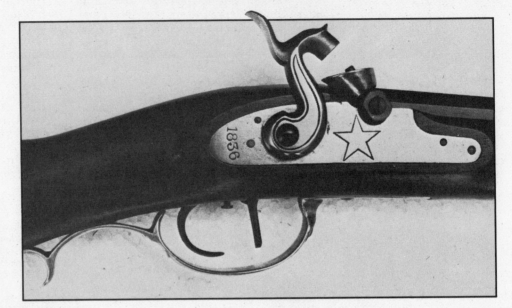

A Lone Star and the date 1836 mean a lot in Texas—the Alamo Rifle's lockplate needs no other embellishment.

CVA's scaled-down 410 side-by-side caplock shotgun is ideal for women, children, and muzzleloaders who don't like recoil.

The small and graceful 5-shot Pocket Police 36 is now being offered by CVA with something the originals never had—a brass frame.

The demand for an inexpensive young beginner's rifle has prompted CVA to come out with a 50-caliber Blazer II, a shorter and lighter version of last year's Blazer.

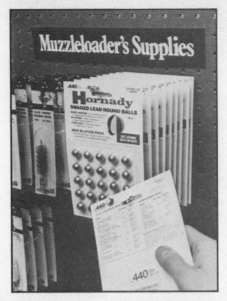

Hornady's new convenience in round ball packaging puts the complete line of balls, from .310 to .450, in handy pop-out blister packs.

Filling a long-standing need for muzzle-loading hunters, Kane has developed camouflaged wrap-around Gun Chaps for CVA and Thompson/Center styled muzzleloaders. The camo-covers are available in brown, green and orange camouflage, plus white for hunting in snow country.

The Texas sesquicentennial has not been lost on the black powder world, as **Trail Guns Armory** is importing a special limited edition of their Alamo 50 percussion longrifle, slicked up with sterling silver furniture and a browned barrel and lock, which will be stamped with the Texas star and the year of independence, 1836. True to form, only 1,836 of these rifles will be produced and the Governor of Texas already has his! Going along with the 150th Anniversary rifle is a special limited edition silver-plated Texas flask, depicting the surrender of Santa Anna to General Sam Houston on April 21, 1836. The flask may be purchased separately from the rifle and will only be available for a one-year period.

Accessories seem to be taking on a new importance this year. **Warren Muzzleloading** has a number of unique items for the hunter, including a short, easy-to-pack short-starter and a miniature brass funnel for filling your powder flask without spilling those little black grains all over the cat. **Mountain State Muzzleloading** has come up with some handy black powder cleaning aids, such as a stiff wire "breech brush" (used with a ramrod for getting to the bottom of the barrel) and a phosphorus bronze cleaning brush for the hard to reach crevices of flintlocks. **Ox-Yoke Originals** now offers a handy cloth Kit Bag containing everything the shooter might wish to take afield for cleaning his muzzleloader. **F.P.F. Company** has developed Deadeye Dan's Quick Loader, which has to be the fastest reloading device I have ever used: 17 seconds to fire and reload my 54 Ozark Mountain Hawken! For bench shooting, **Butler Creek** has Gunpowder Pour Spouts to fit both the old and the new Pyrodex moisture-proof containers; the firm also manufactures unbreakable brass ramrods in a variety of lengths. Too heavy for field use, they will last the benchrest shooter forever. And finally, filling a need for the black powder hunter who must use camouflage when pursuing sharp-eyed critters such as turkey and varmints, **Kane Gun Chaps** has at last come out with a camo cover for some of the more popular black powder rifles, such as the Thompson/Center Hawken and the CVA Hawken and Frontier. **Hodgdon** has a free six-page brochure that gives Pyrodex load's for muzzleloaders and cartridge guns.

Obviously, this seems to be the year of specialization for the muzzle-loading shooter, especially the hunter. ●

the simple Ethan Allen rifles of 1836, has undergone yet another change of ownership. This time the address might stay around awhile and the guns will definitely take a design change for the better, at least as far as the hunter is concerned. Joe Estes and his wife Sharon are the new owners of this historic firm and one of their first acts was to take the basic Great Plains Rifle and adapt it to today's black powder hunter. That means rifling the barrel to a 1 in 30-in. twist for my favorite Buffalo Bul-

let, shortening the barrel length to 28 inches, improving the steel, and adding adjustable Williams sights. The "1 N 30" hunting rifle (as it is unceremoniously called) will still feature hand rubbed premium curly maple stocks and the ruggedly simple Mowrey/Ethan Allen percussion action. Of course, the regular Squirrel Rifle, Plains Rifle and 12-gauge shotgun will still remain. But the "1 N 30" hunting rifle, available in 45, 50 and 54 caliber, is destined to be the star of the new owner's line.

The importance of the file in Ferlach cannot be exaggerated.

The Gunmakers of Austria

by STUART M. WILLIAMS

FOR OVER 3000 years, Austria has served as the arsenal and weapons purveyor to a great part of Central and Southern Europe. She has enjoyed such a position due to abundant deposits of high-grade iron ore. This ore is of such a chemical consistency that it makes up into iron and steel that is readily hardened. The Roman legions that subdued all the Mediterranean world and most of Europe were armed with slashing and stabbing weapons and protected with breastplates and helmets made from iron ore from the provinces of Styria and Carinthia—approximately cen-

tral and southeastern Austria. Today, Styria is the site of Steyr-Daimler-Puch, makers of the renowned Mannlicher-Schoenauer and Steyr-Mannlicher rifles, and Carinthia is the site of Ferlach, one of the foremost gunmaking centers of the world.

Ferlach has in fact been an important gunmaking center since its foundation over four centuries ago. At the time of the Emperor Maximilian I in the early 16th century, Carinthia, the southern borderland of Austria, was under constant threat from the Venetians in the southwest and the Turks in the southeast. Therefore, the capital of Carinthia—Klagenfurt—was walled and garrisoned and fully provisioned as a fortress city. Klagen-

furt, of course, required a great variety of armaments. A register of the citizens of Klagenfurt from the 16th century indicated that there were large numbers of barrel forgers, barrel borers, lockmakers, powder makers, cutlers, and gunsmiths.

In order to create the best possible conditions for the gunmaking industry, the village of Ferlach was chosen as an ideal site in which to establish the industry. Situated in the lowest part of the Rosental (Valley of the Roses), Ferlach was protected by the high Carinthian Alps in the south, the Drava River with its vertical cliffs in the north, the foothills of the Carinthian Alps in the east, and the soaring, fortified Hollenburg Castle in the west. Ferlach was placed in a natural fortress.

Abundant snowfall in the Carinthian Alps delivered strong currents to the local streams throughout the year, which in turn powered the hammer works and the smithies. Wood from the huge surrounding forests provided the smithies with charcoal. Pig iron came from the nearby iron foundries. In other words, as a site for gunmaking Ferlach could not have been better.

A history of gunmaking in Ferlach is not the purpose of this article, but it is interesting—and important—to note a few highlights.

Originally, gunmakers in Ferlach worked in small shops. This system required an extensive division of labor. There were lockmakers, barrel forgers, barrel borers, stockmakers, and toolmakers—in fact, every specialized skill required to make all sorts of guns, both sporting and military. At the time of the Thirty Years War gunmaking in Ferlach experienced a great boom, so that it was necessary to form a gunmakers' guild. Through the rigorous testing of a controller, called an *Armaturenmeister*, the quality of Ferlach guns was continually improved. All guns that passed the test were marked with the official Ferlach stamp. In this way the name Ferlach was spread abroad throughout Europe.

Ferlach enjoyed its heyday during the reign of Empress Maria Theresa (1740-1780) when the entire Austrian army was equipped with Ferlach-made guns. During the Napoleonic Wars (1800-1814), the Ferlach gun industry delivered over 300,000 military guns, an astonishing volume.

During this period a traveler to Ferlach observed: "With few exceptions all the inhabitants of Ferlach devote themselves to gunmaking. One hears an eternal din of hammering and beating, and sees hardworking people in every shop. One workman makes only iron ramrods; another only bayonets; another locks for muskets, carbines, and pistols; and still another trigger mechanisms. Some make files, some bore barrels, some grind and shape barrels, and some polish them. The large bellows and grinding machines are all powered by water. All finished parts are turned over to the Chief Supervisor, who takes the workers' invoices and pays them and arranges the parts in a specific order in a special building. There one can see a huge cabinet full of thousands of locks, and another one filled with trigger mechanisms, and so forth. When a certain lot of guns is finished, they are loaded and fired under the observation of experts to ascertain their quality. Those which betray the slightest fault are sold at a lower price . . ."

From a peak of production during the Napoleonic Wars, the output of the Ferlach gunmakers has gone into a long and irregular decline. In the 1870s it averaged about 10,000 guns a year, but went up to an average of about 15,000 a year during the period 1892-1913. All guns produced during the latter period were hunting guns. By 1924 annual production had declined to about 7000. By 1934, in the depths of the worldwide depression, production sank to 2398 guns. Today the annual output averages about 1400 guns. These are exclusively hunting guns and 80% of them are exported.

Concurrent with declining production has been a decline in the number of gunmakers. From a high of about 300 during Napoleonic days, there are today only 17 licensed master gunmakers in Ferlach. They employ about 150 shop workers and about as many who do piece work at home.

Sixteen of these master gunmakers

This worker in Josef Hambrusch's shop polishes the chambers of an over-under shotgun—by hand.

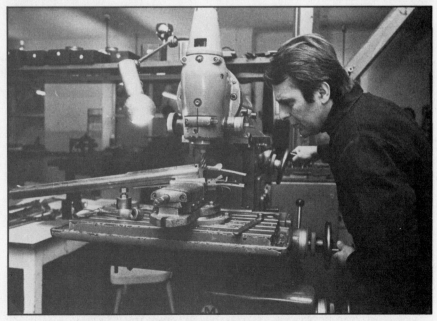

Milling away excess metal on the receiver of a drilling is accomplished in the co-op shop.

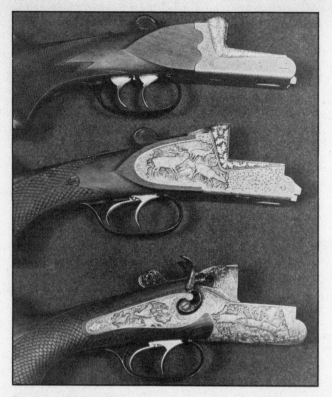

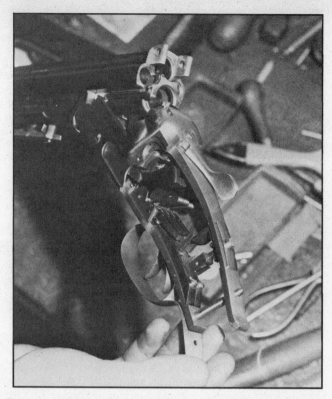

Receivers of three different Hambrusch guns, a boxlock over-under, a sidelock over-under rifle, and a *Hahnbüchsflinte* (over-under hammer gun). All might be in production at once.

This unusual gun is a *Bockdoppelflinte mit seitlichem Kugellauf*—an over-under shotgun with side rifle barrel.

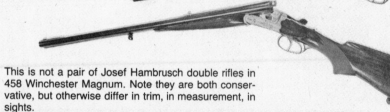

This is not a pair of Josef Hambrusch double rifles in 458 Winchester Magnum. Note they are both conservative, but otherwise differ in trim, in measurement, in sights.

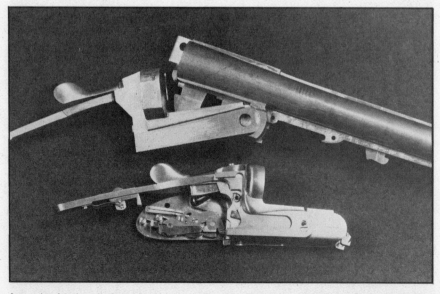

A couple of actions in the white with a set of double rifle barrels. This is the complex gunbuilding for which Ferlach exists.

are joined together in a cooperative (*Genossenschaft*). This enables them to purchase expensive machinery which would be beyond the budgetary reach of any single gunmaker. All this machinery is housed in one large shop, where it is accessible on a time-share basis to all 16 members of the co-op. The 70 workers at the cooperative machine center turn out semi-finished parts and components—barrels, receivers, bolts, locks, etc.—which are then turned over to the individual master gunmakers for further refinement and perfecting.

There is one gunmaker whose operation is so big that he has his own fully equipped factory, and who is therefore not a member of the Ferlach gunmakers' cooperative. That maker is Franz Sodia. His factory accounts for approximately half the production of the Ferlach gunmakers.

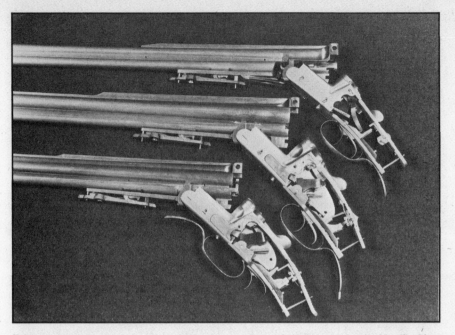

These three guns are, from top: a *Bergstutzen,* a *Bochbüchsflinte,* and a double rifle. Very different guns, with very like work.

The old-timey over-under hammer action is still in demand by Ferlach's customers. This one is by Hambrusch.

As the annual production of the Ferlach gunmakers has declined, they have of necessity put more emphasis on very expensive luxury guns in order to maintain their income. Josef Hambrusch—considered by many connoisseurs to be the foremost Ferlach master—made up for King Faisal of Saudi Arabia a magnificently engraved and gold-inlaid double rifle at a cost of $170,000—a Ferlach record. In particular, the gunmakers of Ferlach have come to concentrate on break-open multiple-barrel combination guns of a wide variety of configurations, with two, three, four or even more sets of interchangeable barrels.

For example, when I visited Johann Fanzoj, one of the premier Ferlach masters, he and his associates were building up an over-under rifle in 8x68S (which corresponds ballistically to the 300 Weatherby Magnum), with additional sets of barrels in 12 gauge, 12 gauge and 243, and 12 gauge and 22 Hornet. This nice little assortment of playthings was being prepared for a plutocratic German industrialist. For a professional hunter in Africa Johann was building a regal

side-by-side double rifle with three sets of barrels in 470 Nitro Express, 375 H&H Magnum, and 6.5x55, opulently ornamented with lavish engraving and gold inlay on the sidelock plates. Indeed, as the brochure of the Ferlach gunmakers' cooperative states, "where else in the world can you buy a precisely made and beautifully decorated gun with seven different interchangeable sets of barrels and four interchangeable scopes with mounts, suitable for hunting everything from squirrels to elephants?"

For most gun lovers the Ferlach exotica will forever remain "the stuff that dreams are made of," and nothing more. They are impractical for most North American hunting and beyond the financial reach of all but a few of us anyway. Nevertheless, they are some of the most fascinating guns in the world, so I am going to give a brief listing of some of the more important Ferlach designs.

The most common is, of course, the *Bockbüchsflinte,* a shotgun-over-rifle combination gun in either boxlock or sidelock configuration. The *Bock-Drilling* is the same shotgun-over-rifle combination with the addition of a third barrel offset to the right-hand side midway between the other two and chambered for a small game or varmint cartridge such as the 22 Rimfire Magnum or 22 Hornet. Then there is the *Hahnbüchsflinte,* which is similar to the *Bockbüchsflinte* except that it has external hammers. There are, of course, the conventional over-under and side-by-side double rifles, and the *Drilling,* which is in this country perhaps the best-known of all the Germanic combination guns. The *Doppelbüchs-Drilling* is another three-barrelled gun, but unlike the *Drilling* it combines two rifle barrels and one shotgun barrel. Some makers put the two rifle barrels side-by-side with the shotgun barrel below; other makers put the shotgun barrel top right and the rifle barrels top left and bottom center. There is, finally, the *Vierling,* a four-barrelled gun which can take several forms. In one form there are over-under shotgun barrels and side-by-side rifle barrels, or vice versa. In another form the bottom barrel is a shotgun barrel and the other three are rifle barrels. Occasionally a four-barrelled shotgun is made up.

Most of these guns will seem to most American gun-lovers to be mere curiosities, which, like music boxes or cuckoo clocks, represent the very quintessence and triumph of Germanic gadgetry. However, there are at least a couple of Ferlachian designs that are quite practical for North

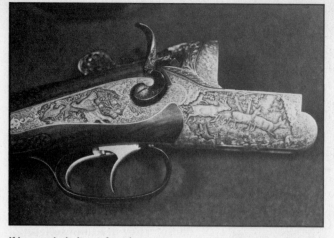

If he can help it, an Austrian engraver never portrays an animal at rest.

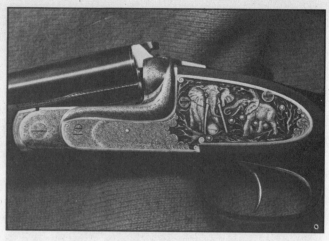

This Joseph Fanzoj heavy double rifle shows its opulent pachyderms in full relief inlaid gold.

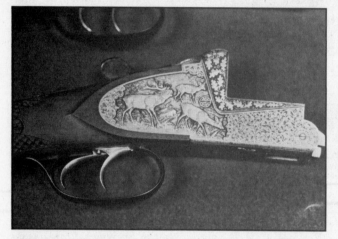

A magnificent stag roaring near his herd of hinds is a very common engraving motif at Ferlach and the oak leaf and scroll are nigh on to universal.

The Hubertus motif is perhaps the most commonly used motif among Ferlach engravers. The hunter (St. Hubert-to-be) has a crossbow, the stag always has a cross over his head.

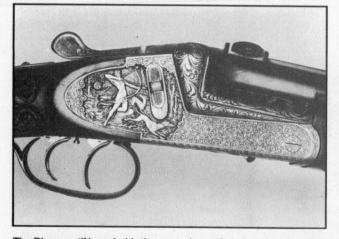

The Diana motif is probably the second most frequently used motif by the Ferlach engravers. The lady always uses a bow and sleek gaze hounds, but never a *Lodenmantel*.

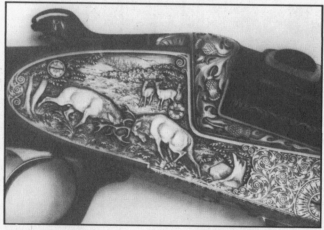

These energetic fighting stags are high-class subjects at Ferlach—difficult to do well.

American hunting conditions. One which has intrigued me for years is the *Bergstutzen,* an over-under double rifle that combines a small-caliber upper barrel (22 Long Rifle, 22 Magnum, 22 Hornet, 222) with a larger caliber lower barrel. The barrels are regulated to shoot to the same point at a given distance, which is usually 80 meters. Consider the versatility of such a gun chambered for the 22 Magnum over the 308 or 30-06 for eastern woods hunting of turkeys, squirrels, and whitetail deer. Or perhaps you do most of your hunting in the Rocky Mountain States, where you might encounter mule deer, antelope, prairie dogs, and coyotes all in the same area in the same day. Wouldn't a 222 over a 270 be absolutely devasting in such circumstances? The *Bergstutzen*

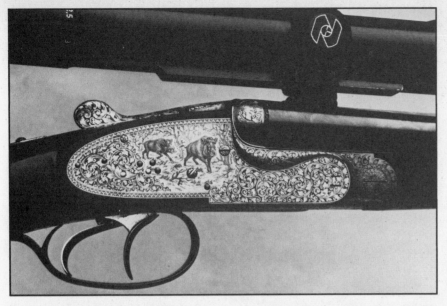

In the small shop of Gottlieb Köthe at Graz, an engraver named Strolz does a very un-Austrian thing—*bulino* figures and world-class scroll.

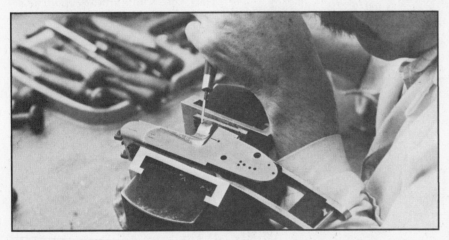

A Ferlach engraver begins work on a sidelock double. He'll cover the whole action.

This Ferlach engraver is working from a painting, possibly a scene furnished by his customer.

is a rifle for all seasons.

Most endearing and practical of all the Ferlach guns for the American hunter, however, is the *Pirschstutzen* or *Kipplaufbüchse*. The *Kipplaufbüchse* is a light, break-open single shot rifle that is specially designed for the rigors of hunting such high mountain species as red stag, Alpine ibex, chamois, and the various wild sheep and goats. Generally chambered for a flat-shooting cartridge such as the 270, the 7mm Remington Magnum, the 6.5x57R, or the 6.5x68R, and equipped with a barrel of 22-24 inches, the *Kipplaufbüchse* will weigh—without scope—about 6½-7 pounds. If the barrel is made of superhard but lightweight Böhler Antinit NG stainless steel or even lighter Böhler Super Blitz steel, the weight can be reduced to 6-6½ pounds. Generally the barrel will be octagonal with a full-length integral rib. A less expensive option is a one-third octagonal two-thirds round barrel.

A well-made *Kipplaufbüchse* is light and incisive and dynamic as a conductor's baton. It just seems to come alive in your hands. I picked up one on a recent visit to the display rooms of Josef Hambrusch, and it was love at first heft. Handling and caressing that lovely instrument of game dispatch filled my head with fantasies of long ascents into high and lonely crags; of sure shots across great crevasses and up into lofty rimrocks; and heavy-horned trophies collapsing and going into long slides down steep snowchutes and moraines. What's more, the price was quite reasonable—about $1800 at the current (November, 1984) rate of exchange. Try getting a fully custom-made, engraved rifle for that price in the U.S.

It should be emphasized that almost all Ferlach guns are custommade to the customer's order as to stock design and measurements, caliber or gauge, barrel length, choke, engraving coverage and motifs, and so on endlessly. Only a very few are made up on speculation or for the big German gun dealers such as Eduard Kettner and Waffen Frankonia.

What's more, a Ferlach gun is extremely labor-intensive. It has an inordinate amount of handwork devoted to it. The same can be said of any fine custom gun, but that is doubly and trebly so in the case of Ferlach guns. That is essentially because of the rather basic—and if I may say so, obsolete—machinery available in the Ferlach gunmakers' cooperative machine shop. Much of it dates from the days of the Third Reich, when Hitler provided large amounts of machinery

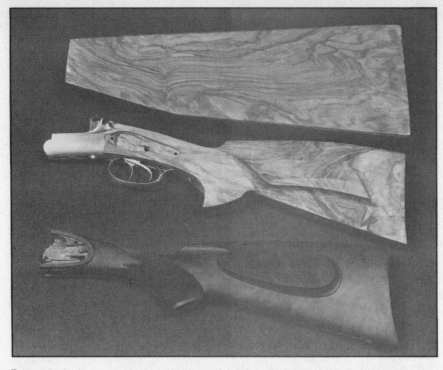

Buttstocks in three stages of completion. Note the usual cheekpiece on the rough-shapen stock—it's typical of Ferlach stock styling.

The rasp is, of course, the most important stockmaster's tool in Ferlach, just as the file shapes the most metal.

to the Ferlach gunmakers. Some of it is even older—I saw a foot-powered lathe on my most recent visit to Ferlach. In all fairness, though, I have to say that I also saw a couple of the most sophisticated computer numerical-controlled machining centers.

When all is said and done, however, the preeminent tool in Ferlach is the file. Enter any workshop in Ferlach and you will see from 10 to 20 workmen filing away incessantly. Arrayed on the workbench before each one will be 40 to 50 files of all shapes and sizes. Johann Fanzoj says that filing is the foremost skill and the indispensable skill of a Ferlach gunmaker. Whenever anyone applies for a job in his shop, he hands him a formless lump of steel and tells him to file it into a perfect cube. Few there are who can pass this test.

I think that it is fair to say that guns are built in Ferlach much as they were a half-century ago. The designs are the same, the insistence on perfection of fit and finish and flawless function is the same, the loving attention to detail is the same, and the many, many dedicated hours of handwork are the same. Only a few of the materials (e.g., superior steels) have changed. Of very few gunmakers—whether small custom shops or large factories—can the same claims be made.

The workshops of Ferlach are provided with a regular supply of thoroughly skilled workers by the Ferlach Higher Technical Institute. The school offers five-year programs in Firearms Theory and Design; Mechanical Drawing, Drafting, and Design; General Gunmaking and Stockmaking; Metalsmithing and Tool and Die Making; and Engraving, inclusive of gold- and silversmithing. The school has its own dormitory and dining room, and draws students from throughout the German-speaking countries as well as other parts of the world.

No coverage of the gunmakers of Ferlach would be complete without some mention of the Ferlach engravers. The Ferlach gunsmithing school has been training engravers for nearly 90 years, and in that time it has turned out some exceptional talents. The best known of these to American gun lovers are Rudolf Kornbrath, the late Albin Obiltschnig, and his son Hans Obiltschnig, all of whom practiced their art in this country at one time or another, and who have exerted considerable influence on American gun engravers. There are others of an equally high level of command of their art who are all but unknown in this country because they have never left Ferlach. Among them are Johann Singer, Alois Maurer, Franz Mack, and Reinhard Phillip.

Ferlach engraving is immediately recognizable to the sophisticated gun lover. It is distinguished first and foremost by deep-relief engraving of a very limited number of motifs, surrounded by scroll and/or oak leaves. Some of the motifs which one sees over and over again in infinite variations on Ferlach guns are those of St. Hubert confronting the stag with the crucifix between its antlers, and of Diana, goddess of the chase, shooting an arrow at a fleeing stag or exulting over a freshly killed stag. Another very popular motif is a roaring stag with enormous antlers and his herd of hinds. Likewise, there are many scenes of chamois or roe deer or wild boar, always running. Of course, the engraver will attempt to accommodate the client's wishes if at all possible in the amount and shape of the space at his disposal, and will copy suitable drawings, paintings, or photographs if feasible.

To the casual observer there is a high degree of sameness to Ferlach engraving. It is true that the motifs and the style are very much the same from one engraver to another. However, to the experienced eye aided with a loupe, there are significant differences in the work of the various Ferlach engravers. The real test is in the realism and fidelity to anatomical detail of human and animal figures, especially those in motion.

The engravers of Ferlach are properly the subject of a book-length treatment, and precisely such a book has been written. It is entitled *Künstlerische Waffengravuren Ferlacher Meister*, is nearly all photos with little text, and is published by Journal-Verlag Schwend of Vienna. Highly recommended.

Not all fine Austrian guns are made in Ferlach, nor are all fine Austrian gunmakers located in Ferlach. There are, in fact, several very fine gunmakers in other parts of Austria whose work is at least as good as that of the Ferlach masters, but very different.

One of these is Helmut Dschulnigg of Salzburg. Dschulnigg is justly renowned for his very elegant and well-stocked store, in which he carries not only a comprehensive line of guns, scopes, binoculars, and hunting accessories, but also a line of extremely fine hunting clothing and boots. In fact, the Dschulnigg store in Salzburg has some of the most beautifully designed and tailored and most practi-

Inletting a lower tang on an over-under double rifle, a Ferlach worker takes it one stroke at a time.

The tedious business of inletting the sideplates of a *Hahnbüchsflinte* at the Josef Hambrusch shop must remove only enough wood. Too much would weaken the stock.

Fish-scale carving on forend and grip is another hallmark of Ferlach gunmakers.

Rifling the large-caliber rifle barrel of a Bock-Drilling is a co-op shop job, working on one of the older, but versatile, machines.

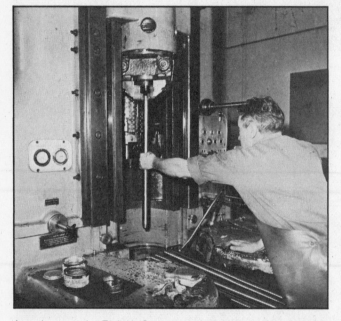

A workman at the Ferlach *Genossenschaft* (co-op) puts a barrel in position to be rifled in a cold hammer-forging machine, also community property.

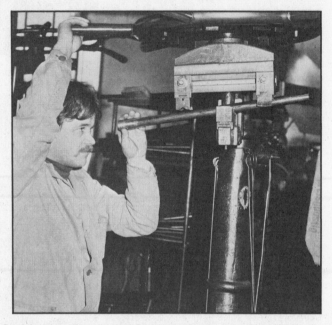

Straightening a barrel at the *Genossenschaft* workshop is still the old familiar scene—everyone has done it this way for 150 years or so.

This workman crowns the muzzle of a *Kipplaufbüchse* at Josef Hambrusch's shop, a job of metalworking a simple lathe can handle.

cal hunting clothing I have seen any-where. An indispensable part of a complete visit to Salzburg is to take in a couple of concerts and at least one opera (Mozart, of course). Equally indispensable is a visit to Waffen Dschulnigg. The elegance of the decor, the very evident quality of the merchandise, and the solicitous attention of the staff immediately put you on notice that you have entered into a very exclusive inner sanctum of the world of the shooting sports.

As far as the Dschulnigg guns are concerned, they are a world apart from the Ferlach guns. Dschulnigg specializes in bolt-action rifles, and, since 90% of his gun customers are Americans, his rifles are designed and built along very American lines, but with a definite Austrian flair. Back in the 1950s and '60s, a typical Dschulnigg rifle would be accoutred with a Monte Carlo comb, roll-over cheekpiece, white spacers, cow-catcher forend tip set on at a 45 degree angle, sharply recurved pistol grip, and lacquer finish—a complete rococo catastrophe. Dschulnigg became known more or less as the Winslow or the Weatherby of Europe. However, Dschulnigg guns have changed with the times. He can now turn out stocks as conservative as any made by the purist practitioner of the American classic style.

One Dschulnigg specialty that has not changed is deep-relief, precisely detailed, and utterly realistic stock carving. A typical Dschulnigg carved stock will have the off side of the buttstock adorned with a game scene surrounded with oak leaves, and the forend and grip lavishly carved with oak leaves. Dschulnigg gets a surprising number of orders for such stocks from Americans.

Dschulnigg rifles used to be built around FN Mauser or pre-64 Model 70 Winchester actions, but nowadays are generally built around Sako or highly refined military Mauser actions. Prices are modest compared with quality.

Dschulnigg rifles are known throughout Europe—and much farther abroad—for beauty, accuracy, and durability. Mr. Dschulnigg has the opportunity—rare among gunmakers—to test his products on a regular basis in Alaska and Africa, British Columbia and Mongolia and throughout Europe, so he is able to make regular improvements to them.

The list of Dschulnigg's clientele reads like an international Who's Who. Former and present clients include Clark Gable, Gary Cooper, David Niven, the Aga Khan, the Duke of

Peter Hambrusch affixes a scope by means of a Suhl-type claw mount, the most popular mount type in Ferlach.

Before a Ferlach gun is shipped, it is extensively fired for accuracy and/or patterning, and must pass rigorous standards.

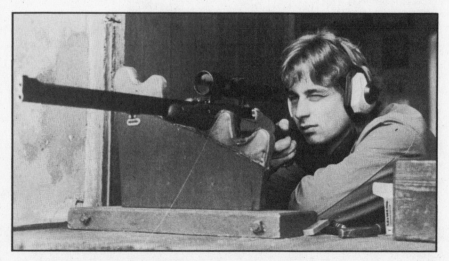
Gunmakers do their own shooting tests. Commonly, iron sights on rifles are set for 80 meters, shotguns patterned at 35 meters.

Helmut Dschulnigg's gun and hunting clothing emporium is a Mecca for continent-trotting sportsmen of the well-heeled varieties.

Dschulnigg's repeating sporters are not so wild as once, but their surfaces are still opulent, still carved to within an inch of their lives.

At Steyr-Daimler-Puch, more business-like guns are produced. This is the SSG with Cycolac stock.

The Voere 2117L, made by Voere of *Kufstein GmbH*, is a handy 22 semi-auto with 20-in. barrel, 10-shot clip and as (differently) Austrian as Ferlacher guns.

Edinburgh, and former Prince Abdorreza Pahlavi of Iran. One very satisfied client—an American doctor—has in 30 years hard usage killed over 1000 head of game with his Dschulnigg 270.

I have saved until last the Austrian gunmaker who may be the best of them all, and that is Gottlieb Köthe of Graz. I consider Köthe a real discovery. To find his shop I had to follow along a series of labyrinthine alleys in the wonderful old section of Graz, asking directions as I went. Finally I found the place, and the sensation I had as I entered his shop was akin to what Balboa must have felt when he first saw the Pacific. Neatly racked against the wall were ten of the most splendid double shotguns I have ever seen. I will go on record right now: Gottlieb Köthe's shotguns are as fine as anything coming out of the "best" London shops, and perhaps finer. The balance is impeccable, the fit of wood to metal and metal to metal is perfection itself, the woodwork is as good as anything coming out of Europe, and the quality of the wood is as good as anything I have seen anywhere. He goes in person to Yugoslavia and Turkey to buy his walnut, and it is magnificent stuff indeed.

Köthe makes other types of guns, but the overwhelming bulk of his production has been sidelock double shotguns. He and his two associates make just five guns a year, devoting a minimum of 800 hours to each gun. They make all parts of the gun except the barrels—which they obtain from Böhler in blank form—right there in the shop. The engraving is farmed out to a Herr Strolz, who does absolutely splendid work that is totally different from that of the Ferlach masters. It is in fact quite Italianate, combining delicate tight scroll and arabesque with *bulino* game scenes.

As Gottlieb put it, "Everybody has heard of Holland and Purdey, but nobody has heard of Gottlieb Köthe, so I have to try harder." His work certainly shows it. Waiting time is 1½ to 2 years, and costs range from $8000 upwards. The guns are well worth it.

The name Austria evokes thoughts of ivory-white Lipizzaner stallions and great slabs of *Sachertorte* smothered under mounds of whipped cream, of the Radetzky March and *The Sound of Music,* of the serene songs of Haydn and Mozart, and of some of the most exhilarating ski runs in the world. To knowledgeable hunters and gun-lovers, however, the name Austria suggests some of the very finest firearms being made anywhere. ●

by BOB ARGANBRIGHT

Our HOLSTER industry was revolutionized in 1983 by the padded nylon holster, made by Michael's of Oregon (Uncle Mike's). Many thought nylon a passing fad, but in just three years the soft nylon holster is established firmly in the marketplace. Most major holster manufacturers and many accessory manufacturers have jumped on the nylon bandwagon and nylon holsters are available from many sources.

What may have considerable affect on the nylon business is U.S. Patent #4,485,947 (Dec. 4, 1984) held by Michael's of Oregon. This patent covers the unique sandwich construction of their padded holsters. The validity of the patent is being tested by litigation between Michael's of Oregon and the Hunter Company, while Safariland is introducing their own line of padded nylon holsters under licensing agreement with Michael's of Oregon. No doubt there will be further developments.

Padded nylon construction offers some things leather doesn't. According to the patent, the object was to provide a holster that would hold handguns of different sizes within a defined range snugly while minimizing blue wear and maximizing protection. While a properly fitted and lined leather holster minimizes blue wear, that is a holster that fits only one frame size and barrel length of handgun, and such holsters are quite expensive.

The soft nylon holster sandwich offers a soft fabric inner layer to minimize blue wear, a central lining of a yieldably firm elastimer, such as a closed-cell foam, to provide a relaxed (contracted) shape memory, and an outer layer of a durable, wear and abrasion-resistant fabric which provides "outside world" protection.

The different manufacturers will argue the virtues of Cordura nylon versus ballistic nylon (Michael's of Oregon uses Cordura, Bianchi International uses ballistic nylon), it appears that either offers scratch, tear and scuff resistance superior to leather. The nylon construction is water resistant, important with some concealment holsters. Bianchi indicates a 20 percent weight reduction compared to leather, and also points out that the

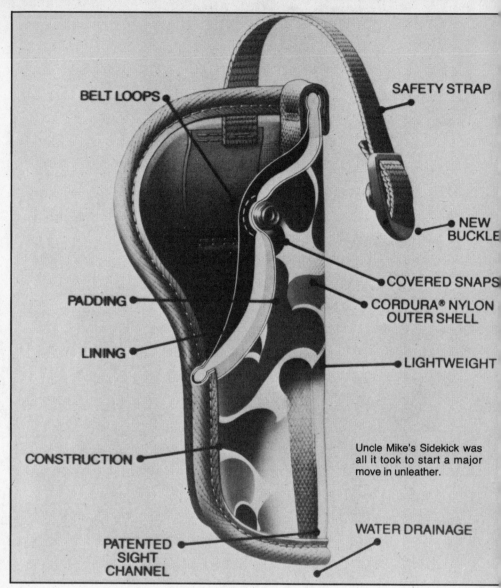

BELT LOOPS

SAFETY STRAP

NEW BUCKLE

PADDING

COVERED SNAPS

CORDURA® NYLON OUTER SHELL

LINING

LIGHTWEIGHT

CONSTRUCTION

Uncle Mike's Sidekick was all it took to start a major move in unleather.

PATENTED SIGHT CHANNEL

WATER DRAINAGE

The NYLON REVOLUTION

nylon holsters are "silent in use," whereas leather has a tendency to "creak.'

Finally, there is the cost. The padded nylon holsters sell for half, or less, of the cost of leather counterparts. Remember, too, the nylon product is designed so one holster fits several handgun models.

Michael's, Bianchi and Roy's Custom Leather Goods offer complete lines of padded nylon holsters, with each offering hip, shoulder and ankle holsters in various colors such as black, tan and camouflage. Uncle Mike's offers 11 different sizes in their basic hip holster, four sizes in a belt slide holster, seven sizes in a vertical

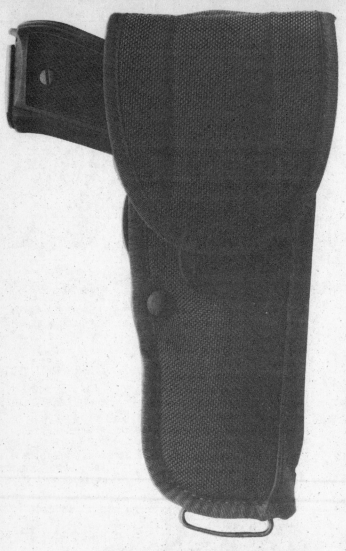

Unleather holsters are here to stay because they're good.

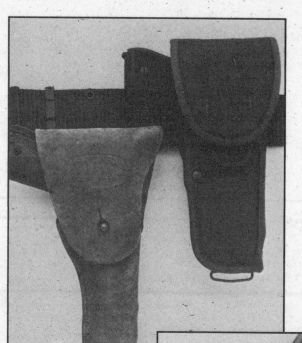

The M-12 hip holster by Bianchi International is the new official standard-issue holster of the United States Armed Forces.

The Model 1916 leather rig for the Model 1911 has been obsoleted by Bianchi's M-12 in nylon.

Apart from all the carrying options, some of which can be seen here, the M-12 also carries a cleaning rod.

The M-12 is what they call *modular*—can be worn right, left, flapless, shoulder, whatever.

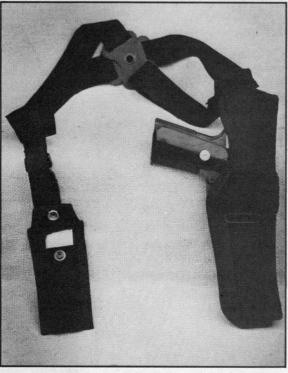

This spring-loaded shoulder holster is padded in nylon, shown here with a Colt 45 Auto, and with the associated rigging. It's a Bianchi.

This close-up shows the open front of the Bianchi International spring-loaded shoulder holster.

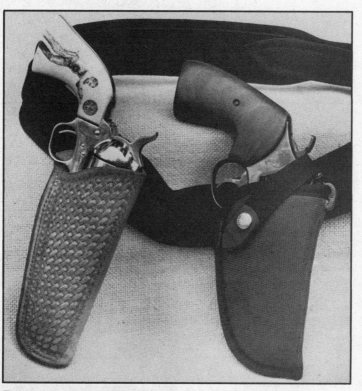

This leather rig is S.D. Myres "Threepersons." The Bianchi Ranger in nylon offers the same carry.

shoulder holster, two sizes in a vertical shoulder holster for scoped handguns, four sizes in a horizontal shoulder holster, and three sizes in ankle holsters.

The adoption of a Bianchi padded nylon holster by the U.S. government is big news. Bianchi's rig is designed for the newly adopted 9mm handgun. A four-year development program by Bianchi led to the M-12 holster. The contract provides for several hundred thousand holsters over the next three years to replace the M1916 holster which was originally designed in 1909 for the use of mounted cavalry troops. John Bianchi estimates that follow-on orders to the original contract will be for hundreds of thousands more.

The M-12 holster is worth a look. Weighing eight ounces, the M-12 is of modular design. It may be worn with or without the flap, right- or left-handed, on wide or narrow belts, cross- or side-draw. With the use of optional accessories it can carry on chest, shoulder or thigh. There is a cleaning rod inserted along the front edge of the holster. The M-12 holster is silent in use, an important consideration in some military applications. The commercial version of this holster is cataloged as the UM-84 and is available for most popular semi-auto handguns. I have selected the UM-84 as the field holster for my personal Colt Officers ACP lightweight Model 45, in order to maximize protection of the pistol and to get the weight savings. Combined with CCI Blazer hollow point ammunition, which is loaded in aluminum cases, I have a minimum weight package for survival/backpacking purposes.

In conventional hip holsters, the offerings of Uncle Mike's, Bianchi or Roy's Custom Leather Goods are all excellent. The original Uncle Mike's Sidekick version had the back side of the male portion of the snap for the retaining strap exposed on the inside of the holster, which was a possible source of excessive blue wear. This has been corrected in their current production. In addition, the retaining strap has been improved by making it adjustable from the front side of the holster. Roy's Pistol Packer differs from its competition in the use of leather for the belt loop and the lining material. Unique in nylon hip holsters is the Brauer Brothers' Blake-Break version, which includes a conventional thumb-break retaining strap. While all of these are excellent holsters, if I had to choose only one, I would go with Bianchi's Ranger

#4000, a high quality padded nylon version of the classic Threepersons holster first produced by Tio Sam Myres almost 60 years ago. A nice feature of all of these hip holsters is the adjustable retaining strap. The concept of one holster fitting numerous guns requires a retaining strap that is adjustable for length. This feature would be an improvement on many leather holsters, as it is not unusual to find that your pet handgun with minor modifications such as custom stocks or sights, seats in a leather holster just differently enough from the stock version to prevent snapping the retaining strap/thumb break.

Both Uncle Mike's and Bianchi offer pancake-style nylon holsters (Uncle Mike's calls theirs a belt slide) made of padded nylon. These offer all the advantages of the pancake design, such as high ride and improved weight distribution for large handguns, which equates to user comfort, plus the advantages of padded nylon, as discussed earlier. An interesting feature of Uncle Mike's belt slides is their ambidextrous design. By including a reversible thumb-break strap and belt loops which may be used from either side, the same holster may be worn for use by either hand. I like to remove the thumb-break completely and wear this holster on the inside of the belt, using the belt tension for securing the handgun. The double belt loop allows the gun to be worn with butt turned to the front, the old cavalryman's draw. A pet project, still in the planning stage, is a budget version of Magnaport's Predator. This will be a 4⅝-inch Ruger Blackhawk in 41 Magnum caliber with action tune, porting, interchangeable front sight blades, and stainless steel lockplating by Magnaport. Either the Bianchi Intl. Shadow #4500 or Uncle Mike's Sidekick Belt Slide will be an excellent choice in a field holster for this revolver. One disadvantage of the one holster for several sizes of handguns approach shows up when the pancake styles are used with auto pistols. If your purpose is to select a holster for self-defense purposes, one should be picked which doesn't allow the pistol to seat so deeply that one cannot acquire a proper shooting grip with first hand contact.

Possibly the greatest advantages of the padded nylon holster is found in the shoulder holsters. As indicated earlier, Uncle Mike's offers 13 different sizes of shoulder holsters. While models are offered for concealed carry, it is the shoulder holsters developed for the large-framed, long-bar-

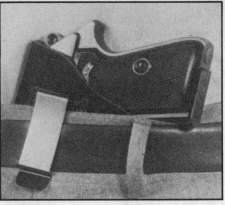

Inside-The-Pant from Uncle Mike's (here for a southpaw) has little bulk, fine comfort, but Arganbright favors not the belt clip.

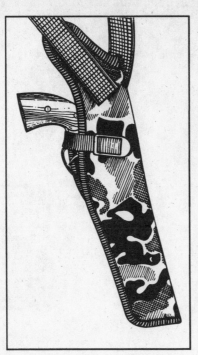

Uncle Mike's shoulder rigs for big revolvers see a lot of use in the hunting mode.

Other belt gear is in nylon, like this 12-round pouch, a handy, quiet way to tote spare cartridges from Michaels.

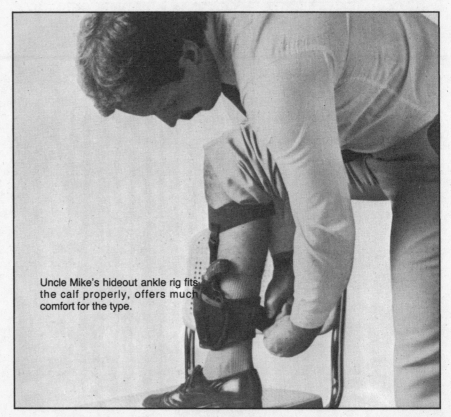

Uncle Mike's hideout ankle rig fits the calf properly, offers much comfort for the type.

reled revolvers and single shot pistols so popular with handgun hunters, that offer definite advantages over their leather counterparts. These specialty handguns are too bulky to carry comfortably in hip holsters. Two examples that merit examination are Roy's Sudden Thunder Shoulder Systems and Bianchi's Ranger Hunting Model 4100. Roy's version is a standard shoulder holster design, a simple pouch holster carried back under the offside arm. The holster is reinforced at stress points with leather, and the over-the-shoulder harness is of heavily padded nylon construction. This increases user comfort considerably when wearing one of these heavy handguns in the field for hours at a time. The Sudden Thunder rig is now available with an optional extra-cost offside piece consisting of a padded harness, cartridge loops or magazine case, and belt tie down. This provides the same dual suspension harness arrangement as their all-leather Hidden Thunder system, distributing the weight evenly over both shoulders for increased user comfort. This is a superior harness design. Sudden Thunder is available in black, brown, or either of two camouflage patterns.

Bianchi approaches the comfort problem differently in the 4100 holster. Being designed specifically for hunting purposes and totally ignoring concealment, the Hunting model is similar to a belt holster worn in high cross-draw position, with the support split between a waist belt and an over-the-shoulder strap which angles across the body and supports the gun from the strong side shoulder. The shoulder strap has a heavily padded area that is adjustable for proper position and ensures maximum comfort. The 4100 is available in black or camouflage and with or without a removable flap. A nice feature is the "adjustable positioner" built into the pouch, which allows quick conversion from medium- to large-frame revolvers. This is the holster I will be using with my Ruger Super Blackhawk this fall while chasing the elusive whitetail buck around eastern Missouri.

As this is written, Bianchi is the only manufacturer of a spring-loaded front break padded nylon holster. This 4601 vertical shoulder holster was introduced at the 1985 SHOT Show. The version I tested, for up to five-inch large frame autos (Colt 45) or four-inch large frame revolvers (Smith & Wesson K and L frames), works well and offers all of the advantages of the padded nylon construction in a concealable holster. Available for handguns ranging in size from the S&W two-inch snubs to the Colt auto, this rig has a unique single point harness attachment which allows it to be converted from right- to left-hand use. The cost savings are very significant in the shoulder holster, as conventional leather models can run close to $100 for a large hunting handgun.

I don't like ankle holsters. Their disadvantages far outweigh their advantages. They are uncomfortable, insecure, very slow to draw from, and tactically unsound. However, if you must use an ankle holster, some of the best are available in padded nylon. Uncle Mike's, available in black only, is constructed of a thinner closed-cell foam to keep the holster as slim as possible. The adjustable thumb break is metal-reinforced for ease of release, and the leg piece is cut on a contour so that it will fit the taper of the calf of the leg properly. Concealment holsters (shoulder, ankle, inside the pants) constructed of padded nylon are not affected by moisture or mildew, a definite advantage over leather.

Uncle Mike's produces an Inside-The-Pant model. Available in black only, this deep pouch holster is constructed of a soft, pliable laminate which adds very little bulk to the gun. The soft, non-abrasive outer surface is of a synthetic suede-like material that tends to cling to the trousers, preventing slippage, yet is comfortable against the skin. This material offers maximum user comfort, an important consideration with a holster worn inside the waistband. Unfortunately, this holster is supplied with a metal belt clip. While holster manufacturers continue to produce this style of holster with belt clips in place of a belt loop, even the best belt clip can release when the gun is grabbed, allowing the holster to be drawn with the gun. With a belt loop and one-way snap, Uncle Mike's Inside-The-Pant holster could be the best on the market. If a metal clip does not bother you, this is the concealment holster for you.

Uncle Mike's has recently added a complete line of Cordura accessories to their Sidekicks. These include speedloader pouches, a pouch for single auto-pistol magazine or large folding knife, cartridge slides for both rifle and revolver cartridges, a very neat folding cartridge carrier for either rifle or handgun cartridges, and an ammunition pouch for 22 rimfire or pellets. All are available in the same color choices as Sidekick belts and holsters. These accessories are constructed of two layers of Cordura nylon and the flaps are secured with Velcro. I have used the folder pouch and the folding cartridge carriers and I am satisfied with them.

Any of the padded nylon hip holsters work best when mated with a proper belt. Both Uncle Mike's and Bianchi offer excellent nylon belts. If selecting an Uncle Mike's belt, one should get the Deluxe model, as the standard belt is too light and narrow to provide the necessary support. The Bianchi belt is available with or without elastic cartridge loops and is 2¼ inches wide. While the elastic cartridge loops will fit cartridges from 22 rimfire through 458 Magnum, I find it very tedious inserting the centerfire rounds in the contracted loops. I would use the belt without loops and add a nylon cartridge carrier.

There is a Law Enforcement system in padded nylon from Bianchi. This includes a two-inch Sam Browne belt, a thumb-break version of the Ranger #4000, speedloader pouch, cartridge box, handcuff case, Mace holder, flashlight holder, side-handle baton holder, key holder, and keepers, all available in black only.

With the recent management decision at Smith & Wesson to concentrate on handgun production, the S&W holster operation has been phased out. This includes their line of nylon holsters. While there were rumors of the S&W holster line being purchased by another holster maker, this has not happened.

Just as S&W drops out of the nylon holster market, Safariland enters. By the time you are reading this, Safariland will be offering shoulder and ankle holsters in padded nylon, under a licensing agreement with Michael's of Oregon. I will be curious to see what affect the consumer acceptance of these synthetic holsters will have on future holster design. Safariland has recently purchased the Rogers Holster Company, including their patented hot synthetic molding process. Safariland is combining this rigid synthetic liner with leather to produce high quality "Safarilaminate" holsters which seem to offer the best of both leather and synthetic holsters. These leather holsters are waterproof because of the synthetic liner, and the hot molded liner won't stretch, thereby maintaining the proper friction fit after years of use.

In another three years, we will all know a lot more. For now, it's a mixed marketplace, but nylon is looking good. ●

WHILE HISTORIANS cannot agree on who invented the pistol or when or where, on one thing they do agree: it was the Germans who brought the pistol to war as a weapon of cavalry. In fact, Field Marshal Viscount Montgomery goes so far as to credit them with inventing it: ". . . the javelin was replaced as the weapon of light cavalry by the pistol—a German invention."[1]

We know that small numbers of "hand gonnes" were used in the battles of Crecy (1346) and Agincourt (1415), but with no influence on the outcome in either case.[2] The French and the Italians were active in the early development of a *bonbarde portative*. The city of Perugia in 1364 ordered the construction of 500 "little bombards of only a palm's length,"

but nothing further is known of them.[3]

It is doubtful if any of those weapons were handguns in today's meaning of the word. Rather, both the Perugia and the Crecy-Agincourt examples most likely were small hand cannons, perhaps similar in style to the famous "Tannenberg Hand Gonne," the earliest known hand-held firearm. This was a heavy, solid brass tube of 66-caliber, 12¼ inches long, with a socket recessed in the breech end to accommodate a straight wood shaft, a "tiller" stock some 39 inches long.

The Tannenberg gun, documented as having been used by Lord Hartmund in defense of his castle against a besieging force in the year 1399, was dug up from the mud 450 years

later when the castle moat was being excavated. It is now in the German National Museum in Nürnberg. Replicas have been sold by a historical foundation in the United States.[4]

Although the Tannenberg gun physically could be held in one hand, its use required both hands, the other being necessary to apply the burning match, or fuse, to the touch hole. The later invention of the serpentine to hold the match and carry it to the powder made possible a true one-hand firearm, but the pistol was still not a practical weapon for the horseman until the invention in Nürnberg about 1515 of the wheel-lock firing system. European armies were apparently quick to recognize its merits, for we know that only five years later, in 1520, German cavalry was already

𝕰arly 𝕯ays of the 𝕻istol

From knightly cavalry to cowboy in just three centuries

by FIELDING GREAVES

making common use of pistols, although lance and sword were still their primary weapons.[5]

The French general and military writer, Francois de La Noue, known as "Bras de Fer" because of the iron hook that served as his artificial arm, in his 1587 book *Political and Military Discourses* acknowledges that the Germans were the first to use the pistol in war: "We must grant them the honor of being the first that brought the pistol into use, which when a man can well handle I take to be very dangerous. The Germans among all sorts of horsemen that use this weapon do carry away the prize."[6]

By 1544 and the battle of Renty against French King Henry II, the German states had made the pistol the primary weapon of their cavalry.

habitually advanced "on a trot or soft pace," whereas "the charge of the lancers is terrible and resolute."[8]

In England, meanwhile, King Henry VIII (509-1547) had imported some Dutch gunsmiths, and by the latter part of his reign some of his cavalry were armed with pistols. His daughter, Elizabeth, hastily raising troops to meet the expected landings by the Spanish Armada in 1588, formed three new types of units, one of which was a body of light cavalrymen, each armed with a spear and a single pistol.[9]

In France, the King's Musketeers, made famous in the fiction of Alexandre Dumas, were a mounted unit. Under Louis XII they had been armed with muskets, whence their name. Later, under Louis XIII (1610-1643),

vor of the headlong charge with the sword, the pistol being reserved for use in the thick of the melee when the cavalry was actually in among the enemy.[13] In England, Oliver Cromwell soon followed suit, as did other nations, and it was not long before the caracole had disappeared from the battlefields of Europe.[14]

Troopers of Cromwell's cavalry, known as "Ironsides" for the heavy cuirass they wore, were usually armed with a sword and a pair of pistols, while their officers often carried carbines. A letter from Cromwell to the young men and women of Norwich on how they might spend the money they had raised to equip soldiers suggested: "Employ your twelve score pounds to buy pistols and saddles, and I will provide four score horses."[15] In

German *reiters*, with pistol holsters hung from saddle pommel, firing pistols at marks and in combat. From engraving in *The Art of Mounted Warfare*, published in 1616 at Frankfurt-am-Main.

Cavalry troopers called *Reiters* each carried a pair of large, heavy pistols in paired holsters attached to the saddle pommel, sometimes with a third pistol tucked into a boot top. Their tactics were developed to defeat the typical infantry of the day, the square of the mercenary Swiss pikemen. Those tactics included a characteristic maneuver called the *caracole*. In the caracole, each rank in turn rode forward at a trot or gentle canter to within close pistol range, halted and fired, then wheeled aside, circling to the rear to reload, form up again and repeat the action.[7]

Keeping just beyond reach of the long Swiss pikes, they easily tore up the ranks of pikemen. They were also said to be effective against cavalry armed only with the sword. Commentators of the time noted, however, that they could not stand against the headlong charge of lancers, for the reiters

they were equipped with swords and pistols and eventually came to be called "pistoleers" by the French.[10]

Meanwhile, just as the Swiss pikemen had been the mercenary infantry of Europe, so the German Reiters became the mercenary cavalry on the continent.[11] However, progress was afoot in the infantry as well, and while pistols were added to the cavalry's weaponry, increasing numbers of harquebuses were being added to the squares of pikemen. The leisurely pace of the reiters' attack left them as vulnerable to gunfire as the infantry square. As an ever larger proportion of harquebusiers were added to the squares of pikemen, reiter casualties climbed steeply, and the force soon lost its effectiveness.[12]

It was not surprising, therefore, that when Gustavus Adolphus of Sweden (1611-1632) reorganized his cavalry he abandoned the caracole in fa-

July 1645, the going price for "troop saddles with furniture" was about 16 shillings apiece, while "holsters for holding pistols, a necessary adjunct to the saddle, cost half a crown a pair."[16]

An idea of the melee tactics of Cromwell's time can be gleaned from the instructions Major-General Sir Thomas Morgan issued to his cavalry in Scotland, that "no man should fire till he came within a horse's length of the enemy, and then to throw their pistols in their faces, and so fall on with the sword."[17]

While military pistols of the era were all single shot weapons, inventors had not been idle. Arms historian W.H.B. Smith has recorded that a pre-Cromwellian revolver, from the reign of Charles I (1625-1647), is in the Tower Collection in London. In 1661, a patent was granted to the Marquis of Worcester for a revolver. The *Diary* of Samuel Pepys records under date of

July 3, 1662 a reference to a "gun to discharge seven times." And one Abraham Hill on March 4, 1664, filed specifications at the patent office for a gun or pistol to carry seven or eight charges in the stock.[18] The era of repeating arms had already begun.

Pistols played an important role in the history of America from the time of the first English settlement at Jamestown. In 1608, the year after the founding of the colony, Captain John Smith with 15 companions had gone upriver to barter for corn at the Indian village of Chief Opechancanough of the Pamunkey tribe. Seeing that some 50 or 60 warriors were preparing to jump his party, Smith forestalled them, whipping out his pistol and pressing it against the chief's chest with one hand while grasping Openchancanough's long hair with the other, taking him hostage and using him to extricate himself and his men from a perilous situation.[19]

In the early 1600s in New Netherlands, the Dutch settlers were selling firearms, including pistols, to the Indians. In New England also, firearms were traded with the Indians. The 1628 and 1629 records of the Massachusetts Bay Company noted the importation of pistols for use by their hired soldiers, and the Company's records also revealed that "about that same time, Indians residing near the villages were well supplied with both pistols and bullet molds."[20]

Along with the blunderbuss and the musket, the pistol was in fact an accepted and commonplace weapon in the New World. At a time when every able-bodied man was considered part of the militia, every man was expected to arm himself. A Congressional report has noted: "In 1623, Virginia forbade its colonists to travel unless they were 'well armed;' in 1631 it required colonists to engage in target practice on Sunday and to 'bring their peeces to church.' In 1658 it required every householder to have a functioning firearm within his house and in 1673 its laws provided that a citizen who claimed he was too poor to purchase a firearm would have one purchased for him by the government, which would then require him to pay a reasonable price when able to do so. In Massachusetts, the first session of the legislature ordered that not only freemen, but also indentured servants, own firearms, and in 1644 it imposed a stern six-shilling fine upon any citizen who was not armed."[21]

In America as in Europe, the pistol was the preferred weapon for mounted troops. The New York provincial law of 1667 required that one-third of each militia band be a mounted unit, armed and ready for service on one hour's notice. New York's militia regulations of 1691 specified that ". . . every soldier belonging to the Horse, shall, when and where commanded, appear and be provided with a good serviceable Horse of his own, covered with a good Saddle, with Holsters, Breast-plate and Crupper, and a Case of good Pistols, Hanger, Sword or Rapier, and half a pound of Powder, with twelve serviceable Bullets . . ."[22]

Up to the time of the French and Indian War (1755), the pistols in the New World had been a miscellany from many countries of Europe.[23] From this time on, however, they were chiefly "those manufactured in England or whose locks were made there," according to W.H.B. Smith.[24]

Some few were manufactured by German gunsmiths who in the 1730s had settled in and around Lancaster, Pennsylvania. These were the gunsmiths who made the famous Pennsylvania rifles, and a few of those skilled craftsmen produced pistols bearing some aspects of resemblance to their long guns.[25]

It was not only land forces that were armed with pistols. Seamen of the mid-1700s were also generally armed not only with a cutlass, but also with a pistol, the latter usually

Captain John Smith with his pistol takes Chief Opechancanough hostage in 1608. The fighting shown in the background did not take place on this occasion. The vignette is one of eight designed and engraved by Robert Vaughan of London for Smith's map of "Ould Virginia" in the *Generall Historie of Virginia* (London, 1624).

tucked into the waistband of their trousers.[26]

At Lexington, "where first the embattled farmers stood, and fired the shot heard 'round the world," that first shot, according to eyewitnesses, was not fired by one of the Minutemen with his musket or rifle, but rather came from a pistol in the hand of British Major Pitcairn. When the Americans refused to disperse, according to contemporary reports, he cursed them, drew one of his pair of pistols and fired it, leading a charge that caused them to fall back on positions at Concord.[27] That brace of Highlander flintlock pistols carried that day by

This large sea service pistol actually belonged to Oliver Hazard Perry, who won a big fight carrying pistols. (Courtesy U.S. Naval Academy Museum)

John Paul Jones, commanding *Bon Homme Richard* vs. *Serapis* in the 1779 action off Flamborough Head, was shown with five pistols tucked into his sash.

This Michael J. McAfee drawing of a 1775 officer in the field shows him with pistol, knife and hanger. From *Military Collector & Historian*, Summer 1976. Reproduced by permission of The Company of Military Historians.

Major Pitcairn can be seen at the Historical Society Museum in Lexington, Massachusetts.

After the failure of the British mission at Concord—the Americans having successfully spirited away the munitions the British sought to capture—the redcoats had to fight their way back to Boston with the colonials harassing them most of the way. At the tiny village of Menotomy, one of the Americans determined to block their way was 80-year-old Sam Whittemore, a stubborn old man who was set on making the British pay dearly for their raid. Armed with a saber, a musket and a pair of pistols, he waited until the enemy were almost upon him, then killed one with his musket and another one or two with his pistols, before being shot in the face. As he lay beside the road, passing redcoats repeatedly bayonetted him. Despite a serious head wound and thirteen bayonet wounds, says historian Major John Galvin, Whittemore survived, eventually living to be almost a hundred years old.[28]

While most of the Continental Army and local militia forces were equipped with muskets, and some carried their Pennsylvania rifles, officers were often armed with pistols. This was also true of naval officers. An interesting old engraving of John Paul Jones, on deck in the swirling smoke of the 1779 action off Flamborough Head between *Bon Homme Richard* and *Serapis,* shows him with no less than five pistols tucked into his sash.[29]

Origin of the term "Pistol"

The origin of the name "pistol" is still a puzzler after all these years. Some claim it can be traced to the name of the home city of its supposed inventor, Camillio Vitelli, of Pistoia, Italy, about 1540. But we know that cannot be, for the pistol was already in common use by German cavalry nearly a quarter of a century earlier.

Others suggest the name derives from the fact that the pistol's usual bore diameter in its earliest days was equal to that of a common small coin of that era, the *pistole*.

The name is also said to come from the Czech *pistala,* meaning "pipe," while yet another explanation holds that the pistol takes its name from the cavalry practice of carrying those early handguns in a pair of holsters hung from the *pistallo* (pommel) of the saddle.[37]

It was not the military alone, but civilians as well who were often armed with the pistol. Historian Douglas Southall Freeman, in his comprehensive biography of George Washington, remarks with surprise at the large number of firearms kept by city dwellers of the Revolutionary era. In the 1775 siege of Boston, the British commander, General Gage, promised that any Bostonians who wished to leave the city might do so, provided they first turned in their firearms. He broke that promise, but not before the gulled Bostonians had surrendered a total of 2,674 firearms, or one gun for every 5.6 inhabitants of the city. Boston then having a population of 15,000. Doubtless, Freeman added, many weapons remained concealed.[30]

Of the total turned in by those Boston citizens, Frothingham in his contemporaneous book *The Siege of Boston* reported that 634 were pistols, or one in every four surrendered firearms.[31]

Most accounts of the Revolutionary War, according to historian George Neumann, "give little attention to the pistol—probably because it was decidedly inaccurate except at close range, and not included in battlefield tactics. Yet the handgun did see considerable service as a personal weapon. It was considered normal for civilians to carry pocket pistols for protection when traveling. Among military personnel, officers, mounted troops and seamen used them as standard arms."[32]

"As an evidence of the extent to which the flintlock pistol contributed to later American history," writes historian W.H.B. Smith, "consider the fact that some 70,000 men shipped out of New England ports alone aboard privateersmen during the War of 1812, and that it was customary for such men to carry at least two heavy belt pistols, as close quarter arms for boarding ships."[33]

Meanwhile, in the infant United States, the wide popularity and availability of pistols can be imagined when one looks at the list of early American gunsmiths. By far the majority of those gunsmiths made long guns—muskets, rifles and fowling pieces. Nevertheless, pistols were such an ordinary part of everyday life in America that by 1800 and earlier, in the city of Philadelphia alone, there had been no less than 21 gunsmithing establishments that specialized in making pistols.[34]

As the colonies grew from primitive settlements to commercially successful trading colonies to independent and united states, always along the western frontiers could be found the fur traders and trappers, pushing ahead, deep into the wilderness, ahead of the advancing frontier. Arms historian Carl Russell notes that "As trade items, pistols did not figure importantly, but as personal side arms the trader and trapper found them indispensable, and their ubiquity in the fur fields—at least as far back as the mid-eighteenth century—can be proved."[35]

Thus from earliest Colonial times, and from our first beginnings as a nation, pistols have played an important role in our history and our society. Since muskets, blunderbusses, rifles, and pistols were all commonplace weapons of our early history, it is clear that when the framers of our Second Amendment wrote into the Constitution an acknowledgement of the fundamental "right of the people to keep and bear arms," their use of the term "arms" was intended to encompass all of those popular and widely owned firearms, as well as swords, hangers, cutlasses, spontoons, pikes, dirks and other ordinary and usual weapons of the time. In the only 20th century United States Supreme Court case which considered the Second Amendment, the high court noted that all constitutional sources "show plainly enough that the militia comprised all males physically capable of acting in concert for the common defense . . . [and that] these men were expected to appear bearing arms supplied by themselves and of the kind in common use at the time."[36]

Over the years the pistol has seen many developments: wheel-lock to flintlock to caplock to self-contained cartridge; muzzleloader to breechloader; single shot, double barrel, revolver, semi-automatic. Still today, as it has for hundreds of years, the pistol remains the ultimate close combat arm for most military officers and many soldiers. It is the standard for practically every police force in the world, and the preferred weapon for home protection by our own armed citizenry. ●

Notes

1 Viscount Bernard Montgomery, *A History of Warfare,* NY, World Publishing Co. 1968, p. 231.

2 Charles Firth, *Cromwell's Army,* London, Matheun & Co. Ltd., 1961, p. 112.

3 Lynn Montross, *War Through the Ages,* NY, Harper & Bros., 1944, p. 181.

4 The American Historical Foundation, Richmond, Virginia.

5 W.H.B. Smith, *The Book of Pistols and Revolvers,* NY, Castle Books, 1968, p. 10.

6 Charles Firth, *Cromwell's Army,* London, Matheun & Co. Ltd., 1961, p. 128.

7 Firth, p. 129; Smith, p. 10; Montgomery, p. 231-2; Montross, p. 238-9; W.W. Greener, *The Gun and Its Development,* NY, Bonanza Books, p. 63.

8 Firth, p. 129.

9 Smith, p. 10; Firth, p. 112; Greener, p. 212.

10 Vezio Melegari, *The World's Great Regiments,* NY, G.P. Putnam's Sons, 1969, p. 84.

11 Montross, p. 239.

12 Montross, p. 236, 242.

13 Montgomery, p. 271.

14 Montgomery, p. 280.

15 Firth, p. 118-19.

16 Firth, p. 241.

17 Firth, p. 141.

18 Smith, p. 13.

19 Carl Bridenbaugh, *Early Americans,* NY, Oxford Univ. Press, 1981, p. 19-20.

20 Smith, p. 13.

21 Senate Judiciary Committee report, Feb. 1982, "The Right to Keep and Bear Arms," (Subcommittee on the Constitution), p. 3.

22 Alan & Barbara Aimone, "New York's Provincial Militia," in *Miliary Collector & Historian* (Journal of The Company of Military Historians), Summer 1981, p. 58.

23 Warren Moore, *Weapons of the American Revolution,* NY, Promontory Press, 1967, p. 13-53. Geo. C. Neumann, *History of Weapons of the American Revolution,* NY: Bonanza Books, 1967, p. 150-51.

24 Smith, p. 15.

25 M.L. Brown, "The Pennsylvania-Kentucky Pistol," *American Rifleman,* April 1981, p.35.

26 *Military Collector & Historian,* Winter 1979, p. 163.

27 Smith, p. 14-15.

28 Maj. John R. Glavin, *The Minutemen* NY, Hawthorn Books, Inc., p. 229-230.

29 Olive Warner, *Great Sea Battles,* NY, The Macmillan Co. 1963, p. 102.

30 Douglas Southall Freeman, *George Washington,* Vol. III, p. 576n.

31 Moore, p viii; Smith, p.15.

32 Neumann, p. 150.

33 Smith, p. 15-16.

34 A. Merwyn Carey, *American Firearms Makers,* NY, Thomas Y. Crowell Co., 1953.

35 Carl P. Russell, *Guns on the Early Frontiers,* NY, Bonanza Books, 1957, p. 82-83.

36 Senate Judiciary Committee, "The Right to Keep and Bear Arms," Feb. 1982, p. 10.

37 Montross, p. 238; Smith, p. 10-11; Greener, p. 97; *Encyclopedia Britannica* (1961), vol. 17, p. 961; Robet Held, *The Age of Firearms,* NY: Harper & Bros., 1957, p. 55; *American Heritage Dictionary of the English Language* (1973), p. 998.

P.P.C.'s Lug Recess Insert . . .

P.P.C.'s Gilkerson's Locking Lug Recess Insert improves feeding, smoothes bolt operation and improves safety should a case rupture—and gives better accuracy, too.

AN ACCURACY BREAK-THROUGH

by ED MATUNAS

NOT MUCH has happened lately in the evolution of the turnbolt rifle. We have better barrel uniformity, bedding methods, lock times and so on, yet no *basic* change has occurred. Now, P.P.C. Corporation has a patented product some of us believe a basic improvement for the turning bolt. Like most really good ideas, what is now called the "Gilkerson P.P.C. Locking Lug Recess Insert" is simplicity to the point of "Why hasn't someone thought of it sooner?"

Consider a standard bolt gun's locking lug recess. As the bolt moves forward, the lugs (on most bolts) lay horizontally, right and left. As the handle turns the lugs into battery, they become oriented vertically.

When a fresh cartridge is being chambered, the lug recesses, top and bottom, are open. Sometimes—not often—a cartridge nose is deformed when it hits the edges of this recess and, under such circumstances, improper bolt manipulation can result in a jam. This area accumulates all kinds of trash, too.

When the bolt is in battery, the recesses are open to its left and right. Should a cartridge rupture, the lug recesses are the beginning of an escape route that allows bits of brass and hot gasses to escape.

P.P.C.'s Lug Recess Insert fills the locking lug recesses and turns with the bolt head in and out of battery. That protects the feeding cartridge bullet nose, even prevents certain types of jamming; and with the lugs up and down, the Insert greatly reduces or eliminates solid particles escaping rearward should a case rupture.

And there is more. By filling receiver voids, the Lug Recess Insert helps keep the lug area clean to smooth out bolt operation. In several versions, there is a Teflon or graphite impregnation of the insert which actually lubricates the turning of the bolt.

There are three proposed materials from which the Lug Recess Insert might be manufactured. It has not at this writing gone into general production. Type A is urethane impregnated with Teflon and has a Durometer hardness of 80. Type B is Nylatron, a graphite-impregnated nylon. Type C will have the thicker sections made of stainless steel.

The feature that may get the most attention is the Lug Recess Insert's claimed accuracy-improvement capability. Because it butts snugly against barrel and receiver, and because it snugly encircles the bolt head, it has the ability to dampen—or at least alter—barrel vibrations so that barrel movement occurs at a reduced level. Due to this increased accuracy capability and the added safety features, both U.S. and overseas manufacturers are interested.

I installed a pre-production sample insert—a Type A unit of urethane impregnated with Teflon—in a Remington Model Seven in caliber 7mm-08. The rifle was tested with a specific lot of ammo prior to the installation and it showed an average accuracy for ten

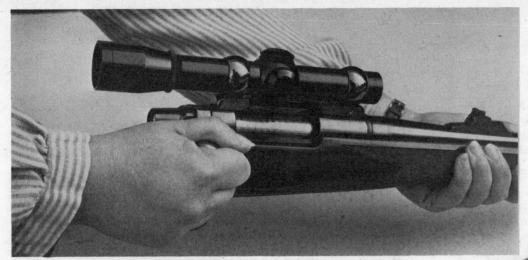

In use the Lug Recess Insert cannot be seen, but smoother bolt operation is noticeable, as is improved accuracy

The Lug Recess Insert snugly fits over the bolt head and lugs. It is shown here with the bolt only, but in use the inset stays in place in the reciever.

A view from the rear showing the close fit of the insert over the bolt head and lugs.

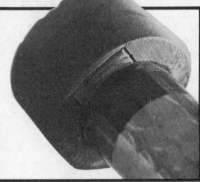

Matunas' extensive tests conclusively demonstrated the Insert's effect in this Remington Model Seven 7mm-08.

5-shot groups at 100 yards of 1¾ inches. The same lot of ammo averaged 1⅜ inches when fired with the insert in place. Another lot of ammo that had previously averaged 1½ inches averaged 1¼ inches with the insert. Accuracy was thus improved by 21% and 19% respectively.

To see if results were consistent, the insert was removed and the rifle once again tested with the original lots of ammo. The results were almost identical to the original testing. Then, once again, the insert was replaced, with average accuracy improving 22% and 19% respectively. It would seem that the insert does indeed dampen barrel vibrations in a manner conducive to accuracy improvement.

I experienced no difficulty with the sample unit. The manufacturer suggests that some sort of detent may be added to the insert to prevent it from turning inadvertently during cleaning procedures, etc.

Installation of the insert requires a 0.010-in. to 0.012-in. undercut in the lug recesses. For factory firearms, this simply means increasing the dimension of the lug recess area. For installation in existing rifles, the barrel must be removed and the undercut made. The Lug Recess Insert is then snapped into place. Should it ever be necessary to remove the insert, it can be pulled from the receiver with a dental pick without further disassembly. Whether a new unit can be then put into place (without disassembly) will depend upon the specific rifle and

the final production versions of the insert.

The insert's future, I guess, may rest with the reception it gets when the public sees it. Since installation requires the removal of the barrel from the receiver, the unit's greatest appeal will be to rifle manufacturers, and barrelsmiths who can fit it when fitting a new barrel. It's a very simple, apparently risk-free, way to get a major improvement though, however it turns out.

●

HAND LOADING UPDATE

by DEAN A. GRENNELL

IN TERMS of thrillingly new and radically innovative gadgetry, the past twelve-months have not exactly been the vintage of the century, but we do have some new stuff to discuss.

Arcadia Machine & Tool (aka **AMT**) has introduced a device they call the AMT Autoscale. It could be termed an automated powder dispenser. It incorporates a tubular powder reservoir, a scale and a pair of electrically powered powder tricklers; one coarse and the other fine.

A well-prepared but unillustrated set of instructions accompanies the Autoscale. After completing the simple assembly, you level it up on the working surface, pour powder into the tube, set the poise and rotor on the beam of the scale for the desired charge weight and press a small button on top of the unit. That starts both of the trickler tubes to rotating, dribbling granules into the pan. As the charge accumulates enough weight to commence moving the beam, the coarse trickler shuts off and the fine trickler continues until the pointer comes up to the witness line, after which the fine one shuts off, also. At that point, you remove the pan, dump the charge into a waiting case by means of the indispensable powder funnel and repeat the operation, as required.

You can adjust the coarse trickler so the fine trickler merely rounds out the charge, which is faster, by means of a small knurled knob with a two-pointed arrow indicating F and S for fast and slow. All in all, it should take a lot of the painful drudgery out of making up weighed powder charges. Typically, the Autoscale may take anywhere from 20 to 40 seconds to weigh out each charge, depending upon variables such as the charge weight and the adjustment of the F/S knob.

I regret to have to report that it does not work overly well with the finer granulations of powder, including ball, spherical or globular types. With any of those, the coarse trickler

will seize up and stop inside of the first half-dozen charges. After a few more, the fine trickler will also come to a stop. With the small granulations of extruded powders like IMR-4227, the coarse trickler cuts out fairly soon, although the fine trickler continues to operate. That permits the use of a dipper to dump in most of the charge for a useful savings of time. With powder granules as large as IMR-4198, happily, there seems to be no further problems with jamming the coarse trickler. I can report that, with the F/S knob adroitly positioned, my Autoscale dispenses 48.2 grains of IMR-4198 in just half a minute, give or take the odd nanosecond.

At last you can buy your very own robot to weigh out rifle charges with patience and precision. It's the AMT Autoscale.

I dare to hope that a little more expenditure on R&D will result in an Autoscale capable of handling granulations even as fine as Accurate Arms #9, so that handgun handloaders can share in the technological breakthrough. AA-9 is so pesky-fine that you can only dispense up to about ten charges out of a **RCBS** Little Dandy before the rotor freezes up solid and you sigh and make a reach for the pipe wrench.

Speaking of the Little Dandy—well named, if ever an artifact was—RCBS has finally adopted my helpful suggestion that eliminates the need to hunt for a slot-head screwdriver every time you wish to change the rotor. When the Dandy first appeared, I

liked every single thing about it except for that miserable little slot-head screw.

A recent letter from Ken Alexander confides that Little Dandies are now being shipped with the screwdriverless screws. Having platoons of automatic screw machines at their disposal, they found it more practical to knurl the heads instead of using hex stock, but the new ones work just fine.

If you climbed aboard the Little Dandy bandwagon, early-on, the new knurled-head screws are available for retrofitting, and I have cheering news for you. Because it was my idea, Alexander says that RCBS will supply the replacement screws to my readers at no cost—within the contiguous 48 states. All you need to do is to write to Ken Alexander, at the usual address of Omark/RCBS Operations, tell him how many of the Part No. 86042 rotor guide screws you need—one for each of the Little Dandy measures you own—and add the magic phrase "Uncle Dino says it's on the house."

As long as you're writing, Alexander's interested in one more bit of information. There is some talk of offering blank rotors, with a small punch-mark to indicate the point for drilling, so that buyers can create their own custom rotors for the Little Dandy. If that stirs any interest for you, mention it.

Meanwhile, after a long interlude of R&D, RCBS hopes to get their hand priming tool on the market soon. It's called the Posi-Prime, made from an aluminum casting, ergonomically-contoured and accepting universal shell holders, such as you probably have on hand at present. Projected

lowing calibers: 32 S&W Long/32 H&R Magnum (RN, SWC); 357 Magnum/38 Special (RN, SWC, WC); 9mm Luger (RN); 380 ACP (RN); 45 ACP (RN, SWC).

Further news from RCBS is that they will offer shotshell loading dies for use in most of their current line of presses and they have modified the RS-2 press to RS-3 configuration by incorporating a removable bushing that will accommodate the shotshell dies. Initially, the shotshell dies will be available in the hotly-popular 12-gauge size, but they plan to add other gauges, as well. Price on the die sets and other needed tooling has not even been established on a tentative basis, to the present.

Late in 1985, **Redding Reloading** completed arrangements to buy out **SAECO**, thus adding equipment for casting and lube/sizing bullets to their already extensive line. The SAECO tooling and equipment has

main in production and I view that as good news, being very partial to that goodly device. The SAECO casting furnace will also continue in production and, again, it's an excellent design.

In the meantime, the up-and-coming Redding line goes forward and they've just added a new reloading press for metallics that they call The Boss. It features compound leverage and a semi-automated priming arm. It's an O-frame design, with the frame of cast iron and the frame is offset 36 degrees to offer accessability and visibility. It has a stop feature that prevents the ram from going over top dead center. Suggested retail price is about $85.

Redding continues to devote a lot of effort to custom reloading dies, including their unique carbide dies that feature inserts of titanium carbide in place of tungsten carbide. They have a new line of what they term Profile Crimp dies, available in a large and growing number of popular handgun calibers. The PC die is a sort of compromise between the conventional roll-crimp die and the taper-crimp die. And at present, Redding well may be the world's only source for carbide dies to load the 10mm Auto or Bren Ten round.

C-H Tool & Die now offers loading dies for the 50-caliber Browning machine gun (BMG) cartridge and can supply presses to handle the assignment. Don't be too quick to snort derisively. A growing number of civilian shooters, these latter days, have taken a keen interest in the cartridge. In terms of sheer capability, it sort of makes rounds such as the 458 and 460 Magnums look like squib loads for that old 22 Hamilton you once got for selling tins of Cloverine salve. At 1500 yards, the 50 BMG is just barely getting its second wind. Candidly, I have fired a great many thousands of rounds of 50 BMG, but never one from the shoulder, to date. I'm told it's an arresting experience and I can well believe that. There is a growing clan of die-hard aficionados hell-bent on exploring the joys and delights of working with this last frontier of big rifle cartridges. Marty Liggins, of Accurate Arms, is sort of their high priest and general factotum. He can be reached at the address listed in the directory for Accurate Arms.

Candidly, the outer limit of my own masochism can be pegged at firing hot 45-70 loads in a #3 Ruger carbine. If you go on and compute the foot-pounds of free recoil to which you are subjected, the term for that is *mathochism*.

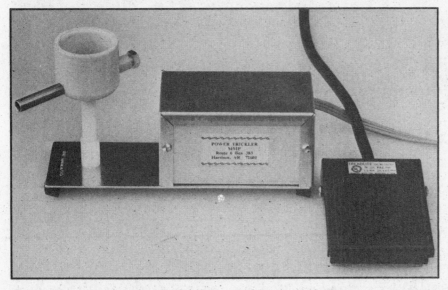

Modern Machine Products (MMP) has this powered powder trickler, with foot switch—it's no robot, but it works.

price will be in the $15-$20 brackets, without shell holders.

Also new from RCBS are T/C die sets and no, it doesn't stand for Thompson/Center, but for *taper crimp*. To further compound the confusion, T/C sets are available in tungsten carbide, but that's not what it stands for, either. Heretofore, RCBS has offered taper-crimp dies in some calibers, for use after the bullet has been seated by means of a conventional seating die. The difference is that the new sets, designated as T/C, supply one or more seating stems to fit the T/C die, so the bullet can be seated and taper-crimped in one operation.

In the initial offering, the T/C dies and die sets will be offered in the fol-

already been moved from the former location in Torrance, California, to the Redding headquarters in Cortland, New York.

The SAECO line dates back a long way. They took over the line of Cramer bullet moulds from pre-WW II days and still had some of the old Cramer cavity-cutters or cherries on hand when I first visited their plant in the mid-'60s. The initials stood for Santa Anita Engineering Company.

Redding honcho Richard Beebe told me they plan to bring back several earlier SAECO products, such as their remarkably handy little cast bullet hardness tester. Besides the moulds, the SAECO lube/sizer will re-

New knurled Little Dandy rotor guide screw (lower) is free when properly requested. Grennell's prototype screw is installed in the measure, here.

The RCBS "Posi-Prime" uses standard shell holders, offers ergonomic curves and surfaces.

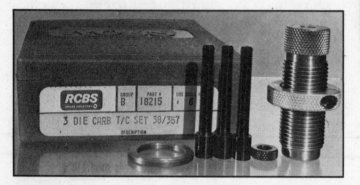

The RCBS Taper-Crimp seating die is available by itself or in die sets, as here.

Back in the other Hartford—not Connecticut but Wisconsin—my old friend Dick Lee continues to pull rabbits from his **Lee Precision** hat for the fascination of the nation's reloaders. His latest offering is the Lee hand tool, calculated to fill the gap between the celebrated Lee Loader kits and his latterday turret presses, progressives and the like. The Lee hand press comes as a complete kit for the given caliber, with nothing else that absolutely has to be purchased. The tab is remarkably painless.

The Lee hand press has roughly the size and bulk of a six-inch Ruger Security-Six. As noted on the shipping carton, it can muster more force than some bench-type reloading presses. It is well suited for attending to assorted reloading chores while unable to sit at the usual bench. If you wish to reload at the shooting site, it is uncommonly well adapted for that.

I have worked with several comparable items of equipment down the years, including the English Pak-Tool, the Decker press and its succes-sor, the Huntington Die Specialties (HDS) press and, more recently, the Lee Hand Press. I'm not sure if you're familiar with the Hindu goddess, Siva. She has something like three arms sprouting from each shoulder and impresses me as the logical person to explore the greatest delights of presses such as the ones just listed. Those of us with the usual complement of two arms, ending in a hand on each, may instead find some amount of challenge. That is particularly true when it comes to seating the bullet. It is possible to do so with precision and aplomb, but it isn't necessarily the simplest project you've ever tackled. If you manage to iron out the minor intricacies, any such systems, including the Lee Hand Press, offer useful capability for reloading at the shooting site.

Up in the fine old Hibernian borough of Murphy in Oregon, the folks at **Hensley & Gibbs** have brought forth a few new bullet designs. They're always up to something in Murphy. One such was produced by Wayne Gibbs at my helpful suggestion. It is but a portion of their long-established #251 design for the 38 Special. It is now officially designated the H&G #333 and it produces a tiny upstart of a 38 wadcutter with a single grease groove, measuring about .285-inch in length and scaling about 66.5 grains in typical alloys.

The H&G #333 comes out of the mould at a diameter that makes it a simple matter to lube-size it to your choice of .356-inch or .358-inch, for use in the 9mm or 38, 357, whatever. To date, there has been remarkably little research plowed into ultra-light-weight bullets for various handguns and rifles. The field offers occasional rewards for exploratory efforts, but not everything you plant, I can confide, comes up roses. Every now and then you get a bumper crop of burdocks.

In the Smith & Wesson Model 547, a 9mm revolver, the H&G #333, sized to .356-inch, can be loaded ahead of 5.1 grains of Bullseye. It zips out of the three-inch barrel at close around 1530 fps of muzzle velocity and what that full-diameter flat nasal area can do in yielding test media is absorbingly fascinating. In stiff clay, you get a crater about 3.5 inches deep by 3.5 inches in diameter. Call it about the size of a restaurant cup in the distant days when a nickel bought a lot of coffee.

A friend and associate, over in Plymouth, England, has another of the H&G #333 moulds and, at last report, was using the wee bullets out of his S&W Model 19 to detonate two-liter beverage bottles filled with water and similar exercises in pure research. Another associate, closer to home, has created a concept he terms the 357 Quadraximum, in which four of the H&G #333s are stuffed down the maw of a 357 R-Max—the bottom two sized to .356-inch—to create a load that makes four holes, fairly close to the point of aim, at a single tug of the trigger.

For my own part, I regard the H&G #333 as having sprung the lid of a whole treasure chest of possibilities, which I have not even begun to explore. Preliminary research suggests the possibility of isolating a charge that makes it a short-range tack-driver at moderate velocities in a good 38

Special. If you do not view ultimate accuracy as the primal criterion, you can shove the tiny pellets from various muzzles at remarkably impressive velocities. As you get up around 2300 fps, they will create some of the sharpest, cleanest holes in the target you've ever seen. That is not impossible to achieve in a long-barreled 357 Magnum.

Never underestimate the value of creative disgruntlement as a force for ongoing progress. As I suspect many another reloader has, I've often encountered a situation in which the case neck did not have quite enough flare to accommodate the base of the bullet I'd hoped to seat in it. If you horse-down on the press handle, it will only ruin the case mouth and/or the bullet, usually both.

The solution was obvious and not in the least original. At least as early as 1960, Dick Lee was offering tapered expanders for use with his Lee Loader kits for shotshells. I still have an example, somewhere around the shop. What I did was to fire up the lathe and knock forth a tapered expanding plug

with an included angle of 10 degrees, putting a handle on it for convenient use. It might or might not prove necessary to dump the charge back into the measure before improving the neck flare; no big matter. After treatment, the charge could be dispensed again and the dilatory bullet would slide home as docile as any little lamb that ever bleated.

Quite manifestly, here was a product that the world's reloaders might use with suitable gratitude. I've neither the facilities nor time to produce such things in quantity, so I sent a sample down to **Paco Kelly** and he discussed it with his associate, Ed Wosika. They decided to put them into the growing line of Paco loading equipment. Their version is double-ended, with an included angle of 12 degrees instead of 10 and it will handle any case necks from 17 through 50. They're calling it the Nexpander and projected retail price is $16.

Lyman has a number of new products, including a carbide cutter for their power case trimmer, at a suggested retail price of $39.95, and now

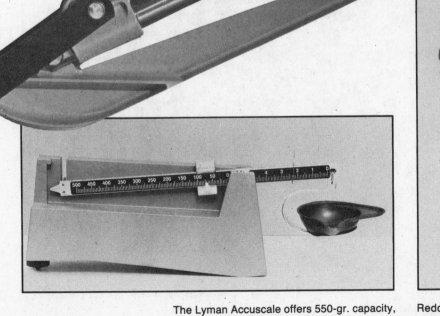

New hand press from Lee Precision is about the size of a service revolver and can be used nearly anywhere.

The Lyman Accuscale offers 550-gr. capacity, standard features, under $40.

Redding's new press, the Boss, offers compound leverage, price under $90.

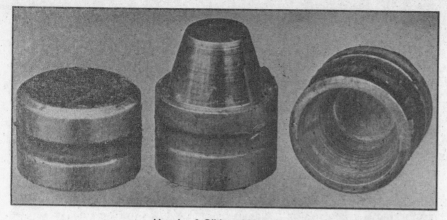

Hensley & Gibbs #333 as cast and lube/sized at left and (center, right) after swaging in the die set from Corbin.

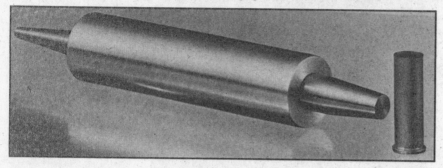

Paco's Nexpander will flare case mouths from 17- to 50-caliber to ease starting the bullet in the case.

offers nine of the most popular collets at no extra cost, when purchased with the Lyman Power Trimmer through the end of 1986. There's the Lyman Accuscale with 500-grain capacity, priced just under $40, and the Lyman Magdipper, a 20-pound, thermostatically-controlled electric casting furnace for those who prefer to dip with a ladle. Available in a choice of 110V or 220V, the Magdipper retails at $134.95 and it's admirably low-slung and compact, with a flanged holder to pre-warm the next mould you plan to use. Lyman also has brass polishing cloths and lead removing cloths, a growing line of case polishing and cleaning items and an inside case neck cleaner/lubricator set.

An eminently useful item of handloading equipment is the chronograph that tells you just how effective and efficient any given handload is. There are few if any areas in the handloading arts where progress has been swifter and more decisive. In the 30-odd years of my handloading career, I've seen chronographs progress from about the level of Ford's prototype to the Ferrari or a bit beyond and you

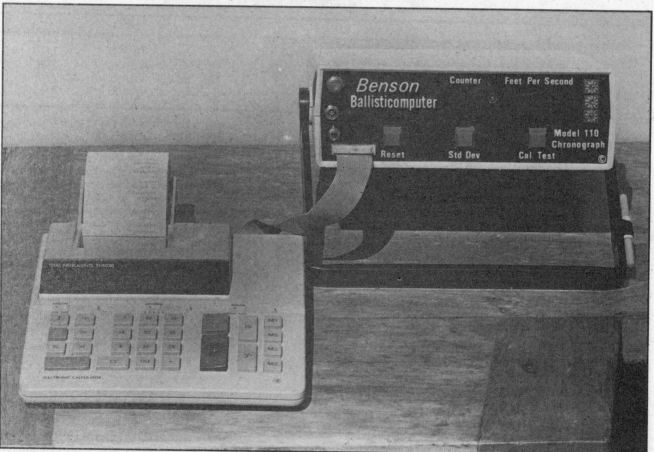

Grennell's new friend, the Ballisticomputer, does not smoke or complain during range testing stints. See text.

can be certain I'm grateful for the improved technology.

Several new chronograph systems have hit the market within the past year. I've been working with one of them and, in my humble opinion, it's a real doozy. I speak of the **Benson Ballisticomputer,** which does just about everything you might possibly wish, with the possible exception of polishing the silverware in its spare time.

A longtime bane of skyscreen systems has been that you often have to whiz the bullet pretty close over the slits in order to secure a reading. With various guns and various loads—particularly if the gun is scoped—that can and all too often does result in cruel damage to one or both screens and a screen is not a cheap item to replace. The Benson will catch and clock a bullet that is well up there, out of potentially harmful trajectories. There is good reason to hope one set of screens will last you a long time.

Screen-spacing is five feet and the screens can be mounted to an aluminum I-beam or similar arrangement. I'm still working mine off a camera tripod because I've not yet been able to steal enough time to build a proper mounting base for it. If, before you start to fire a test series, you take just a bit of time and program the three small dials on the readout box for the bullet weight in grains, the readout unit will for each shot, come up with: (1) the number of the shot (1, 2, 3, etc.); (2) the velocity of the bullet, between the start and stop screens; (3) the kinetic energy of the bullet in foot-pounds. After firing a given number of shots, press the button marked "Std Dev" and it will tell you the number of shots, the average velocity, the average energy and the standard deviation.

You don't even have to bother writing down all that useful dope. The Benson Ballisticomputer does it for you, with a printout unit that's part of the system. It prints out on a strip of adding machine tape and, if you wish, you can key in the line number from your data sheet for identification at a later time. It's sort of like having a secretary accompany you to the range, except it's no fun to put it on your lap. The saving of time, however, is purely wonderful and time, on a test session, is like 25-karat gold and precious jewels. I have come to regard my Benson with an absurd degree of infatuation.

At a less sophisticated—and less expensive— level of powder dispensing, **MMP** has brought forth a powered powder trickler that operates from a foot switch. Thus, if you wish to produce weighed powder charges, you can use a dipper or similar device to dump nearly all the charge into the pan of the scale. Then you settle back and tap the foot switch until the beam comes up to the line. At that point, funnel the charge into the waiting case and repeat the process, as necessary.

Del Ramsey, honcho of MMP— **Modern Machine Products**—is reported to have come up with a further goodie since the power trickler. It's a case trimmer head for any given caliber. What it does is to trim the case neck to the desired length, removing both the inside and outside burrs as it does so. I have worked with his power trickler and can report that it performs quite well, even on finely granulated globular (Ball, Spherical, etc.) powders. I've only heard about his trimmer heads, but I think they have the sound of a good idea.

Corbin Manufacturing & Supply now has a set of bullet swaging dies for making up nesting bullets. The basic concept is quite fascinating, if you happen to have that sort of mind. From the side, it looks like a fairly typical semi-wadcutter, except that the bullet base has a hollow cavity that's a female match for the nose shape.

Working with a set of these dies in .358-inch diameter, I've converted some of the Hensley & Gibbs #333 bullets—discussed previously—over to the new shape. The net effect shows a lot of intriguing promise, I think. For one thing, given the proper powder charge in, for example, the 38 Special, single bullets ought to perform like the super-accurate squib load of all time. Hodgdon's HP38 looks like the promising powder for this application, so far. It is also a simple matter to load two of them into a single 38 Special case, or three into a 357 Magnum, or four into a 357 Remington Maximum and so on.

Creative dissatisfaction, gentle reader, is the basic key to progress. As you go about your handloading activities, keep on asking yourself: "What is it that I don't much like about the way this works? What could be done to make it work better?" As you stalk resolutely about the problem, kicking at the tires, now and then a small light bulb may flare above your head, as they do in the comic strips, and you will trap the secret of some new gizmo that will lighten the labor and gladden the hearts of handloaders, all across the land mass of our planet.

It's always a goal worth striving for, take my sincere word . . . ●

BREN TEN NEWS

The latest word is that **Israeli Military Industries (IMI)** has taken over the Bren Ten pistol and plans to continue producing it. Having done some work with the pistol and cartridge, I can report that I've been favorably impressed. The big deficiency to the present has been a bullet in the requisite .400-inch diameter in JHP persuasion, capable of expansion upon impact. Norma can supply the 200-grain FMJ bullets used in their factory load as components, and **Corbin Manufacturing & Supply** can furnish dies for the Corbin CSP-1 bulletmaking press that will produce an excellent JHP bullet from 44 jackets and prepared lead cores.

One of the initial problems was that, as with the 41 Magnum bullets, you have to start out with 44 jackets. Now, Corbin can furnish a jacket draw-die that positions the 44 jacket to exquisite precision and takes it down to the right size for 10mm (call it caliber 40) in just one pass, leaving the jacket mouth perfectly square and even all around. Originally, it was necessary to draw it to .41-in., then re-draw it to .40-in. and that left uneven jacket mouths that looked mawkish and hampered performance.

Chosen weights for the finished bullets, as in any home swaging operation, are variable over a broad range. I had excellent results with JHP bullets at about 165 grains. What also worked extremely well was to put the Sierra 170-grain JHC bullet for the 41 Magnum through the same draw-die, then give it a light "bump" in the 10mm nose-forming die.

Load data for the Bren Ten has not been widely available. Working with Marty Liggins of Accurate Arms, I compiled 28 different loads that work the action of a pair of 5-inch Bren Tens quite reliably. Some of the loads use the 200-grain FMJ bullets available from Norma; others are for lighter bullets from the Corbin press and dies.
Dean Grennell.

REVOLVERS chambered for the 45 Automatic cartridge seem to be contradictions in terms. The 45 Automatic Colt Pistol (ACP) cartridge was developed specifically to function in semi-automatic pistols, and seems a strange choice for revolver use. Yet, hundreds of thousands of revolvers have been chambered for this round.

Such revolvers have been made for almost seven decades, and a considerable number are still in service. Revolvers chambering the 45 ACP cartridge have proven to be useful, with advantages not fully duplicated by other revolver/cartridge combinations.

It is interesting that such a versatile combination started out strictly as an emergency measure during America's 1917 entry into World War I when U.S. forces were found woefully short of firearms of all types and, going into trench warfare, American leaders thought a larger percentage of troops should be armed with pistols. From 10% the number was upped to 60% and finally to 72%.

Stocks of the recently-adopted Colt 1911 pistol were small. Various estimates of the total number of 45 pistols available on April 6, 1917—the date we entered the war—run between 50,000 and 75,000. Arrangements were made with other firms to begin production, but manufacture could not keep up with the accelerating demand.

Colt and Smith & Wesson already had machinery in place for the production of large-frame revolvers capable of handling a 45-caliber cartridge. Use of a separate rimmed revolver round would have been unacceptable, yet the use of revolvers seemed to be the quickest method to increase the number of available sidearms.

The problem was already on the way to being solved. Smith & Wesson had, since at least early 1916, been working on a revolver for the rimless 45 Automatic cartridge. The final adaptation was achieved by a simple but ingenious invention of Joseph H. Wesson, son of Smith & Wesson founder D. B. Wesson. It came to be called the "half-moon clip." It was not the first revolver loading device—

Colt and Webley as well as others had offered "loaders" before—but it was the first to adapt true rimless cartridges to revolver use.

The device, for which Wesson received U.S. Patent 1,231,106, is a thin semicircle of flat spring steel, with recesses to fit 45 ACP extractor grooves. Each accepts three rounds, holding them against the firing pin blow and allowing extraction of the empty cases.

The importance of this simple device can hardly be overstated. By permitting the use of the standard pistol cartridges in revolvers, it substantially increased the number of sidearms available to U.S. forces after our entry into the war. Amazing coordination was achieved between the War Department, Smith & Wesson and Colt; contracts were awarded to both manufacturers for revolvers that could use common half-moon clips and the service ammunition.

Both 1917 versions had 5½-in. barrels, with an over-all length of 10¾-in. The Smith & Wesson weighed about 36 ounces; the Colt, with a

The 1917s introduced half-moon clips to use 45 Auto cartridges, and ushered in the 45 ACP revolver, still a useful tool.

somewhat larger frame and thicker barrel, tipped the scales at 40 ounces. Finishes varied. Most of the wartime Colts came with a pale greyish blue. The Smith & Wesson products sported a darker finish. None were up to commercial standards.

Colt's revolver was based on the New Service, introduced in 1897. The Smith & Wesson was a modification of that firm's 1907 New Century. The ejector rod shroud of the New Century was omitted, perhaps because of military fears that the revolver might be disabled if the recess plugged with mud.

Colt and Smith & Wesson arms were of roughly similar size but were different mechanically. The cylinder latch of the Colt was drawn to the rear to release the cylinder, which turned clockwise. To open the Smith & Wesson cylinder (which rotated counterclockwise) the latch was pushed forward. The mechanical differences did not significantly affect operation, and the revolvers could be issued interchangeably.

All Smith & Wesson revolvers were made with a step in the chamber, allowing the cartridge to headspace on the case mouth in the same manner as the automatic pistol. This feature permitted the use of loose rounds if the special clips were not available. After firing single rounds, however, empty cases had to be poked or pried from the chambers.

A small number of early Colts lacked the stepped chamber and could only be used with the half-moon clips. The step was soon added, and later Colts and all Smith & Wessons could use either loose or clipped cartridges.

The number of Colts with tapered, rather than stepped, chambers has been reported as 50,000. If this were so, then about one of three 1917 Colts should have the unstepped chambers. Observation of a large number of these revolvers does not bear out this ratio. It is possible that a large number had stepped cylinders fitted later. This seems unlikely, as the original versions were perfectly serviceable when used with clips. It seems more likely that the estimate is in error.

Whether of Colt or Smith & Wesson manufacture, the 45 revolvers were designated Model 1917. Besides the difference in visual appearance, they were additionally marked on the left side of the barrel—as COLT D.A. 45 or S. & W. D.A. 45. Both types were marked "UNITED STATES PROPERTY" on the bottom of the barrels. The designation U.S. ARMY MODEL 1917 appears in four lines on the butt, the Colt reading from the front and the Smith & Wesson reading from the rear.

There has been some confusion caused by the numbers on the 1917 revolvers. The numbering system apparently was this:

The butt number of the Smith & Wesson is both the military serial number and the manufacturer's serial number, as the firm began a new model line with the 1917. Smith & Wesson revolvers bear this same number on the bottom of the barrel (beneath the ejector rod) and on the rear face of the cylinder. An additional assembly number, not related to the serial number, was stamped on the frame inside the crane recess, and on the crane.

REVOLVERS
For the
45ACP

For six decades, this handy chambering has remained in use for good reasons.

by JOHN MALLOY

Colt numbered the butt with the military serial number and placed the factory serial number—a larger number—on the crane and frame. In addition, an assembly number appears near the serial number on the crane and frame; on many specimens this same number is also on the bottom of the barrel, near the "UNITED STATES PROPERTY" marking.

The abundance of numbers has caused some confusion as to the actual serial numbers of particular revolvers and of the total number of revolvers made.

From several sources, there were over 150,000 made by each manufacturer by the end of the contracts in 1919. A total of about 268,000 were completed before the Armistice of November 11, 1918.

Smith & Wesson numbers run in a separate serial range beginning with number 1. The final number has been published in the BATF "Curios and Relics" list as 163,476 and should be considered correct for collectors' purposes.

Colt revolvers were numbered within the existing New Service revolver series. Numbers from different sources vary; 151,700 is probably close to the total production. Observed specimens have been in a factory serial number range of about 130,000-250,000. The exact boundary numbers are uncertain.

The 1917 revolvers earned a reputation for reliability and were desirable personal items. Many "went home" with the troops.

Quantities were sold by the DCM to

NRA members after the war at a cost of $16.15. A large number went into government storage as a substitute-standard sidearm, to be called to duty again a generation later.

After completion of the military contracts, both Colt and Smith & Wesson chose to continue manufacture of the new revolvers for the civilian market.

Colt made a commercial model with better finish and without provision for a butt lanyard swivel. These post-war versions were marked in one line on the left side of the barrel: COLT MODEL 1917 .45 AUTO CTGE. In the middle 1920s, the "Model 1917" designation was dropped and the revolver was continued simply as a 45 ACP variation of the company's established New Service series.

45 ACP double-action revolvers can handle a great variety of loads: (left to right) military ball, commercial SWC, handloads that will not feed through a semi-auto, shotshells made from rifle brass, BBM shotshell and 45 Auto Rim.

New Service revolvers were nicely blued, with checkered walnut grips, and were available in barrel lengths of 4½, 5½, or 7½ inches. Contact surfaces of triggers and hammers were checkered. Interestingly, the commercial New Service retained the butt swivel used by the military 1917, but which was absent from the short-lived civilian 1917.

The New Service line included a target version, and the 45 ACP chambering was added about 1925. Available with a 6- or 7½-in. barrel, the New Service Target featured adjustable sights, checkered wood grips and a hand-finished action. There was no butt swivel. The hammer, trigger and the front and rear surfaces of the grip frame were checkered.

Smith & Wesson 1917 revolvers were numbered reading forward; Colts read toward the rear.

In 1932, a deluxe target version was announced. Based on a rounded-grip variant of the New Service frame, it was called the Shooting Master. Introduced in 38 Special caliber, it was made available in 45 ACP the following year, 1933. The Shooting Master was considered the top of the contemporary Colt line. It featured checkered grips of selected walnut, adjustable sights and checkering on the grip frame, hammer, and trigger. The top and back of the frame were stippled to prevent light reflection. A prestige item, its parts were held to minimum tolerance and the actions were hand-finished. Barrel length was 6 inches.

The adjustable sights of these target models worked well, but may seem very basic to today's shooters. Elevation adjustments were made at the front sight, windage at the rear. They were screw adjustable, but without today's familiar clicks; turns had to be counted. When final adjustment was reached, a binding screw locked the sight in place.

Smith & Wesson also continued civilian production of their 1917 revolvers after the war. The connection with distinguished military service seemed good enough to retain, and the revolver was cataloged as the Model 1917 Army. Post-war Smith & Wesson 1917s had bright blue finish and checkered grips, but otherwise were the same as their wartime predecessors. The "United States Property" marking was omitted, of course.

A Smith & Wesson source has reported in print a total production of 210,320 1917 revolvers. If 163,476 of these were indeed wartime contract production, then 46,844 were commercial pieces. Of these, 25,000 were reportedly made for a Brazilian government contract in 1938.

The 45 ACP revolvers were popular enough so that in 1920, Peters Cartridge Company introduced the 45 Auto Rim, a cartridge that allowed single-round loading and ejection without using clips. It has an extra-thick rim to fill the .090-in. space taken up by the half-moon clips. The 45 Auto Rim was eventually offered by other major ammunition manufacturers.

Because the Auto Rim round did not have to function through a self-loading pistol, lead bullets of different shapes and weights were offered, as well as the conventional jacketed round nose. The cartridge is still manufactured with a 230-grain round-nosed lead bullet.

When the United States entered World War II, a large portion of American industry was devoted to

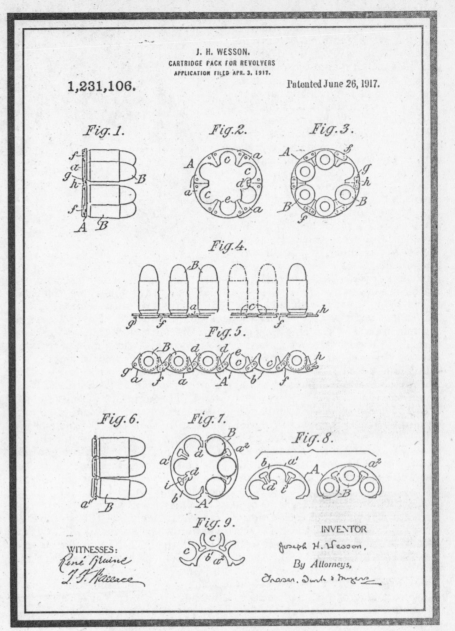

Joseph Wesson explored ways to adapt 45 Automatic cartridges to revolver. Figures 7 and 8 show the basic concept of the half-moon clip. (U.S. Patent Office)

military production. As did most firearms manufacturers, Colt suspended commercial production for the duration, devoting their facilities to the production of current military weapons. And after the war, Colt did not resume production of either the Single Action Army or the large-frame New Service and Shooting Master revolvers. The Government Model 45 automatic was a mainstay of the postwar line, but Colt no longer made a revolver capable of handling the 45 ACP cartridge.

Smith & Wesson, on the other hand, put greater emphasis on their line of large-frame revolvers in the postwar years. The basic 1917 45 became the

1950 Army, improved with a new short-action mechanism, larger "Magna" stocks and a new hammer shape that allowed easier single-action cocking. The butt swivel was eliminated and the sights were Patridge type. A study of catalog illustrations indicates that the barrel markings remained S&W DA 45 for a time (perhaps until the stock of 1917 barrels on hand was used up) then changed to 45 CAL. MODEL 1950. These 1950 revolvers bore an "S" prefix to the serial number.

Interest in competitive target shooting increased in the years after the war, and the final stage of a conventional pistol match required a 45.

With Colt's New Service Target and Shooting Master no longer available, Smith & Wesson introduced a match-grade 45 ACP revolver, the 1950 Target. It featured a slim 6½-in. barrel with ejector-rod shroud, wider hammer spur and a micrometer rear sight adjustable for both windage and elevation. At 11¾ inches in length, it weighed 39 ounces. With its crisp "wish-off" trigger, it soon became the gun to beat in early 1950s target shooting.

Some shooters wanted a heavier revolver. A new version, the Model 1955 Target, was introduced. Noticeable changes were a much heavier 6½-in. barrel with a broad thick rib, wider trigger and hammer, and larger "target" stocks. Weight increased to 45 ounces. For some time, an optional muzzle brake was available.

The 1955 Target introduced a new "U"-shaped mainspring. Ease of cocking was praised by contemporary experts, but the new system apparently gave misfire problems with some ammunition. A change was soon made back to the traditional flat spring and strain screw.

In 1957, Smith & Wesson began designating their revolvers by model numbers as well as name designations. The 1950 Army was Model 22, and the 1950 Target was Model 26. The 1955 Target became the Model 25.

The 1950 and 1955 Target revolvers were manufactured concurrently for several years—until the end of the decade—then the earlier target arm was discontinued. The 1950 Army stayed in the line until 1967. The 1955 Target revolver held a certain following and remained in production for another 15 years.

It is interesting to note that apparently a few Model 25 45 ACP revolvers were made with 8⅜-in. barrels. Reportedly, revolvers bearing serial numbers 25, 2500 and 25,000 were given this treatment. Small quantities of revolvers were made up on special order in 45 Colt caliber. These were not catalog items, but required recognition in factory nomenclature. The 1955 Target 45 ACP still appeared in the catalog as Model 25, but Smith & Wesson's identification became Model 25-2.

Until 1979, the standard barrel length for all of Smith & Wesson's large-frame revolvers had been 6½-in. In that year, standard length was reduced to six inches. This change perhaps was initiated by the growing popularity of NRA Police Combat competitive shooting during the 1970s. Rules for such matches re-

stricted barrel length to six inches, and most of the big-frame "Smiths" were thus excluded. Whatever the reason, production of 6½-in. barrels was discontinued, and—subject to stock on hand—the six-in. barrel was phased in as the standard length.

On the occasion of the firm's 125th Anniversary in 1977, Smith & Wesson had brought out a commemorative version of the Model 25 chambered for—of all things—their competitor's old cartridge, the 45 Colt. Few of the limited run got into the hands of shooters, but the acceptance of this combination indicated a commercial demand. In 1979, the 45 Colt chambering was added as a catalog item, Model 25-5. The new 45 Colt version was well received and soon outsold the 45 ACP chambering and the Model 25-2 was dropped from the line in 1982.

The last production run of about 2000 45 ACP 1955 Target revolvers was reportedly acquired by John Jovino, a large New York gun distributor. The big 45 serves as the basis for a

custom short-barrel holster revolver. This "Effector" revolver has a 2½-in. barrel and small grip. For undercover use, it is an interesting combination of compactness and power.

The postwar years had seen growing interest in the shooting sports. From the standpoint of shooter interest in the 45 ACP revolver, some factors had been both good and bad.

Smith & Wesson had, as mentioned, introduced three new models—the 1950 Army, 1950 Target and 1955 Target. Added to these new items were thousands of surplus 1917 Colt and Smith & Wesson revolvers which came on the market during the late 1950s and 1960s. Many new shooters, your writer included, began competitive shooting with surplus 1917s. Large numbers of 455 Webley revolvers were also converted to use 45 ACP cartridges with half-moon clips. These revolvers initially were priced at $14.95 for the latest Mark VI and $12.95 for the earlier "birds-head-grip" variations. American ingenuity soon proved that anyone with

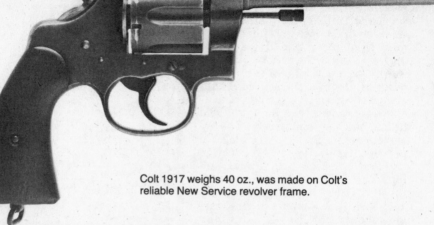

Colt 1917 weighs 40 oz., was made on Colt's reliable New Service revolver frame.

Smith & Wesson 1917 is lighter than the Colt 1917, was made on their New Century frame.

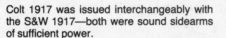

Colt 1917 was issued interchangeably with the S&W 1917—both were sound sidearms of sufficient power.

access to a lathe could have a serviceable 45 revolver at such prices. Simply surfacing the rear of the cylinder for extra clearance allowed use of the 45 Auto cartridges in half-moon clips. Loading and ejection were actually easier and faster with a converted Webley than with a 1917. Many, perhaps most, of the surplus Webleys coming into the country were converted to 45 ACP.

Surplus Smith & Wesson 455 revolvers produced for England—including the "Hand Ejector" and the prized "Triple-Lock" versions—were kept in service by similar conversions.

During this time, all these guns were kept fed at low cost by the large quantities of cheap 45 ACP surplus ammunition.

Other factors, however, were serving to lessen the popularity of the 45 ACP revolver.

From a target shooter's standpoint, the spectacular advances in accurizing techniques for the Colt 45 automatic were in part responsible. Revolver shooters in competition had always had an extra operation to master; cocking the hammer was something of a disadvantage during Timed- and Rapid-fire stages. Now the revolver no longer offered any real accuracy advantage.

For service and field use, the 45 revolver was being outclassed by the growing popularity of the 357 Magnum cartridge. The 357 could be accommodated in a more compact frame and could use 38 Special ammunition for a lower power level. The versatile 357 rapidly became the standard for law enforcement, personal protection and sporting use, and by the end of 1967, only one 45 ACP revolver model—the Smith & Wesson 1955 Target—was still in production.

However, the 45 ACP revolver was to have another mild spurt of popularity. Oddly enough, the major factor was America's revived interest in the single-action revolver.

The postwar years saw the rise in popularity of the western movie, and a new factor—the television west-ern—had been added. Interest in the Old West brought about an unprecedented and unanticipated demand for "western-style" firearms.

Perhaps as early as 1951 reproductions of the Colt single action were being made by Great Western Arms Company of North Hollywood, California. In those carefree days, they were sold primarily by mail order. Close copies of the Colt, they had slightly longer frames and cylinders, and featured floating firing pins. They were made in traditional revolver calibers until 1962.

Toward the end of their manufacture, Great Western listed the 45 ACP among the calibers offered. This writer has never seen one in that caliber, and probably only a small number were made. By 1963, parts kits and individual parts—including 45 ACP cylinders—were advertised, but Great Western revolvers were no longer offered for sale.

Still, the 45 ACP in a single action revolver was the extension of an idea that had been tried by Colt—without commercial success—almost 40 years before.

Headspacing the cartridge case mouth on a step in the chamber had allowed the use of loose rounds in the 1917s when no clips were available. However, extraction of the rimless cases was a problem—they had to be pried or poked out.

The rod ejector of the single action did not require a rim. In 1924, Colt had added the 45 ACP cartridge to its single-action chamberings. It was the only rimless round so honored.

The new loading offered no real advantages over the traditional 45 Colt, however, and only a small number were made. Authorities have stated the prewar total to be only 44 revolvers, although over the years, others apparently had 45 ACP cylinders fitted.

Colt's 45 ACP single action had not been a commercial success, but it had worked well. What had been lacking was an advantage to such a chambering. The quantities of cheap surplus ammunition available through the decade of the 1960s provided that advantage.

The single-action revolver had made its real comeback in 1953 when Ruger's 22-caliber Single-Six was introduced to an enthusiastic public. The firm's successful Blackhawk centerfire series followed in 1955. Colt could hardly sit by and let others cash in on popularity rightfully belonging to the original. Within the year, the company announced the reintroduction of the Colt Single Action.

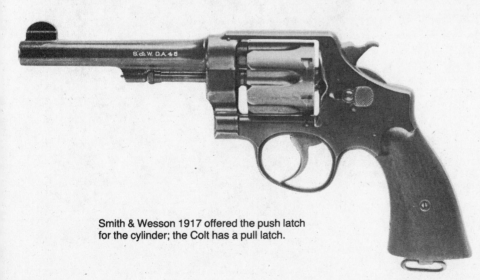

Smith & Wesson 1917 offered the push latch for the cylinder; the Colt has a pull latch.

functioned smoothly, and shot well. They were offered in combinations, with an extra cylinder adapted to military cartridges. And their 45 Colt could be had with a 45 ACP cylinder.

There is some speculation as to whether the extra cylinders were made by Sauer or supplied by another maker. Their chambers were rougher, with tool marks evident. The outside surfaces were unfluted and not as well finished. Several I have seen required polishing of the chambers or minor hand fitting for satisfactory performance. There seemed to be no question, however, as to their strength and safety.

The most common version of the Hawes revolver was the Western

The low prices of converted Webleys introduced many shooters to the versatility of the 45 ACP revolver.

Surplus Webley revolvers—the large Mark VI (above) and the earlier Marks with "birdshead" grips—were converted to 45 ACP by the thousands.

The ease of cylinder removal made the single action a natural for interchangeable cylinders. By the early 1960s, both Colt and Ruger offered dual-cylinder revolvers in 22LR/ 22WMR.

In 1966, a custom conversion of a Ruger Blackhawk 357 to 45 caliber was described in the shooting press. Of particular interest, the conversion was made with two cylinders—for both 45 Colt and 45 ACP cartridges.

In 1968, Hawes Firearms Company of Los Angeles introduced a line of imported single-action revolvers made by J. P. Sauer & Sohn of West Germany. The guns were slightly-lengthened visual and mechanical copies of the Colt, with the addition of floating firing pins. They were nicely made,

Half-moon clips designed for the 1917 revolvers work perfectly in the Webley. Loading is simple and fast; so was the conversion in a lathe.

Marshal, with blued finish, 6-in. barrel and grips of laminated rosewood. It was 11⅜-in. long and, with the unfluted 45 ACP cylinder, weighed about 40 ounces.

Other variations of the Marshal series differed primarily in finish. The Montana Marshal had brass grip frames; the Texas Marshal was nickel-plated; and the Federal Marshal had a case-hardened frame. The gaudy Silver City Marshal was nickel-plated and had pearl grips on a brass grip frame.

They were mechanically the same. And were apparently all available in the 45 Colt/45 ACP combination until about 1979.

The fixed sights of the Western Marshal would seem to be a serious drawback to the actual usefulness of a dual-caliber combination. However, point of impact of a large-caliber revolver bullet is a function of barrel time and amount of recoil. In practice, factory 45 Colt and 45 ACP ammunition available at the time made 25-yard groups which centered within a few inches of each other. For plinking, informal target shooting or personal protection, the fixed sights were adequate.

Indeed, the point of impact established, practical accuracy was good. A 1971 pistol match fired with a Hawes 45 ACP Western Marshal (more or less as a stunt) produced a score only slightly below the writer's 45 average for that year. Still, to make full use of a dual-caliber revolver, adjustable sights are required.

Sturm, Ruger & Company had offered the adjustable-sight Blackhawk as a 357/9mm "Convertible" since 1967, and it had been well received. While they retained traditional single-action operation, the Ruger revolvers were modernizations of the original Colt design. All centerfire versions featured fully-adjustable rear sights.

In 1971, Ruger introduced the Blackhawk series in 45 Colt and offered a Convertible model with a fitted extra 45 ACP cylinder. Made on the Super Blackhawk-size frame, the new 45 Convertibles were offered in two barrel lengths. The short 4⅝-in. version weighed 38 ounces. The longer variant, with a 7½-in. barrel, weighed 40 ounces.

A nice feature of these revolvers is often overlooked: when the cylinder pin is drawn all the way forward, it remains in the frame and will not fall out. This clever design eliminated the greatest inconvenience of interchangeable cylinders. Ruger Convert-

ible cylinders are fitted to a particular revolver and are hand numbered on the front or rear face with the last three digits of the serial number.

The 45 Colt/45 ACP Convertible revolvers were introduced in 1971. In 1973, the entire single-action line was changed.

At that time, increasing attention was being paid to the possibility of accidental discharge of traditional single-action revolvers. The New Model Blackhawk series introduced in 1973 featured a completely redesigned action with transfer-bar ignition. The new revolvers could be safely loaded and carried with a full six rounds. The action has only one notch—full cock—and is loaded with the hammer down. The previous models were subsequently called Old Model Blackhawks.

The 45 Colt/45 ACP Convertibles were included in the New Model lineup. The serial number prefix "45" had (logically) been used for the original 45s. The new models bore a "46" designation. The procedure of numbering the extra 45 ACP fitted cylinder to the revolver was continued.

One change is worthy of note: Whereas the Old Model cylinder had extended rearward to the frame, the New Model cylinder allowed a gap so the loaded chambers can be seen from the side.

Neither the 45 Colt/45 ACP Convertible nor the standard 45 Blackhawk have appeared in Ruger catalogs since 1982. However, caliber variations drift in and out of the Ruger lineup with little fanfare, and a company representative I talked to does not consider the single-action 45s discontinued.

Although not sold in the large numbers of the Rugers, the Seville single-action revolver made by United Sporting Arms of Arizona offered a 45 Colt/45 ACP combination from the latter 1970s through 1983. The Seville is similar in general appearance to Ruger's Super Blackhawk. It is a modern single action and features a fully adjustable rear sight. Variations ranged from a 7½-in. barrel down to a short-barrel Sheriff's Model. Finishes were blue or stainless.

The Seville used the patented Ruger transfer-bar ignition system under license from Sturm, Ruger & Company. However, on July 1, 1984, the license agreement was dissolved as part of bankruptcy proceedings involving United Sporting Arms.

The latest regular production 45 ACP revolver is the Dakota, first offered in that caliber in 1982. While

the other single actions sought to improve on the basic Colt mechanism, the Dakota prides itself on being faithful to the original design.

Dakota revolvers are manufactured in Italy by Armi Jaeger and imported by EMF Company of Santa Ana, California. EMF, incorporated in 1956, for several years owned Great Western Arms, the manufacturer of the first postwar single-action revolver to chamber the 45 ACP cartridge.

Although previously imported by Intercontinental Arms of Los Angeles, no 45 ACP Dakotas were actually offered by that firm. A source previously associated with Intercontinental recalls, however, that a few were made up on special order. For this purpose, a 357 cylinder was bored and chambered to 45 ACP and fitted to a 45 Colt-barrelled frame.

EMF began marketing the Dakota in 1972 and has been the exclusive importer since about 1977. In 1982, the firm offered the 45 Colt/45 ACP multi-cylinder version, first with a choice of 5½- or 7½-in. barrels. A 4¾-in. barrel was added to the line in 1983. The short barrel is often advertised as 4⅝-in., but is actually the original Colt length of 4¾-in.

The Dakota is an almost identical Colt copy; indeed, many of the parts will interchange. The standard finish—a case-hardened frame with blued barrel and cylinder—also looks "Colt." However, there are some differences. The grip frames are brass and hold a one-piece walnut grip. Since the Gun Control Act of 1968, safety devices have been added. The present type—the one used for the 45 Colt/45 ACP versions—consists of a lugged cylinder pin and a hammer notched on the right side to receive this lug. When the cylinder pin is turned 180°, its lug then prevents the hammer going forward far enough to fire. In the "fire" position, a red dot is visible on the left side of the cylinder pin. This safety is positive, and in home or camp would keep a child or inexperienced person out of trouble. For field use it is awkward, and a traditional 5-shot carry would be preferable.

EMF reports that each 45 ACP cylinder is fitted to its revolver. They are not, however, numbered to the gun, as is Ruger's practice. The barrel, even on the multi-cylinder version, is marked DAKOTA CAL. 45 COLT.

The fixed sights, as with the Hawes, are not a disadvantage for casual two-caliber use. Some 25-yard groups fired using both factory 45 Colt and 45 ACP ammunition have proven to be

For competitive shooting, the Smith & Wesson 1950 Target revolver was the gun to beat in the early '50s.

(Above) 45 ACP revolvers, generally the Smith & Wesson Model 25-2, are still used regularly for conventional competition.

only slightly larger than those fired from one cylinder.

Colt never used the 45 ACP chambering in postwar regular-production Single Actions, but did use it for some custom and limited-run pieces. In 1967, 45 ACP was chosen as the caliber for a pair of revolvers known as the "Charter Oak" Colts. The grips were carved from fragments of the original Charter Oak. These highly-decorated, gold-inlaid custom pieces bore the special serial numbers 1ACP and 2ACP.

Early in 1984, Colt brought out a limited-production "Armory Edition" Single Action and 45 ACP was chosen as its caliber. Of the total production of 500, half were finished in nickel, the other 250 were blue with case-hardened frames. All had ivory grips.

Contrary to the usual practice,

Generally used for snake protection, 45 revolver shot loads can also bag small game. Revolver is a Colt 1917 with replacement grips and grip adapter.

these dual-cylinder custom guns have 45 ACP as the primary caliber, and come with an extra cylinder for 45 Colt cartridges! The 4¾-in. barrels bear this one-line legend on the left side: COLT SINGLE ACTION ARMY 45 ACP. The revolvers come with a presentation case and a book, *The Colt Armory*.

Since the introduction of 45 ACP revolvers in 1917, their spurts of popularity have been due to several factors:

After World War I, the revolvers using the military pistol cartridge were a combat-proven novelty.

A generation later, in the years following World War II, civilian target shooting grew and 45 revolvers were favored for accuracy.

By the beginning of the 1960s, the availability of low-priced surplus 45 ammunition and 1917 revolvers and converted Webleys brought the combination back to public attention.

The same quantities of cheap 45 ACP ammo made practical the introduction of that caliber in the new dual-cylinder single-action revolvers.

None of these factors exist today. Still, revolvers chambered for the 45 Automatic cartridge are currently being produced, and existing ones remain in use.

What does this unlikely combination offer today's shooters?

For conventional target shooting, the 45 ACP revolver, almost always in the form of the Smith & Wesson Model 25, is still seen regularly on the target range. A small but dedicated group of target shooters prefers "wheelguns" over semi-automatics for conventional pistol competition.

They realize they pay a price in time, but are willing to master the extra skill of cocking the hammer to obtain certain advantages. Revolvers never smokestack or fail to feed, and there is virtually no worry of an alibi. Clean, undented cases may be dropped straight into a container on the bench. There are no concerns about cases going into a neighbor's pistol box or being stepped on during a brass scramble.

Perhaps the absence of such distractions allows better concentration and may be worth points to some shooters.

For Hunter's Pistol Silhouette competition, revolvers are very popular, although generally in flatter-shooting calibers. Still, an occasional Ruger Blackhawk or Smith & Wesson Model 25 in 45 ACP caliber is seen on the silhouette range. The cartridge is capable of fine accuracy and has plenty of

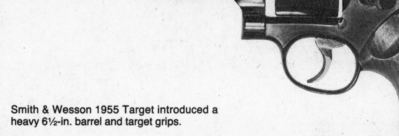

Smith & Wesson 1950 Target introduced micrometer rear sight and reintroduced the ejector rod shroud.

Smith & Wesson 1955 Target introduced a heavy 6½-in. barrel and target grips.

Smith & Wesson 1955 Target, Model 25-2. After November, 1979, the barrel length was reduced to 6-in.

Ruger Blackhawk offered a really rugged single-action to 45 shooters.

This is a convertible Ruger New Model Blackhawk. All 45 ACP cylinders are numbered with the last 3 digits of the serial number.

The 45 ACP revolver can be successful in Hunters Silhouette shooting. This is an Old Model Blackhawk with Ruger conversion unit.

The single-action revolver, with its rod ejector, does not require a rimmed cartridge and is suitable for 45 ACP, but not 45 Auto Rim. Revolver is EMF Dakota.

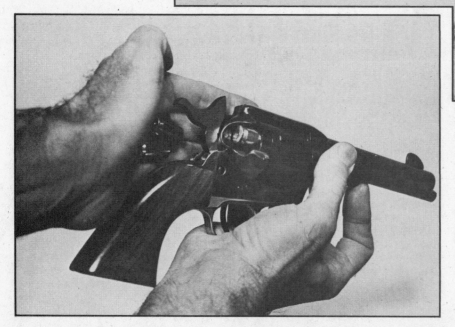

Hawes Western Marshal was made by Sauer of Germany. The 45 ACP cylinder is unfluted.

EMF Dakota is a close copy of Colt SAA, 4¾-in. barrel. Even those with ACP cylinder have 45 Colt barrel legend.

The Ruger Blackhawk Old Model with 4⅝-in. barrel makes a well-balanced handy 45 ACP revolver.

power for toppling rams. High trajectory is its only real disadvantage.

Service use of the 45 ACP revolver has been largely limited to military use. However, 1917s were used to some extent by prison guards and Post Office employees and even, reportedly, the Border Patrol.

I know of no case of adoption by any Police Department. However, where discretion was allowed in choice of sidearms, double-action 45 ACP revolvers have seen police use. Such revolvers have been described by officers as the ideal police arms for urban situations. They have good short range stopping power and limited penetration. The 45 ACP is about the maximum that can be handled effectively in rapid fire by most men.

The 45 ACP chambering in a semi-automatic pistol has recently been accepted for police use in several areas. In the double-action revolver, traditional revolver safety and quickness can offer extra advantages. There is a psychological advantage to the big revolver. That large bore and the big fat bullets—plainly visible in their gaping chambers—can have a calming effect on potentially dangerous situations.

The same characteristics that make the 45 ACP revolver a satisfactory arm for police use also make it a good choice for personal protection. Such revolvers, mostly surplus 1917s, rest in the dresser drawers of many American homes.

For hunting, either double- or single-action 45 ACP revolvers can be used for small to medium game or pests at reasonable ranges.

At the upper end of safe handloads, the short round approaches the 45 Colt cartridge in power. Low power loads can be tailored to specific needs. Effective bullet shapes that would not feed through a semi-automatic action may be used.

A 45 ACP revolver can be effective as a short-range shotgun. Probably not long after World War I, someone realized that 30-06 cases cut just short of cylinder length could be used to produce shot loads for 1917 revolvers. A shell so loaded held almost as much shot as a 2½-in. 410 shell, and countless snakes and a goodly quantity of small game have been killed with them.

Revolver shot shooting developed into a modest sport in its own right, and many 45 ACP Smith & Wessons and Colts were converted to smoothbores, often with choke devices, and used for game and clay target shooting. BUT this practice lasted only un-

Colt's Armory Single Action Army 45 ACP comes with book, presentation box, and extra 45 Colt cylinder. Pictured version has nickel finish and ivory grips.

FACTORY-PRODUCED 45 ACP REVOLVERS

Company	Model	Remarks
Colt	1917	Over 150,000 made 1917-1919; some civilian production to mid-1920s
	New Service	Standard commercial version of 1917 frame; 45 ACP ca. 1925 to WWII
	New Service Target	Target version of New Service; 45 ACP ca. 1925 to WWII
	Shooting Master	Deluxe target version of New Service; 45 ACP 1933-WWII
	Single Action Army	A few made in 45 ACP after 1924; some recent special versions in 45 ACP
Smith & Wesson	1917	163,476 made 1917-1919; commercial production to WWII
	1950 Army	1917 with improved action 1950-1967; became Model 22 in 1957
	1950 Target	Target version of 1950 Army, 1950–ca. 1960; became Model 26 in 1957
	1955 Target	Heavy-barrel target version 1955-1982; became Model 25 in 1957
Great Western	Single Action	Close copy of Colt SAA; small number in 45 ACP ca. 1962
Hawes	Western Marshal	Close copy of Colt SAA 1968-1980; 45 Colt/45 ACP combination offered
Ruger	Blackhawk	Modernized single action revolver; 45 Colt/45 ACP Convertible offered 1971-72
	New Model Blackhawk	Blackhawk improved with transfer-bar ignition; 45 Colt/45 ACP convertible offered 1973-1982
United Sporting Arms	Seville	Modern single-action revolver; 45 Colt/45 ACP offered late 1970s-1983
EMF	Dakota	Copy of Colt SAA; 45 Colt/45 ACP offered 1982-present

til the mid-1950s. Federal legislation outlawing "sawed-off shotguns" was applied to such harmless sport.

It remained legal to use shot in a rifled revolver bore. Even though rifling enlarges and distorts the pattern, such use is still practical at close range against snakes and rodents. The 45 ACP revolver, with its big bore and relatively shallow rifling, disturbs shot patterns less than smaller calibers.

Most shot loads have been assembled from handmade components. Cut-down rifle cases generally require either sizing or thinning of the forward part to pass the step in the chamber. Once formed, they are good for many loadings. Wads may be punched from cardboard with a sharpened 45 case, preferably one of the military steel ones.

Fortunately for today's shooters, especially for those who do not handload, there is another option. Loaded 45 ACP shotshells are marketed by BBM of West Springfield, Massachusetts. Called "Hardcaps," these ingenious shot loads look like military ball rounds, and were developed specifically for semi-automatic functioning. They work perfectly in both double-action and single-action revolvers, however.

Accessories specifically designed for 45 ACP revolvers remain on the market. Although half-moon clips are traditional for loading the double-actions, HKS Products of Florence, Kentucky makes a speedloader for the 45 Auto Rim cartridge in Smith & Wesson revolvers. For those using the ACP round who do not favor the half-moon clip, a special two-shot clip, called (naturally) the "third-moon" clip is available from Ranch Products of Malinta, Ohio. Clipped cartridges can be packed in the divided plastic boxes favored by many handloaders, or kept in belt loops.

The same company has recently introduced a "full-moon" clip, holding six cartridges. Loading six rounds *and* the loading device simultaneously is considered by some to be the fastest revolver speedloading technique of all.

So, the unlikely combination of a revolver chambering for the 45 Automatic cartridge is still with us after nearly seven decades. Hundreds of thousands have been made, and large numbers are still in service. Never dominating any single facet of pistol shooting, 45 ACP revolvers have given their owners a certain versatility that no other handgun/cartridge combination can fully duplicate. ●

Shotgun Review

by **LARRY S. STERETT**

THE PAST year has seen some woeful changes in the shotgun field. After 115 years, Harrington & Richardson is no more. H&R was one of the leading manufacturers of economical, single shot break-action shotguns, from 10 gauge down to the 410 bore. Such shotguns have always found a ready market as a "first gun," among farmers wanting a "barn gun," and even among waterfowlers wanting an economical 10 gauge and willing to settle for a single shot. Now the H&R shotguns have gone the way of similar shotguns manufactured by such firms as Crescent Davis, Winchester, and even Savage.

Savage Industries has indeed stopped production of their single-shots. The machinery and the rights for manufacturing those shotguns have been sold to Pakistani interests, we are told. Shotguns manufactured there may eventually be available in the U.S. under the Savage label at, we also hear, very low prices. For now, however, the Savage/Stevens single shot shotguns, of which the 9478 was the last of the line, are no more.

The economical single shot break-action shotgun is not extinct, however, and several firms have or will have such shotguns available. Kassnar is importing a Korean-manufactured single shot that closely resembles the late Winchester Model 37. Available in 12 or 20 gauge, with barrel lengths of 26, 28, and 30 inches, Full or Modified choke, this shotgun should be welcomed, if the price is reasonable. And F.I.E. Corp. continues with the CBC singles from Brazil.

Although excellent shotguns are manufactured in the U.S., increasing numbers of foreign-manufactured shotguns are being imported. The trend, however, seems to be for such manufacturers to set up their own distributing firm in the U.S. Beretta U.S.A. was one of the first, followed by firms such as Perazzi U.S.A., Marocchi U.S.A., and Valmet Inc., and more recently by the Zoli Group U.S.A., Inc. There are sure to be others in the future, to give the American shotgunner more shotguns from which to choose.

Here's what's new and reportable this year:

The Ithacagun Mag 10 offers a brown-green Camo-Seal finish for the turkey hunter in all of us.

Richland's Model 783 features a single non-selective trigger and interchangeable stainless steel choke tubes.

Mossberg's Model 712 12-gauge auto shotgun and 24-in. Accu II choke barrel has a Speedfeed stock and camo finish option.

Franchi's new Model 80 gas-operated autoloader comes in two finish grades. It's a cousin of the SPÁS-12, shoots standard 12s only.

Armsport

This Miami-based firm always has something new, and now it's a Tri-Barrel shotgun in 12 gauge, with side-by-side barrels over a single, providing a choice of Improved Cylinder, Modified, or Full choke patterns in one shotgun. There's a 10-gauge Magnum over-under Goose Gun with Boss-type action, double triggers and extractors, with 32-in. barrels choked Full/Full. A new Browning-style over-under 410 has been added, and it is not the folding Italian-design commonly seen advertised by other firms. The Armsport 410 is an actual scaled conventional design with a choice of single selective or double triggers.

Bauska Arms

Now there's a Brno distributor in Montana. Available shotguns include the 12-gauge ZP 149 and 349 in plain and engraved grades; this is a side-by-side sidelock with double triggers, demibloc barrel construction, double underbolts and Purdey-type top bolt. There are four 12-gauge over-under shotguns as well, starting with the time-tested ZH Series with double triggers in which the rear trigger can be used as a non-selective single trigger; barrel length on the field gun is 27½ inches, and barrels on the ZH are interchangeable. The Brno 500 is a field grade with double triggers, and the same barrel length and weight as the ZH, but with automatic ejectors and a shallower receiver. The CZ 581 in 12 gauge features 28-in. barrels, selective automatic ejectors, stock with cheekpiece and raised ventilated rib.

Beretta

The 680 Series of over-under competition guns is now the 682, and it has some excellent features, such as the movable trigger which provides adjustment for length of pull. This year the gas-operated autoloader for trap and skeet competition has been redesigned slightly and given a face-lift. The new model—A.303—does not have the magazine cutoff feature, nor the elaborate scroll etching on the receiver, but the forearm has been widened to a beavertail design with wraparound checkering.

Dr. Franco Beretta/ Double M Sporting

The shotguns of Dr. Franco Beretta (not Pietro Beretta) are available in Standard and Deluxe field models, plus American trap and Skeet versions, including a 4-barrel Skeet set; four grades are available for these latter models. The Alpha Three is a side-by-side with 28-in. barrel available in 12, 16, or 20 gauge, double triggers and an Anson & Deeley action, while the Beta Three is a single barrel single shot available in 12, 16, 20, 24, 28, 32 gauge and 410 bore. Two over-under 410s—America and Europa— with 26-in. barrels are available. The Alpha Two is an over-under in 12, 16 or 20 gauge with 28-in. barrels, automatic ejectors and a single trigger, as is the Gamma model. The Gamma has underbolt locking; the Alpha Two has crossbolt locking; both are available in Standard and Deluxe grades, where the difference is in the style and amount of engraving. Both have select Italian walnut stocks and forearms.

The clay target line is the Black Diamond, in which locking is via twin steel bolts projecting forward from the face of the standing breech. A single trigger is standard, with the barrel selector located on the rear shank of the trigger. The trap gun is available only in 12 gauge in either over-under or as a combo with 30-in. over-under barrels and a 34-in. single barrel.

American Arms/Diarm

From the Basque country of Spain come nine new over-unders, and three side-by-sides. In addition, American Arms is distributing three AYA shotguns—the #4A, #2, and #117 side-by-sides.

The AYA 4A and No. 2 shotguns are available in 12, 20, and 28 gauge, plus the 410 bore, with the #117 available only in 12 and 20 gauge. All three models are chambered for 3-in. shells; the 4A has double triggers, while the No. 2 and No. 117 have single selective triggers. Barrels measured 25 inches on the 12- and 20-gauge models, but the 12 gauge is also available at 28 inches.

Diarm side-by-side models include the boxlock York in 12, 20, 28 and 410 bores, and the Shogun in 10 gauge, both with double triggers, plus the sidelock Derby in the same gauges as the York, but with an English stock and choice of single or double triggers. All three models are chambered for magnum length shells.

The over-under field gun line includes the Lince in choice of 12 or 20

gauge and blue or white receiver finish; the Bristol in the same gauges with false sideplates; the Sir with functioning sidelocks and single nonselective trigger; the sidelock Royal, also with single non-selective trigger; and the sidelock Excelsior with single non-selective trigger. All six models are chambered for 3-in. shells, and have selective automatic ejectors, with barrel lengths ranging from 24 to 28 inches on the 12-gauge models, and 24 to 26 inches on the 20-gauge models.

The trap and Skeet guns are available only in 12 gauge, and include the boxlock FS 200, the FS 300 with engraved false sideplates, and the sidelock FS 400. Barrel lengths are 30 and 32 inches on the trap guns, and 26 inches on the Skeet guns; all three models are chambered for standard length shells. Selective automatic ejectors are standard, as is a palm swell on the right side of the pistol grip. The FS 200 and FS 300 have single selective trigger; the FS 400 has a single non-selective trigger. Chokes on the Skeet gun are Skeet/Skeet, and Modified/Full or Improved Modified/ Full on the trap guns. Stocks on all models are of hand-finished Spanish walnut with hand checkering.

Mario Beschi

Thad Scott is importing the shotguns of Armi Mario Beschi in the deluxe grades starting at $3750. These top of the line shotguns are hand-built to the customer's specifications, and Thad says the Linea 105 Imperial side-by-side in 12 or 20 gauge is equal to a best English gun. Featuring demiblock barrels and hand-fitted Holland & Holland type sidelocks, the 105 Imperial has a splinter forearm and straight grip stock of selected root walnut, single trigger, and a receiver which is fully engraved; even the interior surfaces of the sidelock plates are engine turned or jeweled. Engraved hunting scenes are available, as are gold inlays, and each shotgun is accompanied with a numbered guarantee certificate signed by the artist.

Browning

The Classic and Gold Classic series have been expanded to include the over-under shotgun in 20 gauge with 26-in. barrels choked Improved Cylinder and Modified. Highly figured, dense grained walnut is used for the hand checkered English-style stock and schnabel forearm. In addition to the engraving on the Classic guns, the Gold Classics feature an inlaid 18-Karat bust of John M. Browning, the

words "Browning Gold Classic" and individual game species scenes in 18-Karat gold, such as a pointer and two flying quail. Also new is an Upland Special version of the gas-operated B-80 autoloader; featuring a 22-in. barrel chambered for standard length shells in 12 or 20 gauge, with Invector chokes, and a weight of from 5½ to 6⅝ pounds, this B-80 has a straight grip walnut stock and forearm.

For the first time ever, Browning has a new Youth or Ladies gun. Labeled the BPS Youth, this latest version of an old favorite features a 22-in. 20 gauge Invector barrel chambered for 3-in. shells; weighing approximately 6¾ pounds, it features a select walnut regular pistol grip stock with a length of pull of 13¼ inches, complete with a ventilated black rubber recoil pad.

Excam

New from this firm is the Senator line of Angelo Zoli folding shotguns featuring an under lever for opening in place of the conventional top lever. Available in 12 or 20 gauge or 410 bore, with barrel lengths of 28 and 26 inches, respectively, chambered for 3-in. shells, the Senator features ventilated top and side ribs, walnut stock and forearm, and an automatic tang safety. Chokes are Full and Modified and the barrel bores and receiver are chrome plated. Weight of the Senator ranges from 6 to 7 pounds.

Frigon Guns

New from Frigon are the FS-4, FTC, and FT1, consisting of a 4-barrel Skeet set in 12, 20, 28 and 410; a 12-gauge trap combo with over-under barrels and top barrel single; and a single barrel trap gun, respectively. Manufactured by Armi Marocchi of Italy, the Frigon guns feature walnut, quick-change pistol grip Monte Carlo buttstocks with a palm swell for right-hand shooters, and ventilated side ribs on all over-under barrels but the 410 bore, which has no side ribs. Barrel lengths and chokes depend on the model and gauge; each of the over-under barrel assemblies in the Skeet set comes with individual forearm.

Hastings

Remington has introduced screw-in choke tubes for some Model 870 and 1100 shotguns this past year, but this Nebraska firm has ventilated rib 12-gauge barrels of 4130 chrome molybdenum steel for both Remington shotguns available, complete with three choke tubes, in lengths of 24, 26, 28, and 30 inches. In addition, this firm has a rifled slug barrel available in 12 gauge to fit the same Remington shotguns. Available in 22 and 24-in. lengths, complete with rifle-type sights, the barrels have a rifling twist of 1 turn in 34 inches, with a bore diameter of 0.727-in. and lands of 0.716-in.

Heckler & Koch

This firm has been distributing the Benelli autoloader in the U.S. for several years, but it is now available in a new improved form as the Benelli Super 90. Featuring a matte black finish and conventional pistol grip stock and forearm of fiberglass-reinforced polymer, it has a redesigned trigger guard assembly and one-piece alloy receiver unlike the previous upper/lower design. The barrel, chambered for 3-in. shells, has a length of 19¾ inches, and it's fitted with rifle-type sights. The magazine capacity is 7 rounds, and there's an external shell release for quick shell exchanges, if desired, plus a free shell carrier. In addition, an M16-type pistol grip stock in molded rubber is available as an accessory.

Ithacagun

The factory on Gunshop Hill in Ithaca has a couple of new versions of old favorites. The Standard Mag 10 is now available in the 30-in. vent barrel version with interchangeable, out-of-sight choke tubes; a coin can be used to change tubes, and Improved Cylinder, Modified, and Full choke tubes are available. In addition, the rust resistant baked-in Camo-Seal finish is now available in a brown/green pattern on the Mag 10 Standard Vent full choke 26- and 32-in. barrels, the Model 37 Featherlight 12-gauge vent-rib 26-in. Full choke barrel chambered for 3-in. shells, plus the Model 51A 12-gauge Waterfowler (30-in. barrel) and Turkey (26-in. barrel) guns chambered for 3-in. shells, with ventilated ribs and full chokes.

Kassnar Imports

The Windsor Grade over-under shotguns have been given a new schnabel forearm, and the finish changed from a high gloss to an oil finish. The Churchill ICT screw-in choke tubes have been changed to the concealed design, rather than the original design which projected beyond the muzzle. In Windsor side-by-side models the Windsor II is now available with the ICT tubes in 12 gauge only, while an entire line of Windsor Flyweight shotguns has been added in both side-by-side (Windsor I and II) and over-under

models (Windsor III and IV). These shotguns feature 25-in. barrels in the 12 gauge models and 23-in. barrels in the 16, 20 and 28 gauge (side-by-side only) sizes, plus the 410 bore, and a choice of fixed chokes or ICT tubes in the 12 gauge.

The Omega folding single barrel shotgun line remains unchanged; the Churchill gas-operated autoloader and pump-action shotguns are no longer cataloged, and neither are the Omega pump-action shotguns. However, the Omega double gun line has been expanded to include 20 and 28-gauge guns in Standard Grade side-by-side and Deluxe Grade over-under models. Barrel lengths are 26 inches for all models, except for the 20-gauge

Bernardelli's new Anti-Riot B4 12-gauge autoloader-pump has folding buttstock, carrying handle-sight assembly, and a detachable box magazine.

Mossberg's Model 500 Bullpup has molded stock assembly; will come in two barrel lengths and handle all 12-gauge shotshells.

The La Paloma/Benelli 12-gauge Slug gun has a rifled barrel and adjustable rifle-type sights; barrel length is 21½ inches.

Here is a shorter, lighter version of Browning's reliable gas automatic shotgun—the B-80 Upland Special with 22-in. barrel and Invector choke system.

over-under version choked Modified and Full.

La Paloma Marketing

New from this Arizona firm, which distributes the famous 12-gauge BRI Sabot Slug loads, is a new 12-gauge Slug gun. Featuring a rifled barrel, permanently attached to a Benelli 122 Slug receiver, the new shotgun features rifle-type sights, select walnut beavertail forearm and stock with semi-Monte Carlo and cheekpiece. With BRI slugs, this shotgun is reported to have produced some phenomenally-small groups.

Laurona

Screw-in multi-chokes are now available on the Model 83MG-12 and 83MG-20 Super Game over-under

shotguns, plus the Models 85MS-12 and 85MS-20 Super Game over-unders, and the under barrel of the 85MS Super Trap and 85MS Super Pigeon guns. In addition, the 83MG-12 and 85MS-12 over-unders can be obtained with a spare set of 20 gauge barrels, equipped with Multi-choke tubes. Two choke tubes are provided with each barrel assembly, and extra tubes are available.

The Laurona shotguns, which have underbolt locking, and selective automatic ejectors, plus an excellent black chrome finish, now have a new selective single trigger mechanism incorporation with the slide safety on the upper tang. This selector features a spring-loaded ball plunger to prevent the slide from moving accidentally.

Marlin Firearms

The Marlin shotgun line has almost become extinct. Only the bolt action 12 gauge Model 55 Goose Gun remains; the excellent 120 Magnum and the Model 5510 Supergoose 10 gauge have been discontinued. With a two-shot box magazine and 36-inch full choke barrel chambered for 3-inch shells, the 55 is still an economical waterfowl gun, but so was the Supergoose.

Mossberg

Some of our shotgun manufacturers may be having problems, but Mossberg seems to be full speed ahead. Replacing the Model 5500 is the new gas-operated Model 712 autoloading shotgun which can handle all 12-

gauge loads from standard length (2¾ inches) containing 1 ounce of shot to magnum length (3 inches) containing 2 ounces of shot—the patent S & W offered in its last long gun year. Available in four versions—Standard with fixed choke or Accu II flush-type screw-in choke tubes, Slugster with 24-in. barrel having rifle-type sights, Camo/Speedfeed which features a special synthetic stock and black finish.

With a walnut stock and forearm, bright bluing, gold-plated trigger, and a few other touches, the 712 becomes the Regal 712; barrel choices include fixed choke (Modified) 28-in. or Accu II in 28- or 24-in. lengths. Other members of the Regal Series include the Regal 500 in 12 or 20 gauge, with the same barrel and choke combinations as the Regal 712.

length of 18½ inches and 8-shot with 20-in. barrel.

Navy Arms

Val Forgett's firm has seven shotguns—four over-under, one side-by-side, and two single shots. Manufactured in Italy, the shotguns feature chrome-lined barrels, and are available in 12 and 20 gauges, plus 410 bore, depending on the model. The

Valmet's new 412 Series trap and Skeet shotguns, top to bottom: over-under trap, single barrel trap, and Skeet over-under.

The Model 66C by Felix Sarasqueta offers scroll engraving and false sideplates Damasque-inlaid with 18K gold. Showy.

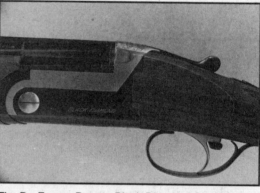

The Dr. Franco Beretta Black Diamond Grade I trap gun. That's the barrel selector on the trigger. Not showy.

forearm with camouflage finish, and a Junior version with shortened buttstock and 24-in. barrel—the 712 has a 5-shot shell capacity, and a new gas regulating system.

The Speedfeed stock and forearm are also available on the 12-gauge Model 500 pump gun in Slugster, Accu II and regular vent rib models with 30-in. Full choke barrel, in addition to the Combo Shooting System, and 18 versions of law enforcement and security shotguns. This stock, which carries four extra 12-gauge shells—two on each side—is built of plastic to withstand extreme conditions of cold and wet; it comes with a 5-year unconditional replacement guarantee, and is available in camo or

The Mossberg Select Series shotguns include the 12 and 20-gauge Model 3000 slide action in choice of Standard (blue finish) or Waterfowler (dull matte finish) with 15 different barrel length/choke/gauge combinations, plus the Model 1000 and Model 1000 Super gas-operated autoloaders in 32 different barrel length/choke/gauge combinations.

First shown more than three years ago, and changed considerably since, the 12-gauge Model 500 Bullpup created a lot of interest at the '86 Shot Show. Featuring a compact, molded stock of space-age materials, and incorporating sights into the carrying handle, the Bullpup will be available in two versions—6-shot with barrel

single shot is a folding design available in all three chamberings, while the over-under Model 83/93 is available in 12 or 20 gauge, with double triggers, and 28-in. fixed choke barrels chambered for 3-in. shells. The Model 95/96 is available in 12 gauge only with the same features as the 83/93, except for a single trigger and five interchangeable screw-in choke tubes. There's also the Model 410 over-under, which has 26-in. barrels chambered for 3-in. shells; chokes are Full/Full or Skeet/Skeet, and a single non-selective trigger is standard. For side-by-side lovers, the Model 100/150 is available in 12 or 20 gauge with double triggers and fixed choke barrels with 3-in. chambers. Deluxe grades of many of the models are available; stocks and forearms are of European walnut, except for the standard single shot which has a beechwood stock and forearm.

Perazzi

This firm has become known for its competition—trap, Skeet, and live pigeon—over-under shotguns during the past two decades, and to a lesser degree for its game or field guns. Now two new game models—MX20 and MX5—have been introduced, in addition to four variations—MX3 Special, TM1 Special, MX8 Special, and Grandamerica Special—of previously available models.

The MX20 is a 20-gauge built on a 20-gauge frame, and is available with 28-gauge and 410-bore barrels also. Chambered for standard length shells, the 26-in. barrels do not have side ribs, but are available with fixed chokes (MX20) or interchangeable choke tubes (MX20C). A single selective trigger is standard, as is a schnabel forearm. The buttstock may be obtained with a pistol grip or straight grip. The MX5 is available in three versions, two in 12 gauge with choice of fixed chokes of interchangeable choke tubes, or with 20-gauge barrels on the 12-gauge frame. The 12-gauge barrels are chambered for standard length shells, while the MX5 20GA is chambered for 3-in. shells. Like the MX20, the MX5 has a single non-detachable, selective trigger assembly, and the same stock and forearm styles. Barrel lengths are 26 inches, except for 27 inches on the MX5C versions.

Precision Sports

Parker-Hale has been a name meaning quality sporting arms to British shooters for many decades and now shotguns bearing the Parker-Hale name are available to U.S. shooters. Crafted in Spain by Ignacio Ugartechea in the classic tradition of English gunmaking, the side-by-side shotguns, known as the 600 Series, are available in field grade boxlock and "best" grade hand-detachable sidelock models. Extractor and ejector versions are available, as are English and American style stocks. Barrel lengths range from 25 to 28 inches, and gauges from 12 to 28, plus 410 bore. Stocks are hand-rubbed, oil-finished walnut, an automatic safety is standard, and weights vary from 5¼ to 5½ pounds for the 410 and the 28 gauge to approximately 7 pounds for the heaviest 12-gauge model. For those inclined toward Churchill-type

ribs on their side-by-side shotguns, the Models 645E-XXV and 680E-XXV should fill the ticket. Featuring 25-in. barrels that are available in all five chamberings, these shotguns offer the ultimate style in English bird guns.

Proofmark, Ltd.

This Illinois firm is now distributing the over-under line of Armi Bettinsoli Tarcisio. These guns, available to European shooters for over 25 years, are completely manufactured in the Bettinsoli factory, using a combination of computer controlled machinery and hand craftsmanship. Available only in 12-gauge at present, and two series—Caccia (field) and Trap—the Bettinsoli shotguns have receivers machined from steel forgings, tri-alloy barrels with chrome-lined bores and chambers, ventilated top and side ribs, single selective triggers, interchangeable firing pins, replaceable hinge pins, select European walnut stocks with hand-cut checkering, and engraving according to the grade. The field gun is available in two grades—840-EM and 845-EM with Interchoke tubes—while the trap gun is available in Senior Lux and Maxim 2 grades. Additional grades are available on special order, including a Maxim 3 with gold inlaid frame, and Skeet versions of the two trap guns will be available. Barrel lengths on current models measure approximately 27½ inches. Weight of the Bettinsoli shotguns is from 7 to 8 pounds, and each shotgun carries a three-year warranty.

Quality Arms

Quality Arms has the French-manufactured Bretton, the world's lightest over-under at 4½ pounds in 12 gauge. Available in 12 or 20 gauge, with the 16 gauge available on special order, the Bretton is a delightful upland game gun.

Quality also will keep in stock selected models of Bernardelli guns, as will others.

Remington

The big news from Ilion are the REM chokes for several versions of the Model 870 and 1100 shotguns. These screw-in choke tubes are available only in 12 gauge at present, and they fit flush with the muzzle. Not all barrels can be obtained with REM chokes; they are available only in 21, 26, and 28-in. barrels. Complete coverage of all the new products at Remington will be provided elsewhere in this edition by the Editor, so it suf-

fices to say the 12-gauge Model 870 Wingmaster has been restyled slightly with cut checkering, plus there are two new 'deer guns' with non-reflective Parkerized finish on metal parts and oil-finished hardwood stocks and forearms. Both models have Improved Cylinder choke barrels—21-in. on the 1100 and 20-in. on the 870—with 3-in. chambers and rifle-type sights; the shotguns come with recoil pads and padded slings of Du Pont "Cordura" nylon.

Richland Arms

New from Blissfield are two over-unders—the 757 and 783—and a single shot—the 80LS. The 757 is available in 12 gauge only with a choice of 26- or 28-in. barrels having fixed chokes or as the 7570 with interchangeable choke tubes in 26-in. barrels. All versions have 3-in. chambers and ventilated top and side ribs. Double triggers and extractors are standard on the 757, while the 783 features a single non-selective trigger and extractors. Barrel lengths on the 783 are 26, 28, and 30 inches, with 3-in. chambers and ventilated top and side ribs, and all barrels have interchangeable stainless steel choke tubes. Five choke tubes are furnished per shotgun, with wrench and case. The stocks and forearms are of European walnut with hand checkering, and the 783 is fitted with a recoil pad. The 80LS is a single shot in 12 or 20-gauge or 410 bore, with Full choke barrel in a choice of 26- or 28-in. length.

Sauer-Franchi

Sauer shotguns are not exactly new to U.S. shooters, having been imported by the Weatherby firm several years ago, nor are Franchi shotguns new. New to U.S. shooters is the combination of Sauer-Franchi shotguns now being distributed by Sigarms. Seven different over-under models are available, carrying retail price tags from $785 for the Standard to $1520 for the Diplomat. Available only in 12-gauge, chambered for standard length shells, all shotguns have a ventilated top rib and walnut stock and forearm. Five of the models—Standard, Regent, Favorit, Diplomat, and Sporting S—have single selective triggers, while the trap and Skeet guns have single non-selective triggers. Double triggers are available for some of the sporting models. The receivers are machined from a drop forging, locking is via underbolt, and barrel lengths and chokes depend on the model.

Savage Industries

The Stevens pump action shotguns, Savage/Stevens guard guns, and Stevens/Fox side-by-side shotguns are still being produced at Westfield, or by the time you read this in a new 240,000 square foot manufacturing facility in western Massachusetts. The Model 67-T has been discontinued, while the 67VR-T, 67VRT-K and 67VRT-Y are available with interchangeable choke tubes. The 67VR-T and 67VRT-K are available in a choice of 12 or 20 gauge with 28-in. barrels, while the 67VRT-Y is available only in 20 gauge with a 22-in. barrel and shortened buttstock for

Shotguns of Ulm

The big news here is the KS-5, a single barrel 12-gauge trap gun. More economical than the K-80, the KS-5 is a product of high-tech computer-controlled manufacturing. Available with a 32- or 34-in. barrel, tapered step ventilated rib, optional screw-in choke tubes, adjustable trigger, interchangeable buttstock assembly with palm swell on both sides of the grip, and underbolt locking, the KS-5 features a single action design with a single centrally-mounted, spiral spring powered hammer. The impact point of the shot charge can be changed on the KS-5 via muzzle hang-

410, which is available with a 26-in. barrel; the bores are chrome-plated. A walnut-stained stock and forearm are standard on the single shot, with the other two models having European walnut stocks; all three have cut checkering on the pistol grip and forearm. Automatic safeties are standard, as are double triggers on the doubles; chokes are Modified/Full.

Springfield Armory

Taking on an importing role, this Illinois source for military-type long guns will be a major distributor of Bernardelli guns. That definitely includes the sporting line.

The Bernardelli over-unders have

Winchester Model 23 Classics come 12, 20, 28 and 410, shown here. The 28 and 410 frames are scaled to the barrels.

With longer forcing cone, backboring and ports, the 34-in. Winchoke barrel graces the Winchester 12-gauge Diamond Grade "Over Single" trap gun.

Hastings 870 and 1100 barrels come with three choke tubes—Improved Cylinder, Modified, and Full.

The new Winchester Custom Two Barrel Hunting Set comes with interchangeable 20- and 28-gauge barrels, each with its own forend, in leather luggage.

youth use. The 67VRT-K has a new laminated camo stock, making it ideal for turkey hunters. In the side-by-side line the Fox-B with double triggers has returned, and is available in 12 or 20 gauge with barrel lengths of 24 to 30 inches, depending on the gauge, or in 410 bore with 26-in. Full choke barrels. The only other change is a new Monte Carlo stock on the Model 24/24C in the rifle/shotgun over-under line.

ers, and several options, such as a release trigger, are available.

Sovereign

Imported by Southern Gun & Tackle Distributors, this line consists of an over-under and side-by-side manufactured in Brescia, Italy, by Fausti Stefano in 12 and 20 gauges, and a folding single shot in 12, 16, and 20 gauge, plus 410 bore. All barrel lengths are 28 inches, except for the

monobloc barrel construction. Barrel lengths range from 25½ inches to 29½ inches. The Model 115 is available in a sporting version with single selective trigger and multichoke barrels, and trap/Skeet versions with single non-selective trigger. A choice of pistol grip or straight stock is available. A Monotrap version of the 115 will be available.

A wide range of side-by-side shotguns includes boxlock and sidelock models. The Elio is a lightweight double with Anson-Deeley action and Purdey locks; it weighs about 6¼ pounds. For slug shooters there's the Slug gun featuring the same type action as the Elio, with coin-finished receiver and rifle-type sights. The Elio and Slug guns are available only in 12 gauge. The most reasonably priced side-by-side is the Urberto 1, sold for years as the Gamecock in gauges from 12 to 28 with barrel lengths and chokes depending on the customer's perferences. Double triggers are standard on all models, including the Roma 6, the premier of the Bernardelli boxlock side-by-sides.

A new Bernardelli shotgun drawing lots of attention at the '86 Shot Show was the B4 Anti-Riot Gun. Available in two versions—B4-8 pump and B4 gas-operated autoloader/pump—the new shotgun features a folding buttstock assembly, a rotating breech bolt, detachable 5-shot box magazine, and a carrying handle/sight assembly, similar to those on the M16. (Larger capacity magazines will probably be available.) The barrel is protected by a perforated handguard.

Stoeger Industries

The IGA line now includes four models—the over-under with a choice of single non-selective or double triggers in 12, 20 or 28 gauge, and 410 bore, plus the double trigger side-by-side in the same gauges, and the Coach Gun side-by-side in 12 or 20 gauge with 20-in. barrels. All four models are chambered for 2¾-in. shells, the 410s are chambered for 3-in. shells. Chokes and barrel lengths depend on the gauges. Automatic tang safeties are standard on the side-by-sides with manual safeties on the over-under models.

U.S. Repeating Arms

A new five-shot version of the 12-gauge pump action Winchester Defender shotgun is available for home security and law enforcement use, in addition to the eight-shot versions already available. The barrel length of the latest Defender is 18 inches, with a choice of muzzle bead or rifle-type sights. Also added to the sporting line is a new XTR field grade version of the Winchester Model 1300 pump action; featuring a stock and forearm of American walnut with a high luster finish and deep-cut, wrap-around checkering for better handling, the 1300 XTR comes with a 28-in. Winchoke barrel and three choke tubes—Improved Cylinder, Modified, and

Full. All Winchester 1300, Ranger, and Defender shotguns are now chambered for 3-in. shells in both 12 and 20 gauge.

Valmet

New for clay target shooters from Valmet are the 412 trap and Skeet guns in over-under and single barrel configurations. Guaranteed for five years, the new ST guns have elongated forcing cones, stainless steel recessed screw-in choke tubes, semi-fancy grade American walnut stocks designed for the American shooter with palm swells on the pistol grip for right- and left-hand shooters, stepped ventilated rib on the trap guns, and a mechanical trigger mechanism. Barrel lengths range from 28 inches on the Skeet model to 34 inches on the single barrel trap gun, with weights of 8 and 9 pounds, respectively.

The field grade 412 Series over-unders have been upgraded with 3-in. chambers, stainless steel recessed choke tubes, a restyled forearm, double palm swell on the pistol grip, and a non-glare, matte nickel finished receiver. Four barrel lengths—24, 26, 28, and 30 inches—are available, and weights of the field guns range from 7¼ to 7½ pounds.

Winchester Olin

The new Winchester shotguns are many. There's a new Quail Special over-under in 12 gauge with Winchoke barrels of 25½ inches, quail scene engraving on the receiver, and a straight grip stock and forearm of extra fancy American walnut with fine hand checkering. There's also a Golden Quail side-by-side based on the Model 23 action; available in 12 gauge and 410 bore with straight grip stock and barrels measuring 25½ inches. The Golden Quail model has a gold quail head on the bottom of the receiver with the words "Golden Quail" "One of 500" underscored.

For duck hunters having a preference for a lighter gun, there's a new 23 Light Duck which features 28-in. Full choke barrels chambered for 3-in. shells, extra fancy American walnut pistol grip stock and beavertail forearm, and the words "Light Duck" embossed in gold on the bottom of the receiver. Another side-by-side "One of 500" is the Custom Two-Barrel Hunting Set with interchangeable 28 and 20-gauge barrels measuring 25½ inches long, and choked Improved Cylinder/Modified; each barrel assembly is fitted with its own beavertail forearm of extra fancy American walnut. The forearms and pistol grip

buttstock are hand checkered at 28 lines-per-inch in a fleur-de-lis pattern. The receiver has gold inlays consisting of a flying pheasant on the left side, a flying quail on the right, and the famous Labrador Retriever, King Buck, with a mallard on the bottom. Each set comes in a full handmade leather carrying case, complete with Parker-Hale oil bottle and snap caps. Another limited production gun is the Two-Barrel Hunting Set, featuring 28-in. Winchoke 12-gauge and 26-in. Winchoke 20-gauge over-under barrels. There are no gold inlays on the receiver, nor an extra forearm, but the receiver is engraved, and the pistol grip stock and forearm are of full fancy American walnut with custom hand checkering. Total production is 250 guns, and each set comes with a special custom two-barrel carrying case.

The Model 23 Classic side-by-side is now available in a Series with 26-in. ventilated rib barrels in 12, 20 and 28 gauge, plus 410. There are fancy American walnut pistol grip stocks and beavertail forearms, and engraved receivers, with gold inlays—a pheasant on the 12- and 20-gauge guns, and a quail on the 410 and 28 gauge. Weights for this series range from 5¾ pounds for the 410 to 7 pounds for the 12-gauge version.

In the Diamond Grade target line, there's a new Over Single 12-gauge with 34-in. Winchoke barrel. Featuring a lengthened forcing cone and ported barrel, with raised ventilated rib, the Over Single is available with a choice of straight or Monte Carlo stock.

Zoli Group U.S.A.

Thirty different shotguns manufactured by Angelo Zoli are distributed in the U.S. by this firm. Included are over-under, side-by-side, pump action, autoloader, and single shot models from 12-gauge down to 410. Some models have been available for several years through other distributors, but new is the Patricia, a handmade side-by-side 410 with 28-in. barrel chambered for 3-in. shells, with a single selective trigger, boxlock action, English-style fancy walnut stock and splinter forearm, and a weight of 5½ pounds. The St. George Trap gun is now available as an "unsingle" or "monotrap" with an under barrel and a high trestle-style ventilated rib. There's even an Alley Cleaner in 12 gauge and 20; it has 20-in. barrels, having fixed or screw-in Multi-choke tubes, a single selective trigger. The very unusual grip slants forward. ●

HANDGUNS TODAY:

AUTOLOADERS

by J. B. WOOD

THE AUTOMATIC pistol scene has lately been marked by continuing trends and a few surprises. In the full-sized military and police pistols, recent government requirements induced designers to include certain points in most of the currently-made large autos: Double-column large-capacity magazines, double-action trigger systems, and side-button magazine releases. Other features frequently seen are manual and automatic firing-pin blocks, and hammer-lowering devices.

Space-age plastics have seen more use in recent times, and many manufacturers are offering standard models in a choice of regular steel or stainless. Three European makers have turned out, for the first time, stainless steel pistols. All three are medium-frame 380 autos; in time, I'm sure someone will make a full-sized stainless pistol. On this side of the ocean, we have long since solved the problems of the early stainless guns, and now use differing alloys in mating parts to eliminate or reduce friction galling. Now, stainless steel seems to be the wave of the U.S. future.

One of the surprises this year was the return of the 32 Automatic. For quite a while, the experts had been telling us that the 380 was the absolute minimum for effective personal protection. Then, Winchester developed the 32 ACP Silvertip cartridge. Aluminum-cased and lead-cored, the hollow point Silvertip bullet expands reliably, and the 32 is now an acceptable cartridge for defense. As a result of this, several makers have designed small pistols in this caliber, with more to come.

In no particular order, let's look now at the new items that have appeared in the past year:

Smith & Wesson now has a stainless steel version of their small 9mm, called the Model 669. The big news, though, is the availability of the first S&W 45 Auto, the Model 645. Made only in stainless, with an eight-round magazine capacity, the Model 645 weighs just 37½ ounces, and is only slightly larger than the standard 9mm S&W pistols. There is a rumor

The 9mm Glock 17, the service sidearm of Austria, is now being imported into the U.S. The magazine and lower frame are tough plastic.

The BRNO CZ-85, a world-class 9mm, is now imported by Bauska Arms.

J. B. Wood tries Holmes' 9mm MP-83 pistol. The MP-83 is one of several assault pistols now actively marketed.

There are both full-size and compact versions of the Bernardelli 9mm PO18 pistol, now being imported by Springfield Armory.

The prototype of the new Iver Johnson 9mm DA pistol. It has not yet been given a name or model designation.

ized, and that process is still going on at this writing. The final pattern may differ from any illustrations shown in advance, even here.

From **Beretta,** the news is mostly that several previously-announced guns will now be available on the market. Gearing up for the large U.S. military contract on the Model 92F occupied the factory in the past year, but now a few new models will begin to make an appearance. Included in this group will be the smaller version of the military pistol, the Model 92F Compact. Also, the Model 87BB, the 22LR version of the Model 85BB. The Model 86 has arrived, a combination of the Model 85BB in 380 chambering and the tip-up barrel of the small pocket pistols. Other news is that the 25-caliber Model 20 has been discontinued. From now on, the small 25 Auto will have the same configuration as the 22-caliber Model 21, and will share its model designation.

It has been known for some time that **Heckler & Koch** discontinued the Model HK4. Now, they have announced its replacement, a 380 Auto called the K3, a small-frame gun that is a lot like the famed P7. The design of the K3 is still being finalized, and at the time I'm writing this, I'm not sure whether a photo of the K3 will be available to show with this report. Meanwhile, at the factory in Oberndorf, work is continuing with prototypes of the P7M7, the long-awaited 45 version of the P7. According to word from H&K, the current experimental pistols in 45 have a different gas-locking system, functioning on a hydraulic principle. No time estimate was given on commercial availability. For those who keep notes on military contracts, a version of the 9mm P7 has been adopted as a standard sidearm by certain units of the Army of Norway.

There are no new pistols from **SIG/ Sauer** but there are some interesting new options and accessories available from **Sigarms.** By mid-to-late 1986, a side-button magazine release was to be standard on the P220. There is speculation that the stainless P230SL may become available with an optional alloy frame, but this has not been confirmed. The 9mm P226 is now offered in two more finishes: A satin nickel, and a new "X-Finish," a tough epoxy that is impervious to acid, salt water, and other corrosives. A 20-round magazine is now available for the P226. A certain U.S. government agency (which I can't name here) is switching to the P226, and their guns are being equipped with Tritium

that in the future there may be a single action version, the Model 647, especially tuned for competition shooting. So far, there's no official confirmation on this from Smith & Wesson.

At **Colt,** the newest auto pistols are the stainless steel version of the Officer's ACP and the 380 Mustang. I looked at the prototype of the Mustang in January of last year, and have been shooting a regular-production Mustang for several months, and I like it. The smallest locked-breech 380 currently made, it is essentially a reduced-size version of the Colt 380 **GM,** a half-inch less in length and in

height. My Mustang handles the Winchester Silvertip load with perfect reliability, and its all-steel construction keeps the recoil moderate in spite of the pistol's tiny dimensions.

Two years ago, **Sturm, Ruger & Company** announced a new 9mm pistol called the P-85. Early information and photos detailed all of the features expected in a modern military or police automatic—double action, large capacity magazine, firing-pin-block safety, and so on. The original announcement, though, was a little too soon. Bill Ruger and his design team decided that there would be a few changes before the pattern was final-

Beretta's Model 86 combines the features of the 380 Model 85BB and the small 22 and 25 Beretta pistols. The tip-up barrel is shown open.

Colt's Mustang, a reduced-size 380 GM, is the smallest locked-breech pistol in current production.

The Detonics Pocket 380, slimmer than the Pocket 9, has the modified guard hook now used on all Detonics.

night-sights. Sometime next year, this option will become available for civilian and police use.

The most important news from **Interarms** is the return to the U.S. market of the famous **Walther** PPK, banned from importation in 1968 because it lacked just $\frac{1}{10}$-in. in vertical measurement. Made in America by Interarms under Walther license, the PPK is available now in stainless steel, and will later be offered in regular blue steel. The excellent **Star** pistols are still among the Interarms imports, including the fine Star Model 30M and 30PK. Equally fine are the guns in the **Astra** line, and there are some new pieces here: The Astra A-60 is a new version of the 380 Constable, with a 13-round magazine and an ambidextrous safety. Also, the regular 380 Constable is now available in stainless steel, and the 22LR version, in blue steel, is now offered in a Sport Model, with a 6-in. barrel.

The Astra A-80 has now been released and the addition of manual firing-pin-block safety on the slide. Other features are the same as the A-80, including a large-capacity magazine—15 rounds in 9mm or 38 Super, 9 rounds in 45 Auto. I noticed that the **Bernardelli** target and medium-frame pistols were absent from the Interarms catalog, but were still included in their price list.

On this same note, there is a new principal importer for the 9mm Bernardelli pistol, the PO18—and for the rest of the line as well. Designed around five years ago, the outstanding PO18 has a 16-round magazine, double action, a sear-block safety, and all-steel construction. It is made in full-sized and compact configurations. There has been some importation by **Mandall's** in Arizona during the past year, but the new primary source will be **Springfield Armory** in Illinois. Another notable gun from Springfield Armory is a new Officer's Model, a smaller version of their GM-pattern 45 Auto.

The small double action 9mm from **Iver Johnson,** announced last year, is scheduled for production in mid-1986. Flat, compact, and all-steel, this neat little pistol has, so far, no official name or model designation. For those who came in late, the gun is just 6½ inches long, weighs 26 ounces, and has a 6-round magazine. It will be available in bright or matte blue, and the price has not been announced. The prototypes I have handled feel good in the hand, and the general design is very similar to the 380 IJ Pony.

For those who like the **Detonics** Pocket 9, but would like something with a little less bark for a wife's or girlfriend's purse, there is now the Detonics Pocket 380. It's slimmer and lighter, but otherwise is very much like the Pocket 9. Both guns, I've noticed, now have a much less obtrusive "hook" at the lower front of the trigger guard.

The **Arminex** Trifire, perhaps the ultimate update of the old 1911-GM design, will soon undergo two very slight design changes. The beryllium alloy trigger will be replaced with one

Left and right view of the Falcon "Portsider," a mirror-image version of the 1911-pattern pistol for left-handers, in stainless steel.

of HTS aluminum alloy, and the trigger guard "hook" will be eliminated. The latter feature will be good news for those who would like to carry the Trifire in a standard holster. A new pocket pistol, Sleeping Beauty, will soon be rolling into production. It has a slight external resemblance to the Walther TPH, and is about the same size. The trigger system is DA-only, and the caliber is 32 Auto.

Another new 32 Auto was recently announced, this one single action and striker-fired. It's from **Davis Industries,** previously notable for a tiny and well-made copy of the Remington double derringer. I haven't yet fired the Davis P-32, but the prototypes I examined were nice-looking guns. The Davis P-32 joins a list of new 32 pistols that include the Seecamp and Sleeping Beauty, and there is likely to be more. Also, now that we have the Winchester Silvertip, a lot of the old 32 automatics have suddenly become viable defense pieces.

While we're in the area of medium- and small-frame pistols, a few random notes: In Garden Grove, Califor-

nia, the people at **American Arms** are still turning out the nicely-made Eagle, a 380 in stainless based on the Walther PPK. A 22LR version is still planned, but is further down the road. **Precision Small Parts** of Charlottesville, Virginia, still has an arrangement with FN to make a copy of the Baby Browning, but production is still on hold. At **Steel City Arms** in Pittsburgh, the serious illness of head man Chuck Bailey caused a long delay in the production of Double Deuce, a neat little 22LR stainless DA auto. All is well now, and the guns are beginning to be seen in stores. On the drawing board at Steel City is a new small 9mm DA in stainless, the War Eagle.

Shooters who are left-handed, and who lamented the passing of the **Randall** mirror-image 45, take heart: It's still there, but it has a new name: The **Falcon.** Available now is the left-hand version, which they're calling the Portsider. Also offered will be a limited edition of one hundred sets, with one left and one right gun. Later, it's planned to offer the smaller ver-

sion that Randall called the Curtis Le May. The full address is Falcon Firearms, Box 3748, Granada Hills, California 91344. They also offer several stainless steel components for GM-pattern pistols, including magazines, extractors, and match-grade barrels.

For those who feel that the CZ75 is the ultimate 9mm DA design, there is good news from Montana. **Bauska Arms,** already well-known for precision custom rifle barrels, is now importing the CZ75, the ambidextrous CZ80, and an excellent smaller pistol, the 32 CZ83. The latter is double action, with a 15-round magazine, ambidextrous magazine release, ambidextrous sear-block safety, and an external slide latch. As with all Czech pistols, it is beautifully made. For more information and prices, the address is: Bauska Arms Corporation, Box 1995, Kalispell, Montana 59903. **Stoeger Arms** has announced that the **Llama** Omni will soon be available in a new 9mm version, the Model 82. In this gun, the one adopted by the Spanish Army, the trigger linkage is simplified, the hammer spur is re-

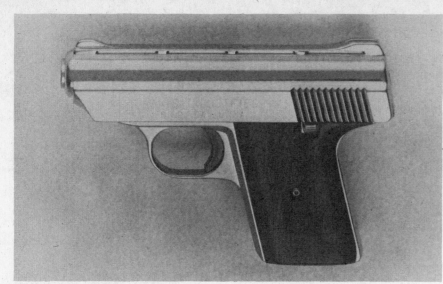

A new small automatic in 32 chambering, the Davis is single-action, striker-fired, and has a sear-block safety.

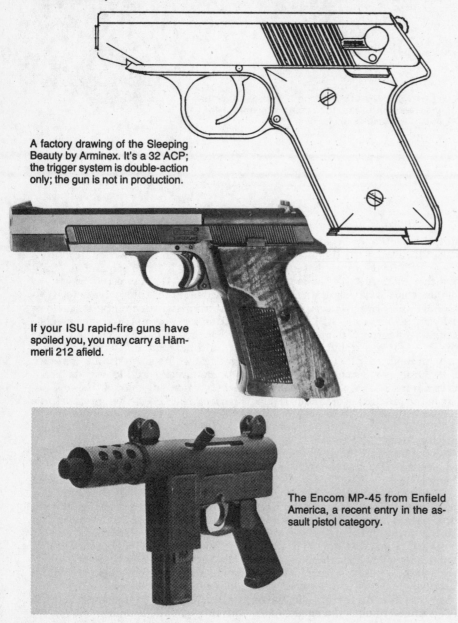

A factory drawing of the Sleeping Beauty by Arminex. It's a 32 ACP; the trigger system is double-action only; the gun is not in production.

If your ISU rapid-fire guns have spoiled you, you may carry a Hämmerli 212 afield.

The Encom MP-45 from Enfield America, a recent entry in the assault pistol category.

shaped, and the slide shape and grips are different. According to Stoeger, the new Model 82 is expected to be available on the U.S. market early in 1987. Meanwhile, the original 9mm and 45 versions of the Omni are still available.

Almost every shooter knows the **Hämmerli** name, and when it's mentioned, most will think of the famed Model 208, winning international matches in the hands of shooters like Eric Buljung or Silvia Kaposztai. For those who want the same precision quality at slightly less cost, Hämmerli recently added the Model 215. Not quite as pretty outside, but just as finely finished inside. I'm not a serious target shooter, and I'm pleased that there is now the Hämmerli Model 212, the shorter version that's called the Hunter's Pistol. I've been shooting a Model 212 for the past year, and it's enough to say that it shoots like a Hämmerli. The U.S. importer is Mandall's, in Scottsdale, Arizona.

In the category of Assault Pistols, **Bill Holmes** is still making the MP-83 and MP-22 in Fayetteville, Arkansas. In California, the regular production of the **Göncz** assault pistol is now under way. Now that I have had an opportunity to shoot a Göncz pistol, and take it apart, I understand why John Göncz calls them hi-tech arms. All parts are machined from the best steels, and tolerances are to .0005 of an inch. This is far better than you expect in guns of this type. The Göncz has beautiful balance, it's accurate, and the functioning of my 9mm is flawless.

A new gun on the assault pistol scene is the **Encom,** available in 9mm or 45 as the MP-9 and MP-45. The gun has an external resemblance to the KG-99, but it's all-steel, and is a four-piece modular design. Magazines are available in 10, 30, 40, and 50-round capacity, and a kit is offered that will convert it to a carbine. Since the collapsible stock is attached to the sleeve of an 18½-in. barrel, everything stays in legal length. An impressive array of other accessories is available. The Encom pistols are marketed by Enfield America, Inc., Box 5314, Atlanta, GA 30307.

In firearms manufacturing, Murphy's Third Law definitely applies: Everything will take longer than you figured it would. Other automatics that fit this dictum are the new double action Browning HP, the Bren Ten, and the Walther Model 88. All of these, I imagine, will be worth the waiting.

●

What's A Gun Without A Ghost?

Shooting is more satisfying if you take someone unseen along.

by ROGER BARLOW

WHAT I FIND wrong with a new gun—no matter how much it costs, how expensive its rich cowhide case may be or even how many more or less useful accessories may be in the case—is that a new gun is just that, a *new* gun. A gun with no ghost, no ghosts at all. Without a ghost in its case, even a new Holland & Holland Royal or a fully engraved Winchester 21, stocked from a blank that could have qualified for a Rolls-Royce instrument panel, is just another fine

WINTER 1909 "POP"

gun and sort of dead.

In my view, there is no way to breathe life into a gun except by endowing it with a friendly, entertaining ghost or two. Indeed, if you have never hunted with a gun having a companionable shade in its case you are missing out on one of the truly important as well as rewarding aspects of this sport.

Many men buying new guns seem to be rather lonely in field and wood and so they apparently find it desirable to go hunting in the company of other hunters, men who are usually also carrying new guns. Now this is surely a bastardized form of this noble activity which, in its purest aspect, is best experienced and savored in solitude—the hunter alone with his quarry, be it gopher, grouse or grizzly. The only companion appropriate to the elemental form of man's ancient sport of hunting is, quite obviously, a ghost. And, on some occasions, a dog. Sometimes, the ghost can be the ghost of a dog, of course.

When I go into the woods after ruffed grouse, carrying my father's old $50 double-barreled Baker sidelock, his ghost is unquestionably my pleased and amiable companion. And so the day is more rewarding than if I carried a new $12,000 Purdey.

The Purdey I *do* shoot with was new 105 years ago and I acquired it, along with the appreciative shade of its original owner, for a mere $400, proving that it was no wonder Abercrombie & Fitch went broke inasmuch as they

often failed to recognize the real value of some of their better ghosts, despite their knack of rarely pricing their *guns* too low.

Think about it for a moment. What would add the most flavor to *your* next hunt—to have a shiny new bolt action rifle resting across your knees on a snowy November day as you sit on a log overlooking a deer trail, or to have, instead, a weathered old single shot Sharps, first used by a Mountain Man in the 1870s and as full of character and history as the Old West itself? Yes, I'd say you would have to look mighty far and fairly wide to find yourself better deer hunting companions than such a classic old rifle and such an experienced shade. A ghost, you might say, with spirit.

As a bird shooter, one of my own favorite guns is a 155-year-old single barrel muzzleloader by Joseph Manton. Now *there's* a ghost to add flavor to any day in the coverts no matter how the birds fly. Manton was the most famous and convivial of all the world's great gunmakers and also the very good friend of Col. Peter Hawker, that most indefatigable shooting man and diarist of 19th century England who may very well have invented the copper percussion cap. His ghost, too, is as likely as not to turn up wherever a Joe Manton gun is being used by a friendly and perceptive modern sportsman. The Colonel wasn't one to pass up any opportunity to go shooting when he lived, so I don't presume the irascible old soldier would let the mere circumstances of dying change his way of life.

Of course, fate has played some cruel pranks upon ghosts as well as mortals. A good many of the sporting Kings of England sent numerous friends, relatives and enemies (they were, all too often, impossible to tell apart for certain) to the Tower of London where they were invariably turned into ghosts in due time, with or without due process. Fate eventually turned the tables and now some of the shades of those same sporting-minded Kings are themselves unwilling residents in the Tower, for that is where most of the Royal Weapons of old are now stored or kept on display.

This is true because once as I stood there in the Tower without a guard in sight, admiring with larcenous thoughts an ornate wheellock pistol (once a favorite toy of Henry VIII) I clearly heard a ghostly but imperious voice whisper, "For God's sake, varlet, stop your drooling and get on with it. Steal it quickly and get me out of here!" Just as I was about to smash and grab, thereby rendering a service almost certain to get me a Shady Knighthood (Sir Varlet!) or, more likely, a stretch in Dartmoor, I was saved from my natural instincts by the sudden arrival of a parish priest with a troop of Boy Scouts in tow.

No doubt about it, many of the most fascinating ghosts are found in the company of the most expensive damn guns you ever saw. Of course, it is only to be expected that the likes of the ghost of Napoleon Bonaparte would by now be accustomed to the Good Life and not very likely to be found slum-

ducks begin to move because, what with Josephine not liking guns around the house plus all those unfinished wars going on, he never did get around to trying out the gun when he first got it! I hand him back his own gun with a courteous "Après vous," and so we take turns clobbering a few mallards. In between opportunities, we quietly discuss various matters of mutual interest, then as the sun breaks through the rising mists and the morning flight peters out, he thanks me and allows that he would have gotten into a hell of a lot less trouble and had a lot more fun out of life if only he had spent less time making war and more time making love and shooting ducks.

That's pretty sound reasoning from one who was there and advice well worth listening to if any of you younger fellows are thinking of having a try at conquering Europe or the Middle East. Who wants to end up as did Napoleon and have to spend eternity in the Metropolitan Museum (in a glass case yet) hoping some nut like me will find an imaginary forgotten Rembrandt for ransom?

Some years ago I was put in touch with an elderly Scotsman, said to be willing to part with a fine Damascus barreled, trigger plate MacNaughton because the infirmities of old age now prevented him from shooting with his beloved old companion. He had already turned down more than one offer from nearby gun dealers and collectors, and I'm sure he only accepted my modest bid because I assured him I was personally going to hunt with that gun every season rather than merely displaying it in a cabinet or use it for trading purposes. I believe the canny old Scot was ensuring that his ghost would be able to hunt in the company of that favorite gun, as well as getting them both to a climate more gentle than Scotland's, which is, indeed, often cold and damp enough to make a ghost shiver. (Which largely explains the sounds of rattling bones in old castles in the late night.)

Anyway, I myself propose to make similar arrangements for my own favorite guns so as to insure a useful working life for them beyond my own time in the company of appreciative friends with whom the ghost of Roger Barlow will also be on congenial terms and sure of a welcome as a hunting companion.

Give this some thought: If Henry VIII couldn't take *his* with him, neither are you likely to do so. Better start making some suitable plans for your beloved firearms—and do your own ghost a favor! •

ming around in the company of a relic of the Death Valley Gun Works. Of course not. Napoleon's ghost is in the Metropolitan Museum of New York, sealed up in that glass display case housing the magnificent Boutet flintlock double with the extra set of barrels with percussion locks.

Nevertheless, imposing an address as the Metropolitan Museum may be, it has always struck me as a lousy place for an active spirit with a gun like that. So I often fantasize a rescue operation. As the Met isn't likely to part with that gun for a dime less than $350,000 cash or heating oil, and as I'll always be two decimal places short of being able to write that sort of a check, I figure the only hope is for me to find a small but rare lost Rembrandt gathering dust in Grandpa's attic (Granny never *did* like that fancy frame) which just might constitute an offer to trade they couldn't refuse.

So I next imagine myself in a duck blind out on Gardiner's Island some cold misty dawn, admiring that intricately carved and inlaid stock in the half-light (while trying to keep the

priming powder dry) when I feel a tap on my shoulder. I turn to find a shadowy figure there in a three-cornered hat and a beat-up old army coat. He asks if, as a special favor, he might have the first shot when the

Barlow with a Bretton 20, a gun he hopes to accompany as Ken Warner hunts with it down the years.

This is a detailed air-soft replica of the Colt 45 Automatic—the Daisy 7045.

This Daisy look-alike of the 44 Magnum Smith & Wesson shoots 25-caliber plastic pellets.

Millions of Americans cut their shooting teeth on the Daisy Model 25. This collector's edition of that classic BB gun commemorates Daisy's 100th Anniversary.

by J. I. GALAN

The legendary Mauser Broomhandle loads from a stripper clip, and shoots plastic pellets at around 150 fps.

This air-soft replica of the Beretta 93R machine pistol is rechargeable via a special air pump, or from a can of compressed air. It shoots hard.

The Crosman 338 Auto is CO$_2$-powered, a BB-repeating copy of the famous Walther P-38.

The SMG 17 exhibits superb workmanship throughout. It has a cyclic rate of 600 BBs per minute—full-auto.

AIR GUN UP-DATE

THE AIRGUN industry is in high gear. Some segments of the firearms industry seem to be in troubled waters, but airgun manufacturers are having a field day. In recent memory there has not been such a wide selection of airguns available to the consumer as now. From youth-type BB plinkers to world-class match rifles, the variety of models and types of airguns has never been greater.

All indications are that the "airgun boom" is really just beginning, particularly in the U.S., where all airguns have traditionally been lumped together in the same category as BB guns, regardless of their mechanical sophistication and level of power. American shooters are finally learning to recognize and respect the many advantages that airguns have to offer.

There is a healthy demand for airgun scopes and other special sights, airgun lubrication and maintenance products, slings, targets, airgun ammo, etc. Custom airgunsmiths are now multiplying faster than fleas on a barnyard dog, offering all kinds of special action tune-ups, custom stock work and other modifications to factory standard airguns. The results are sometimes impressive.

So it's time for a broad look at what's new to see the latest arrivals in a field whose potential is only beginning to be realized.

Air-Soft guns

A lot has been happening. The popularity of air-soft guns has exceeded all expectations, according to some of the major importers and distributors of these unique adult plinkers born in Japan.

Last year, for instance, the **Daisy Mfg. Co.** introduced four air-soft handgun models, all detailed replicas of famous firearms. This year Daisy has added eight new models to their Soft Air Gun (as they prefer to call them) line. Their new handguns are copies of the Colt 45 Auto, the Beretta 92, and the Smith & Wesson 44 Magnum "Dirty Harry" revolver.

There is also a copy of the Remington 870 Wingmaster shotgun, and then, the last four entries are just what aspiring Rambos would want — incredibly faithful copies of the Mini-Uzi, the Heckler & Koch MP5K, the long-barreled KG-9, and a cut-down version of the Ruger Mini-14 carbine — submachine guns for everybody. All shoot 25-caliber plastic ammo (either round shot or pellets) loaded in plastic cases. The latter eject very realistically.

Foreign Exchange Enterprises (P.O. Box 724, Hayward, CA 94543)

The Crosman-Skanaker CO_2 Match pistol is state-of-the-art competition for German-made world-class pellet pistols.

The EM-GE Model LP-101 is a quality air pistol from Germany at a very affordable price.

Top marks go to Daisy for their superb Model 92, a CO_2-powered semi-auto pistol producing around 400 fps with 177-cal. pellets.

This Japanese-made air-soft replica of the Remington 870 shotgun is distributed by Daisy. It loads and functions just like the real one.

The Crosman A.I.R. 17 has broken all previous sales records for Crosman Air Guns.

This Uzi air-soft gun is another Daisy import.

and **The Command Post, Inc.**, (P.O. Box 1500, Crestview, FL 32536) also carry very complete lines of air-soft guns and accessories. Among the models sold by Foreign Exchange are air-soft copies of the Colt M-16A1 and XM177E2 that, in addition to shooting 25-caliber BBs, are capable of firing cap-loaded brass cartridges that cycle the action semi-automatically, just like the originals. Accessories include extra magazines for most of the models they sell, noise targets, plastic BBs in various colors, and special safety masks for playing survival games.

Handguns

Not much has happened with precision pistols in recent years, with a couple of notable exceptions. For each new air pistol these last five years or so, there have been at least three new air rifles. That has changed for the time being, however. Several new air pistols (not counting air-soft models) have appeared almost at once. Some manufacturers haven't been as idle as we thought.

The **Beeman** P1 (covered in some detail in last year's GUN DIGEST) is now available in 20 and 22 calibers. Barrel kits in either caliber are around $70, enabling those who already own a 177-caliber P1 to convert it to one of the larger bores; however, switching loses the dual-power feature of this pistol.

If the Beeman P1 was made to look and feel like the venerable Colt 45 Automatic, how about being able to shoot 177 pellets from the *real* Colt autoloader? Well, that's exactly what a company named **Game Blaser U.S.A., Inc.** (308 Leisure Lane, Victoria, TX 77904) has done. Their CO_2 conversion kit enables owners of the big Colt to convert their pistol to shoot 177 pellets at about 360 fps at the muzzle. The kit includes a slide with barrel to replace the Colt's. A standard 12-gram CO_2 bulb provides enough power for approximately 100 shots in this kit. Pellets are loaded singly into a pivoting chamber located toward the rear of the slide. Retail price of the German-made Blaser CO_2 conversion kit is $129.95.

Crosman Air Guns has two new CO_2 pistols, one at each end of the price scale. At the plinking level, the Crosman 338 Auto is a 20-shot BB repeater that is an exact replica of the Walther P-38. Muzzle velocities are in the 370 fps range with one 12-gram CO_2 Powerlet, which gives enough juice for up to 80 shots. Short on price and long on fun, the 338 will probably do very well among backyard plinkers of all ages.

At the world-class air pistol level, Crosman is introducing a CO_2-type powered handgun designed in cooperation with Sweden's Olympic pistol gold medalist **Ragnar Skanaker.** The Crosman-Skanaker Match pistol is a state-of-the-art machine with enough refinements to satisfy the most fastidious Olympic shooter. Its arrival signals a strong message to Feinwerkbau and Walther that Crosman is very serious.

Crosman's arch-rival in the airgun marketplace has traditionally been the **Daisy Mfg. Co.** The latter company has not been out to lunch, either, judging by the number of new airguns it has introduced in its 100th Anniversary year. Daisy has introduced the Model 92, a CO_2-powered 177 pellet semi-auto styled after the big Beretta 92 9mm pistol. It has a rifled bore and a 10-round magazine capacity. Muzzle velocity is listed at 400 fps, which is plenty for any shooting activity around the house, including "hits" on dirty rats and mice.

Many of you have no doubt heard of the so-called Survival Game, by now. All indications are that this game, which is basically a shoot-em-up duel between two opposing bands of would-be guerrillas, is really gaining in popularity all across America. The basic gun used up to now to "kill" one's opponents in this game has been the CO_2-powered Nel-Spot 007 pistol, which shoots 68-caliber water-soluble paint balls. The **National Survival Game, Inc.** (Box 1439 Main Street, New London, NH 03257), the original promoters, have just introduced their own paint pistol model, which they graphically call the Splatmaster. This new gun features a tough synthetic body with a camo finish, a new valve design, dual cocking system for fast repeat shots, and three different power settings. The Splatmaster is also much lighter than its competitors, and it comes with a set of safety goggles. Although the Splatmaster is really a special-purpose handgun, it can still be used for some wild plinking in places where the vivid paint splashes it creates don't have to be cleaned up!

Long Guns

Nearly all of the new models in this category belong to the magnum airsporter class. This means muzzle velocities of at least 800 fps in 177 caliber and upwards of 630 fps in 22 caliber.

Although a fair number of air rifles have appeared recently, there are only a few models that truly deserve to be called "new." The remainder are basically upgraded versions of existing models. In some cases, the only new thing is a different model designation.

BSA of America (P.O. Box 532277, Grand Prairie, TX 75053) is the distributor for the entire line of BSA airguns here in the U.S. One air rifle from this well-respected British company truly deserving of the adjective "new" is the Model VS2000. This full-sized adult air rifle utilizes a side-lever cocking mechanism, and has a nine-shot interchangeable magazine that enables the shooter to fire repeat shots much faster than with a conventional single-shot air rifle. The VS2000 has enough power for taking small game at up to 30 or 40 yards; like all BSA air rifles, it is available either in 177 or 22.

The BSA Airsporter "Stutzen" is basically a Mannlicher-style version of an old favorite. The full-length stock with schnabel forend imparts a definitive continental flavor to the Stutzen. Its handling characteristics, too, are just like those of a centerfire rifle. Like the full-sized Airsporter, the shorter barreled Stutzen also fits in the magnum category in both calibers.

BSA has also taken their only air pistol offering ever, the Scorpion, and converted it into a nifty little carbine by adding a synthetic thumbhole stock to it. The result is called the Shadow and looks like it will have good acceptance. The powerplant has not been altered to give higher velocities, but 500-525 fps in 177 and 400 fps or so in 22 is entirely adequate at short ranges.

Crosman Air Guns has announced they're the exclusive U.S. distributors of the **Anschütz 380 Match** rifle. This model won an impressive share of world-class matches, including the first U.S. woman's Olympic gold medal. Crosman also has the Model 3100, a spring-piston barrel cocker made in Spain. However, at this writing we only know its power will be in the medium-level airsporter class, in the 600-730 fps range in 177 caliber.

The Crosman A.I.R. 17 single-pump pneumatic rifle, I am told, seems to be breaking all previous sales records for Crosman. This AR-15/M-16 look-alike was introduced only a few months ago and Crosman apparently can't make enough of them. Although it has a smoothbore, the A.I.R. 17 can still produce creditable short-range accuracy with pellets.

In the long gun department, **Dai-**

sy's star entry is the Model 25 Centennial BB gun, a collector's edition of the all-time Daisy best-seller, the Model 25 trombone-actioned BB repeater. The Model 25 was originally introduced in 1913, and the Centennial model is an exact recreation of the original version, chosen to commemorate Daisy's 100th Anniversary in 1986. It has an American walnut stock with a bronze centennial medallion. There's no doubt that this special issue of the Model 25 will appeal to a lot of adults.

Dynamit Nobel of America needs no introduction. Their extensive line of top-quality **RWS** adult airguns and accessories has few equals. This year the long-awaited RSW Model 38 magnum air rifle seems to be finally rolling off the production line in Germany. The Model 38 comes with an elegant walnut stock, complete with pistol grip checkering and a rubber recoil pad. Muzzle velocity is reported to be in the 930-plus class in 177 caliber and around 700 fps in 22 caliber. That's a real hard-hitter.

There is a new pneumatic rifle from the Far East being imported by **Kassnar** (P.O. Box 6097, Harrisburg, PA 17112). This multi-pump rifle is made in Korea and features a wooden stock patterned after that of the famous G.I. M-1 Carbine. At this writing, we only know the muzzle velocity will put this rifle in the magnum category. Retail price is expected to be in the $110 to $125 bracket.

Marksman Products (5622 Engineer Dr., Huntington Beach, CA 92649) has come a long way. Their line of adult airguns and accessories has grown steadily and this year they have launched three new high performance airsporters. Models 55 and 70 are BSF designs now being produced by Weihrauch, after their recent acquisition of BSF. Both models are barrel cockers of magnum velocity. The Model 55 is available in 177 only; the 70 in 22. The Marksman Model 29 is none other than the BSA Meteor, also available in 22 caliber as the Model 30.

Among the many accessories sold by Marksman, there are now four new air rifle telesights. All of them feature 1-in. diameter tubes, range focus, duplex reticles, pellet drop compensators and, most important, when mounted on a spring-piston rifle, they're all recoil-proof.

There is a new company called **Spain America Enterprises, Inc.** (8581 N.W. 54 St., Miami, FL 33166) that's importing four Spanish-made spring-piston air rifles. Two of the models, the K-47 and K-92, have a

Don Robinson (Pennsylvania House, 36 Fairfax Crescent, Southowram, Halifax, W. Yorksh. HX 3 9SQ, England) works up these remarkable custom-stock air-rifles—at left is a Webley Omega in French walnut; center is a Feinwerkbau in bubinga; at right a BSF in crotch maple.

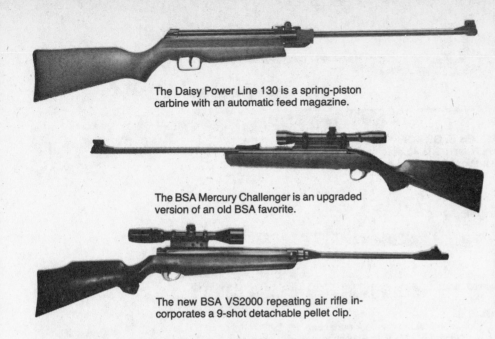

The Daisy Power Line 130 is a spring-piston carbine with an automatic feed magazine.

The BSA Mercury Challenger is an upgraded version of an old BSA favorite.

The new BSA VS2000 repeating air rifle incorporates a 9-shot detachable pellet clip.

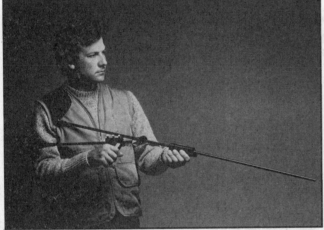

There's no doubt that the Omega File Z-Gun—a blowgun—is a deadly looking contraption. It shoots very well, too.

side-lever mechanism and are made by Norica, a company with a good track record in the airgun business. Available only in 177 caliber, with fully adjustable sights and adjustable triggers, these models go about 650 fps and carry a suggested retail price of only $77.00 — excellent value, considering the quality and features.

Miscellaneous and Special Airguns

This is the "whatever doesn't fit anything else category." And one such gun this year is called the Model SMG 17 Automatic, from **Tippmann Arms Co.** (4402 New Haven Ave., Fort Wayne, IN 46803). The model designation really gives it away, if you read it carefully. This gun is a CO_2-powered BB submachine gun with a magazine capacity for 300 BBs and a cyclic rate of fire of 600 rounds per minute. It utilizes a blowback(!) bolt system with mechanical BB feed which, according to Mr. Tippmann himself, duplicates very closely the actual firing characteristics of a real submachine gun. Muzzle velocity is indicated at around 400 fps, and the gun can be powered by either a 10-ounce bottle of CO_2 or by a special adapter that takes a standard 12-gram CO_2 cartridge. The latter no doubt will be the favored mode, due to its compactness, even if it gives fewer bursts per charge.

The prototype I saw at the SHOT Show exhibited a superb level of workmanship throughout, which reflects its projected retail price tag of $250 to $300. General specs are: overall length 20½-in. (28-in. with folding stock extended), weight 5 lbs. and barrel length 13¾-in. Of course, the Tippmann SMG 17 is completely legal to own despite its full-auto mecha-

nism, simply because it is not a firearm.

One rather unique gun which *is* classified as a firearm by BATF deserves, in my opinion, to be included in this article simply because it shoots airgun ammo. The new gun is a target pistol made by Cabañas, S.A. in Mexico and sold in the U.S. by **Mandall Shooting Supplies, Inc.** (3616 N. Scottsdale Rd., Scottsdale, AZ 85252). (See the test report on two similar Cabañas rifles in the 1985 GUN DIGEST.) The Cabañas guns are technically halfway between a rimfire cartridge gun and an airgun. They fire a slightly oversize 177 (actually around 188-in.) round lead shot powered by a 22 rimfire blank. They can also fire some of the heavier types of 177-caliber pellets, such as Beeman Kodiak and Ram Jet, quite well. The new pistol exhibits quality workmanship throughout and, like the rifles in the Cabañas line, is single shot only. Muzzle velocity is in the 1,000 fps range; however, being classified as a firearm, this pistol can be purchased only through a licensed firearms dealer.

Finally, there is the Z-Gun. This strange-looking device is really an old-fashioned dart-shooting blowgun refined and upgraded to the Nth degree by the addition of a sleek shoulder stock with pistol grip *and* a military-type sight vaguely reminiscent of those used on some anti-tank guns. I've had a chance to test the Z-Gun and can personally attest to its uncanny increase in precision over standard tube-only blowguns, at ranges of up to 15 yards. It would be hard to go back to shooting regular blowguns. The Z-Gun is produced by a company by the curious name of **The Omega File,** and at the time of this writing they're based in Orange, CA although they're scheduled to move operations to another state by the time this appears in print. Although its price is a robust $49.95, the quality, finish and superior accuracy make it a worthwhile investment for those seeking the ultimate in blowgun technology.

Already there are — as might be expected — ominous signs that some of the same forces at work trying to outlaw firearms are beginning to take pot shots at airguns, as well. Sooner or later we may have to stand and fight for our right to own and enjoy airguns. Now that we once again have a regular magazine in the U.S. devoted solely to airguns — *Airgun News & Report* (P.O. Box 711, Comanche, TX 76442) — there will be a central reporting agency. And the new magazine is, of course, itself evidence the boom (Phut? Hiss? Snap?) is here. ●

CHARLES E. GRACE
This 7x57 on a G33-40 action has Grace stock and mounts, Rabourn bolt and safety, Pell octagonal barrel, weighs 6 lb., 2 oz. as shown, including scope.

VIC OLSON
This 338 on a 98 Mauser has four-panel bolt, Model 70-type safety, is stocked from blank in English walnut with extra-capacity magazine. All work by Olson.

CUSTOM GUNS

LARRY BRACE
Stock and finish of this 7mm Remington Magnum on an FN Mauser and English walnut is by Brace; metalsmith was Stephen R. Heilman. (Mike Catlin photo)

STAN MC FARLAND
The 7mm Express Remington (280) in this G33-40 is stocked in California English hard enough to hold 32 l.p.i. checkering.

S.L. BILLEB
This darkly figured walnut surrounds a 25-06 with Hobaugh barrel and skeleton fittings done for Hank Williams, Jr.

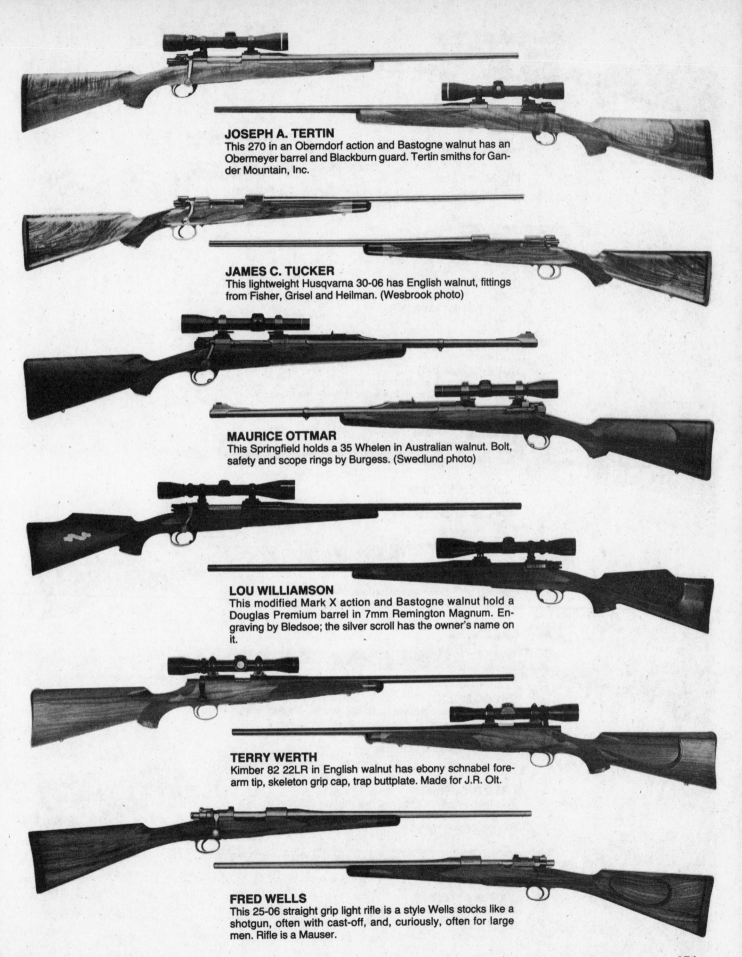

JOSEPH A. TERTIN
This 270 in an Oberndorf action and Bastogne walnut has an Obermeyer barrel and Blackburn guard. Tertin smiths for Gander Mountain, Inc.

JAMES C. TUCKER
This lightweight Husqvarna 30-06 has English walnut, fittings from Fisher, Grisel and Heilman. (Wesbrook photo)

MAURICE OTTMAR
This Springfield holds a 35 Whelen in Australian walnut. Bolt, safety and scope rings by Burgess. (Swedlund photo)

LOU WILLIAMSON
This modified Mark X action and Bastogne walnut hold a Douglas Premium barrel in 7mm Remington Magnum. Engraving by Bledsoe; the silver scroll has the owner's name on it.

TERRY WERTH
Kimber 82 22LR in English walnut has ebony schnabel forearm tip, skeleton grip cap, trap buttplate. Made for J.R. Olt.

FRED WELLS
This 25-06 straight grip light rifle is a style Wells stocks like a shotgun, often with cast-off, and, curiously, often for large men. Rifle is a Mauser.

JERE D. EGGLESTON
This Mauser goes 7 lb., 6 oz. as you see it in California circassian stock. All metal by Dave Talley.

FRANK WELLS
Pre-'64 Model 70 in 270 and English walnut make up this nice classic with full coverage wraparound checkering.

DEAN ZOLLINGER
That's a 26-in. barrel on this 257 Weatherby Magnum in a Mauser action (Fadala photo)

ROBERT M. WINTER
Here's a southpaw 375 H&H on a Mathieu action. The octagon barrel is by Ralph Carter; the wood is Bastogne; the scope is Kahles in EAW mounts.

GEORGE BEITZINGER
Winchester Model 70 375 H&H in California English has quarter-rib, barrel bands, G&H side mount—the trimmings, you could say.

GARNET BRAWLEY
This 280 on a Model 70 action wears a Marquart barrel and English walnut and an early Al Biesen checkering pattern.

GREGG BOEKE
This long Mannlicher-style stock in California English walnut embraces a Mauser in 270. Boeke did all the work.

FRED D. SPEISER
This high-wall Winchester single shot was rebarreled in 25 Krag and altered by Bill Hobaugh. Engraved by Acevado. Stock is English walnut.

JAMES A. TERTIN
SKB Skeet set—20 ga. barrel shown—was stocked in French walnut, checkered 24 l.p.i. Tertin works at Gander Mountain.

LARRY BRACE
This AE Grade Fox 16-bore got the rust blue and the English walnut in fine old style.

R.H. DEVEREAUX
This lightened SAKO L-579 has a 20-in. barrel .500-in. at the muzzle. Stock is Kevlar. It's a 284 Winchester and goes 6 lb. 2 oz. as you see it here.

SHANE CAYWOOD
A Zimmerman (Wildflecken, W. Germany) barreled action was stocked Bavarian style from the block to customer order. It's a 7x65R, engraved by Grant.

WALTER H. LITTLE
Bain & Davis in San Gabriel, CA, offers this Little stock design for the Mini-14, lowering it into the wood, altering the gun as needed.

JIM COFFIN
Red-orange French walnut was chosen for the 270 on a Mauser G33-40. Checkering is 24 l.p.i.

DAVE TALLEY
This is a shortened (⅝-in.) 1909 Peruvian Mauser turned into a G33-40 for the 250 Savage and finished up in all detail.

BUTCH SEARCY
A rebarreled Ruger over-under looks like this in the white— 375 H&H is often chosen for this conversion.

KOCH-PETERSON
This is the KP-33 Mauser, shown here in left-hand version, as made by Crandall Tool & Machine Co. in Cadillac, MI, to the Koch-Peterson specs.

RIFLE REVIEW

by LAYNE SIMPSON

Some new that's REALLY new

THERE'S lots of cream to be skimmed from the rifle churn this year. Without doubt, the most exciting news for 1986 is the return of the pre-64 Model 70 in its original form. And surprising enough, it is not being made by you-know-who. The synthetic stock bandwagon is getting quite crowded as two more major rifle makers hop aboard and several new smaller shops hang on for the ride. Left-hand shooters will rejoice at the sight of yet another big game rifle with its bolt over on their side. Also just for them is the revival of an old custom rifle not made since the 1950s.

And who says you can't shoot a 5-pound 338 Magnum and survive to tell about it? Tiny Tim? Rifles without the game-spooking sparkle are definitely in vogue and a rifle maker who has always dazzled us with brilliance has now bowed to the trend. We have another new lightweight mountain rifle and it is handsome indeed. And, if you didn't buy one of our finest bolt-action 22 rimfire sporters before it was discontinued, its reintroduction will surely dry up those tears. Its less expensive mates are back for another try, too. Last but not least, from behind the Iron Curtain comes a bolt-action rifle we've been wanting for such a long time.

So, without further ado, here is what looks good to these eyes in 1986.

Bishop/Searcy custom 35 Whelen zips the Speer 250-grain spitzer out the muzzle over 2500 fps and usually puts three into less than 1½ inches.

Alpha Arms

The Alpha Alaskan with its laminated wood stock and stainless steel barreled action is now available in a left-hand version. The same applies to Alpha's other two models the Custom and Grand Slam. Two other new options from Dallas are the synthetic stock and octagon barrel with integral quarter rib, sling swivel eye and express sights, all available on all three models. Also, Nitex and Teflon metal finishes are now offered to those who choose to spend a bit less money than the stainless steel Alpha costs.

Alpha Arms boasts of the longest list of calibers available from any rifle company, everything from 17 Remington to 458 Winchester Magnum. The 17, 222 and 223 Remington chamberings are now available in a new single shot bolt-action. Its receiver has a solid bottom for increased rigidity. Varmint shooters love the rifle while metallic silhouette shooters and benchresters are taking serious looks at the action. Four actions are now available from Alpha—short, medium, standard and magnum. All Alpha rifles now have Douglas Premium Grade barrels and come with a custom sling and hard gun case at no extra cost.

A-Square

A-Square rifles are bound to recoil less than others simply because of their great mass and weight. A heavy caliber tips the scale at 12½ pounds and the surface area of its recoil pad is about 40 percent greater than is commonly seen. Two actions are available, P-17 Enfield and Remington Model 700. Twenty-two different chamberings include such stump pullers as the 416 Hoffman, 450 Ackley Magnum, 460 A-Square and 500 A-Square. This company also manufactures solid bullets in eight calibers, from 7mm to 500. Of monolithic construction, they are true solids.

B.E.L.L.

I'll sneak this one in here because of the number of letters I have received from readers who own rifles in 25-20 single shot and in three old wildcats formed from the same case—the 17 Landis Woodsman, 22-3000 and 22-3000 R2. Winchester discontinued the 25-20 single shot many years ago and the cases are scarce as hens' lips. The last I heard they were bringing about $2 apiece from collectors. Thank goodness B.E.L.L. is now making these cases and as a bonus, they should be strong and everlasting, something that cannot be said for the old Winchester brass.

Bishop

Finally, I have my Bishop custom rifle. Actually, I should call it the Bishop/Searcy rifle since Butch Searcy performed all the metal work. Butch turned down one of Sam May's 22-in. Apex barrels to Model 70 Featherweight contour and installed a quarter rib with single leaf, custom front sight and barrel band type sling swivel stud. Next, he took a Mark X Mauser action, square-bridged it for Kimber's quick-detach rings, added a three-position Model 70 type safety and attached one of Dave Talley's custom bolt handles. Last but certainly not least, the fellows at Bishop carved out a European-style stock for the barreled action.

With an old favorite Redfield 1-4x scope, four cartridges and sling, it weighs 8½ pounds. The trim little rifle pushes Speer's 250-grain spitzer to 2540 fps and most always puts three into less than an inch and a half. It's a 35 Whelen. Nice rifle.

BRNO

Bauska Arms of Kalispell, Montana is now the U.S. importer and distributor of BRNO (pronounced BUR-no) shotguns, double rifles, bolt-action rifles and the CZ75 handgun. The Super Express over-under features Holland & Holland type sidelocks and is available in 7x65R, 9.3x47R, 375 H&H and 458 Winchester Magnum. Other niceties include engraved sideplates, select walnut, set trigger and automatic ejectors. All this for slightly over $2000.

Also available are combination guns in 5.6x52R (22 Savage) over 12-gauge; 5.6x50R Magnum over 12-

Happiness is a peaceful mountain, a big buck in yon meadow, a Timber Rattler rifle in 270 and a Schmidt & Bender scope.

The Euromark from Weatherby is a Mark V barreled action with classic-style stock—and no white line spacers.

New from Alpha Arms is the left-hand Grand Slam. The southpaw option is also available on Custom and Alaskan grade rifles.

Remington's Custom Shop now offers left-hand rifles with the short Model 700 action.

Kimber's Model 82 heavy barrel rifle offers the entire 222 Remington family of cartridges, including 221 Fireball, 223, 222 Magnum, 17 Remington, 17 Mach IV, 6.5 TCU, 7mm TCU, 5.6x50mm Magnum and 257 Kimber.

A new option for the Ruger Model 77 Ultra Light is this laminated wood stock—pre-camouflaged, one might say.

The Browning 1886 45-70 lever-action repeater was introduced at the 1986 SHOT Show with 2,000 already sold.

gauge; and 7x57R over 16-gauge. Or, for $2799, you can buy an eight-barrel set including the above three barrels plus five more chambered as follows; 7x57R over 12; 12 over 12 Field; 12 over 12 Trap; 12 over 12 Skeet and 16 over 16 Field. According to my calculator you pay about $550 for the stock, forearm, receiver and one set of barrels and a little over $300 for each additional set of barrels. Amazing!!

The famed BRNO bolt-action rifles are quite reasonably priced too, from $239 for the ZKM 452 22 Rimfire to $599 for the ZKK 602 in 8x68S, 375 H&H or 458 Winchester Magnum. In between those are the ZKB 680 Fox (22 Hornet and 222 Remington), ZKK 601 (243, 308 and 223) and ZKK 600 (30-06, 270, 7x57mm and 7x64mm). In addition, the 680, 600, 601 and 602 actions are available. With a slight

available in a limited edition series. For '86 it's the Big Horn Grade in 270 with engraving on its receiver, barrel reinforce and trigger guard. The sheep head is in 24-Karat gold.

Buckland Gun Shop

Back in October of '85, I bench-tested one of Kenny Jarrett's Timber Rattler rifles. It was a 280 Ackley Improved with fiberglass stock, Model 700 action and Hart barrel. Three-shot groups with a maximum load of IMR-4831 behind the Nosler 140-grain Ballistic Tip averaged an incredible 0.400-in. The Oehler 33 said slightly over 3100 fps. The rifle was one of his switch-barrel guns so I took the 280 barrel off and put the 220 Swift barrel on. It averaged 0.310-in. for FIVE-shot groups.

Jarret is a benchrest shooter who

antee half-inch, 5-shot groups from the one chambered to 6mm PPC.

Heym

The Paul Jaeger shop, importers of Heym bolt-action and double rifles, has relocated from Jenkinstown, PA, to Grand Junction, TN. The new SR20 Classic rifle is available with left- or right-hand action in six American calibers, eight metrics and the 375 H&H. The 5.6x57mm looks interesting. The safety has three positions and trigger options are single, single set and double set. Conetrol, Redfield, Weaver and EAW scope mounts are available. Rings are offered in three diameters, 1-inch, 26mm and 30mm.

Also new is the Heym Model 88 double rifle in 375 H&H, 458 Winchester Magnum and 470 Nitro Express.

Marlin's new Model 45 carbine shoots 45 ACPs as fast as you can pull its trigger.

modification to its bolt the 602 action will handle such boomers as the 416 Rigby and 505 Express. Les Bauska, by the way, is the fellow who makes barrels in every caliber from 17 to 600.

Browning

This is absolutely the last time I will mention in this column a new rifle that was publicized to the skies, written up in at least two major publications and even cataloged by the vendor, and was sold out before the first production rifle reached American soil. So it was with Browning's reproduction of the Winchester Model 1886 lever-action.

On the bright side, the new A-Bolt 22 Rimfire is promised to be in good supply by late '86. For the money, it's a very nice little rifle, all 5 pounds, 9 ounces of it. Its classic style stock is adorned with cut checkering and its safety is on the tang. The bolt rotates 60 degrees and both five and 15-shot detachable magazines are standard equipment.

The A-Bolt centerfire rifle is now

builds rifles for his fellow competitors and for we folk who hunt varmints and big game. His technique is the same for both types of rifles. That's why the 280 and the Swift shot so well. That's also why it takes several weeks of egg money to buy a Jarrett rifle.

Fiberlite

Fiberlite offers seven rifles with synthetic stocks in any caliber from 17 Remington to 338 Winchester Magnum. Barreled-action options include the Remington Model Seven, Remington Model 700, Winchester Model 70, Ruger Model 77 and Ruger Model 77 Ultra Light. Three grades are available, Hunter, Swat and Model 700B. The latter has a Teflon coated Model 700 action, Shilen stainless steel barrel and Shilen trigger. If you prefer, they'll do all the above to *your* barreled action.

Heckler & Koch

The new H-K heavy barrel rifle is here with fiberglass stock, Hart barrel and made in the U.S.A. They guar-

press. It is guaranteed to shoot two lefts and two rights into 2¾ inches at 100 meters.

Kimber

Kimber's block-busting news for '86 is their new big game rifle. Its action and barrel are exact duplicates of the pre-64 Model 70 Featherweight. In fact, component parts will eventually be available to those Model 70 owners in desperate need of such hard-to-find items as extractors, guard screws, firing pins and ejectors. Also, once production catches up with the initial demand, actions and barreled actions will be made available to the custom gun-making trade.

Back in January I examined three prototypes of the new Model P-64-70 rifle and they were most handsome. The barreled actions were pure Model 70 and the stocks were pure Kimber, meaning, classic beyond reproach. Both short and long action rifles will be available in several grades ranging from standard to Super America. Some of the first chamberings available will be the old classics: 270, 280,

The new Model 700 Mountain Rifle has a 22-in. barrel and weighs 6¾ pounds. It's available in 270, 280 and 30-06.

The Model 700 Custom KS has a Kevlar-reinforced fiberglass stock and weighs less than 6½ pounds. Its cartridges are 270, 280, 30-06, 7mm Remington Magnum, 300 Winchester Magnum and 375 H&H.

257 Roberts, and 7x57 as well as the wildcat 338-06.

Kimber now offers as standard the Model 84 baby Mauser rifle in the entire 222 Remington family of cartridges—222 Remington, 221 Fireball, 223 Remington, 222 Remington Magnum, 17 Remington, 17 Mach IV, 6x45mm and 6x47mm. Available on special order are the 6.5 TCU, 7mm TCU, 5.6x50mm Magnum and 257 Kimber. During the past season I took a Rio Grande gobbler and two whitetails with the 257. It works on deer only if you put your bullet where it's supposed to go.

Years ago, Lenard Brownell stocked a Kimber Model 82 in full-stock style. The new Limited Edition Model 82 Brownell is a copy of that fine rifle and will be enscribed with his name. It has a butter knife bolt handle, AAA grade walnut and express sights. Only 500 will be made.

The other Model 82s are now called 82B because of their new cocking system, faster lock time and swept back bolt handle. All Kimber stocks now have higher grade wood and custom sling swivel bases.

K.D.F.

Phil Koehne, chief honcho at Kleinguenther Distinctive Firearms now offers a fiberglass stock on the Texas-assembled rifle. He guarantees the rifle to place five shots into minute-of-angle. The receiver rests atop pillar-type bedding and lock time is said to be 1.5 milliseconds.

A new option is electroless nickel plating on all metal. The new 411 KDF Magnum cartridge is a necked-down 458 Winchester Magnum case. It propels 300- and 400-grain bullets at bone-smashing velocities. The new Recoil Arrestor muzzle brake is said to reduce its rearward shove and muzzle jump by 60 to 80 percent. The brake is also available for other rifles.

Robert Kleinguenther Co.

Robert Kleinguenther, formerly with KDF, now has his own shop in Seguin, Texas. Bob builds custom rifles around any available action, including the Models 70, 700, 77 and Mark X. Recently I tested a RKC rifle in 300 Weatherby Magnum. When shooting the 300 at benchrest its forearm rises from the front sandbag about an inch. Recoil is comparable to an 8-pound 243. That's because of his K-RT muzzle brake. He says it reduces recoil and muzzle jump by around 90 percent. I'd say his statement is no brag. On the less positive side, the brake increases muzzle blast by an earful of decibels and it kicks up dust and debris when the rifle is fired from the prone position.

Another RKC development I've been impressed with is his new Rust-Pruf metal finish. It looks like a matte blue job. I swabbed the barrel and receiver with salt water, deer blood, Coke (the old formula) and sweat and stood the rifle in a corner. It has yet to rust. Good stuff.

Kleinguenther is offering several plans: he will build you a complete rifle or he will install the K-RT, Rust-Pruf or his new weatherproof wood stock on your barreled action.

Marlin

Last year's Model 9 carbine now has a big bore mate, the Model 45 in 45 ACP. Its Micro-Groove barrel is 16½ inches short and the detachable magazine holds 7 rounds. At 6¾ pounds and 35½ inches over-all, the carbine is a lot of fun in an economical little package. The Model 15 single shot rifle has been dropped as has the Model 1894 in 41 Magnum.

The new Model 70P Papoose is a 7-shot takedown version of Marlin's best-selling Model 70 autoloader. Its 16½-in. barrel is detached by turning a threaded sleeve at the action face. It weighs a mere 3¾ pounds. Standard equipment includes a 4x scope and padded case, the latter with built-in flotation cells in case Papoose falls overboard. Considering its low price I expect this little takedown rifle will sell like syrup at a pancake show.

Remington

Lots of good things happened in Ilion since we last met. Fact is, it's difficult to decide which of the new offerings from the boys in green is the most exciting. For starters, they've unveiled the most handsome and best-feeling stock ever worn by a production grade Model 700. Called the Mountain Rifle it has a thin 22-in. barrel in 280, 270 or 30-06. Yep, the 280 Remington, one of our all-time best big game cartridges is back for another try. The Mountain Rifle is advertised at 6¾ pounds but my 280 weighs 3 ounces less.

Drop the Mountain Rifle barreled action in a Kevlar-reinforced fiberglass stock and you've got the new Model 700 Custom KS, at 6 pounds, 6 ounces. Its color is grey and its calibers are 270, 280, 30-06, 7mm Remington Magnum, 300 Winchester Magnum and 375 H&H. Presently the 700 CKS is only available by special order from Remington's Custom Shop, which tells me that you can probably get other calibers as well, like the 22-250, 223 and 6mm Remington, for examples.

Several of my elk hunting buddies will be happy to see the 8mm Remington Magnum back in the lineup. It's now available in two versions from Tim McCormack and his fellow artisans in the Custom Shop. Both are Model 700 Safari grade rifles, one with Monte Carlo stock, the other with classic wood. And speaking of the Model 700 Classic rifle, with this and one other exception it has been dropped. The limited edition Classic is still available, this year in 264 Winchester Magnum. When do we get the 8x57mm, 6.5 Remington Magnum, 338-06 and 35 Whelen?

Last year I and hundreds of other varmint shooters asked for the Sportsman 78 in 223 Remington. Now

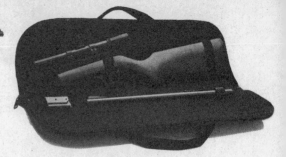

The Marlin Papoose is a cute little 22 takedown rifle that comes in a case that floats.

The Browning A-Bolt in 22 rimfire is a nice little rifle for the money.

we've got it. Also, left-hand shooters had been asking for short-action Model 700s from the Custom Shop. Now they can have them.

Last but certainly not least, Remington is back in the bolt-action 22 rimfire business. Remember the 40-XB sporter? It's back, but now it's called the 40-XR and this time it's a single shot rather than a repeater. The Grade II I examined was most handsome and I expect Grades I, III and IV are likewise. Also reintroduced for '86 are the mini-788 rifles, probably the strongest 22 rimfires ever built. The Model 541-T is the deluxe grade with walnut stock and cut checkering. The Sportsman 581-S is the same without the frills.

Royal Arms

The old Mathieu action that Roy Weatherby used in building left-hand rifles prior to introducing his Mark V is once again available. Royal Arms calls it the Model 80 action. Their other two custom turn-bolt actions are the Model 70 single shot and Model 80 with three-position safety. Also available is the BRNO magnum Mauser action with double square bridge receiver.

Their Trophy Hunter rifle is the Mark X barreled action in a Kevlar reinforced fiberglass stock. Its calibers are 270 and 30-06. The 375 H&H and 458 Winchester magnum rifles have the BRNO action and express open sights.

Ruger

The Model 77 International with Mannlicher-type stock is now available in a long action version. Its new cartridges are 270 and 30-06. New chamberings for the No. 1B single shot are the 270 and 300 Weatherby Magnums. And, the XGI, it is said, will eventually be available in 243 Winchester.

Back in January, Ruger displayed pilot models of a new option for the Models 77 Ultra Light, 77/22 and 10/

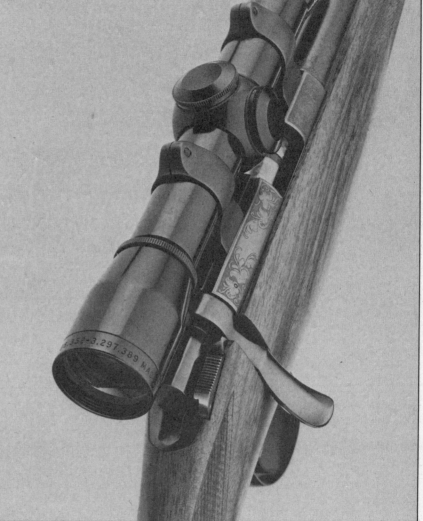

Close-up of the Kimber Model 82 Brownell Grade showing the butter knife bolt handle and engraved receiver.

22 rifles. All wore stocks of laminated wood. And the Number 3 single shot has quietly disappeared from Ruger's latest catalog. Must be gone for now.

Savage

The Savage Model 110 is now available with a laminated wood stock. It looks quite similar to the stock now offered by Ruger. Both look quite similar to the stock in Fajen's catalog.

Thompson Center

The TCR '83 shooting system, as T/C calls their single shot rifle, now offers the versatility of ten interchangeable barrels. The 22 Hornet, 223, 22-250, 243, 270, 7mm Remington Magnum, 222, 308 and 30-06 barrels are joined by a new mate, the 12-gauge slug barrel. The new barrel has open sights but you can mount a scope

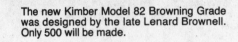

The new Kimber Model 82 Browning Grade was designed by the late Lenard Brownell. Only 500 will be made.

The Remington 40-XR 22 rimfire sporter is back, this time as a single shot only. This is the Grade II.

Back for another try is the Remington Model 541-T, probably the strongest 22 Rimfire ever built.

The Remington Model 581 Sportsman has the same barreled action as the 541-T but a hardwood stock and no frills.

on its monobloc, just like the other barrels. It's 22 inches long and cylinder bored as a barrel for shooting slugs ought to be. The chamber takes 2¾-in. shells and the barrel requires a special forend because of its larger diameter.

The Contender Carbine family keeps on growing, too. Joining the 22 LR, 22 Hornet, 223, 7mm TCU, 7-30 Waters and 30-30 are new 21-in. barrels in 222, 357 Maximum and 410 gauge, the latter with vented rib. Now all they need do is add a sling swivel stud to the TCR '83 and Contender Carbine buttstocks and an Uncle Mike's barrel band out front.

Ultra Light Arms

New for '86 is the Ultra Brake, developed by U.L.A. for reducing recoil and muzzle jump (in case you muster up enough nerve to squeeze the trigger on their 5-pound 338 Winchester Magnum). With 2½x Mini in U.L.A. mounts, nylon sling and three 250-grain loads the Model 28 rifle weighs less than seven pounds. That checks out at over a ¼-ton of punch for every pound of rifle you carry. The cute little beast is also available in three other new magnum chamberings—264

Winchester, 7mm Remington and 300 Winchester.

For those who prefer the old standards, the new Model 24 is available in 25-06, 270, 280, 338-06, 30-06 and 280 Ackley Improved, with 22 or 24-in. barrel. New chamberings for the Model 20 short action rifle are 22 Hornet, 17 Remington and two fine old wildcats, the 257 and 7x57 Ackley Improved. Another new item is the solid-bottomed single shot benchrest action with bolt face for the 222, 308 and PPC size cartridges. It's practically identical to the Remington 40x action but weighs about 12 ounces less.

Some hunters don't like the safety on late Model 700s because when on safe it doesn't lock the bolt from rotation. The U.L.A. two-position, three-function safety is one answer. It replaces the Model 700 safety lever. Back is safe, forward is fire and down unlocks the bolt so the rifle can be unloaded with the safety on. It will cost you $20 for the safe lever, or $35 installed. It also works on the Models 600, 660, 721, 722 and Seven triggers.

USRAC

Remember the Winlite shotgun with its barrel wrapped in several

miles of fiberglass filament? The scattergun is long dead but the name is back, except this time it's a Model 70 option. It's called Winlite because of the fiberglass stock. The color is brown and the 270 and 30-06 with 22-in. barrels weigh 6½ pounds. The 7mm Remington, 300 Winchester and 338 Winchester Magnums are 2 inches longer and weigh 7 pounds.

A new cartridge for the Model 70 Featherweight is the 6.5x55 Swedish Mauser. Norma and Old Western Scrounger sell the ammunition. Last year USRAC made a limited number of Model 70 Featherweights in what they call a legendary caliber, the 280 Remington. During '86, a few Model 70 carbines will be chambered to another one, the fine little 250-3000 Savage. The 358 Winchester next year?

The 308 joins the 25-06, 270 and 30-06 as a new choice in the Model 70 XTR Sporter. And, in case you've forgotten, any Model 70 in the USRAC line is available without the stock.

The new 120th Anniversary Commemorative carbine in 44-40 is a beautiful little Model 94 variation. Its receiver has the horse and rider and a gold etched portrait of Oliver Winchester. A new option with the Ranger Model 94 carbine are scope mounts and a 4x Bushnell scope. The quick-handling Trapper has a new cartridge too, the 44 Remington Magnum. Its magazine will hold nine 44 Specials, if you prefer.

Have you tried the 7-30 Waters? Mine is the most accurate Model 94 I have ever fired. Knocks a whitetail silly too.

Weatherby

Those jet-setters who were taken aback when Roy produced the Fibermark and Fiberguard rifles are in for another surprise. The new Euromark is Roy's first Mark V with a stock more classic in style. The highly figured American walnut stock has a hand-rubbed oil finish, solid recoil pad, cut checkering and ebony fore-end tip, all without a trace of white-line spacers. However, the time-proven Mark V action and white diamond inlet in the grip cap keep us from forgetting the rifle is Weatherby.

The Euromark also has a checkered bolt knob and the nicest checkering on any Weatherby rifle. It is fine in line and without the skip-a-line spacing. In fact, the Euromark is the best looking rifle in Roy Weatherby's stable. All the Weatherby big game cartridges are there, from 240 to 460, plus the 30-06. ●

THE WORLD'S BEST-KEPT
GUN SECRET

Left to right: 234 Sisk Magnum; 23 Ackley Long; 234 RCBS Huntington; 23 Ackley Short; 234/22 High Power. All loaded with 76-grain Barnes bullets.

by JOHN A. MASTERS

EXAMINE THE gun literature, and you can find information on bores from 17 to 30 caliber without a great deal of trouble. Except 23 caliber.

When you do find dope on the 23, you find it in the reports of such old masters as Ralph Sisk, P. O. Ackley and Fred Huntington, all men who know case design, bullet design, and both rifle and cartridge performance. There is always an attempt by writers to find who "originated" a particular cartridge. Ralph Sisk, in this case, was among the first to make 23-caliber bullets in the early 1950s. He built a rifle for a cartridge he called the 234 Sisk Magnum, a necked down and shortened 300 H&H Magnum.

I was in Iowa Park, where the Sisk factory was located, in about 1952. While gathering material for a series of stories I did on Sisk and his bullets, he introduced me to the cartridge. His frank and avowed purpose was to get around—just barely around—the restrictions against 22-caliber centerfire rifles in the Western states.

Sisk built his 23 bullets with thick jackets, to insure that they would hold together and expand, rather than disintegrate, as high-speed varmint bullets are designed to do. He felt that his 75-grain 23-caliber bullet, moving in excess of 3500 fps, was sufficiently strong medicine for anything up through elk, and proceeded to prove

EDITOR'S NOTE: It is with considerable regret we announce that John Masters died March 21, 1986. The circumstances were such that he could call to say good-bye and he did, which made for an interesting phone call, which was normal for John.
K.W.

Ralph Sisk's own 234 Magnum on Mauser action which more or less started Masters.

234/22 High Power on 99 Savage has a Fajen stock and fore-end, and now three barrels.

The 234 RCBS Huntington on Remington 722 action and stock gets Masters' vote as the best all-around 23.

it to be so.

P. O. Ackley issued his first reloading manual in 1959, and therein he had loads for two 23-caliber cartridges, which he called the 23 Short and the 23 Long. Since he had already developed the cartridge designs and had worked up and tested the loads, it is a reasonable assumption that he was working on the 23 quite some time before 1959. Fred Huntington met up with Sisk in Douglas, Wyoming, saw his rifle and became interested in the caliber. The best he recalls, the meeting was in the "early 1950s."

It is known that Gardiner, Barnes and others made bullets in the caliber. In Huntington's carefully kept records, Hemsted bullets are mentioned. These historical notes are accurate, but make no claim to being complete.

I fell into Ralph Sisk's rifle early in 1983 by the simple expedient of visiting a gun shop the day someone traded it in. It came complete with a set of dies made by Huntington in 1961, 40 fire-formed cases, and a single box of Barnes 76-grain bullets. The rifle had

been built on a magnum Mauser action, with a 25-inch heavy sporter barrel. I topped it with a Redfield mount and a fine old Stith 6x Bearcub Double that has a very fine crosswire.

The boxes the cases came in were labelled "55 grains of H-450 and a 76 grain bullet." After scouring the area, I finally found three pounds of H-450, which is no longer made. I started at 45 grains, and worked up in one grain increments until I reached 55. By the usual pressure indications, that was still a mild load, but it was a superbly accurate one. After talking with Bruce Hodgdon, I learned that his H-4831 had about the same burning rate, and could likely be used with equally good results. As the table shows, the charge weights of H-450 and H-4831 are quite similar.

Knowing that just 100 bullets wouldn't even get me off the ground, I began the search for more, and struck pay dirt at once. Randy Brooks of Barnes Bullets had a thousand on hand, and he also had a burning interest in an FN Mauser 30-06 I owned. We made an old-fashioned hoss trade, and my bullet problem was whipped.

After studying Ackley's old manual, and talking with Fred Huntington about his own experiments with the 23, I decided to build another rifle. Fred knew Bill Hobaugh of Phillipsburg, Montana, would build 23 barrels. A single phone call took care of getting the barrel underway.

In the meantime, I started working up H-4831 loads for the Sisk magnum, and began the job of making more cases. It turned out that Ralph Sisk had come very close to the 264 Winchester Magnum with his case design. All I had to do was run 264 Magnum cases in the die and trim them.

I was describing this process to Del Lippard of Capital Gunsmiths in Austin, Texas.

"What bore diameter did you say the gun was," he asked me.

"The bullets mike .234-in., and I think the bore diameter is .230-in.," I told him.

He went to the back of his shop and rummaged around in a rack of old barrels for perhaps 15 minutes. When he returned, he had a Savage 99 takedown barrel that was stamped "22HP," but a 227 Hornady bullet designed for the 22 High Power would drop right through it.

Del formed a lead slug and rammed it through the bore. His mike told the story: the barrel was 23 caliber. It had come in with several dozen other barrels he had gotten in a lot he had purchased when a local elderly gunsmith retired and sold out. We then poured a chamber cast, and found that the chamber was for the High Power case. The frosting on the cake came when that barrel easily fitted and headspaced to my own takedown 22 High Power Savage Model 99.

The exterior of the barrel has some service marks but the bore was near perfect. It had been rebored fairly recently, it seemed, but where and by whom, we'll never know.

An interesting thing about the gun is that with the 234 barrel in place, I can shoot regular 22 High Power loads. The 228 bullet evidently upsets enough to engage the rifling. While the rifle with either barrel is capable of only hunting accuracy, it is my favorite companion on a lot of trips. With the 234 76-grain bullet at a respectable 2800 fps, I can take deer, antelope or javelina easily at up to 150 yards.

To round out this takedown gun, I have sent a shot out 22 Savage barrel to Robert West in Eugene, Oregon. He is going to rebore that one to 25 caliber and rechamber, or at least clean up the chamber, to produce a 25-35 barrel. Thus I will have three barrels to shoot off a single stock, action and fore-end.

Redfield once made a "Little Blue Peep" that popped up on the back of their scope mount base when you removed the scope in its rings. A call to Redfield, and a search by their Customer Service Department uncovered one of the peeps, which I have installed on the back of the mount. When I get my 25-35 barrel, I will sight in the peep, and be able to quickly change to any one of three barrels. This rig rides in a fitted case in my old '72 Scout, known as the "Wander Wagon." I have ammo, all the barrels, and a small spanner wrench all in the same case.

Actually, the deadliest of the three cartridges is the 234. I had a good chance to find out how deadly shortly after I got the barrel and worked up loads.

A local rancher had a flock of Spanish goats, which he ran in some really rough hill and canyon country. He used one of his billys as a Judas goat when he was loading sheep, and the critter stayed around a long time and got to be a very large Spanish goat indeed. But he also got very smart; when my friend would round up his goats, the old billy would refuse to be penned and, time after time, broke free with other goats following and headed back into the brush.

I was given the job of rubbing out the old rebel. With the 99 Savage and the 234 barrel, I spent the better part of three days in a 400-acre pasture before I brought the rogue down. The shot was about 80 yards, through a thin screen of underbrush. I drilled him solidly in the boiler room—the heart-lung area—and he went down like a pole-axed steer. He made one feeble attempt to regain his feet.

He weighed just over 200 pounds, which in my judgment put him in the mule deer class so far as required killing power is concerned. The Barnes 76-grain semi-spitzer went in between ribs, made a mess of the lungs and the lower part of the heart, and made a 50-cent piece-sized exit, taking a piece of rib with it. Without question, the same hit would have taken a deer, an antelope, or a mule deer just as certainly.

Fred Huntington shares that opinion of his own particular choice, his 243 RockChucker case necked to 234. Fred has perhaps the most extensive hunting experience with the cartridge and bullet, and he has furnished the writer with massive laboratory testing results reflecting extensive development work.

Ackley's 230 Short is substantially the 250-3000 case necked down and blown out slightly. It seems from his data to do just about as well as the Huntington case velocity wise. His 230 Long is a necked-down and shortened 30-06, which is very similar to a case Huntington experimented with and concluded was no advantage over his necked-down 6mm Remington case.

The Sisk case—the one I started with—is notably over bore capacity.

Masters takes his friends to the range in batches and this is the 23-caliber batch with the Savage 99 waiting its turn.

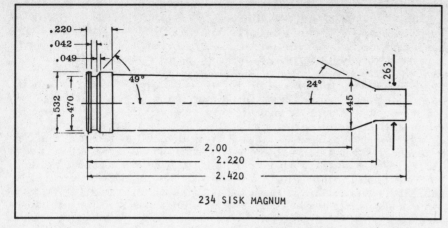

234 SISK MAGNUM

Sisk left the taper in his belted 234 Magnum. There's all the powder capacity the 23-caliber bore can stand.

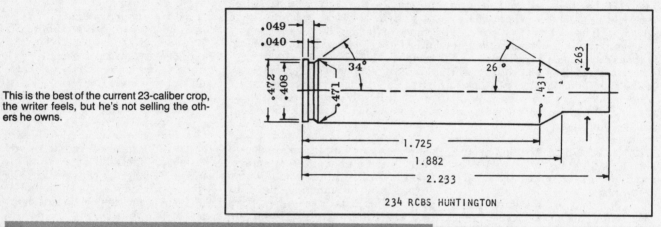

This is the best of the current 23-caliber crop, the writer feels, but he's not selling the others he owns.

234 RCBS HUNTINGTON

BALLISTICS AND LOADING DATA

Cartridge	Bullet	Powder/Weight	Velocity	Remarks	Source
234 Sisk	76 Barnes	55/H-450	3688	Mild load	Author
234 Sisk	76 Barnes	54/H-4831	3600	Mild load	Author
23 Long					
Ackley	60	45/4064	3989	Handbook for	Ackley
	70	47/4350	3578	Shooters and	Ackley
	75	46/4350	3509	Reloaders	Ackley
				(1959)	
234 Huntington					
RCBS	72 Gardiner	47/H-380	3600	Test load*	Huntington
	76 Gardiner	46/H-380	3380	Test load*	Huntington
	79 Hemsted	43/4320	3500	Test load*	Huntington
	83 Hemsted	40/4310	3100	Test load*	Huntington
23 Short					
Ackley	60	39/4320	3597	Handbook for	Ackley
	60	47/4831	3950	Shooters and	Ackley
	70	47/4350	3578	Reloaders	Ackley
	75	45/4831	3187	(1959)	Ackley
	75	46/4350	3509		Ackley
234/22 HP	76 Barnes	28/4895	2800	Necked down 25-35 case	Author
	76 Barnes	28/4320	2812	Necked down 25-35 case	Author
	76 Barnes	29/H-380	2833	Necked down 25-35 case	Author

*All test loads fired from a 23-inch Hobaugh barrel on a Mauser action, and a 1:10 twist. The loads are for the particular gun tested, and should be approached from below and worked up to in half-grain increments.

Ralph Sisk himself told me he suspected barrel life would be in the neighborhood of 300 rounds.

So my new Hobaugh barrel, fitted to a Remington 722 action, is chambered for the Huntington case.

I now feel I have three rifles in 23 caliber that will adequately cover the full capability of the bore size, truly "big game" rifles.

The 99 Savage with the 234 barrel in place is an excellent light rifle, capable of taking the whitetails and javelina that represent the greatest part of my hunting.

The 234 Huntington cartridge will do quite well for long range whitetail hunting, but it comes into its own in the antelope and mule deer country of the Big Bend of Texas. Fred Huntington's carefully documented loads indicate a consistent 3400-3500 fps from the cartridge, and with the beautifully constructed, thick-jacketed Barnes bullets, that is enough medicine for a 350-400-yard shot on either animal.

The Sisk 234 Magnum is a real barn-burner. Ackley rates a 23-caliber of its class, using properly constructed bullets, as superior to the 25-caliber magnums as a long range big game rifle, and he contends, again emphasizing proper bullet design, that the cartridge is sufficient for any

North American big game. I firmly agree, with one reservation. I would prefer a bigger rifle on any dangerous game.

Last fall, in Biddie Martin's country bordering on Hell's Half Acre in the Big Bend Region of Texas, I made the second longest shot I have ever made with a gun and it was a 23.

Biddie was guiding me along the one watered canyon he has on the place. We were on the shallow sloping side of the canyon, and the opposite side rose from the trickle of water in steps or ledges covered with *sotol*—the favorite food of mule deer. There

Spotting while the rangemaster tries out the 234 RCBS on a metallic ram target, Masters was told it equals the 7mm-08 in power on the target.

were clumps of greasewood, agarita, and a stunted mountain juniper.

We stopped on a point, where we had the sun quartering in from our left, got out and stretched our legs, and I fired up the little Coleman one-lunger and started water for a pot of coffee. Biddie leaned over the hood of the Wander Wagon, and glassed the opposite side of the canyon. He found the buck lying bedded down in the shade of a juniper clump.

All we could see was one antler, but we made it to have 6 points, and where the boss of the antler joined the skull looked as big as my arm. I studied him through the 6x Stith. The buck was unaware of us, and there was no hurry in the shot. Biddie and I guessed together he was between four and five hundred yards, but as we looked and thought about it, we shortened it up to maybe 375 yards.

The buck then made it easy. I was down over the hood, legs spread, with

my hunting coat as a solid pad. He unhurriedly stood up, stretched, and unconcernedly relieved himself. I was sighted in an inch and a half high at a hundred yards. I laid the horizontal hair halfway between the point of his elbow and the line of his back, and squeezed the shot off.

There is virtually no recoil to the rifle. I never lost him in the scope, but as I automatically jacked another round home, I knew it wouldn't be necessary. The buck had "popped his feet together" as a hard-hit animal often does, and had gone down solidly. We watched him until we were sure he was dead before retracing our route to get to the floor of the canyon and come up alongside.

The entrance hole was directly behind the elbow; there was no exit hole. I found the bullet under the skin on the other side at a slightly raking angle. It had opened up to about two diameters, and when weighed still had 67 of its original 76 grains. The little slug had literally exploded the heart.

Now I know 23-caliber rifles have several desirable things in common:

The recoil, even in the Sisk Magnum, is negligible. The muzzle blast is not severe.

And in actual drop tests fired over a long period of time, I have found Ackley was right. The 234 Sisk Magnum is flatter shooting than even the 250 Magnums. Admittedly, we are talking inches and fractions of an inch, but it shoots flatter, nevertheless.

And it shoots flatter than the factory 6mm cartridges. Or even Roy

Weatherby's 240 Magnum, which is a fine cartridge indeed.

If you don't mind making up wildcat cases, working up loads, and getting your reloading supplies from less convenient sources, the 23 caliber is your baby.

I think Fred Huntington's cartridge, which is simply the 6mm Remington necked down and blown out to a slightly sharper shoulder, is the finest of the lot. Ralph Sisk's magnum has a lot of emotional appeal, but the gain in velocity, while considerable, is bought at the expense of short barrel life.

Ackley's 23 Long is in the same class with the Huntington cartridge, and his 23 Short is an absolutely perfect choice for a light rifle that a woman or a young hunter will find comfortable to handle and shoot. The 234 based on the 22 Savage High Power Case came about simply because I fell into the barrel. It is useful, but not a cartridge I would start out to build a rifle for.

What I am going to do next is something only a died-in-the-wool rifle nut would understand: I am going to make a 23-caliber rifle up on the new 22 Cheeta case that Jim Carmichel and Fred Huntington sort of co-authored. The use of a small rifle primer in the 308 BR case evidently offers some real advantages. Carmichel reports a dramatic gain in velocity consistency, and in the early going, feels there is some evidence of extended barrel life. And all because of the more uniform "cooler" ignition deriving from the small rifle primer.

If you decide you want a 23 caliber, Bill Hobaugh of Phillipsburg, Montana, will build the barrel, and fit and chamber it to your action. He can do about anything you want in the way of a cartridge. Robert West of Eugene, Oregon, will likewise chamber and fit, but you have to get your own barrel. He doesn't offer the 23 bore. Randy Brooks of Barnes Bullets will supply your bullet needs. And there may be others. Fred Huntington is still in it with his Huntington Specialties Company, and he will supply dies for anything you choose.

It may cost a bit more to get the rifle and supplies laid down, but like the lady in the cosmetic ads on TV—it's worth it. You will have a nearly unique rifle caliber. You will have a rifle and cartridge that has been used by the most renowned of the old masters. And you will have a rifle of low recoil, low muzzle blast, but with a tremendous trajectory and an awesome killing power.

That's a lot to get in just one rifle. ●

HANDGUNS TODAY:

SIXGUNS AND OTHERS

by HAL SWIGGETT

Never before have I seen so much to write about: Ruger has a new double-action revolver; Mitchell Arms sells an all-new single shot; Baford Arms also has an all-new single shot; Manurhin (long noted for fine autoloading pistols) is showing a double-action revolver; Texas Longhorn Arms—another all new single shot pistol; Smith & Wesson has commemoratives galore; Thompson/Center shows new innovations; Colt has a new revolver; it goes on and on—so:

Ruger

It's been a busy year for Sturm, Ruger & Company. A handful of new revolver listings: GP-100 double action, blue Redhawk, Single Six Bisley, Blackhawk Bisley and Super Redhawk. Counting them takes five fingers.

The very special GP-100 is covered at length in TESTFIRE, so look for that detailed description on page 212.

That Redhawk in blue is a welcome sight because there are those among us (I'm a charter member) who still believe guns should be blue. Put another way, we are not enamored by stainless steel and all its brilliance in spite of satin finishing. I've spent a good deal of time with a 5½-in. 41 blue Redhawk, serial number 501-72103 for the curious, and am discovering those touters of the 41 Magnum might not be wrong after all. More about that at another time.

Bisley models were announced last year but not held in hand for honest reporting. Two sizes are offered. The small frame Single Six houses either 22 Long Rifle or 32 Magnum. My test version is 22 Long Rifle. I've been hard-pressed to find a reason for it being offered with only a fixed sight and now find the new catalog makes both fixed and adjustble sights available. Thank you S, R & C. Trigger pull on number 261-03035 is barely over 5 pounds. The "fixed" rear sight is that for elevation only. Windage is quickly handled. Barrel length is 6½ inches and the one I'm shooting weighs 42 ounces. It has "killed" tiny rocks at 15 to 20 paces and football-sized specimens out to near 100 which means it would easily do the same on small game.

The Bisley Blackhawk comes in 357 Magnum, 41 Magnum and 44 Magnum. Test revolver number 85-44678 is a 44 and weighs 49 ounces. Only 7½-inch barrels are offered. A bit more description here and it fits both Bisleys. The trigger guard has been altered a bit, the hammer is set lower, the grip frame given a distinctive look and lengthened. Grip panels are Goncalo Alves. Though it is labeled Blackhawk the frame lays claim to being Super Blackhawk and says so on the side. Trigger pull is typically Ruger, heftier than necessary but within the standards established for their guns.

There is still another option: both

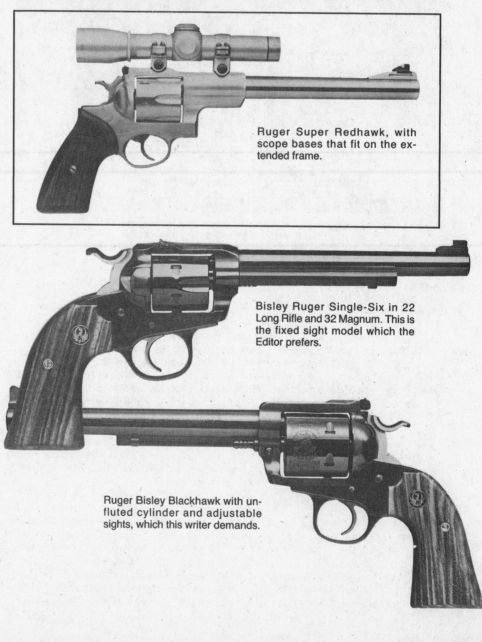

Ruger Super Redhawk, with scope bases that fit on the extended frame.

Bisley Ruger Single-Six in 22 Long Rifle and 32 Magnum. This is the fixed sight model which the Editor prefers.

Ruger Bisley Blackhawk with unfluted cylinder and adjustable sights, which this writer demands.

Single Six and Blackhawk are offered with fluted cylinders or with unfluted cylinders roll marked in a classic styling reminiscent of the turn-of-the-century Bisley era.

Super Redhawk is self-describing. It is a Super Redhawk. It has all of the design features of GP-100, including the live rubber wood-paneled grip plus an extended length frame that serves as the scope mount base. There is no rib on the barrel. Two barrel lengths are available: 7½-in. revolvers weigh 53 ounces, 9½-in. are 5 ounces heavier. The stainless steel Super Redhawk is satin polished. You are going to like this Super Redhawk. If you shoot with scopes, you are going to love it. The rear scope base sits directly over the center of the cylinder, which places the center of the scope over the forcing cone, which means it is a balancing beauty.

will be chambered. The gun, according to Gwinn, is virtually indestructible due to its 3 square inches of locking surface.

The "Mean Little Machine" shown in Houston at the SHOT Show was scope mounted. Conventional sights are also offered. The price—an amazing $175 with 10-in. barrel. Extra barrels will be $60 to $75 according to length.

Don Mitchell's superbly reproduced "gun that won the West" single actions have a bright blue finish with color case-hardened forged steel frames with solid brass backstraps and trigger guards. Calibers are 22, 357 Magnum, 44 Magnum and 45 Colt. Barrel lengths are 4¾ to 7½ inches except for the Special Silhouette Model which is 10 or 12 inches. This one also has an 18-in. barrel available along with a shoulder stock.

3½-in. barrel is chambered to take 44 Special and 2½-in. 410. If that doesn't get your attention lend your eyes to the rest of the story as Paul Harvey might say. Insert barrels are simply dropped in, same as a cartridge, thereby changing caliber. Some are shorter than the host barrel and others the same length or longer. Yes, longer by 2⅝ inches. These lengthier versions are ingeniously designed, —are you ready—to function as a scope mount base. The scope, —Baford uses a tiny Hutson 1¾x—attaches to the mount using the rail system and a single screw. The base of this rail has a hole through which the barrel goes then a cap that screws on the threaded barrel end, and firmly snugs the parts together. Strange as it sounds it seems to work.

Scoped barrels are 22 Long Rifle, 22 Magnum, 25 Auto, 32 (it doesn't say

Here are the differences between the Super Blackhawk and Bisley: different grip shape, hammer, trigger guard and trigger. Bisley on left.

Ruger GP-100 double-action revolver, first in the announced "New Generation."

Manurhin M73 Sport 5¼-in. 32 S&W double-action revolver is beautifully made, polished to a very fine blue finish and shoots.

which one), and 32 Magnum. Conventional barrels include 22 Short, 22 Magnum, 25 Auto, 32 ACP, 32 S&W, 32 Magnum, 380 Auto, 38 Super Auto, 38 Special, 38 S&W, 30 Luger and 9mm.

Accuracy with the scoped barrel will surprise you. At least it surprised me. The only scope barrel submitted for testing was 22 Magnum and it easily handled soft drink cans out to 25 yards. The others? There is no way to know because there are no sights on Thunder. Point and shoot. The octagon barrel is grooved full length on top, for looks I guess. I find it possible to look down the top with none of the barrel visible then lining up the target with the center of the hammer and hitting closer than I had any right to on targets at 10 steps. I had only four

Do you agree that Ruger has given us a handful this time around?

Mitchell Arms

Mean Little Machine! That's what Mack Gwinn, designer of Mitchell Arms new single shot pistol, calls his handiwork. It's different. That's for sure. It looks mean. That too is for sure. Interchangeable barrels of most any caliber, rifle or handgun are or

Baford Arms

"The World's Most Versatile Compact Firearm Capable Of Firing 15 Different Calibers From The Same Derringer." That is the claim of Baford Arms for their Thunder derringer. Weighing in at 8½ ounces, that's right, a fraction over ½-pound, the extra barrels to test; 32, 9mm and 22 plus the 22 Magnum scope barrel and, of course, 44 Special and 410 2½-in. in the host. May I put it this way? The short barrels are not intended as one-holers.

Manurhin

There is a new kid on the block. Manurhin, long noted for making those fine Walther pistols, now offers a top quality double-action revolver. Their line is complete in Europe but for import to the United States only the MR 73 Sport is being made available. Calibers are 32 Long and 357 Magnum. Barrel lengths are 4, 5¼, 6 and 8 inches. GUN DIGEST's test revolver, serial number Y31858, is in 32 Long, with 5¼-in. barrel and weighs 37½ ounces. The ejection rod is enclosed in a full length under-barrel lug that not only adds weight but a handsome appearance. The undercut front sight is of target style, sits on a serrated ramp which is atop a full-length solid rib. The rear sight blade is exceptionally wide, features a square notch, is fully adjustable and, like the front, is finished flat black.

Cylinder lockup is extremely tight. Single-action trigger pull is 56 ounces and crisp as breaking glass. Double-action a custom-like 8¼ pounds.

I've had this revolver only a few days and fired just one 50-round box of Federal match wadcutters through it. Accuracy is superb as I had expected since the overall fit and finish would allow nothing else. Something kept gnawing at me. It was as if I had handled this double-action revolver before yet it was entirely new to me—then came the dawn. I do not mean to detract from the beautifully manufactured Korth revolver made in Germany and priced to sell for at least twice the price but this Manurhin feels and sounds (that's right—sounds—because it has a distinctive ring to its falling hammer in dry firing) for all the world like my Korth.

Texas Longhorn Arms

"Home of the right-hand single action" is the way Bill Grover describes his Texas Longhorn Arms gunmaking company. At the moment we're not interested in his made-for-right-handed-shooters single-action but an entirely new single shot 22 pistol he is putting out. It's so new it doesn't have a name. All I've seen are the two prototypes currently in existence though production will be well under way as you read this. As for the right-handed single-action, see page 172.

Made from 17-4 P.H. stainless steel

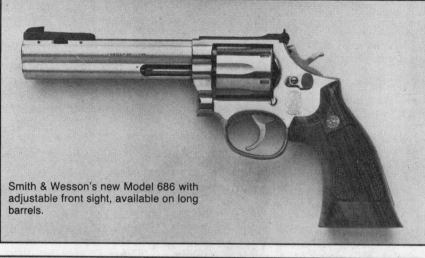

Smith & Wesson's new Model 686 with adjustable front sight, available on long barrels.

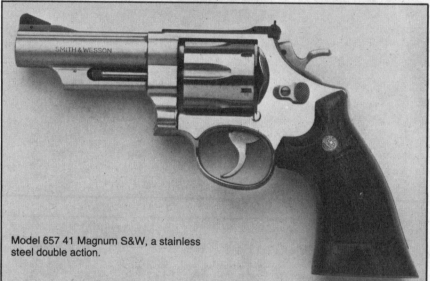

Model 657 41 Magnum S&W, a stainless steel double action.

with satin finish, the weight, with 6-in. barrel, is 17 ounces. Front to back it is 8½ inches and stands 3½ inches tall. Both prototypes let off cleanly at 3 pounds trigger pull. There is a transfer bar safety system and a spring-loaded shell extractor. The 1-piece grip is fancy walnut and made for shooting with either hand. The fore-end is also fancy walnut. Grover makes all his own stocks.

Keith DeHart is the designer. He and Grover teamed up to put this little jewel on the market. Each pistol will be machined from a block of steel and all parts hand-fit to perfection. This little rascal intrigues me to the point I have Number 1 and Number 2 on order. Number 1 will be 22 Long Rifle and Number 2 22 Magnum. These are the only cartridges for which it will be chambered.

Smith & Wesson

Smith & Wesson is loaded with goodies, particularly for the reminisc-ing shooter, though we ought not forget three new revolver models.

Model 657, a 41 Magnum, is stainless steel with a blue micrometer click rear sight. Up front there is a serrated black ramp. The target hammer, smooth combat trigger and checkered Goncalo Alves target stocks add to its distinctive good looks. Barrel lengths are 4, 6, and 8⅜ inches. Weight with 6-in. barrel is 48 ounces.

Models 586 and 686 are 357 Magnum with semi-target hammer and smooth combat trigger. Stocks are checkered Goncalo Alves. The rear sight is S&W micrometer click with optional plain or white outline notch. The front sight is four-position positive click adjustable. Barrel lengths are 4, 6, and 8⅜ inches; however the four-position front sight is available only on the two longer versions. Model 586 is S&W Bright Blue. Model 686 is satin stainless steel.

S&W special editions are several. First, because he was a very dear friend, is the Elmer Keith Commemorative Model 29. This is a 4-in. S&W Bright Blue with red ramp front sight and adjustable rear with white outline. Keith's portrait and signature are on the right sideplate. Rounded service stocks are featured—Keith's preference—rather than customary target stocks. There are two editions. Only 2,500 total will be made. The Deluxe version, numbered EMK001 through EMK0100, is more ornate and wears ivory stocks. There is considerably more gold embellishment than on the standard version though both have Elmer's portrait and signature in 22K gold-plate. They read "Elmer Keith Commemorative 44 Magnum 1899-1984" on the barrel and "1st Outstanding Handgunner—Salmon—Idaho" on the cylinder. Standard models will be numbered EMK0101 through EMK2500. Both configurations are available in blue velvet-lined mahogany presentation case with a brass plate centered on the cover reading "Elmer Keith Commemorative."

The Model 27 Limited Edition Commemorative 357 Magnum honors the 50th anniversary of the cartridge and gun. Engraved and 22K gold-filled in one-of-a-kind styling created especially for this commemorative the sideplate reads "THE FIRST MAGNUM—April 8, 1935," the date on which this model was originally announced and presented to J. Edgar Hoover. The barrel is inscribed "1935—50th ANNIVERSARY—1985 S&W 357 Magnum." Only 2,500 of these commemoratives will be made, each in a finely fitted presentation case decorated with a brass plate bearing the inscription "The First Magnum 50th Anniversary 1935-1985" with space provided for the collector's name.

And Texas has been honored as it celebrates its 150th year of independence. Designated the Texas Wagon Train Commemorative Model 544, the 5-in. barrel is marked "1836 Texas 1986" and gold-filled. The usual S&W sights are installed, red ramp front and fully adjustable rear, along with smooth Goncalo Alves target

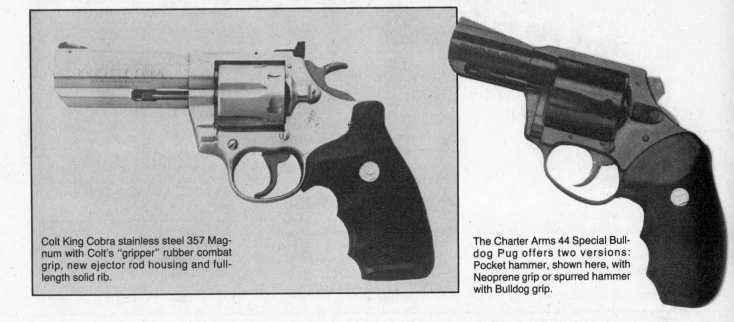

Colt King Cobra stainless steel 357 Magnum with Colt's "gripper" rubber combat grip, new ejector rod housing and full-length solid rib.

The Charter Arms 44 Special Bulldog Pug offers two versions: Pocket hammer, shown here, with Neoprene grip or spurred hammer with Bulldog grip.

Taurus Model 66 6-in. 357 Magnum is a real S&W Model 19 look-alike and shoot-alike.

Ike Garcia has big hands and liked Taurus' thick grip.

Elmer Keith Commemorative Deluxe version with ivory grip. It's a S&W M29 44 Magnum, of course.

S&W Model 27 Limited Edition Commemorative honoring 50th Anniversary of the gun and the 357 Magnum cartridge.

Texas Wagon Train Commemorative is 44-40 only, a Model 544 S&W with a 5-in. barrel.

stocks. The sideplate is roll stamped with the outline of Texas and the Texas Wagon Train logo, all in a gold-filled circle. The accompanying presentation case displays a rustic "barnboard" finish and expansively branded with distinguishing insignias plus "1836—TEXAS—1986." Only 7,800 of these will be produced—and now the really good part—in 44-40.

Thompson/Center

All sorts of exciting things from Thompson/Center this time around. Remember those early barrels marked 45 Colt/410? They are back in two 10-in. versions—standard bull barrel or with vent rib. Both have T/C's internal screw-in choke. Also added to the list of chamberings is the new 32 H&R Magnum in the 10-in. bull barrel. This one zips Federal's 85-grain bullet out at 1,250 fps. Silhouette shooters, along with varmint hunting enthusiasts, will like the 6mm TCU now being offered in the Super 14 barrel.

Claiming it better than stainless steel, T/C has a new Contender in Armour/Alloy II. Described as a technologically advanced plating process more rust resistant than most stain-less steels and harder—59 Rockwell as compared to 42 Rockwell for 410 stainless. The finish is non-glare, satin silver in appearance. Eight of their most popular chamberings are offered in 10-in. barrel, five in 14-in. There is a catch: Armour Alloy II frames and barrels will not interchange with standard blued Contender models.

"Ultimate" sights are now available for Contender barrels. It takes both front and rear and between them they leave nothing whatever to be desired in open sights. The front offers four blade selections (.060, .080, .100 and .120 wide) and the rear four notch widths of those same measurements for a combination of 16 possible settings. Each "click" of the rear elevation screw moves the point of impact .470 at 100 yards for 10-in. barrels and .330 on 14-in. This amounts to less than one inch of movement at 200 yards for either length.

T/C grips have long been a point of contention for Contender shooters. They may have solved the problem. Called "Competitor" the new grip combines wood, soft rubber and air. A rubber insert along the back includes a sealed-in air pocket protecting the web area of the hand. I haven't tried one but it looks and sounds great. Heavy-kicking T/C chamberings do tend to tenderize a hand.

T/C's carbine shooting system on the Contender frame maybe has outgrown this section but since its heart is the pistol frame here's what happened! The BATF stepped in and ruled buttstocks and fore-ends could not be sold without a frame and barrel. This to try and avoid the installation of 10- or 14-in. barrels on the carbine stock. The carbine is now marketed as a complete rifle. I was, maybe, a step ahead. I had already put together a buttstock, fore-end, 223, 7-30 Waters and 45 Winchester Magnum barrels in a single case and kept them together as a unit. Don't raise your eyebrows. I know 45 Winchester Magnum barrels are not long enough but mine has 2⅛ inches of tube welded out front to legalize it for the carbine stock so I could have a heavy caliber for hog hunting should the occasion arise.

As might have been expected, T/C has already improved this carbine system. New for this year is a 3-in. 410 barrel with full length vent rib. It's pretty enough to frame and hang on the wall. But I won't have to as there is room in my case. If it runs or flies, I'll be T/C ready.

Colt

King Cobra is its name and it's the newest in the Colt line in stainless steel with 4- and 6-in. barrel lengths featuring both a full-length barrel rib and ejector rod housing. There's a red insert front sight, adjustable white outline rear sight and Colt rubber grip. Weight is 42 ounces in 4-in. and 4 ounces heavier for the 6-in. The King Cobra might be well classed as a working man's Python. It has a bit of the looks and feel to be sure. Caliber is 357 Magnum only.

Since 1986 is Colt's 150th Anniversary and Texas shares the same year of birth as Colt, there are several Colt guns dolled up to fit the occasion. Colt's Ultimate Python is being turned out as part of a set designated

Double Diamond and so inscribed on the barrel. Quantity is limited to 1,000. There is a 150th Anniversary Single Action 45 that is hand-engraved over half its surface. The 150th Colt logo etched with 24K gold-plating is on the backstrap. Only 1,000 of these will be made.

Then there is the 150th Anniversary Engraving Sampler. This one features the four most sought after styles of engraving performed by Colt: Henshaw, Nimschke, Helfricht and Colt Contemporary. Each Sampler will include ivory grips and a letter of authentication.

Colt has designated the Python as their 150-year Double Diamond model, part of a stainless steel set with an Officers ACP.

Only 1,000 of these long-barreled 150th Anniversary Commemorative single-action 45s will be produced.

The 150th Anniversary Colt Engraving Sampler shows four most-sought-after styles of engraving.

Allen Firearms

Santa Fe-based Allen Firearms has added an interesting single action to their line. It's called The Phantom and is specially designed for silhouette shooting. Sights are target types, fully adjustable. Barrel length is 10 inches and the frame is a bit heavier than their other single actions. The trigger guard is sort of hooked in front providing a place to use the index finger of the supporting hand. "Anatomical" is their description of the grip. Calibers are 44 Magnum and 357 Magnum. I may have to try one.

Altamont

My 6-in. stainless steel Colt Python has become even more handsome in its new outfit, a set of ivory polymer grips from Altamont. Made from their own bonded ivory composite, the grips look like ivory, feel like ivory, scrimshaw like ivory yet are far more durable and decidedly less expensive. Altamont also works with walnut, all of the exotic woods, micarta and elephant ivory. Scrimshaw, carving, inlay is all done in-house and they can fit most any handgun from single actions through combat wraparounds.

American Derringer Corp.

American Derringer is growing in size as a business and in size as a product. Now there is a 6-in. barreled version chambered for 3-in. 410 or 45 Colt. Stainless steel, over-under barrels, satin or high polish finish, 21 ounces, rosewood grips with stag optional for a slight extra charge. And, made exclusively for American Derringer by Eley in England, they offer a 410 buckshot shell featuring three 000 buck pellets. Fired from a pistol they are said to penetrate approximately 700 pages in a telephone directory at 10 feet. These 410 buckshot shells can be used in any 2½- or 3-in. 410 in good condition.

Armscor Precision

Arms Corporation of the Phillippines is our newest entry in the handgun field. This new company lists a single revolver in two versions. Model 100P is service oriented with round butt, fixed sight, solid rib and half-shroud protecting ejector rod. Model 100TC is square butt, adjustable sight, ventilated rib and full-length shroud. These are 6-shot double-action revolvers chambered for 22 Long Rifle, 22 Magnum and 38 Special. Barrel lengths are 2, 3, 4 and 6 inches. Grips are mahogany and checkered.

Astra

The Astra double-action revolver line, imported by Interarms, continues to expand. Two stainless steel models, 4-in. 357 Magnum and 6-in. 44 Magnum, have been added along with a convertible 9mm Parabellum/357 Magnum 3-in. fixed sight service model. I carry regularly a big 44 Magnum Astra customized by Jovino to 2¾ inches and round-butted, then electroplated by Jim Riggs. It is a handful of mighty dependable protection should the need to use it ever rear its ugly head.

Century Mfg. 45-70

The Model 100 45-70 single-action revolver distributed by Century Gun Distributing, Inc. is a bronze beauty. It weighs 6½ pounds with its 8-in. barrel. The cylinder is 2⅝ inches long and 2¼ inches in diameter. Cylinder wall thickness is .228-in. It is a fraction over 3½ inches from the top strap to the bottom of the frame. That top strap is ¾-inch wide. Massive as this Century single action is, the trigger lets go at a mighty sweet 52 ounces. Model 100's deep blue/black barrel, ejector rod housing, cylinder and sights are in stark contrast to the polished bronze frame, backstrap, trigger guard, hammer and trigger. Earl Keller, designer of this huge single action, recommends it as strong enough for 405-grain bullets loaded over rifle charges listed as Government loads in manuals. He has proofed it with considerably stouter powder charges but doesn't recommend their constant use.

Mack Gwinn says his "Mean Little Machine" from Mitchell Arms is "virtually indestructible."

"Thunder" by Baford Arms is a multi-interchangeable caliber single shot pistol. Extra barrels (calibers) slip inside the host 44 Special/410 barrel. Some are even designed for scope mounting.

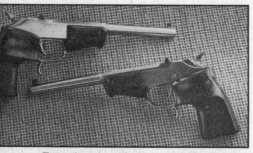

Texas Longhorn Arms new single shot rimfire pistols, all stainless steel with fancy walnut fore-end and grip.

Armour/Alloy II is T/C's new finish. It is claimed to give 30% longer barrel life than stainless steel.

Single shot Pachmayr conversion anchors to Model 1911 through the magazine well.

This is Swiggett's Dominator from Pachmayr with 308 barrel up.

I have shot none of my handloads in this single action. I do shoot mighty heavy 45-70 loads in a custom SSK 12½-in. barrel used on a T/C frame. I have shot Winchester and Remington 405-grain and Federal 300-grain. All do well in this 6½-pound bronze single action. There is, as might be expected, practically no recoil.

Barrel lengths include 6½, 8, 10, 12, 14 and 16 inches. Do not be surprised if this same single-action revolver is offered in full length 444 Marlin and 375 Winchester one of these days.

Charter Arms

Bulldog Pug is the name of Charter Arms' new model. It is 5-shot, 44 Special, service blue and fixed sight. Barrel length is 2½ inches. There are a pair actually. One has the conventional hammer and Bulldog walnut grip. The other wears a bobbed hammer and Neoprene grip. Both have a shrouded ejector with a full ramp, snag free, front sight.

FIE

Remember the "Yellow Rose" 24 KT gold-plated 22 single action we told about last year? It has grown up. FIE's Hombre line of big bore single actions, made in Germany by the Hans Weihrauch Company, is available in three calibers, 45 Colt, 357 Magnum and 44 Magnum, and three finishes. Not only are blue guns with color case-hardened frames and the same with brass back strap and trigger guard available but now there is a 24KT gold-plated big bore Hombre in all three calibers and both barrel lengths, 6 or 7½ inches.

Freedom Arms

Billed as "The World's Most Powerful Revolver" Freedom Arms 454 Casull single action is the only gun personally known by this writer to be the same, after several years of production, as it was first shown to the public. There is no gun built any place in this world that can compare with the excellent workmanship put into each 454 Casull single-action revolver. Jan Libourel, writing in *Guns & Ammo*, described it as, ". . . slick as a Ferrari and tough as a tank." I wish I'd thought of that. For the shooter wanting Freedom Arms quality in a less powerful handgun, the company now offers the big single action in 45 Colt and 44 Magnum. I can, I think, understand the 44 Magnum but not the 45 Colt since that favored old-timer chambers and shoots mighty sweet in the 454.

Gunworks Ltd.

The X-Caliber single shot interchangeable-barreled pistol is back with us. This is the Sterling X-Caliber but now under the guiding hands of Gunworks. The only difference I can see is in the trigger guard. Original X-Caliber pistols had an enlarged front with a hole through it for attaching a shooting lanyard. This new one has a conventional trigger guard. Sighting equipment is original, too; however, Williams, Millett, Micro and Lyman are offered as optionals. Barrels are drilled and tapped for B-Square and Bushnell scope mounts according to their literature. Custom grips by Herrett and Badger are also listed. Barrel lengths are 8, 10 and 14 inches. Calibers include 22 LR, 22 Magnum, 357 Magnum, 357 Remington Magnum 30-30, 7mm International Remington and 44 Magnum.

Gunworks also catalogs a 15-ounce, bottom-hinged, 357 Magnum or 9mm Magnum derringer of over-under configuration. It is electroless nickel finished with wood grips. Each pistol is shipped with a tool kit and in a pant/boot holster.

Heritage 1 45-70

Last year gremlins sneaked in and removed Phelps Mfg., Inc. as the manufacturers of Heritage 1 revolvers. As a result it was impossible to find Gene Phelps or his Heritage 1 45-70 revolver in our Directory of the Arms Trade.

Hope this helps. The Heritage 1 is a six-pound single action of mammoth proportions, obviously, since its cylinder houses six 45-70 cartridges.

K & K Ammo Wrist Band

I shoot a lot of single shot pistols. One of the handiest gadgets I've seen in a long time is the K & K Ammo Wrist Band. It is sized for your wrist—no Velcro fastener—and places three cartridges literally at your fingertips. Mine are for 300 Savage and 45-70, two wrist bands, as not only are they made to your size they are sewn specifically for your cartridge. Actually there are two models: one places five rounds around the wrist and the other three rounds inside the wrist.

Mag-na-port S&W M629 Stalker

Smith & Wesson Model 29 enthusiasts seemed a bit miffed when their favored double-action wasn't included in Larry Kelly's Stalker series. Fret no more, fellows, it's available with 8⅜-in. barrel, SSK full-length ventilated rib, Mag-na-port's own inverted crown, 2x Leupold Silver scope and 1¼-in. nylon web sling. This S&W Stalker is made up from a stainless Model 629. The finish is Kelly's Velvet Hone. Pachmayr Presentation grips round out this highly-tuned, specialized hunting handgun.

M.O.A. Maximum

Richard Mertz raised a few eyebrows at the SHOT Show by having his M.O.A. Maximum on display—chambered for the 460 Weatherby Magnum. When asked if it had been shot he said, "No, but I plan to." I hope I talked him out of it. His falling block single shot pistol is chambered for most any caliber you can think of and is made available with sights or drilled and tapped for scope mounting. I used one on a Kansas prairie dog shoot a couple of summers back. Chambered for 223 Remington it consistently knocked them over out to 200 yards using a 4x Leupold scope.

North American Arms

North American's big 450 Magnum Express is going strong. It's based on an extended length 45 Winchester Magnum case and obviously shoots the parent cartridge except that to do so a separate cylinder has to be installed. After all, this is a semi-automatic round and seats on the case mouth. North American is now offering a 45 Colt cylinder making it possible to shoot all three cartridges in the same revolver.

(Right) Wichita International single shot pistol is designed for silhouette shooters and hunters.

(Below) Remington XP-100 "Varmint Special" adds the 221 Remington option to what has been almost completely a pipsqueak 221 from the beginning.

American Derringer offers a 6-in. 45 Colt/410 model now, with its own distinctive grip shape.

For those not familiar with the 450 Magnum Express, which was introduced a couple of years ago, it is stainless steel, matte finished, and with 7½-inch barrel. Though the 45 Winchester Magnum cartridge is powerful, it in no way compares with what happens when the case is lengthened and heavier bullets utilized over a full charge of powder. It's a hunters' handgun, this 450 Magnum Express.

Pachmayr

When is a semi-automatic pistol a single shot on purpose? When it's a Pachmayr Dominator. The bolt-action receiver/barrel assembly rather easily attaches to a Colt frame once the slide and ejector are removed, and may be chambered for 223 Remington, 7mm-08 Remington, 44 Remington Magnum or the 308 Winchester. I've been testing it in 308.

The Dominator is designed for silhouette shooting and hunting. Mine was mounted on a MK IV 38 Super frame, topped with a Burris 5x scope, and put to work. Shooting Frontier, Federal and Winchester factory ammo loaded with both 150- and 180-grain bullets proved to be a handful. Recoil maybe wasn't excessive, but the Colt grip made it seem so. I talked to Robert Kleinguenther at Kleinguenther Firearms about installing his Recoil Tamer. What a difference it made. Muzzle jump was reduced to very little and recoil to practically nothing.

The Dominator is an ingeniously designed barrel/bolt assembly that attaches through the magazine well. The only problem I had to overcome was the tendency to hold the pistol in my left hand, gripping the frame, and trying to open the bolt. It can't be done because the bolt slide is that frame. Once I got my act together, all went well. Lift the bolt, after cocking the pistol, and pull the slide back. Pour out the empty. This proved to be easier for me than trying to remove it with my fingers. The cartridge fits into a sort of shell holder bolt face. This too poses no problem once the technique is mastered.

Once Kleinguenther's Recoil Tamer was installed, shooting got serious. There is little a rifle can do at 100 yards that this Pachmayr Dominator can't hang close to. I missed three turkey gobblers before connecting but I'm a neck shooter and couldn't blame that performance on the pistol. A whitetail buck dropped in his tracks from a broken neck at about 90 yards.

Remington

Remington's great bolt-action single shot pistol, the XP-100, has come of age. Hatched in 1963 in 221 Fireball, it has been rechambered, rebarreled, reworked in general to about anything any shooter could dream up because of its inherent accuracy plus the almost total disinterest in 221 Fireball. Lots of encouragement and other assorted harassment has gone into the announcement that there is now an XP-100 Varmint Special

Ivory polymer grip from Altamont looks like the real thing, feels like the real thing, is more durable than the real thing, yet costs considerably less.

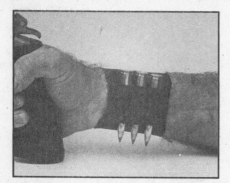

K&K Ammo Wrist Bands, handy for single shot shooters, are sized to fit each wrist and cartridge. Two styles: Three cartridges inside the wrist or five around.

The MTM Case Gard 806 handgun case will hold them all up to 6-in. barrels for about ten bucks.

chambered for 223 Remington. Several writer-types provided the encouragement and harassment.

A few years ago Remington did make the XP-100 available in 7mm Remington BR, but no loaded ammo was furnished. It was a case-making and handloading situation straight down the line. This Varmint Special is similar to the XP-100 Silhouette 7mmBR in that it too has a 14½-in. barrel and the specially-contoured, one-piece Du Pont "Zytel" structural nylon stock. Delivered minus sights, the receiver is drilled and tapped for scope mounting. My test XP-100 Varmint Special 223 Remington was topped with Simmons Outdoor Corporation's new 4x handgun scope. The two are proving exceptionally compatible. The XP-100 in 7mm-08 and 35 Remington is also available from Remington's Custom Shop. This version is walnut stocked.

RG Industries

The bad news is that the Rohm family has totally dropped the handgun business in the United States and left. Word is they even scrapped the spare parts. All those RG guns are true orphans. The other word is that lawyers, courts and impossible insurance rates made the game not worth the candle.

There is no good news.

Rossi

Here is one you have to see. The Rossi Sportsman 22, imported by Interarms, is stainless steel with a 4-in. barrel, red insert front sight, blue fully-adjustable rear sight, and a price you will have to see to believe. My wife fell in love with the Rossi Model 851 4-in. 38 Special added to the line last year and I had to send a check rather than return the revolver. My point, whittled down to fit in a tiny nutshell, is foreign-made revolvers aren't what they used to be. Look them over then pass them up if you don't like the gun, but do not fail to look at them just because they are foreigners. You could be the loser. This new Sportsman 22 for instance. It is well-made, ideally suited to small game hunting, camping, backpacking, plinking—anyplace a 22 can be used. I hope my wife doesn't see it because it weighs 30 ounces, exactly the same as her M851 38 Special.

Taurus

Model 85 is Taurus' new double-action revolver. It's 38 Special, 5-shot, 21 ounces and stainless steel. Up front there is a serrated ramp with a notch rear sight. Stocks are Brazilian hardwood and checkered.

This past year I've been shooting a Model 66, 6-in. 357 Magnum that is so much like S&Ws Model 19 I'd be hard-pressed to tell them apart in the dark except for the grip. The Taurus Model 66 has thicker wood—just a lot more than necessary. I've threatened to take a pocketknife to it several times. The revolver shoots like a winner. I put 110-, 125-, 140-, 158- and 180-grain factory loads through it and all but the 110 and 180 shot about the same. The 110 wasn't so accurate as the others and the 180 kicks more than seems necessary.

Dan Wesson Arms

Look over any list of winners in silhouette production gun matches and you will find Dan Wesson leads the pack. That in itself testifies to the revolver's capabilities and quality so there is nothing I can say other than to report a couple of new calibers. The 32 Magnum is chambered in the same versions as the 357 except there will be no barrels longer than 8 inches. Their big 44 Magnum gun, with no changes other than caliber, will be available in 45 Colt. I've often wondered why this hadn't been done.

Wichita

The International Handgun Metallic Silhouette Association talked Wichita Arms into building a single shot pistol exclusively for them. It was designed by members to be sold to members. Nolan Jackson said, "O.K., I'll do it." About a year later word leaked out that this pistol was available to anyone directly from Wichita Arms.

It looks a lot like the Merrill but with a good many innovations of its own. There is no thumb-activated safety on the left side. When the barrel latch is moved to the rear the hammer is automatically placed on quarter-cock which keeps the hammer off the firing pin. Finish of this stainless steel pistol is dull gray—no shine whatever. The schnabel-tipped fore-end and grip panels are walnut. There is a decided swell at the grip bottom forming a base for the hand.

Barrel length is 10½ inches and the weight 59½ ounces. Trigger pull is excellent at 50 ounces. The rear sight is fully adjustable and of Wichita's own design. The barrel latch is deeply cut with four grooves for a positive grip. The barrel pivots only enough to allow the empty to be removed and a fresh cartridge inserted.

Called Wichita International, this pistol is chambered for 22 Long Rifle, 22 Magnum Rimfire, 357 Magnum, 357 Remington Maximum, 30-30, 7R (30-30 case necked down to 7mm) and 32 H&R Magnum. Barrels are not interchangeable. ●

WHEN IT comes to ribs, gunmakers have left Adam in the dust. He contributed only one, and that merely helped create Woman. Big deal.

The gunmakers who spurred the history and development of sporting arms—ah, they've contributed ribs. Oh, how they've contributed ribs! And theirs serve more important purposes, too—everything from helping a hunter get on grouse swivel-hipping through the thicket to assisting an Olympic Skeet or trap shooter win the coveted gold. Indeed, the different rib designs and the theories behind them are an interesting study, *even* leaving women out.

Sporting guns have worn various types of top ribs ever since gunmakers began joining side-by-side tubes with strips of metal running from breech to muzzle betwixt the tandem. The first gunmakers credited with the use of a rib on doubles are the Mantons of London, namely, John and Joseph, who plied their innovations during the early decades of the 19th century when flinters were in their vintage years. Initially, the top rib (like that on the bottom) merely fixed the side-by-side barrels as rigidly and neatly as possible.

Trapshooters will go to unbelievable extremes in rib designs. Here Zutz shoots a Holmes conversion of a Remington 1100.

Like so many sportsmen today, wingshots of the embryonic 19th century didn't especially enjoy the broad "sight picture" presented by the horizontal double. This displeasure was apparently accompanied by an actual tendency for low shooting with many of the early doubles. It was 1806 when the inventive Joseph Manton gave the sporting world his "elevating rib," and that may very well have been the first attempt to use barrel-top ribs for improved pointing accuracy with shotguns.

Careful readers will note that the Manton concept was termed the eleva*ting* rib, not the eleva*ted* rib. The adjective "elevate" was not used to describe the rib's height above the barrels, but was instead chosen to indicate the rib's influence on pattern placement. Manton's elevating rib was an angled accouterment that started well above the barrels at their breech end and terminated lower, down between the muzzles. If the shooter's line of vision went flush down the elevating rib, the barrels pitched upward somewhat to overcome the complaint about the low-shooting tendency of early side-by-sides. In concept, this is not unlike the radically pitched ribs found on some modern trap guns which are purposely engineered to send their patterns high for a rising target. But mention of modern competition ribs takes us too far ahead of our story.

The Manton elevating rib was more than just an answer for that time. It opened the door to further thinking about the role of top ribs, and since then the theorists and merchants have not been lacking for ideas. The results have given us ribs that range from the simple to the sublime, the classical to the comical. Unfortunately, the myriad variations have led many shooters to be more interested in the cosmetics than in practical application. And although ribs are supposed to expedite fast, accurate gun *pointing,* they have often been misused by unknowing sportsmen who erroneously apply them as precise sighting equipment for deliberate, riflelike *aiming.* Thus, any discussion of ribs must be predicated on how said dinguses fit into the parameters of wing-gunning technique.

Essentially, the rib's *raison d'être* is leading the shooter's eye to the muzzle. That may be a letdown for some of you fancy thinkers out there, but that's it. In classic shotgunning, the shooter isn't supposed to look sharply at the upper surface of his gun; his eyes are always to be focused on the moving target, the gun being seen only as a fuzzy blur. All pointing is supposed to be done with the muzzle blur only as the shooter employs hand-to-eye coordination. If the gun is mounted properly, if the shooter has his head down snuggly so his master eye looks directly over the center of

The evolution

of the

RIB

by Don Zutz

the breech, and if the shooter keeps his head thus positioned to retain alignment over the gun's center line—that should be all the accuracy one needs to hit with the smoothbore and its expanding pattern. Getting one's eye from breech to muzzle quickly and smoothly, therefore, is vitally important, because the muzzle is the shooter's main reference point. That's the rib's main role.

The reason ribs became popular with the advent of side-by-sides should be obvious to anyone who has held the undersides of a set of such tubes to the sky—plain, nicely blued barrels practically disappear due to reflected skylight, and the shooter visual line runs from breech to muzzles regardless of the light conditions.

Costing less to make than a hollow rib, the modern "flat" rib is more commonly used today. As its name implies, the flat rib is . . . well, flat on top. Its surface is matted or knurled to produce a visual effect under all sky conditions. On some wide-ribbed clay target guns, the use of deep longitudinal grooves has been tried effectively, Browning's Broadway being a case in point.

On classic side-by-sides, flat-topped ribs were attached to run straight from the breech to a point even with or slightly above the top line of the muzzles. On over-unders and repeat-

near the muzzles. This bellied form of rib tends to make the middle of the barrel assembly disappear to the eye while emphasizing the start of the rib and the muzzles. The eye virtually jumps from breech to muzzles when a swamped rib is in place. The hollow rib is normally employed when the swamped concept is applied, and this writer feels it is one of the fastest concepts yet devised for the horizontal double. Unfortunately few of the current gunmakers still apply the swamped rib. French Darnes have generally had it and a number of European and British gunmakers will install such a rib on special order.

It wasn't only shotguns that were

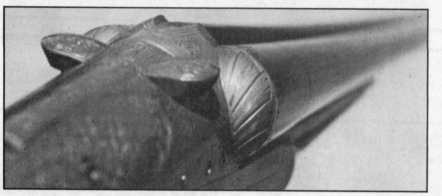

A top view of a broad, hollow rib with its concave surface.

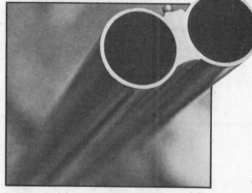

The business-end view of a hollow rib as put on a Neumann 24-gauge.

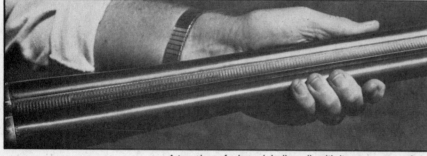

The French Darne employs a swamped rib shown here at its relative high breech starting point. The rib thereupon swoops downward to virtually disappear, leaving breech and muzzles standing out sharply.

The terminus of a swamped, hollow rib between the tubes of a Darne. The eye-to-muzzle jump can be fast and accurate.

can't find the muzzles. The rib, with its dark grooves on either side and its variously file-cut or machine-knurled surface, insures dark longitudinal lines to lead one's eye to the muzzles.

Gunmakers overcame the vanishing effect of skylight on blue steel by using methods that created shadows. One such device was called the "hollow" rib, which isn't hollow at all but is instead concave. With the sides of the hollow rib higher than the curved center, and often with a type of machine or hand matting on its surface, it is almost certain that some kind of

ers, of course, the flat ribs originally attached just above the muzzle to retain the trimmest profile. Because of its direct, straightline dash from breech to muzzle—without any ramp or hump effect—this application of the flat-topped rib has historically been known as the "straight" rib, a designation that is still apropos.

Some gunmakers attempted to expedite eye-to-muzzle contact on side-by-sides with a so-called "swamped rib." Beginning high at the breech, the swamped rib gets its moniker by swooping down and running deeply between the barrels only to rise again

given ribs. Many heavy-caliber big game rifles, be they doubles or bolt actions, were made with ribs running from the breech to the rear sight, which was normally an express-type (Gibbs) blade for fast shooting on relatively close-range, massive beasts. The rib's job, as on a scattergun, was to guide the hunter's eye as quickly as possible to the rear sight. Thus, the rifle's elevated rib plays more roles than just that of a sight mount, shotgun-like roles, in fact.

The first ribs were attached to double shotguns by soft-soldering after the void between barrels had received some connections of tinned iron, and soft-soldering remains a, if not *the*, major method of attachment. Early on, the great W.W. Greener warned against the higher temperatures of hard-soldering because of what the heat could do to the barrels. In *The Gun And Its Development*, Greener cautioned that, "This (hard-soldering) is most injurious, as the (twist and Damascus) barrels are made crooked by the process, and cannot again be straightened effectively . . . With (fluid) steel barrels the result is even more disastrous, the heat required being more than sufficient to ruin the qualities of some steels used for barrels." Soft-soldering isn't without its

The M12s with ventilated ribs and the original "duckbill" ramp had the studs milled onto the barrel, and the rib was attached by means of dovetailing. Milling of this sort is now too expensive for the popular market.

Two companies that led the way in putting accessory ribs on originally plain-barreled guns were Simmons and Poly-Choke. Simmons used a variety of stud designs, all of which were soft-soldered to the barrel and accommodated the rib via dovetailed tops. Poly-Choke employed an innovative method: Its rib was a 1-piece affair that was held in place by, of all things, a strong rubber cement.

Remington at one time set a novel

them—so be it. For neat appearance and obvious craftsmanship, however, it is difficult to match a well-soldered rib or one carefully machined on the barrel.

When the British first began making over-unders, they wanted to preserve the trimmest possible profile. Full-length raised ribs, which gave O-Us a deep, slab-sided appearance, were anathema to the British gunmakers' collective sense of aesthetics. To keep the gun slender, but to provide some forward guidance for the eye, the British cleverly adopted short, or false, ribs which mounted to nothing more than a low, relatively narrow rib extending just briefly

The relatively high (for a side-by-side), thin rib as developed by Robert Churchill on the controversial XXV gun.

The most commonly used rib on side-by-sides today is a straight, flat type.

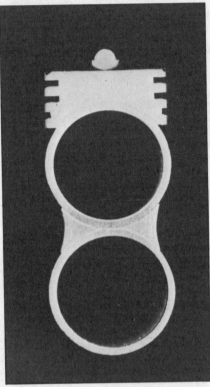

The barrel-width rib of a Japanese Shadow Indy had milled ventilations for cooling, but that style didn't last.

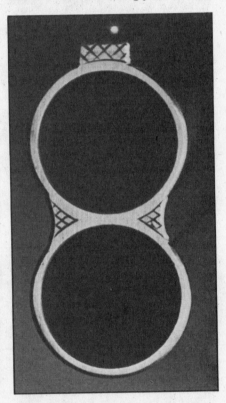

The Europeans—and most others—still prefer a classically trim rib on field guns. This one is on a Merkel.

faults, of course. It will let go, and it is susceptible to the heat of blueing plus the chemical action of blueing salts. But, although not perfect, soft-soldering continues to be the most widespread method of affixing ribs to gun barrels.

At one time, before the cost of production was increased markedly by inflated wages, some single-barreled guns had their ribs or rib studs machined integrally with the barrel. Such integrally milled ribs were put on both the solid-ribbed and the first ventilated-ribbed Winchester Model 12s, and these are classic milling jobs.

nylon ventilated rib on the stubby barrel of the Model 600 bolt-action carbine, and still puts same on the rakish Model XP-100 bolt-action handgun. Since one cannot solder nylon to steel, Remington held it in place with flat-head screws extending down though the nylon rib studs to engage the threaded interior of small, round studs soft-soldered to the barrel top.

Finally, there are some ribs around today that clamp directly to the existing ventilated rib for added height. They are hardly aesthetic, but if a trap shooter breaks the hundred with

ahead of the breech. These abbreviated ribs are akin to those found on rifles with express sights. Anyone who has ever gotten his head down properly on a shotgun so equipped can attest to the fact that such short ribs do provide visual direction to the muzzle despite their brevity. To a degree, these ribs served the same purpose as the matted receiver tops found on modern repeaters: they get the eye started in the correct direction.

With rare exception, early ribs were attached low to the barrel so they wouldn't upset the classically slender profiles of sporting guns.

Perazzi high-ribbed trap guns were intended to permit a naturally upright posture, a concept enforced by the success of California money shooter Dan Bonillas, shown here.

An Olympic rib on the Ljutic Bi-Gun teamed with a high Monte Carlo comb moves the bore axis lower for straightline recoil effect.

Mossberg's Model 500 trap gun also illustrates the use of a lofty rib and high Monte Carlo comb to depress the bore axis for straightline recoil, here in a repeater.

Distinctly different ideas are in this pair of Rottweils. The upper trap gun, a combo set, has high ribs on both barrel assemblies and the single shot barrel is in the Ungun mode with the lower lock being used to keep the recoil in straightline. The lower gun is a field grade with the classic low, trim rib made only to lead the hunter's eye quickly to the muzzle.

Some minor tinkering went on, of course, but the variations didn't produce bulkier, deeper guns. In the 1920s, Britain's Robert Churchill introduced his dynamic XXV gun, and its 25-inch barrels, which were then radically short, sported the so-called "Churchill rib," which was an extremely narrow metal ribbon that arrowed from breech to muzzles. Churchill's rib not only tried to eliminate shooting low and behind, but its slender top also gave the optical illusion of longer barrels. This same type of Churchill rib is now being put on Iberian copies of the XXV, a foremost copy being that from AyA.

Gunmaking great W.W. Greener also made a broad "pigeon" rib with deep longitudinal lines for competitive box pigeon shooters. This was of the straight, flat variety, and it seems to have caught on. The Greener pigeon rib certainly didn't upset aesthetics.

Even the 20th century advent of the raised ventilated rib didn't unduly change gun lines at first. Most ventilated ribs took the form of straight, flat ribs which didn't bulge above the normal line of point running from breech top to muzzles. Even the single-barreled trap guns of said era—the Parkers, Smiths, Ithacas, and Bakers—had conservative ventilated ribs slanting from breech to bead.

The ventilated rib wasn't developed purely for cosmetic purposes, of course. Nor was it made solely to provide the shooter's eye with a raceway to the muzzle, although that was still a major part of the game. For ventilated ribs were also devised to diffuse rising heat waves so that gunners didn't have to view targets through the flickering mirage-type conditions that develop along barrel tops on hot days and/or from sustained firing. The growing popularity of trapshooting undoubtedly prompted increased use of the vent rib as did Skeet shooting which began in the 1920s. Live pigeon competitors apparently did not get excited about ventilated ribs until the 1970s, as they remained very faithful to the trim double and the straight rib.

Perhaps the first noteworthy departure from the normal conservatively low ventilated rib was that put on Winchester's Model 12 trap guns in 1918. This rib sat on milled rib supports that were expensively machined directly on the barrel top, the rib floating on dovetailed slots cut into the supports. What was unique about the Winchester rib was that it sat higher than ribs on other repeaters, ending in what has become known as a "duckbill ramp" on the receiver. The ramp had a V-notch, while the rib generally wore a red bead front sight and a silver metal middle bead noticeably smaller than the front globe. The double beads, along with the rib's height, were also advanced as cures for canting; one careful look down the rib would tell the gunner if he were holding the piece straight or crooked. The height and the ramp all added depth and clutter to the Model 12—but the gun won! Oh, how it won! And since it's virtually impossible to argue against success, the concept of added rib height and an eye-catching ramp was firmly established and accepted among tournament shooters.

The most popular over-under among trap shooters in the '30s was the Browning Belgian-made Superposed, and it didn't have the straight, flat rib, either. The Superposed's ventilated rib was elevated with a breech end that swept upward in a smooth curve to act as an eye-leading ramp. Nor was the ventilated rib that Remington put on its Skeet and trap grade Model 31 pumps perfectly straight, having instead a mildly angular ramp leading to a slightly lofted rib.

But even the rib designs of the Model 12, Superposed, and Model 31 were basically conservative in nature compared to what has happened since the 1960's. Ribs have gone wild! They've been stretched in all directions. Some have such high supports that they look like the Golden Gate bridge, others are as broad as the barrel, and still others reach from the muzzle clear over the receiver and practically into the shooter's pupil. Still others lie flat along the barrel until, at some point far forward of the breech, they suddenly vault abruptly and run the remaining length of the barrel like a high picket fence. Strange as these newfangled ribs may appear to the classicist, however, today's breed of gunner swears by them, finds theoretical strengths in them and, more importantly, wins major tournaments with them.

The latter-day rib revolution began rather quietly in the 1960s, coming to life almost simultaneously in two different parts of the world: Brescia in Italy and Reno in Nevada.

The Italian contribution comes from Perazzi, and its inception was founded on solid theory. In 1964, Ennio Mattarelli of Italy had won the Olympic gold medal in trapshooting (trench) with a Perazzi Mirage, an over-under with a low-mounted, straight rib. The 1968 Olympics were to be held in Mexico City, however, and that meant a torrid sun and blaz-

ing temperatures to intensify heat waves. Perazzi's answer was a higher rib which began with a step just ahead of the chamber contour. This rib became popular among stateside trap shooters and Olympic trench gunners as the MX-8 (so named for Mexico, 1968, not for any intercontinental ballistics missile) because it does in fact do a better job of reducing shimmer and haze.

The other gunmaker who had a

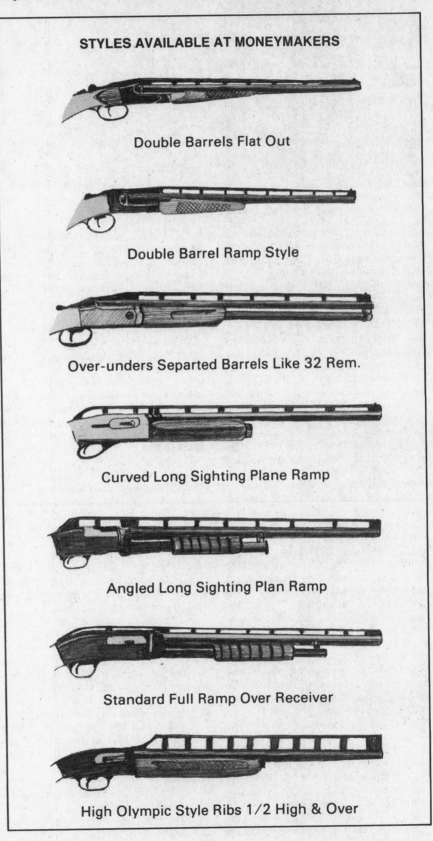

STYLES AVAILABLE AT MONEYMAKERS

Double Barrels Flat Out

Double Barrel Ramp Style

Over-unders Separted Barrels Like 32 Rem.

Curved Long Sighting Plane Ramp

Angled Long Sighting Plan Ramp

Standard Full Ramp Over Receiver

High Olympic Style Ribs 1/2 High & Over

The duckbill ramp on Winchester's Model 12 was one of the first lofty variations in ribs, and it proved to be a winner in both Skeet and trap.

definite impact on rib evolution was Al Ljutic, whose machine shop was then across the highway from Harold's Gun Club just north of Reno. A trap shooter himself, Ljutic began making totally customized single shots that became famous as the Mono Gun. In the hands of Dan Orlich, the Ljutic won all sorts of major trap championships and scored perfect 100s from the maximum 27-yard handicap stripe. Part of the Mono Gun's design included a high-sitting, full-length ventilated rib swept gracefully over the rounded rear of the gun's receiver.

It would seem that lofty ribs were accepted by the public mainly because they were a part of a package that won tournaments. For at the same time that Perazzi and Ljutic were becoming household names among trap shooters, both Simmons Gun Specialties of Olathe, Kansas, and Herter's, Inc., of Waseca, Minnesota, were ready and willing to put full-length ribs on just about any shotgun ever made, and their offerings didn't attract as much attention. The tournament shooters hardly noticed the Simmons and Herter accessory ribs.

As the rib revolution snowballed, the vent rib was assigned new tasks. Whereas old-line gunmakers had kept the rib low near the bore axis(es) and had utilized it almost solely to expedite eye-to-muzzle linkage, modern thinkers began using the rib for such things as increased heat wave disruption and, of all things, recoil reduction! For a short time, it was thought that an ultra-wide rib would force the convection currents away from the main line of view, and some radically wide ribs—such as those on the Browning Broadway and Shadow

Indy—were made. That of the Indy, a Japanese-made trap gun, had a barrel-width top plus milled grooves along each side to enhance air circulation for cooling and heat wave dissipation. While the broader ribs did contribute in the form of a wider shimmer-free area, they were not accepted by shooters, most of whom felt the wider ribs made the guns too muzzle heavy and didn't provide adequate pointing precision. This latter aspect seemed more important than the former in explaining the demise of the Broadway concept, as many trap shooters tend to be "aimers" who favor a sharper rib profile.

The raised rib's role in recoil management is of recent origins, dating back little more than a decade. It begins with the generalization that a barrel which is in a straightline position relative to the shooter's shoulder and has its bore axis running below the comb line will give less sensible recoil than a bore axis running above the comb/shoulder level. For this reason, the under barrel of an over-under is generally set to fire first.

To take advantage of this principle, guns thinkers and tinkerers began increasing rib height so that both bore axes would be lowered to get that less-noticeable, straightline recoil. This meant that the gun's comb would have to be elevated, of course, sometimes markedly so. The accompanying photo of a Mossberg trap model pump gun is a case in point: the comb line is high, thanks to an almost gargantuan Monte Carlo, to keep the shooter's eye in line with the extremely high VR. Lots of other gunmakers went the same route, including Ljutic and Perazzi, both of whom employ high comb lines with steep rib designs

to lower the bore axes of over-unders and single shots for straightline recoil. Such tall ribs are variously known as Olympic, Competition, or Tournament styles. Whatever. Suffice it to say that there is method behind this seeming madness, and the high ribs and combs have caught on, to a degree, among serious clay target and live pigeon gunners despite their tall, top-heavy appearance and dubious aesthetics.

At least two companies are offering high ribs that the shooter can attach to his own gun for extra height. One of these is Allen Timney, the well-known triggersmith, who advertises a rib named the "Piggyback" for the existing ribs on Remington 870s, 1100s, and 3200s plus the Beretta autos and the BT-99. Timney makes three different rib heights (½-, ⅝-, and ¾-inch), all of which are machined from aircraft aluminum to scale less than 3½ ounces. At this writing, the Timney ribs run $85 to $95. Information

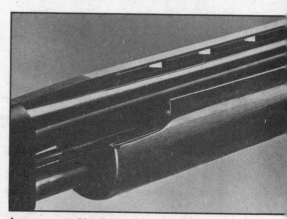

As an eye-catching feature, many repeaters today have inclined ramps leading to the rib. This puts the rib slightly above receiver height.

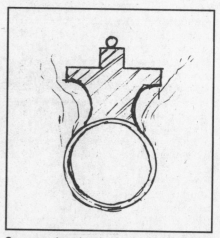

Cross section sketch of writer's idea of the optimum competition rib with a broad plane to force rising heat outward and a narrow rib riding piggyback to present a sharper pointing plane.

comes from the company at 13524 Edgefield St., Cerritos, CA 90701.

The second company selling a latch-on rib is J.L. White Enterprises, 118 McHugh St., Ft. Collins, CO 80524. Known as the HI-RIB X2, this unit is made to fit most shotguns that already have factory installed ventilated ribs, and it comes with a companion cheek pad to help elevate the shooter's eye. The price as I write is $94.95.

Around 1980-81, Perazzi began advancing two other reasons for lofted ribs. First, by raising the rib and comb lines, Perazzi argued, a gunmaker could let the shooter stand with a comfortable, erect posture so that his body could pivot around its

about ribs have liberalized the modern shotgunner's thinking and have provided momentum for further change. A place like Moneymaker Guncraft of 1420 Military Ave., Omaha, NE 68131 has rib designs that might well have been thought radical 20-25 years ago. Along with the conventional "flat out" rib, Moneymaker has a list of possibilities including a high-sitting Olympic rib; a curved long-angle sighting plane that runs high and all the way to the tail of the receiver; an abruptly started rib with a steeply angled ramp known as the long angle rib; and, finally, a raised, ramp-style rib that elevates the pointing plane of a side-by-side. All these Moneymaker ribs can be ordered with

without bulky ramps and/or notches often have the rib extension run full-length over the receiver and practically into the gunner's on-side eye.

In general, field guns have not yet been defaced by gargantuan appendages. Winchester's Model 23 side-by-side have a curiously high ramp, but it doesn't spoil the 23's aesthetics. The fact is, of course, that there is no real need for rib designs that combat heat and recoil in bird guns, as shooting afield isn't as fast and furious as the sustained firing of tournaments. And insofar as all this pre-mounting and riflelike aiming is concerned—forget it! Hunters start with a lowered gun and do their best work with smooth, coordinated, hand-to-eye coordination that emphasizes quick muzzle pointing, not a precise aim started with a static, pre-mounted gun. Ribs that sit higher than those of the Remington Model 1100 and 870 will never be needed in waterfowl blinds, quail covers, or cottontail thickets.

But tournament shooters and gun tinkerers will continue to experiment wildly, searching for that slight advantage which will give them one more target. My own feeling is that the optimum competition rib hasn't yet been developed, but when it comes along it will have a barrel-width surface topped by a higher, narrower strip. *(One might call it the Zutz rib-on-rib: Editor)* Joining wide and narrow ribs has twofold reasons: First, a broad underrib would force the convection currents of heat outward and away from the viewing/pointing plane so the target's image isn't distorted or shifted by the mirage/shimmer effect. The narrow top rib, riding piggyback, *(Or one could call it the Zutz piggyback: Editor)* is added as a sharper pointing feature for those people who admire the theory behind broad ribs, but don't enjoy pointing with them. A narrow piggyback rib provides the sharpness such seek. To be sure, this double-decker rib *(Or one could call it the Zutz double-decker: Editor)* will be expensive to make, but modern tournament shooters are conditioned to paying. If it gets them another target on the score sheet, they'll gladly cough up the greenbacks.

The role of the women created from Adam's rib has been expanded and remains in an evolutionary state; the same is true of Joe Manton's creation. The important thing to remember is that such ribs are not purely for cosmetics. If they don't serve a purpose, they are worthless. But when the concepts do fit their role, they help bring home everything. ●

The primary job of a rib is to expedite eye-to-muzzle-to-target alignment. Ribs are not to be used like rifle sights for aiming.

natural upright axis (spine). This meant a shooter wouldn't have to scrunch down and crawl the comb to get alignment. Much of the theory was based on the success of American money shooter Dan Bonillas, who employs a very straight, upright stance with virtually no lean or comb crawl. The theory manifests itself in the Perazzi DB-81 and TMX guns. For whatever reasons, however, even Bonillas doesn't use the concept and is normally seen shooting with a lower rib. Perhaps this is one place where theory went wild? As a second point, the high Perazzi ribs give improved target visibility by lowering the gun barrel(s) relative to the line of sight, and the muzzle/barrel blob doesn't blot out the low-sitting trap house and/or the clay target or live pigeon during its first yards of flight.

All these variations and theories

a straight 3/8-inch width or with a taper beginning at 3/8-inch and narrowing to 5/16-inch. All ribs are hand filed for straightness, we're told. Why such a repertoire? The people at Moneymaker say the designs were mainly suggested by people who claim they work. So be it.

One interesting trend in the evolution of shotgun ribs is the use of an eye-catching reference point at or near the rib's inception. Here, again, the duckbill ramp of Winchester's Model 12 is a classic example, having a slight V-notch like a rifle's rear sight as well as serving as a stop for the eye. The so-called Olympic rib of today has an abrupt step taper that presents a flat wall to catch the shooter's eye and shouts, "Hey, here's where the rib starts!" And to make it easier for the eyes to find the visual pathway to the muzzle, those ribs

Multi-Coating—
The New Game

by BOB BELL

FIFTY years ago it took only a handful of manufacturers to satisfy the demand for rifle scopes. Now, no one could name all the brands on the market. No doubt a lot of them come out of the same plants in the Far East, wearing whatever name the buyer specifies, but that's no big matter. The thing is, the demand has created the supply, and with so many individuals thinking about a given item, that item has to improve. Thus, in the past few decades, we've been offered variable power scopes that work (if not perfectly, at least well enough for most needs), scopes tough enough for magnum handgun use, high-power action-mounted models, and more.

The facet of the scope field currently attracting attention is multi-coating for lenses. Shooters these days take for granted that a scope's lenses will be coated, but such was not always the case. Lens coating is a comparatively recent thing and a bit of background might be useful for new shooters.

For a scope to function at all, light has to pass through its lenses and be focused by them into an image of use to the shooter. However, all the light which strikes the front lens of a scope does not come out the back end. Some never even gets past the front surface of the objective lens; it's simply reflected away. More is stopped at each lens surface. Some more is absorbed by the lenses themselves. Some is scattered within the tube. For a 700-year period, dating from the time of the first lenses in the mid-13th century, approximately four percent of the light striking any air/glass surface was reflected away. Therefore, early scopes, which often had a dozen such surfaces, transmitted through the ocular lens only 60 percent or so of the light which struck the objective lens.

In the 1930s, Professor A. Smakula of Carl Zeiss in Germany developed a process of depositing a thin coating of low-refracting material on the air/glass surfaces of an optical system. This coating has been described as a material having an intermediate index of refraction between air and the glass on which it is deposited, its purpose being to minimize the change in speed of light between air and the dense medium, thus reducing reflection and increasing light transmission at the interface. Magnesium fluoride was the normal coating material and, when applied to all air/glass surfaces, boosted light transmission from the 60 percent noted to about 86 percent.

Multilayer coating has improved that. Here, several coatings on each surface with alternating high and low refractive indexes further reduce residual reflections and deal with light of different wavelengths. Light transmission in scopes so treated can be well over 90 percent, in some situations reportedly in the high 90s.

Multi-coating is not new, incidentally. In 1939, the Schott Glassworks in Germany was producing two-layer coating and, by 1943, made three layers work. For some years now, Zeiss has been applying up to seven coatings on some optical systems.

All well and good, we shooters think. And doubtless this is a significant improvement, for once light transmission is over 90 percent, if it occurs at all parts of the visual spectrum, there's little need to go higher because the average human eye can-

Tasco 1½-5x snugged low on Model Seven Remington 7mm-08 in Redfield Jr. mount gave Bell an easy kill on whitetail this year past.

not detect differences of less than 10 percent in this factor. However, it should be noted that few if any scope manufacturers, when using the term "multi-coated," actually say how many coatings are used. Two coatings qualify as "multi," but do not give transmission and image quality equal to more coatings. And there can be a question of how many air/glass surfaces are multi-coated. In the '40s and '50s when single coating was becoming the norm in this country, it was not unknown for some scopemakers to coat only the outside objective and ocular lens surfaces, where the resulting color could be seen, and forget about the numerous air/glass surfaces inside the tube. In such cases, the buyer wasn't getting the quality and efficiency he thought he was getting. We're not suggesting anything like that is going on today. But to avoid misunderstandings and let the buyer know the facts, we think it would be nice if each manufacturer specified just how many air/glass surfaces in his scopes are multi-coated and how many coats they have.

Enough of that. Here's this year's rundown, as nearly brand by brand as can be managed:

Redfield, because makers here are usually listed alphabetically, normally comes in the middle of things. But as one of the bigger scope outfits, and because they have a bunch of new scopes this year, we thought we'd start with them.

The Golden Five Star scopes are Redfield's first additions since the Trackers of four years ago. That's understandable, as they also had the Widefield Low Profiles, the Traditionals, and widefield and round-eyepiece versions of the 3-9x Illuminator. The Five Stars replace the Traditionals, except that the 2½x of that line has been kept.

The Five Star series consists of 4x and 6x straight powers, and variables in 2-7x, 3-9x, 4-12x and 6-18x. Apparently they do not share my fondness for the 1½-4½x, though admittedly a 1.7-5x WLP is available.

As with the other Redfields, the Five Stars have one-piece tube construction. The elimination of threaded joints has to add strength and weatherproofness, and in all likelihood makes it easier to maintain lens alignment as the scope is subjected to heavy recoil over the years. Lenses are multi-coated, and the ocular unit is round rather than TV-shaped, for which I'm grateful. Outside diameter of all Five Star eyepieces is 1.5 inches, so all fields are plenty big. Objective diameters are 1.68-in. (43mm) in the

The Burris Mikro pistol scopes are on ⅝-in. tubes in 2x and 3x, weigh 4 oz.

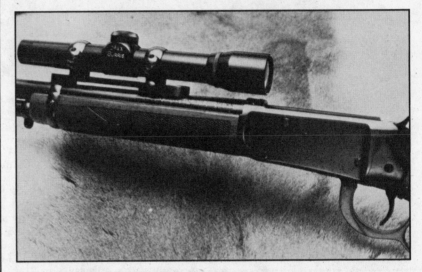
The Burris Gunsite Scout scopes are 2¾x with 7- to 14-in. eye relief for forward mounting.

Smaller Armson O.E.G. models fit 22-cal. rifles and handguns. They are only only 3¾-in. long.

Leupold has ring sets for Ruger No.1 and 77/22 rifles, for rimfire dovetails and for Sako rifles, the latter two in both low and medium heights.

Beeman double-adjustable mounts offer windage correction on grooved receivers, such as 22 rifles and, very likely, air rifles.

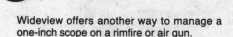

Wideview offers another way to manage a one-inch scope on a rimfire or air gun.

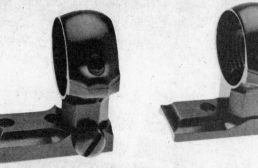

New Millet scope rings are artfully machined to be lighter, but fit Redfield, Burris and Leupold bases.

This is how Clearview handles the rimfire problem—the inserts are for fitting ⅞-and ¾-in. scopes.

6-18x and 4-12x, 1.58-in. (40mm) in the 3-9x and 6x, and 1.42-in. (36mm) in the 2-7x and 4x. These are large enough to give high light transmission without going to needless extremes in the lower magnifications.

All Five Stars come with the 4-Plex reticle, with the Accu-Trac available in all variables except the 2-7x. There are adjustable objectives on the 4-12 and 6-18x, which allow precise focusing for range and thus complete parallax elimination. Tubes are anodized aluminum alloy, thus are corrosion free and scratch resistant. A set of Butler Creek flip-up lens covers is included with each scope.

I've used only the 2-7x, which I feel is the best all-round variable size for big game. Unfortunately, it arrived several months after our season closed, so I couldn't actually hunt with it. Testing was done on a M700 7mm Magnum, and everything checked out well on paper. With luck, I might have a fuller report next year.

Aimpoint has just introduced a new line of mounting systems for their 2000 Series of electronic sights. Mount bases and rings are available for revolvers, autoloading pistols, rifles, and autoloading, pump and over-under shotguns. The Aimpoint sight is now offered in either black matte or brushed aluminum finish for either the Short 2000 or Long 2000 version.

This is the T'SOB mount on a Mag-na-port/ S&W Stalker revolver.

Basic version of each is a no-magnification (1x) unit. The Long 2000 is threaded to accept 3x and 1½-4x attachments. The shorter unit is intended primarily for handgun use, the long one for rifle or slug shooter. All are small, light, and very fast to use.

Armson Inc.'s Occluded Eye Gunsight (OEG), which has been largely oriented toward police and military weapons for some years, now is available in two models for 22 rimfires, one for daylight use, the other for day/night shooting. In use, the OEG presents a bright red dot to the aiming eye while the other eye views the target area normally; the brain unites these views so the dot serves as a reticle. In use, the "off" eye takes advantage of all available light and the dot is easily seen when a conventional scope reticle would be difficult to use.

Armson also offers five riflescopes. Two of these, a 6x and a 3-9x, are also designed for bad light shooting with 56mm objective lenses, which will get as much light to the shooter as most anything around. Armson has mounts for various military-style arms such as the AR-15/M-16, Heckler & Koch, UZI and Mini-14.

Beeman's SS (Short Scopes) were covered at length last year when I detailed how I mounted one on the bolt of an old M94 Winchester, to ride back out of the way when the action was opened, thus making way for the ejecting empty. We won't go into them here, except to say that SS scopes are available in 2½x, 3x, 4x and 1½-4x, with integral mounting clamps. For shooters who want a small scope with more mounting possibilities, Beeman is supplying the MS-1, a 4x built on an inch tube but only 7½ inches in length and 8 oz. in weight. It uses conventional mounts, but extension rings will be necessary in some cases. Beeman also has a line of Blue Ribbon scopes for big game, and Double Adjustable mounts to fit grooved receivers; these have windage adjustments for primary zeroing.

Burris has one of the most extensive scope lines in the country, with single-powers, variables and handgun models in all normal powers, the Automatic Range Compensating reticle for long-distance work, and the like. Nevertheless, they've found room for a couple of new ones this year. One is the Gunsite Scout Scope, influenced by Jeff Cooper's preference for a low-power glass situated ahead of the action opening. The Scout is a 2.75x with eye relief of 7-14 inches, which means its ocular lens can be forward of the bolt on an old 94

Winchester. This makes it easy to grasp Ol' Slabsides around the action, of course, or a 600 Remington, say, but it does make for an odd looking arrangement. It also means the scope's field is reduced from a normal 40 feet to 15. On the other hand, its position makes it easy for the off eye to watch the target, so maybe it all works out.

Handgunners get a couple of new ones this year—the Mikro revolver scopes in 2x or 3x (actually 1.7x and 2.7x). These are built on ⅝-in. tubes with enlarged objective and ocular units. Eye relief is 9-24 inches and fields are 15 and 11 feet. Each weighs 4 oz. and they're just over 9 inches long. Crosswire reticle is it. Internal adjustments are valued at an inch, with a maximum of 70. Steel rings to fit Burris bases come with the package.

Also new are Burris ring mounts for Ruger rifles. You can get either standard front and rear designs for the M77R, 77V and Number 1, or standard front and extension rear for the 77R. All have windage adjustments. The extension unit permits use of the Burris Mini scopes on actions where they otherwise could not be mounted.

Conetrol must have a mount line as extensive as any in the country—or the world, for that matter. Their ultra-streamlined design is available in either bridge or two-piece models, in three price levels, Hunter, Gunnur and Custom. All versions have long been available with 1-inch, 26mm and 26½mm rings. New this year are 30mm rings. These have two screws in each side and come in two heights, 6mm (.236) and 8mm (.315), $37.47 each or $74.94 per pair. All Conetrol bases and rings can be had with special finishes if customer takes them unblued. Cost of special-finish items blued is 1½ times regular price. Bases not normally packaged as a standard two-piece base are available at 1½ times regular cost. This permits the use of a front mount designed for one rifle and a rear unit for a different one, as with a custom rifle or one with an action altered to non-standard dimensions. Nickel-plated Conetrol items are also available at double the cost of blued ones.

Clear View has altered their see-thru mounts to provide easy visual access to the iron sights. Called the Broad View, the new version features extremely wide ovals for the riser sections of the scope rings, to make vision for running shots easier. Scopes with objectives up to 40mm can be accommodated. A 1-inch mount for 22 rifles with grooved receivers also is

available, with insert adapters to handle ⅞- or ¾-in. scopes, and the Clear View Model 101 see-thru mount rings fit almost all Weaver-type bases. Side mounts are offered for both the old M94 Winchester and the new Angle Eject models.

Cougar Optics has for several years been offering a number of big game and handgun scopes. In powers and designs, they essentially cover the needs of most hunters. Full-View wide angle models are available in 4x32, 4x40 and 6x40, plus a 3-9x40 variable. Standard-views are offered in 2.5x32, 4x32, 4x40, 6x40 and 8x40, with a pair of variables in 3-9x40 and 4-12x40. Pistol scopes in either black or silver finish are made in 1.5x20 and 2.5x20 versions. Specifications are conventional, tubes are anodized aluminum alloy, nitrogen filled. Three reticle choices are crosswire, 4 Post-Crosswire and 4 Post-Crosswire-Peep.

Paul Jaeger Inc. is now the exclusive U.S. importer and distributor for the top quality Schmidt & Bender scope line, according to a letter from Dietrich Apel. All non-variable S&B models now have 1-inch steel tubes and black chrome finishes. Most variables have 30mm tubes (some have mounting rails, which eliminates the need for rings). Jaeger routinely stocks 30mm rings and bases to fit most rifles, including units to fit the M77 and No. 1 Rugers. Also available are 30mm rings for Redfield, Burris and Leupold bases.

Schmidt & Bender scopes are available in straight powers from 1½x to 12x, and in variable powers of 1¼-4x, 1½-6x and 2½-10x. Some models can be had with light metal tubes and mounting rails.

Especially interesting are the 1½x15, which has a 90-foot field, so would be an excellent choice on a dangerous-game rifle, and the 1½-6x42. The latter is called the Sniper scope, for good reason. Besides a power spread which is about right for most military applications, its internal elevation adjustments are synchronized with the bullet path of the 7.62x51mm (308 Winchester) using the 150-grain spitzer bullet at conventional velocity. That is, after obtaining a basic zero, instead of making changes in minutes of angle or fractions thereof, changes can be made directly for distances up to 600 meters; that is, you simply set the elevation dial for 1, 2, 3, 4, 5 or 6 hundred meters. The reticle is also designed to serve as a rangefinder, with markings and post thicknesses of specific dimensions. When compared to a target of known size, this lets the shooter calculate range. This scope requires 30mm mounting rings.

Jason Empire's scope line includes several straight 4x's, with objectives of 20mm, 32mm and 40mm, giving the user a choice of sizes depending upon how much light he needs and whether he wants a wide angle or not, plus variables in 3-9x and 4-12x for big game use, 3-7x on a ¾-in. tube for rimfires. One 4x32 is made with its windage turret on the left side to give more clearance for ejecting empties on guns such as the M94. This also helps clear the way for iron sight use. The Jason Golden Stags have multi-coated objective lenses, nitrogen-filled tubes and Dawn-to-Dusk reticles.

Kwik Mounts now have a satin black anodized finish on the units for the Remington 870/1100 and Browning Auto 5 12-gauge models, rather than the Artel epoxy finish of last year. This is intended to give a tougher, non-reflective finish. The Kwik Mount is a U-shaped wrap-around unit that sits low on the action of these models and is held by a pair of bolts that replace the factory pins which hold the trigger housing in place. A base to accept Weaver-type mount rings is an integral part of this Kwik Mount. It is long enough to give good ring separation and positions the scope much nearer the gun than some shotgun mounts. We tried one on an 870 with a 3x Lyman, and found it excellent. So equipped, there's little doubt that a 12-gauge pump gun with perhaps one spare barrel can handle most of the shooting chores a non-guncrank hunter will ever face.

T. K. Lee Co., long renowned for the Floating Dot reticle, went out of business for a bit when Dan Glenn retired, as we mentioned here last year. We hoped someone else would take it over; we're glad to report that has happened. **Gordon Daniel,** an engineer/hunter and longtime shooting buddy of Glenn, is now installing these precise aiming units in many makes and models of scopes—including the Bushnell and Tasco, which weren't formerly handled. As well as dots, Daniel will install just crosshairs, of steel or spider silk, if desired. Turnaround time is about one week. Some scopes are not amenable to reticle changing, so a query wouldn't hurt. The business no longer is located in Birmingham, Alabama, though. Daniel's address is 9264 N. Bellaire St., Denver, CO 80229.

Leupold is another manufacturer

with such an extensive line that it's hard to fit another scope into it. Still, they do so every so often, and this year's entry is a large-objective 6x for the Golden Ring line. It has a 42mm objective lens, compared to the 33mm of their 6x Compact and the 36mm of their older 6x. The 6x42mm gives an exit pupil of 7mm, which means it can deliver all the light the human eye can absorb at maximum dilation. This is the type of scope many European hunters prefer, as they do much of their shooting from stands just before dark at motionless or slowly moving game. Thus a scope with a good twilight factor is the top choice, and for decades they've preferred 6x or 8x scopes with unusually large objectives. This Leupold was designed for the European market, but will serve just as well for American hunters whose needs parallel theirs. The Duplex reticle is slightly heavier in this 6x42mm than normal, to make it more conspicuous in bad light. Scope weight is 11.3 oz., length 12 inches. Tube diameter is the standard one inch.

Also new this year are Leupold mounts for the Ruger No. 1 single shot, the Ruger 77/22, the Sako rifles with integral dovetail bases, and 22 rimfires having grooved receivers. Those for the Rugers are completely interchangeable with Ruger's patented mounting system and are produced under license from Sturm, Ruger & Co. Those for the Sako rifles are available in low and medium heights. The No-Tap rimfire rings also come in those two heights and accept one-inch scopes. The new Ruger and Sako rings allow lower-than-normal mounting of scopes, especially Leupold's great little Compacts.

Lyman Products Corp., long famous as the manufacturer of the renowned Alaskan, Challenger and Super Targetspot scopes, now is out of the scope business, according to a note from Ken Ramage. He says they are still doing some repair on the All-American series, and that John Unertl can do some repair work on the Targetspot series. It's sad to think that there are no more Lyman scopes. They held a special place in the feelings of American hunters, especially older guys who remember the years when the Alaskan was without a doubt one of the top hunting scopes in the world. I finally got an Alaskan a year or so ago—well used, of course, but in good condition. It's now on my pet 284 Mauser, and I can tell you it's one scope I'm not going to part with.

Millett Sights has for several years

been supplying their version of a two-piece pivot-type mount. Its basic design is similar to the long-popular Redfield—in fact, Millett rings can be used with Redfield, Burris or Leupold bases—but there are differences. Due to the sculptured effect of Millett bases, the grooving of inner ring surfaces, and some hollowing out of the vertical pillar of the rings, these are measurably lighter than similar designs from other makers. For example, a low set of Millett rings weighs but 1.5 oz. and the bases for FN-style actions only 1.75 oz. Also, the two halves of a set of rings fit together by a mortise and tenon interlocking system. Units are made in three heights, .145, .265 and .395-in. from the top of the base to the bottom of the inner ring surface. Bases are available for the 700 series of Remington actions, round receiver Ruger 77, Weatherby Mark V and Vanguard, BSA Monarch, the FN series, and, new this year, Model 70 Winchester configurations. Actually, numerous other rifles can be handled by one or the other of these mounts. Mounts are fabricated of heat treated, stress relieved steel, and come standard or engraved.

Also offered is the Scope-Site unit. This consists of a set of open sights (adjustable or fixed rear, blade front with red face), which are integral with the top halves of the scope mounting rings. These serve as emergency sights in case of damage to the scope, or for fast use at close range where for some reason the scope is not suitable. They also could make it easy to find game in the small field of a high power scope, by first using the Scope-Site and then just tilting the head down to pick up the target in the scope. With only a few inches between front and rear sights, any aiming error is multiplied rapidly with range, so such units obviously are not intended for long-distance work. But a Scope-Site could save the day as an emergency backup.

Omark Industries (CCI, Speer, RCBS, Outers and Weaver) has a tremendous number of gun-related items, but so far as this review is concerned, we have to stick to the scope mount stuff. That means Weaver, for Outers took over that extensive mount line when the Weaver scope company went out of existence. Nobody ever accused Weaver mounts of being pretty, so they're rarely used on rifles intended primarily to stand in a fancy gun cabinet and be taken out only to impress visitors. But millions of blood-and-guts hunters have found them just the ticket. They're light,

New Redfield Five-Star scopes include two straight power and four variables, all the way to 6x-18x.

Tasco's EW4x44 Euro-Class scope brings the advantages of the 30mm tube to a matte-finished hunter's scope.

Leupold's 6x42 has a larger-than-standard Duplex reticle to suit its role as a dawn-to-dusk scope.

Swarovski Optik's ZFM 6x42 sniper scope provides a high contrast image even in adverse light conditions and is built to be durable.

Burris ring mounts for Ruger rifles include an extension unit to permit the use of Burris mini-scopes.

Beeman Blue Ribbon Model 66R is marketed for the big game hunter, offers external parallax control.

strong, dependable. They come in various designs—far too many to list here—and are made to fit practically anything a hunter can get to his shoulder. As they used to say around Weaver's El Paso factory, "It's an ugly little mount, but it works." True words.

Simmons has a new line of scopes this year, the Presidential Series. Included are five models. Only one is a straight power, a 4x. There are variables in 2-7x, 3-9x, 4-12x and 6.5-20x. All have 44mm objective lenses, "Simcoat" multi-coating, 360-degree wide angle oculars, polarized and yellow screw-in objective lens filters made of optical glass, speed focusing, quarter-minute click adjustments, and metal sunshades. Objective units are adjustable for parallax elimination, and tubes have an anodized hi-gloss finish. According to Ol' Ernie, 104 separate processes are involved in the multi-coating, all with the ultimate goal of providing shooters with the best possible target image.

The large objective provides fine twilight factors in all these Presidential scopes, ranging from 13+ in the 4x to 30 in the 6.5-20x, but it also adds weight. The 4x, 2-7x and 3-9x go about a pound each, and the 4-12x and 6.5-20x top 19 oz. On a varmint rifle, that's no problem, and the biggest variable is an excellent choice for such use as it gives quick accommodation to all light and mirage problems. On the other hand, the 4x's 15½ oz. can be a bit much for a woods rifle. The big front end also requires medium or high mounting rings on most rifles. We've had the chance to use the 3-9x for several months now, with fine results, so feel sure a lot of shooters will like these Presidentials.

Swift Instruments Inc. has all kinds of optical goods, including a half-dozen big game scopes and two rimfire models. Making up the first group are a 4x and a 3-9x of conventional design with 32mm objectives, full view wide angles in the same powers with 40mm lenses, a 6x and a 12x with 40mm objectives. For 22-cal. shooters, there's a 4x15mm and a 3-7x20mm, both on ¾-in. tubes, adjusted to be parallax free at 50 yards. The centerfire models are adjusted for 100 yards. One-inch mount rings are available in two heights to fit Weaver-style bases. Rimfire models have attached mounts to fit grooved receivers.

Tasco scopes could well be the largest selling make in the country. As with many others, Tascos are made in Japan and marketed out of Miami

and Seattle. Currently, 80 rifle and 15 handgun scopes are catalogued, in models from 1x to 36x, if I didn't miss something along the way. They also sell terrestrial and astronomical telescopes, too. I mention those only because they apparently are included in overall telescope sales listed in a recent Tasco fact sheet—over a half-million in 1985. That's a bunch of scopes, no matter how you look at it. They also sold over a half-million binoculars last year.

As a bit of background on this company which we've rarely mentioned before, it was incorporated in 1954 by George Rosenfield, who previously operated Tanross Supply Co., a wholesale fishing tackle and hardware distributorship. After expanding his line with binoculars, he saw more growth potential in optics, and switched to this field. He shortened the company name to Tasco, began traveling to the Orient to locate manufacturers, and has been largely concentrating on optical goods ever since, though the company also is involved in other fields. Currently, about 225 persons are employed in the Miami 118,000-sq.-ft. complex of offices and warehouses.

I've been using scopes for a number of years, but strangely had never tried

a Tasco. PR person Rita Glassman offered to lend me anything I wanted for testing, so I borrowed a 1.7-5x to try during deer season and a 6-24x for varmints. I put the little variable on a Model Seven Remington 7mm-08 and took it west to Huntingdon County. Legend has it that the name comes from an Indian comment of long ago— "Hunting done"—but that's sure not the case these days. There are more than enough whitetails out yonder, and about an hour past dawn one morning I bounced one out in some heavy cover. Luckily, the little Tasco

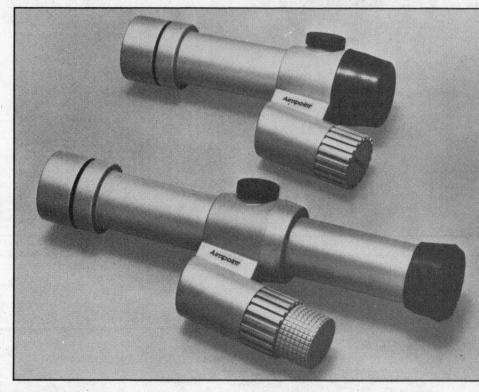

Brushed aluminium finish option and new mounting systems suit Aimpoint sights to handguns, rifles and shotguns, blue or stainless.

was set at 1½x and its big field made it easy to find the running deer and slam a 140-grain Hornady behind the right shoulder from a rearward angle. It went through the neck lengthways and came out in front, for an instant kill. A small variable like this is unbeatable for most deer hunting, I believe. The last 16 or 18 I've killed have been taken with one of this class, set at 1½x.

The 6-24x went onto a Remington 40XB-BR 222. As it arrived in late fall, I had no chance to try it on chucks or prairie dogs, but I have done considerable shooting with it on the bench. I started at 25 yards, as I'm reluctant to stick a collimator's stud in the muzzle of a rifle like this one.

First shot was on paper, and a few adjustments got things centered. While I was there, I fired an 8-shot group, using a different magnification for each shot and covering the whole power spread. The group was scarcely larger in diameter than a single bullet hole, meaning there was no detectable change in point of impact at any setting from 6x to 24x. I then went to 100 yards and did considerable firing, with the purpose of checking the value of the internal adjustments. They consistently checked out at ¼ minute, as listed. With luck, I might be trying

As light and as small as they get, this is the Mark V electronic sight from Action Arms Ltd.

T/C's 4x Short Tube for grooved receivers offers the Electra Dot reticle. There's a version for one-inch rings, too.

this outfit on prairie dogs about the time you're reading this. Its wide magnification choice should make it fully adaptable to the varying mirage conditions the summer sun brings in South Dakota.

Tasco also expects to have another 4-scope line, the Euro-Class, available soon. They will be built on 30mm tubes, the 4x, 6x and 3-9x having 44mm objectives, the 3-12x a 52mm. Tasco mounts will be available.

Thompson/Center added four rifle scopes to their optical line shortly after getting the single shot TCR rifle into production. Their Lobo and Recoil Proof handgun scopes have been available a lot longer, as they were produced to complement the popular

T/C Contender pistol, which has been around for many years now. We've mentioned these at various times, so won't go into them again now.

All T/C rifle scopes are designated as Recoil Proof, which I assume means they are constructed to withstand the same recoil force as the RP pistol scopes. All have Electra Dot reticles, a battery-powered switch-operated unit. Both a center dot and the inner sections of the horizontal and vertical lines are illuminated. The common 1.4V hearing aid battery supplies the power.

The TC4 and TC 3/9V are conventional-size scopes of 4x and 3-9x. The other two rifle scopes are actually the same, except for mounting systems. One has an integral clamping rail for attaching to a grooved receiver, the other takes conventional 1-inch rings. Their power is 4x, field 29 feet, eye relief, 3 inches. Of most interest is their length—7.7 inches—which accounts for the name, 4x Short Tube. The Electra Dot housing just forward of the ocular lens might make an extension mount necessary on some rifles. T/C has their own Detachable Ring Mount now, and it will handle their scopes on T/C firearms, and quite likely on some custom jobs. The rings can be used with Redfield, Burris or Leupold bases.

Weatherby, Inc. begins its fifth decade this year. For some reason I find that hard to accept, but simple arithmetic proves it. They have nothing new in scopes this year, doubtless because their Supreme line was introduced only a couple of years ago and there's no reason whatsoever to change it. As we reported earlier, its five scopes cover the needs of all big game hunting. There are three variables, 1.7-5x20, 2-7x34 and 3-9x44, and a pair of 4x's, one having a 34mm objective, the other a 44mm. The Supremes have a constantly centered, non-magnifying, luminous reticle, binocular-type focusing, multi-coating, and the Autocom system to compensate for bullet drop. I've had considerable experience with the two smaller variables during the past several years, and both have performed flawlessly.

Also deserving mention is the long-popular Mark XXII 4x50 scope intended primarily for the Mark XXII 22 autoloading rifle. It has a grooved dovetail mount as an integral part of its ⅞-in. tube, enlarged ocular and objective units, and Lumi-Plex reticle. The "50" in its designation refers to its relative brightness, incidentally, not the diameter of its front lens, as might be expected. It's a good, bright scope for rimfire use, with a 25-foot field and a large 7mm exit pupil for full light transmission and quick aiming. The Mark XXII has been around so long that it sort of gets taken for granted, but it has lasted because it does the job.

Maynard P. Buehler, Inc. is now in their 41st year of scope mount building. I don't know how many mounts have come out of the Orinda, California plant in those years, but it has to be a trainload. There was a time when Ol' Maynard showed their strength, and his, by installing scopes on assorted 4-bore double rifles and such, then shooting 'em, but he has more sense now. At any rate, anyone who wants to put a glass sight on a rifle or handgun can doubtless do it with a Buehler mount. They come with long and short one-piece bases, two-piece bases, Micro-Dial bases, extension bases, to fit Sako dovetails, and complete custom jobs. The rings come in three heights and assorted diameters up to 30mm. You can get them engraved, too, if that strikes your fancy.

Apollo Optics (Senno Corp.) recently introduced three wide angle waterproof scopes—the Silver Bullet Series—to go with their earlier West-

A shotgun and slugs would not be Dave Wise's first choice for farm country whitetails, he said, but a scope on a Remington 870 in Kwik Mounts' low Saddle mount would work.

Redfield's new Golden Five Star line covers all big game needs. Here, Bob Wise tries the 2-7x on a 7mm Remington Magnum. Butler Creek caps come with the scope; that's a Redfield Jr. mount.

Shepherd's DRS scope is now available in several models. Here, Dave Wise shoots the new 2.5-7.75x version. This size seems more suitable on hunting rifles, Bell feels, even looks OK on Ultralight 77 Ruger.

ern models. The Silver Bullets come in 4x32, 3-9x40 and 4-12x40, either gloss or matte finish. The 4x has half-minute adjustments, the others quarter-minute. Duplex reticles are standard and lenses are multi-coated. The Westerns are made in 4x32 and 3-9x32, and there are two rubber armored scopes, one a 3-9x40 Wide Angle, the other a 4x32 Compact WA. Silver Bullet prices are $99, $124 and $135.

Browning is no longer marketing scopes under their own name as they used to do; however, they do have mounts for installing scopes on their own rifles.

Wideview currently is marketing see-through mounts for more than 40 firearms. Their iron-sight openings are oval shaped—wider than they are high—to give plenty of field. Most versions utilize the factory holes for installation, or the grooved receivers on 22 rifles and air guns. Shotguns with steel receivers must be drilled and tapped. They're also made for some handguns.

Action Arms Ltd.'s Mark V Action Sight is probably the lightest, smallest electronic sight available. Built on a one-inch aluminum tube, it's just over 5 inches long and weighs only 5½ oz. The red dot which serves as the aiming point is powered by two mercury batteries (RM64OH or equivalent), and its intensity can be adjusted to suit ambient light conditions. The Mark V can be installed with many standard mounts, on hunting rifles, revolvers, pistols, military weapons, what have you. It's extremely fast in use, particularly under poor conditions at short range.

Unertl scopes are still available, though they have not been aggressively advertised recently. The target scopes, especially, have long been noted for their extremely high optical quality. We mentioned a bit ago, under the Lyman entry, that Unertl will repair the Lyman Targetspot scopes, but in talking with Mrs. Unertl on the phone just before this was written, she told me the only thing they're doing to the Lymans is replacing reticles.

SSK Industries' T'SOB mount is the rig J. D. Jones uses to install scopes on his Hand Cannons. He tells me he's never had a T'SOB base come off a gun, which indicates they've solved most of the problems inherent in this practice. Anything that'll keep a scope and a 375 JDJ tied together must be doing something right. Their "standard" versions fit most handguns, and true custom mounts can be made to fit anything. The mount base can be extended into a full length ventilated rib on many guns, which gives good versatility in ring placement and also looks nice. There's also a T'LSOB for use on light recoiling calibers.

Zeiss scopes haven't been mentioned in this review for several years, probably because they've made no radical changes in the models that are readily available in this country. Obviously, there's no good reason to do so; the Diatal-Cs cover most hunting situations extremely well. For those who might not be aware of the fact, this line includes 4x, 6x, 10x and 3-9x models, all having *precise* quarter-minute internal adjustments, binocular-type focusing eyepieces, crosshair or Z-Plex reticles, and T-Star multi-layer coating which gives these scopes light transmission ratings well over 90 percent and unsurpassed image accuracy. Multi-coating, incidentally, was a Zeiss development, as was the original single-layer magnesium fluoride coating back in the '30s.

These Diatal-C models are built on one-inch tubes, so can be installed on almost any mount. The 10x has an adjustable objective unit, so can be focused exactly at any range from 40 yards out; the others are set to be parallax free at 100 yards.

I've been using the 4x for four years now, with complete satisfaction. Still, for guys like me who like to ghost through the black timber, it would be nice to have a 1½-4½x Zeiss, or even a 2½x, on a straight inch tube. A 1½x might be even better . . .

Kimber recently sent me a set of the quick detachable mounts designed by stockmaker/gunsmith Len Brownell shortly before his death a few years ago. Kimber's version differs slightly from the original. Instead of having serrations along one edge of each block to engage teeth in a movable locking unit on the scope rings, the current issue has a recoil shoulder at the front of each block to engage the bottom forward edge of each ring. This would seem fully as efficient as the original and a lot easier to manufacture, though perhaps the concept does not seem as sophisticated. The locking units are tightened by finger levers. Blocks are available for many commercial firearms, and custom versions for unusual guns can be had from Ross Billingsley of Dayton, Wyo. A similar mount is made for grooved-receiver rifles such as the Kimber 82 and 84. This Kimber is a sturdy attractive mount, and the bases that go on the action are thin enough that iron sights are usable

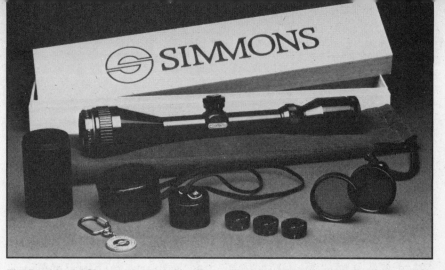

The Presidential Simmons comes with yellow and polarizing filters, built-in sunshades, multi-coating and parallax control.

Swift 3-9x40 is their universal scope—has quadriplex reticle, waterproofing, all Swift features.

Schmidt & Bender scopes from Paul Jaeger, Inc. include a number of 30mm variables and straight scopes from 1.5x to 12x, all with Schmidt & Bender quality.

Pentax makes a full line with five models and sound optics.

when the scope is removed. Its basic dovetail design and the solid bucking-up place to control fore and aft movement means that a good zero can be maintained even when the scope is removed and replaced.

Wally Siebert has for years been significantly increasing the magnification of Lyman AA, Leupold and Unertl medium-power scopes, to make benchrest models out of varmint scopes. Those in the 8x to 12x range can usually be increased to 16x to 24x, and even some high-power target scopes can be boosted. For example, Wally can increase the 36x Leupold to 40x or 45x, if such magnification seems helpful to you. He can also install Superfine Crosshairs, but I'd suggest you don't go for these unless your eyesight is 20/20 or better. Conversely, for those wanting a long eye relief (approximately 10-20 inches) scope for handgun use, Siebert can cut the power of assorted Leupolds and the 12x Redfield in half.

For a long time now, I've been using an 8x Lyman AA which Wally boosted to 16x for me. It has given excellent results on a heavy 222 and a M788 223, particularly on chucks and crows. It also works fine on prairie dogs when mirage is no problem, but at times I find that much magnification unusable on the summer prairie. Of course, that comment applies to any scope of such power. But on those occasions when you're on the shady side of a butte in late afternoon, the higher powers give incredible aiming precision on those small distant targets.

Bausch & Lomb/Bushnell have enough scopes between 'em to handle most any shooting chore. B&L, which got back into the big game scope field a few years ago, covers the bases with a 4x and two variables for large game. A 1½-6x will handle anything from dangerous critters just off the muzzle to distant pronghorns, and there'a a 3-9x because that's what so many hunters want. In addition, a 6-24x takes care of sit-still varmints as far as there's any likelihood of connecting, and doubles for silhouette shooting. Note that the power spread is a 1-4 ratio in two of these, as compared to 1-3 in most switch powers.

The same 1-4 ratio is available in Bushnell's new Sportview Quad Powers, a 2½-10x and a 5-20x. Both have the TAC (Trajectory Adjustment Compensator) reticle for long range shooting, as do the Sportview Rangemasters.

Bushnell's overall line includes six Scopechiefs, nine Banner Standards and Compacts, two Banner Lite-Sites, three Banner Trophy Wide Angles, three Standard Sportviews, nine rimfire scopes, plus three Centurion and two Magnum Phanton handgun models. Hope I didn't miss any; regardless, you get the idea—Bushnell has a bunch of popular scopes. All of the big game models and most of the others have one-piece tubes, the Scopechiefs have multi-coated optics, wide angle versions of some are offered, and several reticles created for ultra-long range shooting are available. Three kinds of mounts—split rings with locking units to fit separate bases, rings with integral bases, and a see-through design—are made for most popular rifles.

Pentax Corp., known for three decades for their excellent single lens reflex cameras, moved into the rifle scope field this year by introducing five big game models. All are built on one-inch tubes, of course. The objective end diameter is 1.52-in. for the 4x, 2-7x and Mini 3-9x, 1.72-in. for the 6x and 3-9x. Ocular end diameter is over 1.5-in. for all except the Mini, which is 1.375-in. Lengths range from 10.4 to 13.4 inches, and weights from 12.2 to 15 oz., all of which means these are about medium in size, among today's hunting scopes.

All have hard anodized finishes, nitrogen filling, and multi-coated lenses. The internal adjustments are rated at ¼ minute in the two 3-9x's, ⅓ in the 6x and 2-7x and ½ minute in the 4x. The latter two values are unusual nowadays, so should be kept in mind when making adjustments.

We haven't used any of these Pentax scopes, so can't give a personal report. Their camera optics have always been praised, so it seems likely they'll be of similar quality in the scopes.

Swarovski Optik's newest AL (American Lightweight) scope is a 3-9x having a 36mm objective lens. It also has a large ocular unit, which results in a large field of view—about 39 feet at bottom power, 13½ feet at 9x. Eye relief is 3½ inches, which means it can be mounted on most magnums without having to worry about recoil delivering a cut eyebrow. A compressible eyepiece helps here too. The tube is hardened aluminum alloy, internal clicks are valued at 7mm (a scant quarter-minute), and weight is 13 oz. Twilight factor ranges from 8.5 to 18, depending on power. It is said to be waterproof, fogproof, and shock and corrosion resistant. Swarovski also currently offers its ZFM 6x42 Military Style Sniper Scope for rifles such as the H&K G-3.

Dave Miller is so well known for the high grade rifles he builds (the other day one was auctioned off for over 200,000 smackers) that his scope mount doesn't attract enough attention. But it is quite a job, essentially hand-fabricated to fit a particular scope to a particular rifle. It cradles the scope solidly but without strain. That's more than a lot of mounts can claim, for if the rifle action is a bit out of true, the mount simply bends the tube to fit. Miller compensates for such inaccuracies by careful measurements before the machining starts. Originally made in a bridge type only, Dave tells me he now makes it in a two-piece version, if desired. I was afraid to ask the price—it was $800 some years ago—but I guess if you can afford the kind of rifle he builds, you can go for the mount too. I would.

Dan Shepherd's Dual Reticle System (DRS) scope line has grown noticeably this year, attracting attention from both sophisticated civilian riflemen and the military. And probably—we might as well say it—scaring off a lot of average-type hunters who are both fascinated and repelled by the options. No space this year to describe its workings; see GD38, 1984, for details.

I'm not a 3-9x fan, no matter who the maker, so was glad to receive a pair of 2.5-7.75x models for testing some months back. This size is a lot more fitting on a hunting rifle. One of these had the DRS reticle for high velocity centerfire loads, so I tried it on a 308 and a 338. The other was intended for rimfire use, up to 250 yards. That's farther than I can get acceptable groups out of a 22LR, but the theory is sound. In this version it boils down to a series of circles, diminishing in size, installed along the vertical crosshair. Separation distance is calibrated with bullet drop, of course.

In just before presstime were a pair of new and bigger variables, in 3-10x. One features the Side II DRS, which adapts to many fast loads. The other has a thin crosshair combined with a 2 MOA open circle, plus MOA reference marks at the top and right side of field. With these the user can actually see the corrections he is making for windage and elevation, and thus be certain he's getting them. Knowing approximate target size, he can use these marks to estimate range, too. That is, if a target 20 inches wide subtends 4 MOA, its distance is 500 yards. I intend to put this one on a heavy M700 223 Remington, so hope I can give some in-field reports next year. ●

MARTIN RABENO

MARTIN RABENO

The Art of The Engraver

BILLY BATES

STEVE LINDSAY

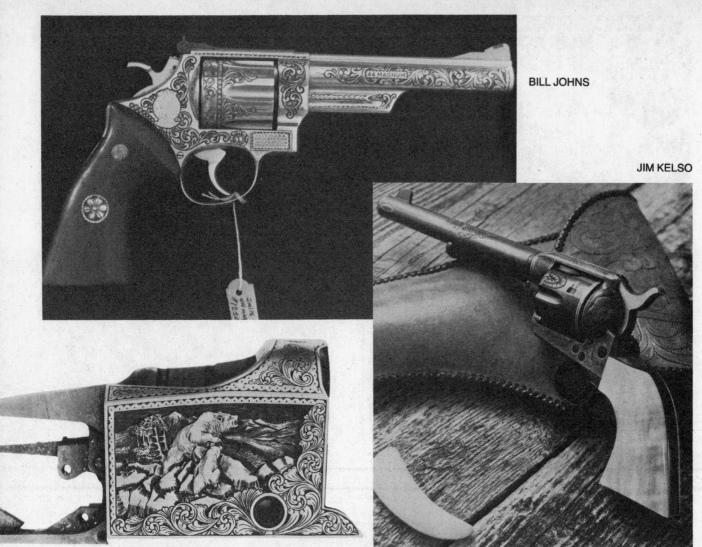

BILL JOHNS

JIM KELSO

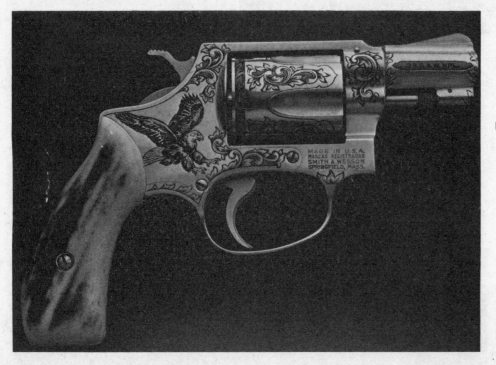

HOWARD V. GRANT

BYRON BURGESS

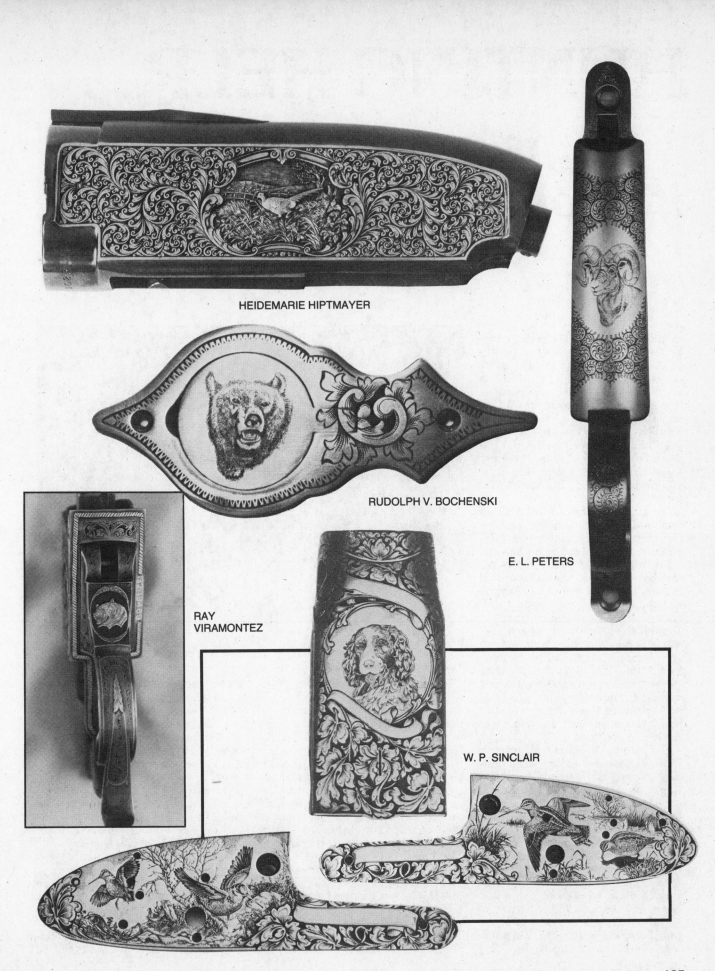

HEIDEMARIE HIPTMAYER

RUDOLPH V. BOCHENSKI

E. L. PETERS

RAY
VIRAMONTEZ

W. P. SINCLAIR

HUNTING HELP . . .

. . . is not always what it should be.

by SIDNEY DU BROFF

THE DEER STOOD grazing maybe 250 yards away. It was a pretty good one, from what I could make out in the glasses. But for me it was no target. It was a European roe deer that might go 60 pounds, not all that much bigger than a good-size dog. I wouldn't have attempted the shot even had there been a scope on the Brno rifle I carried slung over my shoulder. Anything much beyond a 100 yards gets to be kind of tricky for me with iron sights.

My guide, the local forester, in a combination of sign language and bad German, indicated that he was prepared to shoot that roe on my behalf.

I would have liked to see him try the shot. He was, however, interested in more than performing his shooting skill for my benefit. He wanted cash—cold real money and preferably American—in return for which I would be provided with the opportunity to brag about my kill to the folks back home. With just the two of us there, he figured, who was to know different? For how many others had he performed the same service? In this instance, at least, he surely had the wrong customer.

We were in the Balkan Mountains, in Bulgaria, based at one of the prettiest lodges I had ever seen, in a setting enhanced by the trees in the colors of fall. Unfortunately, we were living on Bulgarian sausages, pretty good as sausages go, but definitely not recommended as a steady and exclusive diet. Our guide/interpreter had neglected to bring the rest of the food with us; just as he was meant to insure that a scope-sighted rifle would be provided here, but didn't.

Hunters, I find, are generally people of character. But many of those who are supposed to assist us, as I

This is New Brunswick and the guide with emphysema hands Du Broff his ruffed grouse.

have encountered them over the years in various countries, are often sadly lacking in this essential.

The Bulgarians, who suffered a 500-year Turkish occupation and are eternally grateful to the Russians for having liberated them little more than a century ago, had just opened their doors to the rest of the world. They said they were interested to hear how I rated some of their hunting facilities. When I told them, they got angry at me, taking the position that if you don't like the message, kill the messenger.

Later, near Plovdiv, Bulgaria's second city, I was supposed to be hunting pheasants on a preserve that was part of the local collective farm. Here I was provided with a local "guide," a member of the collective whose services they were no doubt delighted to do without for the day, and probably forever, if they could. He led us over acres of plowed field, where we didn't even see a song bird, let alone a pheasant.

Afterwards, while driving along the road, he did see some pheasants. He promptly loaded a shotgun and shot at them out of the car window.

The Bulgarians are essentially very nice people, but those 500 years of Turkish rule probably taught them to be underhanded as the best way to survive.

While in the Balkans, we might as well stay there for a while. Take Romania, but then who'd want to and who could blame them? They say of Romanians they never tell the truth when a lie will do. I believe it. And the Romanians insist upon it. They revel in their reputation, and go on to add that all Romanians are thieves. I questioned the word "all." It seemed too general, too sweeping, but they assured me it was true (another lie).

That was why, on a visit to the Roumanian Hunting Association in Bucharest, I fell to my knees before a stuffed five-legged roe deer. It was not an act of worship, but merely to get down underneath that roe and feel around its underside to discover where the fifth leg had been sewn on. Actually, I couldn't find the stitches and have to assume that it really did have five legs.

Roumanian hunting was closed to foreigners, because, they said, a German had shot a deer that he wasn't meant to shoot. Had this act so traumatized the Roumanians that they stopped letting foreigners in to shoot their game and swell their coffers? I can believe that the poor fellow shot a deer they thought he should not have shot, but it was probably in frustration, because he couldn't find anything else. Lured by promises of game in abundance, he chose to ignore their well-deserved reputation, and chose instead to believe those who drew the

Roumania is one place, even more so than in Russia, where you do as you are told, or else. It is said that when Stalin died he in fact went to Roumania where he could inflict a form of repression now out of style in Russia.

Knowing how Roumania organizes things, it can be reasonably assumed that they were forced to admit, but only to themselves, that their hunting just wasn't good enough to entice foreigners. It was intended to reopen the season the following year, but they never quite managed it.

I can well understand their muddled state. One of the officials in the Roumanian Hunting Association informed me that Roumanian hunters were permitted to shoot only male hares. I marveled how Roumanian hunters could tell the difference.

Moving the short distance to Yugoslavia, a sister Balkan state, but one on which Roumanians shed little brotherly love, one finds a paradox here: a communist administration in a capitalist economy. At an early date the leaders discovered that communism didn't work, and certainly not in Yugoslavia, where nobody was in favor of it. But they weren't about to do themselves out of jobs and become day-laborers on a road gang in Upper Hercegovina. One of the first capitalist things they did was to inaugurate

his hunting. I was asked to a pheasant hunt in Croatia. The season was already closed, but that didn't matter much because the people who were doing the hunting made the laws, the Party Secretariat. The season might have been closed for most people, but they legislated it open.

The day before the shoot we had a drive around the preserve with the keeper. Why this was necessary I don't know, other than that the keeper wanted us to see the domain he controlled, now mainly bare earth with the occasional left-leaning corn stalk (some of them also leaned right), which looked much like any other field of that make-up in any other place. At that moment in time there did not appear to be many pheasants about, but I had no doubt that by tomorrow there would be an abundant supply, laid out, probably, just before the shooting was to begin.

Now, driving around, we spotted a dog. Dogs aren't allowed on hunting preserves, unless they happen to be hunting dogs, accompanied by a hunter. This dog wasn't a hunting dog, just some old black and white mutt, maybe taking a shortcut back from a visit to a girl dog he knew, definitely not accompanied, and not apparently doing any free-lance hunting. But who could tell what he might come upon, and the idea of not letting stray dogs roam around at will is essentially a good one.

Did I have a gun? the keeper asked. I did, and there was no way of denying that I did. Reluctantly I gave it to him. I dreaded what would follow, though I could not argue with the necessity for it.

Did I have any shells?

I didn't. But I presumed that the keeper did. He didn't, I breathed a sigh of relief, and hoped Old Fido would choose another route in future.

The next morning I was down bright and early, had breakfast and wondered why my Yugoslav guide hadn't also made it down. He came sauntering in as I finished, and announced casually, "No hunting today."

What do you mean, no hunting? It's all arranged.

Not when you're in Yugoslavia. Arrangements are not arrangements. Only occasionally. Not only was I not a member of the Party Secretariat, I wasn't even a member of the Party— not a Croatian, or even a Yugoslav for that matter—but a *Western foreigner American capitalist*. I might learn some deep dark Party secrets, like Rackvitch drinks too much slivovitz, and Holdovitch is a lousy shot, conse-

In Saskatchewan, this is somebody else shooting at Du Broff's moose—got it, too.

posters and wrote the copy for the travel brochures, people who probably had never felt the pressure of gunstock against a shoulder. Even if they had, it wouldn't have made the slightest difference.

a speed trap, 25-mph limit on the only straight stretch of road I had been able to find. After I really revved up and went 40, we settled out of court. The two motorcycle cops solicited a bribe that worked out a bit cheaper than the usual fine for speeding.

The hunting was supposed to be pretty good, at least where Tito did quently they didn't want me.

This is not to say that all the incompetent nincompoops are concentrated on the Balkans. North America has a couple, too, and I met my fair share of them up in Canada. There was this guy in Quebec, a really great hunter, or so he said. He was supposed to be looking after us, but our presence had a disturbing effect, that is, we disturbed his drinking, He wasn't sure what to do with us, so took us a really short distance beyond the outer suburbs of Quebec City. That there were deer here, I have no doubt, but the locals did their hunting at night, with lights, which they felt helped to improve the odds. They had no fear from the local game warden, since he was very local, indeed.

From the car we spotted a grouse. This fellow didn't like getting out of the car, unless it was to go inside somewhere.

"There's one for you," he said. "Get him on the ground."

There is not much fun shooting at a sitting target with a scattergun. I walked him up. He flushed. I fired and missed. That took care of the ruffed grouse hunting in the Province of Quebec. Well, not quite. I was still interested, so our "guide" arranged for us to be driven 100 miles to talk to someone who hunted grouse.

Still in Quebec, and still at a loss to know what to do with us, our "guide" delivered us unto the St. Lawrence River for waterfowl. The idea sounded good; the only trouble was that the millions of waterfowl that come flying down the St. Lawrence hadn't yet begun the journey. Our guide knew it, or, if he didn't, could easily have found out. So we—my poor wife Nedra and I—sat in a boat for three days and waited for some ducks that never appeared, and Nedra got seasick as we bobbed around that choppy river in a little boat.

Where, I wondered, was all this game in which the Province of Quebec was so abundantly endowed? Our "guide" was a source rich in personal hunting experiences, as long as it only required the firing of words. He implored me not to shave, since that would bring bad luck. He cited his father as an example, who insisted upon shaving every day of his life, even when at camp in pursuit of moose; in eight years of trying he never got so much as a shot at a moose. Though I refrained from putting razor to face,

all I succeeded in doing was growing a beard.

In New Brunswick, another time and after woodcock, we had a very conscientious and hardworking guide, but how hard-working can a guide be who suffers from advanced emphysema and has a cigarette poking perpetually out of his face. Even conscientious didn't help.

I felt sorry for the poor man and couldn't drive him beyond his limited functioning capacity. He, I was told, was their best guide. I hate to think what the others were like. I offered him my method of complete and painless termination of the habit that had once enslaved me, but he preferred emphysema and a perpetual cough.

In Saskatchewan, I was after moose, a nice big bull whose rack would be so heavy I'd have trouble hanging it on the wall. I always had the impression that if you went to some good place it was only a question of a little time before you came across one like that or a bit smaller, if you were unlucky.

But my own story is less romantic. We couldn't find a bull moose of any size. For day after day I tramped about, my rifle at the ready. There were tracks, and there were places where moose had bedded down but had since taken up residence elsewhere.

Besides the guide, there was a kind of photographer with me, a man who'd never been moose hunting before, but who was eager to share the experience. Day by day, my resolve to have a big one weakened until it reached the point where any moose would do. Then it happened, but it was a cow. Before I could decide whether I wanted her or not, the photographer grabbed the rifle from my hands, saying, "You don't want a cow anyway," and proceeded to shoot her.

The Swedes have put out the word that they're very efficient. Well, not in everything. Although the trip had been arranged months in advance, the forester in the southern district where I expected to hunt hadn't the vaguest idea I was coming. Suddenly, from his point of view, I appeared, and announced I was looking for a roe deer.

Swedes are extremely ambivalent about people who come from outside to hunt. Those who stand to make money out of it, and don't hunt themselves, are all for it. The local hunters who aren't going to get anything out

of it except competition are against it. Those who hunt, but who will benefit financially are in a serious and unresolvable dilemma, which might be the basis for another Ingmar Bergman film.

My forester was an amiable young fellow who didn't flap. He asked us into his luxurious cabin, where Nedra and I bolted down the forester's wife's

In Roumania, the Hunting Association Officials shoot only male hares, they say.

In East Germany, Du Broff and drilling (at right) did not pose so dashingly as his companion.

homemade coffee cake (Nedra says she didn't bolt). He also had to lend me his rifle. Bringing your rifle into Sweden is probably the most difficult thing anyone is ever called upon to do in life. I also had to take a shooting test. My own rifle, and the forester's, are both Husqvarnas, of Swedish manufacture, mine a 30-06, his a 270, so I had a pretty good idea where all the crucial items were located, except, he warned me, his rifle shot high and to the right.

In the morning we went out together. He came for me while it was still dark. As we drove along the dirt road, a young cow moose (moose are called "elk" in Sweden) loped just ahead of us, no doubt pleased to see her path all lighted up by our headlights. She didn't know it, but in another week she was going to be fair game. We took a stand in a clearing behind some fallen trees and waited. Nothing hap-

Photos by Nedra Du Broff

pened, except, as the light improved, I saw that my forester-companion looked as if he'd fallen out of a twenty-story building on his face. It was much worse than that: he'd been playing soccer.

We didn't see anything, and I let the poor fellow retire to his bed, where he probably should have been in the first place. I went out alone after that. All I saw was a squirrel. I considered bagging him for the pot; he would've been a welcome addition, considering how expensive everything is in Sweden, but thought a 270 wasn't really the ideal squirrel gun.

Later I borrowed the forester's shotgun, a Russian-made over-under and went looking for that squirrel or his brother. We never met up, but I spotted some ducks on the lake that might make several dinners. I stalked them through some thick woods, but they

a hare, and we didn't see him most of the rest of the morning.

To poach a pheasant in the Republic of Ireland is to strike a blow against the British Crown. The only trouble with this concept is that the British Crown has been gone since 1922. The attitude persists. There is usually a little man around with a pheasant under his coat. He is offering it for sale.

When the British left they didn't actually take their pheasants with them, nor did the pheasants die out from loneliness, but generally suffered from a decided lack of proper keepering. The best efforts of the Irish have not succeeded in restoring the pheasant population, bearing in mind the man with the pheasant under his coat. The method now is to lay out a couple of pheasants in the fields, then go look for them.

Northern Ireland has a lot of shoot-

automatic rifle clutched in his hands while fairly large crowds of people crossed the street in both directions within touching distance of him.

In the hotel parking lot in Omagh, I had to open the trunk for the man who did the inspecting. I told him there were guns inside, which at first he thought was a joke in bad taste. But I wanted him to hear about it before his eyes actually fell on the gun cases. It was a performance that I had to repeat each time I returned to the hotel, even though the man knew me and always asked about the day's hunting.

With the forester we went in the Belfast direction, to walk the moors for red grouse. "This is IRA territory," he announced casually.

I peered more intensely out of the window, as if expecting to see something besides the drab, moor-filled landscape, perhaps a sign welcoming

In Portugal, there were shooters and loaders, but not many partridges. There were, however, grocery store quail.

In Portugal, transport from one stand where there was no shooting to the next where there wasn't any either was very grand.

apparently decided to take off before I could pounce.

The ferry boat ride back from Sweden, across the North Sea, was the roughest I had ever endured. Not usually subject to seasickness, I was now. I rang for assistance. No one came.

You don't expect the Irish to be efficient, and they rarely disappoint. Down in County Cork, I said I wanted to go hunting. The proprietor of the hotel where we were staying, a man eager to oblige, produced a dog and a man he called a *ghillie*. The dog was a red setter. When I reached down to pat him he cringed. Later, in the car, when he realized that I wasn't going to hit him, he climbed into my lap. He was in the most acute need of a bath.

Out in the field, the dog sniffed the ground and moved off with eagerness. I could hardly wait to start banging away at woodcock. The ghillie said, "Not much game around."

He was right. The dog took out after

ing, not all of it for sport. I first heard it on arrival at the airport. We were going to a place called Omagh, in County Tyrone. On the map, it looked like a simple matter, but we got funneled onto the road into Dungannon, where we definitely did not want to go, particularly in view of the fact that there was a roadblock up ahead. The driver of each car was requested to open his trunk; in the event of there being a bomb within he got it. I didn't have a bomb, but I did have a scope-sighted 30-06 rifle and a shotgun, all perfectly legal, but I'd probably wind up in the police station having to prove it and I didn't need that, particularly when we didn't want to go anywhere near Dungannon in the first place.

Just before we got to the roadblock a policeman let us make a U-turn out of the line and back toward Omagh. On a corner, a young British soldier crouched behind some shrubs, his

This is, in Portugal, a beater, believe it or not.

Du Broff in the west of Ireland pets the dog that took off after a hare and, intelligently, did not return since there were no woodcock anyway.

us to the domain of the IRA. Nothing but more moor.

Returning after dark, we were on the road back for just a little while, when it became apparent that we were being followed. The car doing the following kept his brights on. As our forester drove faster, so did our tail. He didn't say anything, didn't suggest that the car behind was interested in anything except a drive in the crisp evening air. He just pushed down harder on the accelerator.

Maybe he thought he could outrun our tail, since his was a pretty fast car. We had our guns with us, of course, but our forester didn't suggest loading up, probably thinking that the boys at the rear might be somewhat better armed, perhaps a couple of Armalites at their disposal.

As if to make the point that we couldn't outrun them, they pulled up alongside of us. For some time we drove neck and neck, each of us putting on more speed. In the car opposite, somebody in the back seat lit a piece of twisted newspaper, and kept it burning.

The driver then flicked his lights. Up ahead, just off the road, on the opposite side, there was a truck with his lights on. He flicked them in reply. The other car dropped back and we were allowed to pass on.

Later, back at the hotel, I said to our forester, "We were almost hijacked tonight, weren't we?"

Also present were the hotel owner and a man from the Northern Ireland Tourist Board.

"Of course we were," the forester replied.

The other two looked like they were going to have coronaries. When they had found their voices they attacked our forester, insisting that what had happened had not happened at all. The forester, his veracity questioned, got mad. The three of them shouted at

each other.

The forester said they wanted the car. But if they did, there was nothing to stop them from getting it. What was the significance of the burning paper and the signals from car and truck? Were they trying to see who was inside the car? I don't know the answers, but I am sure that there are those who do.

Portugal, at the time Nedra and I were there, was a relatively tranquil place, ruled by those who never liked bothering with things like elections, since there was a distinct possibility that they might lose. I was after red-legged partridge. That is, I was meant to sit or stand, as the mood took me, in a kind of blind, while the beaters drove the partridge over my head and the heads of those others present—a couple of Frenchmen, the odd Belgian. I also had a gun bearer assigned to me, known as a *secretario*. Nobody objected to having their guns carried for them. It's very European to have somebody else bear the burden of those six or seven pounds. My poor *secretario* wanted only to do his duty, trying to pull the gun from my shoulder. But I clutched it firmly, sorry that I had to hurt his feelings in the process.

The partridge shooting was lousy. So was the snipe shooting. We walked them up one day, then came back the next, accompanied by beaters, who couldn't put up what wasn't there no matter how much noise they made.

Expressing my dissatisfaction, I was asked if I was interested in shooting quail. I was. It could be arranged. They got hold of a dog, a kind of pointer. These quail didn't covey. They didn't fly very well, either. In fact, one of them refused to fly at all. I picked it up, and sent it on its way, not that it was going anywhere or even knew how.

I told a French hunter about these

local quail. He laughed. "They are not wild birds," he said. "They are from the shop, not meant for shooting, but for eating. Like chickens."

In Hungary I was out with a Chief Forester, an elderly man who walked by my side. He stopped, as if suddenly he saw something. He asked for my gun. I handed it to him, waiting for him to shoot whatever it was he saw, that I, looking about, failed to see. But we did not stop. He did not raise the gun. He did not shoot anything. He merely continued to carry it.

As we proceeded through the snow, it came to me that he had no intention of shooting anything, that there was nothing to shoot. He was carrying my gun for me. I felt myself going all red with embarrassment, and I wished I could disappear into the snow.

I could have told him in German

In Yugoslavia, Du Broff learned from this hunting official, and Tito on the wall, that the season is always open for party members, but not always for guests.

that I'd rather carry my own gun, but I didn't think I could explain my feelings about it. I was also afraid that I might offend him, the last thing I wanted to do. When, a little while later we met up with the organizer of the hunt, I said to him, "When I can't carry my own gun anymore, I'll stop hunting."

The organizer was a Hungarian of another era, who thought the Chief Forester should be carrying my gun. For reply, he gave me a dirty look. But he did let the Forester know how I felt on the subject.

We were shooting driven pheasants. The snow was deep. It isn't a problem when you're just standing there. But, for the beaters, the going wasn't particularly easy. After a couple of drives, the Hungarian Revolution was repeated on a small and localized scale. This time, unfortunately, the revolutionaries won, putting an end to the shooting.

In Israel there was little danger that anybody was going to try and carry my gun. In fact, they wouldn't even let me bring one, the laws being what they are regarding arms. Most people there don't own shotguns, but do own machine guns.

The guy in charge was one of those charismatic generals, now retired, who didn't really think he was retired. We met briefly in his Tel Aviv office. He told me to proceed to my hotel and await his instructions. Tel Aviv was not one of the places where I wanted to be. I waited. Nothing happened. I waited some more. Had the general forgotton? I got fed up. I said to hell with it, and packed. Just as I was about to step out of the door, the phone rang. The general had given instructions that I was to proceed to Beersheba, to a specific hotel, where, on a given day and hour, I would meet his men.

They duly appeared. One was a burly game protector who spent his time, not at war, trying to keep the Bedouin from killing all the wildlife they could find for the pot. The rest of the time he was a sniper. The other was a former Irgunist, who said, laconically, "Call me Harry," and advised me against drinking too much water.

In the jeep we drove off the road and onto the trackless desert, which the sniper seemed to know very well. I was given a choice between a 16-gauge pump and a 12-gauge side-by-side double without a safety. I took the double.

We hunted the wadis, for chukar partridge. There'd been a lot of hunting here. But there were some birds. The sniper nailed 'em like he was still at war. We moved to another place. We came upon a Bedouin camp: a man, his veiled wife, his small daughter, who scampered into the tent when Nedra tried to take her picture, eager to avoid the evil eye, and a lot of sheep busily overgrazing the little bit of grass available to them. The sniper chatted with the Bedouin for quite a while, then we found a few more birds in the cactus; that was the morning gone and that was also the end of hunting. The sniper and the Irgunist were off to a seminar on the desert. I'd traveled thousands of miles for half a day of mediocre chukar partridge shooting.

I was also supposed to go after wild boar in the Galilee, in northern Israel.

But by now I'd had enough of the charismatic general and waiting for his instructions and decided against waiting for any more.

In Poland, on the other hand, they seemed to have plenty of time, when we met at the office of the Big Boss Hunter, who served nice cookies and told me how wonderful the hunting was, forgetting to mention the fact that it was only wonderful for those high up in the Party, and other heads of state whom they were eager to impress, as well as those Westerners who had a thousand dollars going up to five thousand they were willing to hand over for a trophy rack.

Later, the hunting man I talked to, not in the Party, not holding a particularly lofty position, told me that he was lucky if he saw just one hare in the course of a whole day of hunting.

When the Poles stopped producing anything, and lived off what the rest of the world supplied to them in the form of gifts, the foresters did quite well out of the situation. Who was to know if there was a deer less, since it was the foresters who were supposed to be looking after them in the first place? Normally, having to account for each rifle shell fired, they could easily claim to have fired it at a fox. And maybe they did, too; even a fox can become a palatable sausage.

In Russia it took a whole week to arrange an interview. It wasn't that I wanted to speak with the Chairman of the Party, but merely with somebody connected to the Hunting Association. And, what was more, my Intourist officials informed me, he wanted to talk to me. So what was standing in the way? Nothing, just bureaucracy.

The embarrassed officials—you usually meet two at a time, since it is accepted practice for one to watch the other—finally arranged the meeting. The man was the editor of their hunting magazine. He had a PhD on bears, which he'd observed, walking the full length of Lake Baikal during a five-year stint. He didn't really approve of hunting; he thought the hunters had it too good.

They confuse the issue by lumping together those who hunt for furs for profit with those who hunt for game for sport. They also have a pollution problem, as well as a poaching problem, with the industry around Baikal threatening species that exist in no other place in the world. The poachers are out for meat for sale, and even in a society that is as much controlled as is the Soviet one, the game thieves still manage to take game illegally.

I asked specifically for an over-un-

der when I was hunting in East Germany, since I'd spent a couple of years trying to get used to one, and now I was a bit concerned that I'd mess things up, using something else. They handed me a side-by-side double, and the thing had a rifle barrel beneath the two smooth bores. The safety was, of all places, on the neck of the stock, at the side. I wasn't pleased. I kept fingering it, telling myself to remember where it was, trying to condition myself to using it.

I waited for some duck to come over. When they did, low and slow, my finger went from the safety on the stock, to the non-existent one at the top, where one would normally find it on a conventional double. It wasn't there, but that didn't stop me from pushing away for all I was worth—as I watched the ducks fly past and fade into the distance.

How come I didn't shoot at the ducks, the forester wanted to know.

"Couldn't find the safety," I confessed.

Then, after deer, I pushed the button where the safety would normally have been, and converted the shotgun to rifle use, with the iron sights now standing upright. I was beginning to feel a little less depressed about this gun. With the forester I took a stand where it was hoped some roe does would be passing. In time one came along. It was a clear and relatively easy shot. The forester told me to hold my fire. I couldn't think why. The roe moved on, finally making it around a bend, partly obscured by some shrubs, and no longer a realistic target.

"Now," the forester said.

Now was not the right time. Before was.

I could not escape the feeling that he didn't want me to make the kill.

Why? I wondered. Perhaps because for some it is an opportunity to exert control, to be able to stage defeat rather than victory provides a greater satisfaction.

For all hunters the next field promises a reward, an abundance of game. And so too does the next country. It drives me on, makes me wonder what I will find over the next border besides incompetents I would rather not have encountered. Maybe this time all will go well, smoothly, with precision, without the drunks, the emphysema sufferers, the foresters who offer to shoot my game for me. There is hope. There is always hope. I will never stop hoping, never stop trying to make it over into the next field, but I've stopped being so *very* disappointed when I get helped again to disaster. ●

SLINGING THE HUNTING RIFLE . . .

. . . can make or break the only shot you get.

by CLARENCE E. ELLIS

From this position to . . .

. . . this takes as much time as getting half-way to shooting position from the muzzle-down carry.

I WAS bellying up a rise among the prickly pear cactus and prairie grass, rifle cradled in my arms, when I saw the black V on my horizon at 10 o'clock. My antelope buck had (a) moved, and (b) spotted me. Maybe he didn't know what I was? I crawled faster and soon made out the buck and four does through the grass. I swear they were laughing hysterically at the sight of me, clad in camouflage and blaze orange trying to sneak up on them. Worse yet, I needed to gain 20 yards so I could shoot over the grass instead of through it. Ignore the cactus! Full speed ahead! Just as I topped my rise and wrapped my arm into a hasty sling arrangement, the buck turned to leave his rise (and my view). The 100-grain Hornady from my 257 spoiled his plans. I paced the distance at 230 meters.

Would I have put the bullet into his heart without using a sling? Probably not, although I might have hit him. If there's anything I dislike more than missing, it's wounding an animal. I've only missed three of the 34 big game animals I've shot at, used a finishing shot on eight, but only had to track two wounded animals of that eight. That's not luck. I'm a good shot, and pick my shots carefully.

Not long ago I was perusing my

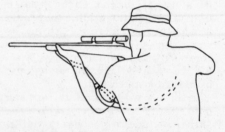

The military sling is tight around the bicep and over the forearm and hand, but loose behind the bicep.

The hasty or CW sling must be tight everywhere or it has no value.

The D sling must also be tight everywhere to be of value.

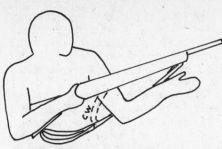

Pass the left arm between rifle and hasty or CW sling . . .

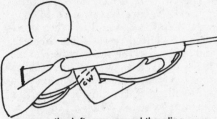

. . . wrap the left arm around the sling . . .

. . . bring the left hand between rifle and sling

The sling must be tight, so it has to be adjusted for clothing changes.

The author's old muzzle-down carry with the hasty sling.

Halfway from carry to shooting position with the hasty sling or CW sling.

notes on big game I've shot, and realized that up to 1982 I used a sling to steady my aim twice when shooting at game (I used a rest for two other shots). That is remarkable because I've been a competitive shooter since 1958, and know the value of a sling. During those 24 years I took 11 head of game ranging from fox to elk, at ranges from 40 to 500 yards. More remarkable is that from 1982 to 1984 I used a sling for 15 of 20 head of game, at ranges from 40 to 430 yards. My average without sling was 119 yards; the maximum was 200 yards. My average range with rest was 183 yards, with hasty sling 150 and 230 yards. My average range since 1982, with sling, has been 251 yards. Why the difference?

My first hunting rifle carried the same military sling I'd used on a National Match M-1 in the Air Force. Shot a couple of deer offhand at 40 and 60 yards with that rig. No reason to use the sling.

My next rifle was carrying weight instead of 10 pounds. I used it and an improvised benchrest for my longest shot ever—a whitetail buck. I used a hasty sling for a 150-yard shot on a spike elk. I took two other elk from sitting at 125 and 150 yards, and a fox from standing at 175 yards.

During this period I was becoming displeased with the way my Brownell sling kept slipping off my shoulder when I was carrying a pack, which is almost always. I also built an ultralight 257 rifle during this period and couldn't see a ¼-pound leather strap on a 5¾-pound rifle, so I made a carrying strap from nylon webbing left over from some climbing gear. Nylon slides off the shoulder easier than does leather. With the 257 I took Catalina goat and mouflon sheep from standing at 90 and 125 yards, and a mule deer from a rest at 300 yards as well as the previously mentioned antelope.

Up to this time I'd missed only two critters, one under circumstances unfit to print, and one because of an unseen branch. Three took finishing shots.

Now we come to the change. First, I could finally afford to hunt beyond my home state—and did. Second, my playing with carrying methods had given me a system immune to slipping off the shoulder. This is nothing more than using an assault rifle sling. Because the sling goes over my head and rests on my left shoulder it cannot slip off regardless of size or type of pack. The rifle hangs in front of me upside down. Yes, it certainly seemed strange at first.

Carry position with the D sling . . .

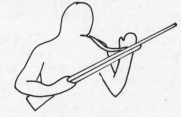

. . . then twist the rifle upright . . .

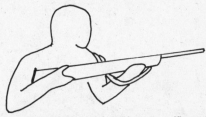

. . . and insert the left hand between rifle and sling.

The sling will be tight across the shoulders.

In less time, the D sling allows going from the carry position . . .

. . . to shooting position.

It didn't take too long to realize I could use this rig as a hasty sling and be into the sling quicker than with the muzzle down, left shoulder carry I used with the Brownell sling. This new arrangement has so well suited me I am not sure I used the sling for steadying my aim on three offhand shots or not.

In my personal and biased opinion, a rifle without a sling is not a hunting rifle. A rifle with only a carrying strap that cannot be used as a hasty sling—a Cobra sling, for instance—is not owned by a shooter.

There are four different sling techniques to steady a hunting rifle. The military sling suffers the drawback that the brass hooks can come undone, it's a bit heavy and it is the slowest to get into. The Brownell sling became my next sling as it did not suf-

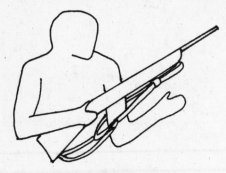

Drop left arm through the military loop . . .

fer from these problems, but I only used it as a hasty sling. As I've already said, either of the above tends to slide off my shoulder when carrying the rifle slung while carrying a pack. The consequence was that I rarely slung the rifle, and I became more fatigued. Even that little bit of fatigue can dull your sharpness, and you will notice less and thus be a less successful hunter. My way of using an assault rifle sling, which I call the D sling, was devised to correct this defect. And Jeff Cooper has reported on the fourth, which he calls the CW sling, in the July 1984 *American Rifleman*.

The CW sling can even make a Cobra sling useful. When I first tried it, I got two surprises. When wrapping my arm into it, I decided it was only a hasty sling until I put the sights on a target. This is a far steadier device than the traditional hasty sling. The second surprise wasn't pleasant. When I tried to carry the rifle muzzle down, it wouldn't hang that way. It would hang slightly muzzle up. Did that on a couple of my rifles. Perhaps Cooper's test rifle with its scope forward balances differently.

When the question rose in my mind, "Is there a real difference in terms of *hunting* accuracy between the various methods and between them and no sling?," I decided to find out. I set up a test using animal silhouettes as targets. I used two rifles initially, a Remington 581 with a Leupold Compact 4x scope and a Remington 540 X with a Weaver T-8 scope. The 581 weighs about 6 pounds and the 540 about 9 pounds. This covers the weight range of most hunting rifles. With each rifle I used each of the four holding methods (no sling, military, hasty, and D; the CW was tested later) in each of prone, sitting, kneeling, and standing. The range was 50 yards and the ammo Federal Champion standard velocity 22 Long Rifle. Ten shots were fired with each combination. Firing 160 careful shots takes both time and effort, so I fired the two rifles on different days. I hit a calm day with the 581 and a gusty day with the 540. My prone target was a crow; sitting was a cottontail's head; kneeling was the cottontail's chest; and standing was a prairie dog's body.

Although the results are far from conclusive, they show the military

. . . tighten keeper with the right hand . . .

sling superior in prone, with the D sling a close second. There should be no misses with either. The hasty sling was a little better than no sling. All three slings were nearly equal in sitting, and better than no sling. Kneeling was similar except that sling use gave a greater advantage. In the standing position the D sling was the same as no sling, and the other slinging methods were poorer. It would seem that if you can rest your left elbow on something, a sling will be of considerable benefit, and the less the inherent stability of the position, the more the sling will allow you to achieve maximum possible stability. The more stable the position, the less the possible increase in stability. When your left elbow is flopping around in the breeze, it would accom-

plish little to join the rifle more snugly to that arm. The advantage of the D sling in standing seems to be from its crossing the left shoulder, and in effect, partially hanging the rifle from a semi-stable object.

The hasty sling was poor with the heavy rifle, but quite acceptable with the light rifle. The heavy rifle shot fairly accurately with no sling, but the light rifle could not be shot really well without a sling.

The CW sling article appeared after my test. Naturally I wanted to compare it, but range and weather problems prevented re-running the test, and I balked at the other swivel on the 581. I devised a different test, using an old Nylon 66 and the Weaver T-8, and Weihrauch HW 55 air rifle with a Beeman 4x scope. With a thought to the carrying problem I placed rear swivels in the usual spot, on the bottom of the pistol grip, at the location of the front receiver screw, and on the Nylon 66, on the front of the trigger

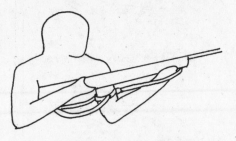

. . . wrap the left hand under the sling.

guard. This way I could compare the CW, TG, PG, D, and hasty. The HW 55 was used for actual shooting, the Nylon 66 was dry fired. I didn't bother with standing, and the HW 55 shoots so well, I discarded prone because any difference was discernible only under a microscope.

A brief discussion of the effects of sling geometry is in order here. Military and target slings pull forward on the left bicep. The elbow is forward of the sling attachment on the bicep, so the sling tends to slide down the bicep toward the elbow, loosening as it goes. This is countered by tightening the loop around the bicep, which puts pressure on the brachial artery. The sling stays put longer, but you pick up your pulse beat. The gain exceeds the loss. With the hasty sling, the pull is on the left rear of the elbow, the sling wants to slide down, and nothing can stop it. The CW sling pulls forward on the bicep, as does the military, but since both attachment points of the sling are in front of the elbow, with one almost directly above it, the sling does not tend to slide down. Pressure on the brachial artery is not great, because there is no need for a tight loop. The pistol grip placement in use is essentially the same as the hasty. No merit there. The trigger guard placement has merit. On any given rifle it might be the better location for both shooting and carrying purposes. The D sling, in contrast to the others, pulls forward on the back of the shoulders, does not pick up pulse, and doesn't slide anywhere.

Certainly, the hunter who is in practice with the military sling will find it does the job admirably, and is vastly superior if you must fire a string of shots from a rifle with recoil, as in high power competition. It *will* stay in place. The CW and D might do well in this situation; the others wouldn't. Most hunters don't maintain that level of practice, will find it too slow, and will seldom need to fire a long string while hunting. The hasty sling does OK in sitting and kneeling (the most useful hunting positions) and is fast with little practice, but in no way equals the CW or D. There

In firing position the rear part of the sling may be loose.

may be a few rifles which are difficult to modify for the CW swivel placement, so the hasty still has a limited place. A plain carrying strap of leather or nylon will suffice for it or the CW sling. The D sling is the only method to show any value for standing shots. It is also faster than the CW or hasty. It is the only method suited for use with a frame pack. Neither the D and CW require much practice to maintain proficiency and speed.

I would judge from my shots on game, and my shooting tests, that I should use a sling or rest for all shots over 250 yards. For small animals, such as coyotes, I should do so beyond 150 yards. For antelope-size stuff, about 200 yards.

Of the 17 critters I took using a sling, two were with the hasty sling and 15 were with the D sling. Of the two with the hasty sling, I could have had time to use the military sling on one, a spike elk I pulled a successful

sneak on. The other, the pronghorn mentioned, I barely had time for the shot with the hasty sling.

Of the critters I took using the D sling, I could have done as well with either the military or hasty sling on a springbok and a vaal rhebok, both at 250 yards. For me the military sling would have been too slow to get a shot, but the hasty would have done OK on the following: mountain reedbuck at 100 yards and black bear at 80 yards. The military would have been OK on a blesbok I took at 430 yards, as would have the CW. The hasty wouldn't have cut the mustard. The speed and steadiness of the D sling was needed on a mountain reedbuck at 350 yards, pronghorn ante-

Author's mountain reedbuck took a fast sitting 280 shot at about 350 yards. The D sling was used.

lope at 280 and 375 yards, mountain goat at 280 yards, nyala at 320 yards, Kodiak bear at 230 yards, and coyote at 240 yards. The CW *might* have been too slow for the Kodiak and the mountain reedbuck, but would certainly have worked for the others.

I sincerely doubt if I'd have taken more than four of the 17 without a sling, and would have tried a shot on only six of them at the most. Given the limited opportunities most of us have to take game, it seems ridiculous to me to reduce the opportunities by not being proficient in the use of a shooting sling. This is even more true now that we have two very different, but very effective methods, one of which should suit anybody's needs. The CW won't solve my problems with slippery, narrow shoulders, so I'll use the D sling. Try both, and use the best for you. ●

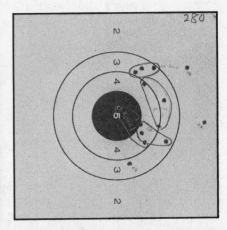

A composite group fired at 100 yards with that 280 and D sling—3 shots per position—includes a good bench group and a bad prone group, but the hunting positions look fine. Total group measures 6½-in.

The author packing out an elk hindquarter and wishing he could sling his rifle.

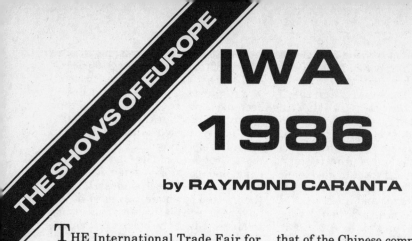

IWA 1986

by RAYMOND CARANTA

THE International Trade Fair for Hunting and Sporting Arms and Accessories—IWA '86—was as usual bigger than ever. In 1986, there were 461 exhibitors; among them 31 countries. Forty percent of the products offered were arms and ammunition; 17 percent accessories; 15 percent sporting clothes; 8 percent were gifts for hunters and shooters; and the rest optical equipment.

This year's show saw three celebrations: Walther celebrated their 100th anniversary, as did Breda Meccanica Bresciana, a reputable Italian company, while Colt had its 150th.

The most impressive display was that of the Chinese company Norinco which introduced a comprehensive line of self-loading semi-military and sporting rifles, a selection of single barrel and over-under shotguns still under the Soviet technical influence, plus target and sporting pistols. Among these, the small Model 77, chambered in 32 ACP and cocked by squeezing the trigger guard, drew much curiosity. The Brazilian exhibitions, which were considered minor only a few years ago, now attract great interest and show spectacular improvements in workmanship.

In the field of handguns, Astra displayed two nice stainless steel 15-shot 9mm Luger automatic pistols; Llama their Spanish Army Model 82 featuring one of the best grips in the market; Star a "practical pistol" set available in 9mm Luger or 45 ACP; Benelli a *superb* new 22 Long Rifle top level competition automatic pistol. Colt showed their King Cobra revolver; FEG their production double-action 9mm pistol which is imported to the United States; Mauser showed artistic Luger variations; and Smith & Wesson had three new variations on hand.

Two most marked achievements, from the technical standpoint, were probably the Ruger GP-100 357 revolver detailed elsewhere in this edition and the French Unique DES/32 target pistol. This Unique automatic pistol, in 32 S&W Long wadcutter, is intended for the centerfire "Sporting pistol" competition under ISU regulations.

In addition to the usual sophistications common to pistols of this class, the DES/32 is fitted with a trigger setting device enabling the shooter to select a crisp, direct "American style" pull for the slow fire event and, for the swiveling silhouette, convert it into a

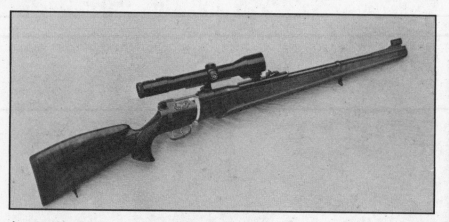

A custom Mauser rifle on 66 S action seen at IWA 86.

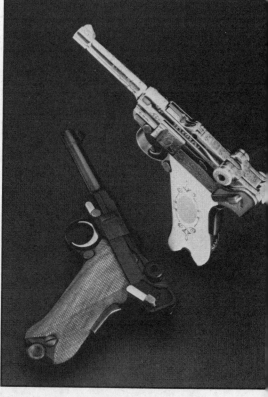

Mauser showed it could still make that special Luger very special indeed.

(Left) The Zeiss Diavari-C 1.5-4.5x18 scope was displayed at IWA '86 despite its 1-inch tube.

clever three-stage pull.

At the 9th Salon International De L'Arme Ancienne Et De Collection is the most famous exhibition of antique guns in France. It remains at Saint Germain-en-Laye, now in the suburbs, still by Yves de Montais.

The French market in antiques is quite flourishing in spite of the general depression. And antique guns remain highly respectable. Current laws on modern guns are more and more restricting plain citizens while guns made before 1870 can be freely sold and owned with no future limitations in sight. Moreover, a new French law now allows the free sale of more modern collectors arms such as American Smith & Wesson No. 3 revolvers of all types, Austrian Mannlichers or German Borchardt, Bergmann or Schwarzlose pistols. So the market is lively.

Eighteenth century pairs of quality flintlock pistols were sold at $4,000 to $7,500. Renaissance matchlocks reached $8,500. Civil War Colt revolvers sold between $850 and $1,200, antique Winchester rifles between $850 and $4,000. Single-action pinfire Lefaucheux revolvers exceeded $500. Cased duelling or target percussion pistols were practically all above $6,000.

EXA is a typically Italian gun show, held in Brescia since 1980. At first, EXA was for professionals; and it was rather small. Five years later, EXA was opened to the general public and got big. It has 231 booths, which is quite important for Europe. There were 143 exhibitors for 172 firms. Nearly 4,000 professional visitors came, and the public attendance reached a highly respectable figure—over 16,000 people. ●

Steve Vogel of Sturm, Ruger was seen field stripping the new GP-100 Ruger revolver at IWA '86.

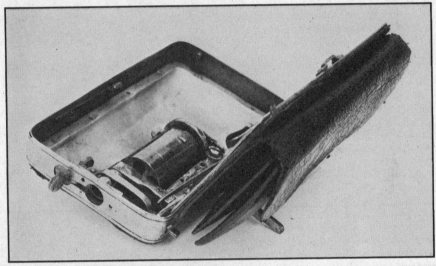

(Above) At Ste.-Germaine-en-Laye such delights as this 19th century pinfire revolver in a wallet could be seen.

The Belgian Browning B125 over-under is replacing the old B15 model in several versions.

GRANNY'S COLT
Is It For Me

by CHARLIE SMITH

I HAVE an anniversary of sorts this year. Thirty years ago, I was a freckled nine-year-old growing up in east Arkansas cotton country. My world centered around a crossroads tavern run by my mom, my Grandma—Granny—and me.

Rural taverns being what they were, Granny felt it necessary to keep a handgun close by. In 1957, the trigger return spring broke in her old Owl-Head 38, so Granny rode a taxi to Highfill's Trading Post in nearby Paragould. There, Melvin Highfill sold her a brand new Colt Detective Special and a box of ammo for 60 dollars. Highway robbery was what Granny called it, but since she could pay it out five dollars a week, the deal was struck.

For the next 14 years it made the daily rounds from home to the store every morning with Granny. There it lay—ready—under the cash register. At 10 PM when the store closed, Granny would drop the blue 38 into her apron pocket for the walk home. In those years it was never used. Perhaps the fact that Granny in earlier years had shot one holdup man and one hell-raising drunk helped discourage would-be troublemakers.

Though I had my own arsenal—two Iver Johnsons, one a single shot 20-gauge, one a 22 revolver and a J.C. Higgins 22 rifle—I often stood and stared at the mirror-bright Colt. I thought that the glittering blue finish and the dark grips were beautiful. Right there my lifelong love of guns began. But stare was all I did. For to touch it without Granny's permission meant a thrashing that was not soon forgotten. Granny had never heard of child abuse laws and she could get my attention.

Perhaps twice a year, Granny and I would take a Sunday stroll into the back pasture and fire off a few round nose 38 shells at stray Prince Albert cans. That tough old lady has been gone for 16 years and I miss that woman. She left me a lot of memories and that blue Colt 38.

By the time she passed away, I was toting a gun for a living as a full-time

The 2-in. barrel is good snake medicine in real close and Grandma's Colt did a lot of this.

policeman and the Detective Special rode many a mile in pockets, boots, and waistbands. Once I learned how to shoot a handgun, I was always amazed at just how well that snubnose shot. I could sometimes shoot 2-inch groups at 25 yards and truthfully, I cannot shoot a 4-inch gun any better.

Over the years the little Colt logged even more miles as a field gun. It has now bagged rabbits, snakes, squirrels, several wild dogs, and a sack full of bullfrogs. Early on, it gave me my greatest handgunning triumph. The Colt had not been fully entrusted to my care yet, but Granny sometimes let me—in my late teens—tote it on weekend fishing trips. Johnny De-Bons and I were hiking through a

(Above) A 30-year veteran, whether stuffed with Plus Ps or shot cartridges, the old Colt still perks.

(Left and below) Braced two-hand hold will put 6 wadcutters in the black at 20 yards today.

poor unlucky animal ran into my bullet. Johnny crossed the distance at a run, hoisted the squirrel in the air, and exclaimed in surprise, "You shot him right through the neck!"

With an air of mastery, and a look of total unconcern, I blew imaginary smoke from the barrel, holstered the gun and said, "You don't ruin as much meat if you shoot 'em through the neck."

Two decades have come and gone, and that remains my single greatest act of one-upmanship.

Like many shooters I am fickle, and it seems each new product of the gun-makers art is just what I've been waiting for. Chief Special Smiths were carried for their smaller size. Sometimes a Walther PPK 380 served as an off-duty gun. I am not sure why, except I read a bit of James Bond in those days. Charter Arms revolvers and custom 9mms came and went. When each new face left, the Detective Special was still there, waiting to work until something new came along.

One of the hazards of being a small-town cop is that everyone recognizes you as such even when you are not in uniform. Even though there were no regulations in those days, I quickly learned never to go anywhere unarmed.

About 5 one morning, I stopped at an all-night grocery to get supplies for a fishing trip. The clerk had just caught three local thugs shoplifting, which was a mistake—they were giving him a good going over. When I walked in, the battered shopkeeper saw me and yelled for help. Seeing no weapon, the three left the frightened clerk and turned toward me. But when the hollowpoint-loaded Colt appeared from under my shirt and centered on the chest of the leader, things changed real quick. Everyone got very friendly and stayed that way while help was summoned.

Thirty years have taken their toll. The grips are worn smooth in places. The blue, once bright, is dull and lightly pitted from sweat and Arkansas humidity. No money has been wasted on fancy accessories, and the only action job is that which three decades of use provides.

I have no doubt spent more on leather than Granny paid for the Colt in the first place. Shoulder holsters, FBI hip holsters, ankle rigs, new generation nylon holsters—they have all carried the "Dick" Special at various times. Today those that get the most use are a 6-dollar inside-the-belt holster that is used when I am wearing a

small woodlot on our way to a bass pond, when Johnny spotted the head of a fox squirrel peeking over a limb in the top of a tall oak tree. Johnny was a great shotgunner and a passable rifle shot, but he had little use for a belt-gun.

Since squirrel season was in, Johnny taunted me to try for the small target. Bracing myself on a tree trunk, I

squeezed off a round single-action. At a range of 30 yards, the bullet struck perhaps an inch below the squirrel's head.

In surprise or fear the squirrel raced down the tree trunk and hit the ground running all-out for a big den tree. In desperation, I pointed the revolver and fired one quick round double-action. At about 35 yards that

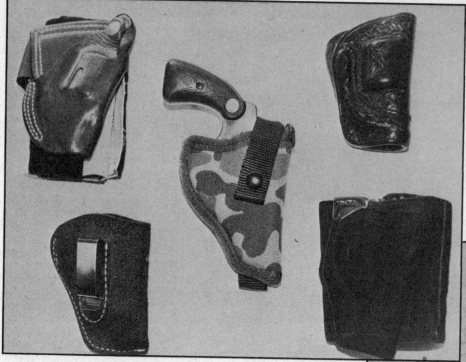

Holsters that have toted the Colt include—upper left, JackAss ankle holster; upper right, Bucheimer Sheriff's model; lower right, Renegade Cozy Partner ankle holster; lower left, inside the belt holster; center, Uncle Mike's Nylon holster. Author has spent a lot more on holsters than Grandma did on the Colt.

In an ankle holster, Grandma's Colt often backed up the author's service revolver. Indeed, it backed up his lawman work out of lots of holsters.

jacket and a Renegade Cozy Partner ankle holster that is used when I work in jeans and sportshirt. When I take the 38 along to the woods, an Uncle Mike's nylon holster is lightweight, quiet, and secure.

I have wasted no time developing special loads for this gun. For practice I still load a hardcast SWC bullet over 3.0 grains of Bullseye. In years past for a defense load, I seated the Speer 146-grain HP half-jacket over 5.0 grains of Unique. These loads are right out of my old *Speer Loading Manual.* Today's loading books tone those loads down, so I do not recommend them. But they have been safe in my gun. Today I usually carry the Colt loaded with Federal +P HPs for what Major Nonte used to call serious social work.

I have made no count of the rounds that have gone through the weapon. Wadcutters, hot handloads, service velocity rounds, and +P loads have all been handled with ease. I know that several thousand cartridges have been fired with no ill effect. Not bad for a bellygun.

For my money, the old-style Detective Special was the best snubnose revolver ever made. Smith's Chief Special is a tad smaller and may have an edge for pocket carry. But the Colt has better sights, a good grip that is hand-filling without noticable bulk, and that extra sixth shot. Today's shooters know and like the New Model Detective Special that was first introduced in 1972. I have owned two, and neither one was as good as the old one. In my eye they are oversize, blocky, and just do not have the smooth lines of their sire.

Colt once had a great ad that showed a cowboy sitting along by a campfire, his Colt Single Action revolver in hand. The caption read, "A Colt says: embers, shadows, snapped twig, confidence."

In spite of what we say about sport, that ad got directly to the heart of why most of us own handguns. That one small revolver has given me confidence around campfires, in dark alleys, in distant motel rooms, and on lonely county roads for 16 years now.

In fact, as I type these words it is after midnight. I am in my office ¼-mile from my home at the end of a lane. To my right, serving as a paperweight, is the holstered Colt waiting to slip on my belt for the walk home. Paranoid? Perhaps.

Except for my hunting guns and any test arms that I am working with, my good guns—my old Colt 357 service revolver, my first NRA 45 auto, my 1893 Marlin 30-30, and the like—are locked away. All except that oily, worn, non-chic, snub-nose 38 Colt.

As I approach my fifth decade, I find that the things that I am used to give me the most pleasure. I am comfortable with them. My wife, my beagle, and my old Chevy pickup come to mind. And I am comfortable with the Colt. It is a lightweight, compact, reasonably potent sidearm. I like it a lot. It is one good gun. ●

BROWNING'S T-BOLT I LIKE

by G.N. TED DENTAY

WHEN dozens of guns go through your hands every year and you keep on turning back to the old standby, you could call it your one good gun. In my case, it's a much-battered-and-used southpaw's Browning T-Bolt which is more than an assembly of steel and wood to me. It's the memories, the whiffs of my history sticking like glue to it. And the certainty that there are going to be more experiences attached to it.

My T-Bolt began life with me as a good deal. When people were discovering that T-Bolts were eminently collectable, I discovered the last bargain. No one wanted the left-handed rifle, so I got it for $95 when they were already $200 and more on the open market. A *goood* deal.

Since that time, a lot of ammo has gone up its spout. Some years saw 10,000 rounds consumed in the ceaseless quest for dragonflies. Other years

whole area for hours.

The most fun was undoubtedly when we, being Canadians and 100 miles or so above U.S. law, got hold of a couple of cartons of Gevelot 22 Long Rifle tracers. We awaited dusk with delicious anticipation of the fiery streaks crossing the pond. It didn't matter much if we connected with the darting insect life. Watching the bullet's track was harmless fun enough. There were perfect sandbank butts behind the pond which would satisfy any safety requirements incumbent upon us. The little red-tipped 22s worked flawlessly out of the T-Bolt, but they wouldn't function reliably in a Gevelot semi-auto.

Then there was the season in which the T-Bolt accounted for dozens of dead rats.

Our office was in the second story of a commercial office. Next door there was a construction yard, in which

inch barrel, but it killed with a well-placed shot, unlike the 6mm round-ball and conical-bullet Flobert caps we'd tried before.

When sunset wrapped its roseate mantle around the area, the aluminum-sashed window would quietly slide back and the muzzle of the rifle would poke out an inch or two. Then the carnage would begin. The brown carpet of rats would predictably flow over the dog's dishes and the diminutive report of the T-Bolt would make itself known.

It took only a few moments of quickly working the action before there were three or four twitching bodies on the ground and an equivalent pile of gleaming brass empties on the carpeted office floor. Then the rest of the lemming-like rush would get the message and melt back into the gathering shadows and the dog would get to eat what balance of his food the miserable creatures had left.

Winter came with monotonous regularity, putting a crimp into usual shooting activities. So, with cross-country skis and snowshoes, we safaried out for icicle shooting. Ice makes the finest of biodegradable targets.

Trap and Skeet shooters like to see the black puff of dust remaining

Dentay's gun is a southpaw, but otherwise, this is it.

saw a versimillitude of assorted 22 BB and CB caps for the famous rat hunts. And then, to balance everything out, there were the years of hypervelocity 22s like Stinger and Yellowjacket. They were best at assassinating huge icicles which coated rock faces in winter.

It's hard to say how many rounds in total went into knocking dragonflies out of the sky. Ten years worth of consumption must have totalled in excess of 100,000 rounds. I think we managed a total of ten confirmed kills so the dragonfly population wasn't much reduced.

Hot, lazy summer days spent stretched out comfortably on a hillside overlooking a waterlily-strewn pond. That's the stuff of memories. Darting, dodging metallic-hued dragonflies jinking around small fountains of water thrown up by impacting bullets. They always seemed to be able to predict the Long Rifle's trajectories, but it just added to the fun. The tang of powder smoke hung over the

hundreds of pieces of forms, timbers and scaffolding were stored. In the middle of this mess was an office trailer and beneath it the residence-of-record for a large, and unpleasant German shepherd dog.

Every evening when the workmen left, a large helping of kibble mixed with canned food was deposited into his feed bowl. And every evening, when the workmen left, a horde of rats would emerge from under the piles of scaffolding and descend upon the hapless creature's food.

Now, we had no love lost for this miserable example of the canine world, but we couldn't bear to see food stolen out from under its very cowardly nose. So the decision was made to snipe the rats from 50 yards. The technical problem was that we couldn't use standard velocity ammunition of any kind because people lived nearby. We quickly settled on CCI's Mini-Caps, the low-velocity 22 Short lookalike. Its report was absolutely minimal out of the T-Bolt's 22-

where once a clay pigeon flew. We delighted in the fountains of glittering ice-shards tumbling in the winter's sun following a direct hit with any of the more potent crop of hyper-velocity 22s. No pre-Cambrian rock face was safe and that little T-Bolt took more than its fair share.

After such honorable service, totalling hundreds of thousands of rounds, you'd think the T-Bolt would receive a reasonable retirement. It hasn't. Now it sits behind the door of the new farmhouse, ready to do service in supplying pheasant, pigeon and rabbit for the pot. The experiences of low velocity ammunition and the best of the hyper-velocity gives it the flexibility needed in a constant companion.

Even at that, things don't really change much. That new place has its very own pond, complete with dragonflies. There aren't too many rats around, but the icicles come out with predictable regularity each winter. The T-Bolt has not retired; it may not ever . . . not ever.
●

TESTFIRE

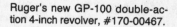

Ruger's new GP-100 double-action 4-inch revolver, #170-00467.

Ruger's First-Born In The New Family

STURM, Ruger & Company introduced their GP-100 as part of a "New Generation of Double-Action Revolvers." Their intention is to have three frame sizes to handle all popular handgun calibers from 22 through 44 Magnum. First out is what I take to be the middle-sized version as it is chambered for 357 Magnum—a mighty popular round among law enforcement agencies, hunters of small to medium-sized game, and plinkers.

A sturdy looking handgun, the GP-100 barrel measures .750-in. in diameter and 1.330 inches from top of the solid rib to the bottom of the ejector housing which extends to the muzzle. This extra weight makes the GP-100 a pleasure to hold because, even in the 4-in. barrel, it is a bit muzzle heavy. The 6-in. version should be rock

Front sight is changeable in the same manner as the Redhawk's, but it's a different sight.

steady. Serial number 170-00467 weighs in at 40½ ounces on my postal scale.

Spring-loaded lock on front of crane fits into slot in frame for positive cylinder lockup front and back.

The frame is Redhawk all the way except that the width has been increased in the barrel support area. Made from A.I.S.I. 4130 chrome-molybdenum alloy steel, GP-100's side walls are solid and integral to provide extra strength and rigidity compared to removable sideplates.

Sights are Redhawk except that the front has no colored insert and the blade is cut to a slightly different angle. Rear is fully adjustable with white outlined notch. The hammer differs only slightly from the Redhawk outline. The trigger may be a little more slender and just a hair longer.

The long ejector shroud provides desirable muzzle weight. Right side is clean.

The exclusive Ruger lock system bolts the crane into frame at front, locks cylinder at rear, a successful mechanical engineering solution.

Rear sight is white-outlined, with blade corners rounded. It has a good roomy square notch, too.

Trigger pull is traditional Ruger at 5½ pounds single action and 12½ pounds when pulling through. I do wish the factories could see their way clear to 3½ to 4 pound triggers so they could be used universally without extra work. Hammer fall seemed faster than on a 5½-in. blue Redhawk being handled at the same time. It was finally determined to be an optical illusion because of an ever-so-slight change in hammer shape which appears to allow ⅛-in. less drop on the GP-100.

The grip is definitely not Redhawk. It feels good. No, it's better than that, it feels great! Not even the most faint-hearted of shooters can claim the necessity of a rubber-cushioned grip on a 357 Magnum weighing near 41 ounces but that is what my test GP-100 wears and it is a pleasure to hold. The grip consists of live rubber with Goncalo Alves wood panels. Its configuration is made possible by the GP-100's total lack of a grip frame. An extension of the revolver frame provides length enough, and width, to house the hammer strut, mainspring, and mainspring seat. No more. This allows a wrap-around grip, even one-piece should the shooter desire, of smaller dimensions than required by a normal grip frame. There is a small disassembly pin positioned in a slot at the bottom of the right grip. With this tiny pin the revolver can be completely disassembled for cleaning.

I do not know from where they came but in removing the grips four tiny pieces of metal fell out. One was lost before they were packaged for photography.

It isn't often I am fascinated by a grip and, to be totally unsubtle (if there is such a word) there are few I really like. My habit, for the past 20-plus years, is to wear a thin buckskin glove on my right hand. I go through them so fast I wish I could buy a couple of dozen right-hand gloves or else find a left-hander who wears a size 7 Cadet so we could share a pair. With this new GP-100 grip I have precisely the same feel as with the buckskin on a conventional grip. Also, this new format will allow the shooter's imagination to run wild as he designs whatever seems best for him at the moment.

Ruger built this GP-100 to withstand most any punishment dealt its direction. Punishment in the form of heavy loads as marketed by ammunition factories for whatever caliber identified on the revolver plus any and all +P loads such as 38 Special in the 357 Magnum. Handloads are not included here for obvious reasons. The shooting world is full of "if a little is good a lot is better" handloaders.

Quoting from page 5 of Ruger's press release: "Actual destructive testing has demonstrated that the GP-100 revolver will withstand tremendous abuse and rough handling under the most severe conditions and still continue to function reliably.

"The simple mechanism and ease of maintenance inherent in this revolver are of particular interest to police users who have found that revolvers of older, conventional design can often be rendered totally unusable by mud or sand, effectively disarming the police officer on the spot and requiring the services of a gunsmith to restore the revolver to working condition. The Ruger GP-100 revolver withstands such treatment and continues to function with equanimity,

The grip of the GP-100 incorporates a variety of functions—mainspring seat, trigger guard latch, and grip panel locator. It permits the installation of customized wrap-around grip panels as well.

This is the basic first-run right-side barrel marking.

RUGER GP100®

.357 MAGNUM CAL.

as field maintenance is readily accomplished."

They said it—and after carefully looking over the GP-100, handling it three evenings while watching TV, firing 100 rounds (one box of 125-grain Federal and one box of Winchester 145-grain Silvertip) and spending most of a morning photographing the revolver (deadlines are totally unforgiving) I not only believe the press release but lean a bit towards thinking them a mite modest. There is a feel to the GP-100 that can't be put into words. It's a shooter's revolver. Weight, balance, grip, rugged good looks, things felt during handling and shooting that can't be put into words. I've never seen the day, and hope I never do, when I would highly praise a 357 Magnum. I'm a field shooter—a hunter with handguns—and this praise is for a revolver—not the caliber. If it carries over into 41s and 44s, and there is no reason it shouldn't, double-action handgun hunters just might find their dreams come true.

Let's go back to that press release a moment: Weight, empty—41 ounces (170-00467 weighs 40½ ounces); Finish—satin polished and blued; Overall length, 4-inch—9.375 inches; Sight radius, 4-inch—5.52 inches; Trigger pull, single-action (approx.)—4.5 pounds +−1.5 pounds (Testfire's barely under max at 5½ pounds), double-action—14 pounds max (ours 12½ pounds).

Hal Swiggett

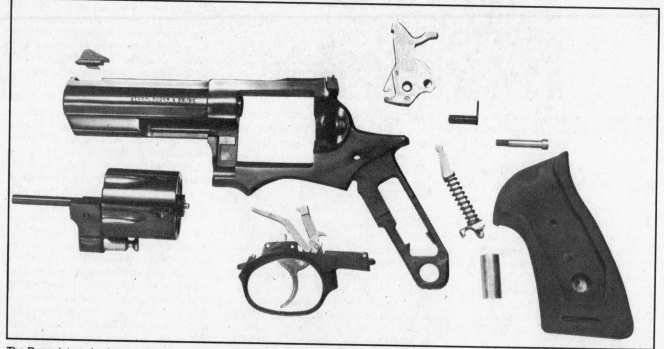

The Ruger integral subassemblies and simple takedown has been proven in previous Ruger designs. The Ruger GP-100 can be field-stripped in a matter of seconds, without the use of special tools.

Illustration by Yhai Siriwat

THE FIRST ALL-PLASTIC PISTOL

by

R.A. LESMEISTER

The 1914 Mauser look is intentional; inside, its all different.

QUESTION: What is super light, fits in the palm of the hand, uses no pins or screws in its construction and floats?

No, not Ivory Soap! It's the new all-plastic pistol designed and manufactured by David Byron and Byron's, Inc. of Casselberry, Florida. With an all-plastic frame, plastic internal workings and ceramic barrel, the yet-to-be named pistol weighs a mere 3½ ounces. Based on a scaled down version of the classic Mauser Model 1914, this 22 Long Rifle autoloader is constructed of four different kinds of plastic from one basic polymer family. (Polymer is just an expensive name for plastic.)

The polymer used is thermoplastic. It is heated and injected into moulds to shape the internal parts, the frame and even the barrel. Once cooled, the parts are ready to be assembled. No after-fitting, finishing or hand work other than assembly is required. Even the barrel's rifling is completed in the injection process.

This sounds easy, but the computer analysis and machining of the moulds cost upwards of a million dollars. The basic resins cost three to four times the price of the finest tool steel and the other tooling is much more expensive than that used in the manufacture of conventional arms. The toler-

ances on all parts are kept to .001-in. and that costs money.

Byron is starting with a 22 LR pistol. Larger calibers will come once maximum stress has been calculated for the 22. By starting with the thinnest possible cross sections and wall thicknesses of polymer for the 22, all he has to do is add to that thickness to achieve strength for larger calibers such as the 9mm or 45 ACP. By doubling the thickness of the polymer, you actually get four times the strength.

The add-on feature on extras that the pistol can be offered with are limitless. Fixed and adjustable rear sights will be offered and different front sight blades of various colors can be molded with the barrel. In fact, the colors the pistol can be molded in are endless and only limited by the imagination of the person requesting. The only color—or non-color—the gun can't be molded in is clear. The base resin in the polymer can't be bleached because it would degrade the properties of the polymer itself. The basic polymer the pistol is made from has a tensile strength over 1,000,000 pounds per square inch.

A plastic pistol is so light, recoil could have been a problem. Byron conceived a patented system to compensate for that. There's also an inter-

nal counter-torque system to keep the pistol from turning in the hand as the bullet exits the barrel and bolt assembly retreats. That was a major problem to be overcome. The bolt assembly is lighter than the 22 LR bullet and unretarded would accelerate backwards faster than the bullet can exit the barrel. This problem, not prevalent in conventional arms, has been solved by Byron's unique design. It *looks* like a conventional arrangement, but it is not.

During the time the plastic pistol was being conceived, Byron was also working on a detector system so his design wouldn't end up by being the skyjacker's dream gun. Every plastic pistol made will have a special implant in it that can be detected by Byron's patented detector. This all-plastic pistol will be the only firearm the FAA need not worry about, because Byron's detector and others will be able to pick up the implant in the pistol from a distance of 10 feet.

From a sketch on a piece of scratch paper in 1979 to complete computer analysis in the spring of 1986, the all-plastic pistol has grown from an idea to a reality and David Byron has taken this idea and placed it on the range. It works. Don't be too anxious to put your orders in just yet; Uncle Sam gets his first. ●

SPECIAL REPORT

Bill Grover poses as if firing my 1880 45 Colt single action.

Switches gun to left hand and opens right-side loading gate.

He right-handedly ejects empties, gun still in left hand.

Sam Colt Was

by HAL SWIGGETT

Grover aims his right-hand six-gun.

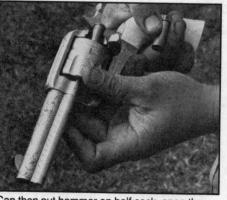

Can then put hammer on half cock, open the loading gate and eject empties without changing hands.

He can load with the left hand, the gun still in his right.

Then close it up and proceed easier than Colt's would let him.

Switches hands again and loads with left—some stay with the left and load right-handed.

Regardless, loading gate gets closed with the right hand as switch to the shooting hand takes place.

Back in the right hand, the hammer goes to full cock, and then is lowered on empty chamber.

Left-Handed

Since Samuel Colt built his first single-action revolver, we have been shooting six-guns designed for left-handed shooters and most of us never knew the difference. Bill Ruger added additional enthusiasm for single actions by making good guns available to one and all at a price easily affordable. This at a time when Colt was dropping back on production.

Ruger single actions retained the basic single-action design as introduced by Colt. Now, after all these years, we know why: Both men are (were) southpaws.

Think on it, to use a phrase favored by long-time friend Bill Jordan. I'm sitting here with a 5½-in. 45 Colt single action made in 1880 that is part of my collection and in above average condition. It's as close as I can come to one of Sam's first single actions. Maybe you do it differently, but I shoot with my right hand, then place the revolver frame in my left as I right-handedly open the loading gate and bring the hammer to half-cock. I keep the frame in my left hand as I eject empties with the right forefinger as I rotate the cylinder with my left thumb and forefinger. Loading is done that same way. Drop a cartridge in the cylinder with the right hand as it is turned with the left forefinger on the bottom. (Single actions were intended to be five-shooters, *not* six-shooters.

To load, insert a cartridge, skip a chamber, fill the next four, close the gate, bring the hammer to full cock then lower it. The hammer will then be on the empty chamber and loaded as the gun was designed to be handled.) Notice, please, that the loading gate is closed with the right forefinger then the revolver grip changed to that right hand to be cocked and the hammer lowered.

Enter Bill Grover and his Texas Longhorn Arms, Inc., home of the right-handed single-action six-gun. Bill figured out that single-action revolvers were designed for left-handed shooters and set about to design one for the majority of us handgunners.

The first time I met Grover his opening comment was "Was Sam Colt left-handed?"

The only response I could think of was, "I don't know, I never met the man."

Bill was so convinced he was right he stuck to his right-handed single action and put it into production. Craig A. Doherty from Zuni, New Mexico read about Grover and got to thinking about his own guns. It also started him on a research project to determine if Samuel Colt was in fact left-handed. The company Colt founded couldn't answer his question and Colt's historian told Doherty the question had never come up. He did

however refer him on to the Connecticut State Library where most of Colt's personal papers are held. No help here either. Doherty was finally directed to Larry Wilson, author of *The Book of Colt Firearms* and was able to confirm definitely that the Colonel was left-handed as Bill Grover had thought obvious from his design.

Now we know for sure Colt and Ruger single actions are designed for left-handed shooters because both men shot from that side.

Bill Grover and his Texas Longhorn Arms right-handed single action has made it possible for most of us to shoot his single action, open the gate with our right thumb, bring the hammer to half-cock with that same thumb, eject the empties with the left forefinger, drop fresh cartridges in the cylinder with the left hand, close the gate with the right thumb, bring the hammer to full cock, then lower it on the empty chamber without changing hands.

The accompanying photos show Grover shooting, unloading, loading, and readying the revolver for further use with my 1880 Colt. It took six pictures because of the hand changing. You will notice only four photos with his right-hand six-gun since there is no changing of hands required.

It has taken more than 135 years but thanks to Bill Grover we right-handers now have a six-gun. ●

Filling in
REMINGTON'S SCORECARD

THERE have been years when Remington introduced heavy hitters like the Model Seven and years when two or three new ammo options were all writers saw at the Annual Seminar. This year there were no *new* guns, but there were 17 or 18 new line items.

You really can't tell that many players without a scorecard. Remington's plan for the future seems to include keeping as many pieces on the board as possible.

In bolt-action centerfire rifles, there's a new Classic Magnum—264 Winchester this time; the Sportsman 78 can be had in 223; and the appealing-to-writers centerpiece, the Model 700 Mountain Rifle, a 6¾-pound long-action, choice of 270 Winchester, 280 Remington, 30-06 Remington, points out that what a hunter does most with a rifle is carry it.

Following up recent shotgunner success, Ilion is now making Model 870 and 1100 Deer Guns dull—that is, non-reflective. And they are flossying up the workhorse 870 with better checkering and such. And the smooth-bore *pièce-de-résistance* is the Rem-Choke, screw-in tubes that are better because, Remington says, "There are advantages, sometimes, in not being first." No Remington spokesman said those advantages were better than being first.

Rimfire bolt-gunners can pick between two new ones. The 581S is in the utility role; the 541T is a classier sporter. Together with a new Custom Shop rimfire, these add up to a full range of 22 sporters.

In that Custom Shop, Remington is now prepared to offer short-action 700s in both left- and right-hand versions with a full range of chamberings, either way. The 8mm Remington Magnum is back in Safari Grade. The new 700 Mountain Rifle already has a Custom Shop option—a DuPont (who else?) Kevlar stock. An XP-100 with walnut stock and choice of 7mm-08 and 35 Remington chambers is another Custom item. And the 40X Sporter is back as the single shot 40XR, a highly finished 22 rifle.

There is now a regular line XP-100 in 223, a hoped-for item among many XP-100 shooters; the new bullet knife is the R1263; and Ed Matunas describes all the new ammo in the "Ammunition, Ballistics and Components" section in this issue.

Taken all together in an uncertain market, this litany of product introduction describes a company anxious to please and willing to invest. The name is Remington.

Ken Warner

Sportsman 78

Model 700 Mountain Rifle

Model 700 Classic

Model 870 Wingmaster

Model 1100 SP Deer Gun

Model 800 SP Deer Gun

GROOVES IDENTIFY CHOKE CONSTRICTION

.050" THICK TUBE WALL DIA.

REMINGTON

IMP. CYL.

Cut-Away: "Rem" Choke Seating Inside Barrel

FLUSH MATING — TUBE TO BARREL BORE

STRONG REAR THREADING

RECESSED NOTCHES FOR INSTALLATION WRENCH

Model XP-100 Custom Pistol

Model XP-100 "Varmint Special"

Model 700 Custom KS Mountain Rifle

Model 700 Custom Grade II Left Hand

40XR Custom Sporter—Grade II

Model 581 Sportsman

Model 541-T

THE NRA FRONT
. . . not exactly quiet

Vice President of the United States George Bush spoke to the assembled members of NRA.

LATE REPORT: Startling developments at NRA Headquarters in May saw G. Ray Arnett leave under a cloud. Not all Arnett-fired staffers came back. ILA leader Cassidy was named acting boss. There will be, no doubt, more. *KW*

NRA President James E. Reinke is a worldwide hunter and long-time anti-gun control activist.

J. Warren Cassidy directs the Institute for Legislative Action, another political heavyweight.

ONLY a minor amount of skirmish and backbite marked the 1986 Annual Meetings of the National Rifle Association of America, a refreshing change from the past several years. One could this year concentrate on the Exhibit Hall in good conscience.

For instance, we finally got to handle the long-looked-for Ruger P-85, that self-same gun you see on our cover. It's an elegant little gun and not near as big as it looks. The gun Ruger will make and the gun you see here will no doubt differ in some details, the actual shape of the trigger for one, but the gun is at last a prototypical reality.

Another elegant little gun one could handle in New Orleans was the Ultra-Light rifle. It's mentioned here because photos don't do it justice—it has to be fondled to be believed. So does the USAS-12, a drum-fed "operational" 12-gauge shotgun. "USAS" stands for "Universal Sporting Automatic Shotgun"—an inside joke.

In the Millett Sights display was their "Mountain Survival Stock" with such bells and whistles as removable buttplate, hollow butt storage for a furnished (extra cost) survival bag, special sling system and a compass in the grip cap. Very slick. It's a drop-in for popular bolt rifles.

On one ballistic front, the former Oro-Tech, proprietors of Golden Powder, were announcing themselves to be now "Golden Powder of Texas" and saying this time was the charm. And at Norma, the management was happy, pointing to such interesting loads as their 170-gr. 280 Remington.

The NRA Meetings are a place where other groups meet. For example, the Ruger Collectors Assn. auctioned a number of things, including the GUN DIGEST cover gun for 1953 orginally presented to John Amber—it brought $7,900.

One group didn't meet in New Orleans but the American Custom Gunmakers Guild's new president Steve Billeb was there. He tells us the Guild will be doing a John Amber commemorative rifle, but still is considering what to do with the quarter-million dollar annuity which passed to the Guild on Amber's death.

NRA's Meeting attracts the kind of people who believe armed citizens OK. For instance, it attracted Vice President George Bush, who said, "Whatever the good intentions, depriving Americans of their constitutional right to keep and bear arms is wrong."

It sounded very good.

Ken Warner

The Ruger P85 9mm pistol holds 15 rounds, offers all the current bells and whistles in a notably neat and sturdy package. This is a production prototype.

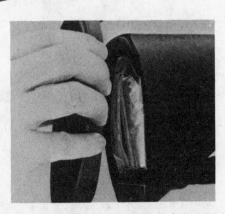

Imported by Gilbert Equipment Co., the USAS-12 also has bells and whistles—and 28 12-gauge cartridges in that drum.

Millett Sights is offering this Mountain Survival stock as a drop-in for popular rifles.

Mountain Survival has its own no-nonsense slinging system.

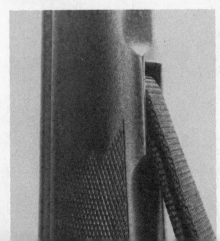

This hollow butt will hold plenty, notably a high-tech bivouac sack.

Those who have used compasses in knife handles will believe a compass in a grip cap a useful idea.

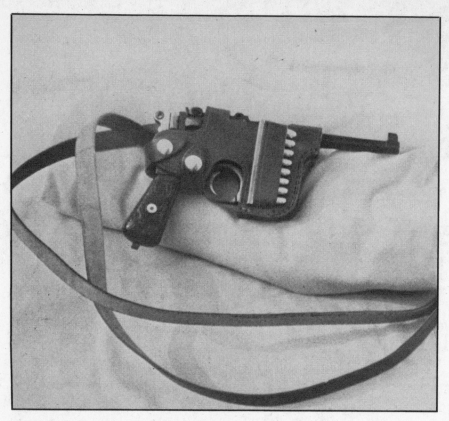

This Bolo Mauser in its new shoot-through holster is a warlord special you can buy today.

IT'S odd to think the influence of Richard Milhous Nixon now touches shooters and gun collectors, but it's so. What began as Nixon's China initiative has now unlocked the last great treasuries of surplus arms and the guns of 70 years of strife on Mainland China are coming out. In fact, they're here.

Since China was the principal market for the big Mauser and Mauser-type pistols for 20 years before World War II, there are lots of broomhandle Mausers to come. They have led very difficult lives, to be sure, and do not come to us unblemished, but they come to us at very attractive prices.

To be specific, right now for less than $500 you can get a very shoot-able Mauser, an associated (and now legal) shoulder-stock-cum-holster, and correct if not original leather trimmings. The gun's bore will be shiny-bright, and it will function and shoot. Under a creditable re-blue will be those pits and stains of the dirty decades, but it won't be a bad-looking gun.

This all doubtless dismays those collectors of military Mausers who have been lovingly tending, and no doubt occasionally improving, those pistols garnered during two World Wars in Europe. They successfully lobbied to get the restrictions on the

The Return of the

Terry MacFarlane works the East Coast gun shows reacquainting shooters with the Mauser system.

holster-stocks lifted; they kept the flame in good faith; and now comes the flood.

It's a fun flood, though. Your reporter was introduced to it by old gun show buddy Terry MacFarlane (Aquia Antiques, Box 448, Garrisonville, VA 22564; 703-659-7403) who has replaced his customary clutter of 19th century military long arms with the shakings of the Chinese Mauser tree. He finds it really satisfying to own, to shoot, to know so many authentic (again, if not wholly original) and significant Mausers. He also likes the money to be made by providing good shootable guns at affordable prices.

One of the chief importers, and MacFarlane's principal source is Sporting Goods Export Co. (Box 948, Rutherfordton, NC 28139; 704-287-2818). This firm manages the rebarreling, barrel sleeving, restoration work and test-firing, and has a lot of pistols to work with, it seems.

It wouldn't do to be buying one of these at $350 or $450 thinking you were buying some Waffen SS sergeant's personal mint sidearm, of course. At that price and bought for what it is, however, a shootable Broomhandle is worth it now in 1986 and 1987.   *Ken Warner*

Broomhandles

Bolos or military or commercial, when it comes to the ex-China guns, what you sees is what you gets.

(Above) The returnees can get pretty fancy, but the box is a standard item these days, as are all the other trimmings.

(Below) The extras are all on hand, too, all properly made, all functional, all priced so you can afford them.

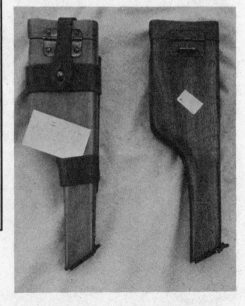

HOLLAND & HOLLAND

Celebrates Everything

DON'T get the idea Holland & Holland is (the British would say "are") about to make a run at the world shotgun market. There are any number of factories in the world which make more 12-gauge firearms in a day than H&H will make by 1990.

When, however, we come to the tip-top of the financial heap, there we will certainly see the gunmakers of Bruton St. They have put together some dandies here lately.

Prices are so astronomical they won't bear discussing. What may be discussed, however, are the concepts—the super gun idea, the limited run of yesteryear designs, the "affordable" boxlock. Things are happening in Blighty, and these are the evidence.

Beyond the guns, we have a super book on the firm's history. And beyond the book, there is a video tape entitled "Game Shooting" and described as "The Definitive Instruction Video."

There is doubtless still room for the $400 Remington 1100 and even the $2,800 replica Parker gun on the world market, but those who make $20,000 guns might be taking notice. We are, here and now.

Ken Warner

Intending to make a capstone to 150 years of fine gun making, Holland & Holland created the Saurian, an all-out Royal hammerless ejector 4-bore gun. The theme is the dinosaur and its relatives; the execution is as near flawless as can be; the mounting and presentation of related fossils, a gun case, a cartridge box (100 rounds) furnished—all make a landmark.

In their own (i.e., the shared Webley & Scott works) Birmingham factory, Holland & Holland is now making an H&H boxlock gun. Price: about £5,000.

The H&H boxlock can be finished up bright or case-colored. This is the bright one.

(Above) These hammer guns—nine 12-bores and six 20s—are H&H Sesquicentennials. The long action flats permit a half bar-in-wood design.

(Right) This is Number 9 of the Sesquicentennial hammer guns and very handsome indeed.

(Left) Another Sesquicentennial stunt was The Set of Three—a 10-bore percussion gun, a 12-bore hammer gun and a 20-bore hammerless Royal, H&H numbers 41020, 41021 and 41022.

Besides all that and the videotape to come, H&H got up an official history of the 150 years.

THE SHOOTING FIELD

One hundred and fifty years
with HOLLAND & HOLLAND

WAFER-FLOAT
That Rifle's Barrel

By JOE LARIMORE

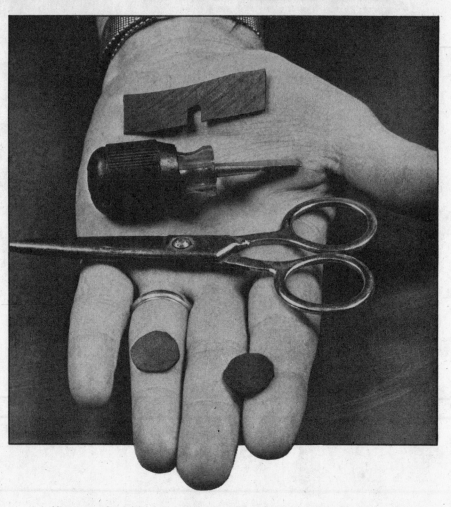

Here are wafers of the type used here, all the tools one needs to wafer-float, and a wafer of a type which might be more appealing.

IN THE PAST, free-floating a rifle barrel was a matter of cutting out the barrel groove to move the stock away from the barrel. Here, we're going to deal with gaining the same effect by reversing the process and moving the barrel very slightly away from the stock, in a much less complicated procedure. The wafering idea does not replace conventional floating, but it is an alternative means to the same end.

Here's how it worked for me. The Remington 350 Magnum was a beautiful rifle. I bought it primarily because of the tastefully laminated stock. The recoil was sufficiently powerful to loosen the rear sight after only three shots, so I could never shoot it accurately. I replaced the iron sights with a scope and virtually welded it into position. Still, accuracy was no more than mediocre, at best.

Oh, sure, I knew vaguely about glass-bedding and I had carefully studied an article on free-floating, but I rationalized away my failure to achieve accuracy by deciding the barrel was simply too short to stabilize a 200-grain slug at 2710 fps (feet per second).

In any event, I traded the 350 for an equally beautiful Ruger M-77 in 243

AUTHOR'S NOTE

The shooter who elects to try this method owes it to himself to read or reread the 1978 GUN DIGEST article on free-floating by Tom Hayes, as that article offers the depth which is absent from this article.

caliber partially because of that round's reputation for accuracy and killing power on whitetail deer, and partially because the heavier calibers aren't all that much fun to shoot when one has only a 128-pound frame.

Upon arriving home with the 243, I assured my wife that henceforth no coyote or other chicken-stealing varmint would dare come within four hundred yards of our house. Testfiring results were completely disappointing, however, and I reasoned that the fault lay in the scope I was using. The new scope had more clarity and magnification than the old and I knew that at long last success was to be mine. By now you've probably guessed that accuracy wasn't improved one iota and that my morale was running lower than my shoetops.

I had expended 60 rounds and was still getting a six-inch pattern at 100 yards. You know how difficult it would be to kill a coyote even at only 200 yards with that sort of scatter?

At that point, I began thinking in terms of glass-bedding. Since deer season was only two weeks away and most gunsmiths seem to have a long waiting list, bedding did not seem to be the answer if I wanted to use the rifle that year. Thus, free-floating the barrel seemed the only viable alternative, as lawyers are wont to say.

After 90 minutes of dowel and sandpaper, as prescribed, I had two skinned knuckles but had removed only a small portion of the walnut needed to gain free-float. At such times, I put a project aside to look at the overall situation.

Firmly ensconced in my favorite chair, I nursed a pipe full of good tobacco and a cup of steaming creek-bank coffee, hooded my eyelids and proceeded to think. Now, I mused, back in the old days when we lost or broke an ammo-belt-holding-pawl-spring in flight on the 50-caliber machine gun, we replaced the spring with a triangular shaped wedge cut from the forward corner of a boot's rubber heel. No esthetics, perhaps, but it served the purpose. And, I continued to muse, isn't it a doggone shame that my present problem isn't as simple as replacing that pawl-spring?

Suddenly, I realized that it really was that simple and I raced for the storage area where we save odds and ends such as the rubber washers our son used to repair leaky faucets. There, I found two small black and wonderful little rubber wafers $1/16$-inch thick and ½-inch in diameter. I remember thinking of them as being completely invaluable.

On the M-77 the barrel lug fits rather neatly into a depression carved into the stock. From the forward end of the magazine a screw extends diagonally forward to engage the lug and hold it there snugly. In this depression, I carefully placed my rubber wafers—one on each side of the screw. Locking metal and wood together with the retaining screws, I immediately determined that the space between stock and barrel would accommodate four, but not five, thicknesses of ordinary notebook paper all the way back to near the chamber. This, I exulted, is free-float the lazy man's way.

But would it shoot? The first projectile was six inches low and an inch to the left. After appropriate clicks, the second hit was almost dead in the center. The third was less than an inch from the second. For a novice, that is acceptable accuracy, at 100 yards in 12-18 mph winds. I haven't felt the need for more adjustment.

Well, then what does one gain by wafer-floating rather than cutting wood? Well:

Speed. In ten minutes or less—the length of time it takes to separate steel from wood and then rejoin them, plus five seconds for laying the two wafers—you've gone from out-of-the-box to free-floated-barrel accuracy.

Economy. There is no need to buy dowel, sandpaper, wood finisher or paint brush, or to expend valuable time and gasoline in shopping for them.

Ease. Can be accomplished with one screw driver and two rubber wafers which, in a pinch, could be cut from a discarded inner tube with a pocket knife or a wife's best sewing scissors.

Beauty. If you are not an accomplished wood worker, you will mar that stock to some extent by sanding and resealing. Such marring, however slight, could seriously affect the value of your gun if you decide to part with it at a later date, particularly if your prospective buyer is a collector. Free-floating by wafer will leave no such defects.

There you have it, and I wish you every good result. I believe wafer-floating has a place in your collection of things to remember, and consider trying. ●

Instant accuracy with wafering is demonstrated by the two holes connected by the dime.

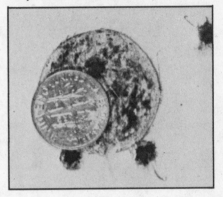

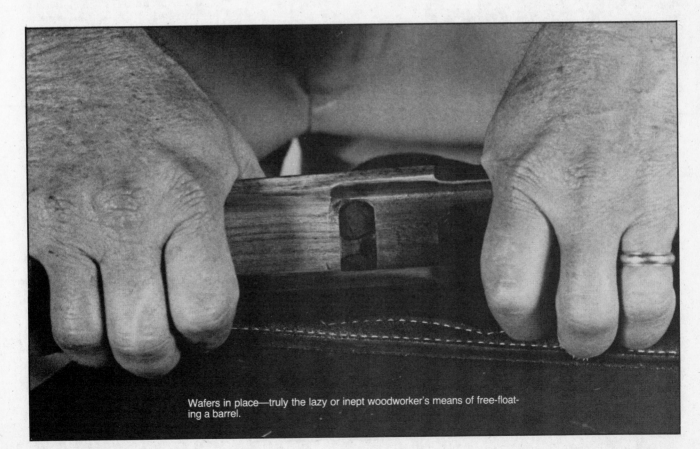

Wafers in place—truly the lazy or inept woodworker's means of free-floating a barrel.

The Significance of
GERTRUDE HURLBUTT

(Above) The gathered Hurlbutt celebrants clearly appear to enjoy her day at the Rivanna club in Charlottesville, VA. (Tom Gathright photo)

(Left) Stalwarts in plus-fours, argyles, stalk Rivanna amidst such vintage machinery as 1929 and 1931 Buicks. (Luther Gore photo)

Double guns and pants bloused very high recall the days when they called chicks "flappers."

GUN CLUBS should celebrate something, and Gertrude Hurlbutt is important.

The solemn practice of commemorating Gertrude Hurlbutt and her contribution to the shooting sports might be spreading. It has gotten to Charlottesville, VA, in fine style on the premises of the Rivanna Rifle & Pistol Club.

The occasion is marked by 1920s attire, transportation, and even firearms. It is also marked by favorable local publicity. It is also marked by a real keen party.

The drink of the day is near beer which, for anyone under 50, may be described as the Volstead Commission's gift to Repeal. It may also be described as a thirst-quenching but otherwise unsatisfactory substitute for beer. Volstead? Well, the legislation which imposed the prohibition of alcoholic beverages all across the United States was the Volstead Act.

And there is competition. The ladies compete for best lady's costume, the men for best men's costume; boys and girls compete separately. And anyone who wishes may shoot in the Hurlbutt Trophy shoot, but they can win only in 1920s attire.

That's a Skeet program, of course. Why "of course?" Well, in 1926, there was a national contest to find a new name for "shooting around the clock." The winner of the contest was Gertrude Hurlbutt of Dayton, Montana. Her name for the new game was *Skeet*.   *Ken Warner*

Ammunition, Ballistics and Components

Remington's newest 280 load has 140-grain bullet, bests the 270 Winchester's long range performance, albeit only by a small amount.

by EDWARD A. MATUNAS

THIS YEAR, keeping abreast of ammo developments has been even more fun and educational than usual. I was able to discover a very clean-burning 1½-ounce 12-gauge load while ridding the air of some Asian feathered species. I watched a particular bullet style partially misbehave and partially do a fine job (more on this under the Norma heading). But best of all, in the company of fine writer types, I had the opportunity to participate in a very thorough wringing out of Remington's newest big game load. Boar, black buck antelope, axis, fallow and whitetail deer, aoudad sheep and several large nilgai were all bagged by our group when putting the new ammo to the test. A writer's niche in life can sometimes be very, very enjoyable. Too, I watched one of my sons put it all together and take his first two deer just weeks apart. Now that's the stuff it's all about; bullets working, hunters performing, and great times in the field.

But not everything went smoothly. I was greatly disappointed by the sorrowful performance of one of the newer ammo brand's soft point ammunition. And I watched in amazement as lot after lot of a long-favored 7mm bullet turned in deplorable accuracy. The only measurable difference I could find between the last good lot and these terrible lots was a change in ogive. But there's more to putting a good bullet together than can be easily measured or detected by the shooter's eye.

And then there were the sub-standard velocities, well below advertised levels, of a number of loads in an imported line and even in one domestic loading; centerfire cartridges all.

All in all, it has been an interesting year, though there were not as many new items to test as in the past sever-

Animals taken with the new Remington 140-grain 280 load and mountain rifle include a long list of exotic and standard types of big game. Shown is an aoudad sheep taken by the author with one shot at 125 yards.

This very fine axis deer trophy was taken with a single shot from a 280 Remington using the new 140-grain loading.

Remington's two new handgun loads with lead semi-wadcutter bullets: A 200-grain 44 Special and a 158-grain 38 Special +P.

A 165-grain bullet is now available for the 308 Winchester cartridge if you purchase Remington ammo.

al years. Here's a rundown on what *is* new since our last discussion:

Remington

At a recent Remington seminar, a good number of outdoor writers had the opportunity to bag a goodly number of exotic species, as well as whitetail and javelina, with the newest Remington centerfire rifle load, a 280 Remington round loaded with a 140-grain spitzer. Ammo and writers proved up to the task and an impressive number of one-shot kills were recorded. The new bullet proved at its best on thin-skinned, light to medium big game.

This new 280 load is bound to turn the heads of diehard 270 and 30-06 users. Its 140-grain bullet exits the muzzle at a sizzling 3000 feet per second (fps) to arrive at the 500-yard mark still going more than 1900 fps. Now, if the 270's 500-yard velocity doesn't come to mind, let me assure you it's more than 100 fps slower, while the 30-06 150-grain bullet arrives at that distant mark almost 300 fps slower.

Velocity is not everything, you say. Well, then consider that this 140-grain 280 Remington load starts out with almost 2800 foot pounds (ft. lbs.) of energy and gets out to 500 yards with over 1100 ft. lbs. of that energy. The 270 has just over 900 at the same range, while the 30-06 doesn't even come up to this level (130 and 150-grain bullets respectively). And if that's not enough to get your attention, the 140-grain new 280 Remington round flattens trajectory to a point somewhat better than the fabled 270 Winchester 130-grain load.

In my opinion the 280 Remington with 140- and 150-grain loads, could well become our most popular hunting round *if* shooters will recognize the obvious virtues encompassed by these loads. As 270 fans will discover, the difference between their 130-grain bullet and the 280's 140-grain projectile might not be enough to cause retirement of their favorite rifle. But for those considering the purchase of a new rifle, be it a replacement or addition, the 280 does indeed edge out the 270 Winchester. And that's no small thing.

Also new from Remington is the 165-grain loading for the 308 Winchester. This weight bullet is the ideal selection for the hunter who wants to use one bullet for both light and medium big game. Bullet type is the superb Remington pointed soft point Core-Lokt. This load should prove to have excellent long range potential on game up to the size of elk.

The 38 Special cartridge is now being offered by Remington in a +P version with a 158-grain lead semi-wadcutter. The 44 Special is also now offered in a 200-grain bullet of similar shape. Complete ballistics for these new handgun loads are shown nearby. A 4-in. barrel was used to obtain the 38 Special ballistics and a 6½-in. barrel was used for the 44 Special.

DuPont

It's not often that there is news from DuPont Powder. They simply continue to make some of the finest canister-grade propellants available. Not since the introduction of Hi-Skor 800-X, a number of years ago, have we had the opportunity to review a new propellant. But since our last effort in these pages, DuPont has made available their IMR-7828 as a canister-grade powder.

I did have the fortune of being supplied some of a sample lot of this propellant sometime before it became generally available and, thus, have had ample time to burn up that eight pounds. I have used it with excellent results with the 243 Winchester and Nosler 100-grain bullets, obtaining higher velocities than previously possible at 3055 fps, and this with pressures below 50,000 CUP. I have also been very satisfied with it in the 6mm Remington with 100-grain bullets. It will provide 60 fps or so additional velocity with the 120-grain bullet in the 25-06 Remington compared to other DuPont powders.

But IMR-7828 really shines in the 264 Winchester Magnum where,

Comparative Remington Ballistics

	280 Rem. (new) 140-gr. PSP	270 Win. 130-gr. PSP	30-06 Spring. 150-gr. PSP
	Velocity (fps)		
Muzzle	3000	3060	2910
100 yards	2758	2776	2617
200 yards	2528	2510	2342
300 yards	2309	2259	2083
400 yards	2102	2022	1843
500 yards	1905	1801	1622
	Energy (foot pounds)		
Muzzle	2797	2702	2820
100 yards	2363	2225	2281
200 yards	1986	1818	1827
300 yards	1657	1472	1445
400 yards	1373	1180	1131
500 yards	1128	936	876

Remington Handgun Load Ballistics
38 Special +P 158-grain LSWC

Range (yds.)	Velocity (fps)	Energy (ft. lbs.)	Mid-Range Trajectory (inches)
0	890	278	-
50	855	257	1.4
100	823	238	6.0

44 S&W Special 200-grain LSWC

Range (yds.)	Velocity (fps)	Energy (ft. lbs.)	Mid-range Trajectory (inches)
0	1035	476	-
50	938	391	1.1
100	866	333	4.9

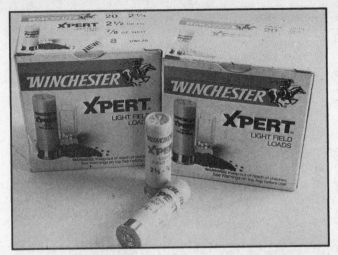

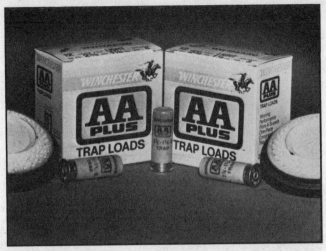

The famous (to older shooters, anyway) Xpert brand is being returned to the Winchester ammo line to replace the now-discontinued Upland brand name.

New from Olin is a trap load modified to improve 16-yard scores. These new "200's" spread their patterns just a bit more to get better results at shorter ranges.

when using 140-grain bullets, a velocity in excess of 3100 fps is possible compared to a previous DuPont maximum of 2875 fps (with IMR-4831). And how about a very, very impressive 2900+ feet per second in the 7mm Remington Magnum with 175-grain bullets?

If you have not already figured it out, IMR-7828 is the slowest burning DuPont powder to date. DuPont's data for this propellant is shown nearby. For complete details refer to DuPont's literature.

Winchester

The biggest news from Winchester this year, in my opinion, is not the announcement of new products, but rather that they have dropped some old ones. Gone, after inventory depletion, will be the 87-grain 250 Savage load, the 256 Winchester cartridge, and the 100-grain 264 Winchester Magnum load.

Also, just a few years after birth, the 180-grain 307 Winchester and the 250-grain 356 Winchester loads are now has-beens. This leaves but one load in each caliber to insure the future of two cartridges that haven't yet had a chance at making it to popularity. My guess would be that both are dying, despite their ballistic superiority over more traditional lever-action carbine rounds.

Also being discontinued is the only varmint load left in Olin's line for the 308 Winchester, the 125-grain pointed soft point. This is part of a continuing and interesting trend. If you would compare the 1986 Winchester catalog with one of not too many years ago, you would be able to note that most of the varmint loads, in calibers which have a reputation for dual varmint/big game applications, have

been discontinued. Gone now, or footnoted for dropping, are the varmint weight bullets for the 250 Savage, 257 Roberts, 264 Winchester, 7mm Remington Magnum, and the 308 Winchester. In fact, the only survivors are the 90-grain 25-06, the 100-grain load for the 270 Winchester and the 125-grain 30-06 loading. (The 110-grain 30-06 varmint load is among those discontinued.) And I'd bet that the 270 Winchester varmint load is out on a limb. I base this wager on the fact that a recently tested lot of this ammo produced a velocity of only 3032 fps (22-in. barrel) against an advertised velocity of 3430 fps. It has been my experience that when a product's performance is allowed to so slip, the manufacturer's interest is on the wane. However, that lot of ammo was accurate!

Also quietly gone from the catalog are the 30-06 220-grain Power Point, the 30-40 Krag 180-grain Silvertip, the 300 Savage 180-grain Silvertip and the 308 Winchester 200-grain Silvertip loads.

While Winchester has dropped the Upland shotshell loads, no loss is really evident, as they have been replaced with the same offerings under the Xpert brand. The Upland name originally replaced the Xpert brand when marketing geniuses decided that the brand Xpert was a poor choice. Now, years later, someone has decided, I guess, that Upland was a poor choice and that Xpert is once again better. Confusing?

Also new in the Winchester catalog is the listing of Super Steel non-toxic game loads, these separated from the expected grouping under Super Steel non-toxic magnum loads. Anti-steel shot persons will find Winchester's suggested applications of steel shot

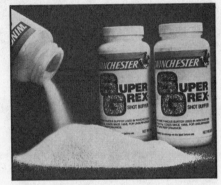

Winchester Super Grex granulated buffer is available now for the first time, packed in 8-oz. plastic bottles.

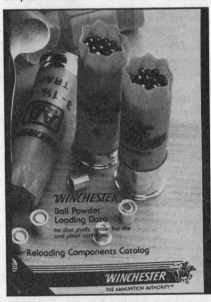

Winchester's Ball Powder data booklet has lost some familiar loads and resurrected some mighty old ones.

for pheasant, woodcock and dove less than to their liking, while steel advocates will take a see-I-told-you-so posture. I just regret seeing the ammo

Federal 257 +P Roberts 117-grain Hi-Shok

Range yards	Velocity fps	Energy ft. lbs.	Mid-Range Trajectory
0	2780	2010	-0-
100	2560	1710	0.6"
200	2360	1445	2.6"
300	2160	1210	6.5"
400	1970	1010	12.6"

Federal Premium 300 Winchester Magnum 180-grain With Nosler Partition Bullet

	Muzzle	100 yds.	200 yds.	300 yds.	400 yds.
Velocity	2960	2750	2540	2340	2160
Energy	3500	3010	2580	2195	1860

folks give support to unilateral applications of steel. Of such things are new regulations made. A few new buffered buckshot loads, one in 10-gauge (No.4 buck) and another in 3-in. 12-gauge (No.000 buck), as well as a 2¾-in. 12-gauge (No.1 buck) complete the shotshell changes for Olin.

In the rimfire category a few items are scheduled for elimination including the 22 Short high velocity hollow point (again), the T22 Short (a standard velocity load) and the 100-pack size of T22 Long Rifle, all per catalog footnotes.

During the past year, Winchester also introduced a new 12-gauge trap load designated AA200 and said to give wider patterns for better 16-yard scores. Too, there was the publication of a revised (ninth) edition of the *Ball Powder Loading Data* booklet, which showed some obvious additions, as well as equally obvious deletions. If you use Ball Powder propellants, be sure you have a copy of this latest data revision. It is available free of charge for single copies by writing to: M. Jordan, Winchester Group, Olin Corp., East Alton, IL 62024.

Federal

Each year, lately, Federal continues to expand. This year the most noteworthy item, in my opinion, is the incorporation of still another Premium load using a Nosler Partition bullet. This latest addition is a 300 Winchester Magnum load using the 180-grain Partition bullet with a muzzle velocity of 2960 fps. Nosler Partition bullets are the very best when it comes to combining positive expansion with very deep penetration. Considering the size game normally hunted with the big 300, this new load should prove popular.

The other new addition to Federal's centerfire rifle ammo line is a 257 Roberts loading. This load will be the only available 257 factory load using a spitzer bullet. As such, it should prove about perfect for long range

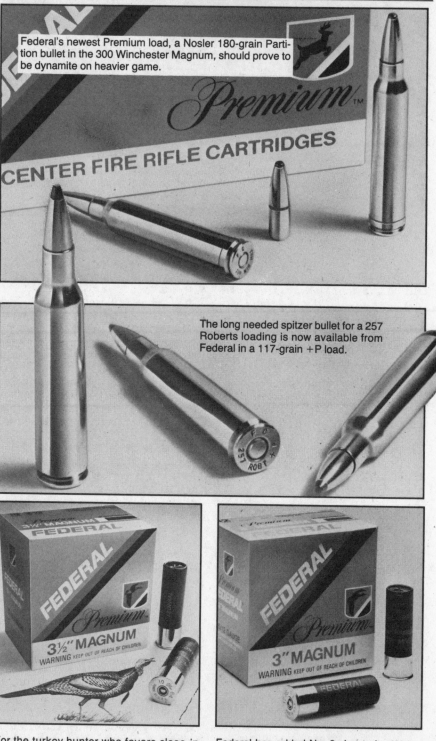

Federal's newest Premium load, a Nosler 180-grain Partition bullet in the 300 Winchester Magnum, should prove to be dynamite on heavier game.

The long needed spitzer bullet for a 257 Roberts loading is now available from Federal in a 117-grain +P load.

For the turkey hunter who favors close-in head shots, Federal's new 2¼ ounces of No. 6 shot in 10-gauge Magnum is just the ticket.

Federal has added No. 2 shot to its 1⅝-oz. 12-gauge Premium 3-in. Magnum shells.

The 1⅜-oz. 12-gauge Federal shell (formerly called Heavy-Weight) is now to be known as a Light Magnum.

Light recoil and a full 1⅛ ounces of shot is made possible with Federal's new reduced-velocity Gold Medal "Extra-Lite" target load.

A new package for Federal's Spitfire hyper-velocity 22 Long Rifle ammo is a reusable plastic "tin."

shooting, especially in that it is a +P loading. The new load should prove effective to about 300 yards, thus adding about 50 yards to this deer and antelope round. However, I do disagree with Federal's comment that the load will prove equally effective for "large game as well as occasional varminting." No way that a bullet designed for deer, with the necessary expansion versus penetration balance, will prove satisfactory for varmints where a very frangible bullet is desired. Ballistics for this new load are shown in the accompanying table.

Federal's shotshell line has a number of new loads. Included in this category are a 10-gauge 3½-in. load with 2¼ ounces of No. 6 shot. That's better than 500 pellets and they are copper plated. Federal suggests this as a turkey load for those hunters who prefer head shots only. Also, the 12-gauge 3-in. Premium 1⅝-ounce load is now available with No. 2 shot. This should prove popular with shooters who have discovered that in many 12-gauge shotguns 1⅝ ounces of shot tend to pattern more evenly than the 1⅞-ounce loads.

Federal's 1⅜-ounce Heavyweight 12-gauge load is now known as the 1⅜-ounce Light Magnum load—exciting, what? It will be packaged in (ugh) a camouflage-pattern box. Pellet sizes are No. 4 (185 pellets), No. 6 (310 pellets), and No. 7½ (480 pellets).

And as you would expect, Federal has once again expanded its steel shot line. The new addition is a worthwhile 12-gauge 3-in. load with 1¼ ounces of shot in steel sizes BB, 1, 2, and 4. Also, No. 6 steel shot has been added to the 20-ga. 1-ounce load.

Also introduced during the past

DuPont IMR 7828 Data (24-in. barrel)

Caliber	Bullet Wt. (grains)	Charge Wt. (grains)	Velocity (fps)	Pressure CUP
243 Win.	95 Nosler	47.0 (C)	3110	48,400
	100 Nosler	47.0 (C)	3050	47,900
	105 Speer	46.0 (C)	2980	48,100
6mm Rem.	100 Sierra	48.0 (C)	3040	48,000
	105 Speer	47.5 (C)	2975	46,400
257 Roberts	117 Sierra	47.0 (C)	2720	42,700
	120 Speer	47.0 (C)	2745	43,900
25-06 Rem.	117 Sierra	55.0	3130	52,100
	120 Speer	55.0	3105	52,800
264 Win.Mag.	140 Sierra	65.0	3115	53,600
270 Win.	150 Hornady	56.5 (C)	2860	50,600
	160 Nosler	56.5 (C)	2780	48,400
280 Rem.	160 Sierra	59.0 (C)	2775	49,100
	175 Hornady	56.0 (C)	2555	44,100
7mm Rem.Mag.	175 Nosler	66.0	2910	52,000
30-06 Spring.	200 Speer	55.0 (C)	2385	44,100
	220 Hornady	55.0 (C)	2285	41,900
300 Win.Mag.	165 Hornady	77.5	3210	53,700
	180 Hornady	74.0	3050	53,900
	200 Nosler	71.0	2900	53,800
	220 Hornady	70.0	2750	53,000
338 Win.Mag.	250 Hornady	74.0 (C)	2565	44,400
	275 Speer	71.0 (C)	2430	43,400

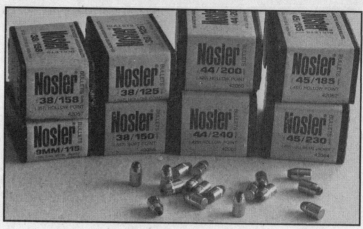

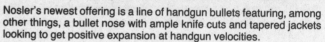

These game farm pheasants succumbed to the cleanest burning 1½-oz. 12-gauge load Matunas ever used—Dan/Arms 2¾-in. Magnum No. 4s.

Nosler's newest offering is a line of handgun bullets featuring, among other things, a bullet nose with ample knife cuts and tapered jackets looking to get positive expansion at handgun velocities.

This Norma bullet weighed 180 grains when fired from a 308 Winchester, but its plastic-tipped Dual (not really) Core bullet proved too fragile, in the author's opinion. Its recovered weight was 112 grains.

year was a new Federal Extra-Lite target load in the Gold Medal line. But instead of reducing the normal 12-gauge shot load of 1⅛ ounces, they instead have reduced the velocity somewhat from the usual 1145 fps. Thus, they have obtained the perceived recoil level of a 1-ounce target load with the higher pellet count of a 1⅛-ounce load. Available in shot sizes 8 and 8½, this load will prove popular with those who like as little recoil as possible.

And finally, the 22 Spitfire is now available in a round container (50 cartridges). This beats the popular (so say the ammo companies) 100-round plastic boxes when you want to get some shells in or out of your pocket. It may be almost as convenient as the standard old tag-board 50-round boxes we all loved so much.

P.P.C. Corp.

Some shooters are aware of what may well be two of the most accurate cartridges around, the 22 PPC and the 6mm PPC. These cartridges have been around for a dozen or so years

and currently hold 52 of 54 benchrest shooting records. The world record aggregate for 25 shots is .145 inches, held by the 6mm PPC.

Dr. Palmisano, one of the co-designers of these cartridges, now owns and operates P.P.C. Corp., 625 E. 24th St., Paterson, NJ 07514. Dr. Palmisano has informed me that factory-loaded cartridges and brass cases will finally be available by the time you read this for the 6mm diameter round. The 22-caliber ammo and brass should be available by September. Rifles will also be available for both calibers at that time. Ammunition and guns will be manufactured for the P.P.C. Corp. by Sako. The P.P.C. Corp. will distribute the entire line of Sako products.

In its factory format the 6mm PPC cartridge will use 70-grain Sierra boat-tail hollow point match bullets. As final testing of the cartridge indicates, the bullet will travel at approximately 3200 fps, give or take a few feet per second. The case will use a small rifle primer and it is anticipated that the CCI benchrest primer will be used. The PPC case, based on the 220 Russian, will be improved somewhat to eliminate an inherent weak point in the head design of the original Russian round. Headstamp will read "6mm PPC - SAKO - USA."

The 22-caliber version of the PPC round will, I am sure, appeal to varmint hunters as well as benchrest fans. It will use a 52-grain Sierra boat-tail hollow point match bullet and the small rifle CCI benchrest primer. Currently, velocities for the factory 22 PPC are anticipated at near 22-250 velocities, i.e. 3500 to 3600 fps. That the 22 PPC is more accurate than any other 22-caliber round has already been established in benchrest competition. Thus, this new cartridge and the available Sako ri-

fles should prove to be the ultimate for varmint hunting.

Just how accurate are the PPC rounds? Well, in addition to those 52 of 54 benchrest records, U.S. shooters have garnered 8 gold and 2 silver Olympic medals thanks to the help of Dr. Palmisano. It is of interest to note that Dr. Palmisano is a technical advisor for the U.S. shooting team.

Winchester passed up the offered opportunity to produce what are perhaps the two most accurate cartridges in the world. But despite this, now, after years of effort, Dr. Palmisano, with Sako's help, will finally be in the position to supply the demand for two very fine and superbly accurate cartridges.

In the works, too, is a new silhouette cartridge based on a 2-in. long version of the PPC 6mm cartridge (the standard length is 1¾ inches). The 2-in. PPC round will use a 6.5mm diameter bullet of 140 grains. Preliminary tests suggests that the best silhouette round of the near future is likely to prove to be the 6.5 x 2" PPC.

Dan/Arms

Dan/Arms continues to import the well-made and well-loaded Dan/Arms shotshells from Denmark. After extensive use, this ammo is proving even better than I reported last year.

For example, many shotgunners are aware of the unburned powder left in the bore and mechanisms after the firing of even a few 1½-ounce loads. During a recent pheasant shoot hosted by Dan/Arms, I used their 1½-ounce loading of No. 4s exclusively. It was a good shoot, with plenty of birds, and I fired almost two boxes of these loads. The shotgun used was then disassembled to rid it of the normal accumulation of crud that occurs with heavy loads. To my surprise, the bore

PPC's Dr. Palmisano preparing to prove, once again, that the PPC cartridges are perhaps the most accurate in the world.

was nearly mirror bright and there was *no* unburned powder or other crud in the action.

I was simply awed by such performance. But I couldn't accept it as standard, so I put additional ammo to the test during some bitter cold New England sea duck hunting. I fired 100 shells in temperatures from −2°F to 23°F. The results were almost identical to the pheasant hunt; and I used ammo from two lots not used on the pheasant shoot.

Every shotgunner can appreciate clean-burning loads, but those who use semi-automatics will be particularly fond of the Dan/Arms 1½-ounce loads.

Dan/Arms has greatly expanded their production facilities and we will soon see the availability of 20-gauge ammo in addition to the currently available 12-gauge loadings. Too, don't be surprised to see Dan/Arms offering load data for their cases in the not-too-distant future.

And all this continues at really bargain pricing. Dan/Arms shotshells are more than worth a try.

Nosler

Nosler is really going all out for the reloaders' bullet business. As you are probably aware, Nosler Partition bul-

lets are the premium choice bullets for many big game hunters. Nosler also offers popular-priced bullets in their Solid Base line, as well as the Ballistic Tip line. This year, we are being treated to still another category of jacketed bullets, this time for handguns.

Nosler has entered the handgun bullet line in style with nine offerings that will cover a very large portion of bullet users' needs. Included are 9mm, 38/357, 44 and 45-caliber bullets. The 9mm bullet is a 115-grain full metal jacket slug which measures as you might expect, .355-in. in diameter. The 38/357 line includes a 125-grain hollow point, a 150-grain soft point, a 158-grain hollow point, a 180-grain *NON*-expanding soft point. The 44 Special line (.429-in.) includes 200 and 240-grain hollow points. The 45-caliber line (for 45 ACP at .451-in.) has a 185-grain hollow point and a 230-grain full metal cased bullet.

The soft nose bullets and hollow points all have tapered jacket walls to promote progressive expansion. Too, the jacket walls incorporate multiple "knife-cut" serrations at the nose to further insure positive expansion. Accuracy will be up to Nosler standards. Some machine-rest 50-yard groups were under ½-inch, Nosler told me.

The 6mmx1.50-in. PPC, center, is flanked by the "tiny" 222 Remington and the 243 Winchester. The PPC cartridges in the 1.50-, 1.75- and 2.0-inch versions are proof that good things do indeed come in little packages.

Norma

In the words of Mike Bussard, Norma's man in the U.S., "Demand for Norma was far greater than we estimated. The pipeline was bone dry. Thus, we have been trying to catch up all year long, somewhat unsuccessfully I might add . . . . Product delivery will be a prime effort for this year." That about says it all. Norma is offering plenty of standard loads, some not so standard and even a few unusual ones. But product availability seems, at best, mighty thin.

When and if Norma catches on to what's required to do business in the U.S. market, loads in such calibers as 22 Savage Hi-Power, 6.5x50 Japanese, 6.5x52 Carcano, 6.5x55 Swedish, 7x64 Brenneke, 7.5x55 Swiss, 7.62x54 Russian, 7.65x53 Argentine, 7.7x58 Japanese, 9.3x57 Mauser and 9.3x62 Mauser will make a goodly number of firearms shootable. Ammo in these calibers has been almost extinct. Too, who else offers pistol ammo for the 10mm Auto? But offering and making available can be far apart. For the life of me, I don't know how the potential annual volume for the odd-balls can be appealing from a marketing point of view.

I am anxious to try some current production Norma ammo and components. I did have the opportunity to watch some 308 Winchester Norma ammo with the 180-grain Dual Core bullet being put to the test. Accuracy was just fine, averaging about 1¾ inches from a Ruger 77 full length stocked carbine. Performance on two deer was, at the same time, both disappointing and satisfying. The first deer was dumped with a neck shot. The vertebrae was missed, but the deer went down. As expected, the heavy bullet exited the neck, but the wound channel was huge. The deer required a mercy shot.

The second deer supplied the answer. It was hit low in the left rear ham as it headed away. Later investigation revealed that the bullet entered the ham and its front section blew up, making a big wound very close to the surface. The rear of the bullet, with no trace of the nose, exited the other side of the ham and re-entered the deer, travelled upward through the paunch, and caused enough damage to bring the deer down some 150 yards or so distant.

This bullet is not constructed with two separated cores as the name "Dual Core" would suggest. It appears to have one homogeneous core, while the jacket has a deep groove. When the rapidly expanding jacket reaches this deep cut, it appears to simply break away, leaving a near-original diameter slug to continue penetration.

Hornady

During the past year, quite a few new bullets have been announced by Hornady, who, it would seem, is bound and determined to maintain the largest bullet line in the component industry. Too, some bullets have been slightly modified. For example, the 220-grain flat point 375 bullet has had its cannelure moved forward .035-in. to permit deeper seating and, hence, positive feeding in lever-action rifles.

A 140-grain 6.5mm bullet is now available in a boat-tail hollow point nose configuration; a match bullet, naturally. Another new boat-tail bullet is the 117-grain spitzer in 25 caliber. And there is a bullet design especially for the 7x30 Waters; a 139-grain flat point Interlock style.

Competitive handgun shooters who favor 32-caliber cartridges, will find the new Hornady 90-grain hollow base wadcutter bullet very appealing. It is a hardened bullet with 5 percent antimony and is dry lubricated. This bullet should prove popular for target work in the 32 S&W Long and be a natural for plinking in the 32 H&R Magnum.

New jacketed handgun bullets were also introduced several months ago, including a 41-caliber 210-grain truncated cone for silhouette shooting. A new full patch pistol bullet introduced is the 124-grain 9mm round nose.

Accurate Brand Powders

Accurate Arms is making serious efforts to get the reloading shooter to use more of their imported (from Israel) powders. To make it easier to remember Accurate nomenclature, all alpha prefixes are being dropped from designations in favor of a 4-digit symbol, i.e. 2230, 5744, 2460 etc. Also, the reloader will now be able to purchase Accurate Powders in one-pound packages. This will make it easier for dealers to stock a larger variety of Accurate Powders without exceeding storage limits and it will also make it less expensive for shooters to try these powders.

The newest Accurate loading data booklet has been expanded to include more data for specific calibers and frequently better identification of the components used (specific brand and style bullets, primers and cases). Also, starting charges as well as maximum charges are now shown for many applications. In addition, new calibers have been included, such as 222 Remington Magnum, 240 Weatherby and 350 Remington Magnum. Test barrel lengths are listed and will prove, in most cases, to be of popular usage.

Shotshell data is still very, very limited, but has been expanded to five loads (from one). The new 24-page data booklet is a must for all Accurate Powder users.

Non-Toxic Components

Last year, when I finally agreed that steel shot reloading had become a practical and *safe* undertaking due to NTC's efforts, I criticized the dearth of loading recipes offered at that time by NTC, a total of seven. It is my pleasure to report that NTC has kept up

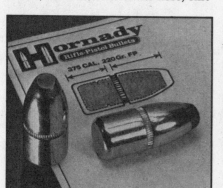
Hornady has relocated the cannelure on their 220-grain 375 bullet to make it better suited for use in Winchester lever-action rifles.

Hornady's 32-caliber 90-grain hollow base wadcutter is sure to prove a winner with 32-caliber target shooters and plinkers.

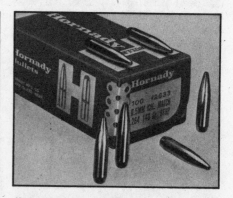
If you shoot targets with a .264-in. rifle bore, then Hornady's newest match bullet in this diameter, a 140-grain boat-tail hollow point, is worth investigating.

the effort and now offers greatly expanded data for the steel shot reloader. Their first issue of supplemental data tripled their original offering, bringing the total number of recipes to 21. Not even satisfied with that effort, the second supplemental issue of data brought about almost another doubling of recipes. I currently have data on hand for 40 different loads.

Too, NTC continues to broaden its basic component line to include new wad sizes and additional sizes of steel shot. If you don't have their current literature and are considering steel shot reloading, write: Jack Rench, NTC Inc., P.O. Box 4202, Portland, OR 97208.

Hercules

The folks at Hercules have not yet decided whether Reloader II, or a similar powder, should be returned to the canister powder market. So another year slips by without a new propellant from the Kenvil, New Jersey, plant.

Speer and Omark

Speer component and CCI loaded ammunition in handgun calibers which feature full metal cased bullets, now incorporate a new style bullet jacket. Instead of the jacket being formed of a separate-from-the-core unit, the jacket is now plated to the lead core. This results in the elimination of the exposed core at the bullet's base. Speer and CCI refer to these bullets as "totally jacketed bullets."

A similar bullet-producing method has been used in the past on at least one very accurate style varmint and target bullet. Thus, if any changes in accuracy occur with these new bullets, it should be for the better.

Hodgdon

In a major break from tradition, Hodgdon Powder Co. has decided to publish a data book with loads not only for their powders, but also for competitors, including DuPont, Hercules and Winchester propellants. The new manual, #25 in a series, should sell for about $14, but the price was not yet firmly established at this writing. The data book should be about 500 to 600 pages long. It should be available by the time you read this. Don't be surprised to find a return of Hodgdon's H450 (kissing cousin to Olin's 785) sometime during 1986.

Miscellaneous

Of course there are other importers or manufacturers of ammunition be-sides those who have received our specific attention. Some are old-line products such as **Lapua** cartridges (Finland) as imported by **Kendall International**, 501 East North Street, Carlisle, KY 40311, or the ubiquitous **PMC** ammo line. These and others oftentimes receive no specific comments due to a lack of new and newsworthy items.

Too, some products, while noteworthy, do not become generally available to most shooters either because of a limited market, limited distribution or other constraints. For instance, the **Barnes** bullet line continues after some 50 years of availability and now there are loaded rounds using these bullets available from Barnes (P.O. Box 215, American Fork, UT 84003).

There are other names, some which have been discussed in these pages in the past and some that will likely see future discussion. The reader should keep in mind his actual needs for accuracy, expansion, safety, range and similar aspects when considering the worth of any ammunition product. And we will continue to try and bring to your attention those items we feel to be worthwhile. ●

Our Ballistics Tables

The following tables have been undergoing changes over the last four years. During this time we have simplified the rimfire cartridge listings, as well as the shotshell load listings. The changes have included making the listings as generic as possible and, hopefully, easier to use and understand. This year our centerfire rifle cartridge listings have seen a similar change. The old headings of "Centerfire Rifle Cartridges," "Norma Rifle Cartridges" and "Weatherby Cartridges" have all been included into one grouping. Gone, too, are the duplication of listings caused by price differences or very slightly different (real or unreal) advertised ballistics, which sometimes were based on questionable variations in bullet ballistic coefficients.

These new centerfire rifle tables will prove easier to use when comparing ballistics of available calibers. We have selected the most popular bullet shapes for our tables, these being a fairly well defined spitzer, or a semi-spitzer, where appropriate. Naturally, exceptionally sharp pointed bullets (such as the Remington Bronze Point) or blunt round nose bullets (such as the Remington round nose Core-Lokt) will produce somewhat higher or lower average ballistics. For specifics on a definitive bullet shape, refer to the readily available manufacturers' ballistics tables which appear in the various catalogs.

The new centerfire rifle cartridge tables have been expanded to include both 400-yard velocities and energies.

This will make comparing long range potential more meaningful.

Finally, the trajectory tables have also been changed. They have been extended to 400 yards and have justifiably been modified where applicable to a common 2-inch high point of impact at 100 yards. This will now allow for a realistic comparison of trajectories for various loads and calibers without the confusion caused by varying sight-in heights. A few cartridges, for which ballistic limitations make a 2-inch high point of impact impractical at 100 yards, are listed with either a 1-inch high or dead-on point of impact at 100 yards. A dash (—) appearing in a trajectory column indicates that the bullet has fallen more than 40 inches below the line of sight. In that holdovers greater than 3 feet or so are impractical in the field, this information is deemed equally impractical and therefore has been eliminated.

We trust you will agree that the improved formats are easier to use and contain more information than ever before. If so, the effort will have been well worth the undertaking.

Ammunition as loaded by Remington, Winchester, Federal, Weatherby and Norma are included in the table. These cover almost all of the loads commonly and not so commonly available. The tables will, of course, be modified and expanded annually as product lines change. Ballistics will be carried for discontinued loads so long as ammunition is generally available in the market-place.

Edward A. Matunas

AVERAGE CENTERFIRE RIFLE CARTRIDGE BALLISTICS AND PRICES

Caliber	Bullet Wgt. Grs.	— VELOCITY (fps) — Muzzle	100 yds.	200 yds.	300 yds.	400 yds.	— ENERGY (ft. lbs.) — Muzzle	100 yds.	200 yds.	300 yds.	400 yds.	— TRAJ. (in.) — 100 yds.	200 yds.	300 yds.	400 yds.	Approx. Price per box
17 Rem.	25	4040	3284	2644	2086	1606	906	599	388	242	143	+2.0	+ 1.7	− 3.7	−17.4	$14.08
22 Hornet	45	2690	2042	1502	1128	948	723	417	225	127	90	+1.0	− 5.3	−27.6	—	26.21*
218 Bee	46	2760	2102	1550	1155	961	778	451	245	136	94	+1.0	− 5.2	−26.3	—	25.93*
222 Rem.	50	3140	2602	2123	1700	1350	1094	752	500	321	202	+2.0	− 0.4	−10.6	−33.1	11.09
222 Rem.	55	3020	2562	2147	1773	1451	1114	801	563	384	257	+2.0	− 0.4	−10.5	−31.8	11.09
222 Rem. Mag.	55	3240	2748	2305	1906	1556	1282	922	649	444	296	+2.0	+ 0.2	− 8.2	−26.3	12.60
223 Rem.	40	3650	3010	2450	1950	1530	1185	805	535	340	205	+2.0	+ 1.0	− 5.9	−22.0	12.12
223 Rem.	55	3240	2747	2305	1906	1556	1282	922	649	444	296	+2.0	+ 0.2	− 8.2	−26.3	12.12
224 Wea. Mag.[2]	55	3650	3192	2780	2403	2056	1627	1244	943	705	516	+2.0	+ 2.0	− 2.4	−12.2	23.95
22-250 Rem.	40	4000	3320	2720	2200	1740	1420	980	660	430	265	+2.0	+ 1.8	− 3.2	−15.5	12.12
22-250 Rem.	53	3710	3190	2740	2250	1790	1615	1200	751	506	377	+2.0	+ 1.0	− 3.5	−16.9	12.32
22-250 Rem.	55	3680	3137	2656	2222	1832	1654	1201	861	603	410	+2.0	+ 1.3	− 4.3	−17.1	13.54+
220 Swift	50	4110	3610	3135	2680	NA	1875	1450	1090	800	NA	+2.0	+ 2.8	+	− 6.9	17.90
22 Savage Hi-Power	71	2790	2295	1885	1560	NA	1225	830	560	383	NA	+2.0	− 0.8	−12.6	—	18.85
243 Win.	80	3350	2955	2593	2259	1951	1993	1551	1194	906	676	+2.0	+ 0.9	− 5.4	−18.6	15.13
243 Win.	85	3320	3070	2830	2600	2380	2080	1770	1510	1280	1070	+2.0	+ 1.2	− 4.5	−14.2	16.67+
243 Win.	100	2960	2697	2449	2215	1993	1945	1615	1332	1089	882	+2.0	+ 0.2	− 7.5	−22.2	16.67+
6mm Rem.	80	3470	3064	2694	2352	2036	2139	1667	1289	982	736	+2.0	+ 1.1	− 4.5	−16.5	15.13
6mm Rem.	100	3100	2829	2573	2332	2104	2133	1777	1470	1207	983	+2.0	+ 0.6	− 6.1	−19.2	15.13
240 Wea. Mag.[2]	87	3500	3202	2924	2663	2416	2366	1980	1651	1370	1127	+2.0	+ 2.2	− 1.8	−10.6	23.95
240 Wea. Mag.[2]	100	3395	3106	2835	2581	2339	2559	2142	1785	1478	1215	+2.0	+ 1.6	− 3.0	−12.8	23.95
25-20 Win.	86	1460	1194	1030	931	858	407	272	203	165	141	+	− 8.2	−23.5	—	24.57*
256 Win.	60	2760	2097	1542	1149	957	1015	586	317	176	122	+1.0	− 5.2	−28.0	—	31.20*
25-35 Win.	117	2230	1866	1545	1282	1097	1292	904	620	427	313	+2.0	− 5.3	−27.4	—	16.75
250-3000 Savage	87	3030	2673	2342	2036	1755	1773	1380	1059	801	595	+2.0	+	− 8.4	−25.2	15.35
250-3000 Savage	100	2820	2504	2210	1936	1684	1765	1392	1084	832	630	+2.0	− 0.6	−10.4	−29.5	15.35
257 Roberts +P	100	3000	2633	2295	1982	1697	1998	1539	1169	872	639	+2.0	− 0.4	− 9.4	−27.2	16.95
257 Roberts	117	2650	2291	1961	1663	1404	1824	1363	999	718	512	+2.0	− 1.0	−15.0	—	17.37
25-06 Rem.	87	3440	2995	2591	2222	1884	2286	1733	1297	954	686	+2.0	+ 1.1	− 5.1	−18.4	18.08
25-06 Rem.	90	3440	3043	2680	2340	2034	2364	1850	1435	1098	827	+2.0	+ 1.2	− 4.2	−16.6	18.08
25-06 Rem.	100	3230	2893	2580	2287	2014	2316	1858	1478	1161	901	+2.0	+ 0.8	− 5.7	−18.9	18.08
25-06 Rem.	120	2990	2730	2484	2252	2032	2382	1985	1644	1351	1100	+2.0	+	− 7.5	−22.0	18.08
257 Wea. Mag.[2]	87	3825	3456	3118	2805	2513	2826	2308	1878	1520	1220	+2.0	+ 2.7	− 0.3	− 7.7	24.95
257 Wea. Mag.[2]	100	3555	3237	2941	2665	2404	2806	2326	1920	1556	1283	+2.0	+ 2.1	− 1.8	−10.5	24.95
257 Wea. Mag.[2]	117	3300	2882	2502	2152	1830	2829	2158	1626	1203	870	+2.0	+ 1.2	− 5.1	−18.9	24.95
6.5x50 Jap.	139	2360	2185	2035	1900	NA	1720	1475	1243	1083	NA	+2.0	− 1.6	−13.4	NA	18.85
6.5x50 Jap.	156	2065	1870	1690	1530	NA	1480	1215	990	810	NA	+2.0	− 4.6	−23.3	NA	18.85
6.5x52 Carcano	156	2430	2210	2000	1800	NA	2045	1690	1385	1125	NA	+2.0	− 2.0	−14.7	NA	18.85
6.5x55 Swedish	140	2855	2665	2500	2350	NA	2530	2210	1930	1677	NA	+2.0	+ 0.6	− 6.7	NA	20.30
6.5x55 Swedish	156	2645	2415	2205	2010	NA	2425	2015	1701	1414	NA	+2.0	− 1.0	−12.1	NA	18.85
6.5 Rem. Mag.	120	3210	2905	2621	2353	2102	2745	2248	1830	1475	1177	+2.0	+ 0.7	− 5.6	−19.3	26.85
264 Win.	100	3320	2926	2565	2231	1923	2447	1901	1461	1105	821	+2.0	+ 0.8	− 5.8	−19.4	21.23
264 Win.	140	3030	2782	2548	2326	2114	2854	2406	2018	1682	1389	+2.0	+ 0.4	− 6.6	−18.4	21.23
270 Win.	100	3430	3021	2649	2305	1988	2612	2027	1557	1179	877	+2.0	+ 1.0	− 4.9	−17.5	16.44
270 Win.	130	3060	2776	2510	2259	2022	2702	2225	1818	1472	1180	+2.0	+ 0.4	− 6.8	−20.8	18.17+
270 Win.	150	2850	2585	2336	2100	1879	2705	2226	1817	1468	1175	+2.0	− 0.4	− 9.2	−25.8	22.25+
270 Wea. Mag.[2]	100	3760	3380	3033	2712	2412	3139	2537	2042	1633	1292	+2.0	+ 2.4	− 0.9	− 8.9	24.95
270 Wea. Mag.[2]	130	3375	3100	2842	2598	2366	3287	2773	2330	1948	1616	+2.0	+ 1.9	− 2.4	−11.6	24.95
270 Wea. Mag.[2]	150	3245	3019	2803	2598	2402	3507	3034	2617	2248	1922	+2.0	+ 1.8	− 3.0	−12.8	24.95
7x30 Waters	120	2700	2300	1930	1600	1330	1940	1405	990	685	470	+2.0	− 2.0	−11.0	−20.0	15.88
7mm-08 Rem.	140	2860	2625	2402	2189	1988	2542	2142	1793	1490	1228	+2.0	− 0.2	− 8.4	−23.9	16.44
7mm Mauser	140	2660	2435	2221	2018	1827	2199	1843	1533	1266	1037	+2.0	− 1.0	−11.1	−29.7	16.73
7mm Mauser	150	2755	2540	2330	2135	NA	2530	2150	1810	1515	NA	+2.0	+	− 8.4	NA	16.90
7mm Mauser	175	2440	2137	1857	1603	1382	2313	1774	1340	998	742	+2.0	− 2.7	−17.6	—	16.73
7x57R	150	2690	2475	2285	2080	NA	2410	2040	1830	1515	NA	+2.0	+	− 8.4	NA	19.66
280 Rem.	140	3000	2758	2528	2309	2102	2797	2363	1986	1657	1373	—	—	—	—	16.44
280 Rem.	150	2970	2699	2444	2203	1975	2937	2426	1989	1616	1299	+2.0	+ 0.2	− 7.5	−22.4	16.44
280 Rem.	165	2820	2510	2220	1950	1701	2913	2308	1805	1393	1060	+2.0	− 0.6	−10.3	−29.3	16.44
7x64 Brenneke	150	2890	2600	2330	2115	NA	2780	2250	1810	1490	NA	+2.0	+ 0.6	− 8.4	NA	19.66
7x64 Brenneke	170	2500	2355	2200	1915	NA	2865	2094	1694	1466	NA	+2.0	− 1.6	−12.4	NA	19.66
284 Win.	125	3140	2829	2538	2265	2010	2736	2221	1788	1424	1121	+2.0	+ 0.6	− 6.3	−18.7	19.85
284 Win.	150	2860	2595	2344	2108	1886	2724	2243	1830	1480	1185	+2.0	− 0.2	− 8.8	−25.2	19.85
7mm Rem. Mag.	125	3310	2976	2666	2376	2105	3040	2428	1972	1567	1230	+2.0	+ 1.0	− 4.9	−17.0	20.37
7mm Rem. Mag.	150	3110	2830	2568	2320	2085	3221	2667	2196	1792	1448	+2.0	+ 0.6	− 6.1	−19.3	22.25+
7mm Rem. Mag.	160	2950	2730	2520	2320	2120	3090	2650	2250	1910	1600	+2.0	+ 0.4	− 7.1	−21.6	26.92+
7mm Rem. Mag.	175	2860	2645	2440	2244	2057	3178	2718	2313	1956	1644	+2.0	+	− 7.9	−22.7	20.37
7mm Wea. Mag.[2]	139	3400	3138	2892	2659	2437	3567	3039	2580	2181	1832	+2.0	+ 2.1	− 2.1	−11.1	24.95
7mm Wea. Mag.[2]	160	3200	3004	2816	2637	2464	3637	3205	2817	2469	2156	+2.0	+ 1.7	− 3.0	−12.6	34.95
30 Carbine[1]	110	1990	1567	1236	1035	923	967	600	373	262	208	+1.0	−11.5	—	—	26.40*
30 Rem.	170	2120	1822	1555	1328	1153	1696	1253	913	666	502	+2.0	− 5.7	−27.8	—	17.31
30-30 Win.	55	3400	2693	2085	1570	1187	1412	886	521	301	172	+2.0	+	−10.2	−35.0	14.33
30-30 Win.	125	2570	2090	1660	1320	1080	1830	1210	770	480	320	+2.0	− 2.4	−19.4	—	13.41
30-30 Win.	150	2390	1973	1605	1303	1095	1902	1296	858	565	399	+2.0	− 4.2	−25.6	—	13.41
30-30 Win.	170	2200	1895	1619	1381	1191	1827	1355	989	720	535	+2.0	− 4.8	−25.1	—	18.84+
300 Savage	150	2630	2311	2015	1743	1500	2303	1779	1352	1012	749	+2.0	− 1.6	−13.9	−36.6	16.61
300 Savage	180	2350	2137	1935	1745	1570	2207	1825	1496	1217	985	+2.0	− 2.6	−19.7	—	16.61
303 Savage	190	1890	1612	1372	1183	1055	1507	1096	794	591	469	+2.0	− 8.8	−38.1	—	18.61
30-40 Krag	180	2430	2213	2207	1813	1632	2360	1957	1610	1314	1064	+2.0	− 2.2	−15.0	−38.5	17.32
307 Win.	150	2760	2321	1924	1575	1289	2538	1795	1233	826	554	+2.0	− 1.4	−15.4	—	16.25
307 Win.	180	2510	2179	1874	1599	1362	2519	1898	1404	1022	742	+2.0	− 2.6	−17.1	—	16.25
308 Win.	55	3770	3215	2726	2286	1888	1735	1262	907	638	435	+2.0	+ 1.4	− 4.2	−15.8	18.24
308 Win.	110	3180	2666	2206	1795	1444	2470	1736	1188	787	509	+2.0	+	− 9.3	−29.5	16.44
308 Win.	125	3050	2697	2370	2067	1788	2582	2019	1659	1186	887	+2.0	+	− 8.2	−24.6	16.44
308 Win.	150	2820	2533	2263	2009	1774	2648	2137	1705	1344	1048	+2.0	− 0.6	10.0	−28.1	16.44
308 Win.	165	2700	2520	2330	2160	1990	2670	2310	1990	1700	1450	+2.0	+	− 8.4	−24.3	18.17+
308 Win.	180	2620	2393	2178	1974	1782	2743	2288	1896	1557	1269	2.0	− 1.2	−11.7	−31.3	16.44
308 Win.	200	2450	2208	1980	1767	1572	2665	2165	1741	1386	1097	+2.0	− 2.2	−15.4	−39.7	16.44
30-06 Spring.	55	4080	3485	2965	2502	2083	2033	1483	1074	764	530	+2.0	+ 1.9	− 2.1	−11.7	18.24
30-06 Spring.	110	3330	2799	2325	1901	1532	2708	1913	1321	882	573	+2.0	+ 0.4	− 7.7	−25.6	16.44
30-06 Spring.	125	3140	2780	2447	2138	1853	2736	2145	1662	1269	953	+2.0	+ 0.4	− 7.1	−22.4	16.44
30-06 Spring.	130	3205	2875	2506	2263	NA	2965	2390	1895	1480	NA	+2.0	+ 1.2	− 4.9	NA	16.57
30-06 Spring.	150	2910	2617	2342	2083	1843	2820	2281	1827	1445	1131	+2.0	− 0.2	− 8.5	−24.6	18.17+
30-06 Spring.	165	2800	2534	2283	2047	1825	2872	2352	1909	1534	1220	+2.0	− 0.6	− 9.9	−27.5	18.17+
30-06 Spring.	180	2700	2469	2250	2042	1846	2913	2436	2023	1666	1362	+2.0	− 0.8	−10.5	−28.6	22.25+
30-06 Spring.	200	2640	2390	2220	1860	NA	3095	2535	2218	1384	NA	+2.0	− 1.2	−11.8	NA	16.57
30-06 Spring.	220	2410	2130	1870	1632	1422	2837	2216	1708	1301	758	+2.0	− 2.7	−20.5	NA	16.44
7.5x55 Swiss	180	2650	2460	2250	2060	NA	2800	2380	2020	1690	NA	+2.0	− 0.2	− 9.2	NA	19.66
7.62x54R Russ.	180	2575	2360	2165	1975	NA	2650	2270	1875	1560	NA	+2.0	− 0.6	−10.4	NA	20.11
308 Norma Mag.	180	3020	2780	2580	2385	NA	3645	3095	2670	2270	NA	+2.0	+ 1.4	− 5.9	NA	23.30
300 H&H Mag.	180	2880	2640	2412	2196	1990	3315	2785	2325	1927	1583	+2.0	− 0.2	− 8.3	−23.7	20.96
300 Win. Mag.	150	3290	2951	2636	2342	2068	3605	2900	2314	1827	1424	+2.0	+ 0.9	− 5.3	−17.8	21.51
300 Win. Mag.	180	2960	2745	2540	2344	2157	3501	3011	2578	2196	1859	+2.0	+	− 7.3	−20.9	25.84+
300 Win. Mag.	200	2830	2680	2530	2380	2240	3560	3180	2830	2520	2230	+2.0	+ 0.6	− 6.2	−19.1	23.42+
300 Win. Mag.	220	2680	2448	2228	2020	1823	3508	2927	2424	1993	1623	+2.0	− 1.0	−11.0	−29.5	21.51

AVERAGE CENTERFIRE RIFLE CARTRIDGE BALLISTICS AND PRICES (continued)

Caliber	Bullet Wgt. Grs.	— VELOCITY (fps) — Muzzle	100 yds.	200 yds.	300 yds.	400 yds.	— ENERGY (ft. lbs.) — Muzzle	100 yds.	200 yds.	300 yds.	400 yds.	— TRAJ. (in.) — 100 yds.	200 yds.	300 yds.	400 yds.	Approx. Price per box
300 Wea. Mag.[2]	110	3900	3441	3028	2652	2305	3714	2891	2239	1717	1297	+2.0	+ 2.6	− 0.6	− 9.2	24.95
300 Wea. Mag.[2]	150	3600	3297	3015	2751	2502	4316	3621	3028	2520	1709	+2.0	+ 2.3	− 1.2	− 9.2	24.95
300 Wea. Mag.[2]	180	3300	3077	2865	2663	2470	4352	3784	3280	2834	2438	+2.0	− 2.6	− 3.0	−12.4	34.95
300 Wea. Mag.[2]	220	2905	2498	2126	1787	1490	4122	3047	2207	1560	1085	+2.0	− 0.1	− 9.9	−22.3	24.95
7.7x58 Jap.	130	2950	2635	2340	2065	NA	2513	2005	1581	1230	NA	+2.0	+ 0.2	− 7.9	NA	20.10
7.7x58 Jap.	180	2495	2290	2100	1920	NA	2485	2100	1765	1475	NA	+2.0	+ 1.2	−12.2	NA	20.10
7.65x53 Argen.	150	2660	2390	2120	1870	NA	2355	1895	1573	1224	NA	+2.0	− 0.2	− 9.1	NA	18.86
303 British	180	2460	2124	1817	1542	1311	2418	1803	1319	950	687	+2.0	− 2.8	−21.3	—	16.92
8mm Rem. Mag.	185	3080	2761	2464	2186	1927	3896	3131	2494	1963	1525	+2.0	+ 0.4	− 7.0	−21.7	25.47
8mm Rem. Mag.	220	2830	2581	2346	2123	1913	3912	3254	2688	2201	1787	+2.0	− 0.4	− 9.1	−25.5	25.47
8mm Mauser	170	2360	1969	1622	1333	1123	2102	1463	993	651	476	+2.0	− 4.1	−24.9	—	16.95
8x57 JS Mauser	165	2855	2525	2225	1955	NA	2985	2335	1733	1338	NA	+2.0	+	− 8.0	NA	17.22
8x57 JS Mauser	196	2525	2195	1895	1625	NA	2780	2100	1560	1150	NA	+2.0	− 2.0	−15.7	NA	17.22
32-20 Win.	100	1210	1021	913	834	769	325	231	185	154	131	+	−32.3	—	—	24.79+
32 Win. Spl.	170	2250	1921	1626	1372	1175	1911	1393	998	710	521	+2.0	− 4.7	−24.7	—	13.79
338 Win. Mag.	200	2960	2658	2375	2110	1862	3890	3137	2505	1977	1539	+2.0	+	− 8.2	−24.3	25.35
338 Win. Mag.	225	2780	2572	2374	2184	2003	3862	3306	2816	2384	2005	+2.0	− 1.4	−11.1	−27.8	25.36
340 Wea. Mag.[2]	200	3260	3011	2775	2552	2339	4719	4025	3420	2892	2429	+2.0	+ 1.6	− 3.3	−13.5	41.95
340 Wea. Mag.[2]	210	3250	2991	2746	2515	2295	4924	4170	3516	2948	2455	+2.0	+ 1.7	− 3.3	−13.8	41.95
340 Wea. Mag.[2]	250	3000	2806	2621	2443	2272	4995	4371	3812	3311	2864	+2.0	+ 1.0	− 5.0	−16.8	41.95
348 Win.	200	2520	2215	1931	1672	1443	2820	2178	1656	1241	925	+2.0	− 2.2	−15.9	—	29.85
351 Win. S.L.	180	1850	1556	1310	1128	1012	1368	968	686	508	409	+	−13.6	—	—	42.35*
35 Rem.	150	2300	1874	1506	1218	1039	1762	1169	755	494	359	+2.0	− 5.1	−27.8	—	15.19
35 Rem.	200	2080	1698	1376	1140	1001	1921	1280	841	577	445	+2.0	− 5.3	−32.1	—	15.19
356 Win.	200	2460	2114	1797	1517	1284	2688	1985	1434	1022	732	+2.0	− 3.0	−18.9	—	22.90
356 Win.	250	2160	1911	1682	1476	1299	2591	2028	1571	1210	937	+2.0	− 4.7	−23.7	—	22.90
358 Win.	200	2490	2171	1876	1610	1379	2753	2093	1563	1151	844	+2.0	− 2.6	−17.5	—	22.90
357 Magnum	180	1550	1160	980	860	770	960	535	383	295	235	+	−23.4	—	—	25.07*
350 Rem. Mag.	200	2710	2410	2130	1870	1631	3261	2579	2014	1553	1181	+2.0	− 1.2	−12.1	−32.9	27.09
9.3x57 Mauser	286	2065	1820	1580	1400	NA	2715	2100	1622	1274	NA	+2.0	− 2.8	−25.9	—	21.63
9.3x62 Mauser	286	2360	2090	1830	1580	NA	3545	2770	2177	1622	NA	+2.0	− 2.0	−23.2	—	21.63
375 Win.	200	2200	1841	1526	1268	1089	2150	1506	1034	714	527	+2.0	− 5.2	−27.4	—	19.75
375 Win.	250	1900	1647	1424	1239	1103	2005	1506	1126	852	676	+2.0	− 7.9	−34.8	—	19.75
375 H&H Mag.	270	2690	2420	2166	1928	1707	4337	3510	2812	2228	1747	+2.0	− 1.0	−11.5	−31.4	25.20
375 H&H Mag.	300	2530	2171	1843	1551	1307	4263	3139	2262	1602	1138	+2.0	− 2.6	−17.1	—	25.20
378 Wea. Mag.[2]	270	3180	2976	2781	2594	2415	6062	5308	4635	4034	3495	+2.0	+ 1.6	− 3.4	−13.2	41.95
378 Wea. Mag.[2]	300	2925	2576	2252	1952	1680	5698	4419	3379	2538	1881	+2.0	+	− 8.7	−26.9	49.95
38-40 Win.	180	1160	999	901	827	764	538	399	324	273	233	+	−23.4	—	—	31.60*
38-55 Win.	255	1320	1190	1091	1018	963	987	802	674	587	525	+	−18.1	—	—	18.35
44-40 Win.	200	1190	1006	900	822	756	629	449	360	300	254	+	−33.3	—	—	32.70*
44 Rem. Mag.	240	1760	1380	1114	970	878	1650	1015	661	501	411	+	−17.6	—	—	31.15*
444 Marlin	240	2350	1815	1377	1087	941	2942	1755	1010	630	472	+2.0	− 5.8	−32.7	—	18.30
444 Marlin	265	2120	1733	1405	1160	1012	2644	1768	1162	791	603	+2.0	− 6.8	−33.4	—	18.53
45-70 Gov.	300	1880	1650	1425	1235	1105	2355	1815	1355	1015	810	+	−12.8	—	—	18.45
45-70 Gov.	405	1330	1168	1055	977	918	1590	1227	1001	858	758	+	−24.6	—	—	18.72
458 Win. Mag.	500	2040	1823	1623	1442	1237	4620	3689	2924	1839	1469	+2.0	− 5.6	−26.4	—	52.00
458 Win. Mag.	510	2040	1770	1527	1319	1157	4712	3547	2540	1970	1239	+2.0	− 6.4	−27.3	—	34.45
460 Wea. Mag.[2]	500	2700	2404	2128	1869	1635	8092	6416	5026	3878	2969	+2.0	− 0.6	−10.7	−31.3	49.95

From 24" barrel except as noted (1 = 20" bbl.; 2 = 26" bbl.). Energies and velocities based on most commonly used bullet profile. Variations can and will occur with different bullet profiles and/or different lots of ammunition as well as individual barrels. Trajectory based on scope reticle 1.5" above center of bore line. + indicates bullet strikes point of aim.

NOTES: * = 50 cartridges to a box pricing (all others 20 cartridges to a box pricing)
NA = Information not available from the manufacturer.
— = Trajectory falls more than 40 inches below line of sight.
+ = Premium priced ammunition.

Please note that the actual ballistics obtained in your gun can vary considerably from the advertised ballistics. Also, ballistics can vary from lot to lot, even within the same brand. All prices were correct at the time this table was prepared. All prices are subject to change without notice.

CENTERFIRE HANDGUN CARTRIDGES—BALLISTICS AND PRICES

Caliber	Bullet Gr.	Bullet Style	Velocity (fps) Muzzle	Velocity (fps) 50 yds.	Energy (ft. lbs.) Muzzle	Energy (ft. lbs.) 50 yds.	Barrel Length in inches	Approx. price/box
22 Rem. Jet	40	JSP	2100	1790	390	285	8⅜	$36.13
221 Rem. Fireball	50	JSP	2650	2380	780	630	10½	12.80*
223 Rem.	55	JSP	NA	NA	NA	NA	14½	12.60*
25 Auto	45	LE	815	729	66	53	2	16.95
25 Auto	50	FMC	760	707	64	56	2	16.04
30 Luger	93	FMC	1220	1110	305	253	4½	25.95
30 Carbine	110	JHP, FMC	1740	1552	740	588	10	10.97*
32 S&W	85, 88	LRN	680	645	90	81	3	15.48
32 S&W Long	98	LRN, LWC	705	670	115	98	4	16.04
32 H&R Mag.	85	JHP	1100	1020	230	195	4½	21.20
32 H&R Mag.	95	LSWC	1030	940	225	190	4½	15.37
32 Short Colt	80	LRN	745	665	100	79	4	15.39
32 Long Colt	82	LRN	755	715	100	93	4	16.04
32 Auto	60	STHP	970	895	125	107	4	20.60
32 Auto	71	FMC	905	855	129	115	4	18.38
380 Auto	85, 88	JHP	1000	921	189	160	3¾	20.35
380 Auto	95	FMC	955	865	190	160	3¾	18.79
38 Auto	130	FMC	1040	980	310	275	4½	20.48
38 Super Auto +P	115	JHP	1300	1147	431	336	5	23.10
38 Super Auto +P	125	STHP	1240	1130	427	354	5	24.56
38 Super Auto +P	130	FMC	1215	1099	426	348	5	19.85
9mm Luger	95	JSP	1350	1140	385	275	4	23.84
9mm Luger	115	JHP	1160	1060	345	285	4	22.81
9mm Luger	115	STHP	1225	1095	383	306	4	24.80
9mm Luger	123, 124	FMC	1110	1030	339	292	4	22.81
9mm Win. Mag.	115	FMC	1475	1264	555	408	5	NA
38 S&W	146	LRN	685	650	150	135	4	17.25
38 Short Colt	125	LRN	730	685	150	130	4	NA
38 Special	148	LWC	710	634	166	132	4V	18.05
38 Special	110	STHP	945	894	218	195	4V	19.51
38 Special	158	LRN, LSWC	753	721	200	182	4V	17.33
38 Special	95	JHP	1175	1044	291	230	4V	23.95
38 Special +P	110	JHP	995	926	242	210	4V	21.99
38 Special +P	125	JSP, JHP	945	898	248	224	4V	21.92
38 Special +P	158	LSWC, LHP	890	855	278	257	4V	19.23
357 Magnum	110	JHP	1295	1094	410	292	4V	24.11
357 Magnum	125	JHP. JSP	1450	1240	583	427	4V	24.11
357 Magnum	145	STHP	1290	1155	535	428	4V	26.25
357 Magnum	158	JSP, LSWC, JHP	1235	1104	535	428	4V	24.11
357 Magnum	180	JHP	1090	980	475	385	4V	25.07
357 MAXIMUM	158	JHP	1825	1588	1168	885	10½	11.57*
357 MAXIMUM	180	JHP	1555	1328	966	705	10½	11.57*
10mm Auto	165	JHP	1400	NA	719	NA	NA	12.65*
10mm Auto	200	FMC	1200	NA	635	NA	NA	12.65*
41 Rem. Mag.	175	STHP	1250	1120	607	488	4V	34.15
41 Rem. Mag.	210	LSWC	965	898	434	376	4V	27.07
41 Rem. Mag.	210	JHP, JSP	1300	1162	788	630	4V	31.71
44 Special	200	LSWC HP, STHP	900	830	360	305	6½	25.21
44 Special	246	LRN	755	725	310	285	6½	24.27
44 Rem. Mag.	180	JHP	1610	1365	1036	745	4V	11.49*
44 Rem. Mag.	210	STHP	1250	1106	729	570	4V	34.25
44 Rem. Mag.	220	FMC	1390	1260	945	775	6½V	34.89
44 Rem. Mag.	240	LSWC	1000	947	533	477	6½V	26.28
44 Rem. Mag.	240	LSWC/GC	1350	1186	971	749	4V	30.80
44 Rem. Mag.	240	JHP, JSP	1180	1081	741	623	4V	12.60*
45 Auto	185	JWC	770	707	244	205	5	26.36
45 Auto	185	JHP	940	890	363	325	5	27.35
45 Auto	230	FMC	810	776	335	308	5	25.11
45 Auto Rim.	230	LRN	810	770	335	305	5½	26.68
45 Win. Mag.	230	FMC	1400	1232	1001	775	5	27.05
45 Colt	225	JHP. LHP	900	860	405	369	5½	10.75*
45 Colt	250, 255	LRN	860	820	420	380	5½	24.64

Notes: Blanks are available in 32 S&W, 38 S&W and 38 Special. V after barrel length indicates test barrel was vented and produced results approximating a revolver with its cylinder to barrel gap.

Abbreviations: JSP (jacketed soft point); LE (lead expanding); FMC (full metal case); JHP (jacketed hollow point); LRN (lead round nose); LWC (lead wadcutter); LSWC (lead semi-wadcutter); STHP (silvertip hollow point); LHP (lead hollow point); LSWCHP (lead semi-wadcutter hollow point); LSWC/GC (lead semi-wadcutter with gas check); JWC (jacketed wadcutter)

*20 rounds per box; all others 50 rounds per box

RIMFIRE AMMUNITION—BALLISTICS AND PRICES

Cartridge Type	Bullet Wt. Grs.	Bullet Type	Velocity (fps) 22½" Barrel Muzzle	Velocity (fps) 22½" Barrel 50 Yds.	Velocity (fps) 22½" Barrel 100 Yds.	Energy (ft. lbs.) 22½" Barrel Muzzle	Energy (ft. lbs.) 22½" Barrel 50 Yds.	Energy (ft. lbs.) 22½" Barrel 100 Yds.	Velocity (fps) 6" Barrel Muzzle	Velocity (fps) 6" Barrel 50 Yds.	Energy (ft. lbs.) 6" Barrel Muzzle	Energy (ft. lbs.) 6" Barrel 50 Yds.	Approx. Price Per Box 50 Rds.	Approx. Price Per Box 100 Rds.
22 CB Short (CCI & Win.)	29	solid	727	667	610	34	29	24	706	—	32	—	NA	13.20(2)
22 CB Long (CCI only)	29	solid	727	667	610	34	29	24	706	—	32	—	NA	5.10
22 Short Match (CCI only)	29	solid	830	752	695	44	36	31	786	—	39	—	NA	5.30
22 Short Std. Vel. (Rem. only)	29	solid	1045	—	810	70	—	42	865	—	48	—	2.49	NA
22 Short H. Vel. (Fed., Rem., Win.)	29	solid	1095	—	903	77	—	53	—	—	—	—	2.49	NA
22 Short H. Vel. (CCI only)	29	solid	1132	1004	920	83	65	55	1065	—	73	—	NA	5.00
22 Short H. Vel. HP (Rem. only)	27	HP	1120	—	904	75	—	49	—	—	—	—	2.70	NA
22 Short H. Vel. HP (CCI only)	27	HP	1164	1013	920	81	62	51	1077	—	69	—	NA	5.30
22 Long Std. Vel. (CCI only)	29	solid	1180	1038	946	90	69	58	1031	—	68	—	NA	5.30
22 Long H. Vel. (Fed., Rem.)	29	solid	1240	—	962	99	—	60	—	—	—	—	2.70	NA
22 LR Pistol Match (Win. only)	40	solid	—	—	—	—	—	—	1060	950	100	80	11.55	NA
22 LR Match (Rifle) (CCI only)	40	solid	1138	1047	975	116	97	84	1027	925	93	76	NA	8.75
22 LR Std. Vel.	40	solid	1138	1046	975	115	97	84	1027	925	93	76	2.85	5.70(3)
22 LR H. Vel.	40	solid	1255	1110	1017	140	109	92	1060	—	100	—	2.85	5.70
22 LR H. Vel. HP	36-38	HP	1280	1126	1010	131	101	82	1089	—	95	—	3.16	6.32
22 LR-Hyper Vel. (Fed., Rem., Win.,(4))	33-34	HP	1500	1240	1075	165	110	85	—	—	—	—	3.19	NA
22 LR-Hyper Vel.	36	solid	1410	1187	1056	159	113	89	—	—	—	—	3.10	NA
22 Stinger (CCI only)	32	HP	1640	1277	1132	191	115	91	1395	1060	138	80	3.60	NA
22 Win. Mag. Rimfire	40	FMC or HP	1910	1490	1326	324	197	156	1428	—	181	—	7.67	NA
22 LR Shot (CCI, Fed., Win.)	—	#11 or #12 shot	1047	—	—	—	—	—	950	—	—	—	5.82	NA
22 Win. Mag. Rimfire Shot (CCI only)	—	#11 shot	1126	—	—	—	—	—	1000	—	—	—	4.35(1)	NA

Please Note: The actual ballisctics obtained from your gun can vary considerably from the advertised ballistics. Also, ballistics can vary from lot to lot even within the same brand. All prices were correct at the time this chart was prepared. All prices are subject to change without notice.

(1) 20 per box. (2) per 250 rounds. (3) also packaged 200 rounds per box. (4) also packaged 250 rounds per box.

SHOTSHELL LOADS AND PRICES

Winchester-Western, Remington-Peters, Federal

Dram Equivalent	Shot Ozs.	Load Style	Shot Sizes	Brands	Average Price Per Box	Nominal Velocity (fps)
10 Gauge 3½" Magnum						
4½	2¼	Premium(1)	BB, 2, 4, 6	Fed., Win.	$32.32	1205
4¼	2	H.V.	BB, 2, 4, 5, 6	Fed., Rem.	29.89	1210
Max.	1¾	Slug, rifled	Slug	Fed.	7.22	1280
Max.	54 pellets	Buck, Premium(1)	00.4 (Buck)	Fed., Win.	6.84	1100
Max.	1¾	Steel shot	BB, 2	Win.	NA	1260
4¼	1⅝	Steel shot	BB, 2	Fed.	26.61	1285
12 Gauge 3" Magnum						
4	1⅞	Premium(1)	BB, 2, 4, 6	Fed., Rem., Win.	21.26	1210
4	1⅝	Premium(1)	2, 4, 5, 6	Fed., Rem., Win.	19.71	1280
4	1⅞	H.V.	BB, 2, 4	Fed., Rem.	18.72	1210
4	1⅝	H.V.	2, 4, 6	Fed., Rem.	17.29	1280
4	Variable	Buck, Premium(1)	000,00,1,4	Fed., Rem., Win.	5.14	1210 to 1225
3½	1⅜	Steel shot	BB, 1, 2, 4	Fed.	18.83	1245
3½	1¼	Steel shot	BB, 1, 2, 4	Rem., Win.	17.33	1375
4	2	Premium(1)	BB, 2, 4, 6	Fed.	22.80	1175
12 Gauge 2¾" Hunting & Target						
3¾	1½	Premium(1), Mag.	BB, 2, 4, 5, 6	Fed., Rem., Win.	18.57	1260
3¾	1½	H.V., Mag.	BB, 2, 4, 5, 6	Fed., Rem.	15.63	—
3¾	1¼	H.V., Premium(1)	2, 4, 6, 7½	Fed., Rem.	13.85	1330
3¾	1¼	H.V., Promo.	BB, 2, 4, 5, 6 7½, 8, 9	Fed., Rem., Win.	12.50	1330
3¼	1¼	Std. Vel., Premium(1)	7½, 8	Fed., Rem.	12.10	1220
3¼	1⅛	Std. Vel., Premium(1)	7½, 8	Fed., Rem.	11.70	1255
3¼	1¼	Std. Vel.	6, 7½, 8, 9	Fed., Rem., Win.	11.15	1220
3¼	1⅛	Std. Vel.	4, 5, 6, 7½, 8, 9	Fed., Rem., Win.	10.17	1255
3¼	1	Std. Vel., Promo	6, 7½, 8	Fed., Rem., Win.	10.00	1290
Max.	1¼	Slug, rifled, Mag.	Slug	Fed.	5.18	1490
Max.	1	Slug, rifled	Slug	Fed., Rem., Win.	4.17	1560
4	Variable	Buck, Mag., Premium(1)	00, 1, 4 (Buck)	Fed., Rem., Win.	4.52	1075 to 1290
3¾	Variable	Buck, Premium(1)	000, 00, 0, 1, 4 (Buck)	Fed., Rem., Win.	4.25	1250 to 1325
3¾	1⅜	H.V.	2, 4, 6	Fed.	14.61	1295
3¼	1¼	Pigeon	6, 7½, 8	Fed., Win.	14.00	1220
3	1⅛	Trap & Skeet	7½, 8, 9	Fed., Rem., Win.	7.00	1200
2¾	1⅛	Trap & Skeet	7½, 8, 8½, 9	Fed., Rem., Win.	7.00	1145
2¾	1	Trap & Skeet	7½, 8, 8½	Fed., Rem., Win.	7.00	1180
3¾	1¼	Steel shot	BB, 1, 2, 4, 6	Fed., Win.	17.33	1275
3¾	1⅛	Steel shot	1, 2, 4, 6	Fed., Rem., Win.	15.95	1365

Dram Equivalent	Shot Ozs.	Load Style	Shot Sizes	Brands	Average Price Per Box	Nominal Velocity (fps)
16 Gauge 2¾"						
3¼	1¼	H.V., Mag., Premium(1)	2, 4, 6	Fed., Rem., Win.	15.37	1260
3¼	1⅛	H.V., Promo.	4, 5, 6, 7½, 9	Fed., Rem., Win.	12.16	1295
2¾	1⅛	Std. Vel.	4, 6, 7½, 8, 9	Fed., Rem., Win.	10.17	1185
2½	1	Std. Vel., Promo.	6, 7½, 8	Fed., Win.	NA	1165
Max.	⅘	Slug, rifled	Slug	Fed., Rem., Win.	4.17	1570
Max.	12 pellets	Buck	1 (Buck)	Fed., Rem., Win.	3.61	1225
3¼	1¼	Premium, Mag.	2, 4, 6	Win.	15.37	1260
20 Gauge 3" Magnum						
3	1¼	Premium(1)	2, 4, 6	Fed., Rem., Win.	14.44	1185
3	1¼	H.V.	2, 4, 6, 7½	Fed., Rem.	12.68	1185
Max.	18 pellets	Buck	2 (Buck)	Fed.	4.52	—
Max.	1	Steel shot	4, 6	Fed., Win.	15.20	1330
20 Gauge 2¾" Hunting & Target						
2¾	1⅛	Premium(1), Mag.	4, 6, 7½	Fed., Rem., Win.	14.57	1175
2¾	1⅛	H.V., Mag.	4, 6, 7½	Fed., Rem.	12.80	1175
2¾	1	H.V., Premium(1)	4, 6	Fed., Rem.	11.98	1220
2¾	1	H.V., Promo.	4, 5, 6, 7½, 8, 9	Fed., Rem., Win.	11.14	1220
2½	1	Std. Vel., Premium(1)	7½, 8	Fed., Rem.	9.55	1165
2½	1	Std. Vel.	4, 5, 6, 7½, 8, 9	Fed., Rem., Win.	10.59	1165
2½	⅞	Promo.	6, 7½, 8	Fed., Win.	NA	1210
2¼	⅞	Std. Vel., Promo.	6, 7½, 8	Rem., Win.	NA	1155
Max.	¾	Slug, rifled	Slug	Fed., Rem., Win.	3.81	1570
Max.	20 pellets	Buck	3 (Buck)	Fed., Rem., Win.	4.52	1200
2½	⅞	Skeet	8, 9	Fed., Rem., Win.	5.86	1200
2¾	¾	Steel shot	4, 6	Fed., Win.	14.05	1425
28 Gauge 2¾" Hunting & Target						
2¼	¾	H.V.	6, 7½	Fed., Rem., Win.	11.23	1295
2	¾	Skeet	9	Fed., Rem., Win.	6.93	1200
410 Bore Hunting & Target						
Max.	11/16	3" H.V.	4, 5, 6, 7½, 8	Fed., Rem., Win.	10.44	1135
Max.	½	2½" H.V.	4, 6, 7½	Fed., Rem., Win.	8.86	1135
Max.	½	2½" Target	9	Fed., Rem., Win.	5.73	1200
Max.	⅕	Slug, rifled	Slug	Fed., Rem., Win.	3.61	1815

(1)Premium shells usually incorporate high antimony extra hard shot and a granulated polyethelene buffer to increase pattern density at long ranges. In general, prices are per 25-round box. Rifled slugs and buckshot prices are per 5-round pack. Premium buckshot prices per 10-round pack. Not every brand is available in every shot size. Price of Skeet and trap loads may vary widely.

CONVERSION KIT

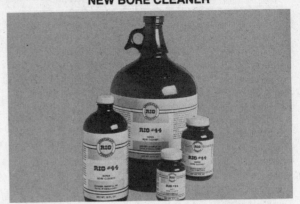

The Pachmayr Dominator Conversion Kit is available in four powerful chamberings, 223 Remington, 7mm-08 Remington, 308 Winchester and 44 Mag.

Virtually any 1911 Colt-type autoloading pistol can be quickly and easily converted to accept this unique, single-shot bolt-action-type mechanism. No special gunsmithing is required.

The Dominator is available in two configurations, a micro-adjustable "iron" sight version and a "scope" model (which is predrilled and tapped for a scope mount). Prices start at $299.50. And there's more good news, no FFL is required to order factory-direct from Pachmayr. A special 56-page Dominator reloading manual is also available from Pachmayr Gun Works at $5.95.

PACHMAYR GUN WORKS

NEW BORE CLEANER

RIG #44 has been chemically formulated to clean, condition and protect all firearms. In addition, RIG #44 was developed to meet the needs of today's shooter and sportsman by cleaning and protecting the bores of handguns, rifles or shotguns in one simple, easy procedure. RIG #44 removes powder residue, as well as built-up lead and carbon deposits, copper fouling, and it leaves a protective film. RIG #44 is another high quality RIG product that was designed to help the hunter and target shooter maintain the accuracy needed from his firearms. RIG #44 is available in 2oz., 4oz., 16oz., and 1-gallon bottles. Contains no water or ammonia!

RIG #44 is now available at your local sporting firearms dealer or write directly to RIG.

RIG PRODUCTS

NEW ADJUSTABLE PISTOL SIGHT

MMC's New Mini-Sight combines adjustable, precision sighting, with compact size. Designed primarily for pocket autos, the Mini-Sight is also compatible with many large frame autos. The Mini-Sight is especially adaptable to Browning's P-35 fixed sight model. It works with factory front sight and requires no machining.

Those familiar with MMC products will notice the similarity of the Mini-Sight to that of MMC's Std. Adj. Sight. Depending on model, the Mini-Sight is some 25% smaller than the Standard Adjustable.

Police officers will quickly recognize the value of having an accurate, compact, adjustable rear sight on their backup or duty weapon. Retail price: $49.99. Write/call for free catalog.

MINIATURE MACHINE CO. (MMC)

SCREWDRIVER SET

Throw away that ill-fitting screwdriver. The Magna-Tip® Super-Set gives you 39 custom, true hollow-ground, graduated screwdriver bits that fit 99.9% of all gun screw slots.

This unique system has nine different blade *widths* ranging from .120″ to .360″, each with three to six blade *thicknesses* from .020″ through .050″ in .005″ increments spread from narrowest/thinnest through widest/thickest.

The *Master Super-Set* includes 39 Custom Gunsmith bits *and* 10 Allen *and* three Phillips bits *plus* two Handles, Tray and Case. Suggested retail price: $63.75. A *Basic Set* of 39 Custom Gunsmith Bits, one Handle, Tray and Case sells for a suggested retail price of $52.77.

BROWNELLS, INC.

See manufacturers' addresses following this section.

SHOOTER'S MARKETPLACE

REPLACEMENT MAGAZINES

D&E Magazines, Mfg. is internationally acclaimed for their steel fabricated pistol and rifle clips, featuring standard and extended sizes for new and "hard to find" models.

Throughout the years, D&E has manufactured hundreds of different magazines for both modern and obsolete firearms.

Their magazines are even recommended by law enforcement agencies due to the durable *steel construction*. They last and last!

For answers to your needs, please send a self-addressed stamped envelope. For the pro or serious amateur, D&E has an up-dated production price list of all their products for which there is a $3 charge. Anyone can order direct.

D&E MAGAZINES MFG.

DROP-IN BARRELS

The QUADRA-LOK® from CENTAUR SYSTEMS, INC., is a *new* and definitely revolutionary competition barrel system for the 1911 45 auto and certain copies. In addition to the system pictured, CENTAUR offers a more sophisticated version—the QUADRA-LOK® II "SUPER BULLSEYE"—for serious 50-yard hole punching. Features of both systems include: *NO* fitting required; guaranteed zero clearance "lock-up"; will *NOT* shoot loose; stainless barrel and slide stop; button rifled; variable rate captive recoil system with buffer and choice of springs; 5"/6"/COMMANDER lengths; 45 ACP/38 Super/9mm; optional QUADRA-PORT and QUADRA-COMP.

From $139.95 retail (5" with std. slide stop and recoil system).

CENTAUR SYSTEMS, INC.

BORE CLEANER

SHOOTER'S CHOICE MC#7 is the world's first one-step bore cleaner and conditioner for smokeless and black powder firearms.

Available from Venco Industries in 2oz., 4oz., and 16oz. bottles, SHOOTER'S CHOICE MC#7 was developed by a precision benchrest shooter and a chemical engineer. More than 3 years of intensive research, development and field testing were devoted to this remarkable formula.

Independent evaluations have shown MC#7 to be the superior product in its field. SHOOTER'S CHOICE MC#7 effectively dissolves and removes virtually all forms of barrel fouling including powder, copper, lead, carbon and plastic shotgun wad fouling. Satisfaction guaranteed.

VENCO INDUSTRIES (SHOOTER'S CHOICE)

DELUXE WATERFOWL CALLS

The P.S. Olt Company is now offering two attractive gift sets containing duck and goose calls. Furnished with a quality custom-imprinted and compartmented presentation box, the gift sets make ideal presents for special occasions. The GS-1 Gift Set contains specially selected Model 800 Goose and DR-115 Duck Calls. Both calls are hand-crafted in American Walnut with Red Cedar tonal parts. The Model 800 and DR-115 are widely used by professional callers.

The GS-2 Gift Set is priced somewhat less than the GS-1, and contains the popular Model #66 Duck and #77 Goose Calls in American Walnut complete with Red Cedar tonal parts.

Price: the GS-1 sells for $38.95. The GS-2 goes for $31.95. Send 50¢ for catalog.

P.S. OLT COMPANY

See manufacturers' addresses following this section.

LEARN GUN REPAIR

Learn gun repair. Modern School has been teaching gun repair the home study way since 1946 to over 43,000 students. All courses are Nationally Accredited and Approved for GI benefits. Courses are complete and include all lessons (including how to get your FFL). Tool Kit, Powley Calculator and Powley Computer, Gun Digest, Numrich Arms Catalog, Mainspring Vise, School Binders, Brownells Catalog, Pull & Drop Gauge, Trigger Pull Gauge, Two Parchment Diplomas ready for framing, Free Consultation Service plus much more. Get into a career where you can start your own business and make money in your spare time too. No previous experience is needed. Write or call for free information. No obligation. No salesman will call.

MODERN GUN REPAIR SCHOOL

NEW S/A RIMFIRE

New from F.I.E., the "Yellow Rose" is the only six-shooter available in the U.S.A. with 100% plating of *genuine 24kt. GOLD*. This 22 rimfire single action is a true reproduction of early "Scout" revolvers. It features a patented hammer block safety and drift adjustable rear sight.

The "Yellow Rose," like all other Buffalo Scouts, will fire any 22 S/L/LR and can be converted easily to 22 Mag. using the extra cylinder.

The "Yellow Rose" weighs in at 31oz. It is available upon special request with a velvet lined genuine American Walnut display case and colorful hand scrimshawed genuine ivory polymer grips. The manufacturer's suggested retail price for the "Yellow Rose" is $149.95. Write for *free* catalog.

F.I.E. CORPORATION

CUSTOM RIFLES

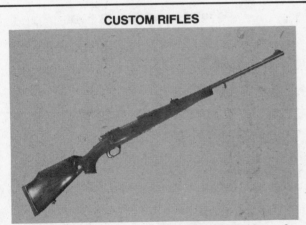

The *"Deer Series,"* a new bolt-action rifle from the Rahn Gun Works is now available for delivery.

It's the first of four series from Rahn. All models feature a Mauser action, choice of domestic or Circassian walnut stock, sling swivels, precision sights, and jeweled bolt guide and release.

Hand checkering is at 22 lines per inch. The floor plate is tastefully engraved by hand.

The Deer Series is available in 270, 25-06 or 308 calibers.

The *Elk, Safari* and *Himalayan* series, to be introduced this fall, will expand available calibers to 14. All guns are built at the Rahn Gun Works in Litchfield, Michigan. Suggested retail price (Deer Series rifle): $750. Write for free catalog.

RAHN GUN WORKS, INC.

BULLET CASTING FLUX

Marvelux® is far and away the most popular—and successful—bullet casting flux on the market.

Marvelux® is non-corrosive to iron and steel and does not produce corrosive fumes as does salammoniac. Reduces dross formation dramatically while increasing fluidity of bullet alloys, making it easier to obtain well-filled-out bullets.

Marvelux® is well suited to any lead-alloy melt intended for casting bullets or swaging cores. Nonsmoking, flameless and odorless. Marvelux® has proven to be superior to beeswax, tallow, parafin and other fluxes.

Available in ½-lb. can, $3.56; 1-lb. can, $5.85; and 4-lb. can, $14.90. From your Dealer or Brownells, Inc., who acquired the Marvelux® Company.

BROWNELLS, INC.

See manufacturers' addresses following this section.

COMPACT SPOTTING SCOPES

The new Kowa TS-9 Compact Spotting Scope features outstanding performance, at an affordable price. A 50mm objective lens allows exceptional brightness, clarity and sharpness.

Two special lightweight models are available, one in standard gray-crackle finish (TS-9C), the other in green armored rubber (TS-9R) for field protection.

A 20x eyepiece is standard with a 15x and 11-33x Zoom as options. TS-9 Scopes can also use interchangeable eyepieces from Kowa's High Quality Traditional Line. Eyepieces available are 9x, 12x Wide Angle, 15x, 24x, 36x and 15x-30x Zoom.

Manufacturer's suggested retail price: TS-9C $115.95, TS-9R (Rubber Armored) $134.95. Optional 15x Eyepiece $24.95.

KOWA OPTIMED

PROFESSIONAL HUNTER BULLETS

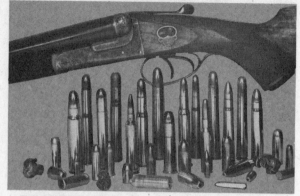

Bill McBride, of Professional Hunter Supplies, has been making, testing and supplying bullets for heavy, dangerous game in Africa. These bullets have been, and are being, used by personnel in Parks and Wildlife elephant control in Africa. The bullets are also used by various professional hunters doing safari work in Zimbabwe, Zambia and Tanzania. Bullets incorporating ideas from these people have been tried and are being used on actual dangerous game.

Professional Hunter Supplies offers various Solids and Soft Nose bullets in most calibers from 7mm through 50 caliber, including 12 bore. Customer specifications may be special ordered. Prices start at $22.50 per 25 bullets.

Write Bill McBride for a free brochure.

PROFESSIONAL HUNTER SUPPLIES

SEE-THROUGH SCOPE MOUNTS

The J.B. Holden Co. introduced the patented, one-piece Ironsighter® scope mounts 20 years ago. Now this two-way sighting method is accepted as standard everywhere. You "See-Thru" the Ironsighter® to use your iron sights. Or use your scope. And Ironsighters® are made of the highest-tensile strength aluminum alloy available.

New *w-i-d-e* apertures make the 700 Series Ironsighter® scope mounts easier than ever to "See-Thru." They actually deliver *twice* the viewing area of other models.

Ironsighters® are made in models to fit just about everything from 22s to big centerfires to muzzle-loaders. See your dealer, or drop Holden a line for a complete list.

J.B. HOLDEN CO.

POWERED ENGRAVING TOOL

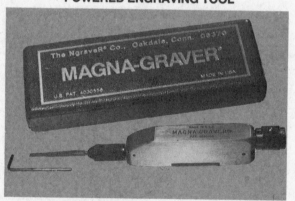

The ability to engrave in metal was brought to the masses by The NgraveR® Company with the introduction 10 years ago of their flex-shaft powered impact tool.

The latest version, the MagnaGraver®, has new needle bearings, heavier output shaft, and improved spring assembly. The result is a longlasting tool with 50% greater impact. Satisfied owners in 50 States and most foreign countries attest to the MagnaGraver® being the lowest cost and most versatile engraving handpiece available. Weighs 5oz., with gold anodize and black oxide finish, comes in a fitted metal case. Operates from any standard flex-shaft machine. With wrench and instructions, the MagnaGraver® retails for $185. The standard M/100 impact tool is $170.

THE NGRAVER® COMPANY

See manufacturers' addresses following this section.

SHOOTER'S MARKETPLACE

CARTRIDGES FOR COLLECTORS

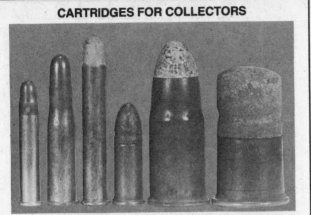

Tillinghast's famous CARTRIDGES FOR COLLECTORS LIST is $1.00 postpaid. It contains over 650 cartridges for sale—Patent Ignition, rimfires, pistol, rifle, shotgun; ammunition price guides, books, catalogs. America's largest supplier of antique collector's cartridges for 45 years. Our ANTIQUE AMMUNITION AUCTION SERVICE is available to buyers, sellers and estates. Get our latest auction brochure or our consignment sheet for auction.

WANTED—cartridge collections, accumulations, box lots, rare singles of all types. We purchase gun catalogs, gun powder tins, gun and ammunition related advertising. Send $1.00 for a current CARTRIDGES FOR COLLECTORS LIST, a real "BARGIN," or $4.00 for the next five cartridge lists.

JAMES C. TILLINGHAST

SNUB NOSE 38 REVOLVER

F.I.E. presents a dependable 2″, 38 Spl., double action, 6-shot revolver . . . the "Titan Tiger." This American-made revolver features an ordnance steel barrel and swing-out cylinder with 1-stroke shell ejection and solid frame walls to provide greater strength. The "Titan Tiger" weighs only 26 ozs. in 2″ or 30 ozs. in 4″. It's ideal for security or home defense and easily fits a belt holster or shoulder rig. Features an internal hammer-block safety and thumb latch release.

"Titan Tigers" come with brown wrap-around composition checkered grips. Hardwood grips are available as an option at modest cost. The "Titan Tiger" comes in bright blue.

Suggested retail price: $149.95.

Write for *free* catalog.

F.I.E. CORPORATION

RIFLE BARREL LINE

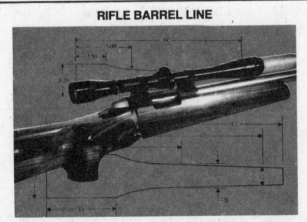

Shilen rifle barrels enjoy a worldwide reputation. The Lone Star line of economical chrome-moly replacement barrels offers the full accuracy potential of calibers used for medium to small game. Pre-threaded and crowned, Lone Star barrels are available for most popular actions. Chrome-moly Match Grade barrels, from 17 to 45 caliber, are recommended when outstanding accuracy is required. Hand-lapped stainless Match Grade barrels are manufactured to the same exacting standards but provide extended life. Shilen SELECT Match Grade barrels are used by leading competitive riflemen.

Shilen Rifles, Inc., is extremely proud to be an Official Supplier to the U.S. Shooting Team. Write for more information.

SHILEN RIFLES, INC.

DRILL & TAP KIT

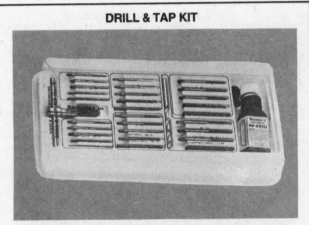

The most frequently used drills and taps in *any* gunshop—large or small—are the ones used by gunsmiths and serious hobbyists to mount sights and scopes. Brownells No. 2 Drill & Tap Kit includes tap-hole and clearance drill, plus the tapper, plug and bottom taps needed for these jobs. Included is a professional-type T-handled tap wrench, a reference chart giving tap-hole drill and clearance drill size for each tap, and a 2-oz. bottle of Do-Drill.

Taps that are included in the Brownells No. 2 Drill & Tap Kit are carbon steel (so when you break one in the hole, you can shatter the stub with a punch and remove the pieces). Drills are made of standard, replaceable, high-speed steel.

Suggested retail price: $36.16.

BROWNELLS, INC.

See manufacturers' addresses following this section.

BORE CLEANER

J-B Non-Embedding Bore Cleaner was developed for the removal of lead, metal and powder fouling from rifle, pistol and shotgun bores. It is especially suited to small caliber, high pressure, high velocity calibers (such as those used in bench rest competition) which have a tendency to foul quickly.

J-B Non-Embedding Bore Cleaner will quickly and safely remove fouling without injuring the finest bore and restore a barrel to its full potential.

J-B Non-Embedding Bore Cleaner is a proven product having been used for more than 30 years by many top competitive shooters, as well as military organizations worldwide.

Manufacturer's suggested retail price: $3.75 per 2 oz. jar.

J-B BORE CLEANER

NEW GREEN BERET BOOKS

LET THE GREEN BERETS lead and protect you with never-before-revealed outdoor savvy. Gathered from around the world, several Green Berets teamed up to write with *easy-to-read* illustrations, and teach:
- Secrets of Green Beret Super-Shooting
- Best Choices for Personal Firearms
- How to Go Anywhere and Never Get Lost
- How to Build Furnished Shelter With a Chainsaw
- Team Operations for Survival
- Easy Methods in Hand-to-Hand Combat
- New Methods in Combat Gunnery . . . and much more!

NOT in book stores. Sold by mail order only, with *MONEY-BACK GUARANTEE,* postage paid. Send check $19.95/set (both volumes), or $12.95 ea.

PATHFINDER PUBLICATIONS

WALNUT STOCK BLANKS

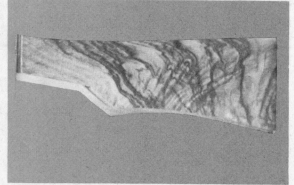

Looking for walnut gun stock blanks? I specialize in Claro, English and Bastogne. My wood is air dried for 2 years or more to eliminate brashiness and color change. Twenty-four years same location. Full fiddle Claro rifle blank at $75. Bastogne and English priced from $50 to $500. All wood guaranteed money back, no hassle. Let me know the type of wood you want, the grade, and budget needs and I will send Polaroids of exact blanks available for purchase. Also, if you are in need of that spectacular "One in a million" blank, I'm your man.

I also have on hand many beautiful two-piece, Mannlicher length and Jaeger pattern blanks, plus many other odd-balls. Stock photos at no cost. Send a S.A.S.E.

JACK BURRES WALNUT

CHRONOGRAPH SYSTEM

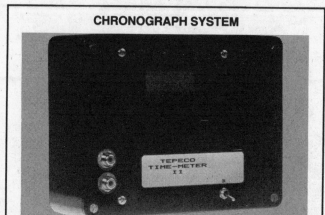

Tepeco Time-Meter II features a liquid crystal display of time-of-flight in microseconds. An ordinary calculator division converts to fps, or velocity tables are provided. The counter is fully automatic, no resetting necessary. Tepeco Photo-Detectors permit shot groups as velocities are checked. A precision crystal of 1 million cycles per sec. is used, allowing measurements of smaller velocity changes at high velocities. Six AA batteries provide 100 hours life. Weight: 1½ lbs.; Size: approx. 7"×5¼"×2½".

The Photo-Detectors automatically adjust to light intensity, and are powered by the Chronograph. Calibers of 17 and larger; velocity capability is 200-5,000 fps.

Manufacturer's suggested price $121.95.

TEPECO

See manufacturers' addresses following this section.

SHOOTER'S MARKETPLACE

ECONOMICAL HANDGUN CASE

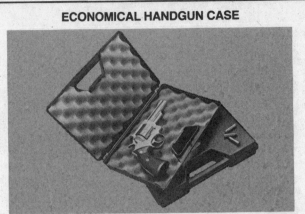

The CASE GARD 806 Handgun Case is a new addition to MTM Molded Products' extensive line of shooters' accessories. The economical 806 has a rugged and durable polypropylene shell, and thick foam inserts which secure the contents. A 2-piece handle assures the case cannot open when carried; additional security is provided by the MTM Snap-lok latch. Measuring a generous 12¼"×8⅜"×2⁵⁄₁₆", the unit will accommodate any handgun with a barrel length of 6" or less. Designed to enable shooters to transport their handgun in absolute security, the CASE GARD 806 provides handgun protection not offered by conventional pistol blankets. At only $10.95, the 806 is fully covered by MTM's 3-Yr. Guarantee. Write for more information.

MTM MOLDED PRODUCTS COMPANY

LIGHTWEIGHT 25 AUTO

F.I.E. now offers a uniquely beautiful and practical addition to their 25 automatic pistol series . . . the "Gold Titan 25."

All external parts are completely layered in genuine 24kt. GOLD, highlighted by a deep blue frame. European Walnut grips are standard.

The "Titan 25" also features an ordnance steel, proof-tested, barrel and slide. The external ring-type hammer allows for quick easy reference to the hammer position in daylight as well as darkness.

Disassembly is simple! Feeding and ejection are reliable! This sleek, compact, durable and lightweight, (only 12ozs.) "Gold Titan 25" also has a positive trigger block safety. Suggested list: $94.95. Write for *free* catalog!

F.I.E. CORPORATION

FIREARMS ENGRAVING SCHOOL

Revealed on video for the first time ever, "The Secrets of the Graveur" (Engraver). An Old World craft comes alive in the privacy of your home as it is shown in its most detailed and definitive forms. Join an elite group of men and women who hold the internationally recognized title of "Master." Experience the tremendous personal pride and satisfaction as you progress at your own rate through the individual projects and see before your very own eyes the making of a "Master Craftsman."

Special on-site and video correspondence courses designed to get *you*, the student, engraving in as short a time as possible. Free information.

Demo tapes are available. Call or write for additional details.

ROBERT E. MAKI—SCHOOL OF FIREARMS ENGRAVING

STOCK BEDDING COMPOUND

Introduced by Brownells as an update of their well known Acraglas® Stock Bedding Compound, Acraglas Gel® Stock Bedding Compound has a smooth consistency that will not drip, run or leach out from between wood and metal after being put into the gunstock. Acraglas Gel® is formulated with nylon derivatives for greater "thin strength," shock resistance and stability over normal temperature extremes. Shrinkage is less than ¹⁄₁₀ of 1%. Readily blends with atomized metals. Easy to use, 1-to-1 mix.

Acraglas Gel® 2-Gun 4-oz. Kit sells for $8.25. Larger 16-oz. Shop Kit is $24.10. Kits contain two-part epoxy, stock-matching dye, mixing sticks and dish, release agent and detailed instructions. Available from your dealer or Brownells.

BROWNELLS, INC.

SHOOTER'S MARKETPLACE

50-ROUND BANANA POWER MAGS

Ram-Line has designed a unique high-capacity magazine to fit the Ruger 10/22 and 77/22 rifles.

Compactness of the new 50-rounder keeps its size comparable to existing 25-round mags. The 30-round version is about ½ the size of previous models.

Levers, windows and windups are eliminated by the proven, patent pending, split-follower design which allows side-by-side bullet stacking for double capacity and ease of loading.

Mags are made of a high impact aerospace polymer and are available in a semi-transparent or black color. Suggested list prices are:

50-round, $38.50
30-round Black, $17.95
30-round Clear, $19.95

RAM-LINE, INC.

KEVLAR RIFLE STOCK

A laminated Kevlar Riflestock for the more popular bolt-action rifles. Not a copy of the factory riflestock, but a classic style either with or without cheekpiece. Straight line for minimum recoil and faster scope alignment. A sure grip forend and pistol grip area for complete control. Standard finish consists of either green or tan camo pattern in a flat finish. An aluminum stabilizing rod surrounds the entire action for exceptional strength.

No drop-in stock. Each barreled action is bedded to its own stock for maximum accuracy and maximum strength.

No fancy brochure—just a clean, classic, very functional riflestock for the person who wants one of the best. Call or write for more information.

GAME HAVEN (Buck Heide)

SCOPE MOUNT FOR HK AUTOS

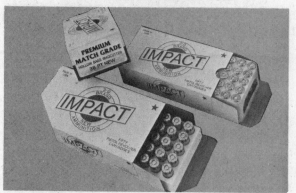

Wasp Shooting Systems offers a new all-steel scope mounting system for the HK 91/93/94 rifles. This design allows full use of iron sights, yet mounts the scope as low as possible for a proper shooting position. Popular red-dot sights, as well as standard scopes, fit the mount. Scopes attach with standard 1″ rings (not included). Wasp's mount is quickly and securely attached to the weapon with your HK sight adjustment tool (no extra tools needed). The bilateral clamping design clamps securely and does not affect weapon function.

Professionaly designed and manufactured from solid steel stock for rugged reliability. Retail $68 and shipping. Accessories catalog $2. Law enforcement, dealer discounts available.

WASP SHOOTING SYSTEMS

NEW HANDGUN AMMUNITION

3-D recently introduced their factory-new line of ammunition under the name "IMPACT." This line was developed to meet a wide range of SHOOTER'S needs; from Law Enforcement training and street carry to the Competitive and Hunting Shooter.

3-D's goals include providing a high quality, factory-new ammunition with a consistent quality control program and reasonable pricing.

3-D's "IMPACT" line includes the following: 38 Spc-Match Grade, Lead & Jacketed (125, 148 & 158); 357 Mag-Copper Plated & Jacketed (125 & 158); 45 ACP Copper Plated & Jacketed (200 & 230); 44 Mag-Copper Plated & Jacketed (200 & 240); & 9mm-Lead, Copper Plated, & Jacketed (115 & 125). For more information, write the manufacturer.

3-D INV., INC.

See manufacturers' addresses following this section.

SHOOTER'S MARKETPLACE

GUN CASES

These genuine leather trunk cases feature a hardwood frame, brass fittings and combination locks. Rifle, shotgun and pistol cases are standard. Custom archery/fishing cases are also available.

Velvet lining, an accessory compartment, and Velcro fastening straps are standard. French-cut or British-blocked cases can be made for an extra $30. A canvas shipping sleeve with a quilted lining is also optional for an extra $30.

Color choices include brown, burgundy, grey or mustard with either matching or contrasting stitching. A suede case with stitched leather trim is also available in the same color choices.

Shotgun case: $180; Rifle Case: $250; Pistol Case: $65. Write for free catalog.

RAHN GUN WORKS

LIGHTWEIGHT AUTOLOADING SHOTGUN

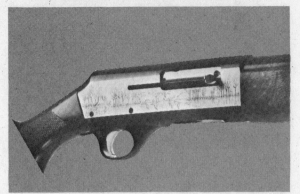

F.I.E. imports one of America's best selling 12 or 20 gauge ultralight autoloading shotguns, the Franchi 48/AL. This Franchi's universal design allows all model 48 vent rib barrels ever manufactured to instantly interchange. No tools needed!

The model 48 is the *lightest autoloader available in the world*. Choose the ultralight 12 gauge at 6 lbs.-4ozs. or the 20 gauge at 5 lbs.-2ozs.

There are two Franchi 48s: the "Standard" model with a beautiful deep blue receiver matching the vent rib barrel, or the "Hunter" model with its fully etched hunting scenes and vent rib barrel. Suggested list price: $499.95 for the Standard Model, $524.95 for the Hunter Model.

Write for *free* catalog!

F.I.E. CORPORATION

HIGH-TECH GUN GREASE

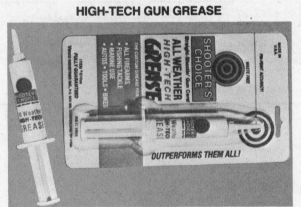

SHOOTER'S CHOICE announces a new addition to its gun care product line, an All Weather, High-Tech GUN GREASE that has been specially formulated to provide shooters with a custom grease that outperforms them all.

SHOOTER'S CHOICE is the ultimate synthetic grease chemically engineered to meet the most demanding need for lubrication and protection of all firearms. Perfect for tools, fishing gear, etc.

SHOOTER'S CHOICE ALL WEATHER GREASE will not gum up under high humidity. It has a wide operating range of from −65° to +350°F.

SHOOTER'S CHOICE GUN GREASE is supplied in a convenient plastic syringe applicator. For further information contact the manufacturer.

VENCO INDUSTRIES (SHOOTER'S CHOICE)

COMBO CLEANING ROD

This beautifully constructed five-piece stainless steel RIG-ROD can be used for all Handguns and Rifles of 25 caliber and up. It can be used on all Shotguns with the enclosed brass adapter for brushes and patch pullers. The rod is made of #303 stainless steel, the handle is made of unbreakable Celcon* and swivels on the Rod.

One of the benefits of the new multi-piece RIG-ROD is the fact that it can be conveniently stored or taken anywhere on a moment's notice.

The RR-32-5HD comes packed in a zip-lock plastic case with a brass bore guide and a brass shotgun brush adapter. It's available at your local dealer or write direct.

*Trademark of the Celanese Corporation.

RIG PRODUCTS

SHOOTING ACCESSORIES

Parker-Hale's famous quality shooting accessories are once again available in the U.S., imported from England by Precision Sports, a Division of Cortland Line Company.

British-made throughout, the following Parker-Hale accessories provide the knowledgeable shooter with a standard of excellence equal to his choice of fine guns.

- Presentation Cleaning Sets
- Snap Caps
- Rosewood Shotgun Rods
- Steel Rifle Rods
- Phosphor Bronze Brushes
- Jags, Loops, and Mops
- Youngs "303" Cleaner
- Express Oil
- Rangoon Oil
- 009 Nitro Solvent
- Black Powder Solvent
- Comet Super Blue

PARKER-HALE/PRECISION SPORTS

CHECKERING TOOLS

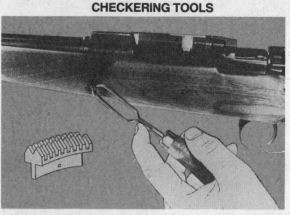

FULL-VIEW checkering tools have been on the market since 1949. The tool features a split shank (which allows the gunsmith to fully view his work at all times), and an adjustable head which lets him checker at any desired angle. FULL-VIEW cutters are made of the highest quality tool steel and come in sizes 16, 18, 20, 22, 24, 26, 28, and 32 lines per inch. The teeth are self-cleaning and cut equally well backwards and forwards.

FULL-VIEW checkering tools include holders; spacing, single line, superfine, skip-line, and border cutters; and short corner tools. A special checkering kit sells for $19 (plus $1.50 for shipping). Send for free descriptive folder complete with prices and hints for better checkering.

W.E. BROWNELL CHECKERING TOOLS

MANUFACTURERS ADDRESSES

W.E. BROWNELL CHECKERING TOOLS
Dept. GD87
3356 Moraga Pl.
San Diego, CA 92117

BROWNELLS, INC.
Dept. GD87
222 West Liberty
Montezuma, IA 50171

JACK BURRES WALNUT
Dept. GD87
10333 San Fernando Rd.
Pacoima, CA 91331 (818-899-8000)

CENTAUR SYSTEMS, INC.
Attn: Mktg. Dir., Dept. GD87
15127 NE 24th, Suite 114
Redmond, WA 98052-5530 (206-392-8472)

D&E MAGAZINES MFG.
Dept. GD87
P.O. Box 4876-N
Sylmar, CA 91342

F.I.E. CORPORATION
Dept. DB-87
4530 N.W. 135th St.
Opa Locka, FL 33054

GAME HAVEN (Buck Heide)
Dept. GD87
13750 Shire Rd.
Wolverine, MI 49799 (616-525-8238)

J.B. HOLDEN CO.
Dept. GD87
P.O. Box 320
Plymouth, MI 48170

J-B BORE CLEANER
Dept. GD87
299 Poplar St.
Hamburg, PA 19526

KOWA OPTIMED, INC.
Dept. GD87
20001 S. Vermont Ave.
Torrance, CA 90502

MAKI SCHOOL OF FIREARMS ENGRAVING
Dept. GD87
P.O. Box 947
Northbrook, IL 60065 (312-724-8238)

MINIATURE MACHINE CO. (MMC)
Dept. GD87
210 E. Poplar
Deming, NM 88030 (505-546-2151)

MODERN GUN REPAIR SCHOOL
Dept. GAN86
2538 N. 8th Street
Phoenix, AZ 85006 (602-990-8346)

MTM MOLDED PRODUCTS COMPANY
Dept. GD87
P.O. Box 14117
Dayton, OH 45414 (513-890-7461)

THE NGRAVER® COMPANY
Dept. GD87
879 Raymond Hill Rd., D.
Oakdale, CT 06370

P.S. OLT COMPANY
Dept. GD87
P.O. Box 550
Pekin, IL 61554

PACHMAYR GUN WORKS
Dept. GD87
1220 South Grand Ave.
Los Angeles, CA 90015

PARKER-HALE/PRECISION SPORTS
Dept. GD-41
P.O. Box 708-5588
Cortland, NY 13045-5588

PATHFINDER PUBLICATIONS
Dept. GD87
150 Hamakua Dr., Suite 401
Kailua/Oahu, HI 96734

PROFESSIONAL HUNTER SUPPLIES
Dept. GD87
444½ Main St., P.O. Box 608
Ferndale, CA 95536

RAHN GUN WORKS, INC.
Dept. GD87
P.O. Box 327
Litchfield, MI 49252 (517-542-3247)

RAM-LINE, INC.
Dept. GD87
406 Violet St.
Golden, CO 80401

RIG PRODUCTS
Dept. GD87
87 Coney Island Dr.
Sparks, NV 89431

SHILEN RIFLES, INC.
Dept. GD87
205 Metro Park Boulevard
Ennis, TX 75119 (214-875-5318)

TEPECO
Dept. GD87
P.O. Box 342
Friendswood, TX 77546

3-D INV., INC.
Dept. GD87
Box J, Main St.
Doniphan, NE 68832

JAMES C. TILLINGHAST
P.O. Box 19GD
Hancock, NH 03449-019G (603-525-6615)

VENCO INDUSTRIES (Shooter's Choice)
Dept. GD87
P.O. Box 598
Chesterland, OH 44026 (216-729-9392)

WASP SHOOTING SYSTEMS
Dept. GD87
Box 241
Lakeview, AR 72642

THE COMPLETE COMPACT CATALOG

GUNDEX®

A listing of all the guns in the catalog, by name and model, alphabetically and numerically.

This feature of our catalog speeds up the chore of finding the basic facts on a given firearm for the experienced. And it may make the contents of the catalog far more available to the inexperienced.

That is our intention.

To use it, you need the manufacturer's name and model designation. That designation might be a number, as in Winchester Model 94, or it might be a name, as in Colt Python. And you need to know the alphabet.

The manufacturers are listed alphabetically and the entry under each manufacturer is arranged in the quickest way—numbers are in numerical order, names are alphabetical.

It's all very straightforward. It is all pretty voluminous, as well. There are over 1200 entries and at about 230 lines per page, what with headings and all, the GUNDEX® is eight pages long.

We have tried to make it easy to find, too—just look for the black GUNDEX® label along the edge of the page, flip to there, and get your page number in short order.

GUNDEX

GUNDEX

AMT LIGHTNING AUTO PISTOL
Caliber: 22 LR, 10-shot magazine.
Barrel: Tapered — 6½″, 8½″, 10½″, 12½″; Bull — 5″, 6½″, 8½″, 10½″, 12½″.
Weight: 45 oz. (6½″ barrel). **Length:** 10¾″ over-all (6½″ barrel).
Stocks: Checkered wrap-around rubber.
Sights: Blade front, fixed rear; adjustable rear available at extra cost.
Features: Made of stainless steel. Uses Clark trigger with adjustable stops; receiver grooved for scope mounting; trigger guard spur for two-hand hold; interchangeable barrels. Introduced 1984. From AMT.
Price: 5″ bull, 6½″ tapered or bull, fixed sight $235.95
Price: 8½″, tapered or bull, fixed sight $235.95
Price: 12½″, tapered or bull, fixed sight $248.95
Price: For adjustable rear sight add $25.00

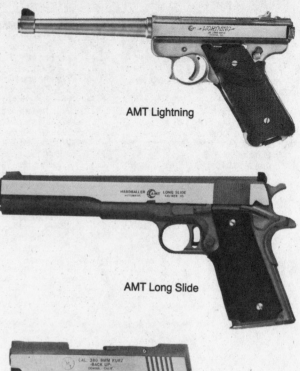
AMT Lightning

AMT Long Slide

AMT "BACKUP" AUTO PISTOL
Caliber: 22 LR, 8-shot magazine; 380 ACP, 5-shot magazine
Barrel: 2½″
Weight: 18 oz. **Length:** 4.25″ over-all.
Stocks: Checkered Lexon.
Sights: Fixed, open, recessed.
Features: Concealed hammer, blowback operation; manual and grip safeties. All stainless steel construction. Smallest domestically-produced pistol in 380. From AMT.
Price: 22 LR or 380 ACP $249.95

AMT 45 ACP HARDBALLER LONG SLIDE
Caliber: 45 ACP.
Barrel: 7″.
Length: 10½″ over-all.
Stocks: Wrap-around rubber.
Sights: Fully adjustable rear sight.
Features: Slide and barrel are 2″ longer than the standard 45, giving less recoil, added velocity, longer sight radius. Has extended combat safety, serrated matte rib, loaded chamber indicator, wide adjustable trigger. From AMT.
Price: $575.00

AMT Backup

AMERICAN ARMS EAGLE 380
Caliber: 380 ACP, 6-shot magazine.
Barrel: 2½″.
Weight: 20 oz. **Length:** 6¼″ over-all.
Stocks: Checkered walnut.
Sights: Fixed.
Features: Double action, stainless steel construction, firing pin lock safety. Comes with fitted carrying case, belt buckle and one magazine. Introduced 1984. From American Arms Corp.
Price: $289.00
Price: As above, except with black rubber grips $300.00

AMT 45 ACP HARDBALLER
Caliber: 45 ACP.
Barrel: 5″.
Weight: 39 oz. **Length:** 8½″ over-all.
Stocks: Wrap-around rubber.
Sights: Adjustable.
Features: Extended combat safety, serrated matte slide rib, loaded chamber indicator, long grip safety, beveled magazine well, adjustable target trigger. All stainless steel. From AMT.
Price: $550.00
Price: Government model (as above except no rib, fixed sights) $440.00

ARMINEX TRIFIRE AUTO PISTOL
Caliber: 9mm. Para. (9-shot), 38 Super. (9-shot), 45 ACP (7-shot).
Barrel: 5″, 6″.
Weight: 38 oz. **Length:** 8″ over-all.
Stocks: Contoured smooth walnut.
Sights: Interchangeable post front, rear adjustable for windage and elevation.
Features: Single action. Slide mounted firing pin block safety. Specially contoured one-piece backstrap. Convertible by changing barrel, slide, magazine, recoil spring. Introduced 1982. Made in U.S. by Arminex Ltd.
Price: Standard Model (5″ bbl.) $396.00
Price: Target Model (6″ bbl.) $448.00
Price: Presentation Model (same as Standard but with ambidextrous safety, smooth burl walnut grips, wood presentation case) $444.00

Arminex Trifire

CAUTION: PRICES CHANGE. CHECK AT GUNSHOP.

ASTRA A-90 DOUBLE-ACTION AUTO PISTOL
Caliber: 9mm Para. (15-shot), 45 ACP (9-shot).
Barrel: 3.75″.
Weight: 40 oz. **Length:** 7″ over-all.
Stocks: Checkered black plastic.
Sights: Square blade front, square notch rear drift-adjustable for windage.
Features: Double or single action; loaded chamber indicator; combat-style trigger guard; optional right-side slide release (for left-handed shooters); automatic internal safety; decocking lever. Introduced 1985. Imported from Spain by Interarms.
Price: Blue **$395.00**

Astra A-90 Pistol

ASTRA CONSTABLE AUTO PISTOL
Caliber: 22 LR, 10-shot, 380 ACP, 7-shot.
Barrel: 3½″
Weight: 26 oz.
Stocks: Moulded plastic
Sights: Adj. rear.
Features: Double action, quick no-tool takedown, non-glare rib on slide. 380 available in blue, stainless steel, or chrome finish. Engraved guns also available—contact the importer. Imported from Spain by Interarms.
Price: Blue, 22 . . . . **$265.00**
Price: Chrome, 22 . . . . **$285.00**
Price: Blue, 380 . . . . **$265.00**
Price: Chrome, 380 . . . . **$285.00**
Price: Stainless, 380 . . . . **$345.00**

Astra A-60 Double Action Pistol
Similar to the Constable except in 380 only, with 13-shot magazine, slide-mounted ambidextrous safety. Available in blued steel only. Introduced 1980.
Price: **$345.00**

Auto-Ordnance 1911A1

AUTO-ORDNANCE 1911A1 AUTOMATIC PISTOL
Caliber: 9mm Para., 38 Super, 9-shot, 45 ACP, 7-shot magazine.
Barrel: 5″.
Weight: 39 oz. **Length:** 8½″ over-all.
Stocks: Checkered plastic with medallion.
Sights: Blade front, rear adj. for windage.
Features: Same specs as 1911A1 military guns—parts interchangeable. Frame and slide blued; each radius has non-glare finish. Made in U.S. by Auto-Ordnance Corp.
Price: 45 cal., about **$324.95**
Price: 9mm, 38 Super, about **$349.95**

BEEMAN SP DELUXE PISTOL
Caliber: 22 LR, single shot.
Barrel: 8″, 10″, 12″, 15″.
Weight: 50 oz. **Length:** 18″ over-all.
Stocks: European walnut, anatomically-shaped with adjustable palm rest.
Sights: Blade front, notch rear adjustable for windage and elevation.
Features: Two-stage trigger; loaded chamber indicator; grooved for scope mount. Detachable fore-end and barrel weight. Standard version available without fore-end and barrel weight. Imported by Beeman. Introduced 1984.
Price: Standard, right or left-hand **$249.50**
Price: Deluxe (with fore-end), illus. **$299.50**

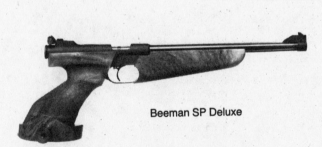

Beeman SP Deluxe

Bernardelli Model 80

BERNARDELLI MODEL 80 AUTO PISTOL
Caliber: 22 LR (10-shot); 380 ACP (7-shot).
Barrel: 3½″.
Weight: 26½ oz. **Length:** 6½″ over-all.
Stocks: Checkered plastic with thumbrest.
Sights: Ramp front, white outline rear adj. for w. & e
Features: Hammer block slide safety; loaded chamber indicator; dual recoil buffer springs; serrated trigger; inertia type firing pin. Imported from Italy by Interarms.
Price: Model 80, 22 . . . . **$215.00**
Price: Model 80, 380 . . . . **$220.00**
Price: Model 90 (22 or 32, 6″ bbl.) **$245.00**

CAUTION: PRICES CHANGE. CHECK AT GUNSHOP.

BERETTA MODEL 84/85 DA PISTOLS
Caliber: 380 ACP, 13-shot magazine, 22 LR, 8 shot (M87BB).
Barrel: 3¾″
Weight: About 23 oz. **Length:** 6½″ over-all.
Stocks: Smooth black plastic (wood optional at extra cost).
Sights: Fixed front and rear.
Features: Double action, quick take-down, convenient magazine release. Introduced 1977. Imported from Italy by Beretta USA.
Price: M-84 (380 ACP) $495.00
Price: With wood grips $510.00
Price: M-84, nickel, wood grips $550.00
Price: M-85W, 380 ACP, wood grips, 9-shot mag $460.00
Price: M-85, nickel, wood grips $500.00
Price: M-86, 8-shot, walnut grips $400.00
Price: M-87, 22 LR $435.00

Beretta Model 84

BERETTA MODEL 950 BS AUTO PISTOL
Caliber: 22 Short, 7 shot, 25 ACP, 9 shot.
Barrel: 2½″, 4″ (22 Short only).
Weight: 8 oz. (22 Short, 10 oz.). **Length:** 4½″ over-all.
Stocks: Checkered black plastic.
Sights: Fixed.
Features: Thumb safety and half-cock safety; barrel hinged at front to pop up for single loading or cleaning. From Beretta U.S.A.
Price: Blue, 25 .... $190.00
Price: Blue, 22, 4″ $200.00
Price: Nickel, 22 or 25 .... $208.00
Price: EL model (gold etching) $220.00

Beretta Model 950 BS-4

Beretta Model 21 Pistol
Similar to the Model 950 BS except chambered for 22 LR, 2.5″ barrel, 4.9″ over-all length, double-action, 7-round magazine, walnut grips. Introduced 1985.
Price: $230.00

BERETTA MODEL 92F PISTOL
Caliber: 9mm Parabellum, 15-shot magazine.
Barrel: 4.92″
Weight: 33½ oz. **Length:** 8.54″ over-all.
Stocks: Checkered black plastic; wood optional at extra cost.
Sights: Blade front, rear adj. for w.
Features: Double-action. Extractor acts as chamber loaded indicator, squared trigger guard, grooved front and back straps, inertia firing pin. Matte finish. Introduced 1977. Imported from Italy by Beretta USA.
Price: With plastic grips $685.00
Price: With wood grips $700.00

Beretta Model 92F

BERSA MODEL 224 AUTO PISTOL
Caliber: 22 LR, 11-shot.
Barrel: 4″.
Weight: 26 oz.
Stocks: Target-type checkered nylon with thumbrest.
Sights: Blade front, square notch rear adjustable for windage.
Features: Blow-back action; combat-type trigger guard; magazine safety; blue finish. Imported from Argentina by Outdoor Sports Headquarters. Introduced 1984.
Price: Model 224 .... $169.00
Price: Model 226 (6″ barrel) $159.00
Price: Model 223DA (3½″ bbl., wood grips) $220.00

Bersa Model 224

BERSA MODEL 383 AUTO PISTOL
Caliber: 380 ACP, 9-shot.
Barrel: 3½″.
Weight: 25 oz.
Stocks: Target-type checkered black nylon.
Sights: Blade front, square notch rear adjustable for windage.
Features: Blow-back action; magazine safety; combat-type trigger guard; blue finish. Imported from Argentina by Outdoor Sports Headquarters. Introduced 1984.
Price: Model 383 .... $169.00
Price: Model 383DA $220.00

Consult our Directory pages for the location of firms mentioned.

CAUTION: PRICES CHANGE. CHECK AT GUNSHOP.

Bren Ten Standard

BREN TEN STANDARD MODEL
Caliber: 10mm Auto, 11-shot capacity.
Barrel: 5″.
Weight: 39 oz. **Length:** 8.37″ over-all.
Stocks: Textured black nylon (Hogue Combat).
Sights: Adjustable; replaceable, 3-dot combat-type.
Features: Full-size combat pistol, with selective double or single action. Has reversible thumb safety and firing pin block. Blued slide, natural stainless frame. Introduced 1983. From Dornaus & Dixon Enterprises, Inc.
Price: Standard model **$500.00**
Price: Military & Police (matte black finish) **$550.00**
Price: Dual-Master (same as Standard except comes with extra 45 ACP slide and barrel, better finish, engraving, wood grips, wood case) **$800.00**
Price: Jeff Cooper Commemorative (same as Standard except has extra fine finish, 22K gold-filled engraving, details, cartridges, laser engraved Herrett's grips and wood case) **$2,000.00**
Price: 45 ACP conversion kit (5″ bbl.) **$150.00**

Bren Ten Special Forces Model
Similar to the Pocket Model except has standard size grip frame with 11-shot capacity; weight is 33 oz. with 4″ barrel. Available in either all black or natural light finish. Introduced 1984.
Price: Black finish **$600.00**
Price: Light finish **$650.00**

Bren Ten Pocket Model
Similar to the Standard Bren Ten except smaller. Has 4″ barrel giving 7.37″ over-all length, and weighs 28 oz. Fires full load 10mm Auto cartridge with 9 round capacity. Has hard chrome slide, stainless frame.
Price: **$600.00**

BRNO CZ 75

BRNO CZ 75 AUTO PISTOL
Caliber: 9mm Para., 15-shot magazine.
Barrel: 4.7″.
Weight: 35 oz. **Length:** 8″ over-all.
Stocks: Checkered wood.
Sights: Blade front, rear adj. for w.
Features: Double action; blued finish. Imported from Czechoslovakia by Bauska Arms Corp.
Price: **$635.00**

BRNO CZ 83 DOUBLE ACTION PISTOL
Caliber: 32, 15-shot; 380, 13-shot.
Barrel: 3.7″.
Weight: 26.5 oz. **Length:** 6.7″ over-all.
Stocks: Checkered black plastic.
Sights: Blade front, rear adj. for w.
Features: Double-action; ambidextrous magazine release and safety. Polished or matte blue. Imported from Czechoslovakia by Bauska Arms Corp.
Price: **$425.00**

BRNO CZ 83

BRNO CZ-85 Auto Pistol
Same gun as the CZ-75 except has ambidextrous slide release and safety levers, is available in 9mm Para. and 7.65, contoured composition grips, matte finish on top of slide. Introduced 1986.
Price: **$655.00**

BROWNING CHALLENGER III SPORTER
Caliber: 22 LR, 10-shot magazine.
Barrel: 6¾″.
Weight: 29 oz. **Length:** 10⅞″ over-all.
Stocks: Smooth impregnated hardwood.
Sights: ⅛″ blade front on ramp, rear screw adj. for e., drift adj. for w.
Features: All steel, blue finish. Wedge locking system prevents action from loosening. Wide gold-plated trigger; action hold-open. Standard grade only. Made in U.S. From Browning.
Price: **$239.95**

Browning Challenger III Sporter

Browning Buck Mark 22 Pistol
Similar to the Challenger III except has black moulded composite grips with skip-line checkering, thumb magazine button, sides of barrel are high-polish blue, rest satin finish. New rear sight screw-adjustable for elevation, drift-adjustable for windage. Introduced 1985.
Price: **$164.95**

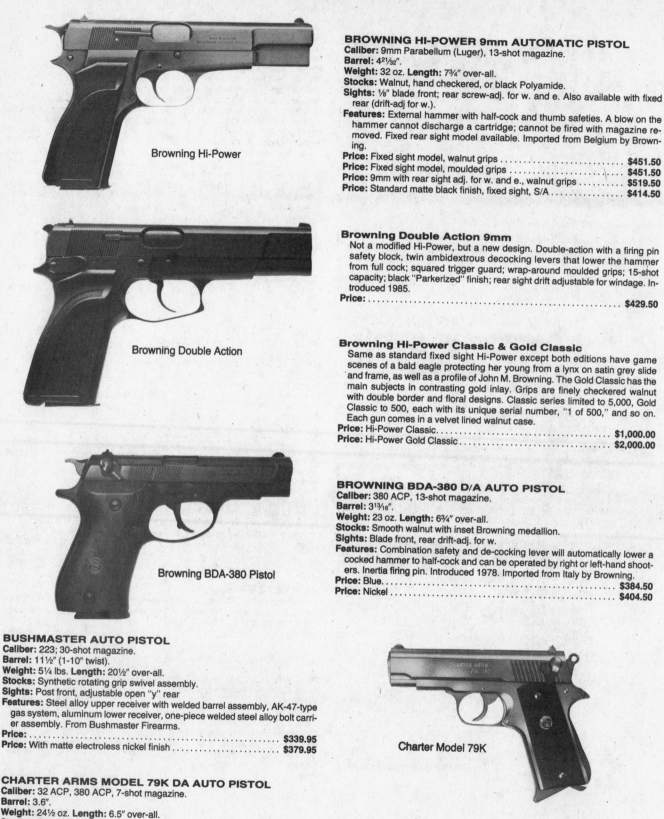

Browning Hi-Power

Browning Double Action

Browning BDA-380 Pistol

Charter Model 79K

BROWNING HI-POWER 9mm AUTOMATIC PISTOL
Caliber: 9mm Parabellum (Luger), 13-shot magazine.
Barrel: 4²¹⁄₃₂".
Weight: 32 oz. **Length:** 7¾" over-all.
Stocks: Walnut, hand checkered, or black Polyamide.
Sights: ⅛" blade front; rear screw-adj. for w. and e. Also available with fixed rear (drift-adj for w.).
Features: External hammer with half-cock and thumb safeties. A blow on the hammer cannot discharge a cartridge; cannot be fired with magazine removed. Fixed rear sight model available. Imported from Belgium by Browning.
Price: Fixed sight model, walnut grips **$451.50**
Price: Fixed sight model, moulded grips **$451.50**
Price: 9mm with rear sight adj. for w. and e., walnut grips **$519.50**
Price: Standard matte black finish, fixed sight, S/A **$414.50**

Browning Double Action 9mm
Not a modified Hi-Power, but a new design. Double-action with a firing pin safety block, twin ambidextrous decocking levers that lower the hammer from full cock; squared trigger guard; wrap-around moulded grips; 15-shot capacity; black "Parkerized" finish; rear sight drift adjustable for windage. Introduced 1985.
Price: **$429.50**

Browning Hi-Power Classic & Gold Classic
Same as standard fixed sight Hi-Power except both editions have game scenes of a bald eagle protecting her young from a lynx on satin grey slide and frame, as well as a profile of John M. Browning. The Gold Classic has the main subjects in contrasting gold inlay. Grips are finely checkered walnut with double border and floral designs. Classic series limited to 5,000, Gold Classic to 500, each with its unique serial number, "1 of 500," and so on. Each gun comes in a velvet lined walnut case.
Price: Hi-Power Classic **$1,000.00**
Price: Hi-Power Gold Classic **$2,000.00**

BROWNING BDA-380 D/A AUTO PISTOL
Caliber: 380 ACP, 13-shot magazine.
Barrel: 3¹³⁄₁₆".
Weight: 23 oz. **Length:** 6¾" over-all.
Stocks: Smooth walnut with inset Browning medallion.
Sights: Blade front, rear drift-adj. for w.
Features: Combination safety and de-cocking lever will automatically lower a cocked hammer to half-cock and can be operated by right or left-hand shooters. Inertia firing pin. Introduced 1978. Imported from Italy by Browning.
Price: Blue. **$384.50**
Price: Nickel **$404.50**

BUSHMASTER AUTO PISTOL
Caliber: 223; 30-shot magazine.
Barrel: 11½" (1-10" twist).
Weight: 5¼ lbs. **Length:** 20½" over-all.
Stocks: Synthetic rotating grip swivel assembly.
Sights: Post front, adjustable open "y" rear.
Features: Steel alloy upper receiver with welded barrel assembly, AK-47-type gas system, aluminum lower receiver, one-piece welded steel alloy bolt carrier assembly. From Bushmaster Firearms.
Price: **$339.95**
Price: With matte electroless nickel finish **$379.95**

CHARTER ARMS MODEL 79K DA AUTO PISTOL
Caliber: 32 ACP, 380 ACP, 7-shot magazine.
Barrel: 3.6".
Weight: 24½ oz. **Length:** 6.5" over-all.
Stocks: Checkered walnut.
Sights: Blade front, rear adj. for w. only.
Features: Double action with hammer block, firing pin and magazine safeties. Stainless steel finish. Introduced 1984. Imported from West Germany by Charter Arms.
Price: 32 or 380 ACP **$390.00**

Charter Arms Model 40 DA Auto Pistol
Similar to the Model 79K except chambered for 22 Long Rifle, 3.3" barrel, 6.3" over-all length, and 21½-oz. weight. Stainless steel finish. Introduced 1984. Imported from West Germany by Charter Arms.
Price: **$319.00**

CAUTION: PRICES CHANGE. CHECK AT GUNSHOP.

CHARTER EXPLORER II & SII PISTOL
Caliber: 22 LR, 8-shot magazine.
Barrel: 8″.
Weight: 28 oz. **Length:** 15½″ over-all.
Stocks: Serrated simulated walnut.
Sights: Blade front, open rear adj. for elevation.
Features: Action adapted from the semi-auto Explorer carbine. Introduced 1980. From Charter Arms.
Price: Black or satin finish $109.00
Price: Extra 6″, 8″ or 10″ barrel $27.00

Charter Explorer Pistol

COLT GOV'T MODEL MK IV/SERIES 80
Caliber: 9mm, 38 Super, 45 ACP, 7-shot.
Barrel: 5″.
Weight: 38 oz. **Length:** 8½″ over-all.
Stocks: Checkered walnut.
Sights: Ramp front, fixed square notch rear.
Features: Grip and thumb safeties, and internal firing pin safety, grooved trigger. Accurizor barrel and bushing.
Price: Blue, 45 ACP $526.50
Price: Nickel, 45 ACP $562.50
Price: 9mm, blue only $534.95
Price: 38 Super, blue only $534.95
Price: Stainless steel, 45 ACP............................. $569.95

Colt Combat Elite MK IV/Series 80
Similar to the Government Model except in 45 ACP only, has stainless frame with ordnance steel slide and internal parts. High profile front, rear sights with three-dot system, extended grip safety, beveled magazine well, Colt checkered rubber grips. Introduced 1986.
Price: .... NA

Colt Stainless MK IV/Series 80

COLT 380 GOVERNMENT MODEL
Caliber: 380 ACP, 7-shot magazine.
Barrel: 3″.
Weight: 21¾ oz. **Length:** 6″ over-all.
Stocks: Checkered composition.
Sights: Ramp front, square notch rear, fixed.
Features: Scaled down version of the 1911A1 Colt G.M. Has thumb and internal firing pin safeties. Introduced 1983.
Price: Blue... $340.50
Price: Nickel... $374.50
Price: Coltguard.. $361.95

Colt 380 Government

COLT COMBAT COMMANDER AUTO PISTOL
Caliber: 45 ACP, 7-shot; 38 Super Auto, 9mm Luger, 9-shot.
Barrel: 4¼″.
Weight: 36 oz. **Length:** 7¾″ over-all.
Stocks: Checkered walnut.
Sights: Fixed, glare-proofed blade front, square notch rear.
Features: Grooved trigger and hammer spur; arched housing; grip and thumb safeties.
Price: Blue, 9mm.. $534.95
Price: Blue, 45 .... $526.50
Price: Blue, 38 super...................................... $534.95
Price: Satin nickel, 45, Series 80 .... $548.95

Colt Lightweight Commander Mark IV/Series 80
Same as Commander except high strength aluminum alloy frame, wood panel grips, weight 27 oz. 45 ACP only.
Price: Blue.. $526.50

Colt Combat Commander

Colt Conversion Unit
Permits the 45 and 38 Super Automatic pistols to use the economical 22 LR cartridge. No tools needed. Adjustable rear sight; 10-shot magazine. Designed to give recoil effect of the larger calibers. Not adaptable to Commander models. Blue finish.
Price: 22 LR, Series 80...................................... $304.50
Price: Fixed sight version, Series 70 .... $304.99
Price: 9mm Series 80 Conversion Unit $304.50

Colt Officers ACP

COLT OFFICERS ACP MK IV SERIES 80
Caliber: 45 ACP, 6-shot magazine.
Barrel: 3½".
Weight: 34 oz. **Length:** 7¼" over-all.
Stocks: Checkered walnut.
Sights: Ramp blade front with white dot, square notch rear with two white dots.
Features: Trigger safety lock (thumb safety), grip safety, firing pin safety; grooved trigger; flat mainspring housing. Also available with lightweight alloy frame and in stainless steel. Introduced 1985.
Price: Matte finish **$516.50**
Price: Satin nickel **$569.95**
Price: L.W., matte finish **$526.50**

Coonan 357 Magnum

COONAN 357 MAGNUM PISTOL
Caliber: 357 Mag., 7-shot magazine.
Barrel: 5".
Weight: 38 oz. **Length:** 8.3" over-all.
Stocks: Smooth walnut.
Sights: Open, adjustable.
Features: Unique barrel hood improves accuracy and reliability. Many parts interchange with Colt autos. Has grip, hammer, half-cock safeties. From Coonan Arms.
Price: Model A **$595.00**
Price: Model B (linkless barrel, interchangeable ramp front sight, new rear sight) **$625.00**

DAVIS P-32 AUTO PISTOL
Caliber: 32 ACP, 6-shot magazine.
Barrel: 2.8".
Weight: 22 oz. **Length:** 5.4" over-all.
Stock: Laminated wood.
Sights: Fixed.
Features: Choices of black Teflon or chrome finish. Announced 1986. Made in U.S. by Davis Industries.
Price: .... **NA**

Davis P-32

DETONICS "COMBAT MASTER" MK VI, MK I
Caliber: 45 ACP, 6-shot clip; 9mm Para., 38 Super, 7-shot clip.
Barrel: 3¼".
Weight: 29 oz. **Length:** 6¾" over-all, 4½" high.
Stocks: Checkered walnut.
Sights: Combat type, fixed and adj. sights avail.
Features: Has a self-adjusting cone barrel centering system, beveled magazine inlet, "full clip" indicator in base of magazine; standard 7-shot (or more) clip can be used in the 45. Throated barrel and polished feed ramp. Mark VI, VII available in 9mm and 38 Super. Introduced 1977. From Detonics.
Price: MK I, matte finish, fixed sights **$610.95**
Price: MK VI, polished stainless, adj. sights **$685.95**

Detonics "Combat Master" MK. I

DETONICS "POCKET 9" DOUBLE ACTION AUTO
Caliber: 9mm Para., 6-shot clip.
Barrel: 3".
Weight: 26 oz. **Length:** 5.7" over-all, 4" high.
Stocks: Black micarta.
Sights: Fixed.
Features: Stainless steel construction; ambidextrous firing pin safety; trigger guard hook for two-hand shooting; double and single action trigger mechanism; snag-free hammer; captive recoil spring; "Chamber Lok" breech system.
Price: About **$457.95**

Detonics "Pocket 9LS" Double Action Auto
Similar to the Pocket 9 except has 4" barrel, is 6⅞" over-all, weighs 28 oz. Other features are the same.
Price: **$457.95**
Price: "Power 9" model (polished slide flats) **$505.95**

Detonics "Pocket 9 LS"

CAUTION: PRICES CHANGE. CHECK AT GUNSHOP.

DETONICS "POCKET 380" DOUBLE ACTION AUTO

Caliber: 380 ACP, 6-shot clip.
Barrel: 3".
Weight: 23 oz. **Length:** 5¾" over-all.
Stocks: Grooved black micarta.
Sights: Fixed.
Features: Stainless steel construction; ambidextrous firing pin safety; trigger guard hook; snag-free hammer; captive recoil spring.
Price: **$457.95**

Detonics "Pocket 380"

DETONICS "SERVICEMASTER" AUTO PISTOL

Caliber: 45 ACP, 7-shot magazine.
Barrel: 4¼".
Weight: 32 oz. **Length:** 7⅞" over-all.
Stocks: Pachmayr rubber.
Sights: Fixed combat.
Features: Stainless steel construction; thumb and grip safeties; extended grip safety.
Price: Matte finish **$685.95**
Price: "Servicemaster II" (polished slide flats) **$762.95**

Detonics "Servicemaster"

Desert Eagle 357

DESERT EAGLE 357 MAGNUM PISTOL

Caliber: 357 Magnum, 10-shot clip.
Barrel: 6", 14" interchangeable.
Weight: 52 oz. (alloy), 60 oz. (steel). **Length:** 10¼" over-all (6" bbl.).
Stocks: Wrap-around soft rubber.
Sights: Blade on ramp front, combat-style rear. Adjustable avail.
Features: Rotating three lug bolt, ambidextrous safety, combat-style trigger guard, adjustable trigger (optional). Military epoxy finish. Contact importer for extra barrel prices. Satin, bright nickel, polished and blued finishes available. Imported from Israel by Magnum Research Inc.
Price: 6" barrel, standard pistol **$559.00**
Price: 6" barrel, alloy frame **$579.00**
Price: 6" barrel, stainless steel frame............................ **$599.00**

ENCOM MP-9, MP-45 ASSAULT PISTOLS

Caliber: 9mm, 45 ACP, 10, 30, 40 or 50-shot magazine.
Barrel: 4½", 6", 8", 10", 18", 18½".
Weight: 6 lbs. (4½" bbl.). **Length:** 11.8" over-all (4½" bbl.).
Stocks: Checkered composition.
Sights: Post front, fixed Patridge rear.
Features: Blowback operation, fires from closed breech with floating firing pin; right or left-hand models available. Made in U.S. From Encom America, Inc.
Price: 9mm or 45 ACP, standard pistol **$275.00**
Price: As above, Mini Pistol (3½" bbl.).......................... **$250.00**
Price: Carbine (18½" bbl., retractable wire stock) **$390.00**

Encom MP-45

Erma KGP22 Pistol

ERMA KGP22 AUTO PISTOL

Caliber: 22 LR, 8-shot magazine.
Barrel: 4".
Weight: 29 oz. **Length:** 7¾" over-all.
Stocks: Checkered plastic.
Sights: Fixed.
Features: Has toggle action similar to original "Luger" pistol. Slide stays open after last shot. Imported from West Germany by Excam. Introduced 1978.
Price: **$230.00**

ERMA KGP38 AUTO PISTOL
Caliber: 380 ACP (5-shot).
Barrel: 4".
Weight: 22½ oz. **Length:** 7⅜" over-all.
Stocks: Checkered plastic. Wood optional.
Sights: Rear adjustable for windage.
Features: Toggle action similar to original "Luger" pistol. Slide stays open after last shot. Has magazine and sear disconnect safety systems. Imported from West Germany by Excam. Introduced 1978.
Price: Plastic grips $230.00

F.I.E. "TZ-75" DA AUTO PISTOL
Caliber: 9mm Parabellum, 15-shot magazine.
Barrel: 4.72".
Weight: 35.33 oz. **Length:** 8.25" over-all.
Stocks: Smooth European walnut.
Sights: Undercut blade front, open rear adjustable for windage.
Features: Double action trigger system; squared-off trigger guard; rotating slide-mounted safety. Introduced 1983. Imported from Italy by F.I.E. Corp.
Price: $349.95
Price: Silver chrome with red outline sights. $399.95

F.I.E. "SUPER TITAN II" PISTOLS
Caliber: 32 ACP, 380 ACP.
Barrel: 3⅞".
Weight: 28 oz. **Length:** 6¾" over-all.
Stocks: Smooth, polished walnut.
Sights: Adjustable.
Features: Blue finish only. 12 shot (32 ACP), 11 shot (380 ACP). Introduced 1981. Imported from Italy by F.I.E. Corp.
Price: 32 ACP $164.95
Price: 380 ACP $194.95

F.I.E. "The Best" A27B

F.I.E. "TITAN II" PISTOLS
Caliber: 32 ACP, 380 ACP, 6-shot magazine; 22 LR, 10-shot magazine.
Barrel: 3⅞".
Weight: 25¾ oz. **Length:** 6¾" over-all.
Stocks: Checkered nylon, thumbrest-type; walnut optional.
Sights: Adjustable.
Features: Magazine disconnector, firing pin block. Standard slide safety. Available in blue or chrome. Introduced 1978. Imported from Italy by F.I.E. Corp.
Price: 32, blue $131.95
Price: 32, chrome $139.95
Price: 380, blue $164.95
Price: 380, chrome $174.95
Price: 22 LR, blue $119.95

F.I.E. "TITAN 25" PISTOL
Caliber: 25 ACP, 6-shot magazine.
Barrel: 2⁷⁄₁₆".
Weight: 12 oz. **Length:** 4⅝" over-all.
Stocks: Smooth walnut.
Sights: Fixed.
Features: External hammer; fast simple takedown. Made in U.S.A. by F.I.E. Corp.
Price: Blue $54.95
Price: Dyna-Chrome $59.95
Price: 24K gold with bright blue frame, smooth walnut grips $79.95

ERMA-EXCAM RX 22 AUTO PISTOL
Caliber: 22 LR, 8-shot magazine.
Barrel: 3¼".
Weight: 21 oz. **Length:** 5.58" over-all.
Stocks: Plastic wrap-around.
Sights: Fixed
Features: Polished blue finish. Double action. Patented ignition safety system. Thumb safety. Assembled in U.S. Introduced 1980. From Excam.
Price: $159.00

F.I.E. "TZ-75"

F.I.E. "THE BEST" A27B PISTOL
Caliber: 25 ACP, 6-shot magazine.
Barrel: 2½".
Weight: 13 oz. **Length:** 4⅝" over-all.
Stocks: Checkered walnut.
Sights: Fixed.
Features: All steel construction. Has thumb and magazine safeties, exposed hammer. Blue finish only. Introduced 1978. Made in U.S. by F.I.E. Corp.
Price: $114.95

F.I.E."Titan II"

F.I.E. "Titan 25"

CAUTION: PRICES CHANGE. CHECK AT GUNSHOP.

Falcon Portsider

Fraser Auto

FALCON PORTSIDER AUTO PISTOL
Caliber: 45 ACP, 7-shot magazine.
Barrel: 5".
Weight: 38 oz. **Length:** 8½" over-all.
Stocks: Checkered walnut.
Sights: Fixed combat.
Features: Made of 17-4 stainless steel. Enlarged left-hand ejection port, extended ejector, long trigger, combat hammer, extended safety, wide grip safety. Introduced 1986. From Falcon Firearms.
Price: $580.00

FRASER AUTOMATIC PISTOL
Caliber: 25 ACP, 6-shot.
Barrel: 2¼".
Weight: 10 oz. **Length:** 4" over-all.
Stocks: Plastic pearl or checkered walnut.
Sights: Recessed, fixed.
Features: Stainless steel construction. Has positive manual safety as well as magazine safety. From Fraser Firearms Corp.
Price: Satin stainless steel, 25 ACP $129.50
Price: Gold plated, with book-type case $247.50
Price: With black Q.P.Q. finish $149.50

Glock 17

GLOCK 17 AUTO PISTOL
Caliber: 9mm Para., 17-shot magazine.
Barrel: 4.48".
Weight: 21.8 oz. (without magazine). **Length:** 7.40" over-all.
Stocks: Black polymer.
Sights: Dot on front blade, white outline rear adj. for w.
Features: Polymer frame, steel slide; trigger safety, mechanical firing pin safety, drop safety; simple take-down without tools; recoil operated action. Adopted by Austrian armed forces 1985. Imported from Austria by Glock, Inc.
Price: With extra magazine, magazine loader, cleaning kit **$443.65**

Consult our Directory pages for the location of firms mentioned.

Goncz High-Tech Pistol

GONCZ HIGH-TECH LONG PISTOL
Caliber: 9mm Para., 30 Mauser, 38 Super, 18- and 32-shot magazine; 45 ACP, 10- and 20-shot magazine.
Barrel: 4", 9.5".
Weight: 3 lbs., 10 oz. (with 4" barrel). **Length:** 10½" over-all (with 4" barrel).
Stock: Alloy grooved pistol grip.
Sights: Front adjustable for elevation, rear adjustable for windage.
Features: Fires from closed bolt; floating firing pin; safety locks the firing pin. All metal construction. Barrel threaded for accessories. Matte black oxide and anodized finish. Designed by Lajos J. Goncz. Introduced 1985. From Goncz Co.
Price: With 9½" barrel $350.00
Price: With 4" barrel $340.00

HAMMERLI MODEL 212 HUNTER'S PISTOL
Caliber: 22 LR.
Barrel: 4.9".
Weight: 31 oz. **Length:** 8.5" over-all.
Stocks: Checkered walnut.
Sights: White dot front adjustable for elevation, rear adjustable for elevation.
Features: Semi-automatic based on the Model 208, intended for field use. Uses target trigger system which is fully adjustable. Comes with tool kit. Imported from Switzerland by Osborne's Supplies. Introduced 1984.
Price: $995.00

Hammerli 212

CAUTION: PRICES CHANGE. CHECK AT GUNSHOP.

Heckler & Koch P7-M8

HECKLER & KOCH P9S DOUBLE ACTION AUTO
Caliber: 9mm Para., 9-shot magazine; 45 ACP, 7-shot magazine.
Barrel: 4".
Weight: 31 oz. **Length:** 7.6" over-all.
Stocks: Checkered black plastic.
Sights: Open combat type.
Features: Double action; polygonal rifling; delayed roller-locked action with stationary barrel. Loaded chamber and cocking indicators; cocking/decocking lever. Imported from West Germany by Heckler & Koch, Inc.
Price: P-9S Combat Model, 9mm **$666.00**
Price: As above, 45 ACP **$732.00**
Price: P9S Target Model, 9mm **$799.00**
Price: As above, 45 ACP **$866.00**
Price: Sports Competition Model with 4" and 5½" barrels, two slides, 9mm only **$1,333.00**

Holmes MP-83

IVER JOHNSON 9mm AUTO PISTOL
Caliber: 9mm Para., 6-shot magazine.
Barrel: 3".
Weight: 26 oz. **Length:** 6½" over-all.
Stocks: Smooth hardwood.
Sights: Blade front, adj. rear.
Features: Ambidextrous safety; polished or matte blue finish. Made in U.S.A. Introduced 1986. From Iver Johnson.
Price: **$350.00**

IVER JOHNSON TP22B, TP25B AUTO PISTOL
Caliber: 22 LR, 25 ACP, 7-shot magazine.
Barrel: 2.85".
Weight: 14½ oz. **Length:** 5.39" over-all.
Stocks: Black checkered plastic.
Sights: Fixed.
Features: Double action; 7-shot magazine. Introduced 1981. Made in U.S. From Iver Johnson's.
Price: Either caliber, blue **$137.00**

HECKLER & KOCH P7-M8 AUTO PISTOL
Caliber: 9mm Parabellum, 8-shot magazine.
Barrel: 4.13".
Weight: 29 oz. **Length:** 6.73" over-all.
Stocks: Stippled black plastic.
Sights: Fixed, combat-type.
Features: Unique "squeeze cocker" in front strap cocks the action. Gas-retarded action. Squared combat-type trigger guard. Blue finish. Compact size. Imported from West Germany by Heckler & Koch, Inc.
Price: P7-M8. . . . . **$612.00**
Price: Extra magazine (8-shot) **$23.00**
Price: P7-M13 (13-shot capacity, matte black finish, ambidextrous magazine release, forged steel frame) **$666.00**
Price: Extra 13-shot magazine. **$39.00**

Heckler & Koch P9S Combat

HOLMES MP-83 ASSAULT PISTOL
Caliber: 9mm (16 or 32 shot), 45 (10 or 20 shot).
Barrel: 6".
Weight: 3½ lbs. **Length:** 14½" over-all.
Stock: Walnut grip and fore-end.
Sights: Post front, open adj. rear.
Features: All steel construction, blue finish. Deluxe package includes gun, foam-lined travel case, Zytel stock, black metal vent. barrel shroud, extra magazine and sling. From Holmes Firearms.
Price: **$450.00**
Price: Deluxe **$525.00**
Price: Caliber conversion kit **$220.00**

Holmes MP-22 Assault Pistol
Similar to the MP-83 except chambered for 22LR, 32-shot capacity. Weighs 2½ lbs., has bolt-notch safety.
Price: **$400.00**
Price: Deluxe **$475.00**

Iver Johnson 9mm

CAUTION: PRICES CHANGE. CHECK AT GUNSHOP.

IVER JOHNSON TRAILSMAN PISTOL
Caliber: 22 LR, 10-shot magazine.
Barrel: 4½" or 6".
Weight: 46 oz. (4½" bbl.) **Length:** 8¾" (4½" bbl.).
Stocks: Checkered composition.
Sights: Fixed, tagret type.
Features: Slide hold-open latch, positive sear block safety, push button magazine release. Made in U.S. Introduced 1984.
Price: Blue only **$170.00**
Price: Model TM22HB (high-polish blue, wood grips) **$190.00**

Iver Johnson Trailsman

IVER JOHNSON MODEL PO380 PONY
Caliber: 380 ACP, 6-shot magazine.
Barrel: 3".
Weight: 20 oz. **Length:** 6" over-all.
Stocks: Checkered walnut.
Sights: Blade front, rear adj. for w.
Features: All steel construction. Inertia firing pin. Thumb safety locks hammer. No magazine safety. Lanyard ring. Made in U.S., available from Iver Johnson's.
Price: Blue. **$253.00**

Jennings J-22 Pistol

JENNINGS J-22 AUTO PISTOL
Caliber: 22 LR, 6-shot magazine.
Barrel: 2½".
Weight: 13 oz. **Length:** 4¹⁵⁄₁₆" over-all.
Stocks: Walnut on chrome or nickel models; checkered black Cycolac on Teflon model.
Sights: Fixed.
Features: Choice of bright chrome, satin nickel or black Teflon finish. Introduced 1981. From Jennings Firearms.
Price: About **$69.95**

KASSNAR PJK-9HP AUTO PISTOL
Caliber: 9mm Para., 13-shot magazine.
Barrel: 4¾".
Weight: 32 oz. **Length:** 8" over-all.
Stocks: Checkered European walnut.
Sights: Ramp front, rear adj. for w.
Features: Single action. Available with or without full length ventilated rib; smooth trigger; lanyard loop on butt; comes with two magazines. Imported from Hungary by Kassnar. Introduced 1986.
Price: With or without rib. **$299.00**

Kassnar PJK-9HP

KORRIPHILA HSP 701 D/A AUTO PISTOL
Caliber: 9mm Para., 38 W.C., 38 Super, 45 ACP, 9-shot magazine in 9mm, 7-shot in 45.
Barrel: 4" (Type I), 5" (Type II, III).
Weight: 35 oz.
Stocks: Checkered walnut.
Sights: Ramp or target front, adj. rear.
Features: Delayed roller lock action with Budichowsky system. Double/single or single action only. Very limited production. Imported from West Germany by Osborne's. Introduced 1986.
Price: **$1,900.00**

Korriphila HSP 701

Korth Auto Pistol

KORTH SEMI-AUTOMATIC PISTOL
Caliber: 9mm Parabellum, 13-shot magazine.
Barrel: 4½".
Weight: 35 oz. **Length:** 10½" over-all.
Stocks: Checkered walnut.
Sights: Combat-adjustable
Features: Double action; 13-shot staggered magazine; forged machined frame and slide. Matte and polished finish. Introduced 1985. Imported from West Germany by Osborne's.
Price: **$2,475.00**

L.A.R. GRIZZLY WIN MAG MK I PISTOL
Caliber: 357 Mag., 45 Win. Mag., 7-shot magazine.
Barrel: 6½″.
Weight: 51 oz. **Length:** 10½″ over-all.
Stocks: Checkered rubber, non-slip combat-type.
Sights: Ramped blade front, fully adjustable rear.
Features: Uses basic Browning/Colt 1911-A1 design; interchangeable calibers; beveled magazine well; combat-type flat, checkered rubber mainspring housing; lowered and back-chamfered ejection port; polished feed ramp; throated barrel; solid barrel bushings. Announced 1983. From L.A.R. Mfg. Inc.
Price: $675.00
Price: Conversion units (9mm Win. Mag., 45 ACP, 357 Mag.) $149.00

L.A.R. Grizzly

L.A.R. Grizzly Win Mag Mk. II Pistol
Similar to the standard Grizzly Win Mag except has fixed rear sight, standard safety, matte Parkerized or blue finish. Other features are the same. Introduced 1986.
Price: $550.00
Price: Conversion units (9mm Win. Mag., 45 ACP, 357 Mag.) $149.00

LLAMA OMNI DOUBLE-ACTION AUTO
Caliber: 9mm (13-shot), 45 ACP (7-shot).
Barrel: 4¼″.
Weight: 40 oz. **Length:** 9mm—8″, 45—7¾″ over-all.
Stocks: Checkered plastic.
Sights: Ramped blade front, rear adjustable for windage and elevation (45), drift-adjustable for windage (9mm).
Features: New DA pistol has ball-bearing action, double sear bars, articulated firing pin, buttressed locking lug and low-friction rifling. Introduced 1982. Imported from Spain by Stoeger Industries.
Price: 45 ACP $499.95
Price: 9mm $545.95

Llama Omni D.A. Pistol

Llama Large Frame Auto

LLAMA LARGE FRAME AUTO PISTOL
Caliber: 45 ACP.
Barrel: 5″.
Weight: 40 oz. **Length:** 8½″ over-all.
Stocks: Checkered walnut.
Sights: Fixed.
Features: Grip and manual safeties, ventilated rib. Imported from Spain by Stoeger Industries.
Price: Blue $284.95
Price: Satin chrome $383.95

Llama Medium Frame

LLAMA MEDIUM FRAME AUTO PISTOL
Caliber: 9mm Para., 9 shot, 45 ACP, 7 shot.
Barrel: 4⁵⁄₁₆″.
Weight: 37 oz.
Stocks: Smooth walnut.
Sights: Blade front, rear adjustable for windage.
Features: Scaled-down version of the Large Frame gun. Locked breech mechanism; manual and grip safeties. Introduced 1985. Imported from Spain by Stoeger Industries.
Price: Blue only $284.95

Llama Small Frame Auto

LLAMA SMALL FRAME AUTO PISTOLS
Caliber: 22 LR, 380.
Barrel: 3¹¹⁄₁₆″.
Weight: 23 oz. **Length:** 6½″ over-all.
Stocks: Checkered plastic, thumb rest.
Sights: Fixed front, adj. notch rear.
Features: Ventilated rib, manual and grip safeties. Model XV is 22 LR, Model IIIA is 380. Both models have loaded indicator; IIIA is locked breech. Imported from Spain by Stoeger Industries.
Price: Blue, 22 LR, 380 .... $241.95
Price: Satin chrome, 22 LR or 380 .... $303.95

CAUTION: PRICES CHANGE. CHECK AT GUNSHOP.

MKE AUTO PISTOL
Caliber: 380 ACP; 7-shot magazine.
Barrel: 4".
Weight: 23 oz. **Length:** 6½" over-all.
Stocks: Hard rubber.
Sights: Fixed front, rear adjustable for windage.
Features: Double action with exposed hammer; chamber loaded indicator. Imported from Turkey by Mandall Shooting Supplies.
Price: $350.00

Manurhin PPK/S

Turkish MKE Pistol

MANURHIN PP AUTO PISTOL
Caliber: 22 LR, 10-shot; 32 ACP, 8-shot; 380 ACP, 7-shot.
Barrel: 3.87".
Weight: 23 oz. (22 LR). **Length:** 6.7" over-all.
Stocks: Checkered composition.
Sights: White outline front and rear.
Features: Double action; hammer drop safety; all steel construction; high-polish blue finish. Each gun supplied with two magazines. Imported from France by Manurhin International.
Price: 22 LR **$429.00**
Price: 32 and 380.. **$419.00**

Manurhin PPK/S Auto Pistol
Similar to the Model PP except has 3.25" barrel and over-all length of 6.12".
Price: 22 LR **$429.00**
Price: 32 and 380.. **$419.00**

Navy Arms Standard Luger

NAVY ARMS LUGER AUTO PISTOL
Caliber: 22 LR, 10-shot magazine.
Barrel: 4".
Weight: 44 ozs. **Length:** 9" over-all.
Stocks: Checkered walnut.
Sights: Fixed.
Features: Blowback toggle action; all-steel construction; made in U.S. From Navy Arms.
Price: Standard Model **$165.00**
Price: War Model (all matte finish) **$165.00**
Price: Naval Model (6" bbl., adj. rear sight).................. **$165.00**
Price: Artillery Model (8" bbl., adj. rear sight on bbl.).............. **$165.00**

Pocket Partner

POCKET PARTNER PISTOL
Caliber: 22 LR, 8-shot magazine.
Barrel: 2¼", 6-groove rifling.
Weight: 10 oz. **Length:** 4¾" over-all.
Stocks: Checkered plastic.
Sights: Fixed.
Features: New design internal hammer. All ordnance steel construction with brushed blue finish. Distributed by Bumble Bee Wholesale, Inc.
Price: About **$99.95**

RAVEN MP-25 AUTO PISTOL
Caliber: 25 ACP, 6-shot magazine.
Barrel: 2⁷⁄₁₆".
Weight: 15 oz. **Length:** 4¾" over-all.
Stocks: Smooth walnut or ivory-colored plastic.
Sights: Ramped front, fixed rear.
Features: Available in blue, nickel or chrome finish. Made in U.S. Available from Raven Arms.
Price: **$69.95**

Raven MP-25

CAUTION: PRICES CHANGE. CHECK AT GUNSHOP.

Ruger Mark II Stainless

RUGER MARK II STANDARD AUTO PISTOL
Caliber: 22 LR, 10-shot magazine.
Barrel: 4¾" or 6".
Weight: 36 oz. (4¾" bbl.). **Length:** 8⁵⁄₁₆" (4¾" bbl.).
Stocks: Checkered hard rubber.
Sights: Fixed, wide blade front, square notch rear adj. for w.
Features: Updated design of the original Standard Auto. Has new bolt hold-
  open device, 10-shot magazine, magazine catch, safety, trigger and new re-
  ceiver contours. Introduced 1982.
Price: Blued (MK 4, MK 6) $180.00
Price: In stainless steel (KMK 4, KMK 6) $240.00

SEECAMP LWS 25, LWS 32 STAINLESS D/A AUTO
Caliber: 25 ACP,8 shot, 32 ACP Win. Silvertip, 6 shot.
Barrel: 2", integral with frame.
Weight: 25 cal. 12 oz., 32 cal. 10.5 oz. **Length:** 4⅛" over-all.
Stocks: Black plastic.
Sights: Smooth, no-snag, contoured slide and barrel top.
Features: Aircraft quality 17-4 PH stainless steel. Inertia operated firing pin.
  Hammer fired double action only. Hammer automatically follows slide down
  to safety rest position after each shot—no manual safety needed. Magazine
  safety disconnector. LWS 25 is satin stainless, LWS 32 is polished. Intro-
  duced 1980. From L.W. Seecamp.
Price: $199.95

Seecamp LWS 25

SIG P-210-1 AUTO PISTOL
Caliber: 7.65mm or 9mm Para., 8-shot magazine.
Barrel: 4¾".
Weight: 31¾ oz. (9mm) **Length:** 8½" over-all.
Stocks: Checkered walnut, with lacquer finish.
Sights: Blade front, rear adjustable for windage.
Features: Lanyard loop; polished finish. Conversion unit for 22 LR available.
  Imported from Switzerland by Osborne's, SIGARMS and Mandall Shooting
  Supplies.
Price: P-210-1 about (Mandall) $1,500.00
Price: P-210-2 Service Pistol (Mandall) $1,600.00
Price: 22 Cal. Conversion unit (Osborne's) $675.00
Price: P-210-1 (Osborne's) $1,450.00
Price: P-210-2 (Osborne's) $1,095.00

SIG P-210-1

SIG P-210-6 AUTO PISTOL
Caliber: 9mm Para., 8-shot magazine.
Barrel: 4¾".
Weight: 36.2 oz. **Length:** 8½" over-all.
Stocks: Checkered black plastic. Walnut optional.
Sights: Blade front, micro. adj. rear for w. & e.
Features: Adjustable trigger stop; target trigger; ribbed front stap; sandblasted
  finish. Conversion unit for 22 LR consists of barrel, recoil spring, slide and
  magazine. Imported from Switzerland by Osborne's and SIGARMS, Inc.
Price: P-210-6 (SIGARMS) $1,526.99
Price: 22 Cal. Conversion unit (Osborne's) $781.00
Price: As above, from SIGARMS $719.00
Price: P-210-6 (Osborne's) $1,295.00

SIG P-210-6

SIG-Sauer P-220

SIG-SAUER P-220 D.A. AUTO PISTOL
Caliber: 9mm, 38 Super; 45 ACP. (9-shot in 9mm and 38 Super, 7 in 45).
Barrel: 4⅜".
Weight: 28¼ oz. (9mm). **Length:** 7¾" over-all.
Stocks: Checkered black plastic.
Sights: Blade front, drift adj. rear for w.
Features: Double action. De-cocking lever permits lowering hammer onto
  locked firing pin. Squared combat-type trigger guard. Slide stays open after
  last shot. Imported from West Germany by SIGARMS, Inc.
Price: $563.99

CAUTION: PRICES CHANGE. CHECK AT GUNSHOP.

SIG-SAUER P-225 D.A. AUTO PISTOL

Caliber: 9mm Parabellum, 8-shot magazine.
Barrel: 3.8″.
Weight: 26 oz. **Length:** 7³⁄₃₂″ over-all.
Stocks: Checkered black plastic.
Sights: Blade front, rear adjustable for windage.
Features: Double action. De-cocking lever permits lowering hammer onto locked firing pin. Squared combat-type trigger guard. Shortened, lightened version of P-220. Imported from West Germany by SIGARMS, Inc.
Price: **$601.99**

SIG-SAUER P-226 D.A. Auto Pistol

Similar to the P-220 pistol except has 15-shot magazine, 4.4″ barrel, and weighs 26½ oz. Imported from West Germany by SIGARMS, Inc.
Price: **$627.99**

SIG-Sauer P226

SIG-SAUER P-230 D.A. AUTO PISTOL

Caliber: 32 ACP (8 shot), 380 ACP (7 shot).
Barrel: 3¾″.
Weight: 16 oz. **Length:** 6½″ over-all.
Stocks: Checkered black plastic.
Sights: Blade front, rear adj. for w.
Features: Double action. Same basic action design as P-220. Blowback operation, stationary barrel. Introduced 1977. Imported from West Germany by SIGARMS, Inc.
Price: **$422.99**
Price: In stainless steel (P-230 SL) **$483.99**

SIG-Sauer P-230 D.A. Pistol

SILE-BENELLI B-76 DA AUTO PISTOL

Caliber: 9mm Para., 8-shot magazine.
Barrel: 4¼″, 6-groove. Chrome-lined bore.
Weight: 34 oz. (empty). **Length:** 8¹⁄₁₆″ over-all.
Stocks: Walnut with cut checkering and high gloss finish.
Sights: Blade front with white face, rear adjustable for windage with white bars for increased visibility.
Features: Fixed barrel, locked breech. Exposed hammer can be locked in non-firing mode in either single or double action. Stainless steel inertia firing pin and loaded chamber indicator. All external parts blued, internal parts hard-chrome plated. All steel construction. Introduced 1979. From Sile Dist.
Price: About **$349.95**

SMITH & WESSON MODEL 439 DOUBLE ACTION

Caliber: 9mm Luger, 8-shot clip.
Barrel: 4″.
Weight: 30 oz. **Length:** 7⅝″ over-all.
Stocks: Checkered walnut.
Sights: Serrated ramp front, square notch rear is fully adj. for w. & e. Also available with fixed sights.
Features: Rear sight has protective shields on both sides of the sight blade. Frame is aluminum alloy. Firing pin lock in addition to the regular rotating safety. Magazine disconnector. Comes with two magazines. Ambidextrous safety standard. Introduced 1980.
Price: Blue, from **$422.00**
Price: Nickel, from **$456.00**
Price: Model 639 (stainless), from **$468.00**

SMITH & WESSON MODEL 459 DOUBLE ACTION

Caliber: 9mm Luger, 14-shot clip.
Barrel: 4″.
Weight: 30 oz. **Length:** 7⅝″ over-all.
Stocks: Checkered high-impact nylon.
Sights: ⅛″ square serrated ramp front, square notch rear is fully adj. for w. & e. Also available with fixed sights.
Features: Alloy frame. Rear sight has protective shields on both sides of blade. Firing pin lock in addition to the regular safety. Magazine disconnector. Comes with two magazines. Ambidextrous safety standard. Introduced 1980.
Price: Blue, from **$459.50**
Price: Nickel, from **$494.00**
Price: Model 659 (stainless), from **$509.00**

Smith & Wesson Model 659

Smith & Wesson Model 469 Mini-Gun

Basically a cut-down version of the Model 459 pistol. Gun has a 3½″ barrel, 12-round magazine, over-all length of 6¹³⁄₁₆″, and weighs 26 oz. Also accepts the 14-shot Model 459 magazine. Cross-hatch knurling on the recurved-front trigger guard and backstrap; magazine has a curved finger extension; bobbed hammer; sandblast blue finish with pebble-grain grips. Ambidextrous safety standard. Introduced 1983.
Price: **$432.50**
Price: Stainless Model 669 (alloy frame) **$475.00**

Smith & Wesson Model 469

SMITH & WESSON MODEL 645 DOUBLE ACTION
Caliber: 45 ACP, 8-shot magazine.
Barrel: 5".
Weight: 37.5 ozs. **Length:** 8⅝" over-all.
Stocks: Checkered high-impact nylon.
Sights: Red ramp front, rear drift-adjustable for windage.
Features: Double action. Made of stainless steel. Has manual hammer-drop, magazine disconnect and firing pin safeties. Cross-hatch knurling on the re-curved front trigger guard and backstrap; bevelled magazine well. Introduced 1985.
Price: $550.00

Smith & Wesson Model 645

Springfield Armory 1911-A1

STAR MODEL 30M & 30 PK DOUBLE-ACTION PISTOLS
Caliber: 9mm Para., 15-shot magazine.
Barrel: 4.33" (Model M); 3.86" (Model PK).
Weight: 40 oz. (M); 30 oz. (PK). **Length:** 8" over-all (M); 7.6" (PK).
Stocks: Checkered black plastic.
Sights: Square blade front, square notch rear click-adjustable for windage and elevation.
Features: Double or single action; grooved front and backstraps and trigger guard face; ambidextrous safety cams firing pin forward; removable back-strap houses the firing mechanism. Model M has steel frame; Model PK is alloy. Introduced 1984. Imported from Spain by Interarms.
Price: Model M or PK $455.00

STAR MODEL PD AUTO PISTOL
Caliber: 45 ACP, 6-shot magazine.
Barrel: 3.94".
Weight: 28 oz. **Length:** 7⁷⁄₁₆" over-all.
Stocks: Checkered walnut.
Sights: Ramp front, fully adjustable rear.
Features: Rear sight milled into slide; thumb safety; grooved non-slip front strap; nylon recoil buffer; inertia firing pin; no grip or magazine safeties. Imported from Spain by Interarms.
Price: Blue. $333.00

STAR BM, BKM AUTO PISTOLS
Caliber: 9mm Para., 8-shot magazine.
Barrel: 3.9".
Weight: 25 oz.
Stocks: Checkered walnut.
Sights: Fixed.
Features: Blue or chrome finish. Magazine and manual safeties, external hammer. Imported from Spain by Interarms.
Price: Blue, BM and BKM. $305.00
Price: Chrome, BM only $315.00

STEEL CITY "DOUBLE DEUCE" PISTOL
Caliber: 22 LR (7-shot), 25 ACP (6-shot).
Barrel: 2½".
Weight: 18 oz. **Length:** 5½" over-all.
Stocks: Rosewood.
Sights: Fixed groove.
Features: Double-action; stainless steel construction with matte finish; ambidextrous slide-mounted safety. From Steel City Arms, Inc.
Price: 22 or 25 cal. $289.95

SPRINGFIELD ARMORY 1911-A1 AUTO PISTOL
Caliber: 9mm or 45 ACP, 8-round magazine.
Barrel: 5".
Weight: 2¼ lbs. **Length:** 8½" over-all.
Stocks: NA.
Sights: Blade front, rear drift-adjustable for windage.
Features: All forged parts, including frame, barrel, slide. All new production. Custom slide and parts available. Introduced 1985. From Springfield Armory.
Price: Complete pistol, Parkerized $362.00
Price: Complete pistol, blued $383.00
Price: Complete parts kit, 45 ACP, Parkerized $305.00
Price: As above, blued $326.00
Price: 45 to 22 or 9mm conversion kit, Parkerized $181.00
Price: As above, blued $186.00

Star Model 30 PK

Star Model PD Pistol

Steel City Double Deuce

CAUTION: PRICES CHANGE. CHECK AT GUNSHOP.

Steyr GB

TARGA MODELS GT32, GT380 AUTO PISTOLS
Caliber: 32 ACP or 380 ACP, 6-shot magazine.
Barrel: 4⅞".
Weight: 26 oz. **Length:** 7⅜" over-all.
Stocks: Checkered nylon with thumb rest. Walnut optional.
Sights: Fixed blade front; rear drift-adj. for w.
Features: Chrome or blue finish; magazine, thumb, and firing pin safeties; external hammer; safety lever take-down. Imported from Italy by Excam, Inc.
Price: 32 cal., blue $133.00
Price: 32 cal., chrome $143.00
Price: 380 cal., blue $161.00
Price: 380 cal., chrome $170.00
Price: 380 cal., chrome, engraved, wooden grips $214.00
Price: 380 cal., blue, engraved, wooden grips $205.00

TARGA GT380XE PISTOL
Caliber: 380 ACP, 11-shot magazine.
Barrel: 3.88".
Weight: 28 oz. **Length:** 7.38" over-all.
Stocks: Smooth hardwood.
Sights: Adj. for windage.
Features: Blue or satin nickel. Ordnance steel. Magazine disconnector, firing pin and thumb safeties. Introduced 1980. Imported by Excam.
Price: 380 cal., blue $205.00

Taurus PT-99AF Auto Pistol
Similar to the PT-92 except has fully adjustable rear sight, smooth Brazilian walnut stocks and is available in polished blue or satin nickel. Introduced 1983.
Price: Polished blue $392.90
Price: Satin nickel $406.00

> Consult our Directory pages for the location of firms mentioned.

Universal Enforcer Model 3000

STEEL CITY "WAR EAGLE" PISTOL
Caliber: 9mm Para., 13-shot magazine.
Barrel: 4".
Weight: NA. **Length:** NA.
Stocks: Rosewood.
Sights: Fixed and adjustable.
Features: Double action; matte-finished stainless steel; ambidextrous safety. Announced 1986.
Price: $389.95

STEYR GB DOUBLE ACTION AUTO PISTOL
Caliber: 9mm Parabellum; 18-shot magazine.
Barrel: 5.39".
Weight: 33 oz. **Length:** 8.4" over-all.
Stocks: Checkered walnut.
Sights: Post front, fixed rear.
Features: Gas-operated, delayed blowback action. Measures 5.7" high, 1.3" wide. Introduced 1981. Imported by Gun South, Inc.
Price: About $595.00

TARGA MODEL GT27 AUTO PISTOL
Caliber: 25 ACP, 6-shot magazine.
Barrel: 2⁷⁄₁₆".
Weight: 12 oz. **Length:** 4⅝" over-all.
Stocks: Checkered nylon.
Sights: Fixed.
Features: Safety lever take-down; external hammer with half-cock. Assembled in U.S. by Excam, Inc.
Price: Blue $58.50
Price: Chrome $64.00

TAURUS MODEL PT-92AF AUTO PISTOL
Caliber: 9mm P., 15-shot magazine.
Barrel: 4.92".
Weight: 34 oz. **Length:** 8.54" over-all.
Stocks: Brazilian walnut.
Sights: Fixed notch rear.
Features: Double action, exposed hammer, chamber loaded indicator. Inertia firing pin. Blue finish. Imported by Taurus International.
Price: $366.90

Taurus PT-99 Pistol

UNIVERSAL ENFORCER MODEL 3000 AUTO
Caliber: 30 M1 Carbine, 5-shot magazine.
Barrel: 11¼" with 12-groove rifling.
Weight: 4 lbs. **Length:** 19" over-all.
Stocks: American walnut with handguard.
Sights: Gold bead ramp front. Peep rear.
Features: Accepts 15 or 30-shot magazines. 4½-6 lb. trigger pull. From Iver Johnson.
Price: Blue finish $225.00

UZI PISTOL
Caliber: 9mm Parabellum.
Barrel: 4.5″.
Weight: 3.8 lbs. **Length:** 9.45″ over-all.
Stocks: Black plastic.
Sights: Post front, open rear adjustable for windage and elevation.
Features: Semi-auto blow-back action; fires from closed bolt; floating firing pin. Comes in a molded plastic case with 20-round magazine; 25 and 32-round magazines available. Imported from Israel by Action Arms. Introduced 1984.
Price: **$579.00**

UZI Pistol

WALTHER PP AUTO PISTOL
Caliber: 22 LR, 8-shot; 32 ACP, 380 ACP, 7-shot.
Barrel: 3.86″.
Weight: 23½ oz. **Length:** 6.7″ over-all.
Stocks: Checkered plastic.
Sights: Fixed, white markings.
Features: Double action, manual safety blocks firing pin and drops hammer, chamber loaded indicator on 32 and 380, extra finger rest magazine provided. Imported from Germany by Interarms.
Price: 22 LR **$550.00**
Price: 32 and 380.. **$530.00**
Price: Engraved models .... **On Request**

Walther American PPK/S Auto Pistol
Similar to Walther PP except made entirely in the United States. Has 3.27″ barrel with 6.1″ length over-all. Introduced 1980.
Price: 380 ACP only **$475.00**
Price: As above, stainless **$515.00**

Walther PP Auto Pistol

Walther American PPK Auto Pistol
Similar to Walther PPK/S except weighs 21 oz., has 6-shot capacity. Made in the U.S. Introduced 1986.
Price: Stainless, 380 ACP only **$515.00**
Price: Blue, 380 ACP only **$475.00**

WALTHER P-38 AUTO PISTOL
Caliber: 22 LR, 30 Luger or 9mm Luger, 8-shot.
Barrel: 4¹⁵/₁₆″ (9mm and 30), 5¹/₁₆″ (22 LR).
Weight: 28 oz. **Length:** 8½″ over-all.
Stocks: Checkered plastic.
Sights: Fixed.
Features: Double action, safety blocks firing pin and drops hammer, chamber loaded indicator. Matte finish standard, polished blue, engraving and/or plating available. Imported from Germany by Interarms.
Price: 22 LR **$690.00**
Price: 9mm or 30 Luger **$640.00**
Price: Engraved models .... **On Request**

Walther P-38 Auto Pistol

Walther P-5 Auto Pistol
Latest Walther design that uses the basic P-38 double-action mechanism. Caliber 9mm Luger, barrel length 3½″; weight 28 oz., over-all length 7″.
Price: **$750.00**

WILKINSON "SHERRY" AUTO PISTOL
Caliber: 22 LR, 8-shot magazine.
Barrel: 2⅛″.
Weight: 9¼ oz. **Length:** 4⅜″ over-all.
Stocks: Checkered black plastic.
Sights: None.
Features: Cross-bolt safety locks the sear into the hammer. Available in all blue finish or blue slide and trigger with gold frame. Introduced 1985.
Price: **$167.95**

Wilkinson "Sherry"

WILKINSON "LINDA" PISTOL
Caliber: 9mm Para., 31-shot magazine.
Barrel: 8⁵/₁₆″.
Weight: 4 lbs. 13 oz. **Length:** 12¼″ over-all.
Stocks: Checkered black plastic pistol grip, maple fore-end.
Sights: Protected blade front, Williams adjustable rear.
Features: Fires from closed bolt. Semi-auto only. Straight blowback action. Cross-bolt safety. Removable barrel. From Wilkinson Arms.
Price: **$368.69**

WILDEY PISTOL
Caliber: 475, 44, 41 Wildey Magnum, 45 Win. Mag., 357 Peterbuilt, 44 Auto Mag.; 7-shot.
Barrel: 6″, 7″, 8″, 10″.
Weight: About 58 oz. (6″ barrel).
Stocks: Black rubber or walnut.
Sights: Interchangeable blade front, Eliason-type rear.
Features: Right or left-hand ejection (bolts), safety and slide lock stop; ambidextrous magazine catch; interchangeable barrels; drilled and tapped for scope mounting; dual cam-up tilt bolt lock; patented auto. gas system; adjustable trigger. Announced 1985. From Wildey, Inc.
Price: **$799.00**

CAUTION: PRICES CHANGE. CHECK AT GUNSHOP.

Air Match 500

AIR MATCH 500 TARGET PISTOL
Caliber: 22 LR, single shot.
Barrel: 10.4″.
Weight: 28 oz.
Stocks: Anatomically shaped match grip of stippled hardwood. Right or left hand.
Sights: Match post front, fully adjustable match rear.
Features: Sight radius adjustable from 14.1″ to 16.1″; easy disassembly for cleaning or adjustment. Comes with case, tools, spare front and rear sight blades. Imported from Italy by Kendall International Arms. Introduced 1984.
Price: $718.75

ALLEN "PHANTOM" SA SILHOUETTE
Caliber: 357 Mag., 44 Mag.
Barrel: 10″.
Weight: NA. **Length:** NA.
Stocks: Walnut target-style.
Sights: Blade on ramp front, fully adj. rear.
Features: Heavier frame than other Allen single actions. Hooked trigger guard. Introduced 1986. Imported by Allen Fire Arms.
Price: $369.00

BEEMAN/AGNER MODEL 80 TARGET PISTOL
Caliber: 22 LR, 5-shot magazine.
Barrel: 5.9″.
Weight: 36 oz. **Length:** 9½″ overall.
Stocks: French walnut briar; anatomically shaped, adjustable.
Sights: Fixed blade front, rear adjustable for windage and elevation; 8¾″ radius.
Features: Security "key" locks trigger, magazine and slide. Design minimizes gun movement; dry-fire button allows trigger practice. Imported from Denmark by Beeman. Introduced 1984.
Price: Right-hand $1,295.00
Price: Left-hand $1,395.00

Beeman/Agner 80

Beeman/Unique 69

Beeman/Unique 2000-U

BEEMAN/UNIQUE D.E.S. 69 TARGET PISTOL
Caliber: 22 LR, 5-shot magazine.
Barrel: 5.91″.
Weight: 35.3 oz. **Length:** 10.5″ over-all.
Stocks: French walnut target style with thumbrest and adjustable shelf; hand checkered panels.
Sights: Ramp front, micro. adj. rear mounted on frame; 8.66″ sight radius.
Features: Meets U.I.T. standards. Comes with 260 gram barrel weight; 100, 150, 350 gram weights available. Fully adjustable match trigger; dry firing safety device. Imported from France by Beeman.
Price: Right-hand.. $599.00
Price: Left-hand $629.00

BEEMAN/UNIQUE MODEL 2000-U MATCH PISTOL
Caliber: 22 Short, 5-shot magazine.
Barrel: 5.9″.
Weight: 43 oz. **Length:** 11.3″ over-all.
Stocks: Anatomically shaped, adjustable, stippled French walnut.
Sights: Blade front, fully adjustable rear; 9.7″ sight radius.
Features: Light alloy frame, steel slide and shock absorber; five barrel vents reduce recoil, three of which can be blocked; trigger adjustable for position and pull weight. Comes with 340 gram weight housing, 160 gram available. Imported from France by Beeman. Introduced 1984.
Price: Right-hand.. $799.00
Price: Left-hand $839.00

BERNARDELLI MODEL 100 PISTOL
Caliber: 22 LR only, 10-shot magazine.
Barrel: 5.9″.
Weight: 37¾ oz. **Length:** 9″ over-all.
Stocks: Checkered walnut with thumbrest.
Sights: Fixed front, rear adj. for w. and e.
Features: Target barrel weight included. Heavy sighting rib with interchangeable front sight. Accessories include cleaning equipment and assembly tools, case. Imported from Italy by Interarms.
Price: With case.. $360.00

Bernardelli Model 100

Chipmunk Silhouette

CHIPMUNK SILHOUETTE PISTOL
Caliber: 22 LR.
Barrel: 14⅞".
Weight: About 2 lbs. **Length:** 20" over-all.
Stock: American walnut rear grip.
Sights: Post on ramp front, peep rear.
Features: Meets IHMSA 22-cal. unlimited category for competition. Introduced 1985.
Price: **$149.95**

COLT GOLD CUP NAT'L MATCH MK IV Series 80
Caliber: 45 ACP, 7-shot magazine.
Barrel: 5", with new design bushing.
Weight: 39 oz. **Length:** 8½".
Stocks: Blue—Checkered walnut, gold plated medallion; stainless has composition grips.
Sights: Ramp-style front, Colt-Elliason rear adj. for w. and e., sight radius 6¾".
Features: Arched or flat housing; wide, grooved trigger with adj. stop; ribbed-top slide, hand fitted, with improved ejection port.
Price: Blue **$687.50**
Price: Stainless **$744.95**

Colt Gold Cup Series 80

DETONICS SCOREMASTER TARGET PISTOL
Caliber: 45 ACP, 451 Detonics Magnum, 7-shot clip.
Barrel: 5" heavy match barrel with recessed muzzle; 6" optional.
Weight: 42 oz. **Length:** 8⅜" over-all.
Stocks: Pachmayr checkered with matching mainspring housing.
Sights: Blade front, Low-Base Bomar rear.
Features: Stainless steel; self-centering barrel system; patented Detonics recoil system; combat tuned, ambidextrous safety; extended grip safety; National Match tolerances; extended magazine release. Comes with two spare magazines, three interchangeable front sights, and carrying case. Introduced 1983. From Detonics.
Price: 45 ACP or 451 Mag., 6" barrel **$1,009.95**
Price: As above, 5" barrel..................................... **$992.95**

FAS 602 MATCH PISTOL
Caliber: 22 LR, 5-shot.
Barrel: 5.6".
Weight: 37 oz. **Length:** 11" over-all.
Stocks: Walnut wrap-around; sizes small, medium or large, or adjustable.
Sights: Match. Blade front, open notch rear fully adj. for w. and e. Sight radius is 8.66".
Features: Line of sight is only ¹¹/₃₂" above centerline of bore; magazine is inserted from top; adjustable and removable trigger mechanism; single lever takedown. Full 5 year warranty. Imported from Italy by Beeman Inc. and Osborne's.
Price: From Beeman .... **$749.00** to **$779.00**
Price: As above, 32 S&W wadcutter (Beeman) .... **$754.00** to **$784.00**
Price: 22LR (Osborne's)..................................... **$775.00**

Detonics "Scoremaster"

FAS 601 Match Pistol
Similar to SP 602 except has different match stocks with adj. palm, shelf, 22 Short only for rapid fire shooting; weighs 40 oz., 5.6" bbl., has gas ports through top of barrel and slide to reduce recoil, slightly different trigger and sear mechanisms.
Price: From Beeman .... **$754.00** to **$784.00**
Price: From Osborne's **$825.00**
Price: FAS 603, 32 S&W wadcutter (Beeman) **$835.00**

HAMMERLI MODEL 150 FREE PISTOL
Caliber: 22 LR. Single shot.
Barrel: 11.3"
Weight: 43 ozs. **Length:** 15.35" over-all.
Stocks: Walnut with adjustable palm shelf.
Sights: Sight radius of 14.6". Micro rear sight adj. for w. and e.
Features: Single shot Martini action. Cocking lever on left side of action with vertical operation. Set trigger adjustable for length and angle. Trigger pull weight adjustable between 5 and 100 grams. Guaranteed accuracy of .78", 10 shots from machine rest. Imported from Switzerland by Osborne's, Mandall Shooting Supplies and Beeman.
Price: About (Mandall)..................................... **$1,500.00**
Price: With electric trigger (Model 152), about (Mandall)......... **$1,650.00**
Price: Model 150 (Osborne's)................................ **$1,295.00**
Price: Model 152 (Osborne's)................................ **$1,395.00**
Price: Model 150 (Beeman) **$1,195.00**
Price: Model 152 (Beeman) **$1,295.00**

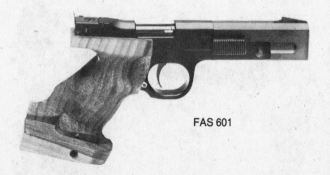

FAS 601

CAUTION: PRICES CHANGE. CHECK AT GUNSHOP.

Hammerli 208

HAMMERLI MODEL 232 RAPID FIRE PISTOL
Caliber: 22 Short, 6-shot.
Barrel: 5″, with six exhaust ports.
Weight: 44 oz. **Length:** 10.4″ over-all.
Stocks: Stippled walnut; wraparound on Model 232-2, adjustable on 232-1.
Sights: Interchangeable front and rear blades, fully adjustable micrometer rear.
Features: Recoil operated semi-automatic; nearly recoilless design; trigger adjustable from 8.4 to 10.6 oz. with three lengths offered. Wraparound grips available in small, medium and large sizes. Imported from Switzerland by Osborne's, Beeman, Mandall. Introduced 1984.
Price: Model 232-1, (Osborne's) $902.00
Price: Model 232-2, (Osborne's) $954.00
Price: Model 232-1 (Beeman) $829.00
Price: Model 232-2 (Beeman) $899.00

HECKLER & KOCH P9S COMPETITION PISTOL
Caliber: 9mm Para.
Barrel: 4″, 5.5″.
Weight: 32 oz. **Length:** 9.1″ over-all.
Stocks: Stippled walnut, target-type.
Sights: Blade front, fully adjustable rear.
Features: Comes with extra standard 4″ barrel, slide and grips, as well as the target gun parts and tools and is fully convertible. Imported from West Germany by Heckler & Koch, Inc.
Price: $1,333.00

MANURHIN MR. 32 MATCH REVOLVER
Caliber: 32 S&W Long, 6-shot.
Barrel: 6″.
Weight: 42 oz. **Length:** 11¾″ over-all.
Stocks: Anatomically shaped grip for target shooting; supplied shaped but not finished; small, medium and large sizes.
Sights: Interchangeable blade front, adjustable underlying micrometer rear.
Features: Target/match 6-shot revolver. Trigger is externally adjustable for weight of pull, and comes with shoe. Imported from France by Manurhin International, Inc. Introduced 1984.
Price: $785.00
Price: Model MR. 38—same as MR. 32 except chambered for 38 Special, 5¾″ barrel. $785.00

MANURHIN MR 73 LONG RANGE/SILHOUETTE REVOLVER
Caliber: 357 Magnum; 6-shot.
Barrel: 9″ (Long Range), 10¾″ (Silhouette).
Weight: 45 oz. (9″ bbl.); 50 oz. (10¾″ bbl.) **Length:** 14″ over-all (9″); 16¾″ (10¾″).
Stocks: Checkered walnut.
Sights: Interchangeable blade front, adjustable micrometer rear.
Features: Trigger externally adjustable for backlash and weight of pull. Single action only. Trigger shoe available. Imported from France by Manurhin International, Inc. Introduced 1984.
Price: $795.00

HAMMERLI STANDARD, MODELS 208 & 211
Caliber: 22 LR.
Barrel: 5.9″, 6-groove.
Weight: 37.6 oz. (45 oz. with extra heavy barrel weight). **Length:** 10″.
Stocks: Walnut. Adj. palm rest (208), 211 has thumbrest grip.
Sights: Match sights, fully adj. for w. and e. (click adj.). Interchangeable front and rear blades.
Features: Semi-automatic, recoil operated. 8-shot clip. Slide stop. Fully adj. trigger (2¼ lbs. and 3 lbs.). Extra barrel weight available. Imported from Switzerland by Osborne's, Mandall Shooting Supplies, Beeman.
Price: Model 208, approx. (Mandall) $1,295.00
Price: Model 211, approx. (Mandall) $1,195.00
Price: Model 215, approx. (Mandall) $1,195.00
Price: Model 208 (Osborne's) $1,029.00
Price: Model 211 (Osborne's) $1,005.00
Price: Model 215 (Osborne's) $835.00
Price: Model 208 (Beeman) $950.00
Price: Model 211 (Beeman) $930.00
Price: Model 215 (Beeman) $779.00

Heckler & Koch P9S Competition

Manurhin MR.32

Manurhin MR 73

MORINI MODEL CM-80 SUPER COMPETITION
Caliber: 22 Long Rifle; single shot.
Barrel: 10″, free floating.
Weight: 30 oz., with weights. **Length:** 21.25″ over-all.
Stocks: Walnut, adjustable or wrap-around in three sizes.
Sights: Match; square notch rear adjustable for w. and e.; up to 15.6″ radius.
Features: Adjustable grip/frame angle, adjustable barrel alignment, adjustable trigger weight (5 to 120 grams), adjustable sight radius. Comes with 20-shot test target (50 meters) and case. Introduced 1985. Imported from Italy by Osborne's.
Price: Standard $810.00
Price: Deluxe $955.00

Morini Model CM-80

COMPETITION HANDGUNS

Remington XP-100 Silhouette

REMINGTON XP-100 SILHOUETTE PISTOL
Caliber: 7mm BR Remington, single-shot.
Barrel: 14¾".
Weight: 4⅛ lbs. **Length:** 21¼" over-all.
Stocks: Brown nylon, one piece, checkered grip.
Sights: None furnished. Drilled and tapped for scope mounts.
Features: Universal grip fits right or left hand; match-type grooved trigger, two-position thumb safety.
Price: About **$405.00**

OLYMPIC RAPID FIRE PISTOL
Caliber: 22 Short.
Barrel: 5", with exhaust ports.
Weight: 43 oz. **Length:** 10.4" over-all.
Stocks: Wrap-around walnut; three sizes.
Sights: Fully adjustable micrometer rear.
Features: Recoil-operated semi-automatic. Trigger adjustable for weight of pull. I.S.U. legal for international competition. Introduced 1985. Imported from Spain by Osborne's.
Price: **$895.00**

RUGER MARK II TARGET MODEL AUTO PISTOL
Caliber: 22 LR only, 10-shot magazine.
Barrel: 6⅞".
Weight: 42 oz. with 6⅞" bbl. **Length:** 11⅛" over-all.
Stocks: Checkered hard rubber.
Sights: .125" blade front, micro click rear, adjustable for w. and e. Sight radius 9⅜". Introduced 1982.
Price: Blued (MK 678) **$215.00**
Price: Stainless, (KMK 678) **$275.00**

Ruger Mark II Bull Barrel
Same gun as the Target Model except has 5½" or 10" heavy barrel (10" meets all IHMSA regulations). Weight with 5½" barrel is 42 oz., with 10" barrel, 52 oz.
Price: Blued (MK-512, MK-10) **$215.00**
Price: Stainless (KMK-512, KMK-10) **$275.00**

Ruger Mark II Target

SIG/HAMMERLI P-240 TARGET PISTOL
Caliber: 32 S&W Long wadcutter, 5-shot.
Barrel: 5.9".
Weight: 49 oz. **Length:** 10" over-all.
Stocks: Walnut, target style with thumbrest. Adjustable palm rest optional.
Sights: Match sights; ⅛" undercut front, ⅛" notch micro rear click adj. for w. and e.
Features: Semi-automatic, recoil operated; meets I.S.U. and N.R.A. specs for Center Fire Pistol competition; double pull trigger adj. from 2 lbs., 15 ozs. to 3 lbs., 9 ozs.; trigger stop. Comes with cleaning kit, test targets. Imported from Switzerland by Osborne's Supplies and Mandall Shooting Supplies.
Price: About (Mandall) **$1,500.00**
Price: 22 cal. conversion unit (Osborne's) **$700.00**
Price: With standard grips (Osborne's) **$1,195.00**
Price: With adjustable grips (Osborne's) **$1,250.00**

SIG/Hammerli P-240

Smith & Wesson 29 Silhouette

SMITH & WESSON MODEL 29 SILHOUETTE
Caliber: 44 Magnum, 6-shot.
Barrel: 10⅝".
Weight: 58 oz. **Length:** 16³⁄₁₆" over-all.
Stocks: Over-size target-type, checkered Goncalo Alves.
Sights: Four-position front to match the four distances of silhouette targets; micro-click rear adjustable for windage and elevation.
Features: Designed specifically for silhouette shooting. Front sight has click stops for the four pre-set ranges. Introduced 1983.
Price: **$455.50**

Smith & Wesson Model 41

SMITH & WESSON 22 AUTO PISTOL Model 41
Caliber: 22 LR, 10-shot clip.
Barrel: 7".
Weight: 43½ oz. **Length:** 12" over-all.
Stocks: Checkered walnut with thumbrest, usable with either hand.
Sights: Front, ⅛" Patridge undercut; micro click rear adj. for w. and e.
Features: ⅜" wide, grooved trigger with adj. stop.
Price: S&W Bright Blue **$485.00**

CAUTION: PRICES CHANGE. CHECK AT GUNSHOP.

SMITH & WESSON 22 MATCH HEAVY BARREL M-41
Caliber: 22 LR, 10-shot clip.
Barrel: 5½" heavy.
Weight: 44½ oz. **Length:** 9".
Stocks: Checkered walnut with modified thumbrest, usable with either hand.
Sights: ⅛" Patridge on ramp base. S&W micro click rear adj. for w. and e.
Features: ⅜" wide, grooved trigger; adj. trigger stop.
Price: S&W Bright Blue, satin matted top area $485.00

Smith & Wesson Model 52

SMITH & WESSON 38 MASTER Model 52 AUTO
Caliber: 38 Special (for Mid-range W.C. with flush-seated bullet only). 5-shot magazine.
Barrel: 5".
Weight: 40.5 oz. with empty magazine. **Length:** 8⅝".
Stocks: Checkered walnut.
Sights: ⅛" Patridge front, S&W micro click rear adj. for w. and e.
Features: Top sighting surfaces matte finished. Locked breech, moving barrel system; checked for 10-ring groups at 50 yards. Coin-adj. sight screws. Dry firing permissible if manual safety on.
Price: S&W Bright Blue $657.50

SOKOLOVSKY 45 AUTOMASTER
Caliber: 45 ACP, 6-shot magazine.
Barrel: 6".
Weight: 3.6 lbs. **Length:** 9½" over-all.
Stocks: Smooth walnut.
Sights: Ramp front, Millett fully adjustable rear.
Features: Intended for target shooting, not combat. Semi-custom built with precise tolerances. Has special "safety trigger" next to regular trigger. Most parts made of stainless steel. Introduced 1985. From Sokolovsky Corp.
Price: $3,000.00

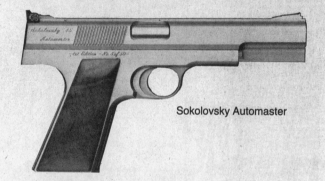

Sokolovsky Automaster

Taurus Model 86 Master

TAURUS MODEL 86 MASTER REVOLVER
Caliber: 38 Spec., 6-shot.
Barrel: 6" only.
Weight: 34 oz. **Length:** 11¼" over-all.
Stocks: Over size target-type, checkered Brazilian walnut.
Sights: Patridge front, micro. click rear adj. for w. and e.
Features: Blue finish with non-reflective finish on barrel. Imported from Brazil by Taurus International.
Price: $245.00
Price: Model 96 Scout Master, same except in 22 cal. $245.00

THOMPSON-CENTER SUPER 14 CONTENDER
Caliber: 22 LR, 222 Rem., 223 Rem., 6mm TCU, 6.5 TCU, 7mm TCU, 30 Herrett, 357 Herrett, 30-30 Win., 35 Rem., 357 Rem. Maximum, 44 Mag. Single shot.
Barrel: 14".
Weight: 45 oz. **Length:** 17¼" over-all.
Stocks: Select walnut grip and fore-end.
Sights: Fully adjustable target-type.
Features: Break-open action with auto safety. Interchangeable barrels for both rimfire and centerfire calibers. Introduced 1978.
Price: $315.00
Price: With Armour Alloy II finish $375.00
Price: Extra barrels $140.00

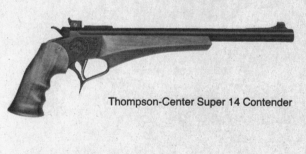

Thompson-Center Super 14 Contender

VIRGINIAN DRAGOON STAINLESS SILHOUETTE
Caliber: 357 Mag., 44 Mag.
Barrel: 7½", 8⅜", 10½", heavy.
Weight: 51 oz. (7½" bbl.) **Length:** 11½" over-all (7½" bbl.).
Stocks: Smooth walnut; also comes with Pachmayr rubber grips.
Sights: Undercut blade front, special fully adjustable square notch rear.
Features: Designed to comply with IHMSA rules. Made of stainless steel; comes with two sets of stocks. Introduced 1982. Made in the U.S. by Interarms.
Price: Either barrel, caliber $425.00

Walther Free Pistol

WALTHER FREE PISTOL
Caliber: 22 LR, single shot.
Barrel: 11.7".
Weight: 48 ozs. **Length:** 17.2" over-all.
Stocks: Walnut, special hand-fitting design.
Sights: Fully adjustable match sights.
Features: Special electronic trigger. Matte finish blue. Introduced 1980. Imported from Germany by Interarms.
Price: $1,295.00

WALTHER GSP MATCH PISTOL
Caliber: 22 LR, 32 S&W wadcutter (GSP-C), 5-shot.
Barrel: 5¾".
Weight: 44.8 oz. (22 LR), 49.4 oz. (32). **Length:** 11.8" over-all.
Stocks: Walnut, special hand-fitting design.
Sights: Fixed front, rear adj. for w. & e.
Features: Available with either 2.2 lb. (1000 gm) or 3 lb. (1360 gm) trigger. Spare mag., bbl. weight, tools supplied in Match Pistol Kit. Imported from Germany by Interarms.
Price: GSP $955.00
Price: GSP-C $1,095.00
Price: 22 LR conversion unit for GSP-C $595.00
Price: 22 Short conversion unit for GSP-C $625.00
Price: 32 S&W conversion unit for GSP-C $725.00

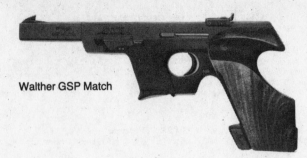

Walther GSP Match

Walther OSP Rapid-Fire Pistol
Similar to Model GSP except 22 Short only, stock has adj. free-style hand rest.
Price: $975.00

DAN WESSON MODEL 40 SILHOUETTE
Caliber: 357 Maximum, 6 shot.
Barrel: 6", 8", 10".
Weight: 64 oz. (8" bbl.) **Length:** 14.3" over-all (8" bbl.).
Stocks: Smooth walnut, target-style.
Sights: ⅛" serrated front, fully adj. rear.
Features: Meets criteria for IHMSA competition with 8" slotted barrel. Blue or stainless steel.
Price: Blue, 6" $426.35
Price: Blue, 8" slotted $450.40
Price: Blue, 10" $456.10
Price: Stainless, 6" $477.30
Price: Stainless, 8" slotted $499.45
Price: Stainless, 10" $511.30

Dan Wesson Model 40

WICHITA MK-40 SILHOUETTE PISTOL
Caliber: 7mm IHMSA, 308 Win. F.L. Other calibers available on special order. Single shot.
Barrel: 13", non-glare blue; .700" dia. muzzle.
Weight: 4½ lbs. **Length:** 19⅜" over-all.
Stocks: Metallic gray fiberthane glass.
Sights: Wichita Multi-Range sighting system.
Features: Aluminum receiver with steel insert locking lugs, measures 1.360" O.D.; 3 locking lug bolts, 3 gas ports; flat bolt handle; completely adjustable Wichita trigger. Introduced 1981. From Wichita Arms.
Price: $720.00

Wichita Silhouette

WICHITA SILHOUETTE PISTOL
Caliber: 7mm IHMSA, 308, 7mm x 308. Other calibers available on special order. Single shot.
Barrel: 14¹⁵⁄₁₆" or 10¾".
Weight: 4½ lbs. **Length:** 21⅜" over-all.
Stocks: American walnut with oil finish, or gray fiberglass. Glass bedded.
Sights: Wichita Multi-Range sight system.
Features: Comes with either right- or left-hand action with right-hand grip. Fluted bolt, flat bolt handle. Action drilled and tapped for Burris scope mounts. Non-glare satin blue finish. Wichita adjustable trigger. Introduced 1979. From Wichita Arms.
Price: Center grip stock $825.00
Price: As above except with Rear Position Stock and target-type Lightpull trigger. (Not illus.) $900.00

Wichita Silhouette/Hunter

WICHITA CLASSIC PISTOL
Caliber: Any, up to and including 308 Win.
Barrel: 11¼", octagon.
Weight: About 5 lbs.
Stock: Exhibition grade American black walnut. Checkered 20 lpi. Other woods available on special order.
Sights: Micro open sights standard. Receiver drilled and tapped for scope mount.
Features: Receiver and barrel octagonally shaped, finished in non-glare blue. Bolt has three locking lugs and three gas escape ports. Completely adjustable Wichita trigger. Introduced 1980. From Wichita Arms.
Price: $1,900.00
Price: Engraved, in walnut presentation case $4,660.00

WICHITA HUNTER, INTERNATIONAL PISTOL
Caliber: 22 LR, 22 Mag., 7mm INT-R, 30-30 Win., 32 H&R Mag., 357 Mag., 357 Super Mag., single shot.
Barrel: 10½".
Weight: International — 3 lbs., 13 oz.; Hunter — 3 lbs., 14 oz.
Stock: Walnut grip and fore-end.
Sights: International — target front, adjustable rear; Hunter has scope mount only.
Features: Made of 17-4PH stainless steel. Break-open action. Grip dimensions same as Colt 45 auto. Safety supplied only on Hunter model. Extra barrels are factory fitted. Introduced 1983. Available from Wichita Arms.
Price: International $484.95
Price: Hunter $484.95
Price: Extra barrels $265.00

CAUTION: PRICES CHANGE. CHECK AT GUNSHOP.

Armscor 38

Astra Model 44, 45 Double Action Revolver
Similar to the 357 Mag. except chambered for 44 Mag. or 45 Colt. Barrel length of 6″ only, giving over-all length of 11⅜″. Weight is 2¾ lbs. Introduced 1980.
Price: **$295.00**
Price: 8½″ bbl. (44 Mag. only) **$305.00**

CHARTER ARMS BULLDOG
Caliber: 44 Special, 5-shot.
Barrel: 2½″, 3″.
Weight: 19 oz. **Length:** 7¾″ over-all.
Stocks: Checkered walnut, Bulldog.
Sights: Patridge-type front, square-notch rear.
Features: Wide trigger and hammer; beryllium copper firing pin.
Price: Service Blue 3″ **$211.00**
Price: Stainless steel **$267.00**
Price: Service blue, 2½″ **$211.00**
Price: Stainless steel, 2½″ **$270.00**
Price: Stainless steel, 3″, neoprene grips **$267.00**

Charter Arms Bulldog Tracker
Similar to the standard Bulldog except chambered for 357 Mag., has adjustable rear sight, 2½″, 4″ or 6″ bull barrel, ramp front sight, square butt checkered walnut grips on 4″ and 6″; Bulldog-style grips on 2½″. Available in blue finish only.
Price: **$214.00**

CHARTER ARMS BULLDOG PUG
Caliber: 44 Spec., 5 shot.
Barrel: 2½″.
Weight: 19 oz. **Length:** 7¼″ over-all.
Stocks: Bulldog walnut or Neoprene.
Sights: Ramp front, notch rear.
Features: Shrouded ejector rod; wide trigger and hammer spur. Introduced 1986.
Price: **$234.00**

CHARTER ARMS TARGET BULLDOG
Caliber: 357 Mag. or 44 Spec., 5 shot.
Barrel: 4″.
Weight: 21 oz. **Length:** 9″ over-all.
Stocks: Square butt.
Sights: Blade front, rear adj. for w. and e.
Features: Shrouded barrel and ejector rod. All-steel frame. Introduced 1986.
Price: 357 Mag. **$232.00**
Price: 44 Spec. **$240.00**

CHARTER ARMS POLICE BULLDOG
Caliber: 32 H&R Mag., 38 Special, 6-shot.
Barrel: 4″, 4″ straight taper bull.
Weight: 21 oz. **Length:** 9″ over-all.
Stocks: Hand checkered American walnut; square butt.
Sights: Patridge-type ramp front, notched rear (adjustable on 32 Mag.).
Features: Spring loaded unbreakable beryllium copper firing pin; steel frame; accepts +P ammunition; full length ejection of fired cases.
Price: Blue, 32 Mag. **$208.00**
Price: Blue, 38 Spec. **$201.00**
Price: Stainless steel, 38 Spec. only **$263.00**

ARMSCOR 38 REVOLVER
Caliber: 38 Spec.
Barrel: 4″
Weight: 32 oz.
Stocks: Checkered Philippine mahogany.
Sights: Ramp front, rear adj. for windage.
Features: Ventilated rib; polished blue finish. Introduced 1986. Imported from the Philippines by Pacific International Merchandising Corp.
Price: **$139.95**

ASTRA 357 MAGNUM REVOLVER
Caliber: 357 Magnum, 6-shot.
Barrel: 3″, 4″, 6″, 8½″.
Weight: 40 oz. (6″ bbl.). **Length:** 11¼″ (6″ bbl.).
Stocks: Checkered walnut.
Sights: Fixed front, rear adj. for w. and e.
Features: Swing-out cylinder with countersunk chambers, floating firing pin. Target-type hammer and trigger. Imported from Spain by Interarms.
Price: 3″, 4″, 6″ **$275.00**
Price: 8½″ **$285.00**
Price: 4″, stainless **$305.00**

Charter Arms Stainless Bulldog

Charter Bulldog Pug

Charter Target Bulldog

Charter Arms Police Bulldog

CHARTER ARMS UNDERCOVER REVOLVER
Caliber: 38 Special, 5 shot; 32 S & W Long, 6 shot.
Barrel: 2″, 3″.
Weight: 16 oz. (2″). **Length:** 6¼″ (2″).
Stocks: Checkered walnut.
Sights: Patridge-type ramp front, notched rear.
Features: Wide trigger and hammer spur. Steel frame. Police Undercover, 2″ bbl. (for 38 Spec. + P loads) carry same prices as regular 38 Spec. guns.
Price: Polished Blue $195.00
Price: 32 S & W Long, blue, 2″ $195.00
Price: Stainless, 38 Spec., 2″................................... $252.00

Charter Stainless Off-Duty

Charter Arms Off-Duty Revolver
Similar to the Undercover except 38 Special only, 2″ barrel, Mat-Black non-glare finish. This all-steel gun comes with Red-Dot front sight and choice of smooth or checkered walnut or neoprene grips. Also available in stainless steel. Introduced 1984.
Price: Mat-Black finish $164.00
Price: Stainless steel... $219.00

Charter Arms Pathfinder
Same as Undercover but in 22 LR or 22 Mag., and has 2″, 3″ or 6″ bbl. Fitted with adjustable rear sight, ramp front. Weight 18½ oz.
Price: 22 LR, blue, 3″ $204.00
Price: 22 LR, square butt, 6″ $237.00
Price: Stainless, 22 LR, 3″ $257.00
Price: 2″, either caliber, blue only $204.00

Charter Arms Police Undercover
Similar to the standard Undercover except 2″ barrel only, chambered for the 32 H&R Magnum and 38 Spec. (6-shot). Patridge-type front with fixed square notch rear. Blue finish or stainless steel; checkered walnut grips. Also available with Pocket Hammer. Introduced 1984.
Price: Standard hammer, 32 Mag., blue $198.00
Price: Pocket hammer, 32 Mag., blue $202.00
Price: Standard hammer, 38 Spec., blue..................... $195.00
Price: Pocket hammer, 38 Spec., blue........................ $198.00
Price: Standard hammer, 38 Spec., stainless................. $252.00
Price: Pocket hammer, 38 Spec., stainless................... $256.00

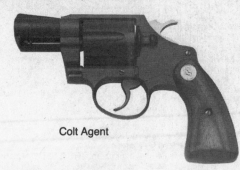

Colt Agent

COLT AGENT L.W.
Caliber: 38 Special, 6-shot.
Barrel: 2″.
Weight: 16¾ ozs. **Length:** 6¾″ over-all.
Stocks: Smooth walnut.
Sights: Fixed.
Features: A no-frills, lightweight version of the Detective Special. Parkerized-type finish. Name re-introduced 1982.
Price: $259.50

Colt Commando Special
Same gun as the Detective Special except comes with rubber grips and matte finish. Introduced 1984.
Price: $299.95

COLT DETECTIVE SPECIAL
Caliber: 38 Special, 6 shot.
Barrel: 2″.
Weight: 21½ oz. **Length:** 6¾″ over-all.
Stocks: Full, checkered walnut, round butt.
Sights: Fixed, ramp front, square notch rear.
Features: Glare-proofed sights, smooth trigger. Nickel finish, hammer shroud available as options.
Price: Blue... $428.50
Price: Nickel $481.50

Colt King Cobra

COLT KING COBRA REVOLVER
Caliber: 357 Magnum, 6 shot.
Barrel: 4″, 6″.
Weight: 42 oz. (4″ bbl.). **Length:** 9″ over-all (4″ bbl.).
Stocks: Checkered rubber.
Sights: Red insert ramp front, adj. white outline rear.
Features: Stainless steel; full length contoured ejector rod housing, barrel rib; matte finish. Introduced 1986.
Price: $389.95

COLT PYTHON REVOLVER
Caliber: 357 Magnum (handles all 38 Spec.), 6 shot.
Barrel: 2½″, 4″, 6″ or 8″, with ventilated rib.
Weight: 38 oz. (4″ bbl.). **Length:** 9¼″ (4″ bbl.).
Stocks: Checkered walnut, target type.
Sights: ⅛″ ramp front, adj. notch rear.
Features: Ventilated rib; grooved, crisp trigger; swing-out cylinder; target hammer.
Price: Blue, 2½″, 4″, 6″, 8″ $687.50
Price: Stainless, 4″, 6″....................................... $775.95
Price: Bright stainless, 2½″, 4″, 6″........................... $786.50

Colt Python 357

CAUTION: PRICES CHANGE. CHECK AT GUNSHOP.

COLT TROOPER MK V REVOLVER
Caliber: 357 Magnum, 6-shot.
Barrel: 4", 6".
Weight: 38 oz. (4"). **Length:** 9" over-all (4").
Stocks: Checkered walnut target-style.
Sights: Orange insert ramp front, adjustable white outline rear.
Features: Vent. rib and shrouded ejector rod. Re-designed action results in short hammer throw, lightened trigger pull and faster lock time. Also has re-designed grip frame. Introduced 1982.
Price: 4" blue $361.50
Price: 4" nickel, ... $395.95
Price: 6", blue $361.50
Price: 6", nickel $398.95

Colt Peacekeeper Revolver
Similar to the Trooper MK V. Available with 4" or 6" barrel. Weighs 42 oz. with 6" barrel; has red insert ramp front sight, white outline fully adjustable rear; rubber "gripper" round bottom combat grips; matte blue finish. Introduced 1985.
Price: 4" or 6" $320.50

COLT DIAMONDBACK REVOLVER
Caliber: 22 LR or 38 Special, 6 shot.
Barrel: 4" or 6" with ventilated rib.
Weight: 31¾ oz. (4" bbl.). **Length:** 9" (4" bbl.)
Stocks: Checkered walnut, target type, square butt.
Sights: Ramp front, adj. notch rear.
Features: Ventilated rib; grooved, crisp trigger; swing-out cylinder; wide hammer spur.
Price: Blue, 4" or 6", 22 or 38 .... $460.50
Price: Nickel, 4" or 6", 22 LR $513.95

F.I.E. "ARMINIUS REVOLVERS"
Caliber: 38 Special, 357 Magnum, 32 S&W, 22 Magnum, 22 LR.
Barrel: 2", 3", 4", 6".
Weight: 35 oz. (6" bbl.). **Length:** 11" (6" bbl. 38).
Stocks: Checkered plastic; walnut optional.
Sights: Ramp front, fixed rear on standard models, w. & e. adj. on target models.
Features: Thumb-release, swing-out cylinder. Ventilated rib, solid frame, swing-out cylinder. Interchangeable 22 Mag. cylinder available with 22 cal. versions. Imported from West Germany by F.I.E. Corp.
Price: .... $99.95 to $224.95

KORTH REVOLVER
Caliber: 22 LR, 22 Mag., 357 Mag., 9mm Parabellum.
Barrel: 3", 4", 6".
Weight: 33 to 38 oz. **Length:** 8" to 11" over-all.
Stocks: Checkered walnut, sport or combat.
Sights: Blade front, rear adjustable for windage and elevation.
Features: Four interchangeable cylinders available. Major parts machined from hammer-forged steel; cylinder gap of .002". High polish blue finish. Presentation models have gold trim. Imported from Germany by Osborne's, Beeman.
Price: Polished (Osborne's) $1,200.00
Price: Matte finish (Osborne's) $1,100.00
Price: From Beeman .... $1,046.00 to $2,096.00

LLAMA COMANCHE III REVOLVERS
Caliber: 357 Mag.
Barrel: 6", 4".
Weight: 28 oz. **Length:** 9¼" (4" bbl.).
Stocks: Checkered walnut.
Sights: Fixed blade front, rear adj. for w. & e.
Features: Ventilated rib, wide spur hammer. Satin chrome finish available. Imported from Spain by Stoeger Industries.
Price: Blue finish $271.95
Price: Satin chrome $324.95

Llama Super Comanche V Revolver
Similar to the Comanche except; large frame, 357 or 44 Mag., 4", 6" or 8½" barrel only; 6-shot cylinder; smooth, extra wide trigger; wide spur hammer; over-size walnut, target-style grips. Weight is 3 lbs., 2 ozs. Blue finish only.
Price: 44 Mag. $358.95
Price: 357 Mag. $378.95

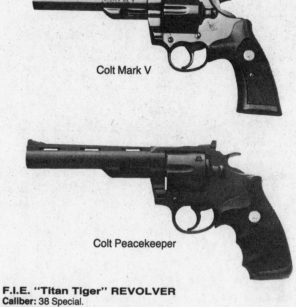

Colt Mark V

Colt Peacekeeper

F.I.E. "Titan Tiger" REVOLVER
Caliber: 38 Special.
Barrel: 2" or 4".
Weight: 27 oz. **Length:** 6¼" over-all. (2" bbl.)
Stocks: Checkered plastic, Bulldog style. Walnut optional ($15.95).
Sights: Fixed.
Features: Thumb-release swing-out cylinder, one stroke ejection. Made in U.S.A. by F.I.E. Corp.
Price: Blue. $129.95

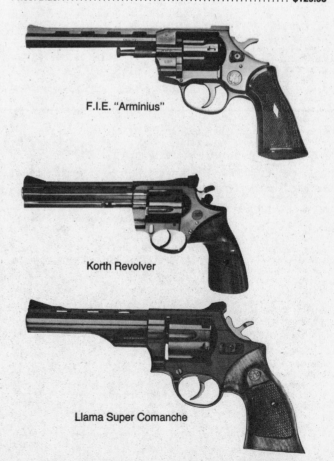

F.I.E. "Arminius"

Korth Revolver

Llama Super Comanche

MANURHIN MR 73 SPORT REVOLVER
Caliber: 32 S&W Long, 357 Magnum, 6-shot.
Barrel: 5.25".
Weight: 37 oz. **Length:** 10.4" over-all.
Stocks: Checkered walnut.
Sights: Blade front, fully adjustable rear.
Features: Double action with adjustable trigger. High-polish blue finish, "Straw" colored hammer and trigger. Comes with sight adjusting tool. Imported from France by Manurhin International, Inc. Introduced 1984.
Price: **$750.00**

ROSSI MODEL 68 REVOLVER
Caliber: 38 Spec.
Barrel: 2", 3".
Weight: 22 oz.
Stocks: Checkered wood.
Sights: Ramp front, low profile adj. rear.
Features: All-steel frame. Thumb latch operated swing-out cylinder. Introduced 1978. Imported from Brazil by Interarms.
Price: 38, blue **$150.00**
Price: M68/2 (2" barrel) **$160.00**

ROSSI MODEL 88, 89 STAINLESS REVOLVERS
Caliber: 32 S&W, 38 Spec., 5-shot.
Barrel: 2", 3".
Weight: 22 oz. **Length:** 7.5" over-all.
Stocks: Checkered wood, service-style.
Sights: Ramp front, square notch rear drift adjustable for windage.
Features: All metal parts except springs are of 440 stainless steel; matte finish; small frame for concealability. Introduced 1983. Imported from Brazil by Interarms.
Price: 3" barrel **$175.00**
Price: M88/2 (2" barrel) **$185.00**
Price: M89 (32 cal.) **$160.00**

ROSSI SPORTSMAN'S 22 REVOLVER
Caliber: 22 LR, 6 shot.
Barrel: 4".
Weight: 30 oz. **Length:** 9" over-all.
Stocks: Checkered wood.
Sights: Orange-insert ramp front, fully adj. square notch rear.
Features: All stainless steel. Shrouded ejector rod; heavy barrel; integral sight rib. Introduced 1986. Imported from Brazil by Interarms.
Price: **$205.00**

RUGER GP-100 REVOLVERS
Caliber: 357 Magnum, 6 shot.
Barrel: 4" (heavy), 6".
Weight: About 40 oz. **Length:** 9.3" over-all (4" bbl.).
Stocks: Ruger Cushioned Grip (live rubber with Goncalo Alves inserts).
Sights: Interchangeable front blade, fully adj. rear
Features: Uses all new action and frame incorporating improvements and features of both the Security-Six and Redhawk revolvers. Full length ejector shroud. Satin and polished blue finish. Introduced 1986.
Price: GP-141 (4" bbl.) **$375.00**
Price: GP-160 (6" bbl.) **$375.00**

RUGER POLICE SERVICE-SIX 107, 108, 707, 708
Caliber: 357 (Model 107, 707), 38 Spec. (Model 108, 708), 6-shot.
Barrel: 2¾" or 4".
Weight: 33½ oz. (4" bbl.). **Length:** 9¼" (4 bbl.) over-all.
Stocks: Checkered rubber or Goncalo Alves.
Sights: Fixed, non-adjustable.
Features: Solid frame; barrel, rib and ejector rod housing combined in one unit. All steel construction Field strips without tools.
Price: Model 107 (357) 2¾" and 4" (SDA 32, SDA 34) **$287.50**
Price: Model 108 (38) 4" (SDA 84) **$287.50**
Price: Mod. 707 (357), Stainless, 4", Goncalo Alves or rubber grips (GF 34, GF 34P) **$310.00**
Price: Mod. 708 (38), Stainless, 4", Goncalo Alves or rubber grips (GF 84, GF 84P) **$310.00**

Rossi Model 88 Stainless

Rossi Model 85 Stainless

ROSSI MODEL 951 REVOLVER
Caliber: 38 Special, 6 shot.
Barrel: 4", vent. rib.
Weight: 30 oz. **Length:** 9" over-all.
Stocks: Checkered hardwood, combat-style.
Sights: Colored insert front, fully adjustable rear.
Features: Polished blue finish, shrouded ejector rod. Medium-size frame. Introduced 1985. Imported from Brazil by Interarms.
Price: M951 .... **$200.00**
Price: M851 (as above, stainless) **$220.00**
Price: M85 (as above, 3" barrel) **$220.00**
Price: M941 (as above, solid rib) **$185.00**
Price: M841 (as above, stainless steel) **$205.00**
Price: M94 (3" barrel, solid rib) **$185.00**

Ruger GP-100

Ruger Model 708

CAUTION: PRICES CHANGE. CHECK AT GUNSHOP.

Ruger Speed-Six

Ruger Redhawk

SMITH & WESSON M&P Model 10 REVOLVER
Caliber: 38 Special, 6 shot.
Barrel: 2″.
Weight: 30½ oz. (4″ bbl.). **Length:** 9¼″ (4″ bbl.).
Stocks: Checkered walnut, Service. Round or square butt.
Sights: Fixed, ramp front, square notch rear.
Price: Blued $282.00
Price: Nickeled $303.00

Smith & Wesson 38 M&P Heavy Barrel Model 10
Same as regular M&P except: 3″ or 4″ heavy ribbed bbl. with ramp front sight, square rear, square butt, wgt. 33½ oz.
Price: Blued $282.00
Price: Nickeled $303.00

SMITH & WESSON 38 M&P AIRWEIGHT Model 12
Caliber: 38 Special, 6 shot.
Barrel: 2″ or 4″.
Weight: 18 oz. (2″ bbl.). **Length:** 6¹⁵⁄₁₆″ over-all (2″ bbl.).
Stocks: Checkered walnut, Magna. Round or square butt.
Sights: Fixed, serrated ramp front, square notch rear.
Price: Blued $320.50

SMITH & WESSON Model 13 H.B. M&P
Caliber: 357 and 38 Special, 6 shot.
Barrel: 3″ or 4″.
Weight: 34 oz. **Length:** 9⁵⁄₁₆″ over-all (4″ bbl.).
Stocks: Checkered walnut, service.
Sights: ⅛″ serrated ramp front, fixed square notch rear.
Features: Heavy barrel, K-frame, square butt (4″), round butt (3″).
Price: Blue, M-13 .... $282.00
Price: Nickel $303.00
Price: Model 65, as above in stainless steel $305.00

SMITH & WESSON MODEL 15 COMBAT MASTERPIECE
Caliber: 38 Special, 6 shot.
Barrel: 2″, 4″,6″, 8⅜″.
Weight: 32 oz. **Length:** 9⁵⁄₁₆″ (4″ bbl.).
Stocks: Checkered walnut. Grooved tangs.
Sights: Front, Baughman Quick Draw on ramp, micro click rear, adjustable for w. and e.
Price: Blued, M-15, 2″ or 4″ $321.00
Price: Nickel M-15, 2″ or 4″ $343.50

RUGER SPEED-SIX Models 207, 208, 737, 738
Caliber: 357 (Model 207), 38 Spec. (Model 208), 6-shot.
Barrel: 2¾″ or 4″.
Weight: 31 oz. (2¾″ bbl.). **Length:** 7¾″ over-all (2¾″ bbl.).
Stocks: Goncalo Alves or checkered rubber with finger grooves.
Sights: Fixed, non-adjustable.
Features: Same basic mechanism as Security-Six. Hammer without spur available on special order. All steel construction. Music wire coil springs used throughout.
Price: Model 207, 357 Mag., 2¾″, 4″, Goncalo Alves or checkered rubber grips (SS 32, SS 32P, SS 34) $292.00
Price: Model 208, 38 Spec. only, 2¾″, Goncalo Alves or checkered grips (SS 82) $292.00
Price: Mod. 737, 357 Mag., stainless, 2¾″, 4″, Goncalo Alves or checkered rubber grips (GS 32, GS 32P, GS 34) $320.00
Price: Mod. 738, 38 Spec. only, stainless, 2¾″, Goncalo Alves grips (GS 82) $320.00

RUGER REDHAWK
Caliber: 41 Mag., 44 Rem. Mag., 6-shot.
Barrel: 5½″, 7½″.
Weight: About 54 oz. (7½″ bbl.). **Length:** 13″ over-all (7½″ barrel).
Stocks: Square butt Goncalo Alves.
Sights: Interchangeable Patridge-type front, rear adj. for w. & e.
Features: Stainless steel, brushed satin finish, or blued ordnance steel. Has a 9½″ sight radius. Introduced 1979.
Price: Blued, 41 Mag., 44 Mag., 5½″, 7½″ $397.00
Price: Blued, 41 Mag., 44 Mag., 7½″, with scope mount, rings $430.00
Price: Stainless, 41 Mag., 44 Mag., 5½″, 7½″ $435.00
Price: Stainless, 41 Mag., 44 Mag., 7½″, with scope mount, rings ... $470.00

S&W Model 10-H.B.

S&W Model 13

SMITH & WESSON MODEL 17 K-22 MASTERPIECE
Caliber: 22 LR, 6-shot.
Barrel: 4″, 6″, 8⅜″.
Weight: 39 oz. (6″ bbl.). **Length:** 11⅛″ over-all.
Stocks: Checkered walnut, service.
Sights: Patridge front with 6″, 8⅜″, serrated on 4″, S&W micro. click rear adjustable for windage and elevation.
Features: Grooved tang, polished blue finish.
Price: 6″ $363.50
Price: 8¾″ bbl. $376.00
Price: Model 48, as above in 22 Mag., 4″ or 6″ $320.50
Price: 8⅜″ bbl. $335.00

SMITH & WESSON 357 COMBAT MAGNUM Model 19
Caliber: 357 Magnum and 38 Special, 6 shot.
Barrel: 2½", 4", 6".
Weight: 36 oz. **Length:** 9⁹⁄₁₆" (4" bbl.).
Stocks: Checkered Goncalo Alves, target. Grooved tangs.
Sights: Front, ⅛" Baughman Quick Draw on 2½" or 4" bbl., Patridge on 6" bbl., micro click rear adjustable for w. and e.
Price: S&W Bright Blue or Nickel, adj. sights, from $285.50

S&W Model 19

SMITH & WESSON MODEL 25 REVOLVER
Caliber: 45 Colt, 6-shot.
Barrel: 4", 6", 8⅜".
Weight: About 46 oz. **Length:** 11⅜" over-all (6" bbl.).
Stocks: Checkered Goncalo Alves, target-type.
Sights: S&W red ramp front, S&W micrometer click rear with white outline.
Features: Available in Bright Blue or nickel finish; target trigger, target hammer. Contact S&W for complete price list.
Price: 4", 6", blue or nickel $371.50
Price: 8⅜", blue or nickel $385.00

S&W Model 25

SMITH & WESSON 357 MAGNUM M-27 REVOLVER
Caliber: 357 Magnum and 38 Special, 6 shot.
Barrel: 4", 6", 8⅜".
Weight: 45½ oz. (6" bbl.). **Length:** 11⁵⁄₁₆" (6" bbl.).
Stocks: Checkered walnut, Magna. Grooved tangs and trigger.
Sights: Serrated ramp front, micro click rear, adjustable for w. and e.
Price: S&W Bright Blue or Nickel, 4", 6" $350.00
Price: 8⅜" bbl., sq. butt, target hammer, trigger, stocks $375.50

SMITH & WESSON HIGHWAY PATROLMAN Model 28
Caliber: 357 Magnum and 38 Special, 6 shot.
Barrel: 4", 6".
Weight: 44 oz. (6" bbl.). **Length:** 11¹⁄₁₆" (6" bbl.).
Stocks: Checkered walnut. Grooved tangs and trigger.
Sights: Front, Baughman Quick Draw, on ramp, micro click rear, adjustable for w. and e.
Price: S&W Satin Blue, sandblasted frame edging and barrel top . . . $305.50
Price: With target stocks $327.00

S&W Model 29

SMITH & WESSON 44 MAGNUM Model 29 REVOLVER
Caliber: 44 Magnum, 44 Special or 44 Russian, 6 shot.
Barrel: 4", 6", 8⅜", 10⅝".
Weight: 47 oz. (6" bbl.), 44 oz. (4" bbl.). **Length:** 11⅜" (6½" bbl.).
Stocks: Oversize target type, checkered Goncalo Alves. Tangs and target trigger grooved, checkered target hammer.
Sights: ⅛" red ramp front, micro click rear, adjustable for w. and e.
Features: Includes presentation case.
Price: S&W Bright Blue or Nickel 4", 6" $409.00
Price: 8⅜" bbl., blue or nickel $423.50
Price: 10⅝", blue only (AF) $455.50
Price: Model 629 (stainless steel), 4", 6" $472.50
Price: Model 629, 8⅜" barrel $488.50

SMITH & WESSON 32 REGULATION POLICE Model 31
Caliber: 32 S&W Long, 6 shot.
Barrel: 2", 3".
Weight: 18¾ oz. (3" bbl.). **Length:** 7½" (3" bbl.).
Stocks: Checkered walnut, Magna.
Sights: Fixed, ¹⁄₁₀" serrated ramp front, square notch rear.
Features: Blued
Price: $313.50

S&W Model 31

SMITH & WESSON 1953 Model 34, 22/32 KIT GUN
Caliber: 22 LR, 6 shot.
Barrel: 2", 4".
Weight: 24 oz. (4" bbl.). **Length:** 8⅜" (4" bbl. and round butt).
Stocks: Checkered walnut, round or square butt.
Sights: Front, serrated ramp, micro. click rear, adjustable for w. & e.
Price: Blued $307.50
Price: Nickeled $332.50
Price: Model 63, as above in stainless, 4" $355.50

Smith & Wesson Model 650/651 Magnum Kit Gun
Similar to the Models 34 and 63 except chambered for the 22 WMR. Model 650 has 3" barrel, round butt and fixed sights; Model 651 has 4" barrel, square butt and adjustable sights. Both guns made of stainless steel. Introduced 1983.
Price: Model 650 . . . . $305.00
Price: Model 651 . . . . $345.00

CAUTION: PRICES CHANGE. CHECK AT GUNSHOP.

SMITH & WESSON BODYGUARD MODEL 38
Caliber: 38 Special; 5 shot, double action revolver.
Barrel: 2″.
Weight: 14½ oz. **Length:** 6⁵⁄₁₆″ over-all.
Stocks: Checkered walnut.
Sights: Fixed serrated ramp front, square notch rear.
Features: Alloy frame; internal hammer.
Price: Blued **$327.50**
Price: Nickeled **$368.00**

SMITH & WESSON 38 CHIEFS SPECIAL & AIRWEIGHT
Caliber: 38 Special, 5 shot.
Barrel: 2″, 3″.
Weight: 19½ oz. (2″ bbl.); 13½ oz. (AIRWEIGHT). **Length:** 6½″ (2″ bbl. and round butt).
Stocks: Checkered walnut, round or square butt.
Sights: Fixed, serrated ramp front, square notch rear.
Price: Blued, standard Model 36 .... **$274.00**
Price: As above, nickel **$296.00**
Price: Blued, Airweight Model 37 .... **$294.00**
Price: As above, nickel **$331.00**

Smith & Wesson 60 Chiefs Special Stainless
Same as Model 36 except: 2″ bbl. and round butt only.
Price: Stainless steel **$332.00**

Smith & Wesson Bodyguard Model 49, 649 Revolvers
Same as Model 38 except steel construction, weight 20½ oz.
Price: Blued, Model 49 .... **$292.00**
Price: Nickeled, Model 49 .... **$316.50**
Price: Stainless Model 649 .... **$346.00**

SMITH & WESSON 41 MAGNUM Model 57 REVOLVER
Caliber: 41 Magnum, 6 shot.
Barrel: 4″, 6″ or 8⅜″.
Weight: 48 oz. (6″ bbl.). **Length:** 11⅜″ (6″ bbl.).
Stocks: Oversize target type checkered Goncalo Alves.
Sights: ⅛″ red ramp front, micro. click rear, adj. for w. and e.
Price: S&W Bright Blue or Nickel 4″, 6″ **$371.00**
Price: 8⅜″ bbl. **$384.50**
Price: Stainless, Model 657, 4″, 6″ **$422.50**
Price: As above, 8⅜″ **$437.50**

SMITH & WESSON MODEL 64 STAINLESS M&P
Caliber: 38 Special, 6-shot.
Barrel: 4″.
Weight: 34 oz. **Length:** 9⁵⁄₁₆″ over-all.
Stocks: Checkered walnut, service style.
Sights: Fixed, ⅛″ serrated ramp front, square notch rear.
Features: Satin finished stainless steel, square butt.
Price: **$305.00**

SMITH & WESSON MODEL 66 STAINLESS COMBAT MAGNUM
Caliber: 357 Magnum and 38 Special, 6-shot.
Barrel: 2½″, 4″, 6″.
Weight: 36 oz. **Length:** 9⁹⁄₁₆″ over-all.
Stocks: Checkered Goncalo Alves target.
Sights: Front, Baughman Quick Draw on ramp, micro clock rear adj. for windage and elevation.
Features: Satin finish stainless steel.
Price: **$329.50**

SMITH & WESSON MODEL 67 K-38 STAINLESS COMBAT MASTERPIECE
Caliber: 38 Special, 6-shot.
Barrel: 4″.
Weight: 32 oz. (loaded). **Length:** 9⁵⁄₁₆″ over-all.
Stocks: Checkered walnut, service style.
Sights: Front, Baughman Quick Draw on ramp, micro click rear adj. for windage and elevation.
Features: Stainless steel. Square butt frame with grooved tangs.
Price: **$339.00**

S&W Model 649

S&W Model 57

Consult our Directory pages for the location of firms mentioned.

S&W Model 586

SMITH & WESSON MODEL 586 Distinguished Combat Magnum
Caliber: 357 Magnum.
Barrel: 4″, 6″, 8⅜″, full shroud.
Weight: 46 oz. (6″), 41 oz. (4″).
Stocks: Goncalo Alves target-type with speed loader cutaway.
Sights: Baughman red ramp front, four-position click-adj. front, S&W micrometer click rear (or fixed).
Features: Uses new L-frame, but takes all K-frame grips. Full length ejector rod shroud. Smooth combat-type trigger, semi-target type hammer. Trigger stop on 6″ models. Also available in stainless as Model 686. Introduced 1981.
Price: Model 586 (blue only) **$340.00**
Price: Model 586, nickel **$340.00**
Price: Model 686 (stainless) **$374.00**
Price: Model 581 (fixed sight, blue), 4″ **$313.50**
Price: Model 581, nickel **$342.00**
Price: Model 681 (fixed sight, stainless) **$324.00**
Price: Model 586, 6″, adj. front sight, blue **$392.00**
Price: As above, 8⅜″ **$403.50**
Price: Model 686, 6″, adj. front sight **$413.50**
Price: As above, 8⅜″ **$426.50**

SMITH & WESSON MODEL 624 REVOLVER
Caliber: 44 Special, 6 shot.
Barrel: 4″ or 6½″.
Weight: 41½ oz. (4″ bbl.). **Length:** 9½″ over-all (4″ bbl.)
Stocks: Checkered Goncalo Alves, target-type.
Sights: Black ramp front, fully adjustable micrometer click rear adj. for w. & e.
Features: Limited production of 10,000 guns. Stainless version of the Model 24. The 6½″ version has target hammer and trigger. Introduced 1985.
Price: 4″ barrel **$449.50**
Price: 6½″ barrel **$463.50**

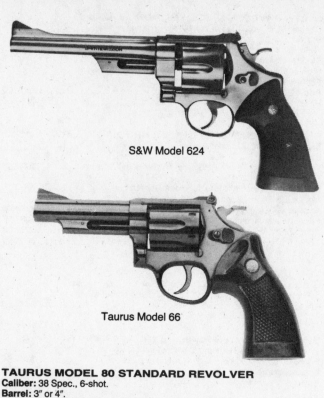

S&W Model 624

TAURUS MODEL 66 REVOLVER
Caliber: 357 Magnum, 6-shot.
Barrel: 3″, 4″, 6″.
Weight: 35 ozs.
Stocks: Checkered walnut, target-type. Standard stocks on 3″.
Sights: Serrated ramp front, micro click rear adjustable for w. and e.
Features: Wide target-type hammer spur, floating firing pin, heavy barrel with shrouded ejector rod. Introduced 1978. From Taurus International.
Price: Blue... **$220.15**
Price: Satin nickel **$230.00**
Price: Model 65 (similar to M66 except has a fixed rear sight and ramp front), blue.. **$204.50**
Price: Model 65, satin nickel **$215.00**

Taurus Model 66

TAURUS MODEL 73 SPORT REVOLVER
Caliber: 32 S&W Long, 6-shot.
Barrel: 3″, heavy.
Weight: 22 oz. **Length:** 8¼″ over-all.
Stocks: Oversize target-type, checkered Brazilian walnut.
Sights: Ramp front, notch rear.
Features: Imported from Brazil by Taurus International.
Price: Blue.. **$186.50**
Price: Satin nickel **$202.80**

TAURUS MODEL 80 STANDARD REVOLVER
Caliber: 38 Spec., 6-shot.
Barrel: 3″ or 4″.
Weight: 31 oz. (4″ bbl.). **Length:** 9¼″ over-all (4″ bbl.).
Stocks: Checkered Brazilian walnut.
Sights: Serrated ramp front, square notch rear.
Features: Imported from Brazil by Taurus International.
Price: Blue...................................... **$180.50**
Price: Satin nickel **$191.50**

TAURUS MODEL 82 HEAVY BARREL REVOLVER
Caliber: 38 Spec., 6-shot.
Barrel: 3″ or 4″, heavy.
Weight: 33 oz. (4″ bbl.). **Length:** 9¼″ over-all (4″ bbl.).
Stocks: Checkered Brazilian walnut.
Sights: Serrated ramp front, square notch rear.
Features: Imported from Brazil by Taurus International.
Price: Blue, about **$180.50**
Price: Satin nickel, about **$191.5**

Taurus Model 82

TAURUS MODEL 83 REVOLVER
Caliber: 38 Spec., 6-shot.
Barrel: 4″ only, heavy.
Weight: 34½ oz.
Stocks: Over-size checkered walnut.
Sights: Ramp front, micro. click rear adj. for w. & e.
Features: Blue or nickel finish. Introduced 1977. Imported from Brazil by Taurus International.
Price: Blue.. **$190.00**
Price: Satin nickel **$199.90**

Taurus Model 83

UBERTI "INSPECTOR" REVOLVER
Caliber: 32 S&W Long, 38 Spec., 6 shot.
Barrel: 3″, 4″, 6″.
Weight: 24 oz. (3″ bbl.). **Length:** 8″ over-all (3″ bbl.).
Stocks: Checkered walnut.
Sights: Blade on ramp front, fixed or adj. rear.
Features: Blue or chrome finish. Introduced 1986. Imported from Italy by Allen Fire Arms.
Price: Blue, fixed sights **$279.00**
Price: Blue, adj. sights **$289.00**
Price: Chrome, fixed sights **$289.00**
Price: Chrome, adj. sights **$309.00**

TAURUS MODEL 85 REVOLVER
Caliber: 38 Spec., 5-shot.
Barrel: 2″, 3″.
Weight: 21 oz.
Stocks: Checkered walnut.
Sights: Ramp front, square notch rear.
Features: Blue, satin nickel finish or stainless steel. Introduced 1980. Imported from Brazil by Taurus International.
Price: Blue.. **$189.90**
Price: Satin nickel **$204.00**
Price: Stainless steel............................... **$240.90**

CAUTION: PRICES CHANGE. CHECK AT GUNSHOP.

Dan Wesson 44 Magnum

DAN WESSON MODEL 41V & MODEL 44V
Caliber: 41 Mag., 44 Mag., six-shot.
Barrel: 4″, 6″, 8″, 10″; interchangeable.
Weight: 48 oz. (4″). **Length:** 12″ over-all (6″ bbl.).
Stocks: Smooth.
Sights: ⅛″ serrated front, white outline rear adjustable for windage and elevation.
Features: Available in blue or stainless steel. Smooth, wide trigger with adjustable over-travel; wide hammer spur. Available in Pistol Pac set also.
Price: 41 Mag., 4″, vent.. $373.40
Price: As above except in stainless $416.05
Price: 44 Mag., 4″, blue.. $373.40
Price: As above except in stainless $416.05

Dan Wesson 9-2, 15-2 & 32M Revolvers
Same as Models 8-2 and 14-2 except they have adjustable sight. Model 9-2 chambered for 38 Special, Model 15-2 for 357 Magnum. Model 32M is chambered for 32 H&R Mag. Same specs and prices as for 15-2 guns. Available in blue or stainless. Contact Dan Wesson for complete price list.
Price: Model 9-2 or 15-2, 2½″, blue $272.50
Price: As above except in stainless $306.55
Price: Model 15-2, 8″, blue...................................... $297.90
Price: As above, with 15″ barrel, blue........................ $365.25

Dan Wesson Model 32M

DAN WESSON MODEL 22 REVOLVER
Caliber: 22 LR, 22 Mag., six-shot.
Barrel: 2½″, 4″, 6″, 8″, 10″; interchangeable.
Weight: 36 oz. (2½″), 44 oz. (6″). **Length:** 9¼″ over-all (4″ barrel).
Stocks: Checkered; undercover, service or over-size target.
Sights: ⅛″ serrated, interchangeable front, white outline rear adjustable for windage and elevation.
Features: Built on the same frame as the Dan Wesson 357; smooth, wide trigger with over-travel adjustment, wide spur hammer, with short double-action travel. Available in brite blue or stainless steel. Contact Dan Wesson for complete price list.
Price: 2½″ bbl., blue $272.50
Price: As above, stainless $306.55
Price: With 4″, vent. rib, blue $300.85
Price: As above, stainless $335.15
Price: Stainless Pistol Pac, 22 LR.............................. $525.95

DAN WESSON MODEL 8-2 & MODEL 14-2
Caliber: 38 Special (Model 8-2); 357 (14-2), both 6-shot.
Barrel: 2½″, 4″, 6″, 8″; interchangeable.
Weight: 30 oz. (2½″). **Length:** 9¼″ over-all (4″ bbl.).
Stocks: Checkered, interchangeable.
Sights: ⅛″ serrated front, fixed rear.
Features: Interchangeable barrels and grips; smooth, wide trigger; wide hammer spur with short double action travel. Available in stainless or brite blue. Contact Dan Wesson for complete price list.
Price: Model 8-2, 2½″, blue $220.75
Price: As above except in stainless $253.65
Price: Model 14-2, 4″, blue...................................... $227.15
Price: As above except in stainless $259.20
Price: Model 714-2 Pistol Pac, stainless $430.65

HANDGUNS—SINGLE ACTION REVOLVERS

Allen Buckhorn

ALLEN BUCKHORN SINGLE ACTION REVOLVERS
Caliber: 44 Magnum, 44-40, 6 shot.
Barrel: 4¾″, 6″, 7½″.
Weight: 44 oz. (6″ bbl.). **Length:** 11¾″ over-all (6″ bbl.).
Stocks: One-piece smooth walnut.
Sights: Blade front, groove rear.
Features: Steel or brass backstrap and trigger guard; color case-hardened frame, blued cylinder and barrel. Imported by Allen Fire Arms.
Price: Fixed sights $299.00
Price: With convertible cylinder................................ $329.00
Price: Target model (ramp front, adj. rear sights, flat-top frame)..... $329.00
Price: Convertible target model................................. $349.00
Price: Buntline (18″ bbl.)....................................... $349.00

ALLEN CATTLEMAN SINGLE ACTION REVOLVERS
Caliber: 22 LR, 22 Mag., 38 Spec., 357 Mag., 44-40, 45 Colt, 6 shot.
Barrel: 4¾″, 5½″, 7½″.
Weight: 38 oz. (5½″ bbl.). **Length:** 10¾″ over-all (5½″ bbl.).
Stocks: One-piece smooth walnut.
Sights: Blade front, fixed groove rear.
Features: Steel or brass backstrap, trigger guard; color case-hardened frame, blued barrel, cylinder, polished hammer flats. Imported by Allen Fire Arms.
Price: Fixed sights $289.00
Price: Target (flat-top frame, fully adj. rear sight)............ $299.00
Price: Buntline (18″ bbl., 357, 44-40, 45 Colt only)............ $299.00
Price: Sheriff's model (3″ bbl., 44-40)......................... $289.00

Allen Cattleman

CAUTION: PRICES CHANGE. CHECK AT GUNSHOP.

ALLEN 1875 ARMY "OUTLAW" REVOLVER
Caliber: 357 Mag., 44-40, 45 Colt, 6 shot.
Barrel: 7½".
Weight: 44 oz. **Length:** 13¾" over-all.
Stocks: Smooth walnut.
Sights: Blade front, notch rear.
Features: Replica of the 1875 Remington S.A. Army revolver. Brass trigger guard, color case-hardened frame, rest blued. Imported by Allen Fire Arms.
Price: $279.00

Century Model 100

CENTURY MODEL 100 SINGLE ACTION
Caliber: 375 Win., 444 Marlin, 45-70.
Barrel: 6½", 8" (standard), 10", 12". Other lengths to order.
Weight: 6 lbs. (loaded). **Length:** 15" over-all (8" bbl.).
Stocks: Smooth walnut.
Sights: Ramp front, Millett adj. square notch rear.
Features: Highly polished high tensile strength manganese bronze frame, blue cylinder and barrel; coil spring trigger mechanism. Introduced 1975. Made in U.S. From Century Gun Dist., Inc.
Price: 8" barrel $600.00
Price: 10", 12" barrel $665.00

COLT SINGLE ACTION ARMY REVOLVER
Caliber: 357 Magnum, 44 Spec., 44-40, or 45 Colt, 6 shot.
Barrel: 3", 4¾", 5½", 7½", 10", 12".
Weight: 37 oz. (5½" bbl.). **Length:** 10⅞" (5½" bbl.)
Stocks: Black composite rubber with eagle and shield crest.
Sights: Fixed. Grooved top strap, blade front.
Features: Blue with color case-hardened frame or all nickel with walnut stocks. Available in limited quantities through the Colt Custom Shop only.
Price: From $1,000.00

COLT NEW FRONTIER 22
Caliber: 22 LR, 6-shot.
Barrel: 4¾", 6", 7½".
Weight: 29½ oz. (4¾" bbl.). **Length:** 9½" over-all (4¾" bbl.).
Stocks: Black composite rubber.
Sights: Ramp-style front, fully adjustable rear.
Features: Cross-bolt safety. Available in blue only. Re-introduced 1982.
Price: 4¾", 6", 7½", blue...................... $180.95

Colt New Frontier

Dakota Bisley

DAKOTA BISLEY MODEL SINGLE ACTION
Caliber: 22 LR, 22 Mag., 32-30, 32 H&R mag., 357, 30 Carbine, 38-40, 44 Spec., 44-40, 45 Colt, 45 ACP.
Barrel: 4⅝", 5½", 7½".
Weight: 37 oz. **Length:** 10½" over-all with 5½" barrel.
Stocks: Smooth walnut.
Sights: Blade front, fixed groove rear.
Features: Colt-type firing pin in hammer; color case-hardened frame, blue barrel, cylinder, steel backstrap and trigger guard. Also avail. in nickel, factory engraved. Imported by E.M.F.
Price: All calibers, bbl. lengths................... $495.00
Price: Combo models — 22 LR/22 Mag., 32-20/32 H&R, 357/9mm, 44-40/44 Spec., 45 Colt/45 ACP.............. $560.00
Price: Nickel, all cals. $540.00
Price: Engraved, all cals., lengths............... $680.00

DAKOTA 1875 OUTLAW REVOLVER
Caliber: 357, 44-40, 45 Colt.
Barrel: 7½".
Weight: 46 oz. **Length:** 13½" over-all.
Stocks: Smooth walnut.
Sights: Blade front, fixed groove rear.
Features: Authentic copy of 1875 Remington with firing pin in hammer; color case-hardened frame, blue cylinder, barrel, steel backstrap and brass trigger guard. Also available in nickel, factory engraved. Imported by E.M.F.
Price: All calibers.............................. $395.00
Price: Nickel $470.00
Price: Engraved $600.00

Dakota 1890 Police

DAKOTA SINGLE ACTION REVOLVERS
Caliber: 22 LR, 22 Mag., 357 Mag., 30 Carbine, 32-20, 32 H&R Mag., 38-40, 44-40, 44 Spec., 45 Colt, 45 ACP.
Barrel: 3½", 4⅝", 5½", 7½", 12", 16¼".
Weight: 45 oz. **Length:** 13" over-all (7½" bbl.).
Stocks: Smooth walnut.
Sights: Blade front, fixed rear.
Features: Colt-type hammer with firing pin, color case-hardened frame, blue barrel and cylinder, brass grip frame and trigger guard. Available in blue or nickel plated, plain or engraved. Imported by E.M.F.
Price: 22 LR, 30 Car., 357, 44-40, 45 L.C., 4⅝", 5½", 7½".......... $395.00
Price: 22 LR/22 Mag., 45 Colt/45 ACP, 32-20/32 H&R, 357/9mm, 44-40/44 Spec., 5½", 7½"......................... $495.00
Price: 357, 44-40, 45, 12"...................... $450.00
Price: 357, 44-40, 45, 3½"...................... $495.00

Dakota 1890 Police Revolver
Similar to the 1875 Outlaw except has 5½" barrel, weighs 40 oz., with 12½" over-all length. Has lanyard ring in butt. Calibers 357, 44-40, 45 Colt. Imported by E.M.F.
Price: All calibers.............................. $425.00
Price: Nickel $490.00
Price: Engraved $625.00

CAUTION: PRICES CHANGE. CHECK AT GUNSHOP.

F.I.E. "TEXAS RANGER" REVOLVER

Caliber: 22 LR, 22 Mag.
Barrel: 4¾", 6½", 9",.
Weight: 31 oz. (4¾" bbl.). **Length:** 10" over-all.
Stocks: American walnut.
Sights: Blade front, notch rear.
Features: Single-action, blue/black finish. Introduced 1983. Made in the U.S. by F.I.E.

Price: 22 LR, 4¾" $69.95
Price: As above, convertible (22 LR/22 Mag.) $86.95
Price: 22 LR, 6½" $75.95
Price: As above, convertible (22 LR/22 Mag.). $92.95
Price: 22 LR, 9" $84.95
Price: As above, convertible (22 LR/22 Mag.) $102.95

F.I.E. "Texas Ranger"

F.I.E. "Little Ranger" Revolver

Similar to the "Texas Ranger" except has 3¼" barrel, birdshead grips. Introduced 1986. Made in U.S.
Price: 22 LR $75.95
Price: 22 LR/22 Mag. convertible $94.95

F.I.E. "Little Ranger"

F.I.E. "HOMBRE" SINGLE ACTION REVOLVER

Caliber: 357 Mag., 44 Mag., 45 LC.
Barrel: 6" or 7½".
Weight: 45 oz. (6" bbl.).
Stocks: Smooth walnut with medallion.
Sights: Blade front, grooved topstrap (fixed) rear.
Features: Color case hardened frame. Bright blue finish. Super-smooth action. Introduced 1979. Imported from West Germany by F.I.E. Corp.

Price: 357, 45 Colt $179.95
Price: 44 Mag. $179.95
Price: 357, 45 Colt, brass backstrap and trigger guard $199.95
Price: As above, 44 Magnum. $199.95
Price: 357, 45 Colt, 24K gold plated $229.95
Price: As above, 44 Magnum. $229.95

F.I.E. "Hombre"

F.I.E. "Buffalo Scout"

F.I.E. "BUFFALO SCOUT" REVOLVER

Caliber: 22 LR/22 Mag.
Barrel: 4¾".
Weight: 32 oz. **Length:** 10" over-all.
Stocks: Black checkered nylon, walnut optional.
Sights: Blade front, fixed rear.
Features: Slide spring ejector. Blue, chrome, gold or blue with gold backstrap and trigger guard models available.

Price: Blued, 22 LR, 4¾" $62.95
Price: Blue, 22 convertible, 4¾" $79.95
Price: Chrome or blue/gold, 22 LR, 4¾" $74.95
Price: Chrome or blue/gold, convertible, 4¾" $91.95
Price: Gold, 22 convertible, 4¾" $124.95

Freedom Arms 454 Casull

Freedom Arms Mini Revolver

FREEDOM ARMS 454 CASULL

Caliber: 44 Mag., 45 Colt, 454 Casull, 5-shot.
Barrel: 4¾", 6", 7½", 10", 12".
Weight: 50 oz. **Length:** 14" over-all (7½" bbl.).
Stocks: Impregnated hardwood.
Sights: Blade front, notch or adjustable rear.
Features: All stainless steel construction; sliding bar safety system. Made in U.S.A.

Price: Fixed sight $795.00
Price: Adjustable sight $895.00

FREEDOM ARMS MINI REVOLVER

Caliber: 22 Short, Long, Long Rifle, 5-shot, 22 Mag., 4-shot.
Barrel: 1", 1¾", 3".
Weight: 4 oz. **Length:** 4" over-all.
Stocks: Black ebonite.
Sights: Blade front, notch rear.
Features: Made of stainless steel, simple take down; half-cock safety; floating firing pin; cartridge rims recessed in cylinder. Comes in gun rug. Lifetime warranty. Also available in percussion — see black powder section. From Freedom Arms.

Price: 22 LR, 1" barrel $105.35
Price: 22 LR, 1¾" barrel $105.35
Price: 22 LR, 3" barrel $118.70
Price: 22 Mag., 1" barrel $124.00
Price: 22 Mag., 1¾" barrel $124.00
Price: 22 Mag., 3" barrel $137.35

CAUTION: PRICES CHANGE. CHECK AT GUNSHOP.

Freedom Arms Boot Gun

Similar to the Mini Revolver except has 3″ barrel, weighs 5 oz. and is 5⅞″ over-all. Has over-size grips, floating firing pin. Made of stainless steel. Lifetime warranty. Comes in rectangular gun rug. Introduced 1982. From Freedom Arms.
Price: 22 LR **$118.70**
Price: 22 Mag. **$137.35**

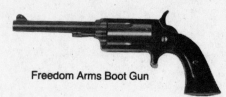

Freedom Arms Boot Gun

MITCHELL SINGLE ACTION ARMY REVOLVERS

Caliber: 22 LR, 357 Mag., 44 Mag., 45 Colt, 6 shot.
Barrel: 4¾″, 5½″, 6″, 6½″, 7½″, 10″, 12″, 18″.
Weight: NA. **Length:** NA.
Stocks: One-piece walnut.
Sights: Serrated ramp front, fixed or adjustable rear.
Features: Color case-hardened frame, brass backstrap, balance blued; hammer block safety. Stainless steel and dual cylinder models available. Imported by Mitchell Arms.
Price: Fixed sight, 22 LR, 4¾″, 5½″, 7½″ **$259.95**
Price: As above, 357, 45 .... **$264.95**
Price: As above, 44 Mag. **$269.95**
Price: Adjustable sight, 22 LR, 4¾″, 5½″, 7½″ **$265.00**
Price: As above, 357, 45 .... **$279.95**
Price: As above, 44 Mag. **$284.95**
Price: Stainless steel, 22 LR, 4¾″, 5½″, 7½″ **$299.00**
Price: As above, 357 Mag. **$319.95**
Price: 44 Mag./44-40, dual cylinder, 4¾″, 6″, 7½″ **$319.95**
Price: 22 LR/22 Mag., dual cylinder, 4¾″, 5½″, 7½″ **$275.00**
Price: Silhouette Model, 44 Mag., 10″, 12″, 18″ **$299.95**

NORTH AMERICAN 450 MAGNUM EXPRESS

Caliber: 450 Magnum Express, 45 Win. Mag., 5 shot.
Barrel: 7½″, 10½″.
Weight: 52 oz. (7½″ bbl.). **Length:** 13½″ (7½″ bbl.).
Stocks: Smooth walnut.
Sights: Blade front, fully adj. rear.
Features: All stainless steel construction. Patented hammer safety. Factory 450 Mag. Exp. ammo available. From North American Arms.
Price: Either caliber **$1,069.40**

NORTH AMERICAN MINI-REVOLVERS

Caliber: 22 S, 22 LR, 22 Mag., 5 shot.
Barrel: 1⅛″, 1⅝″, 2½″.
Weight: 4 oz.
Stocks: Laminated wood.
Sights: Blade front, notch fixed rear.
Features: All stainless steel construction. Polished satin and matte finish. From North American Arms.
Price: 22 Short, 1⅛″ bbl. **$119.95**
Price: 22 LR, 1⅛″ bbl. **$123.95**
Price: 22 LR, 1⅝″ bbl. **$124.95**
Price: 22 Mag., 1⅝″ bbl. **$139.95**
Price: 22 Mag., 2½″ bbl. **$142.95**

North American Mini

PHELPS HERITAGE I, EAGLE I REVOLVERS

Caliber: 444 Marlin, 45-70, 6-shot.
Barrel: 8″ or 12″.
Weight: 5½ lbs. **Length:** 19½″ over-all (12″ bbl.).
Stocks: Smooth walnut.
Sights: Ramp front, adjustable rear.
Features: Single action; polished blue finish; safety bar. From E. Phelps Mfg. Co.
Price: Heritage I (45-70), Eagle I (444 Marlin) 8″ barrel **$650.00**
Price: As above, 12″ barrel. **$675.00**

Phelps Heritage I

RUGER NEW MODEL SUPER BLACKHAWK

Caliber: 44 Magnum, 6-shot. Also fires 44 Spec.
Barrel: 7½″ (6-groove, 20″ twist), 10½″.
Weight: 48 oz. (7½″ bbl.) 51 oz. (10½″ bbl.). **Length:** 13⅜″ over-all (7½″ bbl.).
Stocks: Genuine American walnut.
Sights: ⅛″ ramp front, micro click rear adj. for w. and e.
Features: New Ruger interlocked mechanism, non-fluted cylinder, steel grip and cylinder frame, square back trigger guard, wide serrated trigger and wide spur hammer.
Price: Blue (S-47N, S-411N) **$276.00**
Price: Stainless (KS-47N, KS-411N) **$325.00**

RUGER NEW MODEL BLACKHAWK REVOLVER

Caliber: 30 Carbine, 38 Special, 357 or 41 Mag., 45 Colt, 6-shot.
Barrel: 4⅝″ or 6½″, either caliber, 7½″ (30 Carbine, 45 Colt only).
Weight: 42 oz. (6½″ bbl.). **Length:** 12¼″ over-all (6½″ bbl.).
Stocks: American walnut.
Sights: ⅛″ ramp front, micro click rear adj. for w. and e.
Features: New Ruger interlocked mechanism, independent firing pin, hardened chrome-moly steel frame, music wire springs throughout.
Price: Blue, 30 Carbine (7½″), 357 Mag. (4⅝″, 6½″) **$247.75**
Price: Blue, 357/9mm (4⅝″, 6½″) **$260.00**
Price: Stainless, 357 (4⅝″, 6½″) **$307.50**
Price: Blue, 41 Mag. (4⅝″, 6½″), 45 Colt (4⅝″, 7½″) **$247.75**

Ruger N.M. Blackhawk

CAUTION: PRICES CHANGE. CHECK AT GUNSHOP.

Ruger N.M. Bisley Blackhawk

Ruger Super Single-Six

Ruger Small Frame New Model Bisley Single-Six

Similar to the New Model Single-Six except frame is styled after the classic Bisley "flat-top." Most mechanical parts are unchanged. Hammer is lower and smoothly curved with a deeply checkered spur. Trigger is strongly curved with a wide smooth surface. Longer grip frame designed with a hand-filling shape, and the trigger guard is a large oval. Dovetail rear sight drift-adjustable for windage; front sight base accepts interchangeable square blades of various heights and styles. Weight about 41 oz. Chambered for 22 LR and 32 H&R Mag., 6½" barrel only. Introduced 1985.
Price: **$258.00**

Ruger New Model Single-Six Revolver

Similar to the Super Single-Six revolver except chambered for 32 H&R Magnum (also handles 32 S&W and 32 S&W Long). Weight is about 34 oz. with 6½" barrel. Same barrel lengths as Super Single-Six. Introduced 1985.
Price: **$212.00**

SEVILLE SUPER MAG SINGLE ACTION

Caliber: 357 Maximum, 375 Super Magnum, 6-shot.
Barrel: 7½" (standard), 5½", 6½", 10½" optional.
Weight: 52 oz. **Length:** 14" over-all.
Stocks: Smooth walnut.
Sights: Flourescent insert ramp front, micro. adj. rear. Fixed sights available.
Features: Made of 17-4 PH stainless steel; coil spring action; floating Beryllium copper firing pin, trigger spring; hand-fitted action; brushed satin finish standard, others available. From United Sporting Arms, Inc.
Price: 357 Maximum. **$546.00**
Price: 375 Super Mag. **$568.00**

TEXAS LONGHORN RIGHT-HAND SINGLE ACTION

Caliber: All centerfire pistol calibers.
Barrel: 4¾".
Weight: NA. **Length:** NA.
Stocks: One-piece fancy walnut, or any fancy AAA wood.
Sights: Blade front, grooved top-strap rear.
Features: Loading gate and ejector housing on left side of gun. Cylinder rotates to the left. All steel construction; color case-hardened frame; high polish blue; music wire coil springs. Lifetime guarantee to original owner. Introduced 1984. From Texas Longhorn Arms.
Price: South Texas Army Limited Edition — hand-made, only 1,000 to be produced; "One of One Thousand" engraved on barrel; comes with glass-covered display case **$1,500.00**

Texas Longhorn Sesquicentennial Model Revolver

Similar to the South Texas Army Model except has ¾-coverage Nimschke-style engraving, antique golden nickel plate finish, one-piece elephant ivory grips. Comes with hand-made solid walnut presentation case, factory letter to owner. Limited edition of 150 units. Introduced 1986.
Price: **$2,500.00**

Ruger New Model Bisley Blackhawk

Similar to standard New Model Blackhawk except the hammer is lower with a smoothly curved, deeply checkered wide spur, the trigger is strongly curved with a wide smooth surface. Longer grip frame has a hand-filling shape. Adjustable rear sight, ramp-style front. Cylinder is unfluted and is roll-marked with a classic foliate engraving pattern and depiction of the old time Bisley marksman and a Bisley trophy. Chambered for 357, 41, 44 Mags. and 45 Colt; 7½" barrel; over-all length of 13". Introduced 1985.
Price: **$307.00**

RUGER NEW MODEL SUPER SINGLE-SIX CONVERTIBLE REVOLVER

Caliber: 22 LR, 6-shot; 22 Mag. in extra cylinder (stainless model only).
Barrel: 4⅝", 5½", 6½" or 9½" (6-groove).
Weight: 34½ oz. (6½" bbl.). **Length:** 11¹³⁄₁₆" over-all (6½" bbl.).
Stocks: Smooth American walnut.
Sights: Improved Patridge front on ramp, fully adj. rear protected by integral frame ribs.
Features: New Ruger "interlocked" mechanism, transfer bar ignition, gate-controlled loading, hardened chrome-moly steel frame, wide trigger, music wire springs throughout, independent firing pin.
Price: 4⅝", 5½", 6½", 9½" barrel **$207.00**
Price: 5½", 6½" bbl. only, stainless steel (convertible) **$278.00**

Ruger Bisley Single-Six

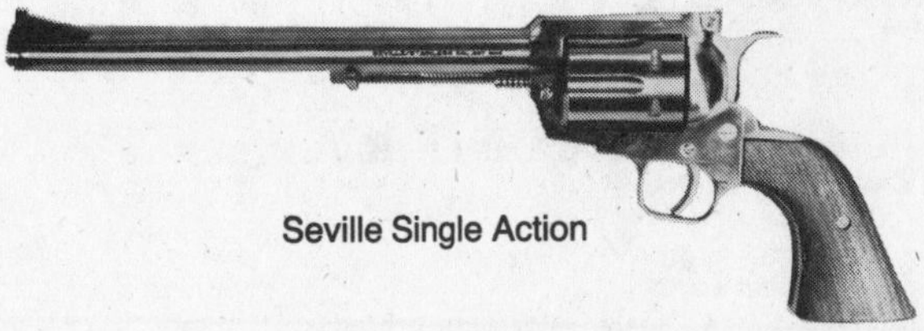

Seville Single Action

TANARMI S.A. REVOLVER MODEL TA76

Caliber: 22 LR, 22 Mag., 6-shot.
Barrel: 4¾".
Weight: 32 oz. **Length:** 10" over-all.
Stocks: Walnut.
Sights: Blade front, rear adj. for w. & e.
Features: Manual hammer block safety; color hardened steel frame; brass backstrap and trigger guard. Imported from Italy by Excam.
Price: 22 LR, blue **$60.00**
Price: Combo, blue **$79.00**
Price: 22 LR, chrome...................................... **$77.00**
Price: Combo, chrome **$92.00**

Texas Longhorn South Texas Army

CAUTION: PRICES CHANGE. CHECK AT GUNSHOP.

Texas Longhorn Arms Texas Border Special
Similar to the South Texas Army Limited Edition except has 3½" barrel, birds-head style grip. Same special features, display case. Introduced 1984.
Price: **$1,500.00**

Texas Longhorn Arms Cased Set
Set contains one each of the Texas Longhorn Right-Hand Single Actions, all in the same caliber, same serial numbers (100, 200, 300, 400, 500, 600, 700, 800, 900). Ten sets to be made (#1000 donated to NRA museum). Comes in hand-tooled leather case. All other specs same as Limited Edition guns. Introduced 1984.
Price: **$5,750.00**
Price: With ¾-coverage "C-style" engraving................... **$7,650.00**

Texas Longhorn Arms West Texas Flat Top Target
Similar to the South Texas Army Limited Edition except choice of barrel length from 7½" through 15"; flat-top style frame; ⅛" contoured ramp front sight, old model steel micro-click rear adjustable for w. and e. Same special features, display case. Introduced 1984.
Price: **$1,500.00**

THE VIRGINIAN DRAGOON REVOLVER
Caliber: 44 Mag.
Barrel: 6", 7½", 8⅜".
Weight: 50 oz. (6" barrel). **Length:** 10" over-all (6" barrel).
Stocks: Smooth walnut.
Sights: Ramp-type Patridge front blade, micro. adj. target rear.
Features: Color case-hardened frame, spring-loaded floating firing pin, coil main spring. Firing pin is lock-fitted with a steel bushing. Introduced 1977. Made in the U.S. by Interarms Industries, Inc.
Price: 6", 7½", 8⅜", blue.................................... **$295.00**
Price: 44 Mag., 6", 7½", 8⅜", stainless **$295.00**
Price: 44 Mag., 7½", 8⅜", 10½" Sil. model **$425.00**

Virginian Dragoon "Deputy" Model
Similar to the standard Dragoon except comes with traditional fixed sights, blue or stainless, in 357 (5" barrel), 44 Mag. (6" barrel). Introduced 1983.
Price: **$295.00**

VIRGINIAN 22 CONVERTIBLE REVOLVERS
Caliber: 22 LR, 22 Mag.
Barrel: 5½".
Weight: 38 oz. **Length:** 10¾" over-all.
Stocks: Smooth walnut.
Sights: Ramp-type Patridge front, open fully adjustable rear.
Features: Smaller version of the big-bore Dragoon revolvers; comes with both Long Rifle and Magnum cylinders, the latter unfluted; color case-hardened frame, rest blued. Introduced 1983. Made by Uberti; imported from Italy by Interarms.
Price: Blue, with two cylinders................................ **$219.00**
Price: Stainless with two cylinders **$239.00**

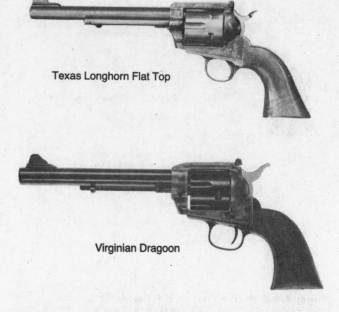

Texas Longhorn Flat Top

Virginian Dragoon

Virginian Dragoon Engraved Models
Same gun as the standard Dragoon except offered only in 44 Mag. 6" or 7½" barrel; choice of fluted or unfluted cylinder, stainless or blued. Hand-engraved frame, cylinder and barrel. Each gun comes in a felt-lined walnut presentation case. Introduced 1983.
Price: **$625.00**

Virginian 22 Convertible

HANDGUNS—MISCELLANEOUS

ALLEN ROLLING BLOCK PISTOL
Caliber: 22 LR, 22 Mag., 357 Mag., single shot.
Barrel: 9⅞", half round, half octagon.
Weight: 44 oz. **Length:** 14" over-all.
Stocks: Walnut grip and fore-end.
Sights: Blade front, fully adj. rear.
Features: Replica of the 1891 rolling block target pistol. Brass trigger guard, color case-hardened frame, blue barrel. Imported by Allen Fire Arms.
Price: **$229.00**

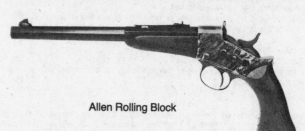

Allen Rolling Block

CAUTION: PRICES CHANGE. CHECK AT GUNSHOP.

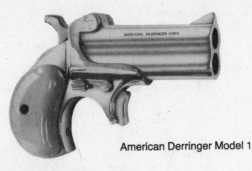

American Derringer Model 1

AMERICAN DERRINGER MODEL 3

Caliber: 38 Special.
Barrel: 2.5".
Weight: 8.5 oz. **Length:** 4.9" over-all.
Stocks: Rosewood.
Sights: Blade front.
Features: Made of stainless steel. Single shot with manual hammer block safety. Introduced 1985. From American Derringer Corp.
Price: **$115.00**

American Derringer Model 6

American Derringer Semmerling

ARM TECH. DERRINGER

Caliber: 22 LR, 22 Mag., 4-shot.
Barrel: 2.6".
Weight: 19 ozs. **Length:** 4.6" over-all.
Stocks: Hard rubber or walnut, checkered or smooth.
Sights: Fixed, non-snagging.
Features: Four barrels with 90° rotating-indexing firing pin system. All stainless steel parts. Double-action only. Blued model available. Introduced 1983. From Armament Technologies Inc.
Price: Stainless, 22 LR, rubber grips **$184.50**
Price: As above, 22 Mag. **$189.00**
Price: Blued, 22 LR, walnut grips **$174.50**
Price: As above, 22 Mag. **$179.00**

BAFORD ARMS THUNDER DERRINGER

Caliber: 410 2½" and 44 Spec. with insert sleeves for 22 S, LR, 22 Mag., 25 ACP, 32 ACP, 32 H&R Mag., 30 Luger, 380 ACP, 38 Super, 38 Spec., 38 S&W, 9mm.
Barrel: Various lengths according to caliber.
Weight: 8½ oz. **Length:** 5⅞" over-all.
Stocks: Smooth walnut.
Sights: None. Scope and mount available.
Features: Side-swinging barrel with positive lock and half-cock safety. Blued steel frame, barrel, polished stainless hammer, trigger. Introduced 1986.
Price: Base gun in 410, 44 Special **$169.95**
Price: Extra barrel inserts to change caliber, each **$29.95**

AMERICAN DERRINGER MODEL 1

Caliber: 22 LR, 22 Mag., 22 Hornet, 223 Rem., 30 Luger, 30-30 Win., 32 ACP, 38 Super, 380 ACP, 38 Spec., 9 × 18, 9mm Para., 357 Mag., 41 Mag., 44-40 Win., 44 Spec., 44 Mag., 45 Colt, 45 ACP, 410-ga. (2½").
Barrel: 3".
Weight: 15½ oz. (38 Spec.). **Length:** 4.82" over-all.
Stocks: Rosewood, Zebra wood.
Sights: Blade front.
Features: Made of stainless steel with high-polish or satin finish. Two shot capacity. Manual hammer block safety. Introduced 1980. Contact the factory for complete list of available calibers and prices. From American Derringer Corp.
Price: 22 LR or Mag. **$212.00**
Price: 223 Rem. **$369.00**
Price: 38 Spec. **$187.50**
Price: 357 Mag. **$225.00**
Price: 9mm, 380 . . . . **$172.50**
Price: 44 Spec. **$275.00**
Price: 44-40 Win., 45 Colt **$275.00**
Price: 41, 44 Mags. **$369.00**
Price: Lightweight (7½ oz.) Model 7, 38 Spec., 38 S&W, 380, 22 LR only **$199.00**
Price: 45-70 (as above), single shot **$369.00**
Price: 45 Colt, 410, 2½" **$312.00**
Price: 45 ACP **$218.00**

American Derringer Model 4

Similar to the Model 1 except has 4.1" barrel, over-all length of 6", and weighs 16½ oz.; chambered for 3" 410-ga. shotshells or 45 Colt. Can be had with 45-70 upper barrel and 3" 410-ga. or 45 Colt bottom barrel. Made of stainless steel. Manual hammer block safety. Introduced 1985.
Price: 3" 410/45 Colt (either barrel) **$359.00**
Price: 3" 410/45 Colt or 45-70 (Alaskan Survival model) **$369.00**

American Derringer Model 6

Similar to the Model 1 except has 6" barrels chambered for 3" 410 shotshells or 45 Colt, rosewood stocks, 8.2" o.a.l. and weighs 21 oz. Shoots either round for each barrel. Manual hammer block safety. Introduced 1986.
Price: **$375.00**

American Derringer Model 7

Similar to Model 1 except made of high strength aircraft aluminum. Weighs 7½ oz., 4.82" o.a.l., rosewood stocks. Available in 22 LR, 32 S&W Long, 32 H&R Mag., 380 ACP, 38 S&W, 38 Spec., 44 Spec. Introduced 1986.
Price: 22 LR or 38 Spec. **$187.50**
Price: 38 S&W, 380 ACP, 32 S&W Long **$157.50**
Price: 32 H&R Mag. **$172.50**
Price: 44 Spec. **$500.00**

AMERICAN DERRINGER SEMMERLING LM-4

Caliber: 9mm Para., 7-shot magazine, or 45 ACP, 5-shot magazine.
Barrel: 3.625".
Weight: 24 oz. **Length:** 5.2" over-all.
Stocks: Checkered plastic on blued guns, rosewood on stainless guns.
Sights: Open, fixed.
Features: Manually-operated repeater. Height is 3.7", width is 1". Comes with manual, leather carrying case, spare stock screws, wrench. From American Derringer Corp.
Price: Blued **$1,250.00**
Price: Stainless steel **$1,650.00**

Baford Arms Thunder

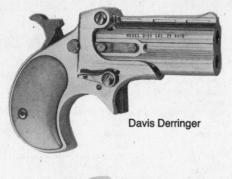

Davis Derringer

F.I.E. Model D-86

GUNWORKS MODEL 9 DERRINGER
Caliber: 38/357 Mag., 9mm/9mm Mag.
Barrel: 3″; button rifled, bottom hinged.
Weight: 15 oz.
Stocks: Smooth wood.
Sights: Millett blaze orange bar front, fixed rear.
Features: All steel; half-cock, through-frame safety; dual extraction; electroless nickel finish; comes with in-pant holster. Made in U.S. by Gunworks, Ltd.
Price: $148.50

LJUTIC LJ II PISTOL
Caliber: 22 Magnum.
Barrel: 2¾″.
Stocks: Checkered walnut.
Sights: Fixed.
Features: Stainless steel; double action; ventilated rib; side-by-side barrels; positive on/off safety. Introduced 1981. From Ljutic Industries.
Price: $799.00

Ljutic Space Pistol

Maximum Single Shot

C. O. P. 357 MAGNUM
Caliber: 38/357 Mag., 4 shots.
Barrel: 3¼″.
Weight: 28 oz. **Length:** 5.5″ over-all.
Stocks: Checkered composition.
Sights: Open, fixed.
Features: Double-action, 4 barrels, made of stainless steel. Width is only one inch, height 4.1″. From M & N Distributors.
Price: About $250.00
Price: In 22 Mag. $250.00
Price: In 22 LR (blued, aluminum frame) $229.95

DAVIS DERRINGERS
Caliber: 22 LR, 22 Mag., 25 ACP, 32 ACP.
Barrel: 2.4″.
Weight: 9.5 oz. **Length:** 4″ over-all.
Stocks: Laminated wood.
Sights: Blade front, fixed notch rear.
Features: Choice of black Teflon or chrome finish; spur trigger. Introduced 1986. Made in U.S. by Davis Industries.
Price: $64.90

F.I.E. MODEL D-86 DERRINGER
Caliber: 38 Special.
Barrel: 3″.
Weight: 14 oz.
Stocks: Checkered black nylon, walnut optional.
Sights: Fixed.
Features: Dyna-Chrome finish. Spur trigger. Tip-up barrel, extractors. Made in U.S. by F.I.E. Corp.
Price: With nylon grips $104.95
Price: With walnut grips $124.95

Gunworks Model 9

LJUTIC RECOILESS SPACE PISTOL
Caliber: 22 Mag., 357 Mag., 44 Mag., 308 Win.; single shot.
Barrel: 13½″.
Weight: 5 lbs. (with scope).
Stocks: Walnut grip and fore-end.
Sights: Scope mounts extra.
Features: Twist-bolt action; button trigger. From Ljutic Industries.
Price: $995.00

MAXIMUM SINGLE SHOT PISTOL
Caliber: 22 Hornet, 223 Rem., 22-250, 6mm BR, 6mm-223, 243, 250 Savage, 6.5mm-35, 7mm TCU, 7mm BR, 7mm-35, 7mm INT-R, 7mm-08, 30 Herrett, 308 Win., 357 Mag., 358 Win., 44 Mag.
Barrel: 10½″, 14″.
Weight: 61 oz. (10½″ bbl.), 78 oz. (14″ bbl.). **Length:** 15″, 18½″ over-all (with 10½″ and 14″ bbl., respectively).
Stocks: Smooth walnut stocks and fore-end.
Sights: Ramp front, fully adjustable open rear.
Features: Falling block action; drilled and tapped for most popular scope mounts; integral grip frame/receiver; adjustable trigger; Douglas barrel (interchangeable); Armoloy finish. Introduced 1983. Made in U.S. by M.O.A. Corp.
Price: Either barrel length............................... $499.00
Price: Extra barrel $129.00
Price: Scope mount $39.00

CAUTION: PRICES CHANGE. CHECK AT GUNSHOP.

RPM XL Pistol

RPM XL SINGLE SHOT PISTOL
Caliber: 22 LR, 22 Mag., 225 Win., 25 Rocket, 6.5 Rocket, 32 H&R Mag., 357
Max., 357 Mag., 30-30 Win., 30 Herrett, 357 Herrett, 41 Mag., 44 Mag., 375
Win., 7mm Merrill, 30 Merrill, 7mm Rocket, 270 Rocket, 45-70.
Barrel: 9″ or 10¾″, 14″; .450″ wide vent. rib, matted to prevent glare.
Weight: About 54 oz. **Length:** 12¼″ over-all (10¾″ bbl.).
Stocks: Smooth walnut with thumb and heel rest.
Sights: Front .125″ blade (.100″ blade optional); rear adj. for w. and e.
Features: Polished blue finish, hard chrome optional. Barrel is drilled and
tapped for scope mounting. Cocking indicator visible from rear of gun. Has
spring-loaded barrel lock, positive thumb safety. Trigger adjustable for
weight of pull and over-travel. For complete price list contact RPM.
Price: Regular ¾″ frame, right hand action $585.00
Price: As above, left hand action $610.00
Price: Wide ⅞″ frame, right hand action only $635.00
Price: Extra barrel, 8″-10¾″ $180.00
Price: Extra barrel, 12″-14″ $250.00

REMINGTON XP-100 "VARMINT SPECIAL"
Caliber: 223 Rem., single shot.
Barrel: 10½″, ventilated rib.
Weight: 60 oz. **Length:** 16¾″.
Stock: Brown nylon one-piece, checkered grip with white spacers.
Sights: Tapped for scope mount.
Features: Fits left or right hand, is shaped to fit fingers and heel of hand.
Grooved trigger. Rotating thumb safety, cavity in fore-end permits insertion
of up to five 38 cal., 130-gr. metal jacketed bullets to adjust weight and bal-
ance. Included is a black vinyl, zippered case.
Price: Including case, about $396.00

Remington XP-100 Varmint Special

Remington XP-100 Custom Long Range Pistol
Similar to the XP-100 "Varmint Special" except chambered for 7mm-08
Rem. and 35 Rem., comes with sights—interchangeable blade on ramp
front, fully adjustable Bo-Mar rear. Custom Shop 14½″ barrel, Custom Shop
English walnut stock. Action tuned in Custom Shop. Weight is under 4½ lbs.
Introduced 1986.
Price: $887.00

TEXAS LONGHORN "THE JEZEBEL" PISTOL
Caliber: 22 Short, Long, Long Rifle, single shot.
Barrel: 6″.
Weight: 15 oz. **Length:** 8″ over-all.
Stocks: One-piece fancy walnut grip (right or left hand), walnut fore-end.
Sights: Bead front, fixed rear.
Features: Top-break action; all stainless steel; automatic hammer block safe-
ty; music wire coil springs. Barrel is half round, half octagon. Announced
1986. From Texas Longhorn Arms.
Price: About $185.00

Texas Longhorn "Jezebel"

TANARMI O/U DERRINGER
Caliber: 38 Special.
Barrel: 3″.
Weight: 14 oz. **Length:** 4¾″ over-all.
Stocks: Checkered white nylon.
Sights: Fixed.
Features: Blue finish; cross-bolt safety; tip-up barrel. Assembled in U.S. by Ex-
cam, Inc.
Price: $80.00

THOMPSON-CENTER ARMS CONTENDER
Caliber: 7mm T.C.U., 30-30 Win., 22 S, L, LR, 22 Mag., 22 Hornet, 6.5 T.C.U.,
223 Rem., 30 & 357 Herrett, 32 H&R Mag., 32-20 Win., 357 Mag., 357 Rem.
Max., also 222 Rem., 41 Mag., 44 Mag., 45 Colt, single shot.
Barrel: 10″, tapered octagon, bull barrel and vent. rib.
Weight: 43 oz. (10″ bbl.). **Length:** 13¼″ (10″ bbl.).
Stocks: Select walnut grip and fore-end, with thumb rest. Right or left hand.
Sights: Under cut blade ramp front, rear adj. for w. & e.
Features: Break open action with auto-safety. Single action only. Interchange-
able bbls., both caliber (rim & centerfire), and length. Drilled and tapped for
scope. Engraved frame. See T/C catalog for exact barrel/caliber availability.
Price: Blued (rimfire cals.) $305.00
Price: Blued (centerfire cals.). $305.00
Price: With Armour Alloy II finish. $365.00
Price: With internal choke. $370.00
Price: As above, vent. rib $380.00
Price: Extra bbls. (standard octagon) $130.00
Price: Bushnell Phantom scope base $9.95
Price: 45/410, vent. rib, internal choke bbl. $145.00

Thompson-Center Contender

CAUTION: PRICES CHANGE. CHECK AT GUNSHOP.

Auto Ordnance 27 A-1

Auto Ordnance Thompson M1

Similar to the Model 27 A-1 except is in the M-1 configuration with side cocking knob, horizontal fore-end, smooth un-finned barrel, sling swivels on butt and fore-end. Matte black finish. Introduced 1985.
Price: **$565.00**

AUTO ORDNANCE MODEL 27 A-1 THOMPSON

Caliber: 45 ACP, 30-shot magazine.
Barrel: 16".
Weight: 11½ lbs. **Length:** About 42" over-all (Deluxe).
Stock: Walnut stock and vertical fore-end.
Sights: Blade front, open rear adj. for w.
Features: Re-creation of Thompson Model 1927. Semi-auto only. Deluxe model has finned barrel, adj. rear sight and compensator; Standard model has plain barrel and military sight. From Auto-Ordnance Corp.
Price: Deluxe **$595.00**
Price: Standard (horizontal fore-end) **$575.00**
Price: 1927A5 Pistol (M27A1 without stock; wgt. 7 lbs.) **$556.00**
Price: Lightweight model **$469.95**

Barrett Light-Fifty

BARRETT LIGHT-FIFTY MODEL 82

Caliber: 50 BMG; 11-shot detachable box magazine.
Barrel: 33".
Weight: 35 lbs. **Length:** 63" over-all.
Stock: Uni-body construction.
Sights: None furnished.
Features: Semi-automatic, recoil operated with recoiling barrel. Three-lug locking bolt; six-port harmonica-type muzzle brake. Bipod legs and M-60 mount standard. Fires same 50-cal. ammunition as the M2HB machine gun. Introduced 1985. From Barrett Firearms.
Price: Parkerized **$3,180.00**
Price: Custom **$4,200.00**

BERETTA AR70 RIFLE

Caliber: 223, 30-shot magazine.
Barrel: 17¾".
Weight: 8¼ lbs. **Length:** 38" over-all.
Stock: Black high-impact plastic.
Sights: Blade front, diopter rear adjustable for windage and elevation.
Features: Matte black epoxy finish; easy take-down. Imported from Italy by Beretta U.S.A. Corp. Introduced 1984.
Price: **$800.00**

BUSHMASTER AUTO RIFLE

Caliber: 223; 30-shot magazine
Barrel: 18½".
Weight: 6¼ lbs. **Length:** 37.5" over-all.
Stock: Rock maple
Sights: Protected post front adj. for elevation, protected quick-flip rear peep adj. for windage; short and long range.
Features: Steel alloy upper receiver with welded barrel assembly, AK-47-type gas system, aluminum lower receiver; silent sling and swivels; bayonet lug; one-piece welded steel alloy bolt carrier assembly. From Bushmaster Firearms.
Price: With maple stock **$384.95**
Price: With nylon-coated folding stock **$394.95**
Price: Matte electroless finish, maple stock **$394.95**
Price: As above, folding stock **$394.95**

Bushmaster Auto Rifle

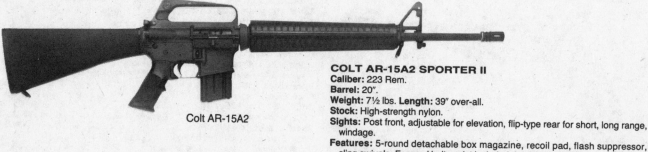

Colt AR-15A2

COLT AR-15A2 SPORTER II

Caliber: 223 Rem.
Barrel: 20".
Weight: 7½ lbs. **Length:** 39" over-all.
Stock: High-strength nylon.
Sights: Post front, adjustable for elevation, flip-type rear for short, long range, windage.
Features: 5-round detachable box magazine, recoil pad, flash suppressor, sling swivels. Forward bolt assist included. Introduced 1985.
Price: **$706.50**

CAUTION: PRICES CHANGE. CHECK AT GUNSHOP.

Colt AR-15 9mm

Colt AR-15 9mm Carbine

Similar to the standard AR-15 with collapsible stock except chambered for 9mm Parabellum. Has 16" barrel, 6-groove, 1-in-10" RH twist; M16A2 pistol grip; 20-round detachable magazine; ribbed round handguard; sight radius of 19¾". Flip rear sight set for 50 and 100 meters. Blow-back system fires from closed bolt. Introduced 1985.
Price: **$695.50**

Colt AR-15A2 H-BAR

Similar to the AR-15A2 Sporter II except has heavy barrel, 800-meter M16A2 rear sight adjustable for windage and elevation, case deflector for left-hand shooters, target-style nylon sling. Introduced 1986.
Price: **$808.50**

Colt AR-15A2 Carbine

Same as standard AR-15A2 except has telescoping nylon-coated aluminum buttstock and redesigned fore-end. Over-all length collapsed is 32", extended 35". Barrel length is 16", weight is 5.8 lbs. Has 14½" sight radius. Introduced 1985.
Price: **$748.95**

Daewoo MAX-2

DAEWOO MAX-1 AUTO RIFLE

Caliber: 5.56mm (223), 30-round magazine.
Barrel: 17".
Weight: 6.5 lbs. **Length:** 38.4" over-all (butt extended).
Stock: Retractable.
Sights: Post front, adjustable peep rear.
Features: Machine-forged receiver; gas-operated action; uses AR-15/M-16 magazines. Introduced 1985. Imported from Korea by Stoeger Industries.
Price: **$625.00**

COMMANDO ARMS CARBINE

Caliber: 45 ACP.
Barrel: 16½".
Weight: 8 lbs. **Length:** 37" over-all.
Stock: Walnut buttstock.
Sights: Blade front, peep rear.
Features: Semi-auto only. Cocking handle on left side. Choice of magazines— 5, 20, 30 or 90 shot. From Commando Arms.
Price: Mark 9 or Mark 45, blue **$219.00**
Price: Nickel plated **$254.00**

Daewoo MAX-2 Auto Carbine

Similar to the MAX-1 except has a folding buttstock giving over-all length of 38.9" (extended), 28.7" (folded). Weight is 7.5 lbs.; barrel length is 18.3". Has hooded post front sight, adjustable peep rear. Uses AR-15/M-16 magazines. Introduced 1985. Imported from Korea by Stoeger Industries.
Price: **$645.00**

FN-LAR Competition

FN-LAR COMPETITION AUTO

Caliber: 308 Win., 20-shot magazine.
Barrel: 21" (24" with flash hider).
Weight: 9 lbs., 7 oz. **Length:** 44½" over-all.
Stock: Black composition butt, fore-end and pistol grip.
Sights: Post front, aperture rear adj. for elevation, 200 to 600 meters.
Features: Has sling swivels, carrying handle, rubber recoil pad. Consecutively numbered pairs available at additional cost. Imported by Gun South, Inc.
Price: **$1,189.00**

FN 308 Model 50-63

Similar to the FN-LAR except has 18" barrel, skeleton-type folding buttstock, folding cocking handle. Introduced 1982. Imported from Belgium by Gun South, Inc. Distr., Inc.
Price: **$1,264.00**

FNC AUTO RIFLE

Caliber: 223 Rem.
Barrel: 18".
Weight: 9.61 lbs.
Stock: Synthetic stock.
Sights: Post front; flip-over aperture rear adj. for elevation.
Features: Updated version of FN-FAL in shortened carbine form. Has 30-shot box magazine, synthetic pistol grip, fore-end. Introduced 1981. Imported by Gun South, Inc.
Price: Standard model **$683.00**
Price: Paratrooper, with folding stock **$713.00**

FNC Auto Rifle

FN-LAR Heavy Barrel 308 Match

Similar to FN-LAR competition except has wooden stock and fore-end, heavy barrel, folding metal bipod. Imported by Gun South, Inc.
Price: With wooden, stock.................................... $1,636.00
Price: With synthetic stock $1,480.00

FN-LAR Paratrooper 308 Match 50-64

Similar to FN-LAR competition except with folding skeleton stock, shorter barrel, modified rear sight. Imported by Gun South, Inc.
Price: $1,264.00

Galil Auto Rifle

GALIL 308 ARM SEMI-AUTO RIFLE

Caliber: 308 Win., 20-shot magazine.
Barrel: 21".
Weight: 8.7 lbs. **Length:** 41.3" over-all (stock extended).
Stock: Tube-type metal folding stock.
Sights: Post-type front, flip-type "L" rear.
Features: Gas operated, rotating bolt. Cocking handle, safety and magazine catch can be operated from either side. Folding bipod, carrying handle. Introduced 1982. Imported from Israel by Action Arms Ltd.
Price: $940.00
Price: As above in 223 (18.1" bbl., 38.6" o.a.l.).................. $875.00

Goncz Carbine

GONCZ HIGH-TECH CARBINE

Caliber: 9mm Para., 30 Mauser, 38 Super, 18- and 32-shot magazine; 45 ACP, 10- and 20-shot magazine.
Barrel: 16.1".
Weight: 4 lbs., 2 oz. **Length:** 31" over-all.
Stock: Grooved alloy pistol grip, black high-impact plastic butt. Walnut optional at extra cost.
Sights: Front adjustable for e., rear adjustable for w.
Features: Fires from closed bolt; floating firing pin; safety locks the firing pin; all metal construction; barrel threaded for accessories. Matte black oxide and anodized finish. Designed by Lajos J. Goncz. Introduced 1985. From Goncz Co.
Price: $375.00
Price: With laser sight system $1,495.00

HECKLER & KOCH HK-91 AUTO RIFLE

Caliber: 308 Win., 5- or 20-shot magazine.
Barrel: 17.71".
Weight: 9½ lbs. **Length:** 40¼" over-all.
Stock: Black high-impact plastic.
Sights: Post front, aperture rear adj. for w. and e.
Features: Delayed roller lock action. Sporting version of West German service rifle. Takes special H&K clamp scope mount. Imported from West Germany by Heckler & Koch, Inc.
Price: HK-91 A-2 with plastic stock............................. $666.00
Price: HK-91 A-3 with retractable metal stock $746.00
Price: HK-91 scope mount with 1" rings........................ $260.00

Heckler & Koch HK-91

Heckler & Koch HK-93 Auto Rifle

Similar to HK-91 except in 223 cal., 16.13" barrel, over-all length of 35½", weighs 7¾ lbs. Same stock, fore-end.
Price: HK-93 A-2 with plastic stock............................. $666.00
Price: HK-93 A-3 with retractable metal stock $746.00

HECKLER & KOCH HK-94 AUTO CARBINE

Caliber: 9mm Parabellum, 15-shot magazine.
Barrel: 16".
Weight: 6½ lbs. (fixed stock). **Length:** 34¾" over-all.
Stock: High-impact plastic butt and fore-end or retractable metal stock.
Sights: Hooded post front, aperture rear adjustable for windage and elevation.
Features: Delayed roller-locked action; accepts H&K quick-detachable scope mount. Introduced 1983. Imported from West Germany by Heckler & Koch, Inc..
Price: HK94-A2 (fixed stock) $562.00
Price: HK94-A3 (retractable metal stock) $636.00
Price: 30-shot magazine $24.00
Price: Clamp to hold two magazines $18.00

Heckler & Koch HK-94

CAUTION: PRICES CHANGE. CHECK AT GUNSHOP.

CENTERFIRE RIFLES—MILITARY STYLE AUTOLOADERS

IVER JOHNSON PM30HB CARBINE
Caliber: 30 U.S. Carbine, 5.7 MMJ.
Barrel: 18" four-groove.
Weight: 6½ lbs. **Length:** 35½" over-all.
Stock: Glossy-finished hardwood or walnut.
Sights: Click adj. peep rear.
Features: Gas operated semi-auto carbine. 15-shot detachable magazine. Made in U.S.A
Price: Blue finish, hardwood stock $203.50
Price: Blue finish, walnut stock $217.50

Iver Johnson PM 30HB

MAS 223 Auto

MAS 223 SEMI-AUTO RIFLE
Caliber: 223, 25-shot magazine.
Barrel: 19.2".
Weight: About 8 lbs. **Length:** 29.8" over-all.
Stock: Rubber-covered adjustable check piece converts to left- or right-hand shooters.
Sights: Adjustable blade front with luminescent spot for night use, aperture adj. rear.
Features: Converts to left- or right-hand ejection. Armored plastic guards vital parts, including sights. Civilian version of the French FAMAS assault rifle. Introduced 1986. Imported from France by Century Arms.
Price: With spare parts kit, bipod sling, spare magazine, about. . . . **$1,495.00**

Mitchell AK-47

MITCHELL AK-47 SEMI-AUTO RIFLE
Caliber: 223, 308, 7.62 x 39, 30-shot magazine.
Barrel: 19.6".
Weight: 9.1 lbs. **Length:** 40.6" over-all with wood stock.
Stock: Teak.
Sights: Hooded post front, open adj. rear.
Features: Gas operated semi-automatic. Last-round bolt hold-open. Imported from Yugoslavia by Mitchell Arms.
Price: Wood stock $495.00
Price: Folding metal stock $525.00

Mitchell M-76

MITCHELL M-76 COUNTER-SNIPER RIFLE
Caliber: 7.9 mm.
Barrel: 21.8". Muzzle brake, flash hider.
Weight: 10.9 lbs. **Length:** 44.6" over-all.
Stock: Teak.
Features: Uses AK-47 action. Optional scope, night sight, mounts available. Imported from Yugoslavia by Mitchell Arms.
Price: $595.00

MITCHELL M-59 SEMI-AUTO RIFLE
Caliber: 7.62 x 39, 10-shot magazine.
Barrel: 18".
Weight: 9 lbs. **Length:** 44" over-all.
Stock: Walnut.
Sights: Hooded post front, open adj. rear.
Features: Gas-operated likeness of the SKS rifle. Imported from Yugoslavia by Mitchell Arms.
Price: $539.95

Ruger Mini-14/5R

Stock: American hardwood, steel reinforced.
Sights: Ramp front, fully adj. rear.
Features: Fixed piston gas-operated, positive primary extraction. New buffer system, redesigned ejector system. Ruger S100RH scope rings included. 20-shot magazines available from Ruger dealers, 30-shot magazine available only to police departments and government agencies.
Price: Mini-14/5R, blued $420.00
Price: K Mini-14/5R, stainless $460.00
Price: K Mini-14/5RF, stainless, folding stock $520.00

RUGER MINI-14/5R RANCH RIFLE
Caliber: 223 Rem., 5-shot detachable box magazine.
Barrel: 18½".
Weight: 6.4 lbs. **Length:** 37¼" over-all.

CAUTION: PRICES CHANGE. CHECK AT GUNSHOP.

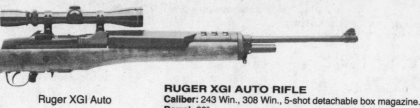

Ruger XGI Auto

Ruger Mini-14/5F Folding Stock

Same as the Ranch Rifle except available with folding stock, checkered high impact plastic vertical pistol grip. Over-all length with stock open is 37¾", length closed is 27½". Weight is about 7¾ lbs.

Price: Blued ordnance steel, standard stock **$390.00**
Price: Stainless **$430.00**
Price: Blued, folding stock **$465.00**
Price: Stainless, folding stock **$494.50**

RUGER XGI AUTO RIFLE

Caliber: 243 Win., 308 Win., 5-shot detachable box magazine.
Barrel: 20".
Weight: 7.9 lbs. **Length:** 39⅞" over-all.
Stock: American hardwood; rubber butt pad.
Sights: Blade front on ramp, folding peep rear adjustable for w. and e.
Features: Uses a Garand-type gas system with fixed cylinder and moving piston with a simplified Garand-type rotating bolt. Ruger integral scope mounting system. Patented recoil buffer system; bolt lock mechanism. Introduced 1985.
Price: **$425.00**

SIG-AMT

SIG PE-57 AUTO RIFLE

Caliber: 7.5mm Swiss, 24-round box magazine.
Barrel: 23.8", with flash suppressor.
Weight: 12.6 lbs. **Length:** 43.6" over-all.
Stock: Black high-impact synthetic butt and pistol grip.
Sights: Folding hooded post front, folding click-adjustable aperture rear.
Features: Semi-automatic, gas-assisted delayed roller-lock action; bayonet lug, bipod, winter trigger, leather sling, maintenance kit, and 6-round magazine included; quick detachable scope mount optional. Imported from Switzerland by Osborne's. Introduced 1984.
Price: About **$1,995.00**

SIG-AMT AUTO RIFLE

Caliber: 308 Win. (7.62mm NATO), 20-shot magazine.
Barrel: 18¾".
Weight: 9½ lbs. **Length:** 39" over-all.
Stock: Walnut butt and fore-end, black grooved synthetic pistol grip.
Sights: Adjustable post front, adjustable aperture rear.
Features: Roller-locked breech system with gas-assisted action; right-side cocking lever; loaded chamber indicator. No tools needed for take-down. Comes with bipod and winter trigger. Spare 5- and 10-shot magazines available. Imported from Switzerland by Osborne's. Introduced 1984.
Price: About **$1,995.00**

Springfield Armory SAR-48

SPRINGFIELD ARMORY SAR-48 RIFLE

Caliber: 7.62mm NATO (308 Win.); 20-round magazine.
Barrel: 21".
Weight: 9.9 lbs. **Length:** 43.3" over-all.
Stock: Fiberglass.
Sights: Adjustable front, adjustable peep rear.
Features: New production. Introduced 1985. From Springfield Armory.
Price: **$899.00**

Springfield Armory M1A

┌─────────────────────────────────┐
│ Consult our Directory pages for │
│ the location of firms mentioned.│
└─────────────────────────────────┘

SPRINGFIELD ARMORY M1A RIFLE

Caliber: 7.62mm Nato (308), 243 Win., 5-, 10- or 20-round box magazine.
Barrel: 25¹⁄₁₆" with flash suppressor, 22" without suppressor.
Weight: 8¾ lbs. **Length:** 44¼" over-all.
Stock: American walnut or birch with walnut colored heat-resistant fiberglass handguard. Matching walnut handguard available.
Sights: Military, square blade front, full click-adjustable aperture rear.
Features: Commercial equivalent of the U.S. M-14 service rifle with no provision for automatic firing. From Springfield Armory. Military accessories available including 3x-9x2 ART scope and mount.
Price: Standard M1A Rifle, about **$782.00**
Price: Match Grade, about **$998.00**
Price: Super Match (heavy Premium barrel), about **$1,125.00**
Price: M1A-A1 Assault Rifle, walnut stock, about **$790.00**
Price: As above, folding stock, about **$857.00**

CAUTION: PRICES CHANGE. CHECK AT GUNSHOP.

Springfield Armory BM-59

SPRINGFIELD ARMORY M1 GARAND RIFLE
Caliber: 308, 30-06, 8-shot clip.
Barrel: 24″.
Weight: 9½ lbs. **Length:** 43½″ over-all.
Stock: Walnut, military.
Sights: Military square blade front, click adjustable peep rear.
Features: Commercially-made M-1 Garand duplicates the original service rifle. Introduced 1979. From Springfield Armory.
Price: Standard, about $696.00
Price: National Match, about $837.00
Price: Ultra Match, about $944.00
Price: Sniper rifle, about $1,065.00
Price: M1-T26 "Tanker," walnut stock, about.................. $732.00
Price: As above, folding stock, about $774.00
Price: Standard M-1 Garand with Beretta-made receiver, about ... $1,510.00

SPRINGFIELD ARMORY BM-59
Caliber: 7.62mm NATO (308 Win.); 20-round box magazine.
Barrel: 17.5″.
Weight: 9¼ lbs. **Length:** 38.5″ over-all.
Stock: Walnut, with trapped rubber butt pad.
Sights: Military square blade front, click adj. peep rear.
Features: Full military-dress Italian service rifle. Available in selective fire or semi-auto only. Refined version of the M-1 Garand. Accessories available include: folding alpine stock, muzzle brake/flash suppressor/grenade launcher combo, bipod, winter trigger, grenade launcher sights, bayonet, oiler. Extremely limited quantities. Introduced 1981.
Price: Standard Italian model, about $1,248.00
Price: Alpine model, about $1,435.00
Price: Alpine Paratrooper model, about $1,624.00
Price: Nigerian Mark IV model, about $1,365.00

STEYR A.U.G. AUTOLOADING RIFLE
Caliber: 223 Rem.
Barrel: 20″.
Weight: 8½ lbs. **Length:** 31″ over-all.
Stock: Synthetic, green. One-piece moulding houses receiver group, hammer mechanism and magazine.
Sights: 1.5x scope only; scope and mount form the carrying handle.
Features: Semi-automatic, gas-operated action; can be converted to suit right or left-handed shooters, including ejection port. Transparent 30- or 40-shot magazines. Folding vertical front grip. Introduced 1983. Imported from Austria by Gun South, Inc.
Price: Right or left-hand model $889.00

Steyr A.U.G. Rifle

Universal 1006 Carbine

Universal Model 5000PT Carbine
Same as standard Model 1003 except comes with "Schmeisser-type paratrooper" folding stock. Barrel length 18″. Over-all length open 36″; folded 27″. Made in U.S.A.
Price: Blue.. $217.50

UNIVERSAL 1003 AUTOLOADING CARBINE
Caliber: 30 M1, 5-shot magazine.
Barrel: 16″, 18″.
Weight: 5½ lbs. **Length:** 35½″ over-all.
Stock: American hardwood stock inletted for "issue" sling and oiler, blued metal handguard.
Sights: Blade front with protective wings, adj. rear.
Features: Gas operated, cross lock safety. Receiver tapped for scope mounts. Made in U.S.A. From Iver Johnson.
Price: $218.00

UZI CARBINE
Caliber: 9mm Parabellum, 45 ACP, 25-round magazine.
Barrel: 16.1″.
Weight: 8.4 lbs. **Length:** 24.4″ (stock folded).
Stock: Folding metal stock. Wood stock available as an accessory.
Sights: Post-type front, "L" flip-type rear adj. for 100 meters and 200 meters. Both click-adjustable for w. and e.
Features: Adapted by Col. Uzi Gal to meet BATF regulations, this semi-auto has the same qualities as the famous submachine gun. Made by Israel Military Industries. Comes in moulded carrying case with sling, magazine, sight adjustment key, and a short "display only" barrel. Exclusively imported from Israel by Action Arms Ltd. 9mm introduced 1980; 45 ACP introduced 1985.
Price: $679.00

UZI Carbine

CAUTION: PRICES CHANGE. CHECK AT GUNSHOP.

CENTERFIRE RIFLES—MILITARY STYLE AUTOLOADERS

Valmet M-76

VALMET M78 SEMI-AUTO
Similar to M76 except chambered for 223, 7.62 x 39 or 308 Win., has 24¼" heavy barrel, weighs 11 lbs., 43¼" over-all; 20- or 30-round magazine; bipod; machined receiver. Length of pull on wood stock dimensioned for American shooters. Rear sight adjustable for w. and e., open-aperture front sight; folding carrying handle. Imported from Finland by Valmet.
Price: **$824.00**

VALMET M-76 STANDARD RIFLE
Caliber: 223, 15 or 30-shot magazine, or 7.62 x 39, 30-shot magazine.
Barrel: 16¾".
Weight: About 8½ lbs. **Length:** 37¾" over-all.
Stock: Wood or folding metal type; composition fore-end.
Sights: Hooded adjustable post front, peep rear with luminous night sight.
Features: Semi-automatic only. Has sling swivels, flash supressor. Bayonet, cleaning kit, 30-shot magazine, scope adaptor cover optional. Imported from Finland by Valmet.
Price: Wood stock **$649.00**
Price: Folding stock **$674.00**

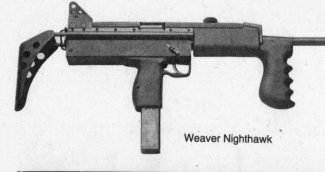

Weaver Nighthawk

WEAVER ARMS NIGHTHAWK
Caliber: 9mm Para., 25-shot magazine.
Barrel: 16.1".
Weight: 7 lbs. **Length:** 26½" (stock retracted).
Stock: Retractable metal frame.
Sights: Hooded blade front, adjustable peep V rear.
Features: Semi-auto fire only; fires from a closed bolt. Has 21" sight radius. Black nylon pistol grip and finger-groove front grip. Matte black finish. Introduced 1983. From Weaver Arms Corp.
Price: **$395.00**

CENTERFIRE RIFLES—SPORTING AUTOLOADERS

Browning Auto Rifle

BROWNING HIGH-POWER AUTO RIFLE
Caliber: 243, 270, 30-06, 308.
Barrel: 22" round tapered.
Weight: 7⅜ lbs. **Length:** 43" over-all.
Stock: French walnut p.g. stock (13⅝"x2"x1⅝") and fore-end, hand checkered.
Sights: Adj. folding-leaf rear, gold bead on hooded ramp front.
Features: Detachable 4-round magazine. Receiver tapped for scope mounts. Trigger pull 3½ lbs. Gold plated trigger on Grade IV. Imported from Belgium by Browning.
Price: Grade I **$552.00**
Price: Grade IV **$1,670.00**

Browning Commemorative BAR
Similar to the standard BAR except has silver grey receiver with engraved and gold inlaid whitetail deer on the right side, a mule deer on the left; a gold-edged scroll banner frames "One of Six Hundred" on the left side, the numerical edition number replaces "One" on the right. Chambered only in 30-06. Fancy, highly figured walnut stock and fore-end. Introduced 1983.
Price: **$3,550.00**

Browning Magnum Auto Rifle
Same as the standard caliber model, except weighs 8⅜ lbs., 45" over-all, 24" bbl., 3-round mag. Cals. 7mm Mag., 300 Win. Mag.
Price: Grade I **$604.00**
Price: Grade IV **$1,720.00**

HECKLER & KOCH HK770 AUTO RIFLE
Caliber: 308 Win., 3-shot magazine.
Barrel: 19.6".
Weight: 7½ lbs. **Length:** 42.8" over-all.
Stock: European walnut. Checkered p.g. and fore-end.
Sights: Vertically adjustable blade front, open, fold-down rear adj. for w.
Features: Has the delayed roller-locked system and polygonal rifling. Magazine catch located at front of trigger guard. Receiver top is dovetailed to accept clamp-type scope mount. Imported from West Germany by Heckler & Koch, Inc.
Price: **$666.00**
Price: HK630, 223 Rem. **$666.00**
Price: HK940, 30-06 .... **$706.00**
Price: Scope mount with 1" rings **$159.00**

Heckler & Koch HK770

CAUTION: PRICES CHANGE. CHECK AT GUNSHOP.

Heckler & Koch SL7

HECKLER & KOCH SL7 AUTO RIFLE
Caliber: 308 Win., 3-shot magazine.
Barrel: 17".
Weight: 8 lbs. **Length:** 39¾" over-all.
Stock: European walnut, oil finished.
Sights: Hooded post front, adjustable aperture rear.
Features: Delayed roller-locked action; polygon rifling; receiver is dovetailed for H&K quick-detachable scope mount. Introduced 1983. Imported from West Germany by Heckler & Koch, Inc.
Price: **$599.00**
Price: Model SL6 (as above except in 223 Rem.) **$599.00**
Price: Quick-detachable scope mount **$159.00**
Price: 10-shot magazine **$27.00**

Marlin Model 45

MARLIN MODEL 9 CAMP CARBINE
Caliber: 9mm Parabellum, 12-shot magazine (20-shot available).
Barrel: 16½", Micro-Groove® rifling.
Weight: 6¾ lbs. **Length:** 35½" over-all.
Stock: Walnut-finished hardwood; rubber butt pad; Mar-Shield® finish.
Sights: Ramp front with bead with Wide-Scan™ hood, adjustable open rear.
Features: Manual bolt hold-open; Garand-type safety, magazine safety; loaded chamber indicator; receiver drilled, tapped for scope mounting. Introduced 1985.
Price: **$259.95**

MARLIN MODEL 45 CARBINE
Similar to the Model 9 except chambered for 45 ACP, 7-shot magazine. Introduced 1986.
Price: **$259.95**

Remington Model Four

REMINGTON MODEL FOUR AUTO RIFLE
Caliber: 243 Win., 270 Win., 280 Rem., 308 Win. and 30-06.
Barrel: 22" round tapered.
Weight: 7½ lbs. **Length:** 42" over-all.
Stock: Walnut, deluxe cut checkered p.g. and fore-end. Full cheekpiece, Monte Carlo.
Sights: Gold bead front sight on ramp; step rear sight with windage adj.
Features: Redesigned and improved version of the Model 742. Positive cross-bolt safety. Receiver tapped for scope mount. 4-shot clip mag. Has cartridge head medallion denoting caliber on bottom of receiver. Introduced 1981.
Price: About **$524.00**
Price: D Grade, about **$2,291.00**
Price: F Grade, about **$4,720.00**
Price: F Grade with gold inlays, about **$7,079.00**

Remington Model 7400 Auto Rifle
Similar to Model Four except also chambered for 6mm Rem., does not have full cheekpiece Monte Carlo stock, has slightly different fore-end design, impressed checkering, no cartridge head medallion. Introduced 1981.
Price: About **$460.00**

Remington "Sportsman" 74 Auto Rifle
Similar to the Model Four rifle except available only in 30-06, 4-shot magazine, 22" barrel, walnut-finished hardwood stock and fore-end, open adjustable sights. Introduced 1984.
Price: About **$385.00**

Valmet Hunter

VALMET HUNTER AUTO RIFLE
Caliber: 223, 15-, 30-shot magazines; 243, 9-shot magazine; 308, 5-, 9- and 20-shot magazines.
Barrel: 20½".
Weight: 8 lbs. **Length:** 42" over-all.
Stock: American walnut butt and fore-end. Checkered palm-swell p.g. and fore-end.
Sights: Blade front, open flip-type rear.
Features: Uses semi-auto Kalashnikov-type gas-operated action with rotating bolt. Stock is adjustable for length via spacers. Optional cleaning kit, sling, ejection buffer, scope mount. Introduced 1986. Imported from Finland by Valmet.
Price: **$639.00**

Voere Model 2185

VOERE MODEL 2185 AUTO RIFLE
Caliber: 222 Rem. 222 Rem. Mag., 243, 308, 7 x 64, 270, 30-06, 9.3 x 62, 2-shot clip.
Barrel: 24".
Weight: NA. **Length:** NA.
Stock: European walnut.
Sights: Hooded bead front, open rear adj. for w. & e.
Features: Hand checkered stock; rotary safety; sling swivels. Muzzle stabilizer available. Imported from Austria by L. Jos. Rahn.
Price: 222, 222 Mag., 243, 308 .... $560.00
Price: 7 x 64, 270, 30-06 .... $660.00
Price: 9.3 x 62 .... $700.00

CENTERFIRE RIFLES—LEVER, SLIDE & MISC.

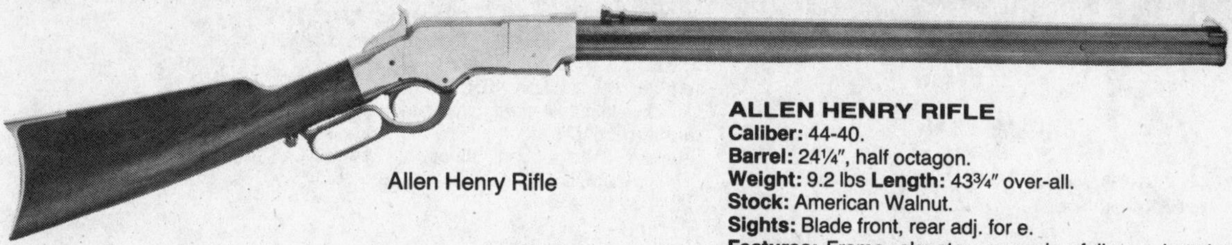

Allen Henry Rifle

ALLEN HENRY RIFLE
Caliber: 44-40.
Barrel: 24¼", half octagon.
Weight: 9.2 lbs **Length:** 43¾" over-all.
Stock: American Walnut.
Sights: Blade front, rear adj. for e.
Features: Frame, elevator, magazine follower, buttplate are brass, balance polished steel. Imported by Allen Fire Arms.
Price: $569.00
Price: Henry Carbine(22¼" bbl.) $569.00

Allen 1866 Rifle

ALLEN MODEL 1866 SPORTING RIFLE
Caliber: 22 LR, 22 Mag., 38 Spec., 44-40.
Barrel: 24¼", octagonal.
Weight: 8.1 lbs. **Length:** 43¼" over-all.

Stock: Walnut.
Sights: Blade front adj. for w., rear adj. for e.
Features: Frame, buttplate, fore-end cap of polished brass, balance blued. Imported by Allen Fire Arms.
Price: $449.00
Price: Yellowboy Carbine (19" round bbl.) $429.00
Price: Yellowboy "Indian" Carbine (engraved receiver, "nails" in wood) $469.00
Price: 1866 "Red Cloud Commemorative" Carbine $469.00
Price: 1866 "Trapper's Model" Carbine (16" bbl., 44-40) $429.00

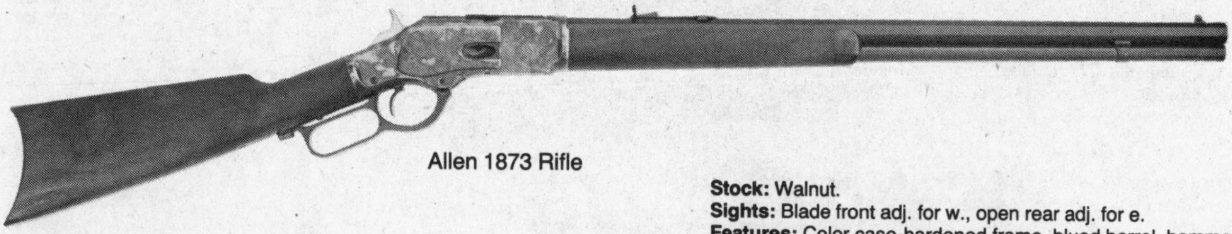

Allen 1873 Rifle

Stock: Walnut.
Sights: Blade front adj. for w., open rear adj. for e.
Features: Color case-hardened frame, blued barrel, hammer, lever, buttplate, brass elevator. Imported by Allen Fire Arms.
Price: $569.00
Price: 1873 Carbine (19" round bbl.) $499.00
Price: 1873 Carbine, nickel plated $569.00
Price: 1873 "Trapper's Model" Carbine (16" bbl., 44-40) $499.00

ALLEN 1873 SPORTING RIFLE
Caliber: 22 LR, 22 Mag., 357 Mag., 44-40.
Barrel: 24¼", octagonal.
Weight: 8.1 lbs. **Length:** 43¼" over-all.

ALLEN CATTLEMAN REVOLVING CARBINE
Caliber: 22 LR/22 Mag., 357 Mag., 44-40, 45 Colt, 6 shot.
Barrel: 18".
Weight: 4.4 lbs. **Length:** 34" over-all.
Stock: Walnut.
Sights: Blade front, groove rear.
Features: Carbine version of the single-action revolver. Brass buttplate, color case-hardened frame, blued cylinder and barrel. Imported by Allen Fire Arms.
Price: $339.00
Price: Buckhorn (44 Mag.) $399.00
Price: As above, convertible (44 Mag./44-40 cylinders) $409.00

ALLEN 1875 ARMY TARGET REVOLVING CARBINE
Caliber: 357 Mag., 44-40, 45 Colt, 6 shot.
Barrel: 18".
Weight: 4.9 lbs. **Length:** 37" over-all.
Stock: Walnut.
Sights: Ramp front, rear adj. for elevation.
Features: Polished brass trigger guard and buttplate, color case-hardened frame, rest is blued. Carbine version of the 1875 revolver. Imported by Allen Fire Arms.
Price: $389.00

CAUTION: PRICES CHANGE. CHECK AT GUNSHOP.

Browning Model 1886

BROWNING MODEL 1886 LEVER ACTION RIFLE
Caliber: 45-70 Govt., 8-round magazine.
Barrel: 26" octagonal.
Weight: 9 lbs. 5 oz. **Length:** 45".

Stock: Straight grip walnut stock and fore-end with matte finish. High grade has Grade III French walnut, fine checkering, high gloss finish.
Sights: Gold bead on elevated ramp front, buckhorn rear with elevator.
Features: Exact replica of John M. Browning's first lever action repeater design to be manufactured. Full-length tubular magazine, loaded through side port. Half-cock safety, metal crescent buttplate. High Grade model has gold plated American bison and elk scenes engraved on gray receiver. Limited production issue (7,000 in Grade I, 3,000 in High Grade). Introduced 1986. Imported from Japan by Browning.
Price: Grade I **$577.95**
Price: High Grade **$934.95**

Browning B-92

BROWNING B-92 LEVER ACTION
Caliber: 357 Mag., 11-shot magazine.
Barrel: 20" round.

Weight: 6 lbs., 6 oz. **Length:** 37½" over-all.
Stock: Straight grip stock and classic fore-end in French walnut with high gloss finish. Steel, modified crescent buttplate. (12¾" x 2 " x 2⅞").
Sights: Post front, classic cloverleaf rear with notched elevation ramp. Sight radius 16⅝".
Features: Tubular magazine. Follows design of original Model 92 lever-action. Introduced 1979. Imported from Japan by Browning.
Price: **$341.50**

Browning BLR

BROWNING BLR LEVER ACTION RIFLE
Caliber: 222, 223, 22-250, 243, 257 Roberts, 7mm-08, 308 Win. or 358 Win. 4-shot detachable mag.
Barrel: 20" round tapered.

Weight: 6 lbs. 15 oz. **Length:** 39¾" over-all.
Stock: Checkered straight grip and fore-end, oil finished walnut.
Sights: Gold bead on hooded ramp front; low profile square notch adj. rear.
Features: Wide, grooved trigger; half-cock hammer safety. Receiver tapped for scope mount. Recoil pad installed. Imported from Japan by Browning.
Price: **$402.95**

Dixie Model 1873

DIXIE ENGRAVED MODEL 1873 RIFLE
Caliber: 44-40, 11-shot magazine.
Barrel: 20", round.
Weight: 7¾ lbs. **Length:** 39" over-all.
Stock: Walnut.
Sights: Blade front, adj. rear.
Features: Engraved and case hardened frame. Duplicate of Winchester 1873. Made in Italy. From Dixie Gun Works.
Price: **$550.00**
Price: Plain, blued carbine **$495.00**

E.M.F. HENRY CARBINE
Caliber: 44-40 or 44 rimfire.
Barrel: 21".
Weight: About 9 lbs. **Length:** About 39" over-all.
Stock: Oil stained American walnut.
Sights: Blade front, rear adj. for e.
Features: Reproduction of the original Henry carbine with brass frame and buttplate, rest blued. From E.M.F.
Price: Standard **$600.00**
Price: Engraved **$1000.00**

MARLIN 336CS LEVER ACTION CARBINE
Caliber: 30-30 or 35 Rem., 6-shot tubular magazine
Barrel: 20" Micro-Groove®.
Weight: 7 lbs. **Length:** 38½".
Stock: Select American black walnut, capped p.g. with white line spacers. Mar-Shield® finish.
Sights: Ramp front with Wide-Scan™ hood, semi-buckhorn folding rear adj. for w. & e.
Features: Hammer block safety. Receiver tapped for scope mount, offset hammer spur; top of receiver sand blasted to prevent glare.
Price: Less scope **$295.95**

Marlin Model 336 Extra-Range Carbine
Similar to the standard Model 336CS except chambered for 356 Win.; has new hammer block safety, rubber butt pad, 5-shot magazine. Comes with detachable sling swivels and branded leather sling. Introduced 1983.
Price: **$323.95**

Marlin 336TS Lever Action Carbine
Same as the 336CS except: straight stock; cal. 30-30 only. Squared finger lever, 18½" barrel, weight 6½ lbs. Hammer block safety.
Price: **$295.95**

Marlin 30AS Lever Action Carbine
Same as the Marlin 336CS except has walnut-finished hardwood p.g. stock, 30-30 only, 6-shot. Hammer block safety.
Price: **$282.95**

CAUTION: PRIGES CHANGE. CHECK AT GUNSHOP.

Marlin 1894S

Marlin Model 1894CS Carbine

Similar to the standard Model 1894S except chambered for 38 Special/357 Magnum with 9-shot magazine, 18½" barrel, hammer block safety, brass bead front sight. Introduced 1983.

Price: **$315.95**

MARLIN 1894S LEVER ACTION CARBINE

Caliber: 44 Magnum, 10-shot tubular magazine
Barrel: 20" Micro-Grove®.
Weight: 6 lbs. **Length:** 37½".
Stock: American black walnut, straight grip and fore-end. Mar-Shield® finish.
Sights: Wide-Scan™ hooded ramp front, semi-buckhorn folding rear adj. for w. & e.
Features: Hammer block safety. Receiver tapped for scope mount, offset hammer spur, solid top receiver sand blasted to prevent glare.
Price: **$315.95**

Marlin 1895SS

MARLIN 444SS LEVER ACTION SPORTER

Caliber: 444 Marlin, 5-shot tubular magazine
Barrel: 22" Micro-Groove®.
Weight: 7½ lbs. **Length:** 40½".
Stock: American black walnut, capped p.g. with white line spacers, rubber rifle butt pad. Mar-Shield® finish; q.d. swivels, leather carrying strap.
Sights: Hooded ramp front, folding semi-buckhorn rear adj. for w. & e.
Features: Hammer block safety. Receiver tapped for scope mount, offset hammer spur, leather sling with detachable swivels.
Price: **$339.95**

MARLIN 1895SS LEVER ACTION RIFLE

Caliber: 45-70, 4-shot tubular magazine.
Barrel: 22" round.
Weight: 7½ lbs. **Length:** 40½".
Stock: American black walnut, full pistol grip. Mar-Shield® finish; rubber butt-pad; q.d. swivels; leather carrying strap.
Sights: Bead front with Wide-Scan hood, semi-buckhorn folding rear adj. for w. and e.
Features: Hammer block safety. Solid receiver tapped for scope mounts or receiver sights, offset hammer spur.
Price: **$339.95**

NAVY ARMS HENRY CARBINE

Caliber: 44-40 or 44 rimfire.
Barrel: 24".
Weight: About 8¼ lbs. **Length:** 39" over-all.
Stock: Oil stained American walnut.
Sights: Blade front, rear adj. for e.
Features: Reproduction of the original Henry carbine with brass frame and buttplate, rest blued. Will be produced in limited edition of 1,000 standard models, plus 50 engraved guns. Made in U.S. by Navy Arms.
Price: Standard **$595.00**
Price: Engraved **$1,500.00**

Navy Arms Henry

Price: Iron Frame rifle (similar to Carbine except has blued frame) . **$795.00**
Price: Military Rifle (similar to Carbine except has sling swivels, different rear sight) **$595.00**
Price: Trapper model (16½" bbl., 7¼ lbs., 34½" o.a.l) **$595.00**

Remington Model Six

REMINGTON MODEL SIX SLIDE ACTION

Caliber: 243, 270, 30-06.
Barrel: 22" round tapered.
Weight: 7½ lbs. **Length:** 42" over-all.
Stock: Cut-checkered walnut p.g. and fore-end, Monte Carlo with full cheekpiece.
Sights: Gold bead front sight on matted ramp, open step adj. sporting rear.
Features: Redesigned and improved version of the Model 760. Has cartridge head medallion denoting caliber on bottom of receiver. Detachable 4-shot clip. Cross-bolt safety. Receiver tapped for scope mount. Also available in high grade versions. Introduced 1981.
Price: About **$484.00**

> Consult our Directory pages for the location of firms mentioned.

Remington Model 7600 Slide Action Rifle

Similar to Model Six except also chambered for 6mm Rem., does not have Monte Carlo stock or cheekpiece no cartridge head medallion. Slightly different fore-end design. Impressed checkering. Introduced 1981.
Price: About **$417.00**

Remington "Sportsman" 76 Pump Rifle

Similar to the Model Six except available only in 30-06, 4-shot magazine, 22" barrel, walnut-finished hardwood stock and fore-end, open adjustable sights. Introduced 1984.
Price: About **$348.00**

CAUTION: PRICES CHANGE. CHECK AT GUNSHOP.

ROSSI SADDLE-RING CARBINE M92 SRC

Caliber: 38 Spec., 357 Mag., 44-40, 44 Mag., 10-shot magazine.
Barrel: 20″.
Weight: 5¾ lbs. **Length:** 37″ over-all.
Stock: Walnut.
Sights: Blade front, buckhorn rear.
Features: Re-creation of the famous lever-action carbine. Handles 38 and 357 interchangeably. Has high-relief Puma medallion inlaid in the receiver. Introduced 1978. Imported by Interarms.

Price:	$237.00
Price: Blue, engraved	$277.00
Price: 44-40	$242.00
Price: 44 Spec./44 Mag.	$252.00
Price: 38/357, 16″ bbl.	$232.00

Rossi Carbine

Rossi Puma M92 SRS Short Carbine
Similar to the standard M92 except has 16″ barrel, over-all length of 33″, in 38/357 only. Has large lever loop, Puma medallion on side of receiver. Introduced 1986.
Price: $232.00

Savage Model 99C

SAVAGE 99C LEVER ACTION RIFLE
Caliber: 243 or 308 Win., detachable 4-shot magazine.
Barrel: 22″, chrome-moly steel.
Weight: 8 lbs. **Length:** 41¾″ over-all.
Stock: Walnut with checkered p.g. and fore-end.
Sights: Ramp front, adjustable ramp rear sight. Tapped for scope mounts.
Features: Grooved trigger, top tang slide safety locks trigger and lever. Black rubber butt pad.
Price: $469.00

Winchester Model 94

WINCHESTER MODEL 94 SIDE EJECT
Caliber: 307 Win., 356 Win., 375 Win., 6-shot magazine.
Barrel: 20″.
Weight: 7 lbs. **Length:** 38⅝″ over-all.
Stock: Monte Carlo-style American walnut. Satin finish.
Sights: Hooded ramp front, semi-buckhorn rear adjustable for w. & e.
Features: All external metal parts have Winchester's deep blue high polish finish. Rifling twist 1 in 12″. Rubber recoil pad fitted to buttstock. Introduced 1983. Made under license by U.S. Repeating Arms Co.
Price: About $319.75

WINCHESTER MODEL 94 SIDE EJECT CARBINE
Caliber: 30-30, (12″ twist), 6-shot tubular magazine.
Barrel: 16″, 20″.
Weight: 6½ lbs. (30-30) **Length:** 37¾″ over-all.
Stock: Straight grip walnut stock and fore-end.
Sights: Hooded blade front, semi-buckhorn rear. Drilled and tapped for receiver sight and scope mount.
Features: Solid frame, forged steel receiver; side ejection, exposed rebounding hammer with automatic trigger-activated safety transfer bar. Introduced 1984.

Price: 30-30, about	$290.00
Price: Trapper model (16″ bbl.), 30-30), about	$290.00
Price: As above, 45 Colt, 44 Mag./44 Spec., about	$315.30

Winchester Model 94 120th Anniversary Edition
Similar to standard Model 94 except chambered for 44-40, has hoop-type finger lever, crescent buttplate, blade front sight. Traditional buttstock and extended fore-end of select walnut with semi-gloss finish, deep-cut checkering. Special 120th Anniversary medallion affixed to left side of receiver which also displays the Horse-and-Rider trademark. Right side has a gold-etched portrait of Oliver F. Winchester with his signature on the tang. Left side of the 20″ barrel has the Winchester name in old-style "lightning" lettering; right side has a rendering of the original factory. Magazine cap, front sight are gold plated. Only 1,000 guns to be made. Introduced 1986.
Price: About $1,136.70

Winchester Model 94XTR

Winchester Model 94XTR Side Eject Carbine
Same as standard Model 94 except has high-grade finish on stock and fore-end with cut checkering on both. Metal has highly polished deep blue finish.
Price: About $316.97

Winchester Model 94XTR Side Eject, 7x30 Waters
Same as Model 94 Side Eject except has 24″ barrel, 7-shot magazine, overall length of 41¾″ and weight is 7 lbs. Barrel twist is 1-12″. Rubber butt pad instead of plastic. Introduced 1984.
Price: About $345.55

Winchester Ranger Side Eject Carbine
Same as Model 94 Side Eject except has 5-shot magazine, American hardwood stock and fore-end, no front sight hood. Introduced 1985.

Price: About	$244.90
Price: With 4 x 32 Bushnell scope, mounts, about	$282.57

CAUTION: PRICES CHANGE. CHECK AT GUNSHOP.

Alpha Custom

ALPHA CUSTOM BOLT ACTION RIFLE
Caliber: 17 Rem., 222, 223 (Short action), 22-250 through 338-284 (Medium action), 25-06 through 35 Whelan (Standard action), 257 Wea. through 338 Win. Mag. (Magnum action).
Barrel: 20″—23″ depending on caliber.
Weight: 6-7 lbs. **Length:** 40″-43″ over-all.
Stock: Classic-style California claro walnut with hand rubbed oil finish, hand checkered 22-24 l.p.i., ebony fore-end tip, custom steel grip cap, Talley inletted swivel studs, solid butt pad.
Sights: None furnished. Drilled and tapped for scope mounting. Custom open sights available.
Features: Three action lengths with three-lug locking system and 60° bolt rotation; three-position Model 70-type safety, pillar bedding system; steel floorplate/trigger guard; satin finish blue. Right or left-hand models available. Introduced 1984. Made in U.S. by Alpha Arms, Inc.
Price: With hard case, Super Sling $1,735.00

Alpha Grand Slam Bolt Action Rifle
Similar to the Custom model except has classic-style stock of Alphawood, Niedner-style grip cap. Weight is about 6½ lbs. Other specs remain the same. Right or left-hand models available. Introduced 1984.
Price: With hard case, Super Sling $1,465.00

Alpha Alaskan

Alpha Alaskan Bolt Action Rifle
Similar to the Custom model except has stainless steel barrel and receiver with all other parts coated with Nitex. Has classic-style Alphawood stock, Niedner-style steel grip cap, barrel band swivel stud, inletted swivel stud on butt. Weight is 6¾ to 7¼ lbs. Same chamberings as Custom. Right or left-hand models available. Introduced 1984.
Price: With hard case, Super Sling $1,675.00

Alpine Custom Grade

ALPINE BOLT ACTION RIFLE
Caliber: 22-250, 243 Win., 264 Win., 270, 30-06, 308, 308 Norma Mag., 7mm Rem Mag., 8mm, 300 Win. Mag., 5-shot magazine (3 for magnum).
Barrel: 23″ (std. cals.), 24″ (mag.).

Weight: 7½ lbs.
Stock: European walnut. Full p.g. and Monte Carlo; checkered p.g. and fore-end; rubber recoil pad; white line spacers; sling swivels.
Sights: Ramp front, open rear adj. for w. and e.
Features: Made by Firearms Co. Ltd. in England. Imported by Mandall Shooting Supplies.
Price: Standard Grade $375.00
Price: Custom Grade (illus.)................................... $395.00

Anschutz 1432D/1532D

ANSCHUTZ 1432D/1532D CLASSIC RIFLES
Caliber: 22 Hornet (1432D), 5-shot clip, 222 Rem. (1532D), 2-shot clip.
Barrel: 23½″; ¹³⁄₁₆″ dia. heavy.
Weight: 7¾ lbs. **Length:** 42½″ over-all.
Stock: Select European walnut with checkered pistol grip and fore-end.
Sights: None furnished, drilled and tapped for scope mounting.
Features: Adjustable single stage trigger. Receiver drilled and tapped for scope mounting. Introduced 1982. Imported from Germany by PSI.
Price: 1432D (22 Hornet) $673.75
Price: 1532D (222 Rem.) $673.75

ARMSPORT 2801 BOLT ACTION RIFLE
Caliber: 243, 308, 30-06, 7mm Rem. Mag., 300 Win. Mag.
Barrel: 24″.
Weight: 8 lbs.
Stock: European walnut with Monte Carlo comb.
Sights: Ramp front, open adj. rear.
Features: Blue metal finish, glossy wood. Introduced 1986. Imported from Italy by Armsport.
Price: $575.00

ANSCHUTZ 1432D/1532D Custom Rifles
Similar to the Classic models except have roll-over Monte Carlo cheekpiece, slim fore-end with Schnabel tip, Wundhammer palm swell on pistol grip, rosewood grip cap with white diamond insert. Skip-line checkering on grip and fore-end. Introduced 1982. Imported from Germany by PSI.
Price: 1432D (22 Hornet) $721.75
Price: 1532D (222 Rem.) $721.75

CAUTION: PRICES CHANGE. CHECK AT GUNSHOP.

Beeman/Krico Model 420

BEEMAN/KRICO MODEL 600/700L DELUXE BOLT ACTION

Caliber: 17 Rem., 222, 223, 22-250, 243, 308, 7x57, 7x64, 270, 30-06, 9.3x62, 8x68S, 7mm Rem. Mag., 300 Win. Mag., 9.3x64.
Barrel: 24″ (26″ in magnum calibers).
Weight: 7.5 lbs. **Length:** 44″ over-all (24″ barrel).
Stock: Traditional European style, select fancy walnut with rosewood Schnable fore-end, Bavarian cheekpiece, 28 lpi checkering.
Sights: Hooded front ramp, rear adjustable for windage.
Features: Butterknife bolt handle; gold plated single-set trigger; front sling swivel attached to barrel with ring; silent safety. Introduced 1983. Made in West Germany. Imported by Beeman.
Price: Model 600, varmint calibers $1,049.50
Price: Model 600, standard calibers $1,049.50
Price: Model 700, magnum calibers $1,049.50

BEEMAN/KRICO MODEL 400 BOLT ACTION RIFLE

Caliber: 22 Hornet, 5-shot magazine.
Barrel: 23.5″.
Weight: 6.8 lbs. **Length:** 43″ over-all.
Stock: Select European walnut, curved European comb with cheekpiece; solid rubber butt pad; cut checkered grip and fore-end.
Sights: Blade front on ramp, open rear adjustable for windage.
Features: Detachable box magazine; action has rear locking lugs, twin extractors. Available with single or optional match and double set trigger. Receiver grooved for scope mounts. Made in West Germany. Imported by Beeman.
Price: $649.50
Price: Model 420 (as above except 19.5″ bbl., full-length Mannlicher-style stock, double set trigger) $749.50

Beeman/Krico Model 620/720 Bolt Action Rifle

Similar to the Model 600/700 except has 20.75″ barrel,. weighs 6.8 lbs., and has full-length Mannlicher-style stock with metal Schnabel fore-end tip; doubel set trigger with optional match trigger available. Receiver drilled and tapped for scope mounting. Imported from West Germany by Beeman.
Price: Model 620 (308 Win.) $995.00
Price: Model 720 (270 Win.) $995.00
Price: Model 720 (30-06) $995.00

Beeman/Krico Model 640 Varmint

BEEMAN/KRICO MODEL 640 VARMINT RIFLE

Caliber: 222 Rem., 4-shot magazine.
Barrel: 23.75″.
Weight: 9.6 lbs. **Length:** 43½″ over-all.
Stock: Select European walnut with high Monte Carlo comb, Wundhammer palm swell, rosewood fore-end tip; cut checkered grip and fore-end.
Sights: None furnished. Drilled and tapped for scope mounting.
Features: Free floating heavy bull barrel; double set trigger with optional match trigger available. Imported from West Germany by Beeman.
Price: $995.00

Beretta 500 Series

BERETTA 500 SERIES BOLT ACTION RIFLE

Caliber: 222, 223 (M500); 243, 308 (M501); 270, 7mm Rem. Mag., 30-06, 375 H&H (M502).
Barrel: 23.62″ to 24.41″.
Weight: 6.4 to 8.4 lbs. **Length:** NA
Stock: Walnut, with oil finish, hand checkering.
Sights: None furnished; drilled and tapped for scope mounting.
Features: Model 500 — short action; 501 — medium action; 502 — long action. All models have rubber butt pad. Imported from Italy by Beretta U.S.A. Corp. Introduced 1984.
Price: Model 500, 501, from . . . . $665.00 to $1,785.00
Price: Model 502, from . . . . $710.00 to $1,785.00

BRNO ZKK 602

BRNO ZKK 531 BOLT ACTION RIFLE

Caliber: 30-06, 270, 7x57, 7x64, 8x57JS, 8x64S, 8x68S, 300 Win. Mag., 338 Win. Mag., 7mm Rem. Mag., 280 Rem. (internal magazine); 243, 308 (detachable box magazine).
Barrel: 23½″.
Weight: NA.
Stock: European walnut.
Sights: Hooded front, open rear adj. for w.
Features: Double set triggers, tang safety, spring-type extractor, sling swivels. Drilled and tapped for scope mounts. Imported from Czechoslovakia by Bauska Arms Corp.
Price: . . . . NA

BRNO ZKK 600, 601, 602 BOLT ACTION RIFLES

Caliber: 30-06, 270, 7x57, 7x64 (M600); 223, 243, 308 (M601); 8x68S, 375 H&H, 458 Win. Mag. (M602), 5-shot magazine.
Barrel: 23½″ (M600, 601), 25″ (M602).
Weight: 6 lbs., 3 oz. to 9 lbs., 4 oz. **Length:** 43″ over-all (M601).
Stock: Walnut.
Sights: Hooded ramp front, open folding leaf adj. rear.
Features: Adjustable set trigger (standard trigger included); easy-release floorplate; sling swivels. Imported from Czechoslovakia by Bauska Arms Corp.
Price: ZKK Standard $479.00
Price: As above, Monte Carlo stock $499.00
Price: ZKK 601 Standard $379.00
Price: As above, Monte Carlo stock $399.00
Price: ZKK 602, Monte Carlo stock $599.00

BRNO ZKB 680 FOX

BRNO ZKB 680 FOX BOLT ACTION RIFLE
Caliber: 22 Hornet, 222 Rem., 5-shot magazine.
Barrel: 23½".
Weight: 5 lbs., 12 oz. **Length:** 42½" over-all.
Stock: Turkish walnut, with Monte Carlo.
Sights: Hooded front, open adj. rear.
Features: Detachable box magazine; adj. double set triggers. Imported from Czechoslovakia by Bauska Arms Corp.
Price: **$399.00**

Browning A-Bolt

BROWNING A-BOLT RIFLE
Caliber: 25-06, 270, 30-06, 7mm Rem. Mag., 300 Win. Mag., 338 Win. Mag.
Barrel: 22" medium sporter weight with recessed muzzle.
Weight: 6½ to 7½ lbs. **Length:** 44¾" over-all. (Magnum and standard), 41¾" (short action).
Stock: Classic style American walnut; recoil pad standard on magnum calibers.

Browning Short Action A-Bolt
Similar to the standard A-Bolt except has short action for 22-250, 243, 257 Roberts, 7mm-08, 308 chamberings. Available in Hunter or Medallion grades. Weighs 6½ lbs. Other specs essentially the same. Introduced 1985.
Price: Medallion, no sights **$446.50**
Price: Hunter, no sights **$379.95**
Price: Hunter, with sights **$424.95**

Features: Short-throw (60°) fluted bolt, 9 locking lugs, plunger-type ejector; adjustable trigger is grooved and gold plated. Hinged floorplate, detachable box magazine (4 rounds std. cals., 3 for magnums). Slide tang safety. Medallion has glossy stock finish, rosewood grip and fore-end caps, high polish blue; Hunter has oil finish stock, matte blue. Introduced 1985. Imported from Japan by Browning.
Price: Medallion, no sights **$446.50**
Price: Hunter, no sights **$379.95**
Price: Hunter, with sights **$424.95**

Browning A-Bolt High Grade Limited Edition Big Horn Sheep Issue
Same specifications as standard A-Bolt except 270 Win. only, stock is high grade walnut, and brass spacers highlight the grip caps and recoil pad; high gloss finish. Deep relief engraving on the receiver, barrel, floorplate and trigger guard serve as a setting for the game species, displayed in 24K gold. Stock has cut skipline checkering with a pearl border design. Limited to only 600 units. Introduced 1986.
Price: **$1,365.00**

Consult our Directory pages for the location of firms mentioned.

CHAMPLIN RIFLE
Caliber: All std. chamberings, including 458 Win. and 460 Wea. Many wildcats on request.
Barrel: Any length up to 26" for octagon. Choice of round, straight taper octagon, or octagon with integral quarter rib, front sight ramp and sling swivel stud.
Weight: About 8 lbs. **Length:** 45" over-all.
Stock: Hand inletted, shaped and finished. Checkered to customer specs. Select French, Circassian or claro walnut. Steel p.g. cap, trap buttplate or recoil pad.
Sights: Bead on ramp front, 3-leaf folding rear.
Features: Right-hand Champlin action, tang safety or optional shroud safety, Canjar adj. trigger, hinged floorplate.
Price: From **$5,400.00**

Champlin

Churchill Regent

CHURCHILL BOLT ACTION RIFLE
Caliber: 25-06, 270, 30-06 (4-shot magazine) 7mm Rem. Mag. (3-shot).
Barrel: 22" (7mm Rem. Mag. has 24").
Weight: 7½-8 lbs. **Length:** 42½" over-all with 22" barrel.
Stock: European walnut, checkered p.g. and fore-end. Regent grade has Monte Carlo, Highlander has classic design.
Sights: Gold bead on ramp front, fully adj. rear.
Features: Positive safety locks trigger; oil-finished wood; swivel posts; recoil pad. Imported by Kassnar Imports, Inc. Introduced 1986.
Price: Highlander, without sights, either cal. **$549.00**
Price: As above, with sights **$584.00**
Price: Regent, without sights **$759.00**
Price: As above, with sights **$789.00**

CAUTION: PRICES CHANGE. CHECK AT GUNSHOP.

Du Biel Modern Classic

Consult our Directory pages for
the location of firms mentioned.

Du BIEL ARMS BOLT ACTION RIFLES

Caliber: Standard calibers 22-250 thru 458 Win. Mag. Selected wildcat calibers available.
Barrel: Selected weights and lengths. Douglas Premium
Weight: About 7½ lbs.
Stock: Five styles. Walnut, maple, laminates. Hand checkered.
Sights: None furnished. Receiver has integral milled bases.
Features: Basically a custom-made rifle. Left or right-hand models available. Five-lug locking mechanism; 36 degree bolt rotation; adjustable Canjar trigger; oil or epoxy stock finish; Presentation recoil pad; jeweled and chromed bolt body; sling swivel studs; lever latch or button floorplate release. All steel action and parts. Introduced 1978. From Du Biel Arms.
Price: Rollover Model, left or right-hand $2,500.00
Price: Thumbhole, left or right hand $2,500.00
Price: Classic, left or right hand $2,500.00
Price: Modern Classic, left or right hand $2,500.00
Price: Thumbhole Mannlicher, left or right hand $2,500.00

DUMOULIN MODEL BAVARIA BOLT ACTION RIFLE

Caliber: 222, 222 Rem. Mag., 223, 270, 280 Rem., 30-06, 6.5x57, 7x57, 7x64, 243, 264 Win., 7mm Rem. Mag., 300 Win., 338 Win., 6.5x68, 8x68S, 25-06, 22-250, 6mm, 300 Wea., 308 Norma, 240 Wea., 375 H&H, 9.3x64, 458 Win. Others on request.
Barrel: 21", 24", 25", octagon.
Weight: About 7 lbs.

Stock: Select walnut with oil finish; hand checkered p.g. and fore-end.
Sights: Blade on ramp front (hooded), classic 2-leaf rear.
Features: Mauser system action; adj. trigger; M70-type safety; Boehler steel barrel, q.d. swivels, front on fore-end or barrel; solid butt pad. Imported from Belgium by Midwest Gun Sport.
Price: About $1,940.00
Price: Model Diane (as above except with round barrel) $1,750.00

DUMOULIN AFRICAN SAFARI RIFLE

Caliber: 264 Win., 7mm Rem. Mag., 300 Win., 338 Win., 6.5x58, 8x68S, 300 H&H, 375 H&H, 9.3x64, 458 Win., 404 Jeffrey, 416 Rigby, 416 Hoffman, 7mm Wea., 300 Wea., 340 Wea. Others on request.
Barrel: 24" to 26".
Weight: 8½-9 lbs. **Length:** 44" over-all with 24" barrel.

Stock: Deluxe European walnut in classic English style; oil finish; recoil lug; buffalo horn grip cap; solid rubber butt pad.
Sights: Hooded front on banded ramp, quarter-rib with 2-leaf rear.
Features: Mauser Oberndorf or modified Sako action; adj. trigger; M70-type or side safety. Custom-built gun. Imported from Belgium by Midwest Gun Sport.
Price: About $2,750.00

Heym Model SR-20L

HEYM MODEL SR-20 BOLT ACTION RIFLES

Caliber: 5.6x57, 243, 6.5x55, 6.5x57, 270, 7x57, 7x64, 308, 30-06 (SR-20L); 9.3x62 (SR-20N) plus SR-20L cals.; SR-20G—6.5x68, 7mm Rem. Mag., 300 Win. Mag., 8x68S, 375H&H.
Barrel: 20½" (SR-20L), 24" (SR-20N), 26" (SR-20G).
Weight: 7-8 lbs. depending upon model.
Stock: Dark European walnut, hand-checkered p.g. and fore-end. Oil finish. Recoil pad, rosewood grip cap. Monte Carlo-style. SR-20L has full Mannlicher-style stock, others have sporter-style with schnabel tip.
Sights: Silver bead ramp front, adj. folding leaf rear.
Features: Hinged floorplate, 3-position safety,. Receiver drilled and tapped for scope mounts. Adjustable trigger. Options available include double-set triggers, left-hand action and stock, Suhler olaw mounts, deluxe engraving and stock carving. Imported from West Germany by Paul Jaeger, Inc.
Price: SR-20L $985.00
Price: SR-20N $875.00
Price: SR-20-G $920.00
Price: Single set trigger, add $70.00

Heym SR-40 Bolt Action Rifle

Same as the SR-20 except has short action, chambered for 222 Rem., 223 Rem., 5.6x50 Mag. Over-all length of 44", weight about 6¼ lbs., 24" barrel. Carbine Mannlicher-style stock. Introduced 1984.
Price: $798.00
Price: Single set trigger, add $70.00

Heym SR-20 Classic

Heym SR-20 Classic

Similar to the standard SR-20N except chambered for 5.6x57, 6.5x57, 6.5x55 SM, 7x57, 7x64, 9.3x62, 243, 270, 308, 30-06 (standard cals.); 6.5x68, 8x68 S, 7mm Rem. Mag., 300 Win. Mag., 375 H&H (magnum cals.). Has 24" barrel (std. cals.), 25" (mag. cals.). Classic-style French walnut stock with cheekpiece, hand checkering, Pachmayr Old English pad, q.d. swivels, oil finish, steel grip cap. Open sights on request. Choice of adjustable, single-set or double-set trigger. Introduced 1985.
Price: SR-20 Classic, right-hand $875.00
Price: SR-20 Classic, left-hand $1,150.00
Price: Magnum calibers, right or left-hand add $45.00
Price: Single set trigger, add $70.00
Price: Open sights, from $125.00

Heym SR-20, SR-40 Left Hand Rifles

All Heym bolt action rifles are available with true left-hand action and stock, in all calibers listed for the right-hand version, for an additional $165.00

KDF K-15 Improved

KDF K-15 Fiberstock "Pro-Hunter" Rifle

Same as K-15 Improved Rifle except standard with Brown Precision fiberglass stock (black, green, gray, brown or camo) wrinkle finish, KDF recoil arrestor installed and choice of parkerized, matte-blue or electroless nickel finish.

Price: Standard calibers **$1,600.00**
Price: Magnum calibers **$1,650.00**

KDF K-15 "Dangerous Game" Rifle

Same as K-15 Improved Rifle except chambered for 411 KDF Magnum caliber. Standard with KDF Recoil Arrestor, choice of iron sights or scope mounts, hinged floorplate, and choice of high-gloss blue, matte blue, parkerized or electroless nickel metal finish.

Price: **$1,800.00**

KDF K-15 IMPROVED RIFLE

Caliber: 243, 25-06, 270, 7x57, 308, 30-06, 4-shot magazine, (standard); 257 Wea., 270 Wea., 7mm Rem. Mag., 300 Win. Mag., 300 Wea., 308 Norma Mag., 375 H&H, 3-shot magazine. Special chamberings avail.
Barrel: 24" (standard), 26" (magnum).
Weight: About 8 lbs. **Length:** 44½" over-all (24" bbl.).
Stock: Oil finished, hand checkered European walnut; recoil pad, swivel studs. Choice of Featherweight Classic with Schnabel or European Monte Carlo with rosewood grip cap, fore-end tip. High luster finish avail.
Sights: None furnished; drilled and tapped for scope mounting. Open sights, rings, bases avail. from KDF.
Features: KDF pillar bedding system; ultra-fast lock time. Three year accuracy guarantee from maker — 3-shot ½" group at 100 yds. From KDF, Inc.
Price: Standard calibers **$1,100.00**
Price: Magnum calibers **$1,150.00**
Price: Special chamberings . . . . **P.O.R.**

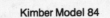

Kimber Model 82

KIMBER MODEL 82 SPORTER

Caliber: 22 Hornet; 3-shot flush-fitting magazine; 218 Bee, 25-20, single shot.
Barrel: 22½", 6 grooves; 1-in-14" twist; 24" heavy.
Weight: About 6¼ lbs. **Length:** 42" over-all.
Stock: Three styles available. "Classic" is Claro walnut with plain, straight comb; "Cascade" has Monte Carlo comb with cheekpiece. "Custom Classic" is of fancy select grade Claro walnut, ebony fore-end tip, Niedner-style buttplate. All have 18 lpi hand cut, borderless checkering, steel grip cap, checkered steel buttplate.

Sights: Hooded ramp front with bead, folding leaf rear (optional).
Features: All steel construction; twin rear horizontally opposed locking lugs; fully adjustable trigger; rocker-type safety. Receiver grooved for Kimber scope mounts. Available in true left-hand version in selected models. Introduced 1982.
Price: Classic stock, no sights (left hand also avail.) **$750.00**
Price: Cascade stock, no sights **$805.00**
Price: Custom Classic, no sights (left hand also avail.) **$995.00**
Price: Kimber scope mounts, from **$48.00**
Price: Open sights fitted (optional) **$55.00**
Price: 218 Bee, Custom Classic, plain or heavy barrel **$995.00**
Price: 25-20, Custom Classic, plain barrel **$995.00**

Kimber Model 84

Kimber Model 82, 84 Super America

Super-grade version of the Model 82. Has a Classic stock only of specially selected, high-grade, California claro walnut, with Continental beaded cheekpiece and ebony fore-end tip; borderless, full-coverage 20 lpi checkering; Niedner-type checkered steel buttplate; comes with barrel quarter-rib which has a folding leaf sight. Round-top receiver on the 1986 model is drilled and tapped to accept Kimber's screw-on scope mount bases. Available in 22 Long Rifle, 22 Magnum, 22 Hornet, 223 Rem.

Price: Model 82, 22 Long Rifle, less 4x scope. **$1,150.00**
Price: Model 82, 22 Hornet, less scope **$1,150.00**
Price: Model 84, 223 Rem. **$1,250.00**

KIMBER MODEL 84 SPORTER

Caliber: 17 Rem., 17 Mach IV, 221 Fireball, 222 Rem., 222 Rem. Mag., 223 Rem., 6x45, 6x47; 5-shot magazine.
Barrel: 22" (Sporter), 24" (Varmint).
Weight: About 6¼ lbs. **Length:** 40½" over-all (Sporter).
Stock: Three styles available. "Classic" is Claro walnut with plain, straight comb; "Cascade" has Monte Carlo comb with cheekpiece. "Custom Classic" is of fancy select grade Claro walnut, ebony fore-end tip, Niedner-style buttplate. All have 18 lpi hand cut, borderless checkering, steel grip cap, checkered steel buttplate.
Sights: Hooded ramp front with bead, folding leaf rear (optional).
Features: All new Mauser-type head locking bolt action; steel trigger guard and hinged floorplate; Mauser-type extractor; fully adjustable trigger; chrome-moly barrel. Round-top receiver drilled and topped for scope mounting. Varmint gun prices same as others. Introduced 1984.
Price: Classic stock, no sights **$850.00**
Price: Cascade stock, no sights **$905.00**
Price: Custom Classic stock, no sights **$1,095.00**
Price: Kimber scope mounts, from **$48.00**
Price: Open sights fitted (optional) **$55.00**

Marathon Sportsman

MARATHON SPORTSMAN BUSH & FIELD RIFLE

Caliber: 243, 308, 7x57, 30-06, 270, 7mm Rem. Mag., 300 Win. Mag.
Barrel: 24".
Weight: 7.9 lbs. **Length:** 45" over-all.
Stock: Select walnut with Monte Carlo and rubber recoil pad.
Sights: Bead front on ramp, open adjustable rear.
Features: Uses the Santa Barbara Mauser action. Triple thumb locking safety blocks trigger, firing pin and bolt. Blue finish. Also available as a kit requiring assembly, wood and metal finishing. Introduced 1984. Imported from Spain by Marathon Products.
Price: Finished **$339.99**
Price: Kit **$209.99**

CAUTION: PRICES CHANGE. CHECK AT GUNSHOP.

CENTERFIRE RIFLES—BOLT ACTIONS

Mossberg Model 1500

Mossberg Model 1550 Rifle
Similar to the M1500 except has removable box magazine. In cals. 243, 270, 30-06 only. Introduced 1986.
Price: .... **NA**

Mossberg Model 1500 Deluxe Rifle
Similar to Standard model except comes without sights, has engine-turned bolt; floorplate has decorative scroll. Stock has skip-line checkering, pistol grip cap with inset S&W seal, white spacers. Sling, swivels and swivel posts are included. Magnum models have vent, recoil pad.
Price: Deluxe, std. cals. **$363.00**
Price: Deluxe, magnum cals. **$386.00**

Mossberg Classic Hunter

Mossberg Model 1500 Varmint Deluxe Rifle
Similar to the standard 1500 except has a 22" heavy barrel and fully adjustable trigger. Chambered for 222, 22-250 and 223. Weighs 9 lbs. 5 oz. Skip-line checkering, q.d. swivels. Introduced 1982.
Price: Blue **$425.00**
Price: Parkerized, oil finished stock **$432.00**

Parker-Hale 81 Classic

PARKER-HALE MODEL 81 CLASSIC RIFLE
Caliber: 22-250, 243, 6mm Rem., 270, 6.5x55, 7x57, 7x64, 308, 30-06, 300 Win. Mag., 7mm Rem. Mag., 4-shot magazine.
Barrel: 24".
Weight: About 7¾ lbs. **Length:** 44½" over-all.

Parker-Hale 81 African

Parker-Hale Model 1100

MOSSBERG M1500 MOUNTAINEER RIFLE
Caliber: 222, 223, 22-250, 243, 25-06, 270, 30-06, 308, 7mm Rem. Mag., 300 Win. Mag., 338 Win. Mag.
Barrel: 22" (24" in magnum calibers.).
Weight: 7½-7¾ lbs. **Length:** 42" over-all (42½" for 270, 30-06, 7mm).
Stock: American walnut with Monte Carlo comb and cheekpiece; 18-line-per-inch checkering on p.g. and fore-end.
Sights: Hooded ramp gold bead front, open round-notch rear adj. for w. & e. Drilled and tapped for scope mounts.
Features: Trigger guard and magazine box are a single unit with a hinged floorplate. Comes with q.d. swivel studs. Composition non-slip buttplate with white spacer. Magnum models have rubber recoil pad. Introduced 1979.
Price: Standard cals., no sights **$341.00**
Price: Magnum cals., no sights **$356.00**
Price: Standard cals., with sights **$365.00**
Price: Magnum cals., with sights **$379.00**

Mossberg Model 1700LS "Classic Hunter"
Similar to the standard Model 1500 except has classic-style stock with tapered fore-end and Schnabel tip, ribbon hand checkering, black rubber butt pad with black spacer; flush mounted sling swivels; removeable 5-shot magazine; jeweled bolt body with knurled bolt knob. Chambered only for 243, 270, 30-06. Introduced 1983.
Price: **$454.00**

Stock: European walnut in classic style with oil finish, hand-cut checkering; palm swell pistol grip, rosewood grip cap.
Sights: None furnished. Drilled and tapped for open sights and scope mounting.
Features: Uses Mauser-style action; one-piece steel, Oberndorf-style trigger guard with hinged floorplate; rubber butt pad; quick-detachable sling swivels. Imported from England by Precision Sports, Inc. Introduced 1984.
Price: **$649.95**
Price: Optional set trigger **$74.95**

Parker-Hale Model 81 African Rifle
Similar to the Model 81 Classic except chambered only for 300 H&H, 308 Norma Mag., 375 H&H and 9.3x64. Has adjustable trigger, barrel band front swivel, African express rear sight, engraved receiver. Classic-style stock has a solid butt pad, checkered p.g. and fore-end. Introduced 1986.
Price: **$789.95**

Parker-Hale Model 1100 Lightweight Rifle
Similar to the Model 81 Classic except has slim barrel profile, hollow bolt handle, alloy trigger guard/floorplate. The Monte Carlo stock has a Schnabel fore-end hand-cut checkering, swivel studs, palm swell pistol grip. Comes with hooded ramp front sight, open Williams rear adjustable for windage and elevation. Same calibers as Model 81. Over-all length is 43", weight 6½ lbs., with 22" barrel. Imported from England by Precision Sports, Inc. Introduced 1984.
Price: **$529.95**
Price: Optional set trigger **$74.95**
Price: Optional Deluxe fancy wood **$64.95**

Parker-Hale 1200 Super

PARKER-HALE MODEL 1200 SUPER BOLT ACTION
Caliber: 22-250, 243, 6mm, 25-06, 270, 6.5x55, 7x57, 7x64, 308, 30-06, 8mm.
Barrel: 24″.
Weight: About 7½ lbs. **Length:** 44½″ over-all.
Stock: European walnut, rosewood grip and fore-end tips, hand-cut checkering; roll-over cheekpiece; palm swell pistol grip; ventilated recoil pad; wraparound checkering.
Sights: Hooded post front, open rear.
Features: Uses Mauser-style action with claw extractor; gold plated adjustable trigger; silent side safety locks trigger, sear and bolt; aluminum trigger guard. Imported from England by Precision Sports, Inc. Introduced 1984.
Price: $549.95
Price: Optional set trigger $74.95

Parker-Hale Model 1200 Super Clip Rifle
Same as the Model 1200 Super except has a detachable steel box magazine and steel trigger guard. Imported from England by Precision Sports, Inc. Introduced 1984.
Price: $579.95
Price: Optional set trigger $74.95

Parker-Hale Model 1100M African Magnum
Similar to the Model 1000 Standard except has 24″ barrel, 46″ over-all length, weighs 9½ lbs., and is chambered for 375 H&H Magnum, 404 Jeffery and 458 Win. Magnum. Has hooded post front sight, shallow V-notch rear, 180° flag safety (low 45° scope safety available). Specially lengthened steel magazine has hinged floorplate; heavily reinforced, glass bedded and weighted stock has a ventilated rubber recoil pad. Imported from England by Precision Sports, Inc. Introduced 1984.
Price: $789.95

Parker-Hale Model 1000 Standard Rifle
Similar to the Model 1200 Super except has standard walnut Monte Carlo stock with satin varnish finish, no rosewood grip/fore-end caps; fitted with checkered buttplate, standard sling swivels. Imported from England by Precision Sports, Inc. Introduced 1984.
Price: $429.95
Price: Optional set trigger $74.95

PARKER-HALE MODEL 2100 MIDLAND RIFLE
Caliber: 22-250, 243, 6mm, 270, 6.5x55, 7x57, 7x64, 308, 30-06.
Barrel: 22″.
Weight: About 7 lbs. **Length:** 43″ over-all.
Stock: European walnut, cut-checkered pistol grip and fore-end; sling swivels.
Sights: Hooded post front, flip-up open rear.
Features: Mauser-type action has twin front locking lugs, rear safety lug, and claw extractor; hinged floorplate; adjustable single stage trigger; silent side safety. Imported from England by Precision Sports, Inc. Introduced 1984.
Price: $299.00

Rahn "Deer Series"

RAHN "DEER SERIES" BOLT ACTION RIFLE
Caliber: 25-06, 308, 270.
Barrel: 24″.
Weight: NA. **Length:** NA.
Stock: Circassian walnut with rosewood fore-end and grip caps, Monte Carlo cheekpiece, semi-Schnabel fore-end; hand checkered.
Sights: Bead front, open adjustable rear. Drilled and tapped for scope mount.
Features: Free floating barrel; rubber recoil pad; one-piece trigger guard with hinged, engraved floorplate; 22 rimfire conversion insert available. Introduced 1986. From Rahn Gun Works, Inc.
Price: $750.00
Price: With custom stock made to customer specs $800.00

Rahn "Himalayan Series" Rifle
Similar to the "Deer Series" except chambered for 5.6x57 or 6.5x68S, short stock of walnut or fiberglass, and floorplate engravings of a yak with scroll border. Introduced 1986.
Price: $800.00
Price: With walnut stock made to customer specs $850.00

Rahn "Safari Series" Rifle
Similar to the "Deer Series" except chambered for 308 Norma Mag., 300 Win. Mag., 8x68S, 9x64. Choice of Cape buffalo, rhino or elephant engraving. Gold oval nameplate with three initials. Introduced 1986.
Price: $900.00
Price: With stock made to customer specs $950.00

Rahn "Elk Series" Rifle
Similar to the "Deer Series" except chambered for 6mmx56, 30-06, 7mm Rem. Mag. and has elk head engraving on floorplate. Introduced 1986.
Price: $785.00
Price: With stock made to customer specs $835.00

Remington 700 Classic

REMINGTON 700 "CLASSIC" RIFLE
Caliber: 264 Win. Mag. only, 4-shot magazine.
Barrel: 24″.
Weight: About 7¾ lbs. **Length:** 44½″ over-all.
Stock: American walnut, 20 l.p.i. checkering on p.g. and fore-end. Classic styling. Satin finish.
Sights: No sights furnished. Receiver drilled and tapped for scope mounting.
Features: A "classic" version of the M700ADL with straight comb stock. Fitted with rubber butt pad on all but magnum caliber, which has a full recoil pad. Sling swivel studs installed. Limited production in 1986 only
Price: About $465.00

CAUTION: PRICES CHANGE. CHECK AT GUNSHOP.

Remington 700 BDL

REMINGTON 700 ADL BOLT ACTION RIFLE

Caliber: 22-250, 243, 25-06, 270, 308 and 30-06.
Barrel: 22″ or 24″ round tapered.
Weight: 7 lbs. **Length:** 41½″ to 43½″.
Stock: Walnut, RKW finished p.g. stock with impressed checkering, Monte Carlo (13⅜″x1⅝″x2⅜″).
Sights: Gold bead ramp front; removable, step-adj. rear with windage screw.
Features: Side safety, receiver tapped for scope mounts.
Price: About **$400.00**
Price: 7mm Rem. Mag., about................................. **$420.00**

Remington 700BDL Left Hand

Same as 700 BDL except: mirror-image left-hand action, stock. Available in 270, 30-06 only.
Price: About **$520.00**
Price: 7mm Rem. Mag., about................................. **$539.00**

Remington 700 Mountain

Remington 700 Custom "KS"

Remington Sportsman 78

Remington Model Seven

Remington 700 BDL Bolt Action Rifle

Same as 700-ADL, except: also available in 222, 223, 6mm, 7mm-08 Rem.; skip-line checkering; black fore-end tip and p.g. cap, white line spacers. Matted receiver top, quick release floorplate. Hooded ramp front sight. Q.D. swivels and 1″ sling.
Price: About **$471.00**
Available also in 17 Rem., 7mm Rem. Mag. and 300 Win. Mag. calibers. 44½″ over-all, weight 7½ lbs.
Price: About **$490.00**
Price: Custom Grade I, about.............................. **$1,131.00**
Price: Custom Grade II, about **$2,056.00**
Price: Custom Grade III, about............................ **$3,181.00**
Price: Custom Grade IV, about............................ **$4,933.00**

Remington 700 BDL Varmint Special

Same as 700 BDL, except: 24″ heavy bbl., 43½″ over-all, wgt. 9 lbs. Cals. 222, 223, 22-250, 243, 6mm Rem., 25-06, 7mm-08 Rem. and 308. No sights.
Price: About **$501.00**

Remington 700 Safari

Same as the 700 BDL except 8mm Rem. Mag., 375 H&H or 458 Win. Magnum calibers only. Hand checkered, oil finished stock in classic or Monte Carlo style with recoil pad installed. Delivery time is about five months.
Price: About **$775.00**

Remington Model 700 "Mountain Rifle"

Similar to the 700BDL except weighs 6¾ lbs., has a 22″ tapered barrel. Redesigned pistol grip, straight comb, contoured cheekpiece, satin stock finish, fine checkering, hinged floorplate and magazine follower, 2-position thumb safety. Chambered for 270 Win., 280 Rem., 30-06, 4-shot magazine. Overall length is 42½″. Introduced 1986.
Price: About **$477.00**

Remington Model 700 Custom "KS" Mountain Rifle

Similar to the 700 "Mountain Rifle" except has Kevlar reinforced resin synthetic stock. Available in both left- and right-hand versions. Chambered for 270 Win., 280 Rem., 30-06, 7mm Rem. Mag., 300 Win. Mag., 375 H&H, all with 24″ barrel only. Weight is 6 lbs., 6 oz. Introduced 1986.
Price: About **$816.00**

Remington "Sportsman" 78 Bolt Action Rifle

Similar to the Model 700 except available only in 223, 243, 308, 270 Win. or 30-06, 4-shot magazine, 22″ barrel, straight comb walnut-finished hardwood stock. Open adjustable sights; weight about 7 lbs. Introduced 1984.
Price: About **$327.00**

REMINGTON MODEL SEVEN BOLT ACTION RIFLE

Caliber: 223 Rem. (5-shot), 243, 7mm-08, 6mm, 308 (4-shot).
Barrel: 18½″.
Weight: 6¼ lbs. **Length:** 37½″ over-all.
Stock: Walnut, with modified Schnabel fore-end. Cut checkering.
Sights: Ramp front, adjustable open rear.
Features: New short action design; silent side safety; free-floated barrel except for single pressure point at fore-end tip. Introduced 1983.
Price: About **$467.00**

CAUTION: PRICES CHANGE. CHECK AT GUNSHOP.

Ruger Model 77R

RUGER 77R BOLT ACTION RIFLE
Caliber: 22-250, 6mm, 243, 308, 220 Swift (Short Stroke action); 270, 7x57, 257 Roberts, 280 Rem., 30-06, 25-06, 7mm Rem. Mag., 300 Win. Mag., 338 Win. Mag. (Magnum action).
Barrel: 22″ round tapered (24″ in 220 Swift and magnum action calibers).
Weight: 6¾ lbs. **Length:** 42″ over-all (22″ barrel).
Stock: Hand checkered American walnut (13¾″x1⅝″x2⅛″), p.g. cap, sling swivel studs and recoil pad.
Sights: None supplied; comes with scope rings.
Features: Integral scope mount bases, diagonal bedding system, hinged floor plate, adj. trigger, tang safety.
Price: With Ruger steel scope rings, no sights (77R) **$440.00**

Ruger Model 77RS Tropical Rifle
Similar to the Model 77RS Magnum except chambered only for 458 Win. Mag., 24″ barrel, steel trigger guard and floorplate. Weight about 8¾ lbs. Comes with open sights and Ruger 1″ scope rings.
Price: **$600.00**

Ruger Model 77RS

Ruger Model 77RS Magnum Rifle
Similar to Ruger 77 except: magnum-size action. Calibers 270, 7x57, 30-06, 243, 308 have 22″ barrel, 25-06, 7mm Rem. Mag., 300 Win., Mag., 338 Win. Mag., with 24″ barrel. Weight about 7 lbs. Integral-base receiver, Ruger 1″ rings and open sights.
Price: Model 77 RS **$474.00**

Ruger International 77

Ruger International Model 77 RSI Rifle
Same as the standard Model 77 except has 18½″ barrel, full-length Mannlicher-style stock, with steel fore-end cap, loop-type sling swivel. Integral base receiver, open sights, Ruger 1″ steel rings. Improved front sight. Available in 22-250, 250-3000, 243, 308, 270, 30-06. Weighs 7 lbs. Length over-all is 38⅜″.
Price: **$480.00**

Ruger 77 Ultra Light

Ruger Model 77RL Ultra Light
Similar to the standard Model 77 except weighs only 6 lbs., chambered for 243, 270, 30-06, 257, 22-250, 250-3000 and 308; barrel tapped for target scope blocks; has 20″ Ultra Light barrel. Over-all length 40″. Ruger's steel 1″ scope rings supplied. Introduced 1983.
Price: Model 77 RL **$455.00**

Ruger 77 Varmint

RUGER MODEL 77V VARMINT
Caliber: 22-250, 220 Swift, 243, 6mm, 25-06, 308.
Barrel: 24″ heavy straight tapered, 26″ in 220 swift.
Weight: Approx. 9 lbs. **Length:** Approx. 44″ over-all (24″ barrel).
Stock: American walnut, similar in style to Magnum Rifle.
Sights: Barrel drilled and tapped for target scope blocks. Integral scope mount bases in receiver.
Features: Ruger diagonal bedding system, Ruger steel 1″ scope rings supplied. Fully adj. trigger. Barreled actions available in any of the standard calibers and barrel lengths.
Price: (Model 77V)... **$440.00**

Sako Hunter

Weight: 5¾ lbs. (short); 6¼ lbs. (med.); 7¼ lbs. (long).
Stock: Hand-checkered European walnut.
Sights: None furnished. Scope mounts included.
Features: Adj. trigger, hinged floorplate. 222 and 223 have short action, 243 and 22-250 have medium action, others are long action. Imported from Finland by Stoeger.

SAKO HUNTER RIFLE
Caliber: 17 Rem., 222, 223 (short action); 22-250, 220 Swift, 243, 6.5x55, 7mm-08, 308 (medium action); 25-06, 270, 30-06, 7mm Rem. Mag., 7x64, 300 Win. Mag., 338 Win. Mag., 375 H&H Mag. (long action).
Barrel: 21¼″—22″ depending on caliber.

Price: Short and medium action **$816.95**
Price: Long action **$834.95**
Price: Magnum cals. **$849.95**
Price: 375 H&H **$866.95**

CAUTION: PRICES CHANGE. CHECK AT GUNSHOP.

Sako Handy Carbine

Sako Carbine
Same action as the Hunter except has full "Mannlicher" style stock, 18½" barrel, weighs 7½ lbs., chambered for 222 Rem., 243, 270, 308 and 30-06. Introduced 1977. From Stoeger.
Price: **$927.95**
Price: 338, 375 H&H **$985.00**

Sako Safari Grade Bolt Action
Similar to the Hunter except available in long action, calibers 300 Win. Mag., 338 Win. Mag. or 375 H&H Mag. only. Stocked in French walnut, checkered 20 l.p.i., solid rubber butt pad; grip cap and fore-end tip; quarter-rib "express" rear sight, hooded ramp front. Front sling swivel band-mounted on barrel.
Price: **$2,245.00**

Sako Handy Carbine
Same 18½" barreled action and calibers as Sako Carbine but with conventional oil-finished stock of the Hunter model. Introduced 1986.
Price: 22-250, 243, 7mm-08, 308 Win. **$816.95**
Price: 25-06, 6.5x55, 270, 7x64, 30-06 . . . . **$834.95**
Price: 7mm Rem. Mag., 300 Win., 338 Win., 375 H&H. **$849.95**
Price: As Handy/Fiberclass with black fiberglass stock, 25-06, 6.5x55, 7x64, 270, 30-06 . . . . **$1,190.00**
Price: As above, 7mm Rem. Mag., 308 Mag., 338 Win., 375 H&H . **$1,225.00**

Sako Fiberclass Sporter
Similar to the Hunter except has a black fiberglass stock in the classic style, with wrinkle finish, rubber butt pad. Barrel length is 23", weight 7 lbs., 2 oz. Long action only. Comes with scope mounts. Introduced 1985.
Price: 25-06, 270, 30-06 . . . . **$1,190.00**
Price: 7mm Rem. Mag., 300, 338 Win. Mag., 375 H&H **$1,225.00**

Sako Super Deluxe Sporter
Similar to Deluxe Sporter except has select European Walnut with high gloss finish and deep cut oak leaf carving. Metal has super high polish, deep blue finish.
Price: **$2,245.00**

Sako Deluxe Sporter

Sako Heavy Barrel
Same as std. Super Sporter except has beavertail fore-end; available in 222, 223 (short action), 220 Swift, 22-250, 243, 308 (medium action). Weight from 8¼ to 8½ lbs. 5-shot magazine capacity.
Price: 222, 223 (short action) **$985.00**
Price: 22-250, 243, 308 (medium action). **$985.00**

Sako Deluxe Sporter
Same action as Hunter except has select wood, rosewood p.g. cap and fore-end tip. Fine checkering on top surfaces of integral dovetail bases, bolt sleeve, bolt handle root and bolt knob. Vent. recoil pad, skip-line checkering, mirror finish bluing.
Price: 222 or 223 cals. **$1,120.00**
Price: 22-250, 243, 308. . . . . **$1,120.00**
Price: 25-06, 270, 30-06 . . . . **$1,120.00**
Price: 7mm Rem. Mag., 300 Win. Mag., 338 Mag., 375 H&H. **$1,145.00**

Sauer Model 90

SAUER 90 RIFLE
Caliber: 222, 22-250, 243, 308 (Junior, Stutzen Junior); 6.5x57, 270, 7x64, 30-06, 9.3x62 (Medium, Stutzen); 6.5x68, 7mm Rem. Mag., 300 Win., 300 Wea., 8x68S, 9.3x64, 375 H&H (Magnum); 458 Win. Mag. (Safari).
Barrel: 20" (Stutzens), 24", 26".

Weight: 7 lbs., 6 oz. (Junior). **Length:** 42½" over-all.
Stock: European walnut with oil finish, recoil pad.
Sights: Post front on ramp, open rear adj. for w.
Features: Detachable 3-4 round box magazine; rear bolt locking lugs; 65° bolt throw; front sling swivel on barrel band. Introduced 1986. Imported from West Germany by SIGARMS.
Price: About. **$1,085.00**
Price: Safari, about. **$1,625.00**

Sauer Model 200

SAUER MODEL 200 RIFLE
Caliber: 243, 308, 25-06, 30-06.
Barrel: 24".
Weight: 6⅔ lbs. (Alloy) to 7¾ lbs. (Steel). **Length:** 44" over-all.
Stock: European walnut with recoil pad; checkered p.g. and fore-end.

Sights: None furnished. Drilled and tapped for iron sights and scope mount.
Features: Easily interchangeable barrels, buttstock and fore-end; removable box magazine; steel and alloy versions; left-hand models available. Introduced 1986. Imported from West Germany by SIGARMS.
Price: Steel, 243, 308, about **$745.00**
Price: Steel, 25-06, 30-06, 270, about **$770.00**
Price: Alloy, 243, 308, about **$785.00**
Price: Alloy, 25-06, 30-06, 270, about **$815.00**
Price: Left-hand, steel, 243, 308, about **$830.00**
Price: Left-hand, steel, 25-06, 30-06, 270, about **$860.00**
Price: Left-hand, alloy, 243, 308, about **$875.00**
Price: Left-hand, alloy, 25-06, 30-06, 270, about **$895.00**

CAUTION: PRICES CHANGE. CHECK AT GUNSHOP.

Savage Model 110D

Savage Model 110K Bolt Action Rifle

Similar to the Model 110D except has laminated camouflage stock, calibers 243, 270, 30-06. Introduced 1986.
Price: **$337.49**

SAVAGE 110E BOLT ACTION RIFLE

Caliber: 270, 308, 30-06, 243, 7mm Rem. Mag., 4-shot.
Barrel: 22″ round tapered, 24″ for magnum.
Weight: 6¾ lbs. **Length:** 43″ (22″barrel).
Stock: Walnut finished hardwood with Monte Carlo; hard rubber buttplate.
Sights: Gold bead removable ramp front, removeable step adj. rear.
Features: Top tang safety, receiver tapped for scope mount.
Price: **$289.00**
Price: Without sights **$280.97**

SAVAGE 110D BOLT ACTION RIFLE

Caliber: 223, 243, 270, 30-06, 4-shot detachable box magazine, 7mm Rem. Mag., 338 Win. Mag. (3-shot).
Barrel: 22″; 24″ in magnum calibers.
Weight: 7lbs. **Length:** 43½″ over-all.
Stock: Select walnut with Monte Carlo, cut checkered p.g. and fore-end. Swivel studs.
Sights: Removable ramp front, open rear adj. for w. & e.
Features: Tapped for scope mounting, free floating barrel, top tang safety, rubber recoil pad on all calibers.
Price: Right hand 110D standard cals.......................... **$369.00**
Price: As above, magnum cals................................. **$435.00**
Price: Left hand 110DL (no 338) **$419.00**

Savage Model 110-V Varmint Rifle

Same as the Model 110D except chambered only for 223 or 22-250, with heavy 26″ barrel, special "varmint" stock. Introduced 1983.
Price: **$385.00**

Shilen DGA Varmint

SHILEN DGA RIFLES

Caliber: All calibers.
Barrel: 24″ (Sporter, #2 weight), 25″ (Varminter, #5 weight).
Weight: 7½ lbs. (Sporter), 9 lbs., (Varminter).
Stock: Selected Claro walnut. Barrel and action hand bedded to stock with free-floated barrel, bedded action. Swivel studs installed.
Sights: None furnished. Drilled and tapped for scope mounting.
Features: Shilen Model DGA action, fully adjustable trigger with side safety. Stock finish is satin sheen epoxy. Barrel and action non-glare blue-black. From Shilen Rifles, Inc.
Price: Sporter or Varminter rifle, from **$1,600.00**

Steyr-Mannlicher Professional

STEYR-MANNLICHER MODEL M

Caliber: 7x64, 7x57, 25-06, 270, 30-06. Left-hand action cals.—7x64, 25-06, 270, 30-06. Optional cals.—6.5x57, 8x57JS, 9.3x62, 6.5x55, 7.5x55.
Barrel: 20″ (full stock); 23.6″ (half stock).
Weight: 6.8 lbs. to 7.5 lbs. **Length:** 39″ (full stock); 43″ (half stock).
Stock: Hand checkered walnut. Full Mannlicher or std. half stock with M.C. and rubber recoil pad.
Sights: Ramp front, open U-notch rear.
Features: Choice of interchangeable single or double set triggers. Detachable 5-shot rotary magazine. Drilled and tapped for scope mounting. Available as "Professional" model with parkerized finish and synthetic stock (right hand action only). Imported by Gun South, Inc.
Price: Full stock (carbine) **$1,095.00**
Price: Half stock (rifle) **$1,016.00**
Price: For left hand action add about **$220.00**
Price: Professional model with iron sights................... **$915.00**

Steyr-Mannlicher "Luxus"

Similar to Steyr-Mannlicher models L and M except has single-set trigger and detachable 3-shot steel magazine. Same calibers as L and M. Oil finish or high gloss lacquer on stock.
Price: Full stock **$1,425.00**
Price: Half stock **$1,355.00**

Steyr-Mannlicher L

STEYR-MANNLICHER MODELS SL & L

Caliber: SL—222, 222 Rem. Mag., 223; SL Varmint—222; L—22-250, 6mm, 243, 308 Win.; L Varmint—22-250, 243, 308 Win.
Barrel: 20″ (full stock); 23.6″ (half stock).
Weight: 6 lbs. (full stock). **Length:** 38¼″ (full stock).
Stock: Hand checkered walnut. Full Mannlicher or standard half-stock with Monte Carlo.
Sights: Ramp front, open U-notch rear.
Features: Choice of interchangeable single or double set triggers. Five-shot detachable "Makrolon" rotary magazine, 6 rear locking lugs. Drilled and tapped for scope mounts. Imported by Gun South, Inc.
Price: Full Stock **$1,095.00**
Price: Half-stock **$1,016.00**

Steyr-Mannlicher Varmint, Models SL and L

Similar to standard SL and L except chambered only for: 222 Rem. (SL), 22-250, 243, 308. Has 26″ heavy barrel, no sights (drilled and tapped for scope mounts). Choice of single or double-set triggers. Five-shot detachable magazine.
Price: **$1,095.00**

CAUTION: PRICES CHANGE. CHECK AT GUNSHOP.

CENTERFIRE RIFLES—BOLT ACTIONS

STEYR-MANNLICHER MODELS S & S/T
Caliber: Model S—300 Win. Mag., 338 Win. Mag., 7mm Rem. Mag., 300 H&H Mag., 375 H&H Mag. (6.5x68, 8x68S, 9.3x64 optional); S/T—375 H&H Mag., 458 Win. Mag. (9.3x64 optional).
Barrel: 25.6".
Weight: 8.4 lbs. (Model S). **Length:** 45" over-all.
Stock: Half stock with M.C. and rubber recoil pad. Hand checkered walnut. Available with optional spare magazine inletted in butt.
Sights: Ramp front, U-notch rear.
Features: Choice of interchangeable single or double set triggers., detachable 4-shot magazine. Drilled and tapped for scope mounts. Imported by Gun South, Inc.
Price: Model S............................. **$1,295.00**
Price: Model ST 375 H&H, 458 Win. Mag.................. **$1,375.00**

Ultra Light Model 20

Ultra Light Arms Model 20S Rifle
Similar to the Model 20 except uses short action chambered for 17 Rem., 222 Rem., 223 Rem., 22 Hornet. Has 22" Douglas Premium No. 1 contour barrel, weighs 4¾ lbs., 41" over-all length.
Price: **$1,300.00**
Price: Model 20S Left Hand (left-hand action and stock) **$1,400.00**

Ultra Light Arms Model 28 Rifle
Similar to the Model 20 except in 264, 7mm Rem. Mag., 300 Win. Mag., 338 Win. Mag. (standard). Improved and other calibers on request. Uses 24" Douglas Premium No. 2 contour barrel. Weighs 5½ lbs., 45" over-all length. K.D.F. or U.L.A. recoil arrestor built in. Any custom feature available on any U.L.A. product can be incorporated.
Price: **$2,150.00**

TIKKA MODEL 55 DELUXE RIFLE
Caliber: 17 Rem., 222, 22-250, 6mm Rem., 243, 308.
Barrel: 23".
Weight: About 6½ lbs. **Length:** 41½" over-all.
Stock: Hand checkered walnut with rosewood fore-end tip and grip cap.
Sights: Bead on ramp front, rear adjustable for windage and elevation.
Features: Detachable 3-shot magazine with 5- or 10-shot magazines available. Roll-over cheekpiece, palm swell in pistol grip. Adjustable trigger. Receiver dovetailed for scope mounting. Imported from Finland by Mandall.
Price: **$650.00**
Price: QD scope mounts............................. **$89.95**

ULTRA LIGHT ARMS MODEL 20 RIFLE
Caliber: 22-250, 243, 6mm Rem., 257 Roberts, 7x57, 7mm-08, 284, 308, standard. Improved and other calibers on request.
Barrel: 22" Douglas Premium No. 1 contour.
Weight: 4½ lbs. **Length:** 41½" over-all.
Stock: Composite Kevlar, graphite reinforced. Dupont Imron paint colors — green, black, brown and camo options. Choice of length of pull.
Sights: None furnished. Scope mount included.
Features: Timney adj. trigger; two-position three-function safety. Benchrest quality action. Matte or bright stock and metal finish. 3" magazine length. Shipped in a hard case. From Ultra Light Arms, Inc.
Price: **$1,300.00**
Price: Model 20 Left Hand (left-hand action and stock) **$1,400.00**
Price: Model 24 (25-06, 270, 280, 30-06, 3⅜" magazine length)... **$1,375.00**
Price: Model 24 Left Hand (left-hand action and stock) **$1,475.00**

Voere Titan

VOERE TITAN BOLT ACTION RIFLE
Caliber: 243, 25-06, 270, 7x57, 308, 30-06, 4-shot magazine (standard); 257 Wea., 270 Wea., 7mm Rem. Mag., 300 Win. Mag., 300 Wea., 308 Norma Mag., 375 H&H, 3-shot magazine (magnum).
Barrel: 24" (standard), 26" (magnum).

Weight: About 8 lbs. **Length:** 44½" over-all (24" bbl.).
Stock: Oil finished, hand checkered European walnut with Monte Carlo. Recoil pad and swivel studs standard.
Sights: None furnished. Drilled and tapped for scope mounts. Open sights, rings, bases avail. from KDF.
Features: Three-lug, front-locking action with ultra-fast lock time. Imported from West Germany by KDF, Inc.
Price: Standard calibers................................. **$799.00**
Price: Magnum calibers................................. **$849.00**

Voere Titan Menor

VOERE TITAN MENOR RIFLE
Caliber: 222 Rem., 223 Rem., 3-shot magazine.
Barrel: 23½".
Weight: About 6 lbs. **Length:** 42" over-all.

Stock: Oil finished, hand checkered European walnut with Monte Carlo, rosewood fore-end tip and grip cap.
Sights: None furnished. Grooved receiver is drilled and tapped for scope mounting. Open sights, rings, bases avail. from KDF.
Features: Rifle carries a three-year guarantee by maker. Competition model available. Introduced 1986. Imported from West Germany by KDF, Inc.
Price: Standard model..................................... **$699.00**
Price: Competition model................................. **$799.00**

VOERE 2155, 2165 BOLT ACTION RIFLE
Caliber: 22-250, 270, 308, 243, 30-06, 7x64, 5.6x57, 6.5x55, 8x57 JRS, 7mm Rem. Mag., 300 Win. Mag., 8x68S, 9.3x62, 9.3x64, 6.5x68.
Stock: European walnut, hog-back style; checkered pistol grip and fore-end.
Sights: Ramp front, open adjustable rear.
Features: Mauser-type action with 5-shot detachable box magazine; double set or single trigger; drilled and tapped for scope mounting. Imported from

Austria by L. Joseph Rahn. Introduced 1984.
Price: Standard calibers, single trigger **$440.00**
Price: As above, double set triggers........................ **$467.00**
Price: Magnum calibers, single trigger....................... **$475.00**
Price: As above, double set triggers........................ **$505.00**
Price: Full-stock, single trigger **$575.00**
Price: As above, double set triggers........................ **$595.00**

Weatherby Euromark

WEATHERBY VANGUARD VGX, VGS RIFLES

Caliber: 22-250, 25-06, 243, 270, and 30-06 (5-shot), 7mm Rem. and 300 Win. Mag. (3-shot).
Barrel: 24″ hammer forged.
Weight: 7⅞ lbs. **Length:** 44½″ over-all.
Stock: American walnut, p.g. cap and fore-end tip, hand inletted and checkered. 13½″ pull.
Sights: Optional, available at extra cost.
Features: Side safety, adj. trigger, hinged floorplate, receiver tapped for scope mounts. Imported from Japan by Weatherby.
Price: VGS **$399.95**
Price: VGX—deluxe wood, different checkering, ventilated recoil pad **$499.95**

Weatherby Mark V Rifle Left Hand

Available in all Weatherby calibers except 224 and 22-250 (and 26″ No. 2 contour 300WM). Complete left handed action; stock with cheekpiece on right side. Prices are $20 higher than right hand models except the 378 and 460WM are unchanged.

Weatherby Fiberguard

WEATHERBY EUROMARK BOLT ACTION RIFLE

Caliber: All Weatherby calibers except 224, 22-250.
Barrel: 24″ or 26″ round tapered.
Weight: 6½ — 10½ lbs. **Length:** 44¼″ over-all (24″ bbl.).
Stock: Walnut, Monte Carlo with extended tail fine-line hand checkering, satin oil finish, ebony fore-end tip and grip cap with maple diamond, solid butt pad.
Sights: Optional (extra).
Features: Cocking indicator; adj. trigger; hinged floor plate; thumb safety; q.d. sling swivels. Introduced 1986.
Price: With 24″ barrel (240, 257, 270, 7mm, 30-06, 300) **$879.95**
Price: 26″ No. 2 Contour barrel **$899.95**
Price: As above, left hand **$899.95**
Price: 340 WM, 26″ **$899.95**
Price: As above, left hand **$914.95**
Price: 378WM, 26″, right or left hand **$1,054.95**
Price: 460WM, 26″, right or left hand **$1,194.95**

Weatherby Vanguard VGL Rifle

Similar to the standard Vanguard except has a short action, chambered for 223, 243, 270, 30-06, 7mm Rem. Mag. with 20″ barrel. Barrel and action have a non-glare blue finish. Guaranteed to shoot a 1½″ 3-shot group at 100 yards. Stock has a non-glare satin finish, hand checkering and a black butt pad with black spacer. Introduced 1984.
Price: **$399.95**

Weatherby Vanguard Fiberguard Rifle

Uses the Vanguard barreled action and a forest green wrinkle-finished fiberglass stock. All metal is matte blue. Has a 20″ barrel, weighs 6½ lbs., measures 40″ in 223, 243, and 308, and 40½″ in 270, 7mm Rem. Mag., 30-06. Accepts same scope mount bases as Mark V action. Introduced 1985.
Price: Right-hand only... **$579.95**

Weatherby Mark V

Weatherby Lazer Mark V Rifle

Same as standard Mark V except stock has extensive laser carving under cheekpiece, on butt, p.g. and fore-end. Introduced 1981.
Price: 22-250, 224 Wea., 24″ bbl. **$914.95**
Price: As above, 26″ bbl. **$929.95**
Price: 240 Wea. thru 300 Wea., 24″ bbl. **$934.95**
Price: As above, 26″ bbl. **$954.95**
Price: 340 Wea. **$954.95**
Price: 378 Wea. **$1,109.95**
Price: 460 Wea. **$1,249.95**

WEATHERBY MARK V BOLT ACTION RIFLE

Caliber: All Weatherby cals., 22-250 and 30-06
Barrel: 24″ or 26″ round tapered.
Weight: 6½-10½ lbs. **Length:** 43¼″-46½″.
Stock: Walnut, Monte Carlo with cheekpiece, high luster finish, checkered p.g. and fore-end, recoil pad.
Sights: Optional (extra).
Features: Cocking indicator, adj. trigger, hinged floorplate, thumb safety, quick detachable sling swivels.
Price: Cals. 224 and 22-250, std. bbl. **$798.95**
Price: With 26″ semi-target bbl................................. **$814.95**
Price: Cals. 240, 257, 270, 7mm, 30-06 and 300 (24″ bbl.) **$819.95**
Price: With 26″ No. 2 contour bbl............................... **$839.95**
Price: Cal. 340 (26″ bbl.)..................................... **$839.95**
Price: Cal. 378 (26″ bbl.)..................................... **$994.95**
Price: Cal. 460 (26″ bbl.)..................................... **$1,134.95**

Weatherby Fibermark Rifle

Weatherby Fibermark Rifle

Same as the standard Mark V except the stock is of fiberglass; finished with a non-glare black wrinkle finish and black recoil pad; receiver and floorplate have low luster blue finish; fluted bolt has a satin finish. Currently available in right-hand model only, 24″ or 26″ barrel, 240 Weatherby Mag. through 340 Weatherby Mag. calibers. Introduced 1983.
Price: 240 W.M. through 300 W.M., 24″ bbl..................... **$949.95**
Price: 240 W.M. through 340 W.M., 26″ bbl..................... **$969.95**

CAUTION: PRICES CHANGE. CHECK AT GUNSHOP.

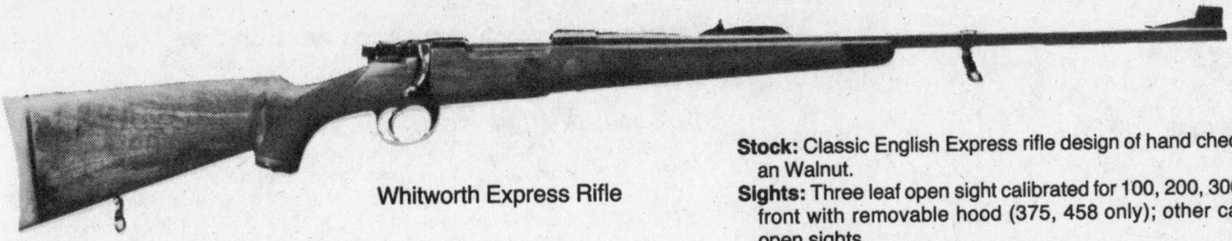

Whitworth Express Rifle

WHITWORTH EXPRESS RIFLE
Caliber: 22-250, 243, 25-06, 270, 7x57, 308, 30-06, 300 Win. Mag., 7mm Rem. Mag., 375 H&H, 458 Win. Mag.
Barrel: 24".
Weight: 7½-8 lbs. **Length:** 44".

Stock: Classic English Express rifle design of hand checkered, select European Walnut.
Sights: Three leaf open sight calibrated for 100, 200, 300 yards on ¼-rib, ramp front with removable hood (375, 458 only); other calibers have standard open sights.
Features: Solid rubber recoil pad, barrel mounted sling swivel, adjustable trigger, hinged floor plate, solid steel recoil cross bolt. Imported by Interarms.
Price: **$525.00**
Price: 375, 458, with express sights **$650.00**
Price: Mannlicher-style carbine, cals. 243, 270, 308, 7x57, 30-06 only, 20" bbl. **$675.00**

Wichita Varmint Rifle

WICHITA CLASSIC RIFLE
Caliber: 17 Rem. thru 308 Win., including 22 and 6mm PPC.
Barrel: 21⅛".
Weight: 8 lbs. **Length:** 41" over-all.
Stock: AAA Fancy American walnut. Hand-rubbed and checkered (20 l.p.i). Hand-inletter, glass bedded, steel grip cap. Pachmayr rubber recoil pad.
Sights: None. Drilled and tapped for scope mounting.
Features: Available as single shot or repeater. Octagonal barrel and Wichita action, right or left-hand. Checkered bolt handle. Bolt is hand-fitted, lapped and jewelled. Adjustable Canjar trigger is set at 2 lbs. Side thumb safety. Firing pin fall is ³⁄₁₆". Non-glare blue finish. Shipped in hard case. From Wichita Arms.
Price: Single shot **$1,900.00**
Price: With blind box magazine **$2,050.00**

WICHITA VARMINT RIFLE
Caliber: 17 Rem. thru 308 Win., including 22 and 6mm PPC.
Barrel: 20⅛".
Weight: 9 lbs. **Length:** 40⅛" over-all.
Stock: AAA Fancy American walnut. Hand-rubbed finish, hand-checkered, 20 l.p.i. pattern. Hand-inletted, glass bedded steel grip cap, Pachmayr rubber recoil pad.
Sights: None. Drilled and tapped for scope mounts.
Features: Right or left-hand Wichita action with three locking lugs. Available as a single shot or repeater with 3-shot magazine. Checkered bolt handle. Bolt is hand fitted, lapped and jeweled. Side thumb safety. Firing pin fall is ³⁄₁₆". Non-glare blue finish. Shipped in hard case. From Wichita Arms.
Price: Single shot **$1,185.00**
Price: With blind box magazine **$1,335.00**

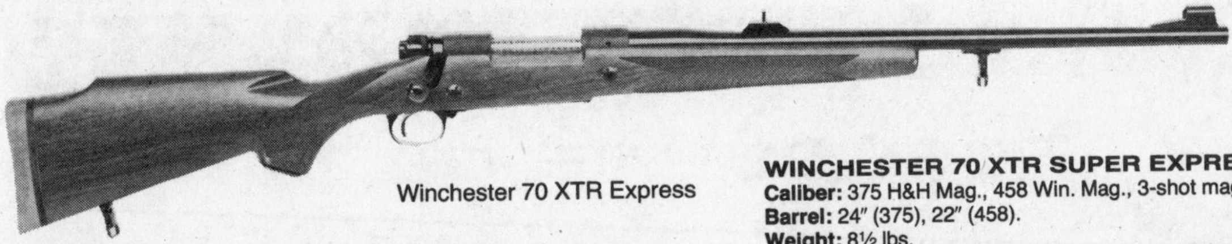

Winchester 70 XTR Express

WINCHESTER MODEL 70 LIGHTWEIGHT CARBINE
Caliber: 270, 30-06 (standard action); 250 Savage, 22-250, 223, 243, 308 (short action), both 5-shot magazine, except 6-shot in 223.
Barrel: 20".
Weight: 6¼ lbs. (std.), 6 lbs. (short). **Length:** 40½" over-all (std.), 40" (short).
Stock: American walnut with satin finish, deep-cut checkering.
Sights: None furnished. Drilled and tapped for scope mounting.
Features: Three position safety; stainless steel magazine follower; hinged floorplate; sling swivel studs. Introduced 1984.
Price: With sights, about **$425.25**
Price: Without sights, about **$442.25**

WINCHESTER 70 XTR SUPER EXPRESS MAGNUM
Caliber: 375 H&H Mag., 458 Win. Mag., 3-shot magazine.
Barrel: 24" (375), 22" (458).
Weight: 8½ lbs.
Stock: American walnut with Monte Carlo cheekpiece. XTR wrap-around checkering and finish.
Sights: Hooded ramp front, open rear.
Features: Two steel crossbolts in stock for added strength. Front sling swivel mounted on barrel. Contoured rubber butt pad. Made under license by U.S. Repeating Arms Co.
Price: About **$831.63**

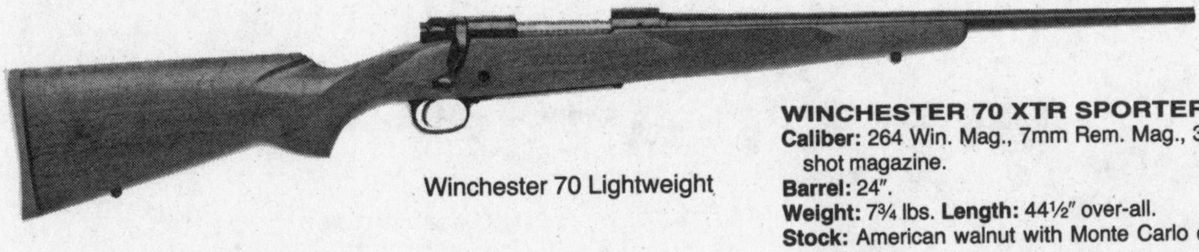

Winchester 70 Lightweight

Winchester 70 XTR Sporter Varmint Rifle
Same as 70 XTR Sporter Magnum except: 223, 22-250 and 243 only, no sights, 24" bbl., 44½" over-all, 7¾ lbs. American walnut Monte Carlo stock with cheekpiece, high luster finish.
Price: About **$470.24**

WINCHESTER 70 XTR SPORTER MAGNUM
Caliber: 264 Win. Mag., 7mm Rem. Mag., 300 Win. Mag., 338 Win. Mag., 3-shot magazine.
Barrel: 24".
Weight: 7¾ lbs. **Length:** 44½" over-all.
Stock: American walnut with Monte Carlo cheekpiece. XTR checkering and satin finish.
Sights: None furnished; optional hooded ramp front, adjustable folding leaf rear.
Features: Three-position safety, detachable sling swivels, stainless steel magazine follower, rubber butt pad, epoxy bedded receiver recoil lug. Made under license by U.S. Repeating Arms Co.
Price: With sights, about **$470.25**
Price: Without sights, about **$487.25**

CAUTION: PRICES CHANGE. CHECK AT GUNSHOP.

Winchester 70 Winlite

Winchester Model 70 Winlite Rifle
Similar to the Model 70XTR Sporter except has brown fiberglass stock. Action bed and fore-end are reinforced Kevlar/Graphite. No sights are furnished but receiver is drilled and tapped for scope mounting. Available in 270, 30-06 (22″ barrel, 4-shot magazine), 7mm Rem. Mag., 338 Win. Mag. (24″ barrel 3-shot magazine). Weight is 6¼-6½ lbs. for 270, 30-06, 6¾-7 lbs. for 7mm Mag., 338. Introduced 1986.

Price: About **$637.25**

Winchester Ranger

Winchester Ranger Rifle
Similar to Model 70 XTR Sporter except chambered only for 270, 30-06, with 22″ barrel. American hardwood stock, no checkering, composition butt plate. Metal has matte blue finish. Introduced 1985.

Price: About **$360.62**
Price: Ranger Youth, 243 only, scaled-down stock **$371.50**

Winchester 70 Featherweight

Winchester Model 70 XTR Featherweight
Available with standard action in 6.5x55, 270 Win., 30-06, short action in 22-250, 223, 243, 308; 22″ tapered Featherweight barrel; classic-style American walnut stock with Schnabel fore-end, wrap-around XTR checkering fashioned after early Model 70 custom rifle patterns. Red rubber butt pad with black spacer; sling swivel studs. Weighs 6¾ lbs. (standard action), 6½ lbs. (short action). Introduced 1984.

Price: About **$487.25**
Price: European Featherweight, 6.5x55, about **$487.25**

Winchester Model 70 XTR Sporter
Same as the Model 70 XTR Sporter Magnum except available only in 308, 25-06, 270 Win. and 30-06, 5-shot magazine.

Price: With sights (except 308), about **$487.25**
Price: Without sights, about **$470.25**

Allen Rolling Block

ALLEN ROLLING BLOCK BABY CARBINE
Caliber: 22 LR, 22 Mag., 357 Mag., single shot.
Barrel: 22″.
Weight: 4.8 lbs. **Length:** 35½ over-all.
Stock: Walnut stock and fore-end.
Sights: Blade front, fully adj. open rear.
Features: Resembles Remington New Model No. 4 carbine. Brass trigger guard and buttplate; color case-hardened frame, blued barrel. Imported by Allen Fire Arms

Price: **$264.00**

ALLEN SHARPS/GEMMER SPORTING RIFLE
Caliber: 45-70.
Barrel: 32″, octagonal.
Weight: 11 lbs. **Length:** 49″ over-all.
Stock: Walnut
Sights: Blade front, buckhorn rear.
Features: Authentic reproduction of 1870s J.P. Gemmer Hawken-Sharps hybrid. Introduced 1986. Imported by Allen Fire Arms.

Price: **$599.00**

Browning Model 1885

BROWNING MODEL 1885 SINGLE SHOT RIFLE
Caliber: 223, 22-250, 30-06, 270, 7mm Rem. Mag., 45-70.
Barrel: 28″.
Weight: About 8½ lbs. **Length:** 43½″ over-all.
Stock: Walnut with straight grip, Schnabel fore-end.
Sights: None furnished; drilled and tapped for scope mounting.
Features: Replica of J.M. Browning's high-wall falling-block rifle. Octagon barrel with recessed muzzle. Imported from Japan by Browning. Introduced 1985.

Price: **$551.50**

CAUTION: PRICES CHANGE. CHECK AT GUNSHOP.

Heym-Ruger HR 30/38

HEYM-RUGER Model HR 30/38 RIFLE
Caliber: 243, 6.5x57R, 7x64, 7x65R, 308, 30-06 (standard); 6.5x68R, 300 Win. Mag., 8x68S, 9.3x74R (magnum).
Barrel: 24″ (standard cals.), 25″ (magnum cals.).
Weight: 6½ to 7 lbs.
Stock: Dark European walnut, hand checkered p.g. and fore-end. Oil finish, recoil pad. Full Mannlicher-type or sporter-style with Schnabel fore-end, Bavarian cheekpiece.
Sights: Bead on ramp front, leaf rear.
Features: Ruger No. 1 action and safety, Canjar single-set trigger, hand-engraved animal motif. Options available include deluxe engraving and stock carving. Imported from West Germany by Paul Jaeger Inc.
Price: HR-30N, round bbl., sporter stock, std. cals. $1,990.00
Price: HR-30G, as above except in mag. cals. $1,990.00
Price: HR-30L, round bbl., full stock, std. cals $2,095.00
Price: For octagon barrel, add $247.00
Price: For sideplates with large hunting scenes, add $640.00

EMF SHARPS "OLD RELIABLE" RIFLE
Caliber: 45-70, 45-120-3¼″ Sharps
Barrel: 28″ full octagon, polished blue.
Weight: 9½ lbs. **Length:** 45″ over-all.
Stock: Walnut with deluxe checkering at p.g. and fore-end.
Sights: Sporting blade front, folding leaf rear. Globe front, Creedmoor rear optional at extra cost.
Features: Falling block, lever action. Color case-hardened hammer, buttplate and action, Seven models of the Sharps are available in M/L configuration. All are available with engraved action for $175.00 extra. From E.M.F.
Price: Old Reliable $377.50
Price: Sporter Rifle $362.50
Price: Military Carbine $345.00
Price: Sporter Carbine $362.50

Ljutic Space Rifle

LJUTIC RECOILESS SPACE RIFLE
Caliber: 22-250, 30-30, 30-06, 308; single-shot.
Barrel: 24″.
Weight: 8¾ lbs. **Length:** 44″ over-all.
Stock: Walnut stock, fore-end and grip.
Sights: Iron sights or scope mounts.
Features: Revolutionary design has anti-recoil mechanism. Twist-bolt action uses six moving parts. Scope and mounts extra. Introduced 1981. From Ljutic Industries.
Price: $3,695.00

Ruger No. 1B Rifle

Ruger No. 1A Light Sporter
Similar to the No. 1-B Standard Rifle except has lightweight 22″ barrel, Alexander Henry style fore-end, adjustable folding leaf rear sight on quarter-rib, dovetailed ramp front with gold bead. Calibers 243, 30-06, 270 and 7x57. Weight about 7¼ lbs.
Price: No. 1-A $575.00
Price: Barrreled action $389.50

RUGER NO. 1B SINGLE SHOT
Caliber: 220 Swift, 22-250, 223, 243, 6mm Rem., 25-06, 257 Roberts, 270, 280, 30-06, 7mm Rem. Mag., 300 Win. Mag., 338 Win. Mag. 270 Wea., 300 Wea.
Barrel: 26″ round tapered with quarter-rib; with Ruger 1″ rings.
Weight: 8 lbs. **Length:** 43⅜″ over-all.
Stock: Walnut, two-piece, checkered p.g. and semi-beavertail fore-end.
Sights: None, 1″ scope rings supplied for integral mounts.
Features: Under lever, hammerless falling block design has auto ejector, top tang safety. Standard Rifle 1B illus.
Price: $575.00
Price: Barreled action $389.50

Ruger No. 1 International

Ruger No. 1V Special Varminter
Similar to the No. 1-B Standard Rifle except has 24″ heavy barrel. Semi-beavertail fore-end, barrel tapped for target scope block, with 1″ Ruger scope rings. Calibers 22-250, 220 Swift, 223, 25-06, 6mm. Weight about 9 lbs.
Price: No. 1-V $575.00
Price: Barreled action $389.50

Ruger No. 1 RSI International
Similar to the No. 1-B Standard Rifle except has lightweight 20″ barrel, full length Mannlicher-style fore-end with loop sling swivel, adjustable folding leaf rear sight on quarter rib, ramp front with gold bead. Calibers 243, 30-06, 270 and 7x57. Weight is about 7¼ lbs.
Price: No. 1-RSI $595.00
Price: Barreled action $389.50

Ruger No. 1H Tropical Rifle
Similar to the No. 1-B Standard Rifle except has Alexander Henry fore-end, adjustable folding leaf rear sight on quarter-rib, ramp front with dovetail gold bead front, 24″ heavy barrel. Calibers 375 H&H (weight about 8¼ lbs.) and 458 Win. Mag. (weight about 9 lbs.).
Price: No. 1-H $575.00
Price: Barreled action $389.50

Ruger No. 1S Medium Sporter
Similar to the No. 1B Standard Rifle except has Alexander Henry style fore-end, adjustable folding leaf rear sight on quarter-rib, ramp front sight base and dovetail-type gold bead front sight. Calibers 7mm Rem. Mag., 338 Win. Mag., 300 Win. Mag. with 26″ barrel, 45-70 with 22″ barrel. Weight about 7½ lbs. in 45-70.
Price: No. 1-S $575.00
Price: Barreled action $389.50

CAUTION: PRICES CHANGE. CHECK AT GUNSHOP.

Ruger No. 3 Carbine

NAVY ARMS ROLLING BLOCK RIFLE
Caliber: 45-70.
Barrel: 30".
Stock: Walnut finished.
Sights: Fixed front, adj. rear.
Features: Reproduction of classic rolling block action. Available in Buffalo Rifle (octagonal bbl.) and Creedmore (half round, half octagonal bbl.) models. Made in U.S. by Navy Arms.
Price: 26", 30" full octagon barrel **$398.00**
Price: Creedmore Model, 30" full octagon **$425.00**
Price: 30", half-round. **$398.00**
Price: 26", half-round. **$395.00**
Price: Half-round Creedmore. **$425.00**

RUGER NO. 3 CARBINE SINGLE SHOT
Caliber: 45-70.
Barrel: 22" round.
Weight: 7¼ lbs. **Length:** 38½".
Stock: American walnut, carbine-type.
Sights: Gold bead front, adj. folding leaf rear.
Features: Same action as No. 1 Rifle except different lever. Has auto ejector, top tang safety, adj. trigger. Drilled and tapped for Ruger bases and Ruger 1" rings.
Price: **$284.00**

SERRIFILE SCHUETZEN RIFLE
Caliber: 32, 33, 38, 41, 44, 45; single shot.
Barrel: To customer specs up to 32"; octagon, half-octagon, round.
Weight: To customer specs.
Stock: Fancy walnut in early Helm pattern.
Sights: None furnished; comes with scope blocks.
Features: Based on a replica Winchester Hi-Wall action with flat top receiver ring, thick or thin wall design, blue or case hardened. Hammer action uses Niedner-type firing pin; hammerless model uses a coil spring striker. Many options in finger levers, buttplates available. Introduced 1984. From Serrifile, Inc.
Price: Hammer model, from $1,853.50

Serrifile Schuetzen

Sharps Model 1875

C. SHARPS ARMS NEW MODEL 1875 RIFLE
Caliber: 22 LR Stevens, 32-40 & 38-55 Ballard, 40-90 3¼", 40-90 2⅝", 40-70 2¹⁄₁₀", 40-70 2¼", 40-70 2½", 40-50 1¹¹⁄₁₆", 40-50 1⅞", 45-90 2⁴⁄₁₀", 45-70 2¹⁄₁₀".
Barrel: 22" to 30", round and octagon depending upon model.
Weight: 8-12 lbs.
Stock: Walnut, straight grip, shotgun butt.
Sights: Blade front, improved Lawrence-pattern buckhorn rear.
Features: Recreation of the 1875 Sharps rifle. Production guns will have case colored receiver. Available in Custom Sporting and Target versions upon request. Announced 1986. From C. Sharps Arms Co.
Price: 1875 Carbine (24" tapered round bbl.) **$550.00**
Price: 1875 Saddle Rifle (26" tapered oct. bbl.) **$725.00**
Price: 1875 Standard Sporter (30" tapered oct. bbl.). **$675.00**
Price: 1875 Deluxe Sporter (30" tapered oct. bbl.). **$775.00**

Consult our directory pages for the location of firms mentioned.

Thompson/Center TCR '83 Hunter

THOMPSON-CENTER CONTENDER CARBINE
Caliber: 22 LR, 22 Hornet, 222 Rem., 223 Rem., 7mm T.C.U., 7 x 30 Waters, 30-30 Win., 357 Rem. Maximum, single shot.
Barrel: 21".
Weight: 5 lbs., 2 oz. **Length:** 35" over-all.
Stock: Checkered American walnut with rubber butt pad.
Sights: Blade front, open adj. rear.
Features: Uses the T/C Contender action. Eight interchangeable barrels available, all with sights, drilled and tapped for scope mounting. Introduced 1985. Offered as a complete Carbine only.
Price: **$345.00**
Price: Extra barrels, each. **$145.00**

THOMPSON/CENTER TCR '83 SINGLE SHOT RIFLE
Caliber: 22 Hornet, 222 Rem., 223 Rem., 22-250, 243 Win., 270, 308, 7mm Rem. Mag., 30-06, 12 ga. slug.
Barrel: 23".
Weight: About 6¾ lbs. **Length:** 39½" over-all.
Stock: American black walnut, checkered p.g. and fore-end.
Sights: Blade on ramp front, open rear adj. for windage only.
Features: Break-open design with interchangeable barrels. Double-set or single-stage trigger function. Cross-bolt safety. Sights removable for scope mounting. Made in U.S. by T/C. Introduced 1983.
Price: Aristocrat **$475.00**
Price: Hunter Field model (single trigger, grooved fore-end, no cheekpiece) **$415.00**
Price: Extra barrel **$175.00**

CAUTION: PRICES CHANGE. CHECK AT GUNSHOP.

ARMSPORT 2783 O-U TURKEY GUN
Caliber/Gauge: 12 ga. (3") over 222 Rem., 270 Win.; 20 ga. over 222, 243, 270.
Barrel: 28" (Full).
Weight: 8 lbs.
Stock: European walnut.
Sights: Blade front, leaf rear.
Features: Ventilated top and middle ribs; flip-up rear sight; silvered receiver. Introduced 1986. Imported from Italy by Armsport.
Price: $1,095.00

BRNO SUPER EXPRESS O/U DOUBLE RIFLE
Caliber: 7 x 65R, 9.3 x 74R, 375 H&H, 458 Win. Mag.
Barrel: 23½."
Weight: 8½ to 9 lbs. **Length:** 40" over-all.
Stock: European walnut with raised cheek piece, skip-line checkering.
Sights: Bead on ramp front, quarter rib with open rear.
Features: Sidelock action with engraved side plates; double set triggers; selective automatic ejectors; rubber recoil pad. Barrels regulated for 100 meters. Imported from Czechoslovakia by Bauska Arms Corp.
Price: 7x65R $2,100.00
Price: 9.3x74R $2,299.00
Price: 375 H&H, 458 Win. Mag............................. $2,599.00

BERETTA EXPRESS S689 DOUBLE RIFLE
Caliber: 30-06, 9.3x74R, 375 H&H, 458 win. Mag.
Barrel: 23".
Weight: 7.7 lbs.
Stock: European walnut, checkered grip and fore-end.
Sights: Blade front on ramp, open V-notch rear.
Features: Boxlock action with silvered, engraved receiver; ejectors; double triggers; solid butt pad. Imported from Italy by Beretta U.S.A. Corp. Introduced 1984.
Price: S689, 30-06, 9.3x74R $2,700.00
Price: SSO, 375 H&H, 458 Win. Mag. $9,375.00

BRNO ZH SERIES 300 COMBINATION GUN
Caliber/Gauge: 5.6x52R/12 ga., 5.6x50R Mag./12, 7x57R/12, 7x57R/16.
Barrel: 23½" (Full).
Weight: 7.9 lbs. **Length:** 40½" over-all.
Stock: Walnut.
Sights: Bead on blade front, folding leaf rear.
Features: Boxlock action; 8-barrel set for combination calibers and o/u shotgun barrels in 12 ga. (Field, Trap, Skeet) and 16 ga. (Field). Imported from Czechoslovakia by Bauska Arms Corp.
Price: $2,799.00

Browning Continental

BROWNING SUPERPOSED CONTINENTAL
Caliber/Gauge: 20 ga. x 20 ga. with extra 30-06x30-06 o/u barrel set.
Barrel: 20 ga.—26½" (Mod. & Full, 3" chambers), vent. rib, with medium raised German nickel silver sight bead. 30-06—24".
Weight: 6 lbs. 14 oz. (rifle barrels), 5 lbs. 14 oz. (shotgun barrels)
Stock: Select high grade American walnut with oil finish. Straight grip stock and Schnabel fore-end with 26 lpi hand checkering.
Sights: Rifle barrels have flat face gold bead front on matted ramp, folding leaf rear.
Features: Action is based on a specially engineered Superposed 20-ga. frame. Single selective trigger works on inertia; let-off is about 4½ lbs. Automatic selective ejectors. Manual top tang safety incorporated with barrel selector. Furnished with fitted luggage-type case. Introduced 1979. Imported from Belgium by Browning.
Price: $4,375.00

BROWNING EXPRESS RIFLE
Caliber: 270 or 30-06.
Barrel: 24".
Weight: About 6 lbs., 14 oz. **Length:** 41" over-all.
Stock: Select walnut with oil finish; straight grip, Schnabel fore-end; hand checkered to 25 lpi.
Sights: Gold bead on ramp front, adjustable folding leaf rear.
Features: Specially engineered Superposed action with reinforced breech face. Receiver hand engraved. Single selective trigger, auto. selective ejectors, manual safety. Comes in fitted luggage case. Imported from Belgium by Browning.
Price: Either caliber $3,125.00

Churchill Regent Combo

CHURCHILL REGENT COMBINATION GUN
Caliber/Gauge: 12 (3") over 222 Rem.
Barrel: 25" (Imp. Mod.)
Weight: 8 lbs. **Length:** 42" over-all.
Stock: Hand checkered European walnut, oil finish, Monte Carlo comb.
Sights: Blade on ramp front, open rear.
Features: Silvered, engraved receiver; double triggers; dovetail scope mount. Imported by Kassnar Imports, Inc. Introduced 1985.
Price: $1,139.00

DUMOLIN "PIONNIER" EXPRESS DOUBLE RIFLE
Caliber: 338 Win., 375 H&H, 458 Win., 470 N.E., 416 Rigby, 416 Hoffman, 500 N.E. Standard calibers also available.
Barrel: 24" to 26".
Weight: About 9½ lbs. **Length:** 45" over-all with 24" barrel.
Stock: Deluxe European walnut in English style with oil finish, beavertail or classic English fore-end. To customer's specifications.
Sights: Bead on ramp front, 2-leaf on quarter-rib.
Features: Box-lock triple lock system with Greener cross-bolt; articulated front trigger; Holland & Holland-type ejectors. Imported from Belgium by Midwest Gun Sport.
Price: About $8,300.00
Price: Standard calibers start at about $5,400.00

Dumoulin "Sidelock Prestige" Double Rifle
Similar to the "Pionnier" except with sidelock action with reinforced 60mm table; internal parts are gold plated to resist corrosion. Choice of traditional chopper lump or "Classic Ernest Dumoulin" barrel system, with quarter-rib, in lengths of 22" to 24" according to caliber. Grand Luxe European walnut; Purdey lock system available on fore-end. All calibers available, special on request. Built to customer specs. Ten grades offered, differing in types, styles of engraving.
Price: About................................ $14,500.00 to $18,000.00

CAUTION: PRICES CHANGE. CHECK AT GUNSHOP.

Heym Model 33 Drilling

HEYM MODEL 33 BOXLOCK DRILLING

Caliber/Gauge: 5.6x50R Mag., 5.6x57R, 6.5x57R, 7x57R, 7x65R, 8x57JRS, 9.3x74R, 222, 243, 270, 308, 30-06; 16x16 (2¾"), 20x20 (3").
Barrel: 25" (Full & Mod.).
Weight: About 6½ lbs. **Length:** 42" over-all.
Stock: Dark European walnut, checkered p.g. and fore-end; oil finish.
Sights: Silver bead front, folding leaf rear. Automatic sight positioner. Available with scope and Suhler claw mounts.
Features: Greener-type crossbolt and safety, double under-lugs. Double set triggers. Plastic or steel trigger guard. Engraving coverage varies with model. Imported from West Germany by Paul Jaeger Inc.
Price: Model 33, from. $3,544.00

Heym 22S Combo

HEYM MODEL 22S SAFETY COMBO GUN

Caliber/Gauge: 16 or 20 ga. (2¾", 3"), 12 ga. (2¾") over 22 Hornet, 22 WMR, 222 Rem., 222 Rem. Mag., 223, 243 Win., 5.6x50R, 6.5x57R, 7x57R, 8x57 JRS.
Barrel: 24", solid rib.
Weight: About 5½ lbs.
Stock: Dark European walnut, hand-checkered p.g. and fore-end. Oil finish.
Sights: Silver bead ramp front, folding leaf rear.
Features: Tang mounted cocking slide, separate barrel selector, single set trigger. Base supplied for quick-detachable scope mounts. Patented rocker-weight system automatically uncocks gun if accidentally dropped or bumped hard. Imported from West Germany. Contact Heym for more data.
Price: Model 22S $1,452.00
Price: Model 22SZ takedown $1,650.00
Price: Scope mounts, add $120.00

HEYM MODEL 37B DOUBLE RIFLE DRILLING

Caliber/Gauge: 7x65R, 30-06, 8x57JRS, 9.3x74R; 20 ga. (3").
Barrel: 25" (shotgun barrel choked Full or Mod.).
Weight: About 8½ lbs. **Length:** 42" over-all.
Stock: Dark European walnut, hand-checkered p.g. and fore-end. Oil finish.
Sights: Silver bead front, folding leaf rear. Available with scope and Suhler claw mounts.
Features: Full side-lock construction. Greener-type crossbolt, double under lugs, cocking indicators. Imported from West Germany by Paul Jaeger, Inc.
Price: Model 37 double rifle drilling $7,172.00
Price: Model 37 Deluxe (hunting scene engraving) from, ... $8,195.00

Heym Model 37

Heym Model 37 Sidelock Drilling

Similar to Model 37 Double Rifle Drilling except has 12x12, 16x16 or 20x20 over 5.6x50R Mag., 5.6x57R, 6.5x57R, 7x57R, 7x65R, 8x57JRS, 9.3x74R, 222, 243, 270, 308 or 30-06. Rifle barrel is manually cocked and uncocked.
Price: Model 37 with border engraving $5,423.00
Price: As above with engraved hunting scenes. $6,446.00

Heym Model 88B

HEYM MODEL 88B SIDE-BY-SIDE DOUBLE RIFLE

Caliber: 7x57, 270, 30-06, 8x57JRS, 300 Win. Mag., 9.3x74R, 375 H&H.
Barrel: 25".
Weight: 7½ lbs. (std. cals), 8½ lbs. (mag.) **Length:** 42" over-all.
Stock: Fancy French walnut, classic North American design.
Sights: Silver bead post on ramp front, fixed or 3-leaf express rear.
Features: Action has complete coverage hunting scene engraving. Available as boxlock or with q.d. sidelocks. Imported from West Germany by Paul Jaeger, Inc.
Price: Boxlock, from. $5,170.00
Price: Sidelock, Model 88B-SS, from $7,249.00
Price: Disengageable ejectors, add $198.00
Price: Interchangeable barrels, add $2,838.00

Heym 88B Safari

HEYM MODEL 88B SAFARI DOUBLE RIFLE

Caliber: 375 H&H, 458 Win. Mag., 470 Nitro Express.
Action: Boxlock with interceptor sear. Automatic ejectors with disengagement sear.
Barrel: 25".
Weight: About 10 lbs.
Stock: Best quality Circassian walnut; classic design with cheekpiece; oil finish, hand-checkering; Presentation butt pad; steel grip cap.
Sights: Large silver bead on ramp front, quarter-rib with three-leaf express rear.
Features: Double triggers; engraved, silvered frame. Introduced 1985. Imported from West Germany by Paul Jaeger, Inc.
Price: 375 and 458. . . . . $6,000.00
Price: 470 Nitro Express $6,800.00
Price: Trap door grip cap $235.00
Price: Best quality leather case. $350.00

CAUTION: PRICES CHANGE. CHECK AT GUNSHOP.

DRILLINGS, COMBINATION GUNS, DOUBLE RIFLES

HEYM MODEL 55B/55SS O/U DOUBLE RIFLE
Caliber: 7x65R, 308, 30-06, 8x57JRS, 9.3x74R; 375 H&H.
Barrel: 25″
Weight: About 8 lbs., depending upon caliber. **Length:** 42″ over-all.
Stock: Dark European walnut, hand-checkered p.g. and fore-end. Oil finish.
Sights: Silver bead ramp front, open V-type rear.
Features: Boxlock or full sidelock; Kersten double crossbolt, cocking indicators; hand-engraved hunting scenes. Options available include interchangeable barrels, Zeiss scopes in claw mounts, deluxe engravings and stock carving, etc. Imported from West Germany by Paul Jaeger, Inc.
Price: Model 55B boxlock $3,839.00
Price: Model 55SS sidelock $6,094.00
Price: Interchangeable shotgun barrels $1,793.00
Price: Interchangeable rifle barrels $2,541.00

PERUGINI-VISINI DOUBLE RIFLE
Caliber: 22 Hornet, 30-06, 7mm Rem. Mag., 7x65R, 9.3x74R, 270 Win., 300 H&H, 375 H&H, 338 Win., 458 Win. Mag., 470 Nitro.
Barrel: 22″-26″.
Weight: 7¼ to 8½ lbs., depending upon caliber. **Length:** 39½″ over-all (22″ bbl.).
Stock: Oil-finished walnut; checkered grip and fore-end; cheekpiece.
Sights: Bead on ramp front, express rear on ¼-rib.
Features: True sidelock action with ejectors; sideplates are hand detachable; comes with leather trunk case. Introduced 1983. Imported from Italy by Wm. Larkin Moore.
Price: $10,500.00

Perugini-Visini O/U Double

Perugini-Visini Boxlock Double

Consult our Directory pages for the location of firms mentioned.

SAUER BBF O/U COMBO GUN
Caliber/Gauge: 16 (2¾″) over 243 or 30-06.
Barrel: 25″.
Weight: About 6 lbs. **Length:** 42″ over-all.
Stock: European walnut, with cheekpiece.
Sights: Post front, folding leaf rear on solid rib.
Features: Double set triggers, sear safety; satin oil finish on wood. Luxus model has better wood with white spacers at p.g. and buttplate, engraving. Introduced in U.S. 1986. Imported from West Germany by SIGARMS.
Price: Standard, About $2,495.00
Price: Luxus, about $2,745.00

Heym Model 55BF/55BFSS O/U Combo Gun
Similar to Model 55B/77B o/u rifle except chambered for 12, 16 or 20 ga. (2¾″ or 3″) over 5.6x50R, 222 Rem., 5.6x57R, 243, 6.5x57R, 270, 7x57R, 7x65R, 308, 30-06, 8x57JRS, 9.3x74R, or 375 H&H. Has solid rib barrel. Available as boxlock or sidelock, with interchangeable shotgun and rifle barrels.
Price: Model 55BF boxlock $3,212.00
Price: Model 55BFSS sidelock $5,467.00

LEBEAU-COURALLY SIDELOCK DOUBLE RIFLE
Caliber: 8x57 JRS, 9.3x74R, 375 H&H, 458 Win.
Barrel: 23½″ to 26″.
Weight: 7 lbs., 8 oz. to 9 lbs., 8 oz.
Stock: Dimensions to customer specs. Best quality French walnut selected for maximum strength, pistol grip with cheekpiece, splinter or beavertail fore-end; steel grip cap.
Sights: Bead on ramp front, express rear on ¼-rib.
Features: Holland & Holland pattern sidelock with ejectors, chopper lump barrels; reinforced action with classic pattern; choice of numerous engraving patterns; can be furnished with scope in fitted claw mounts. Imported from Belgium by Wm. Larkin Moore.
Price: From $20,500.00

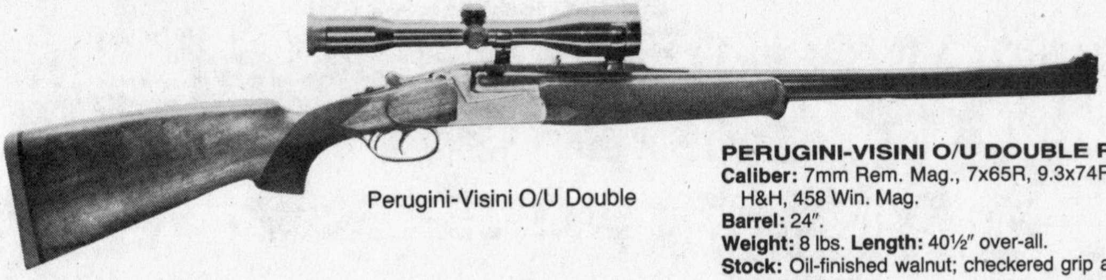

PERUGINI-VISINI O/U DOUBLE RIFLE
Caliber: 7mm Rem. Mag., 7x65R, 9.3x74R, 270 Win., 338 Win. Mag., 375 H&H, 458 Win. Mag.
Barrel: 24″.
Weight: 8 lbs. **Length:** 40½″ over-all.
Stock: Oil-finished walnut; checkered grip and fore-end; cheekpiece, rubber recoil pad.
Sights: Bead on ramp front, express rear on ¼-rib; Swarovski scope and claw mounts optional.
Features: Boxlock action with ejectors; silvered receiver, rest blued; double triggers. Comes with trunk case. Deluxe engraving, better wood, etc. available. Introduced 1983. Imported from Italy by Wm. Larkin Moore.
Price: $4,000.00

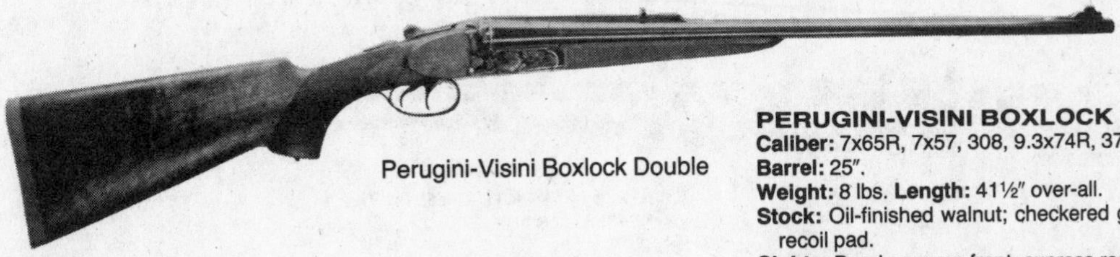

PERUGINI-VISINI BOXLOCK DOUBLE RIFLE
Caliber: 7x65R, 7x57, 308, 9.3x74R, 375 H&H, 444 Marlin, 458 Win. Mag.
Barrel: 25″.
Weight: 8 lbs. **Length:** 41½″ over-all.
Stock: Oil-finished walnut; checkered grip and fore-end; cheekpiece; rubber recoil pad.
Sights: Bead on ramp front, express rear on ¼-rib.
Features: Boxlock action with ejectors; color case-hardened receiver; double triggers. Also available with scope in claw mounts. Comes with trunk case. Introduced 1983. Imported from Italy by Wm. Larkin Moore.
Price: From $3,500.00

SAUER MODEL 3000 DRILLING
Caliber/Gauge: 12 ga., over 30-06, 12 ga. over 243.
Action: Top lever, cross bolt, box lock.
Barrel: 25″ (Mod. & Full).
Weight: 8 lbs. **Length:** 41¾″ over-all.
Stock: American walnut, oil finish. Checkered p.g. and fore-end. Black p.g. cap, recoil pad. 14¼″x2″x1½″.
Sights: Blade front with brass bead, folding leaf rear.
Features: Cocking indicators, tang barrel selector, automatic sight positioner, set rifle trigger, side safety. Blue finish with bright receiver engraved with animal motifs and European-style scrollwork. Imported from West Germany by SIGARMS.
Price: Standard, about $2,635.00
Price: Lux, about $2,920.00

CAUTION: PRICES CHANGE. CHECK AT GUNSHOP.

Savage Model 24-C

SAVAGE MODEL 24-C O/U
Caliber/Gauge: Top bbl. 22 S, L, LR; bottom bbl. 20 gauge cyl. bore.
Action: Take-down, low rebounding visible hammer. Single trigger, barrel selector spur on hammer.

Barrel: 20″ separated barrels.
Weight: 5¾ lbs. **Length:** 35″ (taken down 20″).
Stock: Walnut finished hardwood.
Sights: Ramp front, rear open adj. for e.
Features: Trap door butt holds one shotshell and ten 22 cartridges, comes with special carrying case. Measures 7″x22″ when in case.
Price: $208.39

Savage Model 24-F.G. O/U
Same as Model 24-C except: color case hardened frame, 24″ barrel, stock is walnut finished hardwood, no checkering.
Price: $187.29

Savage Model 24-V
Similar to Model 24-C except: 222 Rem., 223 Rem. or 30-30 and 20 ga; 24″ barrel; stronger receiver; color case-hardened frame; folding leaf rear sight; receiver tapped for scope.
Price: $272.89

Springfield Armory M6

SPRINGFIELD ARMORY M6 SCOUT SURVIVAL RIFLE
Caliber: 22 LR, 22 Mag., 22 Hornet over 410 shotgun.
Barrel: 18″.
Weight: 4 lbs. **Length:** 31½″ over-all.
Stock: Steel, folding, with magazine for 15 22 LR, four 410 cartridges.
Sights: Blade front, military aperture for 22; V-notch for 410.
Features: All metal construction. Designed for quick disassembly and minimum maintenance. Folds for compact storage. Introduced 1982. Made in U.S. by Springfield Armory.
Price: About $115.00

Tikka Model 07

TIKKA MODEL 07 COMBINATION GUN
Caliber/Gauge: 12 (2¾″) over 222 Rem.
Barrel: Shotgun — 25″ (Full), rifle — 22¾″.
Weight: About 7 lbs. **Length:** 40⅝″ over-all.
Stock: Walnut, Monte Carlo-style with palm-swell p.g.
Sights: Blade front, open rear adj. for w.
Features: Exposed hammer; receiver dovetailed for scope mounting; rifle barrel has a muzzle brake. Imported by Kassnar Imports, Inc.
Price: $1,070.00

Valmet 412S Double

VALMET 412S DOUBLE RIFLE
Caliber: 243, 308, 30-06, 375 Win., 9.3x74R.
Barrel: 24″
Weight: 8⅝ lbs.
Stock: American walnut with Monte Carlo style.
Sights: Ramp front, adjustable open rear.
Features: Barrel selector mounted in trigger. Cocking indicators in tang. Recoil pad. Valmet scope mounts available. Interchangeable barrels. Introduced 1980. Imported from Finland by Valmet.
Price: Extractors, 243, 308, 30-06 .... $999.00
Price: With ejectors, 375 Win., 9.3x74R................... $1,099.00
Price: Extra barrels, from $599.00

VALMET 412S COMBINATION GUN
Caliber/Gauge: 12 over 222, 223, 243, 308, 30-06.
Barrel: 24″ (Imp. Mod.).
Weight: 7⅝ lbs.
Stock: American walnut, with recoil pad. Monte Carlo style. Standard measurements 14″x1⅜″x2″x2⅜″.
Sights: Blade front, flip-up-type open rear.
Features: Barrel selector on trigger. Hand checkered stock and fore-end. Barrels are screw-adjustable to change bullet point of impact. Barrels are interchangeable. Introduced 1980. Imported from Finland by Valmet.
Price: $899.00
Price: Extra barrels, from $499.00

A. ZOLI RIFLE-SHOTGUN O/U COMBO
Caliber/Gauge: 12 ga./308 Win., 12 ga./222, 12 ga./30-06.
Barrel: Combo—24″; shotgun—28″ (Mod. & Full).
Weight: About 8 lbs. **Length:** 41″ over-all (24″ bbl.).
Stock: European walnut.
Sights: Blade front, flip-up rear.
Features: Available with German claw scope mounts on rifle/shotgun barrels. Comes with set of 12/12 (Mod. & Full) barrels. Imported from Italy by Mandall Shooting Supplies.
Price: With two barrel sets, without claw mounts $1,495.00
Price: With two barrel sets, scope and claw mounts $1,895.00

CAUTION: PRICES CHANGE. CHECK AT GUNSHOP.

AMT Lightning 25/22

AMT LIGHTNING 25/22 RIFLE
Caliber: 22 LR, 25-shot magazine.
Barrel: NA.
Weight: 6 lbs. **Length:** 26½" (folded).
Stock: Folding stainless steel; finger-grooved vertical pistol grip.
Sights: Ramp front, rear adjustable for windage.
Features: Made of stainless steel with matte finish. Receiver dovetailed for scope mounting. Extended magazine release. Standard or "bull" barrel. Introduced 1984. From AMT.
Price: **$245.00**

AP-74 AUTO RIFLE
Caliber: 22 LR, 32 ACP, 15 shot magazine.
Barrel: 20" including flash reducer.
Weight: 6½ lbs. **Length:** 38½" over-all.
Stock: Black plastic.
Sights: Ramp front, adj. peep rear.
Features: Pivotal take-down, easy disassembly. AR-15 look-alike. Sling and sling swivels included. Imported by EMF.
Price: **$250.00**
Price: With walnut stock and fore-end **$280.00**
Price: 32 ACP **$255.00**
Price: With wood stock and fore-end **$260.00**

Anschutz Model 520/61

ANSCHUTZ DELUXE MODEL 520/61 AUTO
Caliber: 22 LR, 10-shot clip.
Barrel: 24".

Weight: 6½ lbs. **Length:** 43" over-all.
Stock: European hardwood; checkered pistol grip, Monte Carlo comb, beaver-tail fore-end.
Sights: Hooded ramp front, folding leaf rear.
Features: Rotary safety, empty shell deflector, single stage trigger. Receiver grooved for scope mounting. Introduced 1982. Imported from Germany by PSI.
Price: **$276.50**

Auto-Ordnance 1927A-3

AUTO ORDNANCE MODEL 1927A-3
Caliber: 22 LR, 10, 30 or 50-shot magazine.
Barrel: 16", finned.
Weight: About 7 lbs.
Stock: Walnut stock and fore-end.
Sights: Blade front, open rear adjustable for windage and elevation.
Features: Re-creation of the Thompson Model 1927, only in 22 Long Rifle. Alloy receiver, finned barrel.
Price: **$424.75**

BINGHAM PPS-50 CARBINE
Caliber: 22 LR, 50-shot drum.
Barrel: 16.1".
Weight: 6½ lbs. **Length:** 33¾" over-all.
Stock: Beechwood (standard), walnut optional.
Sights: Blade front, folding leaf rear.
Features: Semi-auto carbine with perforated barrel jacket. Standard model has blue finish with oil-finish wood. From Bingham Ltd.
Price: Standard **$229.95**
Price: Deluxe (blue with walnut stock) **$249.95**
Price: Duramil (chrome with walnut stock) **$259.95**

BINGHAM AK-22 CARBINE
Caliber: 22 LR, 15-shot magazine.
Barrel: 17¾".
Weight: 6 lbs., 1 oz. **Length:** 35½" over-all.
Stock: Beechwood (standard), walnut optional.
Sights: Hooded post front, open adjustable rear.
Features: Semi-auto rimfire version of the Soviet assault rifle. A 28-shot "Military Look-Alike" magazine optional. From Bingham Ltd.
Price: Standard **$229.95**
Price: Deluxe (walnut stock) **$249.95**

Browning Auto Rifle

BROWNING AUTOLOADING RIFLE
Caliber: 22 LR, 11-shot.
Barrel: 19¼".
Weight: 4¾ lbs. **Length:** 37" over-all.
Stock: Checkered select walnut (13¾"x1¹³⁄₁₆"x2⅝") with p.g. and semi-beavertail fore-end.
Sights: Gold bead front, folding leaf rear.
Features: Engraved receiver is grooved for tip-off scope mount; cross-bolt safety; tubular magazine in buttstock; easy take down for carrying or storage. Imported from Japan by Browning.
Price: Grade I **$295.50**

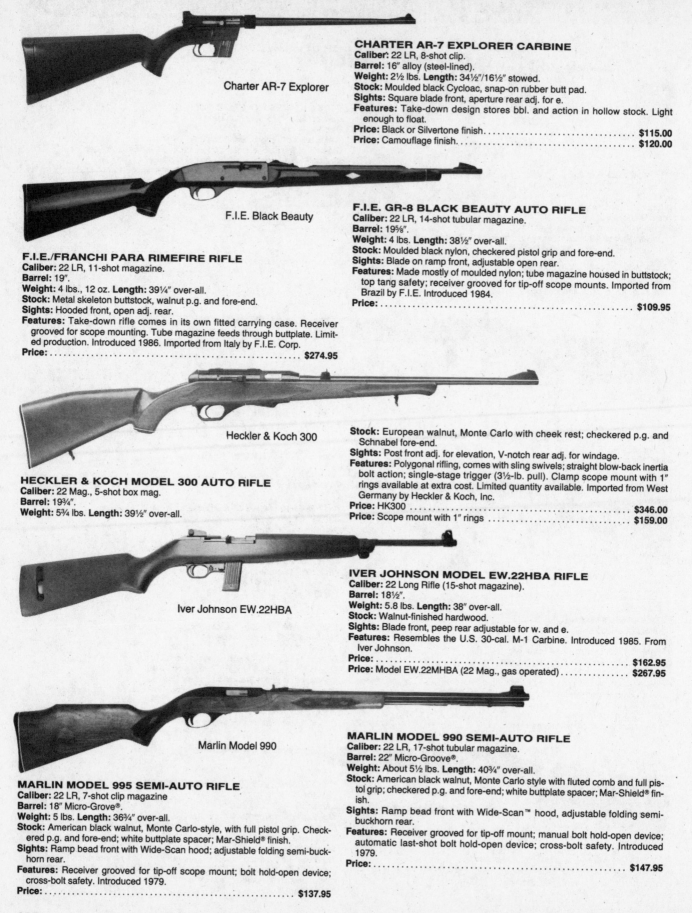

Charter AR-7 Explorer

CHARTER AR-7 EXPLORER CARBINE
Caliber: 22 LR, 8-shot clip.
Barrel: 16" alloy (steel-lined).
Weight: 2½ lbs. **Length:** 34½"/16½" stowed.
Stock: Moulded black Cycloac, snap-on rubber butt pad.
Sights: Square blade front, aperture rear adj. for e.
Features: Take-down design stores bbl. and action in hollow stock. Light enough to float.
Price: Black or Silvertone finish.................................. $115.00
Price: Camouflage finish....................................... $120.00

F.I.E. Black Beauty

F.I.E. GR-8 BLACK BEAUTY AUTO RIFLE
Caliber: 22 LR, 14-shot tubular magazine.
Barrel: 19⅝".
Weight: 4 lbs. **Length:** 38½" over-all.
Stock: Moulded black nylon, checkered pistol grip and fore-end.
Sights: Blade on ramp front, adjustable open rear.
Features: Made mostly of moulded nylon; tube magazine housed in buttstock; top tang safety; receiver grooved for tip-off scope mounts. Imported from Brazil by F.I.E. Introduced 1984.
Price: $109.95

F.I.E./FRANCHI PARA RIMEFIRE RIFLE
Caliber: 22 LR, 11-shot magazine.
Barrel: 19".
Weight: 4 lbs., 12 oz. **Length:** 39¼" over-all.
Stock: Metal skeleton buttstock, walnut p.g. and fore-end.
Sights: Hooded front, open adj. rear.
Features: Take-down rifle comes in its own fitted carrying case. Receiver grooved for scope mounting. Tube magazine feeds through buttplate. Limited production. Introduced 1986. Imported from Italy by F.I.E. Corp.
Price: $274.95

Heckler & Koch 300

Stock: European walnut, Monte Carlo with cheek rest; checkered p.g. and Schnabel fore-end.
Sights: Post front adj. for elevation, V-notch rear adj. for windage.
Features: Polygonal rifling, comes with sling swivels; straight blow-back inertia bolt action; single-stage trigger (3½-lb. pull). Clamp scope mount with 1" rings available at extra cost. Limited quantity available. Imported from West Germany by Heckler & Koch, Inc.
Price: HK300 .... $346.00
Price: Scope mount with 1" rings $159.00

HECKLER & KOCH MODEL 300 AUTO RIFLE
Caliber: 22 Mag., 5-shot box mag.
Barrel: 19¾".
Weight: 5¾ lbs. **Length:** 39½" over-all.

Iver Johnson EW.22HBA

IVER JOHNSON MODEL EW.22HBA RIFLE
Caliber: 22 Long Rifle (15-shot magazine).
Barrel: 18½".
Weight: 5.8 lbs. **Length:** 38" over-all.
Stock: Walnut-finished hardwood.
Sights: Blade front, peep rear adjustable for w. and e.
Features: Resembles the U.S. 30-cal. M-1 Carbine. Introduced 1985. From Iver Johnson.
Price: $162.95
Price: Model EW.22MHBA (22 Mag., gas operated) $267.95

Marlin Model 990

MARLIN MODEL 990 SEMI-AUTO RIFLE
Caliber: 22 LR, 17-shot tubular magazine.
Barrel: 22" Micro-Groove®.
Weight: About 5½ lbs. **Length:** 40¾" over-all.
Stock: American black walnut, Monte Carlo style with fluted comb and full pistol grip; checkered p.g. and fore-end; white buttplate spacer; Mar-Shield® finish.
Sights: Ramp bead front with Wide-Scan™ hood, adjustable folding semi-buckhorn rear.
Features: Receiver grooved for tip-off mount; manual bolt hold-open device; automatic last-shot bolt hold-open device; cross-bolt safety. Introduced 1979.
Price: $147.95

MARLIN MODEL 995 SEMI-AUTO RIFLE
Caliber: 22 LR, 7-shot clip magazine
Barrel: 18" Micro-Grove®.
Weight: 5 lbs. **Length:** 36¾" over-all.
Stock: American black walnut, Monte Carlo-style, with full pistol grip. Checkered p.g. and fore-end; white buttplate spacer; Mar-Shield® finish.
Sights: Ramp bead front with Wide-Scan hood; adjustable folding semi-buckhorn rear.
Features: Receiver grooved for tip-off scope mount; bolt hold-open device; cross-bolt safety. Introduced 1979.
Price: $137.95

CAUTION: PRICES CHANGE. CHECK AT GUNSHOP.

Marlin Model 60

MARLIN 60 SEMI-AUTO RIFLE
Caliber: 22 LR, 17-shot tubular mag.
Barrel: 22″ round tapered.
Weight: About 5½ lbs. **Length:** 40½″ over-all.
Stock: Walnut finished Monte Carlo, full pistol grip; Mar-Shield® finish.
Sights: Ramp front, open adj. rear.
Features: Matted receiver is grooved for tip-off mounts. Manual bolt hold-open; automatic last-shot bolt hold-open.
Price: $109.95

Marlin Model 70

MARLIN MODEL 70 AUTO
Caliber: 22 LR, 7-shot clip magazine.
Barrel: 18″ (16-groove rifling).
Weight: 4½ lbs. **Length:** 36½″ over-all.
Stock: Walnut-finished hardwood with Monte Carlo, full p.g.
Sights: Ramp front, adj. open rear. Receiver grooved for scope mount.
Features: Receiver top has serrated, non-glare finish; cross-bolt safety; manual bolt hold-open.
Price: Less scope $109.95

Marlin 70P Papoose

Marlin Model 70P Papoose
Similar to the Model 70 except is a take-down model with easily removable barrel—no tools needed. Has 16¼″ Micro-Groove® barrel, walnut-finished hardwood stock, ramp front, adjustable open rear sights, cross-bolt safety. Over-all length is 35¼″, weight is 3¾ lbs. Receiver grooved for scope mounting. Comes with 4x scope and mounts. Introduced 1986.
Price: With scope $135.95

Marlin Model 75C

MARLIN MODEL 75C SEMI-AUTO RIFLE
Caliber: 22 LR, 13-shot tubular magazine.
Barrel: 18″.
Weight: 5 lbs. **Length:** 36½″ over-all.
Stock: Walnut-finished hardwood; Monte Carlo with full p.g.
Sights: Ramp front, adj. open rear.
Features: Manual bolt hold-open; automatic last-shot bolt hold-open; cross-bolt safety; receiver grooved for scope mounting.
Price: $109.95

Mitchell AK-22

MITCHELL AK-22 SEMI-AUTO RIFLE
Caliber: 22 LR, 29-shot magazine, 22 Mag., 10-shot magazine.
Barrel: 16½″.
Weight: 3.1 lbs. **Length:** 38″ over-all.
Stock: European walnut.
Sights: Post front, open adj. rear.
Features: Replica of the AK-47 assult rifle. Wide magazine to maintain appearance. Imported from Italy by Mitchell Arms.
Price: 22 LR $249.95
Price: 22 Mag. $265.00

Remington Nylon 66

REMINGTON NYLON 66MB AUTO RIFLE
Caliber: 22 LR, 14-shot tubular mag.
Barrel: 19⅝″ round tapered.
Weight: 4 lbs. **Length:** 38½″ over-all.
Stock: Moulded Mohawk Brown Nylon, checkered p.g. and fore-end.
Sights: Blade ramp front, adj. open rear.
Features: Top tang safety, double extractors, receiver grooved for tip-off mounts.
Price: About $135.00

Remington Nylon 66BD Auto Rifle
Same as the Model 66MB except has black stock, barrel, and receiver cover. Black diamond-shape inlay in fore-end. Introduced 1978.
Price: About $135.00

CAUTION: PRICES CHANGE. CHECK AT GUNSHOP.

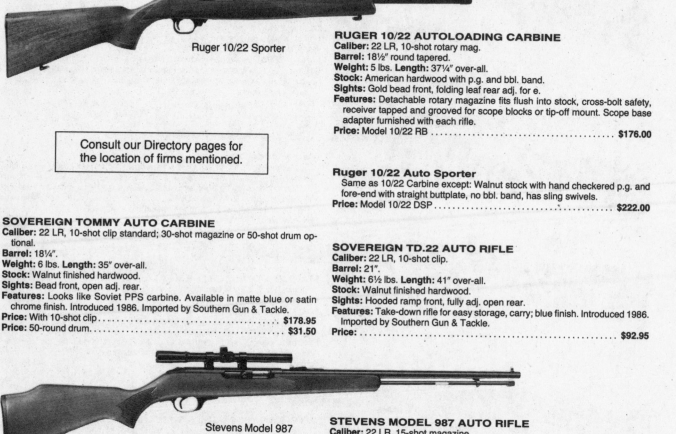

Remington Model 552A

Remington Model 552BDL Deluxe Auto Rifle
Same as Model 552A except: Du Pont RKW finished walnut stock, checkered fore-end and capped p.g. stock. Blade ramp front and fully adj. rear sights.
Price: About **$209.00**

REMINGTON 552A AUTOLOADING RIFLE
Caliber: 22 S (20), L (17) or LR (15) tubular mag.
Barrel: 21" round tapered.
Weight: About 5¾ lbs. **Length:** 40" over-all.
Stock: Full-size, walnut-finished hardwood.
Sights: Bead front, step open rear adj. for w. & e.
Features: Positive cross-bolt safety, receiver grooved for tip-off mount.
Price: About **$183.00**

Ruger 10/22 Sporter

RUGER 10/22 AUTOLOADING CARBINE
Caliber: 22 LR, 10-shot rotary mag.
Barrel: 18½" round tapered.
Weight: 5 lbs. **Length:** 37¼" over-all.
Stock: American hardwood with p.g. and bbl. band.
Sights: Gold bead front, folding leaf rear adj. for e.
Features: Detachable rotary magazine fits flush into stock, cross-bolt safety, receiver tapped and grooved for scope blocks or tip-off mount. Scope base adapter furnished with each rifle.
Price: Model 10/22 RB **$176.00**

> Consult our Directory pages for the location of firms mentioned.

Ruger 10/22 Auto Sporter
Same as 10/22 Carbine except: Walnut stock with hand checkered p.g. and fore-end with straight buttplate, no bbl. band, has sling swivels.
Price: Model 10/22 DSP **$222.00**

SOVEREIGN TOMMY AUTO CARBINE
Caliber: 22 LR, 10-shot clip standard; 30-shot magazine or 50-shot drum optional.
Barrel: 18¼".
Weight: 6 lbs. **Length:** 35" over-all.
Stock: Walnut finished hardwood.
Sights: Bead front, open adj. rear.
Features: Looks like Soviet PPS carbine. Available in matte blue or satin chrome finish. Introduced 1986. Imported by Southern Gun & Tackle.
Price: With 10-shot clip **$178.95**
Price: 50-round drum **$31.50**

SOVEREIGN TD.22 AUTO RIFLE
Caliber: 22 LR, 10-shot clip.
Barrel: 21".
Weight: 6½ lbs. **Length:** 41" over-all.
Stock: Walnut finished hardwood.
Sights: Hooded ramp front, fully adj. open rear.
Features: Take-down rifle for easy storage, carry; blue finish. Introduced 1986. Imported by Southern Gun & Tackle.
Price: **$92.95**

Stevens Model 987

STEVENS MODEL 987 AUTO RIFLE
Caliber: 22 LR, 15-shot magazine.
Barrel: 20".
Weight: About 6 lbs. **Length:** 40½" over-all.
Stock: Walnut finish with Monte Carlo; checkered pistol grip and fore-end.
Sights: Bead front, open adjustable rear.
Features: Top tang safety; metal parts blued.
Price: **$106.50**

Tradewinds Model 260-A

TRADEWINDS MODEL 260-A AUTO RIFLE
Caliber: 22 LR, 5-shot (10-shot mag. avail.).
Barrel: 22½".
Weight: 5¾ lbs. **Length:** 41½" over-all.
Stock: Walnut, with hand checkered p.g. and fore-end.
Sights: Ramp front with hood, 3-leaf folding rear, receiver grooved for scope mount.
Features: Double extractors, sliding safety. Imported by Tradewinds.
Price: **$250.00**

CAUTION: PRICES CHANGE. CHECK AT GUNSHOP.

Voere Model 2005

VOERE MODEL 2005 AUTO RIFLE
Caliber: 22 LR, 5- or 8-shot magazine.
Barrel: 19½".
Weight: 6 lbs. **Length:** 41" over-all.

Stock: European hardwood with Monte Carlo. Butt pad and swivel studs standard.
Sights: Hooded front, open fully adj. rear.
Features: Deluxe model with checkering and raised cheekpiece available. Introduced 1986. Imported from West Germany by KDF, Inc.
Price: Standard $149.00
Price: Deluxe $169.00

Voere 2115

VOERE MODEL 2115 AUTO RIFLE
Caliber: 22 LR, 8 or 15-shot magazine.
Barrel: 18.1".
Weight: 5.75 lbs. **Length:** 37.7" over-all.

Stock: Walnut-finished beechwood with cheekpiece; checkered pistol grip and fore-end.
Sights: Post front with hooded ramp, leaf rear.
Features: Clip-fed autoloader with single stage trigger, wing-type safety. Imported from Austria by L. Joseph Rahn. Introduced 1984.
Price: Model 2115 .... $245.00
Price: Model 2114S (as above except no cheekpiece, checkering or white line spacers at grip, buttplate) $225.00

Weatherby Mark XXII

WEATHERBY MARK XXII AUTO RIFLE, CLIP MODEL
Caliber: 22 LR only, 5- or 10-shot clip.
Barrel: 24" round contoured.
Weight: 6 lbs. **Length:** 42¼" over-all.
Stock: Walnut, Monte Carlo comb and cheekpiece, rosewood p.g. cap and fore-end tip. Skip-line checkering.
Sights: Gold bead ramp front, 3-leaf folding rear.
Features: Thumb operated tang safety. Single shot or semi-automatic side lever selector. Receiver grooved for tip-off scope mount. Single pin release for quick takedown.
Price: $369.95

Weatherby Mark XXII Tubular Model
   Same as Mark XXII Clip Model except: 15-shot tubular magazine.
Price: $369.95

RIMFIRE RIFLES—LEVER & SLIDE ACTIONS

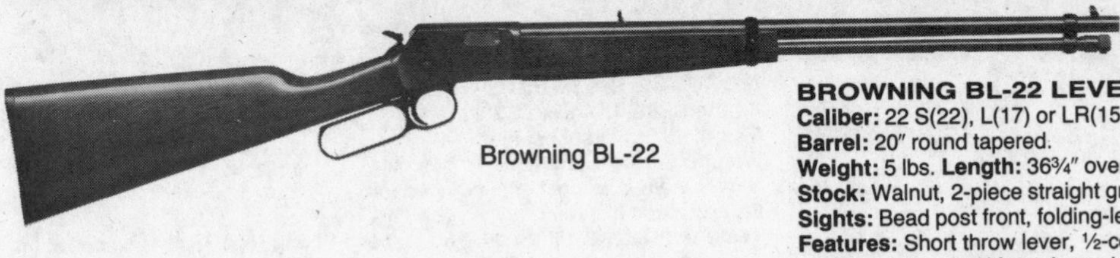

Browning BL-22

BROWNING BL-22 LEVER ACTION RIFLE
Caliber: 22 S(22), L(17) or LR(15). Tubular mag.
Barrel: 20" round tapered.
Weight: 5 lbs. **Length:** 36¾" over-all.
Stock: Walnut, 2-piece straight grip Western style.
Sights: Bead post front, folding-leaf rear.
Features: Short throw lever, ½-cock safety, receiver grooved for tip-off scope mounts. Imported from Japan by Browning.
Price: Grade I $264.50
Price: Grade II, engraved receiver, checkered grip and fore-end $302.50

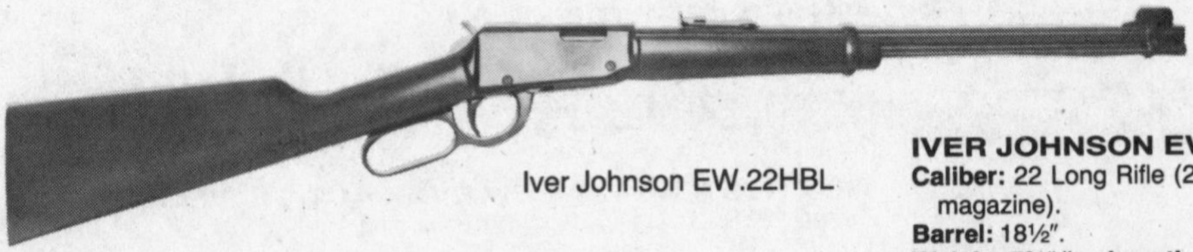

Iver Johnson EW.22HBL

IVER JOHNSON EW.22HBL RIFLE
Caliber: 22 Long Rifle (21 Short, 17 Long, 15 Long Rifle), 22 Mag. (12-shot magazine).
Barrel: 18½".
Weight: 5¾" lbs. **Length:** 36½" over-all.
Stock: Walnut-finished hardwood.
Sights: Hooded ramp front, open adjustable rear.
Features: Polished blue finish. Receiver grooved for scope mounting. Introduced 1985. From Iver Johnson.
Price: 22 Long Rifle $189.95
Price: 22 Magnum $204.95

Marlin 1894M

MARLIN MODEL 1894M CARBINE
Caliber: 22 Mag., 11-shot magazine.
Barrel: 20" Micro-Groove®.

Weight: 6¼ lbs. **Length:** 37½" over-all.
Stock: Straight grip stock of American black walnut, Mar-Shield® finish.
Sights: Ramp front with brass bead, adjustable semi-buckhorn folding rear.
Features: Has new hammer block safety. Side-ejecting solid-top receiver tapped for scope mount or receiver sight; squared finger lever, reversible off-set hammer spur for scope use. Scope shown is optional. Introduced 1983.
Price: $315.95

Marlin Golden 39A

MARLIN GOLDEN 39M CARBINE
Caliber: 22 S(21), L(16), LR(15), tubular magazine.
Barrel: 20" Micro-Grove®.
Weight: 6 lbs. **Length:** 36" over-all.
Stock: American black walnut, straight grip, white line buttplate spacer. Mar-Shield® finish.
Sights: "Wide-Scan"™ ramp front with hood, folding rear semi-buckhorn adj. for w. and e.
Features: Squared finger lever. Receiver tapped for scope mount (supplied) or receiver sight, offset hammer spur, take-down action; gold plated steel trigger.
Price: $281.95

MARLIN GOLDEN 39A LEVER ACTION RIFLE
Caliber: 22 S(26), L(21), LR(19), tubular magazine.
Barrel: 24" Micro-Groove®.
Weight: 6½ lbs. **Length:** 40" over-all.
Stock: American black walnut with white line spacers at p.g. cap and buttplate; Mar-Shield® finish.
Sights: Bead ramp front with detachable "Wide-Scan"™ hood, folding rear semi-buckhorn adj. for w. and e.
Features: Take-down action, receiver tapped for scope mount (supplied), offset hammer spur; gold plated steel trigger.
Price: $281.95

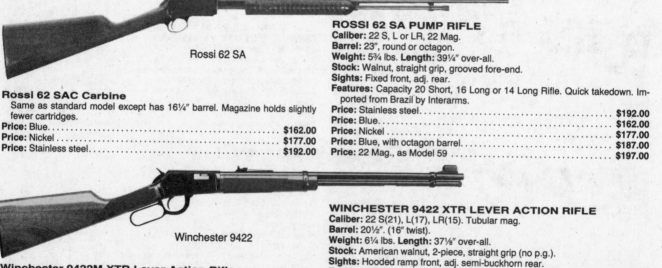

Remington Model 572

Remington Model 572 BDL Deluxe
Same as the 572 except: p.g. cap, walnut stock with RKW finish, checkered grip and fore-end, ramp front and fully adj. rear sights.
Price: About $221.00

REMINGTON 572A FIELDMASTER PUMP RIFLE
Caliber: 22 S(20), L(17) or LR(14). Tubular mag.
Barrel: 21" round tapered.
Weight: 5½ lbs. **Length:** 42" over-all.
Stock: Walnut-finished hardwood with p.g. and grooved slide handle.
Sights: Blade ramp front; sliding ramp rear adj. for w. & e.
Features: Cross-bolt safety, removing inner mag. tube converts rifle to single shot, receiver grooved for tip-off scope mount.
Price: About $192.00

Rossi 62 SA

Rossi 62 SAC Carbine
Same as standard model except has 16¼" barrel. Magazine holds slightly fewer cartridges.
Price: Blue $162.00
Price: Nickel $177.00
Price: Stainless steel $192.00

ROSSI 62 SA PUMP RIFLE
Caliber: 22 S, L or LR, 22 Mag.
Barrel: 23", round or octagon.
Weight: 5¾ lbs. **Length:** 39¼" over-all.
Stock: Walnut, straight grip, grooved fore-end.
Sights: Fixed front, adj. rear.
Features: Capacity 20 Short, 16 Long or 14 Long Rifle. Quick takedown. Imported from Brazil by Interarms.
Price: Stainless steel $192.00
Price: Blue $162.00
Price: Nickel $177.00
Price: Blue, with octagon barrel. $187.00
Price: 22 Mag., as Model 59 .... $197.00

Winchester 9422

Winchester 9422M XTR Lever Action Rifle
Same as the 9422 except chambered for 22 Mag. cartridge, has 11-round mag. capacity.
Price: About $320.27

WINCHESTER 9422 XTR LEVER ACTION RIFLE
Caliber: 22 S(21), L(17), LR(15). Tubular mag.
Barrel: 20½". (16" twist).
Weight: 6¼ lbs. **Length:** 37⅛" over-all.
Stock: American walnut, 2-piece, straight grip (no p.g.).
Sights: Hooded ramp front, adj. semi-buckhorn rear.
Features: Side ejection, receiver grooved for scope mounting, takedown action. Has XTR wood and metal finish. Made under license by U.S. Repeating Arms Co.
Price: About $320.27

CAUTION: PRICES CHANGE. CHECK AT GUNSHOP.

Winchester 9422 Classic
Similar to 9422 XTR except has uncheckered, satin-finished walnut stock with fluted comb, crescent steel buttplate, curved finger lever, and capped pistol grip. Over-all length is 39⅛″, barrel length 22½″, weight is 6½ lbs. In 22 Short, Long, Long Rifle and 22 Magnum. Introduced 1985.
Price: About **$354.45**

Winchester 9422 Classic

RIMFIRE RIFLES—BOLT ACTIONS & SINGLE SHOTS

Anschutz 1416/1516

ANSCHUTZ DELUXE 1416/1516 RIFLES
Caliber: 22 LR (1416D), 5-shot clip, 22 Mag. (1516D), 4-shot clip.
Barrel: 22½″.
Weight: 6 lbs. **Length:** 41″ over-all.
Stock: European walnut; Monte Carlo with cheekpiece, Schnabel fore-end, checkered pistol grip and fore-end.
Sights: Hooded ramp front, folding leaf rear.
Features: Uses Model 1403 target rifle action. Adjustable single stage trigger. Receiver grooved for scope mounting. Imported from Germany by PSI.
Price: 1416D, 22 LR **$372.00**
Price: 1516D, 22 Mag. **$377.75**
Price: 1416D Classic left hand **$424.75**

Anschutz 1418D/1518D Deluxe Rifles
Similar to the 1416D/1516D rifles except has full length Mannlicher-style stock, shorter 19¾″ barrel. Weighs 5½ lbs. Stock has buffalo horn Schnabel tip. Double set trigger available on special order. Model 1418D chambered for 22 LR, 1518D for 22 Mag. Imported from Germany by PSI.
Price: 1418D.. **$528.00**
Price: 1518D.. **$531.50**

Anschutz 1422/1522

ANSCHUTZ 1422D/1522D CLASSIC RIFLES
Caliber: 22 LR (1422D), 5-shot clip, 22 Mag. (1522D), 4-shot clip.
Barrel: 24″.
Weight: 7¼ lbs. **Length:** 43″ over-all.
Stock: Select European walnut; checkered pistol grip and fore-end.
Sights: Hooded ramp front, folding leaf rear.
Features: Uses Match 54 action. Adjustable single stage trigger. Receiver drilled and tapped for scope mounting. Introduced 1982. Imported from Germany by PSI.
Price: 1422D (22 LR) **$606.50**
Price: 1522D (22 Mag.).. **$609.75**

Anschutz 1422D/1522D Custom Rifles
Similar to the Classic models except have roll-over Monte Carlo cheekpiece, slim fore-end with Schnabel tip, Wundhammer palm swell on pistol grip, rosewood grip cap with white diamond insert. Skip-line checkering on grip and fore-end. Introduced 1982. Imported from Germany by PSI.
Price: 1422D.. **$652.50**
Price: 1522D.. **$645.75**

Beeman/Krico 320

BEEMAN/KRICO MODEL 320 BOLT ACTION RIFLE
Caliber: 22 LR, 5-shot magazine.
Barrel: 19.5″.
Weight: 6 lbs. **Length:** 38½″ over-all.
Stock: Select European walnut; full length Mannlicher-style with curved European comb and cheekpiece; cut checkered grip and fore-end.
Sights: Blade front on ramp, open rear adjustable for windage.
Features: Single or double set trigger; blued steel fore-end cap; detachable box magazine. Imported from West Germany by Beeman.
Price: **$549.50**

BEEMAN/KRICO MODEL 300 BOLT ACTION RIFLE
Caliber: 22 LR, 5-shot magazine.
Barrel: 23.5″.
Weight: 6.5 lbs. **Length:** 43″ over-all.
Stock: European walnut with straight American-style comb; cut checkered grip and fore-end.
Sights: Hooded blade front on ramp, open rear adjustable for windage.
Features: Dual extractors; single, match or double set triggers available; detachable box magazine. Imported from West Germany by Beeman.
Price: **$495.50**

BRNO ZKM 452 BOLT ACTION RIFLE
Caliber: 22 LR, 5- or 10-shot magazine.
Barrel: 25″.
Weight: 6 lbs., 10 oz. **Length:** 43½″ over-all.
Stock: Beechwood.
Sights: Hooded bead front, open rear adj. for e.
Features: Blue finish; oiled stock with checkered p.g. Imported from Czechoslovakia by Bauska Arms Corp.
Price: **$239.00**

Browning A-Bolt 22

BROWNING A-BOLT 22 BOLT ACTION RIFLE
Caliber: 22 LR, 5- and 15-shot magazines standard.
Barrel: 22".
Weight: 5 lbs., 9 oz. **Length:** 40¼" over-all.

Stock: Laminated walnut.
Sights: Offered with or without open sights. Open sight model has ramp front and adjustable folding leaf rear.
Features: Short 60-degree bolt throw. Top tang safety. Grooved for 22 scope mount. Drilled and tapped for full size scope mounts. Detachable magazines. Gold-colored trigger preset at about 4 lbs. Imported from Japan by Browning. Introduced 1986.
Price: A-Bolt 22, no sights $299.95
Price: A-Bolt 22, with open sights $309.95

CABANAS MASTER BOLT ACTION RIFLE
Caliber: 177, round ball or pellet; single shot.
Barrel: 19½".
Weight: 8 lbs. **Length:** 45½" over-all.
Stock: Walnut target-type with Monte Carlo.
Sights: Blade front, fully adjustable rear.
Features: Fires round ball or pellet with 22-cal. blank cartridge. Bolt action. Imported from Mexico by Mandall Shooting Supplies. Introduced 1984.
Price: $149.95
Price: Varmint model (21½" barrel, 4½ lbs., 41" o.a.l., varmint-type stock) $109.95

Cabanas Espronceda IV Bolt Action Rifle
Similar to the Leyre model except has full sporter stock, 18¾" barrel, 40" over-all length, weighs 5½ lbs.
Price: $119.95

Cabanas Leyre Bolt Action Rifle
Similar to Master model except 44" over-all, has sport/target stock.
Price: $134.95
Price: Model R83 (17" barrel, hardwood stock, 40" o.a.l.) $79.95
Price: Mini 82 Youth (16½" barrel, 33" o.a.l., 3½ lbs.) $69.95

Chipmunk Rifle

F.I.E. MODEL 122 BOLT ACTION RIFLE
Caliber: 22 S, L, LR, 6-shot magazine.
Barrel: 21".
Weight: 5½ lbs. **Length:** 39" over-all.
Stock: Walnut-finished hardwood.
Sights: Blade front, open rear adj. for w. & e.
Features: Sliding wing-type safety lever, double extractors, red cocking indicator, receiver grooved for scope mounts. Imported from Brazil by F.I.E. Introduced 1986.
Price: $114.95

CHIPMUNK SINGLE SHOT RIFLE
Caliber: 22, S, L, LR, or 22 Mag., single shot.
Barrel: 16⅛".
Weight: About 2½ lbs. **Length:** 30" over-all.
Stock: American walnut, or camouflage.
Sights: Post on ramp front, peep rear adj. for windage and elevation.
Features: Drilled and tapped for scope mounting using special Chipmunk base ($9.95). Made in U.S.A. Introduced 1982. From Chipmunk Mfg.
Price: $119.95
Price: Fully engraved Presentation Model with hand checkered fancy stock $500.00

Iver Johnson Li'l Champ

IVER JOHNSON LI'L CHAMP RIFLE
Caliber: 22 S, L, LR, single shot.
Barrel: 16¼".
Weight: 3 lbs., 2 oz. **Length:** 32½" over-all.
Stock: Moulded composition.
Sights: Blade on ramp front, adj. rear.
Features: Sized for junior shooters. Nickel-plated bolt. Made in U.S.A. Introduced 1986. From Iver Johnson.
Price: $89.00

KDF K-22

KDF K-22 BOLT ACTION RIFLE
Caliber: 22 LR, 22 Mag., 5- or 8-shot magazine.
Barrel: 21½".
Weight: 6½ lbs. **Length:** 40" over-all.
Stock: Oil finished, hand checkered European walnut with Monte Carlo.
Sights: None furnished. Receiver grooved for scope mounts.
Features: Bolt has front-locking lugs; uses KDF pillar bedding system. Introduced 1984. From KDF, Inc.
Price: K-22 Standard, 22 LR $299.00
Price: As above, 22 Mag. $349.00
Price: K-22 Deluxe (22 LR) has rosewood fore-end tip, rubber recoil pad, q.d. sling swivels $449.00

Consult our Directory pages for the location of firms mentioned.

CAUTION: PRICES CHANGE. CHECK AT GUNSHOP.

Kimber Model 82B

KIMBER MODEL 82B BOLT ACTION RIFLE
Caliber: 22 LR, 5-shot detachable magazine.
Barrel: 22"; 6-grooves; 1-in 16" twist; 24" varmint.
Weight: About 6¼ lbs. **Length:** 40½" over-all (Sporter).
Stock: Three styles available. "Classic" is Claro walnut with plain, straight comb; "Cascade" has Monte Carlo comb with cheekpiece; "Custom Classic" is of fancy select grade Claro walnut, ebony fore-end tip, Niedner-style butt-

plate. All have 18 lpi hand cut, borderless checkering, steel grip cap, checkered steel buttplate.
Sights: Hooded ramp front with bead, folding leaf rear (optional).
Features: High quality, adult-sized, bolt action rifle. Barrel screwed into receiver; rocker-type silent safety; twin rear locking lugs. All steel construction. Fully adjustable trigger; receiver grooved for Kimber scope mounts. High polish blue. Barreled actions available. Also available in true left-hand version in selected models. Made in U.S.A. Introduced 1979.
Price: 22 LR Classic stock, no sights, plain or heavy bbl. (left hand avail.) **$750.00**
Price: As above, Cascade stock (left hand avail.) **$805.00**
Price: As above, Custom Classic, plain or heavy bbl. (left hand avail.) **$995.00**
Price: Kimber scope mounts, from **$48.00**
Price: Optional open sights fitted. **$55.00**

Kimber Model 82, 84 Super America
Super-grade version of the Model 82. Has the Classic stock only of specially selected, high-grade, California claro walnut, with Continental beaded cheekpiece and ebony fore-end tip; borderless, full-coverage 20 lpi checkering; Niedner-type checkered steel buttplate; comes with barrel quarter-rib which has a folding leaf sight. Round-top receiver of the 1986 model is drilled and tapped to accept Kimber's screw-on scope mount bases. Available in 22 Long Rifle, 22 Hornet, 223 Rem.

Kimber Super America

Price: Model 82 22 Long Rifle, less scope **$1,150.00**
Price: Model 82 22 Hornet, less scope **$1,150.00**
Price: Model 84, 223 .... **$1,250.00**

MARATHON SUPER SHOT 22 BOLT ACTION
Caliber: 22 LR, single shot.
Barrel: 24".
Weight: 4.9 lbs. **Length:** 41½" over-all.
Stock: Select hardwood.
Sights: Bead front, step-adjustable open rear.
Features: Blued metal parts; receiver grooved for scope mounting. Also avail-

able as a kit, requiring assembly and metal and wood finishing. Introduced 1984. Imported from Spain by Marathon.
Price: Finished **$74.99**
Price: Kit **$55.99**
Price: First Shot (youth model of above with 16½" barrel, 3.8 lbs., 31" o.a.l.), assembled **$74.99**
Price: As above, kit **$55.99**

Marlin Model 780

Marlin 781 Bolt Action Rifle
Same as the Marlin 780 except: tubular magazine holds 25 Shorts, 19 Longs or 17 Long Rifle cartridges. Weight 6 lbs.
Price: **$147.95**

Marlin 782 Bolt Action Rifle
Same as the Marlin 780 except: 22 Rimfire Magnum cal. only, weight about 6 lbs. Sling and swivels attached
Price: **$155.95**

MARLIN 780 BOLT ACTION RIFLE
Caliber: 22 S, L, or LR; 7-shot clip magazine.
Barrel: 22" Micro-Groove.
Weight: 5½ lbs. **Length:** 41".
Stock: Monte Carlo American black walnut with checkered p.g. and fore-end. White line spacer at buttplate. Mar-Shield® finish.
Sights: "Wide-Scan"™ ramp front, folding semi-buckhorn rear adj. for w. & e.
Features: Receiver anti-glare serrated and grooved for tip-off scope mount.
Price: **$141.95**

Marlin Model 783

Marlin 783 Bolt Action Rifle
Same as Marlin 782 except: Tubular magazine holds 12 rounds of 22 Rimfire Magnum ammunition.
Price: **$161.95**

Marlin 25 Bolt Action Repeater
Similar to Marlin 780, except: walnut finished p.g. stock, adjustable open rear sight, ramp front.
Price: **$108.95**

Marlin Model 25M Bolt Action Rifle
Similar to the Model 25 except chambered for 22 Mag. Has 7-shot clip magazine, 22" Micro-Groove® barrel, walnut-finished hardwood stock. Introduced 1983.
Price: **$124.95**

MARLIN 15Y "LITTLE BUCKAROO"
Caliber: 22, S, L, LR, single shot.
Barrel: 16¼" Micro-Groove®.
Weight: 4¼ lbs. **Length:** 33¼" over-all.
Stock: One-piece walnut-finished hardwood with Monte Carlo.
Sights: Ramp front, adjustable open rear.
Features: Beginner's rifle with thumb safety, easy-load feed throat, red cocking indicator. Receiver grooved for scope mounting. Introduced 1984.
Price: Less scope **$105.95**

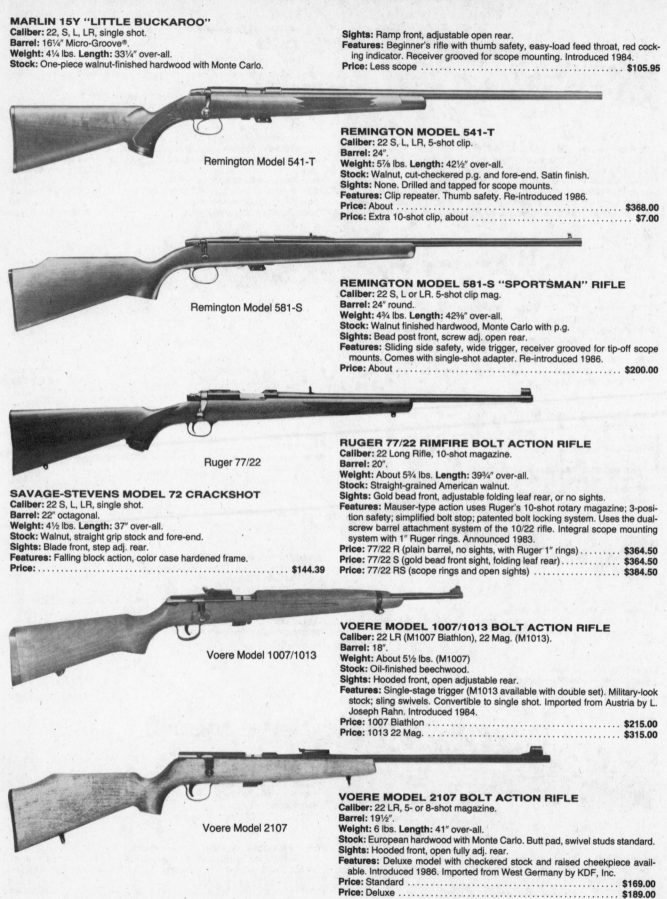

Remington Model 541-T

REMINGTON MODEL 541-T
Caliber: 22 S, L, LR, 5-shot clip.
Barrel: 24".
Weight: 5⅞ lbs. **Length:** 42½" over-all.
Stock: Walnut, cut-checkered p.g. and fore-end. Satin finish.
Sights: None. Drilled and tapped for scope mounts.
Features: Clip repeater. Thumb safety. Re-introduced 1986.
Price: About **$368.00**
Price: Extra 10-shot clip, about **$7.00**

Remington Model 581-S

REMINGTON MODEL 581-S "SPORTSMAN" RIFLE
Caliber: 22 S, L or LR. 5-shot clip mag.
Barrel: 24" round.
Weight: 4¾ lbs. **Length:** 42⅜" over-all.
Stock: Walnut finished hardwood, Monte Carlo with p.g.
Sights: Bead post front, screw adj. open rear.
Features: Sliding side safety, wide trigger, receiver grooved for tip-off scope mounts. Comes with single-shot adapter. Re-introduced 1986.
Price: About **$200.00**

Ruger 77/22

SAVAGE-STEVENS MODEL 72 CRACKSHOT
Caliber: 22 S, L, LR, single shot.
Barrel: 22" octagonal.
Weight: 4½ lbs. **Length:** 37" over-all.
Stock: Walnut, straight grip stock and fore-end.
Sights: Blade front, step adj. rear.
Features: Falling block action, color case hardened frame.
Price: **$144.39**

RUGER 77/22 RIMFIRE BOLT ACTION RIFLE
Caliber: 22 Long Rifle, 10-shot magazine.
Barrel: 20".
Weight: About 5¾ lbs. **Length:** 39¾" over-all.
Stock: Straight-grained American walnut.
Sights: Gold bead front, adjustable folding leaf rear, or no sights.
Features: Mauser-type action uses Ruger's 10-shot rotary magazine; 3-position safety; simplified bolt stop; patented bolt locking system. Uses the dual-screw barrel attachment system of the 10/22 rifle. Integral scope mounting system with 1" Ruger rings. Announced 1983.
Price: 77/22 R (plain barrel, no sights, with Ruger 1" rings) **$364.50**
Price: 77/22 S (gold bead front sight, folding leaf rear) **$364.50**
Price: 77/22 RS (scope rings and open sights) **$384.50**

Voere Model 1007/1013

VOERE MODEL 1007/1013 BOLT ACTION RIFLE
Caliber: 22 LR (M1007 Biathlon), 22 Mag. (M1013).
Barrel: 18".
Weight: About 5½ lbs. (M1007)
Stock: Oil-finished beechwood.
Sights: Hooded front, open adjustable rear.
Features: Single-stage trigger (M1013 available with double set). Military-look stock; sling swivels. Convertible to single shot. Imported from Austria by L. Joseph Rahn. Introduced 1984.
Price: 1007 Biathlon **$215.00**
Price: 1013 22 Mag. **$315.00**

Voere Model 2107

VOERE MODEL 2107 BOLT ACTION RIFLE
Caliber: 22 LR, 5- or 8-shot magazine.
Barrel: 19½".
Weight: 6 lbs. **Length:** 41" over-all.
Stock: European hardwood with Monte Carlo. Butt pad, swivel studs standard.
Sights: Hooded front, open fully adj. rear.
Features: Deluxe model with checkered stock and raised cheekpiece available. Introduced 1986. Imported from West Germany by KDF, Inc.
Price: Standard **$169.00**
Price: Deluxe **$189.00**

CAUTION: PRICES CHANGE. CHECK AT GUNSHOP.

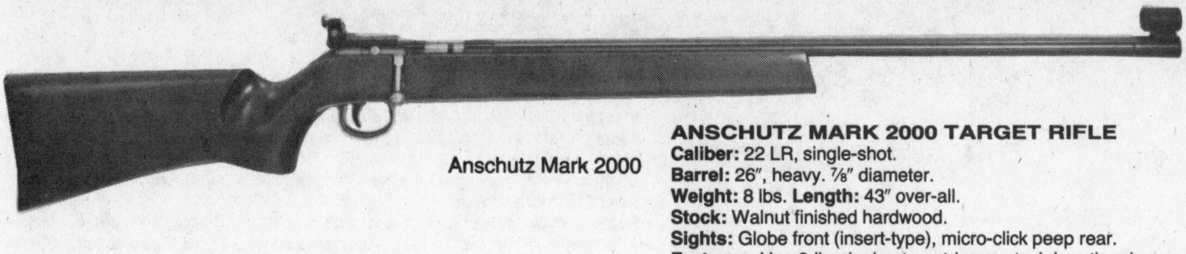

Anschutz Mark 2000

ANSCHUTZ MARK 2000 TARGET RIFLE
Caliber: 22 LR, single-shot.
Barrel: 26″, heavy. ⅞″ diameter.
Weight: 8 lbs. **Length:** 43″ over-all.
Stock: Walnut finished hardwood.
Sights: Globe front (insert-type), micro-click peep rear.
Features: Has 3-lb. single-stage trigger; stock has thumb groove, Wundhammer swell, full length slide rail. Imported from West Germany by PSI.
Price: Without sights $265.00
Price: Sight set #2. . . . . $30.00

ANSCHUTZ MODEL 64-MS, 64-MS LEFT
Caliber: 22 LR, single shot.
Barrel: 21¾″, medium heavy, ⅞″ diameter.
Weight: 8 lbs. 1 oz. **Length:** 39½″ over-all.
Stock: Walnut-finished hardwood, silhouette-type.
Sights: None furnished. Receiver drilled and tapped for scope mounting.
Features: Designed for metallic silhouette competition. Stock has stippled checkering, contoured thumb groove with Wundhammer swell. Two-stage #5091 trigger. Slide safety locks sear and bolt. Introducted 1980. Imported from West Germany by PSI.
Price: Model 64-MS. $450.00
Price: Model 64-MS Left. $498.00
Price: 64-MS FWT (same as 64-MS except weighs about 6¼ lbs, has #5094 trigger. Designed for lightweight-class silhouette shooting) $450.00

ANSCHUTZ 1811 MATCH RIFLE
Caliber: 22 LR. Single Shot.
Barrel: 27¼″ round (1″ dia.)
Weight: 11 lbs. **Length:** 46″ over-all.
Stock: Walnut-finished European hardwood; American prone style with Monte Carlo, cast-off cheek-piece, checkered p.g., beavertail fore-end with swivel rail and adj. swivel, adj. rubber buttplate.
Sights: None. Receiver grooved for Anschutz sights (extra). Scope blocks.
Features: Two-stage #5018 trigger adjustable from 2.1 to 8.6 oz. Extremely fast lock time. Imported from West Germany by PSI.
Price: Right hand, no sights $963.00
Price: M1811-L (true left-hand action and stock) $1,062.00
Price: Anschutz Int'l. sight set $173.40

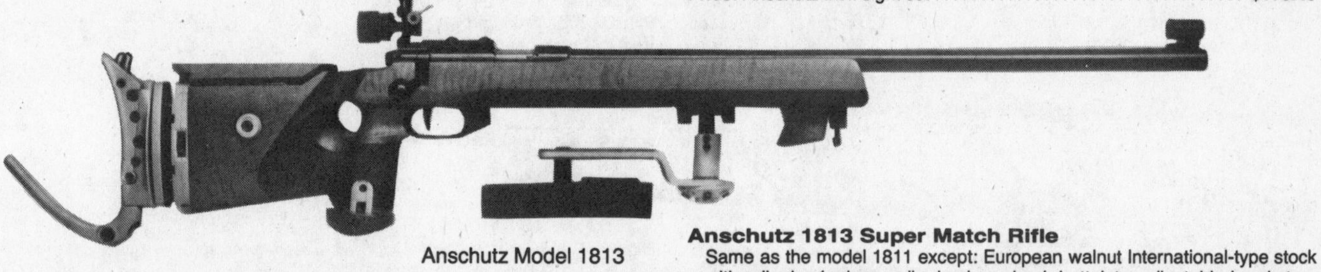

Anschutz Model 1813

Anschutz Model 1810 Super Match II
Similar to the Super Match 1813 rifle except has a stock of European hardwood with tapered fore-end and deep receiver area. Hand and palm rests not included. Uses Match 54 action. Adjustable hook buttplate and cheekpiece. Sights not included. Introduced 1982. Imported from Germany by PSI.
Price: Right-hand $1,232.00
Price: Left-hand $1,289.00
Price: International sight set. $173.40
Price: Match sight set $124.75

Anschutz 1813 Super Match Rifle
Same as the model 1811 except: European walnut International-type stock with adj. cheek-piece, adj. aluminum hook buttplate, adjustable hand stop, weight 15½ lbs., 46″ over-all. Imported from West Germany by PSI.
Price: Right hand, no sights $1,381.00
Price: M1813-L (left-hand action and stock) $1,570.00

Anschutz 1807 Match Rifle
Same as the model 1811 except: 26″ bbl. (⅞″ dia.), weight 10 lbs. 44½″ over-all to conform to ISU requirements and also suitable for NRA matches.
Price: Right hand, no sights. $801.00
Price: M1807-L (true left-hand action and stock) $890.00
Price: Int'l sight set $173.40
Price: Match sight set $124.75

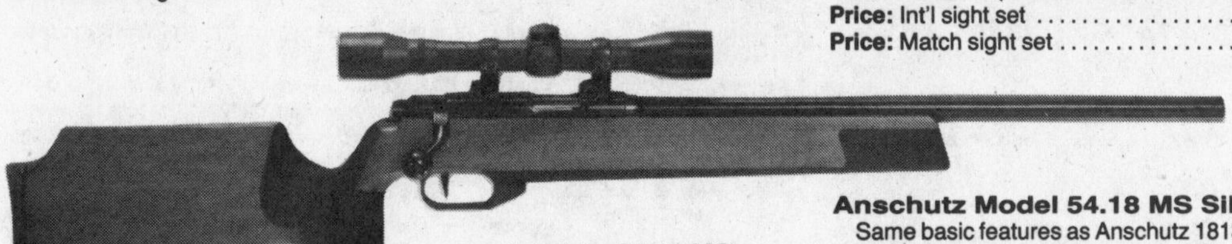

Anschutz 54.18 MS

Anschutz Model 54.18 MS Silhouette Rifle
Same basic features as Anschutz 1813 Super Match but with special metallic silhouette European hardwood stock and two-stage trigger. Has 22″ barrel; receiver drilled and tapped.
Price: $998.00
Price: Model 54.18 MSL (true left-hand version of above) $834.00

ANSCHUTZ 1808ED SUPER RUNNING TARGET
Caliber: 22 LR, single shot.
Barrel: 23½″; ⅞″ diameter.
Weight: 9¼ lbs. **Length:** 42″ over-all.
Stock: European hardwood. Heavy beavertail fore-end, adjustable cheekpiece, buttplate, stippled pistol grip and fore-end.
Sights: None furnished. Receiver grooved for scope mounting.
Features: Uses Super Match 54 action. Adjustable trigger from 14 oz. to 3.5 lbs. Removable sectioned barrel weights. **Special Order Only.** Introduced 1982. Imported from Germany by PSI.
Price: Right-hand. $839.00
Price: Left-hand, 1808EDL. $923.00

ANSCHUTZ MODEL 1403D MATCH RIFLE
Caliber: 22 LR only. Single shot.
Barrel: 26″ round (1¹¹⁄₁₆″ dia.)
Weight: 7¾ lbs. **Length:** 44″ over-all.
Stock: Walnut finished hardwood, cheekpiece, checkered p.g., beavertail fore-end, adj. buttplate.
Sights: None furnished.
Features: Sliding side safety, adj. #5053 single stage trigger, receiver grooved for Anschutz sights. Imported from West Germany by PSI.
Price: Without sights $467.00
Price: 1403DL (left hand stock only). $492.00
Price: Match sight set #6723. . . . . $124.75

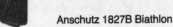

Anschutz 1827B Biathlon

Weight: 9 lbs. with sights. **Length:** 42½" over-all.
Stock: Walnut-finished hardwood; cheekpiece, stippled pistol grip and fore-end.
Sights: Globe front specially designed for Biathlon shooting, micrometer rear with hinged snow cap.
Features: Uses Match 54 action and adjustable trigger; adjustable wooden buttplate, Biathlon butt hook, adjustable hand-stop rail. **Special Order Only.** Introduced 1982. Imported from Germany by PSI.
Price: Right-hand **$1.073.00**
Price: Left-hand **$1,223.00**

ANSCHUTZ 1827B BIATHLON RIFLE
Caliber: 22 LR, 5-shot magazine.
Barrel: 21½".

BSA Martini Match

BSA MARTINI ISU MATCH RIFLE
Caliber: 22 LR, single shot.
Barrel: 28".
Weight: 10¾ lbs. **Length:** 43-44" over-all.
Stock: Match type French walnut butt and fore-end; flat cheekpiece, full p.g.; spacers are fitted to allow length adjustment to suit each shooting position; adj. buttplate.
Sights: Modified PH-1 Parker-Hale tunnel front, PH-25 aperture rear with aperture variations from .080" to .030".

Features: Fastest lock time of any commercial target rifle; designed to meet I.S.U. specs. for the Standard Rifle. Fully adjustable trigger (less than ½ lb. to 3½ lbs.). Mark V has heavier barrel, weighs 12¼ lbs. Imported from England by Freelands Scope Stands.
Price: I.S.U., Standard weight $950.00
Price: Mark V heavy bbl. $1,000.00

Beeman/FWB Free Rifle

BEEMAN/FEINWERKBAU ULTRA MATCH 22 FREE RIFLE
Caliber: 22 LR, single shot.
Barrel: 26.4".
Weight: 17 lbs. (with accessories).
Stock: Anatomically correct thumbhole stock of laminated wood.

Sights: Globe front with interchangeable inserts, micrometer match aperture rear.
Features: Fully adjustable mechanical or new electronic trigger; accessory rails for moveable weights and adjustable palm rest; adjustable cheekpiece and hooked buttplate. Right or left hand. Introduced 1983. Imported by Beeman.
Price: Right hand, electronic trigger $1,595.00
Price: As above, mechanical trigger $1,295.00
Price: Left hand, electronic trigger. $1,730.00
Price: As above, mechanical trigger $1,465.00

BEEMAN/FEINWERKBAU 2000 TARGET RIFLE
Caliber: 22 LR.
Barrel: 26¼"; 22" for Mini-Match.
Weight: 9 lbs. 12 oz. **Length:** 43¾" over-all (26¼" bbl.).
Stock: Standard match. Walnut with stippled p.g. and fore-end; walnut-stained birch for the Mini-Match.

Sights: Globe front with interchangeable inserts; micrometer match aperture rear.
Features: Meets ISU standard rifle specifications. Shortest lock time of any small bore rifle. Electronic or mechanical trigger, fully adjustable for weight, release point, length, lateral position, etc. Available in Standard and Mini-Match models. Introduced 1979. Imported from West Germany by Beeman.
Price: Model 2000 . . . . **$795.00 to $925.00**
Price: Mini-Match. . . . . **$770.00 to $839.00**

Beeman/FWB 2600

BEEMAN/FEINWERKBAU 2600 TARGET RIFLE
Caliber: 22 LR, single shot.
Barrel: 26.3".
Weight: 10.6 lbs. **Length:** 43.7" over-all.
Stock: Laminated hardwood and hard rubber.
Sights: Globe front with interchangeable inserts; micrometer match aperture rear.
Features: Identical smallbore companion to the Beeman/FWB 600 air rifle. Free floating barrel. Match trigger has fingertip weight adjustment dial. Introduced 1986. Imported from West Germany by Beeman
Price: **$878.00**

CAUTION: PRICES CHANGE. CHECK AT GUNSHOP.

COMPETITION RIFLES—CENTERFIRE & RIMFIRE

Beeman/FWB 2000 M.S.

BEEMAN/FWB 2000 METALLIC SILHOUETTE RIFLE
Caliber: 22 LR, single shot.
Barrel: 21.8″.
Weight: 6.8 lbs. **Length:** 39″ over-all.
Stock: Walnut, anatomical grip and fore-end are stippled.
Sights: None furnished; grooved for standard mounts.
Features: Fully adjustable match trigger from 3.5 to 8.5 ozs. Heavy bull barrel. Introduced 1985. Imported by Beeman.
Price: **$795.00**

BEEMAN/KRICO 640 STANDARD SNIPER
Caliber: 308 Win.
Barrel: 20″, semi-bull.
Weight: 7.5 lbs.
Stock: French walnut with ventilated fore-end.
Sights: None furnished.
Features: Five-shot repeater with detachable box magazine. Available with single or double-set trigger. Imported from West Germany by Beeman.
Price: 308 Win. **$1,049.00**
Price: Model 440S, 22 Hornet **$795.00**

BEEMAN/KRICO 340 SILHOUETTE RIFLE
Caliber: 22 Long Rifle, 5-shot clip.
Barrel: 21″, match quality.
Weight: 7.5 lbs. **Length:** 39.5″ over-all.
Stock: European walnut match-style designed for off-hand shooting. Suitable for right- or left-hand shooters. Stippled grip and fore-end.
Sights: None furnished. Receiver grooved for tip-off mounts.
Features: Free-floated heavy barrel; fully adjustable two-stage match trigger or double-set trigger. Meets NRA official MS rules. Introduced 1983. Imported by Beeman.
Price: **$649.50**

Beeman/KRICOtronic 540

Beeman/KRICOtronic 540 Silhouette Rifle
Same basic specs as standard 340 Silhouette rifle except has KRICOtronic electronic ignition system for conventional ammunition. System replaces the firing pin with an electrical mechanism that ignites the primer electrically. Lock time is so fast it is not measureable by present technology. Introduced 1985.
Price: **$795.00**

Beeman/Krico 640 Super

BEEMAN/KRICO 640 SUPER SNIPER
Caliber: 223, 308.
Barrel: 26″. Specially designed match bull barrel, matte blue finish, with muzzle brake/flash hider.
Weight: 9.6 lbs. **Length:** 44¾″ over-all.
Stock: Select walnut with oil finish. Spring-loaded, adj. cheekpiece, adjustable recoil pad. Standard model (640S) is without adjustable stock.
Sights: None furnished. Drilled and tapped for scope mounts.
Features: Match trigger with 10mm wide shoe; single standard or double set trigger available. All metal has matte blue finish. Bolt knob has 1¼″ diameter. Scope mounts available for special night-sight devices. Imported from West Germany by Beeman.
Price: Without scope, mount. **$1,298.50**
Price: Model 640S, as above but without moveable cheekpiece . . . **$1,049.50**

BEEMAN/WEIHRAUCH HW60 TARGET RIFLE
Caliber: 22 LR, single shot.
Barrel: 26.8″.
Weight: 10.8 lbs. **Length:** 45.7″ over-all.
Stock: Walnut with adjustable buttplate. Stippled p.g. and fore-end. Rail with adjustable swivel.
Sights: Hooded ramp front, match-type aperture rear.
Features: Adj. match trigger with push-button safety. Left-hand version also available. Introduced 1981. Imported from West Germany by Beeman.
Price: Right-hand. **$495.00**
Price: Left-hand **$519.00**

Finnish Lion Standard

FINNISH LION STANDARD TARGET RIFLE
Caliber: 22 LR, single-shot.
Barrel: 27⅝″.
Weight: 10½ lbs. **Length:** 44⁹/₁₆″ over-all.
Stock: French walnut, target style.
Sights: None furnished. Globe front, International micrometer rear available.
Features: Optional accessories: palm rest, hook buttplate, fore-end stop and swivel assembly, buttplate extension, 5 front sight aperture inserts, 3 rear sight apertures, Allen wrench. Adjustable trigger. Imported from Finland by Mandall Shooting Supplies.
Price: **$500.00**
Price: Thumbhole stock model **$695.00**
Price: Heavy barrel model (either stock) **$535.00**
Price: Sight set (front and rear) **$100.00**

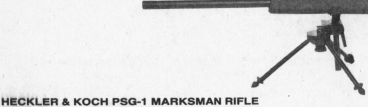

Heckler & Koch PSG-1

HECKLER & KOCH PSG-1 MARKSMAN RIFLE

Caliber: 308, 5- and 20-shot magazines.
Barrel: 25.6″, heavy.
Weight: 17.8 lbs. **Length:** 47.5″ over-all.
Stock: Matte black high impact plastic, adj. for length, pivoting butt cap, verti-cally-adj. cheek-piece; target type pistol grip with adj. palm shelf.
Sights: Hendsoldt 6 x 42 scope.
Features: Uses HK-91 action with low-noise bolt closing device; special fore-end with T-way rail for sling swivel or tripod. Gun comes in special foam-fitted metal transport case with tripod, two 20-shot and two 5-shot magazines, cleaning rod. Imported from West Germany by Heckler & Koch, Inc. Intro-duced 1986.
Price: $5,980.00

HECKLER & KOCH B.A.S.R. BOLT ACTION RIFLE

Caliber: 22 PPC, 22-250, 6mm PPC, 308 Win. 30-06, 300 Win. Mag., blind 4-shot magazine for standard calibers, 3-shot for magnums, or single shot. Other calibers available.
Barrel: 16″-26″ stainless steel.
Weight: To customer specs. **Length:** To customer specs.
Stock: Black high density, urethane foam-filled Kevlar; comes with recoil pad, q.d. swivel studs.
Sights: None furnished; drilled and tapped for scope mounting.
Features: Uses H&K's own action of chrome moly steel with cone breech sys-tem, fluted bolt; fully adjustable trigger; 3-position safety. Guaranteed accu-racy of ½-m.o.a. A custom-made gun. Comes with H&K hardcase, bore guide, cleaning rod. From Heckler & Koch, Inc.
Price: $2,199.00

Remington Model 40-XC

REMINGTON 40-XR RIMFIRE POSITION RIFLE

Caliber: 22 LR, single-shot.
Barrel: 24″, heavy target.
Weight: 10 lbs. **Length:** 43″ over-all.
Stock: Position-style with front swivel block on fore-end guide rail.
Sights: Drilled and tapped. Furnished with scope blocks.
Features: Meets all I.S.U. specifications. Deep fore-end, buttplate vertically adjustable, wide adjustable trigger.
Price: About $711.00

REMINGTON 40-XC NAT'L MATCH COURSE RIFLE

Caliber: 7.62 NATO, 5-shot.
Barrel: 23¼″, stainless steel.
Weight: 10 lbs. without sights. **Length:** 42½″ over-all.
Stock: Walnut, position-style, with palm swell.
Sights: None furnished.
Features: Designed to meet the needs of competitive shooters firing the na-tional match courses. Position-style stock, top loading clip slot magazine, anti-bind bolt and receiver, bright stainless steel barrel. Meets all I.S.U. Army Rifle specifications. Adjustable buttplate, adjustable trigger.
Price: About $970.00

Remington Model 40-XB

REMINGTON 40-XB RANGEMASTER TARGET Centerfire

Caliber: 222 Rem., 22-250, 6mm Rem., 243, 25-06, 7mm Rem. Mag., 30-338 (30-7mm Rem. Mag.), 300 Win. Mag., 7.62 NATO (308 Win.), 30-06. Single shot.
Barrel: 27¼″ round (Stand. dia.—¾″, Hvy. dia.—⅞″).
Weight: Std.—9¼ lbs., Hvy.—11¼ lbs. **Length:** 47″.
Stock: American walnut with high comb and beavertail fore-end stop. Rubber non-slip buttplate.
Sights: None. Scope blocks installed.
Features: Adjustable trigger pull. Receiver drilled and tapped for sights.
Price: Standard s.s., stainless steel barrel, about $896.00
Price: Repeating model, about $964.00
Price: Extra for 2 oz. trigger, about $116.00

Remington Model 40XB-BR

REMINGTON MODEL 40XB-BR

Caliber: 22 BR Rem., 222 Rem., 223, 6mm x47, 6mm BR Rem., 7.62 NATO (308 Win.).
Barrel: 20″ (light varmint class), 26″ (heavy varmint class).

Weight: Light varmint class, 7¼ lbs., Heavy varmint class, 12 lbs. **Length:** 38″ (20″ bbl.), 44″ (26″ bbl).
Stock: Select walnut.
Sights: None. Supplied with scope blocks.
Features: Unblued stainless steel barrel, trigger adj. from 1½ lbs. to 3½ lbs. Special 2 oz. trigger at extra cost. Scope and mounts extra.
Price: About $945.00
Price: Extra for 2-oz. trigger, about $116.00

CAUTION: PRICES CHANGE. CHECK AT GUNSHOP.

SHILEN DGA BENCHREST SINGLE SHOT RIFLE
Caliber: 22, 22-250, 6x47, 308.
Barrel: Select/Match grade stainless. Choice of caliber, twist, chambering, contour or length shown in Shilen's catalog.
Weight: To customer specs.
Stock: Fiberglass. Choice of Classic or thumbhole pattern.
Sights: None furnished. Specify intended scope and mount.
Features: Fiberglass stocks are spray painted with acrylic enamel in choice of basic color. Comes with Benchrest trigger. Basically a custom-made rifle. From Shilen Rifles, Inc.
Price: From **$1,600.00**

SIG SAUER SSG 2000 RIFLE
Caliber: 223, 308, 7.5 Swiss, 300 Weatherby Magnum; 4-shot detachable box magazine.
Barrel: 24″ (25.9″ in 300 W.M.).
Weight: 13.2 lbs. (without scope). **Length:** 47.6″ (24″ barrel).
Stock: Walnut; thumbhole-type with adjustable comb and buttplate; adjustable fore-end rail; stippled grip and fore-end.
Sights: None furnished. Comes with scope mounts.
Features: Uses the Sauer 80/90 rifle action. Available in right- or left-hand models; flash hider/muzzle brake; double-set triggers; push-button sliding safety; EAW scope mount. Choice of Zeiss ZA 8 x 56 or Schmidt & Bender 1½-6 x 42 scope. Introduced 1985. Imported by SIGARMS, Inc.
Price: **$2,848.99**

Steyr SSG Marksman

Steyr-Mannlicher SSG Match
Same as Model SSG Marksman except has heavy barrel, match bolt, Walther target peep sights and adj. rail in fore-end to adj. sling travel. Weight is 11 lbs.
Price: Synthetic half stock. **$1,462.00**
Price: Walnut half stock. **$1,625.00**

STEYR-MANNLICHER MATCH UIT RIFLE
Caliber: 243 Win. or 308 Win., 10-shot magazine.
Barrel: 25.5″.
Weight: 10.9 lbs. **Length:** 44.48″ over-all.
Stock: Walnut with stippled grip and fore-end. Special UIT Match design.
Sights: Walther globe front, Walther peep rear.
Features: Double-pull trigger adjustable for let-off point, slack, weight of first-stage pull, release force and length; buttplate adjustable for height and length. Meets UIT specifications. Introduced 1984. Imported from Austria by Gun South, Inc.
Price: **$2,142.00**

STEYR-MANNLICHER SSG MARKSMAN
Caliber: 308 Win.
Barrel: 25.6″.
Weight: 8.6 lbs. **Length:** 44.5″ over-all.
Stock: Choice of ABS "Cycolac" synthetic half stock or walnut. Removable spacers in butt adjusts length of pull from 12¾″ to 14″.
Sights: Hooded blade front, folding leaf rear.
Features: Parkerized finish. Choice of interchangeable single or double set triggers. Detachable 5-shot rotary magazine (10-shot optional). Drilled and tapped for scope mounts. Imported from Austria by Gun South, Inc.
Price: Synthetic half stock. **$1,040.00**
Price: Walnut half stock. **$1,217.00**

SWISS K-31 TARGET RIFLE
Caliber: 308 Win., 6-shot magazine.
Barrel: 26″.
Weight: 9½ lbs. **Length:** 44″ over-all.
Stock: Walnut.
Sights: Protected blade front, ladder-type adjustable rear.
Features: Refined version of the Schmidt-Rubin straight-pull rifle. Comes with sling and muzzle cap. Imported from Switzerland by Mandall Shooting Supplies.
Price: **$1,000.00**

Tanner Free Rifle

TANNER 300 METER FREE RIFLE
Caliber: 308 Win., 7.5 Swiss; single shot.
Barrel: 28.7″.

Weight: 15 lbs. **Length:** 45.3″ over-all.
Stock: Seasoned walnut, thumb-hole style, with accessory rail, palm rest, adjustable hook butt.
Sights: Globe front with interchangeable inserts, Tanner-design micrometer-diopter rear with adjustable aperture.
Features: Three-lug revolving-lock bolt design; adjustable set trigger; short firing pin travel; supplied with 300-meter test target. Imported from Switzerland by Osborne's Supplies. Introduced 1984.
Price: About. **$2,695.00**

Tanner UIT

TANNER STANDARD UIT RIFLE
Caliber: 308, 7.5mm Swiss, 10-shot.
Barrel: 25.8″.

Weight: 10.5 lbs. **Length:** 40.6″ over-all.
Stock: Match style of seasoned nutwood with accessory rail; coarsely stippled pistol grip; high cheekpiece; vented fore-end.
Sights: Globe front with interchangeable inserts, Tanner micrometer-diopter rear with adjustable aperture.
Features: Two locking lug revolving bolt encloses case head. Trigger adjustable from ½ to 6½ lbs.; match trigger optional. Comes with 300-meter test target. Imported from Switzerland by Osborne's. Introduced 1984.
Price: About. **$2,595.00**

TANNER 50 METER FREE RIFLE
Caliber: 22 LR; single shot.
Barrel: 27.7″.
Weight: 13.9 lbs. **Length:** 43.4″ over-all.
Stock: Seasoned nutwood with palm rest, accessory rail, adjustable hook butt-plate.
Sights: Globe front with interchangeable inserts, Tanner micrometer-diopter rear with adjustable aperture.
Features: Bolt action with externally adjustable set trigger. Supplied with 50-meter test target. Imported from Switzerland by Osborne's Supplies. Introduced 1984.
Price: About **$2,195.00**

TIKKA MODEL 65 WILD BOAR RIFLE
Caliber: 7x64, 308, 30-06, 7mm Rem. Mag., 300 Win. Mag.; 5-shot detachable clip.
Barrel: 20½″.
Weight: About 7½ lbs. **Length:** 41″ over-all.
Stock: Hand checkered walnut; vent. rubber recoil pad.
Sights: Bead on post front, special ramp-type open rear.
Features: Adjustable trigger; palm swell in pistol grip. Sight system developed for low-light conditions. Imported from Finland by Mandall Shooting Supplies.
Price: **$595.00**

Walther U.I.T. Special

Walther Model U.I.T.-E Match Rifle
Similar to the U.I.T. Special model except has state-of-the-art electronic trigger. Introduced 1984.
Price: **$1,250.00**

Walther GX-1 Match Rifle
Same general specs as U.I.T. except has 25½″ barrel, over-all length of 44½″, weight of 15½ lbs. Stock is designed to provide every conceivable adjustment for individual preference and anatomical compatibility. Left-hand stock available on special order. Imported from Germany by Interarms.
Price: **$1,350.00**

WALTHER U.I.T. SPECIAL
Caliber: 22 LR, single shot.
Barrel: 25½″.
Weight: 10 lbs., 3 oz. **Length:** 44¾″.
Stock: Walnut, adj. for length and drop; fore-end guide rail for sling or palm rest.
Sights: Globe-type front, fully adj. aperture rear.
Features: Conforms to both NRA and U.I.T. requirements. Fully adj. trigger. Left hand stock available on special order. Imported from Germany by Interarms.
Price: **$845.00**

Walther U.I.T. Match

Walther U.I.T. Match
Same specifications and features as standard U.I.T. Super rifle but has scope mount bases. Fore-end had new tapered profile, fully stippled. Imported from Germany by Interarms.
Price: **$925.00**

WALTHER RUNNING BOAR MATCH RIFLE
Caliber: 22 LR, single shot.
Barrel: 23.6″.
Weight: 8 lbs. 5 oz. **Length:** 42″ over-all.
Stock: Walnut thumb-hole type. Fore-end and p.g. stippled.
Features: Especially designed for running boar competition. Receiver grooved to accept dovetail scope mounts. Adjustable cheekpiece and butt plate. 1.1 lb. trigger pull. Left hand stock available on special order. Imported from Germany by Interarms.
Price: **$815.00**

> Consult our Directory pages for the location of firms mentioned.

Wichita Silhouette

WICHITA SILHOUETTE RIFLE
Caliber: All standard calibers with maximum over-all cartridge length of 2.800″.
Barrel: 24″ free-floated Matchgrade.
Weight: About 9 lbs.
Stock: Metallic gray fiberthane with ventilated rubber recoil pad.
Sights: None furnished. Drilled and tapped for scope mounts.
Features: Legal for all NRA competitions. Single shot action. Fluted bolt, 2-oz. Canjar trigger; glass-bedded stock. Comes with hard case. Introduced 1983. From Wichita Arms.
Price: **$1,310.00**
Price: Left-hand **$1,410.00**

CAUTION: PRICES CHANGE. CHECK AT GUNSHOP.

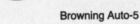

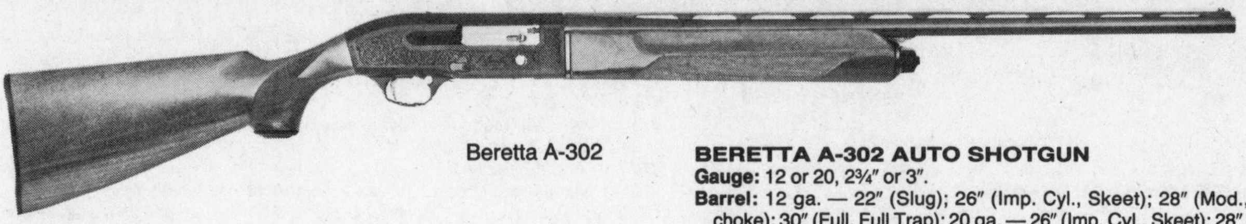

Beretta A-302

BERETTA A-302 AUTO SHOTGUN
Gauge: 12 or 20, 2¾" or 3".
Barrel: 12 ga. — 22" (Slug); 26" (Imp. Cyl., Skeet); 28" (Mod., Full, Multi-choke); 30" (Full, Full Trap); 20 ga. — 26" (Imp. Cyl., Skeet); 28" (Mod., Full).
Weight: About 6½ lbs. (20 ga.).
Stock: European walnut; hand checkered grip and fore-end.
Features: Gas-operated action, alloy receiver with scroll engraving; magazine cut-off, push-button safety. Multi-choke models come with four interchangeable screw-in choke tubes. Introduced 1983. Imported from Italy by Beretta U.S.A.
Price: 12 or 20 ga., standard chokes **$585.00**
Price: Multi-choke, 12 ga. or 20 ga. **$614.00**
Price: 12 ga. trap with Monte Carlo stock (A303) **$690.00**
Price: 12 or 20 ga. Skeet (A303) **$680.00**
Price: Slug, 12 or 20 ga. **$599.00**
Price: Super Lusso (custom gun), 12 or 20 ga. **$2,500.00**

ARMSPORT 2751 GAS AUTO SHOTGUN
Gauge: 12, 3" chamber.
Barrel: 28" (Mod.), 30" (Full).
Weight: 7 lbs.
Stock: European walnut.
Features: Gas-operated action; blued receiver with light engraving. Introduced 1986. Imported from Italy by Armsport.
Price: With fixed chokes **$450.00**
Price: Blue, choke tubes, 28" bbl. **$495.00**
Price: With silvered receiver **$525.00**

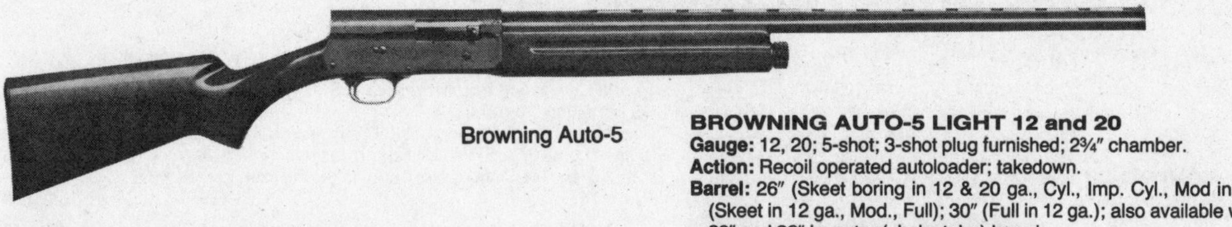

Browning Auto-5

BROWNING AUTO-5 LIGHT 12 and 20
Gauge: 12, 20; 5-shot; 3-shot plug furnished; 2¾" chamber.
Action: Recoil operated autoloader; takedown.
Barrel: 26" (Skeet boring in 12 & 20 ga., Cyl., Imp. Cyl., Mod in 20 ga.); 28" (Skeet in 12 ga., Mod., Full); 30" (Full in 12 ga.); also available with 26", 28", 30" and 32" Invector (choke tube) barrel.
Weight: 12 ga. 7¼ lbs., 20 ga. 6⅜ lbs.
Stock: French walnut, hand checkered half-p.g. and fore-end. 14¼" x 1⅝" x 2½".
Features: Receiver hand engraved with scroll designs and border. Double extractors, extra bbls. interchangeable without factory fitting; mag. cut-off; cross-bolt safety. Buck Special no longer inventoried, but can be ordered as a Buck Special extra barrel, plus an action only. Imported from Japan by Browning.
Price: Vent. rib only **$559.95**
Price: Extra barrels, vent. rib only **$175.00**
Price: Invector model **$589.95**
Price: Extra Invector barrels, vent. rib only **$205.00**

Browning Auto-5 Classic & Gold Classic
Same as the standard Auto-5 Light 12 with 28" (Mod.) barrel. Classic edition has hunting and wildlife scenes engraved on the satin grey receiver, including a portrait of John M. Browning, and is limited to 5,000 guns. Also engraved is "Browning Classic. One of Five Thousand." The Gold Classic has a variation of the engraved scenes but with gold animals and portrait. Only 500 will be made, each numbered "1 of Five Hundred," etc. with "Browning Gold Classic."

Both editions have select, figured walnut, special checkering with carved border, and the semi-pistol grip stock. Scheduled for 1984 delivery. Introduced 1984.
Price: Auto-5 Classic **$1,200.00**
Price: Auto-5 Gold Classic **$6,500.00**

Browning Auto-5 Magnum 12
Same as Std. Auto-5 except: chambered for 3" magnum shells (also handles 2¾" magnum and 2¾" HV loads). 28" Mod., Full; 30" and 32" (Full) bbls. Also available with Invector choke tubes. 14"x1⅝"x2½" stock. Recoil pad. Wgt. 8¾ lbs.
Price: Vent. rib only **$569.95**
Price: Invector model **$599.95**

Browning Auto-5 Magnum 20
Same as Magnum 12 except barrels 28" Full or Mod., or 26" Full, Mod., Imp. Cyl. or Invector. With ventilated rib, 7½ lbs.
Price: **$569.95**
Price: Invector model **$599.95**

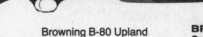

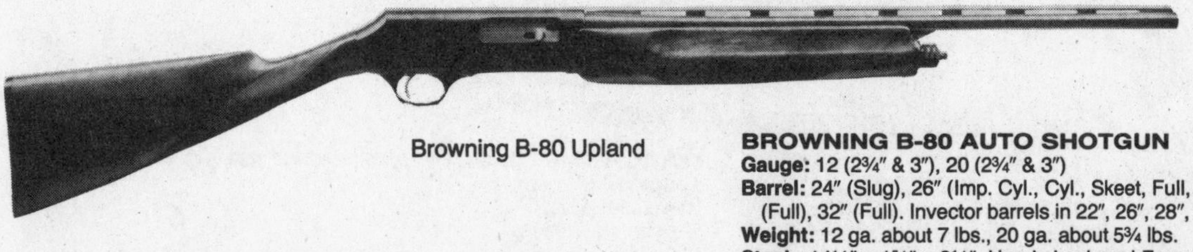

Browning B-80 Upland

BROWNING B-80 AUTO SHOTGUN
Gauge: 12 (2¾" & 3"), 20 (2¾" & 3")
Barrel: 24" (Slug), 26" (Imp. Cyl., Cyl., Skeet, Full, Mod.), 28" (Full, Mod.), 30" (Full), 32" (Full). Invector barrels in 22", 26", 28", 30", 12 or 20 ga.
Weight: 12 ga. about 7 lbs., 20 ga. about 5¾ lbs.
Stock: 14¼" x 1⅝" x 2½". Hand checkered French walnut. Solid black recoil pad.
Features: Vent. rib barrels have non-reflective rib; alloy receiver; cross-bolt safety; interchangeable barrels. Buck Special no longer inventoried, but can be ordered as a Buck Special extra barrel and action only. Introduced 1981. Imported from Belgium by Browning.
Price: Invector, vent. rib, 12 or 20 ga. **$534.50**
Price: Extra Invector barrels **$188.50**
Price: Extra fixed-choke barrels **$105.60**
Price: Extra Buck Special barrel **$188.50**

Browning B-80 Upland Special Auto Shotgun
Same as standard B-80 except has 22" Invector barrel in 2¾" chambering. Straight grip stock with 14" length of pull; 12 and 20 gauge. Introduced 1986.
Price: **$534.50**

Charles Daly Field

CHARLES DALY FIELD AUTO SHOTGUN

Gauge: 12, 2¾" or 3".
Barrel: 27" (Full, Mod., Imp. Cyl., Invector choke tubes), 30" (Extra Full, Full, Mod., Invector choke tubes).
Weight: About 7¼ lbs.
Stock: Walnut, with checkered pistol grip and fore-end, high gloss finish.
Features: Alloy receiver with bright chromed bolt; cross-bolt safety; stainless steel gas piston. Imported from Japan by Outdoor Sports Headquarters. Introduced 1984.
Price: **$386.00**
Price: Super Field (12 ga., 23", straight stock) **$399.50**
Price: Slug gun (12 ga., 20", rifle sights) **$386.00**

COSMI AUTOMATIC SHOTGUN

Gauge: 12 or 20, 2¾" or 3" chamber.
Barrel: 22" to 34". Choke (including choke tubes) and length to customer specs. Boehler steel.
Weight: About 6¼ lbs. (20 ga.)
Stock: Length and style to customer specs. Hand-checkered exhibition grade circassian walnut standard.
Features: Hand-made, essentially a custom gun. Recoil-operated auto with tip-up barrel. Made completely of stainless steel (lower receiver polished); magazine tube in buttstock holds 7 rounds. Double ejectors, double safety system. Comes with fitted leather case. Imported from Italy by Incor Inc.
Price: From **$6,200.00**

F.I.E/Franchi PG-80

Stock: Oil finished European walnut. Prestige model is checkered, Elite is stippled with palm-swell p.g.
Features: Gas-operated action. Prestige model has plain blued receiver, Elite has engraved receiver. Both models have 7mm-wide vent. rib. Gas piston is stainless steel. Introduced 1985. Imported from Italy by F.I.E. Corp.
Price: Prestige **$479.95**
Price: Elite.. **$509.95**
Price: Extra barrels **$144.95**

F.I.E./FRANCHI PG-80 GAS AUTO SHOTGUNS

Gauge: 12, 2¾", 3" chamber.
Barrel: 24" (Slug), 26" (Imp. Cyl.), 26", 28" (Mod.), 28" (Full), 30", 32" (3" Full).
Weight: 7 lbs., 6 oz. **Length:** 50" over-all.

Franchi Model 48/AL

F.I.E./FRANCHI 48/AL AUTO SHOTGUN

Gauge: 12 or 20, 5-shot, 2¾" or 3" chamber.
Action: Recoil-operated automatic.
Barrel: 24" (Imp. Cyl. or Cyl.); 26" (Imp. Cyl. or Mod); 28" (Skeet, Mod. or Full); 30", 32" (Full). Interchangeable barrels.
Weight: 12 ga. 6¼ lbs., 20 ga. 5 lbs. 2 oz.
Stock: Epoxy-finished walnut, with cut-checkered pistol grip and fore-end.
Features: Chrome-lined bbl., easy takedown, 3-round plug provided. Ventilated rib barrel. Imported from Italy by F.I.E.
Price: Vent. rib 12, 20 .... **$439.95**
Price: Hunter model (engraved) **$465.95**
Price: 12 ga. Magnum **$465.95**
Price: Extra barrel **$144.95**

F.I.E./Franchi Slug Gun

Same as Standard automatic except 22" Cylinder bored plain barrel, adj. rifle-type sights, sling swivels.
Price: 12 or 20 ga., standard **$439.95**
Price: As above, Hunter grade **$465.95**
Price: Extra barrel **$144.95**

Ithaca 51A Turkey

ITHACA MODEL 51A WATERFOWLER

Gauge: 12, 3" chamber.
Barrel: 30" (Full).
Weight: About 7½ lbs.
Stock: Checkered walnut.
Features: Matte-finish metal; comes with sling and swivels; ventilated rib.
Price: **$625.00**
Price: As Turkey Gun, 26" bbl., sling and swivels **$625.00**
Price: Camo Vent, 26", 30" (Full) **$700.00**

Ithaca Model 51A Supreme Trap

Same gun as Model 51A Waterfowler with blued metal, fancy American walnut trap stock, 30" (Full).
Price: **$869.00**
Price: With Monte Carlo stock................................. **$905.00**

Ithaca Model 51A Supreme Skeet

Same gun as Model 51 Trap with fancy American walnut stock, 26" (Skeet) barrel, 12 or 20 ga..
Price: **$855.00**

CAUTION: PRICES CHANGE. CHECK AT GUNSHOP.

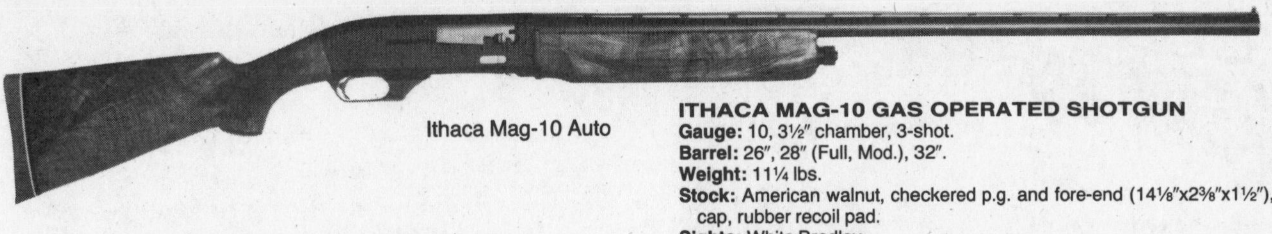

Ithaca Mag-10 Auto

Consult our Directory pages for
the location of firms mentioned.

Ithaca Mag-10 Deerslayer
Similar to the standard Mag-10 except has 22″ barrel, rifle sights.
Price: Std., vent. rib, Vapor Blast finish **$781.00**

ITHACA MAG-10 GAS OPERATED SHOTGUN
Gauge: 10, 3½″ chamber, 3-shot.
Barrel: 26″, 28″ (Full, Mod.), 32″.
Weight: 11¼ lbs.
Stock: American walnut, checkered p.g. and fore-end (14⅛″x2⅜″x1½″), p.g. cap, rubber recoil pad.
Sights: White Bradley.
Features: "Countercoil" gas system. Piston, cylinder, bolt, charging lever, action release and carrier made of stainless steel. ⅜″ vent. rib. Vapor Blast matte finish. Reversible cross-bolt safety. Low recoil force. Supreme has full fancy claro American black walnut.
Price: Standard, plain barrel, 32″ (Full) only **$726.00**
Price: Deluxe, vent. rib, 26″, 32″ only (Full) **$924.00**
Price: Standard, vent. rib **$781.00**
Price: Supreme, vent. rib, 32″ (Full) only **$1,124.00**
Price: Camouflage, 26″ and 32″ (Full), standard vent **$857.00**

KAWAGUCHIYA K.F.C. M-250 AUTO SHOTGUN
K.F.C. Model 250

Gauge: 12, 2¾″.
Barrel: 26″ (Imp. Cyl.), 28″ (Mod.), 30″ (Full); or with Tru-Choke interchangeable choke tube system.

Weight: 7 lbs. **Length:** 48″ over-all (28″ barrel).
Stock: 14⅛″x1½″x2½″. American walnut, hand checkered p.g. and fore-end.
Features: Gas-operated, ventilated barrel rib. Has only 79 parts. Cross-bolt safety is reversible for left-handed shooters. Available with fixed or Tru-Choke interchangeable choke tube system. Introduced 1980. Imported from Japan by La Paloma Marketing.
Price: Standard Grade with Tru-Choke **$565.00**
Price: Deluxe Grade (silvered, etched receiver) with Tru-Choke **$599.00**

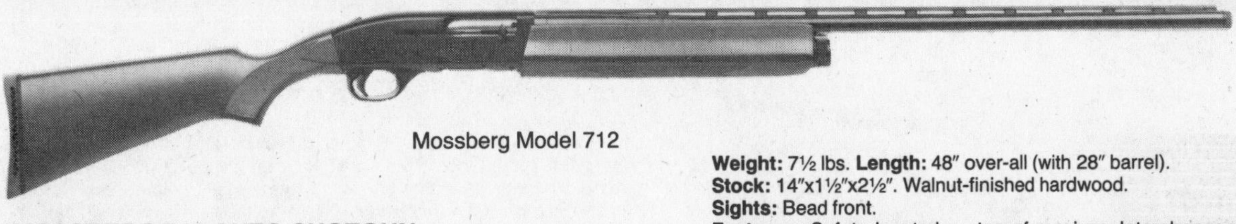

MOSSBERG 712 AUTO SHOTGUN
Mossberg Model 712

Gauge: 12 only, 2¾″ or 3″ chamber.
Barrel: 18½″ (Cyl.), 24″ (Slugster), 26″ (Imp. Cyl.), 28″ (Mod.), 30″ (Full, 2¾″ or 3″).

Weight: 7½ lbs. **Length:** 48″ over-all (with 28″ barrel).
Stock: 14″x1½″x2½″. Walnut-finished hardwood.
Sights: Bead front.
Features: Safety located on top of receiver. Interchangeable barrels and ACCU-CHOKE choke tubes. Introduced 1983.
Price: About **$344.95**
Price: Slug gun, about **$326.95**

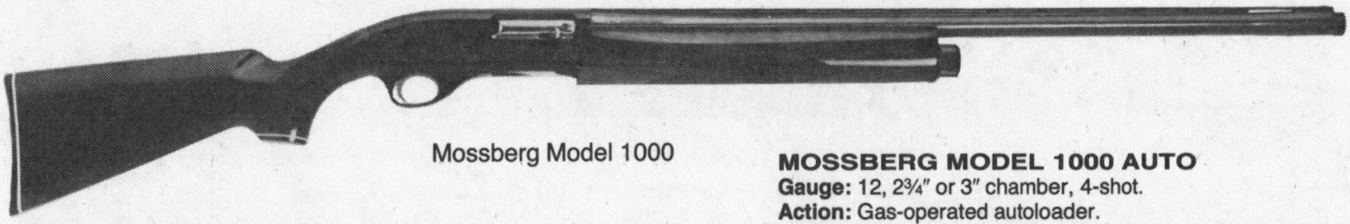

Mossberg Model 1000

Mossberg Model 1000 Trap Shotgun
Similar to the standard Model 1000 except has Monte Carlo trap stock, medium width stepped rib with white middle bead, Bradley front; integral wire shell catcher; specially tuned trigger; 30″ Multi-Choke barrel with Full, Mod. and Imp. Mod. tubes. Steel receiver. Introduced 1983.
Price: **$560.00**

MOSSBERG MODEL 1000 AUTO
Gauge: 12, 2¾″ or 3″ chamber, 4-shot.
Action: Gas-operated autoloader.
Barrel: 26″ (Skeet, Imp. Cyl.), 28″ (Mod. Full). Also available with screw-in Multi-Choke tubes.
Weight: 7½ lbs. (28″ bbl.). **Length:** 48″ over-all (28″ bbl.).
Stock: 14″x1½″x2⅜″, American walnut.
Features: Interchangeable cross-bolt safety, vent. rib with front and middle beads, engraved alloy receiver, pressure compensator and floating piston for light recoil.
Price: **$464.00**

Mossberg Model 1000 Super 12 Shotgun
Similar to the standard Model 1000 auto shotgun except has a new gas metering system to allow the gun to handle any shell from 3-inch mags to 1-oz. 2¾-inch field loads without changing the barrel. Super 12 barrels are not interchangeable with other Model 1000 guns, or vice versa. A longer magazine tube gives four-shot capability. In 12-gauge only, the Super 12 has a 3-inch chamber with choice of 26, 28 or 30-inch Multi-Choke barrel; also available in a Parkerized "Waterfowler" version with 28-inch Multi-Choke barrel.
Price: Super 12 . . . . **$534.00**
Price: Super Waterfowler **$562.00**

Mossberg Model 1000S Super Skeet, 12 & 20
Similar to Model 1000 except has "recessed-type" Skeet choke with a compensator system to soften recoil and reduce muzzle jump. Stock has right-hand palm swell. Trigger is contoured (rounded) on right side; pull is 2½ to 3 lbs. Vent. rib has double sighting beads with a "Bright Point" fluorescent red front bead. Fore-end cap weights (included) of 1 and 2 oz. can be used to change balance. Select-grade walnut with oil finish. Barrel length is 25″, weight 8¼ lbs., over-all length 45.7″. Stock measures 14″x1½″x2½″ with .08″ cast-off at butt, .16″ at toe.
Price: **$657.00**

CAUTION: PRICES CHANGE. CHECK AT GUNSHOP.

Remington Model 1100

Remington 1100 Magnum

Same as 1100 except: chambered for 3″ magnum loads. Available in 12 ga. (30″) or 20 ga. (28″) Mod. or Full., or 12 ga. (28″) with REM Choke tubes; 14″×1½″×2½″ stock with recoil pad, Wgt. 7¾ lbs.

Price: With vent rib, about **$551.00**
Price: As above, 12 ga., 28″ REM Chokes, about **$588.00**
Price: Left hand model with vent. rib, about **$636.00**
Price: As above, 12 ga., 28″ REM Chokes, about **$673.00**

Remington 1100 Small Gauge

Same as 1100 except: 28 ga. 2¾″ (5-shot) or 410, 3″ (except Skeet, 2½″ 4-shot). 45½″ over-all. Available in 25″ bbl. (Full, Mod., or Imp. Cyl.) only.

Price: With vent rib, about. **$550.00**
Price: SA Skeet, about **$578.00**
Price: Tournament Skeet, about **$682.00**

Remington 1100D Tournament Auto

Same as 1100 Standard except: vent, rib, better wood, more extensive engraving.

Price: About. **$2,290.00**

REMINGTON MODEL 1100 AUTO

Gauge: 12, 3-shot plug furnished.
Barrel: 26″ (Imp. Cyl.), 28″ (Mod., Full), 30″ (Full); 26″, 28″ with REM Chokes.
Weight: 7½ lbs.
Stock: 14″x1½″x2½″ American walnut, checkered p.g. and fore-end.
Features: Quickly interchangeable barrels. Matted receiver top with scroll work on both sides of receiver. Cross-bolt safety.

Price: With vent. rib, about. **$505.00**
Price: As above, with REM Chokes, about **$542.00**
Price: Left hand model with vent. rib, about **$586.00**
Price: As above, with REM Chokes, about **$623.00**

> Consult our Directory pages for the location of firms mentioned.

Remington 1100F Premier Auto

Same as 1100D except: select wood, better engraving

Price: About. **$4,720.00**
Price: With gold inlay, about **$7,079.00**

Remington 1100 SP Deer

Remington 1100 LT-20 Youth Gun

Basically the same design as Model 1100, but with special weight-saving features that retain strength and dependability of the standard Model 1100. Has 21″ (Mod., Imp. Cyl.) barrel, weighs 6½ lbs.

Price: About **$505.00**
Price: LT-20 Deer Gun (20″ bbl.), about **$505.00**

Remington Model 1100 "Special Purpose" Deer Gun

Similar to the 1100 "Special Purpose" Magnum except 2¾″ chamber, 21″ Imp. Cyl. barrel with rifle sights. Over-all length is 41½″, weight about 7¾ lbs. Barrel and receiver have non-reflective Parkerized finish, bolt and carrier have dull black oxide finish. Oil-finished stock and fore-end. Comes with recoil pad and padded Cordura nylon sling. Introduced 1986.

Price: About **$505.00**

Remington 1100 SP Magnum

Remington 1100 "Special Purpose" Magnum

Similar to the Model 1100 except chambered for 12-ga., 3″ shells, vent. rib, 26″ or 30″ (both Full) or 26″ REM Choke barrels. All exposed metal surfaces are finished in dull, non-reflective black. Wood has an oil finish. Comes with padded Cordura, 2″ wide sling, quick-detachable swivels. Chrome-lined bores. Dark recoil pad. Introduced 1985.

Price: About **$551.00**
Price: With REM Choke, about **$588.00**

Remington 1100 TA Trap

Remington 1100 TA Trap

Same as the standard 1100 except: recoil pad. 14⅜″x1⅜″x1¾″ stock. Right- or left-hand models. Wgt. 8¼ lbs. 12 ga. only. 30″ (Mod. Trap, Full) vent. rib bbl. Ivory bead front and white metal middle sight.

Price: About **$576.00**
Price: With Monte Carlo stock, about. **$586.00**
Price: 1100TA Trap, left hand, about **$608.00**
Price: With Monte Carlo stock, about. **$621.00**
Price: Tournament Trap, about **$680.00**
Price: Tournament Trap with M.C. stock, better grade wood, different checkering, cut checkering, about **$690.00**

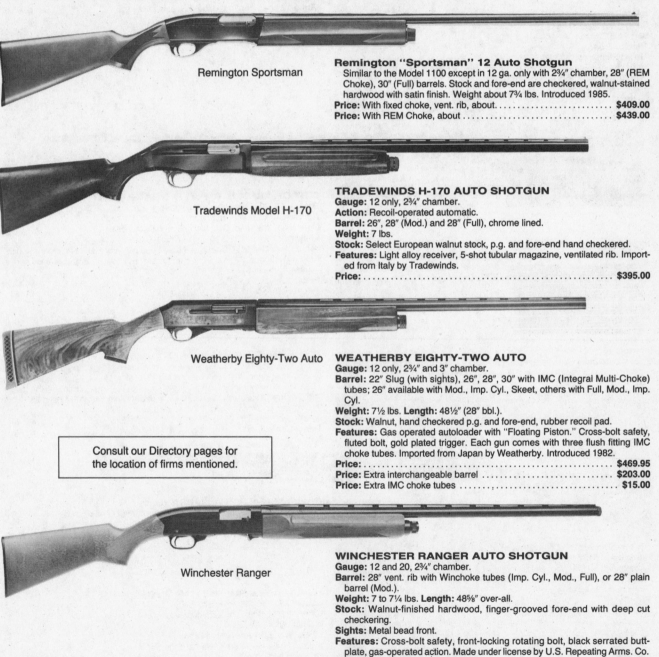

Remington 1100 Special Field

Remington 1100 "Special Field"

Similar to standard Model 1100 except comes with 21" barrel only, choked Imp. Cyl., Mod., Full; 12 ga. weighs 7¼ lbs., LT-20 version 6½ lbs.; has straight-grip stock, shorter fore-end, both with cut checkering. Comes with vent rib only; matte finish receiver without engraving. Introduced 1983.

Price: 12 ga., 21" REM Choke, about **$569.00**
Price: 20 ga., fixed choke, about **$532.00**

Remington 1100 SA Skeet

Same as the 1100 except: 26" bbl., special Skeet boring, vent. rib (high rib on LT-20), ivory bead front and metal bead middle sights. 14"x1½"x2½" stock. 12, 20, 28, 410 ga. Wgt. 7½ lbs., cut checkering, walnut, new receiver scroll.

Price: 12 ga., Skeet SA, about **$563.00**
Price: 12 ga. Left hand model with vent. rib, about **$598.00**
Price: 28 & 410 ga., 25" bbl., about **$578.00**
Price: Tournament Skeet (28, 410), about **$682.00**
Price: Tournament Skeet (12 or 20), about..................... **$668.00**

Remington 1100 Deer Gun

Same as 1100 except: 12 ga. only, 22" bbl. (Imp. Cyl.), rifle sights adjustable for w. and e.; recoil pad with white spacer. Weight 7¼ lbs.

Price: About **$505.00**
Price: Left-hand Deer Gun, about............................... **$586.00**

Remington Sportsman

Remington "Sportsman" 12 Auto Shotgun

Similar to the Model 1100 except in 12 ga. only with 2¾" chamber, 28" (REM Choke), 30" (Full) barrels. Stock and fore-end are checkered, walnut-stained hardwood with satin finish. Weight about 7¾ lbs. Introduced 1985.

Price: With fixed choke, vent. rib, about......................... **$409.00**
Price: With REM Choke, about **$439.00**

Tradewinds Model H-170

TRADEWINDS H-170 AUTO SHOTGUN

Gauge: 12 only, 2¾" chamber.
Action: Recoil-operated automatic.
Barrel: 26", 28" (Mod.) and 28" (Full), chrome lined.
Weight: 7 lbs.
Stock: Select European walnut stock, p.g. and fore-end hand checkered.
Features: Light alloy receiver, 5-shot tubular magazine, ventilated rib. Imported from Italy by Tradewinds.
Price: **$395.00**

Weatherby Eighty-Two Auto

WEATHERBY EIGHTY-TWO AUTO

Gauge: 12 only, 2¾" and 3" chamber.
Barrel: 22" Slug (with sights), 26", 28", 30" with IMC (Integral Multi-Choke) tubes; 26" available with Mod., Imp. Cyl., Skeet, others with Full, Mod., Imp. Cyl.
Weight: 7½ lbs. **Length:** 48½" (28" bbl.).
Stock: Walnut, hand checkered p.g. and fore-end, rubber recoil pad.
Features: Gas operated autoloader with "Floating Piston." Cross-bolt safety, fluted bolt, gold plated trigger. Each gun comes with three flush fitting IMC choke tubes. Imported from Japan by Weatherby. Introduced 1982.

Price: **$469.95**
Price: Extra interchangeable barrel **$203.00**
Price: Extra IMC choke tubes **$15.00**

Consult our Directory pages for the location of firms mentioned.

Winchester Ranger

WINCHESTER RANGER AUTO SHOTGUN

Gauge: 12 and 20, 2¾" chamber.
Barrel: 28" vent. rib with Winchoke tubes (Imp. Cyl., Mod., Full), or 28" plain barrel (Mod.).
Weight: 7 to 7¼ lbs. **Length:** 48⅝" over-all.
Stock: Walnut-finished hardwood, finger-grooved fore-end with deep cut checkering.
Sights: Metal bead front.
Features: Cross-bolt safety, front-locking rotating bolt, black serrated butt-plate, gas-operated action. Made under license by U.S. Repeating Arms. Co.
Price: Vent. rib with Winchoke, about......................... **$310.61**
Price: Deer barrel combo, about................................ **$349.44**
Price: Deer gun, about **$309.74**

Browning BPS Pump

Browning BPS Pump Shotgun (Ladies and Youth Model)

Same as BPS Upland Special except 20 ga. only, 22" Invector barrel, stock has pistol grip with recoil pad. Length of pull is 13¼". Introduced 1986.

Price: $385.95

ARMSPORT 2755 PUMP SHOTGUN

Gauge: 12, 3" chamber.
Barrel: 28" (Mod.), 30" (Full).
Weight: 7 lbs.
Stock: European walnut.
Features: Ventilated rib; rubber recoil pad; polished blue finish. Introduced 1986. Imported from Italy by Armsport.
Price: Fixed chokes $299.00
Price: 28", 30", choke tubes $350.00
Price: Police model with 20" (Imp. Cyl.), black receiver $275.00

BROWNING BPS PUMP SHOTGUN

Gauge: 12 or 20 gauge, 3" chamber (2¾" in target guns), 5-shot magazine.
Barrel: 22", 24", 26", 28", 30", 32" (Imp. Cyl., Mod. or Full). Also available with Invector choke tubes, 12 or 20 ga.; Upland Special has 22" barrel with Invector tubes.
Weight: 7 lbs. 8 oz. (28" barrel). **Length:** 48¾" over-all (28" barrel).
Stock: 14¼"x1½"x2½". Select walnut, semi-beavertail fore-end, full p.g. stock.
Features: Bottom feeding and ejection, receiver top safety, high post vent. rib. Double action bars eliminate binding. Vent. rib barrels only. Introduced 1977. Imported from Japan by Browning.
Price: Grade I Hunting, Upland Special, Invector $385.95
Price: Extra Invector barrel $164.95
Price: Extra fixed-choke barrel $98.85
Price: Buck Special barrel with rifle sights $159.95

Ithaca 37 Field Vent

Ithaca Model 37 Ultralite

Weighs five pounds. Same as standard Model 37 except walnut stock, comes only with 25" vent. rib. Has recoil pad, gold plated trigger, Sid Bell-designed grip cap. Also available as Ultra-Deerslayer with 20" barrel, 20 ga. only.

Price: With choke tubes $522.00
Price: Deerslayer model $450.00
Price: 20 ga., 20" (Special Bore) $480.00

Ithaca Model 37 Supreme

Same as Model 37 except: hand checkered fore-end and p.g. stock, Ithaca recoil pad and vent. rib. Model 37 Supreme also with Skeet (14"x1½"x2¼") or Trap (14½"x1½"x1⅞") stocks available at no extra charge. Other options available at extra charge.

Price: $769.00

ITHACA MODEL 37 FIELD GRADE VENT

Gauge: 12, 20 (5-shot; 3-shot plug furnished).
Action: Slide; takedown; bottom ejection.
Barrel: 25", 28" (Imp. Cyl., Mod., Full choke tubes).
Weight: 12 ga. 6½ lbs., 20 ga. 5¾ lbs.
Stock: 14"x1⅝"x2⅝". Checkered hardwood p.g. stock and ring-tail fore-end.
Features: Ithaca Raybar front sight; cross-bolt safety; action release for removing shells.
Price: $428.00
Price: Deluxe Vent, 12 or 20, fixed chokes $464.00

Ithaca Model 37 Magnum D/X

Same as standard Model 37 except chambered for 3" shells with resulting longer receiver. Stock dimensions are 14"x1⅞"x1½". Grip cap has a Sid Bell-designed flying mallard on it. Has a recoil pad, vent. rib barrel with Raybar front sight. Available in 12 or 20 ga. with 30" (Full), 28" (Mod.) and 26" (Imp. Cyl.) barrel. Weight about 7¼ lbs. Introduced 1978.

Price: $464.00
Price: Camouflage model, 12 ga., 26" (Full) only $500.00

Ithaca 37 English Ultra

Ithaca Model 37 Deerslayer

Same as Model 37 except: 26" or 20" bbl. designed for rifled slugs; sporting rear sight, Raybar front sight: rear sight ramp grooved for Redfield long eye relief scope mount. 12, or 20 gauge. With checkered stock, beavertail fore-end and recoil pad.

Price: $450.00

Ithaca Model 37 English Ultralite

Similar to the standard Model 37 Ultralite except vent. rib barrel has straight-grip stock with better wood. Introduced 1981.

Price: With choke tubes (Full, Mod., Imp. Cyl.). $522.00

LISA MODEL PUMP SLUG SHOTGUN

Gauge: 12, 2¾" chamber, 5 or 8 shot.
Barrel: 21" standard, or to customer specs.
Weight: About 7½ lbs.
Stock: Walnut or select hardwood.
Sights: None furnished. Drilled and tapped for scope mounting.
Features: Free floated barrel (heavy or lightweight); thick action bridge; uses special Pennsylvania Arms slug barrel. Introduced 1986. From Pennsylvania Arms.
Price: From $499.95

CAUTION: PRICES CHANGE. CHECK AT GUNSHOP.

Mossberg Model 3000

Mossberg Model 3000 Waterfowler Pump

Similar to the standard Model 3000 except all exterior metal is Parkerized to reduce glare, bolt is black oxidized, stock has a dull oil finish. Comes with q.d. swivels and a padded, camouflaged sling. Available with 30″ (Full) barrel with 3″ chamber. Introduced 1982.
Price: **$412.00**

MOSSBERG MODEL 3000 PUMP

Gauge: 12 or 20 ga., 3″ chamber.
Barrel: 22″ (Cyl.) with rifle sights, 26″ (Imp. Cyl.), 28″ (Mod.), 30″ (Full), vent. rib or plain. Also available with Multi-Choke system.
Weight: About 7½ lbs. **Length:** 48½″ over-all (28″ bbl.).
Stock: 14″x1⅜″x2¼″. American walnut
Features: Dual action bars for smooth functioning. Rubber recoil pad, steel receiver, chrome plated bolt. Cross-bolt safety reversible for left-handed shooters. Introduced 1980.
Price: **$360.00**

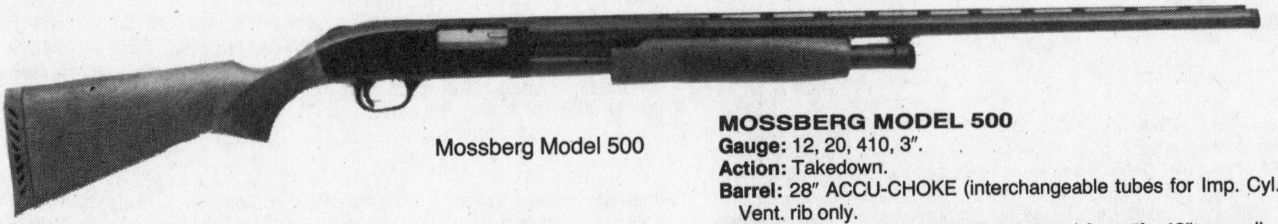

Mossberg Model 500

Mossberg Model 500AHT/AHTD

Same as Model 500 except 12 ga. only with extra-high Simmons Olympic-style free floating rib and built-up Monte Carlo trap-style stock. 30″ barrel (Full), 28″ ACCU-CHOKE with 3 interchangeable choke tubes (Mod., Imp. Mod., Full).
Price: With 30″ barrel, fixed choke **$326.95**
Price: With ACCU-CHOKE barrel, 28″ or 30″ **$346.95**

MOSSBERG MODEL 500

Gauge: 12, 20, 410, 3″.
Action: Takedown.
Barrel: 28″ ACCU-CHOKE (interchangeable tubes for Imp. Cyl., Mod., Full). Vent. rib only.
Weight: 6¾ lbs. (20-ga.), 7¼ lbs. (12-ga.) **Length:** 48″ over-all.
Stock: Walnut-finished hardwood; checkered p.g. and fore-end; recoil pad. (14″x1½″x2½″).
Features: Side ejection; top tang safety; trigger disconnector prevents doubles. Easily interchangeable barrels within gauge.
Price: Vent rib, ACCU-CHOKE, either gauge, about **$315.00**
Price: Extra barrels, from **$31.50**
Price: Youth gun, 20 ga., 13″ stock, 24″ (ACCU-CHOKE), about **$257.95**

Mossberg Model 500ASG Slugster

Same as standard Mossberg Model 500 except has Slugster barrel with ramp front sight, open adj. folding-leaf rear, running deer scene etched on receiver. 12 ga.—18½″, 24″, 20-ga.—24″ bbl.
Price: **$236.95**

Mossberg Model 500 410 Ga.

Similar to Mossberg Model 500 except: 410 bore only, 26″ bbl. (Full); 2½″, 3″ shells; holds six 2¾″ or five 3″ shells. Walnut-finished stock with checkered p.g. and fore-end, fluted comb and recoil pad (14″x1¼″x2½″). Weight about 6 lbs., length over-all 45¾″.
Price: With vent. rib barrel **$221.00**

Remington Model 870

Remington Model 870 Brushmaster Deluxe

Carbine version of the M870 with 20″ bbl. (Imp. Cyl.) for rifled slugs. 40½″ over-all, wgt. 6½ lbs. Recoil pad. Adj. rear, ramp front sights, 12 or 20 ga. Deluxe.
Price: Brushmaster, about **$380.00**
Price: Standard, 12 ga. only, about **$360.00**
Price: Left-hand model, about **$434.00**

REMINGTON 870 PUMP GUN

Gauge: 12, 20, (5-shot; 3-shot wood plug), 3″ chamber.
Action: Takedown, slide action
Barrel: 12, 20, ga., 26″ (Imp. Cyl.); 28″ (Mod. or Full); 12 ga., 30″ (Full); 12 ga., 26″, 28″ (REM CHOKE).
Weight: 7 lbs., 12 ga. (7¾ lbs. with Vari-Weight plug); 6½ lbs., 20 ga.
Length: 48½″ over-all (28″ bbl.).
Stock: 14″x1⅝″x2½″. Checkered walnut, p.g.; fluted extension fore-end; fitted rubber recoil pad.
Features: Double action bars, crossbolt safety. Receiver machined from solid steel. Hand fitted action.
Price: With vent. rib, about **$401.00**
Price: Left hand, vent. rib., 12 ga. only, about **$458.00**
Price: Youth Gun, 21″ vent. rib, Imp. Cyl., Mod., about **$401.00**
Price: 12 ga., 26″, 28″ REM Choke, about **$438.00**
Price: As above with REM Choke, left hand, about **$495.00**

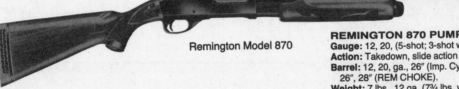

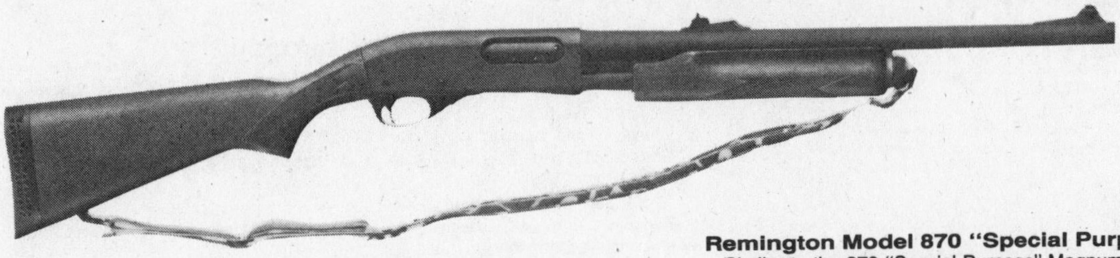

Remington 870 SP Deer

Remington Model 870 "Special Purpose" Deer Gun

Similar to the 870 "Special Purpose" Magnum except comes only with 20″ Imp. Cyl. barrel with rifle sights. Over-all length is 40½″, weight about 7 lbs. Barrel and receiver are Parkerized, bolt and carrier have dull black oxide finish. Oil-finished stock and fore-end. Comes wtih recoil pad and padded Cordura nylon sling. Introduced 1986.
Price: About **$380.00**

Remington 870 "Wingmaster"

Remington Model 870 "Wingmaster"
Similar to the standard Model 870 except has cut checkered stock and fore-end, ivory Bradley-type bead front and middle bead sights. Available in 12 ga. 3" only with 26", 28" REM Choke, or 30" (Full) barrels. Introduced 1986.
Price: 26", 28" REM Choke, about **$489.00**
Price: 30" fixed Full choke, about **$445.00**

Remington 870 Special Field

Remington Model 870 "Special Field"
Similar to the standard Model 870 except comes with 21" barrel only, 3" chamber, choked Imp. Cyl., Mod., Full and REM Choke; 12 ga. weighs 6¾ lbs., Ltwt. 20 weighs 6 lbs.; has straight-grip stock, shorter fore-end, both with cut checkering. Vent. rib barrel only. Introduced 1984.
Price: 12 ga. REM Choke, about. **$465.00**
Price: 20 ga., fixed choke, about. **$429.00**

Remington 870 "Special Purpose" Magnum
Similar to the Model 870 except chambered only for 12-ga., 3" shells, vent. rib. 26" (REM Choke) or 30" (Full) barrels. All exposed metal surfaces are finished in dull, non-reflective black. Wood has an oil finish. Comes with padded Cordura, 2" wide sling, quick-detachable swivels. Chrome-lined bores. Dark recoil pad. Introduced 1985.
Price: About **$401.00**

Remington Model 870 Competition Trap
Same as standard 870 except single shot, gas reduction system, select wood. Has 30" (Full choke) vent. rib barrel
Price: About **$685.00**

Remington 870F High Grade
Same as M870, except select walnut, better engraving
Price: About. **$4,720.00**
Price: With gold inlay, about. **$7,079.00**

Remington 870D High Grade
Same as 870 except: better walnut, hand checkering. Engraved receiver and bbl. Vent. rib. Stock dimensions to order.
Price: About. **$2,290.00**

Remington 870 TA Trap

Remington 870 TA Trap
Same as the M870 except: 12 ga. only, 30" (Mod., Full) vent. rib. bbl., ivory front and white metal middle beads. Special sear, hammer and trigger assy. 14⅜"x1½"x1⅞" stock with recoil pad. Hand fitted action and parts. Wgt. 8 lbs.
Price: Model 870TA Trap, about. **$436.00**
Price: TA Trap with Monte Carlo stock, about **$447.00**

Remington 870 Small Gauges
Exact copies of the large ga. Model 870, except that guns are offered in 28 and 410 ga. 25" barrel (Full., Mod., Imp. Cyl.). D and F grade prices same as large ga. M870 prices.
Price: With vent. rib barrel, about **$429.00**

Remington Sportsman 12

Remington "Sportsman" 12 Pump Shotgun
Similar to the Model 870 except in 12 ga. only with 3" chamber, 28" (REM Choke) or 30" (Full) barrels. Stock and fore-end are walnut-stained hardwood, checkered. Weight about 7½ lbs. Introduced 1984.
Price: 30", fixed choke, about **$275.00**
Price: 28", REM Choke, about. **$305.00**

Stevens 67VR

STEVENS MODEL 67 PUMP SHOTGUN
Gauge: 12, 20 (2¾" & 3"), 410 (2½" & 3").
Barrel: 26" (Full, 410 ga.), 28" (Mod., Full), 30" (Full, 12 ga.), or interchangeable choke tubes.
Weight: 7 lbs. **Length:** 49½" over-all (30" bbl.).
Stock: Walnut-finished hardwood; checkered p.g. and slide handle. 14"x1½"x2½".
Sights: Metal bead front.
Features: Grooved slide handle, top tang safety, steel receiver. From Savage Arms. Introduced 1981.
Price: Model 67 . . . . **$198.61**
Price: Model 67VR (vent. rib). **$214.75**
Price: Model 67 Slug Gun (21" barrel, rifle sights) **$202.29**
Price: Model 67-VRT (as above with vent. rib) **$229.29**
Price: Model 67-VRT-Y (youth gun, 20 ga.) **$229.29**
Price: Model 67-VRT-K (12, 20, choke tubes, laminated camo stock) **$250.29**

CAUTION: PRICES CHANGE. CHECK AT GUNSHOP.

Weatherby Ninety-Two

WEATHERBY NINETY-TWO PUMP
Gauge: 12 only, 3" chamber.
Action: Short stroke slide action.
Barrel: 22" Slug (with sights), 26", 28", 30" with IMC (Integral Multi-Choke) tubes; 26" with Mod., Imp. Cyl., Skeet, others with Full, Mod., Imp. Cyl.
Weight: About 7½ lbs. **Length:** 48⅛" (28" bbl.)
Stock: Walnut, hand checkered p.g. and fore-end, white line spacers at p.g. cap and recoil pad.
Features: Short stroke action, cross-bolt safety. Comes with three flush-fitting IMC choke tubes. Introduced 1982. Imported from Japan by Weatherby.
Price: **$399.95**
Price: Extra interchangeable bbls. **$175.00**
Price: Extra IMC choke tubes **$15.00**

Winchester 1300 XTR

WINCHESTER MODEL 1300 FEATHERWEIGHT PUMP
Gauge: 12 and 20, 3" chamber, 5-shot capacity.
Barrel: 22", vent. rib, with Full, Mod., Imp. Cyl. Winchoke tubes.
Weight: 6⅜ lbs. **Length:** 42⅝" over-all.
Stock: American walnut, with deep cut checkering on pistol grip, traditional ribbed fore-end; high luster finish.
Sights: Metal bead front.
Features: Twin action slide bars; front-locking rotating bolt; roll-engraved receiver; blued, highly polished metal; cross-bolt safety with red indicator. Introduced 1984.
Price: About **$345.45**

Winchester Model 1300XTR Featherweight
Similar to the standard 1300 Featherweight except comes in 12 ga. only with 28" barrel (Winchoke), rubber recoil pad. Weight is 7¼ lbs. with 48⅝" over-all length. Introduced 1986.
Price: About **$364.00**

Winchester Model 1300 Turkey
Similar to the standard Model 1300 Featherweight except 12 ga. only, 30" barrel with Mod., Full and Extra Full Winchoke tubes, matte finish wood and metal, and comes with recoil pad, Cordura sling and swivels.
Price: About **$364.00**

Winchester 1300 Waterfowl

Winchester 1300 Waterfowl Pump
Similar to the 1300 Featherweight except in 3" 12 ga. only, 30" vent. rib barrel with Winchoke system; stock and fore-end of walnut with low-luster finish. All metal surfaces have special non-glare matte finish. Introduced 1985.
Price: About **$364.00**

Winchester Ranger

WINCHESTER RANGER PUMP GUN
Gauge: 12 or 20, 3" chamber, 4-shot magazine.
Barrel: 28" vent rib or plain with Full, Mod., Imp. Cyl. Winchoke tubes, or 30" plain.
Weight: 7 to 7¼ lbs. **Length:** 48⅝" to 50⅝" over-all.
Stock: Walnut finished hardwood with ribbed fore-end.
Sights: Metal bead front.
Features: Cross-bolt safety, black rubber butt pad, twin action slide bars, front-locking rotating bolt. Made under license by U.S. Repeating Arms Co.
Price: Plain barrel, about **$231.00**
Price: Vent. rib barrel, Winchoke, about **$269.80**
Price: Vent. rib. Mod. choke, about............................ **$242.86**

Winchester Ranger Pump Gun Combination
Similar to the standard Ranger except comes with two barrels: 24⅛" (Cyl.) deer barrel with rifle-type sights and an interchangeable 28" vent. rib Winchoke barrel with Full, Mod. and Imp. Cyl. choke tubes. Available in 12 and 20 gauge 3" only, with recoil pad. Introduced 1983.
Price: With two barrels, about **$311.57**

Winchester Ranger Youth Pump Gun
Similar to the standard Ranger except chambered only for 3" 20 ga., 22" vent. rib barrel with Winchoke tubes (Full, Mod., Imp. Cyl.) or 22" plain barrel with fixed Mod. choke. Weighs 6½ lbs., measures 41⅝" o.a.l. Stock has 13" pull length and gun comes with discount certificate for full-size stock. Introduced 1983. Made under license by U.S. Repeating Arms Co.
Price: Vent. rib barrel, Winchoke, about **$275.48**
Price: Plain barrel, Mod. choke, about........................... **$239.88**

Consult our Directory pages for the location of firms mentioned.

ARMSPORT MODEL 2700 O/U
Gauge: 12 or 20 ga.
Barrel: 26″ (Imp. Cyl. & Mod.); 28″ (Mod. & Full); vent. rib.
Weight: 8 lbs.
Stock: European walnut, hand checkered p.g. and fore-end.
Features: Single selective trigger, automatic ejectors, engraved receiver. Imported by Armsport.
Price: $495.00
Price: With extractors only $425.00
Price: With double triggers $375.00
Price: M2733/2735 (Boss-type action, 12, 20, extractors) $495.00
Price: M2741/2743 (as above with ejectors) $550.00
Price: M2730/2731 (as above with single trigger, screw-in chokes) . $650.00
Price: M2705 (410 ga., 26″ Imp. & Mod., double triggers) $399.95
Price: M2720 (as above with single trigger) $465.00

ARMSPORT 2900 TRI-BARREL SHOTGUN
Gauge: 12, 3″ chambers.
Barrel: 28″ (Imp. Cyl. & Mod. & Full).
Weight: 7¾ lbs.
Stock: European walnut.
Features: Top-tang barrel selector; double triggers; silvered, engraved frame. Introduced 1986. Imported from Italy by Armsport.
Price: $895.00

ARMSPORT MODEL 2700 O-U GOOSE GUN
Gauge: 10 ga., 3½″ chambers.
Barrel: 32″ (Full & Full).
Weight: About 9 lbs.
Stock: European walnut.
Features: Boss-type action; double triggers; extractors. Introduced 1986. Imported from Italy by Armsport.
Price: $595.00

ARMSPORT 1225/1226 O-U FOLDING SHOTGUN
Gauge: 12, 20, 3″ chambers.
Barrel: 26″, 28″ (Mod. & Full)
Weight: 6 lbs.
Stock: European walnut.
Features: Top-break folding action; double triggers; extractors; silvered receiver with light engraving. Introduced 1986. Imported from Italy by Armsport.
Price: $295.00

Astra Model 750

Astra Model 650 O/U Shotgun
Same as Model 750 except has double triggers.
Price: With extractors $495.00
Price: With ejectors $630.00

ASTRA MODEL 750 O/U SHOTGUN
Gauge: 12 ga., (2¾″).
Barrel: 28″ (Mod. & Full or Skeet & Skeet), 30″ Trap (Mod. & Full).
Weight: 6½ lbs.
Stock: European walnut, hand-checkered p.g. and fore-end.
Features: Single selective trigger, scroll-engraved receiver, selective auto ejectors, vent. rib. Introduced 1980. From L. Joseph Rahn, Inc.
Price: $735.00
Price: With extractors only $600.00
Price: Trap or Skeet (M.C. stock and recoil pad.) $850.00

Beretta Model 686

BERETTA SO-3 O/U SHOTGUN
Gauge: 12 ga. (2¾″ chambers).
Action: Back-action sidelock.
Barrel: 26″, 27″, 28″, 29″ or 30″, chokes to customer specs.
Stock: Standard measurements—14⅛″x1⁷⁄₁₆″x2⅜″. Straight "English" or p.g.-style. Hand checkered European walnut.
Features: SO-3—"English scroll" floral engraving on action body, sideplates and trigger guard. Stocked in select walnut. SO-3EL—as above, with full engraving coverage. Hand-detachable sideplates. SO-3EELL—as above with deluxe finish and finest full coverage engraving. Internal parts gold plated. Top lever is pierced and carved in relief with gold inlaid crown. Introduced 1977. Imported from Italy by Beretta U.S.A. Corp.
Price: SO-3 .... $6,850.00
Price: SO-3EELL $9,750.00

Beretta SO-4 Target Shotguns
Target guns derived from Model SO-3EL. Light engraving coverage. Single trigger. Skeet gun has 28″ (Skeet & Skeet) barrels, 10mm rib, p.g. stock (14⅛″x2⁹⁄₁₆″x1⅜″). Weight is about 7 lbs. 10 ozs. Trap guns have 30″ (Imp. Mod. & Full or Mod. & Full) barrels, trap stock dimensions, fitted recoil pad, fluted beavertail fore-end. "Skeet" is inlaid in gold into trigger guard. Weight is about 7 lbs. 12 ozs. "Trap" is inlaid in gold into trigger guard. Special dimensions and features, within limits, may be ordered. Introduced 1977.
Price: Skeet or trap $7,400.00
Price: Trap Combo $9,500.00

BERETTA SERIES 680 OVER-UNDER
Gauge: 12 (2¾″).
Barrel: 29½″ (Imp. Mod. & Full, Trap), 28″ (Skeet & Skeet).
Weight: About 8 lbs.
Stock: Trap—14⅜″x1¼″x2⅛″; Skeet—14⅜″x1⅜″x2⁷⁄₁₆″. European walnut with hand checkering.
Sights: Luminous front sight and center bead.
Features: Trap Monte Carlo stock has deluxe trap recoil pad, Skeet has smooth pad. Various grades available—contact Beretta U.S.A. for details. Imported from Italy by Beretta U.S.A. Corp.
Price: M682, Trap or Skeet, from $2,100.00
Price: M682X, Trap or Skeet, from $2,100.00
Price: M682 Field $2,175.00
Price: M685 Field $875.00
Price: M686 Field, from $1,025.00
Price: M687 Field, from $1,175.00

Consult our Directory pages for the location of firms mentioned.

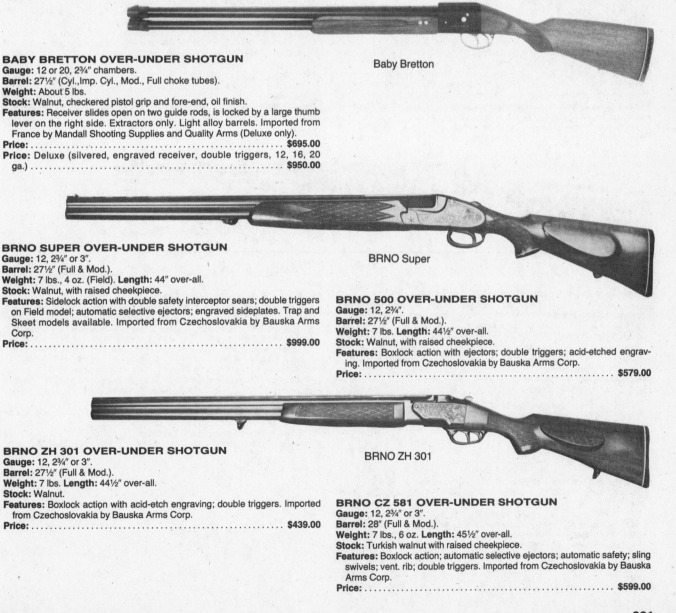

BETTINSOLI MODEL 845 EM OVER-UNDER

Gauge: 12, 2¾″ or 3″ chambers.
Barrel: 27½″ Interchoke (five choke tubes—Full, Mod., Imp. Cyl., Imp. Mod., Skeet).
Weight: About 7 lbs.
Stock: 14½″x1½″x2½″. Hand checkered European walnut; rubber "slip pad."
Features: Boxlock action, single selective trigger, selective automatic ejectors; silver frame with English rose and scroll engraving. Introduced 1986. Imported from Italy. For further information contact Proofmark, Ltd.
Price: **$619.00**
Price: Model 840 EM (as above but with fixed Full & Mod. chokes) . **$529.00**

Bettinsoli Model 845

BERNARDELLI MODEL 190

Gauge: 12 only, 3″ chamber.
Barrel: 28″, 29¾″, choke tubes.
Weight: 7 lbs., 4 oz.
Stock: 14⅜″x1⅜″x2⅜″; European walnut with oil or high-gloss finish.
Features: Engraved, coin-finished receiver; single selective trigger; vent. rib. Imported from Italy by Quality Arms, Inc.
Price: **$950.00**

BETTINSOLI SENIOR LUX OVER-UNDER

Gauge: 12, 2¾″ chambers.
Barrel: 27⅝″, 30″, choked to customer specs.
Weight: About 8 lbs.
Stock: 14½″x1⁷⁄₁₆″x1⅜″. Hand checkered European walnut; oil finish; Monte Carlo; palm swell; rubber magnum "slip pad." Left or right-hand avail.
Features: Blued boxlock action with single selective trigger; automatic selective ejectors. Skeet model available. Comes with fitted Italian luggage-style case. Introduced 1986. Imported from Italy. Contact Proofmark, Ltd. for full information.
Price: **$940.00**
Price: As above except with silvered, engraved frame **$1,800.00**

BABY BRETTON OVER-UNDER SHOTGUN

Gauge: 12 or 20, 2¾″ chambers.
Barrel: 27½″ (Cyl.,Imp. Cyl., Mod., Full choke tubes).
Weight: About 5 lbs.
Stock: Walnut, checkered pistol grip and fore-end, oil finish.
Features: Receiver slides open on two guide rods, is locked by a large thumb lever on the right side. Extractors only. Light alloy barrels. Imported from France by Mandall Shooting Supplies and Quality Arms (Deluxe only).
Price: **$695.00**
Price: Deluxe (silvered, engraved receiver, double triggers, 12, 16, 20 ga.) **$950.00**

Baby Bretton

BRNO SUPER OVER-UNDER SHOTGUN

Gauge: 12, 2¾″ or 3″.
Barrel: 27½″ (Full & Mod.).
Weight: 7 lbs., 4 oz. (Field). **Length:** 44″ over-all.
Stock: Walnut, with raised cheekpiece.
Features: Sidelock action with double safety interceptor sears; double triggers on Field model; automatic selective ejectors; engraved sideplates. Trap and Skeet models available. Imported from Czechoslovakia by Bauska Arms Corp.
Price: **$999.00**

BRNO Super

BRNO 500 OVER-UNDER SHOTGUN

Gauge: 12, 2¾″.
Barrel: 27½″ (Full & Mod.).
Weight: 7 lbs. **Length:** 44½″ over-all.
Stock: Walnut, with raised cheekpiece.
Features: Boxlock action with ejectors; double triggers; acid-etched engraving. Imported from Czechoslovakia by Bauska Arms Corp.
Price: **$579.00**

BRNO ZH 301 OVER-UNDER SHOTGUN

Gauge: 12, 2¾″ or 3″.
Barrel: 27½″ (Full & Mod.).
Weight: 7 lbs. **Length:** 44½″ over-all.
Stock: Walnut.
Features: Boxlock action with acid-etch engraving; double triggers. Imported from Czechoslovakia by Bauska Arms Corp.
Price: **$439.00**

BRNO ZH 301

BRNO CZ 581 OVER-UNDER SHOTGUN

Gauge: 12, 2¾″ or 3″.
Barrel: 28″ (Full & Mod.).
Weight: 7 lbs., 6 oz. **Length:** 45½″ over-all.
Stock: Turkish walnut with raised cheekpiece.
Features: Boxlock action; automatic selective ejectors; automatic safety; sling swivels; vent. rib; double triggers. Imported from Czechoslovakia by Bauska Arms Corp.
Price: **$599.00**

Browning Citori Field

Browning Citori O/U Skeet Models

Similar to standard Citori except: 26", 28" (Skeet & Skeet) only; stock dimensions of 14⅜"x1½"x2", fitted with Skeet-style recoil pad; conventional target rib and high post target rib.

Price: Grade I Invector (high post rib) $968.50
Price: Grade I, 12 & 20 (high post rib) $937.50
Price: Grade I, 28 & 410 (high post rib) $978.50
Price: Grade III, all gauges (high post rib) $1,303.00
Price: Grade VI, all gauges, (high post rib) $1,840.00
Price: Four barrel Skeet set — 12, 20, 28, 410 barrels, with case, Grade I only $3,140.00
Price: Grade III, four-barrel set (high post rib)............... $3,450.00
Price: Grade VI, four-barrel set (high post rib)................ $3,915.00

Browning Citori O/U Trap Models

Similar to standard Citori except: 12 gauge only; 30", 32" (Full & Full, Imp. Mod. & Full, Mod. & Full), 34" single barrel in Combo Set (Full, Imp. Mod., Mod.), or Invector model; Monte Carlo cheekpiece (14⅜"x1⅜"x1⅜"x2"); fitted with trap-style recoil pad; conventional target rib and high post target rib.

Price: Grade I, Invector high post target rib...................... $978.50
Price: Grade I, fixed chokes, high post target rib $937.50
Price: Grade III, Invector, high post target rib $1,303.00
Price: Grade VI, Invector, high post target rib $1,840.00

BROWNING CITORI O/U SHOTGUN

Gauge: 12, 20, 28 and 410.
Barrel: 26", 28" (Mod. & Full, Imp. Cyl. & Mod.), in all gauges, 30" (Mod. & Full, Full & Full) in 12 ga. only. Also offered with Invector choke tubes.
Weight: 6 lbs. 8 oz. (26" 410) to 7 lbs. 13 oz. (30" 12-ga.).
Length: 43" over-all (26" bbl.).
Stock: Dense walnut, hand checkered, full p.g., beavertail fore-end. Field-type recoil pad on 12 ga. field guns and trap and Skeet models.
Sights: Medium raised beads, German nickel silver.
Features: Barrel selector integral with safety, auto ejectors, three-piece takedown. Imported from Japan by Browning.

Price: Grade I, Invector... $875.50
Price: Grade I, 12 and 20, fixed chokes........................... $836.50
Price: Grade III, Invector, 12 and 20............................ $1,185.00
Price: Grade VI, Invector, 12 and 20............................ $1,730.00
Price: Grade I, 28 and 410, fixed chokes......................... $865.50
Price: Grade III, 28 and 410, fixed chokes...................... $1,303.00
Price: Grade VI, 28 and 410, high post rib, fixed chokes......... $1,840.00

Browning Citori Superlight

Browning Superlight Citori Over-Under

Similar to the standard Citori except availiable in 12, 20, 28 or 410 with 24", 26" barrels choked Imp. Cyl. & Mod. or 28" choked Mod. & Full. Has straight grip stock, Schnabel fore-end tip. Superlight 12 weighs 6 lbs., 9 oz. (26" barrels); Superlight 20, 5 lbs., 12 oz. (26" barrels). Introduced 1982.

Price: Grade I only, 12, 20, 28 or 410.......................... $865.50
Price: Grade III, Invector, 12 or 20 .... $1,185.00
Price: Grade III, 28 or 410.................................... $1,303.00
Price: Grade VI, Invector, 12 or 20 .... $1,730.00
Price: Grade VI, 28 or 410.................................... $1,840.00
Price: Grade I Invector $901.50
Price: Grade I Invector, Upland Special (24" bbls.).............. $901.50

Browning Superposed

Browning Over-Under Classic & Gold Classic

Same as the standard Superposed 20-ga. with 26" (Imp. Cyl. & Mod.) barrels except has an upland setting of bird dogs, pheasant and quail on the satin grey receiver. Gold Classic has the animals in inlaid gold. Straight grip stock and Schnabel fore-end are of select American walnut. Classic has pearl borders around the checkering and high gloss finish; Gold Classic has fine checkering and decorative carving with oil finish. Delivery scheduled for 1986. Introduced 1984.

Price: Over-Under Classic $2,000.00
Price: Over-Under Gold Classic............................... $6,000.00

BROWNING SUPERPOSED SUPERLIGHT

Gauge: 12 & 20, 2¾" chamber.
Action: Boxlock, top lever, single selective trigger. Bbl. selector combined with manual tang safety.
Barrel: 26½" (Mod. & Full, or Imp. Cyl. & Mod.)
Weight: 6⅜ lbs., average
Stock: Straight grip (14¼"x1⅝"x2½") hand checkered (fore-end and grip) select walnut.
Features: The Superposed is available in four grades. Pigeon, Pointer, Diana grades have silver grayed receivers with hand-engraved game scenes ascending in artistic design with each successive grade. Midas grade has specially blued steel with deeply hand-carved background and 18 carat gold inlaid pheasants and ducks on the 12 ga., smaller game birds on 20 ga. Lightning has full pistol grip stock, Superlight has straight grip. Basically this gives the buyer a wide choice of engraving styles and designs and mechanical options which would place the gun in a "custom" bracket. Options are too numerous to list here and the reader is urged to obtain a copy of the latest Browning catalog for the complete listing. Imported from Belgium by Browning.

Price: Pigeon Grade, Lightning and Superlight.................. $4,350.00
Price: Pointer Grade, Lightning and Superlight................. $5,350,00
Price: Diana Grade, Lightning and Superlight.................. $6,400.00
Price: Midas Grade, Lightning and Superlight.................. $7,900.00

Browning Limited Edition Waterfowl Superposed

Same specs as the Lightning Superposed. Available in 12 ga. only, 28" (Mod. & Full). Limited to 500 guns, the edition number of each gun is inscribed in gold on the bottom of the receiver with "Black Duck" and its scientific name. Sides of receiver have two gold inlayed black ducks, bottom has two, and one on the trigger guard. Receiver is completely engraved and grayed. Stock and fore-end are highly figured dark French walnut with 24 lpi checkering, hand-oiled finish, checkered butt. Comes with form fitted, velvet-lined, black walnut case. Introduced 1983.

Price: $8,000.00
Price: Similar treatment as above except for the Pintail Duck Issue $7,700.00

CAUTION: PRICES CHANGE. CHECK AT GUNSHOP.

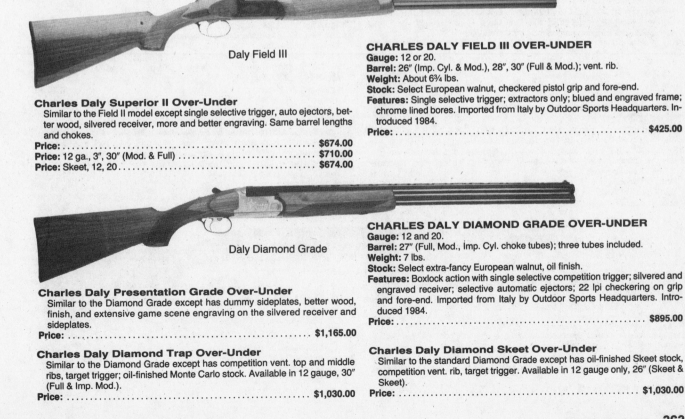

Churchill Monarch

CHURCHILL MONARCH OVER-UNDER SHOTGUNS
Gauge: 12 or 20 (3").
Barrel: 26" (Imp. Cyl. & Mod.), 28" (Mod. & Full). Chrome lined.
Weight: 12 ga.—7½ lbs., 20 ga.—6½ lbs.
Stock: European walnut with checkered p.g. and fore-end.
Features: Single selective trigger; blued, engraved receiver; vent. rib. Introduced 1986. Imported by Kassnar Imports, Inc.
Price: **$529.00**

Churchill Windsor Flyweight

CHURCHILL WINDSOR OVER-UNDER SHOTGUNS
Gauge: 12, 20, 410, 3" chambers.
Barrel: 26" (Skeet & Skeet, Imp. Cyl. & Mod.), 28" (Mod. & Full), 30" (Mod. & Full, Full & Full), 12 ga.; 26" (Skeet & Skeet, Imp. Cyl. & Mod.), 28" (Mod. & Full) 20 ga.; 24", 26" (Full & Full), 410 ga.; or 27", 30" ICT choke tubes.
Stock: European walnut, checkered pistol grip, oil finish.
Features: Boxlock action with silvered, engraved finish; single selective trigger; automatic ejectors on Windsor IV, extractors only on Windsor III. Also available in Flyweight version with 23", 25" barrels, fixed or ICT chokes, straight-grip stock.Imported from Italy by Kassnar. Introduced 1984.
Price: Windsor III, fixed chokes . . . . **$665.00** to **$745.00**
Price: 12 or 20 ga. ICT choke tubes **$745.00**
Price: Windsor IV, fixed chokes. . . . . **$784.00** to **$864.00**
Price: 12 or 20 ga., ICT choke tubes **$864.00**

Churchill Regent Over-Under Shotguns
Similar to the Windsor Grade except better wood with oil finish, better engraving; available only in 12 or 20 gauge (2¾" chambers), 27" barrels, with ICT interchangeable choke tubes (Imp. Cyl., Mod., Full). Regent VII has dummy sideplates. Introduced 1984.
Price: Regent VII, 12 or 20 ga. **$1,144.00**
Price: Regent VII Flyweight, 23", 25", ICT **$1,144.00**

Churchill Regent Trap & Skeet
Similar to the Regent V except Trap has ventilated side rib, Monte Carlo stock, ventilated recoil pad. Oil finished wood, fine checkering, chrome bores. Weight is 8 lbs. Regent Skeet available in 12 or 20 ga., 26" (Skeet & Skeet); oil finished stock measures 14½", 1½" x 2⅜". Both guns have silvered and engraved receivers. Introduced 1984.
Price: Regent Trap (30" Imp. Mod. & Full) **$1,104.00**
Price: Regent Skeet, 12 or 20 ga. **$1,049.00**
Price: Regent Trap (30" ICT) **$1,104.00**

> Consult our Directory pages for the location of firms mentioned.

Daly Field III

CHARLES DALY FIELD III OVER-UNDER
Gauge: 12 or 20.
Barrel: 26" (Imp. Cyl. & Mod.), 28", 30" (Full & Mod.); vent. rib.
Weight: About 6¾ lbs.
Stock: Select European walnut, checkered pistol grip and fore-end.
Features: Single selective trigger; extractors only; blued and engraved frame; chrome lined bores. Imported from Italy by Outdoor Sports Headquarters. Introduced 1984.
Price: **$425.00**

Charles Daly Superior II Over-Under
Similar to the Field II model except single selective trigger, auto ejectors, better wood, silvered receiver, more and better engraving. Same barrel lengths and chokes.
Price: **$674.00**
Price: 12 ga., 3", 30" (Mod. & Full) **$710.00**
Price: Skeet, 12, 20 . . . . **$674.00**

Daly Diamond Grade

CHARLES DALY DIAMOND GRADE OVER-UNDER
Gauge: 12 and 20.
Barrel: 27" (Full, Mod., Imp. Cyl. choke tubes); three tubes included.
Weight: 7 lbs.
Stock: Select extra-fancy European walnut, oil finish.
Features: Boxlock action with single selective competition trigger; silvered and engraved receiver; selective automatic ejectors; 22 lpi checkering on grip and fore-end. Imported from Italy by Outdoor Sports Headquarters. Introduced 1984.
Price: **$895.00**

Charles Daly Presentation Grade Over-Under
Similar to the Diamond Grade except has dummy sideplates, better wood, finish, and extensive game scene engraving on the silvered receiver and sideplates.
Price: **$1,165.00**

Charles Daly Diamond Trap Over-Under
Similar to the Diamond Grade except has competition vent. top and middle ribs, target trigger; oil-finished Monte Carlo stock. Available in 12 gauge, 30" (Full & Imp. Mod.).
Price: **$1,030.00**

Charles Daly Diamond Skeet Over-Under
Similar to the standard Diamond Grade except has oil-finished Skeet stock, competition vent. rib, target trigger. Available in 12 gauge only, 26" (Skeet & Skeet).
Price: **$1,030.00**

Exel Series 100

EXEL SERIES 100 OVER-UNDER SHOTGUNS

Gauge: 12 only; 2¾", 3" chambers.
Barrel: 26" (Imp. Cyl. & Mod., M101), 27⅝" (Imp. Cyl. & Mod., Imp. Cyl. & Imp. Mod., or choke tubes, M102, M104, M105, M106), 29½" (Mod. & Full, choke tubes, M103, M107).

Weight: 6⅞ to 7¾ lbs.
Stock: 14⅜" × 1½" × 2½" (14½" × 1¼" × 1¾" for Trap M107); checkered European walnut.
Features: Single selective trigger, selective auto. ejectors. Virtually any choke combination on special order. M105, 106 come with five choke tubes; M107 Trap has upper barrel Full choke, lower barrel three choke tubes. Made in Spain by Lanber. Imported by Exel Arms.
Price: Model 101, 102 .... **$450.80**
Price: Model 103 .... **$466.91**
Price: Model 104 .... **$543.29**
Price: Model 105 .... **$644.00**
Price: Model 106, 107 .... **$845.25**

Exel Model 305

EXEL SERIES 300 OVER-UNDER SHOTGUNS

Gauge: 12, 20 ga., 2¾" or 3" (20 ga. only) chambers.
Barrel: 28" (Full & Mod.), 29" (Full & Mod. or Full & Imp. Mod.).
Weight: 6½ to 8 lbs.

Stock: 14⅜" x 1⅜" x 2½" (Field), 14⅜" x 1½" x 1⅝" (Monte Carlo). European walnut with checkered grip and fore-end.
Features: Boxlock action with silvered and engraved finish; ventilated rib; full pistol grip stock; automatic selective ejectors. Made in Spain by Laurona; imported by Exel Arms of America. Introduced 1984.
Price: Model 301, 302 .... **$552.92**
Price: Model 303, 304 .... **$622.71**
Price: Model 305, 306, 305A, 306A (choke tubes) **$710.71**
Price: Model 307, 308 .... **$668.31**
Price: Model 309, 310 .... **$726.49**
Price: Model 306T Turkey Gun (matte finish wood, metal, four choke tubes) **$710.71**

F.I.E./FRANCHI DIAMOND GRADE OVER-UNDER

Gauge: 12 ga. only, 2¾" chambers.
Barrel: 28" (Mod. & Full).
Weight: 6 lbs. 13 oz.
Stock: French walnut with cut checkered pistol grip and fore-end.
Features: Top tang safety, automatic ejectors, single selective trigger. Chrome plated bores. Decorative scroll on silvered receiver. Introduced 1982. Imported from Italy by F.I.E. Corp.
Price: Diamond Grade **$850.00**

F.I.E./Franchi Alcione SL Super Deluxe

Similar to the Falconet Super except has best quality hand engraved, silvered receiver, 24K gold plated trigger, elephant ivory bead front sight. Comes with luggage-type fitted case. Has 14K gold inlay on receiver. Same barrel and chokes as on Falconet Super. Introduced 1982.
Price: Alcione Super Deluxe **$1,595.00**

LANBER MODEL 844 OVER-UNDER

Gauge: 12, 2¾" or 3".
Barrel: 28" (Imp. Cyl. & Imp. Mod.), 30" (Mod. & Full).
Weight: About 7 lbs. **Length:** 44⅜" (28" bbl.).
Stock: 14¼" x 1⅝" x 2½". European walnut; checkered grip and fore-end.
Features: Single non-selective or selective trigger, double triggers on magnum model. Available with or without ejectors. Imported from Spain by Lanber Arms of America, and Exel Arms of America. Introduced 1981.
Price: Field, with selective trigger, extractors **$450.80**
Price: As above, 3" Mag., 844 MST **$466.91**

F.I.E./MAROCCINI O/U SHOTGUN

Gauge: 12 or 20 ga., 3".
Barrel: 28" (Mod. & Full); vent. top and middle ribs.
Weight: 7¾ lbs.
Stock: Walnut, hand checkered.
Features: Auto. safety; extractors; double triggers; engraved antique silver receiver. Imported from Italy by F.I.E.
Price: **$399.95**

ARMI FAMARS FIELD OVER-UNDER

Gauge: 12 (2¾"), 20 (3").
Barrel: 26", 28", 30" (Mod. & Full).
Weight: 6½ to 6¾ lbs.
Stock: 14½" x 1½" x 2½". European walnut.
Sights: Gold bead front.
Features: Boxlock action with single selective trigger; automatic selective trigger. Color case-hardened receiver with engraving. Imported from Italy by Mandall Shooting Supplies.
Price: **$750.00**

Lanber Model 2004 Over-Under

Same basic specifications as Model 844 except fitted with LanberChoke interchangeable choke tube system. Available in trap, Skeet, pigeon and field models; ejectors only; single selective trigger; no middle rib on target guns (2008, 2009). Imported from Spain by Lanber Arms of America and Exel Arms of America.
Price: Model 2004 .... **$644.00**
Price: Model 2008 .... **$845.25**
Price: Model 2009 (30" bbl.) **$845.25**

LAURONA SUPER MODEL OVER-UNDERS

Gauge: 12, 20, 2¾" or 3".
Barrel: 26" (Multichokes), 28" (Mod. & Full, Imp. Cyl. & Imp. Mod.), 29" (Multichokes or Full).
Weight: About 7 lbs.
Stock: European walnut. Dimensions vary according to model. Full pistol grip.
Features: Boxlock action, silvered with engraving. Automatic selective ejectors; choke tubes available on most models; single selective or twin single triggers; black chrome barrels. Imported from Spain by International Sporting Goods.
Price: Model 85 MS Super Game **$579.00**

Laurona Super Game

Price: Model 84 S Super Trap **$668.00**
Price: Model 85 MS Super Trap **$688.00**
Price: Model 85 MS Super Pigeon **$683.00**
Price: Model 85 S Super Skeet **$673.00**
Price: Model 85 SM Sporting **$582.00**

CAUTION: PRICES CHANGE. CHECK AT GUNSHOP.

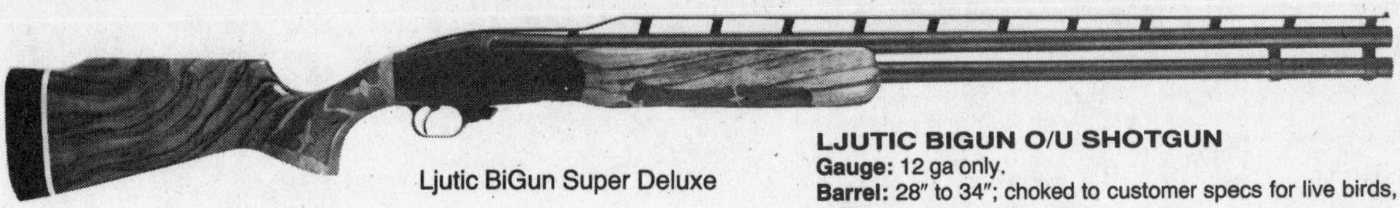

Ljutic BiGun Super Deluxe

Ljutic Four Barrel Skeet Set

Similar to BiGun except comes with matched set of four 28" barrels in 12, 20, 28 and 410. Ljutic Paternator chokes and barrel are integral. Stock is to customer specs, of American or French walnut with fancy checkering.
Price: Four barrel set....................................... $26,995.00

MAROCCHI AMERICA TARGET SHOTGUN

Gauge: 12 or 20, 2¾" chambers.
Barrel: 26" to 29" (Skeet), 27" to 32" (trap), 32" (trap mono, choice of top single or high rib under), 30" (over-under with extra 32" single).
Weight: 7¼ to 8 lbs.
Stock: Hand checkered select walnut with left or right-hand palm swell; choice of beavertail or Schnabel fore-end.
Features: Designed specifically for American target sports. Frame has medium engraving coverage with choice of three finishes. No extra charge for special stock dimensions or stock finish. Comes with fitted hard shell case. Custom engraving and inlays available. Introduced 1983. Imported from Italy by Marocchi U.S.A.
Price: From $2,000.00

LJUTIC BIGUN O/U SHOTGUN

Gauge: 12 ga only.
Barrel: 28" to 34"; choked to customer specs for live birds, trap, International Trap.
Weight: To customers specs.
Stock: To customer specs. Oil finish, hand checkered.
Features: Custom-made gun. Hollow-milled rib, pull or release trigger, push-button opener in front of trigger guard. From Ljutic Industries.
Price: $7,995.00
Price: BiGun Combo (interchangeable single barrel, two trigger guards, one for single trigger, one for doubles) $12,995.00
Price: Super Deluxe LTD TC BiGun $9,984.00
Price: Extra barrels with screw-in chokes or O/U barrel sets $3,995.00

MAROCCHI CONTRAST TARGET SHOTGUN

Gauge: 12 or 20 ga., 2¾" chambers.
Barrel: 26" to 29" (Skeet), 27" to 32" trap.
Weight: 7¼ to 8 lbs.
Stock: Select walnut with hand rubbed wax finish; hand checkered p.g. and fore-end; beavertail or Schnabel fore-end; grip has right or left palm swell.
Features: Lightly engraved frame on standard grade, or can be ordered with custom engraving and inlays in choice of three finishes. Optional different buttstock available. Gun comes with fitted hard shell case. Introduced 1983. Imported from Italy by Marocchi U.S.A.
Price: From $2,000.00

Navy Bird Hunter

NAVY ARMS MODEL 83/93 BIRD HUNTER O-U

Gauge: 12, 20; 3" chambers.
Barrel: 28" (Imp. Cyl. & Mod., Mod. & Full).

Weight: About 7½ lbs.
Stock: European walnut, checkered grip and fore-end.
Sights: Metal bead front.
Features: Boxlock action with double triggers; extractors only; silvered, engraved receiver; vented top and middle ribs. Imported from Italy by Navy Arms. Introduced 1984.
Price: Model 83 (extractors).................................. $320.00
Price: Model 93 (ejectors) $389.00

Navy Arms Model 95/96 Sportsman

Same as the 83/93 Bird Hunter except come with five interchangeable choke tubes. Model 96 has gold-plated single trigger and ejectors.
Price: Model 95 (extractors)................................. $415.00
Price: Model 96 (ejectors) $520.00

NAVY ARMS MODEL 410 O-U SHOTGUN

Gauge: 410, 3" chambers.
Barrel: 26" (Full & Full, Skeet & Skeet).
Weight: 6¼ lbs.
Stock: European walnut; checkered p.g. and fore-end.
Features: Chrome-lined barrels, hard chrome finished receiver with engraving, vent. rib. Single trigger. Imported from Italy by Navy Arms. Introduced 1986.
Price: $299.00

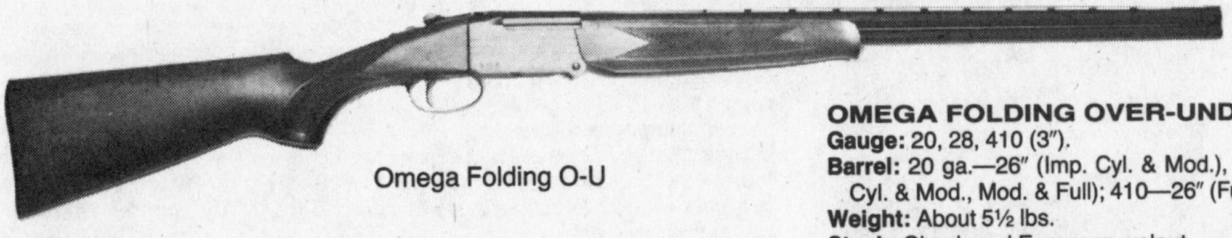

Omega Folding O-U

ROTTWEIL OLYMPIA '72 SKEET SHOTGUN

Gauge: 12 ga. only.
Action: Boxlock.
Barrel: 27" (special Skeet choke), vent. rib. Chromed lined bores, flared chokes.
Weight: 7¼ lbs. **Length:** 44½" over-all.
Stock: French walnut, hand checkered, modified beavertail fore-end. Oil finish.
Sights: Metal bead front.
Features: Inertia-type trigger, interchangeable for any system. Frame and lock milled from steel block. Retracting firing pins are spring mounted. All coil springs. Selective single trigger. Action engraved. Extra barrels are available. Introduced 1976. Imported from West Germany by Dynamit Nobel.
Price: $2,295.00
Price: Trap model (Montreal) is similar to above except has 30" (Imp. Mod. & Full) bbl., weighs 8 lbs., 48½" over-all..................... $2,295.00

OMEGA FOLDING OVER-UNDER SHOTGUNS

Gauge: 20, 28, 410 (3").
Barrel: 20 ga.—26" (Imp. Cyl. & Mod.), 28" (Mod. & Full); 28 ga.—26" (Imp. Cyl. & Mod., Mod. & Full); 410—26" (Full & Full).
Weight: About 5½ lbs.
Stock: Checkered European walnut.
Features: Single trigger; automatic safety; vent rib. Imported from Italy by Kassnar Imports, Inc. Introduced 1986.
Price: .... $377.00 to $392.00

ROTTWEIL 72 AMERICAN SKEET

Gauge: 12, 2¾".
Barrel: 26¾" (Skeet & Skeet).
Weight: About 7½ lbs.
Stock: 14½" x 1⅜" x 1⅜" x ¼". Select French walnut with satin oil finish; hand checkered grip and fore-end; double ventilated recoil pad.
Sights: Plastic front in metal sleeve, center bead.
Features: Interchangeable trigger groups with coil springs; interchangeable buttstocks; special .433" ventilated rib; matte finish silvered receiver with light engraving. Introduced 1978. Imported from West Germany by Dynamit Nobel.
Price: $2,295.00

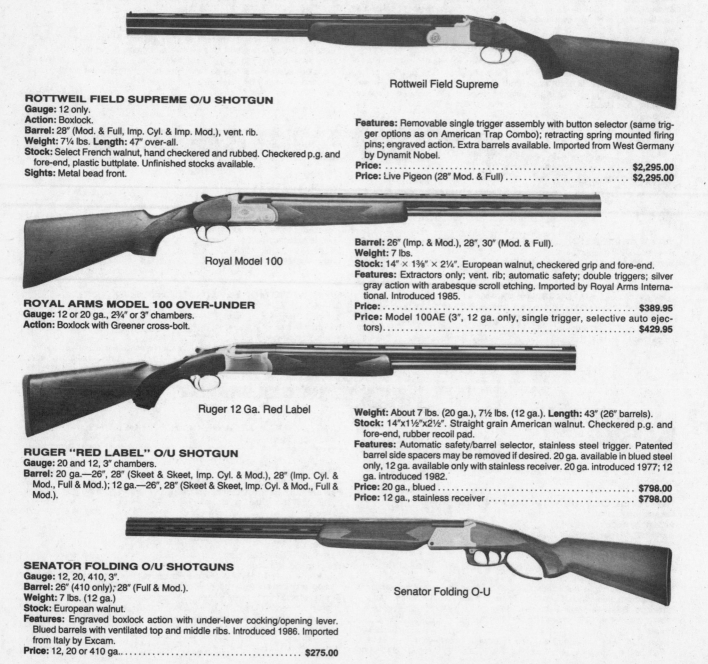

Rottweil American Trap

Rottweil Field Supreme

Royal Model 100

Ruger 12 Ga. Red Label

Senator Folding O-U

ROTTWEIL AMERICAN TRAP COMBO

Gauge: 12 ga. only.
Action: Boxlock
Barrel: Separated o/u, 32" (Imp. Mod. & Full); single is 34" (Full), both with high vent. rib.
Weight: 8½ lbs. (o/u and single)
Stock: Monte Carlo style, walnut, hand checkered and rubbed. Unfinished stocks available. Double vent. recoil pad. Choice of two dimensions.
Sights: Plastic front in metal sleeve, center bead.
Features: Interchangeable inertia-type trigger groups. Trigger groups available: single selective; double triggers;, release/pull; release/release selective. Receiver milled from block steel. Chokes are hand honed, test fired and reworked for flawless patterns. All coil springs, engraved action. Introduced 1977. Imported from West Germany by Dynamit Nobel.
Price: $2,850.00
Price: American Trap O/U (as above except only with o/u bbls.) . . . $2,295.00

ROTTWEIL AAT TRAP GUN

Gauge: 12, 2¾".
Barrel: 32" (Imp. Mod. & Full).
Weight: About 8 lbs.
Stock: 14½"x1⅜"x1⅜"x1⅞". Monte Carlo style of selected French walnut with oil finish. Checkered fore-end and p.g.
Features: Has infinitely variable point of impact via special muzzle collar. Extra single lower barrels available—32" (Imp. Mod.) or 34" (Full). Special trigger groups—release/release or release/pull—also available. Introduced 1979. From Dynamit Nobel.
Price: With single lower barrel $2,295.00
Price: Combo (single and o/u barrels) $2,295.00
Price: Interchangeable trap trigger group $345.00

ROTTWEIL FIELD SUPREME O/U SHOTGUN

Gauge: 12 only.
Action: Boxlock.
Barrel: 28" (Mod. & Full, Imp. Cyl. & Imp. Mod.), vent. rib.
Weight: 7¼ lbs. **Length:** 47" over-all.
Stock: Select French walnut, hand checkered and rubbed. Checkered p.g. and fore-end, plastic buttplate. Unfinished stocks available.
Sights: Metal bead front.

Features: Removable single trigger assembly with button selector (same trigger options as on American Trap Combo); retracting spring mounted firing pins; engraved action. Extra barrels available. Imported from West Germany by Dynamit Nobel.
Price: $2,295.00
Price: Live Pigeon (28" Mod. & Full) $2,295.00

ROYAL ARMS MODEL 100 OVER-UNDER

Gauge: 12 or 20 ga., 2¾" or 3" chambers.
Action: Boxlock with Greener cross-bolt.

Barrel: 26" (Imp. & Mod.), 28", 30" (Mod. & Full).
Weight: 7 lbs.
Stock: 14" × 1⅜" × 2¼". European walnut, checkered grip and fore-end.
Features: Extractors only; vent. rib; automatic safety; double triggers; silver gray action with arabesque scroll etching. Imported by Royal Arms International. Introduced 1985.
Price: $389.95
Price: Model 100AE (3", 12 ga. only, single trigger, selective auto ejectors) $429.95

RUGER "RED LABEL" O/U SHOTGUN

Gauge: 20 and 12, 3" chambers.
Barrel: 20 ga.—26", 28" (Skeet & Skeet, Imp. Cyl. & Mod.), 28" (Imp. Cyl. & Mod., Full & Mod.); 12 ga.—26", 28" (Skeet & Skeet, Imp. Cyl. & Mod., Full & Mod.).

Weight: About 7 lbs. (20 ga.), 7½ lbs. (12 ga.). **Length:** 43" (26" barrels).
Stock: 14"x1½"x2½". Straight grain American walnut. Checkered p.g. and fore-end, rubber recoil pad.
Features: Automatic safety/barrel selector, stainless steel trigger. Patented barrel side spacers may be removed if desired. 20 ga. available in blued steel only, 12 ga. available only with stainless receiver. 20 ga. introduced 1977; 12 ga. introduced 1982.
Price: 20 ga., blued $798.00
Price: 12 ga., stainless receiver $798.00

SENATOR FOLDING O/U SHOTGUNS

Gauge: 12, 20, 410, 3".
Barrel: 26" (410 only), 28" (Full & Mod.).
Weight: 7 lbs. (12 ga.)
Stock: European walnut.
Features: Engraved boxlock action with under-lever cocking/opening lever. Blued barrels with ventilated top and middle ribs. Introduced 1986. Imported from Italy by Excam.
Price: 12, 20 or 410 ga. $275.00

CAUTION: PRICES CHANGE. CHECK AT GUNSHOP.

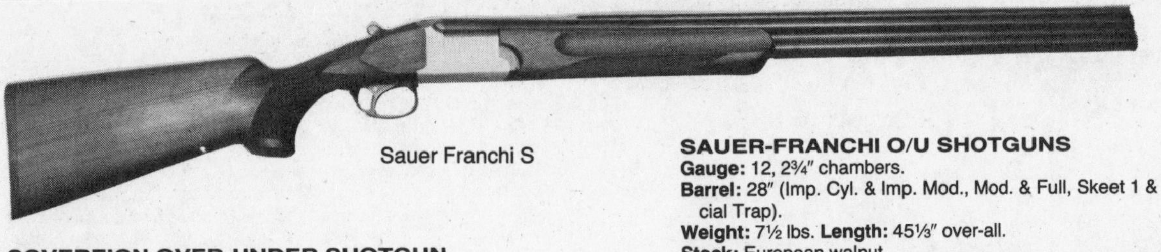

Sauer Franchi S

SOVEREIGN OVER-UNDER SHOTGUN

Gauge: 12 or 20, 2¾" chambers.
Barrel: 28" (Mod. & Full).
Weight: 7 lbs. (12 ga.), 6¾ lbs. (20 ga.).
Stock: 14⅝"x1⅜"x2¼". European walnut with checkered p.g. and fore-end.
Features: Chrome action with engraving; ventilated rib; double triggers. Two frame sizes for each gauge. Introduced 1986. Imported from Italy by Southern Gun & Tackle.
Price: $285.95

SAUER-FRANCHI O/U SHOTGUNS

Gauge: 12, 2¾" chambers.
Barrel: 28" (Imp. Cyl. & Imp. Mod., Mod. & Full, Skeet 1 & Skeet 2); 29" (Special Trap).
Weight: 7½ lbs. **Length:** 45⅓" over-all.
Stock: European walnut.
Features: Blued frame on Standard model, others with silvered, engraved frames; single selective trigger; selective auto. ejectors; vent. rib. Introduced in U.S. 1986. Imported from West Germany by SIGARMS.
Price: Standard, about $785.00
Price: Regent, about $825.00
Price: Favorit, about $875.00
Price: Diplomat, about...................................... $1,520.00
Price: Sporting S, Trap, Skeet models, about $1,375.00

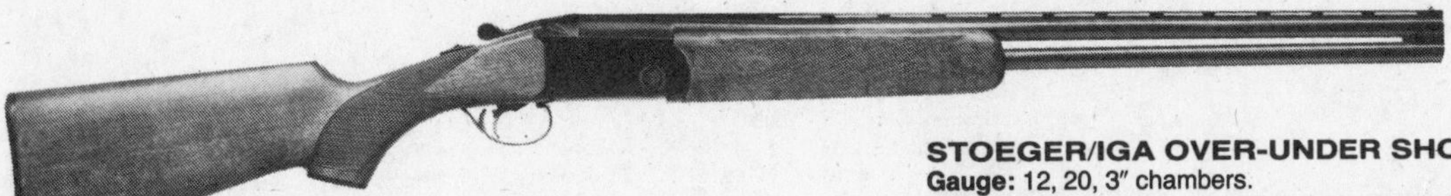

IGA Over-Under

STOEGER/IGA OVER-UNDER SHOTGUN

Gauge: 12, 20, 3" chambers.
Barrel: 26" (Full & Full, Imp. Cyl. & Mod.), 28" (Mod. & Full).
Weight: 6¾ to 7 lbs.
Stock: 14½" x 1½" x 2½". Oil finished hardwood with checkered pistol grip and fore-end.
Features: Manual safety, double triggers, extractors only, ventilated top rib. Introduced 1983. Imported from Brazil by Stoeger Industries.
Price: Double triggers $296.95
Price: Single trigger $341.95

TECHNI-MEC MODEL SPL 640 FOLDING O-U

Gauge: 12, 16, 20, 28, (2¾") 410 (3").
Barrel: 26" (Mod. & Full).
Weight: 5½ lbs.
Stock: European walnut.
Features: Gun folds in half for storage, transportation. Chrome lined barrels; ventilated rib; photo-engraved silvered receiver. Imported from Italy by L. Joseph Rahn. Introduced 1984.
Price: Double triggers $240.00
Price: Single trigger $256.00

TECHNI-MEC MODEL SR 692 EM OVER-UNDER

Gauge: 12, 16, 20, 2¾" or 3".
Barrel: 26", 28", 30" (Mod., Full, Imp. Cyl., Cyl.).
Weight: 6½ lbs.
Stock: 14½" x 1½" x 2½". European walnut with checkered grip and fore-end.
Features: Boxlock action with dummy sideplates, fine game scene engraving; single selective trigger; automatic ejectors available. Imported from Italy by L. Joseph Rahn. Introduced 1984.
Price: $550.00

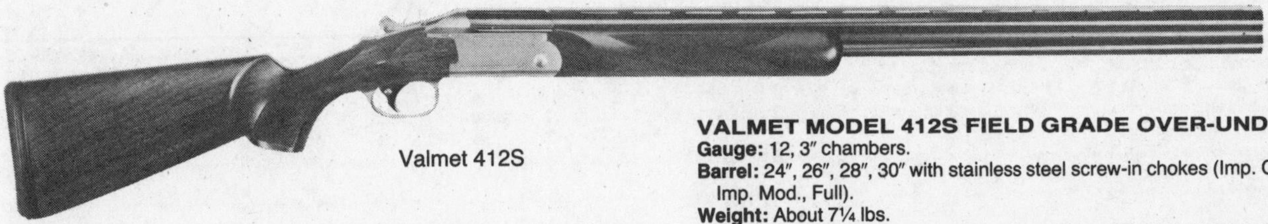

Valmet 412S

WEATHERBY ORION O/U SHOTGUN

Gauge: 12 or 20 ga. (3" chambers; 2¾" on Trap gun).
Action: Boxlock (simulated side-lock).
Barrel: 12 ga. 30" (Full & Mod.), 28" (Full & Mod., Mod. & Imp. Cyl.), 26" (Mod. & Imp. Cyl., Skeet & Skeet); 20 ga. 28" (Full & Mod., Mod. & Imp. Cyl.), 26" (Mod. & Imp. Cyl., Skeet & Skeet).
Weight: 7 lbs., 8 oz. (12 ga. 26").
Stock: American walnut, checkered p.g. and fore-end. Rubber recoil pad. Dimensions for field and Skeet models, 20 ga. 14"x1½"x2½".
Features: Selective auto ejectors, single selective mechanical trigger. Top tang safety, Greener cross-bolt. Introduced 1982. Imported from Japan by Weatherby.
Price: Skeet, fixed choke $859.95
Price: 12 ga. Trap, fixed choke $899.95
Price: 12 or 20 ga., IMC Multi-Choke Field $849.95
Price: IMC Multi-Choke Trap $899.95
Price: Extra IMC choke tubes $15.00

VALMET MODEL 412S FIELD GRADE OVER-UNDER

Gauge: 12, 3" chambers.
Barrel: 24", 26", 28", 30" with stainless steel screw-in chokes (Imp. Cyl., Mod., Imp. Mod., Full).
Weight: About 7¼ lbs.
Stock: American walnut. Standard dimensions-13⁹⁄₁₀"x1½"x2⅝". Checkered p.g. and fore-end.
Features: Free interchangeability of barrels, stocks and fore-ends into double rifle model, combination gun, etc. Barrel selector in trigger; auto. top tang safety; barrel cocking indicators. Introduced 1980. Imported from Finland by Valmet.
Price: Model 412S (ejectors) $799.00
Price: Extra barrels with choke tubes........................... $399.00

Valmet 412 ST Target Series

Both trap and Skeet versions of the 412S gun. Stocks are drilled for insertion of a recoil reducer; quick-change butt stocks; beavertail fore-end; Monte Carlo stock has wider comb and double palm swell; trap stock has Pachmayr pad; wide trigger; barrel indicators near the tang. High vent rib, stepped and tapered on trap gun. Trap guns have choke tubes, 32", 34" barrel (mono), 30", 32" (o/u); weight 9 lbs. Skeet has 28" barrels (12 ga.); weight 8 lbs. Skeet gun also has choke tubes. Introduced 1985.
Price: Trap $899.00
Price: Skeet $899.00
Price: Extra barrels $449.00

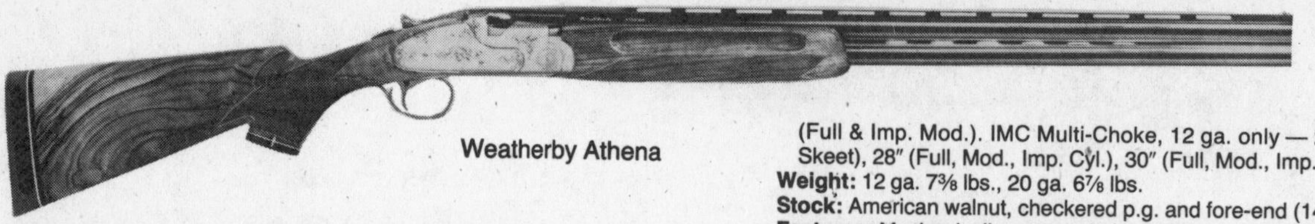

Weatherby Athena

WEATHERBY ATHENA O/U SHOTGUN
Gauge: 12 or 20 ga. (3″ chambers; 2¾″ on Trap gun).
Action: Boxlock (simulated side-lock) top lever break-open. Selective auto ejectors, single selective trigger (selector inside trigger guard).
Barrel: Fixed choke, 12 or 20 ga. — 26″ (Mod. & Imp. Cyl., Skeet & Skeet), 28″ (Mod. & Imp. Cyl., Full & Mod.), 30″ (Full & Mod., Full & Imp. Mod.), 32″ Trap

(Full & Imp. Mod.). IMC Multi-Choke, 12 ga. only — 26″ (Mod., Imp. Cyl., Skeet), 28″ (Full, Mod., Imp. Cyl.), 30″ (Full, Mod., Imp. Mod.).
Weight: 12 ga. 7⅜ lbs., 20 ga. 6⅞ lbs.
Stock: American walnut, checkered p.g. and fore-end (14¼″x1½″x2½″).
Features: Mechanically operated trigger. Top tang safety, Greener cross-bolt, fully engraved receiver, recoil pad installed. IMC models furnished with three interchangeable flush-fitting choke tubes. Imported from Japan by Weatherby. Introduced 1982.
Price: Skeet, fixed choke **$1,329.95**
Price: 12 or 20 ga., IMC Multi-Choke Field **$1,349.95**
Price: IMC Multi-Choke Trap **$1,369.00**
Price: Extra IMC Choke tubes **$15.00**

Winchester 101 Field

Winchester Model 101 Waterfowl Winchoke
Same as Model 101 Field Grade except in 12 ga. only, 3″ chambers, 30″ or 32″ barrels. Comes with four Winchoke tubes: Mod., Imp. Mod., Full, Extra-Full. Blued receiver with hand etching and engraving. Introduced 1981. Manufactured in and imported from Japan by Winchester Group, Olin Corp.
Price: **$1,225.00**

WINCHESTER 101 WINCHOKE O/U FIELD GUN
Gauge: 12, or 20, 3″ chambers.
Action: Top lever, break open. Manual safety combined with bbl. selector at top of receiver tang.
Barrel: 27″, Winchoke interchangeable choke tubes.
Weight: 12 ga. 7 lbs. Others 6½ lbs. **Length:** 44¾″ over-all.
Stock: 14″x1½″x2½″. Checkered walnut p.g. and fore-end; fluted comb.
Features: Single selective trigger, auto ejectors. Hand engraved satin gray receiver. Comes with hard gun case. Manufactured in and imported from Japan by Winchester Group, Olin Corp.
Price: **$1,225.00**
Price: Two Barrel Set (12 and 20) **$2,200.00**

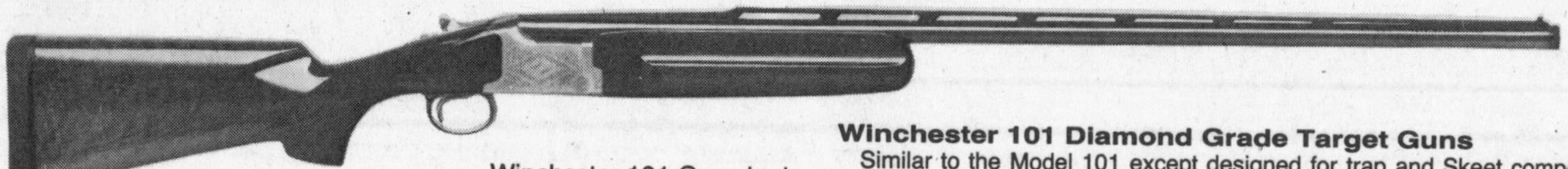

Winchester 101 Oversingle

WINCHESTER MODEL 501 GRAND EUROPEAN O-U
Gauge: 12 ga. (Trap), 12 and 20 ga. (Skeet). 2¾″ chambers.
Barrel: 27″ (Skeet & Skeet), 30″ (Imp. Mod. & Full), 32″ (Imp. Mod. & Full).
Weight: 7½ lbs. (Skeet), 8½ lbs. (Trap) **Length:** 47⅛″ over-all (30″ barrel).
Stock: 14⅛″x1½″x2½″ (Skeet). Full fancy walnut, hand-rubbed oil finish.
Features: Silvered, engraved receiver; engine-turned breech interior. Slide-button selector/safety, selective auto. ejectors. Chrome bores, tapered vent. rib. Trap gun has Monte Carlo or regular stock, recoil pad; Skeet gun has rosewood buttplate. Introduced 1981. Manufactured in and imported from Japan by Winchester Group, Olin Corp.
Price: Trap or Skeet **$1,720.00**
Price: Grand European Featherweight 20 ga., 25½″ (Imp. Cyl. & Mod.). **$1,720.00**

Winchester 101 Diamond Grade Target Guns
Similar to the Model 101 except designed for trap and Skeet competition, with tapered and elevated rib, anatomically contoured trigger and internationally-dimensioned stock. Receiver has deep-etched diamond-pattern engraving. Skeet guns available in 12, 20, 28 and 410 with ventilated muzzles to reduce recoil. Trap guns in 12 ga. only; over-under, combination and single-barrel configurations in a variety of barrel lengths with Winchoke system. Straight or Monte Carlo stocks available. Introduced 1982. Manufactured in and imported from Japan by Winchester Group, Olin Corp.
Price: Trap, o/u, standard and Monte Carlo, 30″, 32″. **$1,720.00**
Price: Trap, single barrel, 32″ or 34″ **$1,820.00**
Price: Trap, o/u-single bbl. combo sets **$2,775.00**
Price: Skeet, 12 and 20 . . . . **$1,720.00**
Price: Skeet, 28 and 410 . . . . **$1,720.00**
Price: Four barrel Skeet set (12, 20, 28, 410) **$4,600.00**
Price: Trap Oversingle, 34″, Monte Carlo or std. stock **$1,900.00**

Winchester Model 101 Pigeon Grade
Similar to the Model 101 Field except comes in two styles: Lightweight-Winchoke (12 or 20 ga., six choke tubes for 12 ga., four for 20, 28 ga., 27″, 28″), Featherweight (12 or 20 ga., Imp. Cyl. & Mod., 25½″), all with 3″ chambers. Vent. rib barrel with middle bead, fancy American walnut. Featherweight has English-style stock. Hard case included. Introduced 1983. Manufactured in and imported from Japan by Winchester Group, Olin Corp.
Price: Featherweight **$1,580.00**
Price: Lightweight-Winchoke **$1,675.00**

Consult our Directory pages for
the location of firms mentioned.

Zanoletti 2000 Field

PIETRO ZANOLETTI MODEL 2000 FIELD O-U
Gauge: 12 only.
Barrel: 28″ (Mod. & Full).
Weight: 7 lbs.
Stock: European walnut, checkered grip and fore-end.
Sights: Gold bead front.
Features: Boxlock action with auto ejectors, double triggers; engraved receiver. Imported from Italy by Mandall Shooting Supplies. Introduced 1984.
Price: **$695.00**

CAUTION: PRICES CHANGE. CHECK AT GUNSHOP.

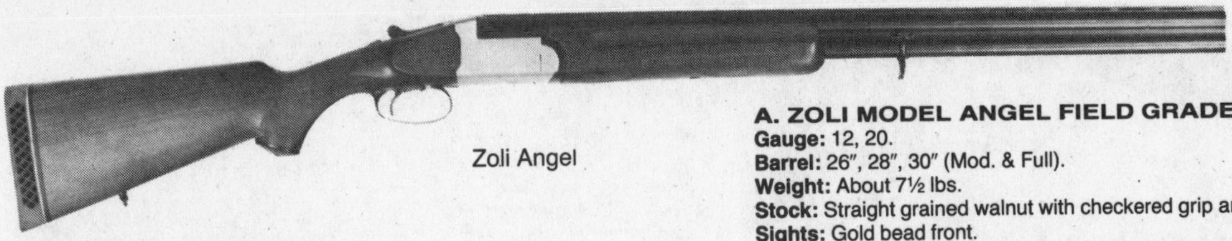

Zoli Angel

A. ZOLI DELFINO S.P. O/U
Gauge: 12 or 20 (3″ chambers).
Barrel: 28″ (Mod. & Full); vent. rib.
Weight: 5½ lbs.
Stock: Walnut. Hand checkered p.g. and fore-end; cheekpiece.
Features: Color case hardened receiver with light engraving; chrome lined barrels; automatic sliding safety; double triggers; ejectors. From Mandall Shooting Supplies.
Price: $795.00

A. ZOLI MODEL ANGEL FIELD GRADE O-U
Gauge: 12, 20.
Barrel: 26″, 28″, 30″ (Mod. & Full).
Weight: About 7½ lbs.
Stock: Straight grained walnut with checkered grip and fore-end.
Sights: Gold bead front.
Features: Boxlock action with single selective trigger, auto ejectors; extra-wide vent. top rib. Imported from Italy by Mandall Shooting Supplies.
Price: $895.00
Price: Condor model $895.00

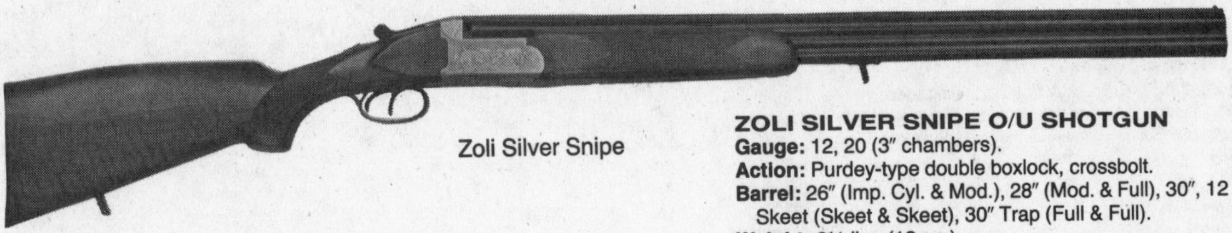

Zoli Silver Snipe

Zoli Golden Snipe O/U Shotgun
Same as Silver Snipe except selective auto. ejectors.
Price: Field $895.00

ZOLI SILVER SNIPE O/U SHOTGUN
Gauge: 12, 20 (3″ chambers).
Action: Purdey-type double boxlock, crossbolt.
Barrel: 26″ (Imp. Cyl. & Mod.), 28″ (Mod. & Full), 30″, 12 only (Mod. & Full); 26″ Skeet (Skeet & Skeet), 30″ Trap (Full & Full).
Weight: 6½ lbs. (12 ga.).
Stock: Hand checkered p.g. and fore-end, European walnut.
Features: Auto. safety (exc. Trap and Skeet), vent rib, single trigger, chrome bores. Imported from Italy by Mandall Shooting Supplies.
Price: Field $795.00

SHOTGUNS—SIDE-BY-SIDES

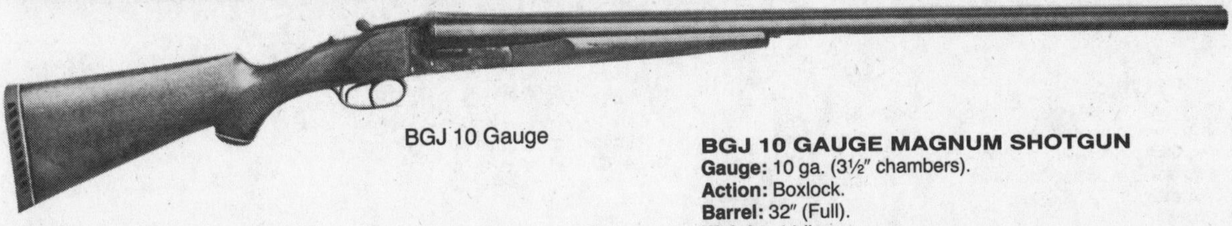

BGJ 10 Gauge

ARMSPORT 1050 SIDE-BY-SIDE SHOTGUNS
Gauge: 12, 20, 410, 3″ chambers.
Barrel: 12 ga.—28″ (Mod. & Full), 20 ga., 410—26″ (Imp. Cyl. & Mod.)
Weight: 5¾-6 lbs.
Stock: European walnut
Features: Double triggers; extractors; silvered, engraved receiver. Introduced 1986. Imported from Italy by Armsport.
Price: 12, 20 ga $399.95
Price: 410 .... $425.00

BGJ 10 GAUGE MAGNUM SHOTGUN
Gauge: 10 ga. (3½″ chambers).
Action: Boxlock.
Barrel: 32″ (Full).
Weight: 11 lbs.
Stock: 14½″x1½″x2⅝″. European walnut, checkered at p.g. and fore-end.
Features: Double triggers; color hardened action, rest blued. Front and center metal beads on matted rib; ventilated rubber recoil pad. Fore-end release has positive Purdey-type mechanism. Imported from Spain by Mandall Shooting Supplies.
Price: $500.00

Bernardelli Series Roma Shotguns
Similar to the Series S. Uberto models except with dummy sideplates to simulate sidelock action. Same gauges and specifications apply.
Price: Roma 3 .... **$1,154.00 to $1,113.92**
Price: As above with ejectors .... **$1,263.00 to $1,243.72**
Price: Roma 4 .... **$1,314.00 to $1,273.22**
Price: As above with ejectors .... **$1,423.00 to $1,401.84**
Price: Roma 6 .... **$1,562.00 to $1,552.88**
Price: As above with ejectors .... **$1,675.00 to $1,682.88**

Bernardelli System Holland H. Side-by-Side
Similar to the Las Palomas model with true sidelock action. Available in 12 gauge only, reinforced breech, three round Purdey locks, automatic ejectors, folding right trigger. Model VB Liscio has color case hardened receiver and sideplates with light engraving, VB and VB Tipo Lusso are silvered and engraved.
Price: VB Liscio .... **$5,700.00 to $5,596.74**
Price: VB .... **$6,400.00 to $6,485.28**
Price: VB Tipo Lusso .... **$7,700.00 to $7,589.76**

BERNARDELLI SERIES S. UBERTO DOUBLES
Gauge: 12, 16, 20, 28; 2¾″, or 3″ chambers.
Barrel: 25⅝″, 26¾″, 28″, 29⅛″ (Mod. & Full).
Weight: 6 to 6½ lbs.
Stock: 14³⁄₁₆″ x 2⅜″ x 1⁹⁄₁₆″ standard dimensions. Select walnut with hand checkering.
Features: Anson & Deeley boxlock action with Purdey locks, choice of extractors or ejectors. Uberto 1 has color case hardened receiver, Uberto 2 and F.S. silvered and differ in amount and quality of engraving. Custom options available. Prices vary with importer and are shown respectively.Imported from Italy by Armes De Chasse and Quality Arms.
Price: S. Uberto 1 .... **$1,081.00 to $1,014.80**
Price: As above with ejectors .... **$1,190.00 to $1,144.60**
Price: S. Uberto 2 .... **$1,130.00 to $1,063.18**
Price: As above with ejectors .... **$1,239.00 to $1,191.80**
Price: S. Uberto F.S. .... **$1,300.00 to $1,243.72**
Price: As above with ejectors .... **$1,409.00 to $1,372.52**

CAUTION: PRICES CHANGE. CHECK AT GUNSHOP.

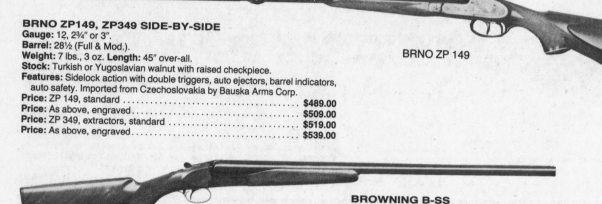

Beretta Model 627 EL

BERETTA 625 SERIES SIDE-BY-SIDES
Gauge: 12 (2¾"), 20 (3").
Action: Beretta patent boxlock; double underlugs and bolts.
Barrel: 12 ga.—26" (Imp. Cyl. & Mod.), 28" (Mod. & Full); 20 ga.—26" (Imp. Cyl. & Mod.), 28" (Mod. & Full).

Weight: 6 lbs. 10 oz. (12 ga.).
Stock: 14⅛"x1⁹⁄₁₆"x2⁹⁄₁₆". "English" straight-type or pistol grip, hand checkered European walnut.
Features: Coil springs throughout action; double triggers (front is hinged); automatic safety; extractors. Concave matted barrel rib. Introduced 1985. Imported by Beretta U.S.A. Corp.
Price: M625, 12 or 20 ga. $935.00
Price: M626, 12 or 20 ga. $1,225.00
Price: M627, from $2,300.00

BRNO ZP149, ZP349 SIDE-BY-SIDE
Gauge: 12, 2¾" or 3".
Barrel: 28½" (Full & Mod.).
Weight: 7 lbs., 3 oz. **Length:** 45" over-all.
Stock: Turkish or Yugoslavian walnut with raised checkpiece.
Features: Sidelock action with double triggers, auto ejectors, barrel indicators, auto safety. Imported from Czechoslovakia by Bauska Arms Corp.
Price: ZP 149, standard $489.00
Price: As above, engraved.............................. $509.00
Price: ZP 349, extractors, standard $519.00
Price: As above, engraved.............................. $539.00

BRNO ZP 149

Browning B-SS

BROWNING B-SS
Gauge: 12, 20 (3").
Action: Top lever break-open action, top tang safety, single trigger.
Barrel: 26" (Mod. and Full or Imp. Cyl. and Mod.), 28" (Mod. and Full), 30" (Full & Full or Mod. & Full).
Weight: 6¾ lbs. (26" bbl., 20 ga.); 7½ lbs. (30" bbl., 12 ga.).
Stock: 14¼"x1⅝"x2½". French walnut, hand checkered. Full p.g., full beavertail fore-end.
Features: Automatic safety, automatic ejectors. Hand engraved receiver, mechanical single selective trigger with barrel selector in rear of trigger guard. Imported from Japan by Browning.
Price: Grade I, 12 or 20 ga. $775.00

Browning B-SS Sidelock
Similar to the B-SS Sporter except gun is a true sidelock. Receiver, fore-end iron, trigger guard, top lever, and tang are all satin grey with rosettes and scroll work. Straight grip stock with checkered butt of French walnut. Double triggers, automatic safety and cocking indicator. Introduced 1984.
Price: 12 or 20 gauge $1,627.50

Browning B-SS Sporter

Browning B-SS Sporter
Similar to standard B-SS except has straight-grip stock and full beavertail fore-end with traditional oil finish. Introduced 1977.
Price: Grade I, 12 or 20 ga. $775.00

Churchill Windsor I

CHURCHILL WINDSOR SIDE-BY-SIDE SHOTGUNS
Gauge: 10 (3½"), 12, 16, 20, 28, 410 (2¾" 16 ga., 3" others).
Barrel: 24" (Mod. & Full), 410 and 20 ga.; 26" (Imp. Cyl. & Mod., Mod. & Full); 28" (Mod. & Full, Skeet & Skeet — 28 ga.); 30" (Full & Full, Mod. & Full); 32" (Full & Full — 10 ga.).
Weight: About 7½ lbs. (12 ga.).
Stock: Hand checkered European walnut with rubber butt pad.
Features: Anson & Deeley boxlock action with silvered and engraved finish; automatic top tang safety; double triggers; beavertail fore-end. Windsor I with extractors only; Windsor II has selective automatic ejectors. Also available in Flyweight versions, 23", 25", fixed or ICT chokes, straight stock. ICT choke tubes also available on Windsor. Imported from Spain by Kassnar. Introduced 1984.

Churchill Regent Side-by-Side Shotguns
Similar to the Windsor Grade except fancy walnut, better checkering and engraving; tapered Churchill rib; 25" (Imp. Cyl. & Mod.) or 28" (Mod. & Full) barrels only; 12 or 20 ga., 2¾" only. Regent VI is full sidelock, with double triggers, automatic selective ejectors, straight English-style stock and splinter fore-end. Imported from Spain by Kassnar. Introduced 1984.
Price: Regent VI. $945.00
Price: Regent VI, ICT $1,084.00

Price: Windor I, 10 ga. $599.00
Price: Windsor I, 12 through 410 ga. .... $449.00 to $465.00
Price: Windsor II, 12 or 20 ga. only.............. $665.00
Price: Windsor II, ICT $729.00

CAUTION: PRICES CHANGE. CHECK AT GUNSHOP.

Hermanos Model 150

DUMOULIN "LIEGE" MODEL DOUBLE
Gauge: 12, 16, 20, 28, 2¾", or 3" chambers.
Barrel: 26" to 32", choked to customer specs.
Weight: 6.4 lbs.
Stock: Circassian or French walnut, to customer specs.
Features: Anson & Deeley boxlock (or sidelock) action. Essentially a custom gun. Imported from Belgium by Midwest Gun Sport.
Price: From **$5,300.00**

CRUCELEGUI HERMANOS MODEL 150 DOUBLE
Gauge: 12, 16 or 20 (2¾" chambers).
Action: Greener triple crossbolt.
Barrel: 20", 26", 28", 30", 32" (Cyl. & Cyl., Full & Full, Mod. & Full, Mod. & Imp. Cyl., Imp. Cyl. & Full, Mod. & Mod.).
Weight: 5 to 7¼ lbs.
Stock: Hand checkered walnut, beavertail fore-end.
Features: Exposed hammers; double triggers; color case hardened receiver; sling swivels; chrome lined bores. Imported from Spain by Mandall Shooting Supplies.
Price: **$399.95**
Price: Model 225 (hammerless version) **$399.95**

Exel Series 200

Exel Models 207, 208, 209, 210 Doubles
Similar to the Models 201, 202, 203 except full sidelock action. Models 207, 208, 209 in 12 ga., 2¾" chambers; 28" (Mod. & Full) for 207 and 208, 26" (Imp. Cyl. & Mod.) for 209, 20 ga., 3", 27" (Mod. & Full) for 210. Selective ejectors, trigger, stock and frame finish to customer specs.
Price: Model 207 . . . . **$611.83**
Price: Model 208, 209, 210 . . . . **$671.52**
Price: Models 211, 212, 213 (similar to above but with better wood, engraving) **$3,100.00**
Price: Model 281, 281A (28 ga., 26" Mod. & Full, Imp. Cyl. & Mod.) . **$471.79**
Price: Model 240, 240A (410, 26" Full & Mod., Imp. Cyl. & Mod.) **$471.79**

EXEL MODELS 201, 202, 203 DOUBLES
Gauge: 12, 2¾" chambers (M201, 202); 20, 3" chambers (M203, M203A).
Barrel: Model 201 — 28" (Full & Mod.); Model 202 — 26" (Imp. Cyl. & Mod.); Model 203 — 27" (Full & Mod.); Model 203A—26" (Imp. Cyl. & Mod.).
Weight: 6½-7 lbs.
Stock: 14⅜" x 1½" x 2½". Walnut, straight or full pistol grip.
Sights: Metal bead front.
Features: Boxlock action with color case hardened finish; double triggers; extractors only; high matted rib; hand checkered stock and fore-end. Made in Spain by Ugartechea; imported by Exel Arms of America.
Price: **$428.91**

Exel Models 204, 205, 206 Doubles
Similar to Models 201, 202, 203 except with silvered and engraved receiver, automatic selective ejectors, single or double triggers. Others specs are the same.
Price: **$626.76**

Ferlib Model FVII

FERLIB MODEL F VII DOUBLE SHOTGUN
Gauge: 12, 20, 28, 410.
Barrel: 25" to 28".
Weight: 5½ lbs. (20 ga.).
Stock: Oil-finished walnut, checkered straight grip and fore-end.
Features: Boxlock action with fine scroll engraved, silvered receiver. Double triggers standard. Introduced 1983. Imported from Italy by Wm. Larkin Moore and Quality Arms, Inc..
Price: 12 or 20 ga. **$3,600.00**
Price: 28 or 410 ga. **$3,550.00**
Price: Extra for single trigger, beavertail fore-end **$310.00**

Garbi Model 51B

GARBI MODEL 51 SIDE-BY-SIDE
Gauge: 12, 16, 20 (2¾" chambers).
Barrel: 28" (Mod. & Full).
Weight: 5½ to 6½ lbs.
Stock: Walnut, to customer specs.
Features: Boxlock action; hand-engraved receiver; hand-checkered stock and fore-end; double triggers; extractors. Introduced 1980. Imported from Spain by L. Joseph Rahn, Inc.
Price: Model 51A, 12 ga., extractors **$540.00**
Price: Model 51B, 12, 16, 20 ga., ejectors **$890.00**

Garbi Model 60

GARBI MODEL 60 SIDE-BY-SIDE
Gauge: 12, 16, 20 (2¾" chambers).
Barrel: 26", 28", 30"; choked to customers specs.
Weight: 5½ to 6½ lbs.
Stock: Select walnut. Dimensions to customer specs.
Features: Sidelock action. Scroll engraving on receiver. Hand checkered stock. Double triggers. Extractors. Imported from Spain by L. Joseph Rahn, Inc.
Price: Model 60A, 12 ga. only **$820.00**
Price: With demi-bloc barrels and ejectors, 12, 16, 20 ga. **$1,195.00**

Garbi Model 71

Garbi Model 62

Similar to Model 60 except choked Mod. & Full, plain receiver with engraved border, demi-bloc barrels, gas exhaust valves, jointed triggers, extractors. Imported from Spain by L. Joseph Rahn.
Price: Model 62A, 12 ga., only $870.00
Price: Model 62B, 12, 16, 20 ga., ejectors $1,170.00

GARBI MODEL 100 DOUBLE

Gauge: 12, 16, 20.
Barrel: 26″, 28″, choked to customer specs.
Weight: 5½ to 7½ lbs.
Stock: 14½x2¼″x1½″. European walnut. Straight grip, checkered butt, classic fore-end.
Features: Sidelock action, automatic ejectors, double triggers standard. Color case-hardened action, coin finish optional. Single trigger; beavertail fore-end, etc. optional. Five other models are available. Imported from Spain by Wm. Larkin Moore.
Price: From $2,100.00

Garbi Model 101 Side-by-Side

Similar to the Garbi Model 100 is available with optional level, file-cut, Churchill or ventilated top rib, and in a 12-ga. pigeon or wildfowl gun. Has Continental-style floral and scroll engraving, select walnut stock. Better overall quality than the Model 100. Imported from Spain by Wm. Larkin Moore.
Price: $3,500.00

Garbi Model 200 Side-by-Side

Similar to the Garbi Model 100 except has barrels of nickel-chrome steel, heavy duty locks, magnum proofed. Very fine continental-style floral and scroll engraving, well figured walnut stock. Other mechanical features remain the same. Imported from Spain by Wm. Larkin Moore.
Price: $4,600.00

GOROSABEL MODEL 503 SIDE-BY-SIDE

Gauge: 12, 16, 20, 28, 410.
Barrel: 26″, 27″, 28″, all standard chokes and combinations.
Stock: Select European walnut, English or pistol grip, sliver or beavertail fore-end; hand checkered.
Features: Anson & Deeley-style boxlock action with scalloped frame and scroll engraving; automatic ejectors. Introduced in U.S. 1986. Imported by Des Moines Imports.
Price: About $959.00
Price: Model 502, as above except less fancy wood, engraving $875.00
Price: Models 500, 501, as above, standard-grade models, about . . . $645.00

GOROSABEL MODEL 505 SIDE-BY-SIDE

Gauge: 12, 20, 2¾″ or 3″ chambers.
Barrel: 26″, 27″, 28″, all standard chokes and combinations
Stock: Select European walnut, English or pistol grip, sliver or beavertail fore-end; hand checkered.
Features: Holland & Holland-style sidelock action; Purdey-style fine scroll and rose engraving. All "Best" gun options. Introduced in U.S. 1986. Imported by Des Moines Imports.
Price: About $1,335.00
Price: Model 504, as above except less fancy wood, has Holland-style large scroll engraving. $995.00

GARBI MODEL 71 DOUBLE

Gauge: 12, 16, 20.
Barrel: 26″, 28″, choked to customer specs.
Weight: 5 lbs., 15 oz. (20 ga.).
Stock: 14½x2¼″x1½″. European walnut. Straight grip, checkered butt, classic fore-end.
Features: Sidelock action, automatic ejectors, double triggers standard. Color case-hardened action, coin finish optional. Five other models are available. Imported from Spain by L. Joseph Rahn and Wm. Larkin Moore.
Price: Model 71, from $1,600.00

GARBI MODEL 102 SHOTGUN

Gauge: 12, 16, 20.
Barrel: 12 ga.-25″ to 30″; 16 & 20 ga.-25″ to 28″. Chokes as specified.
Weight: 20 ga.-5 lbs., 15 oz. to 6 lbs., 4 oz.
Stock: 14½″x2¼x1½″; select walnut.
Features: Holland pattern sidelock ejector with chopper lump barrels, Holland-type large scroll engraving. Double triggers (hinged front) std., non-selective single trigger available. Many options available. Imported from Spain by Wm. Larkin Moore.
Price: From $3,500.00

Garbi Model 103A, B Side-by-Side

Similar to the Garbi Model 100 except has Purdey-type fine scroll and rosette engraving. Better over-all quality than the Model 101. Model 103B has nickel-chrome steel barrels, H&H-type easy opening mechanism; other mechanical details remain the same. Imported from Spain by Wm. Larkin Moore and L. Joseph Rahn, Inc.
Price: Model 103A, from $2,562.00
Price: Model 103B, from $3,400.00

Garbi Model 200

Garbi Model Special Side-by-Side

Similar to the Garbi Model 100 except has best quality wood and metal work. Special game scene engraving with or without gold inlays, fancy figured walnut stock. Imported from Spain by Wm. Larkin Moore.
Price: From $4,600.00

Gorosabel Model 503

Gorosabel Model 504

CAUTION: PRICES CHANGE. CHECK AT GUNSHOP.

LEBEAU-COURALLY MODEL 1225 DOUBLE
Gauge: 12, 20, 28, 2¾", or 3" chambers.
Barrel: 26" to 28", choked to customer specs.
Weight: 6.4 lbs. (12 gauge).
Stock: Grand Luxe walnut, straight English-style, to customer specs.
Features: Holland & Holland sidelock action; automatic ejectors; double trigger; color case-hardened frame with fine English engraving. Imported from Belgium by Midwest Gun Sport.
Price: $9,900.00

Lebeau-Courally Sidelock

LEBEAU-COURALLY SIDELOCK SHOTGUN
Gauge: 12, 16, 20 (standard), 28 (optional).
Barrel: 26" to 30", choked to customer specs.
Weight: 6 lbs., 6 oz. to 8 lbs., 4 oz. (12 ga.)

Mercury Magnum

OMEGA SIDE-BY-SIDE SHOTGUNS
Gauge: 20, 28, 410 (3").
Barrel: 20 ga.—26"(Imp. Cyl. & Mod.); 28 ga.—26" (Mod. & Full); 410—26" (Full & Full).
Weight: 5½ lbs.
Stock: Standard has checkered beechwood, Deluxe has walnut; both have semi-pistol grip.
Features: Blued barrels and receiver; top tang safety. Imported from Italy by Kassnar. Introduced 1984.
Price: Standard.. $270.00 to 313.00
Price: Deluxe $306.00

Navy Model 100

Parker DHE

Consult our Directory pages for the location of firms mentioned.

LEBEAU-COURALLY BOXLOCK SHOTGUN
Gauge: 12, 16, 20, 28.
Barrel: 26" to 30", choked to customer specs.
Weight: 6 lbs., 6 oz. to 8 lbs., 4 oz. (12 ga.)
Stock: Dimensions to customer specs. Select French walnut with hand rubbed oil finish, straight grip (p.g. optional), splinter fore-end (beavertail optional).
Features: Anson & Deeley boxlock with ejectors, Purdey-type fastener; choice of rounded action, with or without sideplates; choice of level rib, file cut or smooth; choice of numerous engraving patterns. Imported from Belgium by Wm. Larkin Moore.
Price: $9,400.00

Stock: Dimensions to customer specs. Best quality French walnut with hand rubbed oil finish, straight grip stock and checkered butt (std.), classic splinter fore-end.
Features: Holland & Holland pattern sidelock ejector double with chopper lump barrels; choice of classic or rounded action; concave or level rib, file cut or smooth; choice of numerous engraving patterns. Can be furnished with H&H type self-opening mechanism. Imported from Belgium by Wm. Larkin Moore.
Price: From $18,700.00

MERCURY MAGNUM DOUBLE BARREL SHOTGUN
Gauge: 10 (3½").
Action: Triple-lock Anson & Deeley type.
Barrel: 32" (Full & Full).
Weight: 10⅛ lbs.
Stock: 14"x1⅝"x2¼" walnut, checkered p.g. stock and beavertail fore-end, recoil pad.
Features: Double triggers, front hinged, auto safety, extractors; safety gas ports, engraved frame. Imported from Spain by Tradewinds.
Price: (10 ga.)... $480.00

NAVY ARMS MODEL 100 FIELD HUNTER
Gauge: 12 and 20, 3" chambers.
Barrel: 28" (Imp. Cyl. & Mod., Mod. & Full).
Weight: About 7 lbs.
Stock: Checkered walnut.
Features: Chrome-lined barrels; engraved hard chrome receiver; gold plated double triggers. Introduced 1985. Imported from Italy by Navy Arms.
Price: Model 100 (extractors)............................. $389.00
Price: Model 150 (ejectors) $464.00

PARKER DHE SIDE-BY-SIDE SHOTGUN
Gauge: 20, 28, 2¾" or 3" chambers.
Barrel: 26" (Imp. Cyl. & Mod., 2¾" chambers), Skeet & Skeet available, 28" (Mod. & Full, 3" chambers only).
Weight: About 6½ lbs. (20 ga.), 5½ lbs. (28 ga.).
Stock: Fancy American walnut, checkered grip and fore-end. Straight stock or pistol grip, splinter or beavertail fore-end; 28 l.p.i. checkering.
Features: Reproduction of the original Parker DHE — most parts interchangeable with original. Double or single selective trigger; checkered skeleton buttplate; selective ejectors; bores hard chromed, excluding choke area. Two-barrel sets available. Hand engraved scroll and scenes on case-hardened frame. Fitted leather trunk included. Introduced 1984. Made by Winchester in Japan. Imported by Parker Div. of Reagent Chemical.
Price: $2,800.00

Parker Hale 645E

PARKER-HALE MODEL "600" SERIES DOUBLES
Gauge: 12, 16, 20, (2¾"), 28, 410 (3").
Barrel: 25", 26", 27", 28" (Imp. Cyl. & Mod., Mod. & Full).
Weight: 12 ga., 6¾-7 lbs.; 20 ga., 5¾-6 lbs.
Stock: 14½"x1½"x2½. Hand checkered walnut with oil finish. "E" (English) models have straight grip, splinter fore-end, checkered butt. "A" (Amercian) modes have p.g. stock, beaver-tail fore-end, butt plate.

PIOTTI MODEL PIUMA SIDE-BY-SIDE
Gauge: 12, 16, 20, 28, 410.
Barrel: 25" to 30" (12 ga.), 25" to 28" (16, 20, 28, 410).
Weight: 5½ to 6¼ lbs. (20 ga.).
Stock: Dimensions to customer specs. Straight grip stock with checkered butt, classic splinter fore-end, hand rubbed oil finish are standard; pistol grip, beavertail fore-end, satin luster finish optional.
Features: Anson & Deeley boxlock ejector double with chopper lump barrels. Level, file-cut rib, light scroll and rosette engraving, scalloped frame. Double triggers with hinged front standard, single non-selective optional. Coin finish standard, color case hardened optional. Imported from Italy by Wm. Larkin Moore.
Price: **$4,000.00**

Piotti King No. 1

PIOTTI KING NO. 1 SIDE-BY-SIDE
Gauge: 12, 16, 20, 28, 410.
Barrel: 25" to 30" (12 ga.), 25" to 28" (16, 20, 28, 410). To customer specs. Chokes as specified.
Weight: 6½ lbs. to 8 lbs. (12 ga., to customer specs.)

Piotti Lunik

Rossi Overland

ROSSI OVERLAND DOUBLE BARREL
Gauge: 12, 20, 410 (3" chambers).
Action: Sidelock with external hammers; Greener crossbolt.
Barrel: 12 ga., 20" (Imp. Cyl., Mod.) 28" (Mod. & Full), 20 ga., 20", 26" (Imp. Cyl. & Mod.), 410 ga., 26" (Full & Full).
Weight: 6½ to 7 lbs.
Stock: Walnut p.g. with beavertail fore-end.
Features: Solid raised matted rib. Exposed hammers. Imported by Interarms.
Price: 12 or 20 .... **$267.00**
Price: 410 .... **$272.00**

Features: Boxlock action; silvered, engraved action; auto. safety; ejectors or extractors. E-models have double triggers, concave rib (XXV models have Churchill-type rib); A-models have single, non-selective trigger, raised matted rib. Made in Spain by Ugartechea. Imported by Precision Sports. Introduced 1986.
Price: 640E (12, 16, 20; 26", 28"), extractors **$449.95**
Price: 640E (28, 410; 27" only), extractors **$499.95**
Price: 640A (12, 16, 20; 26", 28"), extractors **$549.96**
Price: 645E (12, 16, 20; 26", 28"), with ejectors **$559.95**
Price: 645E (28, 410; 27"), with ejectors **$639.95**
Price: 645A (12, 16, 20; 26", 28"), with ejectors **$669.95**
Price: 645E-XXV (12, 16, 20; 25"), with ejectors **$589.95**
Price: 670E (12, 16, 20, 26", 28") sidelock, with ejectors **$2,450.00**
Price: 670E (28, 410; 27") sidelock, with ejectors **$2,600.00**
Price: 680E-XXV (12, 16, 20; 25") sidelock, ejectors, case-color action **$2,350.00**
Price: 680E-XXV (28, 410; 25") sidelock, ejectors, case-color action **$2,500.00**

Piotti Model Monte Carlo Side-by-Side
Similar to the Piotti King No. 1 except has Purdey-style scroll and rosette engraving, no gold inlays, over-all workmanship not as finely detailed. Other mechanical specifications remain the same. Imported from Italy by Wm. Larkin Moore.
Price: **$8,750.00**

Piotti Model King Extra Side-by-Side
Similar to the Piotti King No. 1 except highest quality wood and metal work. Choice of either bulino game scene engraving or game scene engraving with gold inlays. Engraved and signed by a master engraver. Exhibition grade wood. Other mechanical specifications remain the same. Imported from Italy by Wm. Larkin Moore.
Price: **$13,700.00**

Stock: Dimensions to customer specs. Finely figured walnut; straight grip with checkered butt with classic splinter fore-end and hand-rubbed oil finish standard. Pistol grip, beavertail fore-end, satin luster finish optional.
Features: Holland & Holland pattern sidelock action, auto. ejectors. Double trigger with front trigger hinged standard; non-selective single trigger optional. Coin finish standard; color case-hardened optional. Top rib: level, file cut standard; concave, ventilated optional. Very fine, full coverage scroll engraving with small floral bouquets, gold crown in top lever, name in gold, and gold crest in fore-end. Imported from Italy by Wm. Larkin Moore.
Price: **$10,900.00**

Piotti Model Lunik Side-by-Side
Similar to the Piotti King No. 1 except better over-all quality. Has Renaissance-style large scroll engraving in relief, gold crown in top lever, gold name, and gold crest in fore-end. Best quality Holland & Holland-pattern sidelock ejector double with chopper lump (demi-bloc) barrels. Other mechanical specifications remain the same. Imported from Italy by Wm. Larkin Moore.
Price: **$11,600.00**

ROSSI "SQUIRE" DOUBLE BARREL
Gauge: 12, 20, 410 (3" chambers).
Barrel: 12 — 28" (Mod. & Full); 20 ga.—26" (Imp. Cyl. & Mod.), 28" (Mod. & Full); 410—26" (Full & Full).
Weight: About 7½ lbs.
Stock: Walnut finished hardwood.
Features: Double triggers, raised matted rib, beavertail fore-end. Massive twin underlugs mesh with synchronized sliding bolts. Introduced 1978. Imported by Interarms.
Price: 12 or 20 ga. **$292.00**
Price: 410 .... **$297.00**

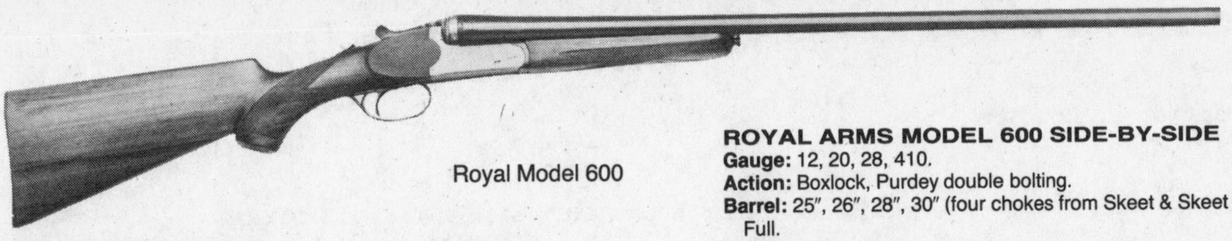

Royal Model 600

ROYAL ARMS MODEL 800 SIDE-BY-SIDE
Gauge: 12, 20, 28, 410.
Action: True quick detachable bar spring sidelocks.
Barrel: 24″, 26″, 28″ (Mod. & Full, Imp. Cyl. & Mod., Imp. Cyl. & Full).
Weight: 7 lbs.
Stock: 15″ x 2½″ x 1½″. Fancy select European walnut; straight grip with fine-line checkering, classic fore-end and butt.
Features: Holland & Holland auto. selective ejectors; gated and fully scroll engraved grayed action; cocking indicators; articulated front trigger; Churchill rib; vented firing pins; auto safety. Introduced 1985. Imported from Spain by Royal Arms International.
Price: All gauges **$899.00**

ROYAL ARMS MODEL 600 SIDE-BY-SIDE
Gauge: 12, 20, 28, 410.
Action: Boxlock, Purdey double bolting.
Barrel: 25″, 26″, 28″, 30″ (four chokes from Skeet & Skeet through Imp. Cyl. & Full.
Weight: 7 lbs., 12 ozs.
Stock: Oil finished European walnut; checkered grip and fore-end.
Features: Double triggers; vent rib; automatic safety; chrome lined barrels. Introduced 1985. Imported from Spain by Royal Arms International.
Price: **$329.95**
Price: Model 600AE (3″, 12 ga. only, single selective trigger, selective auto ejectors) **$419.95**

Savage-Fox B-SE

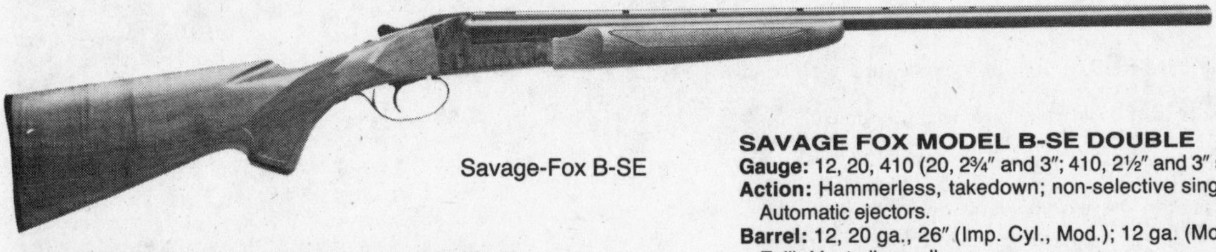

SAVAGE-STEVENS MODEL 311 DOUBLE
Gauge: 12, 20, 410 (12, 20 and 410, 3″ chambers).
Action: Top lever, hammerless; double triggers, auto. top tang safety.
Barrel: 12, 20 ga. 26″ (Imp. Cyl., Mod.); 12 ga. 28″ (Mod., Full); 12 ga. 30″ (Mod., Full); 410 ga. 26″ (Full, Full).
Weight: 7-8 lbs. (30″ bbl). **Length:** 45¾″ over-all.
Stock: 14″x1½″x2½″. Walnut finish, p.g., fluted comb.
Features: Box-type blued frame.
Price: **$278.00**

W&C SCOTT BLENHEIM GAME GUN
Gauge: 12, 16, 20.
Barrel: 25″, 26″, 27″, 28″, 30″ (chokes to order); concave rib standard, flat or Churchill optional.
Weight: 6½ lbs.
Stock: Measurements to order. French walnut with 28 l.p.i. checkering (32 l.p.i. checkering and exhibition grade wood on Deluxe model).
Features: Best quality bar action sidelock ejector, finest rose and scroll engraving; gold name plate. Introduced 1985. Imported from England by British Guns.
Price: Blenheim Deluxe, 12 or 16 ga. **$16,500.00**
Price: As above, 20 ga. **$20,500.00**

SAVAGE FOX MODEL B-SE DOUBLE
Gauge: 12, 20, 410 (20, 2¾″ and 3″; 410, 2½″ and 3″ shells).
Action: Hammerless, takedown; non-selective single trigger; auto. safety. Automatic ejectors.
Barrel: 12, 20 ga., 26″ (Imp. Cyl., Mod.); 12 ga. (Mod., Full); 410, 26″ (Full, Full). Vent. rib on all.
Weight: 12 ga. 7 lbs., 16 ga. 6¾ lbs., 20 ga. 6½ lbs., 410 ga. 6¼ lbs.
Stock: 14″x1½″x2½″. Walnut, checkered p.g. and beavertail fore-end.
Features: Decorated, blued frame; white bead front and middle sights.
Price: **$467.06**
Price: Model B (double triggers) **$369.00**

W&C Scott Bowood DeLuxe Game Gun
Similar to the Chatsworth Grande Luxe except less ornate metal and wood work; checkered 24 lpi at fore-end and pistol grip. Imported from England by L. Joseph Rahn and British Guns.
Price: 12 or 16 ga. **$5,900.00**
Price: 20 or 28 ga. **$6,500.00**

W&C Scott Kinmount Game Gun
Similar to the Bowood DeLuxe Game Gun except less ornate engraving and wood work; checkered 20 lpi; other details essentially the same. Imported from England by L. Joseph Rahn and British Guns.
Price: 12 or 16 ga. **$5,175.00**
Price: 20 or 28 ga. **$5,500.00**

W&C Scott Chatsworth

W&C SCOTT CHATSWORTH GRANDE LUXE DOUBLE
Gauge: 12, 16, 20, 28.
Barrel: 25″, 26″, 27″, 28″, 30″ (chokes to order); concave rib standard, Churchill or flat rib optional.
Weight: About 6½ lbs. (12 ga.).
Stock: 14¾″ x 1½″ x 2¼″, or made to customer specs. French walnut with 32 lpi checkering.

Features: Entirely hand fitted; boxlock action (sideplates optional); English scroll engraving; gold name plate shield in stock. Imported from England by L. Joseph Rahn and British Guns.
Price: 12 or 16 ga. **$7,650.00**
Price: 20 or 28 ga. **$7,800.00**

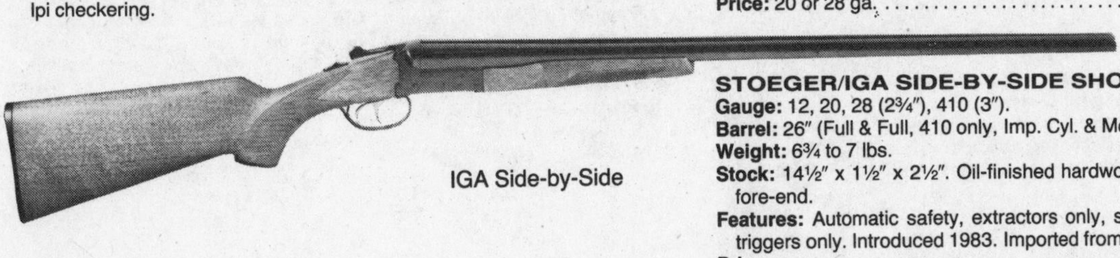

IGA Side-by-Side

STOEGER/IGA SIDE-BY-SIDE SHOTGUN
Gauge: 12, 20, 28 (2¾″), 410 (3″).
Barrel: 26″ (Full & Full, 410 only, Imp. Cyl. & Mod.), 28″ (Mod. & Full).
Weight: 6¾ to 7 lbs.
Stock: 14½″ x 1½″ x 2½″. Oil-finished hardwood. Checkered pistol grip and fore-end.
Features: Automatic safety, extractors only, solid matted barrel rib. Double triggers only. Introduced 1983. Imported from Brazil by Stoeger Industries.
Price: **$229.95**
Price: Coach Gun, 12 or 20 ga., 20″ bbls. **$224.95**

VENTURA REGIS MODEL DOUBLE
Gauge: 12 (2¾"), 20 (3"), 28 (2¾"), 410 (3").
Barrel: 26", 28".
Weight: 6½ lbs. (12 ga.)
Stock: Select figured French walnut, hand checkered English straight or p.g. stock with slender beavertail fore-end.
Features: H & H sidelock with intercepting safeties and triple locks; single selective or double triggers; automatic ejectors; floral engraving. Options include second barrel set, leather trunk case. Introduced 1986. Imported from Italy by Ventura Imports.
Price: .... **$1,448.00 to $1,596.00**

Ventura Regis

SOVEREIGN SIDE-BY-SIDE SHOTGUN
Gauge: 12 or 20, 3" chambers.
Barrel: 28" (Mod. or Full).
Weight: 6 lbs.
Stock: European walnut with checkered p.g. and fore-end.
Features: Chrome-lined bores, automatic safety; chromed, engraved action; double triggers. Introduced 1986. Imported from Italy by Southern Gun & Tackle.
Price: **$335.95**

VENTURA VICTRIX MODEL DOUBLE
Gauge: 12 (2¾"), 20 (3"), 28 (2¾"), 410 (3").
Barrel: 26", 28".
Weight: 6½ lbs. (12 ga.).
Stock: French walnut with hand-checkered p.g. or straight English stock, slender beavertail fore-end.
Features: Anson & Deeley boxlock with triple locks; single selective or double triggers; automatic ejectors. Optional screw-in chokes, leather trunk case. Introduced 1986. Imported from Italy by Ventura Imports.
Price: .... **$796.00 to $876.00**
Price: Victrix Extra Lusso (as above with select wood, full floral engraving) .... **$1,048.00 to $1,148.00**

Ventura Victrix

Winchester Model 23

WINCHESTER MODEL 23 PIGEON GRADE LIGHTWEIGHT
Gauge: 12, 20, 3" chambers
Barrel: 25½" (Imp. Cyl. & Mod.).
Weight: 6¾ lbs. (12 ga.).
Stock: High grade American walnut with English-style straight grip, semi-beavertail fore-end.
Features: Mechanical trigger; tapered ventilated rib; selective ejectors. Receiver, top lever and trigger guard have silver-gray finish with engraved bird scenes. Comes with hard case. Introduced 1981. Manufactured in and imported from Japan by Winchester Group, Olin Corp.
Price: **$1,420.00**

Winchester 23 Winchoke

Winchester Model 23 Pigeon Grade Winchoke
Same features as Model 23 Pigeon Grade Lightweight except has 25½" barrels with interchangeable Winchoke tubes, pistol grip stock. Six choke tubes are supplied with 12 ga. (Skeet, Imp. Cyl., Mod., Imp. Mod., Full, Extra Full), four with 20 ga. (Skeet, Imp. Cyl., Mod., Full). Comes with hard case. Introduced 1983.
Price: **$1,460.00**

Winchester 23 Classic

Winchester Model 23 Classic
Similar to the Model 23 Pigeon Grade Winchoke except has fancy grade American walnut stock with grip cap, 26" barrel choked Imp. Cyl. & Mod. for 12, 20, 28 gauge, Full & Mod. for 410. Blued receiver with scroll engraving, gold inlay on bottom of receiver: pheasant for 12 and 20 gauge; quail on 28 and 410. Ebony inlay in fore-end, gold-initial plate in stock. Introduced 1986.
Price: 12 and 20 gauge **$1,750.00**
Price: 28 and 410 gauge **$1,850.00**

Winchester Model 23 Light Duck
Same basic features as the standard Model 23 Pigeon Grade except has plain, blued frame, 28" barrels choked Full and Full; 20 ga.; 3" chambers. Comes with hard case. Matching serial numbers to previously issued Heavy Duck. Introduced 1983.
Price: **$1,650.00**
Price: Golden Quail (12 ga., 25½", Imp. Cyl. & Mod.) **$1,790.00**
Price: Custom Two Barrel Set (20, 28 ga. bbls., full fancy walnut, leather luggage-style case) **$4,650.00**

CAUTION: PRICES CHANGE. CHECK AT GUNSHOP.

Browning BT-99

EXEL MODEL 51 FOLDING SHOTGUN
Gauge: 410, 3″.
Barrel: 26″ (Mod. & Full).
Weight: 4 lbs.
Stock: Folding. Splinter fore-end.
Features: Non-ejector; case-hardened frame; exposed hammers. Introduced 1985. Imported from Spain by Exel Arms.
Price: $217.00

BROWNING BT-99 COMPETITION TRAP SPECIAL
Gauge: 12 gauge only (2¾″).
Action: Top lever break-open, hammerless.
Barrel: 32″ or 34″ with ¹¹⁄₃₂″ wide high post floating vent. rib. Comes with Invector choke tubes.
Weight: 8 lbs. (32″ bbl.).
Stock: French walnut; hand checkered, full pistol grip, full beavertail fore-end; recoil pad. Trap dimensions with M.C. 14⅜″x1⅜″x1⅜″x2″.
Sights: Ivory front and middle beads.
Features: Gold plated trigger with 3½-lb. pull, deluxe trap-style recoil pad, auto ejector, no safety. Available with either Monte Carlo or standard stock. Imported from Japan by Browning.
Price: Grade I Invector $876.50

FIE Hamilton & Hunter

F.I.E. "S.S.S." SINGLE BARREL
Gauge: 12, 20, 410 (3″).
Action: Button-break on trigger guard.
Barrel: 18½″ (Cyl.).
Weight: 6½ lbs.
Stock: Walnut finished hardwood, full beavertail fore-end.
Features: Exposed hammer. Automatic ejector. Imported from Brazil by F.I.E. Corp.
Price: $99.95

F.I.E. "HAMILTON & HUNTER" SINGLE BARREL
Gauge: 12, 20, 410 (3″).
Barrel: 12 ga. & 20 ga. 28″ (Full); 410 ga. (Full).
Weight: 6½ lbs.
Stock: Walnut stained hardwood, beavertail fore-end.
Sights: Metal bead front.
Features: Trigger guard button is pushed to open action. Exposed hammer, auto ejector, three-piece takedown. Imported from Brazil by F.I.E. Corp.
Price: $89.95
Price: Youth model $89.95

Ithaca 5E Single

ITHACA 5E GRADE SINGLE BARREL TRAP GUN
Gauge: 12 only.
Action: Top lever break open hammerless, dual locking lugs.
Barrel: 32″ or 34″, rampless vent. rib.
Stock: (14½″x1½″x1⅞″). Select walnut, checkered p.g. and beavertail fore-end, p.g. cap, recoil pad, Monte Carlo comb, cheekpiece. Cast-on, cast-off or extreme deviation from standard stock dimensions $100 extra. Reasonable deviation allowed without extra charge.
Features: Frame, top lever and trigger guard extensively engraved and gold inlaid. Gold name plate in stock.
Price: Custom made $7,000.00
Price: Dollar Grade. $9,700.00

Marlin Model 55

LJUTIC MONO GUN SINGLE BARREL
Gauge: 12 ga. only.
Barrel: 34″, choked to customer specs; hollow-milled rib, 35½″ sight plane.
Weight: Approx. 9 lbs.
Stock: To customer specs. Oil finish, hand checkered.
Features: Totally custom made. Pull or release trigger; removable trigger guard contains trigger and hammer mechanism; Ljutic pushbutton opener on front of trigger guard. From Ljutic Industries.
Price: $3,695.00
Price: With Olympic Rib, custom 32″ barrel $3,795.00
Price: As above with screw-in chokes. $3,995.00

MARLIN MODEL 55 GOOSE GUN BOLT ACTION
Gauge: 12 only, (3″ mag. or 2¾″).
Action: Bolt action, thumb safety, detachable 2-shot clip. Red cocking indicator.
Barrel: 36″, Full choke.
Weight: 8 lbs. **Length:** 56¾″ over-all.
Stock: Walnut-finished hardwood, p.g., ventilated recoil pad, leather strap & swivels. Mar-Shield® finish.
Features: Swivels and leather carrying strap. Brass bead front sight, U-groove rear sight.
Price: $180.95

SHOTGUNS—BOLT ACTIONS & SINGLE SHOTS

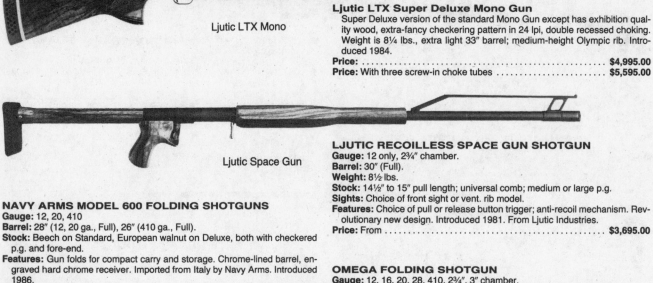

Ljutic LTX Mono

Ljutic Space Gun

Ljutic LTX Super Deluxe Mono Gun
Super Deluxe version of the standard Mono Gun except has exhibition quality wood, extra-fancy checkering pattern in 24 lpi, double recessed choking. Weight is 8¼ lbs., extra light 33″ barrel; medium-height Olympic rib. Introduced 1984.
Price: **$4,995.00**
Price: With three screw-in choke tubes **$5,595.00**

LJUTIC RECOILLESS SPACE GUN SHOTGUN
Gauge: 12 only, 2¾″ chamber.
Barrel: 30″ (Full).
Weight: 8½ lbs.
Stock: 14½″ to 15″ pull length; universal comb; medium or large p.g.
Sights: Choice of front sight or vent. rib model.
Features: Choice of pull or release button trigger; anti-recoil mechanism. Revolutionary new design. Introduced 1981. From Ljutic Industries.
Price: From **$3,695.00**

NAVY ARMS MODEL 600 FOLDING SHOTGUNS
Gauge: 12, 20, 410
Barrel: 28″ (12, 20 ga., Full), 26″ (410 ga., Full).
Stock: Beech on Standard, European walnut on Deluxe, both with checkered p.g. and fore-end.
Features: Gun folds for compact carry and storage. Chrome-lined barrel, engraved hard chrome receiver. Imported from Italy by Navy Arms. Introduced 1986.
Price: Standard model **$158.00**
Price: Deluxe model **$165.00**

OMEGA FOLDING SHOTGUN
Gauge: 12, 16, 20, 28, 410, 2¾″, 3″ chamber.
Barrel: 410 — 26″ (Full); 12, 16, 20, 28 — 28″ (Full); 12 — 30″ (Full).
Stock: Standard has checkered beechwood, Deluxe has checkered walnut.
Sights: Metal bead front.
Features: Standard model has matte chrome receiver, top opening lever; Deluxe has blued receiver, vent. rib. Both guns fold for storage and transport. Imported from Italy by Kassnar. Introduced 1984.
Price: Standard **$185.00**
Price: Deluxe **$242.00**

Omega Single Barrel

OMEGA SINGLE BARREL SHOTGUN
Gauge: 12 (2¾″), 20, 410 (3″).
Barrel: 12 ga.—26″ (Imp.Cyl.), 28″ (Mod.), 28″, 30″ (Full); 20 ga.—26″ (Imp. Cyl.), 28″ (Mod., Full); 410—26″ (Full).
Weight: About 5½ lbs.
Stock: Indonesian walnut.
Features: Rebounding hammer; top lever breaks to either side. Imported by Kassnar Imports, Inc. Introduced 1986.
Price: **$89.00**

SOVEREIGN FOLDING SINGLE BARREL
Gauge: 12, 16, 20, 410, 3″ chamber.
Barrel: 28″ (12, 20, Full or Mod.) 28″ (16, Full) 26″ (410, Full).
Weight: 6 lbs.
Stock: Walnut finished hardwood; cut checkered p.g., fore-end.
Features: Chrome lined barrel, engraved and plated receiver; tang safety; bottom opening lever. Introduced 1986. Imported by Southern Gun & Tackle.
Price: **$94.95**

SHOTGUNS—MILITARY & POLICE

Benelli Super 90

BENELLI SUPER 90 SHOTGUN
Gauge: 12, 3″ chamber, 7-shot magazine.
Barrel: 19¾″ (Cyl.).
Weight: 7 lbs., 4 oz. **Length:** 39¾″ over-all.
Stock: High-impact polymer with sling loop in side of butt; rubberized pistol grip on optional SWAT stock.
Sights: Post front, buckhorn rear adj. for w.
Features: Alloy receiver with rotating locking lug bolt; matte finish; automatic shell release lever. Comes with carrier for speed loading and magazine reducer plug. Optional vent. rib and interchangeable barrels available. Introduced 1986. Imported by Heckler & Koch, Inc.
Price: **$539.00**
Price: Optional pistol grip stock............................... **$76.00**

CAUTION: PRICES CHANGE. CHECK AT GUNSHOP.

F.I.E. SPAS 12

F.I.E. SPAS 12 PUMP/AUTO ASSAULT SHOTGUN
Gauge: 12, 2¾".
Barrel: 21½". Barrel threaded for SPAS choke tubes.
Weight: 9.6 lbs. **Length:** 31¾" (stock folded).

Stock: Folding metal or optional fixed composition.
Sights: Blade front, aperture rear.
Features: Functions as pump and/or gas-operated auto. Has 8-shot magazine. Parkerized alloy receiver, chrome lined bore, resin pistol grip and pump handle. Made in Italy by Franchi. Introduced 1983. Imported by FIE Corp.
Price: $599.95
Price: Mod. or Full choke tube $34.95
Price: Optional fixed stock $64.95

Ithaca 37 M&P

ITHACA MODEL 37 M & P SHOTGUN
Gauge: 12, 2¾" chamber, 5-shot and 8-shot magazine.
Barrel: 18½" (Cyl.), 20" (Cyl.).
Weight: 6½ lbs.
Stock: Oil-finished walnut with grooved walnut pump handle.
Sights: Bead front.
Features: Metal parts are Parkerized. Available with vertical hand grip instead of full butt.
Price: 5-shot, Parkerized, 20" $380.00
Price: 8-shot, Parkerized, 20" only $400.00
Price: Handgrip stock, 5-shot, 18½" $405.00
Price: Handgrip stock, 8-shot, 20" $425.00
Price: M&P II, Handgrip with buttstock $370.00

Ithaca Model 37 LAPD
Similar to the Model 37 DSPS except comes with sling, swivels, sling, rubber recoil pad. Parkerized finish. Rifle-type sights, checkered pistol grip stock, 5-shot magazine.
Price: $430.00

Ithaca 37 DSPS

Ithaca Model 37 DSPS Shotgun
Law enforcement version of the Model 37 Deerslayer. Designed primarily for shooting rifled slugs but equally effective with buckshot. Available in either 5- or 8-shot models. Has 20" barrel, oil-finished stock, adjustable rifle-type sights.
Price: Parkerized, 5-shot $397.00
Price: Parkerized 8-shot $417.00
Price: With Handgrip and buttstock (DSPS II) $407.00

Ithaca Mag-10 Roadblocker

ITHACA MAG-10 ROADBLOCKER
Gauge: 10, 3½" chamber.
Barrel: 22" (Cyl.).

Weight: 10¾ lbs.
Stock: Walnut stock and fore-end, oil finish.
Sights: Bead front.
Features: Non-glare finish on metal parts. Uses Ithaca's Countercoil gas system. Rubber recoil pad. Vent. rib or plain barrel.
Price: Plain barrel $741.00
Price: Vent rib barrel $771.00

Mossberg 500

MOSSBERG MODEL 500 SECURITY SHOTGUNS
Gauge: 12, 20 (2¾"), 410 (3").
Barrel: 18½", 20" (Cyl.).
Weight: 5½ lbs. (410), 7 lbs. (12 ga.).
Stock: Walnut-finished hardwood; synthetic on some models, or folding metal.
Sights: Rifle-type front and rear or metal bead front.
Features: Available in 6- or 8-shot models. Top-mounted safety, double action slide bars, sling swivels, rubber recoil pad. Blue, Parkerized or electroless nickel finishes. Price list not complete—contact Mossberg for full list.
Price: 12 ga., 6-shot, 18½", blue, bead sight, about $178.95
Price: As above, Parkerized, about $215.00
Price: As above, nickel, about $240.00
Price: 12 ga., 8-shot, 20" Parkerized, rifle sights, about $218.00
Price: 20 ga., 6-shot, 18½", blue, bead sight, about $202.00
Price: Model 500 US, Parkerized finish, handguard, about $220.00
Price: Model 500 ATP, blued, bayonet lug, sling, about $245.00

Mossberg Cruiser Persuader Shotgun
Similar to the Model 500 Security guns except fitted with the "Cruiser" pistol grip. Grip and fore-end are solid black. Available in either blue or electroless nickel; 12 gauge only with 18½" (6-shot) or 20" (8-shot) barrel. Folding stock. Muzzle cut with "Muzzle Brake" slots to reduce recoil. Comes with extra long black web sling. Weight is 5¾ lb. (18½"), 6 lb. (20"). Over-all length is 28" with 18½" barrel.
Price: 6-shot, 18½", blue, about $200.00
Price: As above, nickel, about $240.00
Price: 8-shot, 20", blue, about $215.00
Price: As above, nickel, about $240.00

SHOTGUNS—MILITARY & POLICE

Mossberg 500 Bullpup

MOSSBERG 500 BULLPUP
Gauge: 12, 2¾", 6 or 8 shot.
Barrel: 18½", 20".
Weight: NA. **Length:** NA.
Stock: Bullpup design of high-impact plastics.
Sights: Fixed, mounted in carrying handle.
Features: Uses the M500 pump shotgun action. Introduced 1986.
Price: .... **NA**

MOSSBERG 3000 SECURITY SHOTGUN
Gauge: 12, 2¾", 5-shot magazine.
Barrel: 18", 20".
Weight: 6¾ lbs. **Length:** 38¾" over-all (18½" bbl.).
Stock: Plastic Speedfeed (black or camo), folding metal, or pistol grip only.
Sights: Bead front or rifle sights.
Features: Blue/black, Parkerized/camo, Parkerized/black metal and stock finishes.
Price: .... **NA**

Remington 870 Police

REMINGTON MODEL 870P POLICE SHOTGUN
Gauge: 12, 3" chamber.
Barrel: 18", 20" (Police Cyl.), 20" (Imp. Cyl.).
Weight: About 7 lbs.
Stock: Lacquer-finished hardwood or folding stock.
Sights: Metal bead front or rifle sights.
Features: Solid steel receiver, double-action slide bars.
Price: Wood stock, 18" or 20", bead sight, about **$324.00**
Price: Wood stock, 20", rifle sights, about **$349.00**

Savage 69-R/69-RXL

SAVAGE MODEL 69-RXL PUMP SHOTGUN
Gauge: 12 only, 3" chamber.
Barrel: 18¼" (Cyl.).
Weight: 6½ lbs. **Length:** 39" over-all.
Stock: Hardwood, tung-oil finish.
Sights: Bead front.
Features: Top tang safety, 7-shot magazine. Stock has fluted comb and full pistol grip, ventilated rubber pad. QD swivel studs. Introduced 1982.
Price: Either model **$208.39**

STEVENS MODEL 311-R GUARD GUN DOUBLE
Gauge: 12 ga.
Barrel: 18¼" (Cyl. & Cyl.).
Weight: 6¾ lbs. **Length:** 35¼" over-all.
Stock: Hardwood, tung-oil finish.
Sights: Bead front.
Features: Top tang safety, double triggers, color case-hardened frame, blue barrels. Ventilated rubber recoil pad. Introduced 1982.
Price: **$278.00**

Striker 12

STRIKER 12 SPECIAL PURPOSE SHOTGUN
Gauge: 12, 2¾", 12-shot capacity.
Barrel: 18" rifled or smooth, other lengths on request.
Weight: 9 lbs.
Stock: Folding metal buttstock, composition p.g. and front grip.
Features: Semi-auto action; threaded, free-floated barrel of stainless or ordnance steel; sight base designed for optional Armson or laser sight. Made in U.S. Introduced 1986. From Pennsylvania Arms.
Price: **$799.95**

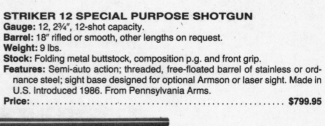

Winchester Defender

WINCHESTER DEFENDER PUMP GUN
Gauge: 12, 3" chamber, 5 or 8-shot capacity.
Barrel: 18" (Cyl.).
Weight: 6¾ lbs. **Length:** 38⅝" over-all.
Stock: Walnut finished hardwood stock and ribbed fore-end.
Sights: Metal bead front.
Features: Cross-bolt safety, front-locking rotating bolt, twin action slide bars. Black rubber butt pad. Made under license by U.S. Repeating Arms Co.
Price: 8-shot, about **$242.80**
Price: 5-shot, about **$236.64**
Price: As above with rifle sights, about **$252.36**

Winchester Pistol Grip Pump Security Shotguns
Same as regular Security Series but with pistol grip and fore-end of high-impact resistant ABS plastic with non-glare black finish. Introduced 1984.
Price: Pistol Grip Defender, about **$242.80**

Winchester "Stainless Marine" Pump Gun
Same as the Defender except has bright chrome finish, stainless-steel barrel, rifle-type sights only. Has special fore-end cap for easy cleaning and inspection.
Price: About **$416.60**

CAUTION: PRICES CHANGE. CHECK AT GUNSHOP.

The following pages catalog the black powder arms currently available to U.S. shooters. These range from quite precise replicas of historically significant arms to totally new designs created expressly to give the black powder shooter the benefits of modern technology.

Most of the replicas are imported, and many are available from more than one source. Thus examples of a given model such as the 1860 Army revolver or Zouave rifle purchased from different importers may vary in price, finish and fitting. Most of them bear proof marks, indicating that they have been test fired in the proof house of their country of origin.

A list of the importers and the retail price range are included with the description for each model. Many local dealers handle more than one importer's products, giving the prospective buyer an opportunity to make his own judgment in selecting a black powder gun. Most importers have catalogs available free or at nominal cost, and some are well worth having for the useful information on black powder shooting they provide in addition to their detailed descriptions and specifications of the guns.

A number of special accessories are also available for the black powder shooter. These include replica powder flasks, bullet moulds, cappers and tools, as well as more modern devices to facilitate black powder cleaning and maintenance. Ornate presentation cases and even detachable shoulder stocks are also available for some black powder pistols from their importers. Again, dealers or the importers will have catalogs.

The black powder guns are arranged in four sections: Single Shot Pistols, Revolvers, Muskets & Rifles, and Shotguns. The guns within each section are arranged roughly by date of the original, with the oldest first. Thus the 1836 Paterson replica leads off the revolver section, and flintlocks precede percussion arms in the other sections.

BLACK POWDER SINGLE SHOT PISTOLS—FLINT & PERCUSSION

Scottish Black Watch

BLACK WATCH SCOTCH PISTOL
Caliber: 577 (.550" round ball).
Barrel: 7", smoothbore.
Weight: 1½ lbs. **Length:** 12" over-all.
Stock: Brass.
Sights: None.
Features: Faithful reproduction of this military flintlock. From Dixie.
Price: $135.00

Dixie Charleville

CHARLEVILLE FLINTLOCK PISTOL
Caliber: 69, (.680" round ball).
Barrel: 7½".
Weight: 48 oz. **Length:** 13½" over-all.
Stock: Walnut.
Sights: None.
Features: Brass frame, polished steel barrel, iron belt hook, brass buttcap and backstrap. Replica of original 1777 pistol. Imported by Dixie.
Price: $135.00

Dixie Queen Anne

DIXIE QUEEN ANNE FLINTLOCK PISTOL
Caliber: 50 (.490" round ball).
Barrel: 7½", smoothbore.
Stock: Walnut.
Sights: None.
Features: Browned steel barrel, fluted brass trigger guard, brass mask on butt. Lockplate left in the white. Made by Pedersoli in Italy. Introduced 1983. Imported by Dixie Gun Works.
Price: $99.95

Lyman Plains Pistol

LYMAN PLAINS PISTOL
Caliber: 50 or 54.
Barrel: 8", 1-in-30" twist, both calibers.
Weight: 50 oz. **Length:** 15" over-all.
Stock: Walnut half-stock.
Sights: Blade front, square notch rear adj. for windage.
Features: Polished brass trigger guard and ramrod tip, color case-hardened coil spring lock, spring-loaded trigger, stainless steel nipple, blackened iron furniture. Hooked patent breech, detachable belt hook. Introduced 1981. From Lyman Products.
Price: Finished $139.95
Price: Kit $109.95

HARPER'S FERRY 1806 PISTOL

Caliber: 58 (.570" round ball).
Barrel: 10".
Weight: 40 oz. **Length:** 16" over-all.
Stock: Walnut.
Sights: Fixed.
Features: Case hardened lock, brass mounted browned bbl. Replica of the first U.S. Gov't.-made flintlock pistol. Imported by Navy Arms, Dixie.
Price: .... $135.00 to $182.00

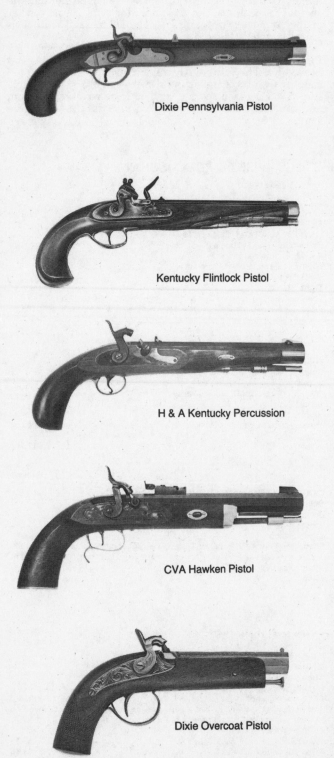

Dixie Pennsylvania Pistol

Kentucky Flintlock Pistol

H & A Kentucky Percussion

CVA Hawken Pistol

Dixie Overcoat Pistol

DIXIE PENNSYLVANIA PISTOL

Caliber: 44 (.430" round ball).
Barrel: 10" (⅞" octagon).
Weight: 2½ lbs.
Stock: Walnut-stained hardwood.
Sights: Blade front, open rear drift-adj. for windage; brass.
Features: Available in flint or percussion. Brass trigger guard, thimbles, nose-cap, wedgeplates; high-lustre blue barrel. Imported from Italy by Dixie Gun Works.
Price: Flint, finished.. $119.95
Price: Percussion, finished...................................... $105.00
Price: Flint, kit.. $85.00
Price: Percussion, kit... $72.50

KENTUCKY FLINTLOCK PISTOL

Caliber: 44, 45.
Barrel: 10⅛".
Weight: 32 oz. **Length:** 15½" over-all.
Stock: Walnut.
Sights: Fixed.
Features: Specifications, including caliber, weight and length may vary with importer. Case hardened lock, blued bbl.; available also as brass bbl. flint Model 1821 ($136.75, Navy). Imported by Armsport, Navy Arms, The Armoury, Dixie.
Price: .... $40.95 to $145.00
Price: In kit form, from .... $90.00 to $112.00
Price: Single cased set (Navy Arms) $234.00
Price: Double cased set (Navy Arms) $394.00

Kentucky Percussion Pistol

Similar to flint version but percussion lock. Imported by The Armoury, Dixie, Navy Arms, CVA, Armsport, Hopkins & Allen.
Price: About .... $97.50 to $133.00
Price: In kit form .... $35.95 to $102.00
Price: Single cased set (Navy Arms) $224.00
Price: Double cased set (Navy Arms) $370.00

CVA HAWKEN PERCUSSION PISTOL

Caliber: 50.
Barrel: 9¾", octagonal, 1" flats; rifled.
Weight: 50 oz. **Length:** 16½" over-all.
Stock: Select walnut.
Sights: Beaded blade front, fully adjustable rear.
Features: Hooked breech, early-style brass trigger. Color case-hardened lock plate; brass wedge plate, nose cap, ramrod thimbles, trigger guard, grip cap; blue barrel and sights.
Price: Finished $118.95
Price: Kit $77.95

CVA COLONIAL PISTOL

Caliber: 45.
Barrel: 6¾", octagonal, rifled.
Length: 12¾" over-all.
Stocks: Selected hardwood.
Features: Case hardened lock, brass furniture, fixed sights. Steel ramrod. Available in percussion only. Imported by CVA.
Price: Finished $73.95
Price: Kit $52.75

DIXIE OVERCOAT PISTOL

Caliber: 39.
Barrel: 4", smoothbore.
Weight: 13 oz. **Length:** 8" over-all.
Stock: Walnut-finished hardwood. Checkered p.g.
Sights: Bead front.
Features: Shoots .380" balls. Breech plug and engraved lock are burnished steel finish; barrel and trigger guard blued.
Price: Engraved model $34.50

CAUTION: PRICES CHANGE. CHECK AT GUNSHOP.

PHILADELPHIA DERRINGER PERCUSSION PISTOL
Caliber: 45.
Barrel: 3⅛″.
Weight: 14 oz. **Length:** 7″ over-all.
Stock: Walnut, checkered grip.
Sights: Fixed.
Features: Engraved wedge holder and bbl. Also available in flintlock version. Imported by CVA.
Price: $66.95
Price: Kit form $44.95

Dixie Philadelphia

Dixie Brass Frame

Hege-Siber Pistol

Le Page Dueling Pistol

MOORE & PATRICK FLINT DUELING PISTOL
Caliber: 45.
Barrel: 10″, rifled.
Weight: 32 oz. **Length:** 14½″ over-all.
Stock: European walnut, checkered.
Sights: Fixed.
Features: Engraved, silvered lock plate, blue barrel. German silver furniture. Imported from Italy by Hopkins & Allen, Dixie and Navy Arms.
Price: .... $200.00 to $295.00

DIXIE LINCOLN DERRINGER
Caliber: 41.
Barrel: 2″, 8 lands, 8 grooves.
Weight: 7 oz. **Length:** 5½″ over-all.
Stock: Walnut finish, checkered.
Sights: Fixed.
Features: Authentic copy of the "Lincoln Derringer." Shoots .400″ patched ball. German silver furniture includes trigger guard with pineapple finial, wedge plates, nose, wrist, side and teardrop inlays. All furniture, lockplate, hammer, and breech plug engraved. Imported from Italy by Dixie Gun Works.
Price: With wooden case $159.95
Price: Kit (not engraved) $59.95

DIXIE PHILADELPHIA DERRINGER
Caliber: 41.
Barrel: 3½″, octagon.
Weight: 8 oz. **Length:** 5½″ over-all.
Stock: Walnut, checkered p.g.
Sights: Fixed.
Features: Barrel and lock are blued; brass furniture. From Dixie Gun Works.
Price: $45.00

DIXIE BRASS FRAME DERRINGER
Caliber: 41.
Barrel: 2½″.
Weight: 7 oz. **Length:** 5½″ over-all.
Stocks: Walnut.
Features: Brass frame, color case hardened hammer and trigger. Shoots .395″ round ball. Engraved model available. From Dixie Gun Works.
Price: Plain model $49.95
Price: Engraved model $59.95
Price: Kit form, plain model $37.50

DIXIE ABILENE DERRINGER
Caliber: 41.
Barrel: 2½″, 6-groove rifling.
Weight: 8 oz. **Length:** 6½″ over-all.
Stocks: Walnut.
Features: All steel version of Dixie's brass-framed derringers. Blued barrel, color case hardened frame and hammer. Shoots .395″ patched ball. Comes with wood presentation case.
Price: $54.95
Price: Kit form $45.00

HEGE-SIBER PISTOL
Caliber: 33, 44.
Barrel: 10″.
Weight: 34 oz. **Length:** 15½″ over-all.
Stock: French walnut, cut-checkered grip.
Sights: Barleycorn front, micro adjustable rear.
Features: Reproduction of pistol made by Swiss watchmaker Jean Siber in the 1800s. Precise lock and set trigger give fast lock time. Has engraving, plum browned barrel, trigger guard. Imported by Navy Arms. Introduced 1984.
Price: British version $865.00

NAVY ARMS LE PAGE DUELING PISTOL
Caliber: 44.
Barrel: 9″, octagon, rifled.
Weight: 34 oz. **Length:** 15″ over-all.
Stock: European walnut.
Sights: Adjustable rear.
Features: Single set trigger. Polished metal finish. From Navy Arms.
Price: $295.00
Price: Single cased set $464.00
Price: Double cased set $785.00
Price: Flintlock, rifled $387.00
Price: Flintlock, smoothbore $387.00
Price: Flintlock, single cased set $559.00
Price: Flintlock, double cased set $975.00

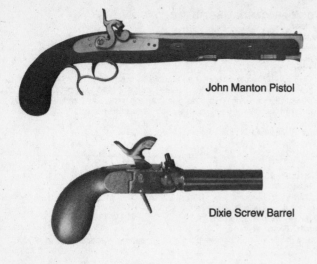

John Manton Pistol

Dixie Screw Barrel

JOHN MANTON MATCH PISTOL
Caliber: 45, uses .440" round ball.
Barrel: 10", rifled.
Weight: 36 oz. **Length:** 15½" over-all.
Stock: European walnut; checkered grip.
Sights: Bead front.
Features: Highly polished steel barrel and lock, brass furniture. From Hopkins & Allen.
Price: Finished gun **$125.00**

DIXIE SCREW BARREL PISTOL
Caliber: .445".
Barrel: 2½".
Weight: 8 oz. **Length:** 6½" over-all.
Stocks: Walnut.
Features: Trigger folds down when hammer is cocked. Close copy of the originals once made in Belgium. Uses No. 11 percussion caps.
Price: **$79.95**

ELGIN CUTLASS PISTOL
Caliber: 44 (.440").
Barrel: 4¼".
Weight: 21 oz. **Length:** 12" over-all.
Stock: Walnut.
Sights: None.
Features: Replica of the pistol used by the U.S. Navy as a boarding weapon. Smoothbore barrel. Available as a kit or finished. Made in U.S. by Navy Arms.
Price: Kit **$78.50**
Price: Finished **$104.95**

Elgin Cutlass Pistol

CLASSIC TWISTER O/U
Caliber: 36.
Barrel: 3⅜".
Weight: 24 ozs.
Stocks: Pearlite.
Sights: None.
Features: Over-under barrels rotate on an axis for two separate shots. Spur trigger. From Navy Arms.
Price: Complete, blued barrel **$84.95**
Price: Kit **$54.00**

NAVY SOUTHERNER DERRINGER
Caliber: 44.
Barrel: 2½".
Weight: 12 ozs. **Length:** 5" over-all.
Stock: Pearlite.
Sights: None.
Features: Blued barrel, brass frame. Uses .440" round ball. From Navy Arms.
Price: Finished **$84.95**
Price: Kit **$54.00**

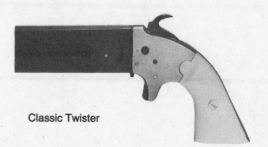

Classic Twister

NAVY ARMS SNAKE EYES
Caliber: 36.
Barrel: 2⅝", double barrel.
Weight: 24 ozs. **Length:** 6¾" over-all.
Stock: Composition pearl.
Sights: None.
Features: Solid brass barrels and receiver. Also comes in kit form, 90% complete with only 14 pieces. From Navy Arms.
Price: Complete **$74.95**
Price: Kit **$54.00**

NAVY ARMS DUCKFOOT
Caliber: 36.
Barrel: 2⅞", three barrels.
Weight: 32 ozs. **Length:** 10½" over-all.
Stock: Walnut.
Sights: None.
Features: Steel barrels and receiver, brass frame. Also comes in kit form, 90% completed, no drilling or tapping. From Navy Arms.
Price: Complete **$69.95**
Price: Kit **$48.95**

Navy Southerner

ETHAN ALLEN PEPPERBOX
Caliber: 36.
Barrel: 3⅛", four smoothbore barrels.
Weight: 38 ozs. **Length:** 9" over-all.
Stock: Walnut.
Sights: None.
Features: Steel barrels, brass receiver. Also comes in kit form, 90% completed. From Navy Arms.
Price: Complete **$79.95**
Price: Kit **$59.25**

CAUTION: PRICES CHANGE. CHECK AT GUNSHOP.

BLACK POWDER SINGLE SHOT PISTOLS—FLINT & PERCUSSION

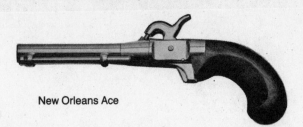

New Orleans Ace

NEW ORLEANS ACE
Caliber: 44.
Barrel: 3½", rifled or smoothbore.
Weight: 16 ozs. **Length:** 9" over-all.
Stock: Walnut.
Sights: None.
Features: Solid brass frame (receiver). Available complete or in kit form. Kit is 90% complete, no drilling or tapping, fully inletted. From Navy Arms.
Price: Complete (smoothbore) **$58.50**
Price: Kit (smoothbore) **$43.25**
Price: Complete (rifled bore) **$64.25**
Price: Kit (rifled bore). **$45.75**

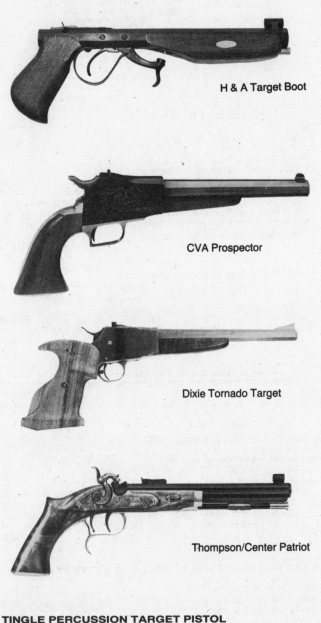

H & A Target Boot

CVA Prospector

Dixie Tornado Target

Thompson/Center Patriot

HOPKINS & ALLEN BOOT PISTOL
Caliber: 45.
Barrel: 6".
Weight: 42 oz. **Length:** 13" over-all.
Stock: Walnut.
Sights: Silver blade front; rear adj. for e.
Features: Under-hammer design. From Hopkins & Allen.
Price: **$71.50**
Price: Kit form **$55.20**
Price: Target version with wood fore-end, ramrod, hood front sight, elevator rear **$89.80**

CVA VEST POCKET DERRINGER
Caliber: 44.
Barrel: 2½", brass.
Weight: 7 oz.
Stock: Two-piece walnut.
Features: All brass frame with brass ramrod. A muzzle-loading version of the Colt No. 3 derringer.
Price: Finished **$40.95**
Price: Kit **$35.95**

CVA PROSPECTOR SINGLE SHOT PERCUSSION PISTOL
Caliber: 44.
Barrel: 8½", octagonal.
Weight: 42 oz. **Length:** 12¾" over-all.
Stocks: One-piece walnut.
Sights: Blade front, hammer notch rear.
Features: Brass backstrap and trigger guard, rest blued. Frame engraved with two different scenes. Introduced 1984.
Price: Finished **$83.95**
Price: Kit **$63.95**

DIXIE TORNADO TARGET PISTOL
Caliber: 44 (.430" round ball).
Barrel: 10", octagonal, 1-in-22" twist.
Stock: Walnut, target-style. Left unfinished for custom fitting. Walnut fore-end.
Sights: Blade on ramp front, micro-type open rear adjustable for windage and elevation.
Features: Grip frame style of 1860 Colt revolver. Improved model of the Tingle and B.W. Southgate pistol. Trigger adjustable for pull. Frame, barrel, hammer and sights in the white, brass trigger guard. Comes with solid brass, walnut-handled cleaning rod with jag and nylon muzzle protector. Introduced 1983. From Dixie Gun Works.
Price: **$145.00**

TINGLE PERCUSSION TARGET PISTOL
Caliber: 44.
Barrel: 10", octagonal.
Weight: 42 oz.
Stocks: Smooth walnut.
Sights: Bead front, rear adj. for w. & e.
Features: Engraved scenes on frame sides; brass backstrap and trigger guard; case-hardened frame and hammer. From E.M.F.
Price: **$150.00**

THOMPSON/CENTER PATRIOT PERCUSSION PISTOL
Caliber: 36, 45.
Barrel: 9¼".
Weight: 36 oz. **Length:** 16" over-all.
Stock: Walnut.
Sights: Patridge-type. Rear adj. for w. and e.
Features: Hook breech system; double set triggers; coil mainspring. From Thompson/Center Arms.
Price: **$215.00**

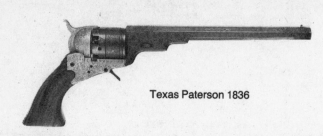

Texas Paterson 1836

TEXAS PATERSON 1836 REVOLVER
Caliber: 36 (.376″ round ball).
Barrel: 7½″.
Weight: 42 oz.
Stocks: One-piece walnut.
Sights: Fixed.
Features: Copy of Sam Colt's first commercially-made revolving pistol. Has no loading lever but comes with loading tool. From Dixie Gun Works, Navy Arms.
Price: **$225.00**
Price: Engraved (Navy Arms) **$500.00**

WALKER 1847 PERCUSSION REVOLVER
Caliber: 44, 6-shot.
Barrel: 9″.
Weight: 72 oz. **Length:** 15½″ over-all.
Stocks: Walnut.
Sights: Fixed.
Features: Case hardened frame, loading lever and hammer; iron backstrap; brass trigger guard; engraved cylinder. Imported by CVA, E.M.F., Navy Arms, Dixie, Armsport, Allen Fire Arms.
Price: About **$250.00**
Price: Single cased set (E.M.F., Navy Arms) .... **$235.00 to $319.00**
Price: Kit (CVA) **$165.95**

Walker 1847

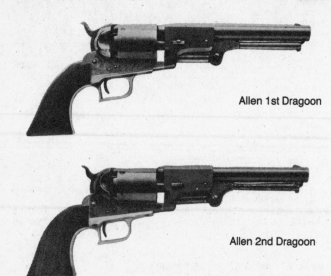

Allen 1st Dragoon

Allen 2nd Dragoon

Dixie Third Dragoon

ALLEN 1st MODEL DRAGOON
Caliber: 44.
Barrel: 7½″, part round, part octagon.
Weight: 66 oz.
Stocks: One piece walnut.
Sights: German silver blade front, hammer notch rear.
Features: First model has oval bolt cuts in cylinder, square-back flared trigger guard, V-type mainspring, short trigger. Ranger and Indian scene on cylinder. Color cased frame, loading lever, plunger and hammer; blue barrel, cylinder, trigger and wedge. Available with old-time charcoal blue or standard blue-black finish. Polished brass backstrap and trigger guard. From Allen Fire Arms.
Price: **$229.00**

Allen 2nd Model Dragoon Revolver
Similar to the 1st Model except this model is distinguished by its rectangular bolt cuts in the cylinder, straight square-back trigger guard, short trigger and flat mainspring with roller in hammer.
Price: **$229.00**
Price: As Confederate Tucker & Sherrard, with 3rd Model loading lever and special cylinder engraving. **$229.00**

Allen 3rd Model Dragoon Revolver
Similar to the 2nd Model except has oval trigger guard, long trigger.
Price: **$229.00**
Price: With silver plated guard and backstrap. **$249.00**

DIXIE THIRD MODEL DRAGOON
Caliber: 44 ((.454″ round ball).
Barrel: 7⅜″.
Weight: 4 lbs., 2½ oz.
Stocks: One-piece walnut.
Sights: Brass pin front, hammer notch rear, or adjustable folding leaf rear.
Features: Cylinder engraved with Indian fight scene. This is the only Dragoon replica with folding leaf sight. Brass backstrap and trigger guard; color case-hardened steel frame, blue-black barrel. Imported by Dixie Gun Works.
Price: **$140.00**

Dixie Baby Dragoon

BABY DRAGOON AND MODEL 1849 REVOLVERS
Caliber: 31.
Barrel: 3″, 4″, 5″; 7 groove, RH twist.
Weight: About 21 oz.
Stocks: Varnished walnut.
Sights: Brass pin front, hammer notch rear.
Features: No loading lever on Allen Baby Dragoon models. Unfluted cylinder with Ranger and Indian scene; cupped cylinder pin; no grease grooves; one safety pin on cylinder and slot in hammer face; straight (flat) mainspring. Silver backstrap and trigger guard. From Allen Fire Arms, Dixie, CVA.
Price: **$199.00**
Price: 6″ barrel, with loading lever (Dixie) **$125.00**
Price: 4″ barrel, brass frame, no loading lever (CVA) **$88.95**
Price: Kit (CVA) **$74.95**

CAUTION: PRICES CHANGE. CHECK AT GUNSHOP.

BLACK POWDER REVOLVERS

Allen Squareback 1851

Dixie 1851 Navy

1851 NAVY-SHERIFF

Same as 1851 Sheriff model except has 4″ barrel. Imported by Allen, CVA, E.M.F., Euroarms of America.
Price: .... $80.00 to $199.00
Price: Kit (CVA) $83.95
Price: Engraved, brass and nickel plated (CVA) $200.00

ARMY 1851 PERCUSSION REVOLVER

Caliber: 44, 6-shot.
Barrel: 7½″.
Weight: 45 oz. **Length:** 13″ over-all.
Stocks: Walnut finish.
Sights: Fixed.
Features: 44 caliber version of the 1851 Navy. Imported by The Armoury, E.M.F.
Price: .... $65.00 to $138.00

CVA 1858 Army

Consult our Directory pages for the location of firms mentioned.

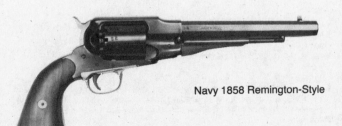

Navy 1858 Remington-Style

NEW MODEL 1858 ARMY PERCUSSION REVOLVER

Caliber: 36 or 44, 6-shot.
Barrel: 6½″ or 8″.
Weight: 40 oz. **Length:** 13½″ over-all.
Stocks: Walnut.
Sights: Blade front, groove-in-frame rear.
Features: Replica of Remington Model 1858. Also available from some importers as Army Model Belt Revolver in 36 cal., shortened and lightened version of the 44. Target Model (Allen, Navy) has fully adj. target rear sight, target front, 36 or 44. Imported by CVA, (as 1858 Remington Army), Dixie, Navy Arms, Hopkins & Allen, The Armoury, E.M.F., Euroarms of America (engraved, stainless and plain), Armsport, Allen.
Price: About $229.00
Price: Single cased set (Navy Arms) $235.00
Price: Double cased set (Navy Arms) $390.00
Price: Nickel finish (E.M.F.) $152.75
Price: Stainless steel (Euroarms, Navy Arms, Allen) ..... $140.00 to $299.00
Price: Target model (Euroarms, Navy Arms, E.M.F., Allen) $95.95 to $185.00
Price: Brass frame, finished (CVA, Navy Arms) .... $99.00 to $122.95
Price: As above, kit (CVA, Navy Arms) .... $80.00 to $101.95

Allen 1861 Navy Percussion Revolver

Similar to 1851 Navy except has round 7½″ barrel, rounded trigger guard, German silver blade front sight, "creeping" loading lever.
Price: $229.00
Price: Stainless $269.00

1851 SHERIFF MODEL PERCUSSION REVOLVER

Caliber: 36, 44, 6-shot.
Barrel: 5″.
Weight: 40 oz. **Length:** 10½″ over-all.
Stocks: Walnut.
Sights: Fixed.
Features: Brass back strap and trigger guard; engraved navy scene; case hardened frame, hammer, loading lever. Imported by E.M.F.
Price: Steel frame $85.00
Price: Brass frame $102.00
Price: Kit, brass or steel frame $65.00

NAVY MODEL 1851 PERCUSSION REVOLVER

Caliber: 36, 6-shot.
Barrel: 7½″.
Weight: 44 oz. **Length:** 13″ over-all.
Stocks: Walnut finish.
Sights: Post front, hammer notch rear.
Features: Brass backstrap and trigger guard; some have 1st model squareback trigger guard, engraved cylinder with navy battle scene; case hardened frame, hammer, loading lever. Imported by The Armoury, Navy Arms, Allen, E.M.F., Dixie, Euroarms of America, Armsport, Hopkins & Allen, CVA.
Price: Brass frame .... $60.00 to $199.00
Price: Steel frame .... $31.50 to $209.00
Price: Stainless Squareback (Allen) $259.00
Price: Kit form .... $60.00 to $119.95
Price: Engraved model (Dixie) $97.50
Price: Also as "Buntline" (Dixie) $166.95
Price: Navy-Civilian model (E.M.F., Allen) $229.00
Price: Single cased set, steel frame (Navy Arms) $218.00
Price: Double cased set, steel frame (Navy Arms) $357.00
Price: London Model with iron backstrap (Allen) $229.00

NAVY ARMS 1858 REMINGTON-STYLE REVOLVER

Caliber: 44.
Barrel: 8″.
Weight: 2 lbs., 13 ozs.
Stock: Smooth walnut.
Sights: Dovetailed blade front.
Features: First exact reproduction — correct in size and weight to the original, with progressive rifling; highly polished with charcoal blue finish. From Navy Arms.
Price: Deluxe model $250.00
Price: As above, single cased set (Navy Arms) $195.00
Price: As above, double cased set (Navy Arms) $310.00
Price: Steel frame, finished (CVA) $167.95
Price: As above, kit (CVA) $126.95

BLACK POWDER REVOLVERS

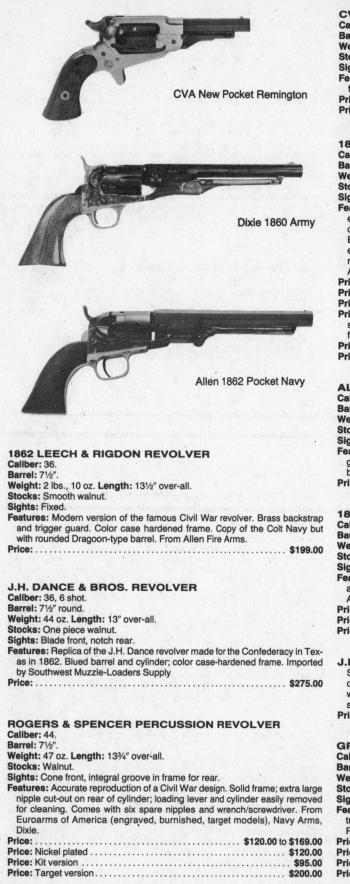

CVA New Pocket Remington

Dixie 1860 Army

Allen 1862 Pocket Navy

1862 LEECH & RIGDON REVOLVER
Caliber: 36.
Barrel: 7½".
Weight: 2 lbs., 10 oz. **Length:** 13½" over-all.
Stocks: Smooth walnut.
Sights: Fixed.
Features: Modern version of the famous Civil War revolver. Brass backstrap and trigger guard. Color case hardened frame. Copy of the Colt Navy but with rounded Dragoon-type barrel. From Allen Fire Arms.
Price: **$199.00**

J.H. DANCE & BROS. REVOLVER
Caliber: 36, 6 shot.
Barrel: 7½" round.
Weight: 44 oz. **Length:** 13" over-all.
Stocks: One piece walnut.
Sights: Blade front, notch rear.
Features: Replica of the J.H. Dance revolver made for the Confederacy in Texas in 1862. Blued barrel and cylinder; color case-hardened frame. Imported by Southwest Muzzle-Loaders Supply
Price: **$275.00**

ROGERS & SPENCER PERCUSSION REVOLVER
Caliber: 44.
Barrel: 7½".
Weight: 47 oz. **Length:** 13¾" over-all.
Stocks: Walnut.
Sights: Cone front, integral groove in frame for rear.
Features: Accurate reproduction of a Civil War design. Solid frame; extra large nipple cut-out on rear of cylinder; loading lever and cylinder easily removed for cleaning. Comes with six spare nipples and wrench/screwdriver. From Euroarms of America (engraved, burnished, target models), Navy Arms, Dixie.
Price: . . . . **$120.00 to $169.00**
Price: Nickel plated **$120.00**
Price: Kit version **$95.00**
Price: Target version **$200.00**

CVA NEW MODEL POCKET REMINGTON
Caliber: 31.
Barrel: 4", octagonal.
Weight: 15½ oz. **Length:** 7½" over-all.
Stocks: Two-piece walnut.
Sights: Post front, grooved top-strap rear.
Features: Spur trigger, brass frame with blued barrel and cylinder. Available finished or in kit form. Introduced 1984.
Price: Finished **$82.95**
Price: Kit **$68.95**

1860 ARMY PERCUSSION REVOLVER
Caliber: 44, 6-shot.
Barrel: 8".
Weight: 40 oz. **Length:** 13⅝" over-all.
Stocks: Walnut.
Sights: Fixed.
Features: Engraved navy scene on cylinder; brass trigger guard; case hardened frame, loading lever and hammer. Some importers supply pistol cut for detachable shoulder stock, have accessory stock available. Imported by E.M.F., CVA, Navy Arms, The Armoury, Dixie (half-fluted cylinder, not roll engraved), Euroarms of America (engraved, stainless steel or burnished steel model), Armsport, Hopkins & Allen, Allen.
Price: About **$229.00**
Price: Single cased set (Navy Arms, E.M.F.) . . . . **$149.00 to $230.00**
Price: Double cased set (Navy Arms) **$385.00**
Price: 1861 Navy: Same as Army except 36 cal., 7½" bbl., wt. 41 oz., cut for stock; round cylinder (fluted avail.), from E.M.F., Allen, CVA (brass frame) . . . . **$99.95 to $245.00**
Price: Kit (CVA, E.M.F.) . . . . **$90.00 to $124.95**
Price: Stainless steel (Euroarms, Allen). . . . . **$200.00 to $269.00**

ALLEN 1862 POCKET NAVY PERCUSSION REVOLVER
Caliber: 36.
Barrel: 4½", 5½", 6½", octagonal, 7 groove, LH twist.
Weight: 27 oz. (5½" barrel)
Stocks: One piece varnished walnut.
Sights: Brass pin front, hammer notch rear.
Features: Rebated cylinder, hinged loading lever, brass backstrap and trigger guard, color cased frame, hammer, loading lever, plunger and latch, rest blued. Has original-type markings. From Allen Fire Arms.
Price: **$199.00**

1862 POCKET POLICE PERCUSSION REVOLVER
Caliber: 36, 5-shot.
Barrel: 4½", 5½", 7½".
Weight: 26 oz. **Length:** 12" (6½" bbl.).
Stocks: Walnut.
Sights: Fixed.
Features: Half-fluted and rebated cylinder; case hardened frame, loading lever and hammer; silver trigger guard and backstrap. Imported by CVA, Navy Arms (5½" only), Euroarms of America (7½" only) Allen (all lengths).
Price: . . . . **$93.95 to $155.00**
Price: Cased with accessories (Navy Arms) **$225.00**
Price: Stainless steel (Allen) **$259.00**

J.H. Dance & Bros. Commemorative Ltd.
Same gun as the standard model except has charcoal blue finish with special commemorative markings and gold inlays. Comes with lined display case with brass inscription plate, leather covered powder flask, bullet mould, screwdriver, nipple wrench, six spare nipples. Only 500 guns to be issued.
Price: **$1,500.00**

GRISWOLD & GUNNISON PERCUSSION REVOLVER
Caliber: 36 or 44, 6-shot.
Barrel: 7½".
Weight: 44 oz. (36 cal.). **Length:** 13" over-all.
Stocks: Walnut.
Sights: Fixed.
Features: Replica of famous Confederate pistol. Brass frame, backstrap and trigger guard; case hardened loading lever; rebated cylinder (44 cal. only). Rounded Dragoon-type barrel. Imported by Navy Arms, Allen, E.M.F.
Price: . . . . **$96.00 to $169.00**
Price: Kit (Navy Arms, E.M.F.). **$73.50**
Price: Single cased set (Navy Arms) **$192.00**
Price: Double cased set (Navy Arms) **$299.00**

CAUTION: PRICES CHANGE. CHECK AT GUNSHOP.

Dixie Spiller & Burr

SPILLER & BURR REVOLVER
Caliber: 36 (.375″ round ball).
Barrel: 7″, octagon.
Weight: 2½ lbs. **Length:** 12½″ over-all.
Stocks: Two-piece walnut.
Sights: Fixed.
Features: Reproduction of the C.S.A. revolver. Brass frame and trigger guard. Also available as a kit. From Dixie, Navy Arms.
Price: .... **$69.95 to $109.00**
Price: Kit form .... **$39.95 to $65.00**

LE MAT CAVALRY MODEL REVOLVER
Caliber: 44/65.
Barrel: 6¾″ (revolver); 4⅞″ (single shot).
Weight: NA.
Stocks: Hand-checkered walnut.
Sights: Post front, hammer-notch rear.
Features: Exact reproduction with all-steel construction; 44-cal. 9-shot cylinder, 65-cal. single barrel; color case-hardened hammer with selector; spur trigger guard; ring at butt; lever-type barrel release. From Navy Arms.
Price: **$500.00**
Price: Army model (round trigger guard, pin-type barrel release) **$500.00**
Price: Naval-style (thumb selector or hammer) **$500.00**

Le Mat Cavalry Model

Dixie "Wyatt Earp"

DIXIE "WYATT EARP" REVOLVER
Caliber: 44.
Barrel: 12″ octagon.
Weight: 46 oz. **Length:** 18″ over-all.
Stocks: Two piece walnut.
Sights: Fixed.
Features: Highly polished brass frame, backstrap and trigger guard; blued barrel and cylinder; case hardened hammer, trigger and loading lever. Navy-size shoulder stock ($45.00) will fit with minor fitting. From Dixie Gun Works.
Price: **$99.95**

E.M.F. 44 BALLISTER REVOLVER
Caliber: 44, 6-shot.
Barrel: 12″.
Weight: 2¾ lbs.
Stocks: Two-piece walnut.
Sights: Fixed.
Features: Barrel and cylinder blued, frame and trigger guard are brass; hammer and loading lever are color case hardened. From E.M.F.
Price: **$99.00**

> Consult our Directory pages for the location of firms mentioned.

Freedom Mini Percussion

FREEDOM ARMS PERCUSSION MINI REVOLVER
Caliber: 22, 5-shot.
Barrel: 1″, 1¾″, 3″.
Weight: 4¾ oz. (1″ bbl.).
Stocks: Simulated ebony, or rosewood (optional).
Sights: Fixed.
Features: Percussion version of the 22 RF gun. All stainless steel; spur trigger. Gun comes with leather carrying pouch, bullet setting tool, powder measure, 20 29-gr. bullets. Introduced 1983. From Freedom Arms.
Price: 1″ barrel **$130.00**
Price: 1¾″ barrel **$130.00**
Price: 3″ barrel **$142.70**

Ruger Old Army

RUGER 44 OLD ARMY PERCUSSION REVOLVER
Caliber: 44, 6-shot. Uses .457″ dia. lead bullets.
Barrel: 7½″ (6-groove, 16″ twist).
Weight: 46 oz. **Length:** 13¾″ over-all.
Stocks: Smooth walnut.
Sights: Ramp front, rear adj. for w. and e.
Features: Stainless steel standard size nipples, chrome-moly steel cylinder and frame, same lockwork as in original Super Blackhawk. Also available in stainless steel in very limited quantities. Made in USA. From Sturm, Ruger & Co.
Price: Stainless steel (Model KBP-7) **$321.00**
Price: Blued steel (Model BP-7) **$251.50**

Navy Brown Bess

NAVY ARMS CHARLEVILLE MUSKET
Caliber: 69
Barrel: 44⅝".
Weight: 8¾ lbs. **Length:** 59⅜" over-all.
Stock: Walnut.
Sights: Blade front.
Features: Replica of Revolutionary War 1763 musket. Bright metal, walnut stock. From Navy Arms.
Price: Finished $370.00
Price: Kit $310.00

SECOND MODEL BROWN BESS MUSKET
Caliber: 75, uses .735" round ball.
Barrel: 42", smoothbore.
Weight: 9½ lbs. **Length:** 59" over-all.
Stock: Walnut (Navy); walnut-stained hardwood (Dixie).
Sights: Fixed.
Features: Polished barrel and lock with brass trigger guard and buttplate. Bayonet and scabbard available. From Navy Arms, Dixie.
Price: Finished . . . . $290.00 to $450.00
Price: Kit . . . . $265.00 to $345.00

Dixie Indian Gun

DIXIE INDIAN GUN
Caliber: 75.
Barrel: 31", round tapered.
Weight: About 9 lbs. **Length:** 47" over-all.
Stock: Hardwood.
Sights: Blade front.
Features: Modified Brown Bess musket; brass furniture, browned lock and barrel. Lock is marked "GRICE 1762" with crown over "GR." Serpent-style sideplate. Introduced 1983.
Price: Complete $375.00
Price: As above, in kit form $360.00

Dixie Tennessee Rifle

DIXIE TENNESSEE MOUNTAIN RIFLE
Caliber: 32 or 50.
Barrel: 41½", 6-groove rifling, brown finish.
Length: 56" over-all.
Stock: Walnut, oil finish; Kentucky-style.
Sights: Silver blade front, open buckhorn rear.
Features: Re-creation of the original mountain rifles. Early Schultz lock, interchangeable flint or percussion with vent plug or drum and nipple. Tumbler has fly. Double-set triggers. All metal parts browned. From Dixie.
Price: Flint or Percussion, finished rifle, 50 cal. $250.00
Price: Kit, 50 cal. $195.00
Price: Left-hand model, flint or perc. $250.00
Price: Left-hand kit, flint or perc., 50 cal. $225.00
Price: Squirrel Rifle (as above except in 32 cal. with ¹³⁄₁₆" barrel), flint or percussion $295.00
Price: Kit, 32 cal., flint or percussion $255.00

KENTUCKY FLINTLOCK RIFLE
Caliber: 44 or 45.
Barrel: 35".
Weight: 7lbs. **Length:** 50" over-all.
Stock: Walnut stained, brass fittings.
Sights: Fixed.
Features: Available in Carbine model also, 28" bbl. Some variations in detail, finish. Kits also available from some importers. Imported by Navy Arms, The Armoury, CVA (45-cal. only), Armsport, Hopkins & Allen.
Price: About $273.75
Price: Kit form (CVA, Hopkins & Allen) . . . . $119.95 to 189.95
Price: Deluxe model, flint or percussion, 50-cal. (Navy Arms) $275.00

Kentucky Percussion Rifle
Similar to flintlock except percussion lock. Finish and features vary with importer. Imported by Navy Arms, The Armoury, CVA, Hopkins & Allen, Armsport (rifle-shotgun combo).
Price: . . . . $54.95 to 250.00
Price: Armsport combo $235.00
Price: 50 cal. (Navy Arms) $259.00

Kentuckian Rifle

KENTUCKIAN RIFLE & CARBINE
Caliber: 44.
Barrel: 35" (Rifle), 27½" (Carbine).

Weight: 7 lbs. (Rifle), 5½ lbs. (Carbine). **Length:** 51" (Rifle) over-all, Carbine 43".
Stock: Walnut stain.
Sights: Brass blade front, steel V-Ramp rear.
Features: Octagon bbl., case hardened and engraved lock plate. Brass furniture. Imported by Dixie.
Price: Rifle or carbine, flint $185.00
Price: As above, percussion $175.00

CAUTION: PRICES CHANGE. CHECK AT GUNSHOP.

Dixie York County

Weight: 7½ lbs. **Length:** 51½" over-all.
Stock: Maple, one piece.
Sights: Blade front, V-notch rear, brass.
Features: Adjustable double-set triggers. Brass trigger guard, patchbox, butt-plate, nosecap and sideplate. Case-hardened lockplate. From Dixie Gun Works.
Price: Percussion $210.00
Price: Flint $215.00
Price: Percussion Kit $149.00
Price: Flint Kit $160.00

YORK COUNTY RIFLE
Caliber: 45 (.445" round ball).
Barrel: 36", rifled, ⅞" octagon, blue.

HATFIELD SQUIRREL RIFLE
Caliber: 36, 45, 50
Barrel: 39½", octagon, 32" on half-stock.
Weight: 8 lbs. (32 cal.).
Stock: American fancy maple fullstock.
Sights: Silver blade front, buckhorn rear
Features: Recreation of the traditional squirrel rifle. Available in flint or percussion with brass trigger guard and buttplate. From Hatfield Rifle Works. Introduced 1983.

Hatfield Squirrel Rifle

Price: Full-stock, flint or percussion Grade I $295.00
Price: As above, Grade II $395.00
Price: As above, Grade III $395.00

CVA Pennsylvania

PECOS VALLEY HALF STOCK PENNSYLVANIA RIFLE
Caliber: 36, 45.
Barrel: 35½"; 1-in-48" twist (36-cal.), 1-in-72" twist (45-cal.).
Weight: About 6½ lbs. **Length:** 50½" over-all.
Stock: Select grade maple with satin finish, 13½" length of pull.
Sights: Silver blade, buckhorn rear
Features: Durrs Egg percussion lock by L&R; Davis double set trigger; brass furniture. Made in U.S. by Pecos Valley Armory. Introduced 1984.
Price: $399.00

CVA PENNSYLVANIA LONG RIFLE
Caliber: 50.
Barrel: 40", octagonal; ⅞" flats.
Weight: 8 lbs., 3 ozs. **Length:** 55¾" over-all.
Stock: Select walnut.
Sights: Brass blade front, fixed semi-buckhorn rear.
Features: Color case-hardened lock plate, brass buttplate, toe plate, patchbox, trigger guard, thimbles, nosecap; blued barrel, double-set triggers; authentic V-type mainspring. Introduced 1983. From CVA.
Price: Finished, percussion $307.95
Price: Finished, flintlock $318.95
Price: Kit, percussion $265.95
Price: Kit, flintlock $275.95

Ozark Taney County

Ozark Mountain Muskrat Rifle
Same as the Taney County rifle except has maple half-stock. Available in right or left hand, flint or percussion.
Price: From $525.00

OZARK MOUNTAIN TANEY COUNTY RIFLE
Caliber: 32, 36, 40.
Barrel: 36".
Weight: 7½ lbs. **Length:** 53" over-all.
Stock: American maple, fullstock design.
Sights: German silver blade front, full buckhorn rear.
Features: Available in flint or percussion, right or left hand; double set trigger.
Price: From $585.00

Oregon Trail Transition

OREGON TRAIL LEMAN PATTERN RIFLES
Caliber: 36, 40, 45, 50, 54, 58.
Barrel: 30" to 39", depending upon style of rifle.
Weight: NA. **Length:** NA.
Stock: Curly maple.

Sights: Steel blade front, semi-buckhorn rear.
Features: Available as various Leman patterns, right- or left-hand—Early Rifle (1⁵⁄₁₆" or 1" × 39" barrel), Transition Rifle (1" × 34" barrel), Indian Trade Rifle (1" or 1¹⁄₁₆" × 30" barrel), Light Rifle (⅞" × 38" barrel). Full stock or half stock, single trigger, brass furniture. Many options available. From Oregon Trail Riflesmiths.
Price: Half stock Leman, percussion, right or left hand $715.00
Price: Half stock, flintlock, right or left hand $725.00
Price: Full stock Indian Trade, Transition, percussion, right or left-hand model $775.00
Price: As above, flintlock, right- or left-hand $785.00

CAUTION: PRICES CHANGE. CHECK AT GUNSHOP.

Mowrey Squirrel Rifle

MOWREY GUN WORKS MODEL "1N30"
Caliber: 45, 50, 54.
Barrel: 45 cal. — 28″, browned octagon, ⅞″ flats; 50, 54 cal. — 28″, browned octagon with 1″ flats.
Weight: 45 cal. — 8 lbs.; 50, 54 cal. — 10 lbs. **Length:** 44″ over-all.
Stock: Curly maple, Premium or Fancy grade.
Sights: White dot blade front, modern fully adj. rear.
Features: Rifling and twist specially designed for conical bullets; steel action and furniture; boxlock action; adj. trigger; oil finish on wood. Made in U.S. Add $38 for fancy wood.
Price: Complete $330.00
Price: Kit (amateur) $250.00
Price: Kit (expert) $190.00

MOWREY ETHAN ALLEN SQUIRREL RIFLE
Caliber: 36 or 45.
Barrel: 28″, browned ocatgon, ¹³⁄₁₆″ flats, 8-groove gain-twist rifling.
Weight: 7½ lbs. **Length:** 43″ over-all.
Stock: Curly maple, Premium or Fancy grade.
Sights: German silver and brass blade front, open, adj. semi-buckhorn rear.
Features: Boxlock action, brass or browned steel frame and furniture; cut-rifled barrel; adj. trigger; hand-rubbed oil finish. Made in U.S. Add $38 for Fancy wood.
Price: Complete, brass or steel $330.00
Price: Kit (amateur) $250.00
Price: Kit (expert) $190.00

Mowrey Ethan Allen Plains Rifle
Similar to the Squirrel Rifle except in 50 or 54 caliber, 32″ browned octagon barrel with 1″ flats, weighs 10 lbs. and has 48″ over-all length. Add $30 for Schuetzen buttplate.
Price: Complete, brass or steel $330.00
Price: Kit (amateur) $250.00
Price: Kit (expert) $190.00

Mowrey Rocky Mountain

ALLEN SQUIRREL RIFLE
Caliber: 32.
Barrel: 28″, octagonal.
Weight: NA. **Length:** NA.
Stock: Walnut.
Sights: Blade front, fully adj. rear.
Features: Color case-hardened lock, brass trigger guard, balance blued. Imported by Allen Fire Arms.
Price: Flintlock $229.00
Price: Percussion. $199.00

MOWREY ETHAN ALLEN ROCKY MOUNTAIN HUNTER
Caliber: 50 or 54.
Barrel: 28″, browned octagon, 1″ flats, 8-groove gain-twist rifling.
Weight: 8 lbs. **Length:** 44″ over-all.
Stock: Curly maple, Premium or Fancy grade.
Sights: Blade front with white dot, modern fully adj. rear.
Features: Steel box-lock action and furniture; adj. trigger; hand-rubbed oil finish. Made in U.S. Add $38 for Fancy wood.
Price: Complete $330.00
Price: Kit (amateur) $250.00
Price: Kit (expert) $190.00

H&A Plainsman Rifle

HOPKINS & ALLEN PLAINSMAN RIFLE
Caliber: 45.
Barrel: 37″.
Weight: 7½ lbs. **Length:** 53″ over-all.
Stock: Walnut.
Sights: Blade front, rear adjustable for w. & e.
Features: Double set triggers, blued barrel has ¹³⁄₁₆″ flats, solid brass barrel rib, engraved percussion lockplate. From Hopkins & Allen.
Price: $292.60

CVA SQUIRREL RIFLE
Caliber: 32.
Barrel: 25″, octagonal; 1¹⁄₁₆″ flats.
Weight: 5 lbs., 12 oz. **Length:** 40¾″ over-all.
Stock: Hardwood.
Sights: Beaded blade front, fully adjustable hunting-style rear.
Features: Available in right or left-hand versions. Color case-hardened lock plate, brass buttplate, trigger guard, wedge plates, thimbles; double-set triggers; hooked breech; authentic V-type mainspring. Introduced 1983. From CVA.

CVA Squirrel Rifle

Price: Finished, percussion, right hand $201.95
Price: Finished, left hand $212.95
Price: Kit, percussion, right hand $143.95
Price: Kit, left hand $153.95
Price: Kit, flintlock $153.95

CAUTION: PRICES CHANGE. CHECK AT GUNSHOP.

Lyman Great Plains

LYMAN GREAT PLAINS RIFLE
Caliber: 50 or 54 cal.
Barrel: 32″, 1-66″ twist.
Weight: 9 lbs.
Stock: Walnut.
Sights: Steel blade front, buckhorn rear adj. for w. & e. and fixed notch primitive sight included.
Features: Blued steel furniture. Stainless steel nipple. Coil spring lock, Hawken-style trigger guard and double set triggers. Round thimbles recessed and sweated into rib. Steel wedge plates and toe plate. Introduced 1979. From Lyman.
Price: Percussion. **$294.95**
Price: Flintlock **$304.95**
Price: Percussion Kit. **$209.95**

CVA KENTUCKY RIFLE
Caliber: 45 (.451″ bore).
Barrel: 33½″, rifled, octagon (⅞″ flats).
Length: 48″ over-all.
Stock: Select hardwood.
Sights: Brass Kentucky blade type front, dovetail open rear.
Features: Available in either flint or percussion. Stainless steel nipple included. From CVA.
Price: Percussion. **$205.95**
Price: Flint. **$217.95**
Price: Percussion Kit. **$119.95**
Price: Flint Kit **$133.95**

PENNSYLVANIA FULL STOCK RIFLE
Caliber: 45 or 50.
Barrel: 32″ rifled, ¹⁵/₁₆″ dia.
Weight: 8½ lbs.
Stock: Walnut.
Sights: Fixed.
Features: Available in flint or percussion. Blued lock and barrel, brass furniture. Offered complete or in kit form. From The Armoury.
Price: Flint. **$235.00**
Price: Percussion. **$210.00**

Lyman Trade Rifle

LYMAN TRADE RIFLE
Caliber: 50 or 54.
Barrel: 28″ octagon, 1-48″ twist.

Weight: 8¾ lbs. **Length:** 45″ over-all.
Stock: European walnut.
Sights: Blade front, open rear adj. for w. or optional fixed sights.
Features: Fast twist rifling for conical bullets. Polished brass furniture with blue steel parts, stainless steel nipple. Hook breech, single trigger, coil spring percussion lock. Steel barrel rib and ramrod ferrules. Introduced 1980. From Lyman.
Price: Percussion. **$209.95**
Price: Kit, percussion **$159.95**
Price: Flintlock **$219.95**

CVA Frontier

CVA FRONTIER RIFLE
Caliber: 45, 50.
Barrel: 28″, octagon; ¹⁵/₁₆″ flats, 1-66″ twist.
Weight: 6 lbs., 14 oz. **Length:** 44″ over-all.
Stock: American hardwood.
Sights: Brass blade front, fully adjustable hunting-style rear.
Features: Available in flint or percussion. Solid brass nosecap, trigger guard, buttplate, thimbles and wedge plates; blued barrel; color case-hardened lock and hammer. Double set triggers, patented breech plug bolster, V-type mainspring. Hooked breech. Introduced 1980.

Price: 50 cal., percussion, complete rifle **$223.95**
Price: Finished, left hand **$234.95**
Price: 50 cal. flint, complete rifle **$234.95**
Price: 45, 50 cal., percussion, kit **$167.95**
Price: Percussion kit, left hand **$170.95**
Price: 50 cal. flint, kit **$177.95**

Oregon Trail "Poor Boy"

OREGON TRAIL "POOR BOY" RIFLE
Caliber: 32, 36, 40, 45, 50, 54, 58.
Barrel: Up to 40″; ¹³/₁₆″, ⅞″, ¹⁵/₁₆″ or 1″ flats.
Weight: NA. **Length:** NA.
Stock: Plain maple; horn heel fitting instead of buttplate.
Sights: Steel blade front, semi-buckhorn rear.
Features: Classic rifle of North Carolina, eastern Tenn. Steel furniture; long tang, single trigger. Buttplate, double set triggers, fancy wood available. Introduced 1986.
Price: Percussion, right- or left-hand **$595.00**
Price: As above, flintlock **$635.00**
Price: As Southern iron-mounted rifle with patch box, buttplate entry thimble, steel nose cap, percussion **$785.00**
Price: As above, flintlock **$795.00**

Consult our Directory pages for the location of firms mentioned.

BLACK POWDER MUSKETS & RIFLES

Navy Country Boy

NAVY ARMS COUNTRY BOY RIFLE
Caliber: 32, 36, 45, 50.
Barrel: 26″.

Weight: 6 lbs.
Stock: Walnut.
Sights: Blade front, adjustable rear.
Features: Octagonal rifled barrel; blue finish; hooked breech; Mule Ear lock for fast ignition. From Navy Arms.
Price: $215.00
Price: Kit $165.00

H&A Pa. Hawken

HOPKINS & ALLEN PA. HAWKEN RIFLE
Caliber: 50.
Barrel: 29″.

Weight: 7½ lbs. **Length:** 44″ over-all.
Stock: Walnut.
Sights: Blade front, open rear adjustable for elevation.
Features: Single trigger, dual barrel wedges. Convertible ignition system. Brass patch box.
Price: With percussion lock $199.50
Price: Conversion kit (percussion to flint). $39.95

Oregon Trail Hawken

TENNESSEE VALLEY TENNESSEE RIFLE
Caliber: 32, 36, 40, 45, 50, 54, 58
Barrel: 42″ standard; shorter lengths available.
Weight: 7½-8 lbs. **Length:** 56″ (with 42″ barrel).
Stock: Maple, walnut or cherry.
Sights: Silver blade front, buckhorn rear.
Features: Steel mounted, double-set triggers standard. Metal parts browned, oil-finished stock. From Tennessee Valley Mfg.
Price: Percussion $410.00
Price: Flintlock $425.00
Price: Left hand, flint or percussion $440.00
Price: Brass-mounted early Lancaster rifle $695.00
Price: Steel-mounted early Virginia rifle. $595.00

OREGON TRAIL HAWKEN FULL STOCK RIFLE
Caliber: 50, 54, 58.
Barrel: 35″, 1″ flats. Other lengths and calibers available.
Weight: NA. **Length:** NA.
Stock: Curly maple.
Sights: Steel blade front, semi-buckhorn rear.
Features: Steel furniture; double set triggers. Tapered barrel, fancy wood optional. Introduced 1986.
Price: Flint or percussion, right- or left-hand $995.00
Price: As half-stock Hawken $895.00

ALLEN SANTA FE HAWKEN RIFLE
Caliber: 54.
Barrel: 32″, octagonal.
Weight: 9.4 lbs. **Length:** 50″ over-all.
Stock: Walnut, with cheekpiece.
Sights: German silver blade front, buckhorn rear.
Features: Browned finish, color-case-hardened lock, German silver ferrule, wedge plates. Imported by Allen Fire Arms.
Price: $299.00

DIXIE DELUX CUB RIFLE
Caliber: 40.
Barrel: 28″.
Weight: 6½ lbs.
Stock: Walnut.
Sights: Fixed.
Features: Short rifle for small game and beginning shooters. Brass patchbox and furniture. Flint or percussion.
Price: Finished $240.00
Price: Kit $195.00

H&A Brush Rifle

HOPKINS & ALLEN BRUSH RIFLE
Caliber: 36 or 45.
Barrel: 25″, octagon, 15/16″ flats.
Weight: 7 lbs.
Stock: Hardwood.
Sights: Silver blade front, notch rear.
Features: Convertible ignition system. Brass furniture. Introduced 1983.
Price: Percussion. $189.00
Price: Flint $200.10
Price: Pre-assembled kit, percussion $129.00
Price: As above, flint $140.10
Price: Kit, percussion. $99.50
Price: Kit, flint $110.60

TRYON RIFLE
Caliber: 50, 54 cal.
Barrel: 34″, octagon; 1-63″ twist.
Weight: 9 lbs. **Length:** 49″ over-all.
Stock: European walnut with steel furniture.
Sights: Blade front, fixed rear.
Features: Reproduction of an American plains rifle with double set triggers and back-action lock. Imported from Italy by Dixie.
Price: $299.00
Price: Kit $249.00

CAUTION: PRICES CHANGE. CHECK AT GUNSHOP.

BLACK POWDER MUSKETS & RIFLES

H&A Heritage

HOPKINS & ALLEN UNDERHAMMER RIFLES
Caliber: 31, 36, 45, 50, 58.
Barrel: 20", 25" 32", 42", octagonal.
Weight: 6½ lbs. **Length:** 37" over-all.

Stock: American walnut.
Features: Blued barrel and receiver, black plastic buttplate. All models available with straight or pistol grip stock. Offered as kits, pre-assembled kits ("white" barrel, unfinished stock), or factory finished. Prices shown are for factory finished guns.
Price: 31, 36, 45, 20" or 25" bbl. × ¹⁵⁄₁₆" $214.50
Price: Heritage, 36, 45, 50-cal. 32" bbl. × ¹⁵⁄₁₆" $226.50
Price: Deerstalker, 58-cal., 28" bbl. × 1⅛" $233.95
Price: Target, 45-cal., 42" bbl. × 1⅛" $245.95

Thompson/Center Renegade

THOMPSON/CENTER RENEGADE RIFLE
Caliber: 50 and 54 plus 56 cal., smoothbore.
Barrel: 26", 1" across the flats.

Weight: 8 lbs.
Stock: American walnut.
Sights: Open hunting (Patridge) style, fully adjustable for w. and e.
Features: Coil spring lock, double set triggers, blued steel trim.
Price: Percussion model $255.00
Price: Flintlock model, 50 cal. only $270.00
Price: Percussion kit $195.00
Price: Flintlock kit $210.00
Price: Left-hand precussion, 50 or 54 cal. $255.00

Thompson/Center Hawken

Thompson/Center Hawken Cougar
Similar to the standard T/C Hawken except stock is of highly figured walnut; all furniture—lock plate, hammer, triggers, trigger plate, trigger guard, fore-end cap, thimbles escutcheons, etc. are of stainless steel with matte finish. Replacing the patch box is a stainless steel medallion cast in deep relief depicting a crouching cougar. Internal parts, breech plug, tang, barrel, sights and under rib are ordnance steel. Barrel, sights and under rib are blued. Buttplate is solid brass, hard chromed to match the stainless parts. Limited production. Introduced 1982. From Thompson/Center Arms.
Price: $350.00

THOMPSON/CENTER HAWKEN RIFLE
Caliber: 45, 50 or 54.
Barrel: 28" octagon, hooked breech.
Stock: American walnut.
Sights: Blade front, rear adj. for w. & e.
Features: Solid brass furniture, double set triggers, button rifled barrel, coil-type main spring. From Thompson/Center Arms.
Price: Percussion Model (45, 50 or 54 cal.) $295.00
Price: Flintlock model (50 cal.) $310.00
Price: Percussion kit $220.00
Price: Flintlock kit $235.00

Thompson/Center Cherokee

THOMPSON/CENTER CHEROKEE RIFLE
Caliber: 32 or 45.
Barrel: 24"; ¹³⁄₁₆" across flats.
Weight: About 6 lbs.

Stock: American walnut. Same as Seneca except minus patch box, toe plate, fore-end cap.
Sights: Open hunting style; round notch rear fully adjustable for w. and e.
Features: Interchangeable barrels. Uses T/C Seneca breech, lock, triggers, sights and stock. Brass buttplate, trigger guard, fore-end escutcheons and lock plate screw bushing. Introduced 1984.
Price: 32 or 45 caliber $250.00
Price: Interchangeable 32 or 45-cal. barrel $115.00
Price: Kit, percussion, 32 or 45 .... $190.00
Price: Kit barrels $75.00

Thompson/Center Seneca

THOMPSON/CENTER SENECA RIFLE
Caliber: 36, 45.
Barrel: 27".
Weight: 6½ lbs.
Stock: American walnut.
Sights: Open hunting style, square notch rear fully adj. for w. and e.
Features: Coil spring lock, octagon bbl. measures ¹³⁄₁₆" across flats, brass stock furniture.
Price: $300.00

Buffalo Hunter Rifle

BUFFALO HUNTER PERCUSSION RIFLE
Caliber: 58.
Barrel: 25½".
Weight: 8 lbs. **Length:** 41½" over-all.
Stock: Walnut finished, hand checkered, brass furniture.
Sights: Fixed.
Features: Designed for primitive weapons hunting. 20 ga. shotgun bbl. also available $90.00. Imported by Dixie.
Price: About **$264.00**

Charles Daly Hawken

CHARLES DALY HAWKEN RIFLE
Caliber: 45, 50, 54.
Barrel: 28" octagonal, ⅞" flats.
Weight: 7½ lbs. **Length:** 45½" over-all.
Stock: European hardwood.
Sights: Blade front, open fully adjustable rear.
Features: Color case-hardened lock uses coil springs; trigger guard, buttplate, fore-end cap, ferrules and ramrod fittings are polished brass. Left-hand model available in 50-cal. only. Imported by Outdoor Sports Headquarters. Introduced 1984.
Price: Right-hand, percussion **$229.95**
Price: Left-hand, percussion (50-cal. only) **$257.00**
Price: Right-hand, flintlock **$255.00**
Price: Left-hand, flintlock (50-cal. only) **$286.00**
Price: Carbine, right hand, 22" bbl., recoil pad **$229.95**

ARMOURY R140 HAWKIN RIFLE
Caliber: 45, 50 or 54.
Barrel: 29".
Weight: 8¾ to 9 lbs. **Length:** 45¾" over-all.
Stock: Walnut, with cheekpiece.
Sights: Dovetail front, fully adjustable rear.
Features: Octagon barrel, removable breech plug; double set triggers; blued barrel, brass stock fittings, color case hardened percussion lock. From Armsport, The Armoury.
Price: **$199.00**

Ozark Hawken Rifle

OZARK MOUNTAIN HAWKEN RIFLE
Caliber: 50, 52, 54, 58.
Barrel: 34".
Weight: About 9½ lbs. **Length:** 50¼" over-all.
Stock: American maple; full and half-stock designs available.
Sights: Blade front, semi-buckhorn rear.
Features: Flint or percussion, right or left hand models (except in flintlock — right-hand only); browned steel furniture.
Price: From **$675.00**

ITHACA-NAVY HAWKEN RIFLE
Caliber: 50 and 54.
Barrel: 32" octagonal, 1-inch dia.
Weight: About 9 lbs.
Stock: Walnut.
Sights: Blade front, rear adj. for w.
Features: Hooked breech, 1⅞" throw percussion lock. Attached twin thimbles and under-rib. German silver barrel key inlays, Hawken-style toe and buttplates, lock bolt inlays, barrel wedges, entry thimble, trigger guard, ramrod and cleaning jag, nipple and nipple wrench. Introduced 1977. From Navy Arms.
Price: Complete, percussion **$375.00**
Price: Kit, percussion **$270.00**

CVA HAWKEN RIFLE
Caliber: 50.
Barrel: 28", octagon; 1" across flats; 1-66" twist.
Weight: 7 lbs. 15 oz. **Length:** 44" over-all.
Stock: Select walnut.
Sights: Beaded blade front, fully adj. open rear.
Features: Fully adj. double set triggers; brass patch box, wedge plates, nose cap, thimbles, trigger guard and buttplate; blued barrel; color case-hardened, engraved lockplate. Percussion or flintlock. Hooked breech. Introduced 1981.
Price: Finished rifle, percussion **$273.95**
Price: Presentation Grade (checkered walnut stock, engraved lock plate) **$650.00**

Kassnar Hawken

HAWKEN RIFLE
Caliber: 45, 50, 54 or 58.
Barrel: 28", blued, 6-groove rifling.
Weight: 8¾ lbs. **Length:** 44" over-all.
Stock: Walnut with cheekpiece.
Sights: Blade front, fully adj. rear.
Features: Coil mainspring, double set triggers, polished brass furniture. Also available with chrome plated bore or in flintlock model from Sile. Introduced 1977. From Kassnar (flint or percussion, right- or left-hand), Dixie (45 or 50 only, walnut stock), Armsport, Hopkins & Allen, 50-cal. only.
Price: .... **$199.00 to $219.00**
Price: True left-hand rifle, percussion (Kassnar) **$234.00**
Price: As above, flintlock (Kassnar) **$254.00**

CAUTION: PRICES CHANGE. CHECK AT GUNSHOP.

BLACK POWDER MUSKETS & RIFLES

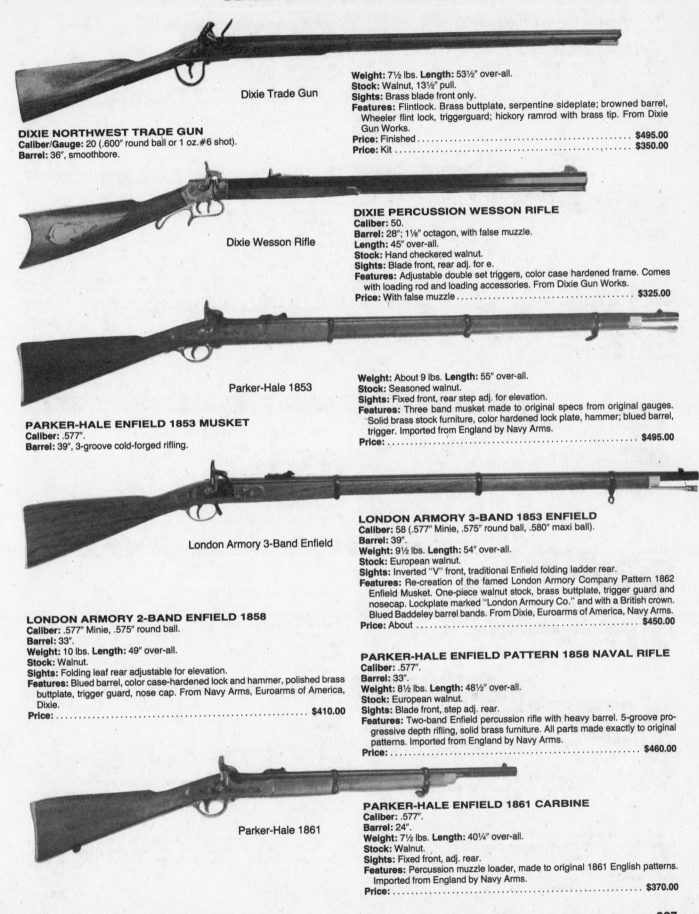

Dixie Trade Gun

DIXIE NORTHWEST TRADE GUN
Caliber/Gauge: 20 (.600" round ball or 1 oz.#6 shot).
Barrel: 36", smoothbore.

Weight: 7½ lbs. **Length:** 53½" over-all.
Stock: Walnut, 13½" pull.
Sights: Brass blade front only.
Features: Flintlock. Brass buttplate, serpentine sideplate; browned barrel, Wheeler flint lock, triggerguard; hickory ramrod with brass tip. From Dixie Gun Works.
Price: Finished $495.00
Price: Kit $350.00

Dixie Wesson Rifle

DIXIE PERCUSSION WESSON RIFLE
Caliber: 50.
Barrel: 28"; 1⅛" octagon, with false muzzle.
Length: 45" over-all.
Stock: Hand checkered walnut.
Sights: Blade front, rear adj. for e.
Features: Adjustable double set triggers, color case hardened frame. Comes with loading rod and loading accessories. From Dixie Gun Works.
Price: With false muzzle $325.00

Parker-Hale 1853

PARKER-HALE ENFIELD 1853 MUSKET
Caliber: .577".
Barrel: 39", 3-groove cold-forged rifling.

Weight: About 9 lbs. **Length:** 55" over-all.
Stock: Seasoned walnut.
Sights: Fixed front, rear step adj. for elevation.
Features: Three band musket made to original specs from original gauges. Solid brass stock furniture, color hardened lock plate, hammer; blued barrel, trigger. Imported from England by Navy Arms.
Price: $495.00

London Armory 3-Band Enfield

LONDON ARMORY 3-BAND 1853 ENFIELD
Caliber: 58 (.577" Minie, .575" round ball, .580" maxi ball).
Barrel: 39".
Weight: 9½ lbs. **Length:** 54" over-all.
Stock: European walnut.
Sights: Inverted "V" front, traditional Enfield folding ladder rear.
Features: Re-creation of the famed London Armory Company Pattern 1862 Enfield Musket. One-piece walnut stock, brass buttplate, trigger guard and nosecap. Lockplate marked "London Armoury Co." and with a British crown. Blued Baddeley barrel bands. From Dixie, Euroarms of America, Navy Arms.
Price: About $450.00

LONDON ARMORY 2-BAND ENFIELD 1858
Caliber: .577" Minie, .575" round ball.
Barrel: 33".
Weight: 10 lbs. **Length:** 49" over-all.
Stock: Walnut.
Sights: Folding leaf rear adjustable for elevation.
Features: Blued barrel, color case-hardened lock and hammer, polished brass buttplate, trigger guard, nose cap. From Navy Arms, Euroarms of America, Dixie.
Price: $410.00

PARKER-HALE ENFIELD PATTERN 1858 NAVAL RIFLE
Caliber: .577".
Barrel: 33".
Weight: 8½ lbs. **Length:** 48½" over-all.
Stock: European walnut.
Sights: Blade front, step adj. rear.
Features: Two-band Enfield percussion rifle with heavy barrel. 5-groove progressive depth rifling, solid brass furniture. All parts made exactly to original patterns. Imported from England by Navy Arms.
Price: $460.00

Parker-Hale 1861

PARKER-HALE ENFIELD 1861 CARBINE
Caliber: .577".
Barrel: 24".
Weight: 7½ lbs. **Length:** 40¼" over-all.
Stock: Walnut.
Sights: Fixed front, adj. rear.
Features: Percussion muzzle loader, made to original 1861 English patterns. Imported from England by Navy Arms.
Price: $370.00

CAUTION: PRICES CHANGE. CHECK AT GUNSHOP.

BLACK POWDER MUSKETS & RIFLES

PARKER-HALE VOLUNTEER RIFLE
Caliber: .451".
Barrel: 32".
Weight: 9½ lbs. **Length:** 49" over-all.
Stock: Walnut, checkered wrist and fore-end.
Sights: Globe front, adjustable ladder-type rear.
Features: Recreation of the type of gun issued to volunteer regiments during the 1860's. Rigby-pattern rifling, patent breech, detented lock. Stock is glass bedded for accuracy. Comes with comprehensive accessory/shooting kit. From Navy Arms.
Price: $600.00

COOK & BROTHER CONFEDERATE CARBINE
Caliber: 58.
Barrel: 24".
Weight: 7½ lbs. **Length:** 40½" over-all.
Stock: Select walnut.
Features: Re-creation of the 1861 New Orleans-made artillery carbine. Color case-hardened lock, browned barrel. Buttplate, trigger guard, barrel bands, sling swivels and nosecap of polished brass. From Euroarms of America.
Price: $190.00

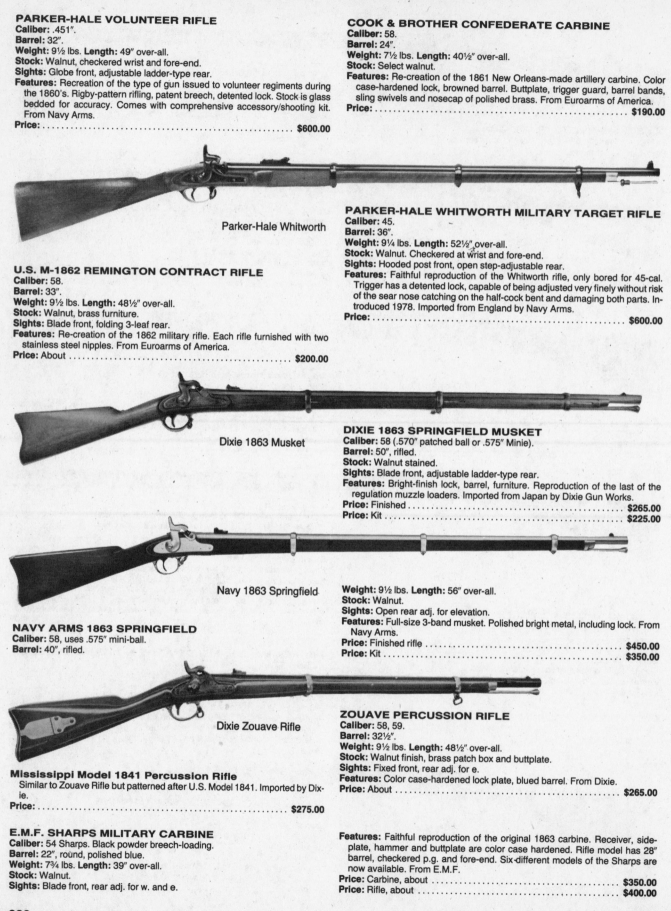

Parker-Hale Whitworth

PARKER-HALE WHITWORTH MILITARY TARGET RIFLE
Caliber: 45.
Barrel: 36".
Weight: 9¼ lbs. **Length:** 52½" over-all.
Stock: Walnut. Checkered at wrist and fore-end.
Sights: Hooded post front, open step-adjustable rear.
Features: Faithful reproduction of the Whitworth rifle, only bored for 45-cal. Trigger has a detented lock, capable of being adjusted very finely without risk of the sear nose catching on the half-cock bent and damaging both parts. Introduced 1978. Imported from England by Navy Arms.
Price: $600.00

U.S. M-1862 REMINGTON CONTRACT RIFLE
Caliber: 58.
Barrel: 33".
Weight: 9½ lbs. **Length:** 48½" over-all.
Stock: Walnut, brass furniture.
Sights: Blade front, folding 3-leaf rear.
Features: Re-creation of the 1862 military rifle. Each rifle furnished with two stainless steel nipples. From Euroarms of America.
Price: About $200.00

Dixie 1863 Musket

DIXIE 1863 SPRINGFIELD MUSKET
Caliber: 58 (.570" patched ball or .575" Minie).
Barrel: 50", rifled.
Stock: Walnut stained.
Sights: Blade front, adjustable ladder-type rear.
Features: Bright-finish lock, barrel, furniture. Reproduction of the last of the regulation muzzle loaders. Imported from Japan by Dixie Gun Works.
Price: Finished $265.00
Price: Kit $225.00

Navy 1863 Springfield

Weight: 9½ lbs. **Length:** 56" over-all.
Stock: Walnut.
Sights: Open rear adj. for elevation.
Features: Full-size 3-band musket. Polished bright metal, including lock. From Navy Arms.
Price: Finished rifle $450.00
Price: Kit $350.00

NAVY ARMS 1863 SPRINGFIELD
Caliber: 58, uses .575" mini-ball.
Barrel: 40", rifled.

Dixie Zouave Rifle

ZOUAVE PERCUSSION RIFLE
Caliber: 58, 59.
Barrel: 32½".
Weight: 9½ lbs. **Length:** 48½" over-all.
Stock: Walnut finish, brass patch box and buttplate.
Sights: Fixed front, rear adj. for e.
Features: Color case-hardened lock plate, blued barrel. From Dixie.
Price: About $265.00

Mississippi Model 1841 Percussion Rifle
Similar to Zouave Rifle but patterned after U.S. Model 1841. Imported by Dixie.
Price: $275.00

E.M.F. SHARPS MILITARY CARBINE
Caliber: 54 Sharps. Black powder breech-loading.
Barrel: 22", round, polished blue.
Weight: 7¾ lbs. **Length:** 39" over-all.
Stock: Walnut.
Sights: Blade front, rear adj. for w. and e.

Features: Faithful reproduction of the original 1863 carbine. Receiver, sideplate, hammer and buttplate are color case hardened. Rifle model has 28" barrel, checkered p.g. and fore-end. Six different models of the Sharps are now available. From E.M.F.
Price: Carbine, about $350.00
Price: Rifle, about $400.00

CAUTION: PRICES CHANGE. CHECK AT GUNSHOP.

C. Sharps 1874

ALLEN ST. LOUIS RIFLE
Caliber: 45, 50, 54, 58.
Barrel: 30″, octagonal.
Weight: NA. **Length:** NA.
Stock: Walnut.
Sights: German silver blade front, adj. rear.
Features: Browned barrel, color case-hardened lock. Percussion or flintlock. Imported by Allen Fire Arms.
Price: Flintlock, 45, 50 . . . . $259.00
Price: As above, 54 . . . . $289.00
Price: Percussion, 45, 50 . . . . $249.00
Price: As above, 54, 58 . . . . $259.00

C. SHARPS ARMS 1874 SPORTING RIFLE
Caliber: 40, 45, 50.
Barrel: 30″, Octagon.
Weight: 9½ lbs.
Stock: American walnut.
Sights: Blade front, Lawrence-style open rear.
Features: Color case-hardened receiver, buttplate and barrel bands, blued barrel. Recreation of the original Sharps rifles. Five other models in many original chamberings available. From C. Sharps Arms Co.
Price: 1874 Military Rifle $685.00
Price: 1874 Carbine $580.00
Price: 1874 Business Rifle $620.00
Price: 1874 Sporting Rifle No. 1 . . . . $775.00
Price: 1874 Sporting Rifle No. 3 . . . . $675.00
Price: 1874 Long Range Express Sporting Rifle $830.00

Dixie Sharps Rifle

Dixie Sharps Rifle
Similar to the E.M.F. Sharps Military Carbine except has 28½″ barrel, checkered half-stock fore-end and stock wrist, flat lockplate. Carbine-style case hardened buttplate. Imported from Italy by Dixie Gun Works.
Price: $349.95
Price: Military Carbine (22″ barrel) $329.95

MAC Silverwolf

Stock: Choice of walnut or maple; soft recoil pad.
Sights: Brass-bead front, adjustable folding leaf rear.
Features: New design uses straight-line ignition with #209 shotshell primer. Fires from an open bolt; has positive safety notch. Fully adjustable trigger. Introduced 1980. Made in U.S. by Michigan Arms Corp.
Price: Blue ordnance steel $398.00
Price: As above except in stainless steel (Silverwolf) $595.00
Price: Friendship Special (select barrel, Lyman globe front, Williams target peep rear, adjustable recoil pad, custom stock, special breech block) $599.00

MAC WOLVERINE RIFLE
Caliber: 45, 50, 54; 20-ga. shotgun.
Barrel: 26″, octagon, 1″ flats.
Weight: 7¾ lbs.

Navy Federal Target

Weight: 13¼ lbs. **Length:** 49½″ over-all.
Stock: European walnut with hook buttplate, Schuetzen-style trigger guard.
Sights: Tunnel front, aperture rear adjustable for windage and elevation.
Features: Hand-built reproduction of 1800s target rifle; quick detachable, five-lever, double-set trigger, adjustable to 4 oz. Color case-hardened furniture. Imported from Italy by Navy Arms. Introduced 1984.
Price: $895.00
Price: Swiss-style palm rest $35.00

NAVY SWISS FEDERAL TARGET RIFLE
Caliber: 45.
Barrel: 32″.

Sanftl Schuetzen

SANFTL SCHUETZEN PERCUSSION TARGET RIFLE
Caliber: 45 (.445″ round ball).
Barrel: 29″, ⅞″ octagon.
Weight: 9 lbs. **Length:** 43″ over-all.
Stock: Walnut, Schuetzen-style.
Sights: Open tunnel front post, peep rear adjustable for windage & elevation.
Features: True back-action lock with "backward" hammer; screw-in breech plug; buttplate, trigger guard and stock inlays are polished brass. Imported from Italy by Dixie Gun Works, Hopkins & Allen.
Price: $595.00

Rigby-style Target

RIGBY-STYLE TARGET RIFLE
Caliber: .451.
Barrel: 32½".
Weight: 7¾ lbs.
Stock: Walnut; hand-checkered pistol grip, fore-end.
Sights: Target front with micrometer adjustment; adjustable vernier peep rear.
Features: Comes cased with loading accessories—bullet starter, bullter sizer, special ramrod. Introduced 1985. From Navy Arms.
Price: $500.00

Morse/Navy Rifle

MORSE/NAVY RIFLE
Caliber: 45, 50 or 58.
Barrel: 26", octagonal.
Weight: 6 lbs. (45 cal.). **Length:** 41½" over-all.
Stock: American walnut, full p.g.
Sights: Blade front, open fixed rear.
Features: Brass action, trigger guard, ramrod pipes. Made in U.S. by Navy Arms.
Price: $167.00
Price: Kit $100.00

CVA EXPRESS RIFLE
Caliber: 50 (.490" ball)
Barrels: 28", round.
Weight: 9 lbs.
Stock: Walnut-stained hardwood.
Sights: Bead and post front, adjustable rear.
Features: Double rifle with twin percussion locks and triggers. Hooked breech. Introduced 1985. From CVA.
Price: Finished $299.95
Price: Kit $269.95
Price: Presentation Express (hand-checkered stock, engraved and polished locks, hammers, tang) $830.00

CVA Blazer II Rifle
Similar to the Blazer except has 24½" barrel, over-all length of 38", and weighs 5¾ lbs. Introduced 1986.
Price: Finished, 50 cal. $89.95
Price: Kit, 50 cal. $69.95

CVA BLAZER RIFLE
Caliber: 50 (.490" ball)
Barrel: 28", octagon.
Weight: 6 lbs., 13 oz.
Stock: Hardwood.
Sights: Brass blade front, fixed semi-buckhorn rear.
Features: Straight-line percussion with pistol-grip stock of modern design. Introduced 1985. From CVA.
Price: Finished $99.95
Price: Kit $79.95

Iver Johnson Double Rifle

IVER JOHNSON O-U MODEL BP.50HB RIFLE
Caliber: 50.
Barrel: 26".
Weight: 8½ lbs. **Length:** 41¼" over-all.
Stock: Checkered walnut
Sights: Blade front with gold bead, folding rear adjustable for w. and e.
Features: Two-shot over-under with two hammers, two triggers. Polished blue finish. Introduced 1985. From Iver Johnson.
Price: $364.95

KODIAK DOUBLE RIFLE
Caliber: 58x58, 50x50 and 58-oal./12 ga. optional.
Barrel: 28", 5 grooves, 1-in-48" twist.
Weight: 9½ lbs. **Length:** 43¼" over-all.
Stock: Czechoslovakian walnut, hand checkered.
Sights: Adjustable bead front, adjustable open rear.
Features: Hooked breech allows interchangeability of barrels. Comes with sling and swivels, adjustable powder measure, bullet mould and bullet starter. Engraved lock plates, top tang and trigger guard. Locks and top tang polished, rest blued. Imported from Italy by Trail Guns Armory, Inc.
Price: 58 cal. SxS $525.00
Price: 50 cal. SxS $525.00
Price: 50 cal. x 12 ga., 58x12. .... $525.00
Price: Spare barrels, 58x12 ga. $294.25
Price: Spare barrels, 12 ga. x 12 ga. $185.00

Kodiak Double Rifle

CAUTION: PRICES CHANGE. CHECK AT GUNSHOP.

Caption: CVA Shotgun

CVA 410 PERCUSSION SHOTGUN
Gauge: 410.
Barrel: 24".
Weight: 6 lbs., 4 oz. **Length:** 38" over-all.
Stock: Hardwood with pistol grip, M.C. comb.
Sights: Brass bead front.
Features: Color case-hardened lock plates; double triggers (front is hinged); brass wedge plates; stainless nipple. Introduced 1986. From CVA.
Price: Finished **$159.95**
Price: Kit **$114.95**

CVA PERCUSSION SHOTGUN
Gauge: 12.
Barrel: 28".
Weight: 6 lbs., 10 oz. **Length:** 44½"over-all.
Stock: Select hardwood; checkered pistol grip and fore-end.
Sights: Brass bead front.
Features: Hooked breech system. Blued barrels and thimbles, polished steel wedge plates, trigger guard, triggers, tang, lock and hammers; engraved lock, hammers, tang and trigger guard. Introduced 1983. From CVA.
Price: Finished **$274.95**
Price: Kit **$209.95**
Price: Presentation Grade (checkered European walnut stock, polished and engraved lock plates, hammers, tang) **$770.00**

Caption: Mowrey Ethan Allen

E.M.F. CLASSIC DOUBLE BARREL SHOTGUN
Gauge: 12.
Barrel: 28".
Weight: 7 lbs., 12 ozs. **Length:** 45" over-all.
Stock: Walnut.
Features: Color case-hardened lock plates and hammers; hand checkered stock. Imported by E.M.F.
Price: **$325.00**
Price: Kit **$250.00**

MOWREY ETHAN ALLEN SHOTGUN
Gauge: 12 or 28.
Barrel: 12 ga. — 32", browned octagon, 1" flats; 28 ga. — 28", browned octagon, 1³⁄₁₆" flats.
Weight: 12 ga. — 8 lbs., 28 ga. — 6½ lbs. **Length:** 48" over-all (12 ga.).
Stock: Curly maple, Premium or Fancy grade; hand-rubbed oil finish.
Sights: ⅛" bead front.
Features: Percussion only; steel or brass boxlock action and furniture; flat shotgun-style butt. Uses standard wads. Made in U.S. Add $38 for Fancy wood.
Price: Complete, brass or steel **$330.00**
Price: Kit (amateur) **$250.00**
Price: Kit (expert) **$190.00**

EUROARMS OF AMERICA MAGNUM CAPE GUN
Gauge: 12.
Barrel: 32" (Cyl.).
Weight: 7½ lbs.
Stock: Walnut.
Features: Single barrel percussion with polished steel lock, blued trigger guard and buttplate; hooked breech for easy takedown. From Euroarms of America.
Price: **$215.00**

> Consult our Directory pages for
> the location of firms mentioned.

MAC WOLVERINE FOWLER SHOTGUN
Gauge: 20.
Barrel: 28".
Weight: 7½ lbs. **Length:** 46" over-all.
Stock: Choice of walnut or curly maple.
Features: Fires from an open bolt, uses #209 shotshell primer for ignition. Modern rifle trigger; O-ring barrel seal; aluminum ramrod drilled and tapped for shotgun and standard blackpowder cleaning accessories. Left-hand model available at no extra charge. Introduced 1985. Made in U.S. by Michigan Arms Corp.
Price: **$395.00**

NAVY ARMS HUNTER SHOTGUN
Gauge: 20.
Barrel: 28½", interchangeable choke tubes (Full, Mod.).
Stock: Walnut, Hawken-style, checkered p.g. and fore-end.
Sights: Bead front.
Features: Chrome-lined barrel; rubber butt pad; color case-hardened lock; double set triggers; blued furniture. Comes with two flush-mounting choke tubes. Introduced 1986. From Navy Arms.
Price: **$245.00**

Caption: Navy T&T Shotgun

NAVY ARMS T&T SHOTGUN
Gauge: 12.
Barrel: 28" (Full & Full).
Weight: 7½ lbs.
Stock: Walnut.
Sights: Bead front.
Features: Color case-hardened locks, blued steel furniture. From Navy Arms.
Price: **$334.00**

BLACK POWDER SHOTGUNS

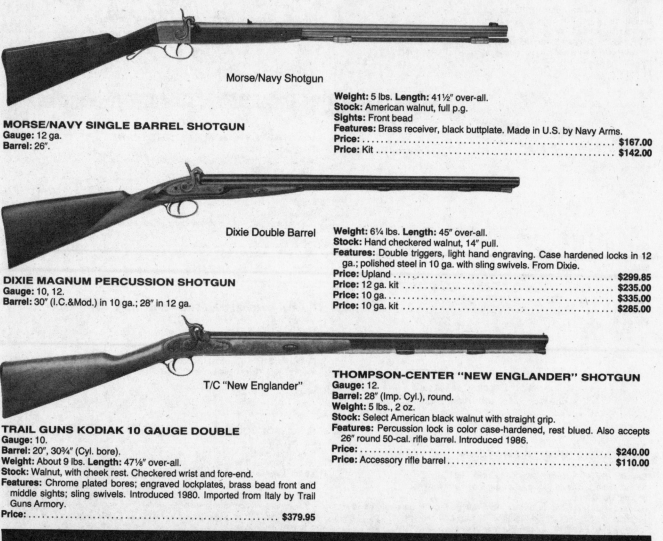

Navy Classic Double

NAVY CLASSIC DOUBLE BARREL SHOTGUN
Gauge: 10, 12.
Barrel: 28″.
Weight: 7 lbs., 12 ozs. **Length:** 45″ over-all.

Stock: Walnut.
Features: Color case-hardened lock plates and hammers; hand checkered stock. Imported by Navy Arms.
Price: 12 ga. $359.00
Price: 10 ga. $359.00
Price: Kit, 12 ga.. . . . . $265.00
Price: Kit, 10 ga. $265.00
Price: Fowler model, 12 ga. only. $249.00

Morse/Navy Shotgun

MORSE/NAVY SINGLE BARREL SHOTGUN
Gauge: 12 ga.
Barrel: 26″.

Weight: 5 lbs. **Length:** 41½″ over-all.
Stock: American walnut, full p.g.
Sights: Front bead
Features: Brass receiver, black buttplate. Made in U.S. by Navy Arms.
Price: $167.00
Price: Kit $142.00

Dixie Double Barrel

DIXIE MAGNUM PERCUSSION SHOTGUN
Gauge: 10, 12.
Barrel: 30″ (I.C.&Mod.) in 10 ga.; 28″ in 12 ga.

Weight: 6¼ lbs. **Length:** 45″ over-all.
Stock: Hand checkered walnut, 14″ pull.
Features: Double triggers, light hand engraving. Case hardened locks in 12 ga.; polished steel in 10 ga. with sling swivels. From Dixie.
Price: Upland $299.85
Price: 12 ga. kit $235.00
Price: 10 ga. $335.00
Price: 10 ga. kit $285.00

T/C "New Englander"

TRAIL GUNS KODIAK 10 GAUGE DOUBLE
Gauge: 10.
Barrel: 20″, 30¾″ (Cyl. bore).
Weight: About 9 lbs. **Length:** 47⅛″ over-all.
Stock: Walnut, with cheek rest. Checkered wrist and fore-end.
Features: Chrome plated bores; engraved lockplates, brass bead front and middle sights; sling swivels. Introduced 1980. Imported from Italy by Trail Guns Armory.
Price: $379.95

THOMPSON-CENTER "NEW ENGLANDER" SHOTGUN
Gauge: 12.
Barrel: 28″ (Imp. Cyl.), round.
Weight: 5 lbs., 2 oz.
Stock: Select American black walnut with straight grip.
Features: Percussion lock is color case-hardened, rest blued. Also accepts 26″ round 50-cal. rifle barrel. Introduced 1986.
Price: $240.00
Price: Accessory rifle barrel $110.00

AIR GUNS—HANDGUNS

AIR MATCH MODEL 600 PISTOL
Caliber: 177, single shot.
Barrel: 8.8″.
Weight: 32 oz. **Length:** 13.19″ over-all.
Power: Single stroke pneumatic.
Stocks: Match-style with adjustable palm shelf.
Sights: Interchangeable post front, fully adjustable match rear with interchangeable blades.
Features: Velocity of 420 fps. Adjustable trigger with dry-fire option. Comes with fitted case. Available with three different grip styles, barrel weight, sight extension. Add $5.00 for left-hand models. Introduced 1984. Imported from Italy by Kendall International Arms.
Price: With adjustable or fixed grip $386.25

Air Match 600

CAUTION: PRICES CHANGE. CHECK AT GUNSHOP.

BEEMAN P1 MAGNUM AIR PISTOL
Caliber: 177, single shot.
Barrel: 8.4".
Weight: 2.5 lbs. **Length:** 11" over-all.
Power: Top lever cocking; spring piston.
Stocks: Checkered walnut.
Sights: Blade front, square notch rear with click micrometer adjustments for w. and e. Grooved for scope mounting.
Features: Dual power: low setting gives 350-400 fps; high setting 500-600 fps. Rearward expanding mainspring simulates firearm recoil. All Colt 45 auto grips fit gun. Optional wooden shoulder stock. Introduced 1985. Imported by Beeman.
Price: **$189.95**

Beeman P1 Magnum

BEEMAN/FEINWERKBAU MODEL 2 CO² PISTOL
Caliber: 177, single shot
Barrel: 10.1".
Weight: 2.5 lbs. **Length:** 16¼" over-all.
Power: Special CO² cylinder.
Stocks: Stippled walnut with adjustable palm shelf.
Sights: Blade front with interchangeable inserts; open micro. click rear with adjustable notch width.
Features: Power adjustable from 360 fps to 525 fps. Fully adjustable trigger; three weights for balance and weight adjustments. Short-barrel Mini-2 model also available. Introduced 1983. Imported by Beeman.
Price: Right hand **$610.00**
Price: Left hand **$650.00**
Price: Mini-2, right hand **$635.00**
Price: Mini-2, left hand **$675.00**

FWB Mini-2

BEEMAN/WEBLEY HURRICANE PISTOL
Caliber: 177 or 22, single shot.
Barrel: 8", rifled.
Weight: 2.4 lbs. **Length:** 11½" over-all.
Power: Spring piston.
Stocks: Thumbrest, checkered high-impact synthetic.
Sights: Hooded front, micro-click rear adj. for w. and e.
Features: Velocity of 470 fps (177-cal.). Single stroke cocking, adjustable trigger pull, manual safety. Rearward recoil like a firearm pistol. Steel piston and cylinder. Scope base included; 1.5x scope **$39.95** extra. Shoulder stock available. Introduced 1977. Imported from England by Beeman.
Price: **$139.50**

Beeman/Webley Hurricane

BEEMAN/WEBLEY TEMPEST AIR PISTOL
Caliber: 177 or 22, single shot.
Barrel: 6.75", rifled ordnance steel.
Weight: 32 oz. **Length:** 9" over-all.
Power: Spring piston.
Stocks: Checkered black epoxy with thumbrest.
Sights: Post front; rear has sliding leaf adjustable for w. and e.
Features: Adjustable trigger pull, manual safety. Velocity 470 fps (177 cal.). Steel piston in steel liner for maximum performance and durability. Unique rearward spring simulates firearm recoil. Shoulder stock available. Introduced 1979. Imported from England by Beeman.
Price: **$109.50**

Beeman/Webley Tempest

BEEMAN/FEINWERKBAU FWB-65 MKII AIR PISTOL
Caliber: 177, single shot.
Barrel: 6.1"; fixed bbl. wgt. avail.
Weight: 42 oz. **Length:** 14.1" over-all.
Power: Spring, sidelever cocking.
Stocks: Walnut, stippled thumbrest; adjustable or fixed.
Sights: Front, interchangeable post element system, open rear, click adj. for w. & e. and for sighting notch width. Scope mount avail.
Features: New shorter barrel for better balance and control. Cocking effort 9 lbs. 2-stage trigger, 4 adjustments. Quiet firing, 525 fps. Programs instantly for recoil or recoilless operation. Permanently lubricated. Steel piston ring. Special switch converts trigger from 17.6 oz. pull to 42 oz. let-off. Imported by Beeman.
Price: Right-hand . . . . **$525.00** to **$623.00**
Price: Left-hand . . . . **$560.00** to **$633.00**
Price: Model 65 Mk.I (7.5" bbl.) . . . . **$515.00** to **$610.00**

FWB 65 Mk. II

CAUTION: PRICES CHANGE. CHECK AT GUNSHOP.

Beeman/Weihrauch HW-70

BENJAMIN SUPER S. S. TARGET PISTOL SERIES 130
Caliber: BB, single shot.
Barrel: 8"; BB smoothbore; 22 and 177, rifled.
Weight: 2 lbs. **Length:** 11" over-all.
Power: Hand pumped.
Features: Bolt action; fingertip safety; adj. power.
Price: M130, BB **$76.00**

Benjamin 232

CROSMAN MODEL 357 AIR PISTOL
Caliber: 177, 6-shot.
Barrel: 4" (Model 357 Four), 6" (Model 357 six), 8" (Model 357 Eight); rifled steel.
Weight: 32 oz. (6") **Length:** 11⅜" over-all.
Power: CO₂ Powerlet.
Stocks: Checkered wood-grain plastic.
Sights: Ramp front, fully adjustable rear.
Features: Average 430 fps (Model 357 Six). Break-open barrel for easy loading. Single or double action. Vent rib barrel. Wide, smooth trigger. Two speed loaders come with each gun. Models Four and Six introduced 1983, Model Eight introduced 1984.
Price: 4" or 6", about **$45.00**
Price: 8", about **$70.00**

> Consult our Directory pages for the location of firms mentioned.

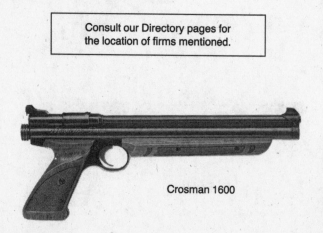

Crosman 1600

BEEMAN/WEIHRAUCH HW-70 AIR PISTOL
Caliber: 177, single shot.
Barrel: 6¼", rifled.
Weight: 38 oz. **Length:** 12¾" over-all.
Power: Spring, barrel cocking.
Stocks: Plastic, with thumbrest.
Sights: Hooded post front, square notch rear adj. for w. and e.
Features: Adj. trigger. 24-lb. cocking effort, 410 f.p.s. M.V.; automatic barrel safety. Imported by Beeman.
Price: From Beeman **$119.50**

BEEMAN/FEINWERKBAU MODEL 90 PISTOL
Caliber: 177, single shot.
Barrel: 7.5", 12-groove rifling.
Weight: 3.0 lbs. **Length:** 16.4" over-all.
Power: Spring piston, single stroke sidelever cocking.
Stocks: Stippled walnut with adjustable palm shelf.
Sights: Interchangeable blade front, fully adjustable open notch rear.
Features: Velocity of 475 to 525 fps. Has new adjustable electronic trigger. Recoilless action, metal piston ring and dual mainsprings. Cocking effort is 12 lbs. Introduced 1983. Imported by Beeman.
Price: . . . . **$685.00 to $715.00**

BENJAMIN 232/237 SINGLE SHOT PISTOLS
Caliber: 177 and 22.
Weight: 32 oz. **Length:** 11¾" over-all.
Power: Hand pumped.
Stocks: Walnut, with walnut pump handle.
Sights: Blade front, open adjustable rear.
Features: Bolt action; fingertip safety; adjustable power.
Price: Model 232 (22 cal.) **$84.45**
Price: Model 237 (177 cal.) **$84.45**

Crosman Model 357

CROSMAN MODEL 1322 AIR PISTOL
Caliber: 22, single shot.
Barrel: 8", button rifled.
Weight: 37 oz. **Length:** 13⅝".
Power: Hand pumped.
Sights: Blade front, rear adj. for w. and e.
Features: Moulded plastic grip, hand size pump forearm. Cross bolt safety. Also available in 177 Cal. as **Model 1377** (same price).
Price: About **$45.00**

CROSMAN 1600 BB PISTOL
Caliber: BB, 17-shot.
Barrel: 7¾".
Weight: 29 oz. **Length:** 11⅜" over-all.
Power: Standard CO₂.
Stocks: Contoured with thumbrest.
Sights: Patridge-type front, fully adj. rear.
Features: Gives about 80 shots per powerlet, slide-action safety, steel barrel, die-cast receiver. Introduced 1983.
Price: About **$30.00**

CAUTION: PRICES CHANGE. CHECK AT GUNSHOP.

CROSMAN MARK II TARGET PISTOL
Caliber: 177 or BB.
Barrel: 7¼", button rifled.
Weight: 44 oz. **Length:** 11⅛" over-all.
Power: Crosman Powerlet CO_2 cylinder.
Features: New system provides same shot-to-shot velocity of 435-485 fps (pellets). Checkered thumbrest grips, right or left. Patridge front sight, rear adj. for w. & e. Adj. trigger.
Price: About **$58.00**

Crosman Mark II

Daisy Softair 04

DAISY SOFTAIR 04
Caliber: 25-cal. plastic pellets.
Barrel: Smoothbore.
Weight: 1.1 lbs. **Length:** 10.5" over-all.
Power: Spring.
Stocks: Woodgrain moulded grip with checkering.
Sights: Blade and ramp front, notched rear.
Features: Fully detailed replica of a classic 44 Magnum, six-shot revolver with swing-out cylinder for easy loading.
Price: About **$44.00**

DAISY MODEL 08 SOFTAIR PISTOL
Caliber: 25 (6mm) plastic pellets; 6-shot clip.
Barrel: Smoothbore.
Weight: NA. **Length:** 9¾" over-all.
Stocks: Woodtone, molded with checkering.
Sights: Post front, notch rear.
Features: Fires 25-cal. plastic pellets loaded into plastic cartridges; semi-auto action ejects spent shells. Introduced 1985.
Price: About **$39.00**

Daisy Softair 08

Daisy Softair 09

DAISY SOFTAIR 09
Caliber: 25-cal. plastic shot.
Barrel: Smoothbore.
Weight: 12 oz. **Length:** 9.5" over-all.
Power: Slide action, spring air.
Stocks: Moulded grip with checkering.
Sights: Blade front, notched rear.
Features: Detailed replica of the official 9mm sidearm recently adopted by the U.S. Armed Forces, the Beretta 9mm. Takes seven-shot clip, ejects spent shells.
Price: About **$44.00**

Daisy Softair 13

DAISY SOFTAIR GUN 13
Caliber: 25-cal. plastic shot.
Barrel: Smoothbore.
Weight: 2.6 lbs. **Length:** 15.5" over-all.
Power: Bolt action, spring air.
Stock: Molded grip and receiver.
Sights: Post front, notched rear.
Features: Replica of the world-famous Israeli semi-automatic assault pistol; loads with 22-shot clip.
Price: About **$83.00**

DAISY MODEL 38 SOFTAIR PISTOL
Caliber: 25 (6mm) plastic pellets; single shot.
Barrel: Smoothbore.
Weight: NA. **Length:** 10" over-all.
Stocks: Molded, grooved plastic.
Sights: Post front, notch rear.
Features: Fires 25-cal. plastic pellets loaded into a pop-up chamber in barrel. Introduced 1985.
Price: About **$39.00**

DAISY SOFTAIR 45
Caliber: 25-cal. plastic shot.
Barrel: Smoothbore.
Weight: 12 oz. **Length:** 8.5" over-all.
Power: Slide cocking, spring air.
Stocks: Moulded grip with checkering.
Sights: Ramp front, notched rear.
Features: Detailed replica of the 45 auto pistol. Holds seven-shot clip, ejects spent shells.
Price: About **$44.00**

CAUTION: PRICES CHANGE. CHECK AT GUNSHOP.

Daisy Softair 57

Daisy Power Line 92

Daisy Model 188

FAS 604

Marksman Model 17

DAISY MODEL 57 SOFTAIR REVOLVER
Caliber: 25 (6mm) plastic pellets; 6-shot.
Barrel: Smoothbore.
Weight: NA. **Length:** 10½" over-all.
Stocks: Molded woodgrain with checkering.
Sights: Blade and ramp front, notch rear.
Features: Fires spring-activated 25-cal. plastic pellets loaded into plastic cartridges. Cylinder swings out for loading. Introduced 1985.
Price: About **$39.00**

DAISY MODEL 59 SOFTAIR PISTOL
Caliber: 25 (6mm) plastic pellets; 10-shot clip.
Barrel: Smoothbore.
Weight: NA. **Length:** 9" over-all.
Stocks: Molded with checkering.
Sights: Blade and ramp front, notch rear.
Features: Fires 25-cal. plastic pellets loaded into plastic cartridges. Clip fed, semi-auto action ejects spent bullets. Introduced 1985.
Price: About **$39.00**

DAISY POWER LINE MODEL 92 PISTOL
Caliber: 177 pellets, 10-shot magazine.
Barrel: Rifled steel.
Weight: 2.15 lbs. **Length:** 8.5" over-all.
Power: CO_2.
Stocks: Cast checkered metal.
Sights: Blade front, adjustable V-slot rear.
Features: Semi-automatic action; 400 fps. Replica of the official 9mm side arm of the United States armed forces.
Price: About **$71.00**

DAISY MODEL 188 BB PISTOL
Caliber: BB.
Barrel: 9.9", steel smoothbore.
Weight: 1.67 lbs. **Length:** 11.7" over-all.
Stocks: Die-cast metal; checkered with thumbrest.
Sights: Blade and ramp front, open fixed rear.
Features: 24-shot repeater. Spring action with under-barrel cocking lever. Grip and receiver of die-cast metal. Introduced 1979.
Price: About **$26.00**

FAS MODEL 604 AIR PISTOL
Caliber: 177, single shot.
Barrel: 7.4", 10-groove rifled steel.
Weight: 2.3 lbs. **Length:** 11.3" over-all.
Power: Single stroke pneumatic.
Stocks: Anatomically shaped stippled walnut; small, medium, large sizes.
Sights: Adjustable.
Features: Top of receiver is cocking arm, requires 13 lbs. effort. Adjustable trigger may be dry-fired without fully cocking pistol. Imported from Italy by Osborne's, Beeman. Introduced 1984.
Price: Beeman .... **$495.00 to $525.00**
Price: Osborne's **$375.00**

HAMMERLI "MASTER" CO_2 TARGET PISTOL
Caliber: 177, single shot.
Barrel: 6.4", 12-groove.
Weight: 38.4 oz. **Length:** 16" over-all.
Power: 12 gram cylinder.
Stocks: Plastic with thumbrest and checkering.
Sights: Ramp front, micro rear, click adj. Adj. sight radius from 11.1" to 13.0".
Features: Single shot, manual loading. Residual gas vented automatically. 5-way adj. trigger. Available from Mandall Shooting Supplies.
Price: **$495.00**

MARKSMAN 17 AIR PISTOL
Caliber: 177, single shot.
Barrel: 7.5".
Weight: 46 oz. **Length:** 14.5" over-all.
Power: Spring air, barrel-cocking.
Stocks: Checkered composition with right-hand thumb rest.
Sights: Tunnel front, fully adj. rear.
Features: Velocity of 330-360 fps. Introduced 1986. Imported from Spain by Marksman Products.
Price: **$75.00**

CAUTION: PRICES CHANGE. CHECK AT GUNSHOP.

Marksman Plainsman

Marksman Model 54 Air Revolver
Similar to the Orion except is 5-shot revolver with 4″ barrel, 9″ over-all length, weighs 21 oz. Velocity of 475-525 fps. Uses same Saxby-Palmer pre-primed cartridge system.
Price: With portable pump, 5 cartridges.........................$260.00

MARKSMAN #1010 REPEATER PISTOL
Caliber: 177, 20-shot repeater.
Barrel: 2½″, smoothbore.
Weight: 24 oz. **Length:** 8¼″.
Power: Spring
Features: Thumb safety. Uses BBs, darts or pellets. Repeats with BBs only.
Price: Matte black finish..$17.00
Price: Model 1020 (as above except fires BBs only)...............$17.00

MAUSER JUMBO AIR PISTOL
Caliber: 177, single shot.
Barrel: 6″, rifled.
Weight: 25 oz. **Length:** 7.25″ over-all.
Power: Spring air.
Stocks: Checkered walnut.
Sights: Blade front, fixed rear.
Features: Velocity of 300-325 fps; extra pellet storage in grip; thumb safety. Imported from West Germany by Marksman Products.
Price:..$74.00

Norica Black Widow

POWER LINE MATCH 777 PELLET PISTOL
Caliber: 177, single shot.
Barrel: 9.61″ rifled steel by Lothar Walther.
Weight: 32 oz. **Length:** 13½″ over-all.
Power: Sidelever, single pump pneumatic.
Stocks: Smooth hardwood, fully contoured with palm and thumb rest.
Sights: Blade and ramp front, match-grade open rear with adj. width notch, micro. click adjustments.
Features: Adjustable trigger; manual cross-bolt safety. MV of 385 fps. Comes with cleaning kit, adjustment tool and pellets.
Price: About...$272.00

MARKSMAN PLAINSMAN 1049 CO₂ PISTOL
Caliber: BB, 100-shot repeater.
Barrel: 5⅞″, smooth.
Weight: 28 oz. **Length:** 9½″ over-all.
Stocks: Simulated walnut with thumbrest.
Power: 8.5 or 12.5 gram CO_2 cylinders.
Features: Velocity of 400 fps. Three-position power switch. Auto. ammunition feed. Positive safety.
Price:..$35.00

MARKSMAN ORION AIR REVOLVER
Caliber: 177, 6-shot.
Barrel: 6″.
Weight: 2 lbs., 3 oz. **Length:** 11″ over-all.
Power: Compressed air cartridges.
Stocks: Composition semi-match style with thumbrest.
Sights: Blade front, fully-adj. rear.
Features: Velocity of 525-575 fps. Single/double action. Power source from Saxby-Palmer pre-primed cartridges; recoilless; comes with compressor unit, 6 cartridges. Gun made in W. Germany, cartridge system from England. Imported by Marksman Products. Introduced 1986.
Price: With table-top pump, 6 cartridges........................$375.00
Price: With portable pump, 6 cartridges.........................$335.00

Marksman 1010

Mauser Jumbo

NORICA BLACK WIDOW AIR PISTOL
Caliber: 177, single shot.
Barrel: 7¾″.
Weight: 3 lbs. **Length:** 15″ over-all.
Power: Spring air, barrel cocking.
Stocks: Target-style of black high-impact plastic.
Sights: Hooded front, open adjustable rear.
Features: Velocity 395 fps. Side mounted automatic safety; receiver grooved for scope mounting. Imported from Spain by Kassnar.
Price:..$74.00

Power Line 777

POWER LINE 717 PELLET PISTOL
Caliber: 177, single shot.
Barrel: 9.61".
Weight: 2.8 lbs. **Length:** 13½" over-all.
Stocks: Molded wood-grain plastic, with thumbrest.
Sights: Blade and ramp front, micro. adjustable notch rear.
Features: Single pump pneumatic pistol. Rifled steel barrel. Cross-bolt trigger block. Muzzle velocity 385 fps. From Daisy. Introduced 1979.
Price: About $64.00

Power Line 717

POWER LINE CO₂ 1200 PISTOL
Caliber: BB, 177.
Barrel: 10½", smooth.
Weight: 1.6 lbs. **Length:** 11.1" over-all.
Power: Daisy CO₂ cylinder.
Stocks: Contoured, checkered molded wood-grain plastic.
Sights: Blade ramp front, fully adj. square notch rear.
Features: 60-shot BB reservoir, gravity feed. Cross-bolt safety. Velocity of 420-450 fps for more than 100 shots.
Price: About $39.00

RWS Model 5G

RWS MODEL 5G AIR PISTOL
Caliber: 177, single shot.
Barrel: 7".
Weight: 2¾ lbs. **Length:** 16" over-all.
Power: Spring air, barrel cocking.
Stocks: Plastic, thumbrest design.
Sights: Tunnel front, micro click open rear.
Features: Velocity of 410 fps. Two-stage trigger with automatic safety. Imported from West Germany by Dynamit Nobel of America.
Price: $130.00

RWS MODEL 5GS AIR PISTOL
Same as the Model 5G except comes with 1.5×15 pistol scope with ramp-style mount, muzzle brake/weight. No open sights supplied. Introduced 1983.
Price: $175.00

RWS Model 10 Match Air Pistol
Refined version of the Model 6M. Has special adjustable match trigger, oil finished and stippled match grips, barrel weight. Also available in left-hand version, and with fitted case.
Price: Model 10 .... $450.00
Price: Model 10, left hand.................................. $480.00
Price: Model 10, with case $470.00
Price: Model 10, left hand, with case $500.00

RWS MODEL 6M MATCH AIR PISTOL
Caliber: 177, single shot.
Barrel: 7".
Weight: 3 lbs. **Length:** 16" over-all.
Power: Spring air, barrel cocking.
Stocks: Walnut-finished hardwood with thumbrest.
Sights: Adjustable front, micro click open rear.
Features: Velocity of 410 fps. Recoilless double piston system, moveable barrel shroud to protect front sight during cocking. Imported from West Germany by Dynamit Nobel of America.
Price: $260.00

SHERIDAN MODEL HB PNEUMATIC PISTOL
Caliber: 5mm; single shot.
Barrel: 9⅜", rifled.
Weight: 36 oz. **Length:** 12" over-all.
Power: Underlever pneumatic pump.
Stocks: Checkered simulated walnut; fore-end is walnut.
Sights: Blade front, fully adjustable rear.
Features: "Controller-Power" feature allows velocity and range control by varying the number of pumps—3 to 10. Maximum velocity of 400 fps. Introduced 1982. From Sheridan Products.
Price: $86.95

RWS Model 10

SHERIDAN MODEL EB CO₂ PISTOL
Caliber: 20 (5mm).
Barrel: 6½", rifled, rust proof.
Weight: 27 oz. **Length:** 9" over-all.
Power: 12 gram CO₂ cylinder.
Stocks: Checkered simulated walnut. Left- or right-handed.
Sights: Blade front, fully adjustable rear.
Features: Turn-bolt single-shot action. Gives about 40 shots at 400 fps per CO₂ cylinder.
Price: $65.25

WALTHER CP CO₂ AIR PISTOL
Caliber: 177, single shot.
Barrel: 9".
Weight: 40 oz. **Length:** 14¾" over-all.
Power: CO₂.
Stocks: Full target type stippled wood with adjustable hand-shelf.
Sights: Target post front, fully adjustable target rear.
Features: Velocity of 520 fps. CO₂ powered; target-quality trigger; comes with adaptor for charging with standard CO₂ air tanks, case, and accessories. Introduced 1983. Imported from West Germany by Interarms.
Price: $565.00
Price: Junior model (modified grip, shorter gas cylinder) $565.00

Sheridan Model HB

CAUTION: PRICES CHANGE. CHECK AT GUNSHOP.

Beeman/FWB 124

BEEMAN/FEINWERKBAU 124/127 MAGNUM
Caliber: 177 (FWB-124); 22 (FWB-127); single shot.
Barrel: 18.3", 12-groove rifling.
Weight: 6.8 lbs. **Length:** 43½" over-all.
Power: Spring piston air; single stroke barrel cocking.
Stock: Walnut finished hardwood.
Sights: Tunnel front; click-adj. rear for w., slide-adj. for e.
Features: Velocity 680-820 fps, cocking effort of 18 lbs. Forged steel receiver; nylon non-drying piston and breech seals. Auto. safety, adj. trigger. Standard model has no checkering, cheekpiece. Deluxe has hand-checkerd p.g. and fore-end, high comb cheekpiece, and buttplate with white spacer. Imported by Beeman.
Price: Standard model **$319.50**
Price: Deluxe model (illus.) **$339.50**

BEEMAN/FEINWERKBAU 300-S SERIES MATCH RIFLE
Caliber: 177, single shot.
Barrel: 19.9", fixed solid with receiver.
Weight: Approx. 10 lbs. with optional bbl. sleeve. **Length:** 42.8" over-all.
Power: Single stroke sidelever, spring piston.
Stock: Match model—walnut, deep fore-end, adj. buttplate.
Sights: Globe front with interchangeable inserts. Click micro. adj. match aperture rear. Front and rear sights move as a single unit.
Features: Recoilless, vibration free. Five-way adjustable match trigger. Grooved for scope mounts. Permanent lubrication, steel piston ring. Cocking effort 9 lbs. Optional 10 oz. bbl. sleeve. Available from Beeman.
Price: Right hand **$735.00**
Price: Left hand **$785.00**

FWB 300-S Universal

BEEMAN/FEINWERKBAU 300-S "UNIVERSAL" MATCH
Caliber: 177, single shot.
Barrel: 19.9".
Weight: 10.2 lbs. (without barrel sleeve). **Length:** 43.3" over-all.
Power: Spring piston, single stroke sidelever.
Stock: Walnut, stippled p.g. and fore-end. Detachable cheekpieces (one std., high for scope use.) Adjustable buttplate, accessory rail. Buttplate and grip cap spacers included.
Sights: Two globe fronts with interchangeable inserts. Rear is match aperture with rubber eyecup and sight viser. Front and rear sights move as a single unit.

Features: Recoilless, vibration free. Grooved for scope mounts. Steel piston ring. Cocking effort about 9½ lbs. Barrel sleeve optional. Left-hand model available. Introduced 1978. Imported by Beeman.
Price: Right-hand **$830.00**
Price: Left-hand **$890.00**

FWB F300S RBTH

BEEMAN/FEINWERKBAU F300-S RUNNING BOAR (TH)
Caliber: 177, single shot.
Barrel: 19.9", rifled.
Weight: 10.9 lbs. **Length:** 43" over-all.

Power: Single stroke sidelever, spring piston.
Stock: Walnut with adjustable buttplate, grip cap and comb. Designed for fixed and moving target use.
Sights: None furnished; grooved for optional scope.
Features: Recoilless, vibration free. Permanent lubrication and seals. Barrel stabilizer weight included. Crisp single-stage trigger. Available from Beeman.
Price: Right-hand **$735.00**
Price: Left-hand **$795.00**

FWB Mini-Match

BEEMAN/FEINWERKBAU 300-S MINI-MATCH
Caliber: 177, single shot.
Barrel: 17⅛".
Weight: 8.8 lbs. **Length:** 40" over-all.

Power: Spring piston, single stroke sidelever cocking.
Stock: Walnut. Stippled grip, adjustable buttplate. Scaled-down for youthful or slightly built shooters.
Sights: Globe front with interchangeable inserts, micro. adjustable rear. Front and rear sights move as a single unit.
Features: Recoilless, vibration free. Grooved for scope mounts. Steel piston ring. Cocking effort about 9½ lbs. Barrel sleeve optional. Left-hand model available. Introduced 1978. Imported by Beeman.
Price: Right-hand **$685.00**
Price: Left-hand **$735.00**

Beeman/Feinwerkbau 600

BEEMAN HW 55 TARGET RIFLES

Model:	55SM	55MM	55T
Caliber:	177	177	177
Barrel:	18½"	18½"	18½"
Length:	43½"	43½"	43½"
Wgt. lbs.:	7.8	7.8	7.8
Rear sight:	All aperture		
Front sight:	All with globe and 4 interchangeable inserts.		
Power:	All spring (barrel cocking). 660-700 fps.		
Price:	$369.50	$399.50	$469.50

Features: Trigger fully adj. and removable. Micrometer rear sight adj. for w. and e. on all. Pistol grip high comb stock with beavertail fore-end, walnut finish stock on 55SM. Walnut stock on 55MM, Tyrolean stock on 55T. Imported by Beeman.

BEEMAN/FEINWERKBAU MODEL 600 AIR RIFLE

Caliber: 177, single shot.
Barrel: 16.6".
Weight: 10.8. **Length:** 43" over-all.
Power: Single stroke pneumatic.
Stock: Special laminated hardwoods and hard rubber for stability.
Sights: Tunnel front with interchangeable inserts, click micrometer match aperture rear.
Features: Recoilless action; double supported barrel; special, short rifled area frees pellet from barrel faster so shooter's motion has minimum effect on accuracy. Fully adjustable match trigger. Trigger and sights blocked when loading latch is open. Imported by Beeman. Introduced 1984.
Price: Right hand **$875.00**
Price: Left hand **$899.50**

BEEMAN/HW77 AIR RIFLE & CARBINE

Caliber: 177 or 22, single shot.
Barrel: 18.5", 12-groove rifling.
Weight: 8.9 lbs. **Length:** 43.7" over-all.
Power: Spring-piston; underlever cocking.
Stock: Walnut-stained beech; rubber buttplate, cut checkering on grip; cheekpiece.
Sights: Blade front, open adjustable rear.
Features: Velocity 830 fps. Fixed-barrel with fully opening, direct loading breech. Extended underlever gives good cocking leverage. Adjustable trig-

Beeman HW77

ger. Grooved for scope mounting. Carbine has 14.5" barrel, weighs 8.7 lbs., and is 39.7" over-all. Imported by Beeman.
Price: Right-hand, rifle or carbine **$359.50**
Price: Left-hand, rifle or carbine **$389.50**

BEEMAN CARBINE MODEL C1

Caliber: 177, single shot.
Barrel: 14", 12-groove rifling.
Weight: 6¼ lbs. **Length:** 38" over-all.
Power: Spring-piston, barrel cocking.
Stock: Walnut-stained beechwood with rubber butt pad.
Sights: Blade front, rear click-adjustable for windage and elevation.
Features: Velocity 830 fps. Adjustable trigger. Receiver grooved for scope mounting. Imported by Beeman.
Price: **$177.50**

Beeman Carbine C1

BEEMAN/WEBLEY OMEGA AIR RIFLE

Caliber: 177.
Barrel: 19¼", rifled.
Weight: 7.8 lbs. **Length:** 43½" over-all.
Power: Spring-piston air; barrel cocking.
Stock: Walnut-stained beech with cut-checkered grip; cheekpiece; rubber butt pad.
Features: Special quick-snap barrel latch; self-lubricating piston seal; receiver grooved for scope mounting. Introduced 1985. Imported from England by Beeman.
Price: **$269.50**

Beeman/Webley Omega

BEEMAN/WEBLEY VULCAN II DELUXE

Caliber: 177 or 22, single shot.
Barrel: 17", rifled.
Weight: 7.6 lbs. **Length:** 43.7" over-all.
Power: Spring piston air, barrel cocking.
Stock: Walnut. Cut checkering, rubber butt pad, checkpiece. Standard version has walnut-stained beech.
Sights: Hooded front, micrometer rear.
Features: Velocity of 830 fps (177), 675 fps (22). Single stage adjustable trigger; receiver grooved for scope mounting. Self-lubricating piston seal. Introduced 1983. Imported by Beeman.
Price: Standard **$198.50**
Price: Deluxe **$245.00**

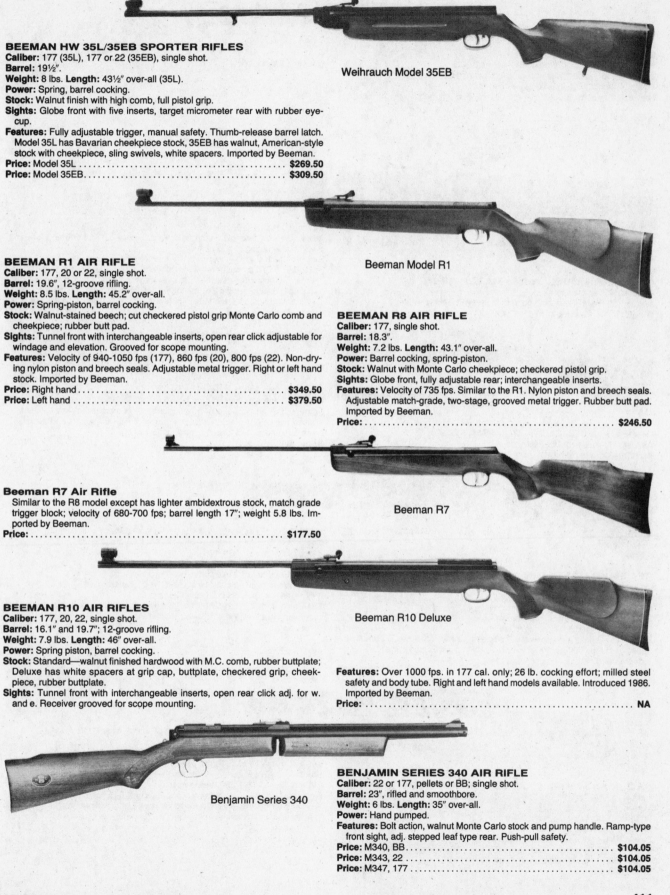

Weihrauch Model 35EB

BEEMAN HW 35L/35EB SPORTER RIFLES
Caliber: 177 (35L), 177 or 22 (35EB), single shot.
Barrel: 19½".
Weight: 8 lbs. **Length:** 43½" over-all (35L).
Power: Spring, barrel cocking.
Stock: Walnut finish with high comb, full pistol grip.
Sights: Globe front with five inserts, target micrometer rear with rubber eye-
    cup.
Features: Fully adjustable trigger, manual safety. Thumb-release barrel latch.
    Model 35L has Bavarian cheekpiece stock, 35EB has walnut, American-style
    stock with cheekpiece, sling swivels, white spacers. Imported by Beeman.
Price: Model 35L **$269.50**
Price: Model 35EB. **$309.50**

Beeman Model R1

BEEMAN R1 AIR RIFLE
Caliber: 177, 20 or 22, single shot.
Barrel: 19.6", 12-groove rifling.
Weight: 8.5 lbs. **Length:** 45.2" over-all.
Power: Spring-piston, barrel cocking.
Stock: Walnut-stained beech; cut checkered pistol grip Monte Carlo comb and
    cheekpiece; rubber butt pad.
Sights: Tunnel front with interchangeable inserts, open rear click adjustable for
    windage and elevation. Grooved for scope mounting.
Features: Velocity of 940-1050 fps (177), 860 fps (20), 800 fps (22). Non-dry-
    ing nylon piston and breech seals. Adjustable metal trigger. Right or left hand
    stock. Imported by Beeman.
Price: Right hand **$349.50**
Price: Left hand **$379.50**

BEEMAN R8 AIR RIFLE
Caliber: 177, single shot.
Barrel: 18.3".
Weight: 7.2 lbs. **Length:** 43.1" over-all.
Power: Barrel cocking, spring-piston.
Stock: Walnut with Monte Carlo cheekpiece; checkered pistol grip.
Sights: Globe front, fully adjustable rear; interchangeable inserts.
Features: Velocity of 735 fps. Similar to the R1. Nylon piston and breech seals.
    Adjustable match-grade, two-stage, grooved metal trigger. Rubber butt pad.
    Imported by Beeman.
Price: **$246.50**

Beeman R7

Beeman R7 Air Rifle
    Similar to the R8 model except has lighter ambidextrous stock, match grade
trigger block; velocity of 680-700 fps; barrel length 17"; weight 5.8 lbs. Imported by Beeman.
Price: **$177.50**

Beeman R10 Deluxe

BEEMAN R10 AIR RIFLES
Caliber: 177, 20, 22, single shot.
Barrel: 16.1" and 19.7"; 12-groove rifling.
Weight: 7.9 lbs. **Length:** 46" over-all.
Power: Spring piston, barrel cocking.
Stock: Standard—walnut finished hardwood with M.C. comb, rubber buttplate;
    Deluxe has white spacers at grip cap, buttplate, checkered grip, cheek-
    piece, rubber buttplate.
Sights: Tunnel front with interchangeable inserts, open rear click adj. for w.
    and e. Receiver grooved for scope mounting.

Features: Over 1000 fps. in 177 cal. only; 26 lb. cocking effort; milled steel
    safety and body tube. Right and left hand models available. Introduced 1986.
    Imported by Beeman.
Price: . . . . **NA**

Benjamin Series 340

BENJAMIN SERIES 340 AIR RIFLE
Caliber: 22 or 177, pellets or BB; single shot.
Barrel: 23", rifled and smoothbore.
Weight: 6 lbs. **Length:** 35" over-all.
Power: Hand pumped.
Features: Bolt action, walnut Monte Carlo stock and pump handle. Ramp-type
    front sight, adj. stepped leaf type rear. Push-pull safety.
Price: M340, BB **$104.05**
Price: M343, 22 . . . . **$104.05**
Price: M347, 177 . . . . **$104.05**

CROSMAN MODEL 66 POWERMASTER
Caliber: 177 (single shot) or BB.
Barrel: 20″, rifled, solid steel.
Weight: 3 lbs., 14 oz. **Length:** 38½″ over-all.
Stock: Wood-grained plastic; checkered p.g. and fore-end.
Sights: Ramp front, fully adjustable open rear.
Features: Velocity about 675 fps. Bolt action, cross-bolt safety. Introduced 1983.
Price: About $40.00

Crosman Model 66

Crosman Model 84

CROSMAN MODEL 84 CO₂ MATCH RIFLE
Caliber: 177, single shot.
Barrel: 20″. Barrel has a chrome shroud to give extra sight radius.
Weight: 9 lbs., 9 oz. **Length:** 45.5″ over-all.

Power: Refillable CO_2 cylinders.
Stock: Walnut; Olympic match design with stippled pistol grip and fore-end, adjustable buttplate and comb.
Sights: Match sights — globe front micrometer adjustable rear.
Features: A CO_2 pressure regulated rifle with adjustable velocity up to 720 fps. Each CO_2 cylinder has more than enough power to complete a 60-shot Olympic match course. Electric trigger adjustable from ½ oz. to 3 lbs. Each gun can be custom fitted to the shooter. Made in U.S.A. Introduced 1984.
Price: About.. $1,379.00

Crosman Model 760

CROSMAN MODEL 760 PUMPMASTER
Caliber: 177 pellets or BB, 200 shot.
Barrel: 19½″, rifled steel.

Weight: 3 lbs., 3 oz. **Length:** 35″ over-all.
Power: Pneumatic, hand pump.
Features: Short stroke, power determined by number of strokes. Walnut finished plastic checkered stock and fore-end. Post front sight and adjustable rear sight. Cross-bolt safety. Introduced 1983.
Price: About $30.00

Crosman Model 781

CROSMAN MODEL 781 SINGLE PUMP
Caliber: 177, BB, 4-shot pellet clip, 195-shot BB magazine.
Barrel: 19½″.
Weight: 2 lbs., 14 oz. **Length:** 35¾″ over-all.
Power: Pneumatic, single pump.
Stock: Wood-grained plastic; checkered p.g. and fore-end.
Sights: Blade front, open adjustable rear.
Features: Velocity of 350-400 fps (pellets). Uses only one pump. Hidden BB reservoir holds 195 shots; pellets loaded via 4-shot clip. Introduced 1984.
Price: About $28.00

CROSMAN MODEL 788 BB SCOUT RIFLE
Caliber: 177, BB.
Barrel: 14″, steel.
Weight: 2 lbs. 7 oz. **Length:** 31″ over-all.
Stock: Wood-grained ABS plastic.
Sights: Blade on ramp front, open adj. rear.
Features: Variable pump power—3 pumps give MV of 330 fps, 6 pumps 437 fps, 10 pumps 500 fps (BBs, average). Steel barrel, cross-bolt safety. Introduced 1978.
Price: About $26.00

Crosman 2100 Classic

CROSMAN MODEL 2200 MAGNUM AIR RIFLE
Caliber: 22, single-shot.
Barrel: 19″, rifled steel.
Weight: 4 lbs., 13 oz. **Length:** 39″ over-all.
Stock: Full-size, wood-grained plastic with checkered p.g. and fore-end.
Sights: Ramp front, open step-adjustable rear.
Features: Variable pump power—3 pumps give 395 fps, 6 pumps 530 fps, 10 pumps 620 fps (average). Full-size adult air rifle. Has white line spacers at pistol grip and buttplate. Introduced 1978.
Price: About $54.00

CROSMAN MODEL 2100 CLASSIC AIR RIFLE
Caliber: 177 pellets or BBs, 200-shot BB magazine.
Barrel: 21″, rifled.
Weight: 4 lbs., 13 oz. **Length:** 39¾″ over-all.
Power: Pump-up, pneumatic.
Stock: Wood-grained checkered ABS plastic.
Features: Three pumps gives about 450 fps, 10 pumps about 795 fps. Cross-bolt safety; concealed reservoir holds over 180 BBs.
Price: About $45.00

CAUTION: PRICES CHANGE. CHECK AT GUNSHOP.

Crosman 6100 Challenger

CROSMAN MODEL 6100 CHALLENGER RIFLE
Caliber: 177, single shot.
Weight: 7 lbs., 12 oz. **Length:** 46″ over-all.
Power: Spring air, barrel cocking.
Stock: Stained hardwood with checkered pistol grip, rubber recoil pad.
Sights: Globe front, open fully adjustable rear.
Features: Average velocity 820 fps. Automatic safety, two-stage adjustable trigger. Receiver grooved for scope mounting. Introduced 1982. Imported from West Germany by Crosman Air Guns.
Price: About **$200.00**

CROSMAN MODEL 6300 CHALLENGER AIR RIFLE
Caliber: 177.
Power: Spring-air, barrel-cocking.
Stock: Stained hardwood.
Sights: Hooded front, micrometer adjustable rear.
Features: Velocity of 680 to 710 fps. Adjustable trigger; automatic safety; comes with mount base for peep sight or scope. Introduced 1985.
Price: About **$126.00**

Crosman Model 6500 Challenger Air Rifle
Similar to the Model 6300 except has tunnel front sight with interchangeable bead for post or aperture inserts; positive barrel locking mechanism; automatic safety; rubber butt pad. Introduced 1985.
Price: About **$140.00**

DAISY MODEL 25 CENTENNIAL
Caliber: BB, 46-shot repeater.
Barrel: Smoothbore steel with removable shot tube.
Weight: 3.25 lbs. **Length:** 37″ over-all.
Power: Spring air.
Stock: American black walnut with hand-rubbed finish, centennial medallion embedded in left side.
Sights: Post front, adjustable v-slot rear.

Daisy Model 25

Features: Authentic styling after 1913 Daisy original. Muzzle velocity up to 340 fps; case-hardened finish lever, blued barrel and receiver parts.
Price: About **$99.00**

Daisy Model 95

DAISY YOUTHLINE RIFLES

Model:	95	111	105
Caliber:	BB	BB	BB
Barrel:	18″	18″	13½″
Length:	35.2″	34.3″	29.8″
Power:	Spring	Spring	Spring
Capacity:	700	650	400
Price: About	$32.00	$29.00	$14.09

Features: Model 95 stock and fore-end are wood; 105 and 111 have plastic stocks.

Daisy 120 Cadet

DAISY/POWER LINE MODEL 120 CADET RIFLE
Caliber: 177, single shot.
Barrel: 15.7″, rifled.

Weight: 5 lbs. **Length:** 36.8″ over-all.
Power: Spring air, barrel cocking.
Stock: Stained hardwood.
Sights: Hooded post front on ramp, open micro-adjustable rear.
Features: Velocity of 500 fps. Lever-type automatic safety, blued steel receiver. Imported from Spain by Daisy. Introduced 1984.
Price: About **$69.00**

Daisy Model 840

DAISY MODEL 840
Caliber: 177 pellet (single-shot) or BB (350-shot).
Barrel: 19″, smoothbore, steel.
Weight: 2.7 lbs. **Length:** 36.8″ over-all.
Stock: Molded wood-grain stock and fore-end.
Sights: Ramp front, open, adj. rear.
Features: Single pump pneumatic rifle. Muzzle velocity 335 fps (BB), 300 fps (pellet). Steel buttplate; straight pull bolt action; cross-bolt safety. Fore-end forms pump lever. Introduced 1978.
Price: About **$41.00**

DAISY/POWER LINE 856 PUMP-UP AIR GUN
Caliber: 177 (pellets), BB, 100-shot BB magazine.
Barrel: Rifled steel with shroud.
Weight: 2¾ lbs. **Length:** 37.4″ over-all.
Power: Pneumatic pump-up.
Stock: Molded woodgrain plastic.
Sights: Ramp and blade front, open rear adjustable for e.
Features: Velocity from 315 fps (two pumps) to 650 fps (10 pumps). Finger grooved fore-end. Cross-bolt trigger-block safety. Introduced 1985. From Daisy.
Price: About **$44.00**

CAUTION: PRICES CHANGE. CHECK AT GUNSHOP.

Power Line Model 860

Daisy Model 900

Power Line Model 922

Daisy Model 953

Daisy Red Ryder

DAISY/POWER LINE 880 PUMP-UP AIR GUN
Caliber: 177 pellets, BB.
Barrel: Rifled steel with shroud.
Weight: 4.5 lbs. **Length:** 37¾" over-all.
Power: Pneumatic pump-up.
Stock: Wood grain molded plastic with Monte Carlo cheekpiece.
Sights: Ramp front, open rear adj. for e.
Features: Crafted by Daisy. Variable power (velocity and range) increase with pump strokes. 10 strokes for maximum power. 100-shot BB magazine. Cross-bolt trigger safety. Positive cocking valve.
Price: About **$62.00**
Price: Model 980 (as above with hardwood stock and fore-end), about **$73.00**

DAISY/POWER LINE MODEL 922
Caliber: 22, 5-shot clip.
Barrel: Rifled steel with shroud.
Weight: 4.5 lbs. **Length:** 37¾" over-all.
Stock: Molded wood-grained plastic with checkered p.g. and fore-end, Monte Carlo cheekpiece.
Sights: Ramp front, full adj. open rear.
Features: Muzzle velocity from 270 fps (two pumps) to 530 fps. (10 pumps).

DAISY/POWER LINE 953
Caliber: 177 pellets.
Barrel: 20.9"; 12-groove rifling, high-grade solid steel by Lothar Walther®, precision crowned; bore sized for precision match pellets.

DAISY/POWER LINE 860 PUMP-UP AIR GUN
Caliber: 177 (pellets), BB, 100-shot BB magazine.
Barrel: Rifled steel with shroud.
Weight: 4.18 lbs. **Length:** 37.4" over-all.
Power: Pneumatic pump-up.
Stock: Molded woodgrain with Monte Carlo cheekpiece.
Sights: Ramp and blade front, open rear adjustble for e.
Features: Velocity from 315 fps (two pumps) to 650 fps (10 pumps). Shoots BBs or pellets. Heavy die cast metal receiver. Cross-bolt trigger-block safety. Introduced 1984. From Daisy.
Price: About **$53.00**

DAISY/POWER LINE 900 PELLET REPEATER
Caliber: 177 pellets, 5-shot clip.
Barrel: Rifled steel.
Weight: 4.3 lbs. **Length:** 38.4" over-all.
Power: Spring air.
Stock: Full length moulded stock with checkering, cheekpiece, white spacers.
Sights: Blade and ramp front, V-slot rear fully adjustable for w. & e.
Features: Easy loading, automatic indexing five-shot clip. Heavy die-cast metal receiver, dovetail mount for scope, heavy die-cast pump lever. Single pump for 545 fps muzzle velocity.
Price: About **$86.00**

Straight pull bolt action. Separate buttplate and grip cap with white spacers. Introduced 1978.
Price: About **$72.00**
Price: Models 970/920 (as above with hardwood stock and fore-end), about.. **$85.00**

Weight: 5.08 lbs. **Length:** 38.9" over-all.
Power: Single-pump pneumatic.
Stock: Full length, select American hardwood, stained and finished; black buttplate with white spacers.
Sights: Globe front with four aperture inserts; precision micrometer adjustable rear peep sight mounted on a standard ⅜" dovetail receiver mount.
Features: Single-shot.
Price: About **$180.00**

DAISY 1938 RED RYDER COMMEMORATIVE
Caliber: BB, 650-shot repeating action.
Barrel: Smoothbore steel with shroud.
Weight: 2.2 lbs. **Length:** 35.4" over-all.
Stock: Wood stock burned with Red Ryder lariat signature.
Sights: Post front, adjustable V-slot rear.
Features: Wood fore-end. Saddle ring with leather thong. Lever cocking. Gravity feed. Controlled velocity. Commemorates one of Daisy's most popular guns, the Red Ryder of the 1940s and 1950s.
Price: About **$49.00**

CAUTION: PRICES CHANGE. CHECK AT GUNSHOP.

Daisy Model 1894

DAISY 1894 SPITTIN' IMAGE CARBINE
Caliber: BB, 40-shot.
Barrel: 17½", smoothbore.
Weight: 3 lbs. **Length:** 38" over-all.
Power: Spring.
Stock: Molded wood-grain stock and fore-end.
Sights: Blade and ramp front, open adjustable rear.
Features: Cocks halfway on forward stroke of lever, halfway on return.
Price: About $58.00

Daisy Softair 12

DAISY SOFTAIR GUN 12
Caliber: 25-cal. plastic shot.
Barrel: Smoothbore.
Weight: 3.25 lbs. **Length:** 18.5" over-all.
Power: Pump or bolt action, spring air.
Stock: Molded grip.
Sights: Blade front, notched rear.
Features: Detailed replica of a famous American-made semi-automatic fire-arm; takes 30-shot clip.
Price: About $79.00

Daisy Softair 14

DAISY SOFTAIR GUN 14
Caliber: 25-cal. plastic shot.
Barrel: Smoothbore.
Weight: 2.9 lbs. **Length:** 26" over-all.
Power: Pump or bolt action, spring air.
Stock: Hardwood stock with molded pistol and pump grips.
Sights: Blade front, adjustable rear peep sight.
Features: Fully-detailed replica of a famous semi-automatic rifle; takes 10-shot clip
Price: About $118.00

Daisy Softair 15

DAISY SOFTAIR 15
Caliber: 25-cal. plastic shot.
Barrel: Smoothbore.
Weight: 2.5 lbs. **Length:** 15.5" over-all.
Power: Pump action, spring air.
Stock: Moulded receiver and grip.
Sights: Post front, 4-way adjustable rear.
Features: Detailed replica of the famous German-made police weapon. 12-shot banana clip, automatically ejects spent shells.
Price: About $66.00

Daisy Softair 870

DAISY SOFTAIR 870
Caliber: 25-cal. plastic shot.
Barrel: Smoothbore.
Weight: 3.6 lbs. **Length:** 40" over-all.
Power: Slide action, spring air.
Stock: Moulded, with checkering.
Sights: Bead front.
Features: Detailed replica of Remington 870 Wingmaster; authentic working action, five-shot magazine, ejects spent shells.
Price: About $89.00

FX-1

FX-1 AIR RIFLE
Caliber: 177, single shot.
Barrel: 18", rifled.
Weight: 6.6 lbs. **Length:** 43" over-all.
Power: Spring-piston, barrel cocking.
Stock: Walnut-stained hardwood.
Sights: Tunnel front with interchangeable inserts; rear with rotating disc to give four sighting notches.
Features: Velocity 680 fps. Match-type adjustable trigger. Receiver grooved for scope mounting. Imported by Beeman.
Price: $146.50

FX-2 Air Rifle
Similar to the FX-1 except weighs 5.8 lbs., 41" over-all; front sight is hooded post on ramp, rear sight has two-way click adjustments. Adjustable trigger. Imported by Beeman.
Price: $116.50

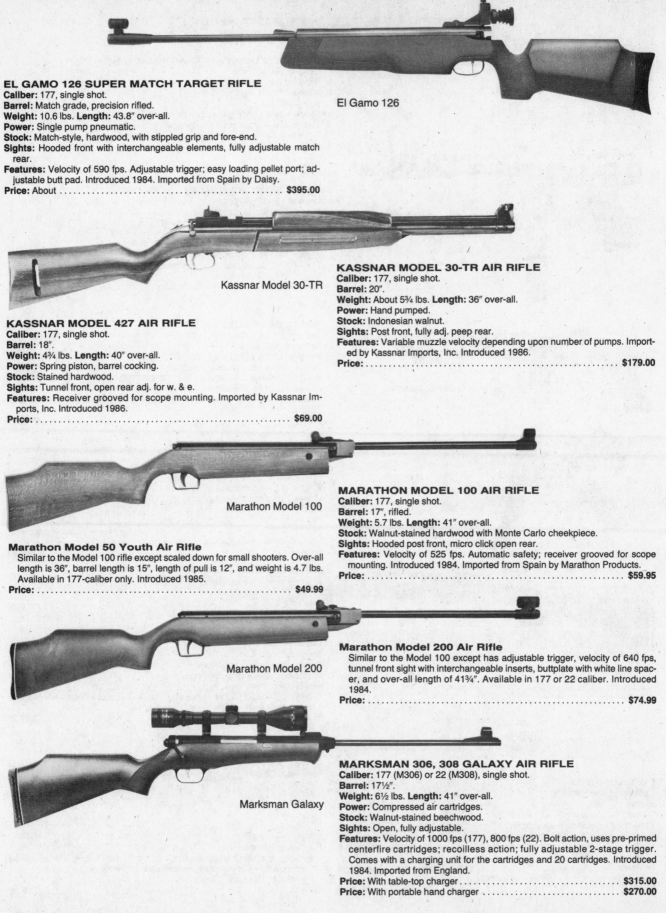

EL GAMO 126 SUPER MATCH TARGET RIFLE

Caliber: 177, single shot.
Barrel: Match grade, precision rifled.
Weight: 10.6 lbs. **Length:** 43.8″ over-all.
Power: Single pump pneumatic.
Stock: Match-style, hardwood, with stippled grip and fore-end.
Sights: Hooded front with interchangeable elements, fully adjustable match rear.
Features: Velocity of 590 fps. Adjustable trigger; easy loading pellet port; adjustable butt pad. Introduced 1984. Imported from Spain by Daisy.
Price: About **$395.00**

El Gamo 126

Kassnar Model 30-TR

KASSNAR MODEL 30-TR AIR RIFLE

Caliber: 177, single shot.
Barrel: 20″.
Weight: About 5¾ lbs. **Length:** 36″ over-all.
Power: Hand pumped.
Stock: Indonesian walnut.
Sights: Post front, fully adj. peep rear.
Features: Variable muzzle velocity depending upon number of pumps. Imported by Kassnar Imports, Inc. Introduced 1986.
Price: **$179.00**

KASSNAR MODEL 427 AIR RIFLE

Caliber: 177, single shot.
Barrel: 18″.
Weight: 4¾ lbs. **Length:** 40″ over-all.
Power: Spring piston, barrel cocking.
Stock: Stained hardwood.
Sights: Tunnel front, open rear adj. for w. & e.
Features: Receiver grooved for scope mounting. Imported by Kassnar Imports, Inc. Introduced 1986.
Price: **$69.00**

Marathon Model 100

MARATHON MODEL 100 AIR RIFLE

Caliber: 177, single shot.
Barrel: 17″, rifled.
Weight: 5.7 lbs. **Length:** 41″ over-all.
Stock: Walnut-stained hardwood with Monte Carlo cheekpiece.
Sights: Hooded post front, micro click open rear.
Features: Velocity of 525 fps. Automatic safety; receiver grooved for scope mounting. Introduced 1984. Imported from Spain by Marathon Products.
Price: **$59.95**

Marathon Model 50 Youth Air Rifle

Similar to the Model 100 rifle except scaled down for small shooters. Over-all length is 36″, barrel length is 15″, length of pull is 12″, and weight is 4.7 lbs. Available in 177-caliber only. Introduced 1985.
Price: **$49.99**

Marathon Model 200

Marathon Model 200 Air Rifle

Similar to the Model 100 except has adjustable trigger, velocity of 640 fps, tunnel front sight with interchangeable inserts, buttplate with white line spacer, and over-all length of 41¾″. Available in 177 or 22 caliber. Introduced 1984.
Price: **$74.99**

Marksman Galaxy

MARKSMAN 306, 308 GALAXY AIR RIFLE

Caliber: 177 (M306) or 22 (M308), single shot.
Barrel: 17½″.
Weight: 6½ lbs. **Length:** 41″ over-all.
Power: Compressed air cartridges.
Stock: Walnut-stained beechwood.
Sights: Open, fully adjustable.
Features: Velocity of 1000 fps (177), 800 fps (22). Bolt action, uses pre-primed centerfire cartridges; recoilless action; fully adjustable 2-stage trigger. Comes with a charging unit for the cartridges and 20 cartridges. Introduced 1984. Imported from England.
Price: With table-top charger **$315.00**
Price: With portable hand charger **$270.00**

CAUTION: PRICES CHANGE. CHECK AT GUNSHOP.

Marksman Model 1740

MARKSMAN 29 AIR RIFLE
Caliber: 177 or 22, single shot.
Barrel: 18.5″.
Weight: 6 lbs. **Length:** 41.5″ over-all.
Power: Spring air, barrel cocking.
Stock: Stained hardwood.
Sights: Blade front, open adj. rear.
Features: Velocity of 790-830 fps (177), 610-640 fps. (22). Introduced 1986. Imported from England by Marksman Products.
Price: Either caliber $140.00

MARKSMAN 70 AIR RIFLE
Caliber: 177 or 22, single shot.
Barrel: 19.75″.
Weight: 8 lbs. **Length:** 45.5″ over-all.
Power: Spring air, barrel cocking.
Stock: Stained hardwood with M.C. cheekpiece, rubber butt pad, cut checkered p.g.
Sights: Hooded front, open fully adj. rear.
Features: Velocity of 910-940 fps (177), 740-780 fps (22); two-stage adj. trigger. Introduced 1986. Imported from West Germany by Marksman Products.
Price: Either caliber $215.00

MARKSMAN 1740 AIR RIFLE
Caliber: 177 or 100-shot BB repeater.
Barrel: 15½″, smoothbore.
Weight: 5 lbs., 1 oz. **Length:** 36½″ over-all.
Power: Spring, barrel cocking.
Stock: Moulded high-impact ABS plastic.
Sights: Ramp front, open rear adj. for e.
Features: Automatic safety; fixed front, adj. rear sight; shoots 177 cal. BB's pellets and darts. Velocity about 475-500 fps.
Price: $35.00
Price: Model 1744 (as above with 4 x 15 scope) $45.80

> Consult our Directory pages for the location of firms mentioned.

Marksman 55 Air Rifle
Similar to the Model 70 except has uncheckered hardwood stock, no cheekpiece, plastic butt plate. Over-all length is 45.25″, weight is 7½ lbs. Available in 177 caliber only.
Price: $185.00

MAUSER MODEL 300 SL AIR RIFLE
Caliber: 177, single shot.
Barrel: 18.9″.
Weight: 8 lbs., 8 oz. **Length:** 43.7″ over-all.
Power: Spring air, under-lever cocking.
Stock: Match style, hardwood, with stippled p.g., rubber butt pad.
Sights: Tunnel front, match aperture rear.
Features: Velocity of 550-600 fps. Dovetail mount for diopter or scope. Automatic safety. Imported from West Germany by Marksman Products.
Price: $260.00

Mauser 300 SL

Norica Model 73

NORICA MODEL 73 AIR RIFLE
Caliber: 177 or 22, single shot.
Barrel: 18″.
Weight: 6¼ lbs. **Length:** 41¾″ over-all.
Power: Spring air, barrel cocking.
Sights: Hooded front with four interchangeable blades, open adjustable rear.
Features: Velocity 610 fps. Adult-size stock with full pistol grip; two-stage trigger; receiver grooved for scope mounting. Imported from Spain by Kassnar. Introduced 1984.
Price: $104.00

Norica Model 80G

NORICA MODEL 80G AIR RIFLE
Caliber: 177 or 22, single shot.
Barrel: 18″.
Weight: 7¼ lbs. **Length:** 43″ over-all.
Power: Spring air, barrel cocking.
Stock: Monte Carlo competition-style.
Sights: Hooded front with four interchangeable blades, fully adjustable diopter rear on ramp.
Features: Velocity 610 fps. Adjustable trigger; target-type buttplate; blued metal. Imported from Spain by Kassnar. Introduced 1984.
Price: $134.00

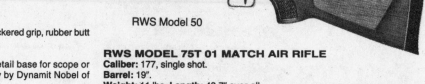

NORICA BLACK WIDOW AIR RIFLE

Caliber: 177 or 22, single shot.
Barrel: 16½".
Weight: 5¼ lbs. **Length:** 37½" over-all.
Power: Spring air, barrel cocking.
Stock: Black stained hardwood.
Sights: Hooded front, open adjustable rear.
Features: Velocity 500 fps. Stocked for young shooters. Receiver grooved for scope mounting. Imported from Spain by Kassnar. Introduced 1984.
Price: **$83.00**

Norica Black Widow

RWS Model 27

RWS MODEL 27 AIR RIFLE

Caliber: 177 or 22, single shot.
Weight: 6 lbs. **Length:** 42" over-all.
Power: Spring air, barrel cocking.
Stock: Walnut-finished hardwood.
Sights: Globe front, micro click rear with four-way blade.
Features: Velocity of 541 fps. Fully adjustable two-stage trigger; dovetail base for peep sight or scope mounting. Small dimensions for young shooters. Imported from West Germany by Dynamit Nobel of America.
Price: **$150.00**

RWS MODEL 45 AIR RIFLE

Caliber: 177 or 22, single shot.
Weight: 7¾ lbs. **Length:** 46" over-all.
Power: Spring air, barrel cocking.
Stock: Walnut-finished hardwood with rubber recoil pad.
Sights: Globe front with interchangeable inserts, micro click open rear with four-way blade.
Features: Velocity of 820 fps (177 cal.), 689 fps (22 cal.). Dovetail base for either micrometer peep sight or scope mounting. Automatic safety. Imported from West Germany by Dynamit Nobel of America.
Price: 177 or 22 .... **$220.00**
Price: With deluxe walnut stock. **$260.00**

RWS Model 45S Air Rifle

Same as the standard Model 45 except comes without sights and has a 4×20 scope, ramp-type mount, muzzle brake/weight, sling and swivels. Introduced 1983.
Price: **$290.00**
Price: As above, without scope, mount, sling, swivels **$210.00**

RWS Model 50

RWS MODEL 50T 01 AIR RIFLE

Caliber: 177, single shot.
Weight: 8 lbs. **Length:** 45" over-all.
Power: Spring air, under-lever cocking.
Stock: Walnut-finished hardwood with cheekpiece, checkered grip, rubber butt pad.
Sights: Globe front, micro click open rear.
Features: Velocity of 750 fps. Automatic safety. Dovetail base for scope or peep sight mounting. Imported from West Germany by Dynamit Nobel of America.
Price: **$310.00**

RWS Model 75KT 01 Running Boar Air Rifle

Similar to the Model 75 Match except has adjustable cheekpiece and buttplate, different stock, sandblasted barrel sleeve, detachable barrel weight, elevated-grip cocking lever, and a 240mm scope mount. Introduced 1983.
Price: **$700.00**

RWS MODEL 75T 01 MATCH AIR RIFLE

Caliber: 177, single shot.
Barrel: 19".
Weight: 11 lbs. **Length:** 43.7" over-all.
Power: Spring air, side-lever cocking.
Stock: Oil finished walnut with stippled grip, adjustable buttplate, accessory rail, Conforms to I.S.U. rules.
Sights: Globe front with 5 inserts, fully adjustable match peep rear.
Features: Velocity of 574 fps. Fully adjustable trigger. Model 75 HV has stippled fore-end, adjustable cheekpiece. Uses double opposing piston system for recoilless operation. Imported from West Germany by Dynamit Nobel of America.
Price: Model 75T 01 .... **$600.00**
Price: Model 75 HVT 01 .... **$700.00**
Price: Model 75T 01 left hand **$640.00**
Price: Model 75 HVT 01 left hand **$740.00**
Price: Model 75 UT 01 (adj. cheekpiece, buttplate, M82 sight) **$700.00**

SHARP-INNOVA AIR RIFLE

Caliber: 177 and 22, single shot.
Barrel: 19.5", rifled.
Weight: 4.4 lbs. **Length:** 34.6" over-all.
Power: Pneumatic, multi-stroke.
Stock: Mahogany.
Sights: Hooded front, adjustable aperture rear.
Features: Velocity of 960 fps with 8 pumps (177). Adjustable trigger. Receiver grooved for scope mount. Introduced 1983. Imported from Japan by Great Lakes Airguns and Beeman.
Price: **$125.00**

SIG-HAMMERLI MILITARY LOOK 420

Caliber: 177 or 22, single shot.
Barrel: 19", rifled.
Weight: About 7 lbs. **Length:** 44¼" over-all.
Stock: Synthetic stock and handguard.
Sights: Open, fully adj.
Features: Side lever cocking; adjustable trigger; rifled steel barrel. Introduced 1977. Imported by Mandall Shooting Supplies.
Price: **$295.00**

CAUTION: PRICES CHANGE. CHECK AT GUNSHOP.

Sharp Ace

SHARP MODEL "ACE" AIR RIFLE
Caliber: 177, 22, single shot.
Weight: 6.3 lbs. **Length:** 38.4" over-all.
Power: Pneumatic, multi-stroke.
Stock: Stained hardwood.
Sights: Hooded ramp front, fully adjustable peep rear.
Features: Velocity of 1019 fps (177-cal.), 892 fps (22-cal.). Receiver grooved for scope mounting. Turn-bolt action for loading. Introduced 1984. Imported from Japan by Great Lakes Airguns and Beeman.
Price: From Great Lakes $216.73
Price: From Beeman $225.00

Sharp Model Ace Hunter Deluxe Air Rifle
Similar to the Ace Target model except comes with a 1" 4x scope, "muzzle brake," sling swivels and leather sling. Has the all metal trigger found on the Target model and the checkered stock. With 12 pumps and RWS Hobby pellets velocity is 1006 fps. Introduced 1985.
Price: From Great Lakes $339.15

Sharp Model Ace Target Standard Air Rifle
Similar to the Model Ace except the under-barrel pump assembly has been rotated about 120° to the side, new one-piece stock, globe front sight takes interchangeable elements, micro. adjustable peep rear. Checkered p.g. and fore-end, adjustable buttplate. Adjustable trigger. Introduced 1985.
Price: From Great Lakes $293.44

Sheridan CO₂

SHERIDAN CO₂ AIR RIFLES
Caliber: 5mm (20 cal.), single shot.
Barrel: 18½", rifled.
Weight: 6 lbs. **Length:** 37" over-all.
Power: Standard 12.5 gram CO_2 cylinder.
Stock: Walnut sporter.
Sights: Open, adj. for w. and e. Optional Sheridan-Williams 5D-SH receiver sight or Weaver D4 scope.
Features: Bolt action single shot, CO_2 powered. Velocity approx. 514 fps., manual thumb safety. Blue or Silver finish. Left-hand models avail. at same prices.
Price: CO₂ Blue Streak $96.20
Price: CO₂ Silver Streak $100.55
Price: CO₂ Blue Streak with receiver sight $114.40
Price: CO₂ Blue Streak with scope $131.90

Sheridan Blue Streak

SHERIDAN BLUE AND SILVER STREAK RIFLES
Caliber: 5mm (20 cal.), single shot.
Barrel: 18½", rifled.
Weight: 5 lbs. **Length:** 37" over-all.
Power: Hand pumped (swinging fore-end).
Features: Rustproof barrel and piston tube. Takedown. Thumb safety. Mannlicher type walnut stock. Left-hand models same price.
Price: Blue Streak $109.85
Price: Silver Streak $113.95

Sterling HR-81 Rifle

STERLING HR-81/HR-83 AIR RIFLE
Caliber: 177 or 22, single-shot.
Barrel: 18½".
Weight: 8½ lbs. **Length:** 42½" over-all.
Power: Spring air, (barrel cocking).
Stock: Stained hardwood, with checkpiece, checkered pistol grip.
Sights: Tunnel-type front with four interchangeable elements, open adjustable V-type rear.
Features: Velocity of 700 fps (177), 600 fps (22). Bolt action with easily accessible loading port; adjustable single-stage match trigger; rubber recoil pad. Integral scope mount rails. Scope and mount optional. Introduced 1983. Made in U.S.A. by Benjamin Air Rifle Co.
Price: HR 81-7 (177 cal., standard walnut stock) $235.85
Price: HR 81-2 (as above, 22 cal.) $245.15
Price: HR 83-7 (177 cal., deluxe walnut stock) $334.75
Price: HR 83-2 (as above, 22 cal.) $338.85
Price: For 4x40 wide angle scope, add $82.35

WALTHER LGR UNIVERSAL MATCH AIR RIFLE
Caliber: 177, single shot.
Barrel: 25.5".
Weight: 13 lbs. **Length:** 44¾" over-all.
Power: Spring air, barrel cocking.
Stock: Walnut match design with stippled grip and fore-end, adjustable cheekpiece, rubber butt pad.
Features: Has the same weight and contours as the Walther U.I.T. rimfire target rifle. Comes complete with sights, accessories and muzzle weight. Imported from West Germany by Interarms.
Price: $765.00

Walther LGR Match Air Rifle
Same basic specifications as standard LGR except has a high comb stock, sights are mounted on riser blocks. Introduced 1977.
Price: $675.00

CAUTION: PRICES CHANGE. CHECK AT GUNSHOP.

Chokes & Brakes

Baker Superior Choke Tubes

Stan Baker's Superior choke tubes can be installed only in single-barrel guns. The external diameter of the barrel is enlarged by swaging, allowing enough for reaming and threading to accept the screw-in WinChoke-style tube. Installation on a single-barrel gun without rib is **$85.00**; with vent rib, cost is **$110.00**. Prices are higher for target guns, so contact Baker for specifics. Price includes honing the bore. Extra choke tubes are $15.95 each. One tube and wrench are provided. Baker also installs WinChoke tubes.

Briley Screw-In Chokes

Installation of these choke tubes requires that all traces of the original choking be removed, the barrel threaded internally with square threads and then the tubes are custom fitted to the specific barrel diameter. The tubes are thin and, therefore, made of stainless steel. Cost of installation for single-barrel guns (pumps, autos) runs **$75.00**; un-single target guns run **$150.00**; over-unders and side-by-sides cost **$150.00** per barrel. Prices include one choke tube and a wrench for disassembly. Extra tubes are **$40.00** each.

Briley also makes "Excentrix" choke tubes that allow horizontal or vertical movement of the pattern up to 11". Add **$35.00** to the prices above. Installation available only from Briley.

Cellini Recoil Reducer

Designed for handgun and rifle applications, the Cellini Reducer is available as a removable factory-installed accessory. Over-all length is 2½", weight is 3.5 ounces, and the unit must be installed by the maker. It is said to reduce muzzle jump to zero, even for automatic weapons. Cost starts at $150. Contact Cellini for full details.

Cutts Compensator

The Cutts compensator is one of the oldest variable choke devices available. Manufactured by Lyman Gunsight Corporation, it is available with a steel body. A series of vents allows gas to escape upward and downward. For the 12-ga. Comp body, six fixed-choke tubes are available: the Spreader—popular with skeet shooters; Improved Cylinder; Modified; Full; Superfull, and Magnum Full. Full, Modified and Spreader tubes are available for 12, or 20, and an Adjustable Tube, giving Full through Improved Cylinder chokes, is offered in 12, or 20 gauges. Cutts Compensator, complete with wrench, adaptor and any single tube **$68.80**; with adjustable tube **$87.80**. All single choke tubes **$18.95** each. No factory installation available.

Emsco Choke

E.M. Schacht of Waseca, Minn., offers the Emsco, a small diameter choke which features a precision curve rather than a taper behind the 1½" choking area. 9 settings are available in this 5 oz. attachment. Its removable recoil sleeve can be furnished in dural if desired. Choice of three sight heights. For 12, 16 or 20 gauge. Price installed, **$29.95**. Not installed, **$22.00**.

Lyman CHOKE

The Lyman CHOKE is similar to the Cutts Comp in that it comes with fixed-choke tubes or an adjustable tube, with or without recoil chamber. The adjustable tube version sells for **$37.95** with recoil chamber, in 12 or 20 gauge. Lyman also offers Single-Choke tubes at **$18.95**. This device may be used with or without a recoil-reduction chamber; cost of the latter is **$8.95** extra. Available in 12 or 20 gauge only. No factory installation offered.

Mag-Na-Port

Electrical Discharge Machining works on any firearm except those having shrouded barrels. EDM is a metal erosion technique using carbon electrodes that control the area to be processed. The Mag-na-port venting process utilizes small trapezoidal openings to direct powder gases upward and outward to reduce recoil.

No effect is had on bluing or nickeling outside the Magna-port area so no refinishing is needed. Cost for the Magna-port treatment is **$53.00** for handguns, **$69.00** for rifles, plus transportation both ways, and **$2.50** for handling.

Poly-Choke

Marble Arms Corp., manufacturers of the Poly-Choke adjustable shotgun choke, now offers two models in 12, 16, 20, and 28 gauge—the Ventilated and Standard style chokes. Each provides nine choke settings including Xtra-Full and Slug. The Ventilated model reduces 20% of a shotgun's recoil, the company claims, and is priced at **$62.50**. The Standard Model is **$56.00**. Postage not included. Contact Marble Arms for more data.

Pro-Choke

Pro-Choke is a system of interchangeable choke tubes that can be installed in any single or double-barreled shotgun, including over-unders. The existing chokes are bored out, the muzzles over-bored and threaded for the tubes. A choice of three Pro-Choke tubes are supplied—Skeet, Imp. Cyl., Mod., Imp. Mod., or Full. Cost of the installation is **$179.95** for single-barrel guns, **$229.95** for doubles. Extra tubes cost **$40** each. Postage and handling charges are **$8.50**.

Pro-Port

A compound ellipsoid muzzle venting process similar to Mag-na-porting, only exclusively applied to shotguns. Like Mag-na-porting, this system reduces felt recoil, muzzle jump, and shooter fatigue. Very helpful for Trap doubles shooters. Pro-Port is a patented process and installation is available in both the U.S. and Canada. Cost for the Pro-Port process is **$110.00** for over-unders (both barrels); **$80.00** for only the bottom barrel; and **$69.00** for single barrel shotguns. Prices do not include shipping and handling.

Walker Choke Tubes

This interchangeable choke tube system uses an adaptor fitted to the barrel without swaging. Therefore, it can be fitted to any single-barreled gun. The choke tubes use the conical-parallel system as used on all factory-choked barrels. These tubes can be used in Winchester, Mossberg, Smith & Wesson, Weatherby, or similar barrels made for the standard screw-in choke system. Available for 10 gauge, 12, 16 and 20. Factory installation (single barrel) with choice of Standard Walker Choke tube is **$105.00**, **$210.00** for double barrels with two choke tubes. A full range of constriction is available. Contact Walker Arms for more data.

Walker Full Thread Choke Tubes

An interchangeable choke tube system using fully threaded inserts. Designed specifically for over-under or side-by-side shotgun barrels, but can be installed in single barrels, and is nearly invisible. No swaging, adaptor or change in barrel exterior dimensions. Available in 12 or 20 gauge. Factory installation cost: **$105.00**, single barrel with one choke tube; **$210.00** for double barrels with two choke tubes. Contact Walker Arms Co. for more data.

CAUTION:　PRICES CHANGE. CHECK AT GUNSHOP.

Micrometer Receiver Sights

BEEMAN/WEIHRAUCH MATCH APERTURE SIGHT
Micrometer ¼-minute click adjustment knobs with settings indicated on scales. Price **$69.95**

BEEMAN/FEINWERKBAU MATCH APERTURE SIGHTS
Locks into one of four eye-relief positions. Micrometer ¼-minute click adjustments; may be set to zero at any range. Extra windage scale visible beside eyeshade. Primarily for use at 5 to 20 meters. Price **$99.95**

BEEMAN SPORT APERTURE SIGHT
Positive click micrometer adjustments. Standard units with flush surface screwdriver adjustments. Deluxe version has target knobs.
Price: Standard **$32.98**
Price: Deluxe **$38.98**

BUEHLER
"Little Blue Peep" auxiliary rear sight used with Buehler scope mounts.
Price **$4.75**

FREELAND TUBE SIGHT
Uses Unertl 1" micrometer mounts. For 22-cal. target rifles, inc. 52 Win., 37, 40X Rem. and BSA Martini. Price **$123.00**

LYMAN No. 57
¼-min. clicks. Stayset knobs. Quick release slide, adjustable zero scales. Made for almost all modern rifles. Price **$49.95**

LYMAN No. 66
Fits close to the rear of flat-sided receivers, furnished with Stayset knobs. Quick release slide, ¼-min. adj. For most lever or slide action or flat-sided automatic rifles. Price **$49.95**

LYMAN No. 66U
Light-weight, designed for most modern shotguns with a flat-sided, round-top receiver. ¼-minute clicks. Requires drilling, taping. Not for Browning A-5, Rem. M11. Price **$49.95**

Millett AR-15 sights.

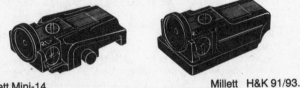

Millett Mini-14.   Millett H&K 91/93.

MILLETT ASSAULT RIFLE SIGHTS
Fully adjustable, heat-treated nickel steel peep aperture receiver sights for AR-15, Mini-14, H&K 91/93. AR-15 rear sight has w. & e. adjustments; nonglare replacement ramp-style front also available. Mini-14 sight has fine w. & e. adjustments; replaces original. H&K sight has a large peep disc with .080" peep; adjustable for w. & e.
Price: Rear sight for above three guns **$45.95**
Price: Front and rear combo for AR-15 .... **$55.95**
Price: Front sight for AR-15 .... **$10.95**

WILLIAMS FP
Internal click adjustments. Positive locks. For virtually all rifles, T/C Contender, Heckler & Koch HK-91, Ruger Mini-14, plus Win., Rem. and Ithaca shotguns. Price **$38.55**
With Twilight Aperture **$39.75**
With Target Knobs **$45.85**
With Target Knobs & Twilight Aperture **$47.05**
With Square Notched Blade **$40.60**
With Target Knobs & Square Notched Blade **$47.90**
FP-GR (for dovetail-grooved receivers, 22s and air guns) **$38.55**

WILLIAMS 5-D SIGHT
Low cost sight for shotguns, 22's and the more popular big game rifles. Adjustment for w. and e. Fits most guns without drilling or tapping. Also for Br. SMLE. Price **$21.90**
With Twilight Aperture **$23.10**
Extra Shotgun Aperture **$5.15**

WILLIAMS GUIDE
Receiver sight for .30 M1 Car., M1903A3 Springfield, Savage 24's, Savage-Anschutz rifles and Wby. XXII. Utilizes military dovetail; no drilling. Double-dovetail W. adj., sliding dovetail adj. for e. Price **$20.75**
With Twilight Aperture **$21.95**
With Open Sight Blade **$19.05**

Sporting Leaf and Open Sights

BINGHAM SPORTING RIFLE SIGHTS
All-steel sights are imported from Europe. Many styles of both front and rear sights available; random sampling listed here.
European express gold bead for European express ramp **$4.25**
European express ramp **$7.50**
Semi-buckhorn rear, with elevator **$6.50**
Rocky Mountain front, blue or bright **$3.95**
European 2-leaf folding express rear (V and U notch) **$12.50**

BINGHAM CLASSIC SIGHTS
All-steel sights for "classic" rifles. Rear sights only. This listing not complete; contact Bingham for full list.
Model 66 folding ladder-type **$19.95**
Model Saddle Ring Carbine (73, 92, 94, etc.) **$14.95**
Elevator, Winchester-type, early series (1876-WW II) **$4.95**

BURRIS SPORTING REAR SIGHT
Made of spring steel, supplied with multi-step elevator for coarse adjustments and notch plate with lock screw for finer adjustments. Price **$13.95**

LYMAN No. 16
Middle sight for barrel dovetail slot mounting. Folds flat when scope or peep sight is used. Sight notch plate adjustable for e. White triangle for quick aiming. 3 heights: A—.400" to .500", B—.345" to .445", C—.500" to .600". Price **$10.50**

MARBLE FALSE BASE #72, #73, #74
New screw-on base for most rifles replaces factory base. ⅜" dovetail slot permits installation of any Marble rear sight. Can be had in sweat-on models also. Price **$5.05**

MARBLE CONTOUR RAMP #14R
For late model Rem. 725, 740, 760, 742 rear sight mounting. ⁹⁄₁₆" between mounting screws. Price **$11.20**

MARBLE FOLDING LEAF
Flat-top or semi-buckhorn style. Folds down when scope or peep sights are used. Reversible plate gives choice of "U" or "V" notch. Adjustable for elevation. Price **$10.00**
Also available with both w. and e. adjustment **$11.70**

MARBLE SPORTING REAR
With white enamel diamond, gives choice of two "U" and two "V" notches of different sizes. Adjustment in height by means of double step elevator and sliding notch piece. For all rifles; screw or dovetail installation. Price: .... **$10.30-$11.70**

MILLETT RIFLE SIGHT
Open, fully adjustable rear sight fits standard ⅜" dovetail cut in barrel. Choice of white outline or target rear blades, .360". Front with white or orange bar, .343", .400", .430", .460", .500", .540".
Price: Rear sight **$47.29**
Price: Front sight **$10.49**

MILLETT RUGER 10/22 SIGHT COMBO
Replacement sight system for the 10/22 rifle has a fully adjustable open rear with deep notch and white outline or target blade. Combo set includes interchangeable white or orange bar front. Also fits Win. 77, 94, Rem. 740-760, 700 old model dovetail rear.
Price: Combo set **$77.69**
Price: Without quick-change front sight feature **$56.69**

Millett Scope-Site.

MILLETT SCOPE-SITE
Open, adjustable or fixed rear sights dovetail into a base integral with the top scope-mount ring. Blaze orange front ramp sight is integral with the front ring half. Rear sights have white outline aperture. Provides fast, short radius, Patridge-type open sights on top of the scope. Can be used with all Millett rings.
Price: Scope-Site ring set, adjustable **$69.95**
Price: As above, fixed **$39.95**
Price: Convertible Top Cap set, adjustable **$56.95**
Price: As above, fixed **$26.95**

CAUTION: PRICES CHANGE. CHECK AT GUNSHOP.

WICHITA MULTI RANGE SIGHT SYSTEM
Designed for silhouette shooting. System allows you to adjust the rear sight to four repeatable range settings, once it is pre-set. Sight clicks to any of the settings by turning a serrated wheel. Front sight is adjustable for weather and light conditions with one adjustment. Specify gun when ordering.
Price: Rear sight **$77.00**
Front sight **$44.00**

WILLIAMS DOVETAIL OPEN SIGHT
Open rear sight with w. and e. adjustment. Furnished with "U" notch or choice of blades. Slips into dovetail and locks with gib lock. Heights from .281" to .531". Price with blade **$11.60**
Less Blade **$7.60**
Extra Blades **$3.70**

WILLIAMS GUIDE OPEN SIGHT
Open rear sight with w. and e. adjustment. Bases to fit most military and commercial barrels. Choice of square "U" or "V" notch blade, ³/₁₆", ¼", ⁵/₁₆", or ⅜" high. Price with blade **$14.00**
Extra blades, each **$4.00**
Price, less blade **$10.00**

Front Sights

LYMAN HUNTING SIGHTS
Made with gold or white beads ¹/₁₆" to ³/₃₂" wide and in varying heights for most military and commercial rifles. Dovetail bases. Price ... **$7.50**

MARBLE STANDARD
Ivory, red, or gold bead. For all American made rifles, ¹/₁₆" wide bead with semi-flat face which does not reflect light. Specify type of rifle when ordering. Price **$6.15**

MARBLE-SHEARD "GOLD"
Shows up well even in darkest timber. Shows same color on different colored objects; sturdily built. Medium bead. Various models for different makes of rifles so specify type of rifle when ordering. Price **$7.65**

MARBLE CONTOURED
Same contour and shape as Marble-Sheard but uses standard ¹/₁₆" or ³/₃₂" bead, ivory, red or gold. Specify rifle type. Price **$7.05**

POLY-CHOKE
Rifle front sights available in six heights and two widths. Model A designed to be inserted into the barrel dovetail; Model B is for use with standard .350 ramp; both have standard ⅜" dovetails. Gold or ivory color ¹/₁₆" bead. Price **$4.95**

WILLIAMS GUIDE BEAD SIGHT
Fits all shotguns, ⅛" ivory, red or gold bead. Screws into existing sight hole. Various thread sizes and shank lengths. Price.............. **$4.05**

Globe Target Front Sights

FREELAND SUPERIOR
Furnished with six 1" plastic apertures. Available in 4½"-6½" lengths. Made for any target rifle. Price **$37.00**
Price with 6 metal insert apertures **$39.00**
Price, front base **$8.00**

FREELAND TWIN SET
Two Freeland Superior or Junior Globe Front Sights, long or short, allow switching from 50 yd. to 100 yd. ranges and back again without changing rear sight adjustment. Sight adjustment compensation is built into the set; just interchange and you're "on" at either range. Set includes 6 plastic apertures. Price with 6 metal apertures **$58.00**

FREELAND MILITARY
Short model for use with high-powered rifles where sight must not extend beyond muzzle. Screw-on base; six plastic apertures. Price .. **$35.00**
Price with 6 metal apertures **$39.00**
Price, front base **$8.00**

LYMAN No. 17A TARGET
Includes 7 interchangeable inserts; 4 apertures, one transparent amber and two posts .50" and .100" in width. Price **$19.95**

Ramp Sights

JAEGER CUSTOM FRONT SIGHT RAMP
Banded style machined from bar stock. Front sights are interchangeable and slide into the ramp, lock with a set screw. Sights available are Silver Bead ($7.50), Sourdough Bead ($9.00), Silver Bead with Folding Night Sight ($20.00), and Reflective Bead (Raybar-type, $9.00).
Price: Ramp with set screw, wrenches **$45.00**
Price: Sight hood **$3.90**

LYMAN SCREW-ON RAMP
Used with 8-40 screws but may also be brazed on. Heights from .10" to .350". Ramp without sight **$13.50**

MARBLE FRONT RAMPS
Available in either screw-on or sweat-on style. 5 heights; ³/₁₆", ⁵/₁₆", ⅜", ⁷/₁₆", ⁹/₁₆". Standard ⅜" dovetail slot. Price **$12.65**
Hoods for above ramps **$2.75**

WILLIAMS SHORTY RAMP
Companion to "Streamlined" ramp, about ½" shorter. Screw-on or sweat-on. It is furnished in ⅛", ³/₁₆", ⁹/₃₂", and ⅜" heights without hood only.
Price **$10.00**

WILLIAMS STREAMLINED RAMP
Hooded style in screw-on or sweat-on models. Furnished in ⁹/₁₆", ⁷/₁₆", ⅜", ⁵/₁₆", ³/₁₆" heights. Price with hood **$15.85**
Price without hood **$13.10**

WILLIAMS SHOTGUN RAMP
Designed to elevate the front bead for slug shooting or for guns that shoot high. Diameters to fit most 12, 16, 20 ga. guns. Fastens by screwclamp, no drilling required. Price, with Williams gold bead **$8.95**
Price, without bead **$6.60**
Price, with Guide Bead **$10.25**

Handgun Sights

BINGHAM PISTOL SIGHTS
All-steel sights of various designs for Colt Government Model and Browning Hi-Power. Low profile "battle sights" (front and rear) for either Colt G.M. or Browning HP. Price **$16.95**
Combat sight set, low profile, white outline for Colt G.M., front and rear **$21.95**
National Match front sight, Colt G.M. **$3.75**
Camp Perry front sight, Colt G.M. **$4.95**

BO-MAR DE LUXE BMCS
Gives ⅜" w. and e. adjustment at 50 yards on Colt Gov't 45, sight radius under 7". For GM and Commander models only. Uses existing dovetail slot. Has shield-type rear blade. Price **$49.50**

BO-MAR LOW PROFILE RIB & ACCURACY TUNER
Streamlined rib with front and rear sights; 7⅛" sight radius. Brings sight line closer to the bore than standard or extended sight and ramp. Weighs 5 oz. Made for Colt Gov't 45, Super 38, and Gold Cup 45 and 38. Price **$79.00**

BO-MAR COMBAT RIB
For S&W Model 19 revolver with 4" barrel. Sight radius 5¾"; weight 5½ oz. Price **$69.00**

BO-MAR FAST DRAW RIB
Streamlined full length rib with integral Bo-Mar micrometer sight and serrated fast draw sight. For Browning 9mm, S&W 39, Colt Commander 45, Super Auto and 9mm. Price **$69.00**

BO-MAR WINGED RIB
For S&W 4" and 6" length barrels—K-38, M10, HB 14 and 19. Weight for the 6" model is about 7¼ oz. Price **$79.00**
For 4", 6" Python **$89.00**

BO-MAR COVER-UP RIB
Adj. rear sight, winged front guards. Fits right over revolver's original front sight. For S&W 4" M-10HB, M-13, M-58, M-64 & 65, Ruger 4" models SDA-34, SDA-84, SS-34, SS-84, GF-34, GF-84. Price.......... **$75.00**

C-MORE SIGHTS
Replacement front sight blades offered in two types and five styles. Made of DuPont Acetal, they come in a set of five high-contrast colors: blue, green, pink, red and yellow. Easy to install. Patridge style for Colt Python (all barrels), Ruger Super Blackhawk (7½"), Ruger Blackhawk (4⅝"); Ramp style for Python (all barrels), Blackhawk (4⅝"), Super Blackhawk (7½" and 10½"). From Mag-num Sales Ltd., Inc. Price, per set.......... **$14.95**

MMC MODEL 84 SIGHT SYSTEM
Replacement sight system for Colt 1911 autos and Browning Hi-Power. Streamlined 1.94" long base covers the dovetail for a custom look. Ideally suited for IPSC, metallic silhouette, bowling pin shooting. Contact MMC for details, full prices.
Complete rear sight **$42.99**
Serrated ramp front **$8.80**
Dot front **$13.50**

MMC COMBAT DESIGN
Available specifically for Colt M1911 and descendants, High Standard autos, Ruger standard autos. Adaptable to other pistols. Some gunsmithing required. Not necessary to replace front sight. Contact MMC for complete details.
Price, less leaf **$28.75**
Plain leaf **$8.55**
White outline leaf **$12.55**
With reflector beads, add **$2.50**

CAUTION: PRICES CHANGE. CHECK AT GUNSHOP.

MMC COMBAT FIXED SIGHT SYSTEM

New sculptured design permits snag-free draw. Improved version of the High Visibility Bar Cross system. Available for Colt 1911-style pistols.
Price: Plain $14.85
Price: White outline $19.05
Price: Dots $19.05

MMC MINI-SIGHT SYSTEM

Miniature-size fully adjustable rear sight. Fits most pocket-size 22, 32 and 380 autos with rear dovetail slot. Sight can also be used on many large-frame autos. Give make and model when ordering.
Price: $49.99

MILLETT SERIES 100 ADJUSTABLE SIGHTS

Replacement sights for revolvers and auto pistols. Positive click adjustments for windage and elevation. Designed for accuracy and ruggedness. Made to fit S&W, Colt, Beretta, SIG Sauer P220, P225, P226, H&K, Ruger, Dan Wesson, Browning, AMT Hardballer. Rear blades are available in white outline or positive black target. All steel construction and easy to install.
Price .... $41.95 to $67.29

MILLETT MARK SERIES PISTOL SIGHTS

Mark I and Mark II replacement combat sights for government-type auto pistols. Mark I is high profile, Mark II low profile. Both have horizontal light deflectors.
Mark I, front and rear $29.39
Mark II, front and rear $41.95

MILLETT FRONT SIGHTS

All-steel replacement front sights with either white or orange bar. Easy to install. For Ruger Redhawk, Security-Six, Police-Six, Speed-Six, Colt Python, Dan Wesson 22 and 15-2. Price .... $11.55 to $13.59

MILLETT DUAL-CRIMP FRONT SIGHT

Replacement front sight for automatic pistols. Dual-Crimp uses an all-steel two-point hollow rivet system. Available in nine heights and four styles. Has a skirted base that covers the front sight pad. Easily installed with the Millett Installation Tool Set. Available in Blaze Orange Bar, White Bar, Serrated Ramp, Plain Post. Price $13.59

MILLETT STAKE-ON FRONT SIGHT

Replacement front sight for automatic pistols. Stake-On sights have skirted base that covers the front sight pad. Easily installed with the Millett Installation Tool Set. Available in seven heights and four styles—Blaze Orange Bar, White Bar, Serrated Ramp, Plain Post. Price $13.59

OMEGA OUTLINE SIGHT BLADES

Replacement rear sight blades for Colt and Ruger single action guns and the Interarms Virginian Dragoon. Standard Outline available in gold or white notch outline on blue metal. Price $5.95

OMEGA MAVERICK SIGHT BLADES

Replacement "peep-sight" blades for Colt, Ruger SAs, Virginian Dragoon. Three models available—No. 1, Plain, No. 2, Single Bar, No. 3 Double Bar Rangefinder. Price, each $6.95

TRIJICON SELF-LUMINOUS SIGHTS

Three-dot sighting system uses self-luminous inserts in the sight blade and leaf. Tritium "lamps" are mounted in a metal cylinder and protected by a polished crystal sapphire. For most popular handguns, fixed or adjustable sights, and some rifles. From Armson, Inc.
Price: .... $34.95 to $139.90

THOMPSON/CENTER "ULTIMATE" SIGHTS

Replacement front and rear sights for the T/C Contender. Front sight has four interchangeable blades (.060", .080", .100", .120"), rear sight has four notch widths of the same measurements for a possible 16 combinations. Rear sight can be used with existing soldered front sights.
Price: Front sight $25.00
Price: Rear sight $55.00

WICHITA SIGHT SYSTEMS

For 45 auto pistols. Target and Combat styles available. Designed by Ron Power. All-steel construction, click adjustable. Each sight has two traverse pins, a large hinge pin and two elevation return springs. Sight blade is serrated and mounted on an angle to deflect light. Patridge front for target, ramp front for combat. Both are legal for ISPC and NRA competitons.
Rear sight, target or combat $54.50
Front sight, patridge or ramp $9.85

WICHITA GRAND MASTER DELUXE RIBS

Ventilated rib has wings machined into it for better sight acquisition. Made of stainless steel, sights blued. Uses Wichita Multi-Range rear sight, adjustable front sight. Made for revolvers with 6" barrel.
Price: Model 301 (adj. sight K-frames with custom bbl. of 1.000"-1.032" dia., L and N frames with 1.062"-1.100" bbl.) $143.00
Price: Model 302 (fixed-sight K-frames; M10, 65, 13 with 1.000" bbl. N-frame with 1.062" bbl.) $143.00
Price: Model 303 (Model 29, 629 with factory bbl., adj. sight K, L, N frames) $143.00
Price: Extra for white outline rear sight $16.00

WICHITA COMBAT V RIBS

Designed by Ron Power, the ventilated rib has a lengthwise V-groove that emphasizes the front sight and reduces glare and distortion. Over-size rear

sight blade for the click-adjustable sight. Made for Browning Hi-Power, Colt Commander, Govt. and Gold Cup models, Ruger Mark I, 4" S&W K-frames—models 10HB, 13, 64HB, 65, 58 with 4" barrel. From Wichita Arms Inc. Price: With sights $99.00
Price: Extra for white outline rear sight $16.00

Sight Attachments

FREELAND LENS ADAPTER

Fits 1⅛" O.D. presciption ground lens to all standard tube and receiver sights for shooting without glasses. Price without lens $44.00
Clear lens ground to prescription $21.00
Yellow or green prescription lens $21.00

MERIT ADAPTER FOR GLOBE FRONT SIGHTS

An Iris Shutter Disc with a special adapter for mounting in Lyman or Redfield globe front sights. Price $46.00

MERIT IRIS SHUTTER DISC

Eleven clicks gives 12 different apertures. No. 3 and Master, primarily target types, 0.22" to .125"; No. 4, ½" dia. hunting type, .025" to .155". Available for all popular sights. The Master Disc, with flexible rubber light shield, is particularly adapted to extension, scope height, and tang sights. All Merit Deluxe models have internal click springs; are hand fitted to minimum tolerance.
Master Deluxe $60.00
No. 4 Hunting Disc $40.00

MERIT LENS DISC

Similar to Merit Iris Shutter (Model 3 or Master) but incorporates provision for mounting prescription lens integrally. Lens may be obtained locally from your optician. Sight disc is 7/16" wide (Mod. 3), or ¾" wide (Master).
Model 3 Deluxe. Price $63.00
Master Deluxe $74.00

MERIT OPTICAL ATTACHMENT

For revolver and pistol shooters, instantly attached by rubber suction cup to regular or shooting glasses. Any aperture .020" to .156". Price, Deluxe (swings aside) $60.00

WILLIAMS APERTURES

Standard thread, fits most sights. Regular series ⅜" to ½" O.D., .050" to .125" hole. "Twilight" series has white reflector ring. .093" to .125" inner hole. Price, regular series ... $3.20. Twilight series $4.40
New wide open 5/16" aperture for shotguns fits 5-D and Foolproof sights. Price $5.75

Shotgun Sights

ACCURA-SITE

For shooting shotgun slugs. Three models to fit most shotguns—"A" for vent. rib barrels, "B" for solid ribs, "C" for plain barrels. Rear sight has windage and elevation provisions. Easily removed and replaced. Includes front and rear sights. Price .... $25.95 to $27.95

MARBLE
FOR DOUBLE BARREL SHOTGUNS (PRESS FIT)

Marble 214—Ivory front bead, 11/64" . . **$3.40; 215**—same with .080" rear bead and reamers . . **$11.15. Marble 220**—Bi-color (gold and ivory) front bead, 11/64" and .080" rear bead, with reamers . . **$12.85; Marble 221**—front bead only . . **$4.90. Marble 223**—Ivory rear .080" . . **$3.15. Marble 224**—Front sight reamer for 214-221 beads . . **$2.45; Marble 226**—Rear sight reamer for 223. Price $2.45

MARBLE
FOR SINGLE OR DB SHOTGUNS (SCREW-ON FIT)

Marble 217—Ivory front bead 11/64" . . **$3.70; Marble 216** . . **$7.65; Marble 218**—Bi-color front, 11/64" . . **$5.35; Marble 219** . . **$9.35; Marble 223T**—Ivory rear .080" Price $5.05
Marble Bradley type sights 223BT—⅛", 5/64" and 11/64" long. Gold, Ivory or Red bead. $3.00

MILLETT SHURSHOT SHOTGUN SIGHT

A sight system for shotguns with a ventilated rib. Rear sight attaches to the rib, front sight replaces the front bead. Front has an orange face, rear has two orange bars. For 870, 1100, or other models.
Price: Front and rear $31.49
Price: Adjustable front and rear $41.95

POLY-CHOKE

Replacement front sights in four styles—Xpert, Poly Bead, Xpert Mid Rib sights, and Bev-L-Block. Xpert Front available in 3x56, 6x48 thread, 3/32" or 5/32" shank length, gold, ivory ($3.00); or Sun Spot orange bead ($4.00); Poly Bead is standard replacement ⅛" bead, 6x48 ($2.00); Xpert Mid Rib in tapered carrier (ivory only) or 3x56 threaded shank (gold only), $3.00; Hi and Lo Blok sights with 6x48 thread, gold or ivory ($3.00) or Sun Spot Orange ($4.00). From Marble Arms.

SLUG SITE

A combination V-notch rear and bead front sight made of adhesive-backed formed metal approx. 7" over-all. May be mounted, removed and remounted as necessary, using new adhesive from the pack supplied.
Price $10.00

SCOPES & MOUNTS
HUNTING, TARGET ■ & VARMINT ■ SCOPES

Maker and Model	Magn.	Field at 100 Yds (feet)	Relative Brightness	Eye Relief (in.)	Length (in.)	Tube Diam. (in.)	W&E Adjustments	Weight (ozs.)	Price	Other Data
Action Arms										
Mark V	0	—	—	—	5⅛	1	Int.	5.5	$183.50	Variable intensity LED red aiming dot. Average battery life up to 500 hours. Waterproof, nitrogen filled aluminum tube. Fits most standard 1″ rings.
Aimpoint										
Mark III	0	—	—	—	6	—	Int.	12	219.95	Illuminates red dot in field of view. No parallax (dot does not need to be centered). Unlimited field of view and eye relief. On/off, adj. intensity. Dot covers 3″ @ 100 yds. Mounts avail. for all sights and scopes. From Aimpoint USA, Inc.
Series 2000S	0	—	—	—	5	1	Int.	5.3	188.95	
Series 2000L	0	—	—	—	7.25	1	Int.	6	209.95	
Apollo										
4x32 Compact	4	29	—	3.3	11.7	1	Int.	10	140.95	Rubber armored, water and fog proof. Come with see through filter caps; ¼-minute click adjustments. [1]Available with matte or gloss finish; multi-coated lenses; duplex reticle; waterproof, shockproof. Limited lifetime warranty. Imported from Japan by Apollo Optics.
3-9x40 Variable	3-9	35.3-13.2	—	3.3-3	12	1	Int.	14	170.95	
Silver Bullet 4x32[1]	4	36	—	3	—	1	Int.	8.5	99.00	
Silver Bullet 3-9x40[1]	3-9	39-15	—	3¾	—	1	Int.	9.9	124.00	
Silver Bullet 4-12x4[1]	4-12	32-11	—	3¾	—	1	Int.	10.5	135.00	
Western 4x32	4	28	—	3	12	1	Int.	9.5	55.10	
Western 3-9x32	3-9	35-13	—	3	13	1	Int.	11.5	74.10	
Armson										
O.E.G.	0	—	—	—	5⅛	1	Int.	4.3	129.90	Shows red dot aiming point. No batteries needed. Standard model fits 1″ ring mounts (not incl.). Other models available for many popular shotguns, para-military rifles and carbines. Also available is a smaller model for rimfire rifles, with dovetail mount.
Armsport										
415	4	19	13.7	3.5	11.5	¾	Int.	6	22.00	[1]Duplex reticle. Crosshair reticle, $90. 4x20, $79, 4x32, $82 (Duplex). [2]Parallax adjustment. [3]For black powder rifles. Polished brass tube with mounts. 4x32 W.A., 4x40 W.A., 6x40 W.A. also avail. Contact Armsport for full details.
3720	3-7	22.5-9.5	43.5-8.1	2.4	11	¾	Int.	8.4	56.00	
2½x32	2.5	32	163.8	3.7	12	1	Int.	9.3	86.00	
4x40[1]	4	29	100	3.5	12.5	1	Int.	9	97.00	
6x32	6	17.8	28	3.2	12	1	Int.	9	86.00	
1.5-4.5x32	1.5-4.5	55.1-20.4	707.6-64	4-3.1	11.8	1	Int.	14.1	124.00	
2-7x32	2-7	50-19	81-22	3.1-2.9	12.2	1	Int.	13.8	124.00	
3-9x40	3-9	35.8-12.7	176.9-19.4	3.1-2.9	12.8	1	Int.	15.2	131.00	
4-12x40 WA[2]	4-12	31-11	36-10.9	2.9-2.8	14.7	1	Int.	16.4	245.00	
4x15 BP-1[3]	4	19	13	3.5	32	¾	Int.	44	110.00	
Bausch & Lomb										
3x-9x 40mm	3.9	36-12	267	3.2	13	1	Int.	16.2	357.95	Contact Bushnell for details.
4x 40 mm	4	28	150	3.2	12¾	1	Int.	14.5	229.95	
1.5-6x	1.5-6	75-18	294-18.4	3.3	10.6	1	Int.	10.5	315.95	
■ 6x-24x	6-24	18-4.5	66.1-4.2	3.1	16.6	1	Int.	20.1	419.95	
Beeman										
Blue Ring 20[1]	1.5	14	150	11-16	8.3	¾	Int.	3.6	49.95	All scopes have 5-pt. reticle, all glass, fully coated lenses. [1]Pistol scope; cast mounts included. [2]Pistol scope; silhouette knobs. [3]Rubber armor coating; built-in double adj. mount, parallax-free setting. [4]Objective focus, built-in double-adj. mount; matte finish. [5]Objective focus. [6]Has 8 lenses; objective focus; milled mounts included. [7]Includes cast mounts. [8]Objective focus; silhouette knobs; matte finish. [9]Has 9 lenses; objective focus. Imported by Beeman.
Blue Ribbon 25[2]	2	19	150	10-24	9 1/16	1	Int.	7.4	119.50	
SS-1[3]	2.5	30	61	3.25	5½	1	Int.	7	129.50	
SS-2[4]	3	34.5	74	3.5	6.8	1.38	Int.	13.6	189.50	
Blue Ribbon 50R[5]	2.5	33	245	3.5	12	1	Int.	11.8	94.50	
Blue Ring 35R[6]	3	25	67	2.5	11¼	¾	Int.	5.1	44.95	
30A[7]	4	21	21	2	10.2	¾	Int.	4.5	29.99	
Blue Ribbon 66R[8]	2-7	62-16	384-31	3	11.4	1	Int.	14.9	168.50	
Blue Ring 45R[9]	3-7	26-12	67-9	2.5	10⅝	¾	Int.	6	69.95	
MS-1	4	23	30	3.5	7.5	1	Int.	8	129.95	
SS-3[4]	1.5-4	44.6-24.6	172-24	3	5.75	⅞	Int.	8.5	169.50	
Blue Ribbon 67R[8]	3-9	435-15	265-29	3	14.4	1	Int.	15.2	229.50	
Blue Ribbon 68R[8]	4-12	30.5-11	150-13.5	3	14.4	1	Int.	15.2	239.50	
Blue Ribbon 54R[5]	4	29	96	3.5	12	1	Int.	12.3	94.50	
SS-2[4]	4	24.6	41	5	7	1.38	Int.	13.7	189.50	
29	4	21	21	2	10.2	¾	Int.	4.5	19.98	
Burris										
4x Fullfield[1]	3.8	37	49	3¼	11¼	1	Int.	11	182.95	½-minute dot $7 extra. LER = Long Eye Relief—ideal for forward mounting on handguns. Plex or cross-hair only. Matte "Satin" finish avail. on 4x, 6x, 2-7x, 3-9x, 4x Mini, 1½-4x LER, 2x LER, 4x LER P.A. at extra cost. [3]3″ dot $6 extra. [2]1″-3″ dot $7 extra. [4]With parallax adjustment $152.95. [5]With parallax adjustment $170.95. [6]With parallax adjustment $183.95. Parallax adjustment adds 5 oz. to weight. [7]Available with Fine Plex crosshair.
2x-7x Fullfield[2] HiLume	2.5-6.8	50-19	81-22	3¼	11⅞	1	Int.	14	240.95	
3x-9x Fullfield[3] HiLume	3.3-8.6	40-15	72-17.6	3¼	12¾	1	Int.	15	254.95	
2¾x Fullfield	2.7	53	49	3¼	10½	1	Int.	9	165.95	
6x Fullfield	5.8	24	36	3¼	13	1	Int.	12	195.95	
1¾-5x Fullfield HiLume	2.5-6.8	70-27	121-25	3¼	10¾	1	Int.	13	213.95	
4x-12x Fullfield[7]	4.4-11.8	28-10½	—	3-3¼	15	1	Int.	18	295.95	
■ 6x-18x Fullfield[7]	6.5-17.6	17-7.5	—	3-3¾	15.8	12	Int.	18.5	302.95	
■ 10x Fullfield[7]	9.8	12½	—	3¼	15	1	Int.	15	238.95	
■ 12x Fullfield[7]	11.8	11	—	3¼	15	1	Int.	15	244.95	
2x LER	1.7	21	—	10-24	8¾	1	Int.	6.8	135.95	
3x LER	2.7	17	—	10-20	8⅞	1	Int.	6.8	145.95	
4x LER[5]	3.7	11	—	10-22	9⅝	1	Int.	8.5	152.95	
5x LER[6]	4.5	8.7	—	12-22	10⅞	1	Int.	9.5	165.95	
7x IER[7]	6.5	6.5	—	10-16	11¼	1	Int.	10	177.95	
10x IER	9.5	4	—	8-12	13.6	1	Int.	14	220.95	
1½x-4x LER	1.6-3.8	16-11	—	11-24	10½	1	Int.	11	222.95	
2x-7x Mini	2.5-6.9	32-14	—	3¾	9⅜	1	Int.	10.5	185.95	
4x Mini[4,7]	3.6	24	—	3¾	8¼	1	Int.	7.8	135.95	
6x Mini	5.5	17	—	3¾	9	1	Int.	7.8	145.95	
3x-9x Mini	3.6-8.8	25-11	—	3¾	9⅞	1	Int.	11.5	188.95	
4-12x Mini	4.5-11.6	19-8	—	3¾	11.2	1	Int.	15	254.95	

CAUTION: PRICES CHANGE. CHECK AT GUNSHOP.

Maker and Model	Magn.	Field at 100 Yds (feet)	Relative Bright-ness	Eye Relief (in.)	Length (in.)	Tube Diam. (in.)	W&E Adjust-ments	Weight (ozs.)	Price	Other Data
Burris (cont'd.)										
2x Mikro	1.7	15	—	7-24	9⅛	⅝	Int.	4	140.95	
3x Mikro	2.7	11	—	8-22	9⅛	⅝	Int.	4	140.95	
2¾xXER Scout	2.7	15	—	7-14	9⅜	1	Int.	7.5	142.95	
Bushnell										All ScopeChief, Banner and Custom models
Scope Chief VI	4	29	96	3½	12	1	Int.	9.3	127.95	come with Multi-X reticle, with or without BDC
Scope Chief VI	3-9	35-12.6	267-30	3.3	12.6	1	Int.	14.3	203.95	(bullet drop compensator) that eliminates hold-
Scope Chief VI	3-9	39-13	241-26.5	3.3	12.1	1	Int.	13	258.95	over. Prismatic Rangefinder (PRF) on some mod-
Scope Chief VI	2½-8	45-14	247-96	3.3	11.2	1	Int.	12.1	179.95	els. Contact Bushnell for data on full line. Prices
Scope Chief VI	1½-4½	73.7-24.5	267-30	3.5-3.5	9.6	1	Int.	9.5	175.95	include BDC—deduct $5 if not wanted. Add $30
Scope Chief VI	4-12	29-10	150-17	3.2	13.5	1	Int.	17	249.95	for PRF. BDC feature available in all Banner
Centurion Handgun 4x32mm	4	10.2	96	10-20	8¾	1	Int.	9.3	129.95	models, except 2.5x. [1]Equipped with Wind Drift Compensator and Parallax-free adjustment.
Centurion H'gun 1.3x[2]	1.3	17	—	7-21	7.9	1	Int.	6.9	109.95	[2]Also available with power booster. [3]4-times
Magnum Phantom 1.3x	1.3	17	—	7-21	7.8	1	Int.	5.5	79.95	zoom ratio. [4]Has battery powered lighted reticle.
Magnum Phantom 2.5x	2.5	9	—	7-21	9.7	1	Int.	6.5	87.95	Contact Bushnell for complete details.
Sportview Quad Power 2.5-10x[3]	2.5-10	45-11	—	3-2	13.5	1	Int.	14.5	109.95	
Sportview Quad Power 5-20x[3]	5-20	22-5.5	—	3.1	13.5	1	Int.	15.5	139.95	
Sportview Rangemaster 3-9x	3-9	38-12	—	3.5	11.75	1	Int.	10	89.95	
■ Sportview Rangemaster 4-12x	4-12	27-9	—	3.2	13.5	1	Int.	14	119.95	
Sportview Standard 4x	4	28	—	4	11.75	1	Int.	9.5	55.95	
Sportview Standard 3-9x	3-9	38-12	—	3.5	11.75	1	Int.	10	75.95	
22 Rimfire 4x	4	28	—	3	11.9	1	Int.	8	51.95	
22 Rimfire 3-7x	3-7	29-13	—	2.5	10	¾	Int.	6.5	55.95	
Banner Lite-Site 1.5-6x	1.5-6	60-15	—	3.2	9.8	1	Int.	12.4	229.95	
Banner Lite-Site 3-9x	3-9	36-12	—	3.3	13.6	1	Int.	14	249.95	
Banner Trophy WA 1.75-5x	1.75-5	68.5-24.5	—	3.2	10.4	1	Int.	10.2	145.95	
Banner Trophy WA 4x	4	34.2	—	3.4	12.4	1	Int.	11.9	137.95	
Banner Trophy WA 3-9x	3-9	39-13	—	3.3	11.8	1	Int.	12.9	153.95	
Banner Standard 2.5x	2.5	45	—	3.5	10.9	1	Int.	8	87.95	
Banner Standard 4x	4	29	—	3.5	12	1	Int.	10	101.95	
Banner Standard 6x	6	19.5	—	3	13.5	1	Int.	11.5	109.95	
Banner Standard 16x	16	7.25	—	3.1	15.4	1	Int.	15.3	179.95	
Banner Standard 3-9x	3-9	43-14	—	3	12.1	1	Int.	14	149.95	
Banner Standard 4-12x	4-12	29-10	—	3.2	13.5	1	Int.	15.5	179.95	
Banner Standard 6-18x	6-18	18-6	—	3.1	14.5	1	Int.	16	199.95	
Colt										All Colt scopes come complete with mount and
AR-15 3x	3	40	—	—	6	—	Int.	—	206.50	allow use of iron sights.
AR-15 4x	4	30	—	—	6	—	Int.	—	227.50	
Cougar										Nitrogen filled, fog proof; ¼-m.o.a. click adjust-
2.5x32	2.5	33	161	3.5	11.7	1	Int.	10.2	85.95	ments; fully coated lenses. Choice of crosshair or
4x32[1]	4	29	64	3.3	11.7	1	Int.	10.2	81.95	four-post crosshair or optional "peep" reticles.
6x40[2]	6	18.5	45	3.2	13	1	Int.	11.6	112.95	[1]Also 4x40 ($105.95) and Full View ($119.95).
8x40	8	13.5	25	3	13	1	Int.	11.6	126.95	[2]Also Full View ($136.95). [3]Also Full View
3-9x40[3]	3-9	35.3-13.2	177-20	3.3-3.0	12	1	Int.	12.7	148.95	($169.95). [4]Also with "Silver" finish, same price.
4-12x40	4-12	29.5-10.3	100-11	3.3-3.0	13.5	1	Int.	13.3	169.95	Imported by Cougar Optics.
Pistol Scopes										
P-1.5x20[4]	1.5	20	177	13.3	8.5	1	Int.	5.8	105.95	
P-2.5x20[4]	2.5	15	64	8	8.7	1	Int.	6.0	111.95	
Davis Optical										Focus by moving non-rotating obj. lens unit. Ext.
Spot Shot 1½"	10,12 15,20 25,30	10-4	—	2	25	.75	Ext.	—	116.00	mounts included. Recoil spring $4.50 extra.
Jason										Constantly centered reticles, ballbearing click
860	4	29	64	3	11.8	1	Int.	9.2	50.00	stops, nitrogen filled tubes, coated lenses. 4-Post
861	3-9	35-13	112-12	3	12.7	1	Int.	10.9	76.00	crosshair about $3.50 extra on models 860, 861,
862	4	19	14	2	11	¾	Int.	5.5	13.50	864, 865.
863C	3-7	23-10	43-8	3	11	¾	Int.	8.4	44.00	
865	3-9	35-13	177-19	3	13	1	Int.	12.2	80.00	
869	4	19	25	2	11.4	¾	Int.	6	23.00	
873	4	29	100	3	12.7	1	Int.	11.1	75.00	
875	3-9	35-13	177-19	3	13	1	Int.	12.2	80.00	
877	4	37	100	3	11.6	1	Int.	11.6	85.00	
878	3-9	42.5-13.6	112-12	2.7	12.7	1	Int.	12.7	110.00	
Kahles										[1]Lightweight model weighs 10.1 oz. [2]Light-
Helia Super 2.5 x 20[1]	2.5	50	64	3.25	9.8	1	Int.	12.6	279.00	weight—11.2 oz. [3]Lightweight—13 oz. [4]Light-
Helia Super 4 x 32[2]	4	30	60	3.25	11.6	1	Int.	15	319.00	weight—16 oz. [5]Lightweight—12.6 oz. [6]Light-
Helia 6 x 42[3]	6	21.1	49	3.25	12.8	1	Int.	17.5	349.00	weight—15.4 oz. [7]Lightweight—15.7 oz.
Helia 8 x 56[4]	8	15.6	49	3.25	14.8	1	Int.	23	389.00	[8]Lightweight—17.8 oz. [9]Calibrated for 7.62
Helia 1.1-4.5 x 20[5]	1.1-4.5	72.2-27	328-18	3.25	10.8	30mm	Int.	15	369.00	NATO ammo, 100 to 800 meters. All scopes have
Helia 1.5-6 x 20[6]	1.5-6	55.6-19.5	784-49	3.25	12.8	30mm	Int.	20	399.00	constantly centered reticles except ZF84; all
Helia 2.2-9 x 42[7]	2.2-9	36.1-13.5	364-21	3.25	13.7	30mm	Int.	20.3	449.00	come with lens caps. 30mm rings available for
Helia 3-12 x 56[8]	3-12	27.1-10	347-21	3.25	15.6	30mm	Int.	24.8	499.00	Redfield, Burris, Leupold bases. Imported from
ZF84 Sniper[9]	6	22.5	49	3.25	12.2	26mm	Int.	16.8	499.00	Austria by Kahles of America. (Del-Sports Inc.).
Kilham										Unlimited eye relief; internal click adjustments;
Hutson Handgunner II	1.7	8	—	—	5½	⅞	Int.	5.1	119.95	crosshair reticle. Fits Thompson/Center rail
Hutson Handgunner	3	8	—	10-12	6	⅞	Int.	5.3	119.95	mounts, for S&W K, N, Ruger Blackhawk, Super, Super Single-Six, Contender

HUNTING, TARGET ■ & VARMINT ■ SCOPES

Maker and Model	Magn.	Field at 100 Yds (feet)	Relative Brightness	Eye Relief (in.)	Length (in.)	Tube Diam. (in.)	W&E Adjustments	Weight (ozs.)	Price	Other Data
Leatherwood										
ART II	3.0-8.8	31-12	—	3.5	13.9	1	Int.	42	675.00	
ART/MPC	3.0-8.7	31-12	—	3.7	14.1	1	Int.	33	349.50	
4x	4.1	27	—	4	12.25	1	Int.	12.3	125.00	
Leupold										
M8-2X EER[1]	1.8	22.0	—	12-24	8.1	1	Int.	6.8	159.65	Constantly centered reticles, choice of Duplex, tapered CPC, Leupold Dot, Crosshair and Dot. CPC and Dot reticles extra. [1]2x and 4x scope have from 12"-24" of eye relief and are suitable for handguns, top ejection arms and muzzleloaders. [2]3x9 Compact, 6x Compact, 12x, 3x9, 3.5x10 and 6.5x20 come with Adjustable Objective. [3]Target scopes have 1-min divisions with ¼ min clicks, and Adjustable Objectives. 50-ft. Focus Adaptor available for indoor target ranges, $40.90. Sunshade available for all Adjustable Objective scopes, $11.40. [4]Also available in matte finish for about $20.00 extra. [5]A.O., $237.50.
M8-2X EER Silver[1]	1.8	22.0	—	12-24	8.1	1	Int.	6.8	177.85	
M8-4X EER[1]	3.5	9.5	—	12-24	8.4	1	Int.	7.6	194.90	
M8-4X EER Silver[1]	3.5	9.5	—	12-24	8.4	1	Int.	8.5	213.15	
M8-2.5X Compact	2.3	42	—	4.3	8.5	1	Int.	7.4	175.80	
M8-4X Compact	3.6	26.5	—	4.1	10.3	1	Int.	8.5	200.80	
2-7x Compact	2.5-6.6	41.7-16.5	—	3.8-3.0	9.9	1	Int.	8.5	253.30	
6x Compact & A.O.	5.7	16	—	3.9	10.7	1	Int.	8.5	204.90	
3-9x Compact & A.O.	3.2-8.5	34.5-13.5	—	3.8-3.1	11	1	Int.	9.5	309.55	
M8-4X[4]	3.6	28	—	4.4	11.4	1	Int.	8.8	200.80	
M8-6X	5.9	18.0	—	4.3	11.4	1	Int.	9.9	214.45	
M8-8X[2]	7.8	14.5	—	4.0	12.5	1	Int.	13.0	285.90	
M8-12X[2]	11.6	9.2	—	4.2	13.0	1	Int.	13.5	289.65	
6.5 x 20 Target AO	6.5-19.2	14.8-5.7	—	5.3-3.7	14.2	1	Int.	16	456.25	
M8-12X Target[3]	11.6	9.2	—	4.2	13.0	1	Int.	14.5	343.60	
M8-24X[3]	24.0	4.7	—	3.2	13.6	1	Int.	14.5	456.25	
M8-36X[3]	36.0	3.2	—	3.4	13.9	1	Int.	15.5	456.25	
Vari-X-II 2X7	2.5-6.6	44.0-19.0	—	4.1-3.7	10.7	1	Int.	10.4	268.50	
Vari-X-II 3X9[4]	3.5-9.0	32.0-13.5	—	4.1-3.7	12.3	1	Int.	13.1	288.40	
Vari-X-II 3X9[2]	3.5-9.0	32.0-13.5	—	4.1-3.7	12.3	1	Int.	14.5	326.35	
Vari-X-III 1.5X5	1.5-4.6	66.0-24.0	—	4.7-3.5	9.4	1	Int.	9.3	294.55	
Vari-X-III 2.5X8[4]	2.7-7.9	38.0-15.0	—	4.2-3.4	11.3	1	Int.	11.0	332.25	
Vari-X-III 3.5X10	3.4-9.9	29.5-10.5	—	4.6-3.6	12.4	1	Int.	13.0	347.50	
Vari-X-III 3.5X10[2]	3.4-9.9	29.5-10.5	—	4.6-3.6	12.4	1	Int.	14.4	386.50	
Vari-X-III 6.5X20[2]	6.5-19.2	14.8- 5.7	—	5.3-3.7	14.2	1	Int.	16	411.60	
Nikon										
4x40	4	26	—	3.4	11.6	1	Int.	13.5	275.00	Multi-coated lenses; ¼-minute windage and elevation adjustments; nitrogen filled; waterproof. From Nikon Inc.
1.5-4.5x20	1.5-4.5	67.5-22.5	—	3.7	10	1	Int.	11.8	315.00	
2-7x32	2-7	43-12	—	4.1	11.4	1	Int.	12.3	348.00	
3-9x40	3-9	34.5-11.5	—	3.5-3.4	12.3	1	Int.	16	355.00	
Pentax										
4x	4	35	—	3¼	11.6	1	Int.	12.2	220.00	Fully coated lenses, fog-proof, water-proof, nitrogen filled. Penta-Plex reticle. Click ¼-m.o.a. adjustments. Imported by Pentax Corp.
6x	6	20	—	3¼	13.4	1	Int.	13.5	250.00	
2-7x	2-7	42.5-17	—	3-3¼	12	1	Int.	14	300.00	
3-9x	3-9	33-13.5	—	3-3¼	13	1	Int.	15	320.00	
3-9x Mini	3-9	26.5-10.5	—	3¾	10.4	1	Int.	13	270.00	
RWS										
100 4x32	4	20	—	10⅞	¾	Int.	6	33.00		Air gun scopes. All have Dyna-Plex reticle. Imported from Japan by Dynamit Nobel of America.
200 3-7x-20	3-7	24-17	—	—	11¼	¾	Int.	6	51.00	
350 4x32	4	28	—	—	10	1	Int.	10	85.00	
400 2-7x32	2-7	56-17	—	—	12¾	1	Int.	12	125.00	
800 1.5x20	1.5	19	—	—	8¾	1	Int.	6½	85.00	
Redfield										
Illuminator Trad. 3-9x	2.9-8.7	33-11	—	3½	12¾	1	Int.	17	378.80	*Accutrac feature avail. on these scopes at extra cost. Traditionals have round lenses. 4-Plex reticle is standard. [1]"Magnum Proof." Specially designed for magnum and auto pistols. Uses "Double Dovetail" mounts. [2]With matte finish $428.95. [3]Also available with matte finish at extra cost. [4]All Golden Five Star scopes come with Butler Creek flip-up lens covers.
Illuminator Widefield 3-9x[2]	2.9-8.7	38-13	—	3½	12¾	1	Int.	17	420.00	
Tracker 4x[3]	3.9	28.9	—	3½	11.02	1	Int.	9.8	117.95	
Tracker 2-7x[3]	2.3-6.9	36.6-12.2	—	3½	12.20	1	Int.	11.6	157.25	
Tracker 3-9x[3]	3.0-9.0	34.4-11.3	—	3½	14.96	1	Int.	13.4	176.90	
Traditional 4x¾"	4	24½	27	3½	9⅜	¾	Int.	—	112.50	
Traditional 2½x	2½	43	64	3½	10¼	1	Int.	8½	155.45	
Golden Five Star 4x[4]	4	28.5	58	3.75	11.3	1	Int.	9.75	169.70	
Golden Five Star 6x[4]	6	18	40	3.75	12.2	1	Int.	11.5	187.60	
Golden Five Star 2-7x[4] Royal	2.4-7.4	42-14	207-23	3-3.75	11.25	1	Int.	12	223.40	
Golden Five Star 3-9x[4]	3.0-9.1	34-11	163-18	3-3.75	12.50	1	Int.	13	241.20	
Golden Five Star 4-12xA.O.[4]	3.9-11.4	27-9	112-14	3-3.75	13.8	1	Int.	16	312.70	
Golden Five Star 6-18xA.O.[4]	6.1-18.1	18.6	50-6	3-3.75	14.3	1	Int.	18	330.60	
Pistol Scopes										
2½xMP[1]	2.5	9	64	14-19	9.8	1	Int.	10.5	171.50	
4xMP[1]	3.6	9	—	12-22	9¹¹⁄₁₆	1	Int.	11.1	183.95	
Low Profile Scopes										
Widefield 2¾xLP	2¾	55½	69	3½	10½	1	Int.	8	194.75	
Widefield 4xLP	3.6	37½	84	3½	11½	1	Int.	10	217.95	
Widefield 6xLP	5.5	23	—	3½	12¾	1	Int.	11	237.70	
Widefield 1¾x5xLP	1¾-5	70-27	136-21	3½	10¾	1	Int.	11½	269.85	
Widefield 2x7xLP*	2-7	49-19	144-21	3½	11¾	1	Int.	13	278.80	
Widefield 3x-9xLP*	3-9	39-15	112-18	3½	12½	1	Int.	14	307.40	
Sanders										
Bisley 2½x20	2½	42	64	3	10¾	1	Int.	8¼	48.50	Alum. alloy tubes, ¼" adj. coated lenses. Five other models are offered; 6x45 at $68.50, 8x45 at $70.50, 2½x7x at $69.50, 3-9x33 at $72.50 and 3-9x40 at $78.50. Rubber lens covers (clear plastic) are $3.50. Write to Sanders for details. Choice of reticles in CH, PCH, 3-post.
Bisley 4x33	4	28	64	3	12	1	Int.	9	52.50	
Bisley 6x40	6	19	45	3	12½	1	Int.	9½	56.50	
Bisley 8x40	8	18	25	3¼	12½	1	Int.	9½	62.50	
Bisley 10x40	10	12½	16	2½	12½	1	Int.	10¼	64.50	
Bisley 5-13x40	5-13	29-10	64-9	3	14	1	Int.	14	86.50	

CAUTION: PRICES CHANGE. CHECK AT GUNSHOP.

Maker and Model	Magn.	Field at 100 Yds (feet)	Relative Brightness	Eye Relief (in.)	Length (in.)	Tube Diam. (in.)	W&E Adjustments	Weight (ozs.)	Price	Other Data
Schmidt & Bender										[1]Heavy duty aluminum. [2]Black chrome finish. [3]For silhouette and varmint shooting. Choice of nine reticles. 30-year warranty. All have 1/3-min. click adjustments, centered reticles, nitrogen filling. Most models avail. in aluminum with mounting rail. Imported from West Germany by Paul Jaeger, Inc.
Vari-M 1¼-4x20[1]	1¼-4	96-16	—	3¼	10.4	30mm	Int.	12.3	402.00	
Vari-M 1½-6x42	1½-6	60-19.5	—	3¼	12.2	30mm	Int.	17.5	440.00	
Vari-M 2½-10x56	2½-10	37.5-12	—	3¼	14.6	30mm	Int.	21.9	512.00	
All Steel 1½x15[2]	1½	90	—	3¼	10	1	Int.	11.8	297.00	
All Steel 4x36[2]	4	30	—	3¼	11.4	1	Int.	14	308.00	
All Steel 6x42[2]	6	21	—	3¼	13.2	1	Int.	17.3	330.00	
All Steel 8x56[2]	8	16.5	—	3¼	14.8	1	Int.	21.9	385.00	
■ All Steel 12x42[3]	12	16.5	—	3¼	13	1	Int.	17.9	368.00	
Shepherd										[1]Also avail. in Rimfire version (#1020). [2]Also avail. as Model 1001 Elite for counter sniper, silhouette shooting with extra-fine crosshair. Models 1001, 1002, 1003, 1020 come with reticle pattern set for shooters choice of ballistics. All except 1001 have Dual Reticle System with instant range finder, bullet drop compensator. Waterproof, nitrogen filled, shock-proof. From Shepherd Scope Ltd.
1003 Centerfire[1]	2.5-7.5	42-14	164-18	2.5-3	11⅝	1	Int.	18	231.55	
1002 Centerfire[2]	3-10	35.3-11.6	178-16	3-3.75	12.8	1	Int.	16.7	280.75	
Deluxe 3-9x	3-9	43.5-15	178-20	3.3	13	1	Int.	13.5	428.00	
Simmons										[1]With ring mount. [2]With ring mount. [3]With rings. [4]3-9x32; also avail. 3-9x40. [5]3-9x32; 3-9x40. [6]4x32; also avail. 4x40 as #1034. [7]3-9x32; also avail. 3-9x40 as #1038. [8]Avail. in brushed aluminum finish as #1052. [9]Avail. with silhouette knobs as #1085, in brushed aluminum as #1088. [10]½-min. dot or Truplex; Truplex reticle also avail. with dot. Sunshade, screw-in lens covers. Parallax adj.; Silhouette knobs; graduated drums. [11]Battery powered, roof prism design. [12]Speed focus, parallax adj., matte finish. [13]"Simcoat" multi-coating on all lenses, 44mm obj. lens, high-gloss finish, parallax adj., polarized and yellow screw-in filters, ¼-min. click adj., leather lens covers incl. Also avail. in wide angle with range finding system. Max-Ilume Mono Tube models have dull finish, speed focus, rubber shock ring, Truplex reticle in all models. All scopes sealed, fog-proof, with constantly centered reticles. Imported from Japan by Simmons Outdoor Corp. **Prices are approximate.**
1002 Rimfire[1]	4	23	—	3	11.5	¾	Int.	6	11.00	
1004 Rimfire[2]	3-7	22.5-9.5	—	3	11	¾	Int.	8.4	27.95	
1007 Rimfire[3]	4	25	—	3	10	1	Int.	9	60.00	
1005 Waterproof	2½	46	—	3	11.5	1	Int.	9.3	54.00	
1006 Waterproof	4	29	—	—	12	1	Int.	9.1	41.00	
1010 Waterproof[4]	3-9	37-12.7	—	3-3¼	12.8	1	Int.	12.8	55.00	
1014 Waterproof	4-12	30-11	—	3-3¼	14	1	Int.	14.9	95.00	
1016 Waterproof	6-18	19-6.7	—	3-3¼	15.7	1	Int.	16.2	122.00	
1024 W.A.	4	37	—	3	11.8	1	Int.	10.5	71.50	
1025 W.A.	6	24.5	—	3	12.4	1	Int.	12	90.00	
1026 W.A.	1½-4½	86-28.9	—	3-3¼	10.6	1	Int.	13.2	97.00	
1027 W.A.	2-7	54.6-18.3	—	3-3¼	12	1	Int.	12.8	97.00	
1028 W.A.[5]	3-9	42-14	—	3-3¼	12.9	1	Int.	12.9	90.00	
1032 Mono Tube[6]	4	37	—	3	12.2	1	Int.	11.5	100.00	
1036 Mono Tube[7]	3-9	42-14	—	3-3¼	13.3	1	Int.	13	130.00	
1040 Mono Tube	2-7	54-18	—	3-3¼	13.1	1	Int.	12.9	146.00	
1049 Compact	2½	37	—	3	9.3	1	Int.	9.1	106.00	
1050 Compact[8]	4	22	—	3	9	1	Int.	9.1	106.00	
1053 Compact	1½-4½	86-28.9	—	3-3¼	10.6	1	Int.	9.1	143.00	
1054 Compact	3-9	40-14	—	3-3¼	10.5	1	Int.	10.5	136.50	
1063 Armored	4	37	—	3	12.4	1	Int.	16	108.00	
1064 Armored	3-9	42-14	—	3-3¼	12.3	1	Int.	17.6	120.25	
1074	6½-20	18-6	—	3	15	1	Int.	16	208.00	
1075	6½-10	22-12	—	3	15	1	Int.	16	208.00	
1076[10]	15	8	—	3	15	1	Int.	16	169.00	
1078[10]	24	6	—	3	15	1	Int.	16	169.00	
1057 Illum.	4	21	—	3	8	1	Int.	11	157.00	
410[11]	4-10	40-15	—	3	12.75	1	Int.	15	157.00	
1073 Sil. Airgun	2-7	54.6-18.3	—	3-3¼	12.1	1	Int.	15.7	128.75	
1080 Handgun	2	18	—	10-20	7.1	1	Int.	8.1	83.00	
1084 Handgun[9]	4	9	—	10-20	8.7	1	Int.	9.5	122.00	
Presidential Series										
1065[13]	4	35	121	3.5	13	1	Int.	15.5	227.50	
1066[13]	2-7	55.1-18.3	484-40	3.3-2.9	12.6	1	Int.	16.6	260.00	
1067[13]	3-9	42-14	216-54	3.3	13	1	Int.	16.2	260.00	
1068[13]	4-12	31-11	121-14	3.9-3.2	14.2	1	Int.	19.1	282.75	
1069[13]	6.5-20	17.8-6.1	46-5	3.4-3.2	15.4	1	Int.	19.4	302.00	
Swarovski Habicht										All models offered in either steel or lightweight alloy tubes except 1.5x20, ZFM 6x42 and Cobras. Weights shown are for lightweight versions. Choice of nine constantly centered reticles. Eyepiece recoil mechanism and rubber ring shield to protect face. Cobra and ZFM also available in NATO Stanag 2324 mounts. Imported by Swarovski America Ltd.
Nova 1.5x20	1.5	61	—	3⅛	9.6	1	Int.	12.7	330.00	
Nova 4x32	4	33	—	3⅛	11.3	1	Int.	13	340.00	
Nova 6x42	6	23	—	3⅛	12.6	1	Int.	14	380.00	
Nova 8x56	8	17	—	3⅛	14.4	1	Int.	17	455.00	
Nova 1.5 6x42	1.5-6	61-21	—	3⅛	12.6	1	Int.	17	470.00	
Nova 2.2-9x42	2.2-9	39.5-15	—	3⅛	13.3	1	Int.	16.5	580.00	
Nova 3-12x56	3-12	30-11	—	3⅛	15.25	1	Int.	19	640.00	
ZFM 6x42	6	23	—	3⅛	12	1	Int.	18	535.00	
Cobra 1.5-14	1.5	50	—	3.9	7.87	1	Int.	10	325.00	
Cobra 3x14	3	21	—	3.9	8.75	1	Int.	11	340.00	
Swift										All Swift Mark I scopes, with the exception of the 4x15, have Quadraplex reticles and are fog-proof and waterproof. The 4x15 has crosshair reticle and is non-waterproof.
600 4x15	4	16.2	—	2.4	11	¾	Int.	4.7	19.98	
650 4x32	4	29	—	3½	12	1	Int.	9	68.00	
651 4x32 WA	4	37	—	3½	11¾	1	Int.	10½	76.50	
653 4x40 WA	4	35½	—	3¾	12¼	1	Int.	12	89.50	
654 3-9x32	3-9	35¾-12¾	—	3	12¾	1	Int.	13¾	92.50	
656 3-9x40 WA	3-9	42½-13½	—	2¾	12¾	1	Int.	14	105.00	
657 6x40	6	18	—	3¾	13	1	Int.	10	78.00	
658 1½-4½x32	1½-4½	55-22	—	3½	12	1	Int.	13	98.00	
Tasco										[1]MAG-IV gives one-third more power. [2]Supercon®, fully coated lenses; waterproof, shockproof, fogproof; includes haze filter caps, lifetime warranty. [3]Trajectory-Range Finding scopes.
WA 1x20 Wide Angle[2,7]	1	98	—	3	9¾	1	Int.	9.5	194.95	
WA 1-3.5x20[2,7] Wide Angle	1-3.5	91-31	—	3½	9¾	1	Int.	10.5	214.95	
WA 4x40 Wide Angle[2,7]	4	36	100	3¼	12⅝	1	Int.	12½	174.95	
WA 3-9x40 Wide Angle[2,7]	3-9	43½-15	178-20	3¼	12⅝	1	Int.	11½	194.95	

Maker and Model	Magn.	Field at 100 Yds (feet)	Relative Brightness	Eye Relief (in.)	Length (in.)	Tube Diam. (in.)	W&E Adjustments	Weight (ozs.)	Price	Other Data
Tasco (cont'd.)										[4]30/30 range finding reticle; rubber covered; built-in mounting rings. Also avail. in wide angle models. [5]Waterproof; anodized finish; 1/4-min. click stops; R.F. reticle. [6]Adj., built-in mount; adj. rheostat, polarizer; 1/2-min. clicks. Avail. to fit Rem. 870, 1100, also with side mounts, in wide angle. [7]World Class Wide Angle®. **Contact Tasco for complete list of models offered.**
WA 2.5x32 Wide Angle[2,7]	2.5	52	44	3 1/4	12	1	Int.	9 1/2	164.95	
WA 2-7x32 Wide Angle[2,7]	2-7	56-17	256-21	3 1/4	11 1/2	1	Int.	11 1/2	194.95	
WA 1 3/4-5x20 Wide Angle[2,7]	1.75-5	72-24	131-16	3 1/4	10 5/8	1	Int.	10 3/4	184.95	
RC 3-9x40 WA[2,4,7]	3-9	43 1/2-15	178-20	3 1/4	—	1	Int.	12 5/8	204.95	
TR 3-12x32 TRF[3]	3-12	34-9	112-7	3	12 1/4	1	Int.	13 3/4	129.95	
TR 4-16x40 TRF[3]	4-16	25 1/2-7	100-6	3	14 1/4	1	Int.	16 3/4	199.95	
W 4x32[5]	4	28	64	3 1/4	11 3/4	1	In.t	9 1/2	66.95	
W 3-12x4 MAG-IV[1]	3-12	34-9	178-11	3	12 3/4	1	Int.	13 3/4	139.95	
EU 4x44[8]	4	29	—	3	12 3/8	30mm	Int.	16	249.95	
EU 6x44[8]	6	24	—	3	12 3/8	30mm	Int.	16	249.95	
EU 3-9x44[8]	3-9	41-14	—	3	12 1/8	30mm	Int.	18.5	279.95	
EU 3-12x52[8]	3-12	33-8.5	—	3	12 1/4	30mm	Int.	18.5	299.95	
IR 4x28P[9]	4	65	—	16-25	9 3/8	1	Int.	13.5	229.95	
SW 2.5-10x32[10]	2.5-10	41-10 1/2	—	3	11 1/4	1	Int.	8.5	129.95	
BDIXCFV Battery Dot[6]	1	—	—		7 1/2	—	Int.	10	179.95	
Thompson/Center										[1]May be used on light to medium recoil guns, including muzzleloaders. Coated lenses, nitrogen filled, lifetime warranty. [2]For heavy recoil guns. Nitrogen filled. Duplex reticle only. Target turrets avail. on 1 1/2x, 3x models. Electra Dot illuminated reticle available in RP 2 1/2x ($35 extra) and RP 3x ($40 extra). [3]Rifle scopes have Electra Dot reticle. [4]Rail model for grooved receivers also available—$165. With Electra Dot reticle.
Lobo 1 1/2 x[1]	1.5	16	127	11-20	7 3/4	7/8	Int.	5	90.00	
Lobo 3x[1]	3	9	49	11-20	9	7/8	Int.	6.3	95.00	
RP 1 1/2 x[2]	1.5	28	177	11-20	7 1/2	1	Int.	5.1	120.00	
RP 2 1/2x[2]	2.5	15	64	11-20	8 1/2	1	Int.	6.5	120.00	
RP 3x[2]	3	13	44	11-20	8 3/4	1	Int.	5.4	120.00	
RP 4x[2]	4	10	71	12-20	9 1/4	1	Int.	10.4	140.00	
TC 4x Rifle[3]	4	29	64	3.3	12 7/8	1	Int.	12.3	150.00	
TC 3/9V Rifle[3]	3-9	35.3-13.2	177-19	3.3	12 7/8	1	Int.	15.5	220.00	
Short Tube 8630[4]	4	29	20	3	7 3/4	1	Int.	10.1	155.00	
Trijicon										Have self-luminous low-light reticle that glow red in poor light, show black in bright light. All have bullet drop compensator. Bar-dot reticle on 4x, 6x, bar-cross on others. From Armson, Inc.
4x40	4	38	100	3	12.2	1	Int.	14.8	259.00	
6x56	6	24	87	3	14	1	Int.	20.1	299.00	
1.5-5x32	1.5-5	50-16	79	4.5-3.5	11.9	1	Int.	14.0	329.00	
2-7x40	2-7	62-16	79	3.3-3	11.9	1	Int.	15.8	359.00	
3-9x56	3-9	35-14	82	3.3-3	14.1	1	Int.	21.3	389.00	
Unertl										[1]Dural 1/4 MOA click mounts. Hard coated lenses. Non-rotating objective lens focusing. [2]1/4 MOA click mounts. [3]With target mounts. [4]With calibrated head. [5]Same as 1" Target but without objective lens focusing. [6]Price with 1/4 MOA click mounts. [7]With new Posa mounts. [8]Range focus until near rear of tube. Price is with Posa mounts. Magnum clamp. With standard mounts and clamp ring $266.00.
■ 1" Target	6,8,10	16-10	17.6-6.25	2	21 1/2	3/4	Ext.	21	154.00	
■ 1 1/4" Target[1]	8,10,12,14	12-16	15.2-5	2	25	3/4	Ext.	21	206.00	
■ 1 1/2" Target	8,10,12,14 16,18,20	11.5-3.2	—	2 1/4	25 1/2	3/4	Ext.	31	235.00	
■ 2" Target[2]	8,10,12, 14,16,18, 24,30,36	8	22.6-2.5	2 1/4	26 1/4	1	Ext.	44	322.00	
■ Varmint, 1 1/4∞3	6,8,10,12	1-7	28-7.1	2 1/2	19 1/2	7/8	Ext.	26	207.00	
■ Ultra Varmint, 2"4	8,10 12,15	12.6-7	39.7-11	2 1/2	24	1	Ext.	34	301.00	
Unertl (cont'd.)										
■ Small Game[5]	4,6	25-17	19.4-8.4	2 1/4	18	3/4	Ext.	16	117.00	
■ Vulture[6]	8	11.2	29	3-4	15 5/8	1	Ext.	15 1/2	231.00	
	10	10.9	18 1/2		16 1/8					
■ Programmer 200[7]	8,10,12 14,16,18, 20,24,30,36	11.3-4	39-1.9	—	26 1/2	1	Ext.	45	403.00	
■ BV-20[8]	20	8	4.4	4.4	17 7/8	1	Ext.	21 1/4	287.00	
Weatherby										Lumiplex reticle in all models. Blue-black, non-glare finish.
Mark XXII	4	25	50	2.5-3.5	11 3/4	7/8	Int.	9.25	85.35	
Supreme 1 3/4-5x20	1.7-5	66.6-21.4	—	3.4	10.7	1	Int.	11	190.00	
Supreme 4x34	4	32	—	3.1	11 1/8	1	Int.	9.6	190.00	
Supreme 2-7x34	2.1-6.8	59-16	—	3.4	11 1/4	1	Int.	10.4	240.00	
Supreme 4x44	3.9	32	—	3	12 1/2	1	Int.	11.6	240.00	
Supreme 3-9x44	3.1-8.9	36-13	—	3.5	12.7	1	Int.	11.6	280.00	
Williams										TNT models
Twilight Crosshair	2 1/2	32	64	3 3/4	11 1/4	1	Int.	8 1/2	115.75	
Twilight Crosshair	4	29	64	3 1/2	11 3/4	1	Int.	9 1/2	124.75	
Twilight Crosshair	2-6	45-17	256-28	3	11 1/2	1	Int.	11 1/2	164.65	
Twilight Crosshair	3-9	36-13	161-18	3	12 3/4	1	Int.	13 1/2	178.00	
Pistol Scopes										
Twilight 1.5x	1.5	19	177	18-25	8.2	1	Int.	6.4	96.95	
Twilight 2x	2	17.5	100	18-25	8.5	1	Int.	6.4	97.95	
Zeiss										All scopes have 1/4-minute click-stop adjustments. Choice of Z-Plex or fine crosshair reticles. Rubber armored objective bell, rubber eyepiece ring. Lenses have T-Star coating for highest light transmission. Z-Series scopes offered in non-rail tubes with duplex reticles only. Imported from West Germany by Zeiss Optical, Inc.
Diatal C 4x32	4	30	—	3.5	10.6	1	Int.	11.3	326.00	
Diatal C 6x32	6	20	—	3.5	10.6	1	Int.	11.3	364.00	
Diatal C 10x36	10	12	—	3.5	12.7	1	Int.	14.1	423.00	
Diatal Z 4x32	4	34.5	—	3.5	10.8	1.02 (26mm)	Int.	10.6	325.00	
Diatal Z 6x42	6	22.9	—	3.5	12.7	1.02 (26mm)	Int.	13.4	375.00	
Diatal Z 8x56	8	18	—	3.5	13.8	1.02 (26mm)	Int.	17.6	425.00	
Diavari 1.5-4.5	1.5-4.5	72-27	—	3.5	11.2	1	Int.	13.4	445.00	
Diavari C 3-9x36	3-9	36-13	—	3.5	11.2	1	Int.	15.2	578.00	
Diavari Z 1.5-6	1.5-6	65.5-22.9	—	3.5	12.4	1.18 (30mm)	Int.	18.5	520.00	
Diavari Z 2.5-10	2.5-10	41-13.7	—	3.5	14.4	1.18 (30mm)	Int.	22.8	610.00	

■ Signifies target and/or varmint scope. Hunting scopes in general are furnished with a choice of reticle—crosshairs, post with crosshairs, tapered or blunt post, or dot crosshairs, etc. The great majority of target and varmint scopes have medium or fine crosshairs but post or dot reticles may be ordered. W—Windage   E—Elevation   MOA—Minute of angle or 1" (approx.) at 100 yards, etc.

CAUTION: PRICES CHANGE. CHECK AT GUNSHOP.

SCOPE MOUNTS

Maker, Model, Type	Adjust.	Scopes	Price	Suitable for
Action Arms	No	1″ split rings.	$32.00	For UZI, Ruger Mk. II, Mini-14, Win. 94, AR-15, Rem. 870, Ithaca 37. From Action Arms.
Aimpoint	No	1″	31.95-47.50	For many popular revolvers, auto pistols, shotguns, military-style rifles/carbines, sporting rifles. Contact Aimpoint for details.
Armson				[1]Fastens with one nut. [2]Models 181, 182, 183, 184, etc. [3]Claw mount. [4]Claw mount, bolt cover still easily removable. From Armson, Inc.
AR-15[1]	No	O.E.G.	28.95	
Mini-14[2]	No	O.E.G.	39.95	
H&K[3]	No	O.E.G.	54.95	
UZI[4]	No	O.E.G.	54.95	
Armsport				[1]Weaver-type rings. [2]Weaver-type base; most popular rifles. Made in U.S. From Armsport.
100 Series[1]	No	1″ rings.	9.50	
104 22-cal.	No	1″.	9.50	
201 See-Thru	No	1″.	11.95	
1-Piece Base[2]	No		4.50	
2-Piece Base[2]	No		2.25	
B-Square				[1]Clamp-on, blue finish. Stainless finish $59.95. [2]For Bushnell Phantom only. [3]Blue finish; stainless finish $59.95. [4]Clamp-on, for Bushnell Phantom only; blue; stainless finish $49.95. [5]Requires drilling & tapping. [6]No gunsmithing, no sight removal; blue; stainless finish $59.95. [7]Clamp-on. [8]Weaver-style rings. Rings not included with Weaver-type bases. Partial listing of mounts shown here. Contact B-Square for more data. B-Square also has mounts for Aimpoint scopes to fit many popular military rifles, shotguns and handguns. Write them for a complete listing.
Pistols				
Colt Python[1]	E	1″	49.95	
Dan Wesson Clamp-On[3,8]	E	1″	49.95	
Hi-Standard Victor	W&E	1″	49.95	
Ruger 22 Auto Mono-Mount[4]	No	1″	39.95	
Ruger Single-Six[5]	No	1″	39.95	
T-C Contender	W&E	1″	49.95	
Rifles				
Daisy 717/722 Champion[2]	No	1″	19.95	
Mini-14[6]	W&E	1″	49.95	
Mini-14[7]	W&E	1″	49.95	
M-94 Side Mount	W&E	1″	49.95	
Ruger 77	W&E	1″	49.95	
SMLE Side Mount	E only	1″	49.95	
T-C Single-Shot Rifle	W&E	1″	49.95	
Rem. Model Seven[8]	No	1″	39.95	
Military				
M1-A	W&E	1″	59.95	
AR-15/16	W&E	1″	49.95	
FN-LAR[8]	E only	1″	99.50	
HK-91/93[8]	E only	1″	69.95	
Shotguns				
Rem. 870/1100	No	1″	39.95	
S&W 1000P	No	1″	39.95	
Beeman				All grooved receivers and scope bases on all known air rifles and 22-cal. rimfire rifles (½″ to ⅝″—6mm to 15mm). [1]Centerfire rifles. Scope detaches easily, returns to zero. [2]Designed specifically for Krico rifles.
Double Adjustable	W&E	1″	24.98	
Deluxe Ring Mounts	No	1″	21.98	
Professional Mounts	W&E	1″	82.50	
Professional Pivot[1]	W	1″	129.50	
Buehler[2]	W	1″	79.00	
Buehler				[1]Most popular models. [2]Sako dovetail receivers. [3]15 models. [4]No drilling & tapping. [5]Aircraft alloy, dyed blue or to match stainless; for Colt Diamondback, Python, Trooper, Ruger Blackhawk, Single-Six, Security-Six, S&W K-frame, Dan Wesson.
One Piece (T)[1]	W only	1″ split rings, 3 heights.	Complete—65.75	
		1″ split rings.	Rings only—91.50	
		26mm split rings, 2 heights	Rings only—48.00	
		30mm split rings, 1 height	Rings only—57.75	
One Piece Micro Dial (T)[1]	W&E	1″ split rings.	Complete—84.25	
Two Piece (T)[1]	W only	1″ split rings.	Complete—65.75	
Two Piece Dovetail (T)[2]	W only	1″ split rings.	Complete—81.00	
One Piece Pistol (T)[3]	W only	1″ split rings.	Complete—65.75	
One Piece Pistol Stainless (T)[1]	W only	1″ stainless rings.	Complete—86.00	
One Piece Ruger Mini-14 (T)[4]	W only	1″ split rings.	Complete—81.00	
One Piece Pistol M83 Blue[4,5]	W only	1″ split rings.	Complete—75.25	
One Piece Pistol M83 Silver[4,5]	W only	1″ stainless rings.	Complete—88.00	
Burris				[1]Most popular rifles. Universal, rings, mounts fit Burris. Universal, Redfield, Leupold and Browning bases. Comparable prices. [2]Browning Standard 22 Auto rifle. [3]Most popular rifles. [4]Grooved receivers. [5]Universal dovetail; accept Burris, Universal, Redfield, Leupold rings. For Dan Wesson, S&W, Virginian, Ruger Blackhawk, Win. 94. [6]Medium standard front, extension rear, per pair. Low standard front, extension rear, per pair. [7]Mini scopes, scopes with 2″ bell, for M77R. Selected rings and bases available with matte Safari finish.
Supreme One Piece (T)[1]	W only	1″ split rings, 3 heights.	1 piece-base—21.95	
Trumount Two Piece (T)	W only	1″ split rings, 3 heights.	2 piece base—19.95	
Browning Auto Mount[2]	No	¾″, 1″ split rings.	17.95	
Sight-Thru Mount[3]	No	1″ Split rings.	17.95	
Rings Mounts[4]	No	¾″, 1″ split rings.	1″ rings—16.95	
L.E.R. Mount Bases[5]	No	1″ split rings.	19.95	
Extension Rings[6]	No	1″ scopes.	33.95	
Ruger Ring Mount[7]	W only	1″ split rings.	39.95	
Bushnell				[1]Most popular rifles. Includes windage adj. [2]V-block bottoms lock to chrome-moly studs seated into two 6-48 holes. Rem. XP-100. [3]Heavy loads in Colt, S&W, Ruger revolvers, Ruger Hawkeye, [4]M94 Win., center dovetail.
Detachable (T) mounts only[1]	W only	1″ split rings, uses Weaver base.	Rings—15.95	
22 mount	No	1″ only.	Rings— 7.95	
All Purpose[2]	No	Phantom.	19.95	
Rigid[3]	No	Phantom.	19.95	
94 Win.[4]	No	Phantom.	19.95	
Clearview				[1]All popular rifles including Sav. 99. Uses Weaver bases. [2]Allows use of open sights. [3]For 22 rimfire rifles, with grooved receivers or bases. [4]Fits 13 models. Broadest view area of the type. [5]Side mount for both M94 and M94-375 Big Bore.
Universal Rings (T)[1]	No	1″ split rings.	19.95	
Mod 101, & 336[2]	No	1″ split rings.	19.95	
Broad-View[4]	No	1″	19.95	
Model 22[3]	No	¾″, ⅞″, 1″	11.95	
94 Winchester[5]	No	1″	19.95	

CAUTION: PRICES CHANGE. CHECK AT GUNSHOP.

Maker, Model, Type	Adjust.	Scopes	Price	Suitable for
Conetrol				[1]All popular rifles, including metric-drilled foreign guns. Price shown for base, two rings. Matte finish. [2]Gunnur grade has mirror-finished rings, satin-finish base. Price shown for base, two rings. [3]Custum grade has mirror-finished rings and mirror-finished, contoured base. Price shown for base, 2 rings. [4]Win. 94, Krag, older split-bridge Mannlicher-Schoenauer, Mini-14, M-1 Garand, etc. Prices same as above. [5]For all popular guns with integral mounting provision, including Sako, BSA, Ithacagun, Ruger, H&K and many others. Also for grooved-receiver rimfires and air rifles. Prices same as above. [6]For XP-100, T/C Contender, Colt SAA, Ruger Blackhawk, S&W. [7]Sculptured 2-piece bases as found on fine custom rifles. Price shown is for base alone. Also available unfinished—**$49.98**. [8]Replaces Ruger rib, positions scope farther back. [9]Horizontally split screw connections; 2 heights.
Huntur[1]	W only	1", 26mm, 26.5mm solid or split rings, 3 heights.	48.93	
Gunnur[2]	W only	1", 26mm, 26.5mm solid or split rings, 3 heights.	59.91	
Custum[3]	W only	1", 26mm, 26.5mm solid or split rings, 3 heights.	74.91	
One Piece Side Mount Base[4]	W only	1", 26mm, 26.5mm solid or split rings, 3 heights.		
Daptar Bases[5]	W only	1", 26mm, 26.5mm solid or split rings, 3 heights.		
Pistol Bases, 2 or 3-ring[6]	W only	1" scopes.		
Fluted Bases[7]	W only	Standard Conetrol rings	74.97	
Ruger No. 1 Base[8]	No	1", 26mm, 26.5mm solid or split rings.	NA	
30mm Rings[9]	—	30mm	74.94	
EAW				Most popular rifles. Elevation adjusted with variable-height sub-bases for rear ring. Imported by Paul Jaeger, Inc., Kahles of America.
Quick Detachable Top Mount	W&E	1"/26mm	150.00	
	W&E	1"/26mm with front extension ring.	155.00	
	W&E	30mm	160.00	
	W&E	30mm with front extension ring.	165.00	
Griffin & Howe				All popular models (Garand $295). All rings $65. Top ejection rings available.
Standard Double Lever (S).	No	1" or 26mm split rings.	175.00	
Holden				[1]Most popular rifles including Ruger Mini-14, H&R M700, and muzzleloaders. Rings have oval holes to permit use of iron sights. [2]For 1" dia. scopes. [3]For 3/4" or 7/8" dia. scopes. [4]For 1" dia. extended eye relief scopes. [5]702—Browning A-Bolt; 709—Marlin 39A. [6]732—Ruger 77/22 R&RS, No. 1 Ranch Rifle; 777 fits Ruger 77R, RS. Both 732, 777 fit Ruger integral bases.
Wide Ironsighter®	No	1" Split rings.	21.36	
Ironsighter Center Fire[1]	No	1" Split rings.	21.36	
Ironsighter S-94	No	1" split rings	26.46	
Ironsighter 22 cal. rimfire				
Model #500[2]	No	1" Split rings.	11.71	
Model #600[3]	No	7/8" Split rings also fits 3/4".	11.71	
Series #700[5]	No	1", split rings.	21.36	
Model 732, 777[6]	No	1", split rings	49.95	
Ironsighter Handguns[4]	No	1" Split rings.	23.40	
Jaeger				All popular models. From Paul Jaeger, Inc.
QD, with windage (S)	W only	1", 3 heights.	190.00	
Kimber				[1]High rings; low rings—**$45.00**; both only for Kimber rifles. [2]For Kimber rifles only. Also avail. for Mauser (FN,98) Rem. 700, 721, 722, 725, Win. M70, Mark X. [3]Vertically split rings; for Kimber and other popular CF rifles.
Standard[1]	No	1", split rings	48.90	
Double Lever[2]	No	1", split rings	69.00	
Non-Detachable[3]	No	1", split rings	48.00	
Kris Mounts				[1]One-piece mount for Win. 94. [2]Most popular rifles and Ruger. [3]Blackhawk revolver. Mounts have oval hole to permit use of iron sights.
Side-Saddle[1]	No	1", 26mm split rings.	11.98	
Two Piece (T)[2]	No	1", 26mm split rings.	7.98	
One Piece (T)[3]	No	1", 26mm split rings.	11.98	
KWIK MOUNT				Wrap-around design; no gunsmithing required. Models for Browning A-5 12 ga., Rem. 870/1100, S&W 916, Savage 67 12 ga., Mossberg 500, Ithaca 37 & 51 12 ga., S&W 1000/3000, Win. 1400. From KenPatable Ent.
Shotgun Mount	No	1"	49.95	
Kwik-Site				[1]Most rifles. Allows use of iron sights. [2]22-cal. rifles with grooved receivers. Allows use of iron sights. [3]Model 94, 94 Big Bore. No drilling or tapping. [4]Most rifles. One-piece solid construction. Use on Weaver bases. 32mm obj. lens or larger. [5]Non-see-through model; for grooved receivers.
KS-See-Thru[1]	No	1"	19.95	
KS-22 See-Thru[2]	No	1"'	17.95	
KS-W94[3]	Yes	1"	39.95	
KSM Bench Rest[4]	No	1"	27.95	
KS-WEV	No	1"	19.95	
KS-WEV-HIGH	No	1"	19.95	
KS-T22 1"[5]	No	1"	17.95	
Leatherwood				[1]Popular bolt actions. [2]With M-16 adaptor. [3]Adaptor base for H&K rail mounts.
M-1A, M-14	W only	ART II, ART/MPC (Weaver rings)	75.00	
AR-15, M-16	No	As above	17.95	
FN-FAL	No	As above	175.00	
SSG	No	As above	50.00	
One-piece Bridge[1]	No	As above	9.95	
Night Vision Adaptor[2]	No	Night vision scopes	37.50	
H&K Adaptor[3]	No	ART II, ART/MPC (Weaver rings)	59.95	
Leupold				[1]Most popular rifles. Also available in 2-piece version, same price. [2]Ruger revolvers, Thompson/Center Contender, S&W K&N Frame revolvers and Colt .45 "Gold Cup" N.M. Available with silver or blue finish. [3]Reversible extended front; regular rear rings, in two heights.
STD Bases (T)[1]	W only	One piece base (dovetail front, windage rear)	Base—19.70	
STD Handgun mounts[2] Base and two rings[2]	No	1"	50.20	
STD Rings		1", 3 ring heights interchangeable with other mounts of similar design.	1" rings—28.40	
Extension-Ring Sets[3]		1"	39.30	
Marlin				Most Marlin lever actions.
One Piece QD (T)	No	1" split rings.	12.10	
Millett				Rem. 40X, 700, 722, 725, Ruger 77 (round top) Weatherby, etc. FN Mauser, FN Brownings, Colt 57, Interarms MkX, Parker-Hale, Sako (round receiver), many others. [1]Fits Win. M70, 70XTR, 670, Browning BBR.
Black Onyx Smooth		1" Low, medium, high	26.95	
Chaparral Engraved		Engraved	39.95	
Universal Two Piece Bases				
700 Series	W only	Two-piece bases	20.95	
FN Series	W only	Two-piece bases	20.95	
70 Series[1]	W only	1", two-piece bases	20.95	

CAUTION: PRICES CHANGE. CHECK AT GUNSHOP.

SCOPE MOUNTS

Maker, Model, Type	Adjust.	Scopes	Price	Suitable for
Redfield				[1]Low, med. & high, split rings. Reversible extension front rings for 1". 2-piece bases for Sako. Colt Sauer bases $39.85. [2]Split rings for grooved 22's. See-thru mounts $16.15. [3]Used with MP scopes for: S&W K or N frame. XP-100, Colt J or I frame. T/C Contender, Colt autos, black powder rifles. [4]One- and two-piece aluminum base; three ring heights.
JR-SR(T)[1]	W only	¾", 1", 26mm.	JR—19.80-26.95 SR—25.85-39.85	
Ring (T)[2]	No	¾" and 1".		
Double Dovetail MP[3]	No	1", split rings.	58.40	
Midline Base & Rings[4]	No	1"	14.25	
See-Thru Rings[4]	No	1"	16.15	
S&K				[1]1903, A3, M1 Carbine, Lee Enfield #1, MK. III, #4, #5, M1917, M98 Mauser, FN Auto, AR-15, AR-180, M-14, M-1, Ger. K-43, Mini-14, M1-A, Krag, AKM, AK-47, Win. 94. [2]Most popular rifles already drilled and tapped. Horizontally and vertically split rings, matte or high gloss.
Insta-Mount (T) base only[1]	W only	Use S&K rings only.	20.00-99.00	
Conventional rings and bases[2]	W only	1" split rings.	50.00	
SKulptured Bases, Rings[2]	W only	1", 26mm, 30mm	From 50.00	
SSK Industries				Custom installation using from two to four rings (included). For T/C Contender, most 22 auto pistols. Ruger and other S.A. revolvers, Ruger, Dan Wesson, S&W, Colt D.A. revolvers. Black or white finish.
T'SOB	No	1"	45.00-145.00	
Sako				Sako, or any rifle using Sako action, 3 heights available, Stoeger, importer.
QD Dovetail	W only	1" only.	99.95	
Simmons				Weaver-type bases. #1401 (low) also in high style (#1403). #1406, 1408 for grooved receiver 22s. Bases avail. for most popular rifles; one- and two-piece styles. Most popular rifles; 1-piece bridge mount. Ring sets—$39.00. [1]For 22 RF rifles.
1401	No	1"	7.00	
1406	No	1"	7.00	
1408	No	1"	16.00	
All Steel Tip-Off[1]	No	1"	7.00	
Tasco				[1]Many popular rifles. [2]For 22s with grooved receivers. [3]Most popular rifles. [4]Most popular rifles. [5]"Quick Peep" 1" ring mount; fits all 22-cal. rifles with grooved receivers. [6]For Ruger Mini-14; also in brushed aluminum. [7]Side mount for Win. 94. [8]Side mount rings and base for Win. 94 in 30-30, 375 Win. [9]Avail. for most rifles. Steel or aluminum rings.
791 and 793 series[1]	No	1", regular or high.	9.95	
797[2]	No	Split rings.	9.95	
798 Quick Peep[3]	No	1" only.	9.95	
799[5]	No	1" only	9.95	
885 BK[8]	No	1" only	23.95	
895[7]	No	1" only	5.95	
896[6]	No	1" only	39.95	
800L Series (with base)[4]	No	1" only. Rings and base.	13.95	
World Class[9]	Yes	1", 26mm, 30mm	Bases—29.95 Rings—39.95	
Thompson/Center				[1]All Contenders except vent. rib. [2]T/C rail mount scopes; all Contenders except vent. rib. [3]All S&W K and Combat Masterpiece, Hi-Way Patrolman, Outdoorsman, 22 Jet, 45 Target 1955. Requires drilling, tapping. [4]Blackhawk, Super Blackhawk, Super Single-Six. Requires drilling, tapping. [5]45 or 50 cal.; replaces rear sight. [6]Rail mount scopes; 54-cal. Hawken, 50, 54, 56-cal. Renegade. Replaces rear sight. [7]Cherokee 32 or 45 cal., Seneca 36 or 45 cal. Replaces rear sight.
Contender 9746[1]	No	T/C Lobo	9.95	
Contender 9741[2]	No	2½, 4 RP	9.95	
Contender 7410	No	Bushnell Phantom 1.3, 2.5x	9.95	
S&W 9747[3]	No	Lobo or RP	9.95	
Ruger 9748[4]	No	Lobo or RP	9.95	
Hawken 9749[5]	No	Lobo or RP	9.95	
Hawken/Renegade 9754[6]	No	Lobo or RP	9.95	
Cherokee/Seneca[7]	No	Lobo or RP	9.95	
Unertl				[1]Unertl target or varmint scopes. [2]Any with regular dovetail scope bases.
Posa (T)[1]	Yes	¾", 1" scopes.	Per set 70.00	
¼ Click (T)[2]	Yes	¾", 1" target scopes.	Per set 66.00	
Weaver				[1]Nearly all modern rifles. Extension rings, 1" $23.45. [2]Most modern big bore rifles. [3]22s with grooved receivers. [4]Same. Adapter for Lee Enfield—$9.65. [5]⅞"—$13.45. 1" See-Thru extension—$23.45. [6]Colt Officer's Model, Python, Ruger B'hawk, Super B'hawk, Security Six, 22 Autos, Mini-14, Ruger Redhawk, S&W N frames. No drilling or tapping. Also in stainless steel—$58.95.
Detachable Mount (T & S)[1]	No	¾", ⅞", 1" 26mm	22.00	
Pivot Mount (T)[2]	No	1"	29.81	
Tip-Off (T)[3]	No	¾", ⅞".	13.31	
Tip-Off (T)[4]	No	1", two-piece.	22.44	
See-Thru Mount[5]	No	1" Split rings ⅞" tip-off Fits all top mounts.	22.00 15.62	
Mount Base System[6]	No	1"	59.51	
Wideview				Models for many popular rifles—$18.95. Low ring, high ring and grooved receiver types—$7.95. From Wideview Scope Mount Corp.
WSM-22	No	1"	10.95	
WSM-94	No	1"	18.95	
WSM-94AE	No	1"	21.86	
Williams				[1]Most rifles, Br. S.M.L.E. (round rec) $3.85 extra. [2]Same. [3]Most rifles including Win. 94 Big Bore. [4]Most rifles. [5]Many modern rifles. [6]Most popular rifles.
Offset (S)[1]	No	⅞", 1", 26mm solid, split or extension rings.	52.95	
QC (T)[2]	No	Same.	41.60	
QC (S)[3]	No	Same.	41.60	
Low Sight-Thru[4]	No	1", ⅞", sleeves $1.80.	17.75	
Sight-Thru[5]	No	1", ⅞", sleeves $1.80.	17.75	
Streamline[6]	No	1" (bases form rings).	18.70	

(S)—Side Mount   (T)Top Mount   22mm—.866"   25.4mm = 1"1.024"   26.5mm = 1.045"   30mm = 1.81"

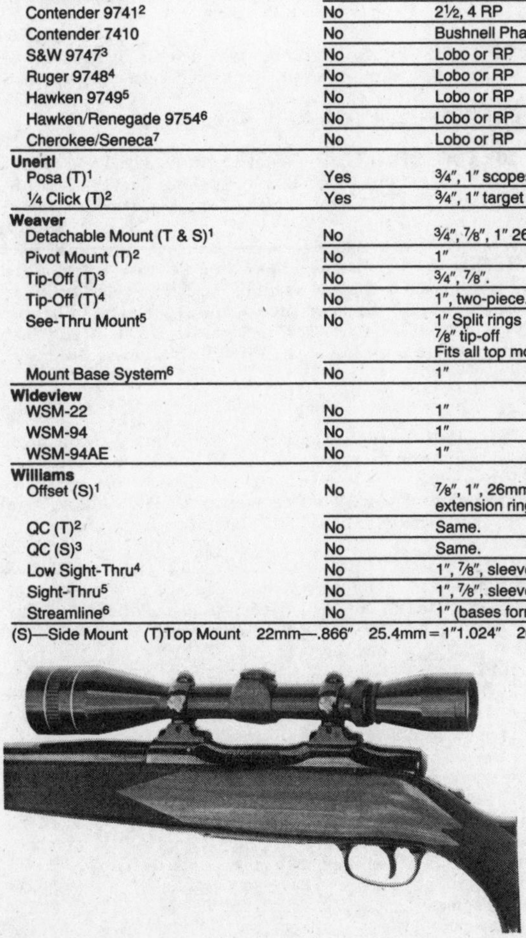

Left: S&K is now offering these new vertically split rings on their SKulptured bases; they'll fit most popular rifles. Right: SSK Industries T'SOB handgun mount uses two to four rings to anchor the scope.

SPOTTING SCOPES

APOLLO 20 X 50 BOBCAT—50mm objective lens. Field of view at 1000 yds. is about 100 ft. Length 9.4", weight 17.5 oz. Tripod socket.
Price: About **$154.95**
Compact tripod, about **$20.00**
BAUSCH & LOMB DISCOVERER—15X to 60X zoom, 60mm objective. Constant focus throughout range. Field at 1000 yds. 40 ft (60X), 156 ft. (15X). Comes with lens caps. Length 17½", wgt. 48½ oz.
Price: **$465.95**
BUSHNELL SPACEMASTER—60MM objective. Field at 1000 yds. 158' to 37'. Relative brightness, 5.76. Wgt., 36 oz. Length closed, 11⅝". prism focusing.
Price: Without eyepiece **$277.95**
15X, 20X, 40X and 60X eyepieces, each **$49.95**
22X wide angle eyepiece **$59.95**
BUSHNELL SPACEMASTER 45°—Same as above except: Wgt., 43 oz., length closed 13". Eyepiece at 45°, without eyepiece.
Price: **$349.95**
BUSHNELL ZOOM SPACEMASTER—15X-45X zoom. 60mm objective. Field at 1000 yards 130'-65'. Relative brightness 9-1.7. Wgt. 36 oz., length 11⅝". Shooter's stand tripod, carrying case.
Price: **$452.95**
BUSHNELL SENTRY®—50mm objective. Field at 1000 yards 120'-45'. Relative brightness 6.25. Wgt., 25½ oz., length 12⅝", without eyepiece.
Price: **$139.95**
20X, 32X and 48X eyepieces, each **$49.95**
BUSHNELL ZOOM SPOTTER—40mm objective. 9X-30X var. power.
Price: **$99.95**

Bushnell Zoom Spotter

BUSHNELL COMPETITOR—40mm objective, 20X. Prismatic. Field at 1000 yards 140'. Minimum focus 33'. Length 9.5", weight 14.5 oz.
Price: With tripod **$99.95**
BUSHNELL TROPHY—12X-36X zoom. Rubber armored, prismatic. 50mm objective. Field at 1000 yards 150' to 80'. Minimum focus 20'. Length with caps 13⅝", weight 38 oz.
Price: With tripod and carrying case **$391.95**
Interchangeable eyepieces—20x, 32x, 48x, each **$49.95**
12-36X zoom eyepiece **$125.95**
COUGAR MODEL 776—60mm objective, 20x, 30x, 40x, 50x eyepieces. Rotating head for straight or 45° viewing. Field at 1,000 yds. 131 ft. (20x), 94 ft. (30x), 65 ft. (40x), 52 ft. (50x). Focus by rotating the objective barrel. Length 12¾", wgt. 4 lbs. From Cougar Optics.
Price: Without eyepiece **$241.50**
Price: Eyepiece **$36.50**
DICKSON 270—20x to 60x variable, 60mm objective, achromatic coated objective lens, complete with metal table tripod with 5 vertical and horizontal adjustments. Turret type, 20x, 30x, 40x 60x
Price: **$249.95**
DICKSON 274A—20x to 60x variable zoom. 60mm achromatic coated objective lens, complete with adjustable metal table tripod.
Price: **$150.00**
DICKSON 274B—As above but with addition of 4 × 16 Finder Scope.
Price: **$161.95**
KOWA TS-1-45—Off-set-type. 60mm objective, 25X, fixed and zoom interchangeable eyepieces; field at 1000 yards 93'; relative brightness 5.8; length 16.5"; wgt. 47.8 oz. Lens shade and caps. Straight-type also available; similar specs **($284.98)**.
Price: **$349.95**
Price: 25X eyepiece **$49.95**
Price: 20X eyepiece (wide angle) **$64.95**
Price: 15X eyepiece **$59.95**
Price: 105X eyepiece **$69.95**

KOWA TSN-1-45°—Off-set-type. 77mm objective, 25X, fixed and zoom eyepieces; field at 1000 yds. 94'; relative brightness 9.6; length 15.4"; wgt. 48.8 oz. Lens shade and caps. Straight-type also available with similar specs and prices.
Price: **$499.95**
Price: 20X-60X zoom eyepiece **$124.95**
Price: 20X eyepiece (wide angle) **$99.95**
Price: 25X, 40X eyepiece **$74.95**
KOWA TS-3—Straight-type. 50mm objective, 20X, standard size, fixed and zoom eyepieces; field at 1000 yds. 120'; relative brightness 6.3; length 13.4"; wgt. 29.4 oz. Lens shade and caps.
Price: **$179.95**
Price: 20X-40X zoom eyepiece **$119.95**
Price: 20X eyepiece **$49.95**
Price: 16X eyepiece (wide angle) **$64.95**
Price: 12X eyepiece **$59.95**
Price: 32X, 48X eyepiece **$54.95**
Price: 84X eyepiece **$69.95**
KOWA TS-4-45—Off-set-type. 50mm objective, 20X, compact size (measures 12.6", wgt. 37 oz.). Other specs are same as Model TS-3. Uses TS-3 eyepieces.
Price: **$279.95**
KOWA TS-8—Straight-type. 50mm objective, 20X, compact model; fixed power eyepieces; field at 1000 yds. 157'; relative brightness 6.3; length 9.25"; wgt. 23.3 oz. Lens caps.
Price: **$139.95**
Price: 10X, 15X eyepieces, each **$34.95**
KOWA TS-9C—Straight-type. 50mm objective, 20X compact model; fixed power eyepieces; objective focusing down to 17 ft.; field at 1000 yds. 157'; relative brightness 6.3; length 9.65"; wgt. 22.9 oz. Lens caps.
Price: **$115.95**
Price: 15X, 20X eyepieces, each **$24.95**
Price: As above, rubber armored (TS-9R) **$129.95**
OPTEX MODEL 420—15x-60x-60 Zoom; 18" overall; weighs 4 lbs. with folding tripod (included). From Southern Precision Instrument
Price: **$135.00**
OPTEX MODEL 421—15x-45x-50 Zoom; 18" over-all; weighs 4 lbs. with folding tripod (included). From Southern Precision Instrument
Price: **$110.00**
OPTEX MODEL 422—8x-25x-30 Zoom. Armour coated; 18" over-all; weighs 3 lbs. with tripod (included). From Southern Precision Instrument
Price: **$100.00**
OPTEX MODEL 423—Same as Model 422 except 12x-40x-40
Price: **$120.00**
REDFIELD 30x CAT SPOTTER—60mm objective, 30x. Field of view 9.5 ft. at 100 yds. Uses catadioptric lens system. Length over-all is 7.5", weight is 11.5 oz. Eye relief 0.5". Also comes in camo armor coating.
Price: **$411.05**
Price: With Armor Camouflage **$424.95**
REDFIELD REGAL II & III—Regal II has 60mm objective, interchangeable 25x and 18x-40x zoom eyepieces. Regal III has 50mm objective, interchangeable 20x and 15x-32x zoom eyepieces, and is shorter and lighter. Field at 1000 yds.—Regal II, 125 ft. @ 25x; Regal III, 157 ft. @ 20x. Both have dual rotation of eyepiece and scope body. With aluminum carrying case, tripod.
Price: Regal II **$521.95**
Price: Regal III **$508.95**
REDFIELD REGAL IV & V—Conventional straight thru viewing. Regal IV has 60mm objective and interchangeable 25x and 20x-60x zoom eyepieces. Regal V has 50mm objective and 20x and 16x-48x zoom eyepieces and is shorter and lighter. Field at 1000 yds.—Regal IV, 94 ft. @ 25x; Regal V, 118 ft. @ 20x. Both come with tripod and aluminum carrying case.
Price: Regal IV **$546.95**
Price: Regal V **$490.95**
REDFIELD REGAL VI—60mm objective, 25x fixed and 20x-60x interchangeable eyepiece. Has 45° angled eyepiece, front-mounted focus ring, 180° tube rotation. Field at 1000 yds., 94 ft. @ 25x; length, 12¼"; weight, 40 oz. Comes with tripod, aluminum carrying case.
Price: Regal VI **$603.95**
SIMMONS 1210—50mm objective, 25x standard, 16, 20, 40, 48, 16-36x zoom eyepieces available. Field at 1000 yds. 22 ft. Length 12.2", weight 32 oz. Comes with tripod, 3x finder scope with crosshair.
Price: About **$150.75**
Price: Fixed eyepieces **$45.50**
Price: Zoom eyepiece **$113.00**
SIMMONS 1215—50mm objective, 25x standard, 16, 20, 40, 48, 16-36x zoom eyepieces available. Field at 1000 yds. 22 ft. Length 12.2", weight 48 oz. Comes with tripod, 3x finder scope with crosshair. Green camo rubber.
Price: About **$207.00**
Price: Fixed eyepieces **$45.50**
Price: Zoom eyepiece **$113.00**

CAUTION: PRICES CHANGE. CHECK AT GUNSHOP.

SIMMONS 1220—60mm objective, 25x standard, 16, 20, 40, 48, 16-36x zoom eyepieces available. Field at 1000 yds. 22 ft. Length 13.8", weight 44 oz. with tripod (included). Has 3x finder scope with crosshairs.
- **Price:** About **$253.00**
- **Price:** Fixed eyepieces **$45.50**
- **Price:** Zoom eyepiece **$113.00**

SWAROVSKI HABICHT HAWK 30x75S TELESCOPE—75mm objective, 30X. Field at 1,000 yds. 90ft. Minimum, focusing distance 90 ft. Length: closed 13 in., extended 20½". Weight: 47 oz. Precise recognition of smallest details even at dusk. Leather or rubber covered, with caps and carrying case.
- **Price:** **$895.00**
  Same as above with short range supplement. Minimum focusing distance 24 to 30 ft. **$935.00**

SWAROVSKI 25-40X75 TELESCOPE—75mm objective, variable power from 25x to 40x with a field of 98 ft. (25x) and 72 ft. (40x). Minimum focusing distance 66 ft. (26 ft. with close focus model). Length closed is 11", extended 15.5"; weight 46 oz. Rubber covered.
- **Price:** Standard **$880.00**
- **Price:** Close focus model **910.00**

SWIFT TELEMASTER M841—60mm objective. 15X to 60X variable power. Field at 1000 yards 160 feet (15X) to 40 feet (60X). Wgt. 3.4 lbs. 17.6" over-all.
- **Price:** **$399.95**
  - Tripod for above **$79.95**
  - Photo adapter **$16.00**
  - Case for above **$57.00**

TASCO 39T COMPACT SPOTTING SCOPE—50mm objective, 20X. With BAK-4 prism. Wgt. 3 lbs. With tripod.
- **Price:** **$179.95**

TASCO 34T RUBBER COVERED SPOTTING SCOPE—50mm objective. 25X. Field at 1000 yds. 136 ft. With tripod and built-in tripod adapter. Weight 29.9 oz. Length 13¾".
- **Price:** **$199.95**

TASCO 21T SPOTTING SCOPE—40mm objective. 20X. Field at 1000 yds. 136 ft. With Tasco 8P tripod. Weight 18.2 oz. Length 12⅜".
- **Price:** **$109.95**

TASCO 25TPC RUBBER COVERED SPOTTING SCOPE—60mm objective. 25X. Field at 1000 yds. 94 ft. Prismatic. With Tasco 25P tripod, olive green to match rubber covering. Weight 38.3 oz. Length 11½".
- **Price:** **$499.95**

TASCO 34TZ RUBBER COVERED—50mm objective. 18-36X zoom. Comes with tripod and built-in tripod adapter. Weight 29.9 oz., length 13¾".
- **Price:** **$239.95**

UNERTL "FORTY-FIVE"—54mm objective. 20X (single fixed power). Field at 100 yds. 10'10"; eye relief 1"; focusing range infinity to 33 ft. Wgt. about 32 oz.; over-all length 15¾". With lens covers.
- **Price:** With multi-layer lens coating **$295.00**
- **Price:** With mono-layer magnesium coating **$225.00**

UNERTL RIGHT ANGLE—63.5mm objective, 24X. Field at 100 yds., 7 ft. Relative brightness, 6.96. Eye relief, ½". Wgt., 41 oz. Length closed, 19". Push-pull and screw-focus eyepiece. 16X and 32X eyepieces **$38.00** each.
- **Price:** **$265.00**

Weatherby Sightmaster 20-60x

Tasco World Class 9000T

Unertl 20x Straight Prismatic

Redfield Regal II

Bushnell Trophy Zoom

SWIFT M844A COMMANDO PRISMATIC SPOTTING SCOPE/ TELEPHOTO LENS, MK.II—60mm objective. Comes with 20X eyepiece; 15X, 30X, 40X, 50X, 60X available. Built-in sunshade. Field at 1000 yds. with 20X, 120 ft. Length 13.7", wgt. 2.1 lbs.
- **Price:** **$260.00**

SWIFT M847 SCANNER—50mm objective. Comes with 25x eyepiece; 20x, 30x, 35x eyepieces available. Field of view at 1000 yds. is 112 ft. (25x). Length 13.6", weight 23 oz.
- **Price:** **$139.50**
  - Each additional eyepiece **$27.50**
  - Tubular case **$25.00**
  - Tripod **$79.95**

SWIFT M700 SCOUT—9X-30X, 30mm spotting scope. Length 15½", weighs 2.1 lbs. Field of 204 ft. (9X), 60 ft. (30X).
- **Price:** **$87.00**

TASCO WORLD CLASS 9000T—60mm objective, 15-60x zoom. Field at 1,000 yd. 160 ft. (15x), 40 ft. (60x). Has tripod mount socket, sun shade, screw-on lens covers. Comes with case, camera adapter, tripod.
- **Price:** **$519.95**
- **Price:** Without tripod **$459.95**

UNERTL STRAIGHT PRISMATIC—Same as Unertl Right Angle except: straight eyepiece and wgt. of 40 oz.
- **Price:** **$225.00**

UNERTL 20X STRAIGHT PRISMATIC—54mm objective. 20X. Field at 100 yds., 8.5 ft. Relative brightness, 6.1. Eye relief, ½". Wgt. 36 oz. Length closed, 13½". Complete with lens covers.
- **Price:** **$190.00**

UNERTL TEAM SCOPE—100mm objective. 15X, 24X, 32X eyepieces. Field at 100 yds. 13 to 7.5 ft. Relative brightness, 39.06 to 9.79. Eye relief, 2" to 1½". Weight 13 lbs. 29⅞" overall. Metal tripod, yoke and wood carrying case furnished (total weight, 67 lbs.)
- **Price:** **$975.00**

WEATHERBY—60mm objective, 20X-60X zoom
- **Price:** Scope only **$323.95**
- **Price:** Scope and tripod **$379.95**
- **Price:** Tripod for above **$69.95**

CAUTION: PRICES CHANGE. CHECK AT GUNSHOP.

PERIODICAL PUBLICATIONS

Airgun World
10 Sheet St., Windsor, Berks., SL4 1BG, England.£11.50 for 12 issues. Monthly magazine catering exclusively to the airgun enthusiast.

Alaska Magazine
Alaska Northwest Pub. Co., Box 4-EEE, Anchorage, AK 99509. $21.00 yr. Hunting, fishing and Life on the Last Frontier articles of Alaska and western Canada.

American Field†
222 W. Adams St., Chicago, IL. 60606. $18.00 yr. Field dogs and trials, occasional gun and hunting articles.

American Firearms Industry
Nat'l. Assn. of Federally Licensed Firearms Dealers, 2801 E. Oakland Park Blvd., Ft. Lauderdale, FL 33306. $20 yr. For firearms dealers & distributors.

American Handgunner*
591 Camino de la Reina, San Diego, CA 92108. $11.95 yr. Articles for handgun enthusiasts, collectors and hunters.

American Hunter (M)
Natl. Rifle Assn., 1600 Rhode Island Ave. N.W., Washington, DC 20036. $15.00 yr. Wide scope of hunting articles.

American Rifleman (M)
National Rifle Assn., 1600 Rhode Island Ave., N.W., Wash., DC 20036. $15.00 yr. Firearms articles of all kinds.

The American Shotgunner
P.O. Box 3351, Reno, NV 89505. $24.00 yr. Official publ. of the American Assn. of Shotgunning. Shooting, reloading, hunting, investment collecting, new used gun classifieds.

American Survival Guide
McMullen Publishing, Inc., 2145 West La Palma Ave., Anaheim, CA 92801. 12 issues $20.98.

American West*
Amer. West Publ. Co., 3033 No. Campbell, Tucson, AZ 85719. $15.00 yr.

AMI
New Fashion Media, Avenue Louise 60, B1050 Brussels, Belgium. Belg. Franc 325, 11 issues. Arms, shooting militaria information; French text.

Angler & Hunter
Ontario's Wildlife Magazine, P.O. Box 1541, Peterborough, Ont. K9J 7H7, Canada.

Arms Collecting (Q)
Museum Restoration Service P.O. Drawer 390, Bloomfield, Ont., Canada K0K IG0 and P.O. Box 70, Alexandria Bay, NY 13607. $10.00 yr. $27.50 3 yrs.

Austrlian Shooters' Journal
Sporting Shooter's Assn. of Australia, Box 1064 G.P.O., Adelaide, SA 5001, Australia. $25.00 yr. locally; $30.00 yr. overseas surface mail only. Hunting and shooting articles.

The Backwoodsman Magazine
Rte. 8, Box 579, Livingston, TX 77351. $11.00 for 6 issues pr. yr.; sample copy $2. Subject incl. muzzle-loading, woodslore, trapping, homesteading, et al.

The Black Powder Report
The Buckskin Press, Inc., P.O. Box 789, Big Timber, MT 59011. $18.00 yr. Shooting, hunting, gun-building and restoration articles; entire section for BP cartridge rifles.

The Blade Magazine*
P.O. Box 22007, Chattanooga, TN 37422. $15.99 yr. Add $13 f. foreign subscription. A magazine for all enthusiasts of the edged blade.

Combat Handguns*
Harris Publications, Inc., 1115 Broadway, New York, NY 10010. Single copy $2.75 U.S.A.; $2.95 Canada.

Competitor USA
SAM Publications Inc., P.O. Box 74515, Dallas, TX 75374. $12.00 yr. Magazine of handgun shooting and competition.

Deer Unlimited*
P.O. Box 509, Clemson, SC 29631. $12.00 yr.

Deutsches Waffen Journal
Journal-Verlag Schwend GmbH, Postfach 100340, D7170 Schwäbisch Hall, Germany. DM76.00 yr. plus DM16.80 for postage. Antique and modern arms. German text.

Ducks Unlimited, Inc. (M)
1 Waterfowl Way at Gilmer, Long Grove, IL 60047

FFL Business News
Nat'l. Assn. of Federally Licensed Firearms Dealers, 2801 E. Oakland Pk. Blvd., Ft. Lauderdale, FL 33306. $6.00 yr. For firearms dealers & distributors.

The Field†
The Harmsworth Press Ltd., Carmelite House, London EC4Y OJA, England. $88.00 yr. Hunting and shooting articles, and all country sports.

Field & Stream
CBS Magazines, 1515 Broadway, New York, NY 10036. $11.94 yr. Articles on firearms plus hunting and fishing.

Fur-Fish-Game
A.R. Harding Pub. Co., 2878 E. Main St., Columbus, OH 43209. $10.00 yr. "Gun Rack" column by Don Zutz.

Gray's Sporting Journal
Gray's Sporting Journal Co., 205 Willow St., So. Hamilton, MA 01982. $24.95 per yr. f. 4 consecutive issues. Hunting and fishing journals.

Gun Owner(Q)
Gun Owners Inc., 1025 Front St., Suite 300, Sacramento, CA 95814. With membership $20 yr.; single copy $3. An outdoors magazine for sportsmen everywhere.

The Gun Report
World Wide Gun Report, Inc., Box 111, Aledo, IL 61231. $25.00 yr. For the antique gun collector.

The Gunrunner
Div. of Kexco Publ. Co. Ltd., Box 565, Lethbridge, Alb., Canada T1J 3Z4. $15.00 yr. Monthly newspaper, listing everything from antiques to artillery.

The Gun Gazette
P.O. Box 2685, Warner Robins, GA 31099. $12.00 yr. Extensive gun show listings, with articles on guns, knives and hunting.

Gun Week†
Second Amendment Foundation, P.O. Box 488, Station C, Buffalo NY 14209. $20.00 yr. U.S. and possessions; $24.00 yr. other countries. Tabloid paper on guns, hunting, shooting and collecting.

Gun World
Gallant Publishing Co., 34249 Camino Capistrano, Capistrano Beach, CA 92624. $17.00 yr. For the hunting, reloading and shooting enthusiast.

Guns & Action
P.O. Box 349, Mt. Morris, IL 61054. $12.00 yr. Defense, adventure, survival articles.

Guns & Ammo
Petersen Pub. Co., 8490 Sunset Blvd., Los Angeles, CA 90069. $13.94 yr. Guns, shooting, and technical articles.

Guns
Guns Magazine, 591 Camino de la Reina, San Diego, CA 92108. $14.95 yr. Articles for gun collectors, hunters and shooters.

Guns Review
Ravenhill Pub. Co. Ltd., Box 35, Standard House, Bonhill St., London E.C. 2A 4DA, England. £12.50 sterling (approx. U.S. $16) USA & Canada yr. For collectors and shooters.

Handloader*
Wolfe Pub. Co. Inc., Box 3030, Prescott, AZ 86302 $16.00 yr. The journal of ammunition reloading.

The IMAS Journal (M)
International Military Arms Society, P.O. Box 122, Williamstown, WV 26187. Military gun collecting articles.

INSIGHTS*
NRA, 1600 Rhode Island Ave. N.W., Washington, DC 20036. Editor Mary E. Shelsby. $5.00 yr. (12 issues). Plenty of details for the young hunter and target shooter.

International Shooting Sport*
International Shooting Union (UIT), Bavariaring 21, D-8000 Munich 2, Fed. Rep. of Germany. Europe: (Deutsche Mark) DM39.00 yr., p.p.; outside Europe: DM45.00. For the International target shooter.

The Journal of the Arms & Armour Society (M)
A.R.E. North (Secy.), Dept. of Metalwork, Victoria and Albert Museum, London, England. $16.00 yr. Articles for the historian and collector.

Journal of the Historical Breechloading Smallarms Assn.
Publ. annually, Imperial War Museum, Lambeth Road, London SE1 6HZ, England. $8.00 yr. Articles for the collector plus mailings of lecture transcripts, short articles on specific arms, reprints, newsletter, etc.; a surcharge is made f. airmail.

Kaliber
Uitgeverij Magnum, Marktstraat 237, 6431 LR Hoensbroek, Netherlands. 6 issues f20.00/Bfr.400. Magazine for the sportshooter.

Knife World
Knife World Publications, P.O. Box 3395, Knoxville, TN 37917. $10.00 yr., $17.00 2 yrs. Published monthly f. knife enthusiasts and collectors. Articles on custom and factory knives; other knife related interests.

Law and Order
   Law and Order Magazine, 1000 Skokie Blvd., Wilmette, IL 60091. $15.00 yr. Articles on weapons for law enforcement, etc.

The List/Guns for Sale
   P.O. Box 7387, Columbia, MO 65205. $8.00 yr. (12 issues); $15.00 2 yrs.

Man At Arms*
   Box 460, Lincoln, RI 02865. $18.00 yr. The magazine of arms collecting-investing, with excellent brief articles for the collector of antique arms and militaria.

MAN/MAGNUM
   S.A. Man (1982) (Pty) Ltd., P.O. Box 35204, Northway, Durban 4065, Rep. of South Africa. R20 f. 12 issues. Africa's only publication on hunting, shooting, firearms, bushcraft, knives, etc.

The Marlin Collector (M)
   R.W. Paterson, 407 Lincoln Bldg., 44 Main St., Champaign, IL 61820.

Muzzle Blasts (M)
   National Muzzle Loading Rifle Assn., P.O. Box 67, Friendship, IN 47021. $16.00 yr. For the black powder shooter.

Muzzleloader Magazine*
   Rebel Publishing Co., Inc., Route 5, Box 347-M, Texarkana, TX 75501. $10.00 U.S., $12.00 foreign yr. The publication for black powder shooters.

National Defense (M)*
   American Defense Preparedness Assn., Rosslyn Center, Suite 900, 1700 North Moore St., Arlington, VA 22209. $25.00 yr. Articles on military-related topics, including weapons, materials technology, management.

National Knife Collector (M)
   Natl. Knife Coll. Assn., P.O. Box 21070, Chattanooga, TN 37421. Membership $15 yr, $40.00 International yr.

National Rifle Assn. Journal (British) (Q)
   Natl. Rifle Assn. (BR.), Bisley Camp, Brookwood, Woking, Surrey, England. GU24, OPB. $14.00 inc. air postage.

National Wildlife*
   Natl. Wildlife Fed., 1412 16th St. N.W., Washington, DC 20036. $12.00 yr. (6 issues); *International Wildlife*, 6 issues, $12.00 yr. Both, $19.00 yr., plus membership benefits. Write to this addr., attn.: Promotion Dept., for the proper information.

New Zealand Wildlife (Q)
   New Zealand Deerstalkers Assoc. Inc., P.O. Box 6514, Wellington, N.Z. $13.00 (N.Z.). Hunting, shooting and firearms/game research articles.

North American Hunter* (M)
   7901 Flying Cloud Dr., P.O. Box 35557, Minneapolis, MN 55435. $18.00 yr. (6 issues). Articles on North American game hunting.

Outdoor Life
   Times Mirror Magazines, Inc., 380 Madison Ave., New York, NY 10017. $11.94 yr. Shooting columns by Jim Carmichel, and others.

Point Blank
   Citizens Committee for the Right to Keep and Bear Arms (sent to contributors) Liberty Park, 12500 NE 10th Pl., Bellevue, WA 98005

The Police Marksman*
   6000 E. Shirley Lane, Montgomery, AL 36117. $15.00 yr.

Police Times/Command (M)
   1100 N.E. 125th St., No. Miami, FL 33161

Popular Mechanics
   Hearst Corp., 224 W. 57th St., New York, NY 10019. $11.97 yr. Hunting, shooting and camping articles.

Precision Shooting
   Precision Shooting, Inc., 37 Burnham St., East Hartford, CT 06108. $15.00 yr. Journal of the International Benchrest Shooters, National Benchrest Shooting Assn., and target shooting in general.

Rendezvous & Longrifles (M)
   Canadian Black Powder Federation Newsletter, P.O. Box 2876, Postal Sta. "A", Moncton, N.B. E1C, 8T8, Canada. 6 issues per yr. w. $15.00 membership.

Rifle*
   Wolfe Publishing Co. Inc., Box 3030, Prescott, AZ 86302. $16.00 yr. The magazine for shooters.

Rod & Rifle Magazine
   Lithographic Serv. Ltd., P.O. Box 38-138, Petone, New Zealand. $30.00 yr. (6 issues) Hunting and shooting articles.

Safari* (M)
   Safari Magazine, 5151 E. Broadway, Suite 1680, Tucson, AZ 85711. $20 (6 times). Official journal of Safari Club International; the journal of big game hunting.

Saga
   Lexington Library, Inc., 355 Lexington Ave., New York, NY 10017. Currently annual. No subscription. $1.75 p. issue U.S.

Schweizer Waffen Magazin
   Orell Füssli Zeitschriften, Postfach CH-8036 Zürich, Switzerland. SF 105.00 (approx. U.S. $46.70 air mail) f. 10 issues. Modern and antique arms. German text.

Second Amendment Reporter
   Second Amendment Fdn., James Madison Bldg., 12500 NE 10th Pl., Bellevue, WA 98005. $15.00 yr. (non-contributors).

Shooting Industry
   Publisher's Dev. Corp., 591 Camino de la Reina, Suite 200, San Diego, CA 92108. $25.00 yr. To the trade $12.50

Shooting Magazine
   10 Sheet St., Windsor, Berks. SL4 1BG England. £11.50 for 12 issues. Monthly journal catering mainly to claypigeon shooters.

The Shooting Times & Country Magazine (England)†
   10 Sheet St., Windsor, Berkshire SL4 1BG, England. £38 (approx. $48.75) yr. (52 issues). Game shooting, wild fowling, hunting, game fishing and firearms articles.

Shooting Times
   PJS Publications, News Plaza. P.O. Box 1790, Peoria, IL 61656. $15.00 yr. Guns, shooting, reloading; articles on every gun activity.

The Shotgun News‡
   Snell Publishing Co., Box 669, Hastings, NE 68901. $15.00 yr.; all other countries $100.00 yr. Sample copy $3.00. Gun ads of all kinds.

Shotgun Sports
   P.O. Box 340, Lake Havasu City, AZ 86403. $20. yr.

Shotgun West
   2052 Broadway, Santa Monica, CA 90404. $8.50 yr. Trap, Skeet and international shooting, scores; articles, schedules.

The Sixgunner (M)
   Handgun Hunters International, P.O. Box 357, MAG. Bloomingdale, OH 43910

The Skeet Shooting Review
   National Skeet Shooting Assn., P.O. Box 28188, San Antonio, TX 78228. $15.00 yr. (Assn. membership of $20.00 includes mag.) Competition results, personality profiles of top Skeet shooters, how-to articles, technical, reloading information.

Soldier of Fortune
   Subscription Dept., P.O. Box 348, Mt. Morris, IL 61054. $26.00 yr. U.S., Can., Mex.; $33.00 all other countries surface mail.

SOF's Combat Weapons (Q)
   P.O. Box 693, Boulder, CO 80306. $3.50 p. issue. Guide to international military firepower.

Sporting Goods Business
   Gralla Pub., 1515 Broadway, New York, NY 10036. Trade journal.

The Sporting Goods Dealer
   1212 No. Lindbergh Blvd., St. Louis, Mo. 63132. $30.00 yr. The sporting goods trade journal.

Sporting Gun
   Bretton Court, Bretton, Peterborough PE3 8DZ, England £16.00 (approx. U.S. $28.00) (airmail £24.00) yr. For the game and clay enthusiasts.

Sports Afield
   The Hearst Corp., 250 W. 55th St., New York, NY 10019. $13.97 yr. Grits Gresham on firearms, ammunition and Thomas McIntyre, Lionel Atwill, Gerald Almy on hunting.

Sports Merchandiser
   A W.R.C. Smith Publication, 1760 Peachtree Rd. NW, Atlanta, GA 30357. Trade Journal.

TACARMI
   Via E. De Amicis, 25;20123 Milano, Italy. $30.00 yr. approx. Antique and modern guns. (Italian text.).

Then And Now*
   P.O. Box 842, Mount Vernon, WA 98273. $15.00 for 6 issues. Magazine for black powder activities; test reports.

Trap & Field
   1000 Waterway Blvd., Indianapolis, IN 46202. $18.00 yr. Official publ. Amateur Trapshooting Assn. Scores, averages, trapshooting articles.

Turkey Call* (M)
   Natl. Wild Turkey Federation, Inc., P.O. Box 530, Edgefield, SC 29824. $15.00 w. membership (6 issues p. yr.)

The U.S. Handgunner* (M)
   U.S. Revolver Assn., 96 West Union St., Ashland, MA 01721. $6.00 yr. General handgun and competition articles. Bi-monthly sent to members.

Waterfowler's World*
   P.O. Box 38306, Germantown, TN 38183. $12.00 yr.

The Weekly Bullet
   Second Amendment Fdn., James Madison Bldg., 12500 NE 10th Pl., Bellevue, WA 98005. $35.00 yr.

Wisconsin Sportsman*
   Wisconsin Sportsman, Inc., P.O. Box 2266, Oshkosh, WI 54903. $9.95. Hunting, hiking, outdoors articles.

---

*Published bi-monthly † Published weekly ‡ Published three times per month. All others are published monthly.
M = Membership requirements; write for details. Q = Published Quarterly.

The Arms Library for

COLLECTOR · HUNTER · SHOOTER · OUTDOORSMAN

A selection of books—old, new and forthcoming—for everyone in the arms field, with a brief description by . . . JOE RILING

IMPORTANT NOTICE TO BOOK BUYERS

Books listed here may be bought from Ray Riling Arms Books Co., 6844 Gorsten St., Philadelphia, PA 19119, phone 215/438-2456. Joe Riling, the proprietor, is the researcher and compiler of "The Arms Library" and a seller of gun books for over 30 years.

The Riling stock includes books classic and modern, many hard-to-find items, and many not obtainable elsewhere. These pages list a portion of the current stock. They offer prompt, complete service, with delayed shipments occurring only on out-of-print or out-of-stock books.

NOTICE FOR ALL CUSTOMERS: Remittance in U.S. funds must accompany all orders. For U.S. add $1.75 per book for postage and insurance. Minimum order $10.00. For U.P.S. add 50% to mailing costs.

All foreign countries add $2.25 per book for postage and handling, plus $3.60 per 10-lb. package or under for safe delivery by registered mail. Parcels not registered are sent at the "buyers risk."

Payments in excess of order or for "Backorders" are credited or fully refunded at request. Books "As-Ordered" are not returnable except by permission and a handling charge on these of $2.00 per book is deducted from refund or credit. Only Pennsylvania customers must include current sales tax.

A full variety of arms books are also available from Rutgers Book Center, 127 Raritan Ave., Highland Park, NJ 08904.

NEW BOOKS

(Alphabetically, no categories)

Advanced Muzzle Loaders Guide, by Toby Bridges, Stoeger Publishing Co., So. Hackensack, NJ, 1985. 256 pp., illus. Paper covers. $11.95.
Touches all bases from "do-it-yourself" to custom rifle makers.

The Adventures of an Elephant Hunter, by James Sutherland, Trophy Room Books, Encino, CA, 1985. 324 pp., illus. $75.00.
Facsimile reprint of a very scarce book on elephant hunting. Limited, numbered edition signed by the publishers.

African Hunter, by Baron Bror von Bliexen-Finecke, St. Martin's Press, New York, NY, 1986. 284 pp., illus. $14.95.
Reprint of the scarce 1938 edition. An African hunting classic.

African Hunter, by James Mellon, Safari Press, Long Beach, CA 1985. 522 pp., illus. $100.00.
A new printing of the most definitive work to appear on African big game hunting in the last 40 years.

Allied Military Fighting Knives and the Men Who Made Them Famous, by Robert A. Buerlein, American Historical Foundation, Richmond, VA, 1985. 183 pp., illus. $34.95.
The background, development and variations of the allied military fighting knives are chronicled, and the tales of the men who used them are told.

The AR-15/M16, A Practical Guide, by Duncan Long, Paladin Press, Boulder, CO, 1985. 168 pp., illus. Paper covers. $16.95.
The definitive book on the rifle that has been the inspiration for so many modern assault rifles.

Archer's Digest, 4th Edition, edited by Roger Combs, DBI Books, Inc., Northbrook, IL, 1986. 256 pp., illus. Paper covers. $12.95.
Authoritative information on all facets of the archer's sport.

Arms Makers of Eastern Pennsylvania: The Colonial Years to 1790, by James B. Whisker and Roy F. Chandler, Acorn Press, Bedford, PA, 1984. Unpaginated. $10.00.
Definitive work on Eastern Pennsylvania gunmakers.

Bear in Their World, by Erwin Bauer, an Outdoor Life Book, New York, NY, 1985. 254 pp., illus. $32.95.
Covers all North American bears, including grizzlies, browns, blacks, and polars.

Beretta Automatic Pistols, by J.B. Wood, Stackpole Books, Harrisburg, PA, 1985. 192 pp., illus. $19.95.
Only English-language book devoted entirely to the Beretta line. Includes all important models.

Beretta: The World's Oldest Industrial Dynasty, by Marco Morin and Robert Held, Acquafresca Deditrice, Chiasso, Switzerland, 1983. 282 pp., illus. $44.95.
The evolution of the Beretta Company with complete coverage of the guns it produced. A bilingual book: Italian and English.

The Best of Babcock, by Havilah Babcock, selected and with and introduction by Hugh Grey, The Gunnerman Press, Auburn Hills, MI, 1985. 262 pp., illus. $19.95.
A treasury of memorable pieces, 21 of which have never before appeared in book form.

The Best of Sheep Hunting, compiled by John Batten, Amwell Press, Clinton, NJ, 1986. 250 pp., illus. $37.50.
An anthology of the finest stories on international sheep hunting ever compiled.

The Bolt Action Volume 2, by Stuart Otteson, Wolfe Publishing Co., Inc., Prescott, AZ, 1985. 289 pp., illus. $22.50.
Covers 17 bolt actions from Newton to Ruger.

Boone and Crockett Club's 18th Big Game Awards 1980-1982, edited by Wm. H. Nesbitt, The Boone and Crockett Club, Alexandria, VA, 1984. 306 pp., illus. $25.00.
Contains tabulations of outstanding North American big game trophies accepted during the 18th award entry period of 1980-82.

The British Falling Block Rifle from 1865, by Jonathan Kirton, Armory Publications, Tacoma, WA, 1985. 247 pp., illus. $39.95.
Covers inventors and producers of British falling-block breechloaders.

Browning .22 Caliber Rifles 1914-1984, by Homer C. Tyler, Homer C. Tyler, Jefferson City, MO, 1985. 304 pp., illus. $39.95.
Serial numbers and annual production figures, grades, special orders and variations, etc.

Campfires and Game Trails: Hunting North American Big Game, by Craig Boddington, Winchester Press, Piscataway, NJ, 1985. 295 pp., illus. $19.95.
How to hunt America's big game species.

Jim Carmichel's Book of the Rifle, by Jim Carmichel, an Outdoor Life Book, New York, NY, 1985. 564 pp., illus. $34.95.
The most important book of the author's career, and the most comprehensive ever published on the subject.

A Century of Sights and Sighting Aids, by Edna Rosalind Park, Alfred J. Parker Ltd., Birmingham, England, 1984. 46 pp., illus. $15.95.
Information on a rare collection of sights collected by the author.

Colt, An American Legend, by R.L. Wilson, Abbeville Press, New York, NY, 1985. 310 pp., illus. $55.00.
Every model Colt has ever produced is shown in magnificent color.

The Colt-Burgess Magazine Rifle, by Samuel L. Maxwell, Sr., Samuel L. Maxwell, Bellvue, WA, 1985. 176 pp., illus. $35.00.
Serial numbers, engraved arms, newly discovered experimental model, etc.

Colt Peacemaker Ready-Reference Handbook, by Keith Cochran, Cochran Publishing Co., Rapid City, ND, 1985. 76 pp., illus. Paper covers. $12.95.
A must book for the SAA collector.

Competitive Shooting, by A.A. Yur'yev, introduction by Gary L. Anderson, NRA Books, The National Rifle Assoc. of America, Wash., DC, 1985. 399 pp., illus. $29.95.
A unique encyclopedia of competitive rifle and pistol shooting.

Custom Knifemaking, by Tim McCreight, Stackpole Books, Inc., Harrisburg, PA, 1985. 224 pp., illus. $14.95.
Ten projects from a master craftsman.

The Deringer in America, Volume 1, The Percussion Period, by R.L. Wilson and L.D. Eberhart, Andrew Mowbray Inc., Lincoln, RI, 1985. 271 pp., illus. $48.00.
A long-awaited book on the American percussion deringer.

The Duck Hunter's Handbook, by Bob Hinman, revised, expanded, updated edition, Winchester Press, Piscataway, NJ, 1985. 288 pp., illus. $15.95.
The duck hunting book that has it all.

NEW BOOKS (cont.)

Dusty Days and Distant Drums, by William R. Rindone, Game Fields Press, Lake Oswego, OR, 1984. 258 pp., illus. $37.50.

An African hunting chronicle.

The Education of Pretty Boy, by Havilah Babcock, The Gunnerman Press, Auburn Hills, MI, 1985. 160 pp., illus. $19.95.

Babcock's only novel, a heartwarming story of an orphan boy and a gun-shy setter.

Elephant, by Commander David Enderby Blunt, The Holland Press, London, England, 1985. 260 pp., illus. $35.00.

A study of this phenomenal beast by a world-leading authority.

English Pistols: The Armories of H.M. Tower of London Collection, by Howard L. Blackmore, Arms & Armour Press, London, England, 1985. 64 pp., illus. $12.95.

All the pistols described and pictured are from this famed collection.

Evolution of the Winchester, by R. Bruce McDowell, Armory Publications, Tacoma, WA, 1986. 200 pp., illus. $37.50.

Historic lever-action, tubular-magazine firearms.

Expert Advice on Gun Dog Training, by David Michael Duffey, revised, expanded, updated edition, Winchester Press, Piscataway, NJ, 1985. 288 pp., illus. $15.95.

America's top professional trainers reveal how you can use their methods.

Sam Fadala's Muzzleloading Notebook, by Sam Fadala, Winchester Press, Piscataway, NJ, 1985. 212 pp., illus. $17.95.

The complete manual by the dean of muzzleloaders.

Firearms of the American West, 1803-1865, by Louis A. Garavaglia and Charles G. Worman, University of New Mexico Press, Albuquerque, NM, 1985. 300 pp., illus. $35.00.

An encyclopedic study tracing the development and uses of firearms on the frontier during this period.

Firearms of the American West, 1866-1894, by Louis A. Garavaglia and Charles G. Wormer, University of New Mexico Press, Albuquerque, NM, 1985. 448 pp., illus. $40.00.

The second volume in this study examines guns as an integral part of the frontier experience in a society where peace officers and judges were few.

Game Guns and Rifles, by Richard Akehurst, Arms & Armour Press, London, England, 1985. 176 pp., illus. $19.95.

Reprint of a classic account on sporting guns.

The Gordon MacQuarrie Trilogy, by Gordon MacQuarrie, compiled and edited by Zack Taylor, Willow Creek Press, Oshkosh, WI, 1985. A three book, slip-cased set. $45.00.

Three-volume set comprising "Stories of the Old Duck Hunters and Other Drivel;" "More Stories of the Old Duck Hunters;" "Last Stories of the Old Duck Hunters."

Great British Gunmakers 1540-1740, by W. Keith Neal and D.H.L. Back, Historical Firearms, London, England, 1984. 479 pp., illus. $125.00.

A limited, numbered edition covering a total of 159 gunmakers.

Grouse Hunter's Guide, by Dennis Walrod, Stackpole Books, Inc., Harrisburg, PA, 1985. 192 pp., illus. $16.95.

Solid facts, observations, and insights on how to hunt the ruffed grouse.

The Gun Digest Book of Assault Weapons, edited by Jack Lewis, DBI Books, Inc., Northbrook, IL, 1986. 256 pp., illus. Paper covers. $12.95.

An in-depth look at the history and uses, test reports on current full- and semi-auto guns in this class.

The Gun Digest Book of 9mm Handguns, by Dean A. Grennell and Wiley Clapp, DBI Books, Inc., Northbrook, IL, 1986. 256 pp., illus. Paper covers. $12.95.

The definitive book on the 9mm pistol.

Handbook of the Pedersen Self-Loading Rifles Model P.A., a facsimile reprint of this Vickers-Armstrongs Ltd. manual, ca. 1930s, by Robert T. Sweeney, San Francisco, CA, 1985. 32 pp., illus. Paper covers. $9.50.

Reprint of an original operator's manual for the British version of a semi-automatic military arm that was a major contender of the Garand rifle.

Historic Pistols: The American Martial Flintlock 1760-1845, by Samuel E. Smith and Edwin W. Bitter, The Gun Room Press, Highland Park, NJ, 1986. 353 pp., illus. $64.50.

Covers over 70 makers and 163 models.

Hunt Elk, by Jim Zumbo, Winchester Press, Piscataway, NJ, 1985. 256 pp., illus. $17.95.

A complete guide by one of America's foremost hunting writers..

Hunting the African Elephant, compiled by Jim Rikhoff, Amwell Press, Clinton, NJ, 1986. 625 pp., illus. $105.00.

An anthology of classics by famous authors and hunters such as Bell, O'Connor, Keith, Dyer, Selous, and others.

Hunting the Elephant in Africa, by Captain C.H. Stigand, St. Martin's Press, New York, NY, 1986. 379 pp., illus. $14.95.

A reprint of the scarce 1913 edition; vintage Africana at its best.

Hunting Predators for Hides and Profits, by Wilf E. Pyle, Stoeger Publishing Co., So. Hackensack, NJ, 1985. 224 pp., illus. Paper covers. $11.95.

The author takes the hunter through every step of the hunting/marketing process.

I Don't Want to Shoot an Elephant, by Havilah Babcock, The Gunnerman Press, Auburn Hills, MI, 1985. 184 pp. illus. $19.95.

Eighteen delightful stories that will enthrall the upland gunner for many pleasurable hours.

The Illustrated Encyclopedia of Ammunition, by Ian V. Hogg, Books Sales, Secaucus, NJ, 1985. 256 pp., illus. $15.98.

A complete and updated illustrated survey of ammunition for small arms, mortar and artillery weapons.

Jane's Directory of Military Small Arms Ammunition, Jane's Publishing Co., Ltd., London, England, 1985. 124 pp., illus. $24.95..

Guide to all currently available military small arms cartridges.

Japanese Handguns, by Frederick E. Leith, Borden Publishing Co., Alhambra, CA, 1985. 160 pp., illus. $14.95.

All identification guide to all models and variations of Japanese handguns.

Jaybirds Go to Hell on Friday, by Havilah Babcock, The Gunnerman Press, Auburn Hills, MI, 1985. 149 pp., illus. $19.95.

Sixteen jewels that re-establish the lost art of good old-fashioned yarn telling.

Keith's Rifles for Large Game, by Elmer Keith, The Gun Room Press, Highland Park, NJ, 1986. 406 pp., illus. $39.95.

Covers all aspects of selecting, equiping, use and care of high-power rifles for hunting big game, especially African.

Know Your Broomhandle Mausers, by R.J. Berger, Blacksmith Corp., Southport, CT, 1985. 96 pp., illus. Paper covers. $6.95.

An interesting story on the big Mauser pistol and its variations.

The Last Book: Confessions of a Gun Editor, by Jack O'Connor, Amwell Press, Clinton, NJ, 1984. 247 pp., illus. $30.00.

Jack's last book. Semi-autobiographical.

"Life Without Fear", by Mike Dalton and Mickey Fowler, ISI Publications, Mission Hills, CA, 1984. 218 pp., illus. Paper covers. $9.95.

Handguns and self defense.

Longrifles of Pennsylvania, Volume 1, Jefferson, Clarion & Elk Counties, by Russel H. Harriger, George Shumway Publisher, York, PA, 1984. 200 pp., illus. $40.00.

First in a series that will treat in great detail the longrifles and gunsmiths of Pennsylvania.

Lords of the Pinnacles: Wild Goats of the World, by Raul Valdez, Wild Sheep & Goat International, Mesilla, NM, 1985. 212 pp., illus. $59.95.

Limited, numbered and signed edition. The first comprehensive survey of the life histories, internal anatomy, and hunting of the wild goats of the world.

The Luger Pistol Model .08, Tables of Dimensions, a facsimile reprint by Joachim Gortz, Munich, Germany, 1981. 30 folio sheets, some folding. Paper covers. $39.50.

Reprint of the "table of dimensions" for the German service pistol which were drawn by the Royal Prussian Infanterie-Konstruktions Bureau at Spandau and distributed to the government owned rifle factories for repair of Luger pitols.

Making Game: An Essay on Woodcock, by Guy De La Valdene, Willow Creek Press, Oshkosh, WI, 1985. 202 pp., illus. $20.00.

The most delightful book on woodcock yet published.

The Man-Eaters of Tsavo, by Lt. Col. J.H. Patterson, St. Martin's Press, New York, NY, 1986. 346 pp., illus. $14.95.

A reprint of the scarce original book on the man-eating lions of Tsavo.

Manufacture of the Model 1903 Springfield Service Rifle, by Fred H. Colvin and Ethan Viall, et al, Wolfe Publishing Co., Inc., Prescott, AZ, 1985. 450 pp., illus. $29.95.

In three parts. Part 1 is a reprint of Colvin & Viall's 1917 work "U.S. Rifles and Machine Guns;" Part 2 is G.P.O. 1911 "Instructions to Bidders . . . Model 1903;" Part 3 is a reprint of two articles on the Springfield from 1928 issues of "Army Ordnance" magazine.

Marsh Tales, by William N. Smith, Tidewater Publishers, Centreville, MD, 1985. 228 pp., illus. $15.95.

Market hunting, duck trapping, and gunning.

Master Tips, by J. Winokur, Potshot Press, Pacific Palisades, CA, 1985. 96 pp., illus. Paper covers. $11.95.

Basics of practical shooting.

Measuring and Scoring North American Big Game Trophies, by Wm. H. Nesbitt and Philip L. Wright, The Boone & Crockett Club, Alexandria, VA, 1986. 176 pp., illus. $15.00.

The Boone and Crocket Club official scoring system, with tips for field evaluation of trophies.

Meat on the Table: Modern Small-Game Hunting, by Galen Geer, Paladin Press, Boulder, CO, 1985. 216 pp., illus. $14.95.

All you need to know to put meat on your table from this comprehensive course in modern small-game hunting.

Modern Waterfowl Guns & Gunning, by Don Zutz, Stoeger Publishing Co., So. Hackensack, NJ, 1985. 224 pp., illus. Paper covers. $11.95.

Up-to-date information on the fast-changing world of waterfowl guns and loads.

Modern Rifles, Shotguns and Pistols, by Ian V. Hogg, Exeter Books, New York, NY, 1985. 112 pp., illus. $7.98.

Describes the most interesting recent developments in the design and manufacture of each of these types of weapons.

Movin' Along with Charley Dickey, by Charley Dickey, Winchester Press, Piscataway, NJ, 1985. 224 pp., illus. $14.95.

More wisdom, wild tales, and wacky wit from the Sage of Tallahassee.

My Health is Better in November, by Havilah Babcock, University of S. Carolina Press, Columbia, SC, 1985. 284 pp., illus. $19.95.

Adventures in the field set in the plantation country and backwater streams of South Carolina.

North American Big Game Animals, by Byron W. Dalrymple, Stackpole Books, Inc., Harrisburg, PA, 1985. 256 pp., illus. $29.95.

The lives of the mammals of North America that over the centuries have commonly been called game animals.

Olson's Encyclopedia of Small Arms, by John Olson, Winchester Press, Piscataway, NJ, 1985. 262 pp., illus. $22.95.

The most complete, authoritative, and up-to-date reference available for shooters, ballisticians, gun collectors, and everyone interested in firearms.

On Bears and Bear Hunting, by Duncan Gilchrist, Amwell Press, Clinton, NJ, 1984. 260 pp., illus. $27.50.

The author's experiences as a bear guide and taker of over 150 bears of all species make this a definitive work on bears.

The Orvis Book of Upland Bird Shooting, by Geoffrey Norman, Winchester Press, Piscataway, NJ, 1985. 155 pp., illus. $15.95.

A marvelously full and helpful look at the compelling world of upland bird shooting.

The Outdoor Life Deer Hunter's Encyclopedia, by John Madson, et al, Stackpole Books, Inc., Harrisburg, PA, 1985. 800 pp., illus. $49.95.

The largest, most comprehensive volume of its kind ever published.

NEW BOOKS (cont.)

Parker, America's Finest Shotgun, by Peter H. Johnson, Stackpole Books, Harrisburg, PA, 1985. 272 pp., illus. $17.95.

A look at one of the rarest and finest shotguns in history.

Precision Handloading, by John Withers, Stoeger Publishing Co., So. Hackensack, NJ, 1985. 224 pp., illus. Paper Covers. $11.95.

An entirely new approach to handloading ammunition.

Recollections of a Longshore Gunner, by 'BB,' The Boydell Press, Suffolk, England, 1979. 86 pp., illus. $11.50.

Wildfowling adventures after geese on the Scottish coast.

Recreating the Double Barrel Muzzle-Loading Shotgun, by William R. Brockway, George Shumway Publisher, York, PA, 1985. 198 pp., illus. Paper covers. $20.00; Cloth. $27.50.

Treats the making of double guns of classic type.

Remington Bullet Knives, by Mel Brewster, Armory Publications, Tacoma, WA 1986. 48 pp., illus. $9.95.

Entire series of bullet knives are shown with all known variations.

Remington Pocket Knife Catalog, 1920, a facsimile reprint by Armory Publications, Tacoma, WA, 1986. 182 pp., illus. Paper covers. $17.95.

Shows entire line of Remington knives for this period.

Ridge Runners & Swamp Rats, by Charles F. Waterman, Amwell Press, Clinton, NJ, 1983. 347 pp., illus. $25.00.

Tales of hunting and fishing.

Shoot to Win, by John Shaw, Blacksmith Corp., Southport, CT, 1985. 160 pp., illus. Paper covers. $9.95.

The lessons taught here are of interest and value to all handgun shooters.

The Shooting Field: One Hundred and Fifty Years with Holland and Holland, by Peter King, Blacksmith Corp., Southport, CT, 1985. 176 pp., illus. $39.95.

History of this famous firm and its guns.

Shotgun Digest, 3rd Edition, edited by Jack Lewis, DBI Books, Inc., Northbrook, IL, 1986. 256 pp., illus. Paper covers. $12.95.

A new look at shotguns.

The Shotgun: History and Development, by Geoffrey Boothroyd, A & C Black Publisher, Ltd., London, England, 1986. 256 pp., illus. $24.95.

From the days of the flintlock, through the percussion era to the early pin-fire breechloaders, and the later hammer centerfire breechloaders.

Skeeter Skelton's Handgun Tales, PJS Publications, Peoria, IL, 1984. 114 pp., illus. $12.50.

Skelton's favorite holsters and handguns, etc.

The SPIW: The Deadliest Weapon that Never Was, by R. Blake Stevens, and Edward C. Ezell, Collector Grade Publications, Inc., Toronto, Canada, 1985. 138 pp., illus. $29.95.

The complete saga of the fantastic flechette-firing Special Purpose Individual Weapon.

Sporting Ammunition, a facsimile reprint of the 1925 Nobel Industries, Ltd. catalog, Begonia Books, Ballarat, Australia, 1985. 119 pp., illus. $29.95.

Covers sporting ammunition manufactured by Eley Bros. Ltd. and Kynoch Ltd.

Steindler's New Firearms Dictionary, by R.A. Steindler, Stackpole Books, Inc., Harrisburg, PA, 1985. 320 pp., illus. $24.95.

Completely revised and updated edition of this standard work.

Sword of the Samurai, by George R. Parulski, Jr., Paladin Press, Boulder, CO, 1985. 144 pp., illus. $20.00.

The classical art of Japanese swordsmanship.

Tales of Quails 'n Such, by Havilah Babcock, University of S. Carolina Press, Columbia, SC, 1985. 237 pp. $19.95.

A group of hunting stories, told in informal style, on field experiences in the South in quest of small game.

Trophy Hunter in Asia, by Elgin T. Gates, Charger Productions Inc., Capistrano Beach, CA, 1982. 272 pp., illus. $19.95.

Fascinating high adventure with one of America's top trophy hunters.

The Turkey Hunter's Book, by John M. McDaniel, Amwell Press, Clinton, NJ, 1980. 147 pp., illus. Paper covers. $9.95.

One of the most original turkey hunting books to be published in many years.

Turkey Hunter's Digest, by Dwain Bland, DBI Books, Inc., Northbrook, IL, 1986. 256 pp., illus. Paper covers. $12.95.

Describes and pictures all varieties of turkey. Offers complete coverage on calls, calling techniques, appropriate guns, bows, cameras and other equipment.

U.S. Military Edged Weapons of the Second Seminole War, 1835-1842, by Ron G. Hickox, Tampa, FL, 1984. 102 pp., illus. Paper covers. $19.95.

A study of U.S. military edged weapons from 1818-1842.

Unrepentant Sinner, by Colonel Charles Askins, Paladin Press, Boulder, CO, 1985. 320 pp., illus. $17.95.

As one of the world's greatest big-game hunters, Askins recalls his adventures.

Victorian Shooting Days, by Derek Johnson, The Boydell Press, Suffolk, England, 1981. 111 pp., illus. $15.95.

Describes the weapons used by these sportsmen, and the author's results of his researches on East Anglian gunsmiths.

The Winchester Book, Silver Anniversary Edition, by George Madis, David Madis Gun Book Distributor, Dallas, TX, 1986. 650 pp., illus. $39.50.

A new revised 25th anniversary edition of this classic book on Winchesters. Complete serial ranges have been added.

Winchester Commemoratives, by Tom Trolard, Commemorative Investment Press, Plano, TX, 1986. 183 pp., illus. $49.95.

The complete pictorial collection of all the Winchester commemoratives.

Winchester's 30-30, Model 94, by Sam Fadala, Stackpole Books, Inc., Harrisburg, PA, 1986. 223 pp., illus. $24.95.

The story of the rifle America loves.

ballistics and handloading

ABC's of Reloading, 3rd Edition, by Dean A. Grennell, DBI Books, Inc., Northbrook, IL, 1985. 288 pp., illus. Paper covers. $12.95.

An all-new book with everything from a discussion of the basics up through and including advanced techniques and procedures.

American Ammunition and Ballistics, by Edward A. Matunas, Winchester Press, Piscataway, NJ, 1979. 288 pp., illus. $18.95.

A complete reference book covering all presently made and much discontinued American rimfire, centerfire, and shotshell ammunition.

The Art of Bullet Casting from Handloader & Rifle Magazines 1966-1981, compiled by Dave Wolfe, Wolfe Publishing Co., Prescott, AZ, 1981. 258 pp., illus. Paper covers. $12.95. Deluxe hardbound. $19.50.

Articles from "Handloader" and "Rifle" magazines by authors such as Jim Carmichel, John Wootters, and the late George Nonte.

Ballistic Science for the Law Enforcement Officer, by Charles G. Wilber, Ph.D., Charles C. Thomas, Springfield, IL, 1977. 309 pp., illus. $45.00.

A scientific study of the ballistics of civilian firearms.

Basic Handloading, by George C. Nonte, Jr., Outdoor Life Books, New York, NY, 1982. 192 pp., illus. Paper covers. $4.50.

How to produce high-quality ammunition using the safest, most efficient methods known.

The Bullet's Flight, by Franklin Mann, Wolfe Publishing Co., Inc., Prescott, AZ, 1980. 391 pp., illus. $22.00.

The ballistics of small arms. A reproduction of Harry Pope's personal copy of this classic with his marginal notes.

Cartridges of the World, 5th Edition, by Frank Barnes, DBI Books, Inc., Northbrook, IL, 1985. 416 pp., illus. Paper covers. $15.95.

Completely updated encyclopedic work on cartridges.

Cast Bullets, by Col. E. H. Harrison, A publication of the National Rifle Association of America, Washington, DC, 1979. 144 pp., illus. Paper covers. $12.95.

An authoritative guide to bullet casting techniques and ballistics.

Computer for Handloaders, by Homer Powley. A slide rule plus 12 page instruction book for use in finding charge, most efficient powder and velocity for any modern centerfire rifle. $6.95.

Discover Swaging, by David R. Corbin, Stackpole Books, Harrisburg, PA, 1979. 283 pp., illus. $18.95.

A guide to custom bullet design and performance.

Firearms Identification, by Dr. J. H. Mathews, Charles C. Thomas, Springfield, IL, 1973. 3 vol. set. A massive, carefully researched, authoritative work published as:

Vol. I **The Laboratory Examination of Small Arms** 400 pp., illus. $56.75.

Vol. II **Original Photographs and Other Illustrations of Handguns** 492 pp., illus. $56.75.

Vol. III **Data on Rifling Characteristics of Handguns and Rifles** 730 pp., illus. $88.00.

Firearms Investigation, Identification and Evidence, by J. S. Hatcher, Frank J. Jury and Jac Weller. Stackpole Books, Harrisburg, PA, 1977. 536 pp., illus. $26.95.

Reprint of the 1957 printing of this classic book on forensic ballistics. Indispensable for those interested in firearms identification and criminology.

Game Loads and Practical Ballistics for The American Hunter, by Bob Hagel, Alfred A. Knopf, NY, NY, 1978. 315 pp., illus., hardbound. $14.95.

Everything a hunter needs to know about ballistics and performance of commercial hunting loads.

The Gun Digest Black Powder Loading Manual, by Sam Fadala, DBI Books, Inc., Northbrook, IL, 1982. 244 pp., illus. Paper covers. $11.95.

Covers 450 loads for 86 of the most popular black powder rifles, handguns and shotguns.

Gun Digest Book of Popular Sporting Rifle Cartridges, by Clay Harvey, DBI Books, Inc., Northbrook, IL, 1984. 320 pp., illus. Paper covers. $13.95.

Provides the hunter/shooter with extensive information on the most popular cartridges introduced during this century.

Handbook for Shooters and Reloaders, by P.O. Ackley, Salt Lake City, UT, 1970, *Vol. I,* 567 pp., illus. $12.50. *Vol. II,* a new printing with specific new material. 495 pp., illus. $12.50.

Handbook of Metallic Cartridge Reloading, by Edward Matunas, Winchester Press, Piscataway, NJ, 1981. 272 pp., illus. $18.95.

Up-do-date, comprehensive loading tables prepared by four major powder manufacturers.

The Handbook of Shotshell Reloading, by Kenneth W. Couger, SKR Industries, San Angelo, TX, 1984. 248 pp., illus. Paper covers. $17.95.

All the present-day methods and techniques and up-to-date advice on reloading equipment and components.

Handloader's Digest, 10th Edition, edited by Ken Warner, DBI Books, Inc., Northbrook, IL, 1985. 320 pp., illus. Paper covers. $13.95.

The big book on handloading with dozens of "how-to" features, covering everything from tools and materials to techniques and tips.

Handloader's Guide, by Stanley W. Trzoniec, Stoeger Publishing Co., So., Hackensack, NJ, 1985. 256 pp., illus. Paper covers. $11.95.

The complete step-by-step fully illustrated guide to handloading ammunition.

Handloading, by Bill Davis, Jr., NRA Books, Wash., D.C., 1980. 400 pp., illus. Paper covers. $15.95.

A complete update and expansion of the NRA Handloader's Guide.

Handloading for Handgunners, by Geo. C. Nonte, DBI Books, Inc., Northbrook, IL, 1978. 288 pp., illus. Paper covers. $11.95.

An expert tells the ins and outs of this specialized facet of reloading.

Handloading for Hunters, by Don Zutz, Winchester Press, Piscataway, NJ, 1977. 288 pp., illus. Paper covers. $11.95.

Precise mixes and loads for different types of game and for various hunting situations with rifle and shotgun.

BALLISTICS & HANDLOADING (cont.)

Hodgdon Data Manual No. 24, Hodgdon Powder Co., Shawnee Mission, KS 1984. 400 pp., illus. $14.95.

Has a new silhouette section and complete data on new H4350 powder.

The Home Guide to Cartridge Conversions, by Maj. George C. Nonte Jr., The Gun Room Press, Highland Park, NJ, 1976. 404 pp., illus. $19.95.

Revised and updated version of Nonte's definitive work on the alteration of cartridge cases for use in guns for which they were not intended.

Hornady Handbook of Cartridge Reloading, Hornady Mfg. Co., Grand Island, NE, 1981. 650 pp., illus. $14.00.

New edition of this famous reloading handbook. Latest loads, ballistic information, etc.

Lyman Cast Bullet Handbook, 3rd Edition, edited by C. Kenneth Ramage, Lyman Publications, Middlefield, CT, 1980. 416 pp., illus. Paper covers. $16.95.

Information on more than 5,000 tested cast bullet loads and 19 pages of trajectory and wind drift tables for cast bullets.

Lyman Black Powder Handbook, ed. by C. Kenneth Ramage, Lyman Products for Shooters, Middlefield, CT, 1975. 239 pp., illus. Paper covers $11.95.

The most comprehensive load information ever published for the modern black powder shooter.

Lyman Pistol & Revolver Handbook, edited by C. Kenneth Ramage, Lyman Publications, Middlefield, CT, 1978. 280 pp., illus. Paper covers. $11.95.

An extensive reference of load and trajectory data for the handgun.

Lyman Reloading Handbook No. 46, edited by C. Kenneth Ramage, Lyman Publications, Middlefield, CT, 1982. 300 pp., illus. $16.95.

A large and comprehensive book on reloading. Extensive list of loads for jacketed and cast bullets.

Lyman Shotshell Handbook, 3rd Edition, edited by C. Kenneth Ramage, Lyman Publications, Middlefield, CT, 1984. 312 pp., illus. Paper covers. $16.95.

Has 2,000 loads, including slugs and buckshot, plus feature articles and a full color I.D. section.

Manual of Pistol and Revolver Cartridges, Volume 1, Centerfire and Metric Calibers, by Hans A. Erlmeier and Jakob H. Brandt, Journal-Verlag, Weisbaden, Germany, 1967. 271 pp., illus. $29.95.

Specifications for each cartridge cataloged; tells bullet and case type with important case dimensions.

Master Index to Handloader and Rifle Magazine, compiled by the staff of Wolfe Publishing Co., Prescott, AZ, 1983. Unpaginated. Paper covers. $8.50.

Covers issues #1-#100 of the *Handloader*; issues #1-#84 of the *Rifle.*

Metallic Cartridge Reloading, edited by Robert S.L. Anderson, DBI Books, Inc., Northbrook, IL, 1982. 320 pp., illus. Paper covers. $13.95.

A true reloading manual with a wealth of invaluable technical data provided by outstanding reloading experts. A must for any reloader. Extensive load tables.

Metallic Reloading Basics, edited by C. Kenneth Ramage, Lyman Publications, Middlefield, CT, 1976. 60 pp., illus. Paper covers. $1.95.

Provides the beginner with loading data on popular bullet weights within the most popular calibers.

Military Ballistics, by C.L. Farrar and D.W. Leeming, Pergamon Press, Oxford, England, 1983. 200 pp., illus. Paper covers. $25.00.

Principles of ballistics, illustrated by reference of military applications.

Modern Handloading, by Maj. Geo. C. Nonte, Winchester Press, Piscataway, NJ, 1972. 416 pp., illus. $15.00.

Covers all aspects of metallic and shotshell ammunition loading, plus more loads than any book in print.

Nosler Reloading Manual Number Two, Nosler Bullets, Inc., Bend, OR, 1981. 308 pp., illus. $8.95.

Thorough coverage of powder data, specifically tailored to the well known Nosler partition and solid base bullets.

Pet Loads, by Ken Waters, Wolfe Publ. Co., Inc., Prescott, AZ, 1979. Unpaginated. In looseleaf form. $29.50.

A collection of the last 13 years' articles on more than 70 metallic cartridges. Most calibers featured with updated material.

Practical Handgun Ballistics, by Mason Williams, Charles C. Thomas, Publisher, Springfield, IL, 1980. 215 pp., illus. $29.50.

Factual information on the practical aspects of ammunition performance in revolvers and pistols.

Rediscover Swaging, by David R. Corbin, Corbin Manufacturing and Supply, Inc., Phoenix, OR, 1983. 240 pp., illus. $18.50.

A new textbook on the subject of bullet swaging.

Reloader's Guide, 3rd Edition, by R.A. Steindler, Stoeger Publishing Co., So. Hackensack, NJ, 1984. 224 pp., illus. Paper covers. $8.95.

Complete, fully illustrated step-by-step guide to handloading ammunition.

Reloading for Shotgunners, 2nd Edition, edited by Robert S.L. Anderson, DBI Books, Inc., Northbrook, IL, 1985. 256 pp., illus. Paper covers. $11.95.

The very latest in reloading information for the shotgunner.

Sierra Bullets Reloading Manual, Second Edition, by Robert Hayden et al, The Leisure Group, Inc., Santa Fe Springs, CA, 1978. 700 pp., illus. Looseleaf binder. $16.95.

Includes all material in the original manual and its supplement updated, plus a new section on loads for competitive shooting.

Sierra Bullets Updated Supplement Reloading Manual, by Robert Hayden, et al, The Leisure Group, Inc., Santa Fe Springs, CA, 1985. Loose-leaf pages in binder. $16.50.

An updated supplement of loose-leaf pages to create a 2nd edition handgun manual for the most comprehensive reloading material ever assembled.

Speer Reloading Manual Number 10, Omark Industries, Inc., Lewiston, ID, 1979, 560 pp., illus. Paper covers. $12.00.

Expanded version with facts, charts, photos, tables, loads and tips.

Why Not Load Your Own? by Col. T. Whelen, A. S. Barnes, New York, 1957, 4th ed., rev. 237 pp., illus. $10.95.

A basic reference on handloading, describing each step, materials and equipment. Loads for popular cartridges are given.

Yours Truly, Harvey Donaldson, by Harvey Donaldson, Wolfe Publ. Co., Inc., Prescott, AZ, 1980. 288 pp., illus. $19.50.

Reprint of the famous columns by Harvey Donaldson which appeared in "Handloader" from May 1966 through December 1972.

COLLECTORS

American Handguns & Their Makers, compiled by J.B. Roberts, Jr. and Ted Bryant, NRA Books, Wash., DC, 1981. 248 pp., illus. Paper covers. $11.95.

First in a series of manuals on gun collecting and the history of firearms manufacturing.

American Percussion Revolvers, by Frank M. Sellers and Samuel E. Smith, Museum Restoration Service, Ottawa, Canada, 1971. 231 pp., illus. $29.95.

The ultimate reference book on American percussion revolvers.

" . . . And Now Stainless", by Dave Ecker with Bob Zwirz, Charter Arms Corp., Bridgeport, CT, 1981. 165 pp., illus. $15.00.

The Charter Arms story. Covers all models to date.

Arms & Accoutrements of the Mounted Police 1873-1973, by Roger F. Phillips and Donald J. Klancher, Museum Restoration Service, Ont., Canada, 1982. 224 pp., illus. $49.95.

A definitive history of the revolvers, rifles, machine guns, cannons, ammunition, swords, etc. used by the NWMP, the RNWMP and the RCMP during the first 100 years of the Force.

Arms & Equipment of the Civil War, by Jack Coggins, Outlet Books, New York, NY, 1983. 160 pp., illus. $7.98.

Lavishly illustrated guide to the principal weapons and equipment of the Civil War used by the forces of the Blue and the Gray.

Arms Makers of Maryland, by Daniel D. Hartzler, George Shumway, York, PA, 1975. 200 pp., illus. $40.00.

A thorough study of the gunsmiths of Maryland who worked during the late 18th and early 19th centuries.

Ballard Rifles in the H.J. Nunnemacher Coll., by Eldon G. Wolff. Milwaukee Public Museum, Wisc., 2nd ed., 1961. Paper, 77 pp. plus 4 pp. of charts and 27 plates. $5.00.

A thoroughly authoritative work on all phases of the famous rifles, their parts, patent and manufacturing history.

Basic Documents on U.S. Martial Arms, commentary by Col. B. R. Lewis, reissue by Ray Riling, Phila., PA., 1956 and 1960. *Rifle Musket Model 1855.* The first issue rifle of musket caliber, a muzzle loader equipped with the Maynard Primer, 32 pp. $2.50. *Rifle Musket Model 1863.* The Typical Union muzzle-loader of the Civil War, 26 pp. $1.75. *Breech-Loading Rifle Musket Model 1866.* The first of our 50 caliber breechloading rifles, 12 pp. $1.75. *Remington Navy Rifle Model 1870.* A commercial type breech-loader made at Springfield, 16 pp. $1.75 *Lee Straight Pull Navy Rifle Model 1895.* A magazine cartridge arm of 6mm caliber. 23 pp. $3.00. *Breech-Loading Arms* (five models)-27 pp. $2.75. *Ward-Burton Rifle Musket 1871-16* pp. $2.50. *U.S. Magazine Rifle and Carbine (cal. 30) Model 1892*(the Krag Rifle) 36 pp. $3.00.

British Military Pistols 1603-1888, by R.E. Brooker, Jr., The Gun Room Press, Highland Park, NJ, 1983. 139 pp., illus. $29.95.

Covers flintlock and percussion pistols plus cartridge revolvers up to the smokeless powder period.

The Broomhandle Pistol 1896-1936, by Wayne R. Erickson and Charles E. Pate, E & P Enterprises, San Antonio, TX, 1985. 300 pp., illus. $49.95.

A new updated publication on the Mauser Broomhandle pistol. Detailed historical and text information, plus a collector's value guide.

The Browning Connection, by Richard Rattenbury, Buffalo Bill Historical Center, Cody, WY, 1982. 71 pp., illus. Paper covers. $10.00.

Patent prototypes in the Winchester Museum.

California Gunsmiths 1846-1900, by Lawrence P. Sheldon, Far Far West Publ., Fair Oaks, CA, 1977. 289 pp., illus. $29.65.

A study of early California gunsmiths and the firearms they made.

Carbines of the Civil War, by John D. McAulay, Pioneer Press, Union City, TN, 1981. 123 pp., illus. Paper covers. $7.95.

A guide for the student and collector of the colorful arms used by the Federal cavalry.

Cartology Savaiog, by Gerald Bernstein, Gerald Bernstein, St. Louis, MO, 1976. 177 pp., illus. Paper covers. $8.95.

An infinite variations catalog of small arms ammunition stamps.

The Cartridge Guide, by Ian V. Hogg, Stackpole Books, Harrisburg, PA, 1982. 160 pp., illus. $24.95.

The small arms ammunition identification manual.

Cartridges of the World, 5th Edition, by Frank Barnes, edited by Ken Warner, DBI Books, Inc., Northbrook, IL, 1985. 416 pp., illus. Paper covers. $15.95.

Complete and authoritative data on rifle and pistol cartridges, shotshells, loads and ammunition components. The "bible" for collectors and reloaders.

A Catalog Collection of 20th Century Winchester Repeating Arms Co., compiled by Roger Rule, Alliance Books, Inc., Northridge, CA, 1985. 396 pp., illus. $29.95.

Reflects the full line of Winchester products from 1901-1931 with emphasis on Winchester firearms.

COLLECTORS (cont.)

Catalogue of the Enfield Pattern Room: British Rifles, Herbert Wooden, Her Majesty's Stationery Office, London, England, 1981. 80 pp., illus. Paper covers. $14.95.

The first exhaustive catalog of a specific section of the collection in the Pattern Room at the Royal Small Arms Factory at Enfield Lock.

Civil War Carbines, by A.F. Lustyik, World Wide Gun Report, Inc., Aledo, Ill, 1962. 63 pp., illus. Paper covers. $3.50.

Accurate, interesting summary of most carbines of the Civil War period, in booklet form, with numerous good illus.

Civil War Guns, by William B. Edwards, Castle Books, NY, 1976. 438 pp., illus. $15.00.

Describes and records the exciting and sometimes romantic history of forging weapons for war and heroism of the men who used them.

A Collector's Guide to Air Rifles, by Dennis E. Hiller, London, England, 1980. 170 pp., illus. Paper covers. $15.95.

Valuations, exploded diagrams and many other details of air rifles, old and new.

A Collector's Guide to Tokarev Pistols, by John Remling, Collector's Services, East Stroudsburg, PA, 1985. 81 pp., illus. Paper covers. $12.95.

Covers all models and variations of this firearm.

The Collector's Handbook of U.S. Cartridge Revolvers, 1856 to 1899, by W. Barlow Fors, Adams Press, Chicago, IL, 1973. 96 pp., illus. $10.95.

Concise coverage of brand names, patent listings, makers' history, and essentials of collecting.

Colonel Colt London, by Joseph G. Rosa, Arms & Armour Press, London, England, 1983. 218 pp., illus. $24.95.

The standard reference volume on the London activities of Samuel Colt.

Colt Engraving, by R.L. Wilson, The Gun Room Press, Highland Park, NJ, 1982. 560 pp., illus. $69.95.

New and completely revised edition of the author's original work on finely engraved Colt firearms.

Colt Firearms from 1836, by James E. Serven, new 8th edition, Stackpole Books, Harrisburg, PA, 1979. 398 pp., illus. $29.95. Deluxe ed. $49.95.

Excellent survey of the Colt company and its products. Updated with new SAA production chart and commemorative list.

The Colt Heritage, by R.L. Wilson, Simon & Schuster, 1979. 358 pp., illus. $75.00.

The official history of Colt firearms 1836 to the present.

Colt Pistols 1836-1976, by R.L. Wilson in association with R.E. Hable, Jackson Arms, Dallas, TX, 1976. 380 pp., illus. $100.00.

A magnificently illustrated book in full-color featuring Colt firearms from the famous Hable collection.

Colt's Dates of Manufacture 1837-1978, by R.L. Wilson, published by Maurie Albert,Coburg, Australia; N.A. distributor I.D.S.A. Books, Hamilton, OH, 1983. 61 pp. $10.00.

An invaluable pocket guide to the dates of manufacture of Colt firearms up to 1978.

Colt's SAA Post War Models, George Garton, Gun Room Press, Highland Park, NJ, 1979. 166 pp., illus. $21.95.

Details all guns produced and their variations.

Colt's Variations of the Old Model Pocket Pistol, 1848 to 1872, by P.L. Shumaker, Borden Publishing, Co., Alhambra, CA, 1966, a reprint of the 1957 edition. 150 pp., illus. $10.95.

A useful tool for the Colt specialist and a welcome return of a popular source of information that had been long out-of-print.

The Colt Whitneyville-Walker Pistol, by Lt. Col. Robert D. Whittington, Brownlee Books, Hooks, TX, 1984. 96 pp., illus. Limited edition. $20.00.

A study of the pistol and associated characters 1846-1851.

Contemporary Makers of Muzzleloading Firearms, by Robert Weil, Screenland Press, Burbank, CA, 1981. 300 pp., illus. $39.95.

Illustrates the work of over 30 different contemporary makers.

Development of the Henry Cartridge and Self-Contained Cartridges for the Toggle-Link Winchesters, by R. Bruce McDowell, A.M.B., Metuchen, NJ, 1984. 69 pp., illus. Paper covers. $10.00.

From powder and ball to the self-contained metallic cartridge.

Early Indian Trade Guns: 1625-1775, by T.M. Hamilton, Museum of the Great Plains, Lawton, OK, 1968. 34 pp., illus. Paper covers. $7.95.

Detailed descriptions of subject arms, compiled from early records and from the study of remnants found in Indian country.

English Gunmakers, by DeWitt Bailey and Douglas A. Nie, ARCO Publishing Co., New York, NY, 1978. 127 pp., illus. $24.95.

The Birmingham and Provincial gun trade in the 18th and 19th centuries.

Fifteen Years in the Hawken Lode, by John D. Baird, The Gun Room Press, Highland Park, NJ, 1976. 120 pp., illus. $17.95.

A collection of thoughts and observations gained from many years of intensive study of the guns from the shop of the Hawken brothers.

Firearms in Colonial America: The Impact on History and Technology 1492-1792, by M.L. Brown, Smithsonian Institution Press, Wash., D.C., 1980. 449 pp., illus. $55.00.

An in-depth coverage of the history and technology of firearms in Colonial North America.

Firearms of the Confederacy, by Claud R. Fuller & Richard D. Steuart, Quarterman Publ., Inc., Lawrence, MA, 1977. 333 pp., illus. $25.00.

The shoulder arms, pistols and revolvers of the Confederate soldier, including the regular United States Models, the imported arms and those manufactured within the Confederacy.

Flayderman's Guide to Antique American Firearms . . . And Their Values, Third Edition, by Norm Flayderman, DBI Books, Inc., Northbrook, IL, 1983. 624 pp., illus. Paper Covers. $19.95.

Updated and expanded third edition of this bible of the antique gun field.

The .45-70 Springfield, by Albert J. Frasca and Robert H. Hall, Springfield Publishing Co., Northridge, CA, 1980. 380 pp., illus. $39.95.

A carefully researched book on the trapdoor Springfield, including all experimental and very rare models.

The 45/70 Trapdoor Springfield Dixie Collection, compiled by Walter Crutcher and Paul Oglesby, Pioneer Press, Union City, TN, 1975. 600 pp., illus. Paper covers. $9.95.

An illustrated listing of the 45-70 Springfields in the Dixie Gun Works Collection. Little known details and technical information is given, plus current values.

French Military Weapons, 1717-1938, Major James E. Hicks, N. Flayderman & Co., Publishers, New Milford, CT, 1973. 281 pp., illus. $22.50.

Firearms, swords, bayonets, ammunition, artillery, ordnance equipment of the French army.

Gas, Air, and Spring Guns of the World, by W.H.B. Smith, Arms & Armour Press, London, England, 1983. 288 pp., illus. Paper covers. $17.50.

The standard work of its kind, invaluable to serious students, gunsmiths, developers, and collectors.

Gun Collector's Digest, 4th Edition, edited by Joseph J. Schroeder, Jr., DBI Books, Inc., Northbrook, IL, 1985. 224 pp., illus. Paper covers. $12.95.

The latest edition of this sought-after series.

Gun Digest Book of Modern Gun Values, 5th Edition, by Jack Lewis, ed. by Harold A. Murtz, DBI Books, Inc., Northbrook, IL, 1985. 432 pp., illus. Paper covers. $14.95.

All-new expanded edition covers the current values of all non-military guns in production from 1900-1983.

The Gun Collector's Handbook of Values, 1983-84, by C.E. Chapel, G.P. Putnam and Son, East Rutherford, NJ, 1984. 462 pp., illus. $19.95.

The 14th revised edition of the best-known price reference for collectors of firearms.

The Gunsmiths and Gunmakers of Eastern Pennsylvania, by James B. Whisker and Roy Chandler, Old Bedford Village Press, Bedford, PA, 1982. 130 pp., illus. Limited, numbered edition. Paper covers. $17.50.

Locates over 2,000 gunsmiths practicing before 1900, with references and documentation.

The Gunsmiths and Gunmakers of Western Pennsylvania, by James B. Whisker and Vaughn E. Whisker, Old Bedford Village Press, Bedford, PA, 1982. 103 pp., illus. Limited, numbered and signed edition. Paper covers. $17.50.

Lists over 650 names of gunsmiths practicing before 1900.

Gunsmiths of Ohio—18th & 19th Centuries: Vol. I, Biographical Data, by Donald A. Hutslar, George Shumway, York, PA, 1973. 444 pp., illus. $35.00.

An important source book, full of information about the old-time gunsmiths of Ohio.

The Hand Cannons of Imperial Japan, 1543-1945, by Harry Derby, Harry Derby, Charlotte, NC, 1982. 300 pp., illus. $37.00.

Superb, comprehensive and definitive study of Japanese handguns beginning with the introduction of the matchlock in Japan and continuing into the post-WW II period.

The Hawken Rifle: Its Place in History, by Charles E. Hanson, Jr., The Fur Press, Chadron, NE, 1979. 104 pp., illus. Paper covers. $6.00.

A definitive work on this famous rifle.

Hawken Rifles, The Mountain Man's Choice, by John D. Baird, The Gun Room Press, Highland Park, NJ, 1976. 95 pp., illus. $17.95.

Covers the rifles developed for the Western fur trade. Numerous specimens are described and shown in photographs.

Historical Hartford Hardware, by William W. Dalrymple, Colt Collector Press, Rapid City, SD, 1976. 42 pp., illus. Paper covers. $5.50.

Historically associated Colt revolvers.

A History of the Colt Revolver, by Charles T. Haven and Frank A. Belden, Outlet Books, New York, NY, 1978. 711 pp., illus. $45.00.

A giant of a book packed with information and pictures about the most cherished American revolver.

A History of the John M. Browning Semi-Automatic .22 Caliber Rifle, by Homer C. Tyler, Jefferson City, MO, 1982. 58 pp., illus. Paper covers. $10.00.

All models and variations are shown. Includes engraved guns.

The History and Development of Small Arms Ammunition, Volume 3, by George A. Hoyem, Armory Publications, Tacoma, WA, 1985. 238 pp., illus. $39.50.

Covers 19th and 20th century British rifle cartridges.

History of Modern U.S. Military Small Arms Ammunition, Vol. 2, 1940-1945, by F.W. Hackley, W.M. Woodin and E.L. Scranton, The Gun Room Press, Highland Park, NJ, 1976. 300 pp., illus. $35.00.

A unique book covering the entire field of small arms ammunition developed during the critical World War II years.

History of Winchester Firearms 1866-1980, by Duncan Barnes, et al,Winchester Press, Piscataway, NJ, 1985. 256 pp., illus. $17.95.

A most complete and authoritative account of Winchester firearms.

How to Buy and Sell Used Guns, by John Traister, Stoeger Publishing Co., So. Hackensack, NJ, 1984. 192 pp., illus. Paper covers. $9.95.

A new guide to buying and selling guns.

Kentucky Rifles and Pistols 1756-1850, compiled by members of the Kentucky Rifle Association, Wash., DC, Golden Age Arms Co., Delaware, OH, 1976. 275 pp., illus. $35.00.

Profusely illustrated with more than 300 examples of rifles and pistols never before published.

Know Your Ruger Single Action Revolvers 1953-1963, by John C. Dougan, edited by John T. Amber, Blacksmith Corp., Southport, CT, 1981. 199 pp., illus. $35.00.

A definitive reference work for the Ruger revolvers produced in the period 1953-1963.

The Krag Rifle Story, by Franklin B. Mallory and Ludwig Olson, Springfield Research Service, Silver Spring, MD, 1979. 224 pp., illus. $20.00.

Covers both U.S. and European Krags. Gives a detailed description of U.S. Krag rifles and carbines and extensive data on sights, bayonets, serial numbers, etc.

Krag Rifles, by William S. Brophy, The Gun Room Press, Highland Park, NJ, 1980. 200 pp., illus. $29.95.

The first comprehensive work detailing the evolution and various models, both military and civilian.

The Krieghoff Parabellum, by Randall Gibson, Randall Gibson, Midland, TX, 1980. 280 pp., illus. $35.00.

A definitive work on the most desirable model Luger pistol.

Lever Action Magazine Rifles Derived from the Patents of Andrew Burgess, by Samuel L. Maxwell Sr., Samuel L. Maxwell, Bellevue, WA, 1976. 368 pp., illus. $29.95.

The complete story of a group of lever action magazine rifles collectively referred to as the Burgess/Morse, the Kennedy or the Whitney.

Levine's Guide to Knives And Their Values, by Bernard Levine, DBI Books, Inc., Northbrook, IL, 1985. 480 pp., illus. Paper covers. $19.95.

An important guide to today's knife values.

Manual of Pistol and Revolver Cartridges, Volume 2, Centerfire U.S. and British Calibers, by Hans A. Erlmeier and Jakob H. Brandt, Journal-Verlag, Weisbaden, Germany, 1981. 270 pp., illus. $35.00.

Catalog system allows cartridges to be traced either by caliber or alphabetically.

Mauser Bolt Rifles, by Ludwig Olson, F. Brownell & Son, Inc., Montezuma, IA, 1976. 364 pp., illus. $32.50.

The most complete, detailed, authoritative and comprehensive work ever done on Mauser bolt rifles.

The Metric FAL, by R. Blake Stevens and Jean E. Van Rutten, Collector Grade Publications, Toronto, Canada, 1981. 372 pp., illus. Paper covers. $50.00.

Volume three of the FAL series. The free world's right arm.

Military Pistols of Japan, by Fred L. Honeycutt, Jr., Julin Books, Lake Park, FL. 1982. 167 pp., illus. $24.00.

Covers every aspect of military pistol production in Japan through WWII.

Military Rifles of Japan, by Fred L. Honeycutt, Jr. and F. Pratt Anthony, Julin Books, Lake Park, FL, 2nd edition, 1983. 206 pp., illus. $29.00.

Limited, signed and numbered edition. Includes the early Murata period, markings, etc.

M1 Carbine, Design, Development and Production, by Larry Ruth, The Gun Room Press, Highland Park, NJ, 1983. 300 pp., illus. Paper covers. $17.95.

The complete history of one of the world's most famous and most produced military firearms.

Modern Guns, Fred Adolph Catalog, reprinted by Armory Publications, Tacoma, WA, 1983. 67 pp., illus. Paper covers. $10.95.

Reprint of a scarce American gun catalog of the early 1900s.

Modern Guns Identification and Values, revised 5th edition, edited by Russell Quertermous and Steve Quertermous, Collector Books, Paducah, KY, 1984. 446 pp., illus. Paper covers. $11.95.

A guide to the current values of modern revolvers, pistols, rifles and shotguns.

More Single Shot Rifles, by James C. Grant, The Gun Room Press, Highland Park, NJ, 1976. 324 pp., illus. $25.00.

Details the guns made by Frank Wesson, Milt Farrow, Holden, Borchardt, Stevens, Remington, Winchester, Ballard and Peabody-Martini.

Simeon North: First Official Pistol Maker of the United States, by S. North and R. North, The Gun Room Press, Highland Park, NJ, 1972. 207 pp., illus. $9.95.

Reprint of the rare first edition.

The Northwest Gun, by Charles E. Hanson, Jr., Nebraska State Historical Society, Lincoln, NB, 1976. 85 pp., illus., paper covers. $6.00.

Number 2 in the Society's "Publications in Anthropology." Historical survey of rifles which figured in the fur trade and settlement of the Northwest.

The P-08 Parabellum Luger Automatic Pistol, edited by J. David McFarland, Desert Publications, Cornville, AZ, 1982. 20 pp., illus. Paper covers. $6.00.

Covers every facet of the Luger, plus a listing of all known Luger models.

The P-38 Pistol: The Contract Pistols 1940-45, Volume Two, by Warren H. Buxton, Ucross Books, Los Alamos, NM, 1984. 247 pp., illus. $45.50.

The production of the pistol in Germany and its occupied areas during the war by firms other than Walther.

Paterson Colt Pistol Variations, by R.L. Wilson and R. Phillips, Jackson Arms Co., Dallas, TX, 1979. 250 pp., illus. $35.00.

A tremendous book about the different models and barrel lengths in the Paterson Colt story.

Peacemaker Evolutions & Variations, by Keith A. Cochran, Colt Collectors Press, Rapid City, SD, 1975. 47 pp., illus. Paper covers. $10.00.

Corrects many inaccuracies found in other books on the Peacemaker and gives much new information regarding this famous arm.

The Pennsylvania-Kentucky Rifle, by Henry J. Kauffman, Crown Publishers, New York, NY 1981. 293 pp., illus. $9.98.

A colorful account of the history and gunsmiths who produced the first American rifle superior to those brought from the Old Country.

Pennsylvania Longrifles of Note, by George Shumway, George Shumway, Publisher, York, PA, 1977. 63 pp., illus. Paper covers. $6.95.

Illustrates and describes samples of guns from a number of Pennsylvania rifle-making schools.

The Pinfire System, by Gene P. Smith and Chris C. Curtis, The Pinfire System, San Francisco, CA, 1983. 216 pp., illus. $50.00.

The first attempt to record the invention, development and use of pinfire cartridge arms and ammunition.

The Plains Rifle, by Charles E. Hanson, Jr., The Gun Room Press, Highland Park, NJ, 1977. 171 pp., illus. $19.95.

Historical survey of popular civilian arms used on the American frontiers, their makers, and their owners.

The Radom Pistol, by Robert J. Berger, Robert J. Berger, Milford, CT, 1981. 99 pp., illus. Paper covers. $10.00.

The complete story of the VIS (Radom) pistol.

The Rare and Valuable Antique Arms, by James E. Serven, Pioneer Press, Union City, TN, 1976. 106 pp., illus. Paper covers. $4.95.

A guide to the collector in deciding which direction his collecting should go, investment value, historic interest, mechanical ingenuity, high art or personal preference.

Reloading Tools, Sights and Telescopes for Single Shot Rifles, by Gerald O. Kelver, Brighton, CO, 1982. 163 pp., illus. Paper covers. $10.00.

A listing of most of the famous makers of reloading tools, sights and telescopes with a brief description of the products they manufactured.

Rifles in Colonial America, Vol. I, by George Shumway, George Shumway, Publisher, York, PA, 1980. 353 pp., illus. $49.50.

An extensive photographic study of American longrifles made in the late Colonial, Revolutionary, and post-Revolutionary periods.

Rifles in Colonial America, Vol. II, by George Shumway, George Shumway, Publisher, York, PA, 1980. 302 pp., illus. $49.50.

Final volume of this study of the early evolution of the rifle in America.

The Ross Rifle Story, by R. Phillips, F. Dupuis, J. Chadwick, John A. Chadwick, Nova Scotia, Canada, 1984. 475 pp., illus. $49.50.

This book explores the myths and folklore surrounding Ross and his rifle and tries to set the record straight.

Ruger Rimfire Handguns 1949-1982, by J.C. Munnell, G.D.G.S. Inc., McKeesport, PA, 1982. 189 pp., illus. Paper covers. $12.00.

Updated edition with additional material on the semi-automatic pistols and the New Model revolvers.

Samuel Colt's New Model Pocket Pistols; The Story of the 1855 Root Model Revolver, by S. Gerald Keogh, S.G. Keogh, Ogden, UT, 1974. 31 pp., illus., paper covers. $5.00.

Collector's reference on various types of the titled arms, with descriptions, illustrations, and historical data.

Savage Automatic Pistols, by James R. Carr. Publ. by the author, St. Charles, Ill., 1967. A reprint. 129 pp., illus. with numerous photos. $30.00.

Collector's guide to Savage pistols, models 1907-1922, with features, production data, and pictures of each.

Scottish Arms Makers, by Charles E. Whitelaw, Arms and Armour Press, London, England, 1982. 363 pp., illus. $29.95.

An important and basic addition to weapons reference literature.

Serial Numbers on U.S. Martial Arms, by Franklin B. Mallory, Springfield Research Service, Silver Spring, MD, 1983. 103 pp., illus. Paper covers. $10.00.

A valuble aid to collectors of U.S. martial arms.

Sharps Firearms, by Frank Seller, Frank M. Seller, Denver, CO, 1982. 358 pp., illus. $39.95.

Traces the development of Sharps firearms with full range of guns made including all martial variations.

Small Arms of the Sea Services, by Robert H. Rankin. N. Flayderman & Co., New Milford, CT, 1972. 227 pp., illus. $14.50.

Encyclopedic reference to small arms of the U.S. Navy, Marines and Coast Guard. Covers edged weapons, handguns, long arms and others, from the beginnings.

Southern Derringers of the Mississippi Valley, by Turner Kirkland. Pioneer Press, Tenn., 1971. 80 pp., illus., paper covers. $2.00.

A guide for the collector, and a much-needed study.

The Springfield 1903 Rifles, by Lt. Col. William S. Brophy, USAR, Ret., Stackpole Books Inc., Harrisburg, PA, 1985. 608 pp., illus. $49.95.

The illustrated, documented story of the design, development, and production of all the models, appendages, and accessories.

Still More Single Shot Rifles, by James J. Grant, Pioneer Press, Union City, TN, 1979. 211 pp., illus. $17.50.

A sequel to the author's classic works on single shot rifles.

The 36 Calibers of the Colt Single Action Army, by David M. Brown. Publ. by the author at Albuquerque, NM, new reprint 1971. 222 pp., well-illus. $65.00.

Edited by Bev Mann of *Guns Magazine*. This is an unusual approach to the many details of the Colt S.A. Army revolver. Halftone and line drawings of the same models make this of especial interest.

Thoughts on the Kentucky Rifle in its Golden Age, by Joe Kindig, George Shumway, Publisher, York, PA, 1984. 561 pp., illus. $75.00.

A new printing of the classic work on Kentucky rifles.

Trade Muskets or Northwest Guns, by Pryor Mt. Bill Newton, Bill Newton, Beaver, WY, 34 pp., illus. Paper covers. $7.50.

The history, patterns and methods of the Whately 1770s and the Barnett, 1830. Workshop manual.

The Trapdoor Springfield, by M.D. Waite and B.D. Ernst, The Gun Room Press, Highland Park, NJ, 1983. 250 pp., illus. $29.95.

The first comprehensive book on the famous standard military rifle of the 1873-92 period.

A Treatise on the British Military Martini: The Martini-Henry 1869-c1900, by B.A. Temple and I.D. Skennerton, B.A. Temple, Burbank, Australia, 1983. 246 pp., illus. $39.95.

The development of the Martini-Henry rifle.

Underhammer Guns, by H.C. Logan. Stackpole Books, Harrisburg, PA, 1965. 250 pp., illus. $10.00.

A full account of an unusual form of firearm dating back to flintlock days. Both American and foreign specimens are included.

U.S. Enfield, by Ian Skennerton, Ian Skennerton, Margate, Australia, 1983. 190 pp., illus. $21.50.

Covers both the British pattern and the U.S. Model 1917 rifles.

U.S. Military Small Arms 1816-1865, by Robert M. Reilly, The Gun Room Press, Highland Park, NJ, 1983. 270 pp., illus. $35.00.

Covers every known type of primary and secondary martial firearms used by Federal forces.

The Virginia Manufactory of Arms, by Giles Cromwell, University Press of Virginia, Charlottesville, VA, 1975. 205 pp., illus. $29.95.

The only complete history of the Virginia Manufactory of Arms which produced muskets, pistols, swords, and cannon for the state's militia from 1802 through 1821.

Walther P-38 Pistol, by Maj. George Nonte, Desert Publications, Cornville, AZ, 1982. 100 pp., illus. Paper covers. $7.50.

Complete volume on one of the most famous handguns to come out of WWII. All models covered.

Walther Models PP and PPK, 1929-1945, by James L. Rankin, assisted by Gary Green, James L. Rankin, Coral Gables, FL, 1974. 142 pp., illus. $20.00.

Complete coverage on the subject as to finish, proof marks and Nazi Party inscriptions.

Walther Volume II, Engraved, Presentation and Standard Models, by James L. Rankin, J.L. Rankin, Coral Gables, FL, 1977. 112 pp., illus. $20.00.

The new Walther book on embellished versions and standard models. Has 88 photographs, including many color plates.

Walther, Volume III, 1908-1980, by James L. Rankin, Coral Gables, FL, 1981. 226 pp., illus. $24.50.

Covers all models of Walther handguns from 1908 to date, includes holsters, grips and magazines.

The Whitney Firearms, by Claud Fuller. Standard Publications, Huntington, W. Va., 1946. 334 pp., many plates and drawings. $40.00.

An authoritative history of all Whitney arms and their maker. Highly recommended. An exclusive with Ray Riling Arms Books Co.

The William M. Locke Collection, compiled by Robert B. Berryman, et al, The Antique Armory, Inc., East Point, GA, 1973. 541 pp., illus. $45.00.

A magnificently produced book illustrated with hundreds of photographs of guns from one of the finest collection of American firearms ever assembled.

The Winchester Book, by George Madis, Art & Reference House, Lancaster, TX, 1980. 638 pp., illus. $39.50.

A greatly enlarged edition of this most informative book on these prized American arms.

Winchester Dates of Manufacture 1849-1984, by George Madis, Art and Reference House, Brownsboro, TX, 1984. 59 pp. $5.95.

A most useful work, compiled from records of the Winchester factory.

The Winchester Handbook, by George Madis, Art & Reference House, Lancaster, TX, 1982. 287 pp., illus. $19.95.

The complete line of Winchester guns, with dates of manufacture, serial numbers, etc.

Winchester: The Golden Age of American Gunmaking and the Winchester 1 of 1000, by R.L. Wilson, Winchester Arms Museum, Cody, WY, 1983. 144 pp., illus. $45.00.

The author traces the evolution of the firm; against this background he then examines the Winchester Model 1873 and 1876, 1 of 100 and 1000 series rifles.

Winchester—The Gun That Won the West, by H.F. Williamson. Combat Forces Press, Washington, D.C., 1952. Later eds. by Barnes, NY. 494 pp., profusely illus., paper covers. $20.00.

A scholarly and essential economic history of an honored arms company, but the early and modern arms introduced will satisfy all but the exacting collector.

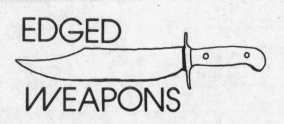

The Robert Abels Collection of Bowie Type Knives of American Interest, by Robert Abels, Robert Abels, Hopewell Junction, NY, 1974. 20 pp., illus. Paper covers. $3.00.

A selection of American Bowie-type knives from the collection of Robert Abels.

American Axes, by Henry Kauffman, The Stephen Green Press, Brattleboro, VT, 1972. 200 pp., illus. $25.00.

A definitive work on the subject. Contains a roster of American axe makers, glossary and notes on the care and use of axes.

American Knives; The First History and Collector's Guide, by Harold L. Peterson, The Gun Room Press, Highland Park, NJ, 1980. 178 pp., illus. $17.95.

A reprint of this 1958 classic. Covers all types of American knives.

American Polearms 1526-1865, by Rodney Hilton Brown, N. Flayderman & Co., New Milford, CT, 1967. 198 pp., illus. $14.50.

The lance, halbred, spontoon, pike and naval boarding weapons used in the American military forces through the Civil War.

American Primitive Knives 1770-1870, by G.B. Minnes, Museum Restoration Service, Ottawa, Canada, 1983. 112 pp., illus. $14.95.

Origins of the knives, outstanding specimens, structural details, etc.

The Ames Sword Co., 1829-1935, by John D. Hamilton, Mowbray Co., Providence, RI, 1983. 255 pp., illus. $45.00.

The story of the most prolific American sword makers over the longest period of time.

The American Sword, 1775-1945, by Harold L. Peterson, Ray Riling Arms Books, Co., Phila., PA, 1980. 286 pp. plus 60 pp. of illus. $35.00.

1977 reprint of a survey of swords worn by U.S. uniformed forces, plus the rare "American Silver Mounted Swords, (1700-1815)."

The Art of Blacksmithing, by Alex W. Bealer, Funk & Wagnalls, New York, NY, revised edition, 1976. 438 pp., illus. $21.95.

Required reading for anyone who makes knives or is seriously interested in the history of cutlery.

The Bayonet An Evolution and History, by R.D.C. Evans and Frederick J. Stephens, Militaria Collector Inc., Northridge, CA, 1985. 200 pp., illus. Paper covers. $19.95.

Traces the story of the bayonet through the centuries from its simple beginnings in 17th century France up to the present age.

The Best of Knife World, Volume I, edited by Knife World Publ., Knoxville, TN, 1980. 92 pp., illus. Paper covers. $3.95.

A collection of articles about knives. Reprinted from monthly issues of *Knife World.*

Blacksmithing for the Home Craftsman, by Joe Pehoski, Joe Pehoski, Washington, TX, 1973. 44 pp., illus. Paper covers. $5.00.

This informative book is chock-full of drawings and explains how to make your own forge.

Blades and Barrels, by H. Gordon Frost, Wallon Press, El Paso, TX, 1972. 298 pp., illus. $19.95.

The first full scale study about man's attempts to combine an edged weapon with a firearm.

Bowie Knives, by Robert Abels, Robert Abels, NY, 1960. 48 pp., illus. Paper covers. $5.00.

A booklet showing knives, tomahawks, related trade cards and advertisements.

Commando Dagger, by Leroy Thompson, Paladin Press, Boulder, CO, 1984. 176 pp., illus. $25.00.

The complete illustrated history of the Fairbairn-Sykes fighting knife.

Custom Knife...II, by John Davis Bates, Jr., and James Henry Schippers, Jr., Custom Knife Press, Memphis, TN, 1974. 112 pp., illus. $20.00.

The book of pocket knives and folding hunters. A guide to the 20th century makers' art.

For Knife Lovers Only, by Harry K. McEvoy, Knife World Publ., Knoxville, TN, 1979. 67 pp., illus. Paper covers. $4.95.

A fascinating and unusual approach to the story of knives.

The German Bayonet, by John Walter, Arms and Armour Press, London, England, 1982. 128 pp., illus. $19.95.

A comprehensive history of the regulation patterns 1871-1945.

Gun Digest Book of Knives, 2nd Edition, by Jack Lewis and Roger Combs, DBI Books, Inc., Northbrook, IL, 1982. 288 pp., illus. Paper covers. $10.95.

Covers the complete spectrum of the fascinating world of knives.

How to Make Knives, by Richard W. Barney & Robert W. Loveless, Beinfield Publ., Inc., No. Hollywood, CA, 1977. 178 pp., illus. $15.00.

A book filled with drawings, illustrations, diagrams, and 500 how-to-do-it photos.

Inscribed Union Swords, 1861-1865, by David V. Stroud, Pinecrest Publishing Co., Kilgore, TX, 1984. 192 pp., illus. Limited, numbered, and signed edition. $27.50.

A definitive work on presentation Union swords.

The Japanese Sword, by Kanzan Sato, Kodansha International Ltd. and Shibundo, Tokyo, Japan, 1983. 210 pp., illus. $19.95.

The history and appreciation of the Japanese sword, with a detailed examination of over a dozen of Japan's most revered blades.

Japanese Swordsmanship, by Gordon Warner and Don. F. Draeger, Weatherhill, New York, NY, 1984. 296 pp., illus. $29.95.

Technique and practice of Japanese swordsmanship.

Kentucky Knife Traders Manual No. 6, by R.B. Ritchie, Hindman, KY, 1980. 217 pp., illus. Paper covers. $10.00.

Guide for dealers, collectors and traders listing pocket knives and razor values.

Knives '87, 7th Edition, edited by Ken Warner, DBI Books, Inc., Northbrook, IL, 1986. 256 pp., illus. Paper covers. $12.95.

Covers trends and technology for both custom and factory knives.

Knife Throwing, Sport...Survival...Defense, by Blackie Collins, Knife World Publ., Knoxville, TN, 1979. 31 pp., illus. Paper covers. $3.00.

How to select a knife, how to make targets, how to determine range and how to survive with a knife.

Knife Throwing a Practical Guide, by Harry K. McEvoy, Charles E. Tuttle Co., Rutland, VT, 1973. 108 pp., illus. Paper covers. $3.95.

If you want to learn to throw a knife this is the "bible".

Knifecraft: A Comprehensive Step-by-Step Guide to the Art of Knifemaking, by Sid Latham, Stackpole Books, Harrisburg, PA, 1978. 224 pp., illus. $24.95.

An exhaustive volume taking both amateur and accomplished knifecrafter through all the steps in creating a knife.

Levine's Guide to Knives And Their Values, by Bernard Levine, DBI Books, Inc., Northbrook, IL, 1985. 480 pp., illus. Paper covers. $19.95.

An important guide to today's knife values and collecting them.

Light But Efficient, by Albert N. Hardin, Jr. and Robert W. Hedden, Albert N. Hardin, Jr., Pennsauken, NJ, 1973. 103 pp., illus. $7.95.

A study of the M1880 Hunting and M1890 intrenching knives and scabbards.

The Modern Blacksmith, by Alexander G. Weygers, Van Nostrand Reinhold Co., NY, 1977. 96 pp., illus. $10.95.

Shows how to forge objects out of steel. Use of basic techniques and tools.

Naval Swords, by P.G.W. Annis, Stackpole Books, Harrisburg, PA, 1970. 80 pp., illus. $12.50.

British and American naval edged weapons 1660-1815.

A Photographic Supplement of Confederate Swords with Addendum, by William A. Albaugh III, Moss Publications, Orange, VA, 1979. 259 pp., illus. $24.95.

A new updated edition of the classic work on Confederate edged weapons.

EDGED WEAPONS (cont.)

The Pocketknife Manual, by Blackie Collins, Blackie Collins, Rock Hill, SC, 1976. 102 pp., illus. Paper covers. $5.50.

Building, repairing and refinishing pocketknives.

Practical Blacksmithing, edited by J. Richardson, Outlet Books, NY, 1978. four volumes in one, illus. $9.98.

A reprint of the extremely rare, bible of the blacksmith. Covers every aspect of working with iron and steel, from ancient uses to modern.

Rice's Trowel Bayonet, reprinted by Ray Riling Arms Books, Co., Phila., PA, 1968. 8 pp., illus. Paper covers. $3.00.

A facsimile reprint of a rare circular originally published by the U.S. Government in 1875 for the information of U.S. Troops.

The Samurai Sword, by John M. Yumoto, Charles E. Tuttle Co., Rutland, VT, 1958. 191 pp., illus. $11.00.

A must for anyone interested in Japanese blades, and the first book on this subject written in English.

The Samurai Sword: An American Perspective, by Gary Murtha, H.S.M. Publications, Independence, MO, 1980. 126 pp., illus. $30.00.

The origin and development of the sword and its historical background.

The Samurai Sword: An American Perspective, Vol. 2, Sword Fittings, by Gary Murtha, R&M Enterprises, Kansas City, MO, 1984. 156 pp., illus. $30.00.

Identification of signatures, family crests, and designs that are encountered on Japanese sword fittings.

Scottish Swords from the Battlefield at Culloden, by Lord Archibald Campbell, The Mowbray Co., Providence, RI, 1973. 63 pp., illus. $5.00.

A modern reprint of an exceedingly rare 1894 privately printed edition.

Secrets of the Samurai, by Oscar Ratti and Adele Westbrook, Charles E. Tuttle Co. Rutland, VT, 1983. 483 pp., illus. $35.00.

A survey of the martial arts of feudal Japan.

The Sword in the Age of Chivalry, by R. Ewar Oakeshott, Arms & Armour Press, London, England, 1982. 160 pp., illus. $32.50.

A classic work—the result of 25 years of research by an authority whose work is acknowledged by scholars all over the world.

Swords and Daggers, by Frederick Wilkinson, Stackpole Books, Inc., Harrisburg, PA, 1985. 80 pp., illus. $10.95.

Included are European weapons, scabbards, Japanese swords, Indian, African, and Asian weapons, and Third Reich daggers, with a guide to their values.

Swords and Other Edged Weapons, by Robert Wilkinson-Latham, Arco Publishing Co., New York, NY, 1978. 227 pp., illus. $8.95.

Traces the history of the "Queen of Weapons" from its earliest forms in the stone age to the military swords of the Twentieth century.

Tomahawks Illustrated, by Robert Kuck, Robert Kuck, New Knoxville, OH, 1977. 112 pp., illus. Paper covers. $10.00.

A pictorial record to provide a reference in selecting and evaluating tomahawks.

U.S. Military Knives, Bayonets and Machetes, Book III, by M. H. Cole, M.H. Cole, Birmingham, AL, 1979. 219 pp., illus. $25.00.

The most complete text ever written on U.S. military knives, bayonets, machetes and bolos.

World Bayonets, 1800-Present, by Anthony Carter, Arms & Armour Press, London, England, 1984. 72 pp., illus. $12.95.

Lavishly illustrated guide to the bayonets of the world.

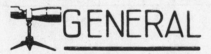

GENERAL

Advanced Muzzleloader's Guide, by Toby Bridges, Stoeger Publishing Co., So. Hackensack, NJ, 1985. 256 pp., illus. Paper covers. $11.95.

The complete guide to muzzle-loading rifles, pistols and shotguns—flintlock and percussion.

The Airgun Book, 3rd Edition, by John D. Walter, Stackpole Books, Harrisburg, PA, 1984. 176 pp., illus. $19.95.

A fully revised assessment of the most recent developments on the airgun scene.

American Gunsmiths, by Frank M. Sellers, The Gun Room Press, Highland Park, NJ, 1983. 349 pp. $39.95.

A comprehensive listing of the American gun maker, patentee, gunsmith and entrepreneur.

American Tools of Intrigue, by John Minnery & Jose Ramos, Desert Publications, Cornville, AZ, 1981. 128 pp., illus. Paper covers. $10.00.

Clandestine weapons which the Allies supplied to resistance fighters.

Be an Expert Shot with Rifle or Shotgun, by Clair Rees, Winchester Press, Piscataway, NJ, 1984. 192 pp., illus. $19.95.

The illustrated self-coaching method that turns shooters into fine marksmen.

Benchrest Actions and Triggers, by Stuart Otteson, Wolfe Publishing Co., Inc., Prescott, AZ, 1983. 61 pp., illus. Paper covers. $9.50.

A combined reprinting of the author's "Custom Benchrest Actions" articles which appeared in *Rifle* magazine.

Black Powder Gun Digest, 3rd Edition, edited by Jack Lewis, DBI Books, Inc., Northbrook, IL, 1982. 256 pp., illus. Paper covers. $11.95.

All new articles, expressly written for the black powder gun buff.

Buckskins and Black Powder, by Ken Grissom, Winchester Press, Piscataway, NJ, 1983. 224 pp., illus. $15.95.

A mountain man's guide to muzzleloading.

Carbine; The Story of David Marshall "Carbine" Williams, by Ross E. Beard, Jr., The Sandlapper Store, Inc., Lexington, SC, 1977. 315 pp., illus. Deluxe limited edition, numbered and signed by the author and "Carbine". $25.00

The story of the man who invented the M1 Carbine and holds 52 other firearms patents.

Colonial Frontier Guns, by T.M. Hamilton, The Fur Press, Chadron, NE, 1980. 176 pp., illus. Paper covers. $12.00.

French, Dutch, and English trade guns before 1780.

Colonial Riflemen in the American Revolution, by Joe D. Huddleston, George Shumway Publisher, York, PA, 1978. 70 pp., illus. $18.00.

This study traces the use of the longrifle in the Revolution for the purpose of evaluating what effects it had on the outcome.

The Complete Black Powder Handbook, by Sam Fadala, DBI Books, Inc. Northbrook, IL, 1979. 288 pp., illus. Paper covers. $12.95.

Everything you want to know about black powder firearms and their shooting.

Complete Book of Shooting: Rifles, Shotguns, Handguns, by Jack O'Connor, Stackpole Books, Harrisburg, PA, 1983. 392 pp., illus. $24.95.

A thorough guide to each area of the sport, appealing to those with a new or ongoing interest in shooting.

The Complete Book of Target Shooting, by Wes Blair, Stackpole Books, Harrisburg, PA, 1984. 416 pp., illus. $24.95.

The encyclopedia of up-to-date shooting information.

The Complete Book of Thompson Patents, compiled by Don Thomas, The Gun Room Press, Highland Park, NJ, 1981. 482 pp., illus. Paper covers. $15.95.

From John Blish's breech closure patented in 1915 to Charles W. Robin's automatic sear release of 1947. Includes all other firearm patents granted to the developers of the famed "Tommy gun."

The Complete Book of Trick & Fancy Shooting, by Ernie Lind, The Citadel Press, Secaucus, NJ, 1977. 159 pp., illus. Paper covers. $6.00.

Step-by-step instructions for acquiring the whole range of shooting skills with rifle, pistol and shotgun.

The Complete Encyclopedia of Arms and Weapons, by Leonid Tarassuk and Claude Blair, Charles Scribner's Sons, New York, N.Y., 1983. 560 pp., illus. $41.50.

Describes armor, crossbows, swords, daggers, cannon, pistols, rifles, bayonets, etc. Comprehensive and arranged alphabetically.

The Complete Guide to Game Care and Cookery, by Sam Fadala, DBI Books, Inc., Northbrook, IL, 1981. 288 pp., illus. Paper covers. $12.95.

A step-by-step journey beginning with meat-hunting philosophy and tactics through what to do with the game once you've brought it down. Includes many recipes.

The Complete Shooter, by Sam Fadala, DBI Books, Inc., Northbrook, IL, 1984. 448 pp., illus. Paper covers. $18.95.

Covers nearly every aspect of shooting, from how to choose the right cartridge/rifle, recoil, defense, varmint, black powder guns, sights, reloading wildcats—nearly everything.

The Complete Survival Guide, edited by Mark Thiffault, DBI Books, Inc., Northbrook, IL, 1983. 256 pp., illus. Paper covers. $11.95.

Covers all aspects of survival from manmade and natural disasters—equipment, techniques, weapons, etc.

Dead Aim, by Lee Echols, Acme Printing Co., San Diego, CA, a reprint, 1972. 116 pp., illus. $9.95.

Nostalgic antics of hell-raising pistol shooters of the 1930's.

The Encyclopedia of Infantry Weapons of World War II, by Ian V. Hogg, Harper & Row, New York, NY, 1977. 192 pp., illus. $15.95.

A fully comprehensive and illustrated reference work including every major type of weapon used by every army in the world during World War II.

Encyclopedia of Modern Firearms, Vol. 1, compiled and publ. by Bob Brownell, Montezuma, IA, 1959. 1057 pp. plus index, illus. $50.00. Dist. by Bob Brownell, Montezuma, IA 50171.

Massive accumulation of basic information of nearly all modern arms pertaining to "parts and assembly". Replete with arms photographs, exploded drawings, manufacturers' lists of parts, etc.

The FP-45 Liberator Pistol, 1942-1945, by R.W. Koch, Research, Arcadia, CA, 1976. 116 pp., illus. $15.00.

A definitive work on this unique clandestine weapon.

Famous Guns & Gunners, by George E. Virgines, Leather Stocking Press, West Allis, WI, 1980. 113 pp., illus. $12.95.

Intriguing and fascinating tales of men of the West and their guns.

Firearms of the American West, 1803-1865, by Louis A. Garavaglia and Charles G. Worman, University of New Mexico Press, Albuquerque, NM, 1983. 300 pp., illus. $35.00.

An encyclopedic study tracing the development of uses of firearms on the frontier during that period.

The German Sniper, 1914-1945, by Peter R. Senich, Paladin Press, Boulder, CO, 1982. 468 pp., illus. $49.95.

The development and application of Germany's sniping weapons systems and tactics traced from WW I through WW II.

Great Sporting Posters, by Sid Latham, Stackpole Books, Harrisburg, PA, 1980. 48 pp., illus. Paper covers. $19.95.

Twenty-three full-color reproductions of beautiful hunting and fishing poster art, mostly of the early 1900s.

Gun Digest 1987, 41st Edition, edited by Ken Warner, DBI Books, Inc., Northbrook, IL, 1986. 496 pp., illus. Paper covers. $16.95.

All-new articles and fully up-dated catalog section in this most famous of gun annuals.

The Gun Digest Book of Assault Weapons, edited by Jack Lewis, DBI Books, Inc., Northbrook, IL, 1986. 256 pp., illus. Paper covers. $12.95.

An in-depth look at the history and uses, test reports.

Gun Digest Book of Holsters and Other Gun Leather, edited by Roger Combs, DBI Books, Inc., Northbrook, IL, 1983. 256 pp., illus. Paper covers. $11.95.

An in-depth look at all facets of leather goods in conjunction with guns. Covers design, manufacture, uses, etc.

GENERAL (cont.)

Gun Digest Book of Metallic Silhouette Shooting, by Elgin Gates, DBI Books, Inc., Northbrook, IL, 1979. 256 pp., illus. Paper covers. $11.95.

Examines all aspects of this fast growing sport including history, rules and meets.

Gun Digest Book of Modern Gun Values, 5th Edition, by Jack Lewis, ed. by Harold A. Murtz, DBI Books, Inc., Northbrook, IL, 1985. 432 pp., illus. Paper covers. $14.95.

All-new expanded edition covers the current values of all non-military guns in production from 1900-1983.

Gun Digest Book of Scopes and Mounts, by Bob Bell, DBI Books, Inc., Northbrook, IL, 1983. 224 pp., illus. Paper covers. $11.95.

Traces the complete history, design, development of scopes and mounts from their beginnings to the current high-tech level of today. Covers the various uses and applications for the modern shooter/hunter.

Gun Digest Book of Sporting Dogs, by Carl P. Wood, DBI Books, Inc., Northbrook, IL, 1985. 256 pp., illus. Paper covers. $11.95.

Investigates various training philosophies, problem dogs, training for versatility, kenneling, etc. Covers most all hunting/sporting dogs.

Gun Talk, edited by Dave Moreton, Winchester Press, Piscataway, NJ, 1973. 256 pp., illus. $9.95.

A treasury of original writing by the top gun writers and editors in America. Practical advice about every aspect of the shooting sports.

Gun Trader's Guide, 11th Edition, by Paul Wahl, Stoeger Industries, So. Hackensack, NJ, 1984. 415 pp., illus. Paper covers. $12.95.

Complete fully illustrated guide to the identification of modern firearms with current market values.

The Gun That Made the Twenties Roar, by Wm. J. Helmer, rev. and enlarged by George C. Nonte, Jr., The Gun Room Press, Highland Park, NJ, 1977: Over 300 pp., illus. $17.95.

Historical account of John T. Thompson and his invention, the infamous "Tommy Gun."

The Gunfighter, Man or Myth? by Joseph G. Rosa, Oklahoma Press, Norman, OK, 1969. 229 pp., illus. (including weapons). Paper covers. $9.95.

A well-documented work on gunfights and gunfighters of the West and elsewhere. Great treat for all gunfighter buffs.

The Gunfighters, by Dale T. Schoenberger, The Caxton Printers, Ltd., Caldwell, ID, 1971. 207 pp., illus. $18.95.

Startling expose of our foremost Western folk heroes.

Guns of the American West, by Joseph G. Rosa, Crown Publishers, New York, NY, 1985. 192 pp., illus. $24.95.

More than 300 photos, line drawings and engravings complement this lively account of the taming of the West.

Guns of the Gunfighters, by the editors of Guns & Ammo, Crown Publishing Co., New York, NY, 1982. 50 pp., illus. Paper covers. $9.98.

A must for Western buffs and gun collectors alike.

Guns Illustrated, 1987, 19th Edition, edited by Harold A. Murtz, DBI Books, Inc., Northbrook, IL, 1986. 320 pp., illus. Paper covers. $14.95.

Packed with timely interesting articles and solid field testing on a wide variety of firearms.

The Gunsmith in Colonial Virginia, by Harold B. Gill, Jr., University Press of Virginia, Charlottesville, VA, 1975. 200 pp., illus. $11.95.

The role of the gunsmith in colonial Virginia from the first landing at Jamestown through the Revolution is examined, with special attention to those who lived and worked in Williamsburg.

Guns & Shooting: A Selected Bibliography, by Ray Riling, Ray Riling Arms Books Co., Phila., PA, 1982. 434 pp., illus. Limited, numbered edition. $75.00.

A limited edition of this superb bibliographical work, the only modern listing of books devoted to guns and shooting.

Hatcher's Notebook, by Maj. Gen. J. S. Hatcher. Stackpole Books, Harrisburg, Pa., 1952. 2nd ed. with four new chapters, 1957. 629 pp., illus. $24.95.

A dependable source of information for gunsmiths, ballisticians, historians, hunters, and collectors.

"Hell, I Was There!", by Elmer Keith, Peterson Publishing Co., Los Angeles, CA, 1979. 308 pp., illus. $19.50.

Adventures of a Montana cowboy who gained world fame as a big game hunter.

Hit the White Part, by Massad Ayoob, Concord, NH, 1982. 107 pp., illus. Paper covers. $7.95.

Second Chance, the art of bowling pin shooting.

How to Make Practical Pistol Leather, by J. David McFarland, Desert Publications, Cornville, AZ. 1982. 68 pp., illus. Paper covers. $8.00.

A guide for designing and making holsters and accessories for law enforcement, security, survival and sporting use.

The Identification and Registration of Firearms, by Vaclav "Jack" Krcma, C. C. Thomas, Springfield, IL, 1971. 173 pp., illus. $25.00.

Analysis of problems and improved techniques of recording firearms data accurately.

Kill or Get Killed, by Col. Rex Applegate, new rev. and enlarged ed. Paladin Press, Boulder, CO, 1976. 421 pp., illus. $19.95.

For police and military forces. Last word on mob control.

The Law Enforcement Book of Weapons, Ammunition and Training Procedures, Handguns, Rifles and Shotguns, by Mason Williams, Charles C. Thomas, Publisher, Springfield, IL, 1977. 496 pp., illus. $40.00.

Data on firearms, firearm training, and ballistics.

Law Enforcement Handgun Digest, 3rd Edition, by Jack Lewis, DBI Books, Inc., Northbrook, IL, 1980. 288 pp., illus. Paper covers. $10.95.

Covers such subjects as the philosophy of a firefight, SWAT, weapons, training, combat shooting, etc.

Lyman Muzzleloader's Handbook, 2nd Edition, edited by C. Kenneth Ramage, Lyman Publications, Middlefield, CT, 1982. 248 pp., illus. Paper covers. $11.95.

Hunting with rifles and shotguns, plus muzzle loading products.

The Manufacture of Gunflints, by Sydney B.J. Skertchly, facsimile reprint with new introduction by Seymour de Lotbiniere, Museum Restoration Service, Ontario, Canada, 1984. 90 pp., illus. $24.50.

Limited edition reprinting of the very scarce London edition of 1879.

Medicolegal Investigation of Gunshot Wounds, by Abdullah Fatteh, J.B. Lippincott Co., Phila., PA, 1977. 272 pp., illus. $35.00.

A much-needed work, clearly written and easily understood, dealing with all aspects of medicolegal investigation of gunshot wounds and deaths.

Military Small Arms of the 20th Century, 5th Edition, by Ian V. Hogg and John Weeks, DBI Books, Inc., Northbrook, IL, 1985. 304 pp., illus. Paper covers. $14.95.

Fully revised and updated edition of the standard reference in its field.

Modern Airweapon Shooting, by Bob Churchill & Granville Davis, David & Charles, London, England, 1981. 196 pp., illus. $20.00.

A comprehensive, illustrated study of all the relevant topics, from beginnings to world championship shooting.

Modern Small Arms, by Major Frederick Myatt, Crescent Books, New York, NY, 1978. 240 pp., illus. $12.98.

An illustrated encyclopedia of famous military firearms from 1873 to the present day.

No Second Place Winner, by Wm. H. Jordan, publ. by the author, Shreveport, LA (Box 4072), 1962. 114 pp., illus. $12.50.

Guns and gear of the peace officer, ably discussed by a U.S. Border Patrolman for over 30 years, and a first-class shooter with handgun, rifle, etc.

Olson's Encyclopedia of Small Arms, by John Olson, Winchester Press, Piscataway, NJ, 1985. 336 pp., illus. $22.95.

The most complete, authoritative, and up-to-date reference available for shooters, ballisticians, gun collectors, and everyone interested in firearms.

Olympic Shooting, by Colonel Jim Crossman, NRA, Washington, DC, 1978. 136 pp., illus. $12.95.

The complete, authoritative history of U.S. participation in the Olympic shooting events from 1896 until the present.

Pistols of the World, Revised Edition, by Ian V. Hogg and John Weeks, DBI Books, Inc., Northbrook, IL, 1982. 304 pp., illus. Paper covers. $12.95.

Revised, single-volume encyclopedia begins in 1870 and follows the development of the hand-held weapon through today. 2000 handguns are described.

E.C. Prudhomme, Master Gun Engraver, A Retrospective Exhibition: 1946-1973, intro. by John T. Amber, The R.W. Norton Art Gallery, Shreveport, LA, 1973. 32 pp., illus., paper covers. $5.00.

Examples of master gun engraving by Jack Prudhomme.

The Quiet Killers II: Silencer Update, by J. David Truby, Paladin Press, Boulder, CO, 1979. 92 pp., illus. Paper covers. $8.00.

A unique and up-to-date addition to your silencer bookshelf.

Shooter's Bible, 1987, No. 78, edited by William Jarrett, Stoeger Publishing Co., So. Hackensack, NJ, 1986. 576 pp., illus. Paper covers. $12.95.

A standard firearms reference book for decades.

The Shooter's Workbench, by John A. Mosher, Winchester Press, Piscataway, NJ, 1977. 256 pp., illus. $22.50.

Accessories the shooting sportsman can build for the range or shop, for transport and the field, and for the handloading bench.

Small Arms Today, by Edward Ezell, Stackpole Books, Harrisburg, PA, 1984. 224 pp., illus. Paper covers. $16.95.

Latest reports on the world's weapons and ammunition.

Small Arms of the World, 12th Edition, by W.H.B. Smith, revised by Edward C. Ezell, Stackpole Books, Harrisburg, PA, 1983. 1,024 pp., illus. $49.95.

An encyclopedia of global weapons—over 3,500 entries.

Sporting Arms of the World, by Ray Bearse, Outdoor Life/Harper & Row, N.Y., 1977. 500 pp., illus. $15.95.

A mammoth, up-to-the-minute guide to the sporting world's favorite rifles, shotguns, handguns.

Street Survival Tactics for Armed Encounters, by Ronald J. Adams, et al, Calibre Press, Northbrook, IL, 1983. 403 pp., illus. $25.95.

Positive tactics to employ on the street to effectively use firearms to defeat assailants.

Stress Fire, Vol. 1: Stress Fighting for Police, by Massad Ayoob, Police Bookshelf, Concord, NH, 1984. 149 pp., illus. Paper covers. $9.95.

Gunfighting for police, advanced tactics and techniques.

Thompson Guns 1921-1945, Anubis Press, Houston, TX, 1980. 215 pp., illus. Paper covers. $10.00.

Facsimile reprinting of five complete manuals on the Thompson submachine gun.

The Trapper's Handbook, by Rick Jamison, DBI Books, Inc., Northbrook, IL, 1983. 224 pp., illus. Paper covers. $11.95.

Gives the ins and outs of successful trapping from making scent to marketing the pelts. Tips and solutions to trapping problems.

A Treasury of Outdoor Life, edited by William E. Rae, Stackpole Books, Harrisburg, PA, 1983. 520 pp., illus. $24.95.

The greatest hunting, fishing, and survival stories from America's favorite sportsman's magazine.

Triggernometry, by Eugene Cunningham. Caxton Printers Lt., Caldwell, ID, 1970. 441 pp., illus. $14.95.

A classic study of famous outlaws and lawmen of the West—their stature as human beings, their exploits and skills in handling firearms. A reprint.

Weapons of the American Revolution, and Accoutrements, by Warren Moore. A & W Books, NY, 1974. 225 pp., fine illus. $15.00.

Revolutionary era shoulder arms, pistols, edged weapons, and equipment are described and shown in fine drawings and photographs, some in color.

The Winchester Era, by David Madis, Art & Reference House, Brownsville, TX, 1984. 100 pp., illus. $14.95.

Story of the Winchester company, management, employees, etc.

You Can't Miss, by John Shaw and Michael Bane, John Shaw, Memphis, TN, 1983. 152 pp., illus. Paper covers. $9.95.

The secrets of a successful combat shooter; tells how to better your defensive shooting skills.

Gunsmithing

The Art of Engraving, by James B. Meek, F. Brownell & Son, Montezuma, IA, 1973. 196 pp., illus. $24.95.
A complete, authoritative, imaginative and detailed study in training for gun engraving. The first book of its kind—and a great one.

Artistry in Arms, The R.W. Norton Gallery, Shreveport, LA., 1970. 42 pp., illus. Paper, $5.00.
The art of gunsmithing and engraving.

Building the Kentucky Pistol, by James R. Johnston, Golden Age Arms Co., Worthington, OH, 1974. 36 pp., illus. Paper covers. $4.00.
A step-by-step guide for building the Kentucky pistol. Illus. with full page line drawings.

Building the Kentucky Rifle, by J.R. Johnston. Golden Age Arms Co., Worthington, OH, 1972. 44 pp., illus. Paper covers. $5.00.
How to go about it, with text and drawings.

Checkering and Carving of Gun Stocks, by Monte Kennedy. Stackpole Books, Harrisburg, PA, 1962. 175 pp., illus. $27.95.
Rev., enlarged clothbound ed. of a much sought-after, dependable work.

Clyde Baker's Modern Gunsmithing, revised by John E. Traister, Stackpole Books, Harrisburg, PA, 1981. 530 pp., illus. $24.95.
A revision of the classic work on gunsmithing.

The Complete Rehabilitation of the Flintlock Rifle and Other Works, by T.B. Tyron. Limbo Library, Taos, NM, 1972. 112 pp., illus. Paper covers. $6.95.
A series of articles which first appeared in various issues of the *American Rifleman* in the 1930s.

Contemporary American Stockmakers, by Ron Toews, The Dove Press, Enid, OK, 1979. 216 pp., illus. $80.00.
The only reference book on its subject. Over 200 detailed photographs of fine rifle stocking.

Do-It-Yourself Gunsmithing, by Jim Carmichel, Outdoor Life-Harper & Row, New York, NY, 1977. 371 pp., illus. $16.95.
The author proves that home gunsmithing is relatively easy and highly satisfying.

Firearms Assembly 3: The NRA Guide to Rifle and Shotguns, NRA Books, Wash., D.C., 1980. 264 pp., illus. Paper covers. $11.50.
Text and illustrations explaining the takedown of 125 rifles and shotguns, domestic and foreign.

Firearms Assembly 4: The NRA Guide to Pistols and Revolvers, NRA Books, Wash., D.C., 1980. 253 pp., illus. Paper covers. $11.50.
Text and illustrations explaining the takedown of 124 pistol and revolver models, domestic and foreign.

Firearms Blueing and Browning, by R.H. Angier. Stackpole Books, Harrisburg, PA, 151 pp., illus. $12.95.
A useful, concise text on chemical coloring methods for the gunsmith and mechanic.

First Book of Gunsmithing, by John E. Traister, Stackpole Books, Harrisburg, PA, 1981. 192 pp., illus. $18.95.
Beginner's guide to gun care, repair and modification.

Gun Care and Repair, by Monte Burch, Winchester Press, Piscataway, NJ, 1978. 256 pp., illus. $15.95.
Everything the gun owner needs to know about home gunsmithing and firearms maintenance.

Gun Digest Book of Exploded Firearms Drawings, 3rd Edition edited by Harold A. Murtz, DBI Books, Inc., Northbrook, IL, 1982. 480 pp., illus. Paper covers. $14.95.
Contains 470 isometric views of modern and collector's handguns and long guns, with parts lists. A must for the gunsmith or tinkerer.

The Gun Digest Book of Firearms Assembly/Disassembly Part I: Automatic Pistols, by J.B. Wood, DBI Books, Inc., Northbrook, IL, 1979. 320 pp., illus. Paper covers. $12.95.
A thoroughly professional presentation on the art of pistol disassembly and reassembly. Covers most modern guns, popular older models, and some of the most complex pistols ever produced.

The Gun Digest Book of Firearms Assembly/Disassembly Part II: Revolvers, by J. B. Wood, DBI Books, Inc., Northbrook, IL, 1979. 320 pp., illus. Paper covers. $12.95.
How to properly dismantle and reassemble both the revolvers of today and of the past.

The Gun Digest Book of Firearms Assembly/Disassembly Part III: Rimfire Rifles, by J.B. Wood, DBI Books, Inc., Northbrook, IL, 1980. 288 pp., illus. Paper covers. $12.95.
A most comprehensive, uniform, and professional presentation available for disassembling and reassembling most rimfire rifles.

The Gun Digest Book of Firearms Assembly/Disassembly Part IV: Centerfire Rifles, by J. B. Wood, DBI Books, Inc., Northbrook, IL, 1980. 288 pp., illus. Paper covers. $12.95.
A professional presentation on the disassembly and reassembly of centerfire rifles.

The Gun Digest Book of Firearms Assembly/Disassembly, Part V: Shotguns, by J.B. Wood, DBI Books, Inc., Northbrook, IL, 1980. 288 pp., illus. Paper covers. $12.95.
A professional presentation on the complete disassembly and assembly of 26 of the most popular shotguns, new and old.

The Gun Digest Book of Firearms Assembly/Disassembly Part VI: Law Enforcement Weapons, by J.B. Wood, DBI Books, Inc., Northbrook, IL, 1981. 288 pp., illus. Paper covers. $12.95.
Step-by-step instructions on how to completely dismantle and reassemble the most commonly used firearms found in law enforcement arsenals.

Gun Digest Book of Gun Care, Cleaning and Refinishing, Book One: Handguns, by J.B. Wood, DBI Books, Inc., Northbrook, IL, 1984. 160 pp., illus. Paper covers. $9.95.
The how, when and why of proper maintenance: revolvers, autoloaders, blackpowder handguns.

Gun Digest Book of Gun Care, Cleaning and Refinishing, Book Two: Long Guns, by J.B. Wood, DBI Books, Inc., Northbrook, IL, 1984. 160 pp., illus. Paper covers. $9.95.
The care and maintenance of long guns with meticulous detail and step-by-step, illustrated, clearly written text.

Gun Digest Book of Gunsmithing Tools and Their Uses, by John E. Traister, DBI Books, Inc., Northbrook, IL, 1980. 256 pp., illus. Paper covers. $10.95.
The how, when and why of tools for amateur and professional gunsmiths and gun tinkerers.

The Gun Digest Book of Pistolsmithing, by Jack Mitchell, DBI Books, Inc., Northbrook, IL, 1980. 288 pp., illus. Paper covers. $11.95.
An expert's guide to the operation of each of the handgun actions with all the major functions of pistolsmithing explained.

Gun Digest Book of Riflesmithing, by Jack Mitchell, DBI Books, Inc., Northbrook, IL, 1982. 256 pp., illus. Paper covers. $11.95.
The art and science of rifle gunsmithing. Covers tools, techniques, designs, finishing wood and metal, custom alterations.

Gun Digest Book of Shotgun Gunsmithing, by Ralph Walker, DBI Books, Inc., Northbrook, IL, 1983. 256 pp., illus. Paper covers. $11.95.
The principles and practices of repairing, individualizing and accurizing modern shotguns by one of the world's premier shotgun gunsmiths.

Gun Owner's Book of Care, Repair & Improvement, by Roy Dunlap, Outdoor Life-Harper & Row, NY, 1977. 336 pp., illus. $12.95.
A basic guide to repair and maintenance of guns, written for the average firearms owner.

Guns and Gunmaking Tools of Southern Appalachia, by John Rice Irwin, Schiffer Publishing Ltd., 1983. 118 pp., illus. Paper covers. $9.95.
The story of the Kentucky rifle.

Gunsmith Kinks, by F.R. (Bob) Brownell. F. Brownell & Son, Montezuma, IA, 1st ed., 1969. 496 pp., well illus. $12.95.
A widely useful accumulation of shop kinks, short cuts, techniques and pertinent comments by practicing gunsmiths from all over the world.

Gunsmith Kinks 2, by Bob Brownell, F. Brownell & Son, Publishers, Montezuma, IA, 1983. 496 pp., illus. $14.95.
An incredible collection of gunsmithing knowledge, shop kinks, new and old techniques, short-cuts and general know-how straight from those who do them best—the gunsmiths.

Gunsmithing, by Roy F. Dunlap. Stackpole Books, Harrisburg, PA, 714 pp., illus. $27.95.
Comprehensive work on conventional techniques, incl. recent advances in the field. Valuable to rifle owners, shooters, and practicing gunsmiths.

Gunsmithing at Home, by John E. Traister, Stoeger Publishing Co., So. Hackensack, NJ, 1985. 256 pp., illus. Paper covers. $11.95.
Over 25 chapters of explicit information on every aspect of gunsmithing.

Gunsmithing: The Tricks of the Trade, by J.B. Wood, DBI Books, Inc., Northbrook, IL, 1982. 256 pp., illus. Paper covers. $11.95.
How to repair and replace broken gun parts using ordinary home workshop tools.

Gunsmiths and Gunmakers of Vermont, by Warren R. Horn, The Horn Co., Burlington, VT, 1976. 76 pp., illus. Paper covers. $6.95.
A checklist for collectors, of over 200 craftsmen who lived and worked in Vermont up to and including 1900.

The Gunsmith's Manual, by J.P. Stelle and Wm.B. Harrison, The Gun Room Press, Highland Park, NJ, 1982. 376 pp., illus. $12.95.
For the gunsmith in all branches of the trade.

Gunstock Finishing and Care, by A. Donald Newell, Stackpole Books, Harrisburg, PA, 1982. 512 pp., illus. $22.95.
The most complete resource imaginable for finishing and refinishing gun wood.

Home Gun Care & Repair, by P.O. Ackley, Stackpole Books, Harrisburg, PA, 1969. 191 pp., illus. Paper covers. $6.95.
Basic reference for safe tinkering, fixing, and converting rifles, shotguns, handguns.

Home Gunsmithing Digest, 3rd Edition, by Tommy L. Bish, DBI Books, Inc., Northbrook, IL, 1984. 256 pp., illus. Paper covers. $11.95.
The know-how supplied by an expert.

How to Build Your Own Wheellock Rifle or Pistol, by George Lauber, The John Olson Co., Paramus, NJ, 1976. Paper covers. $12.50.
Complete instructions on building these arms.

How to Build Your Own Flintlock Rifle or Pistol, by George Lauber, The John Olson Co., Paramus, NJ, 1976. Paper covers. $12.50.
The second in Mr. Lauber's three-volume series on the art and science of building muzzle-loading black powder firearms.

"How to Build Your Own Percussion Rifle or Pistol", by George Lauber, The John Olson Co., Paramus, NJ, 1976. Paper covers, $12.50.
The third and final volume of Lauber's set of books on the building of muzzle-loaders.

Learn Gunsmithing, by John Traister, Winchester Press, Piscataway, NJ, 1980. 202 pp., illus. $16.95.
The troubleshooting method of gunsmithing for the home gunsmith and professional alike.

Lock, Stock and Barrel, by R.H. McCrory. Publ. by author at Bellmore, NY, 1966. 122 pp., illus. $6.00.
A handy and useful work for the collector or the professional with many helpful procedures shown and described on antique gun repair.

Mr. Single Shot's Gunsmithing Idea Book, by Frank DeHaas, Tab Books, Inc., Blue Ridge Summit, PA, 1983. 168 pp., illus. $18.95.
A must-have manual for anyone interested in collecting, repairing, or modifying single-shot rifles.

GUNSMITHING (cont.)

The Modern Kentucky Rifle, How to Build Your Own, by R.H. McCrory. McCrory, Wantagh, NY, 1961. 68 pp., illus., paper bound. $6.00.

A workshop manual on how to fabricate a flintlock rifle. Also some information on pistols and percussion locks.

The NRA Gunsmithing Guide—Updated, by Ken Raynor and Brad Fenton, National Rifle Association, Wash., DC, 1984. 336 pp., illus. Paper covers. $15.95.

Material includes chapters and articles on all facets of the gunsmithing art.

Pistolsmithing, by George C. Nonte, Jr., Stackpole Books, Harrisburg, PA, 1974. 560 pp., illus. $27.95.

A single source reference to handgun maintenance, repair, and modification at home, unequaled in value.

Professional Care and Finishing of Gun Metal, by John E. Traister, Tab Books, Inc., Blue Ridge Summit, PA, 1982. 303 pp., illus. Paper covers. $12.95.

Restore old and antique firearms into handsome workable possessions.

Professional Gunsmithing, by W.J. Howe, Stackpole Books, Harrisburg, PA, 1968 reprinting. 526 pp., illus. $24.95.

Textbook on repair and alteration of firearms, with detailed notes on equipment and commercial gunshop operation.

Recreating the American Longrifle, by William Buchele, et al, George Shumway, Publisher, York, PA, 1983. 175 pp., illus. Paper covers. $20.00; Cloth $27.50.

Includes full-scale plans for building a Kentucky rifle.

Respectfully Yours H.M. Pope, compiled and edited by G.O. Kelver, Brighton, CO, 1976. 266 pp., illus. $16.50.

A compilation of letters from the files of the famous barrelmaker, Harry M. Pope.

The Trade Gun Sketchbook, by Charles E. Hanson, The Fur Press, Chadron, NB, 1979. 48 pp., illus. Paper covers. $4.00.

Complete full-size plans to build seven different trade guns from the Revolution to the Indian Wars and a two-thirds size for your son.

The Trade Rifle Sketchbook, by Charles E. Hanson, The Fur Press, Chadron, NB, 1979. 48 pp., illus. Paper covers. $4.00.

Includes full scale plans for ten rifles made for Indian and mountain men; from 1790 to 1860, plus plans for building three pistols.

handguns

American Pistol and Revolver Design and Performance, by L. R. Wallack, Winchester Press, Piscataway, NJ, 1978. 224 pp., illus. $19.95.

How different types and models of pistols and revolvers work, from trigger pull to bullet impact.

American Police Handgun Training, by Charles R. Skillen and Mason Williams, Charles C. Thomas, Springfield, IL, 1980. 216 pp., illus. $21.50.

Deals comprehensively with all phases of current handgun training procedures in America.

Askins on Pistols and Revolvers, by Col. Charles Askins, NRA Books, Wash., D.C., 1980. 144 pp., illus. Paper covers. $14.95.

A book full of practical advice, shooting tips, technical analysis and stories of guns in action.

The Black Powder Handgun by Sam Fadala, DBI Books, Inc., Northbrook, IL, 1981. 288 pp., illus. Paper covers. $11.95.

The author covers this oldtimer in all its forms: pistols and six-shooters in both small and large bore, target and hunting.

Blue Steel and Gun Leather, by John Bianchi, Beinfeld Publishing, Inc., No. Hollywood, CA, 1978. 200 pp., illus. $12.00.

A complete and comprehensive review of holster uses plus an examination of available products on today's market.

Browning Hi-Power Pistols, Desert Publications, Cornville, AZ, 1982. 20 pp., illus. Paper covers. $6.00.

Covers all facets of the various military and civilian models of this gun.

The Browning High Power Automatic Pistol, by R. Blake Stevens, Collector Grade Publications, Toronto, Canada, 1984. 271 pp., illus. $39.95.

Exhaustive new treatise on this famous automatic pistol.

Colt Automatic Pistols, by Donald B. Bady, Borden Publ. Co., Alhambra, CA, 1974. 368 pp., illus. $18.50.

The rev. and enlarged ed. of a key work on a fascinating subject. Complete information on every automatic marked with Colt's name.

The Colt .45 Auto Pistol, compiled from U.S. War Dept. Technical Manuals, and reprinted by Desert Publications, Cornville, AZ, 1978. 80 pp., illus. Paper covers. $7.50.

Covers every facet of this famous pistol from mechanical training, manual of arms, disassembly, repair and replacement of parts.

Combat Handgun Shooting, by James D. Mason, Charles C. Thomas, Springfield, IL, 1976. 256 pp., illus. $27.50.

Discusses in detail the human as well as the mechanical aspects of shooting.

Combat Handguns, edited by Edward C. Ezell, Stackpole Books, Harrisburg, PA, 1980. 288 pp., illus. $19.95.

George Nonte's last great work, edited by Edward C. Ezell. A comprehensive reference volume offering full coverage of automatic handguns vs. revolvers, custom handguns, combat autoloaders and revolvers—domestic and foreign, and combat testing.

Combat Shooting for Police, by Paul B. Weston. Charles C. Thomas, Springfield, IL, 1967. A reprint. 194 pp., illus. $20.00.

First publ. in 1960 this popular self-teaching manual gives basic concepts of defensive fire in every position.

The Complete Book of Combat Handgunning, by Chuck Taylor, Desert Publications, Cornville, AZ, 1982. 168 pp., illus. Paper covers. $12.95.

Covers virtually every aspect of combat handgunning.

The Defensive Use of the Handgun for the Novice, by Mason Williams, Charles C. Thomas, Publisher, Springfield, IL, 1980. 226 pp., illus. $20.00.

This book was developed for the home owner, housewife, elderly couple, and the woman who lives alone. Basic instruction for purchasing, loading and firing pistols and revolvers.

Fast and Fancy Revolver Shooting, by Ed. McGivern, Anniversary Edition, Winchester Press, Piscataway, NJ, 1984. 484 pp., illus. $15.95.

A fascinating volume, packed with handgun lore and solid information by the acknowledged dean of revolver shooters.

Flattops & Super Blackhawks, by H.W. Ross, Jr., H.W. Ross, Jr., Bridgeville, PA, 1979. 93 pp., illus. Paper covers. $9.95.

An expanded version of the author's book "Ruger Blackhawks" with an extra chapter on Super Blackhawks and the Mag-Na-Ports with serial numbers and approximate production dates.

The Gun Digest Book of Autoloading Pistols, by Dean A. Grennell, DBI Books, Inc., Northbrook, IL, 1983. 288 pp., illus. Paper covers. $11.95.

History, operating principles and firing techniques for rimfire, military/police, competition, hunting, assault autos, value trends.

The Gun Digest Book of Combat Handgunnery, by Jack Lewis and Jack Mitchell, DBI Books, Inc., Northbrook, IL, 1983. 288 pp., illus. Paper covers. $11.95.

From the basics to competition, training and exercises.

Gun Digest Book of Firearms Assembly/Disassembly Part I: Automatic Pistols, by J.B. Wood, DBI Books, Inc., Northbrook, IL, 1979. 320 pp., illus. Paper covers. $12.95.

A thoroughly professional presentation on the art of pistol disassembly and reassembly. Covers most modern guns, popular older models, and some of the most complex pistols ever produced.

Gun Digest Book of Firearms Assembly/Disassembly Part II: Revolvers, by J.B. Wood, DBI Books, Inc., Northbrook, IL, 1979. 320 pp., illus. Paper covers. $12.95.

How to properly dismantle and reassemble both the revolvers of today and of the past.

Gun Digest Book of Gun Care, Cleaning and Refinishing, Book One: Handguns, by J.B. Wood, DBI Books, Inc., Northbrook, IL, 1984. 160 pp., illus. Paper covers. $9.95.

The how, when and why of proper maintenance: revolvers, autoloaders, blackpowder handguns.

The Gun Digest Book of 9mm Handguns, by Dean A. Grennell and Wiley Clapp, DBI Books, Inc., Northbrook, IL, 1986. 256 pp., illus. Paper covers. $12.95

The definitive book on the 9mm pistol.

The Gun Digest Book of Pistolsmithing, by Jack Mitchell, DBI Books, Inc., Northbrook, IL, 1980. 288 pp., illus. Paper covers. $11.95.

An expert's guide to the operation of each of the handgun actions with all the major functions of pistolsmithing explained.

Gun Digest Book of Single Action Revolvers, by Jack Lewis, DBI Books, Inc., Northbrook, IL, 1982. 256 pp., illus. Paper covers. $11.95.

A fond, in-depth look at the venerable "wheelgun" from its earliest days through today's latest developments.

Hallock's .45 Auto Handbook, by Ken Hallock, The Mihan Co., Oklahoma City, OK, 1981. 178 pp., illus. Paper covers. $11.95.

For gunsmiths, dealers, collectors and serious hobbyists.

A Handbook on the Primary Identification of Revolvers & Semi-automatic Pistols, by John T. Millard, Charles C. Thomas, Springfield, IL, 1974. 156 pp., illus. Paper covers. $15.00.

A practical outline on the simple, basic phases of primary firearm identification with particular reference to revolvers and semi-automatic pistols.

Handguns for Self Defence, by Gerry Gore, Macmillan South Africa, Johannesburg, South Africa, 1981. 164 pp., illus. Paper covers. $15.00.

Choosing the gun, basic skills, the draws, stopping power, etc.

Handguns of the World, by Edward C. Ezell, Stackpole Books, Harrisburg, PA., 1981. 704 pp., illus. $39.95.

Encyclopedia for identification and historical reference that will be appreciated by gun enthusiasts, collectors, hobbyists or professionals.

Handloading for Handgunners, by Geo. C. Nonte, DBI Books, Inc., Northbrook, IL, 1978. 288 pp., illus. Paper covers. $11.95.

An expert tells the ins and outs of this specialized facet of reloading.

High Standard Automatic Pistols 1932-1950, by Charles E. Petty, American Ordnance Publ., Charlotte, NC, 1976. 124 pp., illus. $15.00.

A definitive source of information for the collector of High Standard pistols.

The Illustrated Encyclopedia of Pistols and Revolvers, by Major Frederick Myatt, Crescent Books, New York, NY, 1980. 208 pp., illus. $14.95.

An illustrated history of handguns from the 16th century to the present day.

Know Your 45 Auto Pistols—Models 1911 & A1, by E.J. Hoffschmidt, Blacksmith Corp., Southport, CT, 1974. 58 pp., illus. Paper covers. $6.95.

A concise history of the gun with a wide variety of types and copies.

Know Your Walther P.38 Pistols, by E.J. Hoffschmidt, Blacksmith Corp., Southport, CT, 1974. 77 pp., illus. Paper covers. $6.95.

Covers the Walther models Armee, M.P., H.P., P.38—history and variations.

Know Your Walther P.P. & P.P.K. Pistols, by E.J. Hoffschmidt, Blacksmith Corp., Southport, CT, 1975. 87 pp., illus. Paper covers. $6.95.

A concise history of the guns with a guide to the variety and types.

Law Enforcement Handgun Digest, 3rd Edition, by Jack Lewis, DBI Books, Inc., Northbrook, IL, 1980. 288 pp., illus. Paper covers. $10.95.

Covers such subjects as the philosophy of a firefight, SWAT weapons, training, combat shooting, etc.

HANDGUNS (cont.)

The Luger Pistol (Pistole Parabellum), by F.A. Datig. Borden Publ. Co., Alhambra, CA, 1962. 328 pp., well illus. $14.95.

An enlarged, rev. ed. of an important reference on the arm, its history and development from 1893 to 1945.

Luger Variations, by Harry E. Jones, Harry E. Jones, Torrance, CA, 1975. 328 pp., 160 full page illus., many in color. $35.00.

A rev. ed. of the book known as "The Luger Collector's Bible".

Lugers at Random, by Charles Kenyon, Jr., Handgun Press, Chicago, IL. 1st ed., 1970. 416 pp., profusely illus. $25.00.

An impressive large side-opening book carrying throughout alternate facing-pages of descriptive text and clear photographs. A new boon to the Luger collector and/or shooter.

Mauser Pocket Pistols 1910-1946, by Roy G. Pender, Collectors Press, Houston, TX, 1971. 307 pp. $25.00.

Comprehensive work covering over 100 variations, including factory boxes and manuals. Over 300 photos. Limited, numbered ed.

The Mauser Self-Loading Pistol, by Belford & Dunlap, Borden Publ. Co., Alhambra, CA. Over 200 pp., 300 illus., large format. $18.50.

The long-awaited book on the "Broom Handles", covering their inception in 1894 to the end of production. Complete and in detail: pocket pistols, Chinese and Spanish copies, etc.

Modern American Centerfire Handguns, by Stanley W. T. Trzoniec, Winchester Press, Piscataway, NJ, 1981. 260 pp., illus. $24.95.

The most comprehensive reference on handguns in print.

The New Handbook of Handgunning, by Paul B. Weston, Charles C. Thomas, Publisher, Springfield, IL, 1980. 102 pp., illus. $20.00.

A step-by-step, how-to manual of handgun shooting.

The Pistol Book, by John Walter, Arms & Armour Press, London, England, 1983. 176 pp., illus. $19.95.

A concise and copiously illustrated guide to the handguns available today.

The Pistol Guide, by George C. Nonte, Stoeger Publ. Co., So. Hackensack, NJ, 1980. 256 pp., illus. Paper covers. $10.95.

A unique and detailed examination of a very specialized type of gun: the autoloading pistol.

Pistol & Revolver Digest, 3rd Edition, by Dean A. Grennell, DBI Books, Inc., Northbrook, IL, 1982. 288 pp., illus. Paper covers. $11.95.

The latest developments in handguns, shooting, ammunition, and accessories, with catalog.

Pistol & Revolver Guide, 3rd Ed., by George C. Nonte, Stoeger Publ. Co., So. Hackensack, NJ, 1975. 224 pp., illus. Paper covers. $6.95.

The standard reference work on military and sporting handguns.

The Pistols of Germany and Its Allies in Two World Wars, by Jan C. Still, Douglas, AK, 1983. 145 pp., illus. Paper covers. $12.95.

Military pistols of Imperial Germany and her World War I Allies and postwar military, paramilitary and police reworks.

Pistols of the World, Revised Edition, by Ian V. Hogg and John Weeks, DBI Books, Inc., Northbrook, IL, 1982. 306 pp., illus. $12.95.

A valuable reference for collectors and everyone interested in guns.

Police Handgun Manual, by Bill Clede, Stackpole Books, Inc., Harrisburg, PA, 1985. 128 pp., illus. $11.95.

How to get street-smart survival habits.

Quick or Dead, by William L. Cassidy, Paladin Press, Boulder, CO, 1978. 178 pp., illus. $12.95.

Close-quarter combat firing, with particular reference to prominent twentieth-century British and American methods of instruction.

Report of Board on Tests of Revolvers and Automatic Pistols. From the *Annual Report* of the Chief of Ordnance, 1907. Reprinted by J.C. Tillinghast, Marlow, NH, 1969. 34 pp., 7 plates, paper covers. $5.00.

A comparison of handguns, including Luger, Savage, Colt, Webley-Fosbery and other makes.

Revolvers, by Ian V. Hogg, Arms & Armour Press, London, England, 1984. 72 pp., illus. $12.95.

An illustrated guide with prices based on recent auction records.

Revolver Guide, by George C. Nonte, Jr., Stoeger Publishing Co., So. Hackensack, NJ, 1980. 288 pp., illus. Paper covers. $10.95.

Fully illustrated guide to selecting, shooting, caring for and collecting revolvers of all types.

Ruger Automatic Pistols and Single Action Revolvers, Book 3, by Hugo A. Lueders, Blacksmith Corp., Southport, CT, 1983. 95 pp., illus. Paper covers. $17.50.

A key reference for every Ruger enthusiast, collector and dealer.

Shoot a Handgun, by Dave Arnold, PVA Books, Canyon County, CA, 1983. 144 pp., illus. Paper covers. $8.95.

A complete manual of simplified handgun instruction.

Sixgun Cartridges and Loads, by Elmer Keith, reprint edition by The Gun Room Press, Highland Park, NJ, 1984. 151 pp., illus. $19.95.

A manual covering the selection, use and loading of the most suitable and popular revolver cartridges.

Target Pistol Shooting, by K.B. Hinchliffe, David and Charles, London, 1981. 235 pp., illus. $25.00.

A complete guide to target shooting designed to give the novice and expert guidance on the correct techniques for holding, aiming, and firing pistols.

The Walther P-38 Pistol, by Maj. Geo. C. Nonte, Paladin Press, Boulder, CO, 1975. 90 pp., illus. Paper covers. $7.50.

Covers all facets of the gun—development, history, variations, technical data, practical use, rebuilding, repair and conversion.

The Women's Guide to Handguns, by Jim Carmichel, Stoeger Publishing Co., So. Hackensack, NJ, 1984. 190 pp., illus. Paper covers. $8.95.

For women interested in learning how to select, buy, store, carry, care for and use a handgun.

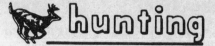

hunting

NORTH AMERICA

Advanced Wild Turkey Hunting & World Records, by Dave Harbour, Winchester Press, Piscataway, NJ, 1983. 264 pp., illus. $19.95.

The definitive book, written by an authority who has studied turkeys and turkey calling for over 40 years.

After Your Deer Is Down, by Josef Fischl and Leonard Lee Rue, III, Winchester Press, Piscataway, NJ, 1981. 160 pp., illus. Paper covers. $10.95.

The care and handling of big game, with a bonus of venison recipes.

Alaska Game Trails with a Master Guide, by Charles J. Keim, Alaska Northwest Publishing Co., Anchorage, AK, 1984. 310 pp., illus. Paper covers. $6.95.

High adventure tales of fair chase with Alaska's first master guide, Hal Waugh.

All About Deer in America, edited by Robert Elman, Winchester Press, Piscataway, NJ, 1976. 256 pp., illus. $15.95.

Twenty of America's great hunters share the secrets of their hunting success.

All About Small-Game Hunting in America, edited by Russell Tinsley, Winchester Press, Piscataway, NJ, 1976. 308 pp., illus. $16.95.

Collected advice by the finest small-game experts in the country.

All About Varmint Hunting, by Nick Sisley, The Stone Wall Press, Inc., Wash., DC, 1982. 182 pp., illus. Paper covers. $8.95.

The most comprehensive up-to-date book on hunting common varmints found throughout North America.

All About Wildfowling in America, by Jerome Knap, Winchester Press, Piscataway, NJ, 1977. 256 pp., illus. $13.95.

More than a dozen top writers provide new and controversial ideas on how and where to hunt waterfowl successfully.

All-American Deer Hunter's Guide, edited by Jim Zumbo and Robert Elman, Winchester Press, Piscataway, NJ, 1983. 320 pp., illus. $29.95.

The most comprehensive, thorough book yet published on American deer hunting.

All Season Hunting, by Bob Gilsvik, Winchester Press, Piscataway, NJ, 1976. 256 pp., illus. $14.95.

A guide to early-season, late-season and winter hunting in America.

American Big-Game Hunting, the Book of the Boone and Crockett Club, edited by Theodore Roosevelt and George Bird Grinnel, a limited edition reprint by the Boone and Crockett Club, Alexandria, VA, 1983. 345 pp., illus. $35.00.

A collection of unique hunting adventures in America by members of the Boone and Crockett Club.

Bear Hunting, by Jerry Meyer, Stackpole Books, Harrisburg, PA, 1983. 224 pp., illus. $14.95.

First complete guide on the how-to's of bear hunting. Information on every type of bear found in the U.S. and Canada.

The Best of Nash Buckingham, by Nash Buckingham, selected, edited and annotated by George Bird Evans, Winchester Press, Piscataway, NJ, 1973. 320 pp., illus. $17.95.

Thirty pieces that represent the very cream of Nash's output on his whole range of outdoor interests—upland shooting, duck hunting, even fishing.

The Best of Jack O'Connor, by Jack O'Connor, Amwell Press, Clinton, NJ, 1984. 192 pp., illus. $27.50.

A collection of Jack O'Connor's finest writings.

Big Game of North America, Ecology and Management, by Wildlife Management Institute, Stackpole Books, Harrisburg, PA, 1983. 512 pp., illus. $29.95.

An outstanding reference for professionals and students of wildlife management.

Big Game Record of British Columbia, compiled by the Trophy Wildlife Records Club of British Columbia, Nanoose, British Columbia, 1983. 216 pp., illus. $35.00.

The official record book for native big game trophies taken in British Columbia.

The Bobwhite Quail Book, Compiled by Lamar Underwood, Amwell Press, Clinton, NJ, 1981. 442 pp., illus. $25.00.

An anthology of the finest stories on Bobwhite quail ever assembled under one cover.

Bobwhite Quail Hunting, by Charley Dickey, printed for Stoeger Publ. Co., So. Hackensack, NJ, 1974. 112 pp., illus., paper covers. $3.95.

Habits and habitats, techniques, gear, guns and dogs.

The Book of the Wild Turkey, by Lovett E. Williams, Jr., Winchester Press, Piscataway, NJ, 1981. 204 pp., illus. $21.95.

A definitive reference work on the wild turkey for hunter, game manager, conservationist, or amateur naturalist.

Bowhunter's Digest, 2nd Edition, by Chuck Adams, DBI Books, Inc., Northbrook, IL, 1981. 288 pp., illus. Paper covers. $11.95.

All-new edition covers all the necessary equipment and how to use it, plus the fine points to improve your skills.

Bugling for Elk, by Dwight Schuh, Stoneydale Press Publishing Co., Stevensville, MT, 1983. 162 pp., illus. $14.95.

A complete guide to early season elk hunting.

The Complete Book of Hunting, by Robert Elman, Abbeville Press, New York, NY, 1982. 320 pp., illus. $29.95.

A compendium of the world's game birds and animals, handloading, international hunting, etc.

The Complete Book of the Wild Turkey, by Roger M. Latham, Stackpole Books, Harrisburg, Pa., 1978. 228 pp., illus. $12.95.

A new revised edition of the classic on American wild turkey hunting.

The Complete Guide to Bird Dog Training, by John R. Falk, Winchester Press, Piscataway, NJ, 1976. 256 pp., illus. $16.95.

How to choose, raise, train, and care for a bird dog.

The Complete Guide to Bowhunting Deer, by Chuck Adams, DBI Books, Inc., Northbrook, IL, 1984. 256 pp., illus. Paper covers. $11.95.

Plenty on equipment, bows, sights, quivers, arrows, clothes, lures and scents, stands and blinds, etc.

The Complete Guide to Game Care and Cookery, by Sam Fadala, DBI Books, Inc., Northbrook, IL., 1981. 288 pp., illus. Paper covers. $12.95.

How to dress, preserve and prepare all kinds of game animals and birds.

The Complete Turkey Hunt, by William Morris Daskal, El-Bar Enterprises Publishers, New York, NY, 1982. 129 pp., illus. Paper covers. $7.95.

Covers every aspect of turkeys and turkey hunting, by an expert.

Confessions of an Outdoor Maladroit, by Joel M. Vance, Amwell Press, Clinton, NJ, 1983. $20.00.

Anthology of some of the wildest, irreverent, and zany hunting tales ever.

Covey Rises and Other Pleasures, by David H. Henderson, Amwell Press, Clinton, NJ, 1983. 155 pp., illus. $17.50.

A collection of essays and stories concerned with field sports.

Coveys and Singles: The Handbook of Quail Hunting, by Robert Gooch, A.S. Barnes, San Diego, CA, 1981. 196 pp., illus. $11.95.

The story of the quail in North America.

Death in the Silent Places, by Peter Hathaway Capstick, St. Martin's Press, New York, NY, 1981. 243 pp., illus. $14.95.

The author recalls the extraordinary careers of legendary hunters such as Corbett, Karamojo Bell, Stigand and others.

Deer and Deer Hunting: The Serious Hunter's Guide, by Dr. Rob Wegner, Stackpole Books, Harrisburg, PA, 1984. 384 pp., illus. $29.95.

In-depth information from the editor of "Deer & Deer Hunting" magazine. Major bibliography of English language books on deer and deer hunting from 1838-1984.

Deer Hunting, by R. Smith, Stackpole Books, Harrisburg, PA, 1978. 224 pp., illus. Paper covers. $10.95.

A professional guide leads the hunt for North America's most popular big game animal.

Deer Hunter's Guide to Guns, Ammunition, and Equipment, by Edward A. Matunas, an Outdoor Life Book, distributed by Stackpole Books, Harrisburg, PA, 1983. 352 pp., illus. $24.95.

Where-to-hunt for North American deer. An authoritative guide that will help every deer hunter get maximum enjoyment and satisfaction from his sport.

The Deer Book, edited by Lamar Underwood, Amwell Press, Clinton, NJ, 1982. 480 pp., illus. $25.00.

An anthology of the finest stories on North American deer ever assembled under one cover.

Deer in Their World, by Erwin Bauer, Stackpole Books, Harrisburg, PA, 1984. 256 pp., illus. $29.95.

A showcase of more than 250 natural habitat deer photographs. Substantial natural history of North American deer.

The Desert Bighorn, edited by Gale Monson and Lowell Sumner, University of Arizona Press, Tucson, AZ, 1980. 392 pp., illus. $35.00.

Life history, ecology and management of the Desert Bighorn.

The Dove Shooter's Handbook, by Dan M. Russell, Winchester Press, Piscataway, NJ, 1974. 256 pp., illus. $12.95.

A complete guide to America's top game bird.

Dove Hunting, by Charley Dickey, Galahad Books, NY, 1976. 112 pp., illus. $6.00.

This indispensable guide for hunters deals with equipment, techniques, types of dove shooting, hunting dogs, etc.

Drummer in the Woods, by Burton L. Spiller, Stackpole Books, Harrisburg, PA, 1980. 240 pp., illus. $15.95.

Twenty-one wonderful stories on grouse shooting by "the Poet Laureate of Grouse".

The Duck Hunter's Book, edited by Lamar Underwood, Amwell Press, Clinton, NJ, 1983. 650 pp., illus. $25.00.

Anthology of the finest duck hunting stories ever written.

The Duck-Huntingest Gentlemen, by Keith C. Russell et al, Winchester Press, Piscataway, NJ, 1980. 284 pp., illus. $17.95.

A collection of stories on waterfowl hunting.

Ducks of the Mississippi Flyway, ed. by John McKane, North Star Press, St. Cloud, MN, 1969. 54 pp., illus. Paper covers. $6.95.

A duck hunter's reference. Full color paintings of some 30 species, plus descriptive text.

Elk Hunting in the Northern Rockies, by Ed. Wolff, Stoneydale Press, Stevensville, MT, 1984. 162 pp., illus. $14.95.

Helpful information about hunting the premier elk country of the northern Rocky Mountain states—Wyoming, Montana and Idaho.

Fair Chase, by Jim Rikhoff, Amwell Press, Clinton, NJ, 1984. 323 pp.,illus. $25.00.

A collection of hunting experiences from the Arctic to Africa, Mongolia to Montana, taken from over 25 years of writing.

For Whom the Ducks Toll, by Keith C. Russell, et al, Winchester Press, Piscataway, NJ, 1984. 288 pp., illus. Slipcased, limited and signed edition. $30.00. Trade edition. $16.95.

A select gathering of memorable waterfowling tales by the author and 68 of his closest friends.

The Formidable Game, by John H. Batten, Amwell Press, Clinton, NJ, 1983. 264 pp., illus. $175.00.

Deluxe, limited, signed and numbered edition. Big game hunting in India, Africa and North America by a world famous hunter.

Fur Trapping in North America, by Steven Geary, Winchester Press, Piscataway, NJ, 1985. 160 pp., illus. Paper covers. $10.95.

A comprehensive guide to techniques and equipment, together with fascinating facts about fur bearers.

A Gallery of Waterfowl and Upland Birds, by Gene Hill, with illustrations by David Maass, Pedersen Prints, Los Angeles, CA, 1978. 132 pp., illus. $44.95.

Gene Hill at his best. Liberally illustrated with fifty-one full-color reproductions of David Maass' finest paintings.

Game in the Desert Revisited, by Jack O'Connor, Amwell Press, Clinton, NJ, 1984. 306 pp., illus. $27.50.

Reprint of a Derrydale Press classic on hunting in the Southwest.

Getting the Most out of Modern Waterfowling, by John O. Cartier, St. Martin's Press, NY, 1974. 396 pp., illus. $17.95.

The most comprehensive, up-to-date book on waterfowling imaginable.

Goose Hunting, by Charles L. Cadieux, A Stonewall Press Book, distributed by Winchester Press, Piscataway, NJ, 1979. 197 pp., illus. $16.95.

Personal stories of goose hunting from Quebec to Mexico.

The Grand Spring Hunt for America's Wild Turkey Gobbler, by Bart Jacob with Ben Conger, Winchester Press, Piscataway, NJ, 1985. 176 pp., illus. $15.95.

The turkey book for novice and expert alike.

Grizzly Country, by Andy Russell. A.A. Knopf, NYC, 1973, 302 pp., illus. $13.95.

Many-sided view of the grizzly bear and his world, by a noted guide, hunter and naturalist.

Grizzlies Don't Come Easy, by Ralph Young, Winchester Press, Piscataway, NJ, 1981. 200 pp., illus. $15.95.

The life story of a great woodsman who guided famous hunters such as O'Connor, Keith, Fitz, Page and others.

The Grizzly Book/The Bear Book, two volume set edited by Jack Samson, Amwell Press, Clinton, NJ, 1982. 304 pp.; 250 pp., illus. Slipcase. $37.50.

A delightful pair of anthologies. Stories by men such as O'Connor, Keith, Fitz, Page, and many others.

Grouse Magic, by Nick Sisley, Nick Sisley, Apollo, PA, 1981. 240 pp., illus. Limited edition, signed and numbered. Slipcase. $30.00.

A book that will enrich your appreciation for grouse hunting and all the aura that surrounds the sport.

Gun Digest 1987 Hunting Annual, 4th Edition edited by Robert S.L. Anderson, DBI Books, Inc., Northbrook, IL, 1986. 256 pp., illus. Paper covers. $13.95.

Well-rounded, fully illustrated collection of expert hunting tips and techniques.

Gun Digest Book of the Hunting Rifle, by Jack Lewis, DBI Books, Inc., Northbrook, IL, 1983. 256 pp., illus. Paper covers. $11.95.

A thorough and knowledgeable account of today's hunting rifles.

Gun Digest Book of Sporting Dogs, by Carl P. Wood, DBI Books, Inc., Northbrook, IL, 1985. 256 pp., illus. Paper covers. $11.95.

Investigates various training philosophies, problem dogs, training for versatility, kenneling, etc. Covers most all hunting/sporting dogs.

Grouse and Woodcock, An Upland Hunter's Book, by Nick Sisley, Stackpole Books, Harrisburg, PA, 1980. 192 pp., illus. $13.95.

Latest field techniques for effective grouse and woodcock hunting.

Hal Swiggett on North American Deer, by Hal Swiggett, Jolex, Inc., Oakland, NJ, 1980. 272 pp., illus. Paper covers. $8.95.

Where and how to hunt all species of North American deer.

Handgun Hunting, by Maj. George C. Nonte, Jr. and Lee E. Jurras, Winchester Press, Piscataway, NJ, 1975. 245 pp., illus. $10.95.

A book with emphasis on the hunting of readily available game in the U.S. with the handgun.

The History of Wildfowling, by John Marchington, Adam and Charles Black, London, England, 1980. 288 pp., illus. $27.50.

Covers decoys, punting, and punt guns.

Horns in the High Country, by Andy Russell, Alfred A. Knopf, NY, 1973. 259 pp., illus. $15.50.

A many-sided view of wild sheep and their natural world.

How to Hunt, by Dave Bowring, Winchester Press, Piscataway, NJ, 1982. 208 pp., illus. Paper covers. $10.95; Cloth. $15.00.

A basic guide to hunting big game, small game, upland birds, and waterfowl.

The Hunter's Book of the Pronghorn Antelope, by Bert Popowski and Wilf E. Pyle, Winchester Press, Piscataway, NJ, 1982. 376 pp., illus. $17.95.

A comprehensive, copiously illustrated volume and a valuable guide for anyone interested in the pronghorn antelope.

A Hunter's Fireside Book, by Gene Hill, Winchester Press, Piscataway, NJ, 1972. 192 pp., illus. $14.95.

An outdoor book that will appeal to every person who spends time in the field—or who wishes he could.

The Hunter's Shooting Guide, by Jack O'Connor, Outdoor Life Books, New York, NY, 1982. 176 pp., illus. Paper covers. $5.95.

A classic covering rifles, cartridges, shooting techniques for shotguns/rifles/handguns.

The Hunter's World, by Charles F. Waterman, Winchester Press, Piscataway, NJ, 1983. 250 pp., illus. $29.95.

A classic. One of the most beautiful hunting books ever produced.

Hunting the American Wild Turkey, by Dave Harbour, Stackpole Books, Harrisburg, PA, 1975. 256 pp., illus. $14.95.

The techniques and tactics of hunting North America's largest, and most popular, woodland game bird.

Hunting America's Game Animals and Birds, by Robert Elman and George Peper, Winchester Press, Piscataway, NJ, 1975. 368 pp., illus. $16.95.

A how-to, where-to, when-to guide—by 40 top experts—covering the continent's big, small, upland game and waterfowl.

Hunting America's Mule Deer, by Jim Zumbo, Winchester Press, Piscataway, NJ, 1981. 272 pp., illus. $17.95.

The best ways to hunt mule deer. The how, when, and where to hunt all seven sub-species.

Hunting Dog Know-How, by D.M. Duffey, Winchester Press, Piscataway, NJ, 1983. 208 pp., illus. Paper covers. $9.95.

Covers selection, breeds, and training of hunting dogs, problems in hunting and field trials.

Hunting Ducks and Geese, by Steven Smith, Stackpole Books, Harrisburg, PA, 1984. 160 pp., illus. $14.95.

Hard facts, good bets, and serious advice from a duck hunter you can trust.

Hunting Moments of Truth, by Eric Peper and Jim Rikhoff, Winchester Press, Piscataway, NJ, 1973. 208 pp., illus. $15.00.

The world's most experienced hunters recount 22 most memorable occasions.

Hunting the Rocky Mountain Goat, by Duncan Gilchrist, Duncan Gilchrist, Hamilton, MT, 1983. 175 pp., illus. Paper covers. $10.95.

Hunting techniques for mountain goats and other alpine game. Tips on rifles for the high country.

Hunting and Stalking Deer Throughout the World, by Kenneth G. Whitehead, Batsford Books, London, 1982. 336 pp., illus. $35.00.

Comprehensive coverage of deer hunting areas on a country-by-country basis, dealing with every species in any given country.

Hunting Trophy Deer, by John Wootters, Winchester Press, Piscataway, NJ, 1983. 265 pp., illus. $15.95.

All the advice you need to succeed at bagging trophy deer.

Hunting Wild Turkeys in the Everglades, by Frank P. Harben, Harben Publishing Co., Safety Harbor, FL, 1983. 341 pp., illus. Paper covers. $8.95.

Describes techniques, ways and means of hunting this wary bird.

Hunting the Woodlands for Small and Big Game, by Luther A. Anderson, A. S. Barnes & Co., New York, NY, 1980. 256 pp., illus. $12.00.

A comprehensive guide to hunting in the United States. Chapters on firearms, game itself, marksmanship, clothing and equipment.

In Search of the Wild Turkey, by Bob Gooch, Greatlakes Living Press, Ltd., Waukegan, IL, 1978. 182 pp., illus. $9.95.

A state-by-state guide to wild turkey hot spots, with tips on gear and methods for bagging your bird.

A Listening Walk . . . and Other Stories, by Gene Hill, Winchester Press, Piscataway, NJ, 1985. 208 pp., illus. $15.95.

Vintage Hill. Over 60 stories.

The Market Hunter, by David and Jim Kimball, Dillon Press Inc., Minneapolis, MN, 1968. 132 pp., illus. $8.95.

The market hunter, one of the "missing chapters" in American history, is brought to life in this book.

Matching the Gun to the Game, by Clair Rees, Winchester Press, Piscataway, NJ, 1982. 272 pp., illus. $17.95.

Covers selection and use of handguns, black-powder firearms for hunting, matching rifle type to the hunter, calibers for multiple use, tailoring factory loads to the game.

Mixed Bag, by Jim Rikhoff, National Rifle Association of America, Wash., DC, 1981. 284 pp., illus. Paper covers $9.95.

Reminiscences of a master raconteur.

Modern Pheasant Hunting, by Steve Grooms, Stackpole Books, Harrisburg, PA, 1982. 224 pp., illus. Paper covers. $8.95.

New look at pheasants and hunters from an experienced hunter who respects this splendid gamebird.

Modern Turkey Hunting, by James F. Brady, Crown Publ., N.Y.C., NY, 1973. 160 pp., illus. $30.00.

A thorough guide to the habits, habitat, and methods of hunting America's largest game bird.

Modern Wildfowling, by Eric Begbie, Saiga Publishing Co., Ltd., Surrey, England, 1980. 171 pp., illus. $27.50.

History of wildfowling, guns and equipment.

More Grouse Feathers, by Burton L. Spiller. Crown Publ., NY, 1972. 238 pp., illus. $15.00.

Facsimile of the original Derrydale Press issue of 1938. Guns and dogs, the habits and shooting of grouse, woodcock, ducks, etc. Illus by Lynn Bogue Hunt.

More Than a Trophy, by Dennis Walrod, Stackpole Books, Harrisburg, PA, 1983. 256 pp., illus. Paper covers. $12.95.

Field dressing, skinning, quartering, and butchering to make the most of your valuable whitetail, blacktail or mule deer.

More Stories of the Old Duck Hunter, by Gordon MacQuarrie, Willow Creek Press, Oshkosh, WI, 1983. 200 pp., illus. $15.00.

Collection of 18 treasured stories of The Old Duck Hunters originally published in major magazines of the 1930s and '40s.

Mostly Tailfeathers, by Gene Hill, Winchester Press, Piscataway, NJ, 1975. 192 pp., illus. $14.95.

An interesting, general book about bird hunting.

Murry Burnham's Hunting Secrets, by Murry Burnham with Russell Tinsley, Winchester Press, Piscataway, NJ, 1984. 244 pp., illus. $17.95.

One of the great hunters of our time gives the reasons for his success in the field.

The Muzzleloading Hunter, by Rick Hacker, Winchester Press, Piscataway, NJ, 1981. 283 pp., illus. $19.95.

A comprehensive guide for the black powder sportsman.

My Lost Wilderness: Tales of an Alaskan Woodsman, by Ralph Young, Winchester Press, Piscataway, NJ, 1983. 193 pp., illus. $15.95.

True tales of an Alaskan hunter, guide, fisherman, prospector, and backwoodsman.

New England Grouse Shooting, by William Harnden Foster, Willow Creek Press, Oshkosh, WI, 1983. 213 pp., illus. $45.00.

A new release of a classic book on grouse shooting.

North American Elk: Ecology and Management, edited by Jack Ward Thomas and Dale E. Toweill, Stackpole Books, Harrisburg, PA, 1982. 576 pp., illus. $39.95.

The definitive, exhaustive, classic work on the North American Elk.

The North American Waterfowler, by Paul S. Bernsen, Superior Publ. Co., Seattle, WA, 1972. 206 pp., Paper covers. $4.95.

The complete inside and outside story of duck and goose shooting. Big and colorful, illus. by Les Kouba.

On Target for Successful Turkey Hunting, by Wayne Fears, Target Communications, Mequon, WI, 1983. 92 pp., illus. Paper covers. $5.95.

Professional turkey hunting advice.

The Old Pro Turkey Hunter, by Gene Nunnery, Gene Nunnery, Meridian, MS, 1980. 144 pp., illus. $12.95.

True facts and old tales of turkey hunters.

1001 Hunting Tips, by Robert Elman, Winchester Press, Piscataway, NJ, 1983. 544 pp., illus. Paper covers. $14.95.

New edition, updated and expanded. A complete course in big and small game hunting, wildfowling and hunting upland birds.

One Man's Wilderness, by Warren Page, Holt, Rinehart and Winston, NY, 1973. 256 pp., illus. $30.00.

A world-known writer and veteran sportsman recounts the joys of a lifetime of global hunting.

Opening Shots and Parting Lines: The Best of Dickey's Wit, Wisdom, and Wild Tales for Sportsmen, by Charley Dickey, Winchester Press, Piscataway, NJ, 1983. 208 pp., illus. $14.95.

Selected by the writer who has entertained millions of readers in America's top sporting publications—49 of his best pieces.

The Outdoor Life Bear Book, edited by Chet Fish, an Outdoor Life book, distributed by Stackpole Books, Harrisburg, PA, 1983. 352 pp., illus. $26.95.

All-time best personal accounts of terrifying attacks, exciting hunts, and intriguing natural history.

Outdoor Yarns & Outright Lies, by Gene Hill and Steve Smith, Stackpole Books, Inc. Harrisburg, PA, 1984. 168 pp.,illus. $12.95.

Fifty or so stories by two wood sports.

The Outlaw Gunner, by Harry M. Walsh, Tidewater Publishers, Cambridge, MD, 1973. 178 pp., illus. $12.50.

A colorful story of market gunning in both its legal and illegal phases.

Pinnell and Talifson: Last of the Great Brown Bear Men, by Marvin H. Clark, Jr., Great Northwest Publishing and Distributing Co., Spokane, WA, 1980. 224 pp., illus. $20.00.

The story of these famous Alaskan guides and some of the record bears taken by them.

Popular Sporting Rifle Cartridges, by Clay Harvey, DBI Books, Inc., Northbrook, IL, 1984. 320 pp., illus. Paper covers. $13.95.

Provides the hunter/shooter with extensive information on most of the cartridges introduced during this century.

The Practical Hunter's Dog Book, Updated and Expanded, by John R. Falk, Winchester Press, Piscataway, NJ, 1984. 336 pp., illus. Paper covers. $11.95.

Everything you need to know from selecting a puppy to basic and advanced training, health care and breeding.

The Practical Hunter's Handbook, by Anthony J. Acerrano, Winchester Press, Piscataway, NJ, 1978. 224 pp., illus. Paper covers. $12.95.

How the time-pressed hunter can take advantage of every edge his hunting situation affords him.

The Practical Wildfowler, by John Marchington, Adam and Charles Black, London, England, 1977. 143 pp., illus. $21.95.

Advice on both the practical and ethical aspects of the sport.

Predator Caller's Companion, by Gerry Blair, Winchester Press, Piscataway, NJ, 1981. 280 pp., illus. $18.95.

Predator calling techniques and equipment for the hunter and trapper.

Ralf Coykendall's Duck Decoys and How to Rig Them, revised by Ralf Coykendall, Jr., Winchester Press, Piscataway, NJ, 1983. 128 pp., illus. Slipcased. $21.95.

For every discriminating book collector and sportsman, a superb new edition of a long out-of-print classic.

Ranch Life and the Hunting Trail, by Theodore Roosevelt, Readex Microprint Corp., Dearborn, MI. 1966 186 pp. With drawings by Frederic Remington. $15.00.

A facsimile reprint of the original 1899 Century Co., edition. One of the most fascinating books of the West of that day.

Records of Alaska Big Game, edited by Norman B. Grant, Alaska Big Game Trophy Club, Anchorage, Alaska, 1971, 111 pp., illus. $95.00.

Contains the recorded and tabulated trophies of Alaskan big game, including the name of the hunter, date and place of hunt, and measurement.

Records of Exotics, Volume 2, 1978 Edition, compiled by Thompson B. Temple, Thompson B. Temple, Ingram, TX, 1978. 243 pp., illus. $15.00.

Lists almost 1,000 of the top exotic trophies bagged in the U.S. Gives complete information on how to score.

Ringneck! Pheasants & Pheasant Hunting, by Ted Janes, Crown Publ., NY, 1975. 120 pp., illus. $8.95.

A thorough study of one of our more popular game birds.

Sheep and Sheep Hunting, by Jack O'Connor, Winchester Press, Piscataway, NJ, 1983. 320 pp., illus. Paper covers. $13.95.

Memorial edition of the definitive book on wild sheep hunting.

Charles Sheldon Trilogy, by Charles Sheldon, Amwell Press, Clinton, NJ, 1983. 3 volumes in slipcase. "The Wilderness of the Upper Yukon," 363 pp., illus.; "The Wilderness of the North Pacific Coast Islands," 246 pp., illus.; "The Wilderness of Denali," 412 pp., illus. Deluxe edition. $205.00.

Custom-bound reprinting of Sheldon's classics, each signed and numbered by the author's son, William G. Sheldon.

Shooting Pictures, by A.B. Frost, with 24 pp. of text by Chas. D. Lanier, Winchester Press, Piscataway, NJ, 1972. 12 color plates. Enclosed in a board portfolio. Ed. limited to 750 numbered copies. $200.00.

Frost's 12 superb 12" by 16" pictures have often been called the finest sporting prints published in the U.S.A facsimile of the 1895-6 edition printed on fine paper with superb color fidelity.

Squirrels and Squirrel Hunting, by Bob Gooch. Tidewater Publ., Cambridge, MD, 1973. 148 pp., illus. $6.

A complete book for the squirrel hunter, beginner or old hand. Details methods of hunting, squirrel habitat, management, proper clothing, care of the kill, cleaning and cooking.

HUNTING (cont.)

Strayed Shots and Frayed Lines, edited by John E. Howard, Amwell Press, Clinton, NJ, 1982. 425 pp., illus. $25.00.

Anthology of some of the finest, funniest stories on hunting and fishing ever assembled.

Successful Deer Hunting, by Sam Fadala, DBI Books, Inc., Northbrook, IL, 1983. 288 pp., illus. Paper covers. $11.95.

Here's all the dope you'll need—where, why, when and how—to have a successful deer hunt.

Successful Turkey Hunting, by J. Wayne Fears, Target Communications, Mequon, WI, 1983. 92 pp., illus. Paper covers. $5.95.

How to be more successful and get more enjoyment from turkey hunting.

Successful Waterfowling, by Zack Taylor, Crown, Publ., NY, 1974. 276 pp., illus. Paper covers. $15.95.

The definitive guide to new ways of hunting ducks and geese.

Through the Brazilian Wilderness, by Theodore Roosevelt, Greenwood Press, Westport, CT, 1982. Reprinting of the original 1914 work. 370 pp., illus. $22.50.

An account of a zoogeographic reconnaissance through the Brazilian hinterland.

Timberdoodle, by Frank Woolner, Crown Publ., Inc., NY, 1974. 168 pp., illus. $15.95.

A thorough, practical guide to the American woodcock and to woodcock hunting.

Topflight; A Speed Index to Waterfowl, by J.A. Ruthven & Wm. Zimmerman, Moebius Prtg. Co., Milwaukee, WI, 1968. 112 pp. $8.95.

Rapid reference for specie identification. Marginal color band of book directs reader to proper section. 263 full color illustrations of body and feather configurations.

Track of the Kodiak, by Marvin H. Clark, Great Northwest Publishing and Distributing Co., Anchorage, AK, 1984. 224 pp., illus. $20.00.

A full perspective on Kodiak Island bear hunting.

The Trophy Hunter, by Col. Allison, Stackpole Books, Harrisburg, PA, 1981. 240 pp., illus. $24.95.

Action-packed tales of hunting big game trophies around the world—1860 to today.

Turkey Hunter's Digest, by Dwain Bland, DBI Books, Inc., Northbrook, IL, 1986. 256 pp., illus. Paper covers. $12.95.

Describes and pictures all varieties of turkey. Offers complete coverage on calls, calling techniques, appropriate guns, bows, cameras and other equipment.

Turkey Hunting, Spring and Fall, by Doug Camp, Outdoor Skills Bookshelf, Nashville, TN, 1983. 165 pp., illus. Paper covers. $12.95.

Practical turkey hunting, calling, dressing and cooking, by a professional turkey hunting guide.

Turkey Hunter's Guide, by Byron W. Dalrymple, et al, a publication of The National Rifle Association, Washington, DC, 1979. 96 pp., illus. Paper covers. $9.95.

Expert advice on turkey hunting hotspots, guns, guides, and calls.

The Whispering Wings of Autumn, by Gene Hill and Steve Smith, Amwell Press, Clinton, NJ, 1982. 192 pp., illus. $17.50.

A collection of both fact and fiction on two of North America's most famous game birds, the Ruffed Grouse and the Woodcock.

White-Tailed Deer: Ecology and Management, by Lowell K. Halls, Stackpole Books, Harrisburg, PA, 1984. 864 pp., illus. $39.95.

The definive work on the world's most popular big-game animal.

The Whitetail Deer Hunter's Handbook, by John Weiss, Winchester Press, Piscataway, NJ, 1979. 256 pp., illus. Paper covers. $12.95.

Wherever you live, whatever your level of experience, this handbook will make you a better deer hunter.

Whitetail: Fundamentals and Fine Points for the Hunter, by George Mattis, World Publ. Co., New York, NY, 1976. 273 pp., illus. $9.95.

A manual of shooting and trailing and an education in the private world of the deer.

Whitetail Hunting, by Jim Dawson, Stackpole Books, Harrisburg, PA, 1982. 224 pp., illus. $14.95.

New angles on hunting whitetail deer.

Wild Sheep and Wild Sheep Hunters of the Old World, by Raul Valdez, Wild Sheep & Goat International, Mesilla,NM, 1983. 207 pp., illus. Limited, signed and numbered edition. $65.00.

A definitive work on Old World sheep hunting.

The Wild Sheep of the World, by Raul Valdez, Wild Sheep and Goat International, Mesilla, NM, 1983. 150 pp., illus. $45.00.

The first comprehensive survey of the world's wild sheep written by a zoologist.

The Wild Turkey Book, edited and with special commentary by J. Wayne Fears, Amwell Press, Clinton, NJ, 1982. 303 pp., illus. $22.50.

An anthology of the finest stories on wild turkey ever assembled under one cover.

AFRICA/ASIA

African Rifles & Cartridges, by John Taylor. The Gun Room Press, Highland Park, NJ, 1977. 431 pp., illus. $21.95.

Experiences and opinions of a professional ivory hunter in Africa describing his knowledge of numerous arms and cartridges for big game. A reprint.

African Hunting and Adventure, by William Charles Baldwin, Books of Zimbabwe, Bulawayo, 1981. 451 pp., illus. $75.00.

Facsimile reprint of the scarce 1863 London edition. African hunting and adventure from Natal to the Zambesi.

African Section Special Field Edition SCI 4th Edition Record Book of Trophy Animals, edited by C.J. McElroy, Safari Club International, Tucson, AZ, 1984. 302 pp., illus. Paper covers. $20.00.

Tabulations of outstanding big game trophies.

Bell of Africa, by Walter (Karamojo) D. M. Bell, Neville Spearman, Suffolk, England, 1983. 236 pp., illus. $35.00.

Autobiography of the greatest elephant hunter of them all.

Big Game Hunting Around the World, by Bert Klineburger and Vernon W. Hurst, Exposition Press, Jericho, NY, 1969. 376 pp., illus. $30.00.

The first book that takes you on a safari all over the world.

Death in the Long Grass, by Peter Hathaway Capstick, St. Martin's Press, New York, NY, 1977. 297 pp., illus. $14.95.

A big game hunter's adventures in the African bush.

The Elephant Hunters of the Lado, by Major W. Robert Foran, Amwell Press, Clinton, NJ, 1981. 311 pp., illus. Limited, numbered, and signed edition, in slipcase. $175.00.

From a previously unpublished manuscript by a famous "white hunter."

Elephant Hunting in East Equatorial Africa, by Arthur H. Neumann, Books of Zimbabwe, Bulawayo, 1982. 455 pp., illus. $85.00.

Facsimile reprint of the scarce 1898 London edition. An account of three years ivory hunting under Mount Kenya.

First Wheel, by Bunny Allen, Amwell Press, Clinton, NJ, 1984. Limited, signed and numbered edition in the NSFL "African Hunting Heritage Series." 292 pp., illus. $100.00.

A white hunter's diary, 1927-47.

Green Hills of Africa, by Ernest Hemingway. Charles Scribner's Sons, NY, 1963. 285 pp., illus. Paper covers. $7.95.

A famous narrative of African big-game hunting, first published in 1935.

A Hunter's Wanderings in Africa, by F. C. Selous, Books of Zimbabwe, Bulawayo, 1981. 455 pp., illus. $85.00.

A facsimile reprint of the 1881 London edition. A narrative of nine years spent among the game of the interior of South Africa.

Hunting in Africa, by Bill Morkel, Howard Timmins, Publishers, Capetown, South Africa, 1980. 252 pp., illus. $25.00.

An invaluable guide for the inexperienced hunter contemplating a possible safari.

Hunting the African Buffalo, edited by Jim Rikhoff, Amwell Press, Clinton, NJ, 1985. 575 pp., illus. $225.00.

Deluxe, limited, signed and numbered edition of the most definitive work on hunting the African Cape buffalo that has ever been compiled.

Hunting on Safari in East and Southern Africa, by Aubrey Wynne-Jones, Macmillan South Africa, Johannesburg, S. Africa, 1980. 180 pp., illus. $42.50.

Every aspect of hunting in East and Southern Africa is covered, from the early planning stages of the hunt itself.

Karamojo Safari, by W.D.M. Bell, Neville Spearman, Suffolk, England, 1984. 288 pp., illus. $35.00.

The true story of Bell's life in Karamojo.

The Recollections of an Elephant Hunter 1864-1875, by William Finaughty, Books of Zimbabwe, Bulawayo, 1980. 244 pp., illus. $85.00.

Reprint of the scarce 1916 privately published edition. The early game hunting exploits of William Finaughty in Matabeleland and Nashonaland.

Rowland Ward's African Records of Big Game, XIX Edition, edited by Edward R. Bryand, Rowland Ward Publications, a division of Game Conservation International, San Antonio, TX, 1984. 640 pp., illus. $100.00.

The premier source book for African trophy hunters.

Safari: The Last Adventure, by Peter Capstick, St. Martin's Press, New York, NY, 1984. 291 pp., illus. $15.95.

A modern comprehensive guide to African safari.

Tanzania Safari, by Brian Herne, Amwell Press, Clinton, NJ, 1982. 259 pp., illus. Limited, signed and numbered edition. Slipcase. $75.00.

The story of Tanzania and hunting safaris, professional hunters, and a little history, too.

Uganda Safaris, by Brian Herne, Winchester Press, Piscataway, NJ, 1979. 236 pp., illus. $12.95.

The chronicle of a professional hunter's adventures in Africa.

The Wanderings of an Elephant Hunter, by W.D.M. Bell, Neville Spearman, Suffolk, England, 1981. 187 pp., illus. $35.00.

The greatest of elephant books by perhaps the greatest elephant hunter of all times, 'Karamojo' Bell.

Wild Ivory, by Horace S. Mazet, Nautilus Books, No. Plainfield, NJ, 1971. 280 pp., illus. $30.00.

The true story of the last of the old elephant hunters.

A White Hunters Life, by Angus MacLagan, an African Heritage Book, published by Amwell Press, Clinton, NJ, 1983. 283 pp., illus. Limited, signed, and numbered deluxe edition, in slipcase. $100.00.

True to life, a sometimes harsh yet intriguing story.

RIFLES

The Accurate Rifle, by Warren Page, Winchester Press, Piscataway, NJ, 1973. 256 pp., illus. Paper covers. $8.95.

A masterly discussion. A must for the competitive shooter hoping to win, and highly useful to the practical hunter.

The AK-47 Assault Rifle, Desert Publications, Cornville, AZ, 1981. 150 pp., illus. Paper covers. $7.50.

Complete and practical technical information on the only weapon in history to be produced in an estimated 30,000,000 units.

American Rifle Design and Performance, by L.R. Wallack, Winchester Press, Piscataway, NJ, 1977. 288 pp., illus. $20.00.

An authoritative, comprehensive guide to how and why every kind of sporting rifle works.

RIFLES (cont.)

Big Game Rifles and Cartridges, by Elmer Keith, reprint edition by The Gun Room Press, Highland Park, NJ, 1984. 161 pp., illus. $19.95.

Reprint of Elmer Keith's first book, a most original and accurate work on big game rifles and cartridges.

The Bolt Action: A Design Analysis, by Stuart Otteson, edited by Ken Warner, Winchester Press, Piscataway, NJ, 1976. 320 pp., illus. Paper covers. $14.95; Cloth. $20.00.

Precise and in-depth descriptions, illustrations and comparisons of 16 bolt actions.

Bolt Action Rifles, revised edition, by Frank de Haas, DBI Books, Inc., Northbrook, IL, 1984. 448 pp., illus. Paper covers. $14.95.

A revised edition of the most definitive work on all major bolt-action rifle designs. Detailed coverage of over 110 turnbolt actions, including how they function, take-down and assembly, strengths and weaknesses, dimensional specifications.

The Book of the Garand, by Maj.-Gen. J.S. Hatcher, The Gun Room Press, Highland Park, NJ, 1977. 292 pp., illus. $15.00.

A new printing of the standard reference work on the U.S. Army M1 rifle.

The Commerical Mauser '98 Sporting Rifle, by Lester Womack, Womack Associates, Publishers, Prescott, AZ, 1980. 69 pp., illus. $20.00.

The first work on the sporting rifles made by the original Mauser plant in Oberndorf.

F.N.-F.A.L. Auto Rifles, Desert Publications, Cornville, AZ, 1981. 130 pp., illus. Paper covers. $7.50.

A definitive study of one of the free world's finest combat rifles.

The Fighting Rifle, by Chuck Taylor, Paladin Press, Boulder, CO, 1983. 184 pp., illus. Paper covers. $12.95.

The difference between assault and battle rifles and auto and light machine guns.

The First Winchester, by John E. Parsons, Winchester Press, Piscataway, NJ, 1977. 207 pp., illus. $35.00.

The story of the 1866 repeating rifle.

A Forgotten Heritage; The Story of a People and the Early American Rifle, by Harry P. Davis, The Gun Room Press, Highland Park, NJ, 1976. 199 pp., illus. $9.95.

Reprint of a very scarce history, originally published in 1941, the Kentucky rifle and the people who used it.

The German Rifle, by John Walter, Arms and Armour Press, London, England, 1982. 160 pp., illus. $16.95.

A comprehensive illustrated history of the standard bolt-action design, 1871-1945.

The Golden Age of Single-Shot Rifles, by Edsall James, Pioneer Press, Union City, TN, 1975. 33 pp., illus. Paper covers. $2.75.

A detailed look at all of the fine, high quality sporting single-shot rifles that were once the favorite of target shooters.

The Great Rifle Controversy, by Edward Ezell, Stackpole Books, Harrisburg, PA, 1984. 352 pp., illus. $29.95.

Search for the ultimate infantry weapon from WW II through Vietnam and beyond.

The Gun Digest Book of Firearms Assembly/Disassembly Part III: Rimfire Rifles, by J.B. Wood, DBI Books, Inc., Northbrook, IL, 1980. 288 pp., illus. Paper covers. $12.95.

A most comprehensive, uniform, and professional presentation available for disassembling and reassembling most rimfire rifles.

The Gun Digest Book of Firearms Assembly/Disassembly Part IV: Centerfire Rifles, by J.B. Wood, DBI Books, Inc., Northbrook, IL, 1980. 288 pp., illus. Paper covers. $12.95.

A professional presentation on the disassembly and reassembly of centerfire rifles.

Gun Digest Book of Gun Care, Cleaning and Refinishing, Book Two: Long Guns, by J.B. Wood, DBI Books, Inc., Northbrook, IL, 1984. 160 pp., illus. Paper covers. $9.95.

The care and maintenance of long guns with meticulous detail and step-by-step, illustrated, clearly written text.

Gun Digest Book of the Hunting Rifle, by Jack Lewis, DBI Books, Inc., Northbrook, IL, 1983. 256 pp., illus. Paper covers. $11.95.

Covers all aspects of the hunting rifle—design, development, different types, uses, and more.

Gun Digest Book of Riflesmithing, by Jack Mitchell, DBI Books, Inc., Northbrook, IL, 1982. 256 pp., illus. Paper covers. $11.95.

Covers major and minor gunsmithing operations for rifles—locking systems, triggers, safeties, rifling, crowning, scope mounting, and more.

Know Your M1 Garand, by E. J. Hoffschmidt, Blacksmith Corp., Southport, CT, 1975, 84 pp., illus. Paper covers. $6.95.

Facts about America's most famous infantry weapon. Covers test and experimental models, Japanese and Italian copies, National Match models.

The M-14 Rifle, facsimile reprint of FM 23-8, Desert Publications, Cornville, AZ, 50 pp., illus. Paper $5.95.

In this well illustrated and informative reprint, the M-14 and M-14E2 are covered thoroughly.

M1 Carbine Owner's Manual, M1, M2 & M3 .30 Caliber Carbines, Firepower Publications, Cornville, AZ, 1984. 102 pp., illus. Paper covers. $9.95.

The complete book for the owner of an M1 carbine.

Modern Military Bullpup Rifles, by T.B. Dugelby, Collector Grade Publications, Toronto, Canada, 1984. 97 pp., illus. $20.00.

The EM-2 concept comes to age.

The Modern Rifle, by Jim Carmichel, Winchester Press, Piscataway, NJ, 1975. 320 pp., illus. $15.95.

The most comprehensive, thorough, up-to-date book ever published on today's rifled sporting arms.

North American FALS, by R. Blake Stevens, Collector Grade Publications, Toronto, Canada, 1979. 166 pp., illus. Paper covers. $20.00.

NATO's search for a standard rifle.

100 Years of Shooters and Gunmakers of Single Shot Rifles, by Gerald O. Kelver, Brighton, CO, 1975. 212 pp., illus. Paper covers. $10.00.

The Schuetzen rifle, targets and shooters, primers, match rifles, original loadings and much more. With chapters on famous gunsmiths like Harry Pope, Morgan L. Rood and others.

The '03 Springfields, by Clark S. Campbell, Ray Riling Arms Books Co., Phila., PA, 1978. 320 pp., illus. $35.00.

The most authoritative and definitive work on this famous U.S. rifle, the 1903 Springfield and its 30-06 cartridge.

The Pennsylvania Rifle, by Samuel E. Dyke, Sutter House, Lititz, PA, 1975. 61 pp., illus. Paper covers. $5.00.

History and development, from the hunting rifle of the Germans who settled the area. Contains a full listing of all known Lancaster, PA, gunsmiths from 1729 through 1815.

The Revolving Rifles, by Edsall James, Pioneer Press, Union City, TN, 1975. 23 pp., illus. Paper covers. $2.50.

Valuable information on revolving cylinder rifles, from the earliest matchlock forms to the latest models of Colt and Remington.

The Rifle Book, by Jack O'Connor, Random House, NY, 1978. 337 pp., illus. Paper covers. $13.95.

The complete book of small game, varmint and big game rifles.

Rifle Guide, by Robert A. Steindler, Stoeger Publishing Co., South Hackensack, NJ, 1978. 304 pp., illus. Paper covers. $9.95.

Complete, fully illustrated guide to selecting, shooting, caring for, and collecting rifles of all types.

Rifle Shooting as a Sport, by Bernd Klingner, A.S. Barnes and Co., Inc., San Diego, CA, 1980. 186 pp., illus. Paper covers. $15.00.

Basic principles, positions and techniques by an international expert.

The Rifleman's Rifle: Winchester's Model 70, 1936-63, by Roger C. Rule, Alliance Books, Inc., Northridge, CA, 1982. 368 pp., illus. $59.95.

The most complete reference book on the Model 70, with much fresh information on the Model 54 and the new Model 70s.

Ned H. Roberts and the Schuetzen Rifle, edited by Gerald O. Kelver, Brighton, CO, 1982. 99 pp., illus. $10.00.

A compilation of the writings of Major Ned H. Roberts which appeared in various gun magazines.

The Ruger No. 1, by J.D. Clayton, edited by John T. Amber, Blacksmith Corp., Southport, CT, 1983. 200 pp., illus. $39.50.

Covers this famous rifle from original conception to current production.

Schuetzen Rifles, History and Loading, by Gerald O. Kelver, Gerald O. Kelver, Publisher, Brighton, CO, 1972. Illus. $10.00.

Reference work on these rifles, their bullets, loading, telescopic sights, accuracy, etc. A limited, numbered ed.

The Sporting Rifle and its Projectiles, by Lieut. James O Forsyth, The Buckeye Press, Big Timber, MT, 1978. 132 pp., illus. $10.00.

Facsimile reprint of the 1863 edition, one of the most authoritative books ever written on the muzzle-loading round ball sporting rifle.

The Springfield Rifle M1903, M1903A1, M1903A3, M1903A4, Desert Publications, Cornville, AZ, 1982. 100 pp., illus. Paper covers. $6.95.

Covers every aspect of disassembly and assembly, inspection, repair and maintenance.

The .22 Rifle, by Dave Petzal, Winchester Press, Piscataway, NJ, 1972. 244 pp., illus. $12.95.

All about the mechanics of the .22 rifle. How to choose the right one, how to choose a place to shoot, what makes a good shot, the basics of small-game hunting.

U.S. Rifle M14, from John Garand to the M21, by R. Blake Stevens, Collector Grade Publications, Toronto, Canada, 1983. 400 pp., illus. $34.95.

The complete history of the M14 rifle.

Henry Wilkinson's Observations on Muskets, Rifles and Projectiles, a facsimile reprint of the scarce 1852 London edition. Reprinted by W.S. Curtis, Bucks, England, 1983. 63 pp., illus. Paper covers. $12.95.

Includes the author's scarce work "Treatise on Elastic Concave Wadding."

The American Shotgun, by David F. Butler, Lyman Publ., Middlefield, CT, 1973. 256 pp. illus. Paper covers. $15.00.

A comprehensive history of the American smoothbore's evolution from Colonial times to the present day.

American Shotgun Design and Performance, by L.R. Wallack, Winchester Press, Piscataway, NJ, 1977. 184 pp., illus. $16.95.

An expert lucidly recounts the history and development of American shotguns and explains how they work.

The Best Shotguns Ever Made in America, by Michael McIntosh, Charles Scribner's Sons, New York, NY, 1981. 185 pp., illus. $17.95.

Seven vintage doubles to shoot and treasure.

The British Shotgun, Volume 1, 1850-1870, by I.M. Crudington and D.J. Baker, Barrie & Jenkins, London, England, 1979. 256 pp., illus. $29.95.

An attempt to trace, as accurately as is now possible, the evolution of the shotgun during its formative years in Great Britain.

Churchill's Game Shooting, edited by Macdonald Hastings, Arms & Armour Press, London, England, 1979. 252 pp., illus. Paper covers. $15.00.

The standard textbook on the successful use of the shotgun.

Combat Shotgun Training, by Charles R. Skillen, Charles C. Thomas, Publisher, Springfield, IL. 1982. 201 pp., illus. $40.00.

Complete, authoritative information on the use of the shotgun in law enforcement.

SHOTGUNS (cont.)

The Double Shotgun, by Don Zutz, Winchester Press, Piscataway, NJ, 1985. 304 pp., illus. $19.95.

Revised, updated, expanded edition of the history and development of the world's classic sporting firearms.

The Golden Age of Shotgunning, by Bob Hinman, Wolfe Publishing Co., Inc., Prescott, AZ, 1982. $17.95.

A valuable history of the late 1800s detailing that fabulous period of development in shotguns, shotshells and shotgunning.

The Gun Digest Book of Firearms Assembly/Disassembly, Part V: Shotguns, by J.B. Wood, DBI Books, Inc., Northbrook, IL, 1980. 288 pp., illus. Paper covers. $12.95.

A professional presentation on the complete disassembly and assembly of 26 of the most popular shotguns, new and old.

Gun Digest Book of Gun Care, Cleaning and Refinishing, Book Two: Long Guns, by J.B. Wood, DBI Books, Inc., Northbrook IL, 1984. 160 pp., illus. Paper covers. $9.95.

The care and maintenance of long guns with meticulous detail and step-by-step, illustrated, clearly written text.

Gun Digest Book of Shotgun Gunsmithing, by Ralph Walker, DBI Books, Inc., Northbrook, IL, 1983. 256 pp., illus. Paper covers. $11.95.

The principles and practices of repairing, individualizing and accurizing modern shotguns by one of the world's premier shotgun gunsmiths.

Gun Digest Book of Trap and Skeet Shooting, by Art Blatt, DBI Books, Inc., Northbrook, IL, 1984. 288 pp., illus. Paper covers. $11.95.

Valuable information for both beginner and seasoned shooter.

Hartman on Skeet, by Barney Hartman, Stackpole Books, Harrisburg, PA, 1973. 143 pp., illus. $10.00.

A definitive book on Skeet shooting by a pro.

How to be a Winner Shooting Skeet & Trap, by Tom Morton, Tom Morton, Knoxville, MD, 1974. 144 pp., illus. Paper covers. $10.95.

The author explains why championship shooting is more than a physical process.

L.C. Smith Shotguns, by Lt. Col. William S. Brophy, The Gun Room Press, Highland Park, NJ, 1979. 244 pp., illus. $29.95.

The first work on this very important American gun and manufacturing company.

A Manual of Clayshooting, by Chris Cradock, Hippocrene Books, Inc., New York, NY, 1983. 192 pp., illus. $24.95.

Covers everything from building a range to buying a shotgun, with lots of illustrations and diagrams.

The Mysteries of Shotgun Patterns, by George G. Oberfell and Charles E. Thompson, Oklahoma State University Press, Stillwater, OK, 1982. 164 pp., illus. Paper covers. $25.00.

Shotgun ballistics for the hunter in non-technical language, with information on improving effectiveness in the field.

The Parker Gun, by Larry L. Baer, The Gun Room Press, Highland Park, NJ, 1983. 240 pp., illus. $29.95.

The only comprehensive work on the subject of America's most famous shotgun.

Plans and Specifications of the L.C. Smith Shotgun, by Lt. Col. William S. Brophy, USAR Ret., F. Brownell & Son, Montezuma, IA, 1982. 247 pp., illus. $19.95.

The only collection ever assembled of all the drawings and engineering specifications on the incomparable and very collectable L.C. Smith shotgun.

The Police Shotgun Manual, by Robert H. Robinson, Charles C. Thomas, Springfield, IL 1973. 153 pp., illus. $21.50.

A complete study and analysis of the most versatile and effective weapon in the police arsenal.

Purdey's, the Guns and the Family, by Richard Beaumont, David and Charles, Pombret, VT, 1984. 248 pp., illus. $28.00.

Records the history of the Purdey family from 1814 to today, how the guns were and are built and daily functioning of the factory.

Reloading for Shotgunners, 2nd Edition, edited by Robert S.L. Anderson, DBI Books, Inc., Northbrook, IL, 1985. 256 pp., illus. Paper covers. $11.95.

The very latest in reloading information for the shotgunner.

Score Better at Skeet, by Fred Missildine, with Nick Karas. Winchester Press, NY 1972. 160 pp., illus. $15.00.

The long-awaited companion volume to *Score Better at Trap.*

Score Better at Trap, by Fred Missildine, Winchester Press, Piscataway, NJ, 1976. 159 pp., illus. $15.00.

An essential book for all trap shooters.

75 Years with the Shotgun, by C.T. (Buck) Buckman, Valley Publ., Fresno, CA, 1974. 141 pp., illus. $10.00.

An expert hunter and trapshooter shares experiences of a lifetime.

The Shotgun Book, by Jack O'Connor, Alfred A. Knopf, New York, NY, 2nd rev. ed., 1981. 341 pp., illus. Paper covers. $9.95.

An indispensable book for every shotgunner containing authoritative information on every phase of the shotgun.

The Shotgun in Combat, by Tony Lesce, Desert Publications, Cornville, AZ, 1979. 148 pp., illus. Paper covers. $8.00.

A history of the shotgun and its use in combat.

Shotgun Digest, 3rd Edition, edited by Jack Lewis, DBI Books, Inc., Northbrook, IL 1986. 256 pp., illus. Paper covers. $12.95.

A new look at shotguns.

Shotgunners Guide, by Monte Burch, Winchester Press, Piscataway, NJ, 1980. 208 pp., illus. $18.95.

A basic book for the young and old who want to try shotgunning or who want to improve their skill.

Shotgunning: The Art and the Science, by Bob Brister, Winchester Press, Piscataway, NJ, 1976. 321 pp., illus. $16.95.

Hundreds of specific tips and truly novel techniques to improve the field and target shooting of every shotgunner.

The Sporting Shotgun: A User's Handbook, by Robin Marshall-Ball, Stonewall Press, Wash., DC, 1982. 176 pp., illus. $23.95.

An important international reference on shotgunning in North America and Europe, including Britain.

Sure-Hit Shotgun Ways, by Francis E. Sell, Stackpole Books, Harrisburg, PA, 1967. 160 pp., illus. $15.00.

On guns, ballistics and quick skill methods.

Skeet Shooting with D. Lee Braun, edited by R. Campbell, Grosset & Dunlap, NY, 1967. 160 pp., illus. Paper covers $5.95.

Thorough instructions on the fine points of Skeet shooting.

Trapshooting with D. Lee Braun and the Remington Pros., ed. by R. Campbell. Remington Arms Co., Bridgeport, CT. 1969. 157 pp., well illus., Paper covers. $5.95.

America's masters of the scattergun give the secrets of professional marksmanship.

The Winchester Model Twelve, by George Madis, David Madis, Dallas, TX, 1984. 176 pp., illus.$19.95.

A definitive work on this famous American shotgun.

Winchester Shotguns and Shotshells, by Ronald W. Stadt, Armory Publications, Tacoma, WA, 1984. 200 pp., illus. $29.50.

From the hammer double to the Model 59.

Wing & Shot, by R.G. Wehle, Country Press, Scottsville, NY, 1967. 190 pp., illus. $24.95.

Step-by-step account on how to train a fine shooting dog.

The World's Fighting Shotguns, by Thomas F. Swearengen, T. B. N. Enterprises, Alexandria, VA 1979. 500 pp., illus. $29.95.

The complete military and police reference work from the shotgun's inception to date, with up-to-date developments.

IMPORTANT NOTICE TO BOOK BUYERS

Books listed here may be bought from Ray Riling Arms Books Co., 6844 Gorsten St., Philadelphia, PA 19119, phone 215/438-2456. Joe Riling, the proprietor, is the researcher and compiler of ''The Arms Library'' and a seller of gun books for over 30 years.

The Riling stock includes books classic and modern, many hard-to-find items, and many not obtainable elsewhere. These pages list a portion of the current stock. They offer prompt, complete service, with delayed shipments occurring only on out-of-print or out-of-stock books.

NOTICE FOR ALL CUSTOMERS: Remittance in U.S. funds must accompany all orders. For U.S. add $1.75 per book for postage and insurance. Minimum order $10.00. For U.P.S. add 50% to mailing costs.

All foreign countries add $2.25 per book for postage and handling, plus $3.60 per 10-lb. package or under for safe delivery by registered mail. Parcels not registered are sent at the ''buyers risk.''

Payments in excess of order or for ''Backorders'' are credited or fully refunded at request. Books ''As-Ordered'' are not returnable except by permission and a handling charge on these of $2.00 per book is deducted from refund or credit. Only Pennsylvania customers must include current sales tax.

A full variety of arms books are also available from Rutgers Book Center, 127 Raritan Ave., Highland Park, NJ 08904.

ARMS ASSOCIATIONS IN AMERICA AND ABROAD

UNITED STATES

ALABAMA

Alabama Gun Collectors Assn.
Dick Boyd, Secy., P.O. Box 5548, Tuscaloosa, AL 35405

ARIZONA

Arizona Arms Assn.,
Clay Fobes, Secy., P.O. Box 17061, Tucson, AZ 85731

CALIFORNIA

Calif. Hunters & Gun Owners Assoc.
V.H. Wacker, 2309 Cipriani Blvd., Belmont, CA 94002
Greater Calif. Arms & Collectors Assn.
Donald L. Bullock, 8291 Carburton St., Long Beach, CA 90808
Los Angeles Gun & Ctg. Collectors Assn.
F.H. Ruffra, 20810 Amie Ave., Apt. #9, Torrance, CA 90503

COLORADO

Pikes Peak Gun Collectors Guild
Charles Cell, 406 E. Uintah St., Colorado Springs, CO 80903

CONNECTICUT

Ye Conn. Gun Guild, Inc.
Robert L. Harris, P.O. Box 8, Cornwall Bridge, CT 06754

FLORIDA

Florida Gun Collectors Assn., Inc.
John D. Hammer, 5700 Mariner Dr., 304-W, Tampa, FL 33609
Tampa Bay Arms Collectors' Assn.
John Tuvell, 2461 — 67th Ave. S., St. Petersburg, FL 33712
Unified Sportsmen of Florida
P.O. Box 6565, Tallahassee, FL 32314

GEORGIA

Georgia Arms Collectors
Cecil W. Anderson, P.O. Box 218, Conley, GA 30027

HAWAII

Hawaii Historic Arms Assn.
John A. Bell, P.O. Box 1733, Honolulu, HI 96806

IDAHO

Idaho State Rifle and Pistol Assn.
Tom Price, 3631 Pineridge Dr., Coeur d'Alene, ID 83814

ILLINOIS

Fox Valley Arms Fellowship, Inc.
16 S. Bothwell St., Palatine, IL 60067
Illinois State Rifle Assn.
520 N. Michigan Ave., Room 615, Chicago, IL 60611
Illinois Gun Collectors Assn.
195 So. Schuyler Ave., Bradley, IL 60915
Mississippi Valley Gun & Cartridge Coll. Assn.
Lawrence Maynard, R.R. 2, Aledo, IL 61231
NIPDEA
c/o Phil Stanger, 1029 Castlewood Lane, Deerfield, IL 60015

Sauk Trail Gun Collectors
Gordell M. Matson, P.O. Box 1057, Milan, IL 61264
Wabash Valley Gun Collectors Assn., Inc.
Eberhard R. Gerbsch, 416 South St., Danville, IL 61832

INDIANA

Indiana Sportsmen's Council-Legislative
Maurice Latimer, P.O. Box 93, Bloomington, IN 47402
Indiana State Rifle & Pistol Assn.
Thos. Glancy, P.O. Box 552, Chesterton, IN 46304
Southern Indiana Gun Collectors Assn., Inc.
Harold M. McClary, 509 N. 3rd St., Boonville, IN 47601

IOWA

Central States Gun Collectors Assn.
Avery Giles, 1104 S. 1st Ave., Marshtown, IA 50158

KANSAS

Four State Collectors Assn.
M.G. Wilkinson, 915 E. 10th, Pittsburg, KS 66762
Kansas Cartridge Coll. Assn.
Bob Linder, Box 84, Plainville, KS 67663
Missouri Valley Arms Collectors Assn.
Chas. F. Samuel, Jr., Box 8204, Shawnee Mission, KS 66208

KENTUCKY

Kentuckiana Arms Coll. Assn.
Tony Wilson, Pres., Box 1776, Louisville, KY 40201
Kentucky Gun Collectors Assn., Inc.
Ruth Johnson, Box 64, Owensboro, KY 42302

LOUISIANA

Washitaw River Renegades
Sandra Rushing, P.O. Box 256, Main St., Grayson, LA 71435

MARYLAND

Baltimore Antique Arms Assn.
Stanley I. Kellert, E-30, 2600 Insulator Dr., Baltimore, MD 21230

MASSACHUSETTS

Bay Colony Weapons Collectors, Inc.
Ronald B. Santurjian, 47 Homer Rd., Belmont, MA 02178
Massachusetts Arms Collectors
John J. Callan, Jr., P.O. Box 1001, Worcester, MA 01613

MICHIGAN

Royal Oak Historical Arms Collectors, Inc.
Nancy Stein, 25487 Hereford, Huntington Woods, MI 48070

MINNESOTA

Minnesota Weapons Coll. Assn., Inc.
Box 662, Hopkins, MN 55343

MISSISSIPPI

Mississippi Gun Collectors Assn.
Mrs. Jack E. Swinney, P.O. Box 1332, Hattiesburg, MS 39401

MISSOURI

Mineral Belt Gun Coll. Assn.
D.F. Saunders, 1110 Cleveland Ave., Monett, MO 65708

MONTANA

Montana Arms Collectors Assn.
Lewis E. Yearout, 308 Riverview Dr. East, Great Falls, MT 59404
The Winchester Arms Coll. Assn.
Lewis E. Yearout, 308 Riverview Dr. East, Great Falls, MT 59404

NEW HAMPSHIRE

New Hampshire Arms Collectors, Inc.
Frank H. Galeucia, Rte. 28, Box 44, Windham, NH 03087

NEW JERSEY

Englishtown Benchrest Shooters Assn.
Michael Toth, 64 Cooke Ave., Carteret, NJ 07008
Experimental Ballistics Associates
Ed Yard, 110 Kensington, Trenton, NJ 08618
Jersey Shore Antique Arms Collectors
Joe Sisia, P.O. Box 100, Bayville, NJ 08721
New Jersey Arms Collectors Club, Inc.
Angus Laidlaw, 230 Valley Rd., Montclair, NJ 07042

NEW YORK

Empire State Arms Coll. Assn.
P.O. Box 2328, Rochester, NY 14623
Hudson-Mohawk Arms Collectors Assn., Inc.
Bennie S. Pisarz, 6 Lamberson St., Dolgeville, NY 13329
Iroquois Arms Collectors Assn.
Kenneth Keller, club secy., (Susann Keller, show secy.) 214 - 70th St., Niagara Falls, NY 14304
Mid-State Arms Coll. & Shooters Club
Jack Ackerman, 24 S. Mountain Terr., Binghamton, NY 13903

NORTH CAROLINA

Carolina Gun Collectors Assn.
Jerry Ledford, 3231 - 7th St. Dr. NE, Hickory, NC 28601

OHIO

Central Ohio Gun and Indian Relic Coll. Assn.
Coyt Stookey, 134 E. Ohio Ave., Washington C.H., OH 43160
Ohio Gun Collectors, Assn.
P.O. Box 24 F, Cincinnati, OH 45224
The Stark Gun Collectors, Inc.
William I. Gann, 5666 Waynesburg Dr., Waynesburg, OH 44688

OKLAHOMA

Indian Territory Gun Collector's Assn.
P.O. Box 4491, Tulsa, OK 74159

OREGON

Oregon Cartridge Coll. Assn.
Richard D. King, 3228 N.W. 60th, Corvallis, OR 97330

Oregon Arms Coll. Assn., Inc.
Ted Dowd, P.O. Box 25103, Portland, OR 97225

PENNSYLVANIA

Presque Isle Gun Coll. Assn.
James Welch, 156 E. 37 St., Erie, PA 16504

SOUTH CAROLINA

Belton Gun Club, Inc.
J.K. Phillips, Route 1, Belton, SC 29627

SOUTH DAKOTA

Dakota Territory Gun Coll. Assn., Inc.
Curt Carter, Castlewood, SD 57223

TENNESSEE

Memphis Antique Weapons Assn.
Jan Clement, 1886 Lyndale #1, Memphis TN 38107
Smoky Mountain Gun Coll. Assn., Inc.
Hugh W. Yarbro, P.O. Box 286, Knoxville, TN 37901
Tennessee Gun Collectors Assn., Inc.
M.H. Parks, 3556 Pleasant Valley Rd., Nashville, TN 37204

TEXAS

Houston Gun Collectors Assn., Inc.
P.O. Box 741429, Houston, TX 77274
Texas State Rifle Assn.
P.O. Drawer 710549, Dallas, TX 75371

WASHINGTON

Washington Arms Collectors, Inc.
J. Dennis Cook, P.O. Box 7335, Tacoma, WA 98407

WISCONSIN

Great Lakes Arms Coll. Assn., Inc.
Edward C. Warnke, 2913 Woodridge Lane, Waukesha, WI 53186
Wisconsin Gun Collectors Assn., Inc.
Lulita Zellmer, P.O. Box 181, Sussex, WI 53089

WYOMING

Wyoming Gun Collectors
Bob Funk, Box 1805, Riverton, WY 82501

NATIONAL ORGANIZATIONS

Amateur Trapshooting Assn.
P.O. Box 458, Vandalia, OH 45377
American Association of Shotgunning
P.O. Box 3351, Reno, NV 89505
American Defense Preparedness Assn.
Rosslyn Center, Suite 900, 1700 N. Moore St., Arlington, VA 22209
American Police Pistol & Rifle Assn.
1100 N.E. 125th St., No. Miami, FL 33161
American Single Shot Rifle Assn.
L.B. Thompson, 987 Jefferson Ave., Salem, OH 44460
American Society of Arms Collectors, Inc.
Robt. F. Rubendunst, 6550 Baywood Lane, Cincinnati, OH 45224
Association of Firearm and Toolmark Examiners
Eugenia A. Bell, Secy., 7857 Esterel Dr., LaJolla, CA 92037
Boone & Crockett Club
205 South Patrick, Alexandria, VA 22314
Cast Bullet Assn., Inc.
Ralland J. Fortier, 14193 Van Doren Rd., Manassas, VA 22111
Citizens Committee for the Right to Keep and Bear Arms
Natl. Hq.: Liberty Park, 12500 N.E. Tenth Pl., Bellevue, WA 98005

Deer Unlimited of America, Inc.
P.O. Box 509, Clemson, SC 29631
Ducks Unlimited, Inc.
One Waterfowl Way, Long Grove, IL 60047
Experimental Ballistics Associates
Ed Yard, 110 Kensington, Trenton, NJ 08618
Handgun Hunters International
J. D. Jones, Dir., P. O. Box 357 MAG, Bloomingdale, OH 43910
International Benchrest Shooters
Evelyn Richards, 411 N. Wilbur Ave. Sayre, PA 18840
International Cartridge Coll. Assn., Inc.
Victor v. B. Engel, 1211 Walnut St., Williamsport, PA 17701
International Handgun Metallic Silhouette Assoc.
Box 1609, Idaho Falls, ID 83401
International Military Arms Society
David M. Armstrong, P.O. Box 122, Williamstown, WV 26187
International Quail Foundation
P.O. Box 550, Edgefield, SC 29824-0550
The Mannlicher Collectors Assn.
Rev. Don L. Henry, Secy., P.O. Box 7144, Salem, OR 97303
Marlin Firearms Coll. Assn., Ltd.
Dick Paterson, Secy., 407 Lincoln Bldg., 44 Main St., Champaign, IL 61820
Miniature Arms Collectors/Makers Society Ltd.
Joseph J. Macewicz, Exec. Secy., 104 White Sand Lane, Racine, WI 53402
National Assn. of Federally Licd. Firearms Dealers
Andrew Molchan, 2801 E. Oakland Park Blvd., Ft. Lauderdale, Fl 33306
National Automatic Pistol Collectors Assn.
Tom Knox, P.O. Box 15738, Tower Grove Station, St. Louis, MO 63163
National Bench Rest Shooters Assn., Inc.
Stella Buchtel, 5735 Sherwood Forest Dr., Akron, OH 44319
National Muzzle Loading Rifle Assn.
Box 67, Friendship, IN 47021
National Reloading Mfrs. Assn.
4905 S.W. Griffith Dr., Suite 101, Beaverton, OR 97005
National Rifle Assn. of America
1600 Rhode Island Ave., N.W., Washington, DC 20036
National Shooting Sports Fdtn., Inc.
Arnold H. Rohlfing, Exec. Director, P.O. Box 1075, Riverside, Ct 06878
National Skeet Shooting Assn.
Ann Myers, Exec. Director, P.O. Box 28188, San Antonio, TX 78228
National Varmint Hunters Assn. (NVHA)
P.O. Box 17962, San Antonio, TX 78217
National Wild Turkey Federation, Inc.
P.O. Box 530, Edgefield, SC 29824
North American Hunting Club
7901 Flying Cloud Dr., P.O. Box 35557, Minneapolis, MN 55435
North-South Skirmish Assn., Inc.
T.E. Johnson, Jr., 9700 Royerton Dr., Richmond, VA 23228
Remington Society of America
Fritz Baehr, 3125 Fremont Ave., Boulder, CO 80302
Ruger Collector's Assn., Inc.
Nancy J. Padua, P.O. Box 211, Trumbull, CT 06611
SAAMI, Sporting Arms and Ammunition Manufacturers' Institute, Inc.
P.O. Box 218, Wallingford, CT 06492
Safari Club International
Holt Bodinson, 5151 E. Broadway, Suite 1680, Tucson, AZ 85711
Sako Collectors Assn., Inc.
Mims C. Reed, Pres., 313 Cooper Dr., Hurst, TX 76053
Second Amendment Foundation
James Madison Building, 12500 N.E. 10th Pl., Bellevue, WA 98005
Slug Shooters International
P.O. Box 402, McHenry, IL 60050
Southern California Schuetzen Society
Rick Van Meter, P.O. Box 11152, Phoenix, AZ 85061
U.S. Revolver Assn.
Chick Shuter, 96 West Union St., Ashland, MA 01721
Winchester Arms Collectors Assoc.
Lewis E. Yearout, 308 Riverview Dr., E., Great Falls, MT 59404
World Fast Draw Assn.
Bob Arganbright, 4704 Upshaw, Northwoods, MO 63121

AUSTRALIA

Sporting Shooters' Assn. of Australia Inc.
Mr. K. MacLaine, P.O. Box 210, Belgrave, Vict. 3160, Australia

CANADA

Alberta

Canadian Historical Arms Society
P.O. Box 901, Edmonton, Alb., Canada T5J 2L8
National Firearms Assn.
Natl. HQ: P.O. Box 1779, Edmonton, Alta. T5J 2P1, Canada

BRITISH COLUMBIA

Historical Arms Collectors Society of B.C.
Ron Tyson, Box 80583, Burnaby, B.C. Canada V5H 3X9

NEW BRUNSWICK

Canadian Black Powder Federation
Mrs. Janet McConnell, P.O. Box 2876, Postal Sta. ''A'', Moncton, N.B. E1C 8T8, Can.

ONTARIO

Ajax Antique Arms Assn.
Monica A. Wright, P.O. Box 145, Millgrove, Ont., L0R 1V0, Canada
The Ontario Handgun Assn.
1711 McCowan Rd., Suite 205, Scarborough, Ont., M1S 2Y3, Canada
Oshawa Antique Gun Coll. Inc.
Monica A. Wright, P.O. Box 145,. Millgrove, Ont., L0R 1V0, Canada
Tri-County Antique Arms Fair
P.O. Box 122, R.R. #1, North Lancaster, Ont., K0C 1Z0, Canada

EUROPE

ENGLAND

Arms and Armour Society of London
A.R.E. North. Dept. of Metalwork, Victoria & Albert Museum, South Kensington, London SW7 2RL
British Cartridge Collectors Club
Peter F. McGowan, 15 Fuller St., Ruddington, Nottingham
Historical Breechloading Smallarms Assn.
D.J. Penn, M.A., Imperial War Museum, Lambeth Rd., London SE1 6HZ, England.Journal and newsletter are $8 a yr. seamail; surcharge for airmail
National Rifle Assn. (British)
Bisley Camp, Brookwood, Woking, Surrey, GU24 OPB, England

FRANCE

Syndicat National de l'Arquebuserie du Commerce de l'Arme Historique
B.P. No 3, 78110 Le Vesient, France

GERMANY (WEST)

Deutscher Schützenbund
Lahnstrasse, 6200 Wiesbaden-Klarenthal, West Germany

NEW ZEALAND

New Zealand Deerstalkers Assn.
Mr. Shelby Grant, P.O. Box 6514, Wellington, New Zealand

SOUTH AFRICA

Historical Firearms Soc. of South Africa
P.O. Box 145, 7725 Newlands, Republic of South Africa
South African Reloaders Assn.
Box 27128, Sunnyside, Pretoria 0132, South Africa

Directory of the Arms Trade

INDEX TO THE DIRECTORY

AMMUNITION (Commercial)

Activ Industries, Inc., P.O. Box 238, Kearneysville, WV 25430/304-725-0451 (shotshells only)
Alberts Corp., 519 East 19th St., Paterson, NJ 07514/201-684-1676
BBM Corp., 221 Interstate Dr., West Springfield, MA 01089/413-737-3118 (45 ACP shotshell)
Bingham Ltd., 1775-C Wilwat Dr., Norcross, GA 30093
C.W. Cartridge Co., 71 Hackensack St., Wood-Ridge, NJ 07075/201-438-5111 (Sharps combustible cartridges)
Cascade Cartridge Inc., (See Omark)
Dynamit Nobel of America, Inc., 105 Stonehurst Court, Northvale, NJ 07647/201-767-1660(RWS)
Eley-Kynoch, ICI-America, Wilmington, DE 19897/302-575-3000
Estate Cartridge Inc., P.O. Box 3702, Conroe, TX 77305 (shotshell)
Federal Cartridge Co., 2700 Foshay Tower, Minneapolis, MN 55402/612-333-8255
Fisher Enterprises, 655 Main St. #305, Edmonds, WA 98020/206-776-4365 (Prometheus airgun pellets)
Frontier Cartridge Division-Hornady Mfg. Co., Box 1848, Grand Island, NE 68801/308-382-1390

Hansen Cartridge Co., 244 Old Post Rd., Southport, CT 06490/203-259-7337
ICI-America, Wilmington, DE 19897/302-575-3000(Eley-Kynoch)
Midway Arms, Inc., 7450 Old Hwy. 40 West, Columbia, MO 65201/314-445-9521
Nevins Ammunition, Inc., 7614 Lemhi Ave., Suite #1, Boise, ID 83709/208-322-8611 (centerfire handgun)
Omark Industries, P.O. Box 856, Lewiston, ID 83501/208-746-2351
P.P.C. Corp., 625 E. 24th St., Paterson, NJ 07514
Precision Prods. of Wash., Inc., N. 311 Walnut Rd., Spokane, WA 99206/509-928-0604 (Exammo)
Prometheus/Titan Black (See Fisher Enterprises)
RWS (See Dynamit Nobel of America)
Remington Arms Co., 1077 Market St., Wilmington, DE 19898
Service Armament, 689 Bergen Blvd., Ridgefield, NJ 07657
Super Vel, FPC, Inc., Hamilton Rd., Rt. 2, P. O. Box 1398, Fond du Lac, WI 54935/414-921-2652
Ten-X Mfg., 2410 East Foxfarm Rd., Cheynne, WY 82001
3-D Inv., Inc., Box J, Main St., Doniphan, NE 68832/402-845-2285
United States Ammunition Co. (USAC), Inc., 1476 Thorne Rd., Tacoma, WA 98421/206-627-8700
Weatherby's, 2781 E. Firestone Blvd., South Gate, CA 90280
Winchester, Shamrock St., East Alton, IL 62024

AMMUNITION (Custom)

A Square Co., Inc., Rt. 4, Simmons Rd., Madison, IN 47250/812-273-3633
Accuracy Systems Inc., 15203 N. Cave Creek Rd., Phoenix, AZ 85032/602-971-1991
Beal's Bullets, 170 W. Marshall Rd., Lansdowne, PA 19050/215-259-1220 (Auto Mag Specialists)
Bell's Gun & Sport Shop, 3309-19 Mannheim Rd., Franklin Park, IL 60131
Brass Extrusion Labs. Ltd., 800 W. Maple Lane, Bensenville, IL 60106
C.W. Cartridge Co., 71 Hackensack St., Wood-Ridge, NJ 07075 (201-438-5111)
Russell Campbell Custom Loaded Ammo, 219 Leisure Dr., San Antonio, TX 78201/512-735-1183
Cartridges Unlimited, Rt. 1, Box 50, South Kent, CT 06785/203-927-3053 (British Express; metric; U.S.)
Cumberland Arms, Rt. 1, Shafer Rd., Blantons Chapel, Manchester, TN 37355
Custom Tackle & Ammo, P.O. Box 1886, Farmington, NM 87499/505-632-3539
Eagle Cap Custom Bullets, P.O. Box 659, Enterprise, OR 97828/503-426-4282
E.W. Ellis Sport Shop, RFD 1, Box 315, Corinth, NY 12822
Ellwood Epps Northern Ltd., 210 Worthington St. W., North Bay, Ont. PIB 3B4, Canada
Estate Cartridge Inc., P.O. Box 3702, Conroe, TX 77305/409-539-9144 (shotshell)
Jack First Distributors, Inc., 44633 Sierra Hwy., Lancaster, CA 93534/805-945-6981
Ramon B. Gonzalez, P.O. Box 370, Monticello, NY 12701/914-794-4515
"Gramps" Antique Cartridges, Ellwood Epps, Box 341, Washago, Ont. L0K 2B0 Canada/705-689-5348
Hardin Specialty Distributors, P.O. Box 338, Radcliff, KY 40160/502-351-6649
R.H. Keeler, 817 "N" St., Port Angeles, WA 98362/206-457-4702
K.K. Arms Co., Star Route Box 671, Kerrville, TX 78028/512-257-4718
KTW Inc., 710 Foster Park Rd., Lorain, OH 44053 216/233-6919 (bullets)
Lindsley Arms Cartridge Co., Inc., P.O. Box 5738, Lake Worth, FL 33466/305-968-1678 (inq. S.A.S.E.)
Lomont Precision Bullets, 4236 West 700 South, Poneto, IN 46781/219-694-6792 (custom cast bullets only)
McConnellstown Reloading & Cast Bullets, Inc., R.D. 3, Box 40, Huntingdon, PA 16652/814-627-5402
Mack's Sport Shop, Box 1155, Kodiak, AK 99615/907-486-4276
North American Arms, 1800 North 300 West, Spanish Fork, UT 84660/801-798-9891
Numrich Arms Corp., 203 Broadway, W. Hurley, NY 12491
Olsen Development Lab., 307 Conestoga Way #37, Edgeville, PA 19403/215-631-1716 (Invicta)
Pearl Armory, Revenden Springs, AR 72460
Robert Pomeroy, Morison Ave., Corinth, ME 04427/207-285-7721 (custom shells)
Precision Ammo Co., P.O. Box 63, Garnerville, NY 10923/914-947-2720
Precision Prods. of Wash., Inc., N. 311 Walnut Rd., Spokane, WA 99206/509-928-0604 (Exammo)
Anthony F. Sailer-Ammunition (AFSCO), 731 W. Third St., Owen, WI 54460/715-229-2516
Sanders Cust. Gun Serv., 2358 Tyler Lane, Louisville, KY 40205
Senica Run, Inc., P.O. Box 3032, Greeley, CO 80633
George W. Spence, 115 Locust St., Steele, MO 63877/314-695-4926 (boxer-primed cartridges)
The 3-D Company, Box J, Main St., Doniphan, NE 68832/402-845-2285 (reloaded police ammo)
R. A. Wardrop, P.O. Box 245, Mechanicsburg, PA 17055/717-766-9663
Zero Ammunition Co., Inc., P.O. Box 1188, Cullman, AL 35056/205-739-1606

AMMUNITION (Foreign)

Action Arms Ltd., P. O. Box 9573, Philadelphia, PA 19124/215-744-0100
Armscor (See Pacific International Merch. Corp.)
Beeman Inc., 47-GDD Paul Drive, San Rafael, CA 94903/415-472-7121
Dan/Arms, 501 Office Center, Suite 128, P.O. Box 5040, Fort Washington, PA 19034/215-646-0720
Dynamit Nobel of America, Inc., 105 Stonehurst Court, Northvale, NJ 07647/210-767-1660(RWS, Geco, Rottweil)
FFV Norma, Inc., 300 S. Jefferson, Suite 301, Springfield, MO 65806/417-865-9314
Fiocchi of America, Inc., 1308 Chase, Springfield, MO 65803/417-864-6970
Hansen Cartridge Co., 244 Old Post Rd., Southport, CT 06490/203-259-7337
Norma, (See Outdoor Sports Headquarters, Inc.)
Hirtenberger Patronen-, Zündhütchen- & Metallwarenfabrik, A.G., Leobersdorfer Str. 33, A2552 Hirtenberg, Austria
Paul Jaeger, Inc., P.O. Box 449, 1 Madison Ave., Grand Junction, TN 38039/901-764-6909 (RWS centerfire ammo)
Kendall International Arms, Inc., 501 East North, Carlisle, KY 40311/606-289-7336 (Lapua)
Lapua (See Kendall International, Inc.)
PMC (See Patton and Morgan Corp.)
Pacific International Merchandising, 2215 "J" St., Sacramento, CA 95816/916-446-2737
Patton and Morgan Corp., 5900 Wilshire Blvd., Suite 1400, Los Angeles, CA 90036/213-938-0143 (PMC ammo)
RWS (Rheinische-Westfälische Sprengstoff) [See Dynamit Nobel of America; Paul Jaeger, Inc.]
Sports Emporium, 1414 Willow Ave., Philadelphia, PA 19126 (Danarms shotshells)

AMMUNITION COMPONENTS—BULLETS, POWDER, PRIMERS

A Square Co., Inc., Rt. 4, Simmons Rd., Madison, IN 47250/812-273-3633 (cust. bull.; brass)
Accurate Arms Co., Inc., (Propellents Div.), Rt. 1, Box 167, McEwen, TN, 37101/615-729-4207/4208 (powders)
Acme Custom Bullets, 5708 Evers Rd., San Antonio, TX 78238/512-680-4828
Alaska Bullet Works, P.O. Box 54, Douglas, AK 99824 (Alaska copper-bond cust.)
Alberts Corp., 519 E. 19th St., Paterson, NJ 07514/201-684-1676 (swaged bullets)
American Bullets, P.O. Box 15313, Atlanta, GA 30333/404-482-4253
Ammo-O-Mart Ltd., P.O. Box 125, Hawkesbury, Ont., Canada K6A 2R8/613-632-9300 (Nobel powder)
Ballistic Prods., Inc., Box 488, 2105 Shaughnessy Circle, Long Lake, MN 55356
Ballistic Research Industries (BRI), 2825 S. Rodeo Gulch Rd. #8, Soquel, CA 95073/408-476-7981 (12-ga. Sabo shotgun slug)
Barnes Bullets, Inc., P.O. Box 215, American Fork, UT 84003/801-756-4222
Bell's Gun & Sport Shop, 3309-19 Mannheim Rd., Franklin Pk., IL 60131/312-678-1900
Bergman and Williams, 2450 Losee Rd., Las Vegas, NV 89030/702-642-1091 (copper tube 308 cust. bull.; lead wire i. all sizes)
Bitterroot Bullet Co., Box 412, Lewiston, ID 83501/208-743-5635 (Coin or stamps) f.50¢ U.S.; 75¢ Can. & Mex.; intl. $3.00 and #10 SASE for lit.
Black Mountain Bullets, Rte. 3, Box 297, Warrenton, VA 22186/703-347-1199 (custom Fluid King match bullets)
B.E.L.L., Brass Extrusion Laboratories, Ltd., 800 W. Maple Lane, Bensenville, IL 60106
Milton Brynin, 214 E. Third St., Mount Vernon, NY 10550/914-664-1311 (cast bullets)
Buffalo Rock Shooter Supply (See Chevron Bullets)
CCI, (See: Omark Industries)
CheVron Bullets, R.R. 1, Ottawa, IL 61350/815-433-2471
Kenneth E. Clark, 18738 Highway 99, Madera, CA 93637/209-674-6016 (Bullets)
Clete's Custom Bullets, RR 6, Box 1348, Warsaw, IN 46580
Cooper-Woodward, P.O. Box 972, Riverside, CA 92502/714-822-4176
Corbin Mfg. & Supply, Inc., P.O. Box 2659, White City, OR 97503/503-826-5211 (bullets)
Cor-Bon Custom Bullets, P.O. Box 10126, Detroit, MI 48210/313-894-2373 (375, 44, 45 solid brass partition bull.)
Custom Bullets by Hoffman, 2604 Peconic Ave. Seaford, NY 11783 (7mm, 308, 257, 224, 270)
Division Lead, 7742 W. 61 Pl., Summit, IL 60502
DuPont, Explosives Dept., Wilmington, DE 19898
Dynamit Nobel of America, Inc., 105 Stonehurst Court, Northvale, NJ 07647/201-767-1660 (RWS percussion caps)
Eagle Bullet Works, P.O. Box 2104, White City, OR 97503/503-826-7143 (Div-Cor 375, 224, 257 cust. bull.)
Eagle Cap Custom Bullets, P.O. Box 659, Enterprise, OR 97828/503-426-4282
Elk Mountain Shooters Supply Inc., 1719 Marie, Pasco, WA 99301 (Alaskan bullets)
Excaliber Wax, Inc., P.O. Box 432, Kenton, OH 43326/419-673-0512 (wax bullets)
Federal Cartridge Co., 2700 Foshay Tower, Minneapolis, MN 55402/612-333-8255 (nickel cases)
FFV Norma, Inc., 300 S. Jefferson, Suite 301, Springfield, MO 65806/417-865-9314 (powder)
Fisher Enterprises, 655 Main St. #305, Edmonds, WA 98020/206-776-4365
Forty Five Ranch Enterprises, 119 S. Main, Miami, OK 74354/918-542-9307
Fowlers, 3731 McKelvey St., Charlotte, NC 28215/704-568-7661 (benchrest bullets)
Glaser Safety Slug, P.O. Box 8223, Foster City, CA 94404/415-345-7677
Godfrey Reloading Supply, Hi-Way 67-111, Brighton, IL 62012 (cast bullets)
Lynn Godfrey, (See: Elk Mtn. Shooters Supply)
GOEX, Inc., Belin Plant, 1002 Springbrook Ave., Moosic, PA 18507/717-457-6724 (black powder)
Green Bay Bullets, P.O. Box 10446, 1486 Servais St., Green Bay, WI 54307-54304/414-497-2949 (cast lead bullets)
Grills-Hanna Bulletsmith Co., Lt., Box 655, Black Diamond, Alb. TOL OHO Canada/403-652-4393 (38, 9mm, 12-ga.)
GTM Co., George T. Mahaney, 15915B E. Main St., La Puente, CA 91744 (all brass shotshells)
Hansen Custom Bullets, 3221 Shelley St., Mohegan, NY 10547
Hardin Specialty Distr., P. O. Box 338, Radcliff, KY 40160/502-351-6649 (empty, primed cases)
Robert W. Hart & Son, Inc. 401 Montgomery St., Nescopeck, PA 18635/717-752-3655
Hercules Inc., Hercules Plaza, Wilmington, DE 19894 (smokeless powder)
Hodgdon Powder Co. Inc., P.O. Box 2932, Shawnee Mission, KS 66201/913-362-9455
Hoffman New Ideas, Inc., 821 Northmoor Rd., Lake Forest, IL 60045/312-234-4075 (practice sub.vel. bullets)
Hornady Mfg. Co., P.O. Drawer 1848, Grand Island, NE 68802/308-382-1390
N.E. House Co., 195 West High St., E. Hampton, CT 06424/203-267-2133 (zinc bases in 30, 38, 44 and 45-cal. only)
Huntington's, P.O. Box 991, 601 Oro Dam Blvd., Oroville, CA 95965/916-534-1210
Jaro Manuf., P.O. Box 6125, 206 E. Shaw, Pasadena, TX 77506/713-472-0471 (bullets)
J&J Custom Bullet, 1210 El Rey Ave., El Cajon, CA 92021 (Power-Pak)
J&P Enterprises, 2999 Dyke Rd., Northpole, AK 99705/907-488-1534 (Grizzly 4-cal. ogive 32&49 mil. bonded core tubing bull.)
Ka Pu Kapili, P.O. Box 745, Honokaa, HI 96272 (Hawaiian Special cust. bullets)
Kendall International Arms, Inc., 501 East North, Carlisle, KY 40311/606-289-7336 (Lapua bull.)

Kodiak Custom Bullets, 8261 Henry Circle, Anchorage, AK 99507
L.L.F. Die Shop, 1281 Highway 99 North, Eugene, OR 97402/503-688-5753
Lage Uniwad Co., 1814 21st St., Eldora, IA 50627/515-858-2634
Lapua (See Kendall International Arms)
Ljutic Ind., Inc., Box 2117, Yakima, WA 98902 (Mono-wads)
Lomont Precision Bullets, 4236 West 700 South, Poneto, IN 46781/219-694-6792 (custom cast bullets)
Paul E. Low Jr., R.R. 1, Dunlap, IL 61525/309-685-1392 (jacketed 44- & 45-cal. bullets)
Lyman Products Corp., Rte. 147, Middlefield, CT 06455
McConnellstown Reloading & Cast Bullets, Inc., R.D. 3, Box 40, Huntingdon, PA 16652/814-627-5402
Mack's Sport Shop, Box 1155, Kodiak, AK 99615/907-486-4276 (cust. bull.)
Marshall Enterprises, 792 Canyon Rd., Redwood City, CA 94062/415-356-1230
Michael's Antiques, Box 233, Copiague, L.I., NY 11726 (Balle Blondeau)
Miller Trading Co., 20 S. Front St., Wilmington, NC 28401/919-762-7107 (bullets)
Morrison Custom Bullet Corp., P.O. Box 5574 Sta. Edmonton, Alb. T6C 3T5 Canada (9mm, 357 handgun)
Muzzleload Magnum Products (MMP), Route 6 Box 383, Harrison, AR 72601/501-741-5019 (sabots f. black powder)
NTC Inc., P.O. Box 4202, Portland, OR 97208
Non-Toxic Components, Inc., P.O. Box 4202, Portland, OR 97208 (steel shot kits)
NORMA (See FFV Norma)
Nosler Bullets Inc., 107 S.W. Columbia, Bend, OR 97702/503-382-5108
Old Western Scrounger, 12924 Hwy A-12, Montague, CA 96064/916-459-5445
Omark Industries, P.O. Box 856, Lewiston, ID 83501/208-746-2351
Oro-Tech Industries, Inc., 1701 W. Charleston Blvd., Suite 510, Las Vegas, NV 89102/702-382-8109 (Golden Powder)
PMC Ammunition, 5400 Wilshire Blvd., Suite 1400, Los Angeles, CA 90036/213-938-3201
Pepperbox Gun Shop, P.O. Box 922, East Moline, IL 61244/309-796-0616 (257, 224 rifle cal. custom swaged bullets)
Pyrodex, See: Hodgdon Powder Co., Inc. (black powder substitute)
Robert Pomeroy, Morison Ave., East Corinth, ME 04427/207-285-7721 (empty cases)
Power Plus Enterprises, 6939 Macon Rd. #15, Columbus, GA 31907/404-561-1717 (12-ga. shotguns slugs; 308, 45 ACP, 357 cust. bull.)
Precision Ammo Co., P.O. Drawer 86, Valley Cottage, NY 10989/914-947-2710
Precision Swaged Bullets, Rte. 1, Box 93H, Ronan, MT 59864/406-676-5135 (silhouette; out-of-prods. Sharps)
Professional Hunter Supplies, P.O. Box 608, Ferndale, CA 95536/707-786-9460 (408, 375, 308, 510 cust. bull.)
Prometheus/Titan Black (See Fisher Enterprises)
Prospect Bullets, D.B.M. Specialty, P.O. Box 58, Holmes, PA 19043/215-586-6240 (9mm, 38 cust.)
Redwood Bullet Works, 3559 Bay Rd., Redwood City, CA 94063 (cust.)
Remington-Peters, 1007 Market St., Wilmington, DE 19898
S&S Precision Bullets, 22963 La Cadena, Laguna Hills, CA 92653/714-768-6836 (linotype cast bull.)
Sansom Bullets, 2506 Rolling Hills, Dr., Greenville, TX 75401 (custom)
Sierra Bullets Inc., 10532 So. Painter Ave., Santa Fe Springs, CA 90670
Speer Products, Box 856, Lewiston, ID 83501
Supreme Products Co., 1830 S. California Ave., Monrovia, CA 91016/800-423-7159/818-357-5395 (rubber bullets)
Swift Bullet Co., Rt. 1, Quinter, KS 67752/913-754-3959 (375 big game, 224 cust.)
Tallon Bullets, 1194 Tidewood Dr., Bethel Park, PA 15102/412-471-4494 (dual. diam. 308 cust.)
Taracorp Industries, 16th & Cleveland Blvd., Granite City, IL 62040/618-451-4400 (Lawrence Brand lead shot)
Traft Gunshop, P.O. Box 1078, Buena Vista, CO 81211/303-395-6034 (cust. bull.)
Trophy Bonded Bullets, P.O. Box 262348, Houston, TX 77207/713-645-4499 (big game 458, 308, 375 bonded cust. bullets only)
Vitt & Boos, 2178 Nichols Ave., Stratford, CT 06497/203-375-6859 (Aerodynamic shotgun slug, 12-ga. only)
Winchester, Shamrock St., East Alton, IL 62024
Worthy Products, Inc., Box 88 Main St., Chippewa Bay, NY 13623/315-324-5450 (slug loads)
Zero Bullet Co. Inc., P.O. Box 1188, Cullman, AL 35056/205-739-1606

ANTIQUE ARMS DEALERS

AD Hominem, R.R. 3, Orillia, Ont., L3V 6H3, Canada/705-689-5303
Antique Arms Co., David F. Saunders, 1110 Cleveland, Monett, MO 65708/417-235-6501
Antique Gun Parts, Inc., 1118 S. Braddock Ave., Pittsburgh, PA 15218/412-241-1811
Armsport, Inc., 3590 N.W. 49th St., Miami, FL 33142/305-635-7850
Beeman Inc., 47 Paul Dr., San Rafael, CA 94903/415-472-7121 (airguns only)
Wm. Boggs, 1243 Grandview Ave., Columbus, OH
Century Arms, Inc., 5 Federal St., St. Albans, VT 05478/802-524-9541
Dave Chicoine, d/b/a Liberty A.S.P., 19 Key St., Eastport, ME 04631/207-853-2327

Chas. Clements, Handicrafts Unltd., 1741 Dallas St., Aurora, CO 80010/303-364-0403
Continental Kite & Key Co. (CONKKO), P.O. Box 40, Broomall, PA 19008/215-356-0711
Peter Dyson Ltd., 29-31 Church St., Honley, Huddersfield, W. Yorksh. HD7 2AH, England/0484-661062 (acc. f. ant. gun coll.; custom-and machine-made)
Ed's Gun House, Box 62, Rte. 1, Minnesota City, MN 55959/507-689-2925
Ellwood Epps Northern Ltd., 210 Worthington St. W., North Bay, Ont. P1B 3B4 Canada
William Fagan, 126 Belleview, Mount Clemens, MI 48043/313-465-4637
Jack First Distributors, Inc., 44633 Sierra Hwy., Lancaster, CA 93534/805-945-6981
N. Flayderman & Co., Squash Hollow, New Milford, CT 06776/203-354-5567
Chet Fulmer, P.O. Box 792, Rt. 2, Buffalo Lake, Detroit Lakes, MN 56501/218-847-7712
Robert S. Frielich, 396 Broome St., New York, NY 10013/212-254-3045
Garcia National Gun Traders, Inc., 225 S.W. 22nd Ave., Miami, FL 33135
Herb Glass, Bullville, NY 10915/914-361-3021
James Goergen, Rte. 2, Box 182BB, Austin, MN 55912/507-433-9280
Griffin's Guns & Antiques, R.R. 4, Peterboro, Ont., Canada K9J 6X5/705-745-7022
The Gun Shop, 6497 Pearl Rd., Parma Heights (Cleveland), OH 44130/216-884-7476
Hansen & Company, 244 Old Post Rd., Southport, CT 06490/203-259-7337
Kelley's Harold Kelley, Box 125, Woburn, MA 01801/617-935-3389
Lever Arms Serv. Ltd., 572 Howe St., Vancouver, B.C., Canada V6C 2E3/604-685-8945
Log Cabin Sport Shop, 8010 Lafayette Rd., Lodi, OH 44254/216-948-1082
Lone Pine Trading Post, Jct. Highways 61 and 248, Minnesota City, MN 55959/507-689-2925
Charles W. Moore, R.D. #1, Box 276, Schenevus, NY 12155/607-278-5721
Museum of Historical Arms, 1038 Alton Rd., Miami Beach, FL 33139/305-672-7480 (ctlg $5)
Muzzleloaders Etc. Inc., 9901 Lyndale Ave. So., Bloomington, MN 55420/612-884-1161
New Orleans Arms Co., 5001 Treasure St., New Orleans, LA 70186/504-944-3371
Old Western Scrounger, 12924 Hwy A-12, Montague, CA 96064/916-459-5445 (write for list; $2)
Pioneer Guns, 5228 Montgomery, (Cincinnati) Norwood, OH 45212/513-631-4871
Pony Express Sport Shop, Inc., 16606 Schoenborn St., Sepulveda, CA 91343/818-895-1231
Martin B. Retting, Inc., 11029 Washington, Culver City, CA 90232/213-837-6111
Ridge Guncraft, Inc., 125 E. Tyrone Rd., Oak Ridge, TN 37830/615-483-4024
San Francisco Gun Exch., 124 Second St., San Francisco, CA 94105/415-982-6097
Santa Ana Gunroom, P.O. Box 1777, Santa Ana, CA 92701/714-541-3035
Don L. Shrum's Cape Outfitters, 412 So. Kingshighway, Cape Girardeau, MO 63701/314-335-4103
S&S Firearms, 74-11 Myrtle Ave., Glendale, NY 11385/212-497-1100
Steves Gun House, Rte. 1, Minnesota City, MN 55959
James Wayne, 308 Leisure Lane, Victoria, TX 77904/512-578-1258
Ward & Van Valkenburg, 114-32nd Ave. N., Fargo, ND 58102
M.C. Wiest, 125 E. Tyrone Rd., Oak Ridge, TN 37830/615-483-4024
Lewis Yearout, 308 Riverview Dr. E., Great Falls, MT 59404

APPRAISERS, GUNS, ETC.

Ad Hominem, R.R. 3, Orillia, ON L3V 6H3, Canada/705-689-5303
Antique Gun Parts, Inc., 1118 So. Braddock Ave., Pittsburgh, PA 15218/412-241-1811
Ahlman's, Rt. 1, Box 20, Morristown, MN 55052/507-685-4244
The Armoury Inc., Route 202, New Preston, CT 06777/203-868-0001
Dave Chicoine, dba Liberty Antique Sixgun, 19 Key St., Eastport, ME 04631/207-853-2327
Chas. Clements, Handicrafts Unltd., 1741 Dallas St., Aurora, CO 80010/303-364-0403
Custom Tackle & Ammo, P.O. Box 1886, Farmington, NM 87499/505-632-3539
D.O.C. Specialists (D.A. Ulrich), 2209 So. Central Ave., Cicero, IL 60650/312-652-3606
Ellwood Epps (Orillia) Ltd., R.R. 3, Hwy. 11 No., Orillia, Ont. L3V 6H3, Canada/705-689-5333
N. Flayderman & Co., Inc., RFD 2, Squash Hollow, New Milford, CT 06776/203-354-5567
"Gramps" Antique Cartridges, Ellwood Epps, Box 341, Washago, Ont. L0K 2B0 Canada/705-689-5348
Griffin & Howe, 589 Broadway, New York, NY 10012/212-966-5323
Kelley's, Harold Kelley, Box 125, Woburn, MA 01801/617-935-3389
Kenneth Kogan, P.O. Box 130, Lafayette Hills, PA 19444/215-233-4509
Lone Pine Trading Post, Jct. Highways 248 & 61, Minnesota City, MN 55959/507-689-2925
Orvis Co. Inc., Rte. 7A, Manchester, VT 05254/802-362-3622
PM Airservices Ltd., P.O. Box 1573, Costa Mesa, CA 92628/714-968-2689
Pony Express Sport Shop, Inc., 16606 Schoenborn St., Sepulveda, CA 91343/818-895-1231
John Richards, Rte. 2, Bedford, KY 40006/502-255-7222
Lewis Yearout, 308 Riverview Dr. East, Great Falls, MT 59404/406-761-0589

AUCTIONEERS, GUNS, ETC.

Alberts Corp., 519 East 19th St., Paterson, NJ 07514/201-684-1676
Richard A. Bourne Co. Inc., Corporation St., Hyannis, MA 02647
Christies-East, 219 E. 67th St., New York, NY 10021
Tom Keilman, 12316 Indian Mount, Austin, TX 78758
Kelley's, Harold Kelley, Box 125, Woburn, MA 01801/617-935-3389
"Little John's" Antique Arms, 777 S. Main St., Orange, CA 92668
Wayne Mock, Inc., Box 37, Tamworth, NH 03886/603-323-8749
Parke-Bernet (see Sotheby's)
Sotheby's, 1334 York Ave. at 72nd St., New York, NY 10021
James C. Tillinghast, Box 19GD, Hancock, NH 03449

BOOKS (ARMS), Publishers and Dealers

Armory Publications, P.O. Box 44372, Tacoma, WA 98444/206-531-4632
Arms & Armour Press, 2-6 Hampstead High Street, London NW3 1QQ, England
Beeman Inc., 47 Paul Dr., San Rafael, CA 94903/415-472-7121 (airguns)
Blacksmith Corp., P.O. Box 424, Southport, CT 06490/203-367-4041
Blacktail Mountain Books, 42 First Ave. West, Kalispell, MT 59901/406-257-5573
Brownlee Books, Box 489, Hooks, TX 75561
DBI Books, Inc., 4092 Commercial Ave., Northbrook IL 60062/312-272-6310
Dove Press, P.O. Box 3882, Enid, OK 73702/405-234-4347
Fortress Publications Inc., P.O. Box 241, Stoney Creek, Ont. L8G 3X9, Canada/416-662-3505
Guncraft Books, Div. of Ridge Guncraft, Inc., 125 E. Tyrone Rd., Oak Ridge, TN 37830/615-483-4024
Gunnerman Books, P.O. Box 4292, Auburn Hills, MI 48057/313-879-2779
Handgun Press, 5832 S. Green, Chicago, IL 60621
Long Survival Publications, P.O. Box 163-GD, Wamego, KS 66547/913-456-7387
Lyman, Route 147, Middlefield, CT 06455
Paladin Press, P.O. Box 1307, Boulder, CO 80306/303-443-7250
Personal Firearms Record Book Co., P.O. Box 2800, Santa Fe, NM 87501/505-983-2381
Petersen Publishing Co., 84990 Sunset Blvd., Los Angeles, CA 99069
Gerald Pettinger Arms Books, Route 2, Russell, IA 50238/515-535-2239
Ray Riling Arms Books Co., 6844 Gorsten St., P.O. Box 18925, Philadelphia, PA 19119/215-438-2456
Rutgers Book Center, Mark Aziz, 127 Raritan Ave., Highland Park, NJ 08904/201-545-4344
Small Arms Press, Box 1316, St. George, UT 84770
Stackpole Books, Cameron & Kelker Sts., Telegraph Press Bldg., Harrisburg, PA 17105
Stoeger Publishing Co., 55 Ruta Court, South Hackensack, NJ 07606
Ken Trotman, 135 Ditton Walk, Unit 11, Cambridge CB5 8QD, England
Winchester Press, 220 Old New Brunswick Rd., Piscataway, NJ 08854/201-981-0820
Wolfe Publishing Co., Inc., 6471 Air Park Dr., Prescott, AZ 86302/602-445-7810

BULLET & CASE LUBRICANTS

C-H Tool & Die Corp., 106 N. Harding St., Owen, WI 54460/715-229-2146
Chopie Mfg. Inc., 700 Copeland Ave., La Crosse, WI 54601/608-784-0926 (Black-Solve)
Clenzoil Corp., P.O. Box 1226, Sta. C, Canton, OH 44708/216-833-9758
Cooper-Woodward, Box 972, Riverside, CA 92502/714-822-4176 (Perfect Lube)
Corbin Mfg. & Supply Inc., P.O. Box 2659, White City, OR 97503/503-826-5211
Fenwal, Inc., 400 Main St., Ashland, MA 01721/617-881-2000
Green Bay Bullets, 1486 Servais St., Green Bay, WI 54304/414-497-2949 (EZE-Size case lube)
Hodgdon Powder Co., Inc., P.O. Box 2932, Shawnee Mission, KS 66201/913-362-9455
Javelina Products, Box 337, San Bernardino, CA 92402/714-882-5847 (Alox beeswax)
Jet-Aer Corp., 100 Sixth Ave., Paterson, NJ 07524
LeClear Industries, 1126 Donald Ave., P.O. Box 484, Royal Oak, MI 48068/313-588-1025
Lyman Products Corp., Rte. 147, Middlefield, CT. 06455 (Size-Ezy)
Marmel Prods., P.O. Box 97, Utica, MI 48087/313-731-8029 (Marvellube, Marvelux)
Micro-Lube, P.O. Box 117, Mesilla Park, NM 88047/505-524-4215
Mirror Lube, 1305 Simpson Way, Suite K, Escondido, CA 92025/619-480-2518
M&N Bullet Lube, P.O. Box 495, 151 N.E. Jefferson St., Madras, OR 97741/503-475-2992
Northeast Industrial, Inc., P.O. Box 249, 405 N. Canyon Blvd., Canyon City, OR 97820/503-575-2513 (Ten X-Lube; NEI mold prep)
Pacific Tool Co., P.O. Box 2048, Ordnance Plant Rd., Grand Island, NE 68801/308-384-2308
RCBS, Inc., Box 1919, Oroville, CA 95965
Radix Research & Marketing, Box 247, Woodland Park, CO 80863/303-687-3182 (Magnum Dri-Lube)
SAECO Rel, 2207 Border Ave., Torrance, CA 90501/213-320-6973
Shooters Accessory Supply (SAS) (See Corbin Mfg. & Supply)
Tamarack Prods., Inc., P.O. Box 224, Barrington, IL 60010/312-526-9333 (Bullet lube)

BULLET SWAGE DIES AND TOOLS

C-H Tool & Die Corp., 106 N. Harding St., Owen, WI 54460/715-229-2146
Lester Coats, 416 Simpson Ave., North Bend, OR 97459/503-756-6995 (lead wire core cutter)
Corbin Mfg. & Supply Inc., P.O. Box 2659, White City, OR 97503/503-826-5211
Hollywood, Loading Tools by M&M Engineering, 10642 Arminta St., Sun Valley, CA 91352/818-842-8376
Huntington Die Specialties, P.O. Box 991, Oroville, CA 95965/916-534-1210
Independent Machine & Gun Shop, 1416 N. Hayes, Pocatello, ID 83201/208-232-1264 (TNT bullet dies)
L.L.F. Die Shop, 1281 Highway 99 North, Eugene, OR 97402/503-688-5753
Rorschach Precision Products, P.O. Box 151613, Irving, TX 75015/214-790-3487
SAS Dies, (See Corbin Mfg. & Supply)
Sport Flite Mfg., Inc., 2520 Industrial Row, Troy, MI 48084/313-280-0648
TNT (See Ind. Mach. & Gun Shop)
Whitney Sales, P.O. Box 875, Reseda, CA 91335/818-345-4212 (tungsten carbide rifle dies)

CARTRIDGES FOR COLLECTORS

AD Hominem, R.R. 3, Orillia, Ont., Canada L3V 6H3/705-689-5303
Ida I. Burgess, Sam's Gun Shop, 25 Squam Rd., Rockport, MA 01966/617-546-6839
Cameron's, 16690 W. 11th Ave., Golden CO 80401/303-279-7365
Chas. E. Duffy, Williams Lane, West Hurley, NY 12419
Tom M. Dunn, 1342 So. Poplar, Casper, WY 82601/307-237-3207
Ellwood Epps (Orillia) Ltd., Hwy. 11 North, Orillia, Ont. L3V 6H3, Canada/705-689-5333
Jack First Distributors, Inc., 44633 Sierra Hwy., Lancaster, CA 93534/805-945-6981
GTM Co., Geo. T. Mahaney, 15915B East Main St., La Puente, CA 91744/818-768-5806
Glaser Safety Slug, Inc., P.O. Box 8223, Foster City, CA 94404/415-345-7677
"Gramps" Antique Cartridges, Box 341, Washago, Ont., Canada L0K 2B0
Griffin's Guns & Antiques, R.R. #4, Peterboro, Ont. K9J 6X5, Canada/705-745-7022
Hansen and Hansen, 244 Old Post Rd., Southport, CT 06490/203-259-7337
Idaho Ammunition Service, 410 21st Ave., Lewiston, ID 83501
Kelley's, Harold Kelley, Box 125, Woburn, MA 01801/617-935-3389
Old Western Scrounger, 12924 Hwy. A-12, Montague, CA 96064/916-459-5445
San Francisco Gun Exchange, 124 Second St., San Francisco, CA 94105/415-982-6097
James C. Tillinghast, Box 405, Hancock, NH 03449/603-525-6615 (list $1)
Lewis Yearout, 308 Riverview Dr. E., Great Falls, MT 59404

CASES, CABINETS AND RACKS—GUN

Alco Carrying Cases, 601 W. 26th St., New York, NY 10001/212-675-5820 (aluminum)
Bob Allen Sportswear, 214 S.W. Jackson, Des Moines, IA 50315/515-283-1988/800-247-8048 (carrying)
Amacker Products Inc., P.O. Box 1432, Tallulah, LA 71282/318-574-4903
The American Import Co., 1453 Mission St., San Francisco, CA 94103/415-863-1506
Armes de Chasse, P.O. Box 827, Chadsford, PA 19317/215-388-1146
Art Jewel Ltd., 421A Irmen Dr., Addison, IL 60101/312-628-6220
Assault Systems of St. Louis, 869 Horan, St. Louis, MO 63026/314-343-3575 (canvas carrying case)
Beeman Precision Arms, Inc., 47-GDD Paul Dr., San Rafael, CA 94903/415-472-7121
Morton Booth Co., Box 123, Joplin, MO 64801
Boyt Co., Div. of Welsh Sportg. Gds., Box 220, Iowa Falls, IA 50126
Brauer Bros. Mfg. Co., 2020 Delmar Blvd., St. Louis, MO 63103/314-231-2864 (soft gun cases)
Brenik, Inc., 925 W. Chicago Ave., Chicago, IL 60622
Browning, Rt. 4, Box 624-B, Arnold, MO 63010
Cap-Lex Gun Cases, Capitol Plastics of Ohio, Inc., 333 Van Camp Rd., Bowling Green, OH 43402
China IM/EX, P.O. Box 27573, San Francisco, CA 94127/415-661-2212 (soft-type cases)
Chipmunk Mfg. Co., 114 E. Jackson, Medford, OR 97501/503-664-5585 (cases)
Dara-Nes Inc., see: Nesci
Dart Mfg. Co., 4012 Bronze Way, Dallas, TX 75237/214-333-4221
Detroit-Armor Corp., 2233 No. Palmer Dr., Schaumburg, IL 60195/312-397-4070 (Saf-Gard steel gun safe)
Doskocil Mfg. Co., Inc., P.O. Box 1246, Arlington, TX 75010/817-467-5116 (Gun Guard carrying)
East-Tenn Mills, Inc., 3112 Industrial Dr., Skyline Industrial Park, Johnson City, TN 37601/615-928-7186 (gun socks)
Ellwood Epps (Orillia) Ltd., R.R. 3, Hwy. 11 North, Orillia, Ont. L3V 6H3, Canada/705-689-5333 (custom gun cases)
Norbert Ertel, P.O. Box 1150, Des Plaines, IL 60018/312-825-2315 (cust. gun cases)
Flambeau Plastics Corp., 801 Lynn, Baraboo, WI 53913
Fort Knox Security Products, 1051 N. Industrial Park Rd., Orem, UT 84057/801-224-7233 (safes)
Gun-Ho Case Mfg. Co., 110 East 10th St., St. Paul, MN 55101
Hansen and Hansen, 244 Old Post Rd., Southport, CT 06490/203-259-7337
Marvin Huey Gun Cases, P.O. Box 22456, Kansas City, MO 64113/816-444-1637 (handbuilt leather cases)
Jumbo Sports Prods., P.O. Box 280-Airport Rd., Frederick, MD 21701

Kalispel Metal Prods. (KMP), P.O. Box 267, Cusick, WA 99119/509-445-1121 (aluminum boxes)
Kane Products Inc., 5572 Brecksville Rd., Cleveland, OH 44131/216-524-9962
Kolpin Mfg., Inc., Box 231, Berlin, WI 54923/414-361-0400
Marble Arms Corp., 420 Industrial Park, Gladstone, MI 49837/906-428-3710
Bill McGuire, 1600 No. Eastmont Ave., East Wenatchee, WA 98801
Merchandise Brokers, P.O. Box 491, Lilburn, GA 30247/404-923-0015 (GunS-linger portable rack)
Nesci Enterprises, Inc., P.O. Box 119, Summit St., East Hampton, CT 06424/203-267-2588 (firearms security chests)
Nortex Industrial Fan Co., 2821 Main St., Dallas TX 75226/214-748-1157 (automobile gun rack)
Paul-Reed, Inc., P.O. Box 227, Charlevoix, MI 49720
Penguin Industries, Inc., Airport Industrial Mall, Coatesville, PA 19320/215-384-6000
Precise, 3 Chestnut, Suffern, NY 10901
Proofmark, Ltd., P.O. Box 183, Alton, IL 62002/618-463-0120 (Italian Emmebi leather cases)
Protecto Plastics, Div. of Penquin Ind., Airport Industrial Mall, Coatesville, PA 19320/215-384-6000 (carrying cases)
Rahn Gun Works, Inc., P.O. Box 327, 535 Marshall St., Litchfield, MI 49252/517-542-3247 (leather trunk cases)
Red Head Brand Corp., 4949 Joseph Hardin Dr., Dallas, TX 75236/214-333-4141
Richland Arms Co., 321 W. Adrian, Blissfield, MI 49228
Saf-T-Case Mfg. Co., 104 S. Rogers, Irving, TX 75060/214-679-8827
San Angelo Co. 1841 Industrial Ave., San Angelo, TX 76904/915-655-7126
Buddy Schoellkopf, 4949 Joseph Hardin Dr., Dallas, TX 75236/214-333-2121
Schulz Industries, 16247 Minnesota Ave., Paramount, CA 90723/213-636-7718 (carrying cases)
Sealine Enterprises, 821 So. 3rd, Kent, WA 98032/206-852-1784 (vaults)
Security Gun Chest, (See Tread Corp.)
Stearns Mfg. Co., P.O. Box 1498, St. Cloud, MN 56301
Tread Corp., P.O. Box 13207, Roanoke, VA 24032/703-982-6881 (security gun chest)
Weather Shield Sports Equipm. Inc., Rte. #3, Petoskey Rd., Charlevoix, MI 49720
Wilson Case Co., 906 Juniata Ave., Juniata, NE 68955/402-751-2145 (cases)
Woodstream Corp., Box 327, Lititz, PA 17543

CHOKE DEVICES, RECOIL ABSORBERS & RECOIL PADS

Action Products Inc., 22 N. Mulberry St., Hagerstown, MD 21740/800-228-7763 (rec. shock eliminator)
Bob Allen Companies, 214 S.W. Jackson St., Des Moines, IA 50302/515-283-2191
Arms Ingenuity Co., Box 1; 51 Canal St., Weatogue, CT 06089/203-658-5624 (Jet-Away)
Armsport, Inc., 3590 N.W. 49th St., Miami, FL 33142/305-635-7850 (choke devices)
Baer Custom Guns, 1725 Minesite Rd., Allentown, PA 18103/215-398-2362 (compensator syst. f. 45 autos)
Stan Baker, 5303 Roosevelt Way NE, Seattle, WA 98105/206-522-4575 (shotgun)
Briley Mfg. Co., 1085-A Gessner, Houston, TX 77055/713-932-6995 (choke tubes)
C&H Research, 115 Sunnyside Dr., Lewis, KS 67552/316-324-5445 (Mercury recoil suppressor)
Vito Cellini, Francesca Inc., 3115 Old Ranch Rd., San Antonio, TX 78217/512-826-2584 (recoil reducer; muzzle brake)
Clinton River Gun Serv. Inc., 30016 S. River Rd., Mt. Clemens, MI 48045 (Reed Choke)
Dahl Gun Shop, 6947 King Ave. West, Billings, MT 59106/406-652-3909
Edwards Recoil Reducer, 269 Herbert St., Alton, IL 62002/618-462-3257
Emsco Variable Shotgun Chokes, 101 Second Ave., S.E., Waseca, MN 56093/507-835-1779
Fabian Bros. Sptg. Goods, Inc., 3333 Midway Dr., Suite 104, San Diego, CA 92110/619-223-3955 (DTA Muzzle Mizer rec. abs.; MIL/brake)
Griggs Recreational Prods. Inc., P.O. Box 789, Bountiful, UT 84010/801-295-9696 (recoil director)
William E. Harper, The Great 870 Co., P.O. Box 6309, El Monte, CA 91734/213-579-3077
I.N.C., Inc., 1133 Kresky #4, Centralia, WA 98531/206-339-2042 (Sorbothane Kick-Eez recoil pad)
La Paloma Marketing, 1735 E. Ft. Lowell Rd., Suite 7, Tucson, AZ 85719/602-881-4750 (Action rec. shock eliminator)
Lyman Products Corp., Rte. 147, Middlefield, CT. 06455 (Cutts Comp.)
Mag-na-port International, Inc., 41302 Executive Drive, Mt. Clemens, MI 48045/313-469-6727 (muzzle-brake system)
Mag-Na-Port of Canada, 1861 Burrows Ave., Winnipeg, Manitoba R2X 2V6, Canada
Marble Arms Corp., 420 Industrial Park, Gladstone, MI 49837/906-428-3710 (Poly-Choke)
Multi-Gauge Enterprises, 433 W. Foothill Blvd., Monrovia, CA 91016/818-357-6117/358-4549 (screw-in chokes)
Pachmayr Gun Works, Inc., 1220 So. Grand Ave., Los Angeles, CA 90015/213-748-7271 (recoil pads)
P.A.S.T. Corp., 210 Park Ave., P.O. Box 7372, Columbia, MO 65205/314-449-7278 (recoil reducer shield)
Poly-Choke (See Marble Arms)
Pro-Port Ltd., 41302 Executive Dr., Mt. Clemens, MI 48045/313-469-7323
Purbaugh, see: Multi-Gauge Enterprises
Supreme Products Co., 1830 S. California Ave., Monrovia, CA 91016/800-423-7159/818-357-5395 (recoil pads)

CHRONOGRAPHS AND PRESSURE TOOLS

B-Square Co., Box 11281, Ft. Worth, TX 76110/800-433-2909
Custom Chronograph Co., Rt. 1, Box 98, Brewster, WA 98812/509-689-2004
D&H Precision Tooling, 7522 Barnard Mill Rd., Ringwood, IL 60072/815-653-9611 (Pressure Testing Receiver)
H-S Precision, Inc., 112 N. Summit St., Prescott, AZ 86302/602-445-0607 (press. barrels)
Paul Jaeger, Inc., P.O. Box 449, 1 Madison Ave., Grand Junction, TN 38039
Oehler Research, Inc., P.O. Box 9135, Austin, TX 78766/512-327-6900
Telepacific Electronics Co., Inc., P.O. Box 1329, San Marcos, CA 92069/714-744-4415
Tepeco, P.O. Box 342, Friendswood, TX 77546/713-482-2702 (Tepeco Speed-Meter)
M. York, 5508 Griffith Rd., Gaithersburg, MD 20760/301-253-4217 (press. tool)

CLEANING & REFINISHING SUPPLIES

A.C. Enterprises, P.O. Box 448, Edenton, NC 27932/919-482-4992
American Gas & Chemical Co., Ltd., 220 Pegasus Ave., Northvale, NJ 07647/201-767-7300 (TSI gun lube)
Anderson Mfg. Co., P.O. Box 536, 6813 S. 220th St., Kent, WA 98032/206-872-7602 (stock finishes)
Armite Labs., 1845 Randolph St., Los Angeles, CA 90001/213-587-7744 (pen oiler)
Armoloy Co. of Ft. Worth, 204 E. Daggett St., Ft Worth, TX 76104/817-461-0051
Beeman Inc., 47 Paul Dr., San Rafael, CA 94903/415-472-7121
Belltown, Ltd., P.O. Box 74, Route 37, Sherman, CT 06784/203-354-5750 (gun clg. cloth kit)
Birchwood-Casey, 7900 Fuller Rd., Eden Prairie, MN 55344/612-927-7933
Blacksmith Corp., P.O. Box 424, Southport, CT 06490/800-531-2665 (Arctic Friction Free gun clg. equip.)
Blue and Gray Prods., Inc., R.D. #6, Box 362, Wellsboro, PA 16901/717-724-1383
Break-Free, Div. of San/Bar Corp., 1035 So. Linwood Ave., Santa Ana, CA 92705/714-953-1900 (lubricants)
Jim Brobst, 299 Poplar St., Hamburg, PA 19526/215-562-2103 (J-B Bore Cleaning Compound)
Browning Arms, Rt. 4, Box 624-B, Arnold, MO 63010
J.M. Bucheimer Co., P.O. Box 280, Airport Rd., Frederick, MD 21701/301-662-5101
Burnishine Prod. Co., 8140 N. Ridgeway, Skokie, IL 60076/312-583-1810 (Stock Glaze)
Call 'N, Inc., 1615 Bartlett Rd., Memphis, TN 38134/901-372-1682 (Gunskin)
Chem-Pak, Inc., 11 Oates Ave., P.O. Box 1685, Winchester, VA 22601/703-667-1341 (Gun-Savr.protect. & lubricant)
Chopie Mfg. Inc., 700 Copeland Ave., La Crosse, WI 54601/608-784-0926 (Black-Solve)
Clenzoil Corp., Box 1226, Sta. C, Canton, OH 44708/216-833-9758
Clover Mfg. Co., 139 Woodward Ave., Norwalk, Ct. 06856/800-243-6492 (Clover compound)
Country Cover Co., Inc., P.O. Box 160, Storrs, CT 06268/203-429-3710 (Masking Gun Oil)
J. Dewey Mfg. Co., 186 Skyview Dr., Southbury, CT 06488/203-264-3064 (one-piece gun clg. rod)
Diah Engineering Co., 5177 Haskell St., La Canada, CA 91011/213-625-2184 (barrel lubricant)
Dri-Slide, Inc., 411 N. Darling, Fremont, MI 49412/616-924-3950
The Dutchman's Firearms Inc., 4143 Taylor Blvd., Louisville, KY 40215/502-366-0555
Forster Products, 82 E. Lanark Ave., Lanark, IL 61046/815-493-6360
Fountain Prods., 492 Prospect Ave., W. Springfield, MA 01089/413-781-4551
Forty-Five Ranch Enterpr., 119 S. Main St., Miami, OK 74354/918-542-9307
Heller & Levin Associates, Inc., 88 Marlborough Court, Rockville Center, NY 11570/516-764-9349
Frank C. Hoppe Division, Penguin Ind., Inc., Airport Industrial Mall, Coatesville, PA 19320/215-384-6000
J-B Bore Cleaner, 299 Poplar St., Hamburg, PA 19526/215-562-2103
Ken Jantz Supply, Rt. 1, Sulphur, OK 73086/405-622-3790
Jet-Aer Corp., 100 Sixth Ave., Paterson, NJ 07524 (blues & oils)
Kellog's Professional Prods., Inc., P.O. Box 1201, Sandusky, OH 44870
K.W. Kleinendorst, R.D. #1, Box 113B, Hop Bottom, PA 18824/717-289-4687 (rifle clg. cables)
Terry K. Kopp, Highway 13, Lexington, MO 64067/816-259-2636 (stock rubbing compound; rust preventative grease)
LPS Chemical Prods., Holt Lloyd Corp., 4647 Hugh Howell Rd., Box 3050, Tucker, GA 30084/404-934-7800
LaPaloma Marketing, Inc., 1735 E. Ft. Lowell Rd., Suite 7, Tucson, AZ 85719/602-881-4750 (Amer-Lene solution)
Mark Lee, P.O. Box 20379, Minneapolis, MN 55420/612-884-4060 (rust blue solution)
LEM Gun Spec., Box 31, College Park, GA 30337/404-761-9054 (Lewis Lead Remover)
Liquid Wrench, Box 10628, Charlotte, NC 28201 (pen. oil)
Lynx Line Gun Prods. Div., Protective Coatings, Inc., 20626 Fenkell Ave., Detroit, MI 48223/313-255-6032
MJL Industries, Inc., P.O. Box 122, McHenry, IL 60050/815-344-1040 (Rust Free)
Marble Arms Co., 420 Industrial Park, Gladstone, MI 49837/906-428-3710
Micro Sight Co., 242 Harbor Blvd., Belmont, CA 94002/415-591-0769 (bedding)
Mount Labs, Inc. (See: LaPaloma Marketing, Inc.)
Nesci Enterprises, Inc., P.O. Box 119, Summit St., East Hampton, CT 06424/203-267-2588

New Method Mfg. Co., P.O. Box 175, Bradford, PA 16701/814-362-6611 (gun blue; Minute Man gun care)

Northern Instruments, Inc., 6680 North Highway 49, Lino Lake, MN 55014 (Stor-Safe rust preventer)

Numrich Arms Co., West Hurley, NY 12491 (44-40 gun blue)

Old World Oil Products, 3827 Queen Ave. No., Minneapolis, MN 55412

Omark Industries, P.O. Box 856, Lewiston, ID 83501/208-746-2351

Original Mink Oil, Inc., P.O. Box 20191, 11021 N.E. Beech St., Portland, OR 97220/503-255-2814

Outers Laboratories; see: Omark Industries

Ox-Yoke Originals, Inc., 130 Griffin Rd., West Suffield, CT 06093/203-668-5110 (dry lubrication patches)

Parker-Hale/Precision Sports, P.O. Box 708, Cortland, NY 13045

Bob Pease Accuracy, P.O. Box 787, Zipp Rd., New Braunfels, TX 78131/512-625-1342

A. E. Pennebaker Co., Inc., P.O. Box 1386, Greenville, SC 29602/803-235-8016 (Pyro Dux)

RBS Industries Corp., 1312 Washington Ave., St. Louis, MO 63103/314-241-8564 (Miracle All Purpose polishing cloth)

Reardon Prod., 103 W. Market St., Morrison, IL 61270 (Dry-Lube)

Rice Protective Gun Coatings, 235-30th St., West Palm Beach, FL 33407/305-845-2383

Richards Classic Oil Finish, John Richards, Rt. 2, Box 325, Bedford, KY 40006/502-255-7222 (gunstock oils, wax)

Rig Products, 87 Coney Island Dr., Sparks, NV 89431/703-331-5666

Rusteprufe Labs., Rte. 5, Sparta, WI 54656/608-269-4144

Rust Guardit, see: Schwab Industries

San/Bar Corp., Break-Free Div., 9999 Muirlands Pkwy., Irvine, CA 92718/714-855-9911 (lubricants)

Saunders Sptg. Gds., 338 Somerset, No. Plainfield, NJ 07060 (Sav-Bore)

Schwab Industries, Inc., P.O. Box 1269, Sequim, WA 98382/206-683-2944

Tyler Scott, Inc., P.O. Box 193, Milford, OH 45150/513-831-7603 (ML black solvent; patch lube)

Secoa Technologies, Inc., 3915 U.S. Hwy. 98 So., Lakeland, FL 33801/813-665-1734 (Teflon coatings)

Shooter's Choice (See Venco Industries)

Silver Dollar Guns, P.O. Box 475, 10 Frances St., Franklin, NH 03235/603-934-3292 (Silicone oil)

TDP Industries, Inc., 603 Airport Blvd., Doylestown, PA 18901/215-345-8687

Taylor & Robbins, Box 164, Rixford, PA 16745 (Throat Saver)

Texas Platers Supply Co., 2453 W. Five Mile Parkway, Dallas, TX 75233

Totally Dependable Products; See: TDP

Treso Ltd., P.O. Box 4640, Pagosa Springs, CO 81157/303-264-2295 (mfg. Durango Gun Rod)

C. S. Van Gorden, 1815 Main St., Bloomer, WI 54724/715-568-2612 (Van's Instant Blue)

United States Products Co., 518 Melwood Ave., Pittsburgh, PA 15213/412-621-2130 (Gold Medallion bore cleaner/conditioner)

Venco Industries, Inc., P.O. Box 598, Chesterland, OH 44026/216-719-9392 (Shooter's Choice bore cleaner & conditioner)

WD-40 Co., P.O. Box 80607, San Diego, CA 92138-9021/619-275-1400

Williams Gun Sight, 7389 Lapeer Rd., Davison, MI 48423 (finish kit)

Winslow Arms Inc., P.O. Box 783, Camden, SC 29020 (refinishing kit)

Wisconsin Platers Supply Co., (See Texas Platers Supply Co.)

Woodstream Corp., P.O. Box 327, Lititz, PA 17543 (Mask)

Zip Aerosol Prods., See Rig

CUSTOM GUNSMITHS

A Square Co., Inc., A. B. Alphin, Rt. 4, Simmons Rd., Madison, IN 47250

Accuracy Systems Inc., 15203 N. Cave Creek Rd., Phoenix, AZ 85032/602-971-1991

Ahlman's Inc., R.R. 1, Box 20, Morristown, MN 55052/507-685-4244

Don Allen Inc., HC55, Box 322, Sturgis, SD 57785/605-347-4686

American Custom Gunmakers Guild, c/o Jan's Secretariat, 220 Division St., Northfield, MN 55057

Amrine's Gun Shop, 937 Luna Ave., Ojai, CA 93023

Antique Arms Co., D. F. Saunders, 1110 Cleveland Ave., Monett, MO 65708/417-235-6501 (Hawken copies)

Armament Gunsmithing Co., Inc., 525 Route 22, Hillside, NJ 07205/201-686-0960

Armament Systems & Procedures, Inc., Box 356, Appleton, WI 54912/414-731-6903

John & Mary Armbrust, John's Gun Shop, 823 S. Union St., Mishawaka, IN 46544/219-255-0973

Armurier Hiptmayer, P.O. Box 136, Eastman, Que. JOE 1P0, Canada/514-297-2492

Armuriers Liegeois-Artisans Reunis "ALAR," rue Masset 27, 4300 Ans, Belgium

Atkinson Gun Co., P.O. Box 512, Prescott, AZ 86301

Ed von Atzigen, The Custom Shop, 890 Cochrane Crescent, Peterborough, Ont., K9H 5N3 Canada/705-742-6693

Creighton Audette, 19 Highland Circle, Springfield, VT 05156/802-885-2331

Richard W. Baber, Hanson's Gun Center, 1440 N. Hancock Ave., Colorado Springs, CO 80903/303-634-4220

Bain and Davis Sptg. Gds., 307 E. Valley Blvd., San Gabriel, CA 91776/213-573-4241

Baer Custom Guns, 1725 Minesite Rd., Allentown, PA 18103/215-398-2362 (rifles)

Stan Baker, 5303 Roosevelt Way NE, Seattle, WA 98105/206-522-4575 (shotgun specialist)

Joe J. Balickie, Rte. 2, Box 56-G, Apex, NC 27502/919-362-5185

Barta's Gunsmithing, 10231 US Hwy., #10, Cato, WI 54206/414-732-4472

Donald Bartlett, 1808 S. 281st Place, Federal Way, WA 98003/206-946-4311

R. J. Beal, Jr., 170 W. Marshall Rd., Lansdowne, PA 19050/215-259-1220

Behlert Custom Guns, Inc., RD 2 Box 36C, Route 611 North, Pipersville, PA 18947/215-766-8681

George Beitzinger, 116-20 Atlantic Ave., Richmond Hill, NY 11419/718-847-7662

Bell's Custom Shop, 3309 Mannheim Rd., Franklin Park, IL 60131/312-678-1900 (handguns)

Bennett Gun Works, 561 Delaware Ave., Delmar, NY 12054/518-439-1862

Gordon Bess, 708 River St., Canon City, CO 81212/303-275-1073

Al Biesen, 5021 Rosewood, Spokane, WA 99208/509-328-9340

Roger Biesen, W. 2039 Sinto Ave., Spokane, WA 99201

Stephen L. Billeb, Box 1176, Big Piney, WY 83113/307-276-5627

E.C. Bishop & Son Inc., 119 Main St., P.O. Box 7, Warsaw, MO 65355/816-438-5121

Bob's Gun & Tackle Shop, 746 Granby St., Norfolk, VA 23510/804-627-8311

Duane Bolden, 1295 Lassen Dr., Hanford, CA 93230/209-582-6937 (rust bluing)

Boone Mountain Trading Post, 118 Sunrise Rd., Saint Marys, PA 15857/814-834-4879

Charles Boswell (Gunmakers), Div. of Saxon Arms Ltd., 615 Jasmine Ave. No., Tarpon Springs, FL 33589/813-938-4882

Art Bourne, (See Guncraft)

Kent Bowerly, H.C.R. Box 1903, Camp Sherman, OR 97730/503-595-6028

Larry D. Brace, 771 Blackfoot Ave., Eugene, OR 97404/503-688-1278

Breckheimers, Rte. 69-A, Parish, NY 13131

A. Briganti, 475 Rt. 32, Highland Mills, NY 10930/914-928-9816

Brown Precision Inc., P.O. Box 270W, 7786 Molinos Ave., Los Molinos, CA 96055 (rifles)

Buckland Gun Shop, Kenny Jarrett, Rt. 1, Box 44, Cowden Plantation, Jackson, SC 29831/803-471-3616 (rifles)

David Budin, Main St., Margaretville, NY 12455/914-568-4103

George Bunch, 7735 Garrison Rd., Hyattsville, MD 20784

Ida I. Burgess, Sam's Gun Shop, 25 Squam Rd., Rockport, MA 01966/617-546-6809 (bluing repairs)

Leo Bustani, P.O. Box 8125, W. Palm Beach, FL 33407/305-622-2710

Cache La Poudre Rifleworks, 168 No. College Ave., Ft. Collins, CO 80524/303-482-6913 (cust. ML)

Cameron's Guns, 16690 W. 11th Ave., Golden, CO 80401

Lou Camilli, 4700 Oahu Dr. N.E., Albuquerque, NM 87111/505-293-5259 (ML)

Dick Campbell, 1198 Finn Ave., Littleton, CO 80124/303-799-0145

Ralph L. Carter, Carter's Gun Shop, 225 G St., Penrose, CO 81240/303-372-6240

Shane Caywood, P.O. Box 321, Hwy. 51 So., Minocqua, WI 54548/715-356-9631

R. MacDonald Champlin, P.O. Box 693, Manchester, NH 03105/603-483-8559 (ML rifles and pistols)

Mark Chanlynn, Rocky Mtn. Rifle Wks. Ltd., 1704-14th St., Boulder, CO 80302/303-443-9189

Dave Chicoine, d/b/a Liberty A.S.P., 19 Key St., Eastport, ME 04631/207-853-2327

F. Bob Chow's Gun Shop, Inc., 3185 Mission St., San Francisco, CA 94110/415-282-8358

Claude Christopher, 1606 Berkley Rd., Greenville, NC 27834/919-756-0872

Classic Arms Corp., P.O. Box 8, Palo Alto, CA 94302/415-321-7243

John Edward Clark, R.R. #4, Tottenham, Ont. L0G 1W0 Canada/416-936-2131 (ML)

Kenneth E. Clark, 18738 Highway 99, Madera, CA 93637/209-674-6016

Clinton River Gun Serv. Inc., 30016 S. River Rd., Mt. Clemens, MI 48045/313-468-1090

Charles H. Coffin, 3719 Scarlet Ave., Odessa, TX 79762/915-366-4729

Jim Coffin, 250 Country Club Lane, Albany, OR 97321/503-928-4391

John Corry, 628 Martin Lane, Deerfield, IL 60015/312-541-6250 (English doubles & repairs)

Crest Carving Co., 14849 Dillow St., Westminster, CA 92683

Crocker, 1510 - 42nd St., Los Alamos, NM 87544 (rifles)

J. Lynn Crook, Rt. 6, Box 295-A, Lebanon, TN 37087/615-449-1930

Cumberland Knife & Gun Works, 5661 Bragg Blvd., Fayetteville, NC 28303/919-867-0009 (ML)

The Custom Gun Guild, 5091-F Buford Hwy., Doraville, GA 30340/404-455-0346

D&D Gun Shop, 363 Elmwood, Troy, MI 48083/313-583-1512

Dahl Gunshop, 6947 King Ave. West, Billings, MT 59106/406-652-3909

Homer L. Dangler, Box 254, Addison, MI 49220/517-547-6745 (Kentucky rifles; brochure $3)

Davis Co., 2793 Del Monte St., West Sacramento, CA 95691/916-372-6789

Jack Dever, 8520 N.W. 90, Oklahoma City, OK 73132/405-721-6393

R. H. Devereaux, D. D. Custom Rifles, 5240 Mule Deer Dr., Colorado Springs, CO 80919/303-548-8468

Ron Dilliott, Rt. 3, Box 340, Scarlett Rd., Dandridge, TN 37725/615-397-9204

Dominic DiStefano, 4303 Friar Lane, Colorado Springs, CO 80907

Dixon Muzzleloading Shop, Inc., RD #1, Box 175, Kempton, PA 19529/215-756-6271 (ML)

William Dixon, Buckhorn Gun Works, Rt. 4 Box 1230, Rapid City, SD 57702/605-787-6289

C. P. Donnelly-Siskiyou Gun Works, 405 Kubli Rd., Grants Pass, OR 97527/503-846-6604

Duncan's Gunworks Inc., 1619 Grand Ave., San Marcos, CA 92069/619-727-0515

David R. Dunlop, Rte. 1, Box 199, Rolla, ND 58367

Jere Eggleston, P.O. Box 50238, Columbia, SC 29250/803-799-3402

Elko Arms, Dr. L. Kortz, 28 rue Ecole Moderne, B-7400 Soignies, H.T., Belgium

William A. Emick, P.O. Box 741, Philipsburg, MT 59858/406-859-3280

Bob Emmons, 238 Robson Rd., Grafton, OH 44044/216-458-5890

Englishtown Sporting Goods, Inc., David J. Maxham, 38 Main St., Englishtown, NJ 07726/201-446-7717

Armas ERBI, S. coop., Avda. Eulogio Estarta, Elgoibar (Guipuzcoa), Spain

Ken Eyster, Heritage Gunsmiths Inc., 6441 Bishop Rd., Centerburg, OH 43011/614-625-6131

Andy Fautheree, P.O. Box 4607, Pagosa Springs, CO 81157/303-731-2502

Ted Fellowes, Beaver Lodge, 9245-16th Ave., S.W., Seattle, WA 98106/206-763-1698 (muzzleloaders)

Fiberpro, Robert Culbertson, 3636 California St., San Diego, CA 92101/619-295-7703 (rifles)

Jack First Distributors Inc., 44633 Sierra Highway, Lancaster, CA 93534/805-945-6981

Marshall F. Fish, Rt. 22 North, RR2 Box 2439, Westport, NY 12993/518-962-4897

Jerry A. Fisher, 1244-4th Ave. West, Kalispell, MT 59901/406-755-7093

Flaig's Inc., 2200 Evergreen Rd., Millvale, PA 15209/412-821-1717

Flynn's Cust. Guns, P.O. Box 7461, Alexandria, LA 71306/318-445-7130

Larry L. Forster, Box 212, 220-1st St. N.E., Gwinner, ND 58040/701-678-2475

Fountain Products, 492 Prospect Ave., West Springfield, MA 01089/413-781-4651

Frank's Custom Rifles, 10420 E. Rusty Spur, Tucson, AZ 85749/602-749-4563

Freeland's Scope Stands, 3737—14th Ave., Rock Island, IL 61201/309-788-7449

Fredrick Gun Shop, 10 Elson Drive, Riverside, RI 02915/401-433-2805

Frontier Arms, Inc., 420 E. Riding Club Rd., Cheyenne, WY 82001

Frontier Shop & Gallery, Depot 1st & Main, Riverton, WY 82501/307-856-4498

Fuller Gunshop, Cooper Landing, AK 99572

Karl J. Furr, 76 East 350 No., Orem, UT 84057/801-225-2603

Gander Mountain, Inc., P.O. Box 128, Wilmot, WI 53192/414-862-2344

Garcia Natl. Gun Traders, Inc., 225 S.W. 22nd Ave., Miami, FL 33135

Jim Garrett, 1413 B. E. Olive Ct., Fort Collins, CO 80524

David Gentry Custom Gunmaker, P.O. Box 1440, Belgrade, MT 59714/406-586-1405 (cust. Montana Mtn. Rifle)

Edwin Gillman, R.R. 6, Box 195, Hanover, PA 17331/717-632-1662

Gilman-Mayfield, 1552 N. 1st, Fresno, CA 93703/209-237-2500

Dale Goens, Box 224, Cedar Crest, NM 87008

Dave Good, 14906 Robinwood St., Lansing, MI 48906/517-321-5392

A. R. Goode, 4125 N.E. 28th Terr., Ocala, FL 32670/904-622-9575

Goodling's Gunsmithing, R.D. #1, Box 1097, Spring Grove, PA 17362/717-225-3350

Gordie's Gun Shop, Gordon Mulholland, 1401 Fulton St., Streator, IL 61364/815-672-7202

Charles E. Grace, 10144 Elk Lake Rd., Williamsburg, MI 49690/616-264-9483

Roger M. Green & J. Earl Bridges, P.O. Box 984, 315 S. 2nd St., Glenrock, WY 82637/307-436-9804

Griffin & Howe, 589 Broadway, New York, NY 10012/212-966-5323

H. L. "Pete" Grisel, 61912 Skyline View Dr., Bend, OR 97701/503-389-2649

Karl Guenther, 165 Granite Springs Rd., Yorktown Heights, NY 10598/914-245-5610

Gun City, 504 Main Ave., Bismarck, ND 58501/701-223-2304

Guncraft, Inc., 117 W. Pipeline, Hurst, TX 76053/817-282-6481

Guncraft (Kamloops) Ltd., 127 Victoria St., Kamloops, B.C. V2C 1Z4, Canada/604-374-2151

The Gun Works, Joe Williams, 236 Main St., Springfield, OR 97477/503-741-4118 (ML)

The Gunworks Inc., 3434 Maple Ave., Brookfield IL 60513/312-387-7888

H-S Precision, Inc., 112 N. Summit, Prescott, AZ 86302/602-445-0607

Hagn Rifles & Actions, Martin Hagn, Cranbrook, B.C. VIC 4H9, Canada/604-426-3334 (s.s. actions & rifles)

Fritz Hallberg, The Outdoorsman, P.O. Box 339, Ontario, OR 97914/503-889-3135

Charles E. Hammans, P.O. Box 788, 2022 McCracken, Stuttgart, AR 72160/501-673-1388

Dick Hanson, Hanson's Gun Center, 521 So. Circle Dr., Colorado Springs, CO 80910/303-634-4220

Harkrader's Cust. Gun Shop, 825 Radford St., Christiansburg, VA 24073

Rob't W. Hart & Son Inc., 401 Montgomery St., Nescopeck, PA 18635/717-752-3655 (actions, stocks)

Hartmann & Weiss KG, Rahlstedter Bahnhofstr. 47, 2000 Hamburg 73, W. Germany

Hubert J. Hecht, Waffen-Hecht, 10112 Fair Oaks Blvd., Fair Oaks, CA 95628/916-966-1020

Edw. O. Hefti, 300 Fairview, College Station, TX 77840/409-696-4959

Stephen Heilmann, P.O. Box 657, Grass Valley, CA 95945/916-272-8758

Iver Henriksen, 1211 So. 2nd St. W, Missoula, MT 59801 (Rifles)

Heppler's Gun Shop, 6000 B Soquel Ave., Santa Cruz, CA 95062/408-475-1235

Wm. Hobaugh, The Rifle Shop, Box M, Philipsburg, MT 59858/406-859-3515

Hoenig and Rodman, 6521 Morton Dr., Boise, ID 83705/208-375-1116

Dick Holland, 422 N.E. 6th St., Newport, OR 97365/503-265-7556

Hollis Gun Shop, 917 Rex St., Carlsbad, NM 88220/505-835-3782

Bill Holmes, Rt. 2, Box 242, Fayetteville, AR 72701/501-521-8958

Steven Dodd Hughes, P.O. Box 11455, Eugene, OR 97440/503-485-8869 (ML; ctlg. $3)

Al Hunkeler, Buckskin Machine Works, 3235 So. 358th St., Auburn, WA 98001/206-927-5412 (ML)

Huntington's, P.O. Box 991, Oroville, CA 95965/916-534-1210

Hyper-Single Precision SS Rifles, 520 E. Beaver, Jenks, OK 74037/918-299-2391

Independent Machine & Gun Shop, 1416 N. Hayes, Pocatello, ID 83201

Paul Jaeger, Inc. P.O. Box 449, 1 Madison Ave., Grand Junction, TN 38039/901-764-6909

R. L. Jamison, Jr., Route 4, Box 200, Moses Lake, WA 98837/509-762-2659

J. J. Jenkins Ent. Inc., 375 Pine Ave. No. 25, Goleta, CA 93017/805-967-1366

Jerry's Gun Shop, 9220 Ogden Ave., Brookfield, IL 60513/312-485-5200

Neal G. Johnson, Gunsmithing Inc., 111 Marvin Dr., Hampton, VA 23666/804-838-8091

Peter S. Johnson, The Orvis Co., Inc., Manchester, VT 05254/802-362-3622

Jos. Jurjevic, Gunshop, 605 Main St., Marble Falls, TX 78654/512-693-3012

Ken's Gun Specialties, K. Hunnell, Rt. 1 Box 147, Lakeview, AR 72642/501-431-5606

Kennedy Gun Shop, Rte. 12, Box 21, Clarksville, TN 37040/615-647-6043

Kennon's Custom Rifles, 5408 Biffle, Stone Mtn., GA 30088/404-469-9339

Stanley Kenvin, 5 Lakeville Lane, Plainview, NY 11803/516-931-0321

Kesselring Gun Shop, 400 Pacific Hiway No., Burlington, WA 98233/206-724-3113

Benjamin Kilham, Kilham & Co., Main St., Box 37, Lyme, NH 03768/603-795-4112

Don Klein Custom Guns, P.O. Box 277, Camp Douglas, WI 54618/608-427-6948

K. W. Kleinendorst, R.D. #1, Box 113B, Hop Bottom, PA 18824/717-289-4687

Terry K. Kopp, Highway 13, Lexington, MO 64067/816-259-2636

J. Korzinek, R.D. #2, Box 73, Canton, PA 17724/717-673-8512 (riflesmith) (broch. $1.50)

Lee Kuhns, 652 Northeast Palson Rd., Paulsbo, WA 98370/206-692-5790

Sam Lair, 520 E. Beaver, Jenks, OK 74037/918-299-2391 (single shots)

Maynard Lambert, Kamas, UT 84036

Harry Lawson Co., 3328 N. Richey Blvd., Tucson, AZ 85716/602-326-1117

John G. Lawson, (The Sight Shop), 1802 E. Columbia, Tacoma, WA 98404/206-474-5465

Mark Lee, P.O. Box 20379, Minneapolis, MN 55420/612-884-4060

Bill Leeper, (See Guncraft)

Frank LeFever & Sons, Inc., R.D. #1, Box 31, Lee Center, NY 13363/315-337-6722

Leland Firearms Co., 13 Mountain Ave., Llewellyn Park, West Orange, NJ 07052/201-964-7500 (shotguns)

Lilja Precision Rifle Barrels, Inc., 245 Compass Creek Rd., P.O. Box 372, Plains, MT 59859/406-826-3084

Al Lind, 7821—76th Ave. S.W., Tacoma, WA 98498/206-584-6363

Robt. L. Lindsay, J & B Enterprises, 9416 Emory Grove Rd., P.O. Box 805, Gaithersburg, MD 20877/301-948-2941 (services only)

Ljutic Ind., Box 2117, Yakima, WA 98904 (shotguns)

Llanerch Gun Shop, 2800 Township Line, Upper Darby, PA 19082/215-789-5462

James W. Lofland, 2275 Larkin Rd., Boothwyn, PA 19061/215-485-0391 (SS rifles)

London Guns, 1528—20th St., Santa Monica, CA 90404/213-828-8486

Longbranch Gun Bluing Co., 2455 Jacaranda Lane, Los Osos, CA 93402/805-528-1792

McCann's Muzzle-Gun Works, Tom McCann, 200 Federal City Rd., Pennington, NJ 08534/609-737-1707 (ML)

McCormick's Gun Bluing Service, 609 N.E. 104th Ave., Vancouver, WA 98664/206-256-0579

Stan McFarland, 2221 Idella Ct., Grand Junction, CO 81506/303-243-4704 (cust. rifles)

Bill McGuire, 1600 N. Eastmont Ave., East Wenatchee, WA 98801

MPI Stocks, P.O. Box 03266, 7011 N. Reno Ave., Portland, OR 97203/503-289-8025 (rifles)

Harold E. MacFarland, Route #4, Box 1249, Cottonwood, AZ 86326/602-634-5320

Nick Makinson, R.R. #3, Komoka, Ont. N0L 1R0 Canada/519-471-5462 (English guns; repairs & renovations)

Monte Mandarino, 136 Fifth Ave. West, Kalispell, MT 59901/406-257-6208 (Penn. rifles)

Lowell Manley, 3684 Pine St., Deckerville, MI 48427/313-376-3665

Mantzoros Cust. Gunsmith, P.O. Box 795, Cooper Landing, AK 99572/907-595-1201

Dale Marfell, 107 N. State St., Litchfield, IL 62056/217-327-3832

Marquart Precision Co., P.O. Box 1740, Prescott, AZ 86302/602-445-5646

Elwyn H. Martin, Martin's Gun Shop, 937 S. Sheridan Blvd., Lakewood, CO 80226/303-922-2184

Mashburn Arms & Sporting Goods Co., Inc., 1218 N. Pennsylvania, Oklahoma City, OK 73107/405-236-5151

Seely Masker, Custom Rifles, 261 Washington Ave., Pleasantville, NY 10570/914-769-2627

E. K. Matsuoka, 2801 Kinohou Place, Honolulu HI 96822/808-988-3008

Geo. E. Matthews & Son Inc., 10224 S. Paramount Blvd., Downey, CA 90241

Maurer Arms, 2154-16th St., Akron, OH 44314/216-745-6864 (muzzleloaders)

John E. Maxson, 3507 Red Oak Lane, Plainview, TX 79072/806-293-9042 (high grade rifles)

R. M. Mercer, 216 S. Whitewater Ave., Jefferson, WI 53549/414-674-3839

Miller Arms, Inc., Dean E. Miller, P.O. Box 260, St. Onge, SD 57779/605-578-1790

Miller Custom Rifles, 655 Dutton Ave., San Leandro, CA 94577/415-568-2447

Miller Gun Works, S. A. Miller, P.O. Box 7326, Tamuning, Guam 96911

David Miller Co., 3131 E. Greenlee Rd., Tucson, AZ 85716/602-326-3117 (classic rifles)

Tom Miller, c/o Huntington, 601 Oro Dam Blvd., Oroville, CA 95965/916-534-8000

Earl Milliron, 1249 N.E. 166th Ave., Portland, OR 97230/503-252-3725

Monell Custom Guns, Red Mill Road, RD #2, Box 96, Pine Bush, NY 12566/914-744-3021

Wm. Larkin Moore & Co., 31360 Via Colinas, Suite 109, Westlake Village, CA 91360/213-889-4160

J. W. Morrison Custom Rifles, 4015 W. Sharon, Phoenix, AZ 85029/602-978-3754

Mitch Moschetti, P.O. Box 27065, Cromwell, CT 06416/203-632-2308

Mountain Bear Rifle Works, Inc., Wm. Scott Bickett, 100-B Ruritan Rd., Sterling, VA 22170/703-430-0420

Larry Mrock, R.F.D. 3, Box 207, Woodhill-Hooksett Rd., Bow, NH 03301/603-224-4096 (broch. $3)

Bruce A. Nettestad, R.R. 1, Box 140, Pelican Rapids, MN 56572/218-863-4301

Newman Gunshop, 119 Miller Rd., Agency, IA 52530/515-937-5775

Paul R. Nickels, P.O. Box 71043, Las Vegas, NV 89170/702-458-7149

Ted Nicklas, 5504 Hegel Rd., Goodrich, MI 48438/313-797-4493

William J. Nittler, 290 More Drive, Boulder Creek, CA 95006/408-338-3376 (shotgun repairs)

Jim Norman, Custom Gunstocks, 11230 Calenda Rd., San Diego, CA 92127/619-487-4173

Nu-Line Guns, 1053 Caulks Hill Rd., Harvester, MO 63303/314-441-4500

Olympic Arms Inc., 624 Old Pacific Hwy. S.E., Olympia, WA 98503/206-456-3471

Vic Olson, 5002 Countryside Dr., Imperial, MO 63052/314-296-8086

Oregon Trail Riflesmiths, Inc., P.O. Box 45212, Boise, ID 83711/208-336-8631

The Orvis Co., Inc., Peter S. Johnson, Rt. 7A, Manchester, VT 05254/802-362-3622

Maurice Ottmar, Box 657, 113 East Fir, Coulee City, WA 99115/509-632-5717

Pachmayr Gun Works, 1220 S. Grand Ave., Los Angeles, CA 90015

Pasadena Gun Center, 206 E. Shaw, Pasadena, TX 77506/713-472-0417

Paterson Gunsmithing, 438 Main St., Paterson, NJ 07501/201-345-4100

John Pell, 410 College Ave., Trinidad, CO 81082/303-846-9406

Penrod Precision, 126 E. Main St., P.O. Box 307, No. Manchester, IN 46962/219-981-8385

A. W. Peterson Gun Shop, 1693 Old Hwy. 441, Mt. Dora, FL 32757 (ML)

Eugene T. Plante, Gene's Custom Guns, 3890 Hill Ave., P.O. Box 10534, White Bear Lake, MN 55110/612-429-5105

Power Custom, Inc., P.O. Box 1604, Independence, MO 64055/816-833-3102

Ridge Guncraft, Inc., 125 E. Tyrone Rd., Oak Ridge, TN 37830/615-483-4024

Rifle Ranch, Jim Wilkinson, Rte. 10, 3301 Willow Creek Rd., Prescott, AZ 86301/602-778-7501

Rifle Shop, Box M, Philipsburg, MT 59858

Rite Bros. Firearms Inc., P.O. Box 2054, Clearbrook, B.C. V2T 1V6, Canada/604-853-5959

J. J. Roberts, 166 Manassas Dr., Manassas Park, VA 22111/703-361-4513

Wm. A. Roberts Jr., Rte. 4, Box 75, Athens, AL 35611/205-232-7027 (ML)

Don Robinson, Pennsylvania Hse., 36 Fairfaix Crescent, Southowram, Halifax, W. Yorkshire HX3 9SQ, England (airifle stocks)

Bob Rogers Guns, P.O. Box 305, Franklin Grove, IL 61031/815-456-2685

Carl Roth, 4728 Pine Ridge Ave., Cheyenne, WY 82001/307-634-3958

Royal Arms, 1210 Bert Acosta, El Cajon, CA 92020/619-448-5466

R.P.S. Gunshop, 11 So. Haskell, Central Point, OR 97502/503-664-5010

Russell's Rifle Shop, Route 5, Box 92, Georgetown, TX 78626/512-778-5338

SSK Industries, Rt. 1, Della Dr., Bloomingdale, OH 43910/614-264-0176

Sanders Custom Gun Serv., 2358 Tyler Lane, Louisville, KY 40205

Sandy's Custom Gunshop, Rte. #1, Box 20, Rockport, IL 62370/217-437-4241

Saratoga Arms Co., 1752 N. Pleasantview Rd., Pottstown, PA 19464/215-323-8326

Roy V. Schaefer, 965 W. Hilliard Lane, Eugene, OR 97404/503-688-4333

SGW, Inc. (formerly Schuetzen Gun Works), see: Olympic Arms

Schumaker's Gun Shop, Rte. 4, Box 500, Colville, WA 99114/509-684-4848

Schwartz Custom Guns, 9621 Coleman Rd., Haslett, MI 48840/517-339-8939

David W. Schwartz Custom Guns, 2505 Waller St., Eau Claire, WI 54701/715-832-1735

Schwarz's Gun Shop, 41-15th St., Wellsburg, WV 26070/304-737-0533

Butch Searcy, 15, Rd. 3804, Farmington, NM 87401/505-327-3419

Shane's Gunsmithing, P.O. Box 321, Hwy. 51 So., Minocqua, WI 54548/715-356-9631

Shaw's, Finest in Guns, 9447 W. Lilac Rd., Escondido, CA 92026/619-728-7070

E. R. Shaw Inc., Small Arms Mfg. Co., Thoms Run Rd., Bridgeville, PA 15017/412-221-4343

George H. Sheldon, P.O. Box 475, Franklin, NH 03235 (45 autos only)

Lynn Shelton Custom Rifles, 1516 Sherry Court, Elk City, OK 73644/405-225-0372

Shell Shack, 113 E. Main, Laurel, MT 59044/406-628-8986 (ML)

Shilen Rifles, Inc., 205 Metro Park Blvd., Ennis, TX 75119/214-875-5318

Harold H. Shockley, 204 E. Farmington Rd., Hanna City, IL 61536/309-565-4524 (hot bluing & plating)

Shootin' Shack, 1065 Silverbeach Rd. #1, Riviera Beach, FL 33403/305-842-0990 ('smithing services)

Walter Shultz, 1752 N. Pleasantview Rd., Pottstown, PA 19464

Silver Dollar Guns, P.O. Box 475, 10 Frances St., Franklin, NH 03235/603-934-3292 (45 autos only)

Simmons Gun Spec., 700 So. Rogers Rd., Olathe, KS 66062/913-782-3131

Simms Hardware Co., 2801 J St., Sacramento, CA 95816/916-442-3800

John R. Skinner, c/o Orvis Co., Manchester, VT 05250

Steve Sklany, 566 Birch Grove Dr., Kalispell, MT 59901/406-755-4527 (Ferguson rifle)

Jerome F. Slezak, 1290 Marlowe, Lakewood (Cleveland), OH 44107/216-221-1668

Art Smith, 4124 Thrushwood Lane, Minnetonka, MN 55345/612-935-7829

John Smith, 912 Lincoln, Carpentersville, IL 60110

Jordan T. Smith, c/o Orvis Co., Manchester, VT 05250

Snapp's Gunshop, 6911 E. Washington Rd., Clare, MI 48617/517-386-9226

Fred D. Speiser, 2229 Dearborn, Missoula, MT 59801/406-549-8133

Spencer Reblue Service, 1820 Tupelo Trail, Holt, MI 48842/517-694-7474 (electroless nickel plating)

Sportsmen's Equip. Co., 915 W. Washington, San Diego, CA 92103/619-296-1501

Sportsmen's Exchange & Western Gun Traders, Inc., P.O. Box 111, 560 S. "C" St., Oxnard, CA 93032/805-483-1917

Jess L. Stark, Stark Mach. Co., 12051 Stroud, Houston, TX 77072/713-498-5882

Ken Starnes, Rt. 1, Box 269, Scroggins, TX 75480/214-365-2312

Steelman's Gun Shop, 10465 Beers Rd., Swartz Creek, MI 48473/313-753-4884

Keith Stegall, Box 696, Gunnison, CO 81230

Date Storey, 1764 S. Wilson, Casper, WY 82601/307-237-2414

Victor W. Strawbridge, 6 Pineview Dr., Dover Point, Dover, NH 03820/603-742-0013

W. C. Strutz, Rifle Barrels, Inc., P.O. Box 611, Eagle River, WI 54521/715-479-4766

Suter's House of Guns, 332 N. Tejon, Colorado Springs, CO 80902/303-635-1475

A. D. Swenson's 45 Shop, P.O. Box 606, Fallbrook, CA 92028

Talmage Ent., 43197 E. Whittier, Hemet, CA 92344/714-927-2397

Target Airgun Supply, P.O. Box 428, South Gate, CA 90280/213-569-3417

Taylor & Robbins, Box 164, Rixford, PA 16745

James A. Tertin, c/o Gander Mountain, P.O. Box 128 - Hwy. W, Wilmot, WI 53192/414-862-2344

Larry R. Thompson, Larry's Gun Shop, 521 E. Lake Ave., Watsonville, CA 95076/408-724-5328

Daniel Titus, 872 Penn St., Bryn Mawr, PA 19010/215-525-8829

Tom's Gunshop, Tom Gillman, 4435 Central, Hot Springs, AR 71913/501-624-3856

Todd Trefts, 217 W. Koch, Bozeman, MT 59715/406-587-3817

Trinko's Gun Serv., 1406 E. Main, Watertown, WI 53094

Dennis A. "Doc" Ulrich, D.O.C. Specialists, Inc., 2209 S. Central Ave., Cicero, IL 60650/312-652-3606

Upper Missouri Trading Co., Inc., Box 181, Crofton, MO 68730

Chas. VanDyke Gunsmith Service, 201 Gatewood Cir. W., Burleson, TX 76028/817-295-7373 (shotgun & recoil pad specialist)

Milton Van Epps, Rt. 69-A, Parish, NY 13131/313-625-7251

Gil Van Horn, P.O. Box 207, Llano, CA 93544

John Vest, P.O. Box 1552, Susanville, CA 96130/916-253-3681

Vic's Gun Refinishing, 6 Pineview Dr., Dover, NH 03820/603-742-0013

Walker Arms Co., Rt. 2, Box 73, Hiwy 80 West, Selma, AL 36701/205-872-6231

Walker Arms Co., 127 N. Main St., Joplin, MO 64801

R. D. Wallace, Star Rt. Box 76, Grandin, MO 63943/314-593-4773

R. A. Wardrop, Box 245, 409 E. Marble St., Mechanicsburg, PA 17055

Weatherby's, 2781 Firestone Blvd., South Gate, CA 90280/213-569-7186

Weaver Arms Co., P.O. Box 8, Dexter, MO 63841/314-568-3800 (ambidextrous bolt action)

J. S. Weeks & Son, 4748 Bailey Rd., Dimondale, MI 48821 (custom rifles)

Terry Werth, 1203 Woodlawn Rd., Lincoln, IL 62656/217-732-3870

Cecil Weems, P.O. Box 657, Mineral Wells, TX 76067/817-325-1462

Wells Sport Store, Fred Wells, 110 N. Summit St., Prescott, AZ 86301/602-445-3655

R. A. Wells Ltd., 3452 N. 1st Ave., Racine, WI 53402/414-639-5223

Terry Werth, 1203 Woodlawn Rd., Lincoln, IL 62656/217-732-9314

Robert G. West, 27211 Huey Lane, Eugene, OR 97402/503-689-6610

Western Gunstocks Mfg. Co., 550 Valencia School Rd., Aptos, CA 95003

Whitefish Sportsman, Pete Forthofer, 711 Spokane Ave., Whitefish, MT 59937/406-862-7252

Duane Wiebe, P.O. Box 497, Lotus, CA 95651/916-626-6240

M. Wiest & Son, 125 E. Tyrone Rd., Oak Ridge, TN 37830/615-483-4024

Dave Wills, 2776 Brevard Ave., Montgomery, AL 36109/205-272-8446

Williams Gun Sight Co., 7389 Lapeer Rd., Davison, MI 48423

Bob Williams, P.O. Box 143, Boonsboro, MD 21713

Williamson-Pate Gunsmith Service, 117 W. Pipeline, Hurst, TX 76053/817-268-2887

Thomas E. Wilson, 644 Spruce St., Boulder, CO 80302 (restorations)

Robert M. Winter, R.R. 2, Box 484, Menno, SD 57045/605-387-5322

Lester Womack, 512 Westwood Dr., Prescott, AZ 86301/602-778-9624

Mike Yee, 29927-56 Pl. S., Auburn, WA 98001/206-839-3991

York County Gun Works, RR 4, Tottenham, Ont., LOG 1WO Canada (muzzleloaders)

Russ Zeeryp, 1601 Foard Dr., Lynn Ross Manor, Morristown, TN 37814

CUSTOM METALSMITHS

Don Allen, Inc., HC55, Box 322, Sturgis, SD 57785/605-347-4686

Alley Supply Co., P.O. Box 848, Gardnerville, NV 89410/702-782-3800

Baer Custom Guns, 1725 Minesite Rd., Allentown, PA 18103/215-398-2362

Al Biesen & Assoc., West 2039 Sinto Ave., Spokane, WA 99201/509-328-6818

Ross Billingsley & Brownell, Box 25, Dayton, WY 82836/307-655-9344

E.C. Bishop & Son Inc., 119 Main St., P.O. Box 7, Warsaw, MO 65355/816-438-5121

Ted Blackburn, 85 E., 700 South, Springville, UT 84663/801-489-7341 (precision metalwork; steel trigger guard)

Gregg Boeke, Rte. 2, Box 149, Cresco, IA 52136/319-547-3746

Larry D. Brace, 771 Blackfoot Ave., Eugene, OR 97404/503,688-1278

A. Briganti, 475 Rt. 32, Highland Mills, NY 10930/914-928-9816

Leo Bustani, P.O. 8125, W. Palm Beach, FL 33407/305-622-2710

C&G Precision, 10152 Trinidad, El Paso, TX 79925/915-592-5496

Clinton River Gun Serv. Inc., 30016 S. River Rd., Mt. Clemens, MI 48045/313-468-1090

Dave Cook, 5831-26th Lane, Brampton, MI 49837/906-428-1235

Crandall Tool & Machine Co., 1540 N. Mitchell St., Cadillac, MI 49601/616-775-5562

Daniel Cullity Restorations, 209 Old County Rd., East Sandwich, MA 02537/617-888-1147

The Custom Gun Guild, Frank Wood, 5091-F Buford Highway, Doraville, GA 30340/404-455-0346

D&D Gun Shop, 363 Elmwood, Troy, MI 48083/313-583-1512

D&H Precision Tooling, 7522 Barnard Mill Rd., Ringwood, IL 60072/815-653-9611

Jack Dever, 8520 N.W. 90th, Oklahoma City, OK 73132/405-721-6393

Ken Eyster Heritage Gunsmiths Inc., 6441 Bishop Rd., Centerburg, OH 43011/614-625-43031

Flaig's Inc., 2200 Evergreen Rd., Millvale, PA 15209/412-821-1717

Fountain Prods., 492 Prospect Ave., W. Springfield, MA 01089/413-781-4651

Frank's Custom Rifles, 10420 E. Rusty Spur, Tucson, AZ 85749/602-749-4563

Fredrick Gun Shop, 10 Elson Dr., Riverside, RI 02915/401-433-2805 (engine turning)

Geo. M. Fullmer, 2499 Mavis St., Oakland, CA 94601/415-533-4193 (precise chambering—300 cals.)

Roger M. Green & J. Earl Bridges, P.O. Box 984, 315 S. 2nd St., Glenrock, WY 82637/307-436-9804

Gentry's The Bozeman Gunsmith, 2010 N. 7th, Bozeman, MT 59715/406-586-1405

Griffin & Howe, 589 Broadway, New York, NY 10012/212-966-5323

Karl Guenther, 165 Granite Springs Rd., Yorktown Heights, NY 10598/914-245-5610

Harkrader's Custom Gun Shop, 825 Radford St., Christiansburg, VA 24073
Robert W. Hart & Son, Inc., 401 Montgomery St., Nescopeck, PA 18635/717-752-3655
Hubert J. Hecht, Waffen-Hecht, 10122 Fair Oaks Blvd., Fair Oaks, CA 95628/916-966-1020
Stephen Heilmann, P.O. Box 657, Grass Valley, CA 95945/916-272-8758
Heppler's Gun Shop, 6000 B Soquel Ave., Santa Cruz, CA 95062/408-475-1235
Klaus Hiptmayer, P.O. Box 136, R.R. 112 #750, Eastman, Que. JOE1PO, Canada/514-297-2492
Hollis Gun Shop, 917 Rex St., Carlsbad, NM 88220/505-885-3782
Huntington's, P.O. Box 991, Oroville, CA 95965
Paul Jaeger, Inc., P.O. Box 449, 1 Madison St., Grand Junction, TN 38039/901-764-6909
R. L. Jamison, Jr., Rt. 4, Box 200, Moses Lake, WA 98837/509-762-2659
Ken Jantz, Rt. 1, Sulphur, OK 73086/405-622-3790
Neil A. Jones, RD #1, Box 483A, Saegertown, PA 16433/814-763-2769
Kennons Custom Rifles, 5408 Biffle Rd., Stone Mountain, GA 30088/404-469-9339
Benjamin Kilham, Kilham & Co., Main St., Box 37, Lyme, NH 03768/603-795-4112
Terry K. Kopp, Highway 13, Lexington, MO 64067/816-259-2636
Ron Lampert, Rt. 1, Box 61, Guthrie, MN 56461/218-854-7345
Mark Lee, P.O. Box 20379, Minneapolis, MN 55420/612-884-4060
Lilja Precision Rifle Barrels, Inc., 245 Compass Creek Rd., P.O. Box 372, Plains, MT 59859/406-826-3084
McIntyre Tools & Guns, P.O. Box 491, State Rd. #1144, Troy, NC 27371/919-572-2603
Miller Arms, Inc., P.O. Box 260, St. Onge, SD 57779/605-578-1790
J. W. Morrison Custom Rifles, 4015 W. Sharon, Phoenix, AZ 85029/602-978-3754
Bruce A. Nettestad, Rt. 1, Box 140, Pelican Rapids, MN 56572/218-863-4301
Vic Olson, 5002 Countryside Dr., Imperial, MO 63052/314-296-8086
Pasadena Gun Center, 206 E. Shaw, Pasadena, TX 77506/713-472-0417
Penrod Precision, 126 E. Main St., P.O. Box 307, No. Manchester, IN 46962/219-982-8385
Precise Chambering Co., 2499 Mavis St., Oakland, CA 94601/415-533-4193
Dave Talley, Rt. 4, Box 366, Leesville, SC 29070/803-532-2700
J. W. Van Patten, P.O. Box 145, Foster Hill, Milford, PA 18337/717-296-7069
Herman Waldron, Box 475, Pomeroy, WA 99347/509-843-1404
R. D. Wallace, Star Rt. Box 16, Grandin, MO 64943/314-593-4773
Fred Wells, Wells Sport Store, 110 N. Summit St., Prescott, AZ 86301/602-445-3655
Terry Werth, 1203 Woodlawn Rd., Lincoln, IL 62656/217-732-3870
John Westrom, Precise Firearm Finishing, 25 N.W. 44th Ave., Des Moines, IA 50313/515-288-8680

DECOYS

Carry-Lite, Inc., 5203 W. Clinton Ave., Milwaukee, WI 53223
Deer Me Products Co., Box 34, 1208 Park St., Anoka, MN 55303/612-421-8971 (Anchors)
Ted Devlet's Custom Purveyors, P.O. Box 886, Fort Lee, NJ 07024/201-886-0196
Flambeau Prods. Corp., 15981 Valplast Rd., Middlefield, OH 44062/216-632-1631
G & H Decoy Mfg. Co., P.O. Box 1208, Henryetta, OK 74437/918-652-3314
Penn's Woods Products, Inc., 19 W. Pittsburgh St., Delmont, PA 15626/412-468-8311
Royal Arms, 1210 Bert Acosta, El Cajon, CA 92020/619-448-5466 (wooden, duck)
Ron E. Skaggs, P.O. Box 34, Princeton, IL 61356/815-875-8207
Woodstream Corp., P.O. Box 327, Lititz, PA 17543

ENGRAVERS, ENGRAVING TOOLS

Abominable Engineering, P.O. Box 1904, Flagstaff, AZ 86002/602-779-3025
John J. Adams, P.O. Box 167, Corinth, VT 05039/802-439-5904
American Derringer Corp., 127 N. Lacy Dr., Waco, TX 76705/817-799-9111
Paolo Barbetti, c/o Stan's Gunshop, 5303 Roosevelt Way N.E., Seattle, WA 98105/206-522-4575
Robert L. Barnard, P.O. Box 93, Fordyce, AR 71742/501-352-5861
Billy R. Bates, 2905 Lynnwood Circle S.W., Decatur, AL 35603/205-355-3690
Joseph C. Bayer, 439 Sunset Ave., Sunset Hill Griggstown, RD 1, Princeton, NJ 08540/201-359-7283
Angelo Bee, 10703 Irondale Ave., Chatsworth, CA 91311/213-882-1567
Sid Bell Originals Inc., R.D. 2, Box 219, Tully, NY 13159/607-842-6431
Jim Bina, 2007 Howard St., Evanston, IL 60202/312-475-6377
Weldon Bledsoe, 6812 Park Place Dr., Fort Worth, TX 76118/817-589-1704
Rudolph V. Bochenski, 1410 Harlem Rd., Cheektowaga, NY 14206/716-896-3619
Carl Bleile, Box 11464, Cincinnati, OH 45211/513-662-0802
C. Roger Bleile, Box 5112, Cincinnati, OH 45205/513-251-0249
Erich Boessler, Gun Engraving Intl., Am Vogeltal 3, 8732 Münnerstadt, W. Germany/9733-9443
Henry "Hank" Bonham, 218 Franklin Ave., Seaside Heights, NJ 08751/201-793-8309
Boone Trading Co., 562 Coyote Rd., Brinnon, WA 98320/206-796-4330 (ivory, scrimshaw tools)
Bryan Bridges, 6350 E. Paseo San Andres, Tucson, AZ 85710
Frank Brgoch, 1580 So. 1500 East, Bountiful, UT 84010/801-295-1885
Dennis B. Brooker, R.R. 1, Box 62, Prole, IA 50229/515-961-8200
Burgess Vibrocrafters (BVI), Rt. 83, Grayslake, IL 60030
Byron Burgess, 710 Bella Vista Dr., Morro Bay, CA 93442/805-772-3974

Brian V. Cannavaro, Gun City U.S.A., 573 Murfreesboro Rd., Nashville, TN 37210/615-256-6127
Winston Churchill, Twenty Mile Stream Rd., RFD Box 29B, Proctorsville, VT 05153/802-226-7772
Clark Engravings, P.O. Box 80746, San Marino, CA 91108/818-287-1652
Frank Clark, 3714-27th St., Lubbock, TX 79410/806-799-3838
Crocker Engraving, 1510 - 42nd St., Los Alamos, NM 87544
Daniel Cullity, 209 Old County Rd., East Sandwich, MA 02537/617-888-1147
Art A. Darakis, RD #2, Box 350, Fredericksburg, OH 44627/216-695-4271
Tim Davis, 230 S. Main St., Eldorado, OH 45321/513-273-4611
Ed Delorge, 2231 Hwy. 308, Thibodaux, LA 70301/504-447-1633
James R. DeMunck, 3012 English Rd., Rochester, NY 14616/716-225-0626 (SASE)
C. Gregory Dixon, RD 1, Box 175, Kempton, PA 19529/215-756-6271
Howard M. Dove, 52 Brook Rd., Enfield, CT 06082/203-749-9403
Mark Drain, S.E. 3211 Kamilche Point Rd., Shelton, WA 98584/206-426-5452
Michael W. Dubber, 3107 E. Mulberry, Evansville, IN 47714/812-476-4036
Henri Dumoulin & Fils, rue du Tilleul 16, B-4411 Milmoret (Herstal), Belgium
Robert Evans, 332 Vine St., Oregon City, OR 97045/503-656-5693
Ken Eyster, Heritage Gunsmiths Inc., 6441 Bishop Rd., Centerburg, OH 43011/614-625-6131
John Fanzoi, P.O. Box 25, Ferlach, Austria 9170
Jacqueline Favre, 3111 So. Valley View Blvd., Suite B-214, Las Vegas, NV 89102/702-876-6278
Armi FERLIB, 46 Via Costa, 25063 Gardone V.T. (Brescia), Italy
Firearms Engravers Guild of America, Robert Evans, Secy., 332 Vine St., Oregon City, OR 97045/503-656-5693
Fountain Prods., 492 Prospect Ave., W. Springfield, MA 01089/413-781-4651
Henry Frank, Box 984, Whitefish, MT 59937/406-862-2681
Leonard Francolini, 56 Morgan Rd., Canton, CT 06019/203-693-2529
GRS Corp., P.O. Box 748, 900 Overland St., Emporia, KS 66801/316-343-1084 (Gravermeister tool)
Donald Glaser, 1520 West St., Emporia, KS 66801
Eric Gold, Box 1904, Flagstaff, AZ 86002
Howard V. Grant, Hiawatha 153, Woodruff, WI 54568/715-356-7146
Griffin & Howe, 589 Broadway, New York, NY 10012/212-966-5323
Gurney Engraving Method, #513-620 View St., Victoria, B.C. V8W 1J6 Canada/604-383-5243
John K. Gwilliam, 218 E. Geneva Dr., Tempe, AZ 85282/602-894-1739
Hand Engravers Supply Co., 4348 Newberry Ct., Dayton, OH 45432/513-426-6762
Jack O. Harwood, 1191 S. Pendlebury Lane, Blackfoot, ID 83221/208-785-5368
Frank E. Hendricks, Master Engravers, Inc., Star Rt. 1A, Box 334, Dripping Springs, TX 78620/512-858-7828
Heidemarie Hiptmayer, R.R. 112, #750, P.O. Box 136, Eastman, Que. J0E 1PO, Canada/514-297-2492
Harvey Hoover, 1263 Nunneley Rd., Paradise, CA 94969/916-872-1154
Ken Hunt, c/o Hunting World, Inc., 16 E. 53rd St., New York, NY 10022/212-755-3400
Jim Hurst, 4537 S. Irvington Ave., Tulsa, OK 74135/918-627-5460
Ken Hurst/Firearm Engraving Co., P.O. Box 249, Route 501, Rustburg, VA 24588/804-332-6440
Ralph W. Ingle, Master Engraver, #4 Missing Link, Rossville, GA 30741/404-866-5589 (color broch. $3)
Paul Jaeger, Inc., P.O. Box 449, 1 Madison Ave., Grand Junction, TN 38039/901-764-6909
Ken Jantz Supply, Rt. 1, Sulphur, OK 73086/405-622-3790 (tools)
Bill Johns, 1113 Nightingale, McAllen, TX 78501/512-682-2971
Steven Kamyk, 9 Grandview Dr., Westfield, MA 01085/413-568-0457
T. J. Kaye, Rocksprings St. Rt., Box 277, Junction, TX 76849/915-446-3091
Lance Kelly, 1824 Royal Palm Dr., Edgewater, FL 32032/904-423-4933
Jim Kelso, Rt. 1, Box 5300, Worcester, VT 05682/802-229-4254
E. J. Koevenig Engraving Service, P.O. Box 55, Rabbit Gulch, Hill City, SD 57745/605-574-2239
John Kudlas, 622-14th St. S.E., Rochester, MN 55901/507-288-5579
Terry Lazette, 142 N. Laurens Dr., Bolivar, OH 44612/216-874-4403
Leonard Leibowitz, 1202 Palto Alto St., Pittsburgh, PA 15212/412-231-5388 (etcher)
Franz Letschnig, Master-Engraver, 620 Cathcart, Rm. 422, Montreal, Queb. H3B 1M1, Canada/514-875-4989
W. Neal Lewis, 9 Bowers Dr., Newnan, GA 30263/404-251-3045
Frank Lindsay, 1326 Tenth Ave., Holdrege, NE 68949/308-995-4623
Steve Lindsay, P.O. Box 1413, Kearney, NE 68847/308-236-7885
London Guns, 1528-20th St., Santa Monica, CA 90404/213-828-8486
Harvey McBurnette, Rt. 4, Box 337, Piedmont, AL 36272
Dennis McDonald, Box 3, Peosta, IA 52068
Lynton S.M. McKenzie, 6940 N. Alvernon Way, Tucson, AZ 85718/602-299-5090
Wm. H. Mains, 3111 S. Valley View Blvd., Suite B-214, Las Vegas, NV 89102/702-876-6278
Robert E. Maki, School of Firearms Engraving, P.O. Box 947, Northbrook, IL 60062/312-724-8238
Laura Mandarino, 136 5th Ave. West, Kalispell, MT 59901/406-257-6208
George Marek, P.O. Box 213, Westfield, MA 01086/413-568-5957
Frank Mele, P.O. Box 361, Somers, NY 10589/914-277-3040
S. A. Miller, Miller Gun Works, P.O. Box 7326, Tamuning, Guam 96911
Cecil J. Mills, 2265 Sepulveda Way, Torrance, Ca 90501/213-328-8088
Frank Mittermeier, 3577 E. Tremont Ave., New York, NY 10465
Mitch Moschetti, P.O. Box 27065, Denver, CO 80227/303-936-1184
Gary K. Nelson, 975 Terrace Dr., Oakdale, CA 95361/209-847-4590
NgraveR Co., 879 Raymond Hill Rd., Oakdale, CT 06370/203-848-8031 (engr. tool)
New Orleans Arms Co., P.O. Box 26087, New Orleans, LA 70186/504-944-3371
New Orleans Jewelers Supply, 206 Chartres St., New Orleans, LA 70130/504-523-3839 (engr. tool)
Hans Obiltschnig, 12. November St. 7, 9170 Ferlach, Austria
Oker's Engraving, 365 Bell Rd., Bellford Mtn. Hts., P.O. Box 126, Shawnee, CO 80475/303-838-6042

Gale Overbey, 612 Azalea Ave., Richmond, VA 23227

Pachmayr Gun Works, Inc., 1220 S. Grand Ave., Los Angeles, CA 90015/213-748-7271

Rex C. Pedersen, 2717 S. Pere Marquette, Ludington, MI 49431/616-843-2061

Marcello Pedini, 5 No. Jefferson Ave., Catskill, NY 12414/518-943-5257

E. L. Peters, P.O. Box 1927, Gibsons, B.C. VON 1VO, Canada/604-886-9665

Paul R. Piquette, 40 Royalton St., Chicopee, MA 01020/413-592-1057

Eugene T. Plante, Gene's Custom Guns, 3890 Hill Ave., P.O. Box 10534, White Bear Lake, MN 55110/612-429-5105

Jeremy W. Potts, 1680 So. Granby, Aurora, CO 80012/303-752-2528

Wayne E. Potts, 912 Poplar St., Denver, CO 80220/303-355-5462

Ed Pranger, 1414-7th St., Anacortes, WA 98221/206-293-3488

Proofmark, Ltd., P.O. Box 183, Alton, IL 62002/618-463-0120 (Italian Bottega Incisioni)

E. C. Prudhomme, #426 Lane Building, 610 Marshall St., Shreveport, LA 71101/318-425-8421

Leonard Puccinelli Design, P.O. Box 3494, Fairfield, CA 94533/415-457-9911

Martin Rabeno, Spook Hollow Trading Co., Box 37F, RD #1, Ellenville, NY 12428/914-647-4567

Jim Riggs, 206 Azalea, Boerne, TX 78006/512-249-8567 (handguns)

J. J. Roberts, 166 Manassas Dr., Manassas Park, VA 22111/703-361-4513

John R. and Hans Rohner, Sunshine Canyon, Boulder, CO 80302/303-444-3841

Bob Rosser, 162 Ramsey Dr., Albertville, AL 35950/205-878-5388

Richard D. Roy, 87 Lincoln Way, Windsor, CT 06095/203-688-0304

Joe Rundell, 6198 Frances Rd., Clio, MI 48420/313-687-0559

Robert P. Runge, 94 Grove St., Ilion, NY 13357/315-894-3036

Shaw-Cullen, Inc., 212 - East 47th St., New York, NY 10017/212-759-8460 (etchers)

Shaw's "Finest In Guns," 9447 W. Lilac Rd., Escondido, CA 92026/619-728-7070

George Sherwood, Box 735, Winchester, OR 97495/503-672-3159

Ben Shostle, The Gun Room, 1201 Burlington Dr., Muncie, IN 47302/317-282-9073

W. P. Sinclair, 36 South St., Warminster, Wiltsh. BA12 8DZ, England

Ron Skaggs, P.O. Box 34, Princeton, IL 61356/815-875-8207

Mark A. Smith, 200 N. 9th, Sinclair, WY 82334/307-324-7929

Ron Smith, 3601 West 7th St., Ft. Worth, TX 76107

R. Spinale, 3415 Oakdale Ave., Lorain, OH 44055/216-246-5344

Robt. Swartley, 2800 Pine St., Napa, CA 94559

George W. Thiewes, 1846 Allen Lane, St. Charles, IL 60174/312-584-1383

Denise Thirion, Box 408, Graton, CA 95444/707-829-1876

Robert B. Valade, 931-3rd. Ave., Seaside, OR 97138/503-738-7672

John Vest, P.O. Box 1552, Susanville, CA 96130/916-253-3681

Ray Viramontez, 4348 Newberry Ct., Dayton, OH 45432/513-426-6762

Vernon G. Wagoner, 2325 E. Encanto, Mesa, AZ 85203/602-835-1307

R. D. Wallace, Star Rt. Box 76, Grandin, MO 63943

Terry Wallace, 385 San Marino, Vallejo, CA 94590

Floyd E. Warren, 1273 State Rt. 305 N.E., Cortland, OH 44410/216-638-4219

Kenneth W. Warren, Mountain States Engraving, 8333 E. San Sebastian Dr., Scottsdale, AZ 85258/602-991-5035

David W. Weber, 1421 East 4th, North Platte, NE 69101/308-534-2525

Rachel Wells, 110 N. Summit St., Prescott, AZ 86301/602-445-3655

Sam Welch, CVSR Box 2110, Moab, UT 84532/801-259-7620

Claus Willig, c/o Paul Jaeger, Inc., P.O. Box 449, 1 Madison Ave. Grand Junction, TN 38039

Mel Wood, P.O. Box 1255, Sierra Vista, AZ 85636/602-455-5541

GAME CALLS

Black Duck, 1737 Davis Ave., Whiting, IN 46394/219-659-2997

Burnham Bros., Box 669, 912 Main St., Marble Falls, TX 78654/512-693-3112

Call'N, Inc., 1615 Bartlett Rd., Memphis, TN 38134/901-372-1682

Faulk's, 616 18th St., Lake Charles, LA 70601

Lohman Mfg. Co., P.O. Box 220, Neosho, MO 64850/417-451-4438

Mallardtone Game Calls, 2901 16th St., Moline, IL 61265/309-762-8089

Phil. S. Olt Co., Box 550, Pekin, IL 61554/309-348-3633

Quaker Boy Inc., 6426 West Quaker St., Orchard Parks, NY 14127/716-662-3979

Penn's Woods Products, Inc., 19 W. Pittsburgh St., Delmont, PA 15626

Scotch Game Call Co., Inc., 6619 Oak Orchard Rd., Elba, NY 14058/716-757-9958

Johnny Stewart Game Calls, Box 7954, Waco, TX 76710/817-772-3261

Sure-Shot Game Calls, Inc., P.O. Box 816, Groves, TX 77619

Thomas Game Calls, P.O. Box 336, Winnsboro, TX 75494

Weems Wild Calls, P.O. Box 7261, Ft. Worth, TX 76111/817-531-1051

GUN PARTS, U.S. AND FOREIGN

American Derringer Corp., 127 N. Lacy Dr., Waco, TX 76705/817-799-9111

Armes de Chasse, P.O. Box 827, Chadds Ford, PA 19317/215-388-1146

Armsport, Inc., 3590 N.W. 49th St., Miami, FL 33142/305-635-7850

Badger Shooter's Supply, 106 So. Harding, Owen, WI 54460/715-229-2101

Behlert Custom Guns, Inc., RD 2, Box 36C, Route 611 North, Pipersville, PA 18947/215-766-8681 (handgun parts)

Can Am Enterprises, Fruitland, ON L0R 1L0, Canada/416-643-4357

Cherokee Gun Accessories, 4127 Bay St. Suite 226, Fremont, CA 94538/415-471-5770

Dave Chicoine, d/b/a Liberty A.S.P., 19 Key St., Eastport, ME 04631/207-853-2327 (S&W only; ctlg. $5)

Crown City Arms, Inc., P.O. Box 550, Cortland, NY 13045/607-753-8238 (rifle, handgun)

Charles E. Duffy, Williams Lane, West Hurley, NY 12491

Falcon Firearms Mfg. Corp., P.O. Box 3748, Granada Hills, CA 91344/818-885-0900 (barrels; magazines)

Federal Ordnance Inc., 1443 Potrero Ave., So. El Monte, CA 91733/213-350-4161

Jack First Distributors Inc., 44633 Sierra Highway, Lancaster, CA 93534/805-945-6981

Forster Products, 82 E. Lanark Ave., Lanark, IL 61046/815-493-6360

Gun City, 504 Main, Bismarck, ND 58501/701-223-2304 (magazines, gun parts)

Gun-Tec, P.O. Box 8125, W. Palm Beach, FL 33407 (Win. mag. tubing; Win. 92 conversion parts)

Hansen and Hansen, 244 Old Post Rd., Southport, CT 06490/203-259-7337

Hastings, Box 224, 822-6th St., Clay Center, KS 67432/913-632-3169

Heller & Levin Associates, Inc., 88 Marlborough Court, Rockville Center, NY 11570/516-764-9349

Walter H. Lodewick, 2816 N.E. Halsey, Portland, OR 97232/503-284-2554 (Winchester parts)

Morgan Arms Co., Inc., 2999 So. Highland Dr., Las Vegas, NV 89109/702-737-5247 (MK-I kit)

Numrich Arms Co., West Hurley, NY 12491

Pacific Intl. Merch. Corp., 2215 "J" St., Sacramento, CA 95816/916-446-2737 (Vega 45 Colt mag.)

Potomac Arms Corp. (See Hunter's Haven)

Pre-64 Winchester Parts Co., P.O. Box 8125, West Palm Beach, FL 33407 (send stamped env. w. requ. list)

Martin B. Retting, Inc., 11029 Washington Blvd., Culver City, CA 90232/213-837-6111

Rock Island Armory, Inc., 111 E. Exchange St., Geneseo, IL 61254/309-944-2109

Royal Ordnance Works Ltd., P.O. Box 3245, Wilson, NC 27893/919-237-0515

Sarco, Inc., 323 Union St., Stirling, NJ 07980

Sherwood Intl. Export Corp., 18714 Parthenia St., Northridge, CA 91324

Simms, 2801 J St., Sacramento, CA 95816/916-442-3800

Clifford L. Smires, R.D. 1, Box 100, Columbus, NJ 08022/609-298-3158 (Mauser rifle parts)

Springfield Sporters Inc., R.D. 1, Penn Run, PA 15765/412-254-2626

Triple-K Mfg. Co., 568-6th Ave., San Diego, CA 92101/619-232-2066 (magazines, gun parts)

GUNS (U.S.-made)

AMT (Arcadia Machine & Tool), 536 N. Vincent Ave., Covina, CA 91722/818-915-7803

Accuracy Systems, Inc., 15203 N. Cave Creek Rd., Phoenix, AZ 85032/602-971-1991

Advantage Arms USA, Inc., 840 Hampden Ave., St. Paul, MN 55114/612-644-5197

Alpha Arms, Inc., 12923 Valley Branch, Dallas, TX 75234/214-243-8124

American Arms, Box 1055, Garden Grove, CA 92643/714-636-5191 (American Arms Eagle 380)

American Arms, Inc., P.O. Box 27163, Salt Lake City, UT 84127/801-971-5006

American Derringer Corp., 127 N. Lacy Dr., Waco, TX 76705/817-799-9111

American Industries, 8700 Brookpark Rd., Cleveland, OH 44129/216-398-8300

ArmaLite, 118 E. 16th St., Costa Mesa, CA 92627

Armament Systems and Procedures, Inc., Box 356, Appleton, WI 54912/414-731-8893 (ASP pistol)

Arminex Ltd., 7882 E. Gray Rd., Scottsdale Airpark, Scottsdale, AZ 85260/602-998-0443 (Excalibur s.a. pistol)

Arm Tech, Armament Technologies Inc., 240 Sargent Dr., New Haven, CT 06511/203-562-2543 (22-cal. derringers)

Armes de Chasse, 3000 Valley Forge Circle, King of Prussia, PA 19406/215-783-6133

Arnett Guns (See Gary DelSignore Weaponry)

Artistic Arms, Inc.,Box 23, Hoagland, IN 46745 (Sharps-Borchardt)

Artistic Firearms Corp., John Otteman, 4005 Hecker Pass Hwy., Gilroy, CA 95020/408-842-4278 (A.F.C. Comm. Rife 1881-1981)

Auto Nine Corp., see: FTL Marketing Corp.

Auto-Ordnance Corp., Box GD, West Hurley, NY 12491/914-679-7225

BJT, 445 Putman Ave., Hamden, CT 06517 (stainless double derringer)

Baford Arms, Inc., 808 E. Cedar St., Bristol TN 37620/615-968-9397

Barrett Firearms Mfg., Inc., 312 S. Church St., Murfreesboro, TN 37130/615-896-2938 (Light Fifty)

Bighorn Rifle Co., P.O. Box 215, American Fork, UT 84003/801-756-4222

Bren Ten (See Dornaus & Dixon Ent.)

Browning (Gen. Offices), Rt. 1, Morgan, UT 84050/801-876-2711

Browning (Parts & Service), Rt. 4, Box 624-B, Arnold, MO 63010/314-287-6800

Bumble Bee Wholesale, Inc., 12521 Oxnard St., North Hollywood, CA 91606/818-985-2939 (Pocket Partner)

Bushmaster Firearms Co., 803 Forest Ave., Portland ME 04103/207-775-3324 (police handgun)

Century Gun Dist., Inc., 1467 Jason Rd., Greenfield, IN 46140/317-462-4524 (Century Model 100 SA rev.)

Challanger Mfg. Corp., 118 Pearl St., Mt. Vernon, NY 10550 (Hopkins & Allen)

Champlin Firearms, Inc., Box 3191, Enid, OK 73702/405-237-7388

Charter Arms Corp., 430 Sniffens Ln., Stratford, CT 06497

Chipmunk Manufacturing Inc., 114 E. Jackson, Medford, OR 97501/503-664-5585 (22 S.S. rifle)

Classic Arms, 815-22nd St., Union City, NJ 08757/201-863-1493

Colt Firearms, P.O. Box 1868, Hartford, CT 06102/203-236-6311

Commando Arms (See Gibbs Guns, Inc.)

Coonan Arms, Inc., 830 Hampden Ave., St. Paul, MN 55114/612-646-6672 (357 Mag. Autom.)

Cumberland Arms, Rt. 1, Shafer Rd., Blanton Chapel, Manchester, TN 37355

The Custom Gun Guild, 5091-F Buford Highway, Doraville, GA 30340/404-455-0346

Davidson Supply, 2703 High Point Rd., Greensboro, NC 27403/800-367-4867

Davis Industries, 13748 Arapahoe Pl., Chino, CA 91710/714-591-4727 (derringer)

Leonard Day & Sons, Inc., P.O. Box 723, East Hampton, MA 01027/413-527-7990 (ML)

Gary DelSignore Weaponry, 3675 Cottonwood, Cedar City, UT 84720/801-586-2505 (Arnett Guns)

Demro Products Inc., 372 Progress Dr., Manchester, CT 06040/203-649-4444 (Wasp, Tac guns)

Detonics Mfg. Corp., 13456 S.E. 27th Pl., Bellevue, WA 98005/206-747-2100 (auto pistol)

Dornaus & Dixon Enterprises, Inc., 15896 Manufacture Lane, Huntingdon Beach, CA 92649/714-891-5090

DuBiel Arms Co., 1724 Baker Rd., Sherman, TX 75090/214-893-7313

Encom America, Inc., P.O. Box 5314, Atlanta, GA 30307/404-525-2811

Excalibur (See Arminex)

F.I.E. Corp. (See Firearms Import & Export Corp.)

FTL Marketing (See Bumble Bee Wholesale, Inc.)

Falcon Firearms Mfg. Corp., P.O. Box 3748, Granada Hills, CA 91344/818-885-0900 (handguns)

Falling Block Works, P.O. Box 3087, Fairfax, VA 22038/703-476-0043

Feather Enterprises, 2500 Central Ave., Boulder, CO 80301/303-442-7021

Federal Eng. Corp., 3161 N. Elston Ave., Chicago, IL 60618/312-267-4151 (XC-220 carbine)

Firearms Imp. & Exp. Corp., P.O. Box 4866, Hialeah Lakes, Hialeah, FL 33014/305-685-5966 (FIE)

Freedom Arms Co., P.O. Box 1776, Freedom, WY 83120 (mini revolver, Casull rev.)

Freedom Arms Marketing (See: L.A.R. Mfg. Co.)

Frontier Shop & Gallery, Depot 1st & Main, Riverton, WY 82501/307-856-4498

Garrett Accur-Light Inc., 1413 B. E. Olive Ct., Fort Collins, CO 80524/303-224-3067

Gibbs Guns, Inc., Rt. 2, Greenback, TN 37742/615-856-2813 (Commando Arms)

Göncz Co., 11526 Burbank Blvd., #18, No. Hollywood, CA 91601/818-505-0408

Golden Age Arms Co., 14 W. Winter St., Delaware, OH 43015

Gunworks Ltd., 10 Aqua Lane, Buffalo, NY 14150/716-877-2565

HJS Industries, Inc., P.O. Box 4351, Brownsville, TX 78520/512-542-3340 (22 4-bbl.; 38 S&W SS derringers)

Harrington & Richardson, Industrial Rowe, Gardner, MA 01440

Hatfield Rifle Works, 2020 Colhoun, St. Joseph, MO 64501/816-279-8688 (squirrel rifle)

A.D. Heller, Inc., Box 268, Grand Ave., Baldwin, NY 11510

Holmes Firearms Corp., Rte. 6, Box 242, Fayetteville, AR 72703

Hopkins & Allen Arms, 3 Ethel Ave., P.O. Box 217, Hawthorne, NJ 07507/201-427-1165 (ML)

Lew Horton Dist. Co. Inc., 175 Boston Rd., Southboro, MA 01772

Hyper-Single Precision SS Rifles, 520 E. Beaver, Jenks, OK 74037/918-299-2391

Ithaca Gun Co., Ithaca, NY 14850

Jennings Firearms Inc., P.O. Box 5416, Stateline, NV 89449/702-588-6884

Jennings-Hawken, 326½-4th St. N.W., Winter Haven, FL 33880 (ML)

Iver Johnson, 2202 Redmond Rd., Jacksonville, AR 72076/501-982-9491

KK Arms Co., Karl Kash, Star Route, Box 671, Kerrville, TX 78028/512-257-4441 (handgun)

Kimber of Oregon, Inc., 9039 S.E. Jannsen Rd., Clackamas, OR 97015/503-656-1704

Kimel Industries, Box 335, Matthews, NC 28105/704-821-7663

L.A.R. Manufacturing Co., 4133 West Farm Rd., West Jordan, UT 84084/801-255-7106 (Grizzly Win Mag pistol)

Law Enforcement Ordnance Corp., Box 649, Middletown, PA 17057/717-944-5500 (Striker-12 shotgun)

Ljutic Ind., Inc., P.O. Box 2117, 732 N 16th Ave., Yakima, WA 98907/509-248-0476 (Mono-Gun)

Loven-Pierson, Inc., 4 W. Main, P.O. Box 377, Apalachin, NY 13732/607-625-2303 (ML)

M & N Distributors, 23535 Telo St., Torrance, CA 90505/213-530-9000 (Budischowsky)

Magnum Sales, Div. of Mag-na-port, 41302 Executive Drive, Mt. Clemens, MI 48045/313-469-7434 (Ltd. editions & customized guns for handgun hunting)

Marlin Firearms Co., 100 Kenna Drive, New Haven, CT 06473

Matteson Firearms Inc., Otsego Rd., Canajoharie, NY 13317/607-264-3744 (SS rifles)

Merrill Pistol, see: Rock Pistol Mfg.

Michigan Arms Corp., 363 Elmwood, Troy, MI 48084/313-583-1518 (ML)

Military Armament Corp., P.O. Drawer 1358, 1481 So. Loop-Suite 4, Stephensville, TX 76401/817-968-7543 (Ingram submach. gun)

Mitchell Arms Inc., 2101 E. 4th St., Suite 201A, Santa Ana, CA 92705/714-964-3678 (AR-50 survival rifle)

M.O.A. Corp., 110 Front St., Dayton, OH 45402/513-223-6401 (Maximum pistol)

O.F. Mossberg & Sons, Inc., 7 Grasso St., No. Haven, CT 06473

Mowrey Gun Works, 1313 Lawsun Rd., Saginaw, TX 76179/817-847-1644

Navy Arms Co., 689 Bergen Blvd., Ridgefield, NJ 07657

North American Arms, 1800 North 300 West, Spanish Fork, UT 84660/801-798-9891

North Georgia Armament, 5265 Jimmy Carter Blvd., Suite 1442, Norcross, GA 30093/404-446-3504

Numrich Arms Corp., W. Hurley, NY 12491

Oregon Trail Riflesmiths, Inc., P.O. Box 45212, Boise, ID 83711/208-336-8631 (ML)

Ozark Mountain Arms, Inc., Rt. 1 Box 44A5, Hwy. 32E, Ashdown, AR 71822/501-898-2345 (ML)

Pecos Valley Armory, 1022 So. Canyon, Carlsbad, NM 88220/505-887-6023 (ML)

Pennsylvania Arms Co., Box 128, Duryea, PA 18642/717-457-4014

Phillips & Bailey, Inc., P.O. Box 219253, Houston, TX 77218/713-392-0207 (357/9 Ultra, rev. conv.)

Precision Small Parts, 155 Carlton Rd., Charlottesville, VA 22901/804-293-6124

Provider Arms, Inc., 261 Haglund Dr., Chesterton, IN 46304/219-879-5590 (ML Predator rifle)

Rahn Gun Works, Inc., P.O. Box 327, 535 Marshall St., Litchfield, MI 49252/517-542-3247

Raven Arms, 1300 Bixby Dr., Industry, CA 91745/213-961-2511 (P-25 pistols)

Remington Arms Co., 1007 Market St., Wilmington, DE 19898

Rock Pistol Mfg., Inc., 150 Viking, Brea, CA 92621/714-990-2444 (Merrill pistol)

Ruger (See Sturm, Ruger & Co.)

Savage Industries, Inc., Springdale Rd., Westfield, MA 01085/413-562-2361

B. Searcy Co., 15, Rd. 3804, Farmington, NM 87401/505-327-3419 (mountain rifle)

L.W. Seecamp Co., Inc., P.O. Box 255, New Haven, CT 06502/203-877-3429

Serrifile, Inc., P.O. Box 508, Littlerock, CA 93543/805-945-0713 (derringer; single shot)

C. Sharps Arms Co., Inc., P.O. Box 885, Big Timber, MT 59011/406-932-4353

Shilen Rifles, Inc., 205 Metro Park Blvd., P.O. Box 1300, Ennis, TX 75119/214-875-5318

Shiloh Products, 181 Plauderville Ave., Garfield, NJ 07026 (Sharps)

The Silhouette, 1409 Benton, Box 1509, Idaho Falls, ID 83401/208-524-0880 (Wichita International pistol)

Six Enterprises, 6564 Hidden Creek Dr., Dan Jose, CA 95120/408-268-8296 (Timberliner rifle)

Smith & Wesson, Inc., 2100 Roosevelt Ave., Springfield, MA 01101

Sokolovsky Corp., Box 70113, Sunnyvale, CA 94086/408-245-9268 (45 Automaster pistol)

Sporting Arms, Inc., 12923 Valley Branch, Dallas, TX 75234/214-243-8124 (Snake Charmer II shotgun)

Springfield Armory, Inc., 420 W. Main St., Geneseo, IL 61254/309-944-5138

SSK Industries, Rt. 1, Della Dr., Bloomingdale, OH 43910/614-264-0176

Steel City Arms, Inc., P.O. Box 81926, Pittsburgh, PA 15217/412-461-3100 (d.a. "Double Deuce" pistol)

Sturm, Ruger & Co., Southport, CT 06490

Tennessee Valley Arms, P.O. Box 2022, Union City, TN 38261/901-885-4456

Texas Longhorn Arms, Inc., P. O. Box 703, Richmond, TX 77469/713-341-0775 (S.A. sixgun)

Thompson-Center Arms, P.O. Box 2426, Rochester, NH 03867/603-332-2394

Tippmann Arms Co., 4402 New Haven Ave., Ft. Wayne, IN 46803/219-422-6448

Traders International, Inc., P.O. Box 595, Indian Trail, NC 28105/704-821-7684

Trail Guns Armoury, 1422 E. Main St., League City, TX 77573/713-332-5833 (muzzleloaders)

Trapper Gun, Inc., 18717 E. 14 Mile Rd., Fraser, MI 48026/313-792-0133 (handguns)

The Ultimate Game Inc., P.O. Box 1856, Ormond Beach, FL 32075/904-677-4358

Ultra Light Arms Co., P.O. Box 1270, Granville, WV 26534/304-599-5687

United Sporting Arms, Inc, 610 Ross Point Rd., Post Falls, ID 83854/208-773-9932 (handguns)

U.S. Repeating Arms Co., P.O. Box 30-300, New Haven, CT 06511/203-789-5000

Universal Firearms, 2202 Redmond Rd., Jacksonville, AR 72076/501-982-9491

Weatherby's, 2781 E. Firestone Blvd., South Gate, CA 90280

Weaver Arms Ltd., P.O. Box 3316, Escondido, CA 92025/619-746-2440

Dan Wesson Arms, 293 So. Main St., Monson, MA 01057

Wichita Arms, 444 Ellis, Wichita, KS 67211/316-265-0661

Wildey, 28 Old Route 7, Brookfield, CT 06804/203-775-4261

Wildey Firearms, 299 Washington St., Newburgh, NY 12550/1-800-243-GUNS

Wilkinson Arms, 26884 Pearl Rd., Parma, ID 83660/208-722-5533

Winchester, (See U.S. Repeating Arms)

York Arms Co., 50 W. State St., Hurricane, UT 84737/801-635-4867

GUNS (Foreign)

Abercrombie & Fitch, 2302 Maxwell Lane, Houston, TX 77023 (Ferlib)

Action Arms, P.O. Box 9573, Philadelphia, PA 19124/215-744-0100

Allen Firearms Co., 2879 All Trades Rd., Santa Fe, NM 87501/505-471-6090 (ML)

American Arms, Inc., 11023 W. 108th Terr., Overland Park, KS 66210

Anschutz (See PSI)

Armoury Inc., Rte. 202, New Preston, CT 06777

Armes de Chasse, P.O. Box 827, Chadds Ford, PA 19317/215-388-1146 (Merkel, Mauser)

Armscor (See Pacific International Merchandising)

Arms Corp. of the Philippines, Pacific Bank Bldg., 6th Fl., #604, Ayala Ave., Makati, Metro Manila, Philippines

Armsport, Inc., 3590 N.W. 49th St., Miami, FL 33142/305-635-7850

Armurerie Liegeois-Artisans Reunis (A.L.A.R.), 27, rue Lambert Masset, 4300 Ans, Belgium

Pedro Arrizabalaga, Eibar, Spain

Bauska Arms Corp., P.O. Box 1995, Kalispell, MT 59903/406-752-2072

Beeman, Inc., 47-GDD Paul Dr., San Rafael, CA 94903/415-472-7121 (FWB, Weihrauch, FAS, Unique, Korth, Krico, Agner, Hammerli firearms)

Benelli Armi, S.p.A. (See: Sile Distributors—handguns; Heckler & Koch—Shotguns)

Beretta U.S.A., 17601 Indian Head Highway, Accokeek, MD 20607/301-283-2191

Bingham Ltd., 1775-C Wilwat Dr., Norcross, GA 30093/404-448-1440

Charles Boswell (Gunmakers), Div. of Saxon Arms Ltd., 615 Jasmine Ave. N., Tarpon Springs, FL 33589/813-938-4882

M. Braun, 32, rue Notre-Dame, 2240 Luxemburg, Luxemburg (all types)

Bretton, 21 Rue Clement Forissier, 42-St. Etienne, France

Britarms/Berdan (Gunmakers Ltd.), See: Action Arms

British Guns, P.O. Box 1924, Corvallis, OR 97339/503-752-5886 (Agent for W.&C. Scott)

Browning (Gen. Offices), Rt. 1, Morgan, UT 84050/801-876-2711

Browning, (parts & service), Rt. 4, Box 624-B, Arnold, MO 63010/314-287-6800

Bumble Bee Wholesale, Inc., 12521 Oxnard St., North Hollywood, CA 91606/818-985-2939 (Valmet auto rifle)

Century Arms Co., 5 Federal St., St. Albans, VT 05478/802-524-9541

Ets. Chapuis, rue de la Chatelaine, 42380 St. Bonnet-le-Chateau, France

Conco Arms, P.O. Box 159, Emmaus, PA 18049/215-967-5477 (Larona)

Connecticut Valley Arms Co., 5988 Peachtree Corners East, Norcross, GA 30071/404-449-4687 (CVA)

Walter Craig, Inc., Box 927, Selma, AL 36701/205-875-7989

Davidson Supply, 2703 High Point Rd., Greensboro, NC 27403/800-367-4867

Des Moines Imports, 21 Glenview Dr., Des Moines, IA 50312/515-279-1987 (Spanish Gorosabel shotguns)

Diana Import, 842 Vallejo St., San Francisco, CA 94133

Charles Daly (See Outdoor Sports HQ)

Dikar s. Coop. (See Connecticut Valley Arms Co.)

Dixie Gun Works, Inc., Hwy 51, South, Union City, TN 38261/901-885-0561 ("Kentucky" rifles)

Double M Shooting Sports, 462 S. Loop Pole Rd., Gylford, CT 06473 (Dr. Franco Beretta)

Dynamit Nobel of America, Inc., 105 Stonehurst Court, Northvale, NJ 07647/201-767-1660 (Rottweil)

E.M.F. Co. Inc. (Early & Modern Firearms), 1900 E. Warner Ave. 1-D, Santa Ana, CA 92705/714-966-0202

Ernest Dumoulin-Deleye, see: Midwest Gun Sport

Henri Dumoulin & Fils, rue du Tilleul 16, B-4411 Milmort (Herstal), Belgium

Peter Dyson Ltd., 29-31 Church St., Honley, Huddersfield, Yorkshire HD7 2AH, England (accessories f. antique gun collectors)

Elko Arms, 28 rue Ecole Moderne, 7400 Soignes, Belgium

Euroarms of American, Inc., P.O. Box 3277, 1501 Lenoir Dr., Winchester, VA 22601/703-661-1863 (ML)

Excam Inc., 4480 E. 11 Ave., P.O. Box 3483, Hialeah, FL 33013

Exel Arms of America, 14 Main St., Gardner, MA 01440/617-632-5008

F.I.E. Corp. (See Firearms Import & Export Corp.)

FTL Marketing (See Bumble Bee Wholesale, Inc.)

J. Fanzoj, P.O. Box 25, Ferlach, Austria 9170

Armi FERLIB di Libero Ferraglio, 46 Via Costa, 25063 Gardone V.T. (Brescia), Italy

Fiocchi of America, Inc., 1308 W. Chase, Springfield, MO 65803/417-864-6970

Firearms Imp. & Exp. Corp., (F.I.E.), P.O. Box 4866, Hialeah Lakes, Hialeah, FL 33014/305-685-5966

Flaig's Inc., 2200 Evergreen Rd., Millvale, PA 15209/412-821-1717

Auguste Francotte & Cie, S.A., rue de Trois Juin 109, 4400 Herstal-Liege, Belgium

Frankonia Jagd, Hofmann & Co., Postfach 6780, D-8700 Wurzburg 1, West Germany

Freeland's Scope Stands, Inc., 3737 14th Ave., Rock Island, IL 61201/309-788-7449

Frigon Guns, 627 W. Crawford, Clay Center, KS 67432/913-632-5607

Renato Gamba, S.p.A., Gardone V.T. (Brescia), Italy (See Steyr Daimier Puch of America Corp.)

Armas Garbi, Urki #12, Eibar (Guipuzcoa) Spain (shotguns, See W. L. Moore)

Gilbert Equipment Co., Inc., 3300 Buckeye Rd. N.W., Suite 220, Atlanta, GA 30341/404-451-5558 (USAS-12 shotgun)

George Granger, 66 Cours Fauriel, 42 St. Etienne, France

Griffin & Howe, 589 Broadway, New York, NY 10012/212-966-5323 (Purdey, Holland & Holland)

Gun South, P.O. Box 129, 108 Morrow Ave., Trussville, AL 35173/205-655-8299 (Steyr, FN, Mannlicher)

Heckler & Koch Inc., 14601 Lee Rd., Chantilly, VA 22021/703-631-2800

Heym, Friedr. Wilh., see: Paul Jaeger, Inc.

HOWCO Dist. Inc., 122 Lafayette Ave., Laurel, MD 20707/301-953-3301

Hunting World, 16 E. 53rd St., New York, NY 10022

IGI Domino Corp., 200 Madison Ave., New York, NY 10016/212-889-4889 (Breda)

Incor, Inc., P.O. Box 132, Addison, TX 75001/214-931-3500 (Cosmi auto shotg.)

Interarmco, See Interarms (Walther)

Interarms Ltd., 10 Prince St., Alexandria, VA 22313 (Mauser, Valmet M-62/S)

International Sporting Goods, 919 Imperial Ave., P.O. Box 496, Calexico, CA 92231/619-357-6641 (Laurona shotguns)

Paul Jaeger Inc., P.O. Box 449, 1 Madison Ave., Grand Junction, TN 38039/901-764-6909 (Heym)

Jenkins Imports Corp., 462 Stanford Pl., Santa Barbara, CA 93111/805-967-5092 (Gebrüder Merkel)

John Jovino Co., 5 Centre Market Pl., New York, NY 10013/212-925-4881 (Terminator)

Kassnar Imports, 5480 Linglestown Rd., Harrisburg, PA 17110

Kawaguchiya Firearms, c/o La Paloma Marketing, 4500 E. Speedway Blvd., Suite 93, Tucson, AZ 85712/602-881-4750

Kendall International, Inc., 501 East North, Carlisle, KY 40311/606-289-7336

Kimel Industries, Box 335, Matthews, NC 28105/704-821-7663

KDF, Inc., 2485 Hwy 46 No., Seguin, TX 78155/512-379-8141

Robert Kleinguenther Firearms, P.O. Box 2020, Seguin, TX 78155

Knight & Knight, 302 Ponce de Leon Blvd., St. Augustine, FL 32084/904-829-9671 (Bernardelli shotguns)

L. A. Distributors, 4 Centre Market Pl., New York, NY 10013

Lanber Arms of America, Inc., 377 Logan St., Adrian, MI 49221/517-263-7444 (Spanish o-u shotguns)

La Paloma Marketing, 1735 E. Ft. Lowell Rd., Suite 7, Tucson, AZ 85719/602-881-4750 (K.F.C. shotguns)

Morris Lawing, P.O. Box 9494, Charlotte, NC 28299/704-375-1740

Leland Firearms Co., 13 Mountain Ave., Llewellyn Park, West Orange, NJ 07052/201-325-3379 (Spanish shotguns)

Llama (See Stoeger)

MRE Dist. Inc., 19 So. Bayles Ave., Pt. Washington, NY 11050/516-944-8200 (IGI Domino)

Magnum Research, Inc., 7271 Commerce Circle West, Minneapolis, MN 55432/612-574-1868 (Israeli Galil)

Mandall Shtg. Suppl. 3616 N. Scottsdale Rd., Scottsdale, AZ 85252/602-945-2553

Mannlicher (See Steyr Daimler Puch of Amer.)

Manurhin, See: Matra-Manurhin

Marocchi USA Inc., 5939 W. 66th St., Bedford Park, IL 60638

Marathon Products Inc., East Haddam Industrial Park, East Haddam, CT 06423/203-873-1478

Matra-Manurhin International, Inc., 1640 W. Oakland Park Blvd., Suite 402, Ft. Lauderdale, FL 33311/305-486-8800

Mauser-Werke Oberndorf, P. O. Box 1349, 7238 Oberndorf/Neckar, West Germany

Mendi s. coop. (See Connecticut Valley Arms Co.)

Merkuria, FTC, Argentinska 38, 17000 Prague 7, Czechoslovakia (BRNO)

Midwest Gun Sport, Belgian HQ, 1942 OakWood View Dr., Verona, WI 53593/608-845-7447 (E. Dumoulin)

Mitchell Arms Corp., 116 East 16th St., Costa Mesa, CA 92627/714-548-7701 (Uberti pistols)

Wm. Larkin Moore & Co., 31360 Via Colinas, Suite 109, Westlake Village, CA 91360/213-889-4160 (AYA, Garbi, Ferlib, Piotti, Lightwood, Perugini Visini)

Navy Arms Co., 689 Bergen Blvd., Ridgefield, NJ 07657

O&L Guns Inc., P.O. Box 1146, Seminole, TX 79360/915-758-2933 (Wolverine rifle)

Odin International, Ltd., 818 Slaters Lane, Alexandria, VA 22314/703-339-8005 (Valmet/military types; CETME; Zastava)

Osborne's, P.O. Box 408, Cheboygan, MI 49721/616-625-9626 (Hammerli; Tanner rifles)

Outdoor Sports Headquarters, Inc., 967 Watertower Lane, Dayton, OH 45449/513-865-5855 (Charles Daly shotguns)

PM Air Services Ltd., P.O. Box 1573, Costa Mesa, CA 92626/714-968-2689

Pachmayr Gun Works, 1220 S. Grand Ave., Los Angeles, CA 90015

Pacific Intl. Merch. Corp., 2215 "J" St., Sacramento, CA 95816/916-446-2737

The Parker Gun, Div. of Reagent Chemical & Research, Inc., 1201 N. Watson Rd., Suite 224, Arlington, TX 76011/817-649-8781

Parker-Hale, Bisleyworks, Golden Hillock Rd., Sparbrook, Birmingham B11 2PZ, England

Perazzi U.S.A. Inc., 206 S. George St., Rome, NY 13440/315-337-8566

E. F. Phelps Mfg., Inc., 700 W. Franklin, Evansville, IN 47710/812-423-2599 (Heritage 45-70)

Precise, 3 Chestnut, Suffern, NY 10901

Precision Sales Intl. Inc., PSI, P.O. Box 1776, Westfield, MA 01086/413-562-5055 (Anschutz)

Precision Sports, P.O. Box 708, Kellogg Rd., Cortland, NY 13045/607-756-2851 (Parker-Hale)

Proofmark, Ltd., P.O. Box 183, Alton, IL 62002/618-463-0120 (Bettinsoli shotguns)

Leonard Puccinelli Design, P.O. Box 3494, Fairfield, CA 94533/415-457-9911 (I.A.B. Rizzini, Bernardelli shotguns of Italy; consultant to Beretta U.S.A.)

Quality Arms, Inc., Box 19477, Houston, TX 77224/713-870-8377 (Bernardelli; Ferlib; Bretton shotguns)

Quantetics Corp., Imp.-Exp. Div., 582 Somerset St. W., Ottawa, Ont. K1R 5K2 Canada/613-237-0242 (Unique pistols-Can. only)

Rahn Gun Works, Inc., P.O. Box 327, 535 Marshall St., Litchfield, MI 49252/517-542-3247

Ravizza Carlo Caccia Pesca, s.r.l., Via Melegnano 6, 20122 Milano, Italy

Richland Arms Co., 321 W. Adrian St., Blissfield, MI 49228

Rottweil, (See Dynamit Nobel of America)

Royal Arms International, 22458 Ventura Blvd., Suite E, Woodland Hills, CA 91364/818-704-5110

Sarco, Inc., 323 Union St., Stirling, NJ 07980/201-647-3800

Sauer (See Sigarms)

Savage Industries, Inc., Springdale Rd., Westfield, MA 01085/413-562-2361

Thad Scott, P.O. Box 412; Hwy 82 West, Indianola, MS 38751/601-887-5929 (Perugini Visini; Bertuzzi; Mario Beschi shotguns)

Service Armament, 689 Bergen Blvd., Ridgefield, NJ 07657 (Greener Harpoon Gun)

Sherwood Intl. Export Corp., 18714 Parthenia St., Northridge, CA 91324

Don L. Shrum's Cape Outfitters, 412 So. Kingshighway, Cape Girardeau, MO 63701/314-335-4103

Sigarms, Inc., 8330 Old Courthouse Rd., Suite 885, Tysons Corner, VA 22180/703-893-1940

Sile Distributors, 7 Centre Market Pl., New York, NY 10013/212-925-4111

Simmons Gun Specialties, Inc., 700 S. Rogers Rd., Olathe, KS 66062/913-782-3131

Sloan's Sprtg. Goods, Inc., 10 South St., Ridgefield, CT 06877

Franz Sodia Jagdgewehrfabrik, Schulhausgasse 14, 9170 Ferlach, (Kärnten) Austria

Southern Gun & Tackle Distributors, P.O. Box 25, Opa-Locka (Miami), FL 33054

Southwest Muzzle Loaders Supply, 201 E. Myrtle, Suite 112/P.O. Box 921, Angleton, TX 77515/409-849-4086

Spain America Enterprises Inc., 8581 N.W. 54th St., Miami, FL 33166

Springfield Armory, 420 W. Main St., Geneseo, IL 61254/309-944-5139 (Bernardelli)

Steyr-Daimler-Puch, Gun South, Inc., Box 6607, 7605 Eastwood Mall, Birmingham, AL 35210/800-821-3021 (rifles)

Stoeger Industries, 55 Ruta Ct., S. Hackensack, NJ 07606/201-440-2700

Taurus International Mfg. Inc., P.O. Box 558567, Ludlam Br., Miami, FL 33155/305-662-2529

Thomas & Barrett, North Frost Center, 1250 Northeast Loop 410, Suite 200, San Antonio, TX 78209/512-826-0943

Loren Thomas Ltd., P.O. Box 18425, Dallas, TX 75218 (Bruchet)

Tradewinds, Inc., P.O. Box 1191, Tacoma, WA 98401

Uberti, Aldo. See: Allen Firearms Co.

Ignacio Ugartechea, Apartado 21, Eibar, Spain
Valmet Sporting Arms Div., 7 Westchester Plaza, Elmsford, NY 10523/914-347-4440 (sporting types)
Valor of Florida Corp., 5555 N.W. 36th Ave., Miami, FL 33142/305-633-0127
Ventura Imports, P.O. Box 2782, Seal Beach, CA 90740 (European shotguns)
Verney-Carron, B.P. 72, 54 Boulevard Thiers, 42002 St. Etienne Cedex, France
Perugini Visini & Co. s.r.l., Via Camprelle, 126, 25080 Nuvolera (Bs.), Italy
Waffen-Frankonia, see: Frankonia Jagd
Waverly Arms Inc., 108 Olde Springs Rd., Columbia, SC 29223/803-736-2861 (Armurerie Vouzelaud; shotguns only)
Weatherby's, 2781 Firestone Blvd., So. Gate, CA 90280/213-569-7186
Whittington Arms, Box 489, Hooks, TX 75561
Winchester, Olin Corp., 120 Long Ridge Rd., Stamford, CT 06904
Zavodi Crvena Zastava (See Interarms)
Zoli Group U.S.A. Inc., P.O. Box 729, 1051 Clinton St., Buffalo, NY 14240/716-852-1445

GUNS (Pellet)

Barnett International, Inc., P.O. Box 934, 1967 Gunn Highway, Odessa, FL 33556/920-2241
Beeman Precision Airguns, 47 Paul Dr., San Rafael, CA 94903/415-472-7121
Benjamin Air Rifle Co., 2600 Chicory Rd., Racine, WI 53403/414-554-7900
Collector's Armoury, Inc., 800 Slaters Lane, Alexandria, VA 22314/703-339-8005
Crosman Airguns, 980 Turk Hill Rd., Fairport, NY 14450/716-223-6000
Daisy Mfg. Co., P.O. Box 220, Rogers, AR 72756/501-636-1200 (also Feinwerkbau)
Dynamit Nobel of America, Inc., 105 Stonehurst Ct., Northvale, NJ 07647/201-767-1660 (Dianawerk)
Great Lakes Airguns, 6175 So. Park Ave., Hamburg, NY 14075/716-648-6666
Harrington & Richardson Arms Co., Industrial Rowe, Gardner, MA 01440 (Webley)
Gil Hebard Guns, Box 1, Knoxville, IL 61448
Interarms, 10 Prince, Alexandria, VA 22313 (Walther)
Kendall International Inc., 501 East North, Carlisle, KY 40311/606-289-7336 (Italian Airmatch)
Mandall Shooting Supplies, Inc., 3616 N. Scottsdale Rd., Scottsdale, AZ 85252/602-945-2553 (Cabanas line)
Marathon Products Inc., East Haddam Industrial Park, East Haddam, CT 06423/203-873-1478
Marksman Products, 5622 Engineer Dr., Huntington Beach, CA 92649/714-898-7535
McMurray & Son, 109 E. Arbor Vitae St., Inglewood, CA 90301/213-412-4187 (cust. airguns)
Paragon Sales & Services, Inc., P.O. Box 2022, Joliet, IL 60434/815-725-9212
Phoenix Arms Co., Phoenix House, Churchdale Rd., Eastbourne, East Sussex BN22 8PX, England (Jackal)
Power Line (See Daisy Mfg. Co.)
Sheridan Products, Inc., 3205 Sheridan, Racine, WI 53403
Smith & Wesson, 2100 Roosevelt Ave., Springfield, MA 01104
Target Airgun Supply, P.O. Box 428, South Gate, CA 90280/213-569-3417

GUNS & GUN PARTS, REPLICA AND ANTIQUE

Antique Arms Co., David E. Saunders, 1110 Cleveland, Monett, MO 65708/417-235-6501
Antique Gun Parts, Inc., 1118 S. Braddock Ave., Pittsburgh, PA 15218/412-241-1811 (ML)
Armoury Inc., Rte. 202, New Preston, CT 06777
Armsport, Inc., 3590 N.W. 49th St., Miami, FL 33142
Artistic Arms, Inc., Box 23, Hoagland, IN 46745 (Sharps-Borchardt replica)
Beeman Precisions Arms, Inc., 47-GDD Paul Dr., San Rafael, CA 94903/415-472-7121
Bob's Place, Box 283J, Clinton, IA 52732 (obsolete Winchester parts only)
Cache La Poudre Rifleworks, 168 No. College Ave., Fort Collins, CO 80524/303-482-6913
Dave Chicoine, d/b/a Liberty A.S.P., 19 Key St., Eastport, ME 04631/207-853-2327(S&W only; ctlg. $5)
Collector's Armoury, Inc., 800 Slaters Lane, Alexandria, VA 22314/703-339-8005
Dixie Gun Works, Inc., Hwy 51, South, Union City, TN 38261/901-885-0561
Federal Ordnance Inc., 1443 Portrero Ave., So. El Monte, CA 91733/213-350-4161
Jack First Distributors, Inc., 44633 Sierra Hwy., Lancaster, CA 93534/805-945-6981
Fred Goodwin, Goodwin's Gun Shop, Silver Ridge, Sherman Mills, ME 04776/207-365-4451 (Winchester rings & studs)
Hansen & Hansen, 244 Old Post Rd., Southport, CT 06490/203-259-7337
Hopkins & Allen Arms, 3 Ethel Ave., P.O. Box 217, Hawthorne, NJ 07507/201-427-1165
Terry K. Kopp, Highway 13, Lexington, MO 64067/816-259-2636 (restoration & pts. 1890 & 1906 Winch.)
The House of Muskets, Inc., P.O. Box 4640, Pagosa Springs, CO 81157/303-731-2295 (ML guns)
Log Cabin Sport Shop, 8010 Lafayette Rd., Lodi, OH 44254/216-948-1082 (ctlg. $30)
Edw. E. Lucas, 32 Garfield Ave., East Brunswick, NJ 08816/201-251-5526 (45/70 Springfield parts; some Sharps, Spencer parts)
Lyman Products Corp., Middlefield, CT 06455

Tommy Munsch Gunsmithing, Rt. 2, Box 248, Little Falls, MN 56345/612-632-5835 (Winchester parts only; list $1.50; oth. inq. SASE)
Numrich Arms Co., West Hurley, NY 12491
Ram Line, Inc., 406 Violet St., Golden, CO 80401/303-279-0886
Replica Models, Inc., 800 Slaters Lane, Alexandria, VA 22314/703-339-8005
S&S Firearms, 88-21 Aubrey Ave., Glendale, NY 11385/212-497-1100
Sarco, Inc., 323 Union St., Stirling, NJ 07980/201-647-3800
C. H. Stoppler, 1426 Walton Ave., New York, NY 10452 (miniature guns)
Upper Missouri Trading Co., Box 191, Crofton, NE 68730/402-388-4844
C. H. Weisz, Box 311, Arlington, VA 22210/703-243-9161
W. H. Wescombe, P.O. Box 488, Glencoe, CA 95232 (Rem. R.B. parts)

GUNS, SURPLUS—PARTS AND AMMUNITION

Can Am Enterprises, Fruitland, Ont. LOR ILO, Canada/416-643-4357 (Enfield rifles)
Century Arms, Inc., 5 Federal St., St. Albans, VT 05478/802-524-9541
Walter Craig, Inc., Box 927, Selma, AL 36701/205-875-7989
Eastern Firearms Co., 790 S. Arroyo Pkwy., Pasadena, CA 91105
Federal Ordnance, Inc., 1443 Potrero Ave., So. El Monte, CA 91733/818-350-4161
Garcia National Gun Traders, 225 S.W. 22nd, Miami, FL 33135
Hansen and Hansen, 244 Old Post Rd., Southport, CT 06490/203-259-7337
Lever Arms Serv. Ltd., 572 Howe St., Vancouver, B.C., Canada V6C 2E3/604-685-8945
Paragon Sales & Services, Inc., P.O. Box 2022, Joliet, IL 60434 (ammunition)
Raida Intertraders S.A., Raida House, 1-G Ave. de la Coronne, B1050 Brussels, Belgium
Sarco, Inc., 323 Union St., Stirling, NJ 07980/201-647-3800 (military surpl. ammo)
Service Armament Co., 689 Bergen Blvd., Ridgefield, NJ 07657
Sherwood Intl. Export Corp., 18714 Parthenia St., Northridge, CA 91324/818-349-7600
Springfield Sporters Inc., R.D. 1, Penn Run, PA 15765/412-254-2626

GUNSMITHS, CUSTOM (see Custom Gunsmiths)

GUNSMITHS, HANDGUN (see Pistolsmiths)

GUNSMITH SCHOOLS

Colorado School of Trades, 1575 Hoyt, Lakewood, CO 80215/303-233-4697
Lassen Community College, P.O. Box 3000, Hiway 139, Susanville, CA 96130/916-257-6181
Robert E. Maki, School of Engraving, P.O. Box 947, Northbrook, IL 60062/312-724-8238 (firearms engraving ONLY)
Modern Gun Repair School, 2538 No. 8th St., Phoenix, AZ 85006/602-990-8346 (home study)
Montgomery Technical College, P.O. Box 787, Troy, NC 27371/919-572-3691 (also 1-yr. engraving school)
Murray State College, Gunsmithing Program, 100 Faculty Dr., Tishomingo, OK 73460/405-371-2371
North American School of Firearms, Curriculum Development Ctr., 4401 Birch St., Newport Beach, CA 92663/714-546-7360 (correspondence)
North American School of Firearms, Education Service Center, Oak & Pawnee St., Scranton, PA 18515/717-342-7701
Penn. Gunsmith School, 812 Ohio River Blvd., Avalon, Pittsburgh, PA 15202/412-766-1812
Piedmont Technical School, P.O. Box 1197, Roxboro, NC 27575
Pine Technical Institute, 1100 Fourth St., Pine City, MN 55063/612-629-6764
Police Sciences Institute, 4401 Birch St., Newport Beach, CA 92660/714-546-7360 (General Law Enforcement Course)
Shenandoah School of Gunsmithing, P.O. Box 300, Bentonville, VA 22610/703-743-5494
Southeastern Community College, Admissions "TF" Gear Ave., West Burlington, IA 52655/319-752-2731
Trinidad State Junior College, 600 Prospect, Trinidad, CO 81082/303-846-5631
Yavapai College, 1100 East Sheldon St., Prescott, AZ 86301/602-445-7300

GUNSMITH SUPPLIES, TOOLS, SERVICES

A.C. Enterprises, P.O. Box 448, Edenton, NC 27932/919-482-4992
Albright Prod. Co., P. O. Box 1144, Portola, CA 96122 (trap buttplates)
Don Allen, Inc., HC55, Box 322, Sturgis, SD 57785/605-347-4686 (stock duplicating machine)
Alley Supply Co., Carson Valley Industrial Park, P.O. Box 848, Gardnerville, NV 89410/702-782-3800 (JET line lathes, mills, etc.)
Ametek, Hunter Spring Div., One Spring Ave., Hatfield, PA 19440/215-822-2971 (trigger gauge)
Anderson Mfg. Co., Union Gap Sta., P.O. Box 3120, Yakima, WA 98903/509-453-2349 (tang safe)
Answer Stocking Systems, 113 N. 2nd St., Whitewater, WI 53190/414-473-4848 (urethane hammers, vice jaws, etc.)
Armite Labs., 1845 Randolph St., Los Angeles, CA 90001/213-587-7744 (pen oiler)
B-Square Co., Box 11281, Ft. Worth, TX 76110/800-433-2909
Jim Baiar, 490 Halfmoon Rd., Columbia Falls, MT 59912 (hex screws)
Behlert Custom Guns, Inc., RD 2 Box 36C, Route 611 North, Pipersville, PA 18947/215-766-8680

Dennis M. Bellm Gunsmithing, Inc., dba P.O. Ackley Rifle Barrels, 2376 S. Redwood Rd., Salt Lake City, UT 84119/801-974-0697 (rifles only)

Al Biesen, W. 2039 Sinto Ave., Spokane, WA 99201 (grip caps, buttplates)

Roger Biesen, 5021 W. Rosewood, Spokane, WA 99208/509-328-9340

Billingsley & Brownell, Box 25, Dayton, Wy 82836/307-655-9344

Blue Ridge Machine and Tool, P.O. Box 536, 2806 Putnam Ave., Hurricane, WV 25526/304-562-3538 (machinery, tools, shop suppl.)

Briganti Custom Gun-Smithing, P.O. Box 56, 475-Route 32, Highland Mills, NY 10930/914-928-9816 (cold rust bluing, hand polishing, metal work)

Brownells, Inc., 222 W. Liberty, Montezuma, IA 50171/515-623-5401

W.E. Brownell Checkering Tools, 3356 Moraga Place, San Diego, CA 92117/619-276-6146

Buehler Scope Mounts, 17 Orinda Way, Orinda, CA 94563/415-254-3201

Burgess Vibrocrafters, Inc. (BVI), Rte. 83, Grayslake, IL 60030

M.H. Canjar, 500 E. 45th, Denver, CO 80216/303-295-2638 (triggers, etc.)

Chapman Mfg. Co., P.O. Box 250, Rte. 17 at Saw Mill Rd., Durham, CT 06422/203-349-9228

Chicago Wheel & Mfg. Co., 1101 W. Monroe St., Chicago, IL 60607/312-226-8155 (Handee grinders)

Dave Chicoine, d/b/a Liberty A.S.P., 19 Key St., Eastport, ME 04631/207-853-2327 (spl. S&W tools)

Chopie Mfg., Inc., 700 Copeland Ave., LaCrosse, WI 54603/608-784-0926

Classic Arms Corp., P.O. Box 8, Palo Alto, CA 94302/415-321-7243 (floorplates, grip caps)

Clover Mfg. Co., 139 Woodward Ave., Norwalk, CT 06856/800-243 6492 (Clover compound)

Clymer Mfg. Co., Inc., 1645 W. Hamlin Rd., Rochester Hills, MI 48063/313-541-5533 (reamers)

Dave Cook, 720 Hancock Ave., Hancock, MI 49930 (metalsmithing only)

Dayton-Traister Co., 9322-900th West, P.O. Box 593, Oak Harbor, WA 98277/206-675-5375 (triggers)

Dem-Bart Hand Checkering Tools, Inc., 6807 Hiway #2, Snohomish, WA 98290/206-568-7356

Dremel Mfg. Co., 4915-21st St., Racine, WI 53406 (grinders)

Chas. E. Duffy, Williams Lane, West Hurley, NY 12491

The Dutchman's Firearms Inc., 4143 Taylor Blvd., Louisville, KY 40215/502-366-0555

Peter Dyson Ltd., 29-31 Church St., Honley, Huddersfield, West Yorksh. HD7 2AH, England/0484-661062 (accessories f. antique gun coll.)

Edmund Scientific Co., 101 E. Gloucester Pike, Barrington, NJ 08007/609-547-3488

Emco-Lux, 2050 Fairwood Ave., P.O. Box 07861, Columbus, OH 43207/614-445-8328

Jack First Distributors, Inc., 44633 Sierra Hwy., Lancaster, CA 93534/805-945-6981

Jerry Fisher, 1244 4th Ave. West, Kalispell, MT 59901/406-755-7093

Forster Products, Inc., 82 E. Lanark Ave., Lanark, IL 61046/815-493-6360

Francis Tool Co., (f'ly Keith Francis Inc.), P.O. Box 7861, Eugene, OR 97401/503-345-7457 (reamers)

G. R. S. Corp., P.O. Box 748, 900 Overlander St., Emporia, KS 66801/316-343-1084 (Gravermeister; Grave Max tools)

Gilmore Pattern Works, P.O. Box 50084, Tulsa, OK 74150/918-245-9627 (Wagner safe-T-planer)

Glendo Corp., P.O. Box 1153, Emporia, KS 66801/316-343-1084 (Accu-Finish tool)

Grace Metal Prod., 115 Ames St., Elk Rapids, MI 49629 (screw drivers, drifts)

Gunline Tools, 2970 Saturn St., Brea, CA 92621/714-993-5100

Gun-Tec, P.O. Box 8125, W. Palm Beach, Fl 33407

Half Moon Rifle Shop, 490 Halfmoon Rd., Columbia Falls, MT 59912/406-892-4409 (hex screws)

Henriksen Tool Co., Inc., P.O. Box 668, Phoenix, OR 97535/503-535-2309 (reamers)

Huey Gun Cases (Marvin Huey), P.O. Box 22456, Kansas City, MO 64113/816-444-1637 (high grade English ebony tools)

Ken Jantz Supply, Rt. 1, Sulphur, OK 73086/405-622-3790

Jeffredo Gunsight Co., 1629 Via Monserate, Fallbrook, CA 92028 (trap buttplate)

Kasenit Co., Inc., P.O. Box 726, Mahwah, NJ 07430/201-529-3663 (surface hardening compound)

Terry K. Kopp, Highway 13, Lexington, MO 64067/816-259-2636 (stock rubbing compound; rust preventive grease)

J. Korzinek, RD#2, Box 73, Canton, PA 17724/717-673-8512 (stainl. steel bluing; broch. $1.50)

John G. Lawson, (The Sight Shop) 1802 E. Columbia Ave., Tacoma, WA 98404/206-474-5465

Lea Mfg. Co., 237 E. Aurora St., Waterbury, CT 06720/203-753-5116

Mark Lee Supplies, P.O. Box 20379, Minneapolis, MN 55420/612-884-4060

Lock's Phila. Gun Exch., 6700 Rowland Ave., Philadelphia, PA 19149/215-332-6225

Longbranch Gun Bluing Co., 2455 Jacaranda Lane, Los Osos, CA 93402/805-528-1792

McIntrye Tools, P.O. Box 491/State Road #1144, Troy, NC 27371/919-572-2603 (shotgun bbl. facing tool)

McMillan Rifle Barrels, U.S. International, P.O Box 3427, Bryan, TX 77805/409-846-3990 (services)

Meier Works, Steve Hines, Box 328, 2102-2nd Ave., Canyon, TX 79015/806-655-9256 (European acc.)

Michaels of Oregon Co., P.O. Box 13010, Portland, OR 97213/503-255-6890

Miller Single Trigger Mfg. Co., R.D. 1, Box 99, Millersburg, PA 17061/717-692-3704

Miniature Machine Co. (MMC), 210 E. Poplar St., Deming, NM 88030/505-546-2151 (screwdriver grinding fixtures)

Frank Mittermeier, 3577 E. Tremont, New York, NY 10465

N&J Sales Co., Lime Kiln Rd., Northford, CT 06472/203-484-0247 (screwdrivers)

Karl A. Neise, Inc., 1671 W. McNab Rd., Ft. Lauderdale, FL 33309/305-979-3900

Olympic Arms Inc., dba SGW, 624 Old Pacific Hwy. S.E., Olympia, WA 98503/206-456-3471

Palmgren Steel Prods., Chicago Tool & Engineering Co., 8383 South Chicago Ave., Chicago, IL 60617/312-721-9675 (vises, etc.)

Panavise Prods., Inc., 2850 E. 29th St., Long Beach, CA 90806/213-595-7621

Pilkington Gun Co., P.O. Box 1296, Muskogee, OK 74402/918-683-9418 (Q.D. scope mt.)

Redman's Rifling & Reboring, Route 3, Box 330A, Omak, WA 98841/509-826-5512 (22 RF liners)

Richland Arms Co., 321 W. Adrian St., Blissfield, MI 49228

Riley's Inc., 121 No. Main St., P.O. Box 139, Avilla, IN 46710/219-897-2351 (Niedner buttplates, grip caps)

Roto/Carve, 6509 Indian Hills Rd., Minneapolis, MN 55435/800-533-8988 (tool)

A.G. Russell Co., 1705 Hiway 71 North, Springdale, AR 72764/501-751-7341 (Arkansas oilstones)

Schaffner Mfg. Co., Emsworth, Pittsburgh, PA 15202 (polishing kits)

SGW, Inc. (formerly Schuetzen Gun Works), See: Olympic Arms

Shaw's, 9447 W. Lilac Rd., Escondido, CA 92026/619-728-7070

James R. Spradlin, Jim's Gun Shop, 113 Arthur, Pueblo, CO 81004/303-543-9462 (rust blues; stock fillers)

L.S. Starrett Co., 121 Crescent St., Athol, MA 01331/617-249-3551

Texas Platers Supply Co., 2453 W. Five Mile Parkway, Dallas, TX 75233 (plating kit)

Teyssier Imported French Walnut, P.O. Box 984, 3155 S. 2nd St., Glenrock, WY 82637/307-436-9804 (blanks)

Timney Mfg. Inc., 3106 W. Thomas Rd., Phoenix, AZ 85017/602-269-6937

Stan de Treville, Box 33021, San Diego, CA 92103/619-298-3393 (checkering patterns)

Turner Co., Div. Cleanweld Prods., Inc., 821 Park Ave., Sycamore, IL 60178/815-895-4545

Twin City Steel Treating Co., Inc. 1114 S. 3rd, Minneapolis, MN 55415/612-332-4849 (heat treating)

Walker Arms Co., Rt. 2, Box 73, Hwy. 80 W, Selma, AL 36701/205-872-6231 (tools)

Weaver Arms Co., P.O. Box 8, Dexter, MO 63841/314-568-3800 (action wrenches & transfer punches)

Will-Burt Co., 169 So. Main, Orrville, OH 44667 (vises)

Williams Gun Sight Co., 7389 Lapeer Rd., Davison, MI 48423

Wilson Arms Co., 63 Leetes Island Rd., Branford, CT 06405/203-488-7297

Wisconsin Platers Supply Co. (See Texas Platers)

W.C. Wolff Co., P.O. Box 232, Ardmore, PA 19003/215-647-1800 (springs)

Woodcraft Supply Corp., 313 Montvale, Woburn, MA 01801

HANDGUN ACCESSORIES

Ajax Custom Grips, Inc., 12229 Cox Lane, Dallas, TX 75244/214-241-6302

Bob Allen Companies, 214 S.W. Jackson St., Des Moines, IA 50302/515-283-2191

American Gas & Chemical Co., Ltd., 220 Pegasus Ave., Northvale, NJ 07647/201-767-7300 (clg. lube)

Armson, Inc., P.O. Box 2130, Farmington Hills, MI 48018/313-478-2577

Armsport, Inc., 3590 N.W. 49th St., Miami, FL 33142/305-635-7850

Assault Accessories, P.O. Box 8994 CRB, Tucson, AZ 85738/602-791-7860 (pistol shoulder stocks)

Baramie Corp., 6250 E. 7 Mile Rd., Detroit, MI 48234 (Hip-Grip)

Bar-Sto Precision Machine, 73377 Sullivan Rd., Twentynine Palms, CA 92277/619-367-2747

Behlert Precision, RD 2 Box 36C, Route 611 North, Pipersville, PA 18947/215-766-8681

Bingham Ltd., 1775-C Wilwat Dr., Norcross, GA 30093 (magazines)

C'Arco, P.O. Box 308, Highland, CA 92346/714-862-8311 (Ransom Rest)

Centaur Systems, Inc., 15127 NE 24th C-3, Redmond, WA 98052/206-392-8472 (Quadra-Lok bbls.)

Central Specialties Co., 200 Lexington Dr., Buffalo Grove, IL 60090/312-537-3300 (trigger locks only)

Dave Chicoine, d/b/a Liberty A.S.P., 19 Key St., Eastport, ME 04631/207-853-2327 (shims f. S&W revs.)

D&E Magazines Mfg., P.O. Box 4876, Sylmar, CA 91342 (clips)

Detonics Firearms Industries, 13456 SE 27th Pl., Bellevue, WA 98005/206-747-2100

Doskocil Mfg. Co., Inc, P.O. Box 1246, Arlington, TX 75010/817-467-5116 (Gun Guard cases)

Essex Arms, Box 345, Island Pond, VT 05846/802-723-4313 (45 Auto frames)

Frielich Police Equipment, 396 Broome St., New York, NY 10013/212-254-3045 (cases)

R. S. Frielich, 211 East 21st St., New York, NY 10010/212-777-4477 (cases)

HKS Products, 7841 Foundation Dr., Florence, KY 41042/606-342-7841 (speedloader)

K&K Ammo Wrist Band, R.D. #1, Box 448-CA18, Lewistown, PA 17044/717-242-2329

Terry K. Kopp, Highway 13, Lexington, MO 64067/816-259-2636

Lee's Red Ramps, 7252 E. Ave. U-3, Littlerock, CA 93543/805-944-4487 (ramp insert kits; spring kits)

Lee Precision Inc., 4275 Hwy. U, Hartford, WI 53027 (pistol rest holders)

Kent Lomont, 4236 West 700 South, Poneto, IN 46781 (Auto Mag only)

Lone Star Gunleather, 1301 Brushy Bend Dr., Round Rock, TX 78664/512-255-1805

Los Gatos Grip & Specialty Co., P.O. Box 1850, Los Gatos, CA 95030 (custommade)

MTM Molded Prods. Co., 3370 Obco Ct., Dayton, OH 45414/513-890-7461

No-Sho Mfg. Co., 10727 Glenfield Ct., Houston, TX 77096/713-723-5332

Harry Owen (See Sport Specialties)

Pachmayr, 1220 S. Grand, Los Angeles, CA 90015 (cases)

Pacific Intl. Mchdsg. Corp., 2215 "J" St., Sacramento, CA 95818/916-446-2737 (Vega 45 Colt comb. mag.)

Poly-Choke Div., Marble Arms Corp., 420 Industrial Park, Gladstone, MI 49837/906-428-3710 (handgun ribs)

Ranch Products, P.O. Box 145, Malinta, OH 43535 (third-moon clips)
Ransom (See C'Arco)
Sile Distributors, 7 Centre Market Pl., New York, NY 10013
Sport Specialties, (Harry Owen), Box 5337, Hacienda Hts., CA 91745/213-968-5806 (.22 rimfire adapters; .22 insert bbls. f. T/C Contender, autom. pistols)
Sportsmen's Equipment Co., 415 W. Washington, San Diego, CA 92103/619-296-1501
Turkey Creek Enterprises, Rt. 1, Box 10, Red Oak, CA 74563/918-754-2884 (wood handgun cases)
Melvin Tyler, 1326 W. Britton, Oklahoma City, OK 73114/800-654-8415 (grip adaptor)
Whitney Sales, P.O. Box 875, Reseda, CA 91335/818-345-4212

HANDGUN GRIPS

Ajax Custom Grips, Inc., 12229 Cox Lane, Dallas, TX 75244/214-241-6302
Altamount Mfg., 510 N. Commercial St., P.O. Box 309, Thomasboro, IL 61878/217-634-3225
Art Jewel Enterprises Ltd., 421A Irmen Dr., Addison, IL 60101/312-628-6220
Barami Corp., 6250 East 7 Mile Rd., Detroit, MI 48234/313-891-2536
Bear Hug Grips, P.O. Box 25944, Colorado Springs, CO 80936/303-598-5675 (cust.)
Beeman Inc., 47 Paul Dr., San Rafael, CA 94903/415-472-7121 (airguns only)
Bingham Ltd., 1775-C Wilwat Dr., Norcross, GA 30093
Boone's Custom Ivory Grips, Inc., 562 Coyote Rd., Brinnon, WA 98320/206-796-4330
Dave Chicoine, d/b/a Liberty A.S.P., 19 Key St., Eastport, ME 04631/207-853-2327 (orig. S&W 1855-1950)
Fitz Pistol Grip Co., P.O. Box 171, Douglas City, CA 96024/916-778-3136
Gateway Shooters' Supply, Inc., 10145-103rd St., Jacksonville, FL 32210/904-778-2323 (Rogers grips)
Herrett's , Box 741, Twin Falls, ID 83301
Hogue Combat Grips, P.O. Box 2038, Atascadero, CA 93423/805-466-6266 (Monogrip)
Paul Jones Munitions Systems, (See Fitz Co.)
Russ Maloni (See Russwood)
Millett Industries, 16131 Gothard St., Huntington Beach, CA 92647/714-842-5575 (custom)
Monogrip, (See Hogue)
Monte Kristo Pistol Grip Co., Box 171, Douglas City, CA 96024/916-778-3136
Mustang Custom Pistol Grips, see: Supreme Products Co.
Pachmayr Gun Works, Inc., 1220 S. Grand Ave., Los Angeles, CA 90015/213-748-7271
Robert H. Newell, 55 Coyote, Los Alamos, NM 87544/505-662-7135 (custom stocks)
Rogers Grips (See Gateway Shooters' Supply)
A. Jack Rosenberg & Sons, 12229 Cox Lane, Dallas, TX 75234/214-241-6302 (Ajax)
Royal Ordnance Works Ltd., P.O. Box 3254, Wilson, NC 27893/919-237-0515
Russwood Custom Pistol Grips, 40 Sigman Lane, Elma, NY 14059/716-592-7131 (cust. exotic woods)
SDA, P.O. Box 424, Fallbrook, CA 92028/619-584-0577
Jean St. Henri, 6525 Dume Dr., Malibu, CA 90265/213-457-7211 (custom)
Sile Dist., 7 Centre Market Pl., New York, NY 10013/212-925-4111
Sports Inc., P.O. Box 683, Park Ridge, IL 60068/312-825-8952 (Franzite)
Supreme Products Co., 1830 S. California Ave., Monrovia, CA 91016/800-423-7159/818-357-5359
Sergeant Violin, P.O. Box 25808, Tamarac, FL 33320/305-721-7856 (wood pistol stocks)
R. D. Wallace, Star Rte. Box 76, Grandin, MO 63943/314-593-4773
Wayland Prec. Wood Prods., Box 1142, Mill Valley, CA 94942/415-381-3543

HEARING PROTECTORS

AO Safety Prods., Div. of American Optical Corp., 14 Mechanic St., Southbridge, MA 01550/617-765-9711 (ear valves, ear muffs)
Bausch & Lomb, 635 St. Paul St., Rochester, NY 14602
Bilsom Interntl., Inc., 11800 Sunrise Valley Dr., Reston, VA 22091/703-620-3950 (ear plugs, muffs)
David Clark Co., Inc., 360 Franklin St., Worcester, MA 01604
Marble Arms Corp., 420 Industrial Park, Gladstone, MI 49837/906-428-3710
North Consumer Prods. Div., 16624 Edwards Rd., P.O. Box 7500, Cerritos, CA 90701/213-926-0545 (Lee Sonic ear valves)
Safety Direct, 23 Snider Way, Sparks, NV 89431/702-354-4451 (Silencio)
Smith & Wesson, 2100 Roosevelt Ave., Springfield, MA 01101
Willson Safety Prods. Div., P.O. Box 622, Reading, PA 19603 (Ray-O-Vac)

HOLSTERS & LEATHER GOODS

Active Leather Corp., 36-29 Vernon Blvd., Long Island City, NY 11106
Alessi Custom Concealment Holsters, 2465 Niagara Falls Blvd., Tonawanda, NY 14150/716-691-5615
Allen Firearms Co., 2879 All Trades Rd., Santa Fe, NM 87501/505-471-6090
Bob Allen Companies, 214 S.W. Jackson, Des Moines, IA 50315/515-283-2191
American Enterprises, 1480 Avocado, El Cajon, CA 92020/619-588-1222
American Sales & Mfg. Co., P.O. Box 677, Laredo, TX 78040/512-723-6893

Andy Anderson, P.O. Box 225, North Hollywood, CA 91603/213-877-2401 (Gunfighter Custom Holsters)
Armament Systems & Procedures, Inc., P.O. Box 356, Appleton, WI 54912/414-731-8893 (ASP)
Rick M. Bachman (see Old West Reproductions)
Barami Corp., 6250 East 7 Mile Rd., Detroit, MI 48234/313-891-2536
Beeman Inc., 47-GDD Paul Dr., San Rafael, CA 94903/415-472-7121
Behlert Precision, RD 2 Box 36C, Route 611 North, Pipersville, PA 18947/215-766-8681
Bianchi International Inc., 100 Calle Cortez, Temecula, CA 92390/714-676-5621
Ted Blocker's Custom Holsters, 409 West Bonita Ave. San Dimas, CA 91773/714-599-4415
Bo-Mar Tool & Mfg. Co., Rt. 12, Box 405, Longview, TX 75605/214-759-4784
Border Guns & Leather, Box 1423, Deming, NM 88031 (Old West cust.)
Eunice Bosselman, P.O. Box 900, Tombstone, AZ 85638
Boyt Co., Div. of Welsh Sptg., P.O. Box 220, Iowa Falls, IA 51026/515-648-4626
Brauer Bros. Mfg. Co., 2020 Delmar, St. Louis, MO 63103/314-231-2864
Browning, Rt. 4, Box 624-B, Arnold, MO 63010
J.M. Bucheimer Co., P.O. Box 280, Airport Rd., Frederick, MD 21701/301-662-5101
Buffalo Leather Goods, Inc., Rt. 4, Box 187, Magnolia, AR 71753/501-234-6367
Cathey Enterprises, Inc., 3423 Milam Dr., P.O. Box 2202, Brownwood, TX 76804/915-643-2553
Cattle Baron Leather Co., Dept. GD, P.O. Box 100724, San Antonio, TX 78201/512-697-8900 (ctlg. $3)
Chace Leather Prods., Longhorn Div., 507 Alden St., Fall River, MA 02722/617-678-7556
Cherokee Gun Accessories, 4127 Bay St., Suite 226, Fremont, CA 94538/415-471-5770
China IM/EX, P.O. Box 27573, San Francisco, CA 94127/415-661-2212
Chas. Clements, Handicrafts Unltd., 1741 Dallas St., Aurora, CO 80010/303-364-0403
Daisy Mfg. Co., P.O. Box 220, Rogers, AR 72756/501-636-1200
Davis Leather Co., G. Wm. Davis, 3930 "F" Valley Blvd., Unit F, Walnut, CA 91789/714-598-5620
Eugene DeMayo & Sons, Inc., 2795 Third Ave., Bronx, NY 10455/212-665-7075
DeSantis Holster Co., 140 Denton Ave., New Hyde Park, NY 11040/516-354-8000
Ellwood Epps Northern Ltd., 210 Worthington St. W., North Bay, Ont. P1B 3B4, Canada (custom made)
Flatbush Country Leather, Box 116, 410 Houghton, Ione, WA 99139/509-442-3448 (made to order only)
GALCO Gun Leather, 4311 W. Van Buren, Phoenix, AZ 85043/602-233-0596
Gunfighter (See Anderson)
Ernie Hill Speed Leather, 3128 S. Extension Rd., Mesa, AZ 85202/602-831-1919
Horsehoe Leather Prods., The Cottage, Sharow, Ripon HG4 5BP, England
Hoyt Holster Co., Inc., P.O. Box 69, Coupeville, WA 98239/206-678-6640
Don Hume, Box 351, Miami, OK 74354/918-542-6604
Hunter Corp., 3300 W. 71st Ave., Westminster, CO 80030/303-427-4626
John's Custom Leather, 525 S. Liberty St., Blairsville, PA 15717/412-459-6802
Jumbo Sports Prods., P.O. Box 280, Airport Rd., Frederick, MD 21701
Kane Products, Inc., 5572 Brecksville Rd., Cleveland, OH 44131/216-524-9962 (GunChaps)
Kirkpatrick Leather Co., P.O. Box 3150, Laredo, TX 78041/512-723-6631
Kolpin Mfg. Inc., P.O. Box 231, Berlin, WI 54923/414-361-0400
Morris Lawing, P.O. Box 9494, Charlotte, NC 28299/704-375-1740
George Lawrence Co., 1435 N.W. Northrup, Portland, OR 97209/503-228-8244
Lone Star Gunleather, 1301 Brushy Bend Dr., Round Rock, TX 78664/512-255-1805
Michael's of Oregon, Co., P.O. Box 13010, Portland, OR 97213/503-255-6890 (Uncle Mike's)
Mixson Leathercraft Inc., 1950 W. 84th St., Hialeah, FL 33014/305-820-5190 (police leather products)
No-Sho Mfg. Co., 10727 Glenfield Ct., Houston, TX 77096/713-723-5332
Kenneth L. Null-Custom Concealment Holsters, R.D. #5, Box 197, Hanover, PA 17331 (See Seventrees)
Old West Reproductions, R. M. Bachman, 1840 Stag Lane, Kalispell, MT 59901/406-755-6902 (ctlg. $3)
Orient-Western, P.O. Box 27573, San Francisco, CA 94127
Pioneer Prods., P.O. Box G, Magnolia, AR 71753/501-234-1566
Pony Express Sport Shop Inc., 1606 Schoenborn St., Sepulveda, CA 91343/818-895-1231
Red Head Brand Corp., 4949 Joseph Hardin Dr., Dallas, TX 75236/214-333-4141
Red River Outfitters, P.O. Box 241, Tujunga, CA 91042/213-352-0177
Rogers Holsters Co., Inc., 1736 St. Johns Bluff Rd., Jacksonville, FL 32216/904-641-9434
Roy's Custom Leather Goods, Hwy, 1325 & Rawhide Rd., P.O. Box G, Magnolia, AR 71753/501-234-1566
Safariland Leather Products, 1941 So. Walker Ave., Monrovia, CA 91016/818-357-7902
Safety Speed Holster, Inc., 910 So. Vail, Montebello, CA 90640/213-723-4140
Buddy Schoellkopf Products, Inc., 4949 Joseph Hardin Dr., TX 75236/214-333-2121
Schulz Industries, 16247 Minnesota Ave., Paramount, CA 90723/213-636-7718
Sile Distr., 7 Centre Market Pl., New York NY 10013/212-925-4111
Milt Sparks, Box 187, Idaho City, ID 83631/208-392-6695 (broch. $2)
Robert A. Strong Co., 105 Maplewood Ave., Gloucester, MA 01930/617-281-3300
Torel, Inc., 1053 N. South St., P.O. Box 592, Yoakum, TX 77995/512-293-2341 (gun slings)
Triple-K Mfg. Co., 568 Sixth Ave., San Diego, CA 92101/619-232-2066
Uncle Mike's (See Michaels of Oregon)

Viking Leathercraft, Inc., P.O. Box 2030, 2248-2 Main St., Chula Vista, CA 92012/619-429-8050
Walt Whinnery, 1947 Meadow Creek Dr., Louisville, KY 40218/502-458-4361
Wildlife Leather Inc., P.O. Box 339, Merrick, NY 11566/516-378-8588 (lea. gds. w. outdoor themes)

Utica Duxbak Corp., 1745 S. Acoma St., Denver, CO 80223/303-778-0324
Waffen-Frankonia, see: Frankonia Jagd
Walker Shoe Co., P.O. Box 1167, Asheboro, NC 27203-1167/919-625-1380 (boots)
Weinbrenner Shoe Corp., Polk St., Merrill, WI 54452
Wolverine Boots & Shoes Div., Wolverine World Wide, 9341 Courtland Dr., Rockford, MI 49351/616-866-1561 (footwear)
Woodstream Corp., Box 327, Lititz, PA 17543 (Hunter Seat)
Woolrich Woolen Mills, Mill St., Woolrich, PA 17779/717-769-6464
Yankee Mechanics, RFD No. 1, Concord, NH 03301/603-225-3181 (hand winches)

HUNTING AND CAMP GEAR, CLOTHING, ETC.

Bob Allen Sportswear, P.O. Box 477, Des Moines, IA 50302/800-247-8048
Eddie Bauer, 15010 NE 36th St., Redmond, WA 98052
L. L. Bean, Freeport, ME 04032
Bear Archery, R.R. 4, 4600 Southwest 41st Blvd., Gainesville, FL 32601/904-376-2327 (Himalayan backpack)
Big Beam, Teledyne Co., 290 E. Prairie St., Crystal Lake, IL 60014 (lamp)
Browning, Rte. 1, Morgan, UT 84050
Brush Hunter Sportswear, Inc., NASCO Ind., 3 NE 21st St., Washington, IN 47501/812-254-4962
Camp-Ways, 1140 E. Sandhill Ave., Carson, CA 90746/213-604-1201
Challanger Mfg. Co., Box 550, Jamaica, NY 11431 (glow safe)
Chippewa Shoe Co., P.O. Box 2521, Ft. Worth, TX 76113/817-332-4385 (boots)
Coleman Co., Inc., 250 N. St. Francis, Wichita, KS 67201
Converse Rubber Co., 55 Fordham Rd., Wilmington, MA 01887 (boots)
Danner Shoe Mfg. Co., P.O. Box 22204, Portland, OR 97222/503-653-2920 (boots)
DEER-ME Prod. Co., Box 34, Anoka, MN 55303/612-421-8971 (tree steps)
Dunham Co., P.O. Box 813, Brattleboro, VT 05301/802-254-2316 (boots)
Durango Boot, see: Georgia/Northlake
Frankonia Jagd, Hofmann & Co., Postfach 6780, D-8700 Wurzburg 1, West Germany
Freeman Ind., Inc., 100 Marblehead Rd., Tuckahoe, NY 10707 (Trak-Kit)
French Dressing Inc., 15 Palmer Heights, Burlington, VT 05401/802-658-1434 (boots)
Game-Winner, Inc., 2625 Cumberland Parkway, Suite 270, Atlanta, GA 30339/404-434-9210 (camouflage suits; orange vests)
Gander Mountain, Inc., P.O. Box 128, Hwy. "W", Wilmot, WI 53192/414-862-2344
Georgia Boot Div., U.S. Industry, 1810 Columbia Ave., Franklin, TN 37064/615-794-1556
Georgia/Northlake Boot Co., P.O. Box 10, Franklin, TN 37064/615-794-1556 (Durango)
Gokeys, 84 So. Wabasha, St. Paul, MN 55107/612-292-3933
Gun Club Sportswear, Box 477, Des Moines, IA 50302
Gun-Ho Case Mfg. Co., 110 E. 10th St., St. Paul, MN 55101
Himalayan Industries, Inc., P.O. Box 7465, Pine Bluff, AR 71611/501-534-6411
Bob Hinman Outfitters, 1217 W. Glen, Peoria, IL 61614
Hunter's Specialties, Inc., 5285 Rockwell Dr. N.E., Cedar Rapids, IA 52402/319-395-0321
Hunting World, 16 E. 53rd St., New York, NY 10022
Kap Outdoors, 1704 Locust St., Philadelphia, PA 19103/215-723-3449 (clothing)
Kenko Intl. Inc., 8141 West I-70 Frontage Rd. No., Arvada, CO 80002/303-425-1200 (footwear & socks)
Langenberg Hat Co., P.O. Box 1860, Washington, MO 63090/314-239-1860
Life Knife Inc., P.O. Box 771, Santa Monica, CA 90406/213-821-6192
Peter Limmer & Sons Inc., Box 66, Intervale, NH 03845 (boots)
Marathon Rubber Prods. Co. Inc., 510 Sherman St., Wausau, WI 54401/715-845-6255 (rain gear)
Marble Arms Corp., 420 Industrial Park, Gladstone, MI 49837
Nelson Recreation Prods., Inc., Fuqua Industries, 14760 Santa Fe Trail Dr., Lenexa, KS 66215/800-255-6061
The Orvis Co., Manchester, VT 05254/802-362-3622 (fishing gear; clothing)
PGB Assoc., 310 E. 46th St., Suite 3E, New York, NY 10017/212-867-9560
Quabaug Rubber Co./Vibram U.S.A., 17 School St. N. Brookfield, MA 01535/617-867-7731 (boots)
Quoddy Moccasins, Div. R. G. Barry Corp., 67 Minot Ave., Auburn, ME 04210/207-784-3555
Ranger Mfg. Co., Inc., P.O. Box 3676, Augusta, GA 30904
Ranger Rubber Co., 1100 E. Main St., Endicott, NY 13760/607-757-4260 (boots)
Red Ball, P.O. Box 3200, Manchester, NH 03105/603-669-0708 (boots)
Red Head Brand Corp., 4949 Joseph Hardin Dr., Dallas, TX 75236/214-333-4141
Refrigiwear, Inc., 71 Inip Dr., Inwood, Long Island, NY 11696
Reliance Prod. Ltd., 1830 Dublin Ave., Winnipeg 21, Man. R3H 0H3 Can. (tent peg)
Safariland Hunting Corp., P.O. Box NN, McLean, VA 22101/703-356-0622 (camouflage rain gear)
Safesport Mfg. Co., 1100 West 45th Ave., Denver, CO 80211/303-433-6506
Saf-T-Bak, see: Kap Outdoors
SanLar Co., Rte. 2, Box 123, Sullivan, WI 53178/414-593-8086 (huntg. sweatsuits)
Servus Rubber Co., 1136 2nd St., Rock Island, IL 61201 (footwear)
Spruce Creek Sportswear, see: Kap Outdoors
Stearns Mfg. Co., P.O. Box 1498, St. Cloud, MN 56301
Teledyne Co., Big Beam, 290 E. Prairie St., Crystal Lake, IL 60014
10-X Mfg. Products Group, 2828 Forest Lane, Suite 1107, Dallas, TX 75234/214-243-4016
Thermos Div., KST Co., Norwich, CT 06361 (Pop Tent)
Norm Thompson, 1805 N.W. Thurman St., Portland, OR 97209
Trim Unlimited, 2111 Glen Forest, Plano, TX 75023/214-596-5059 (electric boat)

KNIVES AND KNIFEMAKER'S SUPPLIES—FACTORY and MAIL ORDER

A.C. Enterprises, P.O. Box 448, Edenton, NC 27932/919-482-4992
Alcas Cutlery Corp., 1116 E. State St., Olean, NY 14760/716-372-3111 (Cutco)
Atlanta Cutlery, Box 839, Conyers, GA 30207/404-922-3700 (mail order, supplies)
Bali-Song, see: Pacific Cutlery Corp.
L. L. Bean, 386 Main St., Freeport, ME 04032/207-865-3111 (mail order)
Benchmark Knives (See Gerber)
Crosman Blades™, The Coleman Co., 250 N. St. Francis, Wichita, KS 67201
Boker, The Cooper Group, 3535 Glenwood Ave., Raleigh, NC 27612/919-781-7200
Bowen Knife Co., P.O. Box 590, Blackshear, GA 31516/912-449-4794
Browning, Rt. 1, Morgan, UT 84050/801-876-2711
Buck Knives, Inc., P.O. Box 1267; 1900 Weld Blvd., El Cajon, CA 92022/619-449-1100 or 800-854-2557
Camillus Cutlery Co., 52-54 W. Genesee St., Camillus, NY 13031/315-672-8111 (Sword Brand)
W. R. Case & Sons Cutlery Co., 20 Russell Blvd., Bradford, PA 16701/814-368-4123
Cattle Baron Leather Co., P.O. Box 100724, Dept. GD, San Antonio, TX 78201/512-697-8900 (ctlg. $3)
Charlton, Ltd., P.O. Box 448, Edenton, NC 27932/919-482-4992
Charter Arms Corp., 430 Sniffens Lane, Stratford, CT 06497/203-377-8080 (Skatchet)
Chicago Cutlery Co., 5420 N. County Rd. 18, Minneapolis, MN 55428/612-533-0472
Chas. Clements, Handicraft Unltd., 1741 Dallas St., Aurora, CO 80010/303-364-0403 (exotic sheaths)
Collins Brothers Div. (belt-buckle knife), See Bowen Knife Co.
Colonial Knife Co., P.O. Box 3327, Providence, RI 02909/401-421-1600 (Master Brand)
Custom Knifemaker's Supply, P.O. Box 308, Emory, TX 75440/214-473-3330
Custom Purveyors, Maureen Devlet's, P.O. Box 886, Fort Lee, NJ 07024/201-886-0196 (mail order)
Dixie Gun Works, Inc., P.O. Box 130, Union City, TN 38261/901-885-0700 (supplies)
Eze-Lap Diamond Prods., Box 2229, 15164 Weststate St., Westminster, CA 92683/714-847-1555 (knife sharpeners)
Gerber Legendary Blades, 14200 S.W. 72nd Ave., Portland, OR 99223/503-639-6161
Golden Age Arms Co., 14 W. Winter St., Delaware, OH 43015/614-369-6513 (supplies)
Gutmann Cutlery Co., Inc., 120 S. Columbus Ave., Mt. Vernon, NY 10553/914-699-4044
H & B Forge Co., Rte. 2 Geisinger Rd., Shiloh, OH 44878/419-895-1856 (throwing knives, tomahawks)
Russell Harrington Cutlery, Inc., Subs. of Hyde Mfg. Co., 44 River St., Southbridge, MA 01550/617-764-4371 (Dexter, Green River Works)
J. A. Henckels Zwillingswerk, Inc., 9 Skyline Dr., Hawthorne, NY 10532/914-592-7370
Imperial Knife Associated Companies, 1776 Broadway, New York, NY 10019/212-757-1814
Indian Ridge Traders, 306 So. Washington, Room 415, Royal Oak, MI 48067/313-399-6034 (mostly blades)
J.A. Blades, Inc., an affiliate of E. Christoper Firearms Co., State 128 & Ferry Street, Miamitown, OH 45041/513-353-1321 (supplies)
Ken Jantz Supply, Rt. 1, Sulphur, OK 73086/405-622-3790 (supplies)
Jet-Aer Corp., 100 Sixth Ave., Paterson, NJ 07524/201-278-8300
KA-BAR Cutlery Inc., 5777 Grant Ave., Cleveland, OH 44105/216-271-4000
KA-BAR Knives, Collectors Division, 434 No. 9th St., Olean, NY 14760/716-372-5611
Keene Corp., Cutting Serv. Div., 1569 Tower Grove Ave., St. Louis, MO 63110/314-771-1550
Kershaw Knives/Kai Cutlery USA Ltd., Stafford Bus. Pk., 25300 SW Parkway, Wilsonville, OR 97070/503-636-0111
Knifeco, P.O. Box 5271, Hialeah Lakes, FL 33014/305-635-2411
Knife and Gun Finishing Supplies, P.O. Box 13522, Arlington, TX 76013/817-274-1282
Koval Knives, 822 Busch Ct. GD, Columbus, OH 43229/614-888-6486 (supplies)
Lamson & Goodnow Mfg. Co., 45 Conway St., Shelburne Falls, MA 03170/413-625-6331
Lansky Sharpeners, P.O. Box 800, Buffalo, NY 14221/716-634-6333 (sharpening devices)
Life Knife Inc., P.O. Box 771, Santa Monica, CA 90406/ 213-821-6192
Al Mar Knives, Inc., P.O. Box 1626, 5755 SW Jean Rd., Suite 101, Lake Oswego, OR 97034/503-635-9229
Matthews Cutlery, P.O. Box 33095, Decatur, GA 30033/404-636-3970 (mail order)
R. Murphy Co., Inc., 13 Groton-Harvard Rd., P.O. Box 376, Ayer, MA 01432/617-772-3481 (StaySharp)
Nordic Knives, 1643-C Copenhagen Dr., Solvang, CA 93463 (mail order)

Normark Corp., 1710 E. 78th St., Minneapolis, MN 55423/612-869-3291
Ontario Knife, Queen Cutlery Co., P.O. Box 500, Franklinville, NY 14737/716-676-5527 (Old Hickory)
Orient-Western, P.O. Box 27573, San Francisco, CA 94127
Pacific Cutlery Corp., 3039 Roswell St., Los Angeles, CA 90085/213-258-7021 (Bali-Song)
Parker Cutlery, 6928 Lee Highway, Chattanooga, TN 37415/615-894-1782
Plaza Cutlery Inc., 3333 Bristol, #161, South Coast Plaza, Costa Mesa, CA 92626/714-549-3932 (mail order)
Queen Cutlery Co., 507 Chestnut St., Titusville, PA 16354/800-222-5233
R & C Knives and Such, P.O. Box 32631, San Jose, CA 95152/408-923-5728 (mail order; ctlg. $2)
Randall-Made Knives, Box 1988, Orlando, FL 32802/305-855-8075 (catlg. $1)
Rigid Knives, P.O. Box 816, Hwy. 290E, Lake Hamilton, AR 71951/501-525-1377
A. G. Russell Co., 1705 Hiwy. 71 No., Springdale, AR 72764/501-751-7341
Bob Sanders, 2358 Tyler Lane, Louisville, KY 40205 (Bahco steel)
San Diego Knives, P.O. Box 326, Lakeside, CA 92040/619-561-5900
Schrade Cutlery Corp., 1776 Broadway, New York, NY 10019/212-757-1814
Sheffield Knifemakers Supply, P.O. Box 141, Deland, FL 32720/904-734-7884
Smith & Wesson, 2100 Roosevelt Ave., Springfield, MA 01101/413-781-8300
Jesse W. Smith Saddlery, N. 307 Haven St., Spokane, WA 99202/509-534-3229 (sheathmakers)
Swiss Army Knives, Inc., P.O. Box 846, Shelton, CT 06484/203-929-6391
Tekna, 1075 Old County Rd., Belmont, CA 94002/415-592-4070
Thompson/Center, P.O. Box 2426, Rochester, NH 03867/603-332-2394
Tru-Balance Knife Co., 2155 Tremont Blvd., N.W., Grand Rapids, MI 49504/616-453-3679
Utica Cutlery Co., 820 Noyes St., Utica, NY 13503/315-733-4663 (Kutmaster)
Valor Corp., 5555 N.W. 36th Ave., Miami, FL 33142/305-633-0127
Washington Forge, Inc., Englishtown, NJ 07727/201-446-7777 (Carriage House)
Wenoka Cutlery, P.O. Box 8238, West Palm Beach, FL 33407/305-845-6155
Western Cutlery Co., 1800 Pike Rd., Longmont, CO 80501/303-772-5900
Walt Whinnery, Walts Cust. Leather, 1947 Meadow Creek Dr., Louisville, KY 40218/502-458-4351 (sheathmaker)
J. Wolfe's Knife Works, Box 1056, Larkspur, CA 94939 (supplies)
Wyoming Knife Co., 101 Commerce Dr., Ft. Collins, CO 80524/303-224-3454

LABELS, BOXES, CARTRIDGE HOLDERS

Milton Brynin, 214 E. Third St., Mount Vernon, NY 10550/914-664-1311
Corbin Mfg. & Supply, Inc., P.O. Box 2659, White City, OR 97503/503-826-5211
Del Rey Products, P.O. Box 91561, Los Angeles, CA 90009/213-823-0494
E-Z Loader, Del Rey Products, P.O. Box 91561, Los Angeles, CA 90009
Hunter Co., Inc., 3300 W. 71st Ave., Westminster, Co 80030/303-472-4626
Peterson Label Co., P.O. Box 186, 23 Sullivan Dr., Redding Ridge, CT 06876/203-938-2349 (cartridge box labels; Targ-Dots)

LOAD TESTING and PRODUCT TESTING, (CHRONOGRAPHING, BALLISTIC STUDIES)

Accuracy Systems Inc., 15203 N. Cave Creek Rd., Phoenix, AZ 85032/602-971-1991
W.W. Blackwell, 9826 Sagedale, Houston, TX 77089/ 713-484-0935 (computer program f. internal ball. f. rifle cartridges)
D&H Precision Tooling, 7522 Barnard Mill Rd., Ringwood IL 60072/815-653-9611 (Pressure testing equipment)
H-S Precision, Inc., 112 N. Summit, Prescott, AZ 86302/602-445-0607
Hutton Rifle Ranch, P.O. Box 45236, Boise, ID 83711/208-343-9841
Kent Lomont, 4236 West 700 South, Poneto, IN 45781/219-694-6792 (handguns, handgun ammunition)
Plum City Ballistics Range, Norman E. Johnson, Rte. 1, Box 29A, Plum City, WI 54761/715-647-2539
Russell's Rifle Shop, Rte. 5, Box 92, Georgetown, TX 78626/512-778-5338 (load testing and chronographing to 300 yds.)
John M. Tovey, 4710 - 104th Lane NE, Circle Pines, MN 55014/612-786-7268
H. P. White Laboratory, Inc., 3114 Scarboro Rd., Street, MD 21154/301-838-6550

MISCELLANEOUS

Action, Mauser-style only, Crandall Tool & Machine Co., 1540 N. Mitchell St., Cadillac, MI 49601/616-775-5562
Action, Single Shot, Miller Arms, Inc., P.O. Box 260, St. Onge, SD 57779 (de-Haas-Miller)
Activator, B.M.F. Activator, Inc., P.O. Box 262364, Houston, TX 77207/713-477-8442
Adapters, Sage Industries, P.O. Box 2248, Hemet, CA 92342/714-925-1006 (12-ga. shotgun; 38 S&W blank)
Adapters for Subcalibers, Harry Owen, P.O. Box 5337, Hacienda Hts., CA 91745/818-968-5806
Airgun Accessories, Beeman Precision Arms, Inc., 47 Paul Dr., San Rafael, CA 94903/415-472-7121 (Beeman Pell seat, Pell Size, etc.)
Air Gun Combat Game Supplies, The Ultimate Game Inc., P.O. Box 1856, Ormond Beach, FL 32075/904-677-4358 (washable pellets, marking pistols/rifles)
Archery, Bear, R.R. 4, 4600 Southwest 41st Blvd., Gainesville, FL 32601/904-376-2327

Arms Restoration, J. J. Jenkins Ent. Inc., 375 Pine Ave. No. 25, Goleta, CA 93017/805-967-1366
Assault Rifle Accessories, Cherokee Gun Accessories, 4127 Bay St. Suite 226, Fremont, CA 94538/415-471-5770
Assault Rifle Accessories, Choate Machine & Tool Corp., P.O. Box 218, Bald Knob, AR 72010 (folding stocks)
Assault Rifle Accessories, Feather Enterprises, 2500 Central Ave., Boulder, CO 80301/303-442-7021
Assault Rifle Accessories, Ram-Line, Inc., 406 Violet St., Golden, CO 80401/303-279-0886 (folding stock)
Barrel Band Swivels, Phil Judd, 83 E. Park St., Butte, MT 59701
Bedding Kit, Fenwal, Inc., Resins Systems Div., 400 Main St., Ashland, MA 01721
Belt Buckles, Bergamot Brass Works, 820 Wisconsin St., Delavan, WI 53115/414-728-5572
Belt Buckles, Herrett's Stocks, Inc., Box 741, Twin Falls, ID 83303/800-635-9334 (laser engr. hardwood)
Belt Buckles, Just Brass Inc., 121 Henry St., P.O. Box 112, Freeport, NY 11520/516-379-3434 (ctlg. $2)
Belt Buckles, Pilgrim Pewter Inc., R.D. 2, Tully, NY 13159/607-842-6431
Benchrest & Accuracy Shooters Equipment, Bob Pease Accuracy, P.O. Box 787, Zipp Road, New Braunfels, TX 78130/512-625-1342
Benchrest Rifles & Accessories, Robert W. Hart & Son Inc., 401 Montgomery St., Nescopeck, PA 18635/717-752-3655
Blowgun, PAC Outfitters, P.O. Box 56, Mulvane, KS 67110/316-777-4909
Cannons, South Bend Replicas Ind., 61650 Oak Rd., S. Bend, IN 44614/219-289-4500 (ctlg. $5)
Cartridge Adapters, Sport Specialties, Harry Owen, Box 5337, Hacienda Hts., CA 91745/213-968-5806 (ctlg. $3)
Case Gauge, Plum City Ballistics Range, Rte. 1, Box 29A, Plum City, WI 54761/715-647-2539
Cased, high-grade English tools, Marvin Huey Gun Cases, P.O. Box 22456, Kansas City, MO 64113/816-444-1637 (ebony, horn, ivory handles)
Cherry Converter, Amimex Inc., 2660 John Montgomery Dr., Suite #3, San Jose, CA 95148/408-923-1720 (shotguns)
Clips, D&E Magazines Mfg., P.O. Box 4876, Sylmar, CA 91342 (handgun and rifle)
Computer & PSI Calculator, Hutton Rifle Ranch, P.O. Box 45236, Boise, ID 83711/208-343-9841
Crossbows, Barnett International, 1967 Gunn Highway, Odessa, FL 33552/813-920-2241
Deer Drag, D&H Prods. Co., Inc., 465 Denny Rd., Valencia, PA 16059/412-898-2840
Defendor, Ralide, Inc., P.O. Box 131, Athens, TN 37303/615-745-3525
Dehumidifiers, Buenger Enterprises, P.O. Box 5286, Oxnard, CA 93030/805-985-0541
Dryer, Thermo-Electric, Golden-Rod, Buenger Enterprises, Box 5286, Oxnard, CA 93030/805-985-0541
E-Z Loader, Del Rey Prod., P.O. Box 91561, Los Angeles, CA 90009/213-823-04494 (f. 22-cal. rifles)
Ear-Valve, North Consumer Prods. Div., 16624 Edwards Rd., Cerritos, CA 90701/213-926-0545 (Lee-Sonic)
Electronic Wall Thickness Tester f. Cases/Bullets/Jackets, The Accuracy Den, 25 Bitterbrush Rd., Reno, NV 89523/702-345-0225
Embossed Leather Belts, Wallets, Wildlife Leather, Inc., P.O. Box 339, Merrick, NY 11566/516-378-8588 (outdoor themes)
Farrsight, Farr Studio, 1231 Robinhood Rd., Greenville, TN 37743/615-638-8825 (clip on aperture)
Flares, Colt Industries, P.O. Box 1868, Hartford, CT 06102
Flares, Smith & Wesson Chemical Co., 2399 Forman Rd., Rock Creek, OH 44084
Frontier Outfitters, Red River Outfitters, P.O. Box 241, Tujunga, CA 91042/213-352-0177 (frontier, western, military Americana clothing)
Game Hoist, Cam Gear Ind., P.O. Box 1002, Kalispell, MT 59901 (Sportsmaster 500 pocket hoist)
Game Hoist, Precise, 3 Chestnut, Suffern, NY 10901
Game Scent, Buck Stop Lure Co., Inc., 3600 Grow Rd., Box 636, Stanton, MI 48888/517-762-5091
Game Scent, Pete Rickard, Inc., Rte. 1, Box 209B, Cobleskill, NY 12043/518-234-2731 (Indian Buck lure)
Game Scent, Safariland Hunting Corp., P.O. Box NN, McLean, VA 22101/703-356-0622 (buck lure)
Gargoyles, Pro-tec Inc., 11108 Northrup Way, Bellevue, WA 98004/306-828-6595
Gas Pistol, Penguin Ind., Inc., Airport Industrial Mall, Coatesville, PA 19320/215-384-6000
Grip Caps, Classic Arms Corp., P.O. Box 8, Palo Alto, CA 94301/415-321-7243
Gun Bedding Kit, Fenwal, Inc., Resins System Div., 400 Main St., Ashland, MA 01721/617-881-2000
Gun Jewelry, Sid Bell Originals, R.D. 2, Box 219, Tully, NY 13159/607-842-6431
Gun Jewelry, Pilgrim Pewter Inc., R.D. 2, Box 219, Tully, NY 13159/607-842-6431
Gun Jewelry, Al Popper, 6l4 Turnpike St., Stoughton, MA 02072/617-344-2036
Gun Jewelry, Sports Style Assoc., 148 Hendricks Ave., Lynbrook, NY 11563
Gun photographer, Mustafa Bilal, 3650 Stoneway Ave. No., Seattle, WA 98103/206-782-1456
Gun photographer, Art Carter, 818 Baffin Bay Rd., Columbia, SC 29210/803-772-2148
Gun photographer, John Hanusin, 3306 Commercial, Northbrook, IL 60062/312-564-2706
Gun photographer, Int. Photographic Assoc., Inc., 4500 E. Speedway, Suite 90, Tucson, AZ 85712/602-326-2941
Gun photographer, Charles Semmer, 7885 Cyd Dr., Denver, CO 80221/303-429-6947
Gun photographer, Weyer Photo Services, Ltd., 333-14th St., Toledo, OH 43624/419-241-5454
Gun photographer, Steve White, 1920 Raymond Dr., Northbrook, IL 60062/312-564-2720

Gun Safety, Gun Alert, Master Products, Inc., P.O. Box 8474, Van Nuys, CA 91409/818-365-0864

Gun Sling, La Paloma Marketing, 1735 E. Ft. Lowell Rd., Suite 7, Tucson, AZ 85719/602-881-4750 (Pro-sling system)

Gun Slings, Torel, Inc., 1053 N. South St., Yoakum, TX 77995

Gun Stock Kits, SDS, P.O. Box 424, Fallbrook, CA 92028/619-584-0577

Gun Vise, Gun-Mate, Inc., Box 2704, Huntington Beach, CA 92647

Hand Exerciser, Action Products, Inc., 22 No. Mulberry St., Hagerstown, MD 21740/301-797-1414

Horsepac, Yellowstone Wilderness Supply, P.O. 129, West Yellowstone, MT 59758/406-646-7613

Horsepacking Equipment/Saddle Trees, Ralide West, P.O. Box 998, 299 Fire-hole Ave., West Yellowstone, WY 59758/406-646-7612

Hugger Hooks, Roman Products, Inc., 4363 Loveland St., Golden, CO 80403/303-279-6959

Insect Repellent, Armor, Div. of Buck Stop, Inc., 3015 Grow Rd., Stanton, MI 48888

Insert Chambers, GTM Co., Geo. T. Mahaney, 15915B E. Main St., La Puente, CA 91744 (shotguns only)

Insert Barrels and Cartridge Adapters, Sport Specialties, Harry Owen, Box 5337, Hacienda Hts., CA 91745/213-968-5806 (ctlg. $3)

Kentucky Rifle Drawings, New England Historic Designs, P.O. Box 171, Concord, NH 03301/603-224-2096

Knife Sharpeners, Lansky Sharpeners, P.O. Box 800, Buffalo, NY 14221/716-634-6333

Light Load, Jacob & Tiffin Inc., P.O. Box 547, Clanton, AL 35045

Locks, Gun, Bor-Lok Prods., 105 5th St., Arbuckle, CA 95912

Locks, Gun, Master Lock Co., 2600 N. 32nd St., Milwaukee, WI 53245

Lugheads, Floorplate Overlays, Sid Bell Originals, Inc., RD 2, Box 219, Tully, NY 13159/607-842-6431

Lug Recess Insert, P.P.C. Corp., 625 E. 24th St. Paterson, NJ 07514

Magazines, San Diego Knives, P.O. Box 326, Lakeside, CA 92040/619-561-5900 (auto pist., rifles)

Magazines, Mitchell Arms Inc., 2101 E. 4th St. Suite 201A, Santa Ana, CA 92705/714-964-3678 (stainless steel)

Magazines, Ram-Line, Inc., 406 Violet St., Golden, CO 80401/303-279-0886

Miniature Cannons, Karl J. Furr, 76 East, 350 North, Orem, UT 84057/801-225-2603 (replicas)

Miniature Guns, Tom Konrad, P.O. Box 118, Shandon, OH 45063/513-738-1379

Miniature Guns, Charles H. Stoppler, 5 Minerva Place, New York, NY 10468

Monte Carlo Pad, Hoppe Division, Penguin Ind., Airport Industrial Mall, Coatesville, PA 19320/215-384-6000

Old Gun Industry Art, Hansen and Hansen, 244 Old Post Rd., Southport, CT 06490/203-259-7337

Pell Remover, A. Edw. Terpening, 838 E. Darlington Rd., Tarpon Springs, FL 33589

Powderhorns, Frontier, 2910 San Bernardo, Laredo, TX 78040/512-723-5409

Powderhorns, Tennessee Valley Mfg., P.O. Box 1125, Corinth, MS 38834

Powderhorns, Thomas F. White, 5801 Westchester Ct., Worthington, OH 43085/614-888-0128

Practice Ammunition, Hoffman New Ideas Inc., 821 Northmoor Rd., Lake Forest, IL 60045/312-234-4075

Pressure Testg. Machine, M. York, 5508 Griffith Rd., Gaithersburg, MD 20760/301-253-4217

Ram Line, Inc., 406 Violet St., Golden, CO 80401/303-279-0886 (accessories)

Ransom Handgun Rests, C'Arco, P.O. Box 308, Highland, CA 92346/714-862-8311

Reloader's Record Book, Reloaders Paper Supply, Don Doerkson, P.O. Box 556, Hines, OR 97738/503-573-7060

Rifle Magazines, Butler Creek Corp., 290 Arden Dr., Belgrade, MT 59714/406-388-1356 (30-rd. Mini-14)

Rifle Magazines, Condor Mfg. Inc., 415 & 418 W. Magnolia Ave., Glendale, CA 91204/818-240-1745 (25-rd. 22-cal.)

Rifle Magazines, Miller Gun Works, P.O. Box 7326, Tamuning, Guam 96911 (30-cal. M1 15&30-round)

Rifle Slings, Bianchi International, 100 Calle Cortez, Temecula, CA 92390/714-676-5621

Rifle Slings, Butler Creek Corp., 290 Arden Dr., Belgrade, MT 59714/406-388-1356

Rifle Slings, Chace Leather Prods., Longhorn Div., 507 Alden St., Fall River, MA 02722/617-678-7556

Rifle Slings, John's Cust. Leather, 525 S. Liberty St., Blairsville, PA 15717/412-459-6802

Rifle Slings, Kirkpatrick Leather Co., P.O. Box 3150, Laredo, TX 78041/512-723-6631

Rifle Slings, Schulz Industr., 16247 Minnesota Ave., Paramount, CA 90723/213-636-7718

RIG, NRA Scoring Plug, Rig Products, 87 Coney Island Dr., Sparks, NV 89431/702-331-5666

Rubber Cheekpiece, W. H. Lodewick, 2816 N.E. Halsey, Portland, OR 97232/503-284-2554

Saddle Rings, Studs, Fred Goodwin, Sherman Mills, ME 04776

Safeties, William E. Harper, The Great 870 Co., P.O. Box 6309. El Monte, CA 91734/213-579-3077 (f. Rem. 870P)

Safeties, Williams Gun Sight Co., 7389 Lapeer Rd., Davison, MI 48423

Safety Slug, Glaser Safety Slug, P.O. Box 8223, Foster City, CA 94404/415-345-7677

Sav-Bore, Saunders Sptg. Gds., 338 Somerset St., N. Plainfield, NJ 07060

Scrimshaw Engraving, C. Milton Barringer, 244 Lakeview Terr., Palm Harbor, FL 33563/813-785-0088

Scrimshaw, G. Marek, P.O. Box 213, Westfield, MA 01086/413-568-9816

Sharpening Stones, A. G. Russell Co., 1705 Hiway 71 North, Springdale, AR 72764/501-751-7341 (Arkansas Oilstones)

Shell Catcher, Condor Mfg. Inc., 415 & 418 W. Magnolia Ave., Glendale, CA 91204/818-240-1745

Shooter's Porta Bench, Centrum Products Co., 443 Century, S.W., Grand Rapids, MI 49503/616-454-9424

Shooting Coats, 10-X Products Group, 2828 Forest Lane, Suite 1107, Dallas, TX 75234/214-243-4016

Shooting Glasses, American Optical Corp., 14 Mechanic St., Southbridge, MA 01550/617-765-9711

Shooting Glasses, Bilsom Intl., Inc., 11800 Sunrise Valley Dr., Reston, VA 22091/703-620-3950

Shooting Glasses, Willson Safety Prods. Division, P.O. Box 622, Reading, PA 19603

Shooting Range Equipment, Caswell Internatl. Corp., 1221 Marshall St. N.E., Minneapolis, MN 55413/612-379-2000

Shotgun Barrel, Pennsylvania Arms Co., Box 128, Duryea, PA 18642/717-457-0845 (rifled)

Shotgun bore, Custom Shootg. Prods., 8505 K St., Omaha, NE 68127

Shotgun Case Accessories, AC Enterprises, P.O. Box 448, Edenton, NC 27932/919-482-4992 (British-made Charlton)

Shotgun Converter, Amimex Inc., 2660 John Montgomery Dr., Suite #3, San Jose, CA 95148/408-923-1720

Shotgun Ribs, Poly-Choke Div., Marble Arms Corp., 420 Industrial Park, Gladstone, MI 49837/906-428-3710

Shotgun Sight, bi-ocular, Trius Prod., Box 25, Cleves, OH 45002

Shotgun Specialist, Moneymaker Guncraft, 1420 Military Ave., Omaha, NE 68131/402-556-0226 (ventilated, free-floating ribs)

Shotshell Adapter, PC Co., 5942 Secor Rd., Toledo, OH 43623/419-472-6222 (Plummer 410 converter)

Shotshell Adapter, Jesse Ramos, P.O. Box 7105, La Puente, CA 91744/818-369-6384 (12 ga./410 converter)

Snap Caps, Edwards Recoil Reducer, 269 Herbert St., Alton, IL 62002/618-462-3257

Sportsman's Chair, Devlet's Custom Purveyors, P.O. Box 886, Fort Lee, NJ 07024/201-886-0196

Springfield Safety Pin, B-Square Co., P.O. Box 11281, Ft. Worth, TX 76110/800-433-2909

Springs, W. C. Wolff Co., Box 232, Ardmore, PA 19003/215-647-1880

Stock Duplicating Machine, Don Allen, Inc., HC55, Box 322, Sturgis, SD 47785/605-347-4686

Supersound, Edmund Scientific Co., 101 E. Gloucester Pike, Barrington, NJ 08007/609-547-3488 (safety device)

Swivels, Michaels, P.O. Box 13010, Portland, OR 97213/503-255-6890

Swivels, Sile Dist., 7 Centre Market Pl., New York, NY 10013/212-925-4111

Swivels, Williams Gun Sight Co., 7389 Lapeer Rd., Davison, MI 48423

Tomahawks, H&B Forge Co., Rt. 2, Shiloh, OH 44878/419-896-2075

Tree Stand, Portable, Advanced Hunting Equipment Inc., P.O. Box 1277, Cumming, GA 30130/404-887-1171 (tree lounge)

Tree Stand, Climbing, Amacker Prods., P.O. Box 1432; 602 Kimbrough Dr., Tallulah, LA 71282/318-574-4903

Tree Steps, Deer Me Products Co., Box 34, 1208 Park St., Anoka, MN 55303/612-421-8971

Trophies, Blackinton & Co., P.O. Box 1300, Attleboro Falls, MA 02763

Trophies, F. H. Noble & Co., 888 Tower Rd., Mundelein, IL 60060

Walking Sticks, Life Knife Inc., P.O. Box 771, Santa Monica, CA 90406/213-821-6192

Warning Signs, Delta Ltd., P.O. Box 777, Mt. Ida, AR 71957

World Hunting Info., Jack Atcheson & Sons, Inc., 3210 Ottawa St., Butte, MT 59701

World Hunting Info., J/B Adventures & Safaris, Inc., 5655 So. Yosemite St., Suite 200, Englewood CO 80111/303-771-0977

World Hunting Info., Wayne Preston, Inc., 3444 Northhaven Rd., Dallas, TX 75229/214-358-4477

MUZZLE-LOADING GUNS, BARRELS or EQUIPMENT

Luther Adkins, Box 281, Shelbyville, IN 46176/317-392-3795 (breech plugs)

Allen Firearms Co., 2879 All Trades Rd., Santa Fe, NM 87501/505-471-6090

Anderson Mfg. Co., Union Gap Sta. P.O. Box 3120, Yakima, WA 98903/509-453-2349 (Flame-N-Go fusil; Accra-Shot)

Antique Arms Co., David F. Saunders, 1110 Cleveland, Monett, MO 65708/417-235-6501

Antique Gun Parts, Inc., 1118 S. Braddock Ave., Pittsburgh, PA 15218/412-241-1811 (parts)

Armoury, Inc., Rte. 202, New Preston, CT 06777

Armsport, Inc., 3590 N.W. 49th St., Miami, FL 33142/305-635-7850

Arm Tech, Armament Technologies Inc., 240 Sargent Dr., New Haven, CT 06511/203-562-2543 (22-cal. derringers)

Bauska Rifle Barrels, Inc., 105-9th Ave. West, Box 511, Kalispell, MT 59901/406-755-2635

Beaver Lodge, 9245 16th Ave. S.W., Seattle, WA 98106/206-763-1698

Beeman Precision Arms, Inc., 47-GDD Paul Dr., San Rafael, CA 94903/415-472-7121

Blackhawk West, Box 285, Hiawatha, KS 66434 (blck powder)

Blue and Gray Prods., Inc. RD #6, Box 362, Wellsboro, PA 16901/717-724-1383 (equipment)

Jim Brobst, 299 Poplar St., Hamburg, PA 19526/215-562-2103 (ML rifle bbls.)

Butler Creek Corp., 290 Arden Dr., Belgrade, MT 59714/406-388-1356 (poly & maxi patch)

Cache La Poudre Rifleworks, 168 N. College, Ft. Collins, CO 80521/303-482-6913 (custom muzzleloaders)

Challenger Mfg. Co., 118 Pearl St., Mt. Vernon, NY 10550

R. MacDonald Champlin, P.O. Box 693, Manchester, NH 03105/603-483-8557 (custom muzzleloaders)

Chopie Mfg. Inc., 700 Copeland Ave., LaCrosse, WI 54601/608-784-0926 (nipple wrenches)

Connecticut Valley Arms Co. (CVA), 5988 Peachtree East, Norcross, GA 30071/404-449-4687 (kits also)

Earl T. Cureton, Rte. 2, Box 388, Willoughby Rd., Bulls Gap, TN 37711/615-235-2854 (powder horns)

Homer L. Dangler, Box 254, Addison, MI 49220/517-547-6745

Leonard Day & Sons, Inc., P.O. Box 723, East Hampton, MA 01027/413-527-7990

Denver Arms, Ltd., P.O. Box 4640, Pagosa Springs, CO 81157/303-731-2295

Dixie Gun Works, Inc., P.O. Box 130, Union City, TN 38261

Dixon Muzzleloading Shop, Inc., RD #1, Box 175, Kempton, PA 19529/215-756-6271

Peter Dyson Ltd., 29-31 Church St., Honley, Huddersfield, W. Yorksh. HD7 2AH, England/0484-661062 (acc. f. ML shooter replicas)

EMF Co., Inc., 1900 E. Warner Ave. 1-D, Santa Ana, CA 92705/714-966-0202

Euroarms of America, Inc., P.O. Box 3277, 1501 Lenoir Dr., Winchester, VA 22601/703-662-1863

F.P.F. Co., P.O. Box 211, Van Wert, OH 45891 (black powder accessories)

Andy Fautheree, P.O. Box 4607, Pagosa Springs, CO 81157/303-731-2502 (cust. ML)

Ted Fellowes, Beaver Lodge, 9245 16th Ave. S.W., Seattle, WA 98106/206-763-1698

Firearms Imp. & Exp. Corp., (F.I.E.), P.O. Box 4866, Hialeah Lakes, Hialeah, FL 33014/305-685-5966

Marshall F. Fish, Rt. 22 N., RR 2 Box 2439, Westport, NY 12993/518-962-4897 (antique ML repairs)

The Flintlock Muzzle Loading Gun Shop, 1238 "G" So. Beach Blvd., Anaheim, CA 92804/714-821-6655

Forster Prods., 82 E. Lanark Ave., Lanark, IL 61046/815-493-6360

Frontier, 2910 San Bernardo, Laredo, TX 78040/512-723-5409 (powderhorns)

Getz Barrel Co., Box 88, Beavertown, PA 17813/717-658-7263 (barrels)

GOEX, Inc., Belin Plant, Moosic, PA 18507/717-457-6724 (black powder)

Golden Age Arms Co., 14 W. Winter St., Delaware, OH 43015 (ctlg. $2.50)

A. R. Goode, 4125 N.E. 28th Terr., Ocala, FL 32670/904-622-9575 (ML rifle barrels.)

Green Mountain Rifle Barrel Co., Inc., RFD 1, Box 184, Center Ossipee, NH 03814/603-539-7721

Guncraft Inc., 117 W. Pipeline, Hurst, TX 76053/817-282-6481

The Gun Works, 236 Main St., Springfield, OR 97477/503-741-4118 (supplies)

Hatfield Rifle Works, 2020 Colhoun, St. Joseph, MO 64501/816-279-8688 (squirrel rifle)

Hopkins & Allen, 3 Ethel Ave., P.O. Box 217, Hawthorne, NJ 07507/201-427-1165

The House of Muskets, Inc., P.O. Box 4640, Pagosa Springs, CO 81157/303-731-2295 (ML bbls. & supplies)

Steven Dodd Hughes, P.O. Box 11455, Eugene, OR 97440/503-485-8869 (cust. guns; ctlg. $3)

JJJJ Ranch, Rte. 1, State Route 243, Ironton, OH 45638/614-532-5298

Jennings-Hawken, 326½-4th St. S.W., Winter Haven, FL 33880

Jerry's Gun Shop, 9220 Odgen Ave., Brookfield, IL 60513/312-485-5200

LaChute Ltd., Box 48B, Masury, OH 44438/216-448-2236 (powder additive)

Morris Lawing, P.O. Box 9494., Charlotte, NC 28299/704-375-1740

Leding Loader, R.R. #1, Box 645, Ozark, AR 72949 (conical ldg. acc. f. ML)

Les' Gun Shop (Les Bauska), 105-9th West, P.O. Box 511, Kalispell, MT 59901/406-755-2635

Lever Arms Serv. Ltd., 572 Howe St., Vancouver, BC V6C 2E3, Canada

Log Cabin Sport Shop, 8010 Lafayette Rd., Lodi, OH 44254/216-948-1082 (ctlg. $3)

Loven-Pierson Inc., 4 W. Main, P.O. Box 377, Apalachin, NY 13732/607-625-2303

Lyman Products Corp., Rte. 147, Middlefield, CT 06455

McCann's Muzzle-Gun Works, 200 Federal City Rd., Pennington, NJ 08534/609-737-1707

McKeown's Sporting Arms, R.R. 4, Pekin, IL 61554/309-347-3559 (E-Z load rev. stand)

Mike Marsh, 6 Stanford Rd., Dronfield Woodhouse, Nr. Sheffield S18 SQJ, England (accessories)

Maurer Arms, 2154-16th St., Akron, OH 44314/216-745-6864 (cust. muzzle-loaders)

Michigan Arms Corp., 363 Elmwood, Troy, MI 48084/313-583-1518

Mountain State Muzzleloading Supplies, Inc., Box 154-1, State Rt. 14 at Boaz, Williamstown, WV 26187/304-375-7842

Mowrey Gun Works, 1313 Lawson Rd. Saginaw, TX 76179/817-847-1644

Muzzleload Magnum Products (MMP), Rt. 6 Box 383, Harrison, AR 72601/501-741-5019 (Premium Universal Powder Solvent)

Muzzleloaders Etc., Inc., Jim Westberg, 9901 Lyndale Ave. S., Bloomington, MN 55420/612-884-1161

Numrich Corp., W. Hurley, NY 12491 (powder flasks)

Olde Pennsylvania, P.O. Box 17419, Penn Hills, PA 15235 (black powder suppl.)

Oregon Trail Riflesmiths, Inc., P.O. Box 45212, Boise, ID 83711

Ox-Yoke Originals, 130 Griffin Rd., West Suffield, CT 06093/203-668-5110 (dry lubr. patches)

Ozark Mountain Arms Inc., Rt. 1 Box 44AS/Hwy. 32, Ashdown, AR 71822/501-898-2345 (rifles)

Pecos Valley Armory, 1022 So. Canyon, Carlsbad, NM 88220/505-887-6023

A. W. Peterson Gun Shop, 1693 Old Hwy. 441 N., Mt. Dora, FL 32757

Phyl-Mac, 609 N.E. 104th Ave., Vancouver, WA 98664/206-256-0579

Provider Arms, Inc., 261 Haglund Rd., Chesterton, IN 46304/219-879-5590 (Predator rifle)

R.V.I., P.O. Box 1439 Stn. A, Vancouver, B.C. V6C 1AO, Canada/604-524-3214 (high grade BP acc.)

Richland Arms, 321 W. Adrian St., Blissfield, MI 49228

H. M. Schoeller, 569 So. Braddock Ave., Pittsburgh, PA 15221

Tyler Scott, Inc. P.O. Box 193, Milford, OH 45150/513-831-7603 (Shooter's choice black solvent; patch lube)

C. Sharps Arms Co., Inc., P.O. Box 885, Big Timber, MT 59011/406-932-4353

Shiloh Products, 181 Plauderville Ave., Garfield, NJ 07026 (4-cavity mould)

Sile Distributors, 7 Centre Market Pl., New York, NY 10013/213-925-4111

C. E. Siler Locks, 7 Acton Woods Rd., Candler, NC 28715/704-667-2376 (flint locks)

South Bend Replicas, Inc., 61650 Oak Rd., South Bend, IN 46614/219-289-4500

Southwest Muzzle Loaders Supply, 201 E. Myrtle, Suite 112, P.O. Box 921, Angleton, TX 77515/409-849-4086

Ken Steggles, see: Mike Marsh

The Swampfire Shop, 1693 Old Hwy. 441 N., Mt. Dora, FL 32757/904-383-0595

Tennessee Valley Arms, P.O. Box 2022, Union City, TN 38261/901-885-4456

Tennessee Valley Mfg., P.O. Box 1125, Corinth, MS 38834 (powderhorn)

Ten-Ring Precision, Inc., 1449 Blue Crest Lane, San Antonio, TX 78232/512-494-3063

Traditions, Inc., Saybrook Rd., Haddam, CT 06438 (guns, kits, accessories)

Upper Missouri Trading Co., Box 191, Crofton, NE 68730/402-388-4844

Warren Muzzle Loading, Hwy. 21, Ozone, AR 72854 (black powder accessories)

J. S. Weeks & Son, 4748 Bailey Rd., Dimondale, MI 48821/517-636-0591 (supplies)

Fred Wells, Wells Sport Store, 110 N. Summit St., Prescott, AZ 86301/602-445-3655

W. H. Wescomb, P.O. Box 488, Glencoe, CA 95232/209-293-7010 (parts)

Thos. F. White, 5801 Westchester Ct., Worthington OH 43085/614-888-0128 (powder horn)

Williamson-Pate Gunsmith Serv., 117 W. Pipeline, Hurst, TX 76053/817-268-2887

Winchester Sutler, Siler Route, Box 393-E, Winchester, VA 22601/703-888-3595 (haversacks)

York County Gun Works, R.R. #4, Tottenham, Ont. LOG 1WO, Canada (locks)

PISTOLSMITHS

Accuracy Systems, Inc., 15203 N. Cave Creek Rd., Phoenix, AZ 85032/602-971-1991

Ahlman's Inc., R.R. #1 Box 20, Morristown, MN 55052/507-685-4243

Armament Gunsmithing Co., Inc., 525 Route 22, Hillside, NJ 07205/201-686-0960

Armson, Inc., P.O. Box 2130, Farmington Hills, MI 48018/313-478-2577

Baer Custom Guns, 1725 Minesite Rd., Allentown, PA 18103/215-398-2362 (accurizing 45 autos and Comp II Syst.; cust. XP100s, P.P.C. rev.)

Bain and Davis Sptg. Gds., 307 E. Valley Blvd., San Gabriel, CA 91776/213-573-4241

Lee Baker, 7252 East Ave. U-3, Littlerock, CA 93543/805-944-4487 (cust. blue)

Bar-Sto Precision Machine, 73377 Sullivan Rd., Twentynine Palms, CA 92277/619-367-2747(S.S. bbls. f. 45 ACP)

Barta's Gunsmithing, 10231 US Hwy. #10, Cato, WI 54206/414-732-4472

R. J. Beal, Jr., 170 W. Marshall Rd., Lansdowne, PA 19050/215-259-1220 (conversions, SASE f. inquiry)

Behlert Custom Guns, Inc., RD 2 Box 36C, Route 611 North, Pipersville, PA 18947/215-766-8681 (short actions)

Bell's Custom Shop, 3309 Mannheim Rd., Franklin Park, IL 60131/312-678-1900

Bob's Gun & Tackle Shop, 746 Granby St., Norfolk, VA 23510/804-627-8311

Bowen Classic Arms Corp., P.O. Box 67, Louisville, TN 37777/615-984-3583

F. Bob Chow, Gun Shop, Inc., 3185 Mission, San Francisco, CA 94110/415-282-8358

Brown Custom Guns, Inc., Steven N. Brown, 8810 Rocky Ridge Rd., Indianapolis, IN 46217/317-881-2771 aft. 5 PM

Leo Bustani, P.O. Box 8125, W. Palm Beach, FL 33407/305-622-2710

Dick Campbell, 1198 Finn Ave., Littleton, CO 80124/303-799-0145 (PPC guns; custom)

Cellini's, Francesca Inc., 3115 Old Ranch Rd., San Antonio, TX 78217/512-826-2584

D&D Gun Shop, 363 Elmwood, Troy, MI 48083/313-583-1512

Dave Chicoine, d/b/a Liberty A.S.P., 19 Key St., Eastport, ME 04631/207-853-2327 (rep. & rest. of early S&W prods.)

Davis Co., 2793 Del Monte St., West Sacramento, CA 95691/916-372-6789

Day Arms Corp., 2412 S.W. Loop 410, San Antonio, TX 78227/512-674-5220

Dominic DiStefano, 4303 Friar Lane, Colorado Springs, CO 80907/303-599-3366 (accurizing)

Duncan's Gunworks Inc., 1619 Grand Ave., San Marcos, CA 92069/619-727-0515

Dan Dwyer, 915 W. Washington, San Diego, CA 92103/619-296-1501

Englishtown Sptg. Gds. Co., Inc., David J. Maxham, 38 Main St., Englishtown, NJ 07726/201-446-7717

Jack First Distributors, Inc., 44633 Sierra Hwy., Lancaster, CA 93534/805-945-6981

Fountain Prods., 492 Prospect Ave., W. Springfield, MA 01089/413-781-4651

Frielich Police Equipment, 396 Broome St., New York, NY 10013/212-254-3045

Giles' 45 Shop, 8614 Tarpon Springs Rd., Odessa, FL 33556/813-920-5366

Gilman-Mayfield, 1552 N. 1st., Fresno, CA 93703/209-237-2500

The Gunworks Inc., John Hanus, 3434 Maple Ave., Brookfield, IL 60513/312-387-7888

Gil Hebard Guns, Box 1, Knoxville, IL 61448

Paul Jaeger, Inc., P.O. Box 449, 1 Madison Ave., Grand Junction, TN 38039/901-764-6909

J. D. Jones, Rt. 1, Della Dr., Bloomingdale, OH 43910/614-264-0176

L. E. Jurras & Assoc., P.O. Box 680, Washington, IN 47501/812-254-7698

Kart Sptg. Arms Corp., 1190 Old Country Rd., Riverhead, NY 11901/516-727-2719 (handgun conversions)

Ken's Gun Specialties, Rt. 1 Box 147, Lakeview, AR 72642/501-431-5606

Benjamin Kilham, Kilham & Co., Main St., Box 37, Lyme, NH 03768/603-795-4112

Terry K. Kopp, Highway 13, Lexington, MO 64067/816-259-2636 (rebblg., conversions)

John G. Lawson, The Sight Shop, 1802 E. Columbia Ave., Tacoma, WA 98404/206-474-5465

Kent Lomont, 4236 West South, Poneto, IN 46781/219-694-6792 (Auto Mag only)

Mag-na-port International, Inc., 41302 Executive Drive, Mt. Clemens, MI 48045/313-469-6727
Robert A. McGrew, 3315 Michigan Ave., Colorado Springs, CO 80910/303-636-1940
Rudolf Marent, 9711 Tiltree, Houston, TX 77075/713-946-7028 (Hammerli)
Elwyn H. Martin, Martin's Gun Shop, 937 So. Sheridan Blvd., Lakewood, CO 80226/303-922-2184
Conley E. Morris, 2135 Waterlevel Hwy., Cleveland, TN 37311/615-476-3984
Nu-Line Guns, 1053 Caulks Hill Rd., Harvester, MO 63303/314-441-4501
Pachmayr Gun Works, 1220 S. Grand Ave., Los Angeles, CA 90015
Paterson Gunsmithing, 438 Main St., Paterson, NJ 07502/201-345-4100
Power Custom, Inc., P.O. Box 1604, Independence, MO 64055/816-833-3102
RPS Gunshop, 11 So. Haskell St., Central Point, OR 97502/503-664-5010
Bob Rogers Gunsmithing, P.O. Box 305, Franklin Grove, IL 61031/815-456-2685 (custom)
SSK Industries (See: J. D. Jones)
L. W. Seecamp Co., Inc., Box 255, New Haven, CT 06502/203-877-3429
Hank Shows, dba The Best, 1078 Alice Ave., Ukiah, CA 95482/707-462-9060
Silver Dollar Guns, P.O. Box 475, 10 Frances St., Franklin, NH 03235/603-934-3292 (45 ACP)
Spokhandguns Inc., Vern D. Ewer, P.O. Box 370, 1206 Fig St., Benton City, WA 99320/509-588-5255
Sportsmens Equipmt. Co., 915 W. Washington, San Diego, CA 92103/619-296-1501 (specialty limiting trigger motion in autos)
Irving O. Stone, Jr., 73377 Sullivan Rd., Twentynine Palms, CA 92277/619-367-2747
Victor W. Strawbridge, 6 Pineview Dr., Dover Pt., Dover, NH 03820
A. D. Swenson's 45 Shop, P.O. Box 606, Fallbrook, CA 92028
Randall Thompson, Highline Machine Co., 654 Lela Pl., Grand Junction, CO 81504/303-434-4971
Trapper Gun, 18717 East 14 Mile Rd., Fraser, MI 48026/313-792-0134
Dennis A. "Doc" Ulrich, 2209 So. Central Ave., Cicero, IL 60650/312-652-3606
Vic's Gun Refinishing, 6 Pineview Dr., Dover, NH 03820/603-742-0013
Walters Industries, 6226 Park Lane, Dallas, TX 75225/214-691-5150

REBORING AND RERIFLING

P.O. Ackley (See Dennis M. Bellm Gunsmithing, Inc.)
Atkinson Gun Co., P.O. Box 512, Prescott, AZ 86301
Dennis M. Bellm Gunsmithing Inc., 2376 So. Redwood Rd., Salt Lake City, UT 84119/801-974-0697 (price list $3; rifle only)
Mark Chanlynn, Rocky Mtn. Rifle Works, Ltd., 1707-14th St., Boulder CO 80302/303-443-9189
Dave Chicoine, d/b/a Liberty A.S.P., 19 Key St., Eastport, ME 04631/207-853-2327 (reline handgun bbls.)
A. R. Goode, 4125 N.E. 28th Terr., Ocala, FL 32760/904-622-9575
H-S Precision, Inc., 112 N. Summit, Prescott, AZ 86302/602-445-0607
Terry K. Kopp, Highway 13, Lexington, MO 64067/816-259-2636 (Invis-A-Line bbl.; relining)
Les' Gun Shop, (Les Bauska), 105-9th West, P.O. Box 511, Kalispell, MT 59901/406-755-2635
Matco, Inc., 126 E. Main St., No. Manchester, IN 46962/219-982-8282
Nu-Line Guns, 1053 Caulks Hill Rd., Harvester, MO 63303/314-441-4500
Redman's Reboring & Rerifling, Route 3, Box 330A, Omak, WA 98841/509-826-5512
Siegrist Gun Shop, 8752 Turtle Rd., Whittemore, MI 48770/517-873-3929
Snapp's Gunshop, 6911 E. Washington Rd., Clare, MI 48617
J. W. Van Patten, P.O. Box 145, Foster Hill, Milford, PA 18337/717-296-7069
Fred Wells, Wells Sport Store, 110 N. Summit St., Prescott, AZ 86301/602-445-3655
Robt. G. West, 27211 Huey Lane, Eugene, OR 97402/503-689-6610

RELOADING TOOLS AND ACCESSORIES

Activ Industries, Inc., P.O. Box 238, Kearneysville, WV 25430/304-725-0451 (plastic hulls, wads)
Advance Car Mover Co., Inc., Rowell Div., P.O. Box 1181, 112 N. Outagamie St., Appleton, WI 54912/414-734-1878 (bottom pour lead casting ladies)
Advanced Precision Prods. Co., 5183 Flintrock Dr., Westerville, OH 43081/614-895-0560 (case super luber)
American Wad Prods. Co., 14729 Spring Valley Rd., Morrison, IL 61270/815-772-3336 (12-ga. shot wad)
Ammo Load Inc., 1560 E. Edinger, Suite G, Santa Ana, CA 92705/714-558-8858
Arcadia Machine & Tool (AMT), 536 No. Vincent Ave. Covina, CA 91722/818-915-7803 (Autoscale)
Benson Ballistics, Box 3796, Mission Viejo, CA 92690
C'Arco, P.O. Box 308, Highland, CA 92346/714-862-8311 (Ransom "Grand Master" progr. loader)
Colorado Sutler Arsenal, 6225 W. 46th Pl., Wheatridge, CO 80033/303-420-6383
Creighton Audette, 19 Highland Circle, Springfield, VT 05156/802-885-2331 (Universal Case Selection gauge)
B-Square Eng. Co., Box 11281, Ft. Worth, TX 76110/800-433-2909
Ballistic Prods., P.O. Box 488, 2105 Shaughnessy Circle, Long Lake, MN 55356/612-473-1550
Ballistic Research Industries (BRI), 2825 S. Rodeo Gulch Rd. #8, Soquel, CA 95073/408-476-7981 (shotgun slug)
Bear Machine Co., 2110 1st Natl. Tower, Akron, OH 44308/216-253-4039
Belding & Mull, Inc., P.O. Box 428, 100 N. 4th St., Philipsburg, PA 16866/814-342-0607
Berdon Machine Co., P.O. Box 9457, Yakima, WA 98909/509-453-0374 (metallic press)

Blackhawk West, R. L. Hough, Box 285, Hiawatha, KS 66434/303-366-3659
Bonanza (See: Forster Products)
Gene Bowlin, Rt. 1, Box 890, Snyder, TX 79549/915-573-2323 (arbor press)
Brown Precision Co., P.O. Box 270W, 7786 Molinos Ave., Los Molinos, CA 96055/916-384-2506 (Little Wiggler)
C-H Tool & Die Corp., 106 N. Harding St., Owen, WI 54460/715-229-2146
Camdex, Inc., 2330 Alger, Troy, MI 48083/313-518-2300
Carbide Die & Mfg. Co., Inc., 15615 E. Arrow Hwy., Irwindale, CA 91706/213-337-2518
Carter Gun Works, 2211 Jefferson Pk. Ave., Charlottesville, VA 22903
Cascade Cartridge, Inc., (See: Omark)
Cascade Shooters, 60916 McMullin Dr., Bend, OR 97702/503-389-5872 (bull. seating depth gauge)
Central Products f. Shooters, 435 Route 18, East Brunswick, NJ 08816 (neck turning tool)
Chevron Case Master, R.R. 1, Ottawa, IL 61350
Lester Coats, 416 Simpson Ave., No. Bend, OR 97459/503-756-6995 (core cutter)
Container Development Corp., 424 Montgomery St., Watertown, WI 53094
Continental Kite & Key Co., (CONKKO) P.O. Box 40, Broomall, PA 19008/215-356-0711 (primer pocket cleaner)
Cooper-Woodward, Box 972, Riverside, CA 92502/714-822-4176 (Perfect Lube)
Corbin Mfg. & Supply Inc., P.O. Box 2659, White City, OR 97503/503-826-5211
Custom Products, RD #1, Box 483A, Saegertown, PA 16443/814-763-2769 (decapping tool, dies, etc.)
J. Dewey Mfg. Co., 186 Skyview Dr., Southbury, CT 06488/203-264-3064
Dillon Precision Prods., Inc., 7442 E. Butherus Dr., Scottsdale, AZ 85260/602-948-8009
Division Lead Co., 7742 W. 61st Pl., Summit, IL 60502
Eagle Products Co., 1520 Adelia Ave., So. El Monte, CA 91733
Edmisten Co. Inc., P.O. Box 1293, Hwy 105, Boone, NC 28607/704-264-1490 (I-Dent-A Handloader's Log)
Efemes Enterprises, P.O. Box 122M, Bay Shore, NY 11706 (Berdan decapper)
Fitz, Box 171, Douglas City, CA 96024 (Fitz Flipper)
Flambeau Prods. Corp., 15981 Valplast Rd., Middlefield, OH 44062/216-632-1631
Forster Products Inc., 82 E. Lanark Ave., Lanark IL 61046/815-493-6360
Francis Tool Co., P.O. Box 7861, Eugene, OR 97401/503-345-7457 (powder measure)
Freechec' (See: Paco)
Geo. M. Fullmer, 2499 Mavis St., Oakland, CA 94601/415-533-4193 (seating die)
Gene's Gun Shop, Rt. 1, Box 890, Snyder, TX 79549/915-573-2323 (arbor press)
Gopher Shooter's Supply, Box 278, Faribault, MN 55021
Hart Products, Rob W. Hart & Son Inc., 401 Montgomery St., Nescopeck, PA 18635/717-752-3655
Hensley & Gibbs, P.O. Box 10, Murphy, OR 97533 (bullet moulds)
Richard Hoch, The Gun Shop, 62778 Spring Creek Rd., Montrose, CO 81401/303-249-3625 (custom Schuetzen bullet moulds)
Hoffman New Ideas Inc., 821 Northmoor Rd., Lake Forest, IL 60045/312-234-4075 (spl. gallery load press)
Hollywood Loading Tools by M&M Engineering, 10642 Arminta St., Sun Valley, CA 91352/818-842-8376
Hornady Mfg. Co., P.O. Drawer 1848, Grand Island, NE 68802/308-382-1390
Hulme see: Marshall Enterprises (Star case feeder)
Huntington, P.O. Box 991, Oroville, CA 95965/916-534-1210 (Compact Press)
Independent Mach. & Gun Shop, 1416 N. Hayes, Pocatello, ID 83201/208-232-1264
Javelina Products, Box 337, San Bernardino, CA 92402 (Alox beeswax)
Neil Jones, RD #1, Box 483A, Saegertown, PA 16433/814-763-2769 (decapping tool, dies)
Paul Jones Munitions Systems (See Fitz Co.)
King & Co., Edw. R. King, Box 1242, Bloomington, IL 61701
Lage Uniwad Co., 1814 21st St., Eldora, IA 50627/515-858-2364 (Universal Shotshell Wad)
Leding Loader, R.R. #1, Box 645, Ozark, AR 72949 (conical loadg. acc. f. ML)
Lee Custom Engineering, Inc. (See Mequon Reloading Corp.)
Lee Precision, Inc., 4275 Hwy. U, Hartford, WI 53027/414-673-3075
L. L. F. Die Shop, 1281 Highway 99 N., Eugene, OR 97402/503-688-5753
Dean Lincoln, Custom Tackle & Ammo, P.O. Box 1886, Farmington, NM 87401 (mould)
Ljutic Industries Inc., P.O. Box 2117, 732 N. 16th Ave., Yakima, WA 98907/509-248-0476 (plastic wads)
Lock's Phila. Gun Exch., 6700 Rowland, Philadelphia, PA 19149/215-332-6225
Lyman Products Corp., Rte. 147, Middlefield, CT 06455
McKillen & Heyer Inc., 37603 Arlington Dr., Box 627, Willoughby, OH 44094/216-942-2491 (case gauge)
Paul McLean, 2670 Lakeshore Blvd., W., Toronto, Ont. M8V 1G8 Canada/416-259-3060 (Universal Cartridge Holder)
M-A Systems, 42417 Third St. East, Lancaster, CA 93535/805-942-6706
MEC, Inc. (See Mayville Eng. Co.)
MTM Molded Products Co., 3370 Obco Ct., P.O. Box 14117, Dayton, OH 45414/513-890-7461
Magma Eng. Co., P.O. Box 161, Queen Creek, AZ 85242
Marmel Prods., P.O. Box 97, Utica, MI 48087/313-731-8029 (Marvelube, Marvelux)
Marquart Precision Co., P.O. Box 1740, Prescott, AZ 86302/602-445-5646 (precision case-neck turning tool)
Marshall Enterprises, 792 Canyon Rd., Redwood City, CA 94062/415-365-1230 (Hulme autom. case feeder f. Star rel.)
Mayville Eng. Co., 715 South St., Mayville, WI 53050/414-387-4500 (shotshell loader)
Mequon Reloading Corp., P.O. Box 253, Mequon, WI 53092/414-673-3060
Merit Gun Slight Co., P.O. Box 995, Sequim, WA 98382/206-683-6127

Multi-Scale Charge Ltd., 55 Maitland St. Suite 310, Toronto, Ont. M4Y 1C9, Canada/416-276-6292

Muzzleload Magnum Products (MMP), Rte. 6 Box 383, Harrison, AR 72601/ 501-741-5019 (Tri-Cut Trimmer; Power Powder Trickler)

Normington Co., Box 6, Rathdrum, ID 83858 (powder baffles)

Northeast Industrial Inc., N.E.I., P.O. Box 249, 405 N. Canyon Blvd., Canyon City, OR 97820/503-575-2513 (bullet mould)

Ohaus Scale, (See RCBS)

Old Western Scrounger, 12924 Hwy. A-12, Montague, CA 96064/916-459-5445 (Press f. 50-cal. B.M.G round)

Omark Industries, Box 856, Lewiston, ID 83501/208-746-2351

P&P Tool Co., 125 W. Market St., Morrison, IL 61270/815-772-7618 (12-ga. shot wad)

Pacific Tool Co., P.O. Box 2048, Ordnance Plant Rd., Grand Island, NE 68801/308-384-2308

Paco, Box 17211, Tucson, AZ 85731 (Freechec' tool for gas checks)

Pak-Tool, Roberts Products, 25238 S. E. 32nd, Issaquah, WA 98027/206-392-8172

Pitzer Tool Mfg. Co., RR #3, Box 50, Winterset, IA 50273/515-462-4268 (bullet lubricator & sizer)

Plum City Ballistics Range, Norman E. Johnson, Rte. 1, Box 29A, Plum City, WI 54761/715-647-2539

Ponsness-Warren, P.O. Box 8, Rathdrum, ID 83858/208-687-2231

Marian Powley, Petra Lane, R.R.1, Eldridge, IA 52748/319-285-9214

Quinetics Corp., P.O. Box 29007, San Antonio, TX 78229/516-684-8561 (kinetic bullet puller)

RCBS, Inc., Box 1919, Oroville, CA 95965/916-533-5191

Ransom (See C'Arco)

Redding Inc., 1089 Starr Rd., Cortland, NY 13045/607-753-3331

Reloaders Paper Supply, Don Doerksen, P.O. Box 556, Hines, OR 97738/503-573-7060 (reloader's record book)

Rifle Ranch, Rte. 10, 3301 Willow Creek Rd., Prescott, AZ 86301/602-778-7501

Rochester Lead Works, 76 Anderson Ave., Rochester, NY 14607/716-442-8500 (leadwire)

Rorschach Precision Prods., P.O. Box 151613, Irving, TX 75015/214-790-3487 (carboloy bull. dies)

Rotex Mfg. Co. (See Texan)

SAECO Rel. 2207 Border Ave., Torrance, CA 90501/213-320-6973

SSK Industries, Rt. 1, Della Drive, Bloomingdale, OH 43910/614-264-0176 (primer tool)

Sandia Die & Cartridge Co., Rte. 5, Box 5400, Albuquerque, NM 87123/505-298-5729

Shannon Associates, P.O. Box 32737, Oklahoma City, OK 73123

Shooters Accessory Supply, (See Corbin Mfg. & Supply)

Jerry Simmons, 715 Middlebury St., Goshen, IN 46526/219-533-8546 (Pope de- & recapper)

J. A. Somers Co., P.O. Box 49751, Los Angeles, CA 90049 (Jasco)

Sport Flite Mfg., Inc., 2520 Industrial Row, Troy, MI 48084/313-280-0648 (swaging dies)

Star Machine Works, 418 10th Ave., San Diego, CA 92101/619-232-3216

Texan Reloaders, Inc., 444 So. Cips St., Watseka, IL 60970/815-432-5065

Trico Plastics, 590 S. Vincent Ave., Azusa, CA 91702

Tru Square Metal Products, P.O. Box 585, Auburn, WA 98002/206-833-2310 (Thumler's tumbler case polishers; Ultra Vibe 18)

WAMADET, Silver Springs, Goodleigh, Barnstaple, Devon, England

Weatherby, Inc., 2781 Firestone Blvd., South Gate, CA 90280/213-569-7186

Weaver Arms Ltd., P.O. Box 3316, Escondido, CA 92025/619-746-2440 (progr. loader)

Webster Scale Mfg. Co., P.O. Box 188, Sebring, FL 33870/813-385-6362

Whits Shooting Stuff, P.O. Box 1340, Cody, WY 82414

L. E. Wilson, Inc. P.O. Box 324, 404 Pioneer Ave., Cashmere, WA 98815/509-782-1328

Zenith Enterprises, 5781 Flagler Rd., Nordland, WA 98358/206-385-2142

RESTS—BENCH, PORTABLE, ETC.

Amacker Products, Inc., 602 Kimbrough, Tallulah, LA 71282/318-574-4903

B-Square Co., P.O. Box 11281, Ft. Worth, TX 76109/800-433-2909 (handgun)

Jim Brobst, 299 Poplar St., Hamburg, PA 19526/215-562-2103 (bench rest pedestal)

Bullseye Shooting Bench, 6100 - 40th St. Vancouver, WA 98661/206-694-6141 (portable)

C'Arco, P.O. Box 308, Highland, CA 92346/714-862-8311 (handgun rest)

Centrum Products Co., 443 Century S.W., Grand Rapids, MI 49503/616-454-9424 (Porta Bench)

Philip Cooley, 34 Bay Ridge Ave., Brooklyn, NY 11220/212-745-9311

Cravener's Gun Shop, 1627 - 5th Ave., Ford City, PA 16226/412-763-8312

Decker Shooting Products, 1729 Laguna Ave., Schofield, WI 54476/715-359-5873 (rifle rests)

Garbini Loga Systems, St. Galler Str. 72, CH-9325 Roggwill TG, Switzerland

The Gun Case, 11035 Maplefield, El Monte, CA 91733

Joe Hall's Shooting Products, Inc., 443 Wells Rd., Doylestown, PA 18901/215-345-6354 (adj. portable)

Harris Engineering, Inc., Barlow, KY 42024/502-334-3633 (bipods)

Rob. W. Hart & Son, 401 Montgomery St., Nescopeck, PA 18635

Tony Hidalgo, 12701 S.W. 9th Pl., Davie, FL 33325/305-476-7645 (adj. shooting seat)

J. B. Holden Co., 295 W. Pearl, P.O. Box 320, Plymouth, MI 48170/313-455-4850

Hoppe's Div., Penguin Industries, Inc., Airport Industrial Mall, Coatesville, PA 19320/251-384-6000 (bench rests and bags)

North Star Devices, Inc., P.O. Box 2095, North St. Paul, MN 55109

Progressive Prods., Inc., P.O. Box 67, Holmen, WI 54636/608-526-3345 (Sandbagger rifle rest)

Protektor Model Co., Galeton,, PA 16922/814-435-2442 (sandbags)

Ransom (See Arco)

San Angelo Mfg. Co., 1841 Industrial Ave., San Angelo, TX 76904/915-655-7126

Suter's, Inc., House of Guns, 332 N. Tejon, Colorado Springs, CO 80902/303-635-1475

Turkey Creek Enterprises, Rt. 1, Box 65, Red Oak, OK 74563/918-754-2884 (portable shooting rest)

Wichita Arms, 444 Ellis, Wichita, KS 67211/316-265-06612

RIFLE BARREL MAKERS

P.O. Ackley Rifle Barrels (See Dennis M. Bellm Gunsmithing Inc.)

Atkinson Gun Co., P.O. Box 512, Prescott, AZ 86301

Jim Baiar, 490 Halfmoon Rd., Columbia Falls, MT 59912/406-892-4409

Bauska Rifle Barrels, Inc., 105-9th Ave. West, Kalispell, MT 59901/406-755-2635

Dennis M. Bellm Gunsmithing Inc., 2376 So. Redwood Rd., Salt Lake City, UT 84119/801-974-0697; price list $3 (new rifle bbls., incl. special & obsolete)

Leo Bustani, P.O. Box 8125, West Palm Beach, FL 33407/305-622-2710 (Win.92 take-down; Trapper 357-44 mag. bbls.)

Ralph L. Carter, Carter's Gun Shop, 225 G St., Penrose, CO 81240/303-372-6240

Mark Chanlynn, Rocky Mtn. Rifle Works, Ltd., 1707-14th St., Boulder, CO 80302/303-443-9189

Charles P. Donnelly & Son, Siskiyou Gun Works, 405 Kubli Rd., Grants Pass, OR 97527/503-846-6604

Douglas Barrels, Inc., 5504 Big Tyler Rd., Charleston, WV 25313/304-776-1341

Douglas Jackalope Gun & Sport Shop, Inc., 1048 S. 5th St., Douglas, WY 82633/307-358-3854

Federal Firearms Co., Inc., P.O. Box 145, Thoms Run Rd., Oakdale, PA 15071/412-221-0300

Getz Barrel Co., Box 88, Beavertown, PA 17813/717-658-7263

A. R. Goode, 4125 N.E. 28th Terr., Ocala, FL 32670/904-622-9575

Green Mountain Rifle Barrel Co., Inc., RFD 1 Box 184, Center Ossipee, NH 03814/603-539-7721

H-S Precision, Inc., 112 N. Summit, Prescott, AZ 86302/602-445-0607

Half Moon Rifle Shop, 490 Halfmoon Rd., Columbia Falls, MT 59912/406-892-4409

Hart Rifle Barrels, Inc., RD 2, Lafayette, NY 13084/315-677-9841

Hastings, Box 224, 822-6th St., Clay Center, KS 67432/913-632-3169 (shotguns ONLY)

Wm. H. Hobaugh, The Rifle Shop, Box M, Philipsburg, MT 59858/406-859-3515

Terry K. Kopp, Highway 13, Lexington, MO 64067/816-259-2636 (22-cal. blanks)

Les' Gun Shop, (Les Bauska), 105-9th West, P.O. Box 511, Kalispell, MT 59901/406-755-2635

Lilja Precision Rifle Barrels, Inc., 245 Compass Creek Rd., P.O. Box 372, Plains, MT 59859/406-826-3084

Marquart Precision Co., P.O. Box 1740, Prescott, AZ 86302/602-445-5646

Matco, Inc., Box 349, 126 E. Main St., No. Manchester, IN 46962/219-982-8282

McMillan Rifle Barrels U.S. International, P.O. Box 3427, Bryan, TX 77805/409-846-3990

Nu-Line Guns, 1053 Caulks Hill Rd., Harvester, MO 63303/314-441-4500

Numrich Arms, W. Hurley, NY 12491

Olympic Arms Inc. dba SGW, 624 Old Pacific Hwy. S.E., Olympia, WA 98503/206-456-3471

John T. Pell Octagon Barrels, (KOGOT), 410 College Ave., Trinidad, CO 81082/303-846-9406

Pennsylvania Arms Co., Box 128, Duryea, PA 18642/717-457-0845 (rifled shotgun bbl. only)

Redman's Rifling & Reboring, Rt. 3, Box 330A, Omak, WA 98841/509-826-5512

Sanders Cust. Gun Serv., 2358 Tyler Lane, Louisville, KY 40205

Gary Schneider, 12202 N. 62d Pl., Scottsdale, AZ 85254/602-948-2525

SGW, Inc., D. A. Schuetz, 624 Old Pacific Hwy. S.E., Olympia, WA 98503/206-456-3471

E. R. Shaw, Inc., Prestley & Thoms Run Rd., Bridgeville, PA 15017/412-221-3636

Shilen Rifles, Inc., 205 Metro Park Blvd., Ennis, TX 75119/214-875-5318

W. C. Strutz, Rifle Barrels, Inc., P.O. Box 611, Eagle River, WI 54521/715-479-4766

Fred Wells, Wells Sport Store, 110 N. Summit St., Prescott, AZ 86301/602-445-3655

Bob Williams, P.O. Box 143, Boonsboro, MD 21713

Wilson Arms, 63 Leetes Island Rd., Branford, CT 06405/203-488-7297

SCOPES, MOUNTS, ACCESSORIES, OPTICAL EQUIPMENT

A.R.M.S., Inc. (Atlantic Research Marketing Systems), 230 W. Center St., West Bridgewater, MA 02379/617-584-7816

Action Arms Ltd., P.O. Box 9573, Philadelphia, PA 19124/215-744-0100

Aimpoint U.S.A., 201 Elden St., Suite 302, Herndon, VA 22070/703-471-6828 (electronic sight)

Alley Suppl. Co., P.O. Box 848, Gardnerville, NV 89410/702-782-3800

American Arms, Inc., P.O. Box 27163, Salt Lake City, UT 84127/801-972-5006

The American Import Co., 1453 Mission, San Francisco, CA 94103/415-863-1506

Anderson Mfg. Co., Union Gap Sta. P.O. Box 3120, Yakima, WA 98903/509-453-2349 (lens cap)

Apolio Optics (See Senno Corp.)

Armsport, Inc., 3590 N.W. 49th St., Miami, FL 33122/305-635-7850
Armson, Inc., P.O. Box 2130, Farmington Hills, MI 48018/313-478-2577 (O.E.G.)
B-Square Co., Box 11281, Ft. Worth, TX 76109/800-433-2909 (Mini-14 mount)
Bausch & Lomb Inc., 1400 Goodman St., Rochester, NY 14602/716-338-6000
Beeman Inc., 47-GDD Paul Dr., San Rafael, CA 94903/415-472-7121
Bennett, 561 Delaware, Delmar, NY 12054/518-439-1862 (mounting wrench)
Billingsley & Brownell, Box 25, Dayton, WY 82836/307-655-9344 (mounts, accessories)
Browning Arms, Rt. 4, Box 624-B, Arnold, MO 63010
Buehler Scope Mounts, 17 Orinda Highway, Orinda, CA 94563/415-254-3201
Burris Co. Inc., 331 E. 8th St., Box 1747, Greeley, CO 80631/303-356-1670
Bushnell Optical Co., 2828 E. Foothill Blvd., Pasadena, CA 91107
Butler Creek Corp., 290 Arden Dr., Belgrade, MT 59714/406-388-1356 (lens caps)
Kenneth Clark, 18738 Highway 99, Madera, CA 93637/209-674-6016
Clear View Mfg. Co., Inc. 20821 Grand River Ave., Detroit, MI 48219/313-535-0033 (mounts)
Colt Firearms, P.O. Box 1868, Hartford CT 06102/203-236-6311
Compass Instr. & Optical Co., Inc., 104 E. 25th St., New York, NY 10010
Conetrol Scope Mounts, Hwy 123 South, Seguin, TX 78155
Cougar Optics, P.O. Box 115, Groton, NY 13071/607-898-5754
D&H Prods. Co., Inc., 465 Denny Rd., Valencia, PA 16059/412-898-2840 (lens covers)
Davis Optical Co., 528 Richmond St., P.O. Box 6, Winchester, IN 47394/317-584-5311
Del-Sports Inc., Main St., Margaretville, NY 12455/914-586-4103 (Kahles scopes; EAW mts.)
Dickson (See American Import Co.)
Flaig's, Babcock Blvd., Millvale, PA 15209
Fontaine Ind., Inc., 11552 Knott St., Suite 1, Garden Grove, CA 92641/714-898-9163
Freeland's Scope Stands, Inc., 3737 14th, Rock Island, IL 61201/309-788-7449
Griffin & Howe, Inc., 589 Broadway, New York, NY 10012/212-966-5323
Heckler & Koch, Inc., 14601 Lee Rd., Chantilly, VA 22021/703-631-2800
H.J. Hermann Leather Co., Rt. 1, P.O. Box 525, Skiatook, OK 74070/918-396-1226 (lens caps)
J.B. Holden Co., 295 W. Pearl, P.O. Box 320, Plymouth, MI 48170/313-455-4850
The Hutson Corp., 105 Century Dr., No., Mansfield, TX 76063/817-477-3421
Import Scope Repair Co., P.O. Box 2633, Durango, CO 81301/303-247-1422
Interarms, 10 Prince St., Alexandria, VA 22313
Paul Jaeger, Inc., P.O. Box 449, 1 Madison Ave., Grand Junction, TN 38039/901-764-6909 (Schmidt & Bender; EAW mts., Noble)
Jason Empire Inc., 9200 Cody, P.O. Box 14930, Overland Park, KS 66214/913-888-0220
Jennison TCS (See Fontaine Ind., Inc.)
Kahles of America, Div. of Del-Sports, Inc., Main St., Margaretville, NY 12455/914-586-4103
Kenko Intl. Inc., 8141 West I-70 Frontage Rd. No., Arvada, CO 80002/303-425-1200
KenPatable Ent. Inc., P.O. Box 19422, Louisville, KY 40219/502-239-5447 (Kwik-Mount)
Kilham & Co., Main St., Box 37, Lyme, NY 03768/603-795-4112 (Hutson handgun scopes)
Kowa Optimed, Inc., 20001 S. Vermont Ave., Torrance, CA 90502/213-327-1913
Kris Mounts, 108 Lehigh St., Johnstown, PA 15905
Kwik-Site, 5555 Treadwell, Wayne, MI 48184/313-326-1500
T.K. Lee, 2830 S. 19th St., Off. #4, Birmingham, AL 35209/205-871-6065
E. Leitz, Inc., 24 Link Dr., Rockleigh, NJ 07647/201-767-1100
Leupold & Stevens Inc., P.O. Box 688, Beaverton, OR 97075/503-646-9171
Jake Levin and Son, Inc., 9200 Cody, Overland Park, KS 66214
W.H. Lodewick, 2816 N.E. Halsey, Portland, OR 97232/503-284-2554 (scope safeties)
Lyman Products Corp., Route 147, Middlefield, CT. 06455
Mandall Shooting Supplies, 7150 E. 4th St., Scottsdale, AZ 85252
Marble Arms Co., 420 Industrial Park, Gladstone, MI 49837/906-428-3710
Marlin Firearms Co., 100 Kenna Dr., New Haven, CO 06473
Millett Industries, 16131 Gothard St., Huntington Beach, CA 92647/714-842-5575 (mounts)
Nikon, Inc., 623 Stewart Ave., Garden City, NY 11530/516-222-0200
Numrich Arms, West Hurley, NY 12491
Nydar, (See Swain Nelson Co.)
Optex (See Southern Precision Instrument Co.)
Orchard Park Enterprise, P.O. Box 563, Orchard Park, NY 14127/716-662-2255 (Saddleproof mount)
Oriental Optical Co., 605 E. Walnut St., Pasadena, CA 91101/213-792-1252 (scope & binocular repairs)
Pachmayr Gun Works, 1220 S. Grand Ave., Los Angeles, CA 90015/213-748-7271
Pentax Corp., 35 Inverness Dr. E., Englewood CO 80112/303-799-8000 (riflescopes)
Pilkington Gun Co., P.O. Box 1296, Muskogee, OK 74402/918-693-9418 (Q. D. mt.)
Pioneer Marketing & Research Inc., 216 Haddon Ave. Suite 522, Westmont, NJ 08108/609-854-2424 (German Steiner binoculars; scopes)
Precise, 3 Chestnut, Suffern, NY 10901
Ram Line, Inc., 406 Violet St., Golden, CO 80401/303-279-0886 (see-thru mt. f. Mini-14)
Ranging, Inc., Routes 5 & 20, East Bloomfield, NY 14443/716-657-6161
Ray-O-Vac, Willson Prod. Div., P.O. Box 622, Reading, PA 19603 (shooting glasses)
Redfield Gun Sight Co., 5800 E. Jewell Ave., Denver, CO 80222/303-757-6411
S & K Mfg. Co., Box 247, Pittsfield, PA 16340/814-563-7808 (Insta-Mount)

SSK Industries, Rt. 1, Della Dr., Bloomingdale, OH 43910/614-264-0176 (bases)
Sanders Cust. Gun Serv., 2358 Tyler Lane, Louisville, KY 40205 (MSW)
Schmidt & Bender, see: Paul Jaeger, Inc.
Seattle Binocular & Scope Repair Co., P.O. Box 46094, Seattle, WA 98146
Senno Corp., S. 323 Grant, P.O. Box 3506, Spokane, WA 99220/800-541-5689
Shepherd Scope Ltd., Box 189, Waterloo, NE 69069/402-779-2386
Sherwood Intl. Export Corp., 18714 Parthenia St., Northridge, CA 91324/818-349-7600 (mounts)
Shooters Supply, 1120 Tieton Dr., Yakima, WA 98902/509-452-1181 (mount f. M14/M1A rifles)
W.H. Siebert, 22720 S.E. 56th St., Issaquah, WA 98027
Simmons Outdoor Corp., 14205 S.W. 119 Ave., Miami, FL 33186/305-252-0477
Southern Precision Inst. Co., 3419 E. Commerce St., San Antonio, TX 78219
Spacetron Inc., Box 84, Broadview, IL 60155(bore lamp)
Steiner (See Pioneer Marketing & Research)
Stoeger Industries, 55 Ruta Ct., S. Hackensack, NJ 07606/201-440-2700
Supreme Lens Covers, (See Butler Creek) (lens caps)
Swain Nelson Co., Box 45, 92 Park Dr., Glenview, IL 60025 (shotgun sight)
Swarovski Optik, Div. of Swarovski America Ltd., One Kenny Dr., Cranston, RI 02920/401-463-6400
Swift Instruments, Inc., 952 Dorchester Ave., Boston, MA 02125
Tasco, 7600 N.W. 26th St., Miami, FL 33122/305-591-3670
Tele-Optics, 5514 W. Lawrence Ave., Chicago, IL 60630/312-283-7757 (optical equipment repair services only)
Thompson-Center Arms, P.O. Box 2426, Rochester, NH 03867/603-332-2394 (handgun scope)
Tradewinds, Inc., Box 1191, Tacoma, WA 98401
Trijicon rifle scopes (See Armson, Inc.)
John Unertl Optical Co., 3551-5 East St., Pittsburgh, PA 15214
United Binocular Co., 9043 S. Western Ave., Chicago, IL 60620
Vissing (See Supreme Lens Covers)
Wasp Shooting Systems, Box 241, Lakeview, AR 72642/501-431-5606 (mtg. system f. Ruger Mini-14 only)
Weatherby's, 2781 Firestone, South Gate, CA 90280/213-569-7186
W.R. Weaver, Omark Industries, Box 856, Lewiston, ID 83501 (mounts & bases only)
Weaver Scope Repair Service, 1121 Larry Mahan Dr., Suite B, El Paso, TX 79925/915-593-1005
Wide View Scope Mount Corp., 26110 Michigan Ave., Inkster, MI 48141/313-274-1238
Williams Gun Sight Co., 7389 Lapeer Rd., Davison, MI 48423
Boyd Williams Inc., 8701-14 Mile Rd. (M-57),Cedar Springs, MI 49319 (BR)
Willrich Precision Instrument Co., 95 Cenar Lane, Englewood, NJ 07631/201-567-1411 (borescope)
Carl Zeiss Inc.,Consumer Prods. Div., Box 2010, 1015 Commerce St., Petersburg, VA 23803/804-861-0033

SIGHTS, METALLIC

Accura-Sites, The Jim J. Tembelis Co., Inc., P.O. Box 114, 216 Loper Ct.,Neenah, WI 54956/414-722-0039
Alley Supply Co., P.O. Box 848, Gardnerville, NV 89410/702-782-3800
Armson, Inc., P.O. Box 2130, Farmington Hills, MI 48018/313-478-2577
B-Square Eng. Co., Box 11281, Ft. Worth, TX 76110/800-433-2909
Beeman Inc., 47 Paul Dr., San Rafael, CA 94903/415-472-7121 (airguns only)
Behlert Custom Sights, Inc., RD 2 Box 36C, Route 611 North, Pipersviflle, PA 18947/215-766-8681
Bingham Ltd., 1775-C Wilwat Dr., Norcross, GA 30093/404-448-1440
Bo-Mar Tool & Mfg. Co., Rt. 12, Box 405, Longview, TX 75605/214-759-4784
Buehler Scope Mounts, 17 Orinda Highway, Orinda, CA 94563/415-254-3201
Burris Co., Inc., 331-8th St., P.O. Box 1747, Greeley, CO 80632/303-356-1670
Farr Studio, 1231 Robinhood Rd., Greeneville, TN 37743/615-638-8825 (sighting aids—clip-on aperture)
Andy Fautheree, P.O. Box 4607, Pagosa Springs, CO 81157/303-731-2502 ("Calif. Sight" f. ML)
Freeland's Scope Stands, Inc., 3734-14th Ave., Rock Island, IL 61201/309-788-7449
Paul Jaeger, Inc., P.O. Box 449, 1 Madison Ave., Grand Junction, TN 38039/901-764-6909
Lee's Red Ramps, 7252 E. Ave. U-3, Littlerock, CA 93543/805-944-4487 (white outline rear sight)
James W. Lofland, 2275 Larkin Rd., Boothwyn, PA 19061/215-485-0391 (single shot replica)
Lyman Products Corp., Rte. 147, Middlefield, CT 06455
Mag-na-port International, Inc., 41302 Executive Drive, Mt. Clemens, MI 48045/313-469-6727
Marble Arms Corp., 420 Industrial Park, Gladstone, MI 49837/906-428-3710
Merit Gunsight Co., P.O. Box 995, Sequim, WA 98382/206-683-6127
Millett Industries, 16131 Gothard St., Huntington Beach, CA 92647/714-842-5575
Miniature Machine Co., 210 E. Poplar, Deming, NM 88030/505-546-2151 (MMC)
Omega Sales, Inc., P.O. Box 1066, Mt. Clemens, MI 48043/313-469-6727
Poly Choke Div., Marble Arms Corp., 420 Industrial Park, Gladstone, MI 49837/906-428-3710
Redfield Gun Sight Co., 5800 E. Jewell St., Denver, CO 80222
S&M Tang Sights, P.O. Box 1338, West Babylon, NY 11704/516-226-4057
Schwarz's Gun Shop, 41-15th St., Wellsburg, WV 26070
Simmons Gun Specialties, Inc., 700 S. Rodgers Rd., Olathe, KS 66062/913-782-3131
Slug Site Co., Ozark Wilds, Versailles, MO 65084/314-378-6430
Tradewinds, Inc., Box 1191, Tacoma, WA 98401
Wichita Arms, 444 Ellis, Wichita, KS 67211/316-265-0661
Williams Gun Sight Co., 7389 Lapeer Rd., Davison, MI 48423

STOCKS (Commercial and Custom)

Accuracy Products, 9004 Oriole Trail, Wonder Lake, IL 60097
Advanced Stocking Systems, see: Answer Stocking Systems
Ahlman's Inc., R.R. 1, Box 20, Morristown, MN 55052
Don Allen Inc., HC55, Box 322, Sturgis, SD 57785/605-347-4686
Angelo & Little Custom Gun Stock Wood, N 4026 Sargent St. Spokane, WA 99212/509-926-0794 (blanks only)
Answer Stocking Systems, 113 N. 2nd St., Whitewater, WI 53190/414-473-4848 (synthetic f. shotguns)
Anton Custom Gunstocks, Paul D. Hillmer, 7251 Hudson Heights, Hudson, IA/319-988-3941
Creighton Audette, 19 Highland Circle, Springfield, VT 05156/802-885-2331
Jim Baiar, 490 Halfmoon Rd., Columbia Falls, MT 599123
Bain & Davis Sporting Goods, Walter H. Little, 307 E. Valley Blvd., San Gabriel, CA 91776/818-573-4241 (cust.)
Joe J. Balickie, Custom Stocks, Rte. 2, Box 56-G, Apex, NC 27502/919-362-5185
Bartas Gunsmithing, 10231 U.S.H.#10, Cato, WI 54206/414-732-4472
Donald Bartlett, 1808 S. 281st. Pl., #115, Federal Way, WA 98003/206-946-4311 (cust.)
Beeman Inc., 47 Paul Dr., San Rafael, CA 94903/415-472-7121 (airguns only)
Dennis M. Bellm Gunsmithing, Inc., 2376 So. Redwood Rd., Salt Lake City, UT 84119/801-974-0697
Al Biesen, West 2039 Sinto Ave., Spokane, WA 99201
Roger Biesen, 5021 W. Rosewood, Spokane, WA 99208/509-328-9340
Stephen L. Billeb, Box 1176, Big Piney, WY 83113/307-276-5627
E.C. Bishop & Son Inc., 119 Main St., Box 7, Warsaw MO 65355/816-438-5121
Gregg Boeke, Rte. 2, Box 149, Cresco, IA 52136/319-547-3746 (cust.)
John M. Boltin, 2008 Havens Dr., North Myrtle Beach, SC 29582/803-272-6581
Kent Bowerly, H.C.R. Box 1903, Camp Sherman, OR 97730/503-595-6028 (custom)
Larry D. Brace, 771 Blackfoot Ave., Eugene, OR 97404/503-688-1278 (custom)
Garnet D. Brawley, P.O. Box 668, Prescott, AZ 86301/602-445-4768 (cust.)
Frank Brgoch, #1580 South 1500 East, Bountiful, UT 84010/801-295-1885 (cust.)
A. Briganti, 475 Rt. 32, Highland Mills, NY 10930/914-928-9816
Brown Precision Co., P.O. Box 270W; 7786 Molinos Ave., Los Molinos, CA 96055/916-384-2506
W. E. Brownell, 3356 Moraga Pl., San Diego, CA 92117/619-276-6146
Jack Burres, 10333 San Fernando Road, Pacoima, CA 91331/818-899-8000 (English, Claro, Bastogne Paradox walnut blanks only)
Calico Hardwoods, Inc., 1648 Airport Blvd., Windsor, CA 95492/707-546-4045 (blanks)
Dick Campbell, 1198 Finn Ave., Littleton, CO 80124/303-799-0145 (custom)
Kevin Campbell, 10152 Trinidad, El Paso, TX 79925/915-592-5496 (cust.)
Shane Caywood, 321 Hwy. 51 So., Minocqua, WI 54548/715-356-9631 (cust.)
Claude Christopher, 1606 Berkley Rd., Greenville, NC 27834/919-756-0872 (rifles)
Winston Churchill, Twenty Mile Stream Rd., RFD, Box 29B, Proctorsville, VT 05153
Clinton River Gun Serv., Inc., 30016 S. River Rd., Mt. Clemens, MI 48045/313-468-1090
Charles H. Coffin, 3719 Scarlet Ave., Odessa, TX 79762/915-366-4729
Jim Coffin, 250 Country Club Lane, Albany, OR 97321/503-928-4391
Reggie Cubriel, 15610 Purple Sage, San Antonio, TX 78255 (cust. stockm.)
The Custom Gun Guild, 5091-F Buford Highway, Doraville, GA 30340/404-455-0346
D&D Gun Shop, 363 Elmwood, Troy, MI 48083/313-583-1512 (cust.)
Dahl's Custom Stocks, Rt. 4, Box 558, Lake Geneva, WI 53147/414-248-2464 (Martin Dahl)
Dahl Gun Shop, 6947 King Ave. West, Billings, MT 59106/406-652-3909
Homer L. Dangler, Box 254, Addison, MI 49220/517-547-6745
Sterling Davenport, 9611 E. Walnut Tree Dr., Tucson, AZ 85715/602-749-5590 (custom)
Jack Dever, 8520 N.W. 90, Oklahoma City, OK 73132/405-721-6393
Charles De Veto, 1087 Irene Rd., Lyndhurst, OH 44124/216-442-3188
William Dixon, Buckhorn Gun Works, Rte. 4 Box 1230, Rapid City, SD 57702/605-787-6289
Duncan's Gunworks Inc., 1619 Grand Ave., San Marcos, CA 92069/619-727-0515 (cust.)
David R. Dunlop, Rte. 1, Box 199, Rolla, ND 58367
Jere Eggleston, P.O. Box 50238, Columbia, SC 29250/803-799-3402 (cust.)
Wm. A. Emick, P.O. Box 741, Philipsburg, MT 59858/406-859-3280 (cust.)
Bob Emmons, 238 Robson Road, Grafton, OH 44044 (custom)
Englishtown Sporting Goods Co., Inc., David J. Maxham, 38 Main St., Englishtown, NJ 07726/201-446-7717 (custom)
Ken Eyster Heritage Gunsmiths Inc., 6441 Bishop Rd., Centerburg, OH 43011/614-625-6131 (cust.)
Reinhart Fajen, Box 338, Warsaw, MO 65355/816-438-5111
Ted Fellowes, Beaver Lodge, 9245 16th Ave. S.W., Seattle WA 98106/206-763-1698
Fiberlite, P.O. Box 1027, Houston, TX 77011/800-752-7005 (synthetic)
Fiberpro, 3636 California St., San Diego, CA 92101/619-295-7703 (blanks; fiberglass; Kevlar)
Jerry A. Fisher, 1244-4th Ave. W., Kalispell, MT 59901/406-755-7093
Flaig's Inc., 2200 Evergreen Rd., Millvale, PA 15209/412-821-1717
Flynn's Cust. Guns, P.O. Box 7461, Alexandria, LA 71301/318-455-7130 (cust.)
Donald E. Folks. 205 W. Lincoln St., Pontiac, IL 61764/815-844-7901 (custom trap, Skeet, livebird stocks)
Larry L. Forster, P.O. Box 212, Gwinner, ND 58040/701-678-2475
Fountain Prods., 492 Prospect Ave., W. Springfield, MA 01089 (cust.)
Frank's Custom Rifles, 10420 E. Rusty Spur, Tucson, AZ 85749/602-749-4563
Freeland's Scope Stands, Inc., 3737 14th Ave., Rock Island, IL 61201/309-788-7443
Game Haven Gunstocks, 13750 Shire Rd., Wolverine, MI 49799/616-525-8238 (Kevlar riflestocks)

Jim Garrett, Garrett Accur-Light Inc., 1413 B. E. Olive Ct., Fort Collins, CO 80524/303-224-3067 (fiberglass)
Dale Goens, Box 224, Cedar Crest, NM 87008
Gordie's Gun Shop, Gordon Mulholland, 1401 Fulton St., Streator, IL 61364/815-672-7202 (cust.)
Gary Goudy, 263 Hedge Rd., Menlo Park, CA 94025/415-322-1338 (cust.)
Charles E. Grace, 10144 Elk Lake Rd., Williamsburg, MI 49690/616-264-9483
Roger M. Green & J. Earl Bridges, 315 S. 2d St., P.O. Box 984, Glenrock, WY 82637/307-436-9804 (Teyssier French walnut blanks)
Greene's Machine Carving, 17200 W. 57th Ave., Golden, CO 80403 (blanks & custom)
Griffin & Howe, 589 Broadway, New York, NY 10012/212-966-5323 (custom)
Karl Guenther, 165 Granite Springs Rd. Yorktown Heights, NY 10598/914-245-5610
Guncraft, Inc., 117 W. Pipeline, Hurst, TX 76053/817-282-6481
The Gunworks Inc., John Smallwood, 3434 Maple Ave., Brookfield, IL 60513/312-387-7888 (cust.)
Half Moon Rifle Shop, 490 Halfmoon Rd., Columbia Falls, MT 59912
Rick J. Halstead, 1100 W. Polk Ave., Lovington, NM 88260/505-396-3746
Harper's Custom Stocks, 928 Lombrano St., San Antonio, TX 78207/512-732-5780
Robert W. Hart & Son, Inc., 401 Montgomery St., Nescopeck, PA 18635/717-752-3655 (cust.)
Hubert J. Hecht, Waffen-Hecht, 10112 Fair Oaks Blvd., Fair Oaks, CA 95628/916-966-1020
Edward O. Hefti, 300 Fairview, College Station, TX 77840/409-696-4959
Heppler's Gun Shop, 6000 B Soquel Ave., Santa Cruz, CA 95062/408-475-1235
Warren Heydenberk, 187 W. Sawmill Rd., Rt. 4, Quakertown PA 18951/215-536-0798 (custom)
Doug Hill, 4518 Skyline Place, Enid, OK 73701/405-242-4455 (cust.)
Klaus Hiptmayer, P.O. Box 136, Eastman, Que., J0E 1P0 Canada/514-297-2492
Hoenig & Rodman, 6521 Morton Dr., Boise, ID 83705/208-375-1116 (stock duplicating machine)
Hollis Gun Shop, 917 Rex St., Carlsbad, NM 88220
Paul Jaeger, Inc., P.O. Box 449, 1 Madison Ave., Grand Junction, TN 38039/901-764-6909
Robert L. Jamison, Rt. 4, Box 200, Moses Lake, WA 98837/509-762-2659 (cust.)
J. J. Jenkins Enterprises, Inc., 375 Pine Ave. #25, Goleta, CA 93117/805-967-1366 (custom)
Johnson Wood Products, I.D. Johnson & Sons, Rte. #1, Strawberry Point, IA 52076/319-933-4930 (blanks)
David Kartak, SRS Box 3042, South Beach, OR 97366/503-867-4951 (custom)
Stanley Kenvin, 5 Lakeville Lane, Plainview, NY 11803/516-931-0321 (custom)
Don Klein, P.O. Box 277, Camp Douglas, WI 54618/608-427-6948
Richard Knippel, 825 Stoddard Ave., Modesto, CA 95350
Harry Lawson Co., 3328 N. Richey Blvd., Tucson, AZ 85716/602-326-1117 (cust.)
Frank LeFever Arms & Sons, Inc., R.D.#1, Box 31, Lee Center, NY 13363/315-337-6722
Al Lind, 7821 76th Ave. S. W., Tacoma, WA 98498/206-584-6361 (cust. stockm.)
Ron Long, 81 Delta St., Denver, CO 80221
MPI Stocks, P.O. Box 03266, 7011 N. Reno Ave., Portland, OR 97203/503-289-8025 (fiberglass)
Monte Mandarino, 136 Fifth Ave. West, Kalispell, MT 59901/406-257-6208 (cust.)
Earl K. Matsuoka, 2801 Kinohou Pl., P.O. Box 61129, Honolulu, HI 96822/808-988-3008 (cust.)
Dennis McDonald, Box 3, Peosta, IA 52068
Bill McGuire, 1600 N. Eastmont Ave., East Wenatchee, WA 98801/509-884-6021
Maurer Arms, Carl R. Maurer, 2154-16th St., Akron, OH 44314/216-745-6864
John E. Maxson, 3507 Red Oak Lane, Plainview, TX 79072/806-293-9042 (custom)
R. M. Mercer, 216 S. Whitewater Ave., Jefferson, WI 53549/414-674-3839 (custom)
Robt. U. Milhoan & Son, Rt. 3, Elizabeth, WV 26143
Miller Arms, Inc., D. E. Miller, P.O. Box 260, St. Onge, SD 57779/605-578-1790
Millet Industries, 16131 Gothard St., Huntington Beach, CA 92647/714-842-5575 (fiber-reinforced rifle stocks)
Earl Milliron Custom Guns & Stocks, 1249 N.E. 166th Ave., Portland, OR 97230/503-252-3725
Monell Custom Guns, Red Mill Road, RD#2, Box 96, Pine Bush, NY 12566/914-744-3021 (custom)
J.W. Morrison Custom Rifles, 4015 W. Sharon, Phoenix, AZ 85029
Ted Nicklas, 5504 Hegel Rd., Goodrich, MI 48438/313-797-4493 (custom)
Paul R. Nickels, P.O. Box 71043, Las Vegas, NV 89170/702-458-7149
Jim Norman, Custom Gunstocks, 11230 Calenda Road, San Diego, CA 92127/619-487-4173
Oakley and Merkley, Box 2446, Sacramento, CA 95811 (blanks)
Vic Olson, 5002 Countryside Dr., Imperial, MO 63052/314-296-8086 (custom)
Maurice Ottmar, Box 657, 113 E. Fir, Coulee City, WA 99115/509-632-5717 (cust.)
Pachmayr Gun Works, 1220 S. Grand Ave., Los Angeles, CA 90015 (blanks and custom jobs)
Pasadena Gun Center, 206 E. Shaw, Pasadena, TX 77506/713-472-0417 (cust.)
Paulsen Gunstocks, Rte. 71, Box 11, Chinook, MT 59523/406-357-3403 (blanks)
Don Robinson, Pennsylvania Hse., 36 Fairfax Crescent, Southowram, Halifax, W. Yorksh. HX3 9SW, England (blanks only)
Carl Roth, Jr., 4728 Pineridge Ave., Cheyenne, WY 82001/309-634-3958
Matt Row, Lock, Stock 'N Barrel, 8972 East Huntington Dr., San Gabriel, CA 91775/818-287-0051
Royal Arms, 1210 Bert Acosta, El Cajon, CA 92020/619-448-5466

STOCKS (Commercial and Custom)—cont'd.

SDS, P.O. Box 424, Fallbrook, CA 92028/619-584-0577 (commercial)
Sage International Ltd., 1856 Star Batt Dr., Rochester, MI 48063/313-852-8733 (telescoping shotgun stock)
Sanders Cust. Gun Serv., 2358 Tyler Lane, Louisville, KY 40205 (blanks)
Saratoga Arms Co., 1752.N. Pleasantview RD., Pottstown, PA 19464/215-323-8386
Roy Schaefer, 965 W. Hilliard Lane, Eugene, OR 97404/503-688-43333 (blanks)
Schwartz Custom Guns, 9621 Coleman Rd., Haslett, MI 48840/517-339-8939
David W. Schwartz, 2505 Waller St., Eau Claire, WI 54701/715-832-1735 (custom)
Shaw's, The Finest in Guns, 9447 W. Lilac Rd., Escondido, CA 92026/619-728-7070
Dan A. Sherk, 1311-105th Ave., Dawson Creek, B.C. V1G 2L9, Canada/604-782-3720 (custom)
Hank Shows, The Best,1078 Alice Ave., Ukiah, CA 95482/707-462-9060
Walter Shultz, 1752 N. Pleasantview Rd., Pottstown, PA 19464
Sile Dist., 7 Centre Market Pl., New York, NY 10013/213-925-4111
Six Enterprises, 6564 Hidden Creek Dr., San Jose, CA 95120/408-268-8296 (fiberglass)
Ed Sowers, 8331 DeCelis Pl., Sepulveda, CA 91343/818-893-1233 (custom hydro-coil gunstocks)
Fred D. Speiser, 2229 Dearborn, Missoula, MT 59801/406-549-8133
Sport Service Center, 2364 N. Neva, Chicago, IL 60635/312-889-1114 (custom)
Sportsmen's Equip. Co., 915 W. Washington, San Diego, CA 92103/714-296-1501 (carbine conversions)
Keith Stegall, Box 696, Gunnison, CO 81230
Talmage Enterpr., 43197 E. Whittier, Hemet, CA 92344/714-927-2397
James C. Tucker, 205 Trinity St., Woodland, CA 95695/916-662-3109 (cust.)
Milton van Epps, Rt. 69-A, Parish, NY 13131/315-625-7251
Gil Van Horn, P.O. Box 207, Llano, CA 93544
John Vest, P.O. Box 1552, Susanville, CA 96130/916-253-3681 (classic rifles)
R. D. Wallace, Star Rt. Box 76, Grandin, MO 63943/314-593-4773 (cust.)
Weatherby's, 2781 Firestone, South Gate, CA 90280/213-569-7186
Cecil Weems, P.O. Box 657, Mineral Wells,.TX 76067/817-325-1462
Frank R. Wells, 10420 E. Rusty Spur, Tucson, AZ 85749/602-749-4563 (custom stocks)
Fred Wells, Wells Sport Store, 110 N. Summit St., Prescott, AZ 86301/602-445-3655
Terry Werth, 1203 Woodlawn Rd., Lincoln, IL 62656/217-732-9314 (cust.)
Western Gunstocks Mfg. Co., 550 Valencia School Rd., Aptos, CA 95003
Duane Wiebe, P.O. Box 497, Lotus, CA 95651
Bob Williams, P.O. Box 143, Boonsboro, MD 21713
Williamson-Pate Gunsmith Service, 117 W. Pipeline, Hurst, TX 76053/817-268-2887
Jim Windish, 2510 Dawn Dr., Alexandria, VA 22306/703-765-1994 (walnut blanks)
Dave Wills, 2776 Brevard Ave., Montgomery, AL 36109/305-272-8446
Robert M. Winter, R.R. 2, Box 484, Menno, SD 57045/605-387-5322
Mike Yee, 29927-56 Pl. S., Auburn, WA 98001/206-839-3991
Russell R. Zeeryp, 1601 Foard Dr., Lynn Ross Manor, Morristown, TN 37814
Dean A. Zollinger, Rt. 2, Box 135-A, Rexburg, ID 83440/208-356-6167

TARGETS, BULLET & CLAYBIRD TRAPS

Amacker Products Inc., P.O. Box 1432, Tallulah, LA 71282/318-574-4903
Beeman Inc., 47-GDD Paul Dr., San Rafael, CA 94903/415-472-7121 (airgun targets, silhouettes and traps)
Bulletboard Target Systems Laminations Corp., Box 469, Neenah, WI 54956/414-725-8368
Caswell International Corp. Inc., 1221 Marshall St. N.E., Minneapolis, MN 55413/612-379-2000 (target carriers; commercial shooting ranges)
J.G. Dapkus Co., P.O. Box 180, Cromwell, CT 06416/203-632-2308 (live bulls-eye targets)
Data-Targ, (See Rocky Mountain Target Co.)
Detroit-Armor Corp., Detroit Bullet Trap Div., 2233 N. Palmer Dr., Schaumburg, IL 60195/312-397-4070 (Shooting Ranges)
The Dutchman's Firearms Inc., 4143 Taylor Blvd., Louisville, KY 40215/502-366-0555
Electro Ballistic Lab., 616 Junipero Serva Blvd., Stanford, CA 94305 (Electronic Trap Boy)
Ellwood Epps Northern Ltd., 210 Worthington St., W., North Bay, Ont. P1B 3B4, Canada (hand traps)
Hunterjohn, P.O. Box 477, St. Louis, MO 63166 (shotgun patterning target)
Jaro Manuf., 206 E. Shaw, Pasadena, TX 77506/713-472-0417 (paper targets)
Laminations Corp. ("Bullettrap"), Box 469, Neenah, WI 54956/414-725-8368
Millard F. Lerch, Box 163, 10842 Front St., Mokena, IL 60448 (bullet target)
MCM (Mathalienne de Construction Mecanique), P.O. Box 18, 17160 Matha, France (claybird traps)
MTM Molded Prods. Co., 3370 Obco Ct., Dayton, OH 45414/513-890-7461
Outers Laboratories, Div. of Omark Industries, Rte. 2, Onalaska, WI 54650/608-783-1515 (claybird traps)
Peterson Label Co., P.O. Box 186, 23 Sullivan Dr., Redding Ridge, CT 06876/203-938-2349 (paste-ons; Targ-Dots)
Remington Arms Co., 1007 Market St., Wilmington, DE 19898 (claybird traps)
Rocky Mountain Target Co., P.O. Box 700, Black Hawk, SD 57718/605-787-5946 (Data-Targ)
Julio Santiago, P.O. Box O, Rosemount, MN 55068/612-890-7631 (targets)
Sheridan Products, Inc., 3205 Sheridan, Racine, WI 54303 (traps)
Trius Prod., Box 25, Cleves, OH 45002/513-914-5682 (claybird, can thrower)
U.S. Repeating Arms Co., P.O. Box 30-300, New Haven, CT 06511/203-789-5000 (claybird traps)
Winchester, Olin Corp., 120 Long Ridge Rd., Stamford, CT 06904

TAXIDERMY

Jack Atcheson & Sons, Inc., 3210 Ottawa St., Butte, MT. 59701
Dough's Taxidermy Studio, Doug Domedion, 5112 Edwards Rd., Medina, NY 14103/716-798-4022 (deer head specialist)
Jonas Bros., Inc., 1037 Broadway, Denver, CO 80203 (catlg. $2)
Kulis Freeze-Dry Taxidermy, 725 Broadway Ave., Bedford, OH 44146
Mark D. Parker, 1233 Sherman Dr., Longmont, CO 80501/303-772-0214

TRAP & SKEET SHOOTERS EQUIP.

A.C. Enterprises, P.O. Box 448, Edenton, NC 27932/919-482-4992
Bob Allen Companies, 214 S.W. Jackson, Des Moines, IA 50315/515-283-2191
The American Import Co., 1453 Mission St., San Francisco, CA 94103/415-863-1506 (Targetthrower)
Anton Custom Gunstocks, Paul D. Hillmer, 7251 Hudson Heights, Hudson, IA 50643/319-988-3941
C&H Research, 115 Sunnyside Dr., Lewis, KS 67552/316-324-5445 (Mercury recoil suppressor)
D&H Prods. Co., Inc., 465 Denny Rd., Valencia, PA 16059/412-898-2840 (snap shell)
Frigon Guns, 627 W. Crawford, Clay Center, KS 67432/913-632-5607
Griggs Recreational Prods. Inc., P.O. Box 789, Bountiful, UT 84010/801-295-9696 (recoil redirector)
Ken Eyster Heritage Gunsmiths, Inc., 6441 Bishop Rd., Centerburg, OH 43011/614-625-6131 (shotgun competition choking)
Hoppe Division, Penguin Inds. Inc., Airport Mall, Coatesville, PA 19320/215-384-6000 (Monte Carlo pad)
Hunter Co., Inc., 3300 W. 71st Ave., Westminster, CO 80030/303-427-4626
Ljutic Industries Inc., P.O. Box 2117; 732 N 16th Ave., Yakima, WA 98907/509-248-0476
MCM (Mathalienne de Construction de Mecanique), P.O. Box 18, 17160 Matha, France (claybird traps)
Meadow Industries, P.O. Box 450, Marlton, NJ 08053/609-953-0922 (stock pad, variable; muzzle rest)
Wm. J. Mittler, 290 Moore Dr., Boulder Creek, CA 95006 (shotgun choke specialist)
Moneymaker Guncraft, 1420 Military Ave., Omaha, NE 68131/402-556-0226 (free-floating, ventilated ribs)
Multi-Gauge Enterprises, 433 W. Foothill Blvd., Monrovia, CA 91061/213-358-4549; 357-6117 (shotgun specialists)
William J. Nittler, 290 Moore Dr., Boulder Creek, CA 95006/408-338-3376 (shotgun barrel repairs)
Outers Laboratories, Div. of Omark Industries, Route 2, Onalaska, WI 54650/608-783-1515 (trap, claybird)
Purbaugh & Sons (See Multi-Gauge) (shotgun barrel inserts)
Remington Arms Co., P.O. Box 1939, Bridgeport, Ct. 06601 (trap, claybird)
Daniel Titus, Shooting Specialties, 872 Penn St., Bryn Mawr, PA 19010/215-525-8829 (hullbag)
Trius Products, Box 25, Cleves, OH 45002/513-941-5682 (can thrower; trap, claybird)
Winchester-Western, New Haven, CT 06504 (trap, claybird)

TRIGGERS, RELATED EQUIP.

Ametek, Hunter Spring Div., One Spring Ave., Hatfield, PA 19440/215-822-2971 (trigger gauge)
NOC, Cadillac Industrial Park, 1610 Corwin St., Cadillac, MI 49601/616-775-3425 (triggers)
M.H. Canjar Co., 500 E. 45th Ave., Denver, CO 80216/303-295-2638 (triggers)
Central Specialties Co., 200 Lexington Dr., Buffalo Grove, IL 60090/312-537-3300 (trigger locks only)
Crown City Arms, Inc., P.O. Box 550, Cortland, NY 13045/607-753-8238
Custom Products, Neil A. Jones, RD #1, Box 483A, Saegertown, PA 16433/814-763-2769 (trigger guard)
Dayton-Traister Co., 9322-900th West, P.O. Box 593, Oak Harbor, WA 98277/206-675-5375 (triggers)
Electronic Trigger Systems, 4124 Thrushwood Lane, Minnetonka, MN 55345/612-935-7829
Flaig's, 2200 Evergreen Rd., Millvale, PA 15209/412-821-1717 (trigger shoes)
Bill Holmes, Rt. 2, Box 242, Fayetteville, AR 72701/501-521-8958 (trigger release)
Neil A. Jones, see: Custom Products
Mad River Metalcraft Inc., 1524 Winding Trail, Springfield, OH 45503/513-399-0948 (bolt shroud safety)
Michaels of Oregon Co., P.O. Box 13010, Portland, OR 97213/503-255-6890 (trigger guards)
Miller Single Trigger Mfg. Co., R.D. 1, Box 99, Millersburg, PA 17061/717-692-3704
Bruce A. Nettestad, Rt. 1, Box 140, Pelican Rapids, MN 56572/218-863-4301 (trigger guards)
Ohaus Corp., 29 Hanover Rd., Florham Park, NJ 07932 (trigger pull gauge)
Pachmayr Gun Works, 1220 S. Grand Ave., Los Angeles, CA 90015 (trigger shoe)
Pacific Tool Co., P.O. Box 2048, Ordnance Plant Rd., Grand Island, NE 68801 (trigger shoe)
Richland Arms Co., 321 W. Adrian St., Blissfield, MI 49228 (trigger pull gauge)
Serrifile Inc., P.O. Box 508, Littlerock, CA 93543/805-945-0713
Timney Mfg. Co., 3106 W. Thomas Rd., Suite 1104, Phoenix, AZ 85017/602-269-6937 (triggers)
Melvin Tyler, 1326 W. Britton Rd., Oklahoma City, OK 73114/800-654-8415 (trigger shoe)
Williams Gun Sight Co., 7389 Lapeer Rd., Davison, MI 48423 (trigger shoe)

Outdoor Life Books offers the 7 x 35 binoculars
good for a wide range of outdoor activities. For
details on ordering, please write: Outdoor Life
Books, P.O. Box 2033, Latham, N.Y. 12111.